KV-418-913

STOKE-ON-TRENT
CITY
LIBRARIES

HORACE BARKS
Reference Library

STATUTORY INSTRUMENTS 1972

PART I
(in two Sections)

SECTION 2

Published by Authority

LONDON
HER MAJESTY'S STATIONERY OFFICE
1972

STOKE-ON-TRENT
CITY
LIBRARIES

24/10/72

© *Crown copyright* 1972

PRINTED AND PUBLISHED BY HER MAJESTY'S STATIONERY OFFICE

To be purchased from
49 High Holborn, LONDON, WC1V 6HB
13a Castle Street, EDINBURGH, EH2 3AR   109 St. Mary Street, CARDIFF, CF1 1JW
Brazennose Street, MANCHESTER, M60 8AS   50 Fairfax Street, BRISTOL, BS1 3DE
258 Broad Street, BIRMINGHAM, B1 2HE   80 Chichester Street, BELFAST, BT1 4JY

or through booksellers

1972

Price for the two Sections: £13·70 net

PRINTED IN ENGLAND

STOKE-ON-TRENT
CITY
LIBRARIES

- 6 NOV 1972

HORACE BARKS
REFERENCE LIBRARY
BIBLIOGRAPHY
SERVICES

SBN 11 840095 9*

Contents of the Volume

PART I, Section 1

PART I, Section 2

PART II

PART III

STATUTORY INSTRUMENTS

1972 No. 318

DEFENCE

The Certificates of Arrest and Surrender (Army) Regulations 1972

Made - - - - *1st March* 1972

Coming into Operation—in accordance with Regulation 1.

The Secretary of State for Defence, in exercise of the powers conferred upon him by section 189(4) of the Army Act 1955(a) and, by virtue of section 44(2) of the Armed Forces Act 1971(b), by section 190A(4) of the Army Act 1955, and of all other powers enabling him in that behalf, hereby makes the following Regulations:—

1.—(1) These Regulations may be cited as the Certificates of Arrest and Surrender (Army) Regulations 1972 and shall come into operation on such date as the Armed Forces Act 1971 comes into force.

(2) The Interpretation Act 1889(c) shall apply to the interpretation of these Regulations as it applies to the interpretation of an Act of Parliament.

2. Where, in pursuance of section 187 of the Army Act 1955, a court of summary jurisdiction has dealt with a person as illegally absent, the certificate which is required by section 189(1) of that Act to be handed over with that person when he is delivered into military custody shall be in the form specified in Part I of the Schedule to these Regulations and shall contain the particulars therein set out as to his arrest or surrender and the proceedings before the court.

3. Where, under section 188 of the Army Act 1955, a person is delivered into military custody without being brought before a court the certificate which is required by section 189(2) of that Act to be handed over with him shall be in the form specified in Part II of the Schedule to these Regulations and shall contain the particulars therein set out relating to his surrender.

4. Where, in pursuance of section 190A of the Army Act 1955, a person suspected of any offence under Part II of that Act has been arrested under a warrant issued by his commanding officer, the certificate which is required by subsection (3) of that section to be handed over with that person when he is delivered into military custody shall be in the form specified in Part III of the Schedule to these Regulations and shall contain the particulars therein set out relating to his arrest and state whether or not the person arrested was at the time of arrest wearing the uniform of any of Her Majesty's military forces.

(a) 1955 c. 18.   (b) 1971 c. 33.   (c) 1889 c. 63.

5. The Certificates of Arrest and Surrender of Deserters and Absentees (Army) Regulations 1956**(a)** and the Certificates of Arrest and Surrender of Deserters and Absentees (Army) (Amendment) Regulations 1961**(b)** are hereby revoked.

Carrington,
One of Her Majesty's Principal
Secretaries of State.

Dated 1st March 1972.

SCHEDULE

PART I

CERTIFICATE IN ACCORDANCE WITH SECTION 189(1) OF THE ARMY ACT 1955

I CERTIFY that on the.................................day of..........................19......,
there was brought before the...
(name and description of court)

Court at..., being a court of summary jurisdiction,
(place)

Number ....

Rank ....

Name ....

Unit or corps..

a member of the regular forces alleged to be an illegal absentee who had

....
(insert as appropriate "been arrested by" or "surrendered to")

....
(insert the name of the person who effected the arrest or to whom surrender was made)

at............................. at..............................on the..........................19...
(place) *(time)* *(date)*

and that he was dealt with in accordance with the provisions of section 187 of the Army Act 1955.

Delete this ⎫ The said member of the regular forces admitted that he had been
paragraph if no ⎬ illegally absent from the said unit or corps
admission made ⎭ at ....
(place from which he absented himself if known)

Dated this   day of   19 .

.... (Signature)

.... (Description)
(As to the persons qualified to sign, see note)

(a) S.I. 1956/657 (1956 I, p. 363).   (b) S.I. 1961/2009 (1961 III, p. 3681).

NOTE

The following persons are authorised to sign under section 30 of the Army and Air Force Act 1961:—

(1) in England, Wales and the Isle of Man, a justice of the peace or the clerk of the court;

(2) in Scotland, the clerk of the court;

(3) in Northern Ireland, a resident magistrate or the clerk of petty sessions for the petty sessions district in which the court sat;

(4) in Jersey and Guernsey, a magistrate or a person for the time being authorised to act as a magistrate;

(5) in Alderney, the chairman of the Court of Alderney or the person for the time being authorised to act as chairman of that court;

(6) in Sark, the Seneschal or the Deputy Seneschal; and

(7) in a colony, protectorate or trusteeship territory under the United Nations, a magistrate or the official (by whatever designation known) who exercises in the court functions similar to those exercised in England by the clerk of a court of summary jurisdiction.

PART II

CERTIFICATE IN ACCORDANCE WITH SECTION 189(2) OF THE ARMY ACT 1955

I certify that...(*full names*)

surrendered himself at...(*place*), at

....................(*hour*), on the...........................day of...............................19...

as being illegally absent from...(*unit*)

at...(*place*) on........................(*date*)

and gave the following particulars:—

No. ....

Rank ....

Name ....

Unit..

Dated this...................................day of...19...

Signature of officer of police in charge of ⎫
  police station where the above-named ⎬...
  person surrendered or was taken on ⎪
  surrender. ⎭

Part III

CERTIFICATE IN ACCORDANCE WITH SECTION 190A(3) OF THE ARMY ACT 1955

I certify that:

Number ....

Rank ....

Full Names....................................

Unit or corps................................

was arrested at...*(place)*

at..............................*(time)* on the.............................day of.......................

19... under a warrant issued by his commanding officer pursuant to section 190A of the Army Act 1955.

He was/was not (*delete as appropriate*) at the time of arrest wearing the uniform of one of Her Majesty's military forces.

Dated this.............................day of..........................19....

Signature of officer of police who causes ⎫
  the above-named person to be deli- ⎬ ....
  vered into military custody. ⎭

EXPLANATORY NOTE

(This Note is not part of the Regulations.)

These Regulations, which replace the Certificates of Arrest and Surrender of Deserters and Absentees (Army) Regulations 1956, prescribe the forms of certificate which must be handed over with a person who is delivered into military custody, being a deserter or absentee from the Army who has been brought before a court of summary jurisdiction or who has surrendered himself to the police or a person suspected of any offence under Part II of the Army Act, 1955 who has been arrested under a warrant issued by his commanding officer.

STOKE-ON-TRENT
CITY
LIBRARIES

STATUTORY INSTRUMENTS

1972 No. 319

CHILDREN AND YOUNG PERSONS

The Community Homes Regulations 1972

Made - - - -	*2nd March* 1972
Laid before Parliament	10*th March* 1972
Coming into Operation	1*st April* 1972

The Secretary of State for Social Services (as respects England, except Monmouthshire) and the Secretary of State for Wales (as respects Wales and Monmouthshire) in exercise of their powers under section 43 of the Children andYoung Persons Act 1969(a) and of all other powers enabling them in that behalf hereby make the following regulations:—

Citation and commencement

1. These regulations may be cited as the Community Homes Regulations 1972, and shall come into operation on 1st April 1972.

Interpretation

2.—(1) In these regulations, unless the context otherwise requires—

"the Act" means the Children and Young Persons Act 1969;

"the Act of 1948" means the Children Act 1948(b);

"community home" means a home provided under section 36 of the Act, and unless the context otherwise implies includes a controlled community home and an assisted community home;

"child" means a person under the age of 18, and a person who has attained the age of 18 and is subject to a care order;

"responsible organisation" means the voluntary organisation responsible for the management, equipment and maintenance of an assisted community home;

"responsible body" means a local authority providing a community home under section 36(2)(*a*) of the Act, a local authority specified in the instrument of management for a controlled home under section 41 of the Act, and a voluntary organisation providing an assisted home under section 42 of the Act;

"local authority home" means a community home provided by the local authority under section 36(2)(*a*) of the Act;

"controlled community home" means a controlled community home designated as such in the regional plan in accordance with section 36(3) of the Act;

(a) 1969 c. 54.　　　　　　　(b) 1948 c. 43.

"assisted community home" means an assisted community home designated as such in the regional plan in accordance with section 36(3) of the Act;

"regional plan" has the meaning assigned to it in section 36(1) of the Act;

"managers" means a body of managers provided for in an instrument of management in accordance with section 39(1) of the Act, exercising the functions of the responsible authority as provided by section 41(2) of the Act as respects a controlled community home, or as the case may be, those of the responsible organisation as provided by section 42(2) of the Act as respects an assisted community home;

"secure accommodation" means accommodation in a community home for the purpose of restricting the liberty of children resident therein in accordance with sections 24(2) and 43(2)(c) of the Act;

"care authority" means a local authority into whose care a person is committed by means of a care order under section 20 of the Act, or who have received a child into care under section 1 of the Act of 1948 or to whose care a child is committed under section 23 of the Act;

"approved school" means a school approved by the Secretary of State under section 79 of the Children and Young Persons Act 1933(a);

"approved probation hostel and approved probation home" means premises approved under section 46(1) of the Criminal Justice Act 1948(b).

(2) The Interpretation Act 1889(c) shall apply to the interpretation of these regulations as it applies to the interpretation of an Act of Parliament.

General provisions governing the conduct of community homes

3.—(1) The responsible body, and in the case of a controlled or assisted community home the managers, shall arrange for the community home under their charge to be conducted so as to make proper provision for the care, treatment and control of the children who are accommodated therein.

(2) In the case of a controlled or assisted community home the managers shall arrange for one or more of their number to visit the home at least once in every month and to report in writing to them on the conduct of the home; and in the case of a local authority home the authority shall arrange for the home to be visited at least once a month and a report made to them in writing upon the home by such persons as they consider appropriate.

Appointment of person in charge

4. The person in charge of a controlled or assisted community home shall be appointed in accordance with the provisions of the instrument of management, and the person in charge of a local authority home shall be appointed by the local authority.

Medical care and hygiene

5. The responsible body shall ensure that arrangements are made—

(a) for providing all children resident in a community home with adequate medical (including where appropriate psychiatric) and dental care;

(b) for maintaining satisfactory conditions of hygiene in the home;

and may for these purposes appoint one or more medical officers.

(a) 1933 c. 12.   (b) 1948 c. 58.
(c) 1889 c. 63.

Notification of death, illness or accident

6. The person in charge of a community home shall as soon as possible notify—

    (*a*) the responsible body and the managers of the death of any child accommodated in the home and the circumstances of the death,

    (*b*) the responsible body and the managers of the outbreak in the home of any infectious disease which in the opinion of the medical officer or other medical practitioner attending the children in the home is sufficiently serious to be so notified, or of any serious injury to or serious illness of any child accommodated in the home,

    (*c*) the child's parent or guardian, the care authority (not being the responsible body), any visitor appointed for the child under section 24(5) of the Act, and any person or organisation having accepted responsibility wholly or partly for the cost of the child's maintenance in the home, of the death of, or of any serious injury to or serious illness of, any child accommodated in the home.

Precautions against fire and accident

7.—(1) The responsible body shall ensure that adequate precautions are taken in a community home against fire and accidents, and in regard to fire if the responsible body are not themselves the local fire authority they shall consult that authority as to the precautions to be taken.

(2) The managers of the community home, or if there are no managers, the local authority providing the home, shall make arrangements to ensure that by means of drills and practices the staff and as far as practicable the children are well versed in procedures in case of fire, and that they know the precautions to be taken for the prevention of accidents.

Religious observance

8. The managers, or if there are no managers, the local authority providing the home, shall ensure that every child resident in the home has so far as practicable in the circumstances the opportunity to attend such religious services and to receive such instruction as are appropriate to the religious persuasion to which the child may belong.

Visits by parents, guardians, relatives and friends.

9. The responsible body shall provide suitable facilities for visits to a community home by parents, guardians, relatives and friends of the children accommodated therein, but the use of such facilities, times of visiting and other arrangements connected with the visits shall be as the managers, or where there are no managers, the local authority, may decide.

Control

10.—(1) The control of a community home shall be maintained on the basis of good personal and professional relationships between the staff and the children resident therein.

(2) The responsible body in respect of a local authority home or controlled community home and the local authority specified in the instrument of management for an assisted community home may approve in respect of each home such additional measures as they consider necessary for the maintenance of control in the home, and the conditions under which such measures may be taken, and in approving such measures and conditions they shall have regard to the purpose and character of the home and the categories of children for which it is provided.

(3) Any approval mentioned in the preceding paragraph shall be given in writing to the person in charge of the home, save that in the case of an assisted community home the approval shall be given to the responsible organisation, and shall be reviewed every twelve months.

(4) Full particulars of any of the measures mentioned in paragraph (2) of this regulation which are used and of the circumstances in which they are used shall be recorded in permanent form by the person in charge of the home and the record shall be kept in the home.

Secure accommodation

11.—(1) The responsible body may make application to the Secretary of State for approval to provide and use in a community home secure accommodation, and if such approval is given the Secretary of State may attach to it such terms and conditions as he thinks fit.

(2) Where secure accommodation has been provided in a home in accordance with approval from the Secretary of State the person in charge of the home may, if he considers it to be necessary in the interests of a child residing in the home or for the protection of other persons, admit a child to such accommodation for one continuous period not exceeding 24 hours or for more than one such continuous period provided that the total time spent in secure accommodation shall not exceed 48 hours in any consecutive period of seven days.

(3) If an extension of the period in secure accommodation is thought necessary by the person in charge of the home, he may apply to the managers, or if there are no managers, to the local authority providing the home, and permission to extend the period to a maximum of 14 continuous days may be given.

(4) If a further period in secure accommodation is thought necessary by the person in charge of the home he may make further application before the expiration of the period of 14 days, and permission may be given to extend the time to a total of 28 continuous days.

(5) Immediately on the managers or the local authority providing the home giving the permission mentioned in the foregoing paragraph they shall inform the care authority (or voluntary organisation having care of the child) that they have given such permission, and the care authority or voluntary organisation may before the expiry of the period of extension—

    (*a*) grant their permission for the period in secure accommodation to continue or to be extended for a specified or an indefinite period,

    (*b*) refuse such permission, in which case the period in secure accommodation shall come to an end not later than 48 hours after notification of the refusal,

and if such grant or refusal has not been notified by the end of the 28th day the period in secure accommodation shall cease forthwith.

(6) If the care authority or voluntary organisation grant permission under paragraph (5) of this regulation they shall review it at intervals not exceeding three months with a view to considering whether to terminate it.

(7) The care authority or the voluntary organisation having care of the child may terminate any permission mentioned in this regulation at any time by notifying the person in charge of the home, and they may communicate their permission, their refusal of permission or their termination of permission to the person in charge of the home in writing or orally and any such oral communication shall take effect immediately but shall be confirmed in writing.

(8) If such permission expires or is refused or terminated the care authority or the voluntary organisation having care of the child shall notify the person in charge of any future arrangements which they are making for the child's accommodation.

(9) For the purpose of giving or withholding permission for extension of time one of the managers or an officer of the local authority, as the case may be, shall be available at all times (including week-ends and public holidays) and the date and times when such manager or officer is available shall be ascertainable from a duty register to be kept in the home.

(10) The care authority or voluntary organisation having the care of the child if they consider it necessary in the interests of the child or for the protection of other persons may decide that a child shall be admitted to secure accommodation and may accordingly arrange for the child to be so accommodated and in such case paragraphs (2) to (9) of this regulation shall not apply but the care authority or voluntary organisation having care of the child shall review their decision at intervals not exceeding three months.

(11) All admissions to, discharges from and permissions in respect of the use of secure accommodation shall be recorded showing the date, and as regards admissions and discharges, the time thereof. The records shall be made by the person in charge of the home and shall be preserved in permanent form and retained in the home.

Obligation to receive children into secure accommodation

12. If a child in care is accommodated elsewhere than in a community home, or if the community home where a child is has no secure accommodation, and if the responsible body, care authority or voluntary organisation having care of the child or person in charge of the home considers it to be necessary in the interests of the child or for the protection of other persons that the child be admitted to secure accommodation, they may apply to the person in charge of a community home having suitable secure accommodation for the child's admission thereto, and the person in charge may if room is available accommodate the child therein, for a consecutive period not exceeding 14 days, provided that:

(a) where a child has been taken into secure accommodation on the application of a person or body other than the care authority or the voluntary organisation having care of the child such person or body shall within 24 hours inform the care authority or the voluntary organisation that the child has been taken into secure accommodation, and the care authority or voluntary organisation before the expiration of the period of 14 days may,

  (i) grant permission for the period in secure accommodation to continue or to be extended for a specified or an indefinite period,

  (ii) refuse to allow the child to be further accommodated in secure accommodation, in which case the child shall not be accommodated for longer than 48 hours after notification of the refusal,

and if such grant or refusal has not been notified within 14 days from the time the child is first accommodated in secure accommodation he shall not be further so accommodated; and the provisions of paragraphs (6) to (8) of regulation 11 shall apply to the foregoing part of this regulation and any reference to permission in those paragraphs shall be construed as permission given under this regulation.

(*b*) a person in charge of a home having secure accommodation shall not refuse an application to accommodate a child in secure accommodation if room is available and arrangements to receive into secure accommodation children from outside the home are sanctioned by the regional plan; but if the person in charge is instructed by the responsible body or the managers to accept the child he shall do so notwithstanding that such arrangements have not been sanctioned.

Review of permission to extend period of time in secure accommodation

13.—(1) Each care authority and each voluntary organisation responsible for the care of children shall appoint a committee, and two or more local authorities and two or more voluntary organisations may combine for the purpose of appointing a joint committee to represent them, for the purpose of reviewing permission given for admission to secure accommodation; and such committees may be appointed in connection with one or more homes.

(2) A committee mentioned in the foregoing paragraph shall have among its members an independent person, and for the purposes of this regulation "an independent person" shall be any person fulfilling the requirements of regulation 3 of the Children and Young Persons (Definition of Independent Persons) Regulations 1971**(a)**.

Care during an interim order or on remand

14. Save for paragraphs (10) and (11) the provisions in regulation 11 of these regulations shall not apply to persons—

(*a*) committed to care during the currency of an interim order as defined in section 20(1) of the Act;

(*b*) committed to care on remand under section 23 of the Act;

(*c*) taken into care and detained under section 29 of the Act.

Directions regarding accommodation of children

15. The Secretary of State may give and revoke directions requiring the responsible body to accommodate in a community home a child in the care of a local authority for whom no places are made available in that home under the regional plan or to take such action in relation to a child accommodated in the home as may be specified in the directions.

Information and records

16. The person in charge of a community home shall give to a person authorised under section 58 of the Act to inspect the home, such information as he may require and as may be relevant to his inspection of the home, its state and management, and of the children and their treatment, and shall further give to such authorised person access to records concerning the home kept therein, and the responsible body shall give to the person access to any records they may keep elsewhere in relation to the home.

Approval of Secretary of State to diminution etc. of buildings, grounds or facilities

17. Where the premises comprising a controlled or assisted community home were formerly used for an approved school, approved probation hostel or approved probation home, the voluntary organisation providing the community home or the trustees in whom the property of the voluntary organisation is

---

(a) S.I. 1971/486 (1971 I, p. 1436).

vested shall not, without the approval of the Secretary of State, do anything by way of diminution or alteration which materially affects the buildings or grounds or other facilities or amenities available for children in such home.

Keith Joseph,
Secretary of State for Social Services.

1st March 1972.

Peter Thomas,
Secretary of State for Wales.

2nd March 1972.

EXPLANATORY NOTE

(*This Note is not part of the Regulations.*)

These Regulations make provision for the conduct of community homes and for securing the welfare of the children in them.

STATUTORY INSTRUMENTS

1972 No. 320

CIVIL AVIATION

The Air Navigation (Restriction of Flying) Regulations 1972

Made - - -	1*st March* 1972
Coming into Operation	1*st April* 1972

The Secretary of State, in exercise of his powers under Article 65 of the Air Navigation Order 1972(**a**) and of all other powers enabling him in that behalf, hereby makes the following Regulations.

1. These Regulations may be cited as the Air Navigation (Restriction of Flying) Regulations 1972, and shall come into operation on 1st April 1972.

2.—(1) Expressions used in these Regulations shall, unless the context otherwise requires, have the same respective meanings as in the Air Navigation Order 1972.

(2) The Interpretation Act 1889(**b**) applies for the interpretation of these Regulations as it applies for the interpretation of an Act of Parliament.

3.—(1) Subject to paragraph (2) of this Regulation, the Air Navigation (Restriction of Flying) Regulations 1970(**c**) are hereby revoked.

(2) Section 38(2) of the Interpretation Act 1889 (which relates to the effect of repeals) shall apply to these Regulations as if these Regulations were an Act of Parliament and as if the Regulations revoked by paragraph (1) of this Regulation were an Act of Parliament thereby repealed.

4.—(1) An aircraft shall not fly at a height of less than 2,000 feet above ground level over any of the areas bounded by circles of two nautical miles radius having their respective centres at the Atomic Energy Establishments specified in the first column of the Schedule hereto:

Provided that nothing in this Regulation shall prohibit—

(*a*) in relation to the Atomic Energy Establishment at Springfields, flight at a height of not less than 1,670 feet above mean sea level for the purpose of landing at Blackpool Airport, or flight, in airspace lying south of a straight line drawn from 53° 46′ 43″N, 02° 44′ 49″W to 53° 45′ 12″N, 02° 50′ 39″W, for the purpose of landing at or taking off from Warton Aerodrome ; or

(*b*) in relation to the Atomic Energy Establishment at Harwell, flight at a height of not less than 1,268 feet above mean sea level for the purpose of making an instrument approach to land on runway 36 at the Royal Air Force Station at Abingdon ; or

(*c*) in relation to the Atomic Energy Establishment at Dounreay, flight for the purpose of landing at or taking off from Dounreay Aerodrome.

(**a**) S.I. 1972/129 (1972 I, p. 366)   (**b**) 1889 c. 63.
(**c**) S.I. 1970/1083 (1970 II, p. 3420).

(2) For the purpose of this Regulation the position of each of the said Atomic Energy Establishments shall be deemed to be that specified in the second column of the Schedule hereto opposite its name.

D. F. Hubback,
A Deputy Secretary,
Department of Trade and Industry.

1st March 1972.

THE SCHEDULE

Atomic Energy Establishment	Position
ALDERMASTON	51°22′00″N 01°08′17″W
CALDER / WINDSCALE	54°25′04″N 03°29′39″W
CAPENHURST	53°15′49″N 02°57′03″W
CHAPELCROSS	55°00′59″N 03°13′29″W
DOUNREAY	58°34′36″N 03°44′28″W
HARWELL	51°34′28″N 01°19′00″W
SPRINGFIELDS	53°46′33″N 02°48′10″W
WINFRITH HEATH	50°41′00″N 02°17′00″W

EXPLANATORY NOTE

(This Note is not part of the Regulations.)

These Regulations revoke and re-enact the substance of the Air Navigation (Restriction of Flying) Regulations 1970.

STATUTORY INSTRUMENTS

1972 No. 321

CIVIL AVIATION

The Rules of the Air and Air Traffic Control Regulations 1972

Made - - - -	*1st March* 1972
Coming into Operation	*1st April* 1972

The Secretary of State in exercise of his powers under Article 61(1) of the Air Navigation Order 1972(a), (hereinafter referred to as "the Order") and of all other powers enabling him in that behalf, hereby makes the following Regulations.

1. These Regulations may be cited as the Rules of the Air and Air Traffic Control Regulations 1972, and shall come into operation on 1st April 1972.

2. The Rules set forth in the Schedule hereto are hereby prescribed as the Rules of the Air and Air Traffic Control.

3.—(1) Subject to the following provisions of this Regulation, the following Regulations are hereby revoked, that is to say:

The Rules of the Air and Air Traffic Control Regulations 1970(b);

The Rules of the Air and Air Traffic Control (Amendment) Regulations 1970(c);

The Rules of the Air and Air Traffic Control (Second Amendment) Regulations 1971(d);

The Rules of the Air and Air Traffic Control (Third Amendment) Regulations 1971(e).

(2) (*a*) Section 38(2) of the Interpretation Act 1889(f) (which relates to the effect of repeals), shall apply to these Regulations as if these Regulations were an Act of Parliament and as if the Regulations revoked by paragraph (1) of this Regulation were Acts of Parliament thereby repealed.

(*b*) These Regulations shall apply to or in relation to any licence or other document issued or granted under any Regulation revoked by these Regulations, as they apply to a licence or other document issued or granted under these Regulations.

(*c*) Any licence or other document issued or granted under any Regulations revoked by these Regulations in force at the date of the coming into operation of these Regulations shall, subject to the provisions of Article 59 of the Order, remain in force and shall have effect for the purposes of these Regulations as if it had been issued or granted under the corresponding provisions thereof:

(a) S.I. 1972/129 (1972 I, p. 366).　　(b) S.I. 1970/1082 (1970 II. p. 3366).
(c) S.I. 1970/1448 (1970 III, p. 4748).　(d) S.I. 1971/1751 (1971 III, p. 4768).
(e) S.I. 1971/1972 (1971 III, p. 5644).　(f) 1889 c. 63.

Provided that any such document which is expressed to remain in force for a definite period shall remain in force, unless renewed, only until the expiration of that period.

D. F. Hubback,
A Deputy Secretary,
1st March, 1972.   Department of Trade and Industry.

THE SCHEDULE

THE RULES OF THE AIR AND AIR TRAFFIC CONTROL ARRANGEMENT OF RULES

SECTION I

INTERPRETATION

1.—(1) In these Rules, unless the context otherwise requires—

"Air traffic control clearance" means authorisation by an air traffic control unit for an aircraft to proceed under conditions specified by that unit.

"Anti-collision light" means a flashing red light showing in all directions for the purpose of enabling the aircraft to be more readily detected by the pilots of distant aircraft.

"Apron" means the part of an aerodrome provided for the stationing of aircraft for the embarkation and disembarkation of passengers, the loading and unloading of cargo and for parking.

"Cloud ceiling" in relation to an aerodrome means the distance measured vertically from the notified elevation of that aerodrome to the lowest part of any cloud visible from the aerodrome which is sufficient to obscure more than one half of the sky so visible.

"Ground visibility" means the horizontal visibility at ground level.

"IFR flight" means a flight conducted in accordance with the Instrument Flight Rules in Section VI of these Rules.

"Manoeuvring area" means the part of an aerodrome provided for the take-off and landing of aircraft and for the movement of aircraft on the surface, excluding the apron and any part of the areodrome provided for the maintenance of aircraft.

"The Order" means the Air Navigation Order 1972.

"Runway" means an area, whether or not paved, which is provided for the take-off or landing run of aircraft.

"VFR Flight" means a flight conducted in accordance with the Visual Flight Rules in Section V of these Rules.

(2) Subject to the provisions of paragraph (1) of these Rules expressions used in these Rules shall, unless the context otherwise requires, have the same respective meanings as in the Order.

(3) The Interpretation Act 1889 applies for the purpose of the interpretation of these Rules as it applies for the purpose of the interpretation of an Act of Parliament.

SECTION II

GENERAL

Application of Rules to aircraft

2. These Rules, in so far as they are applicable in relation to aircraft, shall, subject to the provisions of Rule 30 of these Rules, apply in relation to—

(*a*) all aircraft within the United Kingdom; and

(*b*) all aircraft registered in the United Kingdom, wherever they may be.

Misuse of Signals and Markings

3.—(1) A signal or marking to which a meaning is given by these Rules, or which is required by these Rules to be used in circumstances or for a purpose therein specified, shall not be used except with that meaning, or for that purpose.

(2) A person in an aircraft or on an aerodrome or at any place at which an aircraft is taking off or landing shall not make any signal which may be confused with a signal specified in these Rules, and, except with lawful authority, shall not make any signal which he knows or ought reasonably to know to be a signal in use for signalling to or from any of Her Majesty's naval, military or air force aircraft.

Reporting hazardous conditions

4. The commander of an aircraft shall, on meeting with hazardous conditions in the course of a flight, or as soon as possible thereafter, send to the appropriate air traffic control unit by the quickest means available information containing such particulars of the hazardous conditions as may be pertinent to the safety of other aircraft.

Low Flying

5.—(1) Subject to the provisions of paragraphs (2) and (3) of this Rule:

(*a*) An aircraft other than a helicopter shall not fly over any congested area of a city, town or settlement below—

(i) such height as would enable the aircraft to alight clear of the area and without danger to persons or property on the surface, in the event of failure of a power unit; or

(ii) a height of 1,500 feet above the highest fixed object within 2,000 feet of the aircraft,

whichever is the higher.

(*b*) A helicopter shall not fly below such height as would enable it to alight without danger to persons or property on the surface, in the event of failure of a power unit.

(*c*) Except with the permission in writing of the Authority and in accordance with any conditions therein specified a helicopter shall not fly—

(i) over a congested area of a city, town or settlement below a height of 1,500 feet above the highest fixed object within 2,000 feet of the helicopter; or

(ii) over the area specified, below such height as would enable it to alight clear of the area in the event of failure of a power unit, that is to say the area bounded by straight lines joining successively the following points:

Kew Bridge (51°29′11″N 00°17′10″W).

The Eastern extremity of Brent Reservoir (51°34′18″N 00°13′55″W).

Gospel Oak Station (B.R.) (51°33′18″N 00°08′58″W).

The South East corner of Springfield Park (51°34′09″N 00°03′17″W).

Bromley (Bow) Station (B.R.) (51°31′20″N 00°00′36″W).

The South West corner of Hither Green (51°26′44″N 00°00′38″W).

Herne Hill Station (B.R.) (51°27′12″N 00°06′04″W).

Wimbledon Station (B.R.) (51°25′17″N 00°12′15″W).

The North West corner of Castelnau Reservoir (51°28′52″N 00°14′02″W).

Kew Bridge (51°29′11″N 00°17′10″W).

excluding so much of the bed of the river Thames as lies within that area between the ordinary high water marks on each of its banks.

(*d*) An aircraft shall not fly—

(i) over, or within 3,000 feet of, any assembly in the open air of more than 1,000 persons assembled for the purpose of witnessing or participating in any organised event, except with the permission in writing of the Authority and in accordance with any conditions therein specified and with the consent in writing of the organisers of the event; or

(ii) below such height as would enable it to alight clear of the assembly in the event of the failure of a power unit:

Provided that where a person is charged with an offence under the Order by reason of a contravention of this sub-paragraph, it shall be a good defence to prove that the flight of the aircraft over, or within 3,000 feet of, the assembly was made at a reasonable height and for a reason not connected with the assembly or with the event which was the occasion for the assembly.

(*e*) An aircraft shall not fly closer than 500 feet to any person, vessel, vehicle or structure.

(2)(*a*) The provisions of paragraphs (1)(*a*)(ii) and (1)(*c*)(i) of this Rule shall not apply to an aircraft flying—

(i) on a route notified for the purposes of this Rule, or

(ii) on a special VFR flight as defined in Rule 24 of these Rules in accordance with instructions given for the purposes of that Rule by the appropriate air traffic control unit.

(*b*) Paragraphs (1)(*d*) and (*e*) of this Rule shall not apply to an aircraft in the service of the police authority for any area of the United Kingdom.

(*c*) Paragraphs (1)(*d*) and (*e*) of this Rule shall not apply to the flight of an aircraft over or within 3,000 feet of an assembly of persons gathered for the purpose of witnessing an event which consists wholly or principally of an aircraft race or contest or an exhibition of flying, if the aircraft is taking part in such race, contest or exhibition or is engaged on a flight arranged by, or made with the consent in writing of, the organisers of the event.

(*d*) Paragraph (1)(*e*) of this Rule shall not apply to:

  (i) any aircraft while it is landing or taking off in accordance with normal aviation practice;

  (ii) any glider while it is hill-soaring.

(3) Nothing in this Rule shall prohibit an aircraft from flying in such a manner as is necessary for the purpose of saving life.

(4) Nothing in this Rule shall prohibit any aircraft from flying in accordance with normal aviation practice, for the purpose of taking off from, landing at or practising approaches to landing at, or checking navigational aids or procedures at, a Government aerodrome, an aerodrome owned or managed by the Authority or a licensed aerodrome in the United Kingdom or at any aerodrome in any other country:

Provided that the practising of approaches to landing shall be confined to the airspace customarily used by aircraft when landing or taking off in accordance with normal aviation practice at the aerodrome concerned.

(5) Nothing in this Rule shall apply to any captive balloon or kite.

Simulated instrument flight

6. An aircraft shall not be flown in simulated instrument flight conditions unless—

  (*a*) the aircraft is fitted with dual controls which are functioning properly;

  (*b*) an additional pilot (in this Rule called "a safety pilot") is carried in a second control seat of the aircraft for the purpose of rendering such assistance as may be necessary to the pilot flying the aircraft; and

  (*c*) if the safety pilot's field of vision is not adequate both forward and to each side of the aircraft, a third person, being a competent observer, occupies a position in the aircraft which from his field of vision makes good the deficiencies in that of the safety pilot, and from which he can readily communicate with the safety pilot.

For the purposes of this Rule the expression "simulated instrument flight" means a flight during which mechanical or optical devices are used in order to reduce the field of vision or the range of visibility from the cockpit of the aircraft.

Practice Instrument Approaches

7. Within the United Kingdom an aircraft shall not carry out instrument approach practice when flying in Visual Meteorological Conditions unless—

  (*a*) the appropriate air traffic control unit has previously been informed that the flight is to be made for the purpose of instrument approach practice; and

  (*b*) if the flight is not being carried out in simulated instrument flight conditions, a competent observer is carried in such a position in the aircraft that he has an adequate field of vision and can readily communicate with the pilot flying the aircraft.

SECTION III

LIGHTS AND OTHER SIGNALS TO BE SHOWN OR MADE BY AIRCRAFT

General

8.—(1) For the purposes of this Section of these Rules the horizontal plane of a light shown in an aircraft means the plane which would be the horizontal plane passing through the source of that light, if the aircraft were in level flight.

(2) Where by reason of the physical construction of an aircraft it is necessary to fit more than one lamp in order to show a light required by this Section of these Rules, the lamps shall be so fitted and constructed that, so far as is reasonably practicable, not more than one such lamp is visible from any one point outside the aircraft.

(3) Where in these Rules a light is required to show through specified angles in the horizontal plane, the lamps giving such light shall be so constructed and fitted that the light is visible from any point in any vertical plane within those angles throughout angles of 90° above and below the horizontal plane, but, so far as is reasonably practicable, through no greater angle, either in the horizontal plane or the vertical plane.

(4) Where in these Rules a light is required to show in all directions, the lamps giving such light shall be so constructed and fitted that, so far as is reasonably practicable, the light is visible from any point in the horizontal plane and on any vertical plane passing through the source of that light.

Display of Lights by Aircraft

9.—(1) By night an aircraft shall display such of the lights specified in these Rules as may be appropriate to the circumstances of the case, and shall not display any other lights which might obscure or otherwise impair the visibility of, or be mistaken for, such lights:

Provided that nothing in this paragraph shall prevent the display of an anti-collision light.

(2) A flying machine on a land aerodrome in the United Kingdom at which aircraft normally land or take off at night shall, unless it is stationary on the apron or a part of the aerodrome provided for the maintenance of aircraft, display by night either the lights which it would be required to display if it were flying, or the lights specified in Rule 11(2)(a) or 11(2)(c) of these Rules.

Failure of Navigation Lights

10. In the United Kingdom, in the event of the failure of any light which is required by these Rules to be displayed in flight, if the light cannot be immediately repaired or replaced the aircraft shall land as soon as in the opinion of the commander of the aircraft it can safely do so, unless authorised by the appropriate air traffic control unit to continue its flight.

Flying Machines

11.—(1) A flying machine when flying at night shall display lights as follows:

    (a) in the case of a flying machine registered in the United Kingdom having a maximum total weight authorised of more than 5,700 kg. the system of lights specified in paragraph (2)(b) of this Rule;

    (b) in the case of a flying machine registered in the United Kingdom having a maximum total weight authorised of 5,700 kg. or less, any one of the following systems of lights—

        that specified in paragraph (2)(a) of this Rule; or that specified in paragraph (2)(b); or

        that specified in paragraph (2)(d), excluding sub-paragraph (ii),

    (c) in the case of any other flying machine one of the systems of lights specified in paragraph (2) of this Rule.

(2) The systems of lights referred to in paragraph (1) of this Rule are as follows:

    (a) (i) a green light of at least five candela showing to the starboard side through an angle of 110° from dead ahead in the horizontal plane;

        (ii) a red light of at least five candela showing to the port side through an angle of 110° from dead ahead in the horizontal plane; and

        (iii) a white light of at least three candela showing through angles of 70° from dead astern to each side in the horizontal plane,

all being steady lights;

    (b) (i) the lights specified in sub-paragraph (a) of this paragraph; and

        (ii) an anti-collision light;

    (c) the lights specified in sub-paragraph (a) of this paragraph, but all being flashing lights flashing together;

(*d*) the lights specified in sub-paragraph (*a*) of this paragraph, but all being flashing lights flashing together in alternation with one or both of the following:

(i) a flashing white light of at least twenty candela showing in all directions;

(ii) a flashing red light of at least twenty candela showing through angles of 70° from dead astern to each side in the horizontal plane.

(3) If the lamp showing either the red or the green light specified in paragraph (2)(*a*) of this Rule is fitted more than 2 metres from the wing tip, a lamp may notwithstanding the provisions of Rule 9(1) of these Rules, be fitted at the wing tip to indicate its position showing a steady light of the same colour through the same angle.

Gliders

12. A glider while flying at night shall display either a steady red light of at least five candela, showing in all directions, or lights in accordance with Rule 11(2) and (3) of these Rules.

Free Balloons

13. A free balloon while flying at night shall display a steady red light of at least five candela showing in all directions, suspended not less than 5 metres and not more than 10 metres below the basket, or if there is no basket, below the lowest part of the balloon.

Captive Balloons and Kites

14.—(1) A captive balloon or kite while flying at night at a height exceeding 60 metres above the surface shall display lights as follows:

(*a*) a group of two steady lights consisting of a white light placed 4 metres above a red light, both being of at least five candela and showing in all directions, the white light being placed not less than 5 metres or more than 10 metres below the basket, or if there is no basket, below the lowest part of the balloon or kite;

(*b*) on the mooring cable, at intervals of not more than 300 metres measured from the group of lights referred to in sub-paragraph (*a*) of this paragraph, groups of two lights of the colour and power and in the relative positions specified in that sub-paragraph, and, if the lowest group of lights is obscured by cloud, an additional group below the cloud base; and

(*c*) on the surface, a group of three flashing lights arranged in a horizontal plane at the apexes of a triangle, approximately equilateral, each side of which measures at least 25 metres; one side of the triangle shall be approximately at right angles to the horizontal projection of the cable and shall be delimited by two red lights; the third light shall be a green light so placed that the triangle encloses the object on the surface to which the balloon or kite is moored.

(2) A capitve balloon while flying by day at a height exceeding 60 metres above the surface shall have attached to its mooring cable at intervals of not more than 200 metres measured from the basket, or, if there is no basket, from the lowest part of the balloon, tubular streamers not less than 40 centimetres in diameter and 2 metres in length, and marked with alternate bands of red and white 50 centimetres wide.

(3) A kite flown in the circumstances referred to in paragraph (2) of this Rule shall have attached to its mooring cable either:

(*a*) tubular streamers as specified in paragraph (2) of this Rule, or

(*b*) at intervals of not more than 100 metres measured from the lowest part of the kite, streamers of not less than 80 centimetres long and 30 centimetres wide at their widest part and marked with alternate bands of red and white 10 centi-metres wide.

Airships

15.—(1) Except as provided in paragraph (2) of this Rule, an airship while flying at night shall display the following steady lights:

(*a*) a white light of at least five candela showing through angles of 110° from dead ahead to each side in the horizontal plane;

(b) a green light of at least five candela showing to the starboard side through an angle of 110° from dead ahead in the horizontal plane;

(c) a red light of at least five candela showing to the port side through an angle of 110° from dead ahead in the horizontal plane; and

(d) a white light of at least five candela showing through angles of 70° from dead astern to each side in the horizontal plane.

(2) An airship while flying at night shall display, if it is not under command, or has voluntarily stopped its engines, or is being towed, the following steady lights:

(a) the white lights referred to in paragraph (1)(a) and (d) of this Rule;

(b) two red lights, each of at least five candela and showing in all directions suspended below the control car so that one is at least 4 metres above the other and at least 8 metres below the control car; and

(c) if the airship is making way but not otherwise, the green and red lights referred to in paragraph (1)(b) and (c) of this Rule:

Provided that an airship while picking up its moorings, notwithstanding that it is not under command, shall display only the lights specified in paragraph (1) of this Rule.

(3) An airship, while moored within the United Kingdom by night, shall display the following lights:

(a) when moored to a mooring mast, at or near the rear a white light of at least five candela showing in all directions;

(b) when moored otherwise than to a mooring mast:

(i) a white light of at least five candela showing through angles of 110° from dead ahead to each side in the horizontal plane;

(ii) a white light of at least five candela showing through angles of 70° from dead astern to each side in the horizontal plane.

(4) An airship while flying by day, if it is not under command, or has voluntarily stopped its engines, or is being towed, shall display two black balls suspended below the control car so that one is at least 4 metres above the other and at least 8 metres below the control car.

(5) For the purposes of this Rule:

(a) an airship shall be deemed not to be under command when it is unable to execute a manoeuvre which it may be required to execute by or under these Rules;

(b) an airship shall be deemed to be making way when it is not moored and is in motion relative to the air.

Secondary Surveillance Radar Transponders

16. Every aircraft (not being a glider or a helicopter) when flying within such airspace as may be notified for the purposes of this Rule shall be provided with radio apparatus of a design approved by the Authority capable of replying to an interrogation from secondary surveillance radar units on the surface and set in accordance with such instructions as may be given to the aircraft by the appropriate air traffic control unit:

Provided that where the radio apparatus in the aircraft becomes unserviceable during such a flight the commander of the aircraft shall continue the flight in accordance with such instructions as may be given to him by the appropriate air traffic control unit.

Section IV

General Flight Rules

Weather reports and forecasts

17.—(1) Immediately before an aircraft flies the commander of the aircraft shall examine the current reports and forecasts of the weather conditions on the proposed flight path, being reports and forecasts which it is reasonably practicable for him to obtain, in order to determine whether Instrument Meteorological Conditions prevail or are likely to prevail during any part of the flight.

(2) An aircraft which is unable to communicate by radio with an air traffic control unit at the aerodrome of destination shall not begin a flight to an aerodrome within a control zone if the information which it is reasonably practicable for the commander of the aircraft to obtain indicates that it will arrive at that aerodrome when the ground visibility is less than five nautical miles or the cloud ceiling is less than 1,500 feet, unless the commander of the aircraft has obtained from an air traffic control unit at that aerodrome permission to enter the aerodrome traffic zone.

Rules for avoiding aerial collisions

18.—(1) *General*

> (*a*) Notwithstanding that the flight is being made with air traffic control clearance it shall remain the duty of the commander of an aircraft to take all possible measures to ensure that his aircraft does not collide with any other aircraft.

> (*b*) An aircraft shall not be flown in such proximity to other aircraft as to create a danger of collision.

> (*c*) Aircraft shall not fly in formation unless the commanders of the aircraft have agreed to do so.

> (*d*) An aircraft which is obliged by these Rules to give way to another aircraft shall avoid passing over or under the other aircraft, or crossing ahead of it, unless passing well clear of it.

> (*e*) An aircraft which has the right-of-way under this Rule shall maintain its course and speed.

> (*f*) For the purposes of this Rule a glider and a flying machine which is towing it shall be considered to be a single aircraft under the command of the commander of the towing flying machine.

(2) *Converging*

> (*a*) Subject to the provisions of paragraphs (3) and (4) of this Rule, an aircraft in the air shall give way to other converging aircraft as follows:

>> (i) flying machines shall give way to airships, gliders and balloons;

>> (ii) airships shall give way to gliders and balloons;

>> (iii) gliders shall give way to balloons.

> (*b*) Subject to the provisions of sub-paragraph (*a*) of this paragraph, when two aircraft are converging in the air at approximately the same altitude, the aircraft which has the other on its right shall give way:

>> Provided that mechanically driven aircraft shall give way to aircraft which are towing other aircraft or objects.

(3) *Approaching Head-on*

When two aircraft are approaching head-on or approximately so in the air and there is danger of collision, each shall alter its course to the right.

(4) *Overtaking*

An aircraft which is being overtaken in the air shall have the right-of-way and the overtaking aircraft, whether climbing, descending or in horizontal flight, shall keep out of the way of the other aircraft by altering course to the right, and shall not cease to keep out of the way of the other aircraft until that other aircraft has been passed and is clear, notwithstanding any change in the relative positions of the two aircraft:

Provided that a glider overtaking another glider in the United Kingdom may alter its course to the right or to the left.

(5) *Landing*

An aircraft while landing or on final approach to land shall have the right-of-way over other aircraft in flight or on the ground or water.

(6) *Two or more aircraft landing*

In the case of two or more flying machines or gliders approaching any place for the purpose of landing, the aircraft at the lower altitude shall have the right-of-way, but it shall not cut in front of another aircraft which is on final approach to land or overtake that aircraft:

Provided that:

   (*a*) when an air traffic control unit has communicated to any aircraft an order of priority for landing, the aircraft shall approach to land in that order, and

   (*b*) when the commander of an aircraft is aware that another aircraft is making an emergency landing, he shall give way to that aircraft, and at night, notwithstanding that he may have received permission to land, shall not attempt to land until he has received further permission to do so.

Aerobatic Manoeuvres

19. An aircraft shall not carry out any aerobatic manoeuvre—

   (*a*) over the congested area of any city, town or settlement; or

   (*b*) within controlled airspace except with the consent of the appropriate air traffic control unit.

Right-hand Traffic Rule

20. An aircraft which is flying within the United Kingdom in sight of the ground and following a road, railway, canal or coastline, or any other line of landmarks, shall keep such line of landmarks on its left:

Provided that this rule shall not apply to a helicopter following the Motorway M4 on a route from West Drayton to Osterley Lock.

Notification of Arrival

21.—(1) The commander of an aircraft entering or leaving the United Kingdom on any flight for which a flight plan has been submitted shall take all reasonable steps to ensure upon landing that notice of the arrival of the aircraft is given to the aerodrome of departure:

Provided that notice of arrival need not be given upon completion of a flight between the United Kingdom and the Republic of Ireland or any other country in Europe or in or bordering on the Mediterranean Sea, unless an air traffic control unit at the aerodrome of departure has required it to be given, or unless the aircraft lands at an aerodrome other than its intended destination when it began the flight.

(2) The commander of an aircraft who has caused notice of its intended arrival at any aerodrome to be given to the air traffic control unit or other authority at that aerodrome shall ensure that the air traffic control unit or other authority at that aerodrome is informed as quickly as possible of any change of intended destination and any estimated delay in arrival of 45 minutes or more.

Flight in Notified Airspace

22. In relation to flights in Visual Meteorological Conditions in controlled airspace notified for the purposes of this Rule, the commander of an aircraft shall comply with Rules 28 and 29 of these Rules as if the flights were IFR flights:

Provided that the commander of the aircraft shall not elect to continue the flight in compliance with the Visual Flight Rules for the purposes of Rule 28(3).

Choice of VFR or IFR

23. Subject to the provisions of Rule 22 of these Rules an aircraft shall always be flown in accordance with the Visual Flight Rules or the Instrument Flight Rules:

Provided that in the United Kingdom an aircraft flying at night shall be flown in accordance with the Instrument Flight Rules, or, in a control zone in accordance with the Instrument Flight Rules or the provisions of the proviso to Rule 24(*b*) of these Rules.

VISUAL FLIGHT RULES

24. The Visual Flight Rules shall be as follows:

(a) *Outside controlled airspace*

An aircraft flying outside controlled airspace shall remain at least one nautical mile horizontally and 1,000 feet vertically away from cloud and in a flight visibility of at least five nautical miles:

Provided that at or below 3,000 feet above mean sea level this paragraph shall be deemed to be complied with if the aircraft is flown clear of cloud and in sight of the surface.

(b) *Within controlled airspace*

An aircraft flying within controlled airspace shall remain at least one nautical mile horizontally and 1,000 feet vertically away from cloud and in a flight visibility of at least five nautical miles:

Provided that in a control zone, in the case of a special VFR flight, the aircraft shall be flown in accordance with any instructions given by the appropriate air traffic control unit.

For the purposes of this Rule, "special VFR flight" means a flight made in Instrument Meteorological Conditions or at night in a control zone or in a control zone notified for the purposes of Rule 22 of these Rules, in respect of which the appropriate air traffic control unit has given permission for the flight to be made in accordance with special instructions given by that unit instead of in accordance with the Instrument Flight Rules.

SECTION VI

INSTRUMENT FLIGHT RULES

25. The Instrument Flight Rules shall be as follows:

(a) *Outside controlled airspace*

In relation to flights outside controlled airspace Rules 26 and 27 of these Rules shall apply.

(b) *Within controlled airspace*

In relation to flights within controlled airspace Rules 26, 28 and 29 of these Rules shall apply.

Minimum Height

26. Without prejudice to the provisions of Rule 5 of these Rules, in order to comply with the Instrument Flight Rules an aircraft shall not fly at a height of less than 1,000 feet above the highest obstacle within a distance of five nautical miles of the aircraft unless flying on a route notified for the purposes of this Rule, or otherwise authorised by the competent authority or unless it is necessary to do so in order to take off or land.

Quadrantal Rule and Semi-Circular Rule

27. In order to comply with the Instrument Flight Rules an aircraft when in level flight above 3,000 feet above mean sea level outside controlled airspace shall be flown at a level appropriate to its magnetic track, in accordance with the appropriate table set forth in this Rule.   The level of flight shall be measured by an altimeter set according to the system notified, or in the case of flight over a country other than the United Kingdom, otherwise published by the competent authority, in relation to the area over which the aircraft is flying:

Providing that an aircraft may be flown at a level other than the level required by this Rule if it is flying in conformity with instructions given by an air traffic control unit or in accordance with holding procedures notified in relation to an aerodrome.

TABLE I—*Flights at levels below 25,000 feet*

Magnetic Track	Cruising Level
Less than 90°	Odd thousands of feet.
90° but less than 180°	Odd thousands of feet +500 feet.
180° but less than 270°	Even thousands of feet.
270° but less than 360°	Even thousands of feet +500 feet.

TABLE II—*Flights at levels of 25,000 feet and above*

Magnetic Track	Cruising Level
Less than 180°	25,000 feet. 27,000 feet. 29,000 feet or higher levels at intervals of 4,000 feet.
180° but less than 360°	26,000 feet 28,000 feet. 31,000 feet or higher levels at intervals of 4,000 feet.

Flight Plan and Air Traffic Control Clearance

28.—(1) In order to comply with the Instrument Flight Rules, before an aircraft either takes off from a point within any controlled airspace or otherwise flies within any controlled airspace the commander of the aircraft shall cause a flight plan to be communicated to the appropriate air traffic control unit and shall obtain an air traffic control clearance based on such flight plan.

(2) The flight plan shall contain such particulars of the intended flight as may be necessary to enable the air traffic control unit to issue an air traffic control clearance, or for search and rescue purposes.

(3) The commander of the aircraft shall fly in conformity with

(a) the air traffic control clearance issued for the flight, as amended by any further instructions given by an air traffic control unit; and

(b) the holding and instrument approach procedures notified in relation to the aerodrome of destination, unless he is otherwise authorised by the air traffic control unit there:

Provided that he shall not be required to comply with the foregoing provisions of this paragraph if:

(i) he is able to fly in uninterrupted Visual Meteorological Conditions for so long as he remains in controlled airspace, and

(ii) he has infromed the appropriate air traffic control unit of his intention to continue the flight in compliance with Visual Flight Rules and has requested that unit to cancel his flight plan.

(4) If for the purpose of avoiding immediate danger any departure is made from the provisions of paragraph (3) of this Rule (as is permitted by Article 61(3) of the Order) the commander of the aircraft shall, in addition to causing particulars to be given in accordance with Article 61(4) of the Order, as soon as possible inform the appropriate air traffic control unit of the deviation.

(5) The commander of the aircraft after it has flown in controlled airspace shall, unless he has requested the appropriate air traffic control unit to cancel his flight plan, forthwith inform that unit when the aircraft lands within or leaves the controlled airspace.

Position Reports

29. In order to comply with the Instrument Flight Rules the commander of an aircraft in IFR flight who flies in or is intending to enter controlled airspace shall

report to the appropriate air control unit the time, and the position and altitude of the aircraft at such reporting points or at such intervals of time as may be notified for this purpose or as may be directed by the air traffic control unit.

SECTION VII

AERODROME TRAFFIC RULES

Application of Aerodrome Traffic Rules

30. The Rules in this Section of these Rules which are expressed to apply to flying machines shall also be observed, so far as is practicable, in relation to all other aircraft.

Visual Signals

31. The commander of a flying machine on, or in the traffic zone of, an aerodrome shall observe such visual signals as may be displayed at, or directed to him from the aerodrome by the authority of the person in charge of the aerodrome and shall obey any instructions which may be given to him by means of such signals:

Provided that he shall not be required to obey the signals referred to in Rule 46 of these Rules (Marshalling Signals) if in his opinion it is inadvisable to do so in the interests of safety.

Access to and movement on the Manoeuvring Area and other parts of the aerodrome used by aircraft

32.—(1) A person or vehicle shall not go on to any part of an aerodrome provided for the use of aircraft and under the control of the person in charge of the aerodrome without the permission of the person in charge of the aerodrome, and except in accordance with any conditions subject to which that permission may have been granted.

(2) A vehicle or person shall not go or move on the manoeuvring area of an aerodrome having an air traffic control unit without the permission of that unit, and except in accordance with any conditions subject to which that permission may have been granted.

(3) Any permission granted for the purposes of this Rule may be granted either in respect of persons or vehicles generally, or in respect of any particular person or vehicle or any class of person or vehicle.

Right of Way on the ground

33.—(1) This Rule shall apply to—

(*a*) flying machines; and

(*b*) vehicles

on any part of a land aerodrome provided for the use of aircraft and under the control of the person in charge of the aerodrome.

(2) Notwithstanding any air traffic control clearance it shall remain the duty of the commander of an aircraft to take all possible measures to ensure that his aircraft does not collide with any other aircraft or with any vehicle.

(3)(*a*) Flying machines and vehicles shall give way to aircraft which are taking off or landing.

(*b*) Vehicles, and flying machines which are not taking off or landing, shall give way to vehicles towing aircraft.

(*c*) Vehicles which are not towing aircraft shall give way to aircraft.

(4) Subject to the provisions of paragraph (3) of this Rule and of Rule 35(3)(*b*) of these Rules, in case of danger of collision between two flying machines—

(*a*) when the two flying machines are approaching head-on or approximately so, each shall alter its course to the right;

(b) when the two flying machines are on converging courses, the one which has the other on its right shall give way to the other and shall avoid crossing ahead of the other unless passing well clear of it;

(c) a flying machine which is being overtaken shall have the right-of-way, and the overtaking flying machine shall keep out of the way of the other flying machine by altering its course to the left until that other flying machine has been passed and is clear, notwithstanding any change in the relative positions of the two flying machines.

(5) Subject to the provisions of paragraph (3)(b) of this Rule a vehicle shall—

(a) overtake another vehicle so that the other vehicle is on the left of the overtaking vehicle;

(b) keep to the left when passing another vehicle which is approaching head-on or approximately so.

Dropping of Tow Ropes, etc.

34. Tow ropes, banners or similar articles towed by aircraft shall not be dropped from aircraft except at an aerodrome and:

(a) in accordance with arrangements made with an air traffic control unit at the aerodrome or, if there is no such unit, with the person in charge of the aerodrome or

(b) in the area designated by the marking described in Rule 43(7) of these Rules, and the ropes, banners or similar articles shall be dropped when the aircraft is flying in the direction appropriate for landing.

Aerodromes not having Air Traffic Control Units

35.—(1)(a)An aircraft shall not fly within a zone which the commander of the aircraft knows or ought reasonably to know to be the aerodrome traffic zone of an aerodrome where no air traffic control unit is for the time being notified as being on watch, except for the purpose of taking off or landing at that aerodrome or observing the signals in the signals area with a view to landing there, unless he has the permission of the person in charge of the aerodrome.

(b) An aircraft flying within such a zone for the purpose of observing the signals shall remain clear of cloud and at least 500 feet above the level of the aerodrome.

(2) The commander of an aircraft flying in such a zone or moving on such an aerodrome shall:

(a) conform to the pattern of traffic formed by other aircraft, or keep clear of the airspace in which the pattern is formed;

(b) make all turns to the left unless ground signals otherwise indicate; and

(c) take off and land in the direction indicated by the ground signals or, if no such signals are displayed, into the wind, unless good avation practice demands otherwise.

(3) (a) A flying machine or glider shall not land on a runway at such an aerodrome unless the runway is clear of other aircraft.

(b) Where take-offs and landings are not confined to a runway—

(i) a flying machine or glider when landing shall leave clear on its left any aircraft which has already landed or is already landing or is about to take off; if such a flying machine or glider is obliged to turn, it shall turn to the left after the commander of the aircraft has satisfied himself that such action will not interfere with other traffic movements; and

(ii) a flying machine about to take off shall take up position and manoeuvre in such a way as to leave clear on its left any aircraft which is already taking off or is about to take off.

(4) A flying machine after landing shall move clear of the landing area in use as soon as it is possible to do so.

Aerodromes having Air Traffic Control Units

36.—(1) An aircraft shall not fly within a zone which the commander of the aircraft knows or ought reasonably to know to be the aerodrome traffic zone of an aerodrome where an air traffic control unit is for the time being notified as being on watch, except for the purpose of observing any signals at that aerodrome with a view to landing there, unless he has the permission of the appropriate air traffic control unit.

(2) The commander of an aircraft flying in the aerodrome traffic zone of an aerodrome where an air traffic control unit is for the time being notified as being on watch or moving on such an aerodrome shall—

(*a*) cause a continuous watch to be maintained on the appropriate radio frequency notified for air traffic control communications at the aerodrome, or, if this is not possible, cause a watch to kept for such instructions as may be issued by visual means;

(*b*) not taxi on the apron or manoeuvring area or take off or land anywhere in the zone except with the permission of the air traffic control unit;

(*c*) comply with the provisions of Rule 35(1)(*b*), (2), (3) and (4) of these Rules as if the aerodrome did not have an air traffic control unit, unless he has the permission of the air traffic control unit at the aerodrome, or has been instructed by that unit, to do otherwise.

(3) Without prejudice to the provisions of Rules 21 and 28 of these Rules, the commander of an aircraft shall, immediately upon arrival at, or prior to departure from, an aerodrome within the United Kingdom having an air traffic control unit, ensure that such unit is informed of the flight which he has just made or which he is about to undertake.

Special Rules for certain Aerodromes

37.—(1) The special provisions set out in this Rule shall apply in addition to the other Rules in this Section, in relation to the aerodromes specified in this Rule.

(2) In relation to Glasgow and Prestwick Airports, 'the following special rules shall apply:

Unless it is otherwise authorised by an air traffic control unit at the aerodrome,

(*a*) an aircraft shall not fly at less than 2,000 feet above the notified elevation of the aerodrome within five nautical miles of the notified aerodrome reference point, unless the commander of the aircraft, before so flying, obtains the permission of the air traffic control unit at the aerodrome, and informs the air traffic control unit, on the notified radio frequency appropriate to the circumstances, of the aircraft's position, level and track; and

(*b*) while the aircraft is at less than 2,000 feet above the notified elevation of the aerodrome and within five nautical miles of the notified aerodrome reference point, the commander of the aircraft shall cause a continuous watch to be maintained on that frequency and comply with any instructions which the air traffic control unit at the aerodrome may give in the particular case:

Provided that this paragraph shall not apply to flights made outside the notified hours of watch of the air traffic control unit at the aerodrome.

(3) In relation to Blackpool Airport the following special rules shall apply:

(*a*) an aircraft shall not during the notified hours of watch of the air traffic control unit at the aerodrome fly within the aerodrome traffic zone of Blackpool Airport unless the commander of the aircraft, before so flying, obtains the permission of the air traffic control unit at the aerodrome; and

(*b*) while the aircraft is flying within the said aerodrome traffic zone at any time during the said hours of watch the commander of the aircraft shall cause a continuous watch to be maintained on the radio frequency required by that air traffic control unit, if the aircraft is suitably equipped for that purpose, and comply with any instructions which that air traffic control unit may give in the particular case.

(4) In relation to Glamorgan (Rhoose) Airport, the following special rules shall apply:

Unless it is otherwise authorised by the air traffic control unit at the aerodrome,

    (*a*) an aircraft shall not, during the notified hours of watch of the air control traffic unit at the aerodrome, fly within the relevant airspace unless the commander of the aircraft, before so flying, obtains the permission of the air traffic control unit at the aerodrome, and informs the air traffic control unit, on the notified radio frequency appropriate to the circumstances, of the aircraft's position, level and track;

    (*b*) while the aircraft is within the relevant airspace at any time during the said hours of watch the commander of the aircraft shall cause a continuous watch to be maintained on that frequency and comply with any instructions which the air traffic control unit at the aerodrome may give in the particular case.

For the purposes of this paragraph the "relevant airspace" means the airspace from the surface to flight level 55 within five nautical miles of the notified aerodrome reference point.

(5) In relation to Liverpool Airport the following special rules shall apply:

Unless it is otherwise authorised by the air traffic control unit at the aerodrome,

    (*a*) an aircraft shall not fly within the relevant airspace during the notified hours of watch of the air traffic control unit at the aerodrome unless the commander of the aircraft, before so flying, obtains the permission of the air traffic control unit at the aerodrome and informs the air traffic control unit, on the notified radio frequency appropriate to the circumstances, of the aircraft's position, level and track; and

    (*b*) while the aircraft is within the relevant airspace at any time during the said hours of watch the commander of the aircraft shall cause a continuous watch to be maintained on that frequency and comply with any instructions which the air traffic control unit at the aerodrome may give in the particular case.

For the purposes of this paragraph the "relevant airspace" means the airspace from the surface to 1,250 feet above mean sea level within the area defined by a straight line joining successively the points $53°19'03''N$ $02°36'52''W$ and $53°21'45''N$ $02°39'00''W$ and thence by tangents from those points to the circle with radius of six nautical miles centred on $53°20'20''N$ $02°53'00''W$.

(6) In relation to Southend Airport the following special rules shall apply:

Unless it is otherwise authorised by the air traffic control unit at the aerodrome,

    (*a*) an aircraft shall not, during the notified hours of watch of the air traffic control unit at the aerodrome, fly within eight nautical miles of the notified aerodrome reference point and at less than 6,500 feet above mean sea level, unless the commander of the aircraft, before so flying, obtains the permission of the air traffic control unit at the aerodrome and informs the air traffic control unit, on the notified radio frequency appropriate to the circumstances, of the aircraft's position, level and track; and

    (*b*) while the aircraft is within eight nautical miles of the notified aerodrome reference point, and at less than 6,500 feet above mean sea level at any time during the said hours of watch, the commander of the aircraft shall cause a continuous watch to be maintained on that frequency and comply with any instructions which the air traffic control unit at the aerodrome may give in the particular case:

Provided that except at night the special rules (*a*) and (*b*) shall not apply in relation to an aircraft which remains at least one nautical mile horizontally and 1,000 feet vertically away from cloud and in a flight visibility of at least five nautical miles.

(7) In relation to Gatwick Airport—London, the following special rules shall apply:

Unless it is otherwise authorised by the air traffic control unit at the aerodrome,

    (*a*) an aircraft shall not fly within the relevant airspace unless the commander of the aircraft, before so flying, obtains the permission of the air traffic control unit at the aerodrome and informs the air traffic control unit, on the notified radio frequency appropriate to the circumstances, of the aircraft's position, level and track; and

(b) while the aircraft is within the relevant airspace the commander of the aircraft shall cause a continuous watch to be maintained on that frequency and comply with any instructions which the air traffic control unit at the aerodrome may give in the particular case.

For the purposes of this paragraph the "relevant airspace" means the airspace from the surface to 2,000 feet above the notified elevation of the aerodrome within that part of a circle having a radius of eight nautical miles from 51°08′54″N 00°11′25″W, which lies between two straight lines joining respectively the points 51°10′20″N 00°24′00″W to 51°13′15″N 00°00′45″W and 51°02′48″N 00°19′50″W to 51°05′11″N 00°00′05″W.

(8) In relation to Birmingham Airport, the following special rules shall apply:

Unless it is otherwise authorised by the air traffic control unit at the aerodrome,

(a) an aircraft shall not, during the notified hours of watch of the air traffic control unit at the aerodrome, fly within the relevant airspace unless the commander of the aircraft, before so flying, obtains the permission of the air traffic control unit at the aerodrome and informs the air traffic control unit, on the notified radio frequency appropriate to the circumstances, of the aircraft's position, level and track; and

(b) while the aircraft is within the relevant airspace at any time during the said hours of watch the commander of the aircraft shall cause a continuous watch to be maintained on that frequency and comply with any instructions which the air traffic control unit at the aerodrome may give in the particular case.

For the purposes of this paragraph the "relevant airspace" means the airspace within eight nautical miles of the notified aerodrome reference point—

(i) to the north east of any point on a straight line joining the points 52°35′05″N 01°42′25″W and 52°26′25″N 01°31′55″W from the surface to flight level 35; and

(ii) in the remainder of that area, from the surface to flight level 110.

(9)(a) In relation to Lyneham Aerodrome, the special rules set forth in sub-paragraph (b) of this paragraph shall apply to the airspace (in this paragraph called the "relevant airspace")

(i) from the surface to 3,000 feet above mean sea level within the area defined by straight lines joining successively the following points 51°36′20″N 02°08′38″W to 51°38′12″N 02°03′08″W to 51°37′25″N 01°48′10″W thence by that part of the arc of a circle radius 8 nautical miles centred on 51°31′25″N 01°56′32″W to 51°24′32″N 01°50′05″W thence by a straight line to 51°22′31″N 01°55′40″W and thence by that part of the arc of a circle radius 8 nautical miles centred on 51°29′25″N 02°02′08″W to 51°36′20″N 02°08′38″W; and

(ii) from 3,000 feet above mean sea level to flight level 65 vertically above the area specified in (i) above; and

(iii) from flight level 40 to flight level 65 within the area defined by straight lines joining successively the following points 51°37′25″N 01°48′10″W to 51°36′57″N 01°39′19″W to 51°26′57″N 01°40′43″W to 51°27′13″N 01°45′39″W; thence by that part of the arc of a circle radius 8 nautical miles centred on 51°31′25″N 01°56′32″W to 51°37′25″N 01°48′10″W.

(b) Unless it is otherwise authorised by the air traffic control unit at the aerodrome,

(i) an aircraft shall not fly within the relevant airspace unless the commander of the aircraft, before so flying, obtains the permission of the air traffic control unit at the aerodrome and informs the air traffic control unit, on the notified radio frequency appropriate to the circumstances, of the aircraft's position, level and track; and

(ii) while the aircraft is within the relevant airspace the commander of the aircraft shall cause a continuous watch to be maintained on the notified radio frequency appropriate to the circumstances and comply with any instructions which the air traffic control unit at the aerodrome may give in the particular case:

Provided that this sub-paragraph shall not apply in relation to an aircraft which:

(a) flies in Visual Meteorological Conditions within that part of the relevant airspace specified in sub-paragraph (a)(ii) and (iii) of this paragraph: or

(b) remains in sight of the surface clear of cloud and in a flight visibility of at least one nautical mile and which is not equipped with radio capable of operating on the said radio frequency whilst flying within that part of the relevant airspace—

from the surface to 1,900 feet above mean sea level east of a straight line joining 51°37′37″N 01°51′08″W and 51°29′38″N 01°44′00″W; or from the surface to 1,500 feet above mean sea level south of a straight line joining 51°22′57″N 02°09′40″W and 51°21′57″N 01°57′45″W; or

(c) flies within the airspace from the surface to 1,900 feet above mean sea level within an area comprising a circle of radius 2½ nautical miles centred on 51°30′20″N 01°48′00″W (Wroughton Aerodrome) excluding that part of the circle east of a straight line joining 51°32′42″N 01°46′44″W and 51°29′45″N 01°44′08″W.

(10) In relation to Leeds and Bradford Airport the following special rules shall apply: Unless it is otherwise authorised by the air traffic control unit at the aerodrome,

(a) an aircraft shall not, during the notified hours of watch of the air traffic control unit at the aerodrome, fly within the relevant airspace unless the commander of the aircraft, before so flying, obtains the permission of the air traffic control unit at the aerodrome and informs the air traffic control unit, on the notified radio frequency appropriate to the circumstances, of the aircraft's position, level and track; and

(b) while the aircraft is within the relevant airspace at any time during the said hours of watch, the commander of the aircraft shall cause a continuous watch to be maintained on that frequency and comply with any instructions which the air traffic control unit at that aerodrome may give in the particular case:

Provided that except at night the special rules (a) and (b) shall not apply to an aircraft flying within the relevant airspace which remains at least one nautical mile horizontally and 1,000 feet vertically away from cloud and in a flight visibility of at least five nautical miles.

For the purposes of this paragraph the "relevant airspace" means the airspace from the surface to flight level 85 above the aerodrome within that part of a circle having a radius of eight nautical miles centred on 53°52′00″N 01°39′10″W (Leeds and Bradford Airport) except that part of the circle on the east side of straight lines joining successively the points 54°00′00″N 01°38′45″W, 53°56′20″N 01°33′20″W and 53°53′45″N 01°31′00″W, 53 46′45″N 01°29′00″W.

(11)(a) In relation to Luton Airport, the special rules set forth in sub-paragraph (c) of this paragraph shall, subject to the provisions of sub-paragraph (b) of this paragraph, apply to the airspace (in this paragraph called "the relevant airspace")—

(i) from the surface to 3,500 feet above mean sea level within the area defined by straight lines joining successively the following points:

51°57′31″N	00°21′20″W;	51°55′30″N	00°16′32″W:
51°55′57″N	00°13′33″W;	51°52′03″N	00°11′50″W;
51°51′40″N	00°14′10″W.		

thence by that part of the arc of a circle radius 5 nautical miles centred on 51°52′27″N 00°22′13″W (Luton Airport) to 51°49′20″N 00°28′30″W and thence by straight lines joining successively the following points:

51°49′00″N	00°30′40″W:	51°51′27″N	00°31′46″W;
51°52′10″N	00°27′30″W;	51°57′31″N	00°21′20″W;

and

(ii) from 2,000 feet above mean sea level to 3,500 feet above mean sea level within the areas defined by straight lines joining successively the following points:

51°56′27″N	00°10′22″W;	51°52′32″W;	00°08′45″W;
51°52′03″N	00°11′50″W;	51°55′57″N	00 13′33″W;
51°56′27″N	00°10′22″W and		
51°51′27″N	00°31′46″W;	51°49′00″N	00°30′40″W;
51°48′30″N	00°33′50″W;	51°50′56″N	00°34′50″W;
51°51′27″N	00°31′46″W.		

(b) The relevant airspace shall not include that part of a circle radius 2 nautical miles centred on 51°52′07″N 00°32′50″W (at Dunstable Downs Aerodrome) south of a straight line joining 51°51′48″N 00°29′36″W and 51°50′56″N 00°34′50″W but nevertheless the special rules set forth in sub-paragraph (c) shall be complied with by an aircraft as if it was in the relevant airspace whenever the commander of that aircraft has reason to believe that any other aircraft is, at the time, in the course of landing on runway 08 at Luton Airport.

(c) Unless it is otherwise authorised by the air traffic control unit at Luton aerodrome,

(i) an aircraft shall not fly within the relevant airspace unless the commander of the aircraft, before so flying, obtains the permission of the air traffic control unit at the aerodrome and informs the air traffic control unit, on the notified radio frequency appropriate to the circumstances, of the aircraft's position, level and track; and

(ii) while the aircraft is within the relevant airspace the commander of the aircraft shall cause a continuous watch to be maintained on the notified radio frequency appropriate to the circumstances and comply with any instructions which the air traffic control unit at the aerodrome may give in the particular case:

Provided that sub-paragraphs (i) and (ii) shall not apply to a glider on a flight to or from Dunstable Downs Aerodrome or to an aeroplane which is towing or has released a glider in the course of such a flight, if the following conditions are complied with:

(aa) the commander of the glider or of the aeroplane, as the case may be, has reason to believe that at the time no aircraft is in the course of landing on runway 08 at Luton Airport; and

(bb) the glider or aeroplane, as the case may be, flies within that part of the relevant airspace specified in sub-paragraph (a)(i) of this paragraph north of a straight line joining 51°49′55″N 00°31′05″W, 51°50′18″N 00°29′30″W, 51°52′10″N 00°27′30″W, and specified in sub-paragraph (a)(ii) of this paragraph north of a straight line joining 51°49′08″N 00°34′05″W, 51°49′55″N 00°31′05″W, and remains at least one nautical mile horizontally and 1,000 feet vertically away from cloud and in a flight visibility of at least 5 nautical miles.

SECTION VIII

SPECIAL RULES FOR LOW-LEVEL CROSS-CHANNEL AIR TRAFFIC

38.—(1) Notwithstanding the provisions of Rule 23, during the notified hours of watch of the air traffic control unit at Lydd Airport, the following special rules shall apply to the airspace (in this Rule called "the relevant airspace")

over the sea, between 500 feet and 4,500 feet,
elsewhere, between 1,000 feet and 4,500 feet

above mean sea level within the area defined by straight lines joining successively the following points:

51°30′00″N 00°53′10″E;	51°30′00″N 02°00′00″E;	51°07′00″N 02°00′00″E;
51°00′00″N 01°28′00″E;	50°40′00″N 01°28′00″E;	50°36′20″N 01°18′30″E;
50°57′42″N 00°43′23″E;	51°08′30″N 00°52′00″E;	51°18′50″N 00°53′10″E;
51°26′20″N 00°45′50″E;	and thence by that part of the arc of a circle radius	

eight nautical miles centred on Southend Airport (51°34'15"N 00°42'00"E) to 51°30'00"N 00°53'10"E;

from 4,500 feet to 6,000 feet above mean sea level within that part of the aforesaid area which lies north of a line from 51°26'20"N 00°45'50"E to 51°22'28"N 01°26'51"E and thence to 51°16'00"N 02°00'00"E;

and from the surface—

over the sea, to 500 feet above mean sea level,
elsewhere, to 1,000 feet above mean sea level

within—

    (i) an area comprising two circles each with a radius of five nautical miles whose centres are at 50°57'16"N, 00°56'22"E (Lydd Airport) and 51°04'50"N 01°01'10"E (Ashford Airport) respectively and the area enclosed between those circles and two parallel lines each forming a tangent to both circles; and

    (ii) an area comprising two circles each with a radius of 5 nautical miles whose centres are at 51°20'30"N 01°20'50"E and 51°19'35"N 01°28'35"E respectively and the area enclosed between those circles and two parallel lines each forming a tangent to both circles and an adjoining area defined by straight lines joining successively the following points:

      51°19'35"N 01°13'00"E; 51°20'40"N 01°04'30"E;
      51°24'40"N 01°05'45"E; 51°23'30"N 01°14'15"E

but excluding such parts of that airspace as may from time to time be notified as controlled airspace, including that notified for the purpose of Rule 22 of these Rules.

(2) The commander of an aircraft who intends to fly within the relevant airspace shall before so flying cause to be communicated to the appropriate air traffic control unit a flight plan containing particulars of the time at which and the level and track on which the aircraft is intended to pass through the relevant airspace, and such particulars of the intended flight as may be necessary for search and rescue purposes.

(3) The commander of an aircraft shall, before the aircraft enters the relevant airspace, inform the air traffic control unit serving that part of the relevant airspace which the aircraft is about to enter, on the notified radio frequency appropriate to the circumstances, of the time, position and level at which the aircraft will enter that airspace, and when the aircraft leaves the relevant airspace, shall inform the air traffic control unit serving the area which the aircraft is leaving, on the said frequency, of the time, position and level at which the aircraft is leaving the relevant airspace.

(4) While flying within the relevant airspace, the commander of an aircraft shall—

    (a) cause a continuous watch to be maintained on the notified radio frequency appropriate to the circumstances; and

    (b) measure the level of flight by means of an altimeter set according to the system notified for the relevant airspace; and

    (c) comply with any instructions which the appropriate air traffic control unit may give in the particular case.

(5) Paragraphs (3) and (4)(a) of this Rule shall not apply to aircraft which are not equipped with radio capable of operating on the radio frequency therein referred to. Such aircraft shall not fly within the relevant airspace except in accordance with procedures and on a route notified for that purpose or in conformity with an air traffic control clearance issued for the flight by the appropriate air traffic control unit and when flying within the relevant airspace shall remain in sight of the surface, clear of cloud and in a flight visibility of at least three nautical miles.

(6) These special rules shall not apply in relation to any glider which remains at least one nautical mile horizontally and 1,000 feet vertically away from cloud, in a flight visibility of at least five nautical miles and outside those parts of the relevant airspace between the surface and 4,500 feet above mean sea level which fall within the areas specified in paragraph (1)(i) and (ii) of this Rule.

Section IX

Special Rules for Air Traffic in the Upper Flight Information Regions

39.—(1) The following special rules shall apply to the airspace (in this Rule called "the relevant airspace") from flight level 250 to flight level 460 within the area defined by straight lines joining successively the following points:-

61°00′00″N	06°00′00″W;	61°00′00″N	00°00′00″;
60°00′00″N	00°00′00″;	57°00′00″N	05°00′00″E;
55°00′00″N	05°00′00″E;	52°30′00″N	02°48′30″E;
51°30′00″N	02°00′00″E;	51°07′00″N	02°00′00″E;
51°00′00″N	01°28′00″E;	50°40′00″N	01°28′00″E;
50°00′00″N	00°15′00″W;	50°00′00″N	02°00′00″W;
48°50′00″N	08°00′00″W;	51°00′00″N	08°00′00″W;
52°20′00″N	05°30′00″W;	53°55′00″N	05°30′00″W;
54°57′30″N	05°30′00″W;	55°00′00″N	05°00′00″W;
54°45′00″N	03°42′00″W;	54°50′00″N	03°16′00″W;
55°35′00″N	03°12′00″W;	58°15′00″N	06°00′00″W;
61°00′00″N	06°00′00″W.		

(2) The commander of an aircraft who intends to fly within the relevant airspace shall, before so flying, cause to be communicated to the appropriate air traffic control unit a flight plan containing particulars of the time at which and the level and track on which the aircraft is intended to pass through the relevant airspace, and such particulars of the intended flight as may be necessary for search and rescue purposes.

(3) The commander of an aircraft shall, before the aircraft enters the relevant airspace, obtain the permission of the appropriate air traffic control unit.

(4) While flying within the relevant airspace, the commander of an aircraft shall:

(a) cause a continuous watch to be maintained on the notified radio frequency appropriate to the circumstances; and

(b) measure the flight level by means of an altimeter set to 1013·2 millibars; and

(c) comply with any instructions which the appropriate air traffic control unit may give in the particular case.

(5) These special rules shall not apply in relation to any glider flying within the relevant airspace.

Section X

Aerodrome Signals and Markings; Visual and Aural Signals

General

40.—(1) Whenever any signal specified in this Section of these Rules is given or displayed, or whenever any marking so specified is displayed, by any person in an aircraft, or at an aerodrome, or at any other place which is being used by aircraft for landing or take-off, it shall, when given or displayed in the United Kingdom, have the meaning assigned to it in this Section.

(2) All dimensions specified in this Section of these Rules shall be subject to a tolerance of 10 per cent, plus or minus.

Signals in the Signals area

41.—(1) When any signal specified in the following paragraphs of this Rule is displayed it shall be placed in a signals area, which shall be a square visible in all directions bordered by a white strip 30 centimetres wide the internal sides measuring 12 metres.

(2) A white landing T, as illustrated in this paragraph,

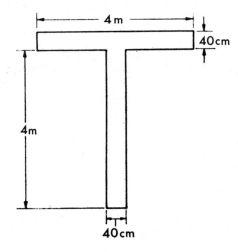

Fig 1

signifies that aeroplanes and gliders taking off or landing shall do so in a direction parallel with the shaft of the T and towards the cross arm, unless otherwise authorised by the appropriate air traffic control unit.

(3) A white disc 60 centimetres in diameter displayed alongside the cross arm of the T and in line with the shaft of the T, as illustrated in this paragraph,

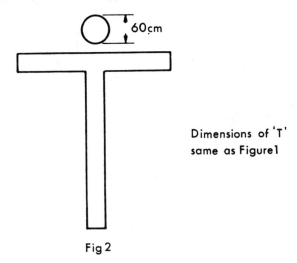

Dimensions of 'T' same as Figure 1

Fig 2

signifies that the direction of landing and take-off do not necessarily coincide.

(4) A white dumb-bell, as illustrated in this paragraph,

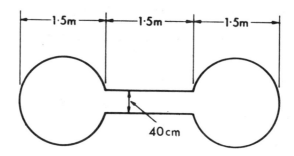

Fig 3

signifies that movements of aeroplanes and gliders on the ground shall be confined to paved, metalled or similar hard surfaces.

(5) A white dumb-bell as described in (4) above but with a black strip 60 centimetres wide across each disc at right angles to the shaft of the dumb-bell, as illustrated in this paragraph,

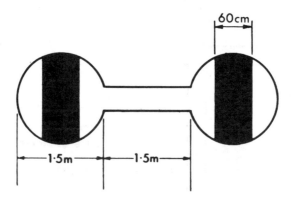

Fig 4

signifies that aeroplanes and gliders taking off or landing shall do so on a runway but that movement on the ground is not confined to paved, metalled or similar hard surfaces.

(6) A red and yellow striped arrow, as illustrated in this paragraph,

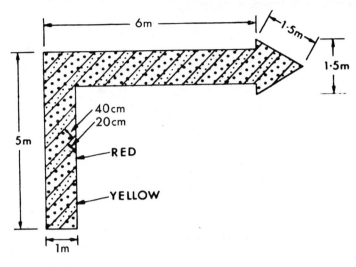

Fig 5

the shaft of which is at least one metre wide placed along the whole or not less than a total of 11 metres of two adjacent sides of the signals area and pointing in a clockwise direction signifies that a right-hand circuit is in force.

(7) A red panel 3 metres square with a yellow strip along one diagonal at least 50 centimetres wide, as illustrated in this paragraph,

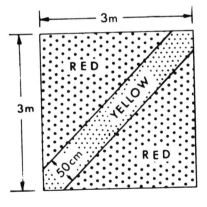

Fig 6

signifies that the state of the manoeuvring area is poor and pilots must exercise special care when landing.

(8) A red panel 3 metres square with a yellow strip, at least 50 centimetre wide, along each diagonal, as illustrated in this paragraph,

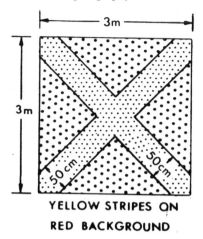

Fig 7

signifies that the aerodrome is unsafe for the movement of aircraft and that landing on the aerodrome is prohibited.

(9) A white letter H, as illustrated in this paragraph,

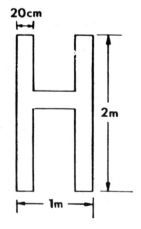

Fig 8

signifies that helicopters shall take off and land only within the area designated by the marking specified in Rule 43(5) of these Rules.

(10) A red letter L displayed on the dumb-bell specified in paragraphs (4) and (5) of this Rule, as illustrated in this paragraph,

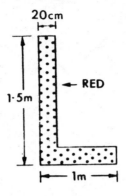

Fig 9

signifies that light aircraft are permitted to take off and land either on a runway or on the area designated by the marking specified in Rule 43(6) of these Rules.

(11) A white double cross, as illustrated in this paragraph,

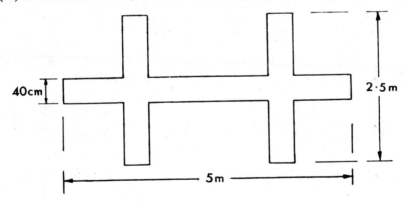

Fig 10

signifies that glider flying is in progress.

Markings for Paved Runways and Taxiways

42 (1) Two or more white crosses, as illustrated in this paragraph,

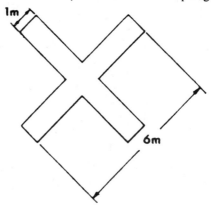

Fig 11

displayed on a runway or taxiway, with the arms of the crosses at an angle of 45° to the centre line of the runway, at intervals of not more than 300 metres signify that the section of the runway or taxiway marked by them is unfit for the movement of aircraft.

(2) A broken white line and a continuous line, as illustrated in this paragraph,

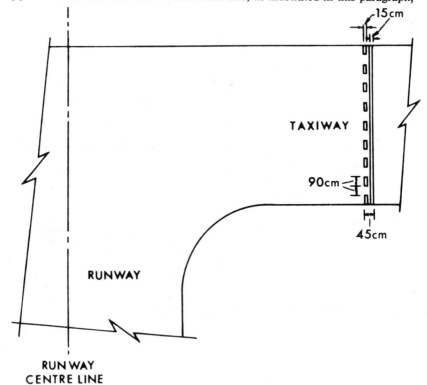

Fig 12

signify a holding position beyond which no part of an aircraft or vehicle shall project in the direction of the runway without permission from an air traffic control unit.

(3) Orange and white markers, as illustrated in this paragraph,

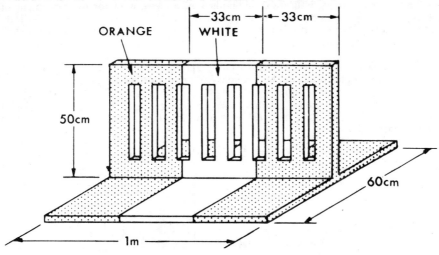

Fig 13

spaced not more than 15 metres apart, signify the boundary of that part of a paved runway, taxiway or apron which is unfit for the movement of aircraft.

Markings on Unpaved Manoeuvring Areas

43.—(1) Markers with orange and white stripes of an equal width of not less than 50 centimetres, with an orange stripe at each end, as illustrated in this paragraph,

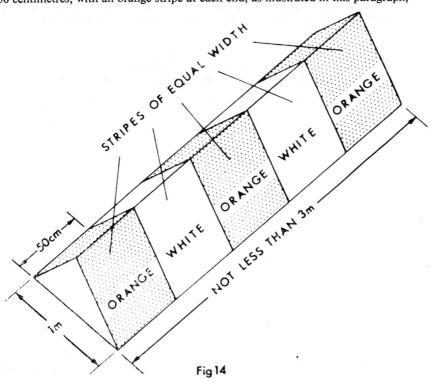

Fig 14

alternating with flags not less than 60 centimetres square showing equal orange and white triangular areas, indicate the boundary of an area unfit for the movement of aircraft and one or more white crosses as specified in Rule 42(1) of these Rules indicate the said area.   The distance between any two successive orange and white flags shall not exceed 90 metres.

(2) Striped markers, as specified in paragraph (1) of this Rule, spaced not more than 45 metres apart, indicate the boundary of an aerodrome.

(3) On structures, markers with orange and white vertical stripes, of an equal width of not less than 50 centimetres, with an orange stripe at each end, as illustrated in this paragraph,

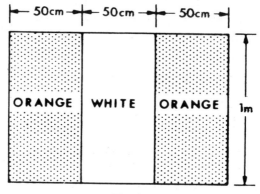

Fig. 15.

spaced not more than 45 metres apart, indicate the boundary of an aerodrome.   The pattern of the marker shall be visible from inside and outside the aerodrome and the marker shall be affixed not more than 15 centimetres from the top of the structure.

(4) White flat rectangular markers 3 metres long and 1 metre wide at intervals not exceeding 90 metres, flush with the surface of the unpaved runway or stopway, as the case may be, indicate the boundary of an unpaved runway or of a stopway.

(5) A white letter H, as illustrated in this paragraph,

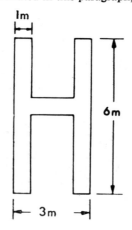

Fig 16

indicates an area which shall be used only for the taking off and landing of helicopters.

(6) A white letter L as illustrated in this paragraph,

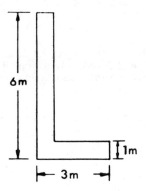

Fig 17

indicates a part of the manoeuvring area which shall be used only for the taking off and landing of light aircraft.

(7) A yellow cross with two arms 6 metres long by 1 metre wide at right angles, indicates that tow ropes and similar articles towed by aircraft shall only be dropped in the area in which the cross is placed.

(8) A white double cross as illustrated in this paragraph,

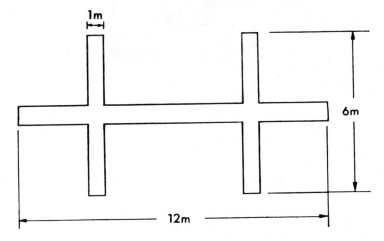

Fig 18

indicates an area which shall be used only for the taking off and landing of gliders.

(9) A white landing T as specified in Rule 41(2) of these Rules placed at the left hand side of the runway when viewed from the direction of landing indicates the runway to be used, and at an aerodrome with no runway it indicates the direction for take-off and landing.

Signals Visible from the Ground

44.—(1) A black ball 60 centimetres in diameter suspended from a mast signifies that the directions of take-off and landing are not necessarily the same.

(2) A checkered flag or board, 1·2 metres by 90 centimetres containing twelve equal squares, 4 horizontally and 3 vertically, coloured red and yellow alternately, signifies that aircraft may move on the manoeuvring area and apron only in accordance with the permission of the air traffic control unit at the aerodrome.

(3) Two red balls 60 centimetres in diameter, disposed vertically one above the other, 60 centimetres apart and suspended from a mast, signify that glider flying is in progress at the aerodrome.

(4) Black arabic numerals in two-figure groups and, where parallel runways are provided the letter or letters L (left), LC (left centre), C (centre), RC (right centre) and R (right), placed against a yellow background, indicate the direction for take-off or the runway in use.

(5) A black letter C against a yellow background, as illustrated in this paragraph,

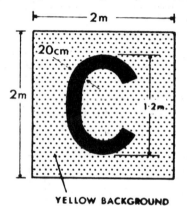

YELLOW BACKGROUND

Fig 19

indicates the position at which a pilot can report to the air traffic control unit or to the person in charge of the aerodrome.

(6) A rectangular green flag of not less than 60 centimetres square flown from a mast indicates that a right hand circuit is in force.

Lights and Pyrotechnic Signals for Control of Aerodrome Traffic

45. Each signal described in the first column of Table A, when directed from an aerodrome to an aircraft or to a vehicle, or from an aircraft, shall have the meanings respectively appearing in the second, third and fourth columns of that Table opposite the description of the signal.

TABLE A

MEANING OF LIGHTS AND PYROTECHNIC SIGNALS (RULE 45)

Characteristic and colour of light beam or pyrotechnic	From an aerodrome		From an aircraft in flight to an aerodrome
	to an aircraft in flight	to an aircraft or vehicle on the aerodrome	
(a) Continuous red light	Give way to other aircraft and continue circling.	Stop.	—
(b) Red pyrotechnic light, or Red flare	Do not land; wait for permission.	—	Immediate assistance is requested.
(c) Red flashes... ...	Do not land; aerodrome not available for landing.	Move clear of landing area.	—
(d) Green flashes ...	Return to aerodrome; wait for permission to land.	To an aircraft: You may move on the manoeuvring area and apron; To a vehicle: You may move on the manoeuvring area.	—
(e) Continuous green light	You may land.	You may take off (not applicable to a vehicle).	—
(f) Continuous green light, or Green flashes, or Green pyrotechnic light	—	—	By night: May I land? By day: May I land in direction different from that indicated by landing T?
(g) White flashes ...	Land at this aerodrome after receiving continuous green light, and then, after receiving green flashes, proceed to the apron.	Return to starting point on the aerodrome.	I am compelled to land.
(h) White pyrotechnic lights Switching on and off the navigation lights Switching on and off the landing lights	—	—	I am compelled to land.

Marshalling Signals (from a marshaller to an aircraft)

46. Each of the signals for the guidance of aircraft manœuvring on or off the ground, described in the first column of Table B, paragraphs (a) to (x) shall, in the United Kingdom, have the meaning set forth in the second column of that Table opposite the description of the signal. By day any such signals shall be given by hand or by circular bats and by night by torches or illuminated wands.

TABLE B—MEANING OF MARSHALLING SIGNALS (RULE 46)

Description of Signal	Meaning of Signal	In Daylight	By Night
(a) Right or left arm down, the other arm moved across body and extended to indicate position of the other marshaller.	Proceed under guidance of another marshaller.		
(b) Arms repeatedly moved upward and backward, beckoning onward.	Move ahead.		

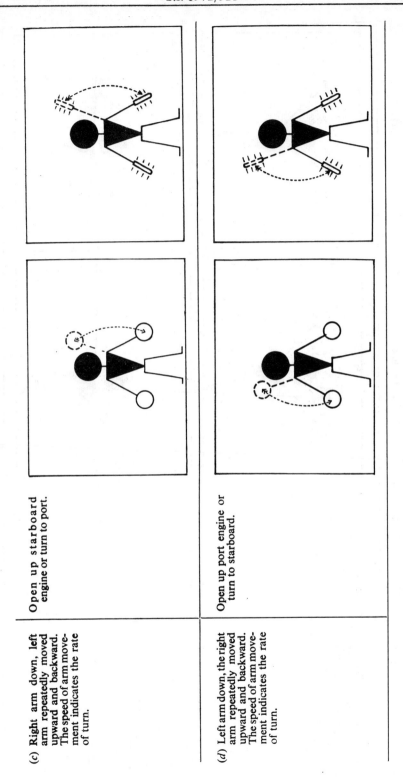

(c) **Right arm down, left arm repeatedly moved upward and backward. The speed of arm movement indicates the rate of turn.**

Open up starboard engine or turn to port.

(d) Left arm down, the right arm repeatedly moved upward and backward. The speed of arm movement indicates the rate of turn.

Open up port engine or turn to starboard.

Description of Signal	Meaning of Signal	In Daylight	By Night
(e) Arms repeatedly crossed above the head. The speed of arm movement indicates the urgency of the stop.	Stop.		
(f) A circular motion of the right hand at head level, with the left arm pointing to the appropriate engine.	Start engines.		

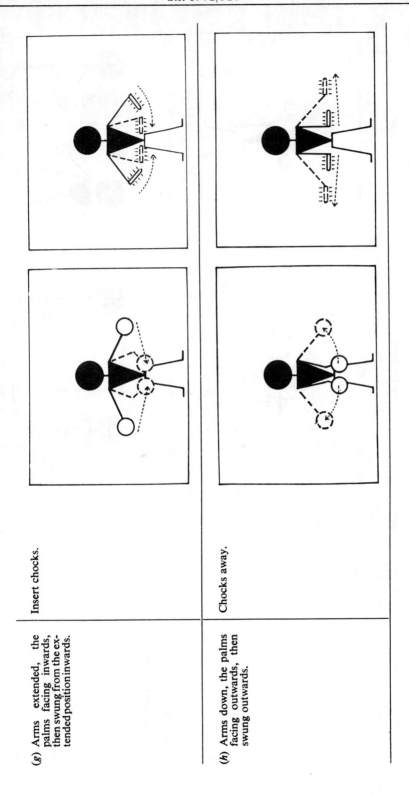

(g) Arms extended, the palms facing inwards, then swung from the extended position inwards.

Insert chocks.

(h) Arms down, the palms facing outwards, then swung outwards.

Chocks away.

Description of Signal	Meaning of Signal	In Daylight	By Night
(j) Either arm and hand placed level with the chest, then moved laterally with the palm downwards.	Cut engines.		
(k) Arms placed down, with the palms towards the ground, then moved up and down several times.	Slow down.		

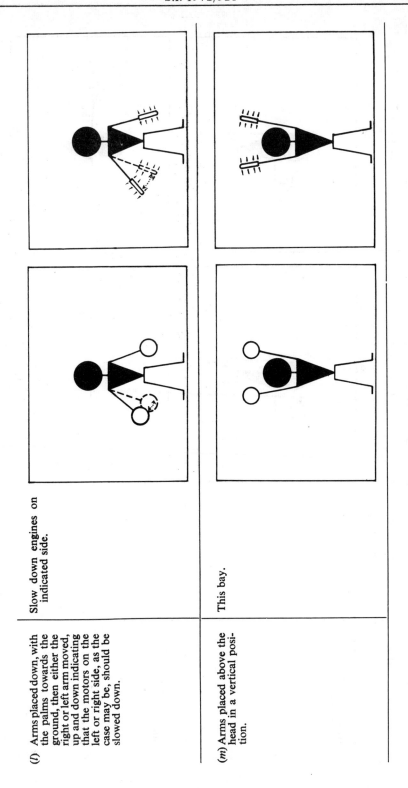

(*l*) Arms placed down, with the palms towards the ground, then either the right or left arm moved, up and down indicating that the motors on the left or right side, as the case may be, should be slowed down.

Slow down engines on indicated side.

(*m*) Arms placed above the head in a vertical position.

This bay.

Description of Signal	Meaning of Signal	In Daylight	By Night
(*n*) The right arm raised at the elbow, with the arm facing forward.	All clear: Marshalling finished.		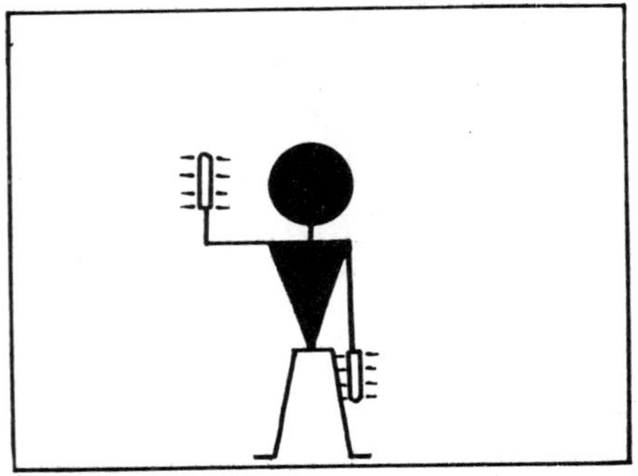
(*o*) Arms placed horizontally sideways.	Hover.		

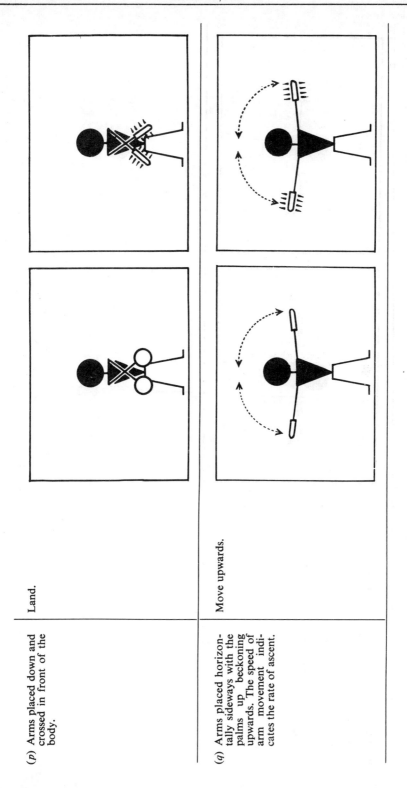

(*p*) Arms placed down and crossed in front of the body.

Land.

(*q*) Arms placed horizontally sideways with the palms up beckoning upwards. The speed of arm movement indicates the rate of ascent.

Move upwards.

Description of Signal	Meaning of Signal	In Daylight	By Night
(r) Arms placed horizontally sideways with the palms towards the ground beckoning downwards. The speed of arm movement indicates the rate of descent.	Move downwards.		

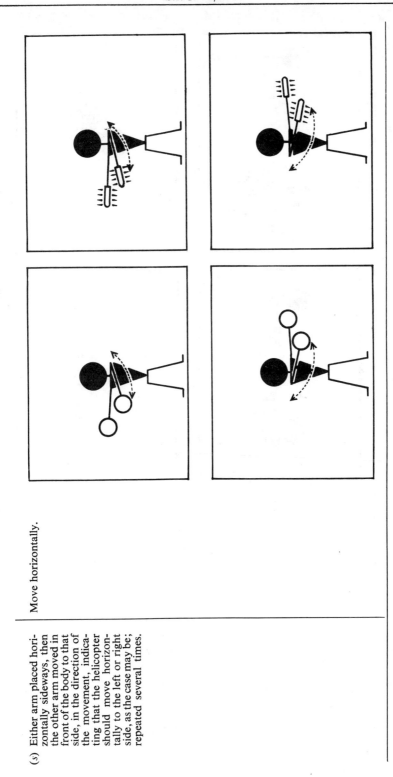

Move horizontally.

(s) Either arm placed horizontally sideways, then the other arm moved in front of the body to that side, in the direction of the movement, indicating that the helicopter should move horizontally to the left or right side, as the case may be; repeated several times.

Description of Signal	Meaning of Signal	In Daylight	By Night
(t) Arms placed down, the palms facing forward, then repeatedly swept up and down to shoulder level.	Move back		
(u) Left arm extended horizontally forward, then right arm making a horizontal slicing movement below left arm.	Release load		

(v) Raise arm, with fist clenched, horizontally in front of body, then extend fingers.

Release brakes

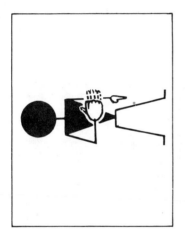

Raise arm and hand, with fingers extended, horizontally in front of body, then clench fist.

Engage brakes

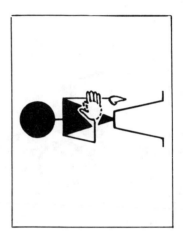

Description of Signal	Meaning of Signal	In Daylight
(w) Left hand overhead with the number of fingers extended, to indicate the number of the engine to be started, and circular motion of right hand at head level.	Start engine(s)	

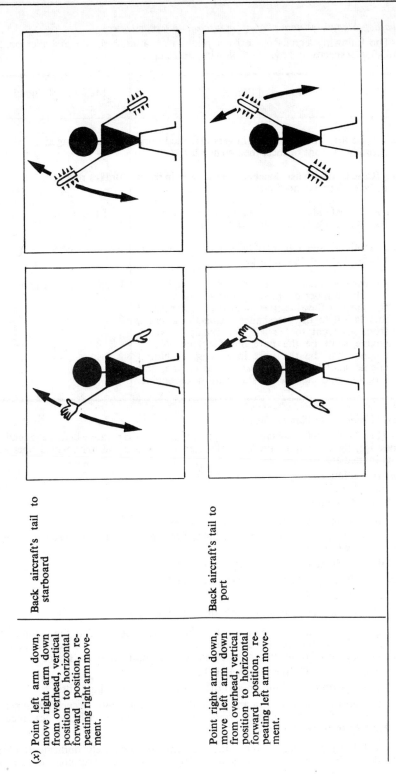

Back aircraft's tail to starboard

Back aircraft's tail to port

(x) Point left arm down, move right arm down from overhead, vertical position to horizontal forward position, repeating right arm movement.

Point right arm down, move left arm down from overhead, vertical position to horizontal forward position, repeating left arm movement.

Marshalling Signals (from a pilot of an aircraft to a marshaller)

47. The following signals made by a pilot in an aircraft to a marshaller on the ground shall respectively have the following meanings:—

Description of Signal	Meaning of Signal
(a) Raise arm and hand with fingers extended horizontally in front of face, then clench fist.	Brakes engaged.
(b) Raise arm with fist clenched horizontally in front of face, then extend fingers.	Brakes released.
(c) Arms extended palms facing outwards, move hands inwards to cross in front of face.	Insert chocks.
(d) Hands crossed in front of face, palms, facing outwards, move arms outwards.	Remove chocks.
(e) Raise the number of fingers on one hand indicating the number of the engine to be started. For this purpose the aircraft engines shall be numbered in relation to the marshaller facing the aircraft, from his right to his left, for example, No. 1 engine shall be the port outer engine, No. 2 engine shall be the port inner engine, No. 3 engine shall be the starboard inner engine, and No. 4 engine shall be the starboard outer engine.	Ready to start engines.

Distress, Urgency and Safety Signals

48.—(1) The following signals, given either together or separately before the sending of a message, signify that an aircraft is threatened by grave and imminent danger and requests immediate assistance:

(a) by radiotelephony:
the spoken word "MAYDAY";

(b) visual signalling:

(i) the signal SOS (. . . — — — . . .);

(ii) a succession of pyrotechnic lights fired at short intervals each showing a single red light;

(iii) a parachute flare showing a red light;

(c) by sound signalling other than radiotelephony:

(i) the signal SOS (. . . — — — . . .);

(ii) a continuous sounding with any sound apparatus.

(2) The following signals, given either together or separately, before the sending of a message, signify that the commander of the aircraft wishes to give notice of difficulties which compel it to land but that he does not require immediate assistance:

(a) a succession of white pyrotechnic lights;

(b) the repeated switching on and off of the aircraft landing lights;

(c) the repeated switching on and off of its navigation lights, in such a manner as to be clearly distinguishable from the flashing navigation lights described in Rule 11 of these Rules.

(3) The following signals, given either together or separately, indicate that the commander of the aircraft has an urgent message to transmit concerning the safety of

a ship, aircraft, vehicle or other property or of a person on board or within sight of the aircraft from which the signal is given:

(*a*) by radiotelephony:
the spoken word "PAN";

(*b*) by visual signalling:
the signal XXX (— . . — — . .— — . . —);

(*c*) by sound signalling other than radiotelephony:
the signal XXX (— . . — — . . — —. . —).

Warning Signals to Aircraft in Flight

49. In the United Kingdom, the following signals shall respectively have the following meanings:

(*a*) (i) by day—a series of projectiles discharged at intervals of ten seconds, each showing on bursting black or white smoke, or

(ii) by night—a series of projectiles discharged at intervals of ten seconds, each showing on bursting white lights or stars, or an intermittent white luminous beam directed at the aircraft,

indicates that the aircraft to which the signal is directed is in the vicinity of such an area as is referred to in Article 65(1)(*c*) of the Order and is required to change its course;

(*b*) by day or by night, a series of projectiles discharged at intervals of ten seconds, each showing on bursting green lights or stars indicates that the aircraft is required to land at the nearest aerodrome in accordance with the provisions of Article 65 of the Order.

SECTION XI

GROUND LIGHTING

Minimum Ground Lighting

50.—(1) The person in charge of any area to which this Rule applies shall cause the lighting specified in Rules 51 to 56, inclusive, of these Rules to be in operation whenever a flying machine or glider, flying for the purpose of the public transport of passengers, is taking off or landing at that area by night and during such period before or after the take off or landing as may be necessary to ensure the safety of the aircraft:

Provided that, if the area is intended for use only by helicopters, there may be in operation in lieu of the lighting specified in Rules 51, 52, 55 and 56 of these Rules, such other lighting as will enable the pilot of a helicopter in flight—

(i) to identify the area;

(ii) to determine the landing direction; and

(iii) to make a safe approach and landing.

(2) The requirements of paragraph (1) of this Rule shall be deemed not to have been contravened if neither the person in charge of the area nor any person acting under his instructions knew or ought reasonably to have known that the aircraft was about to take off or land.

(3) This Rule shall apply to any place, whether or not an aerodrome, intended to be used for the taking off, landing of aircraft or the manoeuvring of aircraft on the ground, but shall not apply to any Government aerodrome, to any aerodrome owned or managed by the Authority, or to any aerodrome licensed for use by night.

Approach Lighting

51. The lighting required by Rule 50 of these Rules shall include lighting to give approach guidance to the runway or landing area intended to be used, which lighting shall consist of either:

2c

(*a*) a line of identical lights each having an intensity of not less than 100 candela of red or white light in the direction of approach, equally spaced at intervals not exceeding 60 metres along the extended centre line of the runway for a distance of not less than 180 metres from the threshold in the direction of approach; or

(*b*) angle of approach lights so arranged as to indicate a sloping path between $2\frac{1}{2}°$ and $4\frac{1}{2}°$ above the horizontal which will provide, for any aircraft approaching to land, safe clearance above all obstacles within three nautical miles of the threshold of the runway and will give a warning by means of red beams of light if the aircraft is below the path. The lights shall indicate the path throughout an angle in azimuth of not less than 12° symmetrically about a line parallel to the direction of landing:

Provided that if the lights specified in Rule 52(1)(*b*) are in operation, the lights specified in sub-paragraph (*b*) of this paragraph shall also be in operation, and not the lights specified in sub-paragraph (*a*) of this paragraph.

Landing Area Lights

52.—(1) Where a runway is not provided, the lighting required by Rule 50 of these Rules shall include either:

(*a*) two lines of white lights parallel to the direction of take-off or landing visible from all directions above the horizontal delineating the landing area intended for use by night, the lights in each line being equally spaced at intervals not exceeding 90 metres. The lines of lights shall not be less than 30 metres nor more than 60 metres apart, and shall be so placed that a line drawn between a light and the opposite light in the parallel line of lights would be at right angles to the direction of use of the landing area; or

(*b*) white lights visible as aforesaid and arranged in the form of a T with the shaft of the T parallel to the direction of use and on the left edge of the area intended for landing when seen from the direction of approach and extending for the whole length of that edge, the lights in the shaft being equally spaced at intervals not exceeding 90 metres, and the cross arm of the T consisting of single lights placed 90 metres on either side of the light in the shaft of the T furthest from the approach end.

(2) Where a runway is provided the lighting required by Rule 50 of these Rules shall include two lines of white lights visible from the direction of approach, placed on the edge of the runway and each extending the whole of the length intended for use, the distance between successive lights in each line being not more than 90 metres so that, so far as is practicable, a line drawn between a light and the opposite light in the parallel line of lights would be at right angles to the axis of the runway.

(3) The lights required by this Rule shall have an intensity of not less than 50 candela.

Guidance Lights on the Manoeuvring Area and other parts of the aerodrome used by aircraft

53. The lighting required by Rule 50 of these Rules shall include either:

(*a*) the delineation of every taxiway intended for use by night by means of lights along its edges, either blue lights on one side and yellow lights on the other or blue lights on both sides. The lights on each side shall have a brightness sufficient to give adequate guidance to a taxying aircraft when the lights are spaced not more than 50 metres apart on straight stretches. On curves the lights shall be at reduced spacing to mark the taxiway edge clearly. If the taxiway is unpaved the lines of lights shall be not less than 15 nor more than 30 metres apart; or

(*b*) where aircraft manoeuvring on the ground are not confined to taxiways, white lights visible from all directions above the horizontal and of an intensity of not less than 10 candela at 5° above the horizontal, spaced at intervals not exceeding 90 metres along the boundary of that part of the aerodrome provided for the use of aircraft and under the control of the person in charge of the aerodrome and intended for use by night.

Areas Unfit for Use

54. The lighting required by Rule 50 of these Rules shall include red lights visible from all directions above the horizontal, sufficient to mark adequately any area unfit for the movement of aircraft at night.

Landing Direction Indicator

55. Where neither the lighting specified in Rule 51(*a*) of these Rules nor that specified in Rule 52(1)(*b*) of these Rules is provided the lighting required by Rule 50 of these Rules shall include—

(*a*) adequate illumination of a landing T as specified in Rule 41(2) of these Rules; or

(*b*) a landing T of the dimensions so specified, consisting of white lights, visible from all directions above the horizontal, of an intensity of not less than 5 nor more than 20 candela placed either in the signals area or between 15 and 30 metres to the left as seen from the direction of approach of the runway at the approach end thereof.

Obstruction Lights

56.—(1) The lighting required by Rule 50 of these Rules shall include the lighting of all obstructions within the area in accordance with the provisions of this Rule.

(2) The lights on an obstruction shall be arranged so as to show not less than 10 candela of red light in all directions in azimuth between 20° below and 60° above the horizontal.

(3) The lights shall be placed within 3 metres of the highest point of the obstruction except that, where the top of a chimney or other obstruction may be obscured by smoke, the lights may be placed instead not more than 7·5 metres below the top of the obstruction.

(4) If the height of an obstruction is more than 45 metres above ground level lights shall be placed on the obstruction between the top and the ground at vertical intervals not exceeding 45 metres.

(5) On any obstruction of more than 45 metres in horizontal extent lights as specified in paragraph (3) of this Rule shall be placed on the highest point of each length of 45 metres of the obstruction, measuring from one end of the obstruction.

(6) For the purposes of this Rule any object, whether permanent or temporary, shall be deemed to be an obstruction if it is likely to endanger aircraft and if it is situated—

(*a*) on that part of the manoeuvring area which is intended for use at night; or

(*b*) within an area extending 60 metres on either side of the centre line of the area intended for landing or take-off at night; or

(*c*) within 60 metres of the area so intended, if the height of the object is more than one quarter of the distance of the object from that area; or

(*d*) within 15 metres of a lighted taxiway; or

(*e*) within an area of the dimensions illustrated in this sub-paragraph,

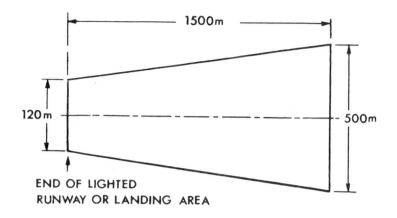

1500m

120m

500m

END OF LIGHTED
RUNWAY OR LANDING AREA

Fig 20

being an area at either end of a lighted runway or lighted landing area and if the height of the object, measured above the level of the nearer end of the runway or landing area, is more than one thirtieth of the distance from the object to the nearest end of the runway or landing area:

Provided that a frangible object not more than 1 metre in height above ground shall not be deemed to be an obstruction by reason of this sub-paragraph; or

(*f*) within one nautical mile of the centre of the area intended for use at night for the taking off, landing or manoeuvring of aircraft on the ground and more than 90 metres above the highest point of the ground within that area.

(7) Nothing in this Rule shall be taken to require the lighting of—

(*a*) any aircraft displaying navigation lights in accordance with Section III of these Rules;

(*b*) in an area set aside for the parking of aircraft, any vehicle which is displaying the lights which are obligatory when it is being driven on a public highway;

(*c*) any obstruction or part of an obstruction which, by reason of the lighting of other obstructions, is not likely to endanger aircraft in flight.

Section XII

Air Traffic Control

Provision of Air Traffic Control Services

57.—(1) At every aerodrome (other than a Government aerodrome or aerodrome owned or managed by the Authority) which is provided with means of two-way radio communication with aircraft and is either situated in a control zone or is an aerodrome in respect of which the Authority has given a direction to the proprietor or person in charge of the aerodrome requiring air traffic control service to be provided there, the person in charge of the aerodrome shall cause air traffic control service to be provided at all times when the aerodrome is open for the take-off and landing of aircraft.

(2) At every aerodrome (other than a Government aerodrome or aerodrome owned or managed by the Authority) which is provided with means of two-way radio communication with aircraft and with equipment for providing holding aid, let-down aid or approach aid by radio or radar the person in charge of the aerodrome shall inform the Authority in advance of any period during which any of the said equipment will be in operation for the purpose of providing holding aid, let-down aid or approach aid and, without prejudice to paragraph (1) of this Rule, cause air traffic control service to be provided at all times when the said equipment is notified as being in operation for any of those purposes.

EXPLANATORY NOTE

(This Note is not part of the Regulations.)

These Regulations consolidate the Rules of the Air and Air Traffic Control Regulations 1970, as amended, with minor drafting amendments, and substitute the Civil Aviation Authority for the Secretary of State.

The Rules of the Air and Air Traffic Control, scheduled to the Regulations, make provision, applying to all civil aircraft within the United Kingdom, and all aircraft registered in the United Kingdom wherever they may be, in respect of:

(*a*) The mis-use of signals and markings (Rule 3).

(*b*) The reporting of hazardous conditions in flight (Rule 4).

(*c*) Low flying (Rule 5).

(*d*) Simulated instrument flight (Rule 6).

(*e*) Practice instrument approaches (Rule 7).

(*f*) Lights and other signals to be shown or made by aircraft (Rules 8 to 15).

(*g*) The carriage of secondary surveillance radar transponders (Rule 16).

(*h*) The use of weather reports and forecasts (Rule 17).

(*i*) Rules for avoiding aerial collisions (Rules 18 to 20).

(*j*) Notification of arrival at planned destination (Rule 21).

(*k*) Visual and instrument flight rules (Rules 22 to 29).

(*l*) Aerodrome traffic rules, including special rules for particular aerodromes (Rules 30 to 37).

(*m*) Rules for low-level cross-Channel air traffic (Rule 38).

(*n*) Rules for air traffic in the Upper Flight Information Regions (Rule 39).

(*o*) Aerodrome signals and markings (Rules 40 to 47).

(*p*) Distress, urgency, safety and warning signals (Rules 48 and 49).

(*q*) Ground lighting (Rules 50 to 56).

(*r*) The provision of air traffic control services (Rule 57).

STATUTORY INSTRUMENTS

1972 No. 322

CIVIL AVIATION
The Air Navigation (General) Regulations 1972

Made - - - -	*1st March* 1972
Coming into Operation	*1st April* 1972

The Secretary of State in exercise of his powers under Articles 9(3), 11(2) and (5), 14, 25(2), 26(1)(*c*), 27(4), 28(1) and (3), 61 and 73 of the Air Navigation Order 1972(a) and of all other powers enabling him in that behalf, hereby makes the following Regulations:

1. These Regulations may be cited as the Air Navigation (General) Regulations 1972, and shall come into operation on the 1st April 1972.

2.—(1) The following Regulations are hereby revoked, that is to say—
The Air Navigation (General) Regulations 1970(b).
The Air Navigation (General) (Amendment) Regulations 1970(c).
The Air Navigation (General) (Second Amendment) Regulations 1970(d).
The Air Navigation (General) (Third Amendment) Regulations 1971(e).
The Air Navigation (General) (Fourth Amendment) Regulations 1971(f).

(2) Section 38(2) of the Interpretation Act 1889(g) (which relates to the effect of repeals), shall apply to these Regulations as if they were an Act of Parliament and as if the Regulations revoked by paragraph (1) of this Regulation were Acts of Parliament thereby repealed.

3.—(1) In these Regulations "the Order" means the Air Navigation Order 1972.

(2) Expressions used in these Regulations shall, unless the context otherwise requires, have the same respective meanings as in the Order.

(3) The Interpretation Act 1889 applies for the purpose of the interpretation of these Regulations as it applies for the purpose of the interpretation of an Act of Parliament.

Load Sheets
4.—(1) Every load sheet required by Article 27(4) of the Order shall contain the following particulars:
  (*a*) the nationality mark of the aircraft to which the load sheet relates, and

---

(a) S.I 1972/129 (1972 I, p. 366)
(c) S.I. 1970/1449 (1970 III, p. 4764).
(e) S.I. 1971/271 (1971 I, p. 929).
(g) 1889 c. 63.

(b) S.I. 1970/1081 (1970 II, p. 3344).
(d) S.I. 1970/1995 (1970 III, p. 6506).
(f) S.I. 1971/1750 (1971 III, p. 4766).

the registration mark assigned to that aircraft by the Authority;

(b) particulars of the flight to which the load sheet relates;

(c) the total weight of the aircraft as loaded for that flight;

(d) the weights of the several items from which the total weight of the aircraft, as so loaded, has been calculated including in particular the weight of the aircraft prepared for service and the respective total weights of the passengers, crew, baggage and cargo intended to be carried on the flight;

(e) the manner in which the load is distributed and the resulting position of the centre of gravity of the aircraft which may be given approximately if and to the extent that the relevant certificate of airworthiness so permits;

and shall include at the foot or end of the load sheet a certificate, signed by the person referred to in Article 27(1) of the Order as responsible for the loading of the aircraft, that the aircraft has been loaded in accordance with the written instructions furnished to him by the operator of the aircraft pursuant to the said Article 27.

(2) For the purpose of calculating the total weight of the aircraft the respective total weights of the passengers and crew entered in the load sheet shall be computed from the actual weight of each person and for that purpose each person shall be separately weighed:

Provided that, in the case of an aircraft of which the maximum total weight authorised exceeds 5,700 kg. or which has a total seating capacity of 12 or more persons, the total weights of the passengers and crew may, subject to the provisions of paragraph (4) of this Regulation, be calculated at not less than the weights shown in Table 1 and the load sheet shall bear a notation to that effect:

Table 1

Males over 12 years of age	75 kg.
Females over 12 years of age	65 kg.

On journeys between the United Kingdom, the Channel Islands and the Isle of Man:

Children aged 3 years or more, but not over 12 years of age	40 kg.
Infants under 3 years of age	10 kg.

On any other journey:

Children aged 2 years or more, but not over 12 years of age	39 kg.
Infants under 2 years of age	8 kg.

(3) (a) For the purpose of calculating the total weight of the aircraft the respective total weights of the baggage and cargo entered in the load sheet shall be computed from the actual weight of each piece of baggage, cargo or cargo container and for that purpose each piece or container shall be separately weighed:

Provided that, in the case of an aeroplane of which the maximum total weight authorised exceeds 5,700 kg. or which has a total seating capacity of 12 or more persons, the total weights of the baggage may, subject to the provisions of paragraph (4) of this Regulation, be calculated at not less than the weights shown in Table 2 and the load sheet shall bear a notation to that effect:

Table 2

1	2	3	
		Hold baggage per piece	
Journey made by the aeroplane	Cabin baggage per passenger*	Scheduled Journey	Holiday Journey
Domestic	3 kg.	10 kg.	13 kg.
European	3 kg.	12 kg.	13 kg.
Intercontinental	3 kg.	14 kg.	16 kg.

*Not infants under 3 years of age on journeys between the United Kingdom, Channel Islands and Isle of Man, or under 2 years of age on any other journey.

(*b*) If Table 2 has been used, subject to the provisions of paragraph (4) for determining the weight of hold baggage, it shall also be used, subject as aforesaid, for determining the weight of the cabin baggage.

(*c*) For the purposes of this Regulation:

(i) A journey made by an aeroplane shall be treated as domestic if it is confined within an area joining successively the following points:

61°00′N 11°00′W   61°00′N 02°00′E
51°05′N 02°00′E   49°30′N 04°00′W
49°30′N 11°00′W   61°00′N 11°00′W

but excluding any journey to or from Shannon.

(ii) A journey made by an aeroplane, not being a domestic journey, shall be treated as European if it is confined within an area joining successively the following points:

66°30′N 30°00′W   66°30′N 39°00′E
30°00′N 39°00′E   30°00′N 11°00′W
24°00′N 11°00′W   24°00′N 30°00′W
66°30′N 30°00′W.

(iii) A journey made by an aeroplane shall be treated as intercontinental if it is neither domestic nor European.

(iv) A journey made by an aeroplane shall be treated as a holiday journey and not as a scheduled journey if it is made for the carriage of passengers each of whom is carried pursuant to an agreement which provides for carriage by air to a place outside Great Britain, and back from that place or from another place to Great Britain (whether or not on the same aeroplane) and for accommodation at a place outside Great Britain.

(4) (*a*) If it appears to the person supervising the loading of the aircraft that any passenger or baggage to be carried exceeds the weights set out in Table 1 or Table 2 of this Regulation he shall, if he considers it necessary in the interests of the safety of the aircraft, or if the Authority has so directed in the particular

case, require any such person or baggage to be weighed for the purpose of the entry to be made in the load sheet.

(b) If any person or baggage has been weighed pursuant to sub-paragraph (a) of this paragraph, the weights entered in the load sheet shall take account of the actual weight of that person or baggage, or of the weight determined in accordance with the respective provisoes to paragraph (2) or (3), whichever weight shall be the greater.

Minimum weather conditions for take-off, approach to landing and landing by public transport aircraft registered in the United Kingdom

5.—(1) In this Regulation—

"approach to landing" means that portion of the flight of the aircraft in which it is descending below a height of 1,000 feet above the critical height of the relevant minimum for landing;

"cloud ceiling" in relation to an aerodrome means the vertical distance from the elevation of the aerodrome to the lowest part of any cloud visible from the aerodrome which is sufficient to obscure more than one-half of the sky so visible;

"critical height" means the minimum height above the elevation of the aerodrome to which an approach to landing can safely be continued without visual reference to the ground;

"minimum weather conditions" in relation to an aerodrome means the cloud ceiling and runway visual range for take-off and the critical height and runway visual range for landing below which the aircraft cannot safely take off or land (as the case may be) at that aerodrome, and the expression "relevant minimum" shall be construed accordingly;

"runway visual range" in relation to a runway or landing strip means the maximum distance in the direction of take-off or landing, as the case may be, at which the runway or landing strip or the markers or lights delineating it can be seen from a point 5 metres above its centre line; and in the case of an aerodrome in the United Kingdom the distance, if any, communicated to the commander of the aircraft by or on behalf of the person in charge of the aerodrome as being the runway visual range shall be taken to be the runway visual range for the time being;

"specified" in relation to an aircraft means specified in or ascertainable by reference to the operations manual relating to that aircraft.

(2) In compliance with Article 25(2) of the Order and paragraph (xiii) of Part A of Schedule 11 thereto, the operator of every aircraft to which that Article applies shall establish and include in the operations manual relating to the aircraft, particulars of minimum weather conditions appropriate to every aerodrome of intended departure or landing and every alternate aerodrome:

Provided that, in respect of aerodromes to be used only on a flight which is not a scheduled journey or any part thereof it shall be sufficient to include in the operations manual data and instructions by means of which the appropriate minimum weather conditions can be calculated by the commander of the aircraft.

(3) The minimum weather conditions specified shall not, in respect of any aerodrome, be less favourable than any declared in respect of that aerodrome by the competent authority, unless that authority otherwise permits in writing.

(4) In establishing minimum weather conditions for the purposes of this Regulation the operator of the aircraft shall take into account the following matters:

(a) the type and performance and handling characteristics of the aircraft and any relevant conditions in its certificate of airworthiness;

(b) the composition of its crew;

(c) the physical characteristics of the relevant aerodrome and its surroundings;

(d) the dimensions of the runways which may be selected for use;

(e) whether or not there are in use at the relevant aerodrome any aids, visual or otherwise, to assist aircraft in approach, landing or take-of, being aids which the crew of the aircraft are trained and equipped to use; the nature of any such aids that are in use; and the procedures for approach, landing and take-off which may be adopted according to the existence or absence of such aids;

and shall establish in relation to each runway which may be selected for use minimum weather conditions appropriate to each set of circumstances which can reasonably be expected.

(5) With reference to Article 28(3) of the Order, an aircraft shall not commence a flight at a time when—

(a) the cloud ceiling or the runway visual range at the aerodrome of departure is less than the minimum respectively specified for take-off; or

(b) according to the information available to the commander of the aircraft it would not be able, without contravening paragraph (6) of this Regulation, to commence or continue an approach to landing at the aerodrome of intended destination at the estimated time of arrival there and at any alternate aerodrome at any time at which according to a reasonable estimate the aircraft would arrive there.

(6) With reference to Article 28(3) of the Order, an aircraft shall not—

(a) commence or continue an approach to landing at any aerodrome if the runway visual range at that aerodrome, established or determined as aforesaid, is at the time less than the relevant minimum for landing; or

(b) continue an approach to landing at any aerodrome by flying below the critical height of the relevant minimum for landing if from that height the approach to landing cannot be completed entirely by visual reference to the ground.

(7) If according to the information available an aircraft would as regards any flight be required by the Rules of the Air and Air Traffic Control to be flown in accordance with the Instrument Flight Rules at the aerodrome of intended landing, the commander of the aircraft shall select prior to take-off an alternate aerodrome unless no aerodrome suitable for that purpose is available.

Weight and Performance: General provisions

6.—(1) The assessment of the ability of an aeroplane to comply with the requirements of Regulations 7 to 11 inclusive (relating to weight and performance) shall be based on the specified information as to its performance:

Provided that, in the case of an aeroplane in respect of which there is in force under the Order a certificate of airworthiness which does not include a performance group classification, the assessment may be based on the best information available to the commander of the aircraft, in so far as the relevant information is not specified.

(2) In assessing the ability of an aeroplane to comply with condition (7) in the Schedule hereto, conditions (4) and (5) of Regulation 8, and conditions (2)(i)(b) and (2)(ii) of Regulation 11, account may be taken of any reduction of the weight of the aeroplane which may be achieved after the failure of a power unit by such jettisoning of fuel as is feasible and prudent in the circumstances of the flight and in accordance with the flight manual included in the certificate of airworthiness relating to the aircraft.

(3) In Regulations 6 to 11 inclusive, and in the Schedule hereto, unless the context otherwise requires:

"specified" in relation to an aircraft means specified in, or ascertainable by reference to—

(a) the certificate of airworthiness in force under the Order in respect of that aircraft; or

(b) the flight manual or performance schedule included in that certificate, or other document, whatever its title, incorporated by reference in that certificate;

"the emergency distance available" means the distance from the point on the surface of the aerodrome at which the aeroplane can commence its take-off run to the nearest point in the direction of take-off at which the aeroplane cannot roll over the surface of the aerodrome and be brought to rest in an emergency without risk of accident;

"the landing distance available" means the distance from the point on the surface of the aerodrome above which the aeroplane can commence its landing, having regard to the obstructions in its approach path, to the nearest point in the direction of landing at which the surface of the aerodrome is incapable of bearing the weight of the aeroplane under normal operating conditions or at which there is an obstacle capable of affecting the safety of the aeroplane;

"the take-off distance available" means either the distance from the point on the surface of the aerodrome at which the aeroplane can commence its take-off run to the nearest obstacle in the direction of take-off projecting above the surface of the aerodrome and capable of affecting the safety of the aeroplane or one and one half times the take-off run available, whichever is the less;

"the take-off run available" means the distance from the point on the surface of the aerodrome at which the aeroplane can commence its take-off run to the nearest point in the direction of take-off at which the surface of the aerodrome is incapable of bearing the weight of the aeroplane under normal operating conditions.

(4) For the purposes of Regulations 6 to 11 inclusive, and of the Schedule hereto:

(a) the weight of the aeroplane at the commencement of the take-off run shall be taken to be its gross weight including everything and everyone carried in or on it at the commencement of the take-off run;

(b) the landing weight of the aeroplane shall be taken to be the weight of the aeroplane at the estimated time of landing allowing for the weight of the fuel and oil expected to be used on the flight to the aerodrome at which it is intended to land or alternate aerodrome, as the case may be;

(c) where any distance referred to in paragraph (3) of this Regulation has been declared in respect of any aerodrome by the authority responsible for regulating air navigation over the territory of the Contracting State in which the aerodrome is situate, and in the case of an aerodrome in the United Kingdom, notified, that distance shall be deemed to be the relevant distance.

(5) Nothing in Regulations 6 to 11 inclusive shall apply to any aircraft flying solely for the purpose of training persons to perform duties in aircraft.

Weight and Performance of Public Transport Aeroplanes having no Performance Group Classification in their Certificates of Airworthiness

7. With reference to Article 28(1) of the Order an aeroplane registered in the United Kingdom in respect of which there is in force under the Order a certificate of airworthiness which does not include a performance group classification shall not fly for the purpose of public transport unless the weight of the aeroplane at the commencement of the take-off run is such that such of the conditions in the Schedule hereto as apply to that aircraft are satisfied.

Weight and Performance of Public Transport Aeroplanes classified as Aeroplanes of Performance Group A in their Certificates of Airworthiness

8. With reference to Article 28(1) of the Order an aeroplane registered in the United Kingdom in respect of which there is in force under the Order a certificate of airworthiness in which the aeroplane is designated as being of performance group A shall not fly for the purpose of public transport unless the weight of the aeroplane at the commencement of the take-off run is such that the following conditions are satisfied:

(1) That weight does not exceed the maximum take-off weight for altitude and temperature specified for the altitude and the air temperature at the aerodrome at which the take-off is to be made.

(2) The take-off run, take-off distance and the emergency distance respectively required for take-off, specified as being appropriate to—

(a) the weight of the aeroplane at the commencement of the take-off run;

(b) the altitude at the aerodrome;

(c) the air temperature at the aerodrome;

(d) the condition of the surface of the runway from which the take-off will be made;

(e) the slope of the surface of the aerodrome in the direction of take-off over the take-off run available, the take-off distance available and the emergency distance available, respectively; and

(f) not more than 50 per cent of the reported wind component opposite to the direction of take-off or not less than 150 per cent of the reported wind component in the direction of take-off,

do not exceed the take-off run, the take-off distance and the emergency distance available, respectively, at the aerodrome at which the take-off is to be made; in ascertaining the emergency distance required, the point at which the pilot is assumed to decide to discontinue the take-off shall not be nearer to the start of the take-off run than the point at which, in ascertaining the take-off run required and the take-off distance required, he is assumed to decide to continue the take-off, in the event of power unit failure.

(3) (*a*) The net take-off flight path with one power unit inoperative, specified as being appropriate to:

> (i) the weight of the aeroplane at the commencement of the take-off run;
>
> (ii) the altitude at the aerodrome;
>
> (iii) the air temperature at the aerodrome; and
>
> (iv) not more than 50 per cent of the reported wind component opposite to the direction of take-off or not less than 150 per cent of the reported wind component in the direction of take-off,

and plotted from a point 35 feet or 50 feet, as appropriate, above the end of the take-off distance required at the aerodrome at which the take-off is to be made to a height of 1,500 feet above the aerodrome, shows that the aeroplane will clear any obstacle in its path by a vertical interval of at least 35 feet, except that if it is intended that the aeroplane shall change its direction of flight by more than 15° the vertical interval shall not be less than 50 feet during the change of direction.

(*b*) For the purpose of sub-paragraph (*a*) hereof an obstacle shall be deemed to be in the path of the aeroplane if the distance from the obstacle to the nearest point on the ground below the intended line of flight of the aeroplane does not exceed:

> (i) a distance of 200 feet plus half the wing span of the aeroplane plus one eighth of the distance from such point to the end of the take-off distance available measured along the intended line of flight of the aeroplane; or
>
> (ii) 5,000 feet,

whichever is the less.

(*c*) In assessing the ability of the aeroplane to satisfy this condition, it shall not be assumed to make a change of direction of a radius less than the radius of steady turn specified.

(4) The aeroplane will, in the meteorological conditions expected for the flight, in the event of any one power unit becoming inoperative at any point on its route or on any planned diversion therefrom and with the other power unit or units operating within the maximum continuous power conditions specified, be capable of continuing the flight, clearing by a vertical interval of at least 2,000 feet obstacles within 10 nautical miles either side of the intended track, to an aerodrome at which it can comply with condition (7) in this Regulation relating to an alternate aerodrome, and on arrival over such aerodrome the gradient of the specified net flight path with one power unit inoperative shall not be less than zero at 1,500 feet above the aerodrome; and in assessing the ability of the aeroplane to satisfy this condition it shall not be assumed to be capable of flying at an altitude exceeding the specified maximum permissible altitude for power unit restarting:

Provided that where the operator of the aeroplane is satisfied, taking into account the navigation aids which can be made use of by the aeroplane on the route, that the commander of the aeroplane will be able to maintain his intended track on that route within a margin of 5 nautical miles, the foregoing provisions of this paragraph shall have effect as if 5 nautical miles were substituted therein for 10 nautical miles.

(5) The aeroplane will, in the meteorological conditions expected for the

flight, in the event of any two power units becoming inoperative at any point along the route or on any planned diversion therefrom more than 90 minutes flying time in still air at the all power units operating economical cruising speed from the nearest aerodrome at which it can comply with condition (7) in this Regulation, relating to an alternate aerodrome, be capable of continuing the flight with all other power units operating within the specified maximum continuous power conditions, clearing by a vertical interval of at least 2,000 feet obstacles within 10 nautical miles either side of the intended track to such an aerodrome, and on arrival over such aerodrome the gradient of the specified net flight path with two power units inoperative shall not be less than zero at 1,500 feet above the aerodrome; and in assessing the ability of the aeroplane to satisfy this condition it shall not be assumed to be capable of flying at an altitude exceeding the specified maximum permissible altitude for power unit restarting:

Provided that where the operator of the aeroplane is satisfied, taking into account the navigation aids which can be made use of by the aeroplane on the route, that the commander of the aeroplane will be able to maintain his intended track on that route within a margin of 5 nautical miles, the foregoing provisions of this paragraph shall have effect as if 5 nautical miles were substituted therein for 10 nautical miles.

(6)   The landing weight of the aeroplane will not exceed the maximum landing weight specified for the altitude and the expected air temperature for the estimated time of landing at the aerodrome at which it is intended to land and at any alternate aerodrome.

(7) (a) The landing distances required, respectively specified as being appropriate to aerodromes of destination and alternate aerodromes, do not exceed at the aerodrome at which it is intended to land or at any alternate aerodrome, as the case may be, the landing distance available on:

  (i) the most suitable runway for a landing in still air conditions; and

  (ii) the runway that may be required for landing because of the forecast wind conditions; provided that if an alternate aerodrome is designated in the flight plan, the specified landing distance required may be that appropriate to an alternate aerodrome when assessing the ability of the aeroplane to satisfy this condition at the aerodrome of destination.

(b) For the purposes of sub-paragraph (a) hereof the landing distance required shall be that specified as being appropriate to:

  (i) the landing weight;

  (ii) the altitude at the aerodrome;

  (iii) the temperature in the specified international standard atmosphere appropriate to the altitude at the aerodrome;

  (iv) (aa) a level surface in the case of runways usable in both directions;

    (bb) the average slope of the runway in the case of runways usable in only one direction; and

  (v) (aa) still air conditions in the case of the most suitable runway for a landing in still air conditions;

    (bb) not more than 50 per cent of the forecast wind component opposite to the direction of landing or not less than 150 per cent of the forecast wind component in the direction of landing in the case of the runway that may be required for landing because of the forecast wind conditions.

Weight and Performance of Public Transport Aeroplanes classified as Aeroplanes of Performance Group C or of Performance Group D in their Certificates of Airworthiness

9.—(1) With reference to Article 28(1) of the Order an aeroplane registered in the United Kingdom in respect of which there is in force under the Order a certificate of airworthiness in which the aeroplane is designated as being of performance group C or of performance group D shall not fly for the purpose of public transport unless the weight of the aeroplane at the commencement of the take-off run is such that the following conditions are satisfied:

(*a*) That weight does not exceed the maximum take-off weight specified for the altitude and the air temperature at the aerodrome at which the take-off is to be made.

(*b*) The take-off run required and the take-off distance required, specified as being appropriate to—

(i) the weight of the aeroplane at the commencement of the take-off run;

(ii) the altitude at the aerodrome;

(iii) the air temperature at the aerodrome;

(iv) the average slope of the surface of the aerodrome in the direction of take-off over the emergency distance available;

(v) not more than 50 per cent of the reported wind component opposite to the direction of take-off or not less than 150 per cent of the reported wind component in the direction of take-off,

do not exceed the take-off run available and the emergency distance available, respectively, at the aerodrome at which the take-off is to be made.

(*c*) The net take-off flight path with all power units operating, specified as being appropriate to—

(i) the weight of the aeroplane at the commencement of the take-off run;
(ii) the altitude at the aerodrome;

(iii) the air temperature at the aerodrome;

(iv) not more than 50 per cent of the reported wind component opposite to the direction of take-off or not less than 150 per cent of the reported wind component in the direction of take-off;

and plotted from a point 50 feet above the end of the take-off distance required at the aerodrome at which the take-off is to be made to the point at which the aeroplane reaches the minimum altitude for safe flight on the first stage of the route to be flown stated in or calculated from the information contained in the operations manual relating to the aircraft, shows that the aeroplane will clear by a safe margin any obstacle the distance from which to the nearest point on the ground below the intended line of flight of the aeroplane does not exceed 200 feet plus half the wing span of the aeroplane. In assessing the ability of the aeroplane to satisfy this condition it shall not be assumed to make a change of direction of a radius less than the specified radius of steady turn.

(*d*) The aeroplane will, if it is designated in its certificate of airworthiness as an aeroplane of performance group C and if it is necessary for it to be flown solely by reference to instruments for any period before reaching the minimum altitude for safe flight on the first stage of the route to be flown, stated in, or calculated from the information contained in, the operations manual, during such period also satisfy condition (3) in Regulation 8.

(*e*) The aeroplane will, in the meteorological conditions expected for the flight, in the event of any one power unit becoming inoperative at any point on its route or on any planned diversion therefrom, and with the other power unit or power units, if any, operating within the specified maximum continuous power conditions:

    (i) in the case of an aeroplane designated as an aeroplane of performance group C, be capable of continuing the flight at altitudes not less than the relevant minimum altitudes for safe flight stated in, or calculated from the information contained in, the operations manual to a point 1,500 feet above an aerodrome at which a safe landing can be made and after arrival at that point be capable of maintaining that height;

    (ii) in the case of an aeroplane designated as an aeroplane of performance group D, be capable of continuing the flight to a point 1,000 feet above a place at which a safe landing can be made:

Provided that in assessing the ability of the aeroplane to satisy this condition it shall not be assumed to be capable of flying at any point on its route at an altitude exceeding the performance ceiling with all power units operating specified as being appropriate to its estimated weight at that point.

(*f*) The landing weight of the aeroplane will not exceed the maximum landing weight specified for the altitude and the expected air temperature for the estimated time of landing at the aerodrome at which it is intended to land and at any alternate aerodrome.

(*g*) Subject to condition (*h*) of this Regulation, the distance required by the aeroplane to land from a height of 50 feet otherwise than in accordance with specified data for short field landing does not, at the aerodrome at which it is intended to land and at any alternate aerodrome, exceed 70 per cent of the landing distance available on the most suitable runway for a landing in still air conditions, and on the runway that may be required for landing because of the forecast wind conditions, and for the purposes of this sub-paragraph the distance required to land from a height of 50 feet shall be taken to be that specified as being appropriate to:

    (i) the landing weight;

    (ii) the altitude at the aerodrome;

    (iii) the expected air temperature for the estimated time of landing at the aerodrome;

    (iv) (*aa*) a level surface in the case of runways usable in both directions;
        (*bb*) the average slope of the runway in the case of runways usable in only one direction; and

    (v) (*aa*) still air conditions in the case of the most suitable runway for a landing in still air conditions;

        (*bb*) not more than 50 per cent of the forecast wind component opposite to the direction of landing or not less than 150 per cent of the forecast wind component in the direction of landing in the case of the runway that may be required for landing because of the forecast wind conditions.

(*h*) As an alternative to condition (*g*) of this Regulation, the distance required by the aeroplane, with all power units operating and with one power unit inoperative, to land in accordance with specified data for short field landing, does not at the aerodrome of intended destination and at any alternate aerodrome exceed the landing distance available on the most suitable runway for a landing in still air conditions and on the runway that may be required for landing because of the forecast wind conditions; and for the purposes of this sub-paragraph the distance required to land from the appropriate heights shall be taken to be that specified as being appropriate to the factors set forth in sub-paragraphs (i) to (v) of condition (*g*) of this Regulation, and the appropriate height shall be:

    (i) for a landing with all power units operating: any height between 30 and 50 feet in the United Kingdom, and 50 feet elsewhere; and

    (ii) for a landing with one power unit inoperative: 50 feet in the United Kingdom and elsewhere:

Provided that if the specified distance required to land with one power unit inoperative from a height of 50 feet at the aerodrome of intended destination exceeds the landing distance available, it shall be sufficient compliance with sub-paragraph (ii) of this sub-paragraph if an alternate aerodrome which has available the specified landing distance required to land with one power unit inoperative from such a height, is designated in the flight plan.

(2) An aeroplane designated as aforesaid as an aeroplane of performance group D shall not fly for the purpose of public transport at night or when the cloud ceiling or visibility prevailing at the aerodrome of departure and forecast for the estimated time of landing at the aerodrome at which it is intended to land and at any alternate aerodrome are less than 1,000 feet and one nautical mile respectively.

(3) The distance required by the aeroplane to land shall not be determined in accordance with condition (*h*) of this Regulation if it is intended to land:

    (*a*) at night; or

    (*b*) when the cloud ceiling or ground visibility forecast for the estimated time of landing at the aerodrome of intended destination and at any alternate aerodrome at which it is intended to land in accordance with specified data for short field landing with all power units operating, are less than 500 feet and one nautical mile respectively.

Weight and Performance of Public Transport Aeroplanes classified as Aeroplanes of Performance Group E in their Certificates of Airworthiness

10.—(1) With reference to Article 28(1) of the Order an aeroplane registered in the United Kingdom in respect of which there is in force under the Order a certificate of airworthiness in which the aeroplane is designated as being of performance group E shall not fly for the purpose of public transport unless the weight of the aeroplane at the commencement of the take-off run is such that the following conditions are satisfied:

    (*a*) That weight for the altitude and the air temperature at the aerodrome at which the take-off is to be made does not exceed the maximum take-off weight specified as being appropriate to:

        (i) the weight at which the aeroplane is capable in the en route configuration and with all power units operating within the specified maximum continuous power conditions, of a rate of climb of 700 feet per minute if it has retractable landing gear and of 500 feet per minute if it has fixed landing gear, and

(ii) the weight at which the aeroplane is capable, in the en route configuration and if it is necessary for it to be flown solely by reference to instruments for any period before reaching the minimum altitude for safe flight on the first stage of the route to be flown, stated in, or calculated from the information contained in, the operations manual relating to the aeroplane and, with one power unit inoperative, of a rate of climb of 150 feet per minute.

(*b*) The distance required by the aeroplane to attain a height of 50 feet, with all power units operating within the maximum take-off power conditions specified, when multiplied by a factor of 1·33 does not exceed the emergency distance available at the aerodrome at which the take-off is to be made. The distance required by the aeroplane to attain a height of 50 feet shall be that appropriate to:

(i) the weight of the aeroplane at the commencement of the take-off run;
(ii) the altitude at the aerodrome;
(iii) the air temperature at the aerodrome;
(iv) not more than 50 per cent of the reported wind component opposite to the direction of take-off or not less than 150 per cent of the reported wind component in the direction of take-off.

(*c*) The aeroplane will, in the meteorological conditions expected for the flight, in the event of any one power unit becoming inoperative at any point on its route or on any planned diversion therefrom, and with the other power unit or power units, if any, operating within the specified maximum continuous power conditions, be capable of continuing the flight at altitudes not less than the relevant minimum altitudes for safe flight stated in, or calculated from the information contained in, the operations manual to a point 1,000 feet above a place at which a safe landing can be made:

Provided that in assessing the ability of the aeroplane to satisfy this condition it shall not be assumed to be capable of flying at any point on its route or on any planned diversion therefrom at an altitude exceeding that at which it is capable of a rate of climb with all power units operating within the maximum continuous power conditions specified of 150 feet per minute and if it is necessary for it to be flown solely by reference to instruments, be capable, with one power unit inoperative, of a rate of climb of 100 feet per minute.

(*d*) The landing weight of the aeroplane for the altitude and the expected air temperature for the estimated time of landing at the aerodrome at which it is intended to land and at any alternate aerodrome will not exceed the maximum landing weight specified:

(i) at which the aeroplane is capable, in the en route configuration and with all power units operating within the specified maximum continuous power conditions, of a rate of climb of 700 feet per minute if it has retractable landing gear and of 500 feet per minute if it has fixed landing gear, and

(ii) at which the aeroplane is capable in the en route configuration and if it is necessary for it to be flown solely by reference to instruments for any period after leaving the minimum altitude for safe flight on the last stage of the route to be flown, stated in, or calculated from the information contained in, the operations manual relating to the aeroplane and with one power unit inoperative, of a rate of climb of 150 feet per minute.

(e) The landing distance required does not, at the aerodrome at which it is intended to land and at any alternate aerodrome, exceed 70 per cent of the landing distance available on the most suitable runway for a landing in still air conditions, and for the purposes of this sub-paragraph the distance required to land from a height of 50 feet shall be taken to be that specified as being appropriate to:

(i) the landing weight;

(ii) the altitude at the aerodrome;

(iii) the temperature in the specified international standard atmosphere appropriate to the altitude at the aerodrome.

(2) An aeroplane designated as aforesaid as an aeroplane of performance group E shall not fly for the purpose of public transport at night or when the cloud ceiling or visibility prevailing at the aerodrome of departure and forecast for the estimated time of landing at the aerodrome at which it is intended to land and at any alternate aerodrome are less than 1,000 feet and one nautical mile respectively:

Provided that the foregoing prohibition shall not apply if the aeroplane is capable in the en route configuration and with one power unit inoperative, of a rate of climb of 150 feet per minute.

Weight and Performance of Public Transport Aeroplanes classified as Aeroplanes of Performance Group X in their Certificates of Airworthiness

11. With reference to Article 28(1) of the Order an aeroplane in respect of which there is in force under the Order a certificate of airworthiness designating the aeroplane as being of performance group X shall not fly for the purpose of public transport unless the weight of the aeroplane at the commencement of the take-off run is such that the following conditions are satisfied:

(1) (i) That weight does not exceed the maximum take-off weight specified for the altitude at the aerodrome at which the take-off is to be made, or for the altitude and the air temperature at such aerodrome, as the case may be.

(ii) The minimum effective take-off runway length required, specified as being appropriate to:

(a) the weight of the aeroplane at the commencement of the take-off run;

(b) the altitude at the aerodrome;

(c) the air temperature at the time of take-off;

(d) the condition of the surface of the runway from which the take-off will be made;

(e) the overall slope of the take-off run available; and

(f) not more than 50 per cent of the reported wind component opposite to the direction of take-off or not less than 150 per cent of the reported wind component in the direction of take-off,

does not exceed the take-off run available at the aerodrome at which the take-off is to be made.

(iii) (a) The take-off flight path with one power unit inoperative, specified as being appropriate to:

> (i) the weight of the aeroplane at the commencement of the take-off run;
>
> (ii) the altitude at the aerodrome; and
>
> (iii) not more than 50 per cent of the reported wind component opposite to the direction of take-off or not less than 150 per cent of the reported wind component in the direction of take-off,

and plotted from a point 50 feet above the end of the minimum effective take-off runway length required at the aerodrome at which the take-off is to be made, shows that the aeroplane will thereafter clear any obstacle in its path by a vertical interval of not less than the greater of 50 feet or 35 feet plus one hundreth of the distance from the point on the ground below the intended line of flight of the aeroplane nearest to the obstacle to the end of the take-off distance available, measured along the intended line of flight of the aeroplane.

(b) For the purpose of sub-paragraph (a) an obstacle shall be deemed to be in the path of the aeroplane if the distance from the obstacle to the nearest point on the ground below the intended line of flight does not exceed:

> (i) a distance of 200 feet plus half the wing span of the aeroplane plus one eighth of the distance from such point to the end of the take-off distance available measured along the intended line of flight; or
>
> (ii) 5,000 feet,

whichever is the less.

(c) In assessing the ability of the aeroplane to satisfy this condition, insofar as it relates to flight path, it shall not be assumed to make a change of direction of a radius less than the radius of steady turn corresponding to an angle of bank of 15°.

(2)(i)(a) Subject to sub-paragraph (b), the weight of the aeroplane at any point on the route or any planned diversion therefrom, having regard to the fuel and oil expected to be consumed up to that point, shall be such that the aeroplane, with one power unit inoperative and the other power unit or units operating within the maximum continuous power conditions specified, will be capable of a rate of climb of at least $K(Vso/100)^2$ feet per minute at an altitude not less than the minimum altitude for safe flight stated in or calculated from the information contained in the operations manual, where Vso is in knots and K has the value of 797—1060/N, N being the number of power units installed.

(b) As an alternative to (a), the aeroplane may be flown at an altitude from which, in the event of failure of one power unit, it is capable of reaching an aerodrome where a landing can be made in accordance with condition (3)(ii) in this Regulation relating to an alternate aerodrome. In that case, the weight of the aeroplane shall be such that, with the remaining power unit or units operating within the maximum continuous power conditions specified, it is capable of maintaining a minimum altitude on the route to such aerodrome of 2,000 feet above all obstacles within 10 nautical miles on either side of the intended track:

Provided that where the operator of the aeroplane is satisfied, taking into account the navigation aids which can be made use of by the aeroplane on the route, that the commander of the aeroplane will be able to maintain his intended track on that route within a margin of 5 nautical miles, the foregoing provisions of this sub-paragraph shall have effect as if 5 nautical miles were substituted therein for 10 nautical miles and

    (*aa*) the rate of climb, specified for the appropriate weight and altitude, used in calculating the flight path shall be reduced by an amount equal to $K(Vso/100)^2$ feet per minute;

    (*bb*) the aeroplane shall comply with the climb requirements of condition 2(i)(*a*) at 1,000 feet above the chosen aerodrome;

    (*cc*) account shall be taken of the effect of wind and temperature on the flight path; and

    (*dd*) the weight of the aeroplane may be assumed to be progressively reduced by normal consumption of fuel and oil.

(ii) An aeroplane having four power units shall, if any two power units become inoperative at any point along the route or any planned diversion therefrom, being a point more than 90 minutes flying time (assuming all power units to be operating) from the nearest aerodrome at which a landing can be made in compliance with condition (3)(ii) of this Regulation relating to an alternate aerodrome, be capable of continuing the flight at an altitude of not less than 1,000 feet above ground level to a point above that aerodrome. In assessing the ability of the aeroplane to satisfy this condition, it shall be assumed that the remaining power units will operate within the specified maximum continuous power conditions, and account shall be taken of the temperature and wind conditions expected for the flight.

(3)(i) The landing weight of the aeroplane will not exceed the maximum landing weight specified for the altitude at the aerodrome at which it is intended to land and at any alternate aerodrome.

(ii) The required landing runway lengths respectively specified as being appropriate to the aerodromes of intended destination and the alternate aerodromes do not exceed at the aerodrome at which it is intended to land or at any alternate aerodrome, as the case may be, the landing distance avilable on:

    (*a*) the most suitable runway for landing in still air conditions; and

    (*b*) the runway that may be required for landing because of the forecast wind conditions,

the required landing runway lengths being taken to be those specified as being appropriate to:

    (*aa*) the landing weight;

    (*bb*) the altitude at the aerodrome;

    (*cc*) still air conditions in the case of the most suitable runway for a landing in still air conditions; and

    (*dd*) not more than 50 per cent of the forecast wind component opposite to the direction of landing or not less than 150 per cent of the forecast wind component in the direction of landing in the case of the runway that may be required for landing because of the forecast wind conditions.

Noise and vibration caused by aircraft on aerodromes

12. With reference to Article 73 of the Order, the conditions under which noise and vibration may be caused by aircraft (including military aircraft) on

Government aerodromes, aerodromes owned or managed by the Authority, licensed aerodromes or on aerodromes at which the manufacture, repair or maintenance of aircraft is carried out by persons carrying on business as manufacturers or repairers of aircraft, shall be as follows, that is to say, that, whether in the course of the manufacture of the aircraft or otherwise—

(a) the aircraft is taking off or landing, or

(b) the aircraft is moving on the ground or water, or

(c) the engines are being operated in the aircraft—

(i) for the purpose of ensuring their satisfactory performance,

(ii) for the purpose of bringing them to a proper temperature in preparation for, or at the end of, a flight, or

(iii) for the purpose of ensuring that the instruments, accessories or other components of the aircraft are in a satisfactory condition.

Certificates of Maintenance and Compliance—issue by maintenance engineers licensed by prescribed countries

13. With reference to Article 9(3) and Article 11(4) of the Order the following countries are hereby prescribed—

Antigua	Kuwait
Australia	Malawi
Bahamas	Malaysia
Barbados	Montserrat
British Honduras	New Zealand
British Virgin Islands	Pakistan
State of Brunei	Republic of Ireland
Burma	Republic of South Africa
Canada	St. Christopher, Nevis and Anguilla
Cayman Islands	St. Lucia
Ceylon	St. Vincent
Dominica	Singapore
Ghana	The Sudan
Grenada	Trinidad and Tobago
Guyana	Turks and Caicos Islands
Hong Kong	Uganda
India	United Republic of Tanzania
Jamaica	Zambia
Kenya	

Radio Navigational Apparatus to be carried in aircraft

14.—(1) This Regulation shall apply to all aircraft of over 2,300 kg. maximum total weight authorised when flying for the purpose of public transport.

(2)(a) For the purpose of Scale B in paragraph 3 of Schedule 6 to the Order radio navigational apparatus shall be provided, subject to the provisions of sub-paragraph (b) of this paragraph, in all aircraft to which this Regulation applies in accordance with the following Table. The numbered areas in column 1 of that Table are more particularly described in paragraph (3) of this Regulation, and the letters in column 2 have the meanings assigned to them by paragraph (4) of this Regulation:

Table

Column 1	Column 2
Area in which the aircraft is flying	*Combination of Apparatus to be carried*
Area 1	Either A, B, C, D or E
Area 2	Either A, C, D or E
Area 3	Either A, C or E
Area 4	D or E
All other areas	E

(*b*) Where not more than one item of apparatus in a combination of apparatus carried in an aircraft pursuant to this Regulation is unserviceable when the aircraft is about to begin a flight, the aircraft may nevertheless take off on that flight if—

   (i) it is not reasonably practicable for the repair or replacement of that item to be carried out before the beginning of the flight; and

  (ii) the aircraft has not made more than one complete flight since the item was last serviceable; and

 (iii) the commander of the aircraft has satisfied himself that taking into account the latest information available as to the route and aerodrome to be used (including any planned diversion), and the weather conditions likely to be encountered, the flight can be made safely and in accordance with any relevant requirements of air traffic control,

and in such case the commander of the aircraft shall cause written particulars of the flight, and the reasons for making it, to be given to the Authority within 10 days thereafter.

(3) The Areas 1 to 4 referred to in Column 1 of the Table in the preceding paragraph are as follows:

(*a*) *Area* 1

    The area enclosed by the notified boundaries of the United Kingdom Flight Information Regions.

(*b*) *Area* 2

    The area enclosed by rhumb lines joining successively the following points, but excluding area 1:

62°00′N 10°00′W	63°00′N 08°00′W	63°00′N 03°00′W
62°00′N 00°45′W	58°50′N 06°00′E	58°50′N 15°00′E
61°45′N 15°00′E	61°45′N 25°00′E	60°15′N 24°00′E
58°20′N 24°00′E	54°15′N 13°45′E	50°45′N 15°00′E
48°00′N 10°00′E	48°00′N 06°20′E	44°00′N 06°20′E
44°00′N 01°30′W	46°00′N 02°00′W	46°00′N 09°00′W
54°34′N 09°00′W	54°34′N 10°00′W	62°00′N 10°00′W

(*c*) *Area* 3

    The area enclosed by rhumb lines joining successively the following points:

61°45′N 15°00′E	61°45′N 12°30′E	63°30′N 12°30′E
63°30′N 18°00′E	65°00′N 14°45′E	66°30′N 16°45′E
66°30′N 27°00′E	65°30′N 28°30′E	61°45′N 25°00′E
61°45′N 15°00′E		

(d) *Area* 4

The area enclosed by rhumb lines joining successively the following points, but excluding areas 1 and 2:

62°00′N 10°00′W	63°00′N 08°00′W	63°00′N 03°00′W
62°00′N 00°45′W	62°00′N 04°00′E	65°00′N 10°00′E
68°30′N 13°00′E	68°30′N 23°00′E	66°30′N 23°00′E
66°30′N 16°45′E	65°00′N 14°45′E	63°30′N 18°00′E
63°30′N 12°30′E	61°45′N 12°30′E	61°45′N 26°00′E
58°20′N 24°00′E	50°30′N 17°30′E	41°30′N 23°15′E
41°30′N 30°00′E	40°00′N 37°00′E	30°00′N 37°00′E
30°00′N 10°00′W	62°00′N 10°00′W.	

(4) Each of the letters in Column 2 of the Table in paragraph (2)(*a*) of this Regulation shall signify the combination of apparatus which is specified opposite that letter in columns 2 and 3 of the following Table. The Roman numerals in column 3 of the last-mentioned Table have the meanings assigned to them by paragraph (5) of this Regulation:

Table

Column 1	Column 2	Column 3
Reference letter of combination of Apparatus	*Single or duplicate Apparatus*	*Items of Apparatus in the combination*
A	Single	(i), (ii), (iii), (iv) and (v)
B	Duplicate	(i)
	Single	(ii)
	Single	(iii)
	Single	(v)
C	Duplicate	(i)
	Single	(ii)
	Single	(iv)
	Single	(v)
D	Single	(iii)
	Duplicate	(iv)
	Single	(v)
E	Duplicate	(iii)
	Single	(iv)
	Single	(v)

(5) The Roman numerals indicating the items of apparatus in column 3 of the Table in the preceding paragraph signify the following—

(i) apparatus which will enable the aircraft to be navigated by means of signals received from radio navigation land stations forming part of the Decca radio navigation system;

(ii) a flight log intended to operate with the apparatus described in the preceding paragraph and to display on a chart to the pilot at the controls of the aircraft a continuous and instantaneous pictorial plot of the path of the aircraft;

(iii) automatic direction finding apparatus which indicates to the pilot at the controls of the aircraft the bearing of any radio station transmitting signals in the low and medium frequency bands received by such apparatus;

   (iv) apparatus capable of giving to the pilot at the controls of the aircraft visual indications of bearings of the aircraft by means of signals received from very high frequency omni-directional radio ranges;

   (v) a VHF receiver capable of receiving signals from a 75MHz marker beacon.

Aeroplanes flying for the purpose of public transport of passengers—Aerodrome facilities for approach to landing and landing

15.—(1) Notwithstanding the provisions of paragraph (2), this Regulation shall apply to every aeroplane registered in the United Kingdom engaging on a flight for the purpose of the public transport of passengers on a scheduled journey and to every aeroplane so registered whose maximum total weight authorised exceeds 5,700 kg. engaging on such a flight otherwise than on a scheduled journey.

(2) For the purposes of Article 26(1)(c) of the Order, the following manning and equipment are prescribed in relation to aerodromes intended to be used for landing or as an alternate aerodrome by aircraft to which this Regulation applies:

   (a) air traffic control service, including the reporting to aircraft of the current meteorological conditions at the aerodrome;

   (b) very high frequency radiotelephony;

   (c) at least one of the following radio navigation aids, either at the aerodrome or elsewhere, and in either case for the purpose of assisting the pilot in locating the aerodrome and in making an approach to landing there:

     (i) radio direction finding apparatus utilising emissions in the very high frequency band;

     (ii) a non-directional radio beacon transmitting signals in the low or medium frequency bands;

     (iii) very high frequency omni-directional radio range;

     (iv) radio navigation land stations forming part of the Decca radio navigation system;

     (v) radar equipment.

It shall be sufficient if the equipment specified in sub-paragraph (c) is provided, even if for the time being it is not in operation.

(3) An aircraft to which this Regulation applies shall not land or make an approach to landing at any aerodrome unless services and equipment according with paragraph (2) of this Regulation are provided and are in operation at that aerodrome, and can be made use of by that aircraft; and, in the case of the navigation aids specified in sub-paragraph (c), items (i) to (iv), instructions and procedures for the use of the aid are included in the operations manual. A person shall be deemed not to have contravened the provisions of this paragraph if he proves that—

   (a) for the time being use could not be made of the radio navigation aids provided under paragraph 2(c) whether by reason of those aids not being in operation or of the unserviceability of apparatus in the aircraft itself, and

   (b) the approach to landing was made in acordance with instructions and procedures appropriate to that circumstance and included in the operations manual.

(4) An aircraft to which this Regulation applies shall, without prejudice to the requirements of Regulation 14, be equipped with the apparatus necessary to enable use to be made of at least one of the navigation aids specified in paragraph 2(c) of this Regulation and in use for landing at the aerodrome, and in particular the equipment for use with the radio navigation land stations referred to in paragraph 2(c)(iv) of this Regulation shall include a flight log designed to operate with that equipment and to display on a chart to the pilot at the controls of the aircraft a continuous and instantaneous pictorial plot of the path of the aircraft. Nothing in this paragraph shall require the duplication of any equipment carried in pursuance of any other provision of the Order or of any regulation made thereunder.

Pilot Maintenance—prescribed repairs or replacements

16. With reference to Article 11(2) of the Order the following repairs or replacements are hereby prescribed:
(1) Replacement of landing gear tyres, landing skids or skid shoes.
(2) Replacement of elastic shock absorber cord units on landing gear where special tools are not required.
(3) Replacement of defective safety wiring or split pins excluding those in engine, transmission, flight control and rotor systems.
(4) Patch-repairs to fabric not requiring rib stitching or the removal of structural parts or control surfaces, if the repairs do not cover up structural damage and do not include repairs to rotor blades.
(5) Repairs to upholstery and decorative furnishings of the cabin or cockpit interior when the repair does not require dismantling of any structure or operating system or interfere with an operating system or affect the structure of the aircraft.
(6) Repairs, not requiring welding, to fairings, non-structural cover plates and cowlings.
(7) Replacement of side windows where that work does not interfere with the structure or with any operating system.
(8) Replacement of safety belts or safety harness.
(9) Replacement of seats or seat parts not involving dismantling of any structure or of any operating system.
(10) Replacement of bulbs, reflectors, glasses, lenses or lights.
(11) Replacement of any cowling not requiring removal of the propeller, rotors or disconnection of engine or flight controls.
(12) Replacement of unserviceable sparking plugs.
(13) Replacement of batteries.
(14) Replacement of wings and tail surfaces and controls, the attachments of which are designed to provide for assembly immediately before each flight and dismantling after each flight.
(15) Replacement of main rotor blades that are designed for removal where special tools are not required.
(16) Replacement of generator and fan belts designed for removal where special tools are not required.

D. F. Hubback,
A Deputy Secretary,
Department of Trade and Industry.

1st March 1972.

SCHEDULE

Regulation 7

WEIGHT AND PERFORMANCE OF PUBLIC TRANSPORT AEROPLANES HAVING NO
PERFORMANCE GROUP CLASSIFICATION IN THEIR CERTIFICATES OF AIRWORTHINESS

Conditions (1) and (2) apply to all aeroplanes to which Regulation 7 applies ;
Conditions (3) to (10) apply to all aeroplanes to which Regulation 7 applies—

  (i) of which the specified maximum total weight authorised exceeds
      5,700 kg., or

  (ii) of which the specified maximum total weight authorised does not
       exceed 5,700 kg. and which comply with neither condition (1)(*a*) nor
       condition (1)(*b*) ;

Conditions (11) to (18) inclusive apply to all aeroplanes to which Regulation 7
applies of which the specified maximum total weight authorised does not exceed
5,700 kg., and which comply with condition (1)(*a*) or condition (1)(*b*) or with both
those conditions.

All aeroplanes

  (1) Either—

    (*a*) the wing loading of the aeroplane does not exceed 20 lb. per square foot ;
         or

    (*b*) the stalling speed of the aeroplane in the landing configuration does not
         exceed 60 knots ; or

    (*c*) the aeroplane, with any one of its power units inoperative and the remain-
         ing power unit or units operating within the maximum continuous power
         conditions specified, is capable of a gradient of climb of at least 1 in 200
         at an altitude of 5,000 feet in the specified international standard atmos-
         phere.

  (2) The weight of the aeroplane at the commencement of the take-off run does
not exceed the maximum take-off weight, if any, specified for the altitude and the
air temperature at the aerodrome at which the take-off is to be made.

*Aeroplanes of a specified maximum total weight authorised exceeding 5,700 kg.
and aeroplanes of a specified maximum total weight authorised not exceeding
5,700 kg. which comply with neither condition (1)(a) nor condition (1)(b).*

  (3) (*a*) The distance required by the aeroplane to attain a height of 50 feet, with
all power units operating within the maximum take-off power conditions specified,
does not exceed the take-off run available at the aerodrome at which the take-off
is to be made.

    (*b*) The distance required by the aeroplane to attain a height of 50 feet with
all power units operating within the maximum take-off power conditions specified,
when multiplied by a factor of either 1·33 for aeroplanes having two power units
or by a factor of 1·18 for aeroplanes having four power units, does not exceed
the emergency distance available at the aerodrome at which the take-off is to be
made.

    (*c*) For the purposes of sub-paragraphs (*a*) and (*b*) the distance required by
the aeroplane to attain a height of 50 feet shall be that appropriate to:

      (i) the weight of the aeroplane at the commencement of the take-off run ;

      (ii) the altitude at the aerodrome ;

      (iii) the air temperature at the aerodrome ;

      (iv) the condition of the surface of the runway from which the take-off
           will be made ;

      (v) the slope of the surface of the aerodrome in the direction of take-off
          over the take-off run available and the emergency distance available,
          respectively ; and

(vi) not more than 50 per cent of the reported wind component opposite to the direction of take-off or not less than 150 per cent of the reported wind component in the direction of take-off.

(4) (a) The take-off flight path with one power unit inoperative and the remaining power unit or units operating within the maximum take-off power conditions specified, appropriate to:

(i) the weight of the aeroplane at the commencement of the take-off run;

(ii) the altitude at the aerodrome;

(iii) the air temperature at the aerodrome;

(iv) not more than 50 per cent of the reported wind component opposite to the direction of take-off or not less than 150 per cent of the reported wind component in the direction of take-off,

and plotted from a point 50 feet above the end of the appropriate factored distance required for take-off under condition (3)(b) of this Regulation at the aerodrome at which the take-off is to be made, shows that the aeroplane will clear any obstacle in its path by a vertical interval of at least 35 feet except that if it is intended that an aeroplane shall change its direction by more than 15° the vertical interval shall be not less than 50 feet during the change of direction.

(b) For the purpose of sub-paragraph (4)(a) an obstacle shall be deemed to be in the path of the aeroplane if the distance from the obstacle to the nearest point on the ground below the intended line of flight does not exceed:

(i) a distance of 200 feet plus half the wing span of the aeroplane plus one-eighth of the distance from such point to the end of the take-off distance available, measured along the intended line of flight; or

(ii) 5,000 feet,

whichever is the less.

(c) In assessing the ability of the aeroplane to satisfy this condition, it shall not be assumed to make a change of direction of a radius less than a radius of steady turn corresponding to an angle of bank of 15°.

(5) The aeroplane will, in the meteorological conditions expected for the flight, in the event of any one power unit becoming inoperative at any point on its route or on any planned diversion therefrom and with the other power unit or units operating within the maximum continuous power conditions specified, be capable of continuing the flight clearing obstacles within 10 nautical miles either side of the intended track by a vertical interval of at least:

(a) 1,000 feet when the gradient of the flight path is not less than zero; or

(b) 2,000 feet when the gradient of the flight path is less than zero,

to an aerodrome at which it can comply with condition (9), and on arrival over such aerodrome the flight path shall have a gradient of not less than zero at 1,500 feet above the aerodrome.

For the purpose of this condition the gradient of climb of the aeroplane shall be taken to be one per cent less than that specified.

(6) The aeroplane will, in the meteorological conditions expected for the flight, at any point on its route or on any planned diversion therefrom be capable of climbing at a gradient of at least 1 in 50, with all power units operating within the maximum continuous power conditions specified, at the following altitudes:

(a) the minimum altitudes for safe flight on each stage of the route to be flown or of any planned diversion therefrom specified in, or calculated from the information contained in, the operations manual relating to the aeroplane; and

(b) the minimum altitudes necessary for compliance with conditions (5) and (7), as appropriate.

(7) If on the route to be flown or any planned diversion therefrom, the aeroplane will be engaged in a flight over water during which at any point it may be more than 90 minutes flying time in still air from the nearest shore, it will in the

event of two power units becoming inoperative during such time and with the other power unit or units operating within the maximum continuous power conditions specified be capable of continuing the flight having regard to the meteorological conditions expected for the flight, clearing all obstacles within 10 nautical miles either side of the intended track by a vertical interval of at least 1,000 feet, to an aerodrome at which a safe landing can be made.

(8) The landing weight of the aeroplane will not exceed the maximum landing weight, if any, specified for the altitude and the expected air temperature for the estimated time of landing at the aerodrome at which it is intended to land and at any alternate aerodrome.

(9) The distance required by the aeroplane to land from a height of 50 feet does not, at the aerodrome at which it is intended to land, exceed 60 per cent of the landing distance available on—

(i) the most suitable runway for a landing in still air conditions ; and

(ii) the runway that may be required for landing because of the forecast wind conditions ; provided that if an alternate aerodrome is designated in the flight plan the landing distance required at the aerodrome at which it is intended to land shall not exceed 70 per cent of that available on the runway.

The distance required to land from a height of 50 feet shall be taken to be that appropriate to—

(a) the landing weight ;

(b) the altitude at the aerodrome ;

(c) the temperature in the specified international standard atmosphere appropriate to the altitude at the aerodrome ;

(d) (i) a level surface in the case of runways usable in both directions ;

(ii) the average slope of the runway in the case of runways usable in only one direction ; and

(e) (i) still air conditions in the case of the most suitable runway for a landing in still air conditions ; and

(ii) not more than 50 per cent of the forecast wind component opposite to the direction of landing or not less than 150 per cent of the forecast wind component in the direction of landing in the case of the runway that may be required for landing because of the forecast wind conditions.

(10) The distance required by the aeroplane to land from a height of 50 feet does not, at any alternate aerodrome, exceed 70 per cent of the landing distance available on—

(i) the most suitable runway for a landing in still air conditions ; and

(ii) the runway that may be required for landing because of the forecast wind conditions.

For the purpose of this condition the distance required to land from a height of 50 feet shall be determined in the manner provided in condition (9).

Aeroplanes of a specified maximum total weight authorised not exceeding 5,700 kg. and which comply with either condition (1)(a) or condition (1)(b), or with both those conditions

(11) If the aeroplane is engaged in a flight at night or when the cloud ceiling or visibility prevailing at the aerodrome of departure and forecast for the estimated time of landing at the aerodrome of destination or at any alternate aerodrome, are less than 1,000 feet and one nautical mile respectively, it will, with any one of its power units inoperative and the remaining power unit or units operating within the maximum continuous power conditions specified, be capable of climbing at a gradient of at least 1 in 200 at an altitude of 2,500 feet in the specified international standard atmosphere.

(12) (a) The distance required by the aeroplane to attain a height of 50 feet with all power units operating within the maximum take-off power conditions specified, does not exceed the take-off run available at the aerodrome at which the take-off is to be made ;

(b) The distance required by the aeroplane to attain a height of 50 feet, with all power units operating within the maximum take-off power conditions specified, when multiplied by a factor of 1·33 does not exceed the emergency distance available at the aerodrome at which the take-off is to be made ;

(c) For the purposes of sub-paragraphs (a) and (b) the distance required by the aeroplane to attain a height of 50 feet shall be that appropriate to:

> (i) the weight of the aeroplane at the commencement of the take-off run ;
>
> (ii) the altitude at the aerodrome ;
>
> (iii) the temperature in the specified international standard atmosphere appropriate to the altitude at the aerodrome, or, if greater, the air temperature at the aerodrome less 15° centigrade ;
>
> (iv) the slope of the surface of the aerodrome in the direction of take-off over the take-off run available and the emergency distance available, respectively ; and
>
> (v) not more than 50 per cent of the reported wind component opposite to the direction of take-off or not less than 150 per cent of the reported wind component in the direction of take-off.

(13) The take-off flight path, with all power units operating within the maximum take-off power conditions specified, appropriate to:

> (i) the weight of the aeroplane at the commencement of the take-off run ;
>
> (ii) the altitude at the aerodrome ;
>
> (iii) the temperature in the specified international standard atmosphere appropriate to the altitude at the aerodrome, or, if greater, the air temperature at the aerodrome less 15° centigrade ; and
>
> (iv) not more than 50 per cent of the reported wind component opposite to the direction of take-off or not less than 150 per cent of the reported wind component in the direction of take-off,

and plotted from a point 50 feet above the end of the factored distance required for take-off under condition (12)(b), at the aerodrome at which the take-off is to be made, shows that the aeroplane will clear any obstacle lying within 200 feet plus half the wing span of the aeroplane on either side of its path by a vertical interval of at least 35 feet. In assessing the ability of the aeroplane to satisfy this condition it shall not be assumed to make a change of direction of a radius less than a radius of steady turn corresponding to an angle of bank of 15°.

(14) The aeroplane will, in the meteorological conditions expected for the flight, in the event of any one power unit becoming inoperative at any point on its route or on any planned diversion therefrom and with the other power unit or units, if any, operating within the maximum continuous power conditions specified, be capable of continuing the flight so as to reach a point above a place at which a safe landing can be made at a suitable height for such landing.

(15) The aeroplane will, in the meteorological conditions expected for the flight, at any point on its route or any planned diversion therefrom, be capable of climbing at a gradient of at least 1 in 50, with all power units operating within the maximum continuous power conditions specified, at the following altitudes:

> (a) the minimum altitudes for safe flight on each stage of the route to be flown or on any planned diversion therefrom specified in, or calculated from, the information contained in the operations manual relating to the aeroplane ; and
>
> (b) the minimum altitudes necessary for compliance with condition (14).

(16) If on the route to be flown or any planned diversion therefrom the aeroplane will be engaged in a flight over water during which at any point it may be

more than 30 minutes flying time in still air from the nearest shore, it will, in the event of one power unit becoming inoperative during such time and with the other power unit or units operating within the maximum continuous power conditions specified, be capable of climbing at a gradient of at least 1 in 200 at an altitude of 5,000 feet in the specified international standard atmosphere.

(17) The landing weight of the aeroplane will not exceed the maximum landing weight, if any, specified for the altitude and the expected air temperature for the estimated time of landing at the aerodrome at which it is intended to land and at any alternate aerodrome.

(18) The distance required by the aeroplane to land from a height of 50 feet does not, at the aerodrome at which it is intended to land and at any alternate aerodrome, exceed 70 per cent, or, if a visual approach and landing will be possible in the meteorological conditions forecast for the estimated time of landing, 80 per cent, of the landing distance available on:

> (i) the most suitable runway for a landing in still air conditions ; and
> (ii) the runway that may be required for landing because of the forecast wind conditions,

the distance required to land from a height of 50 feet being taken to be that appropriate to:

- (a) the landing weight ;
- (b) the altitude at the aerodrome ;
- (c) the temperature in the specified international standard atmosphere appropriate to the altitude at the aerodrome ;
- (d) (i) a level surface in the case of runways usable in both directions ;
  - (ii) the average slope of the runway in the case of runways usable in only one direction ; and
- (e) (i) still air conditions in the case of the most suitable runway for a landing in still air conditions ;
  - (ii) not more than 50 per cent of the forecast wind component opposite to the direction of landing or not less than 150 per cent of the forecast wind component in the direction of landing in the case of the runway that may be required for landing because of the forecast wind conditions.

EXPLANATORY NOTE

(This Note is not part of the Regulations.)

These Regulations consolidate the Air Navigation (General) Regulations 1970, as amended and substitute the Civil Aviation Authority for the Secretary of State. In addition to some minor and drafting amendments the following change is made in Regulation 9 (which governs the weight and performance requirements of public transport aeroplanes having a performance group classification of Group C or Group D in their certificate of airworthiness): an alternative condition governing the landing distance required is introduced, which permits the use of specified short field data when determining the weight of the aeroplane at the commencement of the take-off run.

STOKE-ON-TRENT
CITY
LIBRARIES

STATUTORY INSTRUMENTS

1972 No. 323

CIVIL AVIATION

The Civil Aviation (Births, Deaths and Missing Persons) (Amendment) Regulations 1972

Made - - -	*1st March* 1972
Coming into Operation	*1st April* 1972

The Secretary of State, in exercise of his powers under section 55 of the Civil Aviation Act 1949(**a**) as amended by paragraph 2 of Schedule 10 to the Civil Aviation Act 1971(**b**) and of all other powers enabling him in that behalf hereby makes the following Regulations.

1. These Regulations may be cited as the Civil Aviation (Births, Deaths and Missing Persons) (Amendment) Regulations 1972 and shall come into operation on 1st April 1972.

2. The Interpretation Act 1889(**c**) applies for the purpose of these Regulations as it applies for the purpose of the interpretation of an Act of Parliament.

3. The Civil Aviation (Births, Deaths and Missing Persons) Regulations 1948(**d**) are hereby amended as follows:

(1) In Regulation 2:

(*a*) there shall be inserted the following:

"(1A) "the Authority" means the Civil Aviation Authority" ;

(*b*) the definition of "Minister" shall be deleted ;

(2) For the words "the Minister" wherever they occur there shall be substituted the words "the Authority" and for "he" and "him" wherever those expressions refer to the Minister, there shall be substituted "it" ;

(3) For the words "aircraft registered in Great Britain and Northern Ireland" wherever they occur there shall be substituted the words "aircraft registered in the United Kingdom".

(4) In Regulations 5 and 6 the words "in his Department" shall be deleted and in Regulation 9(1) for the words "in his Department" there shall be substituted the words "pursuant to these Regulations" ;

(5) In Appendices A and B for the words "Section 43 of the Civil Aviation Act 1946" there shall be substituted the words "section 55 of the Civil Aviation Act 1949" ;

D. F. Hubback,
A Deputy Secretary,
Department of Trade and Industry.

1st March 1972.

(**a**) 1949 c. 67.
(**b**) 1971 c. 75.
(**c**) 1889 c. 63.
(**d**) S.I. 1948/1411 (Rev. I, p. 1302: 1948 I, p. 473).

EXPLANATORY NOTE

(This Note is not part of the Regulations.)

In addition to some minor and drafting amendments these Regulations amend the Civil Aviation (Births, Deaths and Missing Persons) Regulations 1948 by substituting the Civil Aviation Authority for the Minister of Civil Aviation.

STATUTORY INSTRUMENTS

1972 No. 325 (C.5)

PENSIONS

The Superannuation Act 1972 (Commencement No. 1) Order 1972

Made	-	-	-	*2nd March* 1972

The Minister for the Civil Service, in exercise of the powers conferred on him by section 30(4) of the Superannuation Act 1972(a), hereby makes the following Order:—

1. This Order may be cited as the Superannuation Act 1972 (Commencement No. 1) Order 1972.

2. The Superannuation Act 1972, except section 21 thereof and paragraphs 68 and 96 of Schedule 6 thereto, shall come into force on 25th March 1972.

Given under the official seal of the Minister for the Civil Service on 2nd March 1972.

(L.S.)

A. W. Wyatt,
Authorised by the Minister
for the Civil Service.

EXPLANATORY NOTE

(This Note is not part of the Order.)

This Order brings into force on 25th March 1972 the whole of the Superannuation Act 1972, except section 21 and paragraphs 68 and 96 of Schedule 6 (which relate to pensions for the employees of the British Airways Board group).

(a) 1972 c. 11.

STATUTORY INSTRUMENTS

1972 No. 328 (S.23)

PENSIONS

The Superannuation (Teaching and Northern Ireland Local Government) Interchange (Scotland) Rules 1972

Made - - -	*25th February* 1972
Laid before Parliament	*13th March* 1972
Coming into Operation	*31st March* 1972

ARRANGEMENT OF RULES

PART I

GENERAL

PART II

TRANSFER FROM TEACHING SERVICE TO NORTHERN IRELAND LOCAL GOVERNMENT SERVICE

PART III

TRANSFER FROM NORTHERN IRELAND LOCAL GOVERNMENT SERVICE TO TEACHING SERVICE

In exercise of the powers conferred on me by sections 2 and 15 of the Superannuation (Miscellaneous Provisions) Act 1948(a) as amended by section 11 of the Superannuation (Miscellaneous Provisions) Act 1967(b), and of all other powers enabling me in that behalf, and with the consent of the Minister for the Civil Service, I hereby make the following rules:—

PART I

GENERAL

Citation and Commencement

1. These rules may be cited as the Superannuation (Teaching and Northern Ireland Local Government) Interchange (Scotland) Rules 1972 and shall come into operation on 31st March 1972.

Revocation

2.—(1) The Superannuation (Teaching and Northern Ireland Local Government) Interchange (Scotland) Rules 1967(c) are hereby revoked:

Provided that the rules hereby revoked shall continue to apply in relation to any person who, before 1st February 1969, became employed in contributing service or became an officer within the meaning of those rules in like manner as they would have applied if these rules had not been made.

(2) Section 38 of the Interpretation Act 1889(d) (which relates to the effect of repeals) shall apply as if these rules were an Act of Parliament and as if the rules revoked by these rules were Acts of Parliament repealed by an Act of Parliament.

Interpretation

3.—(1) In these rules, unless the context otherwise requires—

"the Act of 1939" means the Education (Scotland) (War Service Superannuation) Act 1939(e);

"the Act of 1948" means the Superannuation (Miscellaneous Provisions) Act 1948;

"the Act of 1968" means the Teachers Superannuation (Scotland) Act 1968(f);

"added years" means, in relation to an officer, any additional years of service reckonable by him under regulation 26 of the Local Government Superannuation Regulations or the provisions of the Corporation Superannuation Scheme corresponding thereto and includes any additional years of service which, having been granted under any similar provision contained in any other enactment or scheme, have subsequently become and are reckonable under those Regulations or the Corporation Superannuation Scheme;

"appropriate authority" means, in relation to an officer, either the Northern Ireland Local Government Officers' Superannuation Committee or the Council of the County Borough of Belfast, whichever shall be appropriate;

"benefit" means any superannuation benefit payable to or in respect of any person;

(a) 1948 c. 33.
(c) S.I. 1967/1882 (1967 III, p. 5110).
(e) 1939 c. 96.

(b) 1967 c. 28.
(d) 1889 c. 63.
(f) 1968 c. 12.

"contributing service" and "contributory employee" have the same respective meanings as in the Local Government Superannuation (Scotland) Acts 1937 to 1953(**a**);

"the Corporation Superannuation Scheme" means the superannuation scheme made by the Council of the County Borough of Belfast under section 5A of the Local Government (Superannuation) Act (Northern Ireland) 1950(**b**);

"the Local Government Superannuation Regulations" means the Local Government (Superannuation) Regulations (Northern Ireland) 1962(**c**) as amended (**d**);

"national service", in relation to any person, means service which is relevant service within the meaning of the Reserve and Auxiliary Forces (Protection of Civil Interests) Act 1951(**e**) and any similar service immediately following relevant service entered into with the consent of the body or person by whom he was last employed before undertaking the service;

"officer" means—

(*a*) a person who has been duly admitted to participate in the benefits of the superannuation scheme administered by the Northern Ireland Local Government Officers' Superannuation Committee under the Local Government Superannuation Regulations; or

(*b*) a person to whom the Corporation Superannuation Scheme applies;

"operative date" means the date of the coming into operation of these rules;

"prescribed period" has the meaning assigned to that expression by rule 4;

"reckonable service" means such service as is by virtue of the Teachers Regulations of 1969 reckonable service for all purposes of Part I of the Act of 1968;

"repaid contributions" means any sum paid to a person under a pension scheme applicable to him by way of repayment of contributions (other than voluntary contributions and contributions made or deemed to be made for the purpose of securing benefits for a widow, children or other dependants); and includes both any interest included in such sum and any amount deducted therefrom in respect of liability to income tax arising by reason of the payment;

"the Teachers Regulations of 1957" means the Teachers (Superannuation) (Scotland) Regulations 1957(**f**) as amended (**g**);

"the Teachers Regulations of 1969" means the Teachers Superannuation (Scotland) Regulations 1969(**h**) as amended (**i**);

"the Teachers Schemes" means the Superannuation Scheme for Teachers in Scotland dated 5th June 1919(**j**), the Superannuation Scheme for Teachers (Scotland) 1926(**k**) and the Superannuation Scheme for Teachers (Scotland) 1952(**l**);

"teaching service" means—

(*a*) reckonable service; or

(**a**) 1937 c. 69; 1939 c. 18; 1953 c. 25.　　(**b**) 1950 c. 10 (N.I.).
(**c**) S.R. & O. (N.I.) 1962 No. 210.
(**d**) S.R. & O. (N.I.) 1966 No. 274, 1968 No. 153, 1969 No. 154, 1970 No. 54, 1971 No. 108.
(**e**) 1951 c. 65.　　　　　　　　　　(**f**) S.I. 1957/356 (1957 I, p. 733).
(**g**) S.I. 1958/1595, 1963/2111, 1965/1166, 1966/1229, 1967/1736 (1958 I, p. 1077; 1963 III, p. 4685; 1965 II, p. 3284; 1966 III, p. 3295; 1967 III, p. 4657).
(**h**) S.I. 1969/77 (1969 I, p. 133).
(**i**) S.I. 1969/659, 1971/1995 (1969 II, p. 1820; 1971 III, p. 5683).
(**j**) S. R. & O. 1919/1105 (1919 I, p. 688).　　(**k**) S. R. & O. 1926/363 (1926 p. 449).
(**l**) S.I. 1952/464 (1952 I, p. 873).

(b) service which for the purposes of the Teachers Regulations of 1969 is service as an organiser;

"the Transfer Value Regulations" means the Local Government Superannuation (Transfer Value) (Scotland) Regulations 1954(a);

"voluntary contributions" means—

(a) in relation to employment in teaching service, additional contributions paid or being paid under regulation 31 of the Teachers Regulations of 1969 in respect of a period of previous employment and any contributions being paid as a condition of actual service being increased by the addition thereto of any other period (not being a period of war service or national service); and

(b) in relation to employment as an officer, payments (other than completed payments, that is to say, payments made in respect of a liability which has been wholly discharged) of either of the following categories:—

   (i) additional contributory payments made in accordance with the provisions of the Second Schedule to the Local Government Superannuation Regulations or with the provisions of the Corporation Superannuation Scheme corresponding thereto; or

   (ii) payments in respect of added years.

(2) Any reference in these rules to the provisions of any enactment, rules, regulations or other instrument shall, unless the context otherwise requires, be construed as a reference to those provisions as amended, modified, extended, applied or re-enacted by any subsequent enactment, rules, regulations or instrument.

(3) References in these rules to a rule, Part or paragraph, shall, unless the context otherwise requires, be construed as references to that rule or Part of these rules, or to that paragraph of the rule in which the reference occurs, as the case may be.

(4) The Interpretation Act 1889 shall apply for the interpretation of these rules as it applies for the interpretation of an Act of Parliament.

Prescribed Period

4.—(1) For the purposes of these rules, subject as provided hereafter in this rule, the expression "prescribed period" shall mean—

(a) in the case of a person who, immediately after ceasing to be employed in teaching service or as an officer became engaged in national service, a period of six months after the date of termination of the national service; and

(b) in the case of any other person, a period of twelve months after the date on which he ceased to be employed in teaching service or as an officer.

(2) The Secretary of State in the case of a person becoming employed in teaching service and the appropriate authority in the case of a person becoming an officer may, with the agreement of the other, in any particular case extend the period of six months or twelve months, whichever is appropriate, specified in paragraph (1).

(a) S.I. 1954/1256 (1954 II, p. 1736).

(3) Subject as provided in paragraph (4)—

    (*a*) in reckoning the periods of six months and twelve months specified in paragraph (1) no account shall be taken of any period spent by a person on a course of study or training which he undertook after leaving his former employment; and

    (*b*) if a person left his former employment in order to undertake a course of study or training and on completion of that course became engaged in national service, he shall be deemed for the purposes of paragraph (1) to have left his former employment at the time when he completed the said course of study or training.

(4) The provisions of paragraph (3) shall not apply—

    (*a*) to a person who in his new employment is an officer unless the appropriate authority is satisfied that by reason of his having undertaken the said course of study or training he is better fitted for the duties of his new employment; or

    (*b*) to a person who in his new employment is in teaching service unless—

        (i) before leaving his former employment (or, if between leaving that employment and undertaking the said course of study or training he was engaged in national service, before the end of that service) he gave notice in writing to the appropriate authority of his intention to undertake the said course of study or training; and

        (ii) the Secretary of State is satisfied that by reason of his having undertaken the said course of study or training he is better fitted for the duties of his new employment.

PART II

TRANSFER FROM TEACHING SERVICE TO NORTHERN IRELAND LOCAL GOVERNMENT SERVICE

Application

5.—(1) Except as in paragraph (3) provided, this Part shall apply to a person who—

    (*a*) on or after 1st February 1969 becomes, or has become, an officer within the prescribed period after ceasing to be employed in teaching service;

    (*b*) within three months after becoming an officer, or within such longer period as the appropriate authority may with the agreement of the Secretary of State in any particular case allow, notifies that authority in writing that he desires this Part to apply to him and furnishes that authority with particulars in writing of his teaching service and of any national service in which he has been engaged since ceasing to be employed in teaching service; and

    (*c*) within three months after becoming an officer, or within such longer period as the appropriate authority may in any particular case allow, pays to that authority an amount equal to any repaid contributions paid to him after he last ceased to be employed in teaching service, together with compound interest thereon of an amount determined in accordance with paragraph (2).

(2) For the purposes of paragraph (1)(*c*)—

    (*a*) compound interest shall be paid where the prescribed period exceeds one year and shall be calculated on the amount of the repaid contributions at three per cent per annum with yearly rests from the day one year after that on which the person ceased to be employed in teaching service or from the day on which that amount was paid to him, whichever shall be the later, to the day on which he became an officer; and

(b) if the amount of compound interest calculated as aforesaid exceeds a sum equal to one-half of the difference between the amount of the transfer value payable under rule 6 and the amount of the transfer value which would have been so payable if calculated by reference to the person's age on ceasing to be employed in teaching service, it shall be reduced to that sum.

(3) This Part shall not apply to a person who—

(a) has received payment of any benefit (other than repayment of contributions) under the Teachers Schemes, the Teachers Regulations of 1957 or the Teachers Regulations of 1969; or

(b) is a person in respect of whom a transfer value has been paid otherwise than under these rules by the Secretary of State since he last ceased to be employed in teaching service.

Transfer Value

6.—(1) In respect of a person to whom this Part applies the Secretary of State shall, out of moneys provided by Parliament, pay to the appropriate authority a transfer value of an amount calculated in accordance with the following provisions of this rule.

(2) Subject as hereafter in this rule provided, the transfer value shall be an amount equal to the transfer value which would have been payable under the Transfer Value Regulations if the person, at the date when he ceased to be employed in teaching service, had ceased to be a contributory employee under one local authority and had become such an employee under another local authority and had been entitled to reckon as contributing service within the meaning of those Regulations his reckonable service and his service reckonable for the purposes of Part VII of the Teachers Regulations of 1969 at the length at which it is so reckonable.

(3) For the purposes of paragraph (2) service which is reckoned as contributing service shall be deemed to have been affected or modified in accordance with regulations applicable to such service made under section 110 of the National Insurance Act 1965(**a**), or under any provision corresponding thereto contained in an enactment repealed by that Act, in like manner and to the like extent, as nearly as may be, as it was affected or modified by other such regulations.

(4) In respect of a person to whom either paragraph (2) or paragraph (3) of rule 4 applies the transfer value shall be calculated by reference to his age on the date on which he became an officer.

(5) In calculating the amount of a transfer value there shall be excluded—

(a) any period of war service within the meaning of the Act of 1939 and of national service within the meaning of the Teachers Superannuation (National Service) (Scotland) Rules 1952(**b**) in respect of which, at the time the transfer value is paid, the contributions remain unpaid; and

(b) any period of previous employment and any period additional to actual service in respect of which the person was immediately before

---

(**a**) 1965 c. 51.　　　　　　　　　(**b**) S.I. 1952/518 (1952 I, p. 928).

ceasing to be employed in teaching service paying voluntary contributions and in respect of which, at the time the transfer value is paid, he has not elected to continue to pay such contributions.

(6) The amount of the transfer value payable in respect of a person shall, in lieu of being reduced in accordance with the proviso to paragraph 2 of the First Schedule to the Transfer Value Regulations, be reduced by—

(a) an amount equal to the sum of any repaid contributions paid to him after he last ceased to be employed in teaching service and any compound interest thereon payable under rule 5(1)(c);

(b) an amount equal to any sum which remained to be paid by him on his ceasing to be employed in teaching service towards the discharge of a fixed sum as a condition of any period of service being reckoned for the purposes of the Teachers Regulations of 1969;

(c) an amount equal to the capital value of any voluntary contributions which on his ceasing to be employed in teaching service remained to be paid by him in respect of any period not excluded from the calculation of the amount of the transfer value by paragraph (5)(b); and

(d) an amount equal to any sum payable by the Secretary of State by way of income tax by reason of its payment.

Benefits under Teachers Regulations of 1969

7.—(1) Subject to the provisions of Part III and of interchange rules, no payment of any benefit shall be made under the Teachers Regulations of 1969 to or in respect of any person in respect of any service which is taken into account in calculating the amount of a transfer value under rule 6 other than a payment by way of return of voluntary contributions.

(2) In this rule "interchange rules" means rules made under section 2 of the Act of 1948 and includes provisions similar to those of such rules contained in any instrument made under any other Act.

PART III

TRANSFER FROM NORTHERN IRELAND LOCAL GOVERNMENT SERVICE TO TEACHING SERVICE

Application

8.—(1) Except as provided in paragraph (3) this Part shall apply to a person who—

(a) on or after 1st February 1969 becomes, or has become, employed in teaching service within the prescribed period after ceasing to be an officer;

(b) within three months after becoming employed in teaching service, or within such longer period as the Secretary of State may with the agreement of the appropriate authority in any particular case allow, notifies the Secretary of State in writing that he desires this Part to apply to him and furnishes the Secretary of State with particulars in writing of his service as an officer and of any national service in which he has been engaged since ceasing to be employed in local government service;

(c) within three months after becoming employed in teaching service, or within such longer period as the Secretary of State may in any particular case allow, pays to the Secretary of State an amount equal to any repaid contributions paid to him after he last ceased to be an officer, together with compound interest thereon of an amount determined in accordance with paragraph (2); and

    (*d*) is a person in respect of whom the Secretary of State receives from the appropriate authority a transfer value of an amount determined in accordance with the provisions of rule 9.

(2) For the purposes of paragraph (1)(*c*)—

    (*a*) compound interest shall be paid where the prescribed period exceeds one year and shall be calculated on the amount of the repaid contributions at three per cent per annum with yearly rests from the day one year after that on which the person ceased to be an officer or from the day on which that amount was paid to him, whichever shall be the later, to the day on which he became employed in teaching service; and

    (*b*) if the amount of compound interest calculated as aforesaid exceeds a sum equal to one-half of the difference between the amount of the transfer value payable under rule 9 and the amount of the transfer value which would have been so payable if calculated by reference to the person's age on ceasing to be an officer, it shall be reduced to that sum.

(3) This Part shall not apply to a person who has received payment of any benefit (other than repayment of contributions) under the Local Government Superannuation Regulations or the Corporation Superannuation Scheme.

Transfer Value

9.—(1) Subject as provided hereafter in this rule, the transfer value receivable by the Secretary of State from the appropriate authority in respect of a person to whom this Part applies shall be an amount equal to the transfer value which would have been payable under the Transfer Value Regulations if the person, at the date when he ceased to be an officer, had ceased to be a contributory employee under one local authority and had become such an employee under another local authority and had been entitled to reckon as contributing service or non-contributing service, as the case may be, for the purposes of those Regulations service reckonable as contributing service and non-contributing service for the purposes of the Local Government Superannuation Regulations or the Corporation Superannuation Scheme.

(2) For the purposes of paragraph (1) service which is reckoned as contributing service shall be deemed to have been affected or modified in accordance with regulations applicable to such service made under section 110 of the National Insurance Act 1965, or under any provision corresponding thereto contained in an enactment repealed by that Act, in like manner and to the like extent, as nearly as may be, as the person's service as an officer was affected or modified by regulations in force in Northern Ireland and corresponding to such regulations as aforesaid.

(3) In respect of a person to whom either paragraph (2) or paragraph (3) of rule 4 applies the transfer value shall be calculated by reference to his age on the date on which he became employed in teaching service.

(4) The amount of the transfer value payable in respect of a person shall be reduced by—

    (*a*) an amount equal to the sum of any repaid contributions paid to him after he last ceased to be an officer and any compound interest thereon payable under rule 8(1)(*c*); and (*b*) an amount equal to any sum payable by the appropriate authority by way of income tax by reason of its payment.

Reckoning of Service

10.—(1) Subject as provided hereafter in this rule, in respect of a person to whom this Part applies:—

(*a*) there shall be reckoned as reckonable service—

(i) any period of service which, at the time of his ceasing to be an officer, is reckonable as contributing service for the purposes of the Local Government Superannuation Regulations or the Corporation Superannuation Scheme; and

(ii) one-half of any period of service which, at the time of his ceasing to be an officer, is reckonable as non-contributing service for the purposes of the Local Government Superannuation Regulations or the Corporation Superannuation Scheme; and

(*b*) there shall be reckoned as class C external service for the purposes of the Teachers Regulations of 1969 any period of service which, at the time of his ceasing to be an officer, is reckonable as non-contributing service for the purposes of the Local Government Superannuation Regulations or the Corporation Superannuation Scheme, except in so far as that service is reckoned under this rule or the Teachers Regulations of 1969 as reckonable service or as class A or class B external service for the purposes of the Teachers Regulations of 1969.

(2) Where a person to whom this Part applies has, whilst he was an officer, been employed as a part-time employee, the period of his part-time service shall be treated—

(*a*) for the purposes of determining whether he has served for any minimum period prescribed by the Teachers Regulations of 1969 as necessary for any benefit to be paid to or in respect of him as if it were whole-time service; and

(*b*) for the purpose of calculating the amount of any benefit payable under the Teachers Regulations of 1969, as if it were whole-time service for a proportionately reduced period.

(3) The whole of any period of service to which paragraph (1) applies shall, for the purpose of calculating under section 4(3) of the Act of 1968 the average salary of a person to whom this Part applies, be reckoned as a period of employment in reckonable service and his salary during any period so reckoned shall be such amount as would under the Local Government Superannuation Regulations or the Corporation Superannuation Scheme be taken into account for the purposes of determining the annual average of his remuneration during that period.

(4) Notwithstanding anything in this rule before contained, any service of a person to whom this Part applies, which, under the Local Government Superannuation Regulations or the Corporation Superannuation Scheme, was at the time he ceased to be an officer, service reckonable only for the purpose of calculating the amount of any benefit payable to or in respect of him or only for the purpose of determining whether he was entitled to any pension, shall be reckoned only for the corresponding like purpose under the Teachers Regulations of 1969.

Voluntary Contributions

11.—(1) A person to whom this Part applies may, within three months of becoming employed in teaching service or within such longer period as the

Secretary of State may in any particular case allow, elect to continue to pay voluntary contributions being paid by him immediately before ceasing to be an officer.

(2) If a person elects as aforesaid and—

(*a*) within three months of becoming employed in teaching service, or within such longer period as the Secretary of State may in any particular case allow, pays to the Secretary of State a sum equal to the sum of any payment made to him on or after ceasing to be an officer by way of return of voluntary contributions, any interest added thereto and any deduction therefrom in respect of income tax; and

(*b*) thereafter pays to the Secretary of State any amounts outstanding in respect of voluntary contributions at the times at which they would have been payable if he had remained an officer,

his teaching service shall be affected in the manner prescribed by the following provisions of this rule.

(3) In respect of voluntary contributions paid in respect of added years, those years shall be reckoned as reckonable service.

(4) In respect of voluntary contributions paid otherwise than in respect of added years, the service in respect of which they are paid shall be reckoned for the purposes of the Teachers Regulations of 1969 in the manner in which it would under rule 10 have been so reckoned if the payment of the contributions had been completed immediately before the person ceased to be an officer.

(5) The provisions of regulation 31(5)(*b*), (6), (7) and (10) and regulation 37 of the Teachers Regulations of 1969 shall apply to voluntary contributions payable under this rule as if they were additional contributions payable in respect of previous employment within the meaning of those regulations.

(6) If a person does not elect as aforesaid or if voluntary contributions are repaid to him under regulation 37 of the Teachers Regulations of 1969, as applied by this rule, the period in respect of which such contributions were paid shall be reckoned for the purposes of the Teachers Regulations of 1969 only to the extent, if any, to which it would have been so reckoned if no such payments or contributions had been made in respect thereof.

Commencement of Employment

12. For the purposes of regulation 40(1)(*a*)(ii) of the Teachers Regulations of 1969 the date on which a person to whom this Part applies became an officer shall be deemed to be a date on which he became employed in teaching service.

Return of Contributions

13.—(1) Where a person to whom this Part applies ceases to be employed in teaching service or dies, then, in computing the sum to which he or his personal representatives shall be entitled under the Teachers Regulations of 1969, there shall be included a sum in respect of contributions paid by him in respect of service which by virtue of these rules is reckoned as reckonable service and, in the case of a person who has elected in pursuance of rule 11 to continue paying voluntary contributions, in respect also of voluntary contributions paid by him before becoming employed in teaching service which have either not been returned to him or, if returned, have been paid to the Secretary of State under rule 11 and have not subsequently been again returned.

(2) In computing the amount of the sum so included for the purposes of this rule compound interest shall be calculated—

(a) as respects the period ending immediately before the date on which the person became employed in teaching service, in the manner in which such interest, if any, would have been calculated if the occasion for making the calculation had occurred immediately before that date; and

(b) as respects the period beginning with that date, in accordance with the provisions of Part IV of the Teachers Regulations of 1969.

Modification of Contributions and Benefits by reason of National Insurance

14.—(1) In relation to a person to whom this Part applies—

(a) the following paragraphs of Schedule 5 to the Teachers Regulations of 1969, that is to say—

paragraph 3 (which provides for the reduction of contributions),
paragraph 5 (which provides for the reduction of benefits by fixed annual amounts specified therein) and

paragraph 6 (which provides for the reduction of benefits by annual amounts ascertained by reference to a table)

shall not apply if, on the date on which he ceased to be an officer, neither the provisions of regulation 42 of the Local Government Superannuation Regulations nor the provisions of the Corporation Superannuation Scheme corresponding thereto applied to him;

(b) paragraphs 3 and 6 of the said Schedule 5 shall apply if any benefit payable to him under the Local Government Superannuation Regulations or the Corporation Superannuation Scheme would, by virtue of regulation 42 of those regulations or of the provisions of that scheme corresponding thereto, have been subject to reduction by a fixed annual amount; and

(c) paragraphs 3 and 6 of the said Schedule 5 shall apply if any benefit payable to him under the Local Government Superannuation Regulations or the Corporation Superannuation Scheme would by virtue of regulation 42 of those regulations or of the provisions of that scheme corresponding thereto, have been subject to reduction by an annual amount ascertained by reference to a table.

(2) Where, by virtue of paragraph (1)(c), paragraph 6 of Schedule 5 to the Teachers Regulations of 1969 applies to a person the date of modification for the purposes of the latter paragraph shall be the date which was in relation to him relevant for the purposes of regulation 42 of the Local Government Superannuation Regulations or of the provisions of the Corporation Superannuation Scheme corresponding thereto.

Gordon Campbell,
One of Her Majesty's Principal
Secretaries of State.

St. Andrew's House,
Edinburgh.
22nd February 1972.

Consent of the Minister for the Civil Service given under his Official Seal on 25th February 1972.

(L.S.)

K. H. McNeill,
Authorised by the Minister for
the Civil Service.

EXPLANATORY NOTE

(This Note is not part of the Rules.)

These Rules continue, with minor amendments and in terms of the Teachers Superannuation (Scotland) Act 1968 and the Teachers Superannuation (Scotland) Regulations 1969, the existing arrangements for the preservation of superannuation rights of persons changing employment in either direction between pensionable teaching service in Scotland and pensionable local government service in Northern Ireland, by virtue of the Superannuation (Teaching and Northern Ireland Local Government) Interchange (Scotland) Rules 1967, which are revoked.

The Rules may have retrospective effect in certain cases under the express power of, and subject to the safeguards required by, section 2(5) of the Superannuation (Miscellaneous Provisions) Act 1948.

STATUTORY INSTRUMENTS

1972 No. 329

SOCIAL SECURITY

The Supplementary Benefit (Recovery by Deductions from Earnings) Regulations 1972

Made - - -	*3rd March* 1972
Laid before Parliament	*10th March* 1972
Coming into Operation	*3rd April* 1972

The Secretary of State for Social Services, in exercise of the powers conferred by section 17(1) of the Ministry of Social Security Act 1966(**a**), section 2(6) and (9) of, and paragraph 1(3) of Part I of Schedule 1 to, the Social Security Act 1971(**b**), and of all other powers enabling him in that behalf, hereby makes the following regulations:—

Citation, commencement and interpretation

1.—(1) These regulations may be cited as the Supplementary Benefit (Recovery by Deductions from Earnings) Regulations 1972 and shall come into operation on 3rd April 1972.

(2) In these regulations, unless the context otherwise requires—

"the 1966 Act" means the Ministry of Social Security Act 1966(**a**);

"the 1971 Act" means the Social Security Act 1971(**b**);

"benefit" means benefit under the 1966 Act and includes benefit recoverable under section 2(2) of the 1971 Act;

"the Department" means the Department of Health and Social Security;

"employee" means a person falling within section 2(1) of the 1971 Act who has been without employment by reason of a stoppage of work due to a trade dispute at his place of employment;

"employer" means the employer of an employee;

"Part I" means Part I of Schedule 1 to the 1971 Act;

and other expressions have the same meaning as in the 1966 Act and the 1971 Act.

(3) References in these regulations to any enactment or regulations shall, unless the context otherwise requires, include references to such enactment or regulations, as amended by any subsequent enactment, order or regulations, and to any enactments, orders or regulations which replace them by provisions which deal with the same subject matter and are (so far as material) to the like effect.

(**a**) 1966 c. 20. (**b**) 1971 c. 73.

(4) Any notice or other document required or authorised to be given or sent to any person under the provisions of these regulations shall be deemed to have been given or sent if it was sent by post to that person at his ordinary or last known address or in the case of an employer at the place of business where the employee is ordinarily employed.

(5) The rules for the construction of Acts of Parliament contained in the Interpretation Act 1889(a) shall apply for the purpose of the interpretation of these regulations as they apply for the purpose of the interpretation of an Act of Parliament.

Resumption of work between payment days

2.—(1) This regulation applies where in relation to an employee claiming benefit the following conditions are satisfied—

(*a*) he was entitled to benefit during a stoppage of work due to a trade dispute; and

(*b*) he is a person to whom section 2(2) of the 1971 Act (benefit to be recoverable) would but for this regulation apply; and

(*c*) the Secretary of State had arranged for more than one payment day in the terminal week; and

(*d*) the payment day applicable to that employee in the terminal week was a day other than the earlier or earliest of the several payment days in that week; and

(*e*) work was resumed after the first payment day of the terminal week but, by reason only of the arrangements for payment days made by the Secretary of State, before benefit was paid, or an instrument of payment was issued, to that employee for that week.

(2) Where this regulation has effect the employee shall be entitled to benefit in respect of the terminal week on the same terms as if the payment day applicable to him had been the earlier or earliest of such days relating to that week.

(3) Benefit to which an employee is entitled by virtue of this regulation shall not be recoverable under section 2(2) of the 1971 Act.

(4) In this regulation—

"payment day" means the day of the terminal week on which benefit is paid, or an instrument of payment is issued, to an employee;

"the terminal week" means the period of seven days during which work was resumed by employees after a stoppage of work and ending with the last of the several payment days which by virtue of the arrangements for payment days made by the Secretary of State form a single group.

Earnings not paid weekly

3.—(1) Where a deduction notice is served on the employer of an employee whose earnings are payable otherwise than weekly, Part I shall have effect with the adaptations applicable under the following provisions of this regulation.

(a) 1889 c. 63.

(2) Where the employee's earnings are payable at two-weekly intervals, or at periods of some other multiple of a week, for the purposes of paragraph 4 of Part I the amount of the protected earnings shall be twice, or the other appropriate multiple, as the case may be, of that specified in the deduction notice, and the references to one-tenth shall be treated as references to one-fifth or to the other appropriate multiple of one-tenth, as the case may be, of the notified amount; and in paragraph 6(3) of Part I references to protected earnings and to one-tenth shall be adapted in the same manner.

(3) Where the employee is paid monthly Part I shall be adapted in the same manner as under paragraph (2) but as if he were paid every five weeks.

(4) Where the employee's earnings are payable daily, for the purposes of paragraph 4 of Part I the amount of the protected earnings as specified in the deduction notice shall be divided by five and the references to one-tenth shall be treated as references to one-fiftieth; and in paragraph 6(3) of Part I references to protected earnings and to one-tenth shall be adapted in the same manner.

(5) Where the employee's earnings include any bonus, commission or other similar payment payable on a day or days other than the day (hereinafter in this paragraph called "the normal pay-day") on which the remainder of his wages or salary is normally paid, then in order to calculate the employee's available earnings for the purposes of Part I, any such bonus, commission or other similar payment shall be treated as being payable to him on the next following normal pay-day instead of on the day or days on which they are actually payable.

(6) If any doubt arises in any case to which this regulation applies but for which specific provision is not made, the Secretary of State, on the application of the employer or the employee, shall specify the adaptation of Part I to be made in that case.

Recording and payment of recovered amounts to Secretary of State

4.—(1) The employer shall keep a record on an approved form of the available earnings of each employee in respect of whom a deduction notice is in force and of payments under paragraph (2)(*a*) of this regulation.

(2) (*a*) Within seven working days of each pay-day of the employee the employer shall pay to the Department the amount which he was required to deduct from the employee's available earnings in accordance with paragraph 4 of Part I and also any additional amount which with the consent of the employee he deducted in accordance with paragraph 4(3)(*b*) of Part I.

(*b*) All such payments shall be made to the Department at the regional office and shall be accompanied by a statement of deductions on an approved form.

(3) Where on any pay-day the employer, by reason only of the circumstances mentioned in paragraph 4(4)(*a*) of Part I, makes no deduction from the employee's available earnings he shall within seven working days give notice of that fact on an approved form to the Department at the regional office.

(4) Where a deduction notice is cancelled by virtue of paragraph 2(6) or 3(2) of Part I or ceases to have effect by virtue of paragraph 3(1) of Part I, the employer shall within seven working days return the deduction notice to

the Department at the regional office and where paragraph 3(1) applies shall furnish with that notice a statement on an approved form of the reason for the return of the notice.

(5) In this regulation—

"approved form" means either a form approved by the Secretary of State or such other statement in writing as the Secretary of State may accept as sufficient in the circumstances of any particular case;

"regional office" means such office of the Department as the Secretary of State may direct.

Employees to give notice of cessation or resumption of employment

5.—(1) Where an employee ceases to be in the employment of a person on whom a deduction notice relating to him has been duly served knowing that there has not been deducted from his earnings or otherwise recovered by the Secretary of State the full amount specified in that deduction notice as the amount by reference to which deductions were to be made, he shall notify the Department of his address and of the date of such cessation of employment within one week.

(2) Where on or after such cessation the employee resumes full-time employment, whether with the same or some other employer, he shall within one week notify the Department of the name of the employer and of the address of his place of employment.

Review of determination of protected earnings

6.—(1) A determination of the employee's protected earnings whether made by the Commission in accordance with section 2(4) and (5) of the 1971 Act or on review under this regulation may be reviewed by the Commission—

    (*a*) if the Secretary of State has been notified of any relevant change of circumstances since the determination was made in respect of which a determination on review would result in an increase of £2 or more in the amount of the employee's protected earnings; or

    (*b*) if the Commission are satisfied that the determination was based on a mistake as to the law or was made in ignorance of, or was based on a mistake as to, some material fact; or

    (*c*) where there are exceptional circumstances.

(2) Notice of any determination made by the Commission under paragraph (1) shall be given or sent to the employee in writing.

(3) Where the Commission review the employee's protected earnings under this regulation they shall thereupon give to the Secretary of State notice in writing specifying the amount of the employee's protected earnings as determined on review (hereinafter in this regulation called "the revised protected earnings").

(4) Where the Secretary of State receives notice from the Commission under paragraph (3) he shall thereupon serve on the employer written notice varying the relevant deduction notice by substituting the amount of the revised protected earnings for the amount of the protected earnings as specified in the notice.

(5) Any variation of a deduction notice under paragraph (4) shall take effect either from the end of the period of seven days beginning with the day on which notice of the variation is served on the employer or, within the discretion of the employer, at any earlier time after service of the notice.

Keith Joseph,
Secretary of State for Social Services.

3rd March 1972.

EXPLANATORY NOTE

(This Note is not part of the Regulations.)

These Regulations make provisions for the purposes of section 2 of the Social Security Act 1971. This section, which comes into operation on 3rd April 1972, provides that supplementary benefit awarded to a person during the period of 15 days after his return to full-time employment following a trade dispute shall in certain circumstances be recoverable by deductions from his earnings.

Regulation 1 is formal.

Regulation 2 provides that where by reason of arrangements for dealing with benefit payments in connection with a stoppage of work some claimants are paid for the terminal week before, and some after, resumption of work, the latter also are to qualify (in respect of dependants' requirements) for benefit which is not recoverable under section 2 of the Social Security Act 1971.

Regulation 3 sets out the manner in which an employee's protected earnings (the earnings from which no deductions can be made for the recovery of benefit) are to be calculated where the earnings are payable other than weekly.

Regulation 4 requires employers to keep records where a deduction notice is in force and provides for them to make payments, give notices and return expired deduction notices to the Department of Health and Social Security.

Regulation 5 requires employees, on leaving employment knowing that recoverable benefit has not been fully recovered, to notify the Department of such termination and of subsequent resumption of employment.

Regulation 6 provides for review by the Supplementary Benefits Commission of determinations of protected earnings and for consequential variation of deduction notices.

STATUTORY INSTRUMENTS

1972 No. 330

SOCIAL SECURITY

The Supplementary Benefit (General) Amendment Regulations 1972

Made - - -	*3rd March* 1972
Laid before Parliament	*13th March* 1972
Coming into Operation	*4th April* 1972

The Secretary of State for Social Services, in exercise of the powers conferred by section 17(1) of the Ministry of Social Security Act 1966(a) and by paragraph 2(3) of Schedule 2 to that Act as modified by regulation 2(2) of the Supplementary Benefit (Decimalisation of the Currency) Regulations 1970(b), and of all other powers enabling him in that behalf, hereby makes the following regulations:—

Citation, interpretation and commencement

1. These regulations, which may be cited as the Supplementary Benefit (General) Amendment Regulations 1972, shall be read as one with the Supplementary Benefit (General) Regulations 1966(c) as amended (d) (hereinafter referred to as "the principal regulations") and shall come into operation on 4th April 1972.

Amendment to regulation 5 of the principal regulations

2.—(1) Paragraph (5) of regulation 5 of the principal regulations (review of determinations made by the Commission or an Appeal Tribunal) shall be amended in accordance with the following paragraphs of this regulation.

(2) In sub-paragraph (*d*) for the words "(*c*) or (*e*)" there shall be substituted the words "(*c*), (*e*) or (*g*)".

(3) At the end of sub-paragraph (*d*) there shall be added the word "or" and immediately after that sub-paragraph there shall be inserted the following sub-paragraph:—

"(*e*) the provisions for computing family income supplement under section 2 (prescribed amount) or section 3 (amount of family income supplement) of the Family Income Supplements Act 1970(e) where such change would affect any adjustment of benefit under paragraph 5 of Schedule 2 to the Act (adjustment of benefit to normal earnings) as modified by section 13(2) of the said Act of 1970

(a) 1966 c. 20.　　　　　　　　　　(b) S.I. 1970/1784 (1970 III, p. 5793).
(c) S.I. 1966/1065 (1966 II, p. 2614).
(d) The relevant amending instrument is S.I. 1967/1045 (1967 II, p. 3134).
(e) 1970 c. 55.

(family income supplement to be taken into account);".

Keith Joseph,
Secretary of State for Social Services.
3rd March 1972.

EXPLANATORY NOTE
(*This Note is not part of the Regulations.*)

These Regulations, which amend the Supplementary Benefit (General) Regulations 1966, enable the Supplementary Benefits Commission to review determinations of entitlement to supplementary benefit (including benefit subject to the "wage-stop") solely for the purpose of giving effect to changes in the provisions for computing family income supplements.

STATUTORY INSTRUMENTS

1972 No. 331

CUSTOMS AND EXCISE

The Import Duty Reliefs (No. 1) Order 1972

Made - - - -	*3rd March* 1972
Laid before the *House of Commons*	*10th March* 1972
Coming into Operation	*1st April* 1972

The Lords Commissioners of Her Majesty's Treasury, by virtue of the powers conferred on them by section 5 of the Import Duties Act 1958(a), as extended by section 1(4) of the Finance Act 1971(b), and of all other powers enabling them in that behalf, on the recommendation of the Secretary of State, hereby make the following Order:—

1.—(1) This Order may be cited as the Import Duty Reliefs (No. 1) Order 1972.

(2) The Interpretation Act 1889(c) shall apply for the interpretation of this Order as it applies for the interpretation of an Act of Parliament.

(3) This Order shall come into operation on 1st April 1972.

2.—(1) Subject to the provisions of article 3 below, import duty shall not be chargeable on articles which—

(a) consist wholly or mainly of cotton or silk or of a combination of the two; and

(b) are either handloom fabrics, as defined in paragraph (2) below, or articles made entirely or mainly of such handloom fabrics.

(2) For the purposes of this article, handloom fabrics are fabrics which—

(a) contain more than 50 per cent. by weight of cotton, of silk, or of both together, and do not contain more than 5 per cent. by weight of man-made fibres; and

(b) are of a type traditionally woven on a handloom; and

(c) have been woven on a handloom for which the motive power is provided entirely by the operator, that is to say, where the three primary movements of weaving (namely shedding, picking and beating) are induced by hand or foot and are not in any way power-assisted.

3.—(1) The relief from import duty provided for by article 2 above shall not apply to articles falling within that provision unless—

(a) they are certified, in accordance with paragraph (2) below, to be handloom goods of a country claiming to be a developing country or to be manufactured in such a country from handloom goods of that country, and

(b) they are certified by the Secretary of State to be imported in accordance with arrangements made between Her Majesty's Government in the United Kingdom and the government of that country.

(a) 1958 c. 6.   (b) 1971 c. 68.   (c) 1889 c. 63.

(2) The certificate required for the purposes of paragraph (1)(*a*) above

(*a*) shall be given by or on behalf of, or by a body authorised by, the government of the country where the articles were made, and

(*b*) shall certify that the articles themselves, or the fabrics of which they are made up as mentioned in article 2(1) above, fall within the description of handloom fabrics in article 2(2) above, and

(*c*) shall contain a description of the articles specifying—

    (i) the quantity of handloom fabrics to which the certificate relates or, in the case of made-up articles, the number of articles and the quantity of handloom fabrics of which they are made up; and

    (ii) the name and address of the manufacturer of the articles and, in the case of made-up articles, of the handloom fabrics of which they are made up.

Walter Clegg,

P. L. Hawkins,

Two of the Lords Commissioners
of Her Majesty's Treasury

3rd March 1972.

EXPLANATORY NOTE

(This Note is not part of the Order.)

This Order, which will come into operation on 1st April 1972, provides for certain handloom goods to be relieved from the duties otherwise chargeable under the Import Duties Act 1958.

STATUTORY INSTRUMENTS

1972 No. 332

INDUSTRIAL TRAINING

The Industrial Training Levy (Carpet) Order 1972

Made - - -	*3rd March* 1972
Laid before Parliament	*13th March* 1972
Coming into Operation	*7th April* 1972

The Secretary of State after approving proposals submitted by the Carpet Industry Training Board for the imposition of a further levy on employers in the carpet industry and in exercise of his powers under section 4 of the Industrial Training Act 1964(a) and of all other powers enabling him in that behalf hereby makes the following Order:—

Title and commencement

1. This Order may be cited as the Industrial Training Levy (Carpet) Order 1972 and shall come into operation on 7th April 1972.

Interpretation

2.—(1) In this Order unless the context otherwise requires:—

(*a*) "agriculture" has the same meaning as in section 109(3) of the Agriculture Act 1947(b), or, in relation to Scotland, as in section 86(3) of the Agriculture (Scotland) Act 1948(c);

(*b*) "an appeal tribunal" means an industrial tribunal established under section 12 of the Industrial Training Act 1964;

(*c*) "assessment" means an assessment of an employer to the levy;

(*d*) "the Board" means the Carpet Industry Training Board;

(*e*) "business" means any activities of industry or commerce;

(*f*) "carpet establishment" means an establishment in Great Britain engaged in the sixth base period wholly or mainly in the carpet industry for a total of twenty-seven or more weeks or, being an establishment that commenced to carry on business in the sixth base period, for a total number of weeks exceeding one-half of the number of weeks in the part of the said period commencing with the day on which business was commenced and ending on the last day thereof;

(*g*) "the carpet industry" means any one or more of the activities which, subject to the provisions of paragraph 2 of the Schedule to the industrial training order, are specified in paragraph 1 of that Schedule as the activities of the carpet industry;

(a) 1964 c. 16.   (b) 1947 c. 48.
(c) 1948 c. 45.

(*h*) "charity" has the same meaning as in section 360 of the Income and Corporation Taxes Act 1970(**a**);

(*i*) "emoluments" means all emoluments assessable to income tax under Schedule E (other than pensions), being emoluments from which tax under that Schedule is deductible, whether or not tax in fact falls to be deducted from any particular payment thereof;

(*j*) "employer" means a person who is an employer in the carpet industry at any time in the sixth levy period;

(*k*) "the industrial training order" means the Industrial Training (Carpet Board) Order 1968(**b**);

(*l*) "the levy" means the levy imposed by the Board in respect of the sixth levy period;

(*m*) "notice" means a notice in writing;

(*n*) "the sixth base period" means the period of twelve months that commenced on 6th April 1970;

(*o*) "the sixth levy period" means the period commencing with the day upon which this Order comes into operation and ending on 31st March 1973.

(2) Any reference in this Order to an establishment that commences to carry on business or that ceases to carry on business shall not be taken to apply where the location of the establishment is changed but its business is continued wholly or mainly at or from the new location, or where the suspension of activities is of a temporary or seasonal nature.

(3) The Interpretation Act 1889(**c**) shall apply to the interpretation of this Order as it applies to the interpretation of an Act of Parliament.

Imposition of the Levy

3.—(1) The levy to be imposed by the Board on employers in respect of the sixth levy period shall be assessed in accordance with the provisions of this Article.

(2) The levy shall be assessed by the Board separately in respect of each carpet establishment of an employer, but in agreement with the employer one assessment may be made in respect of any number of such establish· ments, in which case those establishments shall be deemed for the purposes of that assessment to constitute one establishment.

(3) Subject to the provisions of this Article, the levy assessed in respect of a carpet establishment of an employer shall be an amount equal to 0·8 per cent. of the sum of the emoluments of all the persons following, that is to say—

(*a*) any persons employed by the employer at or from that establishment in the sixth base period;

(*b*) any persons deemed to have been so employed under the provisions of the next following paragraph.

(4) In the case where a carpet establishment is taken over (whether directly or indirectly) by an employer in succession to, or jointly with, another person, a person employed at any time in the sixth base period at or from the establishment shall be deemed, for the purposes of this Article, to have been so employed by the employer carrying on the said establishment on the day upon which this Order comes into operation.

(**a**) 1970 c. 10.   (**b**) S.I. 1968/1882 (1968 III, p. 5017).
(**c**) 1889 c. 63.

(5) The amount of the levy imposed in respect of a carpet establishment that ceases to carry on business in the sixth levy period shall be in the same proportion to the amount that would otherwise be due under paragraph (3) of this Article as the number of days between the commencement of the said levy period and the date of cessation of business (both dates inclusive) bears to the number of days in the said levy period.

(6) For the purposes of this Article no regard shall be had to the emoluments of any person wholly engaged in agriculture or in the supply of food or drink for immediate consumption.

(7) There shall be exempt from the levy—

    (a) an employer in whose case the number of all the persons employed by him on 5th April 1971 at or from the carpet establishment or establishments of the employer was less than twenty six;

    (b) a charity.

Assessment Notices

4.—(1) The Board shall serve an assessment notice on every employer assessed to the levy, but one notice may comprise two or more assessments.

(2) The amount of any assessment payable under an assessment notice shall be rounded down to the nearest £1.

(3) An assessment notice shall state the Board's address for the service of a notice of appeal or of an application for an extension of time for appealing.

(4) An assessment notice may be served on the person assessed to the levy either by delivering it to him personally or by leaving it, or sending it to him by post, at his last known address or place of business in the United Kingdom or, if that person is a corporation, by leaving it, or sending it by post to the corporation at such address or place of business or at its registered or principal office.

Payment of the Levy

5.—(1) Subject to the provisions of this Article and of Articles 6 and 7, the amount of each assessment appearing in an assessment notice served by the Board shall be payable to the Board in two instalments equal to one-fifth and four-fifths of the said amount respectively, and the said instalments shall be due respectively one month and seven months after the date of the notice.

(2) An instalment of an assessment shall not be recoverable by the Board until there has expired the time allowed for appealing against the assessment by Article 7(1) of this Order and any further period or periods of time that the Board or an appeal tribunal may have allowed for appealing under paragraph (2) or (3) of that Article or, where an appeal is brought, until the appeal is decided or withdrawn.

Withdrawal of Assessment

6.—(1) The Board may, by a notice served on the person assessed to the levy in the same manner as an assessment notice, withdraw an assessment if that person has appealed against that assessment under the provisions of Article 7 of this Order and the appeal has not been entered in the Register of Appeals kept under the appropriate Regulations specified in paragraph (5) of that Article.

(2) The withdrawal of an assessment shall be without prejudice to the power of the Board to serve a further assessment notice in respect of any

establishment to which that assessment related, and where the withdrawal is made by reason of the fact that an establishment has ceased to carry on business in the sixth levy period, the said notice may provide that the whole amount payable thereunder in respect of the establishment shall be due one month after the date of the notice.

Appeals

7.—(1) A person assessed to the levy may appeal to an appeal tribunal against the assessment within one month from the date of the service of the assessment notice or within any further period or periods of time that may be allowed by the Board or an appeal tribunal under the following provisions of this Article.

(2) The Board by notice may for good cause allow a person assessed to the levy to appeal to an appeal tribunal against the assessment at any time within the period of four months from the date of the service of the assessment notice or within such further period or periods as the Board may allow before such time as may then be limited for appealing has expired.

(3) If the Board shall not allow an application for extension of time for appealing, an appeal tribunal shall upon application made to the tribunal by the person assessed to the levy have the like powers as the Board under the foregoing paragraph.

(4) In the case of an establishment that ceases to carry on business in the sixth levy period on any day after the date of the service of the relevant assessment notice the foregoing provisions of this Article shall have effect as if for the period of four months from the date of the service of the assessment notice mentioned in paragraph (2) of this Article there were substituted the period of six months from the date of the cessation of business.

(5) An appeal or an application to an appeal tribunal under this Article shall be made in accordance with the Industrial Tribunals (England and Wales) Regulations 1965(**a**) as amended by the Industrial Tribunals (England and Wales) (Amendment) Regulations 1967(**b**) except where the establishment to which the relevant assessment relates is wholly in Scotland in which case the appeal or application shall be made in accordance with the Industrial Tribunals (Scotland) Regulations 1965(**c**) as amended by the Industrial Tribunals (Scotland) (Amendment) Regulations 1967(**d**).

(6) The powers of an appeal tribunal under paragraph (3) of this Article may be exercised by the President of the Industrial Tribunals (England and Wales) or by the President of the Industrial Tribunals (Scotland) as the case may be.

Evidence

8.—(1) Upon the discharge by a person assessed to the levy of his liability under an assessment the Board shall if so requested issue to him a certificate to that effect.

(2) The production in any proceedings of a document purporting to be certified by the Secretary of the Board to be a true copy of an assessment or other notice issued by the Board or purporting to be a certificate such as is mentioned in the foregoing paragraph of this Article shall, unless the contrary is proved, be sufficient evidence of the document and of the facts stated therein.

(**a**) S.I. 1965/1101 (1965 II, p. 2805).   (**b**) S.I. 1967/301 (1967 I, p. 1040).
(**c**) S.I. 1965/1157 (1965 II, p. 3266).   (**d**) S.I. 1967/302 (1967 I, p. 1050).

Signed by order of the Secretary of State.
3rd March 1972.

Paul Bryan,
Minister of State,
Department of Employment.

EXPLANATORY NOTE

(This Note is not part of the Order.)

This Order gives effect to proposals submitted by the Carpet Industry Training Board to the Secretary of State for Employment for the imposition of a further levy on employers in the carpet industry for the purpose of raising money towards the expenses of the Board.

The levy is to be imposed in respect of the sixth levy period commencing on the date upon which this Order comes into operation and ending on 31st March 1973. The levy will be assessed by the Board and there will be a right of appeal against an assessment to an industrial tribunal.

STATUTORY INSTRUMENTS

1972 No. 333

CRIMINAL PROCEDURE, ENGLAND AND WALES

The Fixed Penalty (Procedure) (Amendment) Regulations 1972

Made - - -	*3rd March* 1972
Laid before Parliament	*10th March* 1972
Coming into Operation	*1st April* 1972

In exercise of the powers conferred upon me by section 80(11) of the Road Traffic Regulation Act 1967(**a**), I hereby make the following Regulations:—

1. These Regulations may be cited as the Fixed Penalty (Procedure) (Amendment) Regulations 1972 and shall come into operation on 1st April 1972.

2. The Fixed Penalty (Procedure) (Amendment) (No. 4) Regulations 1970(**b**), the Fixed Penalty (Procedure) (Amendment) Regulations 1971(**c**) and the Fixed Penalty (Procedure) (Amendment) (No. 2) Regulations 1971(**d**) are hereby revoked.

3. In these Regulations a reference to the principal Regulations is a reference to the Fixed Penalty (Procedure) Regulations 1970(**e**), as amended(**f**).

4. In a case in which a notice under subsection (2) of section 80 of the Road Traffic Regulation Act 1967, offering the opportunity of the discharge of any liability to conviction of an offence to which that section applies by payment of a fixed penalty, has been given or affixed under the said section before the coming into operation of these Regulations, the principal Regulations shall have effect as if these Regulations had not been made.

5. For Regulation 4 of the principal Regulations (clerk to whom fixed penalty is to be paid) there shall be substituted the Regulation set out in Appendix 1 to these Regulations.

6. After Schedule 2 to the principal Regulations there shall be added the Schedule set out in Appendix 2 to these Regulations.

R. Maudling,
One of Her Majesty's Principal
Secretaries of State.

Home Office,
    Whitehall.
3rd March 1972.

(**a**) 1967 c. 76.
(**b**) S.I. 1970/1209 (1970 II, p. 4013).
(**c**) S.I. 1971/479 (1971 I, p. 1432).
(**d**) S.I. 1971/1505 (1971 III, p. 4209).
(**e**) S.I. 1970/198 (1970 I, p. 869).
(**f**) The relevant amending instruments are S.I. 1971/479, 1505 (1971 I, p. 1432; III, p. 4209).

APPENDIX 1

REGULATION SUBSTITUTED FOR REGULATION 4 OF THE PRINCIPAL REGULATIONS

4. The notice shall provide that any payment of a fixed penalty should be made—

(a) if the offence is alleged to have been committed in an area specified in the first column of Schedule 3 to these Regulations, to the clerk specified opposite thereto in the second column of that Schedule;

(b) if the offence is alleged to have been committed otherwise than in an area so specified, to the clerk to the justices for the petty sessions area in which it is alleged to have been committed.

APPENDIX 2

SCHEDULE ADDED TO THE PRINCIPAL REGULATIONS

SCHEDULE 3

PAYMENT OF FIXED PENALTY IN CERTAIN AREAS

Area in which offence was committed	Clerk to whom payment is to be made
The administrative county of Bedford-shire.	The clerk to the justices for the Bedford petty sessional division.
The Derby county and borough police area.	The clerk to the justices for the county borough of Derby.
That part of the administrative county of Gloucester comprising the petty sessional divisions of Campden, of Chel-tenham, of Newent, of Northleach, of Stow-on-the-Wold, of Tewkesbury and of Winchcombe.	The clerk to the justices for the Cheltenham petty sessional division.
Heathrow Airport	The clerk to the justices for the New Spelthorne petty sessional division.
The Hampshire police area.	The clerk to the justices for the Winchester petty sessional division.
The administrative county of Hereford.	The clerk to the justices for the city of Hereford.
The Kent police area.	The clerk to the justices for the Maidstone petty sessional division.
The Leicester and Rutland police area.	The clerk to the justices for the county borough of Leicester.
The Metropolitan Police District, excluding Heathrow Airport (mentioned above).	The chief clerk at the Marylebone Magistrates' Court.
The Sheffield and Rotherham police area.	The clerk to the justices for the county borough of Sheffield.
That part of the Suffolk police area comprising the petty sessional divisions of Orwell and of Woodbridge.	The clerk to the justices for the Woodbridge petty sessional division.

Area in which offence was committed	Clerk to whom payment is to be made
That part of the Sussex police area comprising the petty sessional divisions of Bexhill and of Burwash.	The clerk to the justices for the Bexhill petty sessional division.
That part of the West Yorkshire police area comprising the county borough of Wakefield, the non-county boroughs of Castleford, of Goole, of Harrogate, of Morley, of Ossett, of Pontefract, of Pudsey and of Ripon, the urban districts of Aireborough, of Featherstone, of Garforth, of Hemsworth, of Horbury, of Horsforth, of Ilkley, of Knaresborough, of Knottingley, of Normanton, of Otley, of Rothwell, of Selby and of Stanley, the rural districts of Goole, of Hemsworth, of Nidderdale, of Osgoldcross, of Ripon and Pateley Bridge, of Selby, of Tadcaster, of Thorne, of Wakefield, of Wetherby, and of Wharfedale and, in the rural district of Skipton, the parishes of Addingham, of Beamsley, of Bolton Abbey, of Draughton and of Hazlewood with Storiths.	The clerk to the justices for the county borough of Leeds.
That part of the West Yorkshire police area comprising the county borough of Barnsley, the urban districts of Adwick-le-Street, of Bentley with Arksey, of Conisbrough, of Cudworth, of Darfield, of Darton, of Dearne, of Dodworth, of Hoyland Nether, of Maltby, of Mexborough, of Rawmarsh, of Royston, of Stocksbridge, of Swinton, of Tickhill, of Wath-upon-Dearne, of Wombwell, of Worsborough and of Penistone, and the rural districts of Doncaster, of Kiveton Park, of Wortley, of Rotherham and of Penistone.	The clerk to the justices for the county borough of Sheffield.
That part of the West Yorkshire police area not mentioned above, excluding the county borough of Doncaster.	The clerk to the justices for the county borough of Bradford.
The administrative county of Wiltshire, excluding the borough of Swindon.	The clerk to the justices for the Trowbridge petty sessional division.

EXPLANATORY NOTE

(This Note is not part of the Regulations.)

These Regulations amend the provisions of the Fixed Penalty (Procedure) Regulations 1970 which specify the clerk to whom a fixed penalty is payable.

Changes are made which affect cases where the offence is alleged to have been committed in the administrative county of Wiltshire, in the Hampshire, the Leicester and Rutland or the West Yorkshire police area or at Heathrow Airport.

STATUTORY INSTRUMENTS

1972 No. 334 (L.4)

COUNTY COURTS

The County Court Funds (Amendment) Rules 1972

Made - - -	*29th February* 1972
Laid before Parliament	*13th March* 1972
Coming into Operation	*4th April* 1972

The Lord Chancellor, in exercise of the powers conferred on him by section 168 of the County Courts Act 1959(a), as amended by section 9 of the Administration of Justice Act 1965(b), and with the concurrence of the Treasury, hereby makes the following Rules:—

1.—(1) These Rules may be cited as the County Court Funds (Amendment) Rules 1972 and shall come into operation on 4th April 1972.

(2) In these Rules a rule referred to by number means the rule so numbered in the County Court Funds Rules 1965(c), as amended (d).

(3) The Interpretation Act 1889(e) shall apply to the interpretation of these Rules as it applies to the interpretation of an Act of Parliament.

2. In Part IV of the Arrangement of Rules in the County Court Funds Rules 1965, as amended,—

(*a*) the words "or through the National Giro" shall be omitted; and

(*b*) for the word "cheque" there shall be substituted the words "payable order".

3. In rule 2(1)—

(*a*) after the definition of "Capital Fund", the following definition shall be inserted:—

"cash account" means the Accountant-General's County Courts Cash Account at the office of Her Majesty's Paymaster-General; and

---

(a) 1959 c. 22.   (b) 1965 c. 2.
(c) S.I. 1965/1500 (1965 II, p. 4343).
(d) The relevant amending instruments are S.I. 1969/1547, 1971/260 (1969 III, p. 5005; 1971 I, p. 900).   (e) 1889 c. 63.

(*b*) the definitions of "the bank", "central control account" and "court's Giro account" shall be omitted.

4. In rule 3, the words from "either" to "or (*b*)" shall be omitted.

5. In rule 4, for the words from "bank" to "may determine)" there shall be substituted the words "cash account".

6. In rule 6, for the words "through the National Giro or by cheque payable" there shall be substituted the words "by crossed payable order"; and the words "and crossed to the payee's official account" shall be omitted.

7. In rule 8(3)(*b*), for the words "cheque or through the National Giro" there shall be substituted the words "payable order".

8. In rule 10—

    (*a*) in paragraph (1), the words "or through the National Giro" shall be omitted;

    (*b*) in paragraph (2)(*b*), for the words "cheque or through the National Giro" there shall be substituted the words "payable order"; and

    (*c*) for paragraph (3), there shall be substituted the following paragraph:—

        "(3) Upon receipt of the request and accompanying documents the registrar shall, subject to the proviso in the last preceding rule, forward the money, less the cost of remittance, if any, by crossed payable order for sums of £2·00 or more and, for smaller sums, by money order, crossed postal order or crossed payable order as he may think fit."

9. In rule 11, for the word "cheque" there shall be substituted the words "payable order"; and the words "or pay that sum through the National Giro" shall be omitted.

10. In rule 12, paragraph (1)(*aa*) shall be omitted.

11. In rules 13(2), 15(*a*)(ii), 16(1) and 23(2)(*a*)(ii), for the words "Head of the County Courts Branch" there shall be substituted the words "Permanent Secretary to the Lord Chancellor".

12. In rule 14—

    (*a*) in paragraph (1), for the words from "bank" to "may determine)" there shall be substituted the words "cash account";

    (*b*) paragraph (3) shall be omitted; and

    (*c*) in paragraph (4), for the words "the bank" there shall be substituted the words "a bank".

13. In rule 15(*a*)(i), the words "in pursuance of rule 14" shall be omitted.

14. In rule 26—

(*a*) paragraph (2) shall be omitted; and

(*b*) in paragraph (4), for the words "cheque, or through the National Giro" there shall be substituted the words "payable order".

15. For rule 28 there shall be substituted the following rule:—

"28. Out of the moneys paid into the cash account the Accountant-General shall pay all moneys relating to funds into an account to be entitled the "Lord Chancellor's Department Deposit Account" at the office of Her Majesty's Paymaster-General and shall draw payable Orders on this account for sums required for the purchase of units."

16. In rules 29, 30, 31(2)(*a*) and 32(1), for the words "County Courts" there shall be substituted the words "Lord Chancellor's Department".

Dated 28th February 1972.

Hailsham of St. Marylebone, C.

We concur,

Dated 29th February 1972.

Walter Clegg,
Tim Fortescue,
Two of the Lords Commissioners of
Her Majesty's Treasury.

EXPLANATORY NOTE

(This Note is not part of the Rules.)

These Rules amend the County Court Funds Rules 1965 by providing for banking facilities for Registrars of County Courts through the Accountant-General's County Courts Cash Account with Her Majesty's Paymaster-General with effect from 4th April 1972. These arrangements will replace the facilities at present provided by joint stock banks and the National Giro. Moneys relating to funds in court will, under Rule 28 as amended, be paid from the cash account into the Lord Chancellor's Department Deposit Account, on which payable orders will be drawn for the purchase of units.

STOKE-ON-TRENT
CITY
LIBRARIES

STATUTORY INSTRUMENTS

1972 No. 335

COAL INDUSTRY

The Redundant Mineworkers (Payments Scheme) Order 1972

Laid before Parliament in draft

Made - - -	*6th March* 1972
Coming into Operation	*16th March* 1972

The Secretary of State, in exercise of his powers under section 3 of the Coal Industry Act 1967(a) (hereinafter referred to as "the Act") as amended by section 2 of the Coal Industry Act 1971(b) and all other powers in that behalf enabling him, hereby makes the following Order, a draft of which has been laid before Parliament and has been approved by a resolution of each House of Parliament in accordance with section 3(4) of the Act:—

Citation, commencement and interpretation

1.—(1) This Order, which may be cited as the Redundant Mineworkers (Payments Scheme) Order 1972, shall come into operation fourteen days after it has been approved by resolution of each House of Parliament.

(2) The Interpretation Act 1889(c) shall apply to the interpretation of this Order as it applies to the interpretation of an Act of Parliament.

Amendment of former Order

2. The Redundant Mineworkers (Payments Scheme) Order 1968(d) as amended (e) is further amended—

(a) by the substitution of paragraphs (4) and (6) to (8) of Article 5 of the Schedule to this Order for paragraph (2) of Article 5 of the Schedule thereto;

(b) by the substitution of paragraphs (1) to (3) of Article 6 of the Schedule to this Order for paragraphs (1) to (4) of Article 6 of the Schedule thereto; and

(c) by the substitution of paragraph (2) of Article 7 of the Schedule to this Order for the same paragraph of the same Article of the Schedule thereto.

(a) 1967 c. 91.
(c) 1889 c. 63.
(e) S.I. 1971/553 (1971 I, p. 1546).

(b) 1971 c. 16.
(d) S.I. 1968/987 (1968 II, p. 2602).

Application of the Scheme

3. The Scheme set out in the Schedule to this Order shall apply to the classes of persons prescribed therein, being persons who at any time between 25th March 1972 and 31st March 1974—

(*a*) were employed at a coal mine or at any place of a class prescribed in the Scheme; and

(*b*) became redundant within the meaning of the Scheme after attaining the age of 55 and before attaining the age of 65 in the case of men or 60 in the case of women.

Dated 6th March 1972.

John Eden,
Minister for Industry,
Department of Trade and Industry.

THE SCHEDULE

THE REDUNDANT MINEWORKERS PAYMENTS SCHEME

Definitions

1. In this Scheme, unless the context otherwise requires:—

"the Board" means the National Coal Board;

"the basic benefit" means the total amount payable under Article 5;

"coal industry employee" has the meaning assigned thereto in Article 2;

"coal industry employer" in relation to any person employed by the Board or by a small mine licensee means the Board or the small mine licensee as the case may be, and in relation to any person who is a workmen's employee means the person or persons responsible for the payment of such person's remuneration;

"disablement pension" means disablement pension under the National Insurance (Industrial Injuries) Act 1965(**a**);

"earnings-related supplement" means an increase of unemployment or sickness benefit under section 2 of the National Insurance Act 1966(**b**) (benefit by way of an earnings-related supplement) but not such an increase as is referred to in section 2(6) of that Act (benefit payable to a widow);

"the former Scheme" means the Redundant Mineworkers Payments Scheme contained in the Schedule to the Redundant Mineworkers (Payments Scheme) Order 1968 as amended;

"house" has the same meaning as in section 58(1) of the Housing (Financial Provisions) Act 1958(**c**);

"industrial accident" means any accident arising out of or in the course of employment;

"industrial disease" means any disease or personal injury for the time being prescribed under section 56 of the National Insurance (Industrial Injuries) Act 1965;

(a) 1965 c. 52.   (b) 1966 c. 6.
(c) 1958 c. 42.

"injury benefit" means industrial injury benefit under the National Insurance (Industrial Injuries) Act 1965;

"invalidity benefit" and "invalidity pension" mean respectively invalidity benefit and invalidity pension under the National Insurance Act 1971(a);

"Mineworkers' Pension Scheme" means the Mineworkers' Pension Scheme established by the Board under powers conferred by the Coal Industry Nationalisation (Superannuation) Regulations 1950(b);

"pre-redundancy earnings" means in relation to any person that person's average weekly earnings as a coal industry employee during the relevant tax year in the grade in which he was employed at the relevant date if he was so employed during that year and had earnings from that employment in not less than 13 weeks of that year, but otherwise the average weekly earnings which it is calculated he would have had if he had been so employed during the whole of that year having such regard as the Secretary of State may consider appropriate to the average weekly earnings of other coal industry employees who were employed in the same grade by that same employer throughout the relevant tax year;

"prescribed place" means a place of a class specified in Appendix 1;

"redundant person" has the meaning assigned thereto in Article 4;

"the relevant date" has the same meaning as in sections 3(4) or 4(2) of the Redundancy Payments Act 1965(c) as the case may be;

"the relevant tax year" means the last complete income tax year before the relevant date;

"sickness benefit" means sickness benefit under the National Insurance Act 1965(d);

"self-employed" means a self-employed person for the purposes of section 1(2)(b) of the National Insurance Act 1965 (description and classification of insured persons);

"small mine licensee" means any individual working coal by virtue of the grant of a gale in the Forest of Dean or in any other part of the Hundred of St. Briavels and any person or body of persons for the time being engaged in coal mining activities by virtue of a licence granted by the Board under section 36(2)(a) of the Coal Industry Nationalisation Act 1946(e);

"special hardship allowance" means an increase of disablement pension under section 14 of the National Insurance (Industrial Injuries) Act 1965 (increase of disablement pension in cases of special hardship);

"the Staff Superannuation Scheme" means the National Coal Board Superannuation Scheme established by the Board under powers conferred by the Coal Industry Nationalisation (Superannuation) Regulations 1946(f);

"supplementary allowance" means supplementary allowance under the Ministry of Social Security Act 1966(g);

"the Supplementary Benefits Commission" has the same meaning as in Section 3 of the Ministry of Social Security Act 1966;

"supplementary pension" means supplementary pension under the Ministry of Social Security Act 1966;

"unemployment benefit" means unemployment benefit under the National Insurance Act 1965;

"week" means a period of seven days beginning with midnight between Saturday and Sunday;

"workmen's employee" means any person who is employed at a coal mine or a prescribed place being a person remunerated out of moneys provided by deductions from the wages of or contributions by employees of a coal industry employer;

and references to any enactment, order, regulation or scheme shall be construed as references to the same as amended from time to time.

(a) 1971 c. 50.
(c) 1965 c. 62.
(e) 1946 c. 59.
(g) 1966 c. 20.

(b) S.I. 1950/376 (1950 I, p. 356).
(d) 1965 c. 51.
(f) S.I. 1946/2198 (1946 I, p. 282).

Eligibility for payment

2. Any person who is or was on the relevant date employed at a coal mine or a prescribed place being either—

(*a*) a person so employed by the Board or by a small mine licensee—

(i) in a grade which renders him eligible for membership of the Mineworkers' Pension Scheme; or

(ii) in a grade which is specified in Appendix 2; or

(*b*) a person so employed as a workmen's employee,

shall, subject as hereinafter provided, and provided he is not eligible for payments under the former Scheme, be eligible for payments under this Scheme and such person is hereafter referred to as a "coal industry employee".

Age and redundancy requirements

3. A coal industry employee shall not be eligible for payments under this Scheme unless—

(*a*) he is a redundant person and, in the case of an employee employed at a prescribed place, became a redundant person by reason of the cessation or reduction of the services or facilities at that place, being services or facilities ancillary to one or more coal mines, in consequence of the closure of one or more such mines or the reduction in the number of persons employed thereat;

(*b*) when he became a redundant person the relevant date fell between 25th March 1972 and 31st March 1974; and

(*c*) on the relevant date he had attained the age of 55 and had not attained the age of 65 in the case of a man or 60 in the case of a woman.

Requirements of a redundant person

4.—(1) A coal industry employee shall be a redundant person within the meaning of this Scheme if he has completed a total period of not less than 10 years' employment with one or more coal industry employers, or with any other employer at a coal mine or at a prescribed place prior to 1st January 1947, and in consequence of his dismissal on the relevant date by a coal industry employer, he either—

(*a*) becomes entitled to receive a redundancy payment under the Redundancy Payments Act 1965 from that employer; or

(*b*) would have become entitled to receive such a payment except only that he had not been continuously employed by one coal industry employer for a period of 104 weeks ending with the relevant date and he had either—

(i) during such period of 104 weeks left the employment of a coal industry employer and not later than one week after leaving such employment had entered into employment with that or any other coal industry employer; or

(ii) become entitled previously to receive such a payment from a coal industry employer and had entered into employment with that or any other coal industry employer not later than 52 weeks after becoming so entitled.

(2) Appendix 3 hereof and not section 8 of the Redundancy Payments Act 1965 (which provides for the calculation of periods of employment) shall apply for the purposes of paragraph (1) of this Article, for ascertaining the length of a coal industry employee's period of employment, and whether or not the period of 104 weeks ending with the relevant date has been continuous.

Basic benefit to be paid

5. Subject as hereinafter provided—

(1) The Secretary of State may pay to any coal industry employee eligible for payments under the foregoing provisions of this Scheme the weekly sum specified

in column 2 of Appendix 4 opposite the amounts specified in column 1 of that Appendix appropriate to the amount of that employee's pre-redundancy earnings.

(2) When the weekly sum payable under paragraph (1) has been paid for 52 weeks it may be supplemented in respect of any subsequent week by such additional weekly sum as the Secretary of State may think appropriate to take account of changes in the cost of living during the period of 12 months ending on the 6th April which immediately precedes the expiry of the said 52 weeks and when the said weekly sum (supplemented as aforesaid) has been paid for a further 52 weeks it may be further supplemented in respect of any subsequent week by such additional weekly sum as the Secretary of State may think appropriate to take account of changes in the cost of living during the period of 12 months ending on the 6th April which immediately precedes the expiry of these further 52 weeks.

(3) Where any coal industry employee eligible for payments under this Scheme is re-employed by a coal industry employer and then ceases to be so employed the Secretary of State in assessing the supplements under paragraph (2) may take account of changes in the cost of living during his period of re-employment by a coal industry employer as well as the changes in the cost of living during a period specified in that paragraph: Provided that this paragraph does not apply to such an employee who is so employed for a period of not less than one year and makes an election under paragraph (4).

(4) A coal industry employee eligible for payments under this Scheme who is re-employed by a coal industry employer for a period of not less than one year and then is dismissed by a coal industry employer by reason of redundancy within the meaning of section 1 of the Redundancy Payments Act 1965, may elect to substitute his date of cessation of that employment as the relevant date for the purpose of calculating his pre-redundancy earnings referred to in paragraph (1) and for the purpose of adjusting his basic benefit under Article 6 provided the said election is made within 26 weeks of such cessation.

(5) Where a coal industry employee makes an election under paragraph (4), the Secretary of State in assessing the supplements under paragraph (2) may take account of changes in the cost of living during the period of 12 months ending on the 6th April which immediately precedes the date on which the weekly sum payable under paragraph (1) has been paid for 52 weeks and the further period of 52 weeks respectively after the date substituted as the relevant date by virtue of the said election under paragraph (4).

(6) Where any coal industry employee was on the relevant date occupying a house as a tenant of or under a licence from the Board and, in consequence of his having ceased to be in their employment, the Board—

    (*a*) in the case of an employee who immediately before such relevant date was not making any payment to them in respect of his occupation of that house, charge that employee any weekly payment in respect of his occupation of that house or any other house; or

    (*b*) in the case of an employee who immediately before such relevant date was making a payment to them in respect of his occupation of that house, increase the weekly amount payable in respect of his occupation of that house or any other house,

then, provided that such employee is eligible for payments under the foregoing provisions of this Scheme, the Secretary of State may pay to him in addition to any sums payable under this Article either—

    (i) a weekly sum equal to the weekly amount of such payment or weekly increase of such payment as the case may be; or

    (ii) the weekly sum of £1,

whichever shall be the less.

(7) A coal industry employee shall remain eligible for payments under paragraph (6) notwithstanding the sale of the house in respect of which the weekly sum is payable or his having moved to another house.

(8) Paragraph (6) shall not apply to any coal industry employee who receives any rent rebate or allowance under any National Rent Rebate and Allowance Scheme.

Adjustment of the basic benefit

6.—(1) Subject to paragraph (3), if in any week in respect of which the basic benefit is payable to any coal industry employee he is entitled to receive any of the payments specified under heads (*a*), (*b*), (*c*), (*d*), (*e*), (*f*), (*g*), (*h*), (*i*) or (*j*) of this Article the basic benefit payable to him in respect of that week shall be reduced or extinguished by making the deduction specified below in relation to that head—

    (i) in respect of—

        (*a*) earnings-related supplement;

        (*b*) injury benefit in excess of the amount of any sickness benefit or invalidity pension which would have been payable to a coal industry employee had he been entitled to receive sickness benefit or invalidity pension in place of that injury benefit;

        (*c*) pension benefits, other than widows' benefits, paid under the Mineworkers' Pension Scheme;

        (*d*) pension benefits, other than widows' benefits, paid before normal retiring age under any scheme, other than the Mineworkers' Pension Scheme or the Staff Superannuation Scheme, established or continued by the Board under the Coal Industry Nationalisation (Superannuation) Regulations 1950;

        (*e*) supplementary allowance or supplementary pension in excess of the amount which the Supplementary Benefits Commission determine would have been paid had the payments under this Scheme been made before the amount of supplementary allowance or supplementary pension was determined;

    by the amount of any such benefits which such employee becomes entitled to receive after the relevant date;

    (ii) in respect of—

        (*f*) special hardship allowance in respect of an industrial accident sustained or an industrial disease developed before the relevant date;

        (*g*) supplementary disablement pension under the National Insurance (Industrial Injuries) Colliery Workers Supplementary Scheme;

    by the amount of any such benefits which such employee becomes entitled to receive taking into account any increases or decreases thereof (but ignoring any general increases in such benefits) after the last week before the relevant date in which such employee is not entitled to sickness, invalidity or injury benefit;

    (iii) in respect of—

        (*h*) workmen's compensation under the Workmen's Compensation Acts 1925 to 1945, the enactments repealed by the Workmen's Compensation Act 1925(**a**), or under any contracting-out scheme duly certified under any of those Acts;

        (*i*) benefit under the Workmen's Compensation (Supplementation) Scheme 1966(**b**);

(**a**) 1925 c. 84.   (**b**) S.I. 1966/165 (1966 I, p. 325).

(j) benefit under the Scheme established by the Board pursuant to a resolution dated 2nd July 1948 for providing benefits to persons in receipt of workmen's compensation or in receipt of benefits under the Pneumoconiosis (Benefit) Scheme 1943(a);

by the amount of any such benefits which such employee becomes entitled to receive taking into account any increases or decreases thereof (but ignoring any general increases in such benefits or any individual variation thereof resulting from a change of category from partial to total, or from lesser to major, incapacity, as the case may be) after the last week before the relevant date in which such employee is not entitled to sickness, invalidity or injury benefit.

(2) Where a coal industry employee eligible for payments under this Scheme has been entitled to receive unemployment benefit and his right to that benefit excluding an earnings-related supplement thereof has become exhausted, so long as he remains unemployed there shall be payable to him, in addition to the basic benefit, a weekly sum equal to the weekly rate of unemployment benefit, excluding an earnings-related supplement thereof, which he would have been entitled to receive but for such exhaustion.

(3) In any week in respect of which a coal industry employee is entitled to receive under paragraph (2) an addition to the basic benefit, the aggregate of the basic benefit and that addition shall be reduced or extinguished by deducting therefrom an amount equal to the aggregate of the amounts referred to in paragraph (1) which such employee is entitled to receive in respect of that same week.

(4) The weekly sum payable by virtue of Article 5(1) in respect of a week commencing after 6th April 1973 to a coal industry employee whose relevant date falls on or after the said date shall be reduced by an amount equal to any increase in the amount of unemployment benefit for a man over the age of 18 with one adult dependant which may have been made during the 12 months immediately preceding 6th April 1973.

(5) Where a coal industry employee makes an election under Article 5(4) paragraph (4) of this Article will not apply and the weekly sum referred to in Article 5(1) shall be reduced by an amount equal to any increase in the amount of unemployment benefit for a man over the age of 18 with one adult dependant which may have been made during the period between 6th April 1972 and the 6th April immediately preceding the date substituted as the relevant date by virtue of an election under Article 5(4).

Limitation of benefits

7.—(1) No payments shall be made under this Scheme to any coal industry employee who receives any payment, other than widow's benefit, under the Staff Superannuation Scheme.

(2) Subject to paragraph (4), no payments shall be made under this Scheme to any coal industry employee in respect of any day in any week unless in respect of such day that employee satisfies the conditions for receipt of unemployment benefit, sickness benefit or invalidity benefit, or would satisfy those conditions but for—

(a) the provisions of regulations made under section 50 of the National Insurance Act 1965 (overlapping benefits); or

(b) the fact that his right to that benefit is exhausted; or

(c) (in the case of unemployment benefit only) the fact that he was employed or self-employed for not more than 21 hours in that week;

(d) being a married woman or widow and having elected not to pay National Insurance contributions;

(a) S.R. & O. 1943/886 (Rev. XXIV, p. 597: 1943 I, p. 1016).

(*e*) (in the case of unemployment benefit only) being self-employed for a period after the relevant date;

and for the purposes of this paragraph, payments in respect of any day shall be one-sixth of the appropriate weekly rate.

(3) No payments shall be made under this Scheme in respect of any week in which a coal industry employee is in the employment of a coal industry employer.

(4) In respect of any week during which a coal industry employee is self-employed or in the employment of a person other than a coal industry employer the amount payable to him under this Scheme shall not exceed—

(*a*) the basic benefit adjusted if appropriate in accordance with the provisions of Article 6; or

(*b*) the sum of £6,

whichever shall be the less.

Duration of benefits

8.—(1) Subject to the following paragraphs of this Article, payments under this Scheme shall first become payable to a coal industry employee in respect of the week commencing next after the relevant date applicable but shall not be payable to any coal industry employee in respect of any week falling after—

(*a*) the attainment by such employee of the age of 65 in the case of a man or 60 in the case of a woman; or

(*b*) 26th March 1977,

whichever shall first occur.

(2) No coal industry employee shall be eligible for payments under this Scheme in respect of an aggregate of more than 156 weeks.

(3) Any week in which a coal industry employee is in the employment of a coal industry employer shall not be taken into account in calculating the period of 156 weeks referred to in paragraph (2) nor the two periods of 52 weeks referred to in Article 5(2).

(4) Any day or week in respect of which a coal industry employee is disqualified under Article 7(2) from receiving payments under this Scheme shall be taken into account in calculating such period of 156 weeks.

Meaning of Employment in Articles 7 and 8

9. For the purposes of Article 7(3) and (4) and Article 8, employment or self-employment in any week for not more than 21 hours shall not be regarded as employment or self-employment as the case may be.

Rounding-off of benefits

10. Where the total weekly sum payable to a coal industry employee under this Scheme exceeds five new pence or a multiple thereof by a fraction of five new pence that fraction shall be disregarded if it is less than two and a half new pence and shall be treated as five new pence if it is two and a half new pence or more.

Time of payment of benefits

11. Sums payable to a coal industry employee under this Scheme may be paid in arrear and at intervals of not more than 6 weeks.

Claims for benefits

12.—(1) Subject to paragraph (2), it shall be a condition of the making of payments under this Scheme to any coal industry employee that a claim for those payments shall be submitted to the Secretary of State not later than 26 weeks after the relevant date.

(2) In any case in which the Secretary of State is satisfied that there is reasonable ground for failing to make a claim within such period as aforesaid he may, from time to time, extend the period within which a claim may be made under paragraph (1) on application being made to him in that behalf and notwithstanding that such period has expired.

Article 1

APPENDIX 1

PRESCRIBED PLACES

Ambulance stations
Civil engineering depots
Coal depots
Coal laboratories
Coal preparation plants
Coal stocking grounds
Electricity distribution installations
Estate and house maintenance depots
Generating plants
Granaries (for foodstuffs for pit ponies)
Medical centres
Mineral processing plants
Pumping stations
Railway sidings and other places associated with the operation of railways
Rescue stations
Road transport depots
Shipping staithes and wharves
Stone and dust disposal and treatment plants
Timber impregnation plants
Training centres
Waterworks
Workshops, stores and plant pool depots

Article 2(*a*)(ii)

APPENDIX 2

GRADES OF EMPLOYMENT IN WHICH A COAL INDUSTRY EMPLOYEE IS ELIGIBLE FOR PAYMENTS UNDER THIS SCHEME

1. Any grade of official to whom the First Schedule of an agreement dated 26th March 1971 (made between the Board of the one part and the National Association of Colliery Overmen, Deputies and Shotfirers of the other part) applies.

2. Any grade of weekly paid industrial staff to whom Schedule 1 or Schedule 4 of an agreement dated 1st May 1968 (made between the Board of the one part and the National Association of Colliery Overmen, Deputies and Shotfirers and the National Union of Mineworkers of the other part) applies.

3. Foreman other than a grade of Foreman under the agreement referred to in paragraph 2.

4. Canteen Manager.

5. Canteen Manageress.

6. Canteen Supervisor.

Article 4(2)

APPENDIX 3

COMPUTATION OF PERIOD OF EMPLOYMENT

Preliminary

1. A coal industry employee's period of employment shall be computed in weeks in accordance with this Appendix, and the period of ten years mentioned in Article 4 of this Scheme shall be taken as 520 weeks.

General provisions as to the period of employment

2.—(1) Except so far as is otherwise provided by the following provisions of this Appendix any week which does not count under paragraphs 3, 4, 5 and 6 of this Appendix breaks the continuity of the period of employment.

(2) During any week which breaks the continuity of the period of employment a coal industry employee shall not be treated as being in the employment of a coal industry employer.

Normal working weeks

3. Any week in which a coal industry employee is employed for 21 hours or more by a coal industry employer shall count in computing a period of employment.

Employment governed by contract

4. Any week during the whole or part of which a coal industry employee's relations with a coal industry employer are governed by a contract of employment which normally involves employment for 21 hours or more weekly shall count in computing a period of employment.

Periods in which there is no contract of employment

5.—(1) If in any week a coal industry employee is for the whole or part of that week:—

   (*a*) incapable of work in consequence of sickness or injury; or

   (*b*) absent from work on account of a temporary cessation of work; or

   (*c*) absent from work in circumstances such that, by arrangement or custom, he is regarded as continuing in the employment of a coal industry employer for all or any purposes,

that week shall, notwithstanding that it does not fall within paragraphs 3 or 4 of this Appendix, count as a period of employment.

(2) Not more than 26 weeks shall count under head (*a*) of the foregoing sub-paragraph between any two periods falling within paragraphs 3 and 4 of this Appendix.

Industrial Disputes

6. If during any week a coal industry employee was for the whole or any part of that week absent from work because he was taking part in a strike that week shall count as a period of employment.

Interpretation

7. In this Appendix, unless the context otherwise requires:—

"period of employment" means period of employment by a coal industry employer and in the case of paragraph 1 by any other employer at a coal mine or at a prescribed place prior to 1st January 1947;

"strike" means the cessation of work by a body of coal industry employees acting in combination or a concerted refusal or refusal under a common understanding of any number of coal industry employees to continue to work for a coal industry employer in consequence of a dispute done as a means of compelling that coal industry employer or any person or body of persons employed or to aid other employees in compelling their employer or any person or body of persons employed to accept or not to accept terms or conditions of or affecting employment.

Article 5(1)

APPENDIX 4

Table of Pre-Redundancy Earnings and Weekly Payments

Column 1		Column 2
Amount of pre-redundancy earnings		Weekly sum payable under Article 5(1)
Exceeding		
£p but not exceeding	£p	£p
0·0	11·50	0·0
11·50	11·75	0·14
11·75	12·00	0·30
12·00	12·25	0·46
12·25	12·50	0·63
12·50	12·75	0·79
12·75	13·00	0·96
13·00	13·25	1·12
13·25	13·50	1·29
13·50	13·75	1·46
13·75	14·00	1·62
14·00	14·25	1·78
14·25	14·50	1·94
14·50	14·75	2·11
14·75	15·00	2·28
15·00	15·25	2·44
15·25	15·50	2·61
15·50	15·75	2·77
15·75	16·00	2·94
16·00	16·25	3·10
16·25	16·50	3·26
16·50	16·75	3·43
16·75	17·00	3·59
17·00	17·25	3·76
17·25	17·50	3·93
17·50	17·75	4·09
17·75	18·00	4·26
18·00	18·25	4·40
18·25	18·50	4·56
18·50	18·75	4·72
18·75	19·00	4·87
19·00	19·25	5·03

APPENDIX 4 (continued)

Column 1		Column 2
Amount of pre-redundancy earnings		Weekly sum payable under Article 5(1)
Exceeding		
£p but not exceeding	£p	£p
19·25	19·50	5·19
19·50	19·75	5·34
19·75	20·00	5·50
20·00	20·25	5·66
20·25	20·50	5·81
20·50	20·75	5·97
20·75	21·00	6·12
21·00	21·25	6·27
21·25	21·50	6·43
21·50	21·75	6·59
21·75	22·00	6·74
22·00	22·25	6·90
22·25	22·50	7·05
22·50	22·75	7·21
22·75	23·00	7·37
23·00	23·25	7·52
23·25	23·50	7·68
23·50	23·75	7·83
23·75	24·00	7·98
24·00	24·25	8·14
24·25	24·50	8·30
24·50	24·75	8·45
24·75	25·00	8·61
25·00	25·25	8·77
25·25	25·50	8·92
25·50	25·75	9·08
25·75	26·00	9·23
26·00	26·25	9·39
26·25	26·50	9·55
26·50	26·75	9·69
26·75	27·00	9·85
27·00	27·25	10·01
27·25	27·50	10·16
27·50	27·75	10·32
27·75	28·00	10·48
28·00	28·25	10·63
28·25	28·50	10·79
28·50	28·75	10·95
28·75	29·00	11·10
29·00	29·25	11·26
29·25	29·50	11·41
29·50	29·75	11·56
29·75	30·00	11·72
30·00	30·25	11·87
30·25	30·50	12·03
30·50	30·75	12·19
30·75	31·00	12·34
31·00	31·25	12·50
31·25	31·50	12·66
31·50	31·75	12·81
31·75	32·00	12·97
32·00	32·25	13·13
32·25	32·50	13·27
32·50	32·75	13·43

APPENDIX 4 (continued)

Column 1			Column 2
Amount of pre-redundancy earnings			Weekly sum payable under Article 5(1)
Exceeding			
£p	but	not exceeding	£p	£p
32·75		33·00	13·59
33·00		33·25	13·74
33·25		33·50	13·90
33·50		33·75	14·06
33·75		34·00	14·21
34·00		34·25	14·37
34·25		34·50	14·52
34·50		34·75	14·68
34·75		35·00	14·84
35·00		35·25	14·98
35·25		35·50	15·14
35·50		35·75	15·30
35·75		36·00	15·45
36·00		36·25	15·61
36·25		36·50	15·77
36·50		36·75	15·92
36·75		37·00	16·08
37·00		37·25	16·24
37·25		37·50	16·39
37·50		37·75	16·55
37·75		38·00	16·70
38·00		38·25	16·85
38·25		38·50	17·01
38·50		38·75	17·16
38·75		39·00	17·32
39·00		39·25	17·48
39·25		39·50	17·63
39·50		39·75	17·79
39·75		40·00	17·95
40·00 and over			18·11

EXPLANATORY NOTE

(This Note is not part of the Order.)

This Order establishes under the Coal Industry Act 1967 and the Coal Industry Act 1971 a scheme for the payment of weekly benefits in certain cases to supplement the income of mineworkers made redundant between 25th March 1972 and 31st March 1974, after attaining the age of 55 and before attaining the age of 65 in the case of men or 60 in the case of women.

The scheme prescribes the classes of persons eligible and sets out the places at which they must be employed in order to qualify.

The amount of benefit is based on pre-redundancy earnings, but is subject to certain specified additions and deductions and no person is eligible for benefit for a total period of more than 156 weeks.

The scheme differs in certain respects from the former scheme. The weekly sum payable to beneficiaries will be supplemented after the fifty-second and one hundred and fourth weeks of benefit to take account of changes in the cost-of-living. The amount of weekly benefit which a beneficiary may retain if he obtains other employment has been increased. In addition there are a number of minor changes from the provisions of the former scheme made under the Coal Industry Act 1967. The order also makes some amendments to the former scheme.

This Order comes into operation on 16th March 1972.

STATUTORY INSTRUMENTS

1972 No. 336

ROAD TRAFFIC

The Cycle Racing on Highways (Special Authorisation) (England and Wales) Regulations 1972

Made - - -	*6th March* 1972
Laid before Parliament	*13th March* 1972
Coming into Operation	*18th March* 1972

The Secretary of State for the Environment (as respects England excluding Monmouthshire) in exercise of his powers under section 12(2) of the Road Traffic Act 1960(a) and the Secretary of State for Wales (as respects Wales and Monmouthshire) in exercise of his powers under the said section 12(2), as read with the Secretary of State for Wales and Minister of Land and Natural Resources Order 1965(b), and of all other enabling powers, and after consultation with representative organisations in accordance with the provisions of section 260(2) of the said Act of 1960, hereby make the following Regulations: —

1.—(1) These Regulations shall come into operation on 18th March 1972 and may be cited as the Cycle Racing on Highways (Special Authorisation) (England and Wales) Regulations 1972.

(2) In these Regulations—

(*a*) "specified events" means the cycle racing events proposed to be held on or between 19th March and 10th September 1972, particulars of which as notified to the Secretary of State for the Environment or, as the case may be, the Secretary of State for Wales by the British Cycling Federation are specified in the Schedule to these Regulations;

(*b*) "the principal Regulations" means the Cycle Racing on Highways Regulations 1960(c), as amended by the Cycle Racing on Highways (Amendment) Regulations 1963(d);

(*c*) expressions to which a meaning is assigned by the principal Regulations shall have that meaning.

(3) The Interpretation Act 1889(e) shall apply for the interpretation of these Regulations as it applies for the interpretation of an Act of Parliament.

(a) 1960 c. 16. (b) S.I. 1965/319 (1965 I, p. 785).
(c) S.I. 1960/250 (1960 III, p. 3047). (d) S.I. 1963/929 (1963 II, p. 1556).
(e) 1889 c. 63.

2.—(1) The principal Regulations shall have effect in their application to any bicycle race comprised in any of the specified events as if in Regulation 5(1)(*a*)(i) for the condition that the number of competitors must not exceed 40 there were substituted the condition that the number of competitors must not exceed,—

(*a*) in the case of a bicycle race comprised in the event specified in the Schedule to these Regulations under the title "Tour of Britain (Milk Race)", 84, and

(*b*) in the case of a bicycle race comprised in any of the other specified events, 60.

(2) The foregoing provisions of this Regulation shall have effect in relation to any bicycle race comprised in any of the specified events notwithstanding that after the coming into operation of these Regulations the title of that event is changed from that specified in column 1 of the Schedule to these Regulations or that some person other than the person specified in column 3 of the said Schedule becomes the promoter of that event.

(3) Save as otherwise provided by the foregoing provisions of these Regulations, the principal Regulations shall apply to a bicycle race comprised in any of the specified events as they apply to any other bicycle race.

Peter Walker,
Secretary of State for the Environment.

6th March 1972.

Peter Thomas,
Secretary of State for Wales.

6th March 1972.

SCHEDULE

CYCLE RACING EVENTS—1972

1. Title of event	2. Proposed time for the holding of the event	3. Name and address of the promoter of the event
1. Grand Prix of Essex	19 March	D. Worsley Esq., Bramble Rise, Colne Engaine, Colchester, Essex.
2. Slimplicity 3-Day Cycle Race	31 March to 2 April (inclusive)	E. Fletcher Esq., c/o 21 Church Lane, Farington Moss, Leyland, Lancs.
3. Deeside Easter 4-Day	31 March to 3 April (inclusive)	G. C. Terry Esq., 74 Richmond Road, Connah's Quay, Deeside, Flintshire, CH5 4JE.
4. Watney Mann 2-Day Road Race	1 to 2 April (inclusive)	T. Lovell Esq., 50 Aldbury Rise, Allesley Park, Coventry.
5. Ras Tri Niwrnod de Cymru	1 to 3 April (inclusive)	R. Phillips Esq., 12 Harriet Town, Troedyrhiw, Merthyr Tydfil.
6. Galena Two Day Road Race	8 to 9 April (inclusive)	B. Edbrooke Esq., 124 School Road, Brislington, Bristol, BS4 4LY.
7. Harp Lager Grand Prix	9 April	L. Docker Esq., 182, Droop Street, Paddington, W10 4DY.
8. Mackeson Tour of Furness	16 April	J. Thorne Esq., 28 Keswick Avenue, Barrow-in-Furness, Lancs.
9. Morecambe and Lakeland 2-Day	22 to 23 April (inclusive)	D. Tunstall Esq., 3 Empsom Road, Kendal, Westmorland.
10. Greenall Whitley International Grand Prix	28 to 30 April (inclusive)	N. Shelmerdine Esq., 1 Fircroft Close, Tilehurst, Reading, RG3 6LJ, Berkshire.
11. International Cycle Sport Grand Prix	6 to 7 May (inclusive)	J. Wilcockson Esq., 39 Bentsbrook Road, North Holmwood, Dorking, Surrey
12. Wills Grand Prix	9 to 14 May (inclusive)	D. Foxwell Esq., 7 Cantell Grove, Whitchurch Green, Bristol 4.
13. Lincoln Grand Prix	14 May	I. Emmerson Esq., 5 Larkin Avenue, Cherry Willingham, Lincoln.
14. Zerny Two Day Road Race	20 to 21 May (inclusive)	D. J. Bishop Esq., 47 Hardwick Street, Marlborough Avenue, Hull.

SCHEDULE—(continued)

1. Title of event	2. Proposed time for the holding of the event	3. Name and address of the promoter of the event
15. Tour of Britain (Milk Race)	29 May to 10 June (inclusive)	P. Liggett Esq., 28 Arlow Road, Winchmore Hill, N. 21.
16. Cutty Sark Grand Prix	25 June	C. W. Messenger Esq., 25 Browning Way, Heston, Middlesex.
17. National Amateur Road Race Championship	2 July	E. Fletcher Esq., c/o 21 Church Lane, Farington Moss, Leyland, Lancs.
18. Five Valleys Road Race	8 July	A. T. Evans Esq., 2, Limeslade Court, The Mumbles, Swansea.
19. The Journal Two Day Cycle Race	15 to 16 July (inclusive)	J. Oxnard Esq., 54, Westmoor Drive, Westmoor, Newcastle-on-Tyne, NE1 20NS.
20. Courage Grand Prix	16 July	N. Shelmerdine Esq., 1 Fircroft Close, Tilehurst, Reading, RG3 6LJ.
21. Tour of the North	25 to 30 July (inclusive)	J. Wilcockson Esq., International Cycle Sport, St. Johns Street, Silsden, Nr. Keighley, Yorks.
22. Tour of the Cotswolds	30 July	R. T. Griffin Esq., 37 Courtenay Street, Cheltenham, Gloucestershire.
23. Bromsgrove Olympique Grand Prix	20 August	G. Calcutt Esq., "Stet", Withybed Lane, Inkberrow, Worcester.
24. Tour of the Peak	10 September	A. Pickburn Esq., 48 Mostyn Road, Hazel Grove, Stockport, Cheshire.

EXPLANATORY NOTE

(This Note is not part of the Regulations.)

The Cycle Racing on Highways Regulations 1960 authorise certain races or trials of speed between bicycles or tricycles, not being motor vehicles, (described in those Regulations as bicycle races) to be held on public highways subject to certain conditions including the condition that the number of competitors taking part must not exceed 40. These Regulations, which apply to England and Wales, provide for varying this condition in the case of any bicycle race (as defined in the 1960 Regulations) which is comprised in the 24 cycle racing events proposed to be held in 1972 which are specified in the Schedule, by increasing to 84 the maximum number of competitors who may take part in the case of the event specified under the title "Tour of Britain (Milk Race)" and to 60 in the case of the other events so specified.

STATUTORY INSTRUMENTS

1972 No. 338

CUSTOMS AND EXCISE
The Origin of Goods (Republic of Ireland) (Amendment) Regulations 1972

Made - - -	*6th March* 1972
Laid before House of Commons	*15th March* 1972
Coming into Operation	1st *April* 1972

The Secretary of State, in exercise of his powers under section 12(2) of the Import Duties Act 1958(**a**), hereby makes the following Regulations:—

1. These Regulations may be cited as the Origin of Goods (Republic of Ireland) (Amendment) Regulations 1972 and shall come into operation on 1st April 1972.

2. The Interpretation Act 1889(**b**) shall apply to the interpretation of these Regulations as it applies to the interpretation of an Act of Parliament.

3. The Origin of Goods (Republic of Ireland) Regulations 1966(**c**), as amended(**d**), shall have effect as if—

(*a*) at the end of Regulation 1 there were added the following:—
"(*c*) in the case of goods of a description specified in Part II of Schedule 3 not being goods of a description specified in Schedule 2, the relevant conditions set out in Part I of Schedule 3 have been fulfilled.";

(*b*) Schedule 2 were amended in the manner specified in Schedule 2 to these Regulations;

(*c*) there were added, as Schedule 3, Schedule 1 to these Regulations.

Anthony Grant,
Parliamentary Under Secretary of State,
Department of Trade and Industry.
6th March 1972.

(**a**) 6 & 7 Eliz. 2. c. 6.   (**b**) 1889 c. 63.
(**c**) S.I. 1966/667 (1966 II, p. 1463).
(**d**) S.I. 1966/1098; 1968/988; 1223 (1966 III, p. 2699; 1968 II, pp. 2612, 2380).

SCHEDULE 1

(Schedule 3 to S.I. 1966/667)

INTRODUCTORY NOTES

1. "the area", except in the next following definition, has the same meaning as in Regulation 5 of these Regulations:

"Commonwealth Preference Area" means the area which is for the time being the Commonwealth Preference Area for the purposes of the Import Duties Act 1958, excluding the United Kingdom and the Republic of Ireland;

"Eastern Area" means Albania, Bulgaria, the People's Republic of China, Czechoslovakia, Eastern Germany (USSR zone and sector of Berlin), Hungary, North Korea, North Vietnam, the People's Republic of Mongolia, Poland, Romania, the Union of Soviet Socialist Republics;

"a restricted territory" means a territory from which exports to the United Kingdom of goods to which Regulation 1(c) of these Regulations applies were on 31st December 1971 subject to quantitative restrictions either on exportation from that territory to the United Kingdom or on importation from that territory into the United Kingdom;

"scheduled material" means material falling within a description of goods specified in Part II of this Schedule but not falling within a description of goods specified in Schedule 2.

2.—(1) Four-figure references are references to headings of the Customs Tariff 1959(a) and any description of goods specified in relation to such heading shall be taken to comprise all goods which would be classified under a description in the same terms in the relevant heading in the said Customs Tariff.

(2) Where in a description of goods the word "Other" appears immediately preceded by a letter or figure in brackets it shall have the same meaning as it has when it appears in the corresponding place in the relevant heading in the Customs Tariff 1959.

3. Regulations 3 and 4 of these Regulations shall apply for the purpose of determining what proportion of the costs of manufacture of goods to which Regulation 1(c) applies is attributable to expenditure within the area in like manner as they apply for determining the same question in relation to goods to which Regulation 1(a) applies.

PART I

1. In the case of fabric woven in the Republic of Ireland and containing 15% or more by weight of scheduled material being yarn spun in the Eastern Area or apparel (excluding shirts (ex61·03) containing not less than one third by weight of wool) and other made up articles containing scheduled material being fabric woven in the Eastern Area, the relevant conditions are as follows:—

(a) the goods were manufactured in the Republic of Ireland and 25% of the costs of their manufacture is attributable to expenditure within the area; and

(b) the scheduled material imported into the Republic of Ireland and used in the manufacture of the goods, has borne duty in the area at a rate which, after account is taken of any drawback or other relief from duty, is not less than the rate shown in the Customs Tariff 1959 as applicable to like material at the time of the importation of the material in question into the area.

For the purposes of this sub-paragraph (in its application in relation to goods to which paragraphs 2 and 3 apply as well as in its application in relation to goods to which this paragraph applies) material which was imported into the area before 1st April 1972 shall be deemed to have borne duty at the rate referred to in this sub-paragraph.

2. In the case of—

(a) fabric woven in the Republic of Ireland and containing less than 15% by weight of scheduled material being yarn spun in a restricted area territory or in the Commonwealth Preference Area;

(a) See S.I. 1971/1971 (1971 III, p. 5330).

(*b*) apparel and other made up articles not containing scheduled material being fabric woven in a restricted territory or in the Commonwealth Preference Area;

(*c*) shirts (ex 61.03) containing not less than one third by weight of wool not being goods falling within paragraph 1 above, the relevant condition or conditions are either (i) the conditions set out in paragraph 1(*a*) above, or (ii) that the goods have undergone a process of manufacture in the Republic of Ireland, and the condition set out in paragraph 1(*b*) above.

3. In the case of other goods, the relevant conditions are that the goods have undergone a process of manufacture in the Republic of Ireland, and the condition set out in paragraph 1(*b*) above.

PART II

Tariff Heading	*Description of Goods*

55.05   Cotton yarn, not put up for retail sale;
    (B) Other

55.06   Cotton yarn, put up for retail sale;
    (B) Other

55.07   Cotton gauze

55.08   Terry towelling and similar terry fabrics, of cotton

55.09   Other woven fabrics of cotton

58.04   Woven pile fabrics and chenille fabrics (other than terry towelling or similar terry fabrics of cotton falling within heading No. 55.08 and fabrics falling within heading No. 58.05);
    (B) Not containing silk or man-made fibres:
        (1) Containing more than 50 per cent. by weight of cotton

58.10   Embroidery, in the piece, in strips or in motifs;
    (B) Not containing silk or man-made fibres:
        (1) Containing woven fabric of which the cotton content exceeds 50 per cent. by weight of the total textile fabric content

59.07   Textile fabrics coated with gum or amylaceous substances, of a kind used for the outer covers of books and the like; tracing cloth; prepared painting canvas; buckram and similar fabrics for hat foundations and similar uses:
    (B) Not containing silk or man-made fibres:
        (1) Containing woven fabric of which the cotton content exceeds 50 per cent. by weight of the total textile fabric content

59.08   Textile fabrics impregnated, coated, covered or laminated with preparations of cellulose derivatives or of other artificial plastic materials:
    (B) Not containing silk or man-made fibres:
        (1) Containing woven fabrics of which the cotton content exceeds 50 per cent. by weight of the total textile fabric content

59.09   Textile fabrics coated or impregnated with oil or preparations with a basis of drying oil:
    (B) Not containing silk or man-made fibres:
        (1) Containing woven fabric of which the cotton content exceeds 50 per cent. by weight of the total textile fabric content

59.11   Rubberised textile fabrics, other than rubberised knitted or crocheted goods:
    (B) Not containing silk or man-made fibres:
        (1) Containing woven fabric of which the cotton content exceeds 50 per cent. by weight of the total textile fabric content

59.12   Textile fabrics otherwise impregnated or coated; painted textile fabrics being theatrical scenery, studio back-cloths or the like:

    (A) Fabrics:

      (2) Not containing silk or man-made fibres:

        (*a*) containing woven fabric of which the cotton content exceeds 50 per cent. by weight of the total textile fabric content

59.13   Elastic fabrics and trimmings (other than knitted or crocheted goods) consisting of textile materials combined with rubber threads:

    (B) Not containing silk or man-made fibres:

      (1) Woven fabric containing more than 50 per cent. by weight of cotton

59.14   Wicks, of woven, plaited or knitted textile materials, for lamps, stoves, lighters, candles and the like; tubular knitted gas-mantle fabric and incandescent gas mantles:

    (B) Not containing silk or man-made fibres:

      (1) Of woven fabric containing more than 50 per cent. by weight of cotton

59.15   Textile hosepiping and similar tubing, with or without lining, armour or accessories of other materials:

    (B) Other:

      (1) Containing woven fabric of which the cotton content exceeds 50 per cent. by weight of the total textile fabric content

59.16   Transmission, conveyor or elevator belts or belting, of textile material, whether or not strengthened with metal or other material;

    (B) Other

      (1) Containing woven fabric of which the cotton content exceeds 50 per cent. by weight of the total textile fabric content

59.17   Textile products and textile articles, of a kind commonly used in machinery or plant:

    (D) Other:

      (2) Other:

        (*a*) Containing woven fabric of which the cotton content exceeds 50 per cent. by weight of the total textile fabric content

61.01   Men's and boys' outer garments:

    (C) Other:

      (1) Containing woven fabric of which the cotton content exceeds 50 per cent. by weight of the garment

61.02   Women's, girls' and infants' outer garments:

    (C) Other:

      (1) Containing woven fabric of which the cotton content exceeds 50 per cent. by weight of the garment

61.03   Men's and boys' under garments, including collars, shirt fronts and cuffs:

    (C) Other:

      (1) Containing woven fabric of which the cotton content exceeds 50 per cent. by weight of the garment

61.04   Women's, girls' and infants' under garments:

    (C) Other:

      (1) Containing woven fabric of which the cotton content exceeds 50 per cent. by weight of the garment

61.05   Handkerchiefs:
        (C) Other:
           (1) Containing woven fabric of which the cotton content exceeds 50 per cent. by weight of the article

61.06   Shawls, scarves, mufflers, mantillas, veils and the like:
        (C) Other:
           (1) Containing woven fabric of which the cotton content exceeds 50 per cent. by weight of the article

61.07   Ties, bow ties and cravats:
        (C) Other:
           (1) Containing woven fabric of which the cotton content exceeds 50 per cent. by weight of the article

61.08   Collars, tuckers, fallals, bodice-fronts, jabots, cuffs, flounces, yokes and similar accessories and trimmings for women's and girls' garments:
        (C) Other:
           (1) Containing woven fabric of which the cotton content exceeds 50 per cent. by weight of the article

61.09   Corsets, corset-belts, suspender-belts, brassieres, braces, suspenders, garters and the like (including such articles of knitted or crocheted fabric) whether or not elastic:
        (C) Other:
           (1) Corsets and similar body-supporting under garments and brassieres not containing embroidery, net, lace or material resembling lace:
              (a) Containing woven fabric of which the cotton content exceeds 50 per cent. by weight of the garment
           (2) Other:
              (a) Containing woven fabric of which the cotton content exceeds 50 per cent. by weight of the article

61.10   Gloves, mittens, mitts, stockings, socks and sockettes, not being knitted or crocheted goods:
        (C) Other:
           (1) Gloves, mittens and mitts wholly or partly cut out of fabric containing cotton and sewn up (but excluding gloves known as astrakhan gloves, mittens and mitts in which the fabric containing cotton is present in the lining only):
              (a) Containing woven fabric of which the cotton content exceeds 50 per cent. by weight of the article

61.11   Made up accessories for articles of apparel (for example dress shields, shoulder and other pads, belts, muffs, sleeve protectors, pockets):
        (C) Other:
           (1) Containing woven fabric of which the cotton content exceeds 50 per cent. by weight of the article

62.01   Travelling rugs and blankets:
        (B) Other:
           (1) Containing woven fabric of which the cotton content exceeds 50 per cent. by weight of the article

62.02   Bed linen, table linen, toilet linen, and kitchen linen; curtains and other furnishing articles:
        (B) Other:
           (1) Bedspreads, sheets, quilts, pillow cases, bolster cases, mattress cases

and face, hand and bath towels, wholly of cotton and not containing embroidery, net lace or material resembling lace

(2) Other:

(*a*) Containing woven fabric of which the cotton content exceeds 50 per cent. by weight of the article

62.04   Tarpaulins, sails, awnings, sunblinds, tents and camping goods:

(B) Other:

(2) Other:

(*a*) Containing woven fabric of which the cotton content exceeds 50 per cent. by weight of the article

62.05   Other made up textile articles (including dress patterns):

(B) Other:

(1) Containing woven fabric of which the cotton content exceeds 50 per per cent. by weight of the article

SCHEDULE 2
(*Amendments of Schedule 2 to* S.I. 1966/667)

1. In Introductory Note (4) for the list of items to be regarded as a single textile material there shall be substituted the following:—

"(*a*) Silk and waste silk.

(*b*) Man-made fibres, continuous, produced by a processs mentioned in Note 1(*a*) to Chapter 51.

(*c*) Man-made fibres, continuous, produced by a process mentioned in Note 1(*b*) to Chapter 51.

(*d*) Man-made fibres, discontinuous, produced by a process mentioned in Note 1(*a*) to Chapter 51.

(*e*) Man-made fibres, discontinuous, produced by a process mentioned in Note 1(*b*) to Chapter 51.

(*f*) Metallised textiles.

(*g*) Wool.

(*h*) Other animal hair.

(*i*) Flax and ramie.

(*j*) Cotton.

(*k*) Other vegetable fibres.".

2. At the end of Introductory Note (8) there shall be substituted a comma for the full stop and there shall be added—

"and which have not benefitted from drawback or other relief from import duty in the Member State of the Association in which the goods underwent their last process of production.".

3. There shall be added the following entries:—

Column 1 Tariff Heading	Column 2 Description of Goods	Column 3 Qualifying Process
§61.03	Men's and boys' shirts containing more than 5% by weight of silk and/or man-made fibres.	Manufacture from fibres, yarns or fabric (ex Chapters 50 to 59) provided that in the case of fabric, it has borne duty in the area at a rate which, after account is taken of any drawback or other relief from duty, is not less than the rate shown in the Customs Tariff 1959 as applicable to like fabrics at the time of the importation of the fabric in question into the area; or from materials not falling in Chapters 50 to 62.
§60.05	Women's and girls' knitted or crocheted dresses, complete and ready to wear containing more than 5% by weight of silk and/or man-made fibres.	Manufacture from fibres or yarns, or (except in the case of lining) from knitted or crocheted fabrics ex. 60.06, provided that, in the case of fabric, it has borne duty on importation into the area at a rate which, after account is taken of any drawback, or other relief from duty, is not less than the rate shown in the Customs Tariff 1959 as applicable to like fabrics at the time of the importation of the fabric in question into the area; or from materials not falling in Chapters 50 to 62.

EXPLANATORY NOTE

(This Note is not part of the Regulations.)

These Regulations amend the Origin of Goods (Republic of Ireland) Regulations 1966.

The principal change is that to be free of import duty on importation from the Republic of Ireland into the United Kingdom certain cotton textiles have in future to qualify as goods of the Republic of Ireland. The Regulations specify the conditions that have to be fulfilled.

STATUTORY INSTRUMENTS

1972 No. 339

POLICE

The Police (Amendment) (No. 2) Regulations 1972

Made - - -	*6th March* 1972
Laid before Parliament	*15th March* 1972
Coming into Operation	*6th April* 1972

In exercise of the powers conferred on me by section 33 of the Police Act 1964(**a**), and after consulting the Police Council for the United Kingdom in accordance with section 4(4) of the Police Act 1969(**b**), I hereby make the following Regulations:—

1. These Regulations may be cited as the Police (Amendment) (No. 2) Regulations 1972.

2. These Regulations shall come into operation on 6th April 1972 and shall have effect—

(*a*) for the purposes of Regulation 4 thereof, as from 15th February 1971;

(*b*) for the purposes of Regulation 5 thereof, as from 6th April 1964;

(*c*) for the purposes of Regulation 6 thereof, as from 6th April 1972;

(*d*) for the purposes of Regulation 7 thereof, as from 10th February 1964.

3. In these Regulations any reference to the principal Regulations is a reference to the Police Regulations 1971(**c**), as amended(**d**).

4. For Regulation 45 of the principal Regulations (compensatory grant) there shall be substituted the following Regulation:—

"Compensatory grant

45.—(1) In each financial year a member of a police force who, during the preceding financial year, has paid income tax or surtax attributable to the inclusion of a rent allowance or compensatory grant in his emoluments in respect of service as a member of that force shall be paid a compensatory grant.

(2) The amount of the compensatory grant made to a member of a police force in any year shall be the aggregate of—

(*a*) the amount by which the income tax in fact deducted from his emoluments in respect of service as a member of that force dur-

---

(**a**) 1964 c. 48.
(**c**) S.I. 1971/156 (1971, p. 439).

(**b**) 1969 c. 63.
(**d**) The amending Regulations are not relevant to the subject matter of these Regulations.

ing the preceding year, according to the tax tables prepared or prescribed by the Commissioners of Inland Revenue, is increased by the inclusion in such emoluments of a rent allowance or any compensatory grant, and

(*b*) the amount by which he satisfies the police authority that any surtax paid by him during the preceding year for any earlier year beginning on or after 6th April 1963 is increased by the inclusion in his emoluments in respect of such service during that earlier year of a rent allowance or any compensatory grant.

(3) The compensatory grant may, except in the circumstances described in paragraph (4), be paid by such instalments throughout the year in which it is payable as the police authority may determine.

(4) Where, in the course of a financial year, a member of a police force leaves the force or dies whilst serving therein, he or his personal representative, as the case may be, shall be paid the whole of the compensatory grant due to the member during that year and, in addition, shall be paid a further compensatory grant equal to that which, had he not left the force or died, would have been due to him in a subsequent year by reason of income tax deducted from, or surtax paid on, his emoluments while in fact a member of the police force.

(5) For the purposes of the preceding provisions of this Regulation—

(*a*) the expression "year" or "financial year" means a year commencing on 6th April and ending on the following 5th April;

(*b*) the expression "income tax" means income tax other than surtax;

(*c*) in the case of a member of a police force whose total income for any year which is chargeable to surtax includes income other than his emoluments in respect of service as a member of that force, any reference to the amount of surtax paid for that year shall be construed as a reference to the amount which would have been so paid had his total chargeable income for that year not included such other income; and

(*d*) where a member of a police force has served more than once in the same force, references in this Regulation to service in the force shall be construed as references to his service therein since his last appointment thereto.".

5.—(1) Where the compensatory grant made to a member of a police force in any financial year beginning on or after 6th April 1964 but before the coming into operation of the principal Regulations was less than it would have been if the Regulation substituted for Regulation 45 of the principal Regulations by the preceding Regulation had been substituted—

(*a*) with effect from 6th April 1964, for Regulation 30 of the Police Regulations 1952(**a**), as amended(**b**), (which applied in respect of the period 6th April 1964 to 1st April 1965);

(*b*) with effect from 1st April 1965, for Regulation 39 of the Police Regulations 1965(**c**), as amended(**b**), (which applied in respect of the period 1st April 1965 to 1st February 1968), and

(*c*) with effect from 1st February 1968, for Regulation 38 of the Police Regulations 1968(**d**), as amended(**b**), (which applied in respect of the

---

(**a**) S.I. 1952/1704 (1952 II, p. 2480).
(**b**) The amending Regulations are not relevant to the subject matter of this Regulation.
(**c**) S.I. 1965/538 (1965 I, p. 1555).　　(**d**) S.I. 1968/26 (1968 I, p. 38).

period 1st February 1968 to 15th February 1971 when the principal Regulations came into operation),

then the member in question shall be entitled to the difference by way of an increase in compensatory grant for the financial year in question.

(2) In this Regulation the expression "financial year" means a year commencing on 6th April and ending on the following 5th April.

6. For Regulation 46 of the principal Regulations (discharge of tax liability in respect of police house or quarters) there shall be substituted the following Regulation:—

"Discharge of tax liability in respect of police house or quarters

46.—(1) Where a member of a police force is provided with a house or quarters free of rent and rates and his liability to pay income tax or surtax is increased—

    (*a*) in consequence thereof, by virtue of section 185 of the Income and Corporation Taxes Act 1970(**a**) or otherwise, or

    (*b*) in consequence of any payment required to be made by this Regulation,

that liability shall be discharged by the police authority in accordance with, and to the extent hereinafter provided in, this Regulation.

(2) A member of a police force shall be reimbursed the amount by which the income tax in fact deducted from his emoluments in respect of service as a member of that force, according to the tax tables prepared or prescribed by the Commissioners of Inland Revenue, is increased—

    (*a*) in consequence of his being provided with a house or quarters free of rent and rates, or

    (*b*) in consequence of any payment under this Regulation.

(3) Where any surtax becomes due and payable for any year by a member of a police force, the liability therefor shall be discharged by the police authority to the extent that he satisfies them that the amount thereof is increased—

    (*a*) in consequence of his having been provided with a house or quarters free of rent and rates during his service as a member of that force or, where he transferred thereto from some other force, during his service as a member of that other force, or

    (*b*) in consequence of any payment under this Regulation by the police authority or, where he transferred as aforesaid, by the police authority maintaining the force from which he transferred, not being a payment under paragraph (4).

(4) Where any liability to surtax would fall to be discharged by a police authority under the preceding paragraph but for the fact that the person concerned has left the police force maintained by them, otherwise than on transfer to another police force, or has died, that liability shall be discharged by the police authority and, to the extent that, in consequence of the discharge of that liability, any further surtax becomes due and payable, liability for that further surtax shall be also so discharged.

(a) 1970 c. 10.

(5) For the purposes of the preceding provisions of this Regulation—

　　(*a*) the expression "income tax" means income tax other than surtax;

　　(*b*) in the case of a member of a police force whose total income for any year which is chargeable to surtax includes income other than emoluments in respect of his service as a member of that force or, where he transferred thereto from some other force, as a member of that other force, any reference to surtax due and payable for that year shall be construed as a reference to the surtax which would have been so due and payable had his total chargeable income for that year not included such other income.".

7.—(1) Where before the coming into operation of these Regulations a member of a police force has paid any income tax (including surtax) which arose in consequence of any house or quarters with which he was provided, free of rent, on or after 10th February 1964, being provided also free of rates, then, to the extent that liability therefor would have fallen to be discharged by a police authority under a Regulation hereinafter mentioned if in paragraph (*a*) of each such Regulation there had been inserted the words "or otherwise" after the words "section 47 of the Finance Act 1963"—

　　(*a*) with effect from 10th February 1964, in the case of Regulation 30A of the Police Regulations 1952, as amended(**a**), (which applied in respect of the period 10th February 1964 to 1st April 1965);

　　(*b*) with effect from 1st April 1965, in the case of Regulation 40 of the Police Regulations 1965, as amended(**b**), (which applied in respect of the period 1st April 1965 to 1st February 1968), and

　　(*c*) with effect from 1st February 1968, in the case of Regulation 39 of the Police Regulations 1968, as amended(**b**), (which applied in respect of the period 1st February 1968 to 15th February 1971), and

　　(*d*) with effect from 15th February 1971 in the case of Regulation 46 of the principal Regulations, as originally made, (which applies in respect of the period 15th February 1971 to 6th April 1972 when Regulation 6 of these Regulations takes effect),

then that police authority shall reimburse the member in question the amount of tax so paid by him.

(2) For the purposes of Regulation 46(1)(*b*) and (2)(*b*) of the principal Regulations, as amended by Regulation 6 of these Regulations, any payment under this Regulation shall be treated as if it were a payment under the said Regulation 46.

R. Maudling,
One of Her Majesty's Principal
Secretaries of State.

Home Office,
　Whitehall.
6th March 1972.

(**a**) The relevant amending Regulations are S.I. 1964/133 (1964 I, p. 246).
(**b**) The amending Regulations are not relevant to the subject matter of this Regulation.

EXPLANATORY NOTE
(This Note is not part of the Regulations.)

These Regulations, first, amend the Police Regulations 1971, which came into operation on 15th February 1971, and, secondly, contain related provisions in respect of periods before that date.

Regulation 4 amends, with effect from 15th February 1971, the provisions of the Regulations of 1971 relating to compensatory grant. It provides that in calculating such grant account shall be taken not only of income tax deducted under the P.A.Y.E. system but also of surtax, so far as it is referable to police emoluments. Regulation 5 contains corresponding provision in respect of the period 6th April 1964 to 15th February 1971.

Regulation 6 amends, with effect from 6th April 1972, the provisions of the Regulations of 1971 relating to the discharge of a policeman's tax liability in respect of a police house provided free of rent and rates. First, it ensures that the tax liability to be discharged by the police authority includes not only the policeman's liability in respect of the annual value of the house but also that arising from the house being provided free of rates. Regulation 7 contains corresponding provision in respect of the period 10th February 1964 to 6th April 1972. Secondly, Regulation 6 distinguishes between income tax deducted under the P.A.Y.E. system and income tax by way of surtax: surtax liability to be discharged by the police authority is limited to liability referable to police emoluments. (Regulation 7 contains no corresponding provision in this regard.)

In so far as Regulation 2 provides that the Regulations shall have retrospective effect (as mentioned above), they are made in exercise of the power conferred by section 33(4) of the Police Act 1964.

STOKE-ON-TRENT
CITY
LIBRARIES

1404

STATUTORY INSTRUMENTS

1972 No. 341

ROAD TRAFFIC
The Public Service Vehicles (International Circulation) Regulations 1972

Made - - -		*7th March* 1972
Laid before Parliament		*13th March* 1972
Coming into Operation		*1st April* 1972

The Secretary of State for the Environment in exercise of the powers conferred on him by section 160(1) of the Road Traffic Act 1960(a) and all other powers him enabling in that behalf, and after consultation with representative organisations in accordance with the provisions of section 260(2) of the said Act of 1960, hereby makes the following Regulations:—

1. These Regulations shall come into operation on 1st April 1972, and may be cited as the Public Service Vehicles (International Circulation) Regulations 1972.

2. The Public Service Vehicles (International Circulation) Regulations 1970(b) are hereby revoked.

3. The Interpretation Act 1889(c) shall apply for the interpretation of these Regulations as it applies for the interpretation of an Act of Parliament, and as if for the purposes of section 38 of that Act these Regulations were an Act of Parliament and the Regulations revoked by Regulation 2 of these Regulations were an Act of Parliament thereby repealed.

4. These Regulations apply to a public service vehicle which—

(1) is brought into Great Britain for the purpose of carrying persons making only a temporary stay therein;

(2) remains in Great Britain for a period of no more than three months from the date of its entry therein;

(3) is used only by persons who are employed to drive the vehicle or to act in the capacity of guide interpreter or organiser and by passengers—

    (i) who during their journey to Great Britain were passengers in that vehicle, commenced their journey at the same point of departure and will return together to that point of departure in that vehicle or will make their return journey by another means, or

    (ii) who are travelling to Great Britain in that vehicle from the same point of departure and will make their return journey in another such vehicle operated by the same carrier under a contract concluded with him before they arrived in Great Brit-

---

(a) 1960 c. 16.
(c) 1889 c. 63.

(b) S.I. 1970/612 (1970 I, p.1946).

ain, or who are returning in that vehicle to the same point in the country from which they started their journey, being passengers who travelled to Great Britain in another vehicle operated by the same carrier and who are making their return journey under a contract concluded with him before they arrived in Great Britain;

For the purpose of this paragraph any part of a journey during which a person travelled by sea or air shall be disregarded for the purpose of ascertaining whether he has been a passenger on a vehicle during a journey;

(4) is registered in the country from which passengers using it commenced their journey to Great Britain; and

(5) is operated by a carrier duly authorised under the law of the country in which it is registered to use it for the carriage of the passengers who are using it on the journey on which it is being used or such parts thereof as are within that country.

5. Save as provided in Regulation 6 of these Regulations, the provisions of Part III of the Road Traffic Act 1960 shall, in relation to vehicles to which these Regulations apply, have effect as though sections 127, 134 and 144 (which subject users of public service vehicles to the holding of public service vehicle licences, road service licences and require the holding of licences by drivers and conductors of such vehicles) were omitted therefrom.

6. In relation to any vehicle to which these Regulations apply and which is—

(1) used only by persons in the circumstances described in paragraph (3)(i) of Regulation 4 of these Regulations, and

(2) is registered in Austria, Belgium, Denmark, Federal Republic of Germany, France, Greece, Republic of Ireland, Italy, Luxembourg, Norway, Portugal, Spain, Sweden, Turkey and Yugoslavia the provisions of Part III of the Road Traffic Act 1960 shall have effect as though sections 134 and 144 (which subject users of public service vehicles to the holding of road service licences and require the holding of licences by drivers and conductors of such vehicles) were omitted therefrom, and as if section 127 were modified to read as follows:—

> "127. No person shall cause or permit a motor vehicle to be used on a road as a public service vehicle unless there is in force in relation to the user of that vehicle an appropriate document carried on the vehicle."

In this paragraph "appropriate document" means a document issued by the competent authority of the country in which the vehicle is registered or any duly authorised agency in the form specified in Part I or Part II of the Schedule to these Regulations and duly completed in accordance with the tenor thereof.

7. None of the provisions of the Public Service Vehicles (Equipment and Use) Regulations 1958(a), as amended(b), shall have effect in relation to a vehicle to which these Regulations apply.

(a) S.I. 1958/926 (1958 II, p. 2036).
(b) S.I. 1966/676, 1968/826 (1966 II, p. 1517; 1968 II, p. 2226).

Signed by authority of the Secretary of State.
7th March 1972.

John Peyton,
Minister for Transport Industries,
Department of the Environment.

SCHEDULE

Part I

(The following is the control document in Annex 1 to Report of the Committee of Deputies of the European Conference of Ministers of Transport presented to and adopted by the Council of Ministers of the said Conference at a meeting in Paris on the 16th June 1971).

(Front)

White paper—30cm x 21 cm or 32 cm x 21 cm

Carnet No.............
Waybill No.............

(Text drafted in the official language(s) of the Member country
where the vehicle employed is registered, and in English and French.)

WAYBILL (1)
(Please use block letters)

Issuing country
(Insert country symbol)

1. Vehicle
   Registration No. ....
   Seating capacity.......................................

2. Transport operator
   Name and first name, or business name and address.......................................
   ....

3. Driver(s) name(s) : 1.......................................　　2. ....

4. Type of service
   (a) closed-door circular tour
   (b) outward journey laden—return trip unladen

5. Journey schedule
   For journeys referred to under 4(b) : Passengers will be left at...
   (name of locality and country)

Part I - *cont.*

Date	Stages day-by-day		Vehicles driven (4)		km per day	Point of entry at the frontier of the Member country concerned
	from	to	laden	unladen		

6. Passenger list (names and initials) (5)

1. ....   21. ....   41. ....
2. ....   to   to
3. ....
to   40. ....   60. ....
20.

7. ....
(date of issue of waybill)

.... (Transport Operator's Signature)

8. Unforseen changes

Inspection visas, if any

Part II

(The following is the control document in Annex 2 to Report of the Committee of Deputies of the European Conference of Ministers of Transport presented to and adopted by the Council of Ministers of the said Conference at a meeting in Paris on the 16th December 1969)

(Front)

(Green Paper—30 cm x 42 cm)

Carnet No...................
Waybill No.................

ISSUING COUNTRY
(Country symbol)

(Text drafted in the official language(s) of the Member country where the vehicle employed is registered. Translations in the other official languages of the EEC should be given at the back)

WAYBILL

(to be completed in block letters)

1. VEHICLE

Registration No..................make...................
Seating capacity......................

2. TRANSPORT OPERATOR

Name and first names, or business name and address...................

3. NAME(S) OF DRIVER(S): 1. .... 2. ....

4. TYPE OF SERVICE | A | B | C1 | C2 | C3 | D | (1) (2)

Supporting documents to be produced for the following services

Services A and B: nil.

Service C1: transport operator's declaration (see item 9).

Service C2: waybill for the earlier trip involving an outward journey laden and a return journey unladen, when the transport operator took the passengers concerned to the country where he is returning to pick them up.

Service C3: letter or photocopy.

Service D: transport licence.

All the above services: if the operator is authorised to pick up of set down passengers on the way in another Member country, the licence enabling him to do this must also be appended.

5. JOURNEY SCHEDULE

Passengers picked up at....................
.... (locality and country)

Instructions

(1) "A", "B", "C1", "C2", "C3" and "D" are the code letters for separate categories of occasional transport services as follows:

Service "A": closed-door circular tours;
Service "B": outward journey laden and return journey unladen;

Service "C1": entry unladen in order to pick up, at the same point, passengers that are covered, as a group, by the contract of carriage referred to under Article 5, paragraph 2(a) of Regulation No. 117/66/EEC, this contract having been entered into before their arrival in the country where they are to be picked up.

Service "C2": entry unladen to pick up, at the same point, passengers who were previously conveyed by the transport operator, in the course of a trip involving a return journey unladen, to the country in which they are to be picked up. They must then be brought out of that country.

6. PASSENGER LIST (name and initials)

1.	21.	41. ....
2.	22.	42. ....
3.	23.	43. ....
4.	24.	44. ....
5.	25.	45. ....
6.	26.	46. ....
7.	27.	47. ....
8.	28.	48. ....
9.	29.	49. ....
10.	30.	50. ....
11.	31.	51. ....
12.	32.	52. ....
13.	33.	53. ....
14.	34.	54. ....
15.	35.	55. ....
16.	36.	56. ....
17.	37.	57. ....
18.	38.	58. ....
19.	39.	59. ....
20.	40.	60. ....

7. INFORMATION CONCERNING SERVICE "D":

....

8. .... (Date at which the way-bill is filled in)

.... (Transport operator's signature)

Part II - *cont.*

Date	Stages day-by-day		Vehicle driven(3)		Points of entry at the frontier of the Member country concerned (with appropriate country symbol)
	from	to	laden	unladen	

Service "C3": entry unladen to pick up, at the same point, passengers who had been invited to visit another Member country, the transport costs being borne by the person inviting them. Such passengers must constitute a group not made up solely for the purpose of the journey.

Service "D": all other services. The type of service must be carefully indicated under item 7.

(2)   Cross out where required.

(3)   Put a cross(x) in the appropriate column to show whether the daily stage at the date indicated is "laden" or "unladen".

9.   TRANSPORT OPERATORS DECLARATION CONCERNING SERVICE "C1":

The above passengers are covered, as a group, by the contract of carriage referred to under Article 5 paragraph 2(*a*) of Regulation No. 117/66/EEC entered into with .... before their

arrival at...

....
(country where these passengers are picked up)

....
(Date)   (Transport operator's
signature)

10.   UNFORESEEN CHANGES

(Inspection visas if any: see back of this page)

INSPECTION VISAS

TRANSLATIONS

(in the other official languages of the EEC)

EXPLANATORY NOTE
(This Note is not part of the Regulations.)

These Regulations revoke the Public Service Vehicles (International Circulation) Regulations 1970 and provide similar qualifying conditions for exemption from the requirements of sections 127, 134 and 144 of the Road Traffic Act 1960 for public service vehicles brought temporarily into Great Britain save that in the case of such vehicles which are registered in Austria, Belgium, Denmark, Federal Republic of Germany, France, Greece, Republic of Ireland, Italy, Luxembourg, Norway, Portugal, Spain, Sweden, Turkey and Yugoslavia, member countries of the European Conference of Ministers of Transport with whom there exists no bilateral agreement as to the international carriage of passengers by road, a control document as prescribed in Part I or Part II of the Schedule is required to be carried on the vehicle. The Regulations also extend from 90 days to three months the period during which a qualifying public service vehicle may remain in Great Britain.

STATUTORY INSTRUMENTS

1972 No. 347

AGRICULTURE

The Price Stability of Imported Products (Rates of Levy) (Cereals) (No. 10) Order 1972

Made – – – –	*7th March* 1972
Coming into Operation	*8th March* 1972

The Minister of Agriculture, Fisheries and Food, in exercise of the powers conferred upon him by section 1(2), (4), (5), (6) and (7) of the Agriculture and Horticulture Act 1964(a) and of all other powers enabling him in that behalf, hereby makes the following order: —

1. This order may be cited as the Price Stability of Imported Products (Rates of Levy) (Cereals) (No. 10) Order 1972, and shall come into operation on 8th March 1972.

2.—(1) In this order—

" the Principal Order " means the Price Stability of Imported Products (Levy Arrangements) (Cereals) Order 1971(b), as amended by any subsequent order and if any such order is replaced by any subsequent order the expression shall be construed as a reference to such subsequent order;

AND other expressions have the same meaning as in the Principal Order.

(2) The Interpretation Act 1889(c) shall apply to the interpretation of this order as it applies to the interpretation of an Act of Parliament and as if this order and the order hereby revoked were Acts of Parliament.

3. In accordance with and subject to the provisions of Part II of the Principal Order (which provides for the charging of levies on imports of certain specified commodities) the rate of levy for such imports into the United Kingdom of any specified commodity as are described in column 2 of the Schedule to this order in relation to a tariff heading indicated in column 1 of that Schedule shall be the rate set forth in relation thereto in column 3 of that Schedule.

4. The Price Stability of Imported Products (Rates of Levy) (Cereals) (No. 9) Order 1972(d) is hereby revoked.

In Witness whereof the Official Seal of the Minister of Agriculture, Fisheries and Food is hereunto affixed on 7th March 1972.

(L.S.)

T. R. M. Sewell,
Assistant Secretary.

(a) 1964 c. 28.   (b) S.I. 1971/631 (1971 I, p. 1660).   (c) 1889 c. 63.
(d) S.I. 1972/299 (1972 I, p. 951).

SCHEDULE

1. Tariff Heading	2. Description of Imports	3. Rate of Levy
	Imports of:—	per ton £
10.01	Denatured wheat	4·50
	Wheat (other than denatured wheat)	7·00
10.03	Barley other than barley having a potential diastatic activity of not less than 170 degrees	2·50
10.04	Oats	5·75
10.05	Maize (other than sweet corn on the cob) ..	4·50
10.07	Grain sorghum	1·75
11.02	Cereal groats, meals, kibbled or cut cereals, rolled, flaked, crushed or bruised cereals and other processed cereals— of barley .. .. of oats .. .. of maize	 5·25 8·75 5·00

EXPLANATORY NOTE

(This Note is not part of the Order.)

This order, which comes into operation on 8th March 1972, supersedes the Price Stability of Imported Products (Rates of Levy) (Cereals) (No. 9) Order 1972. It—

(*a*) increases the rate of levy to be charged on imports of oats to £5·75 per ton;

(*b*) fixes a rate of levy of £8·75 per ton to be charged on imports of processed oats within tariff heading 11.02; and

(*c*) reimposes unchanged the remaining rates of levy in force immediately before the commencement of the order.

STATUTORY INSTRUMENTS

1972 No. 355

DEFENCE

The Royal Air Force Terms of Service (Amendment) Regulations 1972

Made - - -	*25th February* 1972
Laid before Parliament	*16th March* 1972
Coming into Operation	*1st May* 1972

The Defence Council, in exercise of the powers conferred upon them by section 2 of the Armed Forces Act 1966(a) and of all other powers enabling them in that behalf, hereby make the following regulations:—

Citation, Commencement and Interpretation

1.—(1) These Regulations may be cited as the Royal Air Force Terms of Service (Amendment) Regulations 1972 and shall come into operation on the 1st May 1972.

(2) The Interpretation Act 1889(b) shall apply to the interpretation of these Regulations as it applies to the interpretation of an Act of Parliament.

(3) In these Regulations "the Principal Regulations" means the Royal Air Force Terms of Service Regulations 1971(c).

Amendments to the Principal Regulations

2.—(1) The following Regulation shall be substituted for Regulation 4 of the Principal Regulations:—

"**4.**—(1) Subject to Regulation 7, a person in air force service shall, at the end of the period of 9 years beginning with the relevant date and at any time thereafter, have the right exercisable in accordance with Regulation 6 to be transferred to the reserve or, in the case of a woman, to determine her service.

(2) Without prejudice to the generality of the preceding Regulation a person who has attained the age of 17 years 6 months may, after the commencement of these Regulations, be enlisted in the Royal Air Force for a term of not less than 3 years nor more than 9 years air force service from the relevant date with the right, subject to Regulation 7 and exercisable in accordance with Regulation 6, to be transferred to the reserve (or, in the case of a woman, to determine her service) at the end of the period of 3 years beginning with the date of the expiration of his period of training or at any time thereafter and a woman may be enlisted in air force service with the right to determine her service, subject to Regulation 7 and in accordance with the provisions of Regulation 6, at the end of the period of 4 years beginning with the date of her attestation or at any time thereafter.

(a) 1966 c. 45. (b) 1889 c. 63.
(c) S.I. 1971/510 (1971 I, p. 1500).

(3) Subject to Regulation 7, a person who, after the commencement of these Regulations, enlists in the Royal Air Force under the age of 17 years 6 months for a term of air force service expiring on a date falling later than 3 years after the date of his attaining the age of 18 years shall have the right exercisable in accordance with Regulation 6 to be transferred to the reserve (or in the case of a woman, to determine her service) at the end of the period of 3 years beginning with the date of his attaining the age of 18 years or the date of the expiration of his period of training (including, where appropriate, such further period of service as is designated "Improver Service" at the time of attestation) whichever is the later, or at any ume thereafter PROVIDED that the person in question has given notice in writing to his commanding officer not more than 28 days after his attaining the age of 18 years.

(4) Subject to Regulation 7, a person who, after the commencement of these Regulations, enlists in the Royal Air Force for a term of more than 12 years air force service shall have the right exercisable in accordance with Regulation 6 to determine his service at the end of the period of 12 years beginning with the relevant date or at any time thereafter.".

(2) The following Regulation shall be substituted for Regulation 6 of the Principal Regulations : —

"**6.** A right to determine air force service and a right to be transferred to the reserve conferred by Regulation 4 shall be exercised by notice in writing given by the person in question to his commanding officer not less than 18 months before the expiration of the period at the end of which his service is to be determined or as the case may be he is to be transferred to the reserve.".

(3) Regulation 8(1) of the Principal Regulations shall be amended by the substitution for the words "Regulation 4(3)" of the words "Regulation 4(1), (2) or (3)".

(4) The Principal Regulations shall have effect as though—

(*a*) the following provisions were omitted : —

    (i) Regulation 3(3)

    (ii) Regulation 9(3)

    (iii) in Schedule 1, the words "Regulation 6(2)" in Column 1 and all the words opposite thereto in Columns 2 and 3 and the words "The Commander, Far East Air Force for persons enlisted in the R.A.F. (Malaya)" wherever they appear in Column 3;

(*b*) in Schedule 1, for the words "Air Officer Commanding R.A.F. Record and Pay Office", wherever they appear in Column 3, there were substituted the words "Director of Personnel Management 1 (R.A.F.)" and

(*c*) in Regulation 10(1), there were inserted immediately after the words "who has completed 22 years service" the words "in Her Majesty's forces".

Saving

3. The amendments effected by Regulation 2 in so far as they relate to the substituted Regulations 4(2), (3) and (4) of the Principal Regulations shall not affect the term of service (either as respects duration, or as respects liability to air force service or any liability to serve in the reserve) for which any person who is in air force service immediately before the commencement of these Regulations is serving immediately before such commencement.

On behalf of the Defence Council,

Lambton,
D. Spotswood,
Members of the Defence Council.

Dated 25th February 1972.

EXPLANATORY NOTE

(This Note is not part of the Regulations.)

These Regulations amend the Royal Air Force Terms of Service Regulations 1971 by conferring on all persons enlisted in the Royal Air Force at any time after 9 years a right to be transferred to the reserve (or, in the case of women, to determine service) provided 18 months prior notice is given to their commanding officer. Provision is also made for persons over the age of $17\frac{1}{2}$ years to be enlisted in the Royal Air Force after the 1st May 1972 for not more than 9 years air force service with the right to be transferred to the reserve, or as the case may be, to determine service, at any time after 3 years from the end of training (for women on special enlistment the period is 4 years) on similar notice being given. Similar rights are conferred on these enlisting under that age provided they give notice of their intention to take them up within 28 days of reaching the age of 18. Persons may also, after giving 18 months notice, determine service at any time after 12 years.

Amendments are made to the competent air force authorities; to remove the restrictions on enlisting persons under the age of $17\frac{1}{2}$ years for longer than 12 years and on the right to leave on notice for those who have extended their term of service; and to provide that service in any of H.M. Forces will be included in the 22 years service which an airman must complete to be eligible for continuance.

STATUTORY INSTRUMENTS

1972 No. 356

SUGAR

The Sugar (Distribution Payments) (No. 2) Order 1972

Made - - - -	*8th March* 1972
Laid before Parliament -	*8th March* 1972
Coming into Operation -	*9th March* 1972

The Minister of Agriculture, Fisheries and Food in exercise of the powers conferred upon him by sections 14(5) and 33(4) of the Sugar Act 1956(a) having effect subject to the provisions of section 3 of, and Part II of Schedule 5 to, the Finance Act 1962(b), section 22 of the Finance Act 1964(c) and section 52 of the Finance Act 1966(d) and of all other powers enabling him in that behalf, with the concurrence of the Treasury, and on the advice of the Sugar Board hereby makes the following order:—

1.—(1) This order may be cited as the Sugar (Distribution Payments) (No. 2) Order 1972, and shall come into operation on 9th March 1972.

(2) The Interpretation Act 1889(e) shall apply for the interpretation of this order as it applies for the interpretation of an Act of Parliament.

2. Notwithstanding the provisions of article 3 of the Sugar (Distribution Payments) Order 1972(f), the rates of distribution payments payable under and in accordance with the provisions of section 14 of the Sugar Act 1956, having effect as aforesaid, in respect of sugar and invert sugar imported or home produced or used in the manufacture of imported composite sugar products shall on and after 9th March 1972 be those rates specified in the Schedule to this order; and section 10 of the Finance Act 1901(g) (which relates to new or altered customs or excise duties and their effect upon contracts) shall apply accordingly.

In Witness whereof the Official Seal of the Minister of Agriculture, Fisheries and Food is hereunto affixed on 7th March 1972.

(L.S.)

E. J. G. Smith,
Authorised by the Minister.

We concur.
8th March 1972.

Tim Fortescue,
P. L. Hawkins,
Two of the Lords Commissioners of
Her Majesty's Treasury.

(a) 1956 c. 48.   (b) 1962 c. 44.   (c) 1964 c. 49.   (d) 1966 c. 18.
(e) 1889 c. 63.   (f) S.I. 1972/66 (1972 I, p. 158).   (g) 1901 c. 7.

SCHEDULE

PART I

RATES OF DISTRIBUTION PAYMENT FOR SUGAR

Polarisation	Rate of Distribution Payment per ton
Exceeding—	£
99°	34·000
98° but not exceeding 99°	32·062
97° ,, ,, ,, 98°	31·280
96° ,, ,, ,, 97°	30·464
95° ,, ,, ,, 96°	29·648
94° ,, ,, ,, 95°	28·832
93° ,, ,, ,, 94°	28·016
92° ,, ,, ,, 93°	27·200
91° ,, ,, ,, 92°	26·384
90° ,, ,, ,, 91°	25·568
89° ,, ,, ,, 90°	24·752
88° ,, ,, ,, 89°	23·936
87° ,, ,, ,, 88°	23·256
86° ,, ,, ,, 87°	22·576
85° ,, ,, ,, 86°	21·964
84° ,, ,, ,, 85°	21·352
83° ,, ,, ,, 84°	20·740
82° ,, ,, ,, 83°	20·128
81° ,, ,, ,, 82°	19·584
80° ,, ,, ,, 81°	19·040
79° ,, ,, ,, 80°	18·496
78° ,, ,, ,, 79°	17·952
77° ,, ,, ,, 78°	17·408
76° ,, ,, ,, 77°	16·864
Not exceeding 76°	16·320

PART II

RATES OF DISTRIBUTION PAYMENT FOR INVERT SUGAR

Sweetening matter content by weight	Rate of Distribution Payment per cwt.
	£
70 per cent. or more	1·07
Less than 70 per cent. and more than 50 per cent.	0·77
Not more than 50 per cent.	0·37

EXPLANATORY NOTE

(*This Note is not part of the Order.*)

This order provides for increases equivalent to £24 per ton of refined sugar in the rates of distribution payment in respect of sugar and invert sugar which become eligible for such payments on and after 9th March 1972.

STATUTORY INSTRUMENTS

1972 No. 357

SUGAR

The Sugar (Distribution Repayments) (Amendment) Order 1972

Made - - - -	*8th March* 1972
Laid before Parliament	*8th March* 1972
Coming into Operation	*9th March* 1972

The Minister of Agriculture, Fisheries and Food in exercise of the powers conferred upon him by sections 15 and 33(4) of the Sugar Act 1956(**a**), having effect subject to the provisions of section 3 of, and Part II of Schedule 5 to, the Finance Act 1962(**b**), section 22 of the Finance Act 1964(**c**) and section 52 of the Finance Act 1966(**d**) and of all other powers enabling him in that behalf, an order (**e**) having been made under section 14 of the said Act, hereby makes the following order:—

1.—(1)This order may be cited as the Sugar (Distribution Repayments) (Amendment) Order 1972, and shall come into operation on 9th March 1972.

(2) The Interpretation Act 1889(**f**) shall apply for the interpretation of this order as it applies for the interpretation of an Act of Parliament.

2. The Sugar (Distribution Repayments) Order 1972(**g**) shall be amended by adding at the end of article 5(*a*) thereof the words " when sugar duty became chargeable on the said materials ".

3.—(1) Notwithstanding the provisions of article 5(*b*) of the Sugar (Distribution Repayments) Order 1972 the amount of distribution repayment payable in respect of invert sugar, if the relevant drawback is payable thereon as being invert sugar produced in the United Kingdom from materials on which sugar duty has been paid on or after 9th March 1972 shall be calculated thereon at the rate applicable to the invert sugar in accordance with the rates prescribed in the Schedule to this order.

(2) Article 2(1) of the Sugar (Distribution Repayments) Order 1972 shall apply for the interpretation of this article.

In Witness whereof the Official Seal of the Minister of Agriculture, Fisheries and Food is hereunto affixed on 8th March 1972.

(L.S.)

E. J. G. Smith,
Authorised by the Minister.

(**a**) 1956 c. 48.   (**b**) 1962 c. 44.   (**c**) 1964 c. 49.
(**d**) 1966 c. 18.   (**e**) S.I. 1972/356 (1972 I, p. 1417).   (**f**) 1889 c. 63.
(**g**) S.I. 1972/67 (1972 I, p. 162).

THE SCHEDULE

RATES OF DISTRIBUTION REPAYMENT FOR INVERT SUGAR

Sweetening matter content by weight	Rate of Distribution Repayment per cwt.
	£
More than 80 per cent.	1·27
More than 70 per cent. but not more than 80 per cent.	1·07
More than 60 per cent. but not more than 70 per cent.	0·77
More than 50 per cent. but not more than 60 per cent.	0·61
Not more than 50 per cent. and the invert sugar not being less in weight than 14 lb. per gallon	0·37

EXPLANATORY NOTE

(This Note is not part of the Order.)

This order, which is consequent upon the Sugar (Distribution Payments) (No. 2) Order 1972 (S.I. 1972/356), provides for increases equivalent to £24 per ton of refined sugar in the rates of distribution repayment, in respect of sugar and invert sugar produced in the United Kingdom from materials which become eligible for distribution payments on or after 9th March 1972. It also makes provision for continued liability to distribution repayments at the rates previously payable on sugar and invert sugar produced in the United Kingdom from materials which became eligible for distribution payments before 9th March 1972.

STATUTORY INSTRUMENTS

1972 No. 358

SUGAR

The Composite Sugar Products (Distribution Payments—Average Rates) (No. 2) Order 1972

Made -	-	-	*8th March* 1972
Laid before Parliament-			*8th March* 1972
Coming into Operation			*9th March* 1972

Whereas the Minister of Agriculture, Fisheries and Food (hereinafter called " the Minister ") has on the recommendation of the Sugar Board made an order (a) pursuant to the powers conferred upon him by section 9(1) of the Sugar Act 1956(b) having effect subject to section 14(8) of that Act and to the provisions of section 3 of, and Part II of Schedule 5 to, the Finance Act 1962 (c), section 22 of the Finance Act 1964(d) and section 52 of the Finance Act 1966(e), providing that in the case of certain descriptions of composite sugar products distribution payments shall be calculated on the basis of an average quantity of sugar or invert sugar taken to have been used in the manufacture of the products and that certain other descriptions shall be treated as not containing any sugar or invert sugar:

And whereas the Minister has made an order (f) providing for a change in the rates of distribution payments in respect of sugar and invert sugar:

Now, therefore, the Minister on the recommendation of the Sugar Board, and in exercise of the powers conferred upon him by sections 9(1) and 33(4) of the Sugar Act 1956, having effect as aforesaid, and of all other powers enabling him in that behalf, hereby makes the following order:—

1.—(1) This order may be cited as the Composite Sugar Products (Distribution Payments—Average Rates) (No. 2) Order 1972, and shall come into operation on 9th March 1972.

(2) The Interpretation Act 1889(g) shall apply to the interpretation of this order as it applies to the interpretation of an Act of Parliament.

2. Distribution payments payable on or after 9th March 1972 under and in accordance with section 14 of the Sugar Act 1956, having effect as aforesaid, in respect of sugar and invert sugar used in the manufacture of the descriptions of imported composite sugar products specified in the second column of Schedule 1 to this order, being goods which are classified in the tariff headings indicated in relation to them in the first column of the said Schedule shall, notwithstanding the provisions of the Sugar (Distribution Payments) (No. 2) Order 1972(f) and the Composite Sugar Products (Distribution Payments—Average Rates) Order 1972(a) be calculated by reference to the weight of the products and the rates specified in relation thereto in the third column of the said Schedule.

3. Imported composite sugar products other than those of a description specified in Schedules 1 and 2 to this order shall be treated as not containing any sugar or invert sugar for the purposes of distribution payments.

(a) S.I. 1972/68.   (b) 1956 c. 48.   (c) 1962 c. 44.   (d) 1964 c. 49.
(e) 1966 c. 18.   (f) S.I. 1972/356 (1972 I, p. 1417).   (g) 1889 c. 63.

In Witness whereof the Official Seal of the Minister of Agriculture, Fisheries and Food is hereunto affixed on 8th March 1972.

(L.S.)

E. J. G. Smith,
Authorised by the Minister.

SCHEDULE 1

In this Schedule:—

" Tariff heading " means a heading or, where the context so requires, a subheading of the Customs Tariff 1959 (see paragraph (1) of Article 2 of the Import Duties (General) (No. 7) Order 1971)(a).

Tariff heading	Description of Composite Sugar Products	Rate of Distribution Payment
		Per cwt. £
04.02 ..	Milk and cream, preserved, concentrated or sweetened, containing more than 10 per cent. by weight of added sugar	0·75
17.02 (B) (2) and 17.05 (B)	Syrups containing sucrose sugar, whether or not flavoured or coloured, but not including fruit juices containing added sugar in any proportion:—	
	Containing 70 per cent. or more by weight of sweetening matter	1·07
	Containing less than 70 per cent., and more than 50 per cent. by weight of sweetening matter	0·77
	Containing not more than 50 per cent. by weight of sweetening matter	0·37
17.02 (F) ..	Caramel:—	
	Solid	1·70
	Liquid	1·18
17.04 ..	Sugar confectionery, not containing cocoa ..	1·38
18.06 ..	Chocolate and other food preparations containing cocoa and added sugar:—	
	Chocolate couverture not prepared for retail sale; chocolate milk crumb, liquid ..	0·75
	Chocolate milk crumb, solid	0·93
	Solid chocolate bars or blocks, milk or plain, with or without fruit or nuts; other chocolate confectionery consisting wholly of chocolate or of chocolate and other ingredients not containing added sugar ..	0·76
	Other	0·98

(a) S.I. 1971/1971 (1971 III, p. 5330).

SCHEDULE 1—*continued*

Tariff heading	Description of Composite Sugar Products	Rate of Distribution Payment
		Per cwt. £
19.08 ..	Pastry, biscuits, cakes and other fine bakers' wares containing added sugar:—	
	Biscuits, wafers and rusks containing more than 12½ per cent. by weight of added sugar, and other biscuits, wafers and rusks included in retail packages with such goods.. ..	0·42
	Cakes with covering or filling containing added sugar; meringues	0·56
	Other	0·21
20.01 ..	Vegetables and fruit, prepared or preserved by vinegar or acetic acid, containing added sugar:—	
	Containing 10 per cent. or more by weight of added sugar	0·59
	Other	0·12
20.03 ..	Fruit preserved by freezing, containing added sugar	0·21
20.04 ..	Fruit, fruit-peel and parts of plants, preserved by sugar (drained, glacé or crystallised)	1·11
20.05 ..	Jams, fruit jellies, marmalades, fruit puree and fruit pastes, being cooked preparations, containing added sugar	1·06
20.06 ..	Fruit otherwise prepared or preserved, containing added sugar:—	
	Ginger	0·85
	Other	0·21

SCHEDULE 2

Tariff heading	Description of Composite Sugar Products
17.05 (A) and (B)	Sugar and invert sugar, flavoured or coloured.

EXPLANATORY NOTE

(*This Note is not part of the Order.*)

This order provides for increases in the average rates of distribution payments payable in respect of imported composite sugar products of the descriptions specified in Schedule 1 on and after 9th March 1972. These correspond to increases in the rates of distribution payment effected by the Sugar (Distribution Payments) (No. 2) Order 1972 (S.I. 1972/356). Provision is also made for certain imported composite sugar products to be treated as not containing any sugar or invert sugar.

STATUTORY INSTRUMENTS

1972 No. 359 (C.6)

DEFENCE

The Armed Forces Act 1971 (Commencement) Order 1972

Made - - - - *8th March* 1972

The Secretary of State in exercise of his powers under section 78(3) of the Armed Forces Act 1971(a) and of all other powers enabling him in that behalf, hereby makes the following Order:

1. The Armed Forces Act 1971 shall come into force on 1st July 1972.

2. This Order may be cited as the Armed Forces Act 1971 (Commencement) Order 1972.

Dated 8th March 1972.

Carrington,
One of Her Majesty's Principal
Secretaries of State.

EXPLANATORY NOTE

(This Note is not part of the Order.)

This Order brings into force the outstanding provisions of the Armed Forces Act 1971 on 1st July 1972. Section 1 of the Act (which relates to the duration of the Army and Air Force Acts 1955 (cc.18, 19) and the Naval Discipline Act 1957 (c. 53)) and section 78 thereof (which relates to the short title, construction and commencement of the Act) are already in force.

(a) 1971 c. 33.

STATUTORY INSTRUMENTS

1972 No. 360

EDUCATION, ENGLAND AND WALES

The Teachers' Superannuation (Family Benefits) (Amendment) Regulations 1972

Made - - -	*8th March* 1972
Laid before Parliament	*16th March* 1972
Coming into Operation	*17th March* 1972

The Secretary of State for Education and Science, with the consent of the Minister for the Civil Service and after consultation with representatives of local education authorities and of teachers appearing to her to be likely to be affected, in exercise of the powers conferred on her by section 7 of the Teachers' Superannuation Act 1967(a) as read with the Minister for the Civil Service Order 1968(b) hereby makes the following regulations:—

Citation, commencement and interpretation

1.—(1) These regulations may be cited as the Teachers' Superannuation (Family Benefits) (Amendment) Regulations 1972 and shall come into operation on 17th March 1972.

(2) The Teachers' Superannuation (Family Benefits) Regulations 1970 and 1971(c) and these regulations may be cited together as the Teachers' Superannuation (Family Benefits) Regulations 1970 to 1972.

(3) In these regulations "the 1970 Regulations" means the Teachers' Superannuation (Family Benefits) Regulations 1970 and "the 1971 Regulations" means the Teachers' Superannuation (Family Benefits) (Amendment) Regulations 1971(d).

(4) The Interpretation Act 1889(e) shall apply for the interpretation of these regulations as it applies for the interpretation of an Act of Parliament.

Amount of widow's pension

2. In paragraph (2) of regulation 47 of the 1970 regulations as substituted by regulation 13 of the 1971 regulations—

(*a*) the word "or" at the end of sub-paragraph (*b*) shall be omitted;

(a) 1967 c. 12. (b) S.I. 1968/1656 (1968 III, p. 4485).
(c) S.I. 1970/862; 1971/679 (1970 II, p. 2736; 1971 I, p. 1787).
(d) S.I. 1971/679 (1971 I, p. 1787). (e) 1889 c. 63.

(*b*) in sub-paragraph (*c*) after "1st May 1971" there shall be inserted "and before 17th March 1972" and at the end of that sub-paragraph there shall be added—

"or

(*d*) £153 if her husband, on or after 17th March 1972 so ceased or so died."

Amount of short service widow's pension

3. In regulation 50 of the 1970 regulations as substituted by regulation 15 of the 1971 regulations—

(*a*) the word "or" at the end of paragraph (*b*) shall be omitted;

(*b*) in paragraph (*c*) after "1st May 1971" there shall be inserted "and before 17th March 1972" and at the end of that paragraph there shall be added—

"or

(*d*) in column (5) thereof in the case of a widow whose husband, on or after 17th March 1972 so ceased or so died : —"; and

(*c*) there shall be added to the Table as an additional column—

"(5)

Annual Amount

£ 78
£ 90
£ 99
£111
£123
£132
£144 "

Amount of children's pension

4. In paragraph 1 of regulation 53 of the 1970 regulations as substituted by regulation 16 of the 1971 regulations—

(*a*) the word "or" at the end of sub-paragraph (*b*) shall be omitted;

(*b*) in sub-paragraph (*c*) after "1st May 1971" there shall be inserted "and before 17th March 1972" and at the end of that paragraph there shall be added—

"or

(*d*) under letter D, where such contributor or deceased teacher, on or after 17th March 1972 so ceased or so died : —"; and (*c*) there shall be added to columns (2) and (3) of the Table—

"(2)	(3)
D	D
£ 84	£120
£150	£225
£219	£330
£285	£447"

Given under the Official Seal of the Secretary of State for Education and Science on 7th March 1972.

(L.S.)

Margaret H. Thatcher,
Secretary of State for Education
and Science.

Consent of the Minister for the Civil Service given under his Official Seal on 8th March 1972.

(L.S.)

K. H. McNeill,
Authorised by the Minister for the
Civil Service.

EXPLANATORY NOTE

(*This Note is not part of the Regulations.*)

These regulations further amend the Teachers' Superannuation (Family Benefits) Regulations 1970 by raising the minimum of a widow's pension and increasing a short service widow's pension and a children's pension which commence after they come into operation.

STATUTORY INSTRUMENTS

1972 No. 361

INDUSTRIAL TRAINING

The Industrial Training Levy (Food, Drink and Tobacco) Order 1972

Made - - -	*7th March* 1972
Laid before Parliament	*16th March* 1972
Coming into Operation	*10th April* 1972

The Secretary of State after approving proposals submitted by the Food, Drink and Tobacco Industry Training Board for the imposition of a further levy on employers in the food, drink and tobacco industry and in exercise of his powers under section 4 of the Industrial Training Act 1964(a) and of all other powers enabling him in that behalf hereby makes the following Order: —

Title and commencement

1. This Order may be cited as the Industrial Training Levy (Food, Drink and Tobacco) Order 1972 and shall come into operation on 10th April 1972.

Interpretation

2.—(1) In this Order unless the context otherwise requires: —

(*a*) "agriculture" has the same meaning as in section 109(3) of the Agriculture Act 1947(b) or, in relation to Scotland, as in section 86(3) of the Agriculture (Scotland) Act 1948(c);

(*b*) "an appeal tribunal" means an industrial tribunal established under section 12 of the Industrial Training Act 1964;

(*c*) "assessment" means an assessment of an employer to the levy;

(*d*) "the Board" means the Food, Drink and Tobacco Industry Training Board;

(*e*) "business" means any activities of industry or commerce;

(*f*) "charity" has the same meaning as in section 360 of the Income and Corporation Taxes Act 1970(d);

(*g*) "emoluments" means all emoluments assessable to income tax under Schedule E (other than pensions), being emoluments from which tax under that Schedule is deductible, whether or not tax in fact falls to be deducted from any particular payment thereof;

(*h*) "employer" means a person who is an employer in the food, drink and tobacco industry at any time in the fourth levy period;

(a) 1964 c. 16. (b) 1947 c. 48.
(c) 1948 c. 45. (d) 1970 c. 10.

(*i*) "food, drink and tobacco establishment" means an establishment in Great Britain engaged in the fourth base period wholly or mainly in the food, drink and tobacco industry for a total of twenty-seven or more weeks or, being an establishment that commenced to carry on business in the fourth base period, for a total number of weeks exceeding one half of the number of weeks in the part of the said period commencing with the day on which business was commenced and ending on the last day thereof;

(*j*) "the food, drink and tobacco industry" means any one or more of the activities which, subject to the provisions of paragraph 2 of the Schedule to the industrial training order, are specified in paragraph 1 of that Schedule as the activities of the food, drink and tobacco industry;

(*k*) "the fourth base period" means the period of twelve months that commenced on 6th April 1971;

(*l*) "the fourth levy period" means the period commencing with the day upon which this Order comes into operation and ending on 5th April 1973;

(*m*) "the industrial training order" means the Industrial Training (Food, Drink and Tobacco Board) Order 1971(**a**);

(*n*) "the levy" means the levy imposed by the Board in respect of the fourth levy period;

(*o*) "notice" means a notice in writing;

(*p*) other expressions have the same meanings as in the industrial training order.

(2) In reckoning the amount of emoluments for the purposes of this Order no regard shall be had to the emoluments of any person employed as follows: —

(*a*) by a local authority;

(*b*) by a milk marketing board in the provision of—

(i) services of artificial insemination for livestock at a centre providing such services; or

(ii) any services in respect of milk recording;

(*c*) wholly in agriculture;

(*d*) as a member of the crew of an aircraft, as the master or a member of the crew of a ship, or, in the case of a person employed as a seaman, in or about a ship in port by the owner or charterer thereof on work of a kind ordinarily done by a seaman on a ship while it is in port;

(*e*) wholly as a registered dock worker in dock work; or

(*f*) wholly in the supply (including any preparation thereof by the person engaged in such supply) of food or drink to persons, being a supply—

(i) for immediate consumption;

(ii) of hot fried fish or hot chipped potatoes; or

(iii) by means of an automatic vending machine at or in connection with an hotel, restaurant, café, snack bar, canteen, mess room or similar place of refreshment.

(**a**) S.I. 1971/648 (1971 I, p. 1709).

(3) Any reference in this Order to persons employed at or from a food, drink and tobacco establishment shall in any case where the employer is a company be construed as including a reference to any director of the company (or any person occupying the position of director by whatever name he was called) who was, at the material time, in receipt of a salary from the company.

(4) In the case where a food, drink and tobacco establishment is taken over (whether directly or indirectly) by an employer in succession to, or jointly with, another person, a person employed at any time in the fourth base period at or from the establishment shall be deemed, for the purposes of this Order, to have been so employed by the employer carrying on the said establishment on the day upon which this Order comes into operation, and any reference in this Order to persons employed by an employer at or from a food, drink and tobacco establishment in the fourth base period shall be construed accordingly.

(5) Any reference in this Order to an establishment that commences to carry on business or that ceases to carry on business shall not be taken to apply where the location of the establishment is changed but its business is continued wholly or mainly at or from the new location, or where the suspension of activities is of a temporary or seasonal nature.

(6) The Interpretation Act 1889(a) shall apply to the interpretation of this Order as it applies to the interpretation of an Act of Parliament.

Imposition of the levy

3.—(1) The levy to be imposed by the Board on employers in respect of the fourth levy period shall be assessed in accordance with the provisions of this Article.

(2) The levy shall be assessed by the Board separately in respect of each food, drink and tobacco establishment of an employer (not being an employer who is exempt from the levy by virtue of paragraph (5) of this Article), but in agreement with the employer one assessment may be made in respect of any number of such establishments, in which case those establishments shall be deemed for the purposes of that assessment to constitute one establishment.

(3) Subject to the provisions of this Order, the levy assessed in respect of a food, drink and tobacco establishment of an employer shall be an amount equal to 0·7 per cent. of the sum of the emoluments of all the persons employed by the employer at or from that establishment in the fourth base period.

(4) The amount of the levy imposed in respect of a food, drink and tobacco establishment that ceases to carry on business in the fourth levy period shall be in the same proportion to the amount that would otherwise be due under paragraph (3) of this Article as the number of days between the commencement of the said levy period and the date of cessation of business (both dates inclusive) bears to the number of days in the said levy period.

(a) 1889 c. 63.

(5) There shall be exempt from the levy—

  (a) an employer in whose case the sum of the emoluments of all the persons employed by him in the fourth base period at or from the food, drink and tobacco establishment or establishments of the employer (including any persons employed in that period at or from a food, drink and tobacco establishment by an associated company of the employer) is less than £30,000;

  (b) a charity.

Assessment notices

4.—(1) The Board shall serve an assessment notice on every employer assessed to the levy, but one notice may comprise two or more assessments.

(2) The amount of any assessment payable under an assessment notice shall be rounded down to the nearest £1.

(3) An assessment notice shall state the Board's address for the service of a notice of appeal or of an application for an extension of time for appealing.

(4) An assessment notice may be served on the person assessed to the levy either by delivering it to him personally or by leaving it, or sending it to him by post, at his last known address or place of business in the United Kingdom or, if that person is a corporation, by leaving it, or sending it by post to the corporation, at such address or place of business or at its registered or principal office.

Payment of the levy

5.—(1) Subject to the provisions of this Article and of Articles 6 and 7, the amount of each assessment appearing in an assessment notice served by the Board shall be due and payable to the Board one month after the date of a further notice requiring payment of that amount, which notice shall be served by the Board on the person assessed to the levy in the same manner as an assessment notice.

(2) The amount of an assessment shall not be recoverable by the Board until there has expired the time allowed for appealing against the assessment by Article 7(1) of this Order and any further period or periods of time that the Board or an appeal tribunal may have allowed for appealing under paragraph (2) or (3) of that Article or, where an appeal is brought, until the appeal is decided or withdrawn.

Withdrawal of assessment

6.—(1) The Board may, by a notice served on the person assessed to the levy in the same manner as an assessment notice, withdraw an assessment if that person has appealed against that assessment under the provisions of Article 7 of this Order and the appeal has not been entered in the Register of Appeals kept under the appropriate Regulations specified in paragraph (5) of that Article.

(2) The withdrawal of an assessment shall be without prejudice to the power of the Board to serve a further assessment notice in respect of any establishment to which that assessment related.

Appeals

7.—(1) A person assessed to the levy may appeal to an appeal tribunal against the assessment within one month from the date of the service of the assessment notice or within any further period or periods of time that may be allowed by the Board or an appeal tribunal under the following provisions of this Article.

(2) The Board by notice may for good cause allow a person assessed to the levy to appeal to an appeal tribunal against the assessment at any time within the period of four months from the date of the service of the assessment notice or within such further period or periods as the Board may allow before such time as may then be limited for appealing has expired.

(3) If the Board shall not allow an application for extension of time for appealing, an appeal tribunal shall upon application made to the tribunal by the person assessed to the levy have the like powers as the Board under the last foregoing paragraph.

(4) In the case of an establishment that ceases to carry on business in the fourth levy period on any day after the date of the service of the relevant assessment notice the foregoing provisions of this Article shall have effect as if for the period of four months from the date of the service of the assessment notice mentioned in paragraph (2) of this Article there were substituted the period of six months from the date of the cessation of business.

(5) An appeal or an application to an appeal tribunal under this Article shall be made in accordance with the Industrial Tribunals (England and Wales) Regulations 1965(a) as amended by the Industrial Tribunals (England and Wales) (Amendment) Regulations 1967(b) except where the establishment to which the relevant assessment relates is wholly in Scotland in which case the appeal or application shall be made in accordance with the Industrial Tribunals (Scotland) Regulations 1965(c) as amended by the Industrial Tribunals (Scotland) (Amendment) Regulations 1967(d).

(6) The powers of an appeal tribunal under paragraph (3) of this Article may be exercised by the President of the Industrial Tribunals (England and Wales) or by the President of the Industrial Tribunals (Scotland) as the case may be.

Evidence

8.—(1) Upon the discharge by a person assessed to the levy of his liability under an assessment the Board shall if so requested issue to him a certificate to that effect.

(2) The production in any proceedings of a document purporting to be certified by the Secretary of the Board to be a true copy of an assessment or other notice issued by the Board or purporting to be a certificate such as is mentioned in the foregoing paragraph of this Article shall, unless the contrary is proved, be sufficient evidence of the document and of the facts stated therein.

(a) S.I. 1965/1101 (1965 II, p. 2805).   (b) S.I. 1967/301 (1967 I, p. 1040).
(c) S.I. 1965/1157 (1965 II, p. 3266).   (d) S.I. 1967/302 (1967 I, p. 1050).

Signed by order of the Secretary of State.

7th March 1972.

Paul Bryan,
Minister of State,
Department of Employment.

EXPLANATORY NOTE
(This Note is not part of the Order.)

This Order gives effect to proposals submitted by the Food, Drink and Tobacco Industry Training Board to the Secretary of State for Employment for the imposition of a further levy on employers in the industry for the purpose of raising money towards the expenses of the Board.

The levy is to be imposed in respect of the fourth levy period commencing with the date upon which this Order comes into operation and ending on 5th April 1973. The levy will be assessed by the Board and there will be a right of appeal against an assessment to an industrial tribunal.

STATUTORY INSTRUMENTS

1972 No. 362 (S.24)

AGRICULTURE

AGRICULTURAL GRANTS, GOODS AND SERVICES

The Farm Capital Grant (Variation) (Scotland) Scheme 1972

Made - - -	*7th March* 1972
Laid before Parliament	*16th March* 1972
Coming into Operation	*19th March* 1972

In exercise of the powers conferred on me by sections 28 and 29 of the Agriculture Act 1970(**a**) and of all other powers enabling me in that behalf, with the approval of the Treasury, I hereby make the following scheme: —

Citation, commencement, extent and interpretation

1.—(1) This scheme which may be cited as the Farm Capital Grant (Variation) (Scotland) Scheme 1972, shall come into operation on 19th March 1972 and shall apply to Scotland only.

(2) The Interpretation Act 1889(**b**) shall apply for the interpretation of this scheme as it applies for the interpretation of an Act of Parliament.

Variation of the principal scheme

2. The Farm Capital Grant (Scotland) Scheme 1970(**c**), as varied (**d**), shall be further varied as follows: —

    (*a*) by inserting in paragraph 3 thereof immediately after subparagraph (1) the following subparagraph: —

        "(1A) In the case of any work or facility, or part thereof, of a kind specified in paragraph 8, 10, 11, 12 (other than orchard grubbing), 14 or 15 of Schedule 1, the provisions of this paragraph shall not apply to expenditure in respect of any such work or facility unless application for approval of the expenditure for the purposes of a grant under this scheme is made on or before 31st March 1972.";

    (*b*) by adding at the end of paragraph 13 of Schedule 1 thereto the words "provision, replacement or improvement of sheep grids, cattle grids, permanent fences, hedges, walls, gates, shelter belts or shelter hedges, land levelling or grading (including filling in of ditches or ponds), removal of hedges, tree roots, boulders or other like obstructions to cultivation, bracken control, clearance and reclamation of land.";

    (*c*) by substituting in Columns 3 and 5 of the Table at the end of paragraph 1 of Schedule 2 thereto for the figures "50" and "60" where those figures appear in relation to paragraphs 4 and 6 of Schedule 1 thereto (which specify as eligible works and facilities various drainage

---

(**a**) 1970 c. 40.
(**c**) S.I. 1970/1805 (1970 III, p. 5869).
(**b**) 1889 c. 63.
(**d**) S.I. 1971/1076 (1971 II, p. 3208).

works and works for the prevention or mitigation of flooding or erosion of agricultural land) the figures "60" and "70" respectively.

Gordon Campbell,
One of Her Majesty's Principal
Secretaries of State.

St. Andrew's House,
Edinburgh.
3rd March 1972.

We approve,

P. L. Hawkins,
Keith Speed,
Two of the Lords Commissioners
of Her Majesty's Treasury.

7th March 1972.

EXPLANATORY NOTE
(This Note is not part of the Scheme.)

This Scheme, which applies to Scotland only, further varies the Farm Capital Grant (Scotland) Scheme 1970, as varied.

It makes provision for the rate of grant towards expenditure on drainage works and on works for the prevention or mitigation of flooding or erosion of agricultural land to remain at 60 per cent. (or 70 per cent. if the work is in the opinion of the Secretary of State of benefit in the farming of hill land) instead of being reduced to 50 per cent. and 60 per cent. respectively in the case of applications for approval made on or after 19th March 1972, as was previously provided.

The Scheme also provides that grant shall no longer be payable towards expenditure on certain specified works and facilities if application for approval of the expenditure is made after 31st March 1972. However grants for cattle grids, fencing, shelter belts and certain land clearance and reclamation work may still be payable if, in the opinion of the Secretary of State, the work is of benefit in the farming of hill land.

STATUTORY INSTRUMENTS

1972 No. 363 (C.7) (S.25)

LOCAL GOVERNMENT, SCOTLAND

The Sewerage (Scotland) Act 1968 (Commencement) Order 1972

Made - - - *7th March* 1972

In exercise of the powers conferred on me by section 61(2) of the Sewerage (Scotland) Act 1968(a) and of all other powers enabling me in that behalf, I hereby make the following order: —

Citation and Interpretation

1. This order may be cited as the Sewerage (Scotland) Act 1968 (Commencement) Order 1972 and in this order "the Act" means the Sewerage (Scotland) Act 1968.

Commencement Provisions

2.—(1) The provisions of section 18 except in so far as providing for an appointed day on which all special drainage districts and drainage districts shall be dissolved and of section 59(1) of the Act shall come into operation on 16th May 1972.

(2) The day appointed for the dissolution of special drainage districts and drainage districts under section 18 of the Act shall be 16th May 1973.

(3) The provisions of the Act other than those specified in paragraph (1) of this article shall come into operation on 16th May 1973.

Gordon Campbell,
One of Her Majesty's
Principal Secretaries of State.

St. Andrew's House,
Edinburgh.
7th March 1972.

(a) 1968 c. 47.

EXPLANATORY NOTE

(This Note is not part of the Order.)

This Order brings into force on 16th May 1972 the provisions of section 18 of the Sewerage (Scotland) Act 1968 which terminate the power of local authorities to form special drainage districts and drainage districts and the provisions of section 59(1) of the Act necessary for interpretation purposes. The Order appoints 16th May 1973 as the day on which all such districts shall be dissolved, and brings the remaining provisions of the Act into force on that date.

1972 No. 366

FOOD AND DRUGS

The Milk (Northern Ireland) (Amendment) Order 1972

Made - - -	*8th March* 1972
Laid before Parliament	*14th March* 1972
Coming into Operation	*2nd April* 1972

The Minister of Agriculture, Fisheries and Food, in exercise of the powers conferred on him by sections 6 and 7 of the Emergency Laws (Re-enactments and Repeals) Act 1964(a) and of all other powers enabling him in that behalf, hereby makes the following order:—

Citation and commencement

1. This order may be cited as the Milk (Northern Ireland) (Amendment) Order 1972, and shall come into operation on 2nd April 1972.

Amendment of the principal order

2. The Milk (Northern Ireland) Order 1971(b) shall be amended by substituting for the Schedule thereto the Schedule to this order.

In Witness whereof the Official Seal of the Minister of Agriculture, Fisheries and Food is hereunto affixed on 8th March 1972.

(L.S.)

J. M. L. Prior,
Minister of Agriculture, Fisheries and Food.

(a) 1964 c. 60.　　　　　　　(b) S.I. 1971/1037 (1971 II, p. 3105).

SCHEDULE

MAXIMUM PRICES OF MILK

Milk	Maximum Price (Rate per Pint)	
	From 2nd April 1972 to 29th July 1972 inclusive	On and after 30th July 1972
	p	p
Farm bottled milk	5	5½
Pasteurised milk	5	5½

EXPLANATORY NOTE

(This Note is not part of the Order.)

This amending Order, which comes into operation on 2nd April 1972, reduces by ½p per pint, from 2nd April 1972 to 29th July 1972 inclusive, the maximum prices of milk on sales in Northern Ireland.

STATUTORY INSTRUMENTS

1972 No. 367

FOOD AND DRUGS

The Milk (Great Britain) (Amendment) Order 1972

Made - - -	*8th March* 1972
Laid before Parliament	*14th March* 1972
Coming into Operation	*2nd April* 1972

The Minister of Agriculture, Fisheries and Food and the Secretary of State, acting jointly in exercise of the powers conferred on them by sections 6 and 7 of the Emergency Laws (Re-enactments and Repeals) Act 1964(a) and of all other powers enabling them in that behalf, hereby make the following order:—

Citation and commencement

1. This order may be cited as the Milk (Great Britain) (Amendment) Order 1972, and shall come into operation on 2nd April 1972.

Amendment of the principal order

2. The Milk (Great Britain) Order 1971(b) shall be amended by substituting for Schedules 1 and 2 thereto respectively Schedules 1 and 2 to this order.

In Witness whereof the Official Seal of the Minister of Agriculture, Fisheries and Food is hereunto affixed on 8th March 1972.

(L.S.)

J. M. L. Prior,
Minister of Agriculture, Fisheries and Food.

Gordon Campbell,
8th March 1972.   Secretary of State for Scotland.

(a) 1964 c. 60.   (b) S.I. 1971/1038 (1971 II, p. 3108).

SCHEDULE 1

MAXIMUM PRICES OF MILK IN ENGLAND AND WALES

1. Subject to the provisions of this Schedule, the maximum price of milk on a sale in England and Wales shall be a price in accordance with the following table:—

Milk	Maximum Price (Rate per Pint)	
	From 2nd April 1972 to 29th July 1972 inclusive	On and after 30th July 1972
	p	p
Channel Islands milk	6	6½
South Devon milk	6	6½
Untreated Milk Farm Bottled	6	6½
Ultra Heat Treated milk	5½	6
Sterilised milk	5½	6
Homogenised milk	5½	6
Untreated milk	5	5½
Pasteurised milk	5	5½
Milk, other than the above mentioned	5	5½

2. A reasonable charge may be made by the seller in addition to the appropriate maximum price specified in the above table for milk sold by him as Kosher milk or Kedassia milk if—

(a) such milk is sold in a container distinctly labelled "Kosher" or "Kedassia", as the case may be; and

(b) such milk has been prepared for consumption in accordance with the appropriate Jewish practice relating thereto.

SCHEDULE 2

Maximum Prices of Milk in Scotland

1. Subject to the provisions of this Schedule, the maximum price of milk on a sale in Scotland, excluding the islands other than the islands of Islay, Coll and Gigha in the County of Argyll and those in the Counties of Bute and Orkney, shall be a price in accordance with the following table: —

Milk	Maximum Price (Rate per Pint)	
	From 2nd April 1972 to 29th July 1972 inclusive	On and after 30th July 1972
	p	p
Channel Islands milk	6	6½
South Devon milk	6	6½
Premium milk	6	6½
Ultra Heat Treated milk	5½	6
Sterilised milk	5½	6
Homogenised milk	5½	6
Standard milk	5	5½
Pasteurised milk	5	5½
Milk, other than the above mentioned	5	5½

2. A reasonable charge may be made by the seller in addition to the appropriate maximum price specified in the above table for milk sold by him as Kosher milk or Kedassia milk if—

    (a) such milk is sold in a container distinctly labelled "Kosher" or "Kedassia", as the case may be; and

    (b) such milk has been prepared for consumption in accordance with the appropriate Jewish practice relating thereto.

EXPLANATORY NOTE

(This Note is not part of the Order.)

This amending Order, which comes into operation on 2nd April 1972, reduces by $\frac{1}{2}$p per pint, from 2nd April 1972 to 29th July 1972 inclusive, the maximum prices of milk on sales in Great Britain.

STATUTORY INSTRUMENTS

1972 No. 368

AGRICULTURE

AGRICULTURAL GRANTS, GOODS AND SERVICES

The Farm Capital Grant (Variation) Scheme 1972

Made - - - -	*9th March* 1972
Laid before Parliament	*16th March* 1972
Coming into Operation	*19th March* 1972

The Minister of Agriculture, Fisheries and Food and the Secretary of State for Wales, acting jointly, in exercise of the powers conferred on them by sections 28, 29 and 51(1) of the Agriculture Act 1970(a) and of all other powers enabling them in that behalf, with the approval of the Treasury, hereby make the following scheme: —

Citation, commencement, extent and interpretation

1.—(1) This scheme, which may be cited as the Farm Capital Grant (Variation) Scheme 1972, shall come into operation on 19th March 1972 and shall apply to England and Wales and Northern Ireland.

(2) The Interpretation Act 1889(b) shall apply to the interpretation of this scheme as it applies to the interpretation of an Act of Parliament.

Variation of the principal scheme

2. The Farm Capital Grant Scheme 1970(c), as varied(d), shall be further varied as follows: —

(*a*) by substituting in paragraph 3(1)(*a*) thereof for the word " of " the second time that word appears the word " or " ;

(*b*) by inserting in paragraph 3 thereof immediately after sub-paragraph

(1) the following sub-paragraph: —

"(1A) In the case of any work or facility, or part thereof, of a kind specified in paragraph 8, 10, 11, 12 (other than orchard grubbing), 14, 15 or 16 of Schedule 2, the provisions of this paragraph shall not apply to expenditure in respect of any such work or facility unless application for approval of the expenditure for the purposes of a grant under this scheme is made on or before 31st March 1972." ;

(*c*) by adding at the end of paragraph 13 of Schedule 2 thereto the words " provision, replacement or improvement of sheep grids, cattle grids, permanent fences, hedges, walls, gates, shelter belts or shelter hedges, land levelling or grading (including filling in of ditches or ponds), removal of hedges, tree roots, boulders or other like obstructions to cultivation, bracken control." ;

(*d*) by substituting in columns 3 and 5 of the table at the end of paragraph 1 of Schedule 3 thereto for the figures " 50 " and " 60 " where those figures appear in relation to paragraph 4 of Schedule 2 thereto (which specifies as eligible works and facilities field drainage, including under-drainage and ditching) the figures " 60 " and " 70 " respectively.

(a) 1970 c. 40.
(c) S.I. 1970/1759 (1970 III, p. 5741).
(b) 1889 c. 63.
(d) S.I. 1971/1077 (1971 II, p. 3210).

In Witness whereof the Official Seal of the Minister of Agriculture, Fisheries and Food is hereunto affixed on 7th March 1972.

(L.S.)

J. M. L. Prior,
Minister of Agriculture,
Fisheries and Food.

Given under my hand 8th March 1972.

Peter Thomas,
Secretary of State for Wales.

We approve.

9th March 1972.

Keith Speed,
Tim Fortescue,

Two of the Lords Commissioners of
Her Majesty's Treasury.

EXPLANATORY NOTE

(This Note is not part of the scheme.)

This scheme, which applies to England and Wales and Northern Ireland, further varies the Farm Capital Grant Scheme 1970, as varied.

It makes provision for the rate of grant towards expenditure on field drainage to remain at 60 per cent. (or 70 per cent. if the work is in the opinion of the appropriate Minister of benefit in the farming of hill land) instead of being reduced to 50 per cent. and 60 per cent. respectively in the case of applications for approval made on or after 19th March 1972, as was previously provided.

The scheme also provides that grant shall no longer be payable towards expenditure on certain specified works and facilities if application for approval of the expenditure is made after 31st March 1972. However, grant for cattle grids, fencing, shelter belts and certain land clearance and reclamation work may still be payable if, in the opinion of the appropriate Minister, the work is of benefit in the farming of hill land.

STATUTORY INSTRUMENTS

1972 No. 372

AGRICULTURE

The Price Stability of Imported Products (Rates of Levy) (Cereals) (No. 11) Order 1972

Made - - - - - *9th March* 1972
Coming into Operation - 10*th March* 1972

The Minister of Agriculture, Fisheries and Food, in exercise of the powers conferred upon him by section 1(2), (4), (5), (6) and (7) of the Agriculture and Horticulture Act 1964(a) and of all other powers enabling him in that behalf, hereby makes the following order:—

1. This order may be cited as the Price Stability of Imported Products (Rates of Levy) (Cereals) (No. 11) Order 1972, and shall come into operation on 10th March 1972.

2.—(1) In this order—

" the Principal Order " means the Price Stability of Imported Products (Levy Arrangements) (Cereals) Order 1971(b), as amended by any subsequent order and if any such order is replaced by any subsequent order the expression shall be construed as a reference to such subsequent order;

AND other expressions have the same meaning as in the Principal Order.

(2) The Interpretation Act 1889(c) shall apply to the interpretation of this order as it applies to the interpretation of an Act of Parliament and as if this order and the order hereby revoked were Acts of Parliament.

3. In accordance with and subject to the provisions of Part II of the Principal Order (which provides for the charging of levies on imports of certain specified commodities) the rate of levy for such imports into the United Kingdom of any specified commodity as are described in column 2 of the Schedule to this order in relation to a tariff heading indicated in column 1 of that Schedule shall be the rate set forth in relation thereto in column 3 of that Schedule.

4. The Price Stability of Imported Products (Rates of Levy) (Cereals) (No. 10) Order 1972(d) is hereby revoked.

In Witness whereof the Official Seal of the Minister of Agriculture, Fisheries and Food is hereunto affixed on 9th March 1972.

(L.S.)

T. R. M. Sewell,
Assistant Secretary.

(**a**) 1964 c. 28.   (**b**) S.I. 1971/631 (1971 I, p. 1660).   (**c**) 1889 c. 63.
(**d**) S.I. 1972/347 (1972 I, p. 1412).

SCHEDULE

1. Tariff Heading	2. Description of Imports	3. Rate of Levy
	Imports of:—	per ton £
10.01	Denatured wheat .. .. Wheat (other than denatured wheat)..	4·50 7·00
10.03	Barley other than barley having a potential diastatic activity of not less than 170 degrees	2·50
10.04	Oats	6·00
10.05	Maize (other than sweet corn on the cob)	4·50
10.07	Grain sorghum	1·75

11.02	Cereal groats, meals, kibbled or cut cereals, rolled, flaked, crushed or bruised cereals and other processed cereals—
	    of barley .. ..
	    of oats .. ..
	    of maize .. ..
		
		5·25
		8·75
		5·00

EXPLANATORY NOTE
(This Note is not part of the Order.)

This order, which comes into operation on 10th March 1972, supersedes the Price Stability of Imported Products (Rates of Levy) (Cereals) (No. 10) Order 1972.

It—

(*a*) increases the rate of levy to be charged on imports of oats to £6·00 per ton ; and

(*b*) reimposes unchanged the remaining rates of levy in force immediately before the commencement of the order.

STATUTORY INSTRUMENTS

1972 No. 373

COAL INDUSTRY

The Opencast Coal (Rate of Interest on Compensation) Order 1972

Made	-	-	-	9th March 1972
Laid before Parliament				17th March 1972
Coming into Operation				18th March 1972

The Treasury, in exercise of the powers conferred upon them by sections 35(8) and 49(4) of the Opencast Coal Act 1958(a) and of all other powers enabling them in that behalf, hereby make the following Order:—

1. This Order may be cited as the Opencast Coal (Rate of Interest on Compensation) Order 1972, and shall come into operation on 18th March 1972.

2. The Interpretation Act 1889(b) shall apply for the interpretation of this Order as it applies for the interpretation of an Act of Parliament.

3. The rate of interest for the purposes of section 35 of the Opencast Coal Act 1958 shall be $5\frac{1}{4}$ per cent. per annum.

4. The Opencast Coal (Rate of Interest on Compensation) (No. 2) Order 1971(c) is hereby revoked.

Keith Speed,
Tim Fortescue,
Two of the Lords Commissioners
of Her Majesty's Treasury.

9th March, 1972.

EXPLANATORY NOTE

(This Note is not part of the Order.)

Section 35 of the Opencast Coal Act 1958 provides that interest shall be payable in addition to compensation in certain circumstances. This Order reduces the rate of interest from 6 per cent. to $5\frac{1}{4}$ per cent. per annum and revokes the Opencast Coal (Rate of Interest on Compensation) (No. 2) Order 1971.

(a) 1958 c. 69.　　(b) 1889 c. 63.　　(c) S.I. 1971/1551 (1971 III, p. 4363).

STATUTORY INSTRUMENTS

1972 No. 374

INCOME TAX

The Post-War Credit (Income Tax) Regulations 1972

Laid before House of Commons in draft

Made - - - *10th March* 1972

Coming into Operation *1st April* 1972

Whereas a draft of the following Regulations was laid before the Commons House of Parliament and approved by resolution:

Now, therefore, the Lords Commissioners of Her Majesty's Treasury, in exercise of the powers conferred upon them by sections 1, 3 and 5 of the Income Tax (Repayment of Post-War Credits) Act 1959(**a**), and of all other powers enabling them in that behalf, hereby make the following Regulations: —

1. These Regulations may be cited as the Post-War Credit (Income Tax) Regulations 1972, and shall come into force on 1st April 1972.

2.—(1) The Interpretation Act 1889(**b**) applies to these Regulations as it applies for the interpretation of an Act of Parliament.

(2) References in these Regulations to any enactment, regulations, scheme or other instrument shall include references to any such enactment, regulations, scheme or instrument as amended by any subsequent enactment, regulations, scheme or instrument.

(3) In these Regulations,

"post-war credit certificate" means a certificate or amended certificate issued by the Inspector of Taxes under the Post-War Credit (Income Tax) Regulations 1942(**c**); and

"the 1959 Act" means the Income Tax (Repayment of Post-War Credits) Act 1959.

(**a**) 1959 c. 28.   (**b**) 1889 c. 63.
(**c**) S.R. & O. 1942/1111 (Rev. X, p. 325; 1942 I, p. 450).

3. Without prejudice to any other Regulations(**a**) already made under the 1959 Act, a person entitled to a post-war credit shall, for the purposes of section 1(2) of the 1959 Act, be qualified to receive payment on the date specified in Regulation 4 on making to the Commissioners of Inland Revenue a proper application under the said section 1 and producing a post-war credit certificate relevant to his entitlement.

4. The date on which a person within Regulation 3 shall be qualified to receive payment shall depend on the first letter of the surname appearing on the post-war credit certificate which he produces (or if he produces more than one, on any one of them) and shall be the date in 1972 specified in column 2 below corresponding to the position of the said first letter in column 1 : —

Column 1	*Column 2*
A—C	April 1
D—G	May 1
H—L	June 1
M—O	July 1
P—S	August 1
T—Z	September 1

5. Where a written application has been made to the Commissioners of Inland Revenue satisfying them that the applicant is such a society as is mentioned in section 3(1) of the 1959 Act, or is the successor or assignee of such a society within the meaning of sub-section (2) or (3) of the said section, the Commissioners shall as soon as may be after the first day of June 1972, pay to the applicant the balance of the amount payable to such applicant under sub-section (1) of the said section.

6. An applicant for payment of a post-war credit shall verify his application by producing such evidence as the Commissioners of Inland Revenue may require.

P. L. Hawkins,
Tim Fortescue,
Two of the Lords Commissioners
of Her Majesty's Treasury.

10th March 1972.

(**a**) See S.I. 1959/876, 1960/769, 1962/2455 (1959 I, p. 1453; 1960 II, p. 1703; 1962 III, p. 3321).

EXPLANATORY NOTE

(This Note is not part of the Regulations.)

Under Regulations made between 1959 and 1962, a person is entitled to receive payment of his or her post-war credits on age grounds (60 for men, 55 for women) or if certain other conditions are satisfied (e.g. 26 weeks' continuous registered unemployment, 12 weeks' continuous receipt of supplementary benefit, etc.).

The present Regulations provide for the payment of post-war credits to persons who do not satisfy the existing Regulations and who can produce one or more of their post-war credit certificates. Payment will be made on an alphabetic basis, on the dates prescribed in Regulation 4. A properly completed application form will be required.

Regulation 5 provides for the payment to building societies of the balance of the amounts akin to post-war credits which were credited to them during the war years. Three-fifths of the amount due was repayable under Regulations made in 1962.

Regulation 6 lays down requirements for verifying applications for credits.

STATUTORY INSTRUMENTS

1972 No. 375

SOCIAL SECURITY

The National Insurance (Industrial Injuries) (Claims and Payments) Amendment Regulations 1972

Made - - -	10*th March* 1972
Laid before Parliament	17*th March* 1972
Coming into Operation	6*th April* 1972

The Secretary of State for Social Services in exercise of his powers under sections 25(1) and 54(1) of the National Insurance (Industrial Injuries) Act 1965(a) and of all other powers enabling him in that behalf, and after reference to the Industrial Injuries Advisory Council, hereby makes the following regulations: —

Citation, interpretation and commencement

1. These regulations, which may be cited as the National Insurance (Industrial Injuries) (Claims and Payments) Amendment Regulations 1972, shall be read as one with the National Insurance (Industrial Injuries) (Claims and Payments) Regulations 1964(b) as amended(c) (hereinafter referred to as "the principal regulations") and shall come into operation on 6th April 1972.

Amendment of regulation 12 of the principal regulations

2. In the proviso to regulation 12(1) of the principal regulations, for the words "reasonable cause" there shall be substituted the words "good cause".

Amendment of regulation 16 of the principal regulations

3. In regulation 16(10)(a) of the principal regulations, for the words "the last preceding regulation" there shall be substituted the words "regulation 15 of these regulations".

(a) 1965 c. 52.   (b) S.I. 1964/73 (1964 I, p. 115).
(c) There is no amendment which relates expressly to the subject matter of these regulations.

Amendment of regulation 18 of the principal regulations

4. The following amendments shall be made in regulation 18(1) of the principal regulations (suspension of payment of benefit pending appeals or references): —

    (i) after the words "until after the expiration of a period of 21 days from that date" there shall be inserted the words "(or, in the case of an appeal by an insurance officer from the decision of a local tribunal, from the date on which an insurance officer received the record of that decision)";

    (ii) after the words "an appeal from the award or from a decision on which the award was based is brought" there shall be inserted the words "(or in the case of such an appeal by an insurance officer notice of appeal is given or sent to the claimant)",

and the said regulation shall accordingly have effect as set out in the Schedule to these regulations.

Keith Joseph,
Secretary of State for Social Services.

10th March 1972.

THE SCHEDULE   Regulation 4

Containing Regulation 18(1) of the Principal Regulations as amended by these Regulations.*

Suspension of payment of benefit pending appeals or references

18.—(1) So much of a pension or of an allowance (other than injury benefit) or of an increase of disablement benefit as is awarded in respect of a period before the date of the award shall not be payable until after the expiration of a period of 21 days from that date (*or, in the case of an appeal by an insurance officer from the decision of a local tribunal, from the date on which an insurance officer received the record of that decision*) and if before the expiration of that period an appeal from the award or from a decision on which the award was based is brought (*or, in the case of such an appeal by an insurance officer, notice of appeal is given or sent to the claimant*), until after the decision on that appeal is given; and a gratuity or any part thereof shall not be payable until after the expiration of the time limited for an appeal from the award thereof or from a decision on which the award was based, and where any such appeal is brought, until after the decision on that appeal is given:

Provided that—

    (i) this paragraph shall not apply to an award made by an insurance officer of disablement benefit (including any increase thereof) based upon the decision of a medical appeal tribunal or of death benefit (other than a gratuity), or to any award of benefit made by the Commissioner;

    (ii) during the period intervening between the award of a gratuity under section 22 or 23 of the Act or under Schedule 4 of the Act and the date when in accordance with the foregoing provisions of this paragraph such gratuity becomes payable, there shall be paid to the beneficiary on account of such gratuity weekly payments at a rate not exceeding the weekly rate of the contribution which the deceased at his death was, or would but for the relevant accident have been, making towards the maintenance of the beneficiary;

    (iii) payment of benefit shall not be suspended under the provisions of this paragraph if in any case or class of cases the Minister so directs.

---

*The words inserted by these regulations are shown in italics.

EXPLANATORY NOTE

(This Note is not part of the Regulations.)

These Regulations amend regulation 18 of the National Insurance (Industrial Injuries) (Claims and Payments) Regulations 1964, which provides for the suspension of the payment of arrears of benefit that have been awarded, in certain cases, where an appeal has been made against the award within 21 days. The amendment provides that when the benefit is awarded by a local tribunal and an insurance officer appeals, the period of 21 days begins when an insurance officer receives the record of the tribunal's decision (instead of on the date of the decision, as previously) and that the provision for suspension of payment applies if an insurance officer gives or sends notice of his appeal to the claimant within that period (previously it applied only if the claimant received notice of the appeal within the 21 days).

These Regulations also amend paragraph (1) of regulation 12 of the said Regulations in order to secure consistency between that paragraph and paragraph (2) of the said regulation which was so amended by the National Insurance &c. Act 1964 (1964 c. 96).

The amendment to regulation 16 of the said Regulations is of a minor consequential character.

1972 No. 382 (S.26)

FIRE PRECAUTIONS

The Fire Precautions (Hotels and Boarding Houses) (Scotland) Order 1972

Made - - - -	*13th March* 1972
Laid before Parliament	*17th March* 1972
Coming into Operation	*1st June* 1972

In exercise of the powers conferred on me by section 1 of the Fire Precautions Act 1971(**a**), I hereby make the following order:—

1.—(1) This order may be cited as the Fire Precautions (Hotels and Boarding Houses) (Scotland) Order 1972 and shall come into operation on 1st June 1972.

(2) This order extends to Scotland only.

2.—(1) In this order, the expression—

"the Act" means the Fire Precautions Act 1971;

"the first floor" means the floor above the ground floor; and

"guests" means members of the general public, being travellers, holiday-makers or other persons, for whom sleeping accommodation is provided.

(2) The Interpretation Act 1889(**b**) shall apply for the interpretation of this order as it applies for the interpretation of an Act of Parliament.

3. The following use of premises is hereby designated for the purposes of section 1 of the Act (which requires fire certificates for premises put to designated uses) that is to say, use for providing, in the course of carrying on the business of a hotel, or boarding house keeper, sleeping accommodation for staff or sleeping, dining-room, drawing-room, ball-room or other accommodation for guests:

Provided that the provisions of this order shall not have effect in relation to any premises unless either—

(*a*) sleeping accommodation is provided in those premises for more than six persons being staff or guests; or

(*b*) some sleeping accommodation is provided in those premises for staff or guests on any floor above the first floor of the building which constitutes or comprises the premises; or

(*c*) some sleeping accommodation is provided in those premises for staff or guests below the ground floor of the building which constitutes or comprises the premises.

Gordon Campbell,
One of Her Majesty's Principal
Secretaries of State.

St. Andrew's House,
Edinburgh.
13th March 1972.

(**a**) 1971 c. 40.   (**b**) 1889 c. 63.

EXPLANATORY NOTE
(This Note is not part of the Order.)

Section 1 of the Fire Precautions Act 1971 requires that a fire certificate should be obtained in respect of any premises which are put to a designated use.

This Order designates for this purpose the use of premises for a hotel or boarding house if sleeping accommodation is provided there for more than six persons (whether guests or staff) or there is some sleeping accommodation above first-floor or below ground-floor level.

1972 No. 384 (C.8)

PENSIONS

The Superannuation Act 1972 (Commencement No. 2) Order 1972

Made -   -   -   -   *9th March* 1972

The Secretary of State, in exercise of the powers conferred on him by section 30(3) of the Superannuation Act 1972**(a)** and of all other powers enabling him in that behalf, hereby makes the following Order:

1. This Order may be cited as the Superannuation Act 1972 (Commencement No. 2) Order 1972.

2. Section 21 of the Superannuation Act 1972 and paragraphs 68 and 96 of Schedule 6 thereto shall come into force on 1st April 1972.

A. M. Houghton,
An Under Secretary,
9th March 1972.   Department of Trade and Industry.

EXPLANATORY NOTE

(*This Note is not part of the Order.*)

This Order brings into force on 1st April 1972 section 21 of and related paragraphs in Schedule 6 to the Superannuation Act 1972. These provisions are concerned with pensions for the employees of the British Airways Board group.

(a) 1972 c. 11.

STATUTORY INSTRUMENTS

1972 No. 385

CIVIL AVIATION

The Civil Aviation Authority Aerodromes (Designation) (Detention and Sale of Aircraft) Order 1972

Made - - -	*13th March* 1972
Laid before Parliament	*21st March* 1972
Coming into Operation	*1st April* 1972

The Secretary of State in exercise of his powers under section 14(9) of the Civil Aviation Act 1968(**a**), and of all other powers enabling him in that behalf, hereby orders as follows: —

1. This Order may be cited as the Civil Aviation Authority Aerodromes (Designation) (Detention and Sale of Aircraft) Order 1972 and shall come into operation on 1st April 1972.

2. The following aerodromes are hereby designated for the purposes of section 14 of the Civil Aviation Act 1968: —

> Aberdeen
> Benbecula
> Inverness
> Islay (Port Ellen)
> Kirkwall
> Stornoway
> Sumburgh
> Tiree
> Wick

Michael Noble,
Minister for Trade,
Department of Trade and Industry.

13th March 1972.

EXPLANATORY NOTE

(This Note is not part of the Order.)

This Order designates, for the purposes of section 14 of the Civil Aviation Act 1968, the nine aerodromes which, by virtue of the Civil Aviation Authority (Vesting Date) (No. 1) Order 1972 (S.I. 1972/140), will vest in the Civil Aviation Authority on 1st April 1972. Section 14 applies to aerodromes so designated and provides for the detention and sale of aircraft for unpaid airport charges.

(**a**) 1968 c. 61.

STATUTORY INSTRUMENTS

1972 No. 386

EXCHANGE CONTROL

The Exchange Control (Scheduled Territories) Order 1972

Made - - -	10*th March* 1972
Laid before Parliament	28*th March* 1972
Coming into Operation	18*th April* 1972

The Treasury, in exercise of the powers conferred upon them by sections 1(3)(*b*) and 36(5) of the Exchange Control Act 1947(**a**), hereby make the following Order:—

1.—(1) This Order may be cited as the Exchange Control (Scheduled Territories) Order 1972, and shall come into operation on 18th April 1972.

(2) The Interpretation Act 1889(**b**) shall apply for the interpretation of this Order as it applies for the interpretation of an Act of Parliament.

2. Schedule 1 to the Exchange Control Act 1947 (as amended by the Orders hereby revoked) shall be further amended to read as set out in Schedule 1 to this Order.

3. The Orders specified in Schedule 2 to this Order are hereby revoked.

4. This Order shall extend to the Channel Islands, and any reference in this Order to the Exchange Control Act 1947 includes a reference to that Act as extended by the Exchange Control (Channel Islands) Order 1947(**c**).

P. L. Hawkins,
Tim Fortescue,
Two of the Lords Commissioners
of Her Majesty's Treasury.

10th March 1972.

(**a**) 1947 c. 14.   (**b**) 1889 c. 63.
(**c**) S.R. & O. 1947/2034 (Rev. VI, p. 1001: 1947 I, p. 660).

SCHEDULE 1

SCHEDULED TERRITORIES

1. The United Kingdom, the Channel Islands and the Isle of Man.
2. Australia, the Commonwealth of.
3. Bahrain.
4. Bangladesh.
5. Barbados.
6. Botswana.
7. British Solomon Islands, the.
8. Brunei.
9. Ceylon.
10. Cyprus, the Republic of.
11. Fiji.
12. Gambia, the.
13. Ghana.
14. Guyana.
15. Iceland.
16. India (including Sikkim).
17. Ireland, the Republic of.
18. Jamaica.
19. Jordan, the Hashemite Kingdom of.
20. Kenya.
21. Kuwait.
22. Lesotho.
23. Malawi.
24. Malaysia.
25. Malta.
26. Mauritius.
27. New Zealand.
28. Nigeria.
29. Pakistan.
30. Qatar.
31. Sierra Leone.
32. Singapore.
33. South Africa, the Republic of, and the territory of South West Africa.
34. Swaziland.
35. Tanzania, the United Republic of.
36. Tonga.
37. Trinidad and Tobago.
38. Uganda.
39. United Arab Emirates, the.
40. Western Samoa.
41. Yemen, the People's Democratic Republic of.
42. Zambia.
43. Any part of Her Majesty's dominions not mentioned in any of the foregoing paragraphs, except Canada and Southern Rhodesia.

SCHEDULE 2

ORDERS REVOKED

The Exchange Control (Scheduled Territories) Order 1967.	S.I. 1967/1767 (1967 III, p. 4736).
The Exchange Control (Scheduled Territories) (Amendment) Order 1968.	S.I. 1968/333 (1968 I, p. 971).
The Exchange Control (Scheduled Territories) (Amendment) (No. 2) Order 1968.	S.I. 1968/1399 (1968 II, p. 4047).
The Exchange Control (Scheduled Territories) (Amendment) Order 1970.	S.I. 1970/748 (1970 II, p. 2343).
The Exchange Control (Scheduled Territories) (Amendment No. 2) Order 1970.	S.I. 1970/1455 (1970 III, p. 4785).
The Exchange Control (Scheduled Territories) (Amendment) Order 1971.	S.I. 1971/1406 (1971 II, p. 3943).
The Exchange Control (Scheduled Territories) (Amendment) (No. 2) Order 1971.	S.I. 1971/1556 (1971 III, p. 4373).
The Exchange Control (Scheduled Territories) (Amendment) (No. 3) Order 1971.	S.I. 1971/2002 (1971 III, p. 5693).
The Exchange Control (Scheduled Territories) (Amendment) Order 1972.	S.I. 1972/146 (1972 I, p. 501).

EXPLANATORY NOTE

(This Note is not part of the Order.)

This Order consolidates the list of scheduled territories in the First Schedule to the Exchange Control Act 1947. It also amends that list by the inclusion by name of the British Solomon Islands, **Brunei** and the United Arab Emirates all of which were previously included by definition.

STATUTORY INSTRUMENTS

1972 No. 387

PENSIONS

The Pensions Increase (Wheat Commission) Regulations 1972

Made - - -		13*th March* 1972
Laid before Parliament		17*th March* 1972
Coming into Operation		10*th April* 1972

The Minister for the Civil Service, in exercise of the powers conferred on him by section 13(2) and (5) of the Pensions (Increase) Act 1971(a) and of all other powers enabling him in that behalf, hereby makes the following Regulations: —

Citation and commencement

1. These Regulations may be cited as the Pensions Increase (Wheat Commission) Regulations 1972, and shall come into operation on 10th April 1972.

Interpretation

2.—(1) In these Regulations—

"the civil service pension scheme" means the principal civil service pension scheme within the meaning of section 2 of the Superannuation Act 1972(b) and for the time being in force;

"reckonable service" means, in relation to any person, such of his service after 4th May 1940 as is reckonable for the purposes of the Wheat Commission pension scheme;

"the Wheat Commission pension scheme" means the pension scheme established by the Wheat Commission for members of its staff.

(2) The Interpretation Act 1889(c) shall apply for the interpretation of these Regulations as it applies for the interpretation of an Act of Parliament.

Persons to whom the Regulations apply

3.—(1) These Regulations apply to any person who—

(*a*) has after 4th May 1940 served for a continuous period of not less than ten years either in the employment of the Wheat Commission as a participant in the Wheat Commission pension scheme, or partly in such employment as such a participant and partly in the civil service of the State; and

---

(a) 1971 c. 56.   (b) 1972 c. 11.
(c) 1889 c. 63.

(b) either—

    (i) has retired from the service of the Wheat Commission after attaining the age of sixty years or on account of physical or mental infirmity; **or**

    (ii) has retired from the civil service of the State after attaining the age of sixty years or on account of physical or mental infirmity; or

    (iii) having retired from the civil service of the State not earlier than 14th July 1949 in circumstances other than those described in (ii) above, has attained the age of sixty years or satisfies the Minister for the Civil Service that he is disabled by physical or mental infirmity; or

    (iv) having been transferred from the civil service of the State to employment which is approved employment for the purposes of the civil service pension scheme, has retired from such employment after attaining the age of sixty years or on account of physical or mental infirmity; and

(c) has received, or become entitled to receive, retirement benefit under the Wheat Commission pension scheme.

(2) For the purposes of paragraph (1) above, a person shall be deemed to have retired after attaining the age of sixty years if he retired within twelve months before attaining that age in such circumstances that he became entitled immediately after his retirement to retirement benefit under the Wheat Commission pension scheme.

Notional pension and lump sum

4.—(1) There shall be ascribed to each person to whom these Regulations apply a notional pension calculated by multiplying one-eightieth of the average annual amount of the salary and emoluments of his office during the last three years of his reckonable service by the number of completed years of his reckonable service.

(2) Where a person to whom these Regulations apply has retired or been transferred from the civil service of the State in such circumstances that, if the civil service pension scheme applied to him, a lump sum would become payable to him by way of retiring allowance upon his subsequently attaining a particular age or becoming disabled by physical or mental infirmity before that age, there shall be ascribed to him a notional lump sum, treated as if it became payable on his attaining that age or becoming so disabled, as the case may be, and calculated by multiplying three-eightieths of the average annual amount of the salary and emoluments of his office during the last three years of his reckonable service by the number of completed years of his reckonable service.

(3) In calculating, under paragraph (1) above, the notional pension of a person to whom an allowance was payable before the coming into operation of these Regulations under or by reference to the Pensions Increase (Former Wheat Commission Staff) Regulations 1970(a), any fraction of a pound in the resulting sum shall be treated as a whole pound.

(a) S.I. 1970/355 (1970 I, p. 1267).

Payment of benefit equivalent to pension increase

5. The Minister for the Civil Service may, in respect of any period beginning on or after 1st September 1971, pay to any person to whom these Regulations apply an amount equal to the increase which would be payable to him under the Pensions (Increase) Act 1971 if—

(*a*) there were payable to him—

    (i) a superannuation allowance under the civil service pension scheme of an amount equal to the notional pension ascribed to him under Regulation 4(1) above, and

    (ii) in a case where a notional lump sum is ascribed to him under Regulation 4(2) above, a lump sum allowance under the civil service pension scheme of an amount equal to and becoming payable at the same time as that notional lump sum, and

(*b*) any allowance which might (but for the pensions (Increase) Act 1971) have been paid to him under the Pensions Increase (Former Wheat Commission Staff) Regulations 1970 were a relevant increase within the meaning of section 6(10) of that Act.

Given under the official seal of the Minister for the Civil Service on 13th March 1972.

(L.S.)

A. W. Wyatt,
Authorised by the Minister
for the Civil Service.

EXPLANATORY NOTE

(This Note is not part of the Regulations.)

These Regulations provide for the payment of allowances to certain pensioners of the former Wheat Commission, corresponding to the increases provided by the Pensions (Increase) Act 1971.

The allowances will be calculated on a "notional pension" and, in certain circumstances, a "notional lump sum" which correspond broadly to the pension and lump sum a person would have received if he had been subject to the principal civil service pension scheme and entitled to reckon under that scheme his service during which he was subject to the Wheat Commission pension scheme.

Under the power in section 13(5) of the Pensions (Increase) Act 1971 the Regulations provide for allowances payable under the Regulations to take effect from 1st September 1971.

STATUTORY INSTRUMENTS

1972 No. 389 (S.29)

NATIONAL HEALTH SERVICE, SCOTLAND

The Hospital Endowments (Scotland) Act 1971 (Appointed Day) Order 1972

Made - - - *9th March* 1972

In exercise of the powers conferred on me by section 12(1) of the Hospital Endowments (Scotland) Act 1971(*a*), and of all other powers enabling me in that behalf, I hereby make the following order:—

1. This order may be cited as the Hospitals Endowments (Scotland) Act 1971 (Appointed Day) Order 1972.

2. For the purposes of sections 2(1) and 13(2) of the Hospital Endowments (Scotland) Act 1971 "the appointed day" shall be 1st April 1972.

Gordon Campbell,
One of Her Majesty's Principal
Secretaries of State.

St. Andrew's House,
Edinburgh.
9th March 1972.

EXPLANATORY NOTE

(This Note is not part of the Order.)

This Order made under the Hospital Endowments (Scotland) Act 1971 names the appointed day for the purposes of the transfer of relevant endowments to the Scottish Hospital Trust and for the taking effect of the repeals specified in the Act.

(a) 1971 c. 8.

STATUTORY INSTRUMENTS

1972 No. 390 (S.28)

NATIONAL HEALTH SERVICE, SCOTLAND

The Scottish Hospital Trust Regulations 1972

Laid before Parliament in draft

Made - - - - 9*th March* 1972

Coming into Operation 16*th March* 1972

In exercise of the powers conferred on me by sections 2(2)(*c*), 2(3), 5(2) and 6(2) of the Hospital Endowments (Scotland) Act 1971**(a)**, and of all other powers enabling me in that behalf, I hereby make the following regulations:—

PART I

GENERAL

1. These regulations may be cited as the Scottish Hospital Trust Regulations 1972 and shall come into operation on 16th March 1972.

2. In these regulations:—

(*a*) "the Act" means the Hospital Endowments (Scotland) Act 1971; "the Trust" means the Scottish Hospital Trust constituted by and in accordance with section 1(1) of and the Schedule to the Act.

(*b*) Unless the context otherwise requires the several words and expressions to which meanings are assigned in the Act shall have the same meanings in these regulations as they have in the Act.

3. The Interpretation Act 1889**(b)** shall apply for the interpretation of these regulations as it applies for the interpretation of an Act of Parliament and as if these regulations were an Act of Parliament.

PART II

EXCEPTIONS FROM TRANSFERENCE TO THE TRUST OF RELEVANT ENDOWMENTS OF BOARDS OF MANAGEMENT.

4. There shall be excepted from transference to the Trust—

(a) 1971 c. 8.   (b) 1889 c. 63.

(*a*) the relevant endowments of the Boards of Managements for

    (i) Glasgow Homoeopathic Hospitals and

    (ii) the Lews and Harris Hospitals, and

(*b*) the endowments specified in the Schedule to these regulations

PART III

CONDITIONS AFFECTING THE TRANSFERENCE OF RELEVANT ENDOWMENTS

5.—(1) (*a*) At the request of the Board of Management for the Astley Ainslie, Edenhall and Associated Hospitals, the Secretary of State may direct that the Trust shall realise part of the capital of the funds transferred to it under section 2(1) of the Act up to the value of the capital of the funds which at the appointed day where held and administered as a Development Fund in terms of paragraph 11 of the Astley Ainslie, Edenhall and Associated Hospitals Endowment Scheme 1954 approved by the Secretary of State by the National Health Service (Astley Ainslie, Edenhall and Associated Hospitals Endowment Scheme) Approval Order 1954(**a**) (less any outstanding sums borrowed which may have been written off by the appointed day with the approval of the Secretary of State under regulation 7(2) of these regulations).

The amounts so realised shall be transferred to the said Board of Management and shall be applied by them when received to meet capital expenditure on the provision of facilities for the convalescence and rehabilitation of patients in the hospitals or clinics administered by the said Board of Management.

(*b*) At the request of the Board of Management for the Royal Infirmary of Edinburgh and Associated Hospitals the Secretary of State may direct that the Trust shall realise part of the capital of the funds transferred to it under section 2(1) of the Act up to the value of the capital of the funds which at the appointed day were held and administered as the Sir Robert McVitie Grant Dermatological Fund in terms of paragraph 7 of the Royal Infirmary of Edinburgh and Associated Hospitals Endowment Scheme approved by the Secretary of State by the National Health Service (Royal Infirmary of Edinburgh and Associated Hospitals Endowment Scheme) Approval Order 1954(**b**) (less any outstanding sum borrowed which may have been written off as at the appointed day with the approval of the Secretary of State under regulation 7(2) of these regulations).

The amounts so realised shall be transferred to the said Board of Management and shall be applied by them when received to meet capital expenditure for purposes connected with the Dermatological Department of the Royal Infirmary of Edinburgh.

(2) Provided that for the purpose of realisations carried out under this regulation the capital value of the total funds held by the Trust shall be taken to be as at the date of realisation.

PART IV

CAPITAL VALUE OF RELEVANT ENDOWMENTS TRANSFERRED

6.—(1) The capital value of the relevant endowments transferred to the Trust in terms of Section 2(1) of the Act shall be calculated as follows:—

(**a**) S.I. 1954/1295.   (**b**) S.I. 1954/1296.

(*a*) Investments quoted on a Stock Exchange—at middle market value as at the appointed day;

(*b*) Investments not quoted on a Stock Exchange—at independent valuation as at the appointed day;

(*c*) land and heritable property, feu duties and ground annuals—failing agreement between the Trust and the Board concerned, at independent valuation as at the appointed day,

(*d*) Short term loans, bank and cash balances—at amounts outstanding or at credit at commencement of the appointed day;

(*e*) Net borrowing—at actual amount as determined in regulation 7 of these regulations.

(2) Where paragraph (1) of this regulation provides for independent valuation the valuer shall, failing agreement between the Trust and the Board concerned, be appointed by the Secretary of State.

(3) The Trust shall prepare and issue to Boards of Management and Regional Hospital Boards certificates which shall state each Board's share of the total funds represented by the capital value of the relevant endowments transferred to the Trust on the appointed day calculated as provided in paragraph (1) of this regulation.

(4) The Trust shall in like manner issue a certificate to the Board of Management for the Astley Ainslie, Edenhall and Associated Hospitals in respect of the capital value of the funds transferred to the Trust from the Development Fund referred to in the preceding regulation and a certificate to the Board of Management for the Royal Infirmary of Edinburgh and Associated Hospitals in respect of the capital value of the funds transferred to the Trust from the Sir Robert McVitie Grant Dermatological Fund also referred to in the preceding regulation.

(5) Where under a scheme approved by the Secretary of State new Boards of Management are formed by the amalgamation or re-distribution of responsibilities of former Boards, the shares of the former Boards in the funds of the Trust for which such Boards hold certificates issued under paragraph (3) of this regulation shall be assigned to the new Boards in the same proportion as the bed complements, determined by the Secretary of State, of the hospitals affected by such amalgamation or re-distribution have been assigned. The Trust shall issue a certificate to each new Board stating its share of the total funds as provided in paragraph (3) of this regulation, and shall similarly issue a fresh certificate to any Board which continues in existence but whose bed complement has been altered by such re-distribution.

(6) Where under regulation 5 of these regulations part of the capital of the Trust is realised and transferred, the Trust shall withdraw the certificates issued in terms of paragraphs (3) or (5) of this regulation and shall issue to each Board a fresh certificate in which the stated share of the total funds of the Trust shall take account of the capital so realised and transferred: and the Trust shall also withdraw from the Board concerned the certificate issued in terms of paragraphs (4) of this regulation and shall issue a revised certificate in respect of the capital value of the Development Fund or the Sir Robert McVitie Grant Dermatological Fund, as the case may be, transferred to the Trust.

Part V

Arrangements regarding borrowing by Boards of Management and Regional Hospital Boards

7.—(1) Outstanding borrowings from relevant endowments by Boards of Management or Regional Hospital Boards shall be offset by any amounts written off in terms of paragraph (2) of this regulation, and the net amounts resulting shall be assets of the Trust, and shall be repayable over a period not exceeding thirty years from the date of borrowing, or such shorter period as may in any particular case be determined by the Secretary of State having regard to the amount of accumulated revenue balances held by the Board concerned, and with interest at a rate approved by the Secretary of State which shall be not less than 5% per annum.

(2) The Secretary of State may direct that the Trust shall as at the appointed day write off from the relevant endowments of a Board the whole or part of such outstanding borrowings as are referred to in paragraph (1) of this regulation.

(3) Sums borrowed after the appointed day by Boards of Management or Regional Hospital Board against their share of the capital of the Trust shall be repayable over a period not exceeding thirty years, with interest at a rate approved by the Secretary of State which shall not be less than 5% per annum.

(4) The Trust may require notice of borrowing to be given where the sum proposed to be borrowed including any sums borrowed under section 6(1) of the Act within the previous twelve months, exceeds £5,000, as follows:—

(*a*) up to £25,000, six months notice;

(*b*) over £25,000, twelve months notice.

Gordon Campbell,
One of Her Majesty's
Principal Secretaries of State.

St. Andrew's House,
Edinburgh.
9th March 1972.

Regulation 4 SCHEDULE

ENDOWMENTS EXCEPTED FROM TRANSFER TO THE TRUST IN TERMS OF
REGULATION 4(*b*)

Board of Management	*Endowment*
Arran Hospitals	House "Cuilabhaila", Lamlash.
Astley Ainslie and Associated Hospitals	Houses at 4 and 8 Parkgrove Place, Musselburgh.
Banffshire Hospitals	House "Bruxlea", Turriff.
Caithness Hospitals	House "Slateford", George Street, Wick. Tennis Courts and playing fields at Wick (let to Wick Town Council).
Campbeltown and District Hospitals	House at 12 Glebe Street, Campbeltown. Land known as Kintyre Nursery, Campbeltown, extending to 5·87 acres or thereby.
Coatbridge, Airdrie and District Hospitals	Agricultural land extending to 41·731 acres or thereby at Calderbank House, Baillieston, and sheds and buildings thereon.
County and City of Perth General Hospitals	House "Ferndale", situated in the grounds of Hillside Hospital.
Dunoon Hospitals	House known as No. 2 Dunoon General Hospital.
East Fife Hospitals	Houses on first and second flats (right hand side) at 18 and 24 Hunter Street, house on first and second flat (left hand side) at 32 Hunter Street, 46 Forth Park Gardens, 189 Dunnikier Road, and 14 Muirfield Street, all in Kirkcaldy.
Edinburgh Northern Hospitals	Houses and property at 1a, 2, 4, 5, and 7 Rillbank Terrace, 1, 3 and first flat of 4 Rillbank Crescent, 11 and 12 Millerfield Place, and 84 Dudley Avenue, all in Edinburgh.
Edinburgh Southern Hospitals	House at 62 Spring Gardens, Edinburgh. House, 2 shops, and lock-up garages at 1-11 Waverley Park, Edinburgh. Property at 15-17 Carlton Terrace, Edinburgh, occupied as the South Edinburgh School of Nursing. Land at Liberton known as Stenhouse Market Gardens, extending to 27 acres or thereby.
Foresterhill and Associated Hospitals	Ground at 169 Constitution Street, Aberdeen extending to 133 sq. yds. or thereby. Yard at 143 Constitution Street, Aberdeen extending to 1970 sq. yds. or thereby. Land adjoining Insch and District War Memorial Hospital extending to 1·3 acres or thereby.
Glasgow Northern Hospitals	Land bordering 3 sides of the Glasgow Convalescent Home Lenzie extending to 3·4 acres or thereby.

Board of Management—(cont.)	*Endowment*
Moray Hospitals	Houses "Grovelea", 11 Seafield Street, Elgin, and "Limekilns", 22 Springfield Road, New Elgin.
Northern Ayrshire Hospitals	Houses at 2-14 Hill Street and 28 Kirkgate all in Irvine.
Oban and District Hospitals	Land at Benvoulin Lane, Oban, extending to 0·57 acres or thereby, and the houses erected thereon, numbers 1, 2 and 3 Benvoulin Lane, Oban.
Paisley and District Hospitals	Land at Harelaw and Hollybush Farms extending to 173 acres or thereby. Land at Dykebarhill and Oldbar Farms extending to 119 acres or thereby. 2 flats on the ground floor at 29 Calside, Paisley.
Royal Edinburgh and Associated Hospitals	House at 50 Caiystane Avenue, Edinburgh.
Royal Infirmary of Edinburgh and Associated Hospitals	2 houses being centre houses on first and second floors at 114 Lauriston Place, house consisting of 2 flats entered from staircase at 118 Lauriston Place, main door house at 120 Lauriston Place, tenement 5-7 Moncrieff Terrace, east and west flats on top floor and office at 6 Cambridge Street, tenement at 14-18 Marionville Road comprising 8 houses (under exception of top flat west at 16 Marionville Road) all in Edinburgh.
Scottish Borders Hospitals	2 houses at 14 and 16 Duke Street, Galashiels. Field extending to 4·3 acres or thereby at Gordon.
Skye Hospitals	House at Mackinnon Memorial Hospital, Broadford.
Stirling, Falkirk and Alloa Hospitals	2 small triangular plots, extending to 0·829 acre and 0·830 acre or thereby, bordering the Stirling Inner relief road.

EXPLANATORY NOTE

(This Note is not part of the Regulations.)

These regulations make provision in respect of conditions of and exceptions from transference of relevant endowments to the Scottish Hospital Trust, the valuation of endowments transferred, and the arrangements for outstanding and future borrowings by hospital boards against their relevant endowments.

STATUTORY INSTRUMENTS

1972 No. 391 (S.27)

NATIONAL HEALTH SERVICE, SCOTLAND

The Scottish Hospital Trust Scheme 1972

Laid before Parliament in draft

Made -	-	-	-		*9th March* 1972
Coming into Operation					*16th March* 1972

In exercise of the powers conferred on me by section 7(1) of the Hospital Endowments (Scotland) Act 1971(a), and of all other powers enabling me in that behalf, and having given to Boards of Management, Regional Hospital Boards and the Committee of the State Hospital in terms of section 7(2) thereof an opportunity to make representations, I hereby make the following scheme:—

Citation and commencement

1. This scheme may be cited as the Scottish Hospital Trust Scheme 1972 and shall come into operation on 16th March 1972.

Interpretation

2.—(1) In this scheme—

"the Act" means the Hospital Endowments (Scotland) Act 1971 and the "Trust" means the Scottish Hospital Trust constituted under section 1(1) of and the Schedule to the Act.

(2) Unless the context otherwise requires the several words and expressions to which meanings are assigned in the Act shall have the same meanings in this scheme as they have in the Act.

(3) The Interpretation Act 1889(b) shall apply for the interpretation of this scheme as it applies for the interpretation of an Act of Parliament and as if the scheme were an Act of Parliament.

Application of endowment funds

3. Subject to the provisions of paragraph 4(c) and (d) of this scheme the Trust after paying the necessary expenses of management and the burdens and taxes affecting the endowments transferred to them in terms of section 2(1) or accepted by them in terms of section 3(f) of the Act shall distribute at dates in each year to be determined by the Secretary of State the resulting balance of

---

(a) 1971 c. 8.   (b) 1889 c. 63

income among Boards of Management (except those for Glasgow Homoeo-pathic Hospitals and the Lews and Harris Hospitals), Regional Hospital Boards and the State Hospital on the following basis:

    (i) a basic distribution to provide

        (*a*) an annual income of £3 per bed, or, in the case of dental hospitals, per chair, within the complement (as determined annually by the Secretary of State after consultation with Regional Hospital Boards) of hospitals under the management of the Board of Management concerned;

        (*b*) an annual income of £3 per bed within the complement of the State Hospital as agreed by the Secretary of State; and

        (*c*) the following annual sums payable to Regional Hospital Boards;

Regional Hospital Boards	Fixed Annual Sum
	£
Northern	350
North-Eastern	600
Eastern	600
South-Eastern	900
Western	1,200

    (ii) a share of the balance remaining in proportion to its share of the total funds represented by the value of the relevant endowments transferred to the Trust in terms of section 2(1) of the Act for which a Board of Management or Regional Hospital Board may hold certificates issued to it by the Trust in terms of regulation 6 of the Scottish Hospital Trust Regulations 1972**(a)**.

4. (*a*) Subject to sub-paragraphs (*b*), (*c*) and (*d*) of this paragraph, the sums received by Boards of Management and Regional Hospital Boards in terms of this scheme shall be used for such purposes relating to hospital and specialist services within the meaning of section 3(1) of the National Health Service (Scotland) Act 1947**(b)** or to research into any matters as are mentioned in section 17 of that Act as they in their discretion think fit and the sums received by the State Hospital shall be used by that hospital for any purpose for which the hospital was provided including research in connection with any such purpose.

    (*b*) The Boards listed in column 1 of the Schedule to this scheme shall use income for the purposes, and to the extent, specified in column 2 of the Schedule.

    (*c*) Before deciding to expend on any one research project any sum exceeding £2,000 a Board of Management, Regional Hospital Board or State Hospital Management Committee shall consult the Advisory Committee on Medical Research in Scotland or such other body as the Secretary of State may from time to time direct.

(a) S.I. 1972/390 (1972 I, p. 1466)
(b) 1947 c. 27.

(*d*) A Board of Management shall not without the consent of the Regional Hospital Board incur under this scheme expenditure exceeding £2,000 on

(i) any one project involving the acquisition, erection or adaptation of a building, or

(ii) the provision of any one piece of equipment otherwise than by way of replacement.

Gordon Campbell
One of Her Majesty's Principal
Secretaries of State.

St Andrew's House,
Edinburgh.

9th March 1972.

Paragraph 4   SCHEDULE

SPECIAL PROVISIONS FOR USE OF INCOME RECEIVED FROM THE TRUST

BOARD OF MANAGEMENT	*PROVISION*
Foresterhill and Associated Hospitals	In pursuance of the gift of £400 by Sir John Duthie of Cairnbulg Castle, Aberdeenshire, the Board shall in each year apply the sum of £13·75 in the purchase of gifts to be given in the name of his daughter Leslie Elliot Duthie to girl patients in the Royal Aberdeen Childrens Hospital on the 17th day of August, being the birthday of the said Leslie Elliot Duthie.
	The Board shall in all time coming maintain in good order the grave and tombstone of Robert Edwards, late of 13 Ruthriehill Road, Stoneywood.
	The Board shall in all time coming maintain the War Memorial Stone erected in the village of Torphins.
Dundee General Hospitals	The Board shall in each year apply the following sums on prizes for nurses in Dundee Royal Infirmary:—

(*a*) the sum of five pounds to be known as the Miss Duff Memorial Prize;

(*b*) the sum of five pounds to be known as the Ogilvy Dalgleish Prize;

(*c*) the sum of three pounds to be known as the Miss J. H. Nicol Prize; and

(*d*) the sum of five pounds to be known as the Dr. J. S. Y. Rogers Prize.

The Board shall from time to time decide the conditions governing the award of these prizes.

| Astley Ainslie and Associated Hospitals | The Board shall provide for the upkeep in all time coming of the burying ground in the cemetery of South Leith of the family of David Ainslie of Costerton and of the burying ground of and the memorial tombstone to the said David Ainslie in Crichton Churchyard, Midlothian. |

BOARD OF MANAGEMENT   PROVISION

Glasgow Royal Infirmary and   The Board shall in each year apply such sums as
Associated Hospitals   they think fit to the purposes aftermentioned:—

> (a) the provision of medals to be known as the
> Dr. John Burns Medals to be awarded to the
> most distinguished male student in attendance
> at the Royal Infirmary of Glasgow in the
> examinations for clinical medicine, clinical
> surgery, gynaecology and ophthalmology
> respectively;
>
> (b) the provision of medals to be known as the
> Mrs. William R. Herkless Medals to be
> awarded to the most distinguished female
> student in attendance at the Royal Infirmary
> of Glasgow in the examinations for clinical
> medicine, clinical surgery, gynaecology and
> ophthalmology respectively;
>
> (c) the provision of a medal to be known as the
> Graham Medal for a student in the Ear, Nose
> and Throat class in attendance at the Royal
> Infirmary of Glasgow;
>
> (d) the provision of prizes, bursaries, scholar-
> ships or post-graduate teaching for nurses in
> the Royal Infirmary of Glasgow;
>
> (e) the provision of cancer research scholar-
> ships in the Royal Infirmary of Glasgow to be
> known as the McGhie Cancer Research
> Scholarships;
>
> (f) the provision of clinical research scholar-
> ships in the Royal Infirmary of Glasgow to be
> known as the McIntyre Clinical Research
> Scholarships;

Provided always that the Board may in any year, if
they deem it expedient so to do, resolve not to make
an award of any of the said medals, prizes, scholarships or bursaries. The Board shall from time to
time decide the conditions governing the award of the
said medals, prizes, scholarships and bursaries.

Southern Lanarkshire Hospi-   The Board shall in all time coming maintain the
tals   graves and tombstones in Biggar Churchyard of
                        Mrs. Eleanora Thomson or Bell Brown and her
                        husband George Bell Brown, and of the parents of the
                        said Mrs. Eleanora Thomson or Bell Brown.

Dumfries and Galloway Hospi-   The Board shall in each year apply the sum of £3
tals   on a prize or medal for the best practical nurse in the
                        Dumfries and Galloway Royal Infirmary or the
                        General Hospital in Dumfries, to be known as the
                        Mary Dalgleish Prize.

HOSPITAL AUTHORITY	*PROVISION*
Stirling, Falkirk and Alloa Hospitals	The Board shall in each year apply sums for the purposes aftermentioned:—

    (*a*) The provision of a medal for a nurse in Stirling Royal Infirmary, the said medal to be known as the John Risk Medal and the conditions of award to be such as the Board may from time to time determine;

    (*b*) The provision of books for the nurses' library in Stirling Royal Infirmary in memory of the late Dr. C. G. Fletcher.

EXPLANATORY NOTE

(This Note is not part of the Scheme.)

This scheme makes provision in respect of the arrangements under which the income from the endowments transferred to the Scottish Hospital Trust shall be distributed to hospital authorities.

STATUTORY INSTRUMENTS

1972 NO. 392 (S.30)

FIRE PRECAUTIONS

The Fire Precautions (Application for Certificate) (Scotland) Regulations 1972

Made - - - -	13*th March* 1972
Laid before Parliament	17*th March* 1972
Coming into Operation	20*th March* 1972

In exercise of the powers conferred on me by section 5(1) of the Fire Precautions Act 1971(**a**), I hereby make the following regulations:—

1.—(1) These regulations may be cited as the Fire Precautions (Application for Certificate) (Scotland) Regulations 1972 and shall come into operation on 20th March 1972.

(2) These regulations extend to Scotland only.

2. The Interpretation Act 1889(**b**) shall apply for the interpretation of these regulations as it applies for the interpretation of an Act of Parliament.

3. An application for a fire certificate in respect of any premises shall be in the form specified in the Schedule to these regulations or a form to the like effect.

Gordon Campbell,
One of Her Majesty's Principal
Secretaries of State.

St. Andrew's House,
Edinburgh.
13th March 1972.

(**a**) 1971 c. 40.   (**b**) 1889 c. 63.

Regulation 3   SCHEDULE

APPLICATION FOR A FIRE CERTIFICATE

FIRE PRECAUTIONS ACT 1971, s. 5

To the Clerk of the Fire Authority[1]

Dear Sir

I hereby apply for a fire certificate in respect of the premises of which details are given below. I make the application as, or on behalf of, the [2] of the premises.

Yours faithfully

Signature

(Insert description if signing on behalf of a company or some other person)

Address ....

Telephone number......................................   Date................................

---

[1] In the case of Crown premises, application should be made instead to H.M. Inspector of Fire Services.

[2] State whether occupier, manager or as the case may be.

To be completed by the applicant

1. Postal address of the premises to which this application relates

   ....

2. The use or uses to which the premises are to be put and which it is desired to have covered by the fire certificate

   ....

3. Name of the occupier of the premises and trading name (if any)

   ....

4. Name and address of the owner of the premises

   ....

5. If the premises consist of only part of a building, the name and address of the owner of the building and also the name and address of any person having overall management of the building

   ....

6. If the premises consist of a complete building, the number of floors in the building

   ....

7. If the premises consist of only part of a building,

   (*a*) location of the premises within the building

   ....

   (*b*) use or uses of the other parts of the building

   ....

8. Maximum number of (*a*) staff and (*b*) other persons, likely to be in the premises at any one time—

   (*a*) ....   (*b*) ....

9. Approximate date of construction of the premises..

10. Nature and approximate quantity of any explosive or highly flammable materials kept in, on or under the premises or any building containing the premises

EXPLANATORY NOTE

(This Note is not part of the Regulations.)

These Regulations prescribe the form of application for a fire certificate under the Fire Precautions Act 1971.

1972 No. 393

SOCIAL SECURITY

The National Insurance (Industrial Injuries) (Benefit) Amendment Regulations 1972

Made - - -	*10th March* 1972
Laid before Parliament	*22nd March* 1972
Coming into Operation	*14th April* 1972

The Industrial Injuries Joint Authority, in exercise of the powers conferred by section 34(1) of the National Insurance (Industrial Injuries) Act 1965(a) and of all other powers enabling them in that behalf, hereby make the following regulations which have been referred to the Industrial Injuries Advisory Council:—

Citation, interpretation and commencement

1. These regulations, which may be cited as the National Insurance (Industrial Injuries) (Benefit) Amendment Regulations 1972, shall be read as one with the National Insurance (Industrial Injuries) (Benefit) Regulations 1964(b) as amended (c) (hereinafter referred to as "the principal regulations") and shall come into operation on 14th April 1972.

Amendment of the principal regulations

2. After regulation 14 of the principal regulations there shall be inserted the following regulation:—

"Deeming contributions for the maintenance of children or adult dependants of the amount of benefit under the Act abated under section 16(1A) of the Ministry of Social Security Act 1966

14A. Where for any period a person (in this regulation referred to as A) is entitled to, or to an increase in the amount of, any benefit mentioned in section 16(1)(b) of the Ministry of Social Security Act 1966(d) (benefit under the National Insurance (Industrial Injuries) Acts 1965 to 1971) in respect of another person (in this regulation referred to as B) and the amount of, or of the increase in, any such benefit is abated under the provisions of section 16(1A) of the said Act of 1966 (further provision for pre-

---

(a) 1965 c. 52.   (b) S.I. 1964/504 (1964 I, p. 833).
(c) There is no amendment which relates expressly to the subject matter of these
    ·regulations.
(d) 1966 c. 20.

venting duplication of supplementary and other benefits) then in determining for the purposes of Part II of the Act whether A is wholly or mainly maintaining, or is contributing at any weekly rate to the maintenance of, or is or has been contributing at any weekly rate to the cost of providing for, B, the amount by which such benefit for any week has been so abated shall be deemed to be a contribution of that amount for that week made by A for the maintenance of B.".

Given under the official seal of the Industrial Injuries Joint Authority.

(L.S.)

N. *Hanson*,
Secretary,
Industrial Injuries Joint Authority.

10th March 1972.

EXPLANATORY NOTE

(This Note is not part of the Regulations.)

These Regulations are made in consequence of section 3 of the Social Security Act 1971 (c.73) (extension of the provisions of section 16 of the Social Security Act 1966 preventing duplication of social security payments) and provide that, where benefit under the National Insurance (Industrial Injuries) Acts 1965 to 1971 in respect of a child or adult dependant is abated pursuant to the provisions of section 3 of the Social Security Act 1971, the amount by which it is abated is to be deemed to be a contribution of that amount towards the maintenance of the child or adult dependant in question for the purposes of the said Acts of 1965 to 1971.

STATUTORY INSTRUMENTS

1972 No. 394

SOCIAL SECURITY

The National Insurance (General Benefit and Miscellaneous Amendments) Regulations 1972

Made - - - -	13*th March* 1972
Laid before Parliament	22*nd March* 1972
Coming into Operation	14*th April* 1972

The National Insurance Joint Authority, in conjunction with the Treasury so far as relates to matters with regard to which the Treasury have so directed, in exercise of powers conferred under sections 50(1) and 55(1) of the National Insurance Act 1965**(a)** and of all other powers enabling them in that behalf, after considering the report of the National Insurance Advisory Committee on the preliminary draft submitted to them in accordance with section 108 of the said Act of 1965, hereby make the following regulations:—

Citation, commencement and interpretation

1.—(1) These regulations, which may be cited as the National Insurance (General Benefit and Miscellaneous Amendments) Regulations 1972, shall come into operation on 14th April 1972.

(2) Each provision of these regulations which amends other regulations shall be construed as one with the regulations which it amends.

Amendment of the National Insurance (General Benefit) Regulations 1970

2. After regulation 9 of the National Insurance (General Benefit) Regulations 1970**(b)**, as amended **(c)**, there shall be inserted the following regulation:—

"*Deeming benefit under the Act abated under section* 16(1A) *of the Ministry of Social Security Act* 1966 *to be a contribution for the maintenance of children or adult dependants*

9A. Where for any period a person (in this regulation referred to as A) is entitled to, or to an increase in the amount of, any such benefit, allowance or pension as is mentioned in section 16(1)(*a*) of the Ministry of Social Security Act 1966**(d)** (benefits, allowances and pensions under the National Insurance Acts 1965 to 1971) in respect of another person (in this regulation referred to as B) and the amount of, or of the increase in, any such benefit, allowance or pension is abated under the provisions of section 16(1A) of the said Act

---

(a) 1965 c. 51. (b) S.I. 1970/1981 (1970 III, p. 6461).
(c) There is no amendment which relates expressly to the subject matter of these regulations.
(d) 1966 c. 20.

of 1966 (further provision for preventing duplication of supplementary and other benefits), then in determining for the purposes of Part II of the Act whether A is wholly or mainly maintaining, or is contributing at any weekly rate to the maintenance of, or is or has been contributing at any weekly rate to the cost of providing for, B, the amount by which such benefit, allowance or pension for any week has been so abated shall be deemed to be a contribution of that amount for that week made by A for the maintenance of B."

Amendment of the National Insurance (Overlapping Benefits) Regulations 1948

3.—(1) The National Insurance (Overlapping Benefits) Regulations 1948**(a)**, as amended **(b)**, shall be further amended in accordance with the following provisions of this regulation.

(2) At the end of the definition of "dependency benefit" in regulation 1(2) there shall be added the words "and includes child's special allowance".

(3) In regulation 2 (adjustment of personal benefit under the Act where other personal benefit (whether under the Act or otherwise) is payable), in paragraph (4)(b), for the words "and being over seventy years of age" there shall be substituted the words "and being over sixty-five years of age".

Amendment of the National Insurance (Hospital In-Patients) Regulations 1949

4. In the National Insurance (Hospital In-Patients) Regulations 1949**(c)**, as amended (b), at the end of the definition of "dependency benefit" in regulation 1(2) there shall be added the words "and includes child's special allowance".

Given under the official seal of the National Insurance Joint Authority.

(L.S.)   *N. Hanson*,
                                                    Secretary,
                                        National Insurance Joint Authority.

8th March 1972.

                                                P. L. Hawkins,
                                                Tim Fortescue,
                                        Two of the Lords Commissioners
                                           of Her Majesty's Treasury.

13th March 1972.

(a) S.I. 1948/2711 (Rev. XVI, p. 196: 1948 I, p. 2657).
(b) There is no amendment which relates expressly to the subject matter of these regulations.
(c) S.I. 1949/1461 (1949 I, p. 2718).

EXPLANATORY NOTE

(This Note is not part of the Regulations.)

These Regulations amend the National Insurance (General Benefit) Regulations 1970, the National Insurance (Overlapping Benefits) Regulations 1948 and the National Insurance (Hospital In-Patients) Regulations 1949.

Regulation 1 is formal.

Regulation 2, which is made in consequence of section 3 of the Social Security Act 1971 (c.73) (extension of the provisions of section 16 of the Ministry of Social Security Act 1966 preventing duplication of social security payments) and which amends the General Benefit Regulations, provides that where benefit under the National Insurance Acts 1965 to 1971 in respect of a child or adult dependant is abated pursuant to the provisions of section 3 of the Social Security Act 1971, then the amount by which it is abated is to be deemed to be a contribution of that amount towards the maintenance of the child or adult dependant in question for the purposes of the said Acts of 1965 to 1971.

Regulation 3 amends the Overlapping Benefits Regulations, for the removal of doubt adding an express reference to child's special allowance to the definition of "dependency benefit" in regulation 1(2) and amending regulation 2(4)(*b*) so that certain grants payable to persons over age 65 (previously over age 70) are disregarded for adjustment purposes.

Regulation 4 makes an amendment to the definition of "dependency benefit" in regulation 1(2) of the Hospital In-Patients Regulations corresponding to the amendment made to the definition of "dependency benefit" in the Overlapping Benefits Regulations.

The report of the National Insurance Advisory Committee on the preliminary draft of these Regulations (described on its publication as the preliminary draft of the National Insurance (General Benefit and Miscellaneous Amendments) Regulations 1971) dated 27 January 1972 is contained in House of Commons Paper No. 185 (Session 1971-72) published by Her Majesty's Stationery Office.

STATUTORY INSTRUMENTS

1972 No. 395

PENSIONS

The Pensions Increase (Federated Superannuation Scheme for Nurses and Hospital Officers) (Civil Service) Regulations 1972

Made - - - -	*14th March* 1972
Laid before Parliament	*21st March* 1972
Coming into Operation	*12th April* 1972

The Minister for the Civil Service, in exercise of the powers conferred on him by section 13(2) and (5) of the Pensions (Increase) Act 1971(a) and of all other powers enabling him in that behalf, hereby makes the following Regulations:—

Citation and commencement

1. These Regulations may be cited as the Pensions Increase (Federated Superannuation Scheme for Nurses and Hospital Officers) (Civil Service) Regulations 1972, and shall come into operation on 12th April 1972.

Interpretation

2.—(1) In these Regulations—

"the civil service pension scheme" means the principal civil service pension scheme within the meaning of section 2 of the Superannuation Act 1972**(b)** and for the time being in force;

"dependant" has the meaning assigned to it by section 3(6) of the Pensions (Increase) Act 1971;

"F.S.S.N. scheme" means a superannuation scheme operated under the Federated Superannuation Scheme for Nurses and Hospital Officers;

"reckonable service" has the meaning assigned to it by the Schedule to these Regulations.

(2) The Interpretation Act 1889**(c)** shall apply for the interpretation of these Regulations as it applies for the interpretation of an Act of Parliament.'

(3) Any reference in these Regulations to the provisions of any enactment or regulations shall be construed, unless the context otherwise requires, as a reference to those provisions as amended by any subsequent enactment or regulations.

Persons to whom the Regulations apply

3.—(1) These Regulations apply to any person who—

(*a*) either—

(i) has retired from employment in the civil service of the State after attaining the age of sixty years; or

---

(**a**) 1971 c. 56. (**b**) 1972 c. 11.
(**c**) 1889 c. 63.

    (ii) having retired from such employment not earlier than 14th July 1949 before attaining the age of sixty years, has attained that age or satisfies the Minister for the Civil Service that he is disabled by physical or mental infirmity; or

    (iii) has retired from such employment on account of physical or mental infirmity; or

    (iv) has retired from such employment and is a woman who has at least one dependant; and

  (b) at the date of his retirement was subject to an F.S.S.N. scheme and had completed ten years' reckonable service; and

  (c) has received, or become entitled to receive, retirement benefit under that scheme.

(2) Notwithstanding the provisions of paragraph (1)(a)(ii) above, these Regulations shall not apply to any person who, within twelve months after retiring from employment in the civil service of the State, has entered any of the employments specified in paragraph 2 of the Schedule to these Regulations.

(3) For the purposes of paragraph (1) above, a person shall be deemed to have retired after attaining the age of sixty years if he retired within twelve months before attaining that age in such circumstances that he became entitled immediately after his retirement to retirement benefit under an F.S.S.N. scheme.

Notional pension and lump sum

4.—(1) There shall be ascribed to every person to whom these Regulations apply a notional pension calculated by multiplying one-eightieth of the average annual amount of the salary and emoluments of his office during the last three years of his reckonable service by the number of completed years of his reckonable service.

(2) Where a person to whom these Regulations apply has retired from the civil service of the State in such circumstances that, if the civil service pension scheme applied to him, a lump sum would become payable to him by way of retiring allowance upon his subsequently attaining a particular age or becoming disabled by physical or mental infirmity before that age, there shall be ascribed to him a notional lump sum, treated as if it became payable on his attaining that age or becoming so disabled, as the case may be, and calculated by multiplying three-eightieths of the average annual amount of the salary and emoluments of his office during the last three years of his reckonable service by the number of completed years of his reckonable service.

(3) In calculating, under paragraph (1) above, the notional pension of a person to whom an allowance was payable before the coming into operation of these Regulations under or by reference to the Pensions Increase (Federated Superannuation Scheme for Nurses and Hospital Officers) (Civil Service) Regulations 1969(a), any fraction of a pound in the resulting sum shall be treated as a whole pound.

Payment of benefit equivalent to pensions increase

5. The Minister for the Civil Service may, in respect of any period beginning on or after 1st September 1971, pay to any person to whom these Regulations apply

---

(a) S.I. 1969/1293 (1969 III, p. 3833).

an amount equal to the increase which would be payable to him under the Pensions (Increase) Act 1971 if—

(a) there were payable to him—

(i) a superannuation allowance under the civil service pension scheme of an amount equal to the notional pension ascribed to him under Regulation 4(1) above, and

(ii) in a case where a notional lump sum is ascribed to him under Regulation 4(2) above, a lump sum allowance under the civil service pension scheme of an amount equal to and becoming payable at the same time as that notional lump sum, and

(b) any allowance which might (but for the Pensions (Increase) Act 1971) have been paid to him under the Pensions Increase (Federated Superannuation Scheme for Nurses and Hospital Officers) (Civil Service) Regulations 1969 were a relevant increase within the meaning of section 6(10) of that Act.

Given under the official seal of the Minister for the Civil Service on 14th March 1972.

(L.S.)

A. W. Wyatt,
Authorised by the Minister
for the Civil Service.

SCHEDULE

Regulations 2(1) and 3(2)

Meaning of reckonable service

1. Subject to the provisions of this Schedule, a person's reckonable service shall be a period equivalent to the aggregate of any periods of employment—

(a) which he has spent in any employment described in paragraph 2 below, and

(b) which have become reckonable under an F.S.S.N. scheme as described in paragraph 3 below.

2. The employments to which paragraph 1 above relates are—

(a) employment in the civil service of the State;

(b) employment under an authority which was, or was deemed to be, an employing authority for the purposes of the National Health Service (Superannuation) Regulations 1961(a) or the National Health Service (Superannuation) (Scotland) Regulations 1961(b);

(c) employment under an employing authority or a local Act authority within the meaning of section 1(3) of the Local Government Superannuation Act 1937(c) or section 1(6) of the Local Government Superannuation (Scotland) Act 1937(d);

(d) employment in which the person was subject to any regulations or scheme made under section 2 of the Local Government (Superannuation) Act (Northern Ireland) 1950(e), section 61 of the Health Services Act (Northern Ireland)

(a) S.I. 1961/1441 (1961 II, p. 2824).   (b) S.I. 1961/1398 (1961 II, p. 2697).
(c) 1937 c. 68.   (d) 1937 c. 69.
(e) 1950 c. 10 (N.I.).

1948(a) or section 54 of the National Health Service (Isle of Man) Act 1948 (an Act of Tynwald);

(e) employment by a county or district nursing association during any period when a local health authority had arrangements with, or paid contributions to, that association under Part III of the National Health Service Act 1946(f) or Part III of the National Health Service (Scotland) Act 1947(b).

3. For the purposes of paragraph 1 above, a period of employment shall be deemed to have become reckonable under an F.S.S.N. scheme if—

(a) during such period the person was subject to an F.S.S.N. scheme and the contributions authorised or required to be paid by the employer were duly paid, or

(b) such period was taken into account in calculating a sum in the nature of a transfer value paid to that scheme under the National Health Service (Superannuation) Regulations 1961 or any corresponding provision in Scotland, Northern Ireland, or the Isle of Man or under rules made under section 2 of the Superannuation (Miscellaneous Provisions) Act 1948(d):

Provided that—

(i) so much of any period referred to in sub-paragraph (b) as consisted of non-contributing service shall be reckonable under this paragraph at half its actual length, and

(ii) so much of any such period as consisted of part-time service shall be reckonable under this paragraph as though it were whole-time service of a proportionately reduced period.

4. For the purposes of Regulation 3(1)(b) of these Regulations, there may be added to the service described in paragraph 1 above:—

(a) any service which, during such a period of employment as is defined in paragraph 3(b) above, the person was entitled to reckon for the purpose of determining whether he was eligible to receive a pension but not for calculating the amount thereof; and

(b) any period of employment by a county or district nursing association during which a local authority had arrangements with that association under section 1 of the Midwives Act 1936(e) or section 1 of the Maternity Services (Scotland) Act 1937(f).

5. For the purposes of paragraph 3(a) above no account shall be taken of any period of employment preceding a break of twelve months or more during which the person was not in employment described in paragraph 2 above.

(a) 1948 c. 3 (N.I.).   (b) 1946 c. 81.
(c) 1947 c. 27.   (d) 1948 c. 33.
(e) 1936 c. 40.   (f) 1937 c. 30.

EXPLANATORY NOTE
(This Note is not part of the Regulations.)

Certain persons who have retired from the civil service receive superannuation benefits through a scheme operated under the Federated Superannuation Scheme for Nurses and Hospital Officers (F.S.S.N.), such benefits being lump sums or annuities or both provided by means of insurance policies.

These Regulations provide for the payment of allowances corresponding to the increases for which the persons concerned would have been eligible under the Pensions (Increase) Act 1971 if they had been pensionable in the normal way under the principal civil service pension scheme. The allowances will be calculated on a "notional pension" and, in certain circumstances, a "notional lump sum" corresponding broadly to the pension and lump sum a person would have received if he had been subject to the principal civil service pension scheme and entitled to reckon under that scheme his service during which he was subject to an F.S.S.N. scheme.

In accordance with the power conferred by section 13(5)of the 1971 Act, the Regulations provide for the increases to take effect from 1st September 1971.

1972 No. 399

AGRICULTURE

The Price Stability of Imported Products (Rates of Levy) (Eggs) (No. 6) Order 1972

Made - - - *14th March* 1972

Coming into Operation 15*th March* 1972

The Minister of Agriculture, Fisheries and Food, in exercise of the powers conferred upon him by section 1(2), (4), (5), (6) and (7) of the Agriculture and Horticulture Act 1964 **(a)** and of all other powers enabling him in that behalf, hereby makes the following order:—

1. This order may be cited as the Price Stability of Imported Products (Rates of Levy) (Eggs) (No. 6) Order 1972, and shall come into operation on 15th March 1972.

2.—(1) In this order—

" the Principal Order " means the Price Stability of Imported Products (Levy Arrangements) (Eggs) Order 1970 **(b)** as amended **(c)** and as amended by any subsequent order, and if any such order is replaced by any subsequent order the expression shall be construed as a reference to such subsequent order;

AND other expressions have the same meaning as in the Principal Order.

(2) The Interpretation Act 1889 **(d)** shall apply to the interpretation of this order as it applies to the interpretation of an Act of Parliament and as if this order and the order hereby revoked were Acts of Parliament.

3. In accordance with and subject to the provisions of the Principal Order (which provides for the charging of levies on imports of those eggs and egg products which are specified commodities for the purposes of the Agriculture and Horticulture Act 1964) the rate of general levy for such imports into the United Kingdom of any specified commodity as are described in column 2 of the Schedule to this order in relation to a tariff heading indicated in column 1 of that Schedule shall be the rate set forth in relation thereto in column 3 of that Schedule.

4. The Price Stability of Imported Products (Rates of Levy) (Eggs) (No. 5) Order 1972 **(e)** is hereby revoked.

In Witness whereof the Official Seal of the Minister of Agriculture, Fisheries and Food is hereunto affixed on 14th March 1972.

(L.S.)

G. P. Jupe,
Assistant Secretary.

(a) 1964 c. 28.   (b) S.I. 1970/359 (1970 I, p. 1277).
(c) S.I. 1971/947, 1642 (1971 II, p. 2709; III, p. 4505).
(d) 1889 c. 63.   (e) S.I. 1972/277 (1972 I, p. 930).

SCHEDULE

1. Tariff Heading	2. Description of Imports	3. Rate of General Levy
	Imports of:—	
04.05	*Birds' eggs (in shell or not in shell), fresh, dried or otherwise preserved, sweetened or not, other than egg yolks:*	(per 120 eggs)
	A. Eggs in shell:	*p*
	1. Not exceeding 11 lb. in weight per 120 ..	45
	2. Over 11 lb. but not exceeding 12½ lb. in weight per 120	45
	3. Over 12½ lb. but not exceeding 14 lb. in weight per 120	50
	4. Over 14 lb. but not exceeding 15½ lb. in weight per 120	55
	5. Over 15½ lb. but not exceeding 17 lb. in weight per 120	60
	6. Over 17 lb. in weight per 120	60
	B. Eggs not in shell:	(per ton)
	Whole dried	£250
	Whole frozen or liquid	£165

EXPLANATORY NOTE

(This Note is not part of the Order.)

This order, which comes into operation on 15th March 1972, supersedes the Price Stability of Imported Products (Rates of Levy) (Eggs) (No. 5) Order 1972. It—

(*a*) imposes rates of general levy to be charged on imports of eggs in shell in the weight grades specified in the Schedule to the order ; and

(*b*) reimposes unchanged the rates of general levy to be charged on imports of dried frozen or liquid whole egg not in shell.

STATUTORY INSTRUMENTS

1972 No. 400

AGRICULTURE

The Price Stability of Imported Products (Rates of Levy) (Cereals) (No. 12) Order 1972

Made -	-	-	-	14*th March* 1972	
Coming into Operation			15*th March* 1972		

The Minister of Agriculture, Fisheries and Food, in exercise of the powers conferred upon him by section 1(2), (4), (5) and (6) of the Agriculture and Horticulture Act 1964(a) and of all other powers enabling him in that behalf, hereby makes the following order:—

1. This order may be cited as the Price Stability of Imported Products (Rates of Levy) (Cereals) (No. 12) Order 1972, and shall come into operation on 15th March 1972.

2.—(1) In this order—

" the Principal Order " means the Price Stability of Imported Products (Levy Arrangements) (Cereals) Order 1971(b), as amended by any subsequent order and if any such order is replaced by any subsequent order the expression shall be construed as a reference to such subsequent order;

AND other expressions have the same meaning as in the Principal Order.

(2) The Interpretation Act 1889(c) shall apply to the interpretation of this order as it applies to the interpretation of an Act of Parliament.

3. In accordance with and subject to the provisions of Part II of the Principal Order (which provides for the charging of levies on imports of certain specified commodities) the rate of levy for such imports into the United Kingdom of any specified commodity as are described in column 2 of the Schedule to this order in relation to a tariff heading indicated in column 1 of that Schedule shall be the rate set forth in relation thereto in column 3 of that Schedule.

In Witness whereof the Official Seal of the Minister of Agriculture, Fisheries and Food is hereunto affixed on 14th March 1972.

(L.S.)

> *T. R. M. Sewell,*
> Assistant Secretary.

(a) 1964 c. 28.   (b) S.I. 1971/631 (1971 I, p. 1660).   (c) 1889 c. 63.

SCHEDULE

1. Tariff Heading	2. Description of Imports	3. Rate of Levy
11.01	Imports of:— Wheat flours not containing chalk and containing not more than 1 per cent. by weight of fibre at the prescribed standard moisture content ..	per ton £ 1·25

EXPLANATORY NOTE
(This Note is not part of the Order.)

This order, which comes into operation on 15th March 1972, fixes a rate of levy of £1·25 per ton to be charged on imports into the United Kingdom of wheat flours not containing chalk and containing not more than 1 per cent. by weight of fibre at the prescribed standard moisture content.

STATUTORY INSTRUMENTS

1972 No. 403

PLANT BREEDERS' RIGHTS

The Plant Breeders' Rights (Applications in Designated Countries) (Amendment) Order 1972

Made - - -	14*th March* 1972
Coming into Operation	4*th April* 1972

The Minister of Agriculture, Fisheries and Food, the Secretary of State for Scotland and the Secretary of State for the Home Department (being the Secretary of State concerned with agriculture in Northern Ireland), acting jointly, in exercise of the powers conferred on them by paragraph 2(7) of Part I of Schedule 2 to the Plant Varieties and Seeds Act 1964(a), as extended to Northern Ireland by the Plant Varieties and Seeds (Northern Ireland) Order 1964(b) and to the Isle of Man by the Plant Varieties and Seeds (Isle of Man) Order 1969(c), and of all other powers enabling them in that behalf, hereby make the following order: —

Citation, commencement and interpretation

1.—(1) This order may be cited as the Plant Breeders' Rights (Applications in Designated Countries) (Amendment) Order 1972 and shall come into operation on 4th April 1972.

(2) The Interpretation Act 1889(d) shall apply to the interpretation of this order as it applies to the interpretation of an Act of Parliament.

Designated countries in respect of applications for plant breeders' rights

2. The Plant Breeders' Rights (Applications in Designated Countries) Order 1968(e) is hereby amended as follows: —

In Article 2—

(*a*) the word "and" appearing after the word "Germany" shall be omitted; and

(*b*) the words "France and Sweden" shall be added after the word "Denmark".

(a) 1964 c. 14.
(c) S.I. 1969/1829 (1969 III, p. 5701).
(e) S.I. 1968/2077 (1968 III, p. 5620).

(b) S.I. 1964/1574 (1964 III, p. 3543).
(d) 1889 c. 63.

In Witness whereof the Official Seal of the Minister of Agriculture, Fisheries and Food is hereunto affixed on 13th March 1972.

(L.S.)   *J. M. L. Prior,*
                              Minister of Agriculture, Fisheries and Food.

                                              Gordon Campbell,
13th March 1972.   Secretary of State for Scotland.

                                              R. Maudling,
14th March 1972.   Secretary of State for the Home Department.

EXPLANATORY NOTE

(This Note is not part of the Order.)

Paragraph 2 of Part I of Schedule 2 to the Plant Varieties and Seeds Act 1964 enables an application for a grant of plant breeders' rights, made in a country to which that paragraph applies, to be treated as if made in the United Kingdom. This order adds France and Sweden to the countries to which the paragraph applies.

STATUTORY INSTRUMENTS

1972 No. 406

CUSTOMS AND EXCISE

The Import Duty Drawbacks (No. 1) Order 1972

Made - - - -	*16th March* 1972
Laid before the House of Commons	*22nd March* 1972
Coming into Operation	*13th April* 1972

The Lords Commissioners of Her Majesty's Treasury, by virtue of the powers conferred on them by sections 9 and 13 of, and Schedule 5 to, the Import Duties Act 1958(**a**), and of all other powers enabling them in that behalf, on the recommendation of the Secretary of State hereby make the following Order:—

1.—(1) This Order may be cited as the Import Duty Drawbacks (No. 1) Order 1972.

(2) The Interpretation Act 1889(**b**) shall apply for the interpretation of this Order as it applies for the interpretation of an Act of Parliament.

(3) This Order shall come into operation on 13th April 1972.

2. In Schedule 2 to the Import Duty Drawbacks (No. 1) Order 1971(**c**) (which relates to the drawbacks to be allowed on the exportation of goods produced or manufactured from imported articles)—

(*a*) in the entry relating to linseed oil and goods made with linseed oil (other than printers' inks), for paragraphs 3 to 8 there shall be substituted the paragraphs set out in the Schedule to this Order; and

(*b*) in the entry relating to printers' inks and printing ink base, in column 3 (in relation to entry (B) in column 2) for the words " £15·3500 per ton of linseed oil " there shall be substituted the words " £12·4400 per ton of linseed oil ".

Walter Clegg,
Tim Fortescue,
Two of the Lords Commissioners
of Her Majesty's Treasury.

16th March 1972.

(**a**) 1958 c. 6.   (**b**) 1889 c. 63.   (**c**) S.I. 1971/274 (1971 I, p. 939)

SCHEDULE

REVISED PARAGRAPHS 3 TO 8 OF ENTRY FOR LINSEED OIL AND
GOODS MADE THEREWITH (EXCLUDING PRINTERS' INKS)

Exported goods	Imported goods	Rate of drawback
3. Linseed oil fatty acids (being the acids obtained by the hydrolysis of linseed oil).	Linseed oil.	£12·2800 per ton of linseed oil fatty acids.
4. Linoleum, not printed, manufactured on a base of jute canvas, cotton or spun rayon cloth.	Linseed oil.	£2·5900 per ton of linoleum.
5. Linoleum, not printed, manufactured on a base of bitumenised felt.	Linseed oil.	£1·9500 per ton of linoleum.
6. Cork carpets; unpigmented linoleum composition manufactured on a base of flannelette.	Linseed oil.	£2·5000 per ton of cork carpet or linoleum composition.
7. Felt base.	Linseed oil.	£0·3100 per ton of felt base.
8. Blocks, tiles and similar articles, of a kind used for floors, walls or staircases, consisting mainly (by weight) of cement, lime, and plaster, and impregnated with linseed oil, of dimensions not greater than 10 inches in length or width.	Linseed oil.	£1·4100 per ton of blocks, tiles or other articles.

EXPLANATORY NOTE

(This note does not form part of the Order)

This Order revises the rates of drawback of import duty for certain specified linseed oil goods manufactured from imported linseed oil.

STATUTORY INSTRUMENTS

1972 No. 407 (S.31)

CROFTERS, COTTARS AND SMALL LANDHOLDERS, SCOTLAND

The Crofting Counties Agricultural Grants (Scotland) Scheme 1972

Made - - -	*15th March* 1972
Laid before Parliament	*17th March* 1972
Coming into Operation	*19th March* 1972

In exercise of the powers conferred on me by section 22(1) of the Crofters (Scotland) Act 1955(**a**) and section 14(1) of the Crofters (Scotland) Act 1961(**b**), and of all other powers enabling me in that behalf and after consultation with the Crofters Commission and with the approval of the Treasury, I hereby make the following scheme:—

Citation and commencement

1. This scheme may be cited as the Crofting Counties Agricultural Grants (Scotland) Scheme 1972 and shall come into operation on 19th March 1972.

Interpretation

2.—(1) In this scheme, unless the context otherwise requires—

"the Act of 1955" means the Crofters (Scotland) Act 1955;

"the Act of 1961" means the Crofters (Scotland) Act 1961;

"approved" means approved by the Secretary of State in writing, and "approve" and "approval" shall be construed accordingly;

"crofter" includes any grazings committee or grazings constable appointed under section 24 of the Act of 1955 and in the application of this scheme to a grazings committee or a grazings constable any reference to a croft shall be construed as a reference to the common grazings for the management of which the committee or, as the case may be, the grazings constable is responsible;

"eligible occupier" has the meaning assigned to it by paragraph 3 of this scheme;

"operation" means any of the operations specified in the Schedule to this scheme.

(**a**) 1955 c. 21.   (**b**) 1961 c. 58.

(2) The Interpretation Act 1889(**a**) shall apply to the interpretation of this scheme as it applies to the interpretation of an Act of Parliament.

(3) Except insofar as the context otherwise requires, any reference in this scheme to an enactment shall be construed as a reference to that enactment as amended or extended by any other enactment.

Eligible occupier

3.—(1) For the purposes of this scheme, the expression "eligible occupier" means any one of the following occupiers, that is to say—

(*a*) the occupier of a croft who is also the owner thereof and who in the opinion of the Secretary of State is of substantially the same economic status as a crofter;

(*b*) the occupier of a holding, other than a croft, situated in the crofting counties which is either a holding of which the area does not exceed 75 acres (exclusive of any common pasture or grazing held therewith), or a holding the annual rent of which, if it were a croft let to a crofter under the Act of 1955 and the Act of 1961, would not, in the opinion of the Secretary of State, exceed £50, being an occupier who in the opinion of the Secretary of State is of substantially the same economic status as a crofter; or

(*c*) the subtenant of a croft or part of a croft occupying under a sublease intimated to the Crofters Commission under section 11(1) of the Act of 1961 or granted by a crofter with the consent of the Crofters Commission and in accordance with any conditions imposed by them under section 11(3) of the Act of 1961.

(2) Any reference in any other scheme to "an eligible occupier within the meaning of the Crofting Counties Agricultural Grants (Scotland) Scheme 1965" (**b**) shall be deemed to include a reference to an eligible occupier within the meaning of this scheme.

Part I

Grants in respect of Operations

Grants to be made

4.—(1) Subject to the provisions of this scheme, the Secretary of State may make a grant under this part of this scheme to a crofter or eligible occupier towards the approved cost of any operation of a kind specified in the Schedule to this scheme carried out by him or on his behalf for the purpose of aiding and developing agricultural production, in the case of a crofter, on his croft and, in the case of an eligible occupier, on the croft or holding or part of a croft, as the case may be, in respect of which he is the eligible occupier.

(**a**) 1889 c. 63. (**b**) S.I. 1965/1519 (1965 II, p. 4399).

(2) For the purpose of this paragraph, "approved cost" shall mean the cost approved for the purposes of a grant under this part of this scheme and comprising the aggregate of—

(*a*) the expenditure reasonably incurred by the applicant in respect of materials required for the purpose of carrying out the relevant operation and

(*b*) such sum as the Secretary of State may deem it reasonable to allow in respect of the labour necessary for that purpose.

(3) Any application by a crofter or eligible occupier for approval of the cost of any such operation shall be made in such form and manner and at such time as the Secretary of State may from time to time require and the applicant shall furnish all such particulars and information relating to the operation as the Secretary of State may require.

(4) The Secretary of State may, as he thinks fit, either refuse to approve the cost of any such operation or approve it in whole or in part for the purposes of a grant under this part of this scheme and any such approval may be given, and any such grant may be made, subject to such conditions as the Secretary of State thinks fit.

(5) Any approval of cost for the purposes of a grant under this part of this scheme may be varied or withdrawn by the Secretary of State with the applicant's written consent.

Amounts of grant

5.—(1) The amounts of grant payable under this part of this scheme shall be determined in accordance with the provisions of the Schedule to this scheme.

(2) If the Secretary of State is satisfied that any condition subject to which a grant under this part of this scheme may be made has not been complied with in carrying out the relevant operation, he may, notwithstanding the immediately preceding sub-paragraph, either withhold payment of the grant or make payment of a grant of such amount as he may in all the circumstances of the case consider reasonable.

PART II

GRANTS IN RESPECT OF CONTRIBUTIONS

Grants to be made

6.—(1) Subject to the provisions of this scheme, the Secretary of State may make a grant under this part of this scheme to a crofter or eligible occupier in respect of any contribution made by him under any such agreement as is referred to in section 10(1) of the Highways (Provision of Cattle-Grids) Act 1950(**a**) towards the expenses of the provision of a cattle-grid for

---

(**a**) 1950 c. 24.

the purpose of aiding and developing agricultural production, in the case of a crofter, on his croft and, in the case of an eligible occupier, on the croft or holding or part of a croft, as the case may be, in respect of which he is the eligible occupier.

(2) Any application by a crofter or eligible occupier for a grant under this part of this scheme shall be made in such form and manner and at such time as the Secretary of State may from time to time require and the applicant shall furnish all such particulars and information in regard to the cattle-grid provided or proposed to be provided as the Secretary of State may require.

(3) Any grant which may be made under this part of this scheme shall be subject to such conditions as may be intimated in writing to the applicant by the Secretary of State at the time of the making of the grant.

Amounts of grant

7. The amounts of grant payable under this part of this scheme shall be determined in accordance with the provisions of the Schedule to this scheme.

Part III

General

Abatement of grant

8. The Secretary of State may reduce or withhold grant payable under this scheme in any case where assistance in respect of cost towards which grant is payable has been or may be given otherwise than under this scheme.

Recovery of grant

9. Where any condition subject to which a grant has been made under this scheme fails to be complied with by the applicant after the date upon which the grant has been made and the Secretary of State is satisfied at any time that that condition is not being complied with, he may recover the amount of the grant or such part thereof as he may in all the circumstances consider reasonable in like manner as if it were a debt due by the applicant to him.

Crofters Commission to be agents

10.—(1) The Secretary of State hereby appoints the Crofters Commission to be his agents for the purpose of the administration of any grant applied for or made under this scheme so far as it relates to crofts:

Provided that nothing in this sub-paragraph shall be construed as enabling the Crofters Commission to make payment of any grant under this scheme.

(2) In carrying out their functions as agents as aforesaid of the Secretary of State under this scheme, the Crofters Commission shall have the like powers, rights and duties as are conferred by it upon the Secretary of State.

Gordon Campbell,
One of Her Majesty's Principal
Secretaries of State.

St. Andrew's House,
Edinburgh.
13th March 1972.

We approve.

Walter Clegg,
Tim Fortescue,
Two of the Lords Commissioners of
Her Majesty's Treasury.

15th March 1972.

Paragraphs 4(1), 5(1) and 7

SCHEDULE

1. Subject to the provisions of this Schedule and of paragraph 8 of this scheme, the amount of any grant payable under this scheme towards the approved cost of any operation specified in column 1 of this Schedule shall not exceed a sum equal to the percentage of that cost specified in relation to that operation in column 2 of this Schedule.

Column 1	*Column 2*
Operation	*Percentage of Approved Cost*
	per cent
1. Cropping of marginal land.	85
2. Improvement of land by reclamation, regeneration or reconditioning.	85
3. Drainage.	75
4. Bracken cutting.	60
5. Removal of whins, gorse, bushes, scrub, stumps, roots, boulders or other like obstructions to cultivation.	60
6. Provision or improvement of pit or clamp silos.	60
7. Provision of field shelter for cattle or sheep.	60
8. Provision or improvement of fixed equipment for the handling or treatment of sheep or cattle.	60
9. Provision of fencing or cattle-grids.	60
10. Planting of shelter belts.	85
11. Provision of electrical equipment.	60
12. Provision or improvement of roads, bridges or boat slips.	60
13. Provision of water supplies.	60

2. The amount of any grant payable under this scheme towards the approved cost of carrying out any operation which is incidental to the carrying out of an operation of any kind specified in this Schedule or necessary or proper in the carrying out of that operation or for securing the full benefit thereof shall be calculated at the rate of grant appropriate to that operation in accordance with the provisions of this Schedule.

3. In such cases and subject to such conditions as the Secretary of State may from time to time determine, the amount of any cost towards which grant is payable under this scheme shall, if the applicant so elects, be taken for the purpose of determining the amount of the grant as such standard amount as the Secretary of State may from time to time fix with the approval of the Treasury.

EXPLANATORY NOTE

(This Note is not part of the Scheme.)

This Scheme, made with the approval of the Treasury under section 22 of the Crofters (Scotland) Act 1955 and section 14 of the Crofters (Scotland) Act 1961, provides that the Secretary of State may make grants to crofters and certain other occupiers of land in the crofting counties in Scotland (*a*) in respect of specified operations carried out by them for the purpose of aiding and developing agricultural production on crofts and holdings, and (*b*) in respect of contributions made by them under certain arrangements towards the expenses of provision of cattle-grids for the purpose foresaid.

This Scheme differs from the 1965 Scheme (S.I. 1965/1519), as amended by the 1970 Amendment Scheme (S.I. 1970/572), in that it is no longer necessary for a formal offer of grant to have been made by the Secretary of State before grant may be paid under the Scheme. The Scheme also makes provision for payment of grant on the basis of standard costs and for changes in the rates of grant which will apply to applications made on or after 19th March 1972.

STOKE-ON-TRENT
CITY
LIBRARIES

STATUTORY INSTRUMENTS

1972 No. 419

DEFENCE

The Rules of Procedure (Air Force) 1972

Made - - - -	*14th March* 1972
Laid before Parliament	*7th April* 1972
Coming into Operation	*In accordance with Rule* 1

ARRANGEMENT OF RULES

Citation and commencement

Rule

1. Citation and commencement.

Definitions and interpretation

2. Definitions.
3. Interpretation Act 1889.

Arrest and avoidance of delay

4. Avoidance of delay by commanding officers in investigating charges.
5. Eight day delay reports.
6. Arrest not to exceed 72 days without permission from higher authority.

Investigation of charges by commanding officer

7. Methods of investigating charges.
8. Hearing of evidence by commanding officer.
9. Summary of evidence.
10. Abstract of evidence.
11. Investigation before summary dealing by commanding officer.
12. Notice of alibi.
13. Reference of charges to higher authority.

SCHEDULE 1

Forms for commanding officers

SCHEDULE 2

Charge-sheets

SCHEDULE 3

Record of proceedings before an appropriate superior authority

SCHEDULE 4
Court-martial forms

Rule

1. Convening orders.
2. Declarations under Rules 103 and 104.
3. Order to inspect bankers' books and to take copies of entries.
4. Summons to a witness to attend a court-martial.
5. Notices requiring oral evidence to be given in lieu of a written statement.
6. Record of proceedings of a court-martial.
7. Findings.
8. Record of reconsideration of finding under Rule 80(5).
9. Service record of accused.
10. Record of proceedings on revision under section 109 of the Act.
11. Confirmation.
12. Determination by a confirming officer or reviewing authority of a suspended sentence, and direction that sentences are to run concurrently or consecutively.
13. Direction under section 127(4) of the Act.
14. Restitution order.
15. Promulgation.

SCHEDULE 5
Sentences

1. Sentences.
2. Forfeiture of seniority.
3. Consecutive sentences of imprisonment for offences against section 70 of the Act.
4. Order that sentences are to begin to run on the expiry of some other sentence.
5. Determination of a suspended sentence and direction that sentences are to run concurrently or consecutively.
6. Recommendation under section 127(4) of the Act.
7. Restitution order.

SCHEDULE 6
Oaths and affirmations

1. Oaths at investigations by commanding officers and appropriate superior authorities.
2. Oaths at courts martial.
3. Scottish oaths.
4. Manner of administering oaths.
5. Solemn affirmations.

SCHEDULE 7
Petitions

1. Petitions.
2. List of persons to whom petitions may be presented under Rule of Procedure 100.

SCHEDULE 8
Revocation of previous rules

The Secretary of State in exercise of the powers conferred upon him by sections 103, 104, 105 and 106 of the Air Force Act, 1955(a), and of all other powers enabling him in that behalf, hereby makes the following rules:—

CITATION AND COMMENCEMENT

1. These Rules may be cited as the Rules of Procedure (Air Force), 1972, and shall come into operation on such date as the Armed Forces Act 1971(b), comes into force.

DEFINITIONS AND INTERPRETATION

Definitions

2.—(1) In these Rules:

"child" means a person under the age of 14 years;

"convening a fresh court" includes dissolving the existing court;

"member" when used in relation to a court-martial does not include the president;

"sexual offence" means in relation to an offence against section 70 of the Act any offence under the Sexual Offences Act, 1956(c), or the Indecency with Children Act, 1960(d), or any attempt to commit such an offence and shall include any offence of an indecent or unnatural kind under section 66 of the Act or any attempt to commit such an offence under section 68A of the Act or an offence of an indecent kind under section 69 of the Act;

"special finding" means when used in relation to:

(*a*) section 98 of the Act, any finding which a court-martial may make in accordance with that section;

(*b*) section 116 of the Act, a finding in accordance with Sub-section (2) of that section that the accused is not guilty by reason of insanity.

(*c*) Rule 66(3), a finding that the accused is guilty of the charge subject to the exception or variation specified in the finding.

"the Act" means the Air Force Act 1955.

"young person" means a person who has attained the age of 14 years and is under the age of 17 years;

(2) Other expressions in these Rules have the same meanings as if these Rules formed part of the Act.

(3) Any reference in these Rules to an enactment contained in the Act, being an enactment amended by another enactment or by an instrument having effect under an enactment, whether passed or made before or after the coming into effect of this paragraph, shall, unless the contrary intention appears, be construed as referring to that enactment as so amended.

Interpretation Act, 1889

3. The Interpretation Act, 1889(e), shall apply to the interpretation of these Rules as it applies to the interpretation of an Act of Parliament and, in particular, words importing the masculine gender shall include females, and words in the singular shall include the plural, and words in the plural shall include the singular.

(a) 1955 c. 19. (b) 1971 c. 33.
(c) 1956 c. 69. (d) 1960 c. 33.
(e) 1889 c. 63.

ARREST AND AVOIDANCE OF DELAY

Avoidance of delay by commanding officers in investigating charges

4.—(1) When a person is detained by air-force authority in arrest his commanding officer shall, unless it is impracticable, within forty-eight hours of becoming aware that he is so detained have such person brought before him, inform him of the charge against him and begin to investigate it.

(2) Every case of such a person being detained in arrest beyond the period of forty-eight hours referred to in this Rule without such investigation having begun and the reason therefor shall be reported by his commanding officer to higher authority.

Eight day delay reports

5. The report required by section 75(2) of the Act with regard to the necessity for further delay in bringing an accused to trial shall be in the form set out in Schedule 1 to these Rules and shall be signed by his commanding officer. The report shall be sent to the officer who would be responsible for convening a court-martial for the trial of the accused and a copy thereof shall be sent direct to the Director of Legal Services or his representative.

Arrest not to exceed 72 days without permission from higher authority

6. An accused shall not be held in arrest for more than seventy-two consecutive days without a court-martial being convened for his trial, unless the officer who would be responsible for convening the court-martial directs in writing that he shall not be released from arrest. When giving such a direction, such officer shall state his reasons for giving it.

INVESTIGATION OF CHARGES BY COMMANDING OFFICER

Methods of investigating charges

7.—(1) Subject to paragraphs (3) and (4) of this Rule, when a commanding officer investigates a charge he shall first read and, if necessary, explain the charge to the accused and shall then:

    (*a*) hear the evidence himself in accordance with Rule 8; or

    (*b*) cause the evidence to be reduced to writing, in accordance with paragraph (2) of this Rule, and read and consider it:

Provided that:

    (*a*) notwithstanding that he has heard all or part of the evidence himself, he may cause the evidence to be reduced to writing:

    (*b*) after the evidence has been reduced to writing and he has considered it, he may himself hear evidence in accordance with Rule 8; and

    (*c*) before he submits to higher authority a charge against an officer or warrant officer or a civilian to whom Part II of the Act is applied by section 208A or section 209 of the Act or remands a non-commissioned officer or airman for trial by court-martial he shall cause the evidence to be reduced to writing.

(2) Evidence may be reduced to writing in the form of a summary of evidence taken in accordance with Rule 9 or an abstract of evidence made in accordance with Rule 10:

Provided that a summary of evidence must be taken if:—

    (*a*) the maximum punishment for the offence with which the accused is charged is death; or

    (*b*) the accused, at any time before the charge against him is referred to higher authority in accordance with Rule 13 requires in writing that a summary of evidence be taken; or

    (*c*) the commanding officer is of the opinion that the interests of justice require that a summary of evidence be taken.

(3) Where the evidence taken in accordance with paragraph (1) of this Rule discloses an offence other than the offence which is the subject of the investigation, a new charge alleging that offence may be preferred against the accused in addition to, or in substitution for, the original charge and the investigation of the original charge may be treated, for the purposes of these Rules, as the investigation of the added or substituted charge.

(4) Where a civilian, to whom Part II of the Act is applied by section 208A or section 209 of the Act, is charged with an offence with which an appropriate superior authority can deal summarily, it shall not be necessary for his commanding officer to read the charge to the accused: but it shall be a sufficient compliance with the provisions of this Rule if his commanding officer causes to be delivered to the accused a copy of the charge and of the abstract of evidence and considers them together with any statement made by the accused under Rule 10(2), and any statements of witnesses submitted by the accused under Rule 10(3).

Hearing of evidence by commanding officer

8. When a commanding officer investigates a charge by hearing the evidence himself:

    (*a*) each prosecution witness shall give his evidence orally in the presence of the accused, or the commanding officer shall read to the accused a written statement made by the witness:

        Provided that a written statement of a prosecution witness shall not be used if the accused requires that the witness shall give his evidence orally.

    (*b*) the accused shall be allowed to cross-examine any prosecution witness;

    (*c*) the accused may, on his own behalf, give evidence on oath or may make a statement without being sworn;

    (*d*) the accused may call witnesses in his defence, who shall give their evidence orally and in his presence;

    (*e*) the evidence shall not be given on oath unless the commanding officer so directs or the accused so demands;

    (*f*) if the evidence is given on oath, the commanding officer shall, subject to the accused's right to make a statement without being sworn, administer the oath to each witness and to any interpreter in accordance with Rule 34.

Summary of evidence

9. A summary of evidence shall be taken in the following manner and shall be in accordance with the form set out in Schedule 1 to these Rules:

    (*a*) it shall be taken in the presence of the accused by the commanding officer or by another officer on the direction of the commanding officer;

(*b*) the prosecution witnesses shall give their evidence orally and the accused shall be allowed to cross-examine any prosecution witness;

Provided that, if a person cannot be compelled to attend as a prosecution witness or if, owing to the exigencies of the service or on other grounds (including the expense and loss of time involved), the attendance of any prosecution witness cannot, in the opinion of the officer taking the summary (to be certified by him in writing), be readily procured, a written statement of his evidence, purporting to be signed by him, may be read to the accused and included in the summary of evidence; but, if such witness can be compelled to attend, the accused may insist that he shall attend for cross-examination;

(*c*) A child shall not be called as a prosecution witness in any case where the charge being investigated is for a sexual offence and any statement made in writing by or taken in writing from the child which would be admissible if given orally may be read to the accused and included in the summary of evidence:

Provided that this paragraph shall have no application where the child can be compelled to attend and the accused objects to the application of this paragraph or the officer taking the summary of evidence requires the attendance of the child for the purpose of establishing the identity of any person or is satisfied it has not been possible to obtain from the child a statement that may be given in evidence under this paragraph;

(*d*) after all the evidence against the accused has been given, the accused shall be asked:

"Do you wish to say anything? You are not obliged to do so, but, if you wish, you may give evidence on oath, or you may make a statement without being sworn. Any evidence you give or statement you make will be taken down in writing and may be given in evidence."

Any evidence given or statement made by the accused shall be recorded in writing and, immediately thereafter, the record of his evidence or statement shall be read over to him and corrected where necessary and he shall be asked to sign it;

(*e*) the accused may call witnesses in his defence, who shall give their evidence orally;

Provided that, if a person cannot be compelled to attend as a defence witness or if, owing to the exigencies of the service or other grounds (including the expense and loss of time involved), the attendance of any defence witness cannot, in the opinion of the officer taking the summary (to be certified by him in writing), be readily procured, a written statement of his evidence, purporting to be signed by him, may be read to the accused and included in the summary of evidence;

(*f*) neither the accused nor the witnesses for the defence shall be subject to cross-examination;

(*g*) the evidence of each witness (other than the accused) who gives evidence orally shall be recorded in writing and, immediately thereafter, the record of his evidence shall be read over to him, corrected where necessary and signed by him;

(*h*) the record of the evidence may be in narrative form, save that any question put to a witness in cross-examination by the accused, and the answer thereto, shall be recorded *verbatim* if the accused so requires;

(*i*) the oath shall be administered in accordance with Rule 34 by the officer taking the summary of evidence, to each witness before he gives his evidence, and to any interpreter:

Provided that, where any child of tender years, called as a witness, does not, in the opinion of the officer taking the summary, understand the nature of an oath his evidence may be received, though not given upon oath, if, in the opinion of the officer taking the summary, he is possessed of sufficient intelligence to justify the reception of the evidence and understands the duty of speaking the truth; and

(*j*) at the conclusion of the taking of the summary of evidence, the officer taking it shall certify thereon that he has complied with the provisions of this Rule.

Abstract of evidence

10.—(1) An abstract of evidence shall be made in the following way and shall be in accordance with the form set out in Schedule 1 to these Rules:

(*a*) it shall be made by the commanding officer or by another officer on the direction of the commanding officer;

(*b*) the accused should not be present while the abstract of evidence is being made;

(*c*) it shall consist of signed statements by such witnesses as are necessary to prove the charge and such statements of witnesses as are submitted by the accused in accordance with paragraph (3) of this Rule;

Provided that if, in the case of any witness, a signed statement is not readily procurable, a precis of the evidence to be given by that witness may be included instead of a signed statement; and

(*d*) an oath shall not be administered to a witness making a statement for inclusion in an abstract of evidence, but use may be made, where necessary, of sworn statements which are already in existence.

(2) When an abstract of evidence has been made in accordance with paragraph (1) of this Rule, a copy of it shall be handed to the accused and he shall then be cautioned in the following terms:—

"This is a copy of the abstract of evidence in your case; you are not obliged to say anything with regard to it unless you wish to do so, but you should read it and, when you have read it, if you wish to say anything what you say will be taken down in writing and may be given in evidence."

Any statement made by the accused after he has read the abstract of evidence shall be taken down in writing and he shall be asked to sign it.

(3) After the accused has been given an opportunity of making a statement in accordance with paragraph (2) of this Rule, and after his statement (if any) has been recorded, he may submit to the officer making the abstract the statements of any witnesses he wishes to be attached to the abstract of evidence.

(4) Any statement made by the accused in accordance with paragraph (2) of this Rule and any statements of witnesses submitted by him in accordance with paragraph (3) of this Rule shall be attached to the abstract of evidence.

(5) A certificate by the person who recorded the statement made by the accused in accordance with paragraph (2) of this Rule, stating that the accused was duly cautioned in accordance with this Rule, shall be attached to the abstract of evidence and shall thereafter form part of it. This certificate shall be in the form set out in Schedule 1 to these Rules.

Investigation before summary dealing by commanding officer

11. Before a commanding officer deals summarily with a charge after the evidence has been reduced to writing:

(*a*) any prosecution witness who has not given his evidence orally shall do so if the accused requires it; and

(*b*) the commanding officer shall give the accused a further opportunity to give evidence on oath or to make a statement without being sworn and to call witnesses in his defence.

Notice of alibi

12. At the time when he remands the accused for trial by court-martial the accused's commanding officer shall inform the accused of the requirements of section 11 of the Criminal Justice Act, 1967**(a)**, as modified by the Courts-Martial (Evidence) Regulations, 1967**(b)**.

Provided that the accused's commanding officer shall not be required to give this warning in any case where it appears to him that, having regard to the nature of the offence with which the accused is charged, it is unnecessary to do so.

Reference of charges to higher authority

13.—(1) When a commanding officer submits to higher authority a charge against an officer or warrant officer or a civilian to whom Part II of the Act is applied by section 208A or section 209 of the Act, or has remanded a non-commissioned officer or airman for trial by court-martial he shall send to higher authority:—

(*a*) a copy of the charge on which the accused is held;

(*b*) a draft charge-sheet containing the charges upon which the commanding officer considers that the accused should be dealt with summarily or tried by court-martial;

(*c*) the summary or abstract of evidence;

(*d*) a statement of the character and, in the case of a warrant officer, non-commissioned officer or airman, service record of the accused; and

(*e*) a recommendation as to how the charge should be proceeded with.

(2) After a commanding officer has referred a charge to higher authority in accordance with paragraph (1) of this Rule he shall not dismiss it unless it has been referred back to him with a direction to dismiss it.

PREPARATION OF CHARGE-SHEETS AND FRAMING OF CHARGES

Charge-sheets

14.—(1) A charge-sheet shall contain the whole of the issue or issues to be tried at one time and may contain more than one charge if the charges are founded on the same facts or form or are part of a series of offences of the same or a similar character:

(a) 1967 c. 80. (b) S.I. 1967/1807 (1967 III, p. 4830).

Provided that charges under section, 37(1) section 38, section 46(1) (where the charge is connected with a charge under either of the before mentioned provisions) or section 56 of the Act may be included in any charge-sheet, notwithstanding that other charges in that charge-sheet are not founded on the same facts and do not form or are not part of a series of offences of the same or a similar character.

(2) Every charge-sheet shall in its layout follow the appropriate illustration given in Schedule 2 to these Rules.

(3) The commencement of each charge-sheet shall be in the appropriate form set out in Schedule 2 to these Rules and shall state the number, rank, name and unit of the accused and show by the description of the accused or directly by an express averment that he is subject to air-force law or otherwise liable to trial by court-martial.

Charges

15.—(1) Each charge shall state one offence only.

(2) Offences may be charged in the alternative in separate charges but in no case shall they be charged in the alternative in the same charge. When charges are laid in the alternative they should be set out in order of gravity commencing with the most serious.

(3) Each charge shall consist of two parts, namely:—

    (*a*) the statement of the offence, and

    (*b*) the particulars of the act, neglect or omission constituting the offence.

(4) The statement of an offence, if it is not a civil offence, shall be in the appropriate form set out in Schedule 2 to these Rules, if it is a civil offence in such words as sufficiently describe that offence.

(5) The particulars shall state:—

    (*a*) such circumstances respecting the alleged offence as will enable the accused to know every act, neglect or omission which it is intended to prove against him as constituting the offence;

    (*b*) when the offence charged is one which can be committed either in circumstances involving a higher degree of punishment or in circumstances involving a less degree of punishment, facts which it is intended to prove as rendering the accused liable to the higher degree of punishment if convicted; and

    (*c*) any additional facts which it is intended to prove as rendering the accused liable to the punishment of stoppages if convicted.

Joint Charges

16.—(1) Any number of accused may be charged in the same charge-sheet with offences alleged to have been committed by them separately, if the acts on which the charges are founded are so connected that it is in the interests of justice that they be tried together.

(2)(*a*) Any number of accused may be charged jointly in one charge for an offence committed by them jointly.

    (*b*) Where so charged any one or more of such accused may at the same time be charged in the same charge-sheet with any other offence alleged to have been committed by him or them individually or jointly:

Provided that such charges could, if the accused to whom they relate had been tried separately, have been included under Rule 14(1) in the same charge-sheet as the other charges against him.

Construction of charge-sheets and charges

17. In the construction of a charge-sheet or charge there shall be presumed in favour of supporting it every proposition which may reasonably be presumed to be impliedly included, though not expressed therein, and the statement of the offence and the particulars of the offence shall be read and construed together.

ACTION BY HIGHER AUTHORITY ON RECEIPT OF A CHARGE

Action by higher authority on receipt of a charge

18. When a higher authority receives a charge against an accused, he shall, if he does not refer it back to the commanding officer or deal summarily with it himself or himself convene a court-martial to try the accused, refer the charge either to an appropriate superior authority in order that that authority may deal summarily with it or to the officer who would be responsible for convening the appropriate court-martial to try the accused, and shall, when he so refers the charge, send to the appropriate superior authority or other officer concerned the documents mentioned in Rule 13 together with his own recommendations as to how the case should be proceeded with.

INVESTIGATION OF, AND SUMMARY DEALING WITH, CHARGES BY AN APPROPRIATE SUPERIOR AUTHORITY

Documents to be given to officers, warrant officers and civilians dealt with summarily

19. An appropriate superior authority shall ensure before investigating and dealing summarily with a charge that the accused is given, not less than twenty-four hours before the charge is so investigated and dealt with, a copy of the charge-sheet containing the charge upon which he will be so dealt with and a copy of the summary or abstract of evidence.

Investigation of and summary dealings with charges against officers, warrant officers and civilians

20. When an appropriate superior authority investigates and deals summarily with a charge:

(*a*) he shall first read the charge to the accused;

(*b*) the witnesses against the accused need not give their evidence orally if the accused has so agreed in writing but if the accused has not so agreed they shall give their evidence orally in his presence and he shall be allowed to cross-examine them. If the witnesses against the accused do not give their evidence orally the appropriate superior authority shall read the summary or abstract of evidence to the accused if he so requires;

(*c*) the accused in his defence may adduce evidence as to the facts of the case and as to his character and in mitigation of punishment;

(*d*) the accused himself may give evidence on oath, make a statement without being sworn or hand in a written statement;

(*e*) each witness who gives evidence shall give it on oath and the oath shall be administered by the appropriate superior authority to each witness and to any interpreter in accordance with Rule 34;

(f) when an appropriate superior authority awards the punishment of forfeiture of seniority the award shall be in the appropriate form set out in Schedule 5 to these Rules; and

(g) a record shall be made of the proceedings in accordance with the form set out in Schedule 3 to these Rules.

Alternative courses open to an appropriate superior authority

21. An appropriate superior authority shall, if an accused elects to be tried by court-martial or the appropriate superior authority in the course of investigating a charge determines that it is desirable that the charge should be tried by court-martial, either himself convene the court-martial or refer the charge to higher authority in accordance with Rule 18.

CONVENING OF COURTS-MARTIAL

Duties of convening officer when convening courts-martial

22.—(1) Subject to paragraphs (2) and (3) of this Rule when an officer convenes a court-martial he shall:

(a) issue a convening order in the appropriate form set out in Schedule 4 to these Rules;

(b) direct upon what charges the accused is to be tried and ensure that the accused is remanded for trial by court-martial upon those charges either by his commanding officer or by the appropriate superior authority who has investigated them;

(c) if he is of the opinion that charges should be put in separate charge-sheets, so direct and direct the order in which they are to be tried;

(d) direct, if there is more than one accused, whether the accused are to be tried jointly or separately;

(e) appoint the president and member of the court and any waiting members in accordance with Rule 23;

(f) if convening:

(i) a general court-martial; or

(ii) a district or field general court-martial at which he considers there should be a judge advocate;

take the necessary steps to procure the appointment of a judge advocate by or on behalf of the Judge Advocate General and failing such appointment, himself appoint a suitable person so to act;

(g) appoint an officer subject to air-force law or counsel assisted by such an officer to prosecute, or detail a commanding officer to appoint an officer subject to air-force law to prosecute:

Provided that the convening officer may appoint two such officers to prosecute if he thinks fit;

(h) appoint the date, time and place for the trial;

(i) send to the president the charge sheet and the convening order and in any case in which a judge advocate has not been appointed a copy of the summary or abstract of evidence from which any evidence which in his opinion would be inadmissible under the Act at the court-martial has been expurgated;

(*j*) send to each member of the court and to each waiting member a copy of the charge-sheet;

(*k*) send to the prosecutor copies of the charge-sheet and convening order and the original summary or abstract of evidence together with an unexpurgated copy thereof showing the passages (if any) which have been expurgated in any copy sent to the president;

(*l*) send to the judge advocate (if any) copies of the charge-sheet and convening order and an unexpurgated copy of the summary or abstract of evidence;

(*m*) ensure that the accused is given a proper opportunity to prepare his defence in accordance with Rule 25; and

(*n*) take steps in accordance with Rule 91 to procure the attendance at the court-martial of all witnesses to be called for the prosecution and all witnesses whose attendance the accused has reasonably requested in accordance with Rule 25:

> Provided that the convening officer may require the accused to defray or to undertake to defray, as the convening officer thinks fit, the cost of the attendance of a witness whose attendance he has requested and if the accused refuses to defray or to undertake to defray, as the case may be, such cost, the convening officer shall not be obliged to take any further steps to procure the attendance of that witness.

(2) When an officer convenes a field general court-martial he shall not be obliged to comply with paragraphs (*g*), (*i*) (in so far as it relates to the copy of the summary or abstract of evidence sent to the president being expurgated), (*j*), (*k*) and (*l*) of paragraph (*l*) of this Rule, if, in his opinion it is impracticable to do so.

(3) When an officer convenes a court-martial consequent on an order authorising a re-trial made under the Courts-Martial (Appeals) Act, 1968(**a**), by the Courts-Martial Appeal Court or the Defence Council:

(*a*) Sub-paragraph (*b*) of paragraph (1) of this Rule shall not apply but the convening officer shall direct that a charge-sheet shall be prepared in accordance with the provisions of section 19(3) of the said Act and with any directions which may have been given by the Courts-Martial Appeal Court or the Defence Council under sub-section (4) of the said section and that the accused shall be tried on the charge in that charge-sheet.

(*b*) When it is proposed to tender any evidence given by any witness at the original trial as evidence at the re-trial in accordance with the provisions of Part II of Schedule 1 to the said Act the convening officer shall send to the accused as soon as practicable and in any case not less than 24 hours before his trial and also to the president, the judge advocate (if any) and the prosecutor a copy of any such evidence.

Appointment of president and members

23. The convening officer shall:

(*a*) appoint the president of a court-martial by name and appoint the members either by name or by detailing a commanding officer to appoint an officer of a specified rank; and

(*b*) appoint such waiting members as he thinks expedient either by name or by detailing a commanding officer to appoint an officer of a specified rank.

(**a**) 1968 c. 20.

Officers under instruction

24.—(1) Subject to Rule 81, any officer subject to air-force law, the Naval Discipline Act**(a)** or military law may, by direction of the convening officer or at the discretion of the president, remain with a court-martial throughout the proceedings as an officer under instruction.

(2) An officer under instruction, although allowed to be present in closed court, shall take no part in any of the deliberations or decisions of the court.

Preparation of defence

25.—(1) Subject to paragraph (2) of this Rule:

(*a*) an accused who has been remanded for trial by court-martial shall be afforded a proper opportunity for preparing his defence and shall be allowed proper communication with his defending officer or counsel and with his witnesses;

(*b*) a defending officer or counsel shall be appointed to defend an accused who has been remanded for trial by court-martial unless the accused states in writing that he does not wish such an appointment to be made;

(*c*) if the prosecution is to be undertaken by a legally qualified officer or by counsel, the accused shall be notified of this fact in sufficient time to enable him, if he so desires and it is practicable, to make arrangements for a legally qualified officer or counsel to defend him;

(*d*) as soon as practicable after an accused has been remanded for trial by court-martial and in any case not less than twenty-four hours before his trial he shall be given:—

(i) a copy of the charge-sheet;

(ii) an unexpurgated copy of the summary or abstract of evidence showing the passages (if any) which have been expurgated in any copy sent to the president;

(iii) notice of any additional evidence which the prosecution intend to adduce; and

(iv) if the accused so requires, a list of the ranks, names, and units of the president and members who are to form the court and of any waiting members;

(*e*) when an accused is given a copy of the charge-sheet and of the summary or abstract of evidence in accordance with this Rule, he shall:—

(i) if necessary, have the charge explained to him; and

(ii) be informed that, upon his making a written request to his commanding officer not less than twenty-four hours before his trial requiring the attendance at his trial of any witness (other than a witness for the prosecution) whom he desires to call in his defence (such witness to be named by him), reasonable steps will be taken in accordance with these Rules to procure the attendance of any such witness at his trial;

(*f*) when an accused is served with a copy of a written statement which the prosecutor proposes to hand to the court in accordance with section 9 of the Criminal Justice Act, 1967**(b)**, as modified by paragraphs 1 and 2 of the Schedule to the Courts-Martial (Evidence) Regulations, 1967**(c)**, he shall be informed of his right under the said section to require that oral evidence shall be given in lieu of such written evidence;

(a) 1957 c. 53.   **(b)** 1967 c. 80.   **(c)** S.I. 1967/1807 (1967 III, p. 4830).

(g) when it is intended to try two or more accused jointly, notice of this fact shall be given to each such accused when he is given a copy of the charge-sheet. Any such accused may, before trial, by written notice to the convening officer claim to be tried separately on the ground that he would be prejudiced in his defence if he were not tried separately. In such case the convening officer shall, if he is of the opinion that the interests of justice so require, direct that the accused who has so claimed shall be tried separately;

(h) when a charge-sheet contains more than one charge, the accused may, before trial, by written notice to the convening officer, claim to be tried separately on any charge in that charge-sheet on the ground that he would be prejudiced in his defence if he were not tried separately on that charge, and in such case the convening officer shall, if he is of the opinion that the interests of justice so require, direct that the accused shall be tried separately on that charge.

(2) In the case of a field general court-martial the provisions of paragraph (1) of this Rule need only be complied with so far as it is practicable to do so.

ASSEMBLY AND SWEARING OF COURT

Preliminary matters to be considered by court and beginning of trial

26.—(1) Upon a court-martial assembling, the court shall, before opening, satisfy themselves:—

(a) that the court has been convened in accordance with the Act and these Rules;

(b) that the court consists of not less than the legal minimum of officers;

(c) that the president and members are of the required rank;

(d) that the president and members have been duly appointed and are not disqualified under the Act;

(e) if there is a judge advocate, that he has been duly appointed;

(f) that the accused appears from the charge-sheet to be subject to air-force law or otherwise liable to trial by court-martial and to be subject to the jurisdiction of the court; and

(g) that each charge is on its face correct in law and framed in accordance with these Rules.

(2)(a) Where a vacancy occurs through a member of the court being disqualified under the Act or being absent when the court assemble, the president may appoint a duly qualified waiting member to fill that vacancy.

(b) The president may, if the interests of justice so require, substitute a duly qualified waiting member for a member appointed by the convening officer.

(3) If the court are not satisfied on any of the matters mentioned in paragraph (1) above, and are not competent to rectify such matters themselves under the Act or these Rules, they shall, before commencing the trial, report to the convening officer thereon.

(4) When the court have complied with this Rule and are ready to proceed with the trial, the president shall open the court and the trial shall begin.

Objections to the court

27.—(1) The order convening the court and the names of the officers appointed to try the accused shall be read in the hearing of the accused who shall be given an opportunity to object to any of those officers in accordance with section 92 of the Act.

(2) When a court is convened to try more than one accused whether separately or jointly, each accused shall be given an opportunity to object to any officer on the court in accordance with the preceding paragraph and shall be asked separately whether he has any such objection.

(3) An accused shall state the names of all the officers to whom he objects before any objection is disposed of.

(4) If more than one officer is objected to, the objection to each officer shall be disposed of separately and the objection to the lowest in rank shall be disposed of first, except where the president is objected to, in which case the objection to him shall be disposed of before the objection to any other officer.

(5) An accused may make a statement and call any person to make a statement in support of his objection.

(6) An officer to whom the accused has objected may state in open court anything relevant to the accused's objection whether in support or in rebuttal thereof.

(7) An objection to an officer shall be considered in closed court by all the other officers on the court including any officer who has been appointed by the president in accordance with paragraph (9) of this Rule in place of an officer who has retired.

(8) When an objection to an officer is allowed that officer shall forthwith retire and take no further part in the proceedings.

(9) When an officer objected to (other than the president) retires and there is a duly qualified waiting member in attendance, the president should immediately appoint him to take the place of the officer who has retired.

(10) The court shall satisfy themselves that a waiting member who takes the place of a member of the court is of the required rank and not disqualified under the Act and shall give the accused an opportunity to object to him and shall deal with any such objection in accordance with this Rule.

(11) If an objection to the president is allowed, the court shall report to the convening officer without proceeding further with the trial.

(12) If, as the result of the allowances of an objection to a member there are insufficient officers available to form a court in compliance with the Act, the court shall report to the convening officer without proceeding further with the trial and the convening officer may either appoint an officer as a member to fill the vacancy or convene a fresh court to try the accused.

Swearing of court

28.—(1) Immediately after Rule 27 has been complied with, an oath shall be administered to the president and each member of the court in accordance with Rule 34 and in the presence of the accused.

(2) If there is a judge advocate, the oath shall be administered by him to the president first and afterwards to each member of the court. If there is no judge advocate, the oath shall be first administered by the president to the members of the court and then to the president by any member of the court already sworn.

(3) A court may be sworn at one time to try any member of accused then present before them whether they are to be tried jointly or separately.

(4) When a court is convened to try two or more accused separately and one accused objects to the president or to any member of the court, the court, may if they think fit, proceed to determine that objection in accordance with Rule 27, or postpone the trial of that accused and swear the court for the trial of the other accused only.

Swearing of judge advocate

29. After the court have been sworn, an oath shall be administered to the judge advocate (if any) in accordance with Rule 34 and in the presence of the accused.

Swearing of officers under instruction

30. After the court and judge advocate (if any) have been sworn, an oath shall be administered to any officer under instruction in accordance with Rule 34 and in the presence of the accused.

Appointment and swearing of, and objections to interpreters and shorthand writers

31.—(1) A competent and impartial person may be appointed at any time to act as an interpreter or shorthand writer at a trial by court-martial and before he so acts an oath shall be administered to him in accordance with Rule 34 and in the presence of the accused.

(2) Before a person is sworn as an interpreter or as a shorthand writer, the accused shall be given an opportunity to object to him in the same manner as an objection may be taken to a member of the court and, if the court thinks that the objection is reasonable, that person shall not act as interpreter or shorthand writer.

No right of objection to judge advocate, prosecutor and officer under instruction

32. The accused shall have no right to object to a judge advocate, prosecutor or any officer under instruction.

Order of trials

33.—(1) When a court has been convened to try two or more accused separately and has been sworn in accordance with Rule 28(3), the court shall try them in the order indicated by the convening officer or, where he has given no such indication, then in such order as the court thinks fit.

(2) When a court has been convened to try an accused on charges which are included in more than one charge-sheet, the court shall take the charge-sheets in the order indicated by the convening officer or, where he has given no such indication, then in such order as the president thinks fit.

Oaths and solemn affirmations

34.—(1) An oath which is required to be administered under these Rules shall be administered in the appropriate form and in the manner set out in Schedule 6 to these Rules:

Provided that:

    (*a*) if any person desires to swear with uplifted hand in the form and manner in which an oath is usually administered in Scotland he shall be permitted to do so;

    (*b*) the opening words of the oath may be varied to such words and the oath may be administered in such manner as the person taking the oath declares to be binding on his conscience in accordance with his religious beliefs.

(2) Subject to Rule 28(2) every oath shall be administered at a court-martial by the president, a member of the court or the judge advocate.

(3) Where a person is a child or young person the oath shall be in the appropriate form set out in Schedule 6 to these Rules.

(4) Where a person is permitted to make a solemn affirmation instead of swearing an oath, the affirmation shall be in the appropriate form set out in Schedule 6 to these Rules.

(5) The provisions of section 102 of the Act shall apply to proceedings before a commanding officer, the taking of summaries of evidence and proceedings before an appropriate superior authority as they apply to proceedings before a court-martial.

ARRAIGNMENT OF ACCUSED

Arraignment of accused

35.—(1) When the court and judge advocate (if any) have been sworn the accused shall be arraigned.

(2) If there is more than one charge against the accused before the court he shall be required to plead separately to each charge.

(3) If there is more than one charge-sheet against the accused before the court, the court-shall arraign and try the accused upon the charge in the first of such charge-sheets and shall anounce their finding thereon and if the accused has pleaded guilty the court may either proceed to comply with paragraphs (1) and (2) of Rule 45 before they arraign him upon the charge in any subsequent charge-sheet or they may defer compliance with those paragraphs until after the accused has been arraigned and tried upon such charge.

Plea to the jurisdiction of the court

36.—(1) The accused, before pleading to the charge, may offer a plea to the jurisdiction of the court. If he does so:—

    (*a*) the accused may adduce evidence in support of the plea and the prosecutor may adduce evidence in answer thereto; and

    (*b*) the prosecutor may address the court in answer to the plea and the accused may reply to the prosecutor's address.

(2) If the court allow the plea they shall adjourn and report to the convening officer.

(3) When a court report to the convening officer under this Rule, the convening officer shall:—

(a) if he approves the decision of the court to allow the plea, dissolve the court;

(b) if he disapproves the decision of the court;

  (i) refer the matter back to the court and direct them to proceed with the trial; or

  (ii) convene a fresh court to try the accused.

Objection to charge

37.—(1) An accused before pleading to a charge may object to it on the grounds that it is not correct in law or is not framed in accordance with these Rules, and, if he does so, the prosecutor may address the court in answer to the objection and the accused may reply to the prosecutor's address.

(2) If the court uphold the objection, they shall either amend the charge, if permissible under Rule 83, or adjourn and report to the convening officer;

Provided that if there is another charge or another charge-sheet before the court the court may, before adjourning under this Rule, proceed with the trial of such other charge or other charge-sheet.

(3) When a court report to the convening officer under this Rule, the convening officer shall:—

(a) if he approves the decision of the court to allow the objection:

  (i) dissolve the court; or

  (ii) where there is another charge or another charge-sheet before the court to which the objection does not relate and which the court have not tried, direct the court to proceed with the trial of such other charge or charge-sheet only; or

  (iii) amend the charge to which the objection relates if permissible under Rule 84, and direct the court to try it as amended;

(b) if he disapproves the decision of the court to allow the objection:—

  (i) direct the court to try the charge; or

  (ii) where there is another charge or another charge-sheet before the court to which the objection does not relate and which the court have not tried, direct the court to proceed with the trial of such other charge or charge-sheet only: or

  (iii) convene a fresh court to try the accused.

Plea in bar of trial

38.—(1) An accused before pleading to a charge, may offer a plea in bar of trial in reliance upon section 132 or section 134 of the Act. If he does so:—

(a) the accused may adduce evidence in support of the plea and the prosecutor may adduce evidence in answer thereto; and

(b) the prosecutor may address the court in answer to the plea and the accused may reply to the prosecutor's address.

(2) If the court allow the plea they shall adjourn and report to the convening officer:

Provided that if there is another charge or another charge-sheet before the court, the court may, before adjourning under this Rule, proceed with the trial of such other charge or other charge-sheet.

(3) When a court report to the convening officer under this Rule, the convening officer shall:—

    (*a*) if he approves the decision of the court to allow the plea:—

        (i) dissolve the court; or

        (ii) where there is another charge or another charge-sheet before the court to which the plea does not relate and which the court have not tried, direct the court to proceed with the trial of such other charge or charge-sheet only:

    (*b*) if he disapproves the decision of the court to allow the plea:—

        (i) direct the court to try the charge; or

        (ii) where there is another charge or another charge-sheet before the court to which the plea does not relate and which the court have not tried, direct the court to proceed with the trial of such other charge or charge-sheet only; or

        (iii) convene a fresh court to try the accused.

Application by an accused at a joint trial to be tried separately

39. Where two or more accused are charged jointly or are charged in the same charge-sheet with offences alleged to have been committed by them separately, any one of the accused may, before pleading to the charge or charges, apply to the court to be tried separately on the ground that he would be prejudiced in his defence, if he were not tried separately. If the accused makes such an application the prosecutor may address the court in answer thereto and the accused may reply to the prosecutor's address. If the court are of the opinion that the interests of justice so require they shall allow the application and try separately the accused who made it.

Application by an accused at a trial to have a charge tried separately

40. Where a charge-sheet contains more than one charge the accused may, before pleading to the charges, apply to the court to be tried separately on any charge in that charge-sheet on the ground that he would be prejudiced in his defence if he were not tried separately on that charge. If the accused makes such an application the prosecutor may address the court in answer thereto and the accused may reply to the prosecutor's address. If the court are of the opinion that the interests of justice so require they shall allow the application and try the accused separately on the charge to which it relates as if that charge has been inserted in a separate charge-sheet.

Pleas to the charge

41.—(1) After any pleas under Rules 36 and 38, any objection under Rule 37, and any applications under Rules 39 and 40, have beeen dealt with, the accused shall be required (subject to paragraph (2) of this Rule) to plead either guilty or not guilty to each charge on which he is arraigned.

(2) Where a court are empowered by section 98 of the Act to find an accused guilty of an offence other than that charged or guilty of committing the offence in circumstances involving a less degree of punishment or where they could, after hearing the evidence, make a special finding of guilty subject to exceptions or variations in accordance with Rule 66, the accused may plead guilty to such other offence or to the offence charged as having been committed in circumstances involving a less degree of punishment or to the offence charged subject to such exceptions or variations.

Acceptance of pleas of guilty

42.—(1) If an accused pleads guilty to a charge under either paragraph (1) or paragraph (2) of Rule 41, the president or judge advocate shall, before the court decides to accept the plea, explain to the accused the nature of the charge and the general effect of his plea and in particular the difference in procedure when an accused pleads guilty and when an accused pleads not guilty.

(2) A court shall not accept a plea of guilty under either paragraph (1) or paragraph (2) of Rule 41 if:—

    (a) the court are not satisfied that the accused understands the nature of the charge or the effect of his plea; or

    (b) the president having regard to all the circumstances considers that the accused should plead not guilty; or

    (c) the accused is liable if convicted to be sentenced to death.

(3) In the case of a plea of guilty under Rule 41(2), a court shall also not accept the plea unless the convening officer concurs and they are satisfied of the justice of such course. The concurrence of the convening officer may be signified by the prosecutor.

(4) When a plea of guilty under either paragraph (1) or paragraph (2) of Rule 41 is not accepted by the court or the accused either refuses to plead to the charge or does not plead to it intelligibly, the court shall enter a plea of not guilty.

(5) When a court are satisfied that they can properly accept a plea of guilty under either paragraph (1) or paragraph (2) of Rule 41 they shall record a finding of guilty in respect thereof.

Pleas on alternative charges

43.—(1) When an accused pleads guilty to the first of two or more alternative charges, the court, if they accept the accused's plea of guilty, shall record a finding of guilty in respect of the first charge and the prosecutor shall withdraw any alternative charge before the accused is arraigned on it.

(2) When an accused pleads guilty to one of two or more charges which are laid in the alternative other than the first of such charges, the court may:—

    (a) proceed as if the accused had pleaded not guilty to all the charges; or

    (b) with the concurrence of the convening officer (which may be signified by the prosecutor) record a finding of guilty on the charge to which the accused has pleaded guilty and a finding of not guilty on any alternative charge which is placed before it in the charge-sheet. Where the court records such findings, the prosecutor shall before the accused is arraigned on it withdraw any charge which is alternative to the charge of which the court have found the accused guilty and which is placed after it in the charge-sheet.

PROCEDURE AFTER RECORDING A FINDING OF GUILTY

Order of trial where pleas of guilty and not guilty

44. After the court have recorded a finding of guilty, if there is no other charge in the same charge-sheet to which the accused has pleaded not guilty and no other accused who has pleaded not guilty to a charge in that charge-sheet, they shall proceed with the trial as directed by Rule 45. If there is another charge in the charge-sheet to which the accused has pleaded not guilty or there is another accused who has pleaded not guilty to a charge in that charge-sheet, the court shall not comply with Rule 45 until after they have dealt with such other charge or tried such other accused and have announced and recorded their finding in respect thereof.

Procedure of finding of guilty after plea of guilty

45.—(1) After the court have recorded a finding of guilty in respect of a charge to which an accused pleaded guilty, the prosecutor shall, subject to Rule 44, read the summary or abstract of evidence to the court or inform the court of the facts contained therein;

Provided that if the summary or abstract of evidence contains evidence which in the opinion of the convening officer, is inadmissible under the Act, the prosecutor shall not read to the court those parts of the summary or abstract which are inadmissible or inform the court of the facts contained in those parts, and shall not hand the original summary or abstract to the court until the trial is concluded.

(2) If there is no summary or abstract of evidence or the summary or abstract is, in the opinion of the court, inadequate or incomplete, the court shall hear and record in accordance with these Rules sufficient evidence to enable them to determine the sentence.

(3) After paragraphs (1) and (2) of this Rule have been complied with, the accused may:—

(*a*) adduce evidence of character and in mitigation of punishment; and

(*b*) address the court in mitigation of punishment.

(4 After paragraph 3 of this Rule has been complied with the court shall proceed as directed in paragraphs (1), (2), (3) and (4) of Rule 71.

CHANGES OF PLEA

Changes of plea

46.—(1) An accused who has pleaded not guilty may at any time before the court close to deliberate on their finding withdraw his plea of not guilty and substitute a plea of guilty (including a plea of guilty under Rule 41(2)) and in such case the court shall, if they are satisfied that they can accept the accused's changed plea under these Rules; record a finding in accordance with the accused's changed plea and so far as is necessary proceed as directed by Rule 45.

(2) If at any time during the trial it appears to the court that an accused who has pleaded guilty does not understand the effect of his plea or the nature of the charge, the court shall enter a plea of not guilty and proceed with the trial accordingly.

(3) When a court enters a plea of not guilty in respect of any charge under paragraph (2) of this Rule, they shall, if there was a charge laid in the alternative thereto which the prosecutor withdrew under Rule 43, reinstate such alternative charge, arraign the accused thereon and proceed with the trial as if it had never been withdrawn.

PROCEDURE ON PLEAS OF NOT GUILTY

Application for adjournment of trial

47. After a plea of not guilty to any charge has been entered:—

(*a*) the court shall ask the accused whether he wishes to apply for an adjournment on the ground that any of these Rules relating to procedure before trial have not been complied with and that he has been prejudiced thereby or on the ground that he has not had sufficient opportunity for preparing his defence;

(*b*) if the accused applies for an adjournment:—

   (i) the accused may adduce evidence in support of his application and the prosecutor may adduce evidence in answer thereto; and

   (ii) the prosecutor may address the court in answer to the application and the accused may reply to the prosecutor's address;

(*c*) the court may grant an adjournment if they think the interests of justice so require.

Case for the prosecution

48.—(1) The prosecutor may, if he desires, and shall, if required by the court, make an opening address explaining the charge, where necessary, and the nature and general effect of the evidence which he proposes to adduce.

(2) the witnesses for the prosecution shall then be called and give their evidence.

Calling of witnesses whose evidence is not contained in summary or abstract of evidence

49. If the prosecutor intends to adduce evidence which is not contained in any summary or abstract of evidence given to the accused, notice of such intention together with the particulars of the evidence shall, when practicable, be given to the accused a reasonable time before the evidence is adduced. If such evidence is adduced without such notice or particulars having been given, the court may, if the accused so desires, either adjourn after receiving the evidence or allow any cross-examination arising out of that evidence to be postponed, and the court shall inform the accused of his right to apply for such an adjournment or postponement.

Notice to an accused that a witness will not be called by the prosecutor

50. The prosecutor shall not be bound to call all the witnesses against the accused whose evidence is contained in the summary or abstract of evidence nor a witness whom he has notified the accused that he intends to call under Rule 49, but if the prosecutor does not intend to call such a witness to give evidence he shall either tender him for cross-examination by the accused, or give the accused reasonable notice that he does not intend to call the witness and that the accused will be allowed to communicate with him and to call him as a witness for the defence, if he so desires and if the witness is available.

CALLING AND EXAMINATION OF WITNESSES

Swearing of witnesses

51. Save as is otherwise provided by the Act an oath shall be administered to each witness in accordance with Rule 34 before he gives evidence and in the presence of the accused.

Exclusion of witnesses from court

52. During a trial a witness other than the prosecutor or accused shall not, except by leave of the court, be in court while not under examination, and if while he is under examination a discussion arises as to the allowance of a question or otherwise with regard to the evidence the court may direct the witness to withdraw during such discussion.

Examination of witnesses

53.—(1) A witness may be examined by the person calling him and may be cross-examined by the opposite party to the proceedings and on the conclusion of any such cross-examination may be re-examined by the person who called him on matters arising out of the cross-examination.

(2) The person examining a witness shall put his questions to the witness orally and unless an objection is made by the witness, court, judge advocate, prosecutor or by the accused, the witness shall reply forthwith. If such an objection is made, the witness shall not reply until the objection has been disposed of.

(3) The court may allow the cross-examination or re-examination of a witness to be postponed.

Examination of witnesses by court

54.—(1) The president, the judge advocate and, with permission of the president, any member of the court may put questions to a witness.

(2) Upon any such question being answered, the prosecutor and the accused may put to the witness such questions arising from the answer which he has given as seem proper to the court.

Reading back of evidence to witnesses

55.—(1) The record which has been made of the evidence given by a witness shall be read back to him before he leaves the court and when this is done he may ask for the record to be corrected or explain the evidence which he has given. If any such correction is made or explanation given, the prosecutor and the accused may put such questions to the witness respecting the correction or explanation as seem proper to the court.

(2) When a shorthand writer is employed it shall not be necessary to comply with paragraph (1) of this Rule, if, in the opinion of the court and the judge advocate (if any), it is unnecessary to do so:

Provided that if any witness so demands paragraph (1) of this Rule shall be complied with.

Calling of witnesses by court and recalling of witnesses

56.—(1) The court may, at any time before they close to deliberate on their finding or, if there is a judge advocate before he begins to sum up, call a witness or recall a witness, if in the opinion of the court it is in the interests of justice to do so. If the court calls a witness or recalls a witness under this Rule, the prosecutor and the accused may put such questions to the witness as seem proper to the court.

(2) The prosecutor and the accused may, at any time before the court closes to deliberate on their findings or, if there is a judge advocate before he begins to sum up, recall a witness by leave of the court and the prosecutor and the accused may put such questions to the witness as seem proper to the court.

Written statements

57. A written statement which is admissible in accordance with the provision of section 9 of the Criminal Justice Act, 1967**(a)**, as modified by the Courts-Martial (Evidence) Regulations, 1967**(b)**, shall be handed to the court by the prosecutor or the accused, as the case may be, without being produced by a witness.

SUBMISSION OF NO CASE TO ANSWER AND STOPPING OF CASES

Submission of no case to answer and power of court to stop a case

58.—(1) At the close of the case for the prosecution the accused may submit to the court in respect of any charge that the prosecution has failed to establish a *prima facie* case for him to answer and that he should not be called upon to make his defence to that charge.   If the accused makes such a submission, the prosecutor may address the court in answer thereto and the accused may reply to the prosecutor's address.

(2) The court shall not allow the submission unless they are satisfied that:—

(*a*) the prosecution had not established a *prima facie* case on the charge as laid; and

(*b*) it is not open to them on the evidence adduced to make a special finding under either section 98 of the Act or Rule 66(3).

(3) If the court allow the submission they shall find the accused not guilty of the charge to which it relates and announce this finding in open court forthwith; if the court disallow the submission they shall proceed with the trial of the offence as charged.

(4) Irrespective of whether there has been a submission under this Rule or not, the court may at any time after the close of the hearing of the case for the prosecution, and after hearing the prosecutor, find the accused not guilty of a charge, and if they do so shall also announce such finding in open court forthwith.

CASE FOR THE DEFENCE

Explanation to accused of his rights when making his defence

59.—(1) After the close of the case for the prosecution, the president or judge advocate (if any) should explain to the accused that:—

(*a*) if he wishes, he may give evidence on oath as a witness or make a statement without being sworn, but that he is not obliged to do either;

(*b*) if he gives evidence on oath, he will be liable to be cross-examined by the prosecutor and to be questioned by the court and the judge advocate (if any) but that, if he makes a statement without being sworn, no one will be entitled to ask him any questions; and

(*c*) whether he gives evidence or makes a statement or remains silent, he may call witnesses on his behalf both to the facts of the case and to his character.

(a) 1967 c. 80.   **(b)** S.I. 1967/1807 (1967 III, p. 4830).

(2) After the president or judge advocate has complied with paragraph (1) of this Rule, he shall ask the accused if he intends to give evidence on oath or to make a statement without being sworn and if he intends to call any witness on his behalf and, if so, whether he is a witness to fact or to character only.

(3) If the accused intends to call a witness to the facts of the case other than himself, he may make an opening address outlining the case for the defence before the evidence for the defence is given.

Evidence for the defence

60.—(1) After Rule 59 has been complied with the witnesses for the defence (if any) shall be called and give their evidence.

(2) Rules 51, 52, 53, 54, 55, 56 and 57 shall apply to the witnesses and the evidence for the defence as they apply to the witnesses and the evidence for the prosecution.

Evidence in rebuttal

61. After the witnesses for the defence have given their evidence the prosecutor may, by leave of the court, call a witness or recall a witness to give evidence on any matter raised by the accused in his defence which the prosecution could not properly have mentioned to the court before the accused disclosed his defence or which the prosecution could not reasonably have foreseen.

Closing addresses

62.—(1) After all the evidence has been given the prosecutor and the accused may each make a closing address to the court.

(2) The accused shall be entitled to make his closing address after the closing address by the prosecutor.

(3) Where two or more accused are represented by the same defending officer or counsel he may make one closing address only.

(4) Where the accused is not represented by defending officer or counsel, then, whether or not he himself has given evidence, the prosecutor shall not, make a closing address unless the accused has called witnesses as to the facts of the case.

Handing in of a written statement by accused

63. For the purpose of Rule 59, the handing in by the accused of a written statement shall be treated as the calling of a witness by him.

Summing up by judge advocate

Summing up by judge advocate

64. After the closing addresses, if there is a judge advocate, he shall sum up the evidence and advise the court on the law relating to the case in open court.

DELIBERATION ON, AND ANNOUNCEMENT OF, FINDING ON THE CHARGE

Deliberation on finding on the charge

65.—(1) After the closing addresses, or if there is a judge advocate after his summing up, the court shall close to deliberate on their finding on the charge.

(2) While the court are deliberating on their finding on the charge no person shall be present except the president and members of the court and any officer under instruction.

(3) If there is a judge advocate and the court, while deliberating on their finding on the charge require further advice from him, the court shall suspend their deliberation and ask and be given such advice in open court.

Expression of opinions on, and form of, finding

66.—(1) The opinion of the president and each member as to the finding shall be given in closed court, orally, and on each charge separately and their opinions shall be given in order of seniority commencing with the junior in rank.

(2) Save as is otherwise provided in paragraph (4) of this Rule the court shall record on every charge on which a plea of not guilty has been recorded:—

> (*a*) a finding of guilty or a special finding in accordance with section 98 or section 116(2) of the Act or paragraph (3) of this Rule; or

> (*b*) a finding of not guilty or of not guilty and honourably acquitted of the charge.

(3) Where the court are of the opinion as regards any charge that the facts which they find to be proved in evidence differ from the facts alleged in the particulars of the charge, but are nevertheless sufficient to prove the offence stated in the charge and that the difference is not so material as to have prejudiced the accused in his defence, the court may, instead of recording a finding of not guilty, record a finding that the accused is guilty of the charge subject to any exception or variation which they shall specify in the finding.

(4) Where the court have recorded a finding of guilty on a charge which is laid in the alternative they shall find the accused not guilty of any charge alternative thereto which is placed before it in the charge-sheet and record no finding on any charge alternative thereto which is placed after it in the charge-sheet.

Announcement of finding

67.—(1) The finding on each charge shall be announced in open court forthwith.

(2) Every finding which requires confirmation shall be announced as being subject to confirmation.

(3) The finding shall be in the appropriate form set out in Schedule 4 to these Rules.

PROCEDURE AFTER ANNOUNCEMENT OF FINDING

Completion of procedure on plea of guilty before deliberation on sentence

68. After the court have announced their finding on any charge on which the court have entered a plea of not guilty, if there is another charge in the same charge-sheet on which the court have accepted a plea of guilty, the court shall comply with Rule 45(1)(2) in respect of that charge before proceeding further with the trial.

Trial of charges in other charge-sheets before deliberation on sentence

69. Where there is another charge-sheet against the accused before the court, the court shall not comply with Rules 70, 71 and 72 until they have arraigned and tried the accused and have complied with Rule 67 and, if necessary, with Rule 68, in respect of each charge in such other charge-sheet unless that charge-sheet is withdrawn under Rule 82.

Release of accused

70. If the findings on all charges against the accused are not guilty the court shall order the accused to be released and the president and judge advocate (if any) shall date and sign the record of the proceedings. The president or the judge advocate shall then forward it as directed in the convening order.

Accused's record and plea in mitigation

71.—(1) If the findings on a charge against the accused is guilty, or the court makes a special finding in accordance with section 98 of the Act or Rule 66(3) the court before deliberating on their sentence shall whenever possible take evidence of his age, rank and service record. Such service record shall include:—

    (*a*) any recognised acts of gallantry or distinguished conduct on the part of the accused and any decoration to which he is entitled; and

    (*b*) particulars of any offence of which the accused has been found guilty during his service and which is recorded in the service books relating to the accused and of the length of time he has been under arrest awaiting trial or in confinement under a current sentence.

(2) Evidence of the matters referred to in paragraph (1) of this Rule may be given by a witness producing to the court a written statement containing a summary of the entries in the service books relating to the accused after the witness has in court verified such statement and identified the accused as the person to whom it relates. Such statement shall be in the form set out in Schedule 4 to these Rules.

(3) In addition to the evidence contained in the statement referred to in paragraph (2) of this Rule, it shall be the duty of the prosecutor whenever possible to call as a witness an officer to give to the court any information in the possession of the air-force authorities regarding:—

    (*a*) the accused's family background and responsibilities and any other circumstances which may have made him more susceptible to the commission of the offence charged;

    (*b*) his general conduct in the service; and

    (*c*) particulars of offences which do not appear in the statement above referred to of which the accused has been found guilty by a civil court not being offences of which he was found guilty while under the age of 14 years.

Provided that the court shall not be informed of any such civil offence unless the finding is proved in accordance with section 199 of the Act, or the accused has admitted, after the purpose for which such admission is required has been explained to him, that he has been found guilty of the offence.

(4) The accused may cross-examine any witness who gives evidence in accordance with paragraphs (2) and (3) of this Rule and if the accused so requires the service books, or a duly certified copy of the material entries therein, shall be produced, and if the contents of the form are in any respect not in accordance with the service books or such certified copy, the court shall cause the form to be corrected accordingly.

(5) After paragraphs (1), (2), (3) and (4) of this Rule have been complied with the accused may:—

(a) give evidence on oath and call witnesses in mitigation of punishment and to his character; and

(b) address the court in mitigation of punishment.

Request by accused for other offences to be taken into consideration

72.—(1) Before the court close to deliberate on their sentence, the accused may request the court to take into consideration any other offence against the Act committed by him of a similar nature to that of which he has been found guilty, and, upon such a request being made, the court may agree to take into consideration any of such other offences as to the court seems proper.

(2) A list of the offences which the court agrees to take into consideration shall be read to the accused by the president or judge advocate, who shall ask the accused if he admits having committed them. The accused shall sign a list of the offences which he admits having committed and the court shall take the offences in this list into consideration. This list shall be signed by the president or judge advocate and be attached to the record of the proceedings as an exhibit.

DELIBERATION ON SENTENCE

Persons entitled to be present during deliberation on sentence

73. While the court are deliberating on their sentence no person shall be present except the president, members, judge advocate (if any) and any officer under instruction.

Sentence and recommendation to mercy

74.—(1) Subject to the provisions of paragraph (2) of this Rule the court shall award one sentence in respect of all the offences of which the accused is found guilty.

(2) Where the accused is found guilty by a general court-martial or a field general court-martial of two or more offences against s. 70 of the Act, consisting in the commission of civil offences for which a civil court in England could award imprisonment, the court-martial may by its sentence award, for any of the said offences, a term of imprisonment which is to run from the expiry of a term awarded by that sentence for any other of those offences.

(3) Sentences awarded pursuant to paragraphs (1) and (2) of this Rule shall be in the appropriate form set out in Schedule 5 to these Rules.

(4) Where the court order that a sentence of imprisonment or detention is to begin to run from the expiry of some other sentence of imprisonment or detention, the order shall be in the appropriate form set out in Schedule 5 to these Rules.

(5) The opinion of the president and each member as to the sentence shall be given orally and in closed court and their opinions shall be given in order of seniority commencing with the junior in rank.

(6) When the court have agreed to take into consideration an offence which is not included in the charge-sheet, the court shall award a sentence appropriate both to the offence of which the accused has been found guilty and to the other offence which they are taking into consideration, but not greater than the maximum sentence which may be awarded under the Act for the offence of which the accused has been found guilty, save that they may include in their sentence a direction that such deduction shall be made from the pay of the accused as they would have had power to direct to be made if the accused had been found guilty of the offence taken into consideration as well as of the offence of which he has been found guilty.

(7) The court may make a recommendation to mercy and if they do so shall record in the proceedings their reasons for making it.

Postponement of deliberation on sentence

75. Where two or more accused are tried separately by the same court upon charges arising out of the same transaction, the court may, if they think that the interests of justice so require, postpone their deliberation upon the sentence to be awarded to any one or more of such accused until they have recorded and announced their findings in respect of all of such accused.

ANNOUNCEMENT OF SENTENCE AND CONCLUSION OF TRIAL

Announcement of sentence and conclusion of trial

76.—(1) The sentence, and any recommendation to mercy together with the reasons for making it, shall be announced in open court. The sentence shall also be announced as being subject to confirmation.

(2) When paragraph (1) of this Rule has been complied with the president shall announce in open court that the trial is concluded.

(3) Immediately after the conclusion of the trial the president and judge advocate (if any) shall date and sign the record of the proceedings. The president or the judge advocate shall then forward it as directed in the convening order.

GENERAL DUTIES OF THE PRESIDENT, PROSECUTOR AND THE DEFENDING OFFICER OR COUNSEL

General duties of president

77. It shall be the duty of the president to ensure that the trial is conducted in accordance with the Act and these Rules and in a manner befitting a court of justice and in particular:—

> (a) to ensure that the prosecutor and the defending officer or counsel conduct themselves in accordance with these Rules;
>
> (b) to ensure that the accused does not suffer any disadvantage in consequence of his position as such or of his ignorance or of his incapacity to examine or cross-examine witnesses or to make his own evidence clear and intelligible, or otherwise;

(c) to ensure that an officer under instruction does not express an opinion to the court on any matter relating to the trial before the court have come to their finding, nor on sentence before the court have decided upon the sentence;

(d) when there is no judge advocate present, to ensure that a proper record of the proceedings is made in accordance with Rule 92 and that the record of the proceedings and exhibits are properly safeguarded in accordance with Rule 94.

General duties of prosecutor and defending officer or counsel

78.—(1) It shall be the duty of the prosecutor and of the defending officer or counsel to assist the court in the administration of justice, to treat the court and judge advocate with due respect and to present their cases fairly and in particular:—

(a) to conform with these Rules and the practice of the civil courts in England relating to the examination, cross-examination and re-examination of witnesses;

(b) not to refer to any matter not relevant to the charge before the court; and

(c) not to state as a matter of fact any matter which is not proved or which they do not intend to prove by evidence.

(2) Without prejudice to the generality of any of the provisions of paragraph (1) of this Rule, it shall be the duty of the prosecutor to bring the whole of the transaction before the court and not to take any unfair advantage of, or to withhold any evidence in favour of, the accused.

Counsel

79.—(1) Subject to these Rules the following persons shall be allowed to appear as Counsel at a court-martial:—

(a) every person who is qualified as a barrister-at-law or a solicitor according to the law of England or Northern Ireland;

(b) every person who is qualified as an advocate or as a solicitor according to the law of Scotland; and

(c) with the consent of the convening officer, any person who is recognised by him as having in any Commonwealth country or territory outside the United Kingdom rights and duties similar to those of a barrister-at-law or solicitor in England, and as being subject to punishment or disability for a breach of professional rules.

(2) Any right granted by these Rules to the accused at a court-martial to call or examine witnesses or to address the court, any right of the accused to object to the admissibility of evidence at a court-martial and any right granted to the accused by Rules 25(1)(e), (g) and (h), 27, 31, 36, 37, 38, 39, 40, 47, 58, 72, 80(2), 92 and 94(2) may be exercised by his defending officer or his counsel on his behalf, and any reference in these Rules to any address, request, application, claim, submission, objection or plea to the jurisdiction or in bar of trial made, taken or offered at a court-martial by the accused shall be construed as including any address, request, application, claim, submission, objection or plea to the jurisdiction or in bar of trial made, taken or offered at a court-martial by his defending officer to counsel on his behalf.

(3) If the accused is to be defended at his court-martial by counsel not nominated by the convening officer the accused shall give the convening officer notice of this fact not less than 24 hours before his trial.

POWERS AND DUTIES OF THE JUDGE ADVOCATE

General duties of judge advocate

80.—(1) The judge advocate shall be responsible for the proper discharge of his functions to the Judge Advocate General.

(2) The prosecutor and the accused respectively are at all times after the judge advocate is named to act at the trial entitled to his opinion on any question of law or procedure relative to the charge or trial whether he is in or out of court, subject when he is in court to the permission of the court.

(3) On the assembly of the court the judge advocate shall advise the court of any defect in the constitution of the court or in the charge-sheet, and during the trial he shall advise the court upon all questions of law or procedure which may arise. The court shall accept his advice on all such matters unless they have weighty reasons for not doing so, and if the court does not accept it their reasons for not doing so shall be recorded in the proceedings.

(4) After the closing addresses the judge advocate shall sum up the evidence and advise the court upon the law relating to the case before the court close to deliberate on their finding. If in the course of deliberating on their finding the court require further advice from the judge advocate, they shall suspend their deliberation and ask and be given such advice in open court.

(5) If when the court announce a finding of guilty or a special finding under either section 98 of the Act or Rule 66(3) the judge advocate is of the opinion that such finding or special finding is contrary to the law relating to the case, he shall once more, but not more than once more, advise the court what findings are, in his opinion, open to them. The court shall then reconsider their finding in closed court. The record of the proceedings relating to such reconsideration shall be in the form set out in Schedule 4 to these Rules.

(6) The judge advocate shall be present whenever the court are sitting whether in open or closed court, except when the court are deliberating on the finding on the charge or on a revision thereof.

(7) The judge advocate has equally with the president the duty of ensuring that the accused does not suffer any disadvantage in consequence of his position as such or of his ignorance or of his incapacity to examine or cross-examine witnesses, or to make his own evidence clear and intelligible, or otherwise.

(8) The judge advocate shall be responsible for seeing that a proper record of the proceedings is made in accordance with Rule 92 and responsible for the safe custody of the record of the proceedings under Rule 94.

Judge advocate sitting alone

81.—(1) Where there is a judge advocate and:—

    (a) an accused before pleading to a charge offers a plea in bar of trial; or

    (b) during the course of a trial any question as to the admissibility of evidence arises; or (*c*) during a joint trial an application is made by any of the accused for a separate trial; or

(*d*) an application is made by an accused that a charge should be tried separately; or

(*e*) an application is made by a party calling a witness for permission to treat that witness as hostile; or

(*f*) a submission is made to the court in respect of any charge that the prosecution has failed to establish a *prima facie* case for him to answer;

the president may direct that the point at issue shall be determined by the judge advocate in the absence of the president and the members of the court and of any officer under instruction. Where the president so directs he, the members of the court and any officer under instruction shall withdraw from the court.

(2) The judge advocate shall, when the president and members of the court and any officer under instruction have withdrawn in accordance with paragraph (1) of this Rule, hear the arguments and evidence relevant to the point at issue and shall give his ruling upon this point and such reasons therefor as he may consider necessary. After the judge advocate has given his ruling, the president and members of the court and any officer under instruction shall return to the court room and the judge advocate shall announce his ruling to them and the court shall follow his ruling.

(3) When a judge advocate sits alone in accordance with this Rule the proceedings before his shall form part of the proceedings of the court, and section 57(1), section 93, section 94(1)(2) and sections 95, 99, 100, 101, and 102 of the Act and Rules 34, 51, 52, 53, 54, 55, 56, 57, 78, 79, 85, 86, 87, 91, 92, 93, 94, 97, 98 and 106 shall apply to proceedings before the judge advocate sitting alone as they apply to proceedings before the president and members of the court, and anything which is authorised by those sections and those Rules to be done by the court or by the president may be done by the judge advocate when sitting alone.

(4) When a judge advocate is sitting alone in accordance with this Rule and a person subject to air-force law commits an offence against section 57(1) of the Act, the judge advocate shall report the occurrence to the president who shall take such action as he considers appropriate.

(5) The judge advocate shall be responsible for ensuring that the president and members do not see the record of the proceedings before the judge advocate when sitting alone until after the court have announced their finding.

WITHDRAWAL AND AMENDMENT OF CHARGE-SHEETS AND CHARGES

Withdrawal of charge-sheets and charges

82. A court may with the concurrence of the convening officer (which may be signified by the prosecutor) allow the prosecutor to withdraw a charge before the accused is arraigned thereon or a charge-sheet before the accused is arraigned on any charge therein.

Amendment of charge-sheets and charges by the court

83.—(1) At any time during a trial if it appears to the court that there is in the charge-sheet:—

(*a*) a mistake in the name or description of the accused;

(*b*) a mistake which is attributable to a clerical error or omission;
the court may amend the charge-sheet so as to correct the mistake.

(2) If at any time during a trial at which there is a judge advocate it appears to the court, before they close to deliberate on their finding, that it is desirable in the interests of justice to make any addition to, omission from or alteration in a charge which cannot be made under paragraph (1) of this Rule they may, if such addition, omission, or alteration can be made without unfairness to the accused, so amend the charge if the judge advocate concurs.

(3) If at any time during a trial at which there is no judge advocate it appears to the court, before they close to deliberate on their finding, that in the interests of justice it is desirable to make any addition to, omission from or alteration in a charge which cannot be made under paragraph (1) of this Rule, they may adjourn and report their opinion to the convening officer, who may:—

> (*a*) amend the charge if permissible under Rule 84 and direct the court to try it as amended after due notice of the amendment has been given to the accused; or
>
> (*b*) direct the court to proceed with the trial of the charge without amending it; or
>
> (*c*) convene a fresh court to try the accused.

Amendment of charges by convening officer

84. When a court reports to the convening officer under either Rule 37(2) or Rule 83(3), he may amend the charge in respect of which they have reported to him by making any addition to, omission from, or alteration in the charge which, in his opinion, is desirable in the interest of justice and which he is satisfied can be made without unfairness to the accused.

SITTINGS AND ADJOURNMENT OF THE COURT

Sittings of the court

85. Subject to the provisions of the Act and of these Rules relating to adjournment, a trial shall be continued from day to day and the court shall sit for such time each day as may be reasonable in the circumstances:

Provided that the court shall not sit on Sunday, Christmas Day, or Good Friday, unless in the opinion of the court or of the convening officer the exigencies of the service make it necessary to do so.

Adjournment

86.—(1) During a trial the court may adjourn from time to time and from place to place as the interests of justice require.

(2) A court may adjourn at any time to consult the convening officer on a point of law.

(3) If during a trial any reason emerges which makes it advisable that the court should not continue to hear the case, the court shall adjourn and report thereon to the convening officer.

(4) If at any time during a trial the accused becomes ill and it appears to the court that the illness is such that it will be impracticable to continue the trial, the court shall ascertain the facts of the illness and shall then adjourn and report to the convening officer.

View by court

87. If at any time during a trial before the court closes to deliberate on its finding it appears to the court that they should, in the interests of justice, view any place or thing, they may adjourn for this purpose. When the court views any place or thing the president, members of the court, judge advocate (if any), prosecutor, accused and defending officer or counsel (if any) shall be present.

Absence of president, members or judge advocate

88.—(1) If after the commencement of a trial the president dies or is otherwise unable to attend, the court shall adjourn and the senior member shall report to the convening officer.

(2) If after the commencement of a trial any member of the court dies or is otherwise unable to attend, the court, if not thereby reduced below the legal minimum, shall continue with the trial, but if reduced below the legal minimum the court shall adjourn and the president shall report to the convening officer.

(3) If a judge advocate who has been appointed to act at a trial dies or is otherwise unable to attend, the court shall adjourn and report to the convening officer.

(4) If the president or a member of the court is absent during any part of a trial, he shall take no further part in it and the like steps shall be taken as if the president or member, as the case may be, had died.

(5) An officer cannot be added to the court after the accused has been arraigned.

UNFITNESS TO STAND TRIAL AND INSANITY

Unfitness to stand trial and insanity

89.—(1) Where on the trial of a person the question of his fitness to be tried falls to be determined in accordance with the provisions of section 116(4a) of the Act, the court shall take evidence as to his condition. If, after considering the evidence, they are of the opinion that the accused is fit to stand his trial, they shall proceed with the trial; but if they are of the opinion that the accused is unfit to stand his trial, they shall so find and their finding shall be announced in open court forthwith and as being subject to confirmation.

(2) If a court in the course of their deliberation on their finding on a charge find pursuant to section 116(2) of the Act that the accused was not guilty of the offence by reason of insanity, their finding shall be announced in open court forthwith and as being subject to confirmation.

(3) Immediately after a finding has been announced under either paragraph (1) or paragraph (2) of this Rule the president shall announce in open court that the proceedings are terminated and thereupon the president and the judge advocate (if any) shall date and sign the record of the proceedings. The president or judge advocate shall then forward it as directed in the convening order.

INTERVIEWING AND ATTENDANCE OF WITNESSES

Interviewing of witnesses

90.—(1) The prosecution shall not without the consent of the convening officer, or, after the trial has begun, without the consent of the president, interview any witness who was called for the defence at the taking of the summary of evidence, whose statement of evidence was included in the summary of evidence or attached to the abstract of evidence or whose attendance at the trial the accused has requested in accordance with Rule 25(1)(*e*), or who has made a written statement a copy of which the accused has served on the prosecution in accordance with section 9 of the Criminal Justice Act 1967**(a)**, as modified by the Courts-Martial (Evidence) Regulations, 1967**(b)**.

(2) Except as provided in Rule 50, neither the accused, nor any person on his behalf shall without the consent of the convening officer, or, after the trial has begun, without the consent of the president, interview any witness who was called for the prosecution at the taking of the summary of evidence whose statement of evidence was included in the summary of evidence or whose evidence is included in the abstract of evidence, or in respect of whom the prosecution has given the accused notice under Rule 49 that it is intended to call him as a witness at the trial or who has made a written statement a copy of which the prosecution has served on the accused in accordance with section 9 of the Criminal Justice Act, 1967, as modified by the Courts-Martial (Evidence) Regulations, 1967.

Procuring attendance of witnesses

91.—(1) A witness who is subject to air-force law may be ordered by the proper air-force authority to attend at the taking of a summary of evidence or a trial by court-martial.

(2) A witness who is not subject to air-force law may be summoned to attend:—

  (*a*) the taking of a summary of evidence by an order under the hand of the commanding officer of the accused; or

  (*b*) a trial by court-martial by an order under the hand of an officer authorised to convene a court-martial or of a staff officer on his behalf, or, after the assembly of the court, of the president.

(3)(*a*) The summons referred to in paragraph (2) of this Rule shall when it relates to the taking of a summary of evidence be in the appropriate form set out in Schedule 1 to these Rules, and, when it relates to a trial by court-martial be in the appropriate form set out in Schedule 4 to these Rules, and shall be served on the witness either personally or by leaving it with some person at the witness's normal place of abode.

  (*b*) At the time of service of the summons there shall be paid or tendered any expenses which by Queen's Regulations are payable to a witness in respect of his journey to, attendance at and return from the taking of the summary of evidence or the trial, as the case may be; provided that for the purposes of this paragraph:—

    (i) the tender of a warrant or voucher entitling the witness to travel free of charge shall be deemed to constitute tender of his expenses in respect of any travelling authorised by the warrant or voucher; and

---

(a) 1967 c. 80.　　　　　　　　**(b)** S.I. 1967/1807 (1967 III, p. 4830).

(ii) the tender of a written undertaking on behalf of the defence Council to defray at the taking of the summary of evidence or the trial, as the case may be, any other expenses payable under such regulations in respect of the witness's attendance shall be deemed to constitute tender of these expenses.

(4) The provisions of section 101 of the Act shall apply in relation to proceedings at the taking of a summary of evidence as they apply in relation to proceedings at a court-martial, and when so applied they shall be construed as though the words "officer taking the summary of evidence" were substituted for the words "president of the court-martial".

RECORD OF PROCEEDINGS

Record of proceedings

92.—(1) The proceedings of general and district courts-martial shall be recorded in accordance with the following provisions:—

(a) the proceedings of a court-martial shall be recorded in writing in accordance with the appropriate form set out in Schedule 4 to these Rules and in sufficient detail to enable the confirming officer to follow the course of the proceedings and to judge of the merits of the case;

(b) when there is no shorthand writer present the evidence should be taken down in narrative form as nearly as possible in the words used:

Provided that if the court, judge advocate, prosecutor or accused consider it necessary, any particular question and answer shall be taken down *verbatim*;

(c) when an objection, submission or application is made during a trial at which there is no shorthand writer, a record shall be made of the proceedings relating to such objection, submission or application if and in such detail as the court or judge advocate think fit;

Provided that if the prosecutor or accused so requests a note shall be made of the objection, submission or application, the grounds therefor, the advice of the judge advocate (if any) thereon, and the decision of the court;

(d) when any address by the prosecutor or the accused or summing up of the judge advocate is not in writing and there is no shorthand writer present, it shall only be necessary to record so much of such address or summing up as the court or judge advocate think proper;

Provided that if the prosecutor or accused so requests a note shall be made of any particular point in such address or summing up;

(e) there shall not be recorded in the record of the proceedings any matter not forming part of the trial, but if any comment or report seems to the court to be necessary, the president may forward it to the proper air-force authority in a separate document.

(2) When a shorthand writer has been appointed to act at a trial by court-martial in pursuance of Rule 31 a transcript of the shorthand note of the proceedings shall only be made of that portion of the proceedings which relates to any charge upon which the accused has been found guilty and such other portions of the proceedings as may be required by the confirming officer or, in the event of the accused being found not guilty of all the charges, the officer who would have been the confirming officer if the accused had been found guilty of any of the charges.

(3) The proceedings of a field general court-martial shall so far as is practicable be recorded in accordance with the provisions of paragraph (1) of this Rule and the record must in any event contain the names of the president and members constituting the court and the judge advocate (if any), the name and description of the accused, the charge-sheet, all pleas, a brief summary of the evidence and the finding and sentence.

Exhibits

93.—(1) Subject to paragraph (2) of this Rule, any document or thing admitted in evidence shall be made an exhibit.

(2) When an original document or book is produced to the court by a witness, the court may at the request of the witness compare a copy of it or an extract of the relevant parts therefrom with the original, and after they have satisfied themselves, that such copy or extract is correct and the president or the judge advocate has certified thereon that the court have compared it with the original and found it correct, the court may return the document or book to the witness and attach the copy or extract to the record of the proceedings as an exhibit.

(3) Every exhibit shall:—
  (*a*) be marked with a number or letter and be signed by the president or judge advocate or have a label bearing a number or letter and the signature of the president or judge advocate affixed to it.
  (*b*) be attached to or kept with the record of the proceedings, unless in the opinion of the court having regard to the nature of the exhibit or for other good reason it is not expedient to attach it to or keep it with the record.

(4) When an exhibit is not attached to or kept with the record of the proceedings under paragraph (3)(*b*) of this Rule, the president shall ensure that proper steps are taken for its safe custody.

Custody and inspection of record of proceedings during trial

94.—(1) During a trial at which there is no judge advocate, the record of the proceedings and the exhibits shall be deemed to be in the custody of the president. During a trial at which there is a judge advocate the record and the exhibits shall be deemed to be in the custody of the judge advocate, save when he is not present in closed court when they shall be deemed to be in the custody of the president.

(2) With the permission of the court, the prosecutor or the accused may at any reasonable time before the trial is concluded have a particular part of the record of the proceedings read to him, and, if proper precautions are taken for its safety, inspect any exhibit.

CONFIRMATION, REVISION AND PROMULGATION

Confirmation and promulgation

95.—(1) When a confirming officer receives the record of the proceedings of a court-martial and the finding of the court requires confirmation, he shall record his decision thereon and on any sentence and any order which the court may have made under section 138 of the Act, on the record of the proceedings in the appropriate form set out in Schedule 4 to these Rules, and such record of his decision shall form part of the record of the proceedings.

(2) When a court have accepted a plea of guilty made under Rule 41(2), the confirming officer may confirm their finding notwithstanding that the court have accepted the plea without the concurrence of the convening officer if, in the opinion of the confirming officer, it is in the interests of justice to do so.

(3) When a court have rejected a plea to the jurisdiction of the court or a plea in bar of trial or have overruled an objection to a charge, it shall not be necessary for the confirming officer to approve specifically the decision of the court, but his approval shall be implied from his confirming the finding on the charge to which the plea or objection relates. If he disapproves the decision of the court to reject the plea or to overrule the objection, he shall withhold confirmation of the finding on the charge to which the plea or objection relates.

(4) The confirming officer may state his reasons for withholding confirmation in any case, but if he withholds confirmation where the court have rejected a plea to the jurisdiction or a plea in bar of trial or have overruled an objection to the charge, because he disapproves this decision of the court, he shall when recording his decision under paragraph (1) of this Rule state that he has withheld confirmation for this reason.

(5) If the sentence of a court-martial is informally expressed, the confirming officer may in confirming the sentence vary the form thereof so that it shall be properly expressed.

(6) Whenever it appears that there is sufficient evidence or a plea of guilty under either paragraph (1) or paragraph (2) of Rule 41 to justify the finding of the court, such finding and any lawful sentence consequent thereon may be confirmed, and if confirmed shall be valid, notwithstanding any deviation from these Rules, if the accused has not been prejudiced by such deviation.

(7) When a confirming officer has confirmed a finding and sentence of a court or has withheld confirmation thereof, he shall send the record of the proceedings to the commanding officer of the accused for promulgation to the accused of the finding and sentence, or of the fact that confirmation has been withheld, as the case may be. The fact of promulgation shall be recorded on the record of the proceedings in the form set out in Schedule 4 to these Rules. If confirmation has been withheld because the confirming officer disapproves the court's decision to reject a plea to the jurisdiction or a plea in bar of trial or to overrule an objection to the charge, the accused shall be so informed.

Revision

96.—(1) The proceedings and decision of a court on revision shall be recorded on the record of the proceedings in the appropriate form set out in Schedule 4 to these Rules, and the president shall date and sign such record and decision and return it to the confirming officer, after it has been signed by the judge advocate (if any).

(2) When an accused is acquitted on revision the revised finding shall be communicated to the accused in such manner as may be specified by the confirming officer.

LOSS OF PROCEEDINGS

Loss of original record of proceedings before confirmation

97.—(1) If before confirmation the whole or any part of the original record of the proceedings of a court-martial is lost and a copy exists, such copy may, if the president or the judge advocate certifies it to be correct, be accepted and used in lieu of the original.

(2) If before confirmation the whole or any part of the original record of the proceedings of a court-martial is lost and no copy thereof exists, but evidence of the proceedings of the court can be procured to enable the record or part thereof which has been lost to be reconstituted sufficiently to permit the confirming officer to follow the course of the proceedings and to judge of the merits of the case, the record as so reconstituted may, with the consent of the accused, be accepted and used in lieu of the original:

Provided that where part only of the original record of the proceedings of a court-martial has been lost, and the part which remains is sufficient to enable the confirming officer to follow the course of the proceedings and judge of the merits of the case, such remaining part may, with the consent of the accused, be accepted and used as if it were the complete record, and in such case it shall not be necessary to reconstitute the part of the record which has been lost.

(3) If before confirmation the whole or any part of the original record of the proceedings of a court-martial is lost and such loss cannot be made good under either paragraph (1) or paragraph (2) of this Rule, the confirming officer shall withhold confirmation and shall record his decision in the appropriate form set out in Schedule 4 to these Rules.

Loss of original record of proceedings after confirmation

98. If after confirmation the whole or any part of the original record of the proceedings of a court-martial is lost and a copy thereof is certified by the president or the judge advocate to be correct, or a sufficient record of the charge, finding, sentence and proceedings before the court and of the confirmation of the finding and sentence remains or can be reconstituted to permit of the case being reviewed or the sentence reconsidered, such copy or reconstituted record or remaining part of the record may be accepted and used in lieu of the original.

CUSTODY OF THE RECORD AFTER CONFIRMATION

Custody and preservation of record of proceedings after confirmation

99. For the purposes of section 141(1) of the Act the prescribed period during which the record of the proceedings of a court-martial shall be kept in the custody of the Judge Advocate General shall be six years from the conclusion of the trial.

PETITIONS

Petitions

100.—(1) If an accused who has been sentenced by a court-martial or who has been found by a court-martial to be unfit to stand his trial or to be not guilty by reason of insanity wishes to petition before confirmation against the finding or sentence or both, he shall present a petition to the confirming officer in the appropriate form set out in Schedule 7 to these Rules.

(2) If an accused who has been sentenced by a court-martial or who has been found by a court-martial to be unfit to stand his trial or to be not guilty by reason of insanity wishes to petition after promulgation against the finding so as to be able to exercise the rights conferred on him by the Courts-Martial (Appeals) Act, 1968(**a**), if his petition is rejected, he shall present a petition (hereinafter referred to as an "appeal petition") in the appropriate form set out in Schedule 7 to these Rules, within the period prescribed by the Rules(**b**) made under section 49 of the said Act.

(**a**) 1968 c. 20.　　　　　　　　　(**b**) S.I. 1968/1071 (1968 II, p. 2872).

(3) If an accused who has been sentenced by court-martial or who has been found by a court-martial to be unfit to stand his trial or to be not guilty by reason of insanity wishes to petition after promulgation against the finding otherwise than by means of an appeal petition, he shall present a petition to a reviewing authority at any time within six months of promulgation in the appropriate form set out in Schedule 7 to these Rules.

(4) If an accused who has been sentenced by a court-martial wishes to petition after promulgation against the sentence, he shall present a petition to a reviewing authority or an officer authorised to reconsider a sentence of a court-martial under section 114 of the Act at any time within six months of promulgation in the appropriate form set out in Schedule 7 to these Rules.

(5) In any of the circumstances specified in the first column of the list of persons to whom petitions may be presented under this Rule which is set out in Schedule 7 to these Rules, an appeal petition or a petition under paragraph (3) or paragraph (4) of this Rule which is presented to the person specified in relation to those circumstances in the second column of that list shall be treated as having been presented to the authority to whom the petition is addressed.

MISCELLANEOUS PROVISIONS

Notice requiring oral evidence in lieu of written statement

101. A notice under section 9(2)(*d*) of the Criminal Justice Act, 1967**(a)**, as modified by the Courts-Martial (Evidence) Regulations, 1967**(b)**, requiring that oral evidence shall be given in lieu of a written statement shall be in the appropriate form set out in Schedule 4 to these Rules.

Order to inspect bankers' books

102. The powers conferred by section 7 of the Bankers' Books Evidence Act 1879**(c)**, may be exercised for the purposes of a court-martial by order of the convening officer. The order referred to in this Rule shall be in the form set out in Schedule 4 to these Rules.

Exceptions from Rules on account of the exigencies of the service

103.—(1) Where in the opinion of the officer who is or would be responsible for convening a court-martial to try the accused or, if he is not available, of the senior officer on the spot, the exigencies of the service render compliance with all or any of the provisions of the Rules mentioned in paragraph (4) of this Rule impracticable, the officer who is or would be responsible for convening a court-martial to try the accused, or the senior officer on the spot as the case may be, may make a declaration to that effect in the appropriate form set out in Schedule 4 to these Rules.

(2) Any declaration made under paragraph (1) of this Rule by the senior officer on the spot shall be forwarded by him as soon as possible to the officer who is or would be responsible for convening a court-martial to try the accused.

(3) When a declaration has been made under paragraph (1) of this Rule, it shall not be necessary to comply with any provision of these Rules which is mentioned in such declaration and these Rules shall be construed accordingly.

(4) The provisions of these Rules in respect of which a declaration may be made under paragraph (1) of this Rule are:

(a) 1967 c. 80. (b) S.I. 1967/1807 (1967 III, p. 4830).
(c) 1879 c. 11.

(*a*) Provisos (*a*) and (*b*) to Rule 7(2);

(*b*) Rule 9(*b*) in so far as it relates to the accused's right to insist that a witness shall be compelled to attend the taking of a summary of evidence for cross-examination;

(*c*) Rule 19 in so far as it provides that the documents specified therein must be given to the accused not less than twenty-four hours before the appropriate superior authority investigates and deals summarily with the charge;

(*d*) Rule 25(1) paragraphs (*b*) and (*c*) and paragraph (*d*) in so far as it provides that the documents specified therein shall be given to the accused not less than twenty-four hours before his trial.

(5) If an accused is brought to trial by court-martial or is dealt with summarily by an appropriate superior authority, any declaration which has been made in his case under paragraph (i) of this Rule shall be attached to the record of the proceedings of the court-martial or to the record made by the appropriate superior authority as the case may be.

Exceptions from Rules in the interests of security

104.—(1) When in the opinion of the officer who is or would be responsible for convening a court-martial to try the accused, or, if he is not available, of the senior officer on the spot a charge-sheet, summary or abstract of evidence or other document which, or a copy of which, is required under these Rules to be given to an accused contains information the disclosure of which would or might be directly or indirectly useful to an enemy, the officer who is or would be responsible for convening a court-martial to try the accused, or the senior officer on the spot, as the case may be, may make a declaration to that effect in the appropriate form set out in Schedule 4 to these Rules specifying the document concerned.

(2) Any declaration made under paragraph (1) of this Rule by the senior officer on the spot shall be forwarded by him as soon as possible to the officer who is or would be responsible for convening a court-martial to try the accused.

(3) When a declaration has been made under paragraph (1) of this Rule it shall not be necessary to give to the accused any document mentioned in that declaration or any copy of such a document, and it shall be a sufficient compliance with these Rules if the accused is given a proper opportunity to inspect such documents while preparing and making his defence.

(4) If an accused is brought to trial by court-martial or is dealt with summarily by an appropriate superior authority, any declaration which has been made in his case under paragraph (1) of this Rule shall be attached to the record of the proceedings of the court-martial or to the record made by the appropriate superior authority as the case may be.

Deviations from the forms in the Schedules

105. A deviation or omission from a form or form of words set out in a Schedule to these Rules shall not, by reason only of such deviation or omission, render any document, act or proceeding invalid.

Cases not covered by Rules

106. In any case not provided for by these Rules such course shall be adopted as appears best calculated to do justice.

Revocation of previous Rules

107. The Rules and the Order as set out in Schedule 8 to these Rules are hereby revoked.

Dated 14th March 1972.

Carrington,
One of Her Majesty's Principal
Secretaries of State.

SCHEDULES TO RULES OF PROCEDURE (AIR FORCE), 1972
Rules 5, 9, 10, 91

SCHEDULE 1

FORMS FOR COMMANDING OFFICERS

(1) DELAY REPORT.

(2) SUMMARY OF EVIDENCE.

(3) ABSTRACT OF EVIDENCE.

(4) CERTIFICATE TO BE ATTACHED TO AN ABSTRACT OF EVIDENCE AFTER IT HAS BEEN HANDED TO THE ACCUSED.

(5) SUMMONS TO A WITNESS TO ATTEND THE TAKING OF A SUMMARY OF EVIDENCE.

---

(1) DELAY REPORT

Unit Address:

....

....

....

Tel: ....

To: ....
(Convening Officer)

To: Director of Legal Services (RAF)
Ministry of Defence
(or Deputy Director of Legal Services, HQ Command, (overseas) where applicable).

[1]...... EIGHT DAY DELAY REPORT

pursuant to the Air Force Act, 1955, section 75(2)

Number, Rank, Name of accused   ....
                                       ....

Date placed in arrest...19......

Alleged Offence(s)	Date of Alleged Offence(s)
....	....
....	....
....	....
....	....

[2]The accused is in $\frac{close}{open}$ arrest

The reasons for his retention in arrest are   ....

....

....

[2]The $\frac{abstract}{summary}$ of evidence $\begin{cases} \text{was taken on} \\ \text{has not yet been} \\ \text{taken because} \end{cases}$ ....19......

....

[2]Application for trial $\begin{cases} \text{was made on} \\ \text{has not yet been} \\ \text{made because} \end{cases}$ ....19......

....

[2]D.L.S. $\begin{cases} \text{was consulted on} \\ \text{has not yet been consulted because} \end{cases}$ ....19......

....

²D.L.S. advice { was received on ....19......
                { has not been received.

²Action { is being taken } on D.L.S. advice ···
        { has been taken } as follows   ···
                                         ···

²Date of trial { has not yet been fixed.
               { has been fixed as   ···

Reasons for delay since last report ···
                                     ···
                                     ···
                                     ···

Date ....19......   ···
                                                 Officer commanding accused's Unit.
                                                 (*To be signed personally by the C.O.*)

Notes

¹Insert "1st", "2nd", "3rd", "Final" or as the case may be.
²Strike out words not applicable.

(2) SUMMARY OF EVIDENCE

Summary of evidence in the case of.................................(*number, rank, name, unit*).

Taken by (the commanding officer of the accused) (.........................
(*rank, name, unit*) on the direction of the commanding officer of the accused.)

First Witness for the prosecution
.................................(*number, rank, name, unit*), having been duly sworn states:—

(Cross-examined by the accused)
²Question 1 ....
Answer 1   ....

or

(The accused declines to cross-examine this witness)

....
(*Signature and rank (if any) of witness*).

or

... witness for the prosecution
.................................(*number, rank, name, unit*).

A written statement of this witness's evidence purporting to be signed by him has been read to the accused and is included in this summary at page ...... Having regard to..
(*insert grounds for non-attendance of witness—see Rule 9 (b)*) the attendance of this witness cannot in my opinion be readily procured.

[The accused does not demand the attendance of this witness for cross-examination.] [The accused demands the attendance of this witness for cross-examination but the witness is not compellable and has refused to attend.]

....
(*Signature of officer taking the summary of evidence*)

or

.... (*description*)
A written statement of this witness's evidence has been read to the accused and is included in this summary at page ...... (*The accused does not object to the application of Rule of Procedure 9(c).* (*The accused objects to the application of Rule of Procedure 9(c) but the witness is not compellable and has refused to attend*).

....
(*Signature of officer taking the summary of evidence*)

The accused having been duly cautioned in accordance with Rule of Procedure 9(*d*) reserves his defence.

or

The accused having been duly cautioned in accordance with Rule of Procedure 9(*d*) elects [to give evidence on oath] [to make a statement without being sworn] and to call a witness(es)[3].

The accused...(*number, rank, name, unit*) having been duly sworn[1] states:—

First witnesss
for the defence
....
(*Signature and rank* (*if any*) *of accused if he signs*).

... witness for
the defence
....(*number, rank, name, unit*) having been duly sworn[1] states:—

....
(*Signature and rank* (*if any*) *of witness*)

or

... witness for
the defence
....(*number, name, rank, unit*))
A written statement of this witness's evidence purporting to be signed by him has been read to the accused and is included in this summary at page...... Having regard to (*insert grounds for non-attendance of witness, see Rule 9(e)*), the attendance of this witness cannot in my opinion be readily procured.

....
(*Signature of officer taking the summary of evidence*).

Certified that Rule of Procedure 9 has been complied with.
This summary of evidence consisting of.........numbered pages was taken by me at...................................in the presence and hearing of the accused on the.................day(s) of...............................19......

....
(*Signature and rank of officer taking the summary of evidence*).

Notes

[1]When the witness or the accused affirms the words "duly affirmed" should be substituted for the words "been duly sworn" and when a witness is a child who is too young to give evidence on oath or the accused makes a statement without being sworn the words "without being sworn" should be substituted for the words "having been duly sworn".

[2]See however, Rule 9(*h*).

[3]Omit the words "and to call a witness(es)" if they are not applicable.

(3) ABSTRACT OF EVIDENCE

Abstract of evidence in the case of......................................(*number, rank, name, unit*) consisting of the...............(*insert the number of statements*) attached statements and...............(*insert the number of precis*) precis of evidence of witnesses for the prosecution and compiled by me [the commanding officer of the accused] [.................................[2] on the direction of the commanding officer of the accused.]

(Date).....................................   ....
                                                                    (*Signature and rank*)

Notes

[1]Strike out any reference to statements or précis which are not applicable.

[2]Insert name and rank of the officer making the abstract.

(4) CERTIFICATE TO BE ATTACHED TO AN ABSTRACT OF EVIDENCE

Certified that I[1]...;
....[1]
on the................................day of...................................19...
handed to the accused[2]...
a copy of the abstract of evidence relating to him dated the...........................
day of.................................19...... and duly cautioned him in accordance with Rule of Procedure 10(2) and that (on the...................................day of......
.....................19...... he elected to make and sign the statement which is marked ....and attached to this certificate] [he did not make a statement.] [The accused submitted................................statements of evidence for the defence which are marked............................[respectively] and attached to this certificate].
(Dated............................19......   ....
                                                              (*Signature of certifying officer*).

Notes

[1]Insert rank, name and unit of officer signing the certificate.

[2]Insert number, rank, name and unit of the accused.

(5) SUMMONS TO A WITNESS TO ATTEND THE TAKING OF A SUMMARY OF EVIDENCE

To..[1]
WHEREAS a charge has been preferred against...[2]
AND WHEREAS I have directed a summary of the evidence to be taken at.....................
..................................[3] on the....................day of...........................19......

Pursuant to section 103 of the Air Force Act, 1955, and Rule 91 of the Rules of Procedure (Air Force) 1972, made thereunder, YOU ARE HEREBY SUMMONED and required to attend as a witness the taking of the said summary of evidence at ....[3] on the........day of.......................................19......
at........o'clock in the............noon and to bring with you the documents hereinafter mentioned, viz.:[4]..
....
....
....

Whereof you shall fail at your peril.

Given under my hand at...............................on the.............................day
of...................................19......

....
(*Signature, rank and unit*)
Commanding officer of the accused.

Notes

[1]Insert name and address of the person to whom the summons is to be sent.

[2]Insert the number, rank, name and unit of the accused.

[3]Insert the place where the summary of evidence is to be taken.

[4]Specify the documents (if any) which the witness is to bring. If the witness is not required to bring any documents, strike out the words relating to the documents.

Rules 14, 15.

SCHEDULE 2

CHARGE SHEETS

(1) COMMENCEMENT OF A CHARGE-SHEET.

(2) STATEMENTS OF OFFENCES.

(3) ILLUSTRATIONS OF CHARGE-SHEETS.

(1) COMMENCEMENT OF A CHARGE SHEET

1. The accused............(*rank, name, number, unit*) an officer holding a commission in the { Royal Air Force / Royal Air Force Reserve of Officers / Royal Air Force Volunteer Reserve / Royal Auxiliary Air Force / Royal Auxiliary Air Force General List / Royal Auxiliary Air Force Reserve of Officers } subject to air-force law under section 205 (1) (*a*) of the Air Force Act, 1955, is charged with:—

2. The accused............(*rank, name, number, unit*) an officer holding a commission in the Royal Air Force liable to be recalled to air-force service under Her Majesty, subject to air-force law under section 205 (1) (*b*) of the Air Force Act, 1955, is charged with:—

3. The accused............(*rank, name, number, unit*) an officer of the { Royal Air Force Reserve of Officers / Royal Air Force Volunteer Reserve } liable to be called out for training, subject to air-force law under section 205 (1) (*c*) of the Air Force Act, 1955, is charged with:—

4. The accused............(*rank, name, number, unit*) an officer of the Training Branch of the Royal Air Force Volunteer Reserve, subject to air-force law under section 205 (1) (*c*) of the Air Force Act, 1955, is charged with:—

5. The accused............(*rank, name, number, unit*) an officer holding a commission in the { Royal Air Force / Royal Air Force Reserve of Officers / Royal Air Force Volunteer Reserve / Royal Auxiliary Air Force / Royal Auxiliary Air Force General List / Royal Auxiliary Air Force Reserve of Officers } subject to air-force law under section 205 (1) (*d*) of the Air Force Act, 1955, is charged with:—

6. The accused............(*rank, name, number, unit*) an officer (*here insert type of commission*), subject to air-force law under section 205 (1) (*e*) of the Air Force Act, 1955, is charged with:—

7. The accused............(*rank, name, number, unit*) an officer holding a commission { in the Royal Auxiliary Air Force on the active list / on the permanent staff of the Royal Auxiliary Air Force } subject to air-force law under section 205(1)(*f*) of the Air Force Act, 1955, is charged with:—

8. The accused............(*rank, name, number, unit*) an officer in the { Royal Auxiliary Air Force General List / Royal Auxiliary Air Force Reserve of Officers } doing duty with a body of the regular air force { ordered on a duty/service for which he was liable as such an officer, } subject to air-force law under section 205(1)(*f*) of the Air Force Act, 1955, is charged with:—

9. The accused............(*number, rank, name, unit*) { a warrant officer / a non-commissioned officer / an airman } of the regular air force, is charged with:—

10. The accused............(*number, rank, name, unit*) { a warrant officer / a non-commissioned officer / a man } of the air force reserve { called out { on permanent service / in aid of the civil power } / undergoing training / employed in Her Majesty's service in employment of which it is an express condition that while employed therein he is to be subject to air-force law, } subject to air-force law under section 205 (1) (*h*) of the Air Force Act, 1955, is charged with:—

11. The accused............(*number, rank, name, unit*) { a warrant officer / a non-commissioned officer / a man } of the Royal Auxiliary Air Force { embodied / called out for home defence service / undergoing training / attending { a drill / a parade } / serving on the permanent staff of the Royal Auxiliary Air Force } subject to air-force law under section 205 (1) (*i*) of the Air Force Act, 1955, is charged with:—

12. The accused............(*name and unit in which employed*), a pensioner employed in Her Majesty's service in employment of which it is an express condition that while employed therein he is to be subject to air-force law, subject to air-force law under section 205 (1) (*j*) of the Air Force Act, 1955, is charged with:—

13. The accused............(*number, rank, name, unit*) a person serving in a force raised by order of Her Majesty outside the United Kingdom and under the command of an officer holding an air forces commission, subject to air-force law under section 205 (1) (*k*) of the Air Force Act, 1955, is charged with:—

14. The accused............(*number, rank, name, unit*) attached to (*unit*) a member of a Commonwealth Force attached to the United Kingdom air forces, subject to air-force law under section 4 of the Visiting Forces Act, 1933, is charged with:—

15. The accused............(number, rank, name, unit) { an officer / a warrant officer / a non-commissioned officer / an airman } of an air force raised under the law of a colony and subject to air-force law under section 207 (1) of the Air Force Act, 1955, and under (*here set out the section, etc. of the law of the colony subjecting the accused to air-force law*), is charged with:—

16. The accused............ (number, rank, name, unit) { an officer / a warrant officer / a non-commissioned officer / an airman } of an air force raised under the law of a colony and serving with part of the { regular air force / air force reserve / Royal Auxiliary Air Force } and subject to air-force law under section 207 (2) of the Air Force Act, 1955, is charged with:—

17. The accused............(number, rank, name, unit) (*unit to which attached or with which doing duty, etc.*) { an officer / a warrant officer / a non-commissioned officer / an airman } of a force raised under the law of a colony and { attached to / doing duty with / acting as part of / with } any portion of the { regular air force / air force reserve / Royal Auxiliary Air Force } in the United Kingdom, subject to air-force law under section 207 (3) of the Air Force Act, 1955, is charged with:—

18. The accused............(number, rank, name, unit) attached to (unit) a member of Her Majesty's { naval / military } forces attached to the { regular air force / air force reserve / Royal Auxiliary Air Force } subject to air-force law under section 208 of the Air Force Act, 1955, is charged with:—

19. The accused............(name) a person embarked as a passenger on board Her Majesty's (*ship*) aircraft (*type*)............ No............. and liable to trial by court-martial under section 208A of the Air Force Act, 1955, is charged with:—

20. The accused ....(name) a person { employed in the service of / accompanying } { a body / a part of a body / a member of a body / a body / a part of a body } of the regular air force on active service and liable to trial by court-martial under section 209 (1) of the Air Force Act, 1955, is charged with:—

21. The accused............(name) (*here give a description of the person sufficient to show that he falls within a class of persons mentioned in Schedule 5 to the Act*), liable to trial by court-martial under section 209 (2) of the Air Force Act, 1955, is charged with:—
Where the offence has been committed by a person while subject to air-force law, and he has ceased to be subject at the time when he is charged (in accordance with the provisions of section 131 of the Air Force Act, 1955) the commencement of the charge-sheet will run as follows:—

22. The accused............(name) formerly (*number, rank, unit*), an airman of the regular air force (*or other description showing how the accused was subject to air-force law*), liable to trial by court-martial under section 131 of the Air Force Act, 1955, is charged with:—

Air Force Reserve Act, 1950

23. The accused............(*number, rank, name and unit*) being liable to trial by court-martial under the provisions of section {14 (1) / 14 (2) / 17 (2)} of the Air Force Reserve Act, 1950, is charged with:—

Auxiliary Forces Act, 1953

24. The accused............(*number, rank, name and unit*) being liable to trial by court-martial under the provisions of section 27 (1) of the Auxiliary Forces Act, 1953, is charged with:—

National Service Act, 1948 and Air Force Reserve Act, 1950

25. The accused............(*number, rank, name and unit*) being liable to trial by court-martial under the provisions of section 5(4) of the National Service Act, 1948 and of section 14 (1) of the Air Force Reserve Act, 1950, is charged with:—

National Service Act, 1948 and Auxiliary Forces Act, 1953

26. The accused............(*number, rank, name and unit*) being liable to trial by court-martial under the provisions of section 5(4) of the National Service Act, 1948, and of section 27(1) of the Auxiliary Forces Act, 1953, is charged with:—

(2) STATEMENTS OF OFFENCES

AIR FORCE ACT, 1955

Misconduct in action and other offences arising out of air-force service

SECTION 24

(1) {(*a*)/(*b*)} Misconduct in action contrary to section 24(1) {(*a*)/(*b*)} of the Air Force Act, 1955

(2) {(*a*)/(*b*)/(*c*)/(*d*)} [Misconduct in the presence or vicinity of the enemy / Misconduct in action / Misconduct when under orders] contrary to section 24(2) {(*a*)/(*b*)/(*c*)/(*d*)} of the Air Force Act, 1955

SECTION 25

{(*a*)/(*b*)/(*c*)/(*d*)/(*e*)/(*f*)} Assisting the enemy contrary to section 25(1) {(*a*)/(*b*)/(*c*)/(*d*)/(*e*)/(*f*)} of the Air Force Act, 1955

SECTION 26

(1) Obstructing an action or operation contrary to section 26(1) of the Air Force Act, 1955.

(2) Giving a false air signal
Altering an air signal
Interfering with apparatus for giving an air signal
} contrary to section 26(2) of the Air Force Act, 1955.

SECTION 27

(a) Failing to send to a Prize Court papers found on board a prize } contrary to section 27(1)(a) of the Air Force Act, 1955.

(b) Unlawfully agreeing to ransom a prize contrary to section 27(1)(b) of the Air Force Act, 1955.

(c) Restoring
Abandoning
} a prize contrary to section 27(1)(c) of the Air Force Act, 1955.

SECTION 28

(a) Striking
Ill-treating
Unlawful taking from
} a person on board a prize contrary to section 28(a) of the Air Force Act, 1955.

(b) Removing goods out of a prize contrary to section 28(b) of the Air Force Act, 1955.

(c) Breaking bulk with intent contrary to section 28(c) of the Air Force Act, 1955.

SECTION 29

(a) Sleeping
Leaving his place of duty
} { when on guard duty
when on watch
when under orders to regulate traffic
} contrary to section 29(a) of the Air Force Act, 1955.

(b) Striking
Using force against
} a person { on guard duty
on watch
under orders to regulate traffic
} contrary to section 29(b) of the Air Force Act, 1955.

(c) Compelling a person { on guard duty
on watch
under orders to regulate traffic
} to let a person pass contrary to section 29(c) of the Air Force Act, 1955.

2k

SECTION 29A

(a) Failing to attend for a duty / Leaving a duty } contrary to section 29A(a) of the Air Force Act, 1955.

(b) Neglecting to perform / Negligently performing } a duty contrary to section 29A(b) of the Air Force Act, 1955.

SECTION 30

(a) (b) (c) Looting contrary to section 30 {(a) (b) (c)} of the Air Force Act, 1955.

Mutiny and Insubordination

SECTION 31

(1)(a) Mutiny relating to the enemy contrary to section 31(1)(a) of the Air Force Act, 1955.

(1)(b) Incitement to mutiny relating to the enemy contrary to section 31(1)(b) of the Air Force Act, 1955.

(2) Mutiny / Incitement to mutiny } contrary to section 31(2) of the Air Force Act, 1955.

SECTION 32

(a) Failing to suppress or prevent mutiny contrary to section 32(a) of the Air Force Act, 1955.

(b) Failing to report mutiny contrary to section 32(b) of the Air Force Act, 1955.

SECTION 33

(1)(a) Striking / Using violence to / Offering violence to } his superior officer contrary to section 33(1)(a) of the Air Force Act, 1955.

(1)(b) Using threatening / Using insubordinate } language to his superior officer contrary to section 33(1)(b) of the Air Force Act, 1955.

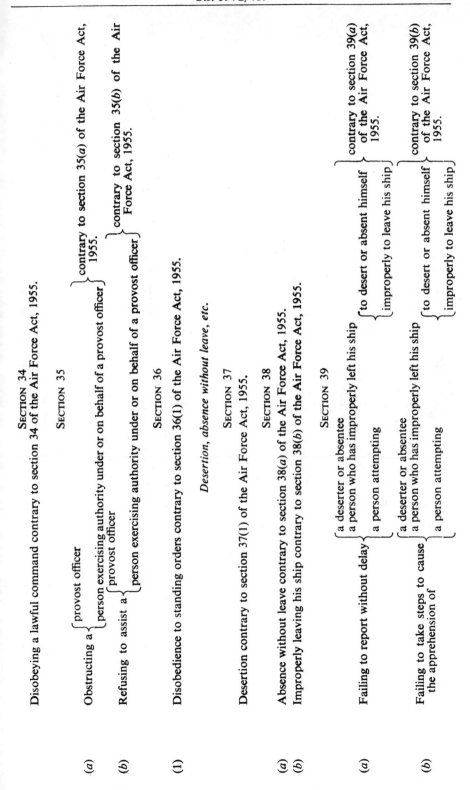

SECTION 34

Disobeying a lawful command contrary to section 34 of the Air Force Act, 1955.

SECTION 35

(a) Obstructing a { provost officer / person exercising authority under or on behalf of a provost officer } contrary to section 35(a) of the Air Force Act, 1955.

(b) Refusing to assist a { provost officer / person exercising authority under or on behalf of a provost officer } contrary to section 35(b) of the Air Force Act, 1955.

SECTION 36

(1) Disobedience to standing orders contrary to section 36(1) of the Air Force Act, 1955.

Desertion, absence without leave, etc.

SECTION 37

Desertion contrary to section 37(1) of the Air Force Act, 1955.

SECTION 38

(a) Absence without leave contrary to section 38(a) of the Air Force Act, 1955.

(b) Improperly leaving his ship contrary to section 38(b) of the Air Force Act, 1955.

SECTION 39

(a) Failing to report without delay { a deserter or absentee / a person who has improperly left his ship / a person attempting } { to desert or absent himself / improperly to leave his ship } contrary to section 39(a) of the Air Force Act, 1955.

(b) Failing to take steps to cause the apprehension of { a deserter or absentee / a person who has improperly left his ship / a person attempting } { to desert or absent himself / improperly to leave his ship } contrary to section 39(b) of the Air Force Act, 1955.

SECTION 40
(DELETE)

SECTION 41
(DELETE)

Malingering and drunkenness

SECTION 42

(1)   Malingering contrary to section 42(1) $\left\{\begin{matrix}(a)\\(b)\\(c)\\(d)\end{matrix}\right\}$ of the Air Force Act, 1955.

SECTION 43

Drunkenness contrary to section 43(1) of the Air Force Act, 1955.

Disorderly conduct

SECTION 43A

(a)   Fighting contrary to section 43A(a) of the Air Force Act, 1955.

(b)   Using threatening, abusive, insulting or provocative $\left\{\begin{matrix}\text{words}\\\text{behaviour}\end{matrix}\right\}$ likely to cause a disturbance contrary to section 43A(b) of the Air Force Act, 1955.

Offences relating to property

SECTION 44

(1)(a) $\left\{\begin{matrix}\text{Wilfully damaging}\\\text{Wilfully causing the loss of}\left\{\begin{matrix}\text{damage of}\\\text{loss of}\end{matrix}\right\}\\\text{Being concerned in the wilful}\end{matrix}\right.$ $\left.\begin{matrix}\text{public property}\\\text{service property}\\\text{property belonging to a person subject to air-force law}\end{matrix}\right\}$ contrary to section 44(1)(a) of the Air Force Act, 1955.

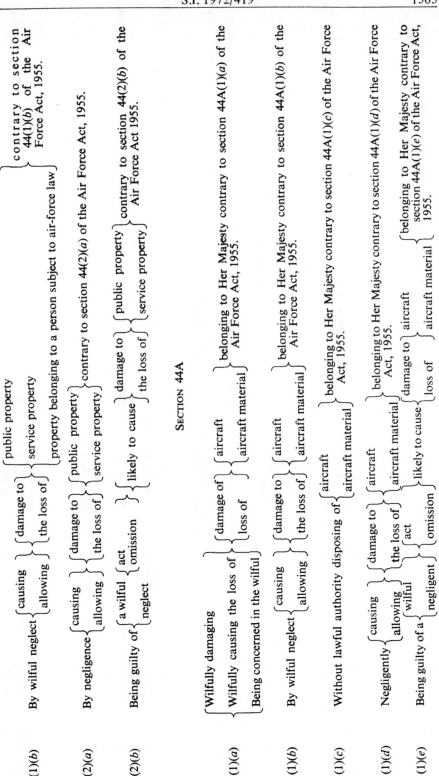

(1)(b)   By wilful neglect {causing / allowing} {damage to / the loss of} {public property / service property} / property belonging to a person subject to air-force law} contrary to section 44(1)(b) of the Air Force Act, 1955.

(2)(a)   By negligence {causing / allowing} {damage to / the loss of} {public property / service property} contrary to section 44(2)(a) of the Air Force Act, 1955.

(2)(b)   Being guilty of {a wilful / neglect} {act / omission} likely to cause {damage to / the loss of} {public property / service property} contrary to section 44(2)(b) of the Air Force Act 1955.

SECTION 44A

(1)(a)   {Wilfully damaging / Wilfully causing the loss of / Being concerned in the wilful {damage of / loss of}} {aircraft / aircraft material} belonging to Her Majesty contrary to section 44A(1)(a) of the Air Force Act, 1955.

(1)(b)   By wilful neglect {causing / allowing} {damage to / the loss of} {aircraft / aircraft material} belonging to Her Majesty contrary to section 44A(1)(b) of the Air Force Act, 1955.

(1)(c)   Without lawful authority disposing of {aircraft / aircraft material} belonging to Her Majesty contrary to section 44A(1)(c) of the Air Force Act, 1955.

(1)(d)   Negligently {causing / allowing} {damage to / the loss of} {aircraft / aircraft material} belonging to Her Majesty contrary to section 44A(1)(d) of the Air Force Act, 1955.

(1)(e)   Being guilty of a {wilful / negligent} {act / omission} likely to cause {damage to / loss of} {aircraft / aircraft material} belonging to section 44A(1)(e) of the Air Force Act, 1955.

(1)(*f*) Wilfully / Negligently } causing the { sequestration / destruction } of aircraft belonging to Her Majesty contrary to section 44A(1)(*f*) of the Air Force Act 1955.

Section 45

Misapplying / Wastefully expending } public property / service property } contrary to section 45 of the Air Force Act, 1955.

Section 46

(1)(*a*) Making away with / Losing / Negligently damaging } his equipment } contrary to section 46(1)(*a*) of the Air-Force Act, 1955.

(*b*) Negligently allowing / to be damaged } a decoration } contrary to section 46(1)(*b*) of the Air Force Act, 1955.

Offences relating to billeting and requisitioning of vehicles

Section 47

(*a*) Obtaining / Ordering / Procuring } a person to obtain } billets contrary to section 47(*a*) of the Air Force Act, 1955.

(*b*) Corruption in relation to a billeting requisition contrary to section 47(*b*) of the Air Force Act, 1955.

(*c*) Wilful damage / Damage by wilful neglect } to { his billet / property in his billet } contrary to section 47(*c*) of the Air Force Act, 1955.

Section 48

(1) { (*a*) / (*b*) } Unlawful requisitioning contrary to section 48(1) { (*a*) / (*b*) } of the Air Force Act, 1955.

(1) (*c*) Corruption in relation to a requisitioning order contrary to section 48(1)(*c*) of the Air Force Act, 1955.

Flying, etc, offences

SECTION 48A

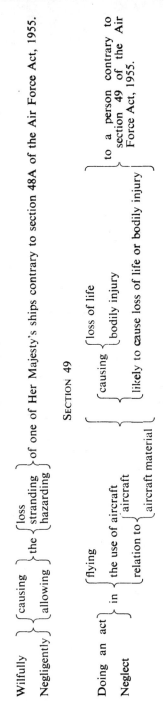

Wilfully / Negligently { causing / allowing } the { loss / stranding / hazarding } of one of Her Majesty's ships contrary to section **48A** of the Air Force Act, 1955.

SECTION 49

Doing an act / Neglect in { the use of aircraft / relation to { flying / aircraft / aircraft material } } { causing { loss of life / bodily injury } / likely to cause loss of life or bodily injury } to a person contrary to section **49** of the Air Force Act, 1955.

SECTION 50

(a) Making / Signing a certificate relating to a ship belonging to Her Majesty without having ensured its accuracy contrary to section 50(a) of the Air Force Act, 1955.

(b) Making / Signing a certificate relating to { aircraft / aircraft material } belonging to Her Majesty without having ensured its accuracy contrary to section 50(b) of the Air Force Act, 1955.

SECTION 51

Unlawful low flying contrary to section 51 of the Air Force Act, 1955.

SECTION 52

Flying an aircraft in a manner causing or likely to cause unnecessary annoyance to a person contrary to section 52 of the Air Force Act, 1955.

Offences relating to and by persons in custody

SECTION 53

(DELETE)

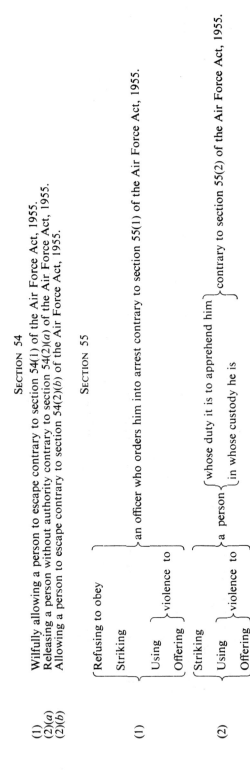

SECTION 54

(1) Wilfully allowing a person to escape contrary to section 54(1) of the Air Force Act, 1955.
(2)(a) Releasing a person without authority contrary to section 54(2)(a) of the Air Force Act, 1955.
(2)(b) Allowing a person to escape contrary to section 54(2)(b) of the Air Force Act, 1955.

SECTION 55

(1) { Refusing to obey / Striking / Using violence to / Offering violence to } an officer who orders him into arrest contrary to section 55(1) of the Air Force Act, 1955.

(2) { Striking / Using violence to / Offering violence to } a person { whose duty it is to apprehend him / in whose custody he is } contrary to section 55(2) of the Air Force Act, 1955.

SECTION 56

Escaping from custody contrary to section 56 of the Air Force Act, 1955.

Offences relating to courts-martial and civil authorities

SECTION 57

(1) { (a) (b) (c) (d) (e) (f) } Contempt of a court-martial contrary to section 57(1) { (a) (b) (c) (d) (e) (f) } of the Air Force Act, 1955.

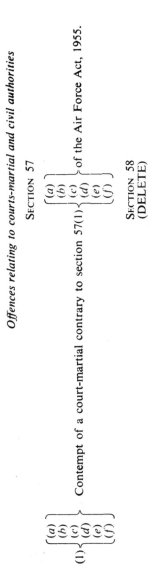

SECTION 58
(DELETE)

Section 59
(DELETE)

Miscellaneous offences

Section 60

Disclosing / Purporting to disclose } information contrary to section 60(1) of the Air Force Act, 1955.

Section 61

Making a false answer on enlistment contrary to section 61 of the Air Force Act, 1955.

Section 62

(a) Making / Signing } a false / Making a false entry in an / Altering / Altering an entry in } official document contrary to section 62(a) of the Air Force Act, 1955.

(b) Suppressing } an official document contrary to section 62(b) of the Air Force Act, 1955.

(c) Defacing / Making away with / Failing to make an entry in an official document with intent to deceive contrary to section 62(c) of the Air Force Act, 1955.

Section 63

Committing an offence against the { person / property } of a member of a civil population outside the United Kingdom contrary to section 63 of the Air Force Act, 1955.

SECTION 63A

Spreading reports relating to operations likely to create despondency or unnecessary alarm contrary to section 63A of the Air Force Act, 1955.

SECTION 64

Scandalous conduct unbecoming the character of an officer contrary to section 64 of the Air Force Act, 1955.

SECTION 65

(a) Striking / Ill-treating { an officer of inferior rank or less seniority / a warrant officer / a non-commissioned officer / an airman } contrary to section 65(a) of the Air Force Act, 1955.

(b) Striking / Ill-treating { a warrant officer / a non-commissioned officer / an airman } of inferior rank or less seniority } contrary to section 65(b) of the Air Force Act, 1955.

SECTION 66

Disgraceful conduct of { a cruel / an indecent / an unnatural } kind contrary to section 66 of the Air Force Act, 1955.

SECTION 67
(DELETE)

SECTION 68

Attempting to commit an offence contrary to section 68 of the Air Force Act, 1955, that is to say (*set out the offence*).

SECTION 68A

SECTION 69

Conduct } to the prejudice of good order and air-force discipline contrary to section 69 of the Air Force Act, 1955.
Neglect }

Civil offences

SECTION 70

Committing a civil offence contrary to section 70(1) of the Air Force Act, 1955, that is to say (*here describe the civil offence in such words as sufficiently describe the offence*).

AIR FORCE RESERVE ACT, 1950

SECTION 14

(1) { Desertion } contrary to section 14(1) of the Air Force Reserve Act, 1950.
    { Absence without leave }

(2) Absence without leave contrary to section 14(2) of the Air Force Reserve Act, 1950.

SECTION 17

(1)(*a*) Failing to comply with { orders / regulations } respecting the payment of the Air Force Reserve contrary to section 17(1)(*a*) of the Air Force Reserve Act, 1950.

(1)(*b*) Failing to attend at a place where it was his duty to be contrary to section 17(1)(*b*) of the Air Force Reserve Act, 1950.

(1)(*c*) Using { threatening / insulting } language to { an officer / a warrant officer / a non-commissioned officer } contrary to section 17(1)(*a*) of the Air Force Reserve Act, 1950.
Behaving in an insubordinate manner

(1)(*d*) { Fraudulently obtaining / Being accessory to the fraudulent obtaining of } { pay / [*other sums*] } contrary to section 17(1)(*d*) of the Air Force Reserve Act, 1950.

(1)(e)   Failing to comply with $\begin{cases}\text{orders} \\ \text{regulations}\end{cases}$ contrary to section 17(1)(e) of the Air Force Reserve Act, 1950.

AUXILIARY FORCES ACT, 1953

SECTION 27

(1) $\begin{cases}\text{Desertion} \\ \text{Absence without leave}\end{cases}$ contrary to section 27(1) of the Auxiliary Forces Act, 1953.

(3) ILLUSTRATIONS OF CHARGE-SHEETS
(i) CHARGE-SHEET

The accused, No. 153 Leading Aircraftman John Smith of No. 2 Squadron, Royal Air Force Station Andover, an airman of the regular air force, is charged with:—

1st Charge.

MALINGERING CONTRARY TO SECTION 42(1)(*b*) OF THE
AIR FORCE ACT, 1955

in that he
at Uxbridge on 1st May 1972, by discharging a rifle wilfully blew off two fingers of his right hand with intent thereby to render himself unfit for service.

2nd Charge
(Alternative to
1st Charge)

NEGLECT TO THE PREJUDICE OF GOOD ORDER AND AIR FORCE
DISCIPLINE CONTRARY TO SECTION 69 OF THE AIR FORCE
ACT, 1955

in that he
at Uxbridge on 1st May 1972, so negligently handled a rifle as to cause it to be discharged, thereby injuring his right hand and rendering himself temporarily unfit for service.

A. B. JONES, Group Captain.
Andover
7th May, 1972.
Commanding Royal Air Force Station,
Andover.[1]

To be tried by District[2] Court-Martial.
C. D. BROWN, Air Vice-Marshal.
Leeds
Commanding No. 06 Group.[3]

9th May 1972.

[1]As to who is a commanding officer for disciplinary purposes see Q.R. 994. It must be made apparent from the description of the commanding officer's appointment which follows his signature, that he is the commanding officer of the unit or station to which the accused, in the heading of the charge sheet, is stated to belong. This fact would not be apparent in the illustration given above if, for example, the word "station" were not included in the description of the commanding officer's appointment, because the accused is described as being of "R.A.F. *Station*, Andover." See also note 1 to R.P. 14.

[2]The type of court will be a general, district or field general court-martial according to the circumstances.

[3]The order for trial may be signed by a staff officer "an officer authorised to sign for" the convening officer, but in that event the staff officer's appointment should be shown (see second illustration charge-sheet).

(ii) CHARGE SHEET

The accused, No 654 Corporal John Robinson, a non-commissioned officer of the air-force reserve called out on permanent service subject to air-force law under section 205(*l*)(*h*) of the Air Force, 1955, and No. 754 Aircraftman William Sprogg, an airman of the Royal Auxiliary Air Force embodied, subject to air-force law under section 205(1)(i) of the Air Force Act, 1955, both of No. 2 Squadron, Royal Air Force Station, Andover are charged with:—

Both accused jointly:

COMMITTING A CIVIL OFFENCE CONTRARY TO SECTION 70(1) OF THE AIR FORCE ACT, 1955, THAT IS TO SAY COMMON ASSAULT

in that they

at Uxbridge on 1st May 1972 assaulted Jack Spratt.

Corporal Robinson only

2nd Charge
STRIKING HIS SUPERIOR OFFICER CONTRARY TO SECTION 33(1)(a) OF THE AIR FORCE ACT, 1955

in that he

at Uxbridge on 1st May, 1972, struck No. 789 Sergeant William Green of No. 2 Squadron Royal Air Force Station Andover.

Aircraftman Sprogg only

3rd Charge.
STRIKING HIS SUPERIOR OFFICER CONTRARY TO SECTION 33(1)(a) OF THE AIR FORCE ACT, 1955,

in that he

at Uxbridge on 1st May, 1972, struck No. 345 Sergeant John Brown of No. 2 Squadron Royal Air Force Station Andover.

Andover
9th May, 1972.

A. B. JONES, Group Captain.
Commanding Royal Air Force Station,
Andover.[1]

To be tried by field general[2] court-martial.[1]

Leeds.
10th May, 1972

J. O. SOPE, Squadron Leader,
Personnel Staff Officer, an officer
authorised to sign for
Air Officer Commanding, No. 06 Group.

Notes

[1]See note 1 to charge-sheet (i) above.

[2]This type of court-martial will be a general, district or a field-general court-martial according to the circumstances.

[3]The order for trial by court-martial should not be entered on the charge-sheet until the convening officer has decided that the accused is to be tried by court-martial.

Rule 20   SCHEDULE 3

RECORD OF PROCEEDINGS BEFORE AN APPROPRIATE SUPERIOR AUTHORITY

ACCUSED'S NUMBER, RANK AND NAME...
    UNIT...

1. *Questions to be put to the accused by the officer dealing with the case before the charge is read.*

Q. Have you received a copy of the charge sheet and [summary] [abstract] of evidence not less than 24 hours ago?

A. ....

Q. Have you had sufficient time to prepare your defence?

A. ....

2. *The officer dealing with the case shall then read the charge(s) to the accused and ask him the following question:—*

Q. Have you agreed in writing that the witnesses against you need not give their evidence in person?

A. ....

3. *If the accused has agreed in writing that the witnesses against him need not give their evidence in person the officer dealing with the case shall read the summary or abstract of evidence to the accused if the accused so requires but, if the accused has not so agreed, the witnesses against him shall give their evidence in person and it shall be recorded on a separate sheet and be attached to this record.*

4. *After the summary or abstract of evidence has been read or the witnesses against the accused have given their evidence, as the case may be, the officer dealing with the case shall say to the accused:—*

Q. Do you wish to give evidence on oath or to make or hand in a statement without being sworn? Your evidence or statement may deal with the facts of the case, with your character and with matters in mitigation of punishment.

A. ....

Q. Do you wish to adduce any other evidence in your defence?

A. ....

5. *If the accused elects to give evidence or to make a statement or to call witnesses the evidence for the defence including any statement made by the accused himself shall be recorded on a separate sheet and attached to this record. The officer dealing with the case shall then: (i) consider all the evidence and determine whether the accused is guilty of the offence or not, and (ii) if he determines that the accused is guilty, examine and consider the accused's record of service. If he intends to award either the punishment of forfeiture of seniority fine, or stoppages or if the finding will involve a forfeiture or in the case of a civilian if he intends to award any punishment he shall not announce and record his finding unless the accused says in answer to the following question that he will accept his award.*

Q. Will you accept my award or do you elect to be tried by court-martial?

A. ....

6. FINDING ....

    AWARD ....

(*Date*)...........................

....
(*Signature, rank and appointment of appropriate superior authority*)

SCHEDULE 4   Rules 22, 67, 71, 80, 91, 92, 95, 96, 101, 102, 103, 104.

COURT-MARTIAL FORMS

(1) CONVENING ORDERS.

(2) DECLARATIONS UNDER RULES 103 AND 104.

(3) ORDER TO INSPECT BANKERS' BOOKS AND TO TAKE COPIES OF ENTRIES.

(4) SUMMONS TO A WITNESS TO ATTEND A COURT-MARTIAL.

(5) NOTICES REQUIRING ORAL EVIDENCE TO BE GIVEN IN LIEU OF A WRITTEN STATEMENT.

(6) RECORD OF PROCEEDINGS OF A COURT-MARTIAL.

(7) FINDINGS.

(8) RECORD OF RECONSIDERATION OF FINDING UNDER RULE 80(5).

(9) SERVICE RECORD OF ACCUSED.

(10) RECORD OF PROCEEDINGS ON REVISION UNDER SECTION 109 OF THE ACT.

(11) CONFIRMATION.

(12) DETERMINATION BY A CONFIRMING OFFICER OR REVIEWING AUTHORITY OF A SUSPENDED SENTENCE, AND DIRECTION THAT SENTENCES ARE TO RUN CONCURRENTLY OR CONSECUTIVELY.

(13) DIRECTION UNDER SECTION 127(4) OF THE ACT.

(14) RESTITUTION ORDER.

(15) PROMULGATION.

---

(1) CONVENING ORDERS
CONVENING ORDERS FOR A [GENERAL] [DISTRICT] COURT-MARTIAL

ORDERS BY...1

    Commanding ....

          (*Place*) ....

Name etc. of accused.   The detail of officers as mentioned below will assemble at.................

....at..............................hours on the...................

....   day of....................19......for the purpose of trying by a [General] [District] Court-Martial the accused person(s) named in the margin.

PRESIDENT

....

MEMBERS[3]

....

....

....

WAITING MEMBERS[3]

....

....

JUDGE ADVOCATE*

The judge advocate has been appointed by or on behalf of the Judge Advocate General of the Forces.

or

....[4] is hereby appointed Judge Advocate.[5]

*Strike out if not applicable.

In the opinion of the convening officer the necessary number of air-force officers having suitable qualifications is not available to form the court and cannot be made available with due regard to the public service.*

An officer of the rank of squadron leader or above having suitable qualifications is not in the opinion of the convening officer available with due regard to the public service.*

The record of the proceedings will be forwarded in an envelope marked confidential to ....
at..Signed this..............................day of
....19......

....
(*Signature, rank and appointment of the convening officer*)
or

....
(*Signature, rank and appointment of the appropriate staff officer*)
an officer authorised to sign for...............................
(*appointment held by the convening officer*).

*Strike out if not applicable.

Notes

[1] Insert rank and name of convening officer.

[2] Insert number, rank, name and unit of the accused. These particulars must agree with his description in the charge-sheet.

³A member or a waiting member may be described either by giving his rank, name and unit or thus: "A..............................(*rank*) to be detailed by the officer commanding.......................................(*unit*)", see Rule of Procedure 23(*a*).

⁴Insert the judge advocate's name and any legal qualifications which he has.

⁵This form of words is appropriate when the judge advocate is appointed by the convening officer, see Rule of Procedure 22(1) (*f*).

CONVENING ORDER FOR A FIELD GENERAL COURT-MARTIAL.

ORDERS BY..¹
Commanding ....
(*Place and date*)..

___

In the opinion of the convening officer it is not possible without serious detriment to the public service that the accused should be tried by a General or District Court-Martial.

Name, etc. of accused.
....

The detail of officers as mentioned below will assemble at ....at...............hours on the..............................day of ....19......for the purpose of trying by a Field General Court-Martial the accused(s) person(s) named in the margin.

PRESIDENT

....
....

MEMBER(S)³

....
....
....
....
....
....

WAITING MEMBER(S)³

....
....

JUDGE ADVOCATE*

The judge advocate has been appointed by or on behalf of the Judge Advocate General of the Forces.

or

....⁴ is hereby appointed Judge Advocate.⁵

In the opinion of the convening officer the necessary number of air-force officers having suitable qualifications is not available to form the court and cannot be made available with due regard to the public service.*

Three officers having suitable qualifications are not in the opinion of the convening officer available without serious detriment to the public service.*

It is not in the opinion of the convening officer practicable to appoint an officer other than himself as President.*

The record of the proceedings will be forwarded to...
Signed this...............................day of...............................19......
....
(*Signature, rank and appointment of the convening officer*)
or

....
(*Signature, rank and appointment of the appropriate staff officer*)
an officer authorised to sign for...............................
(*appointment held by the convening officer*).

Strike out if not applicable

Notes.

[1]Insert rank and name of convening officer.

[2]Insert number, rank, name and unit of the accused.

[3]A member or a waiting member may be described either be giving his rank, name and unit or this: "A.....................(*rank*) to be detailed by the officer commanding.................................(*unit*), see Rule of Procedure 23(*a*).

[4] Insert the judge advocate's name and any legal qualifications which he has.

[5]This form of words is appropriate where the judge advocate is appointed by the convening officer, see Rule of Procedure 22(1)(*f*).

(2) DECLARATIONS UNDER RULES 103 AND 104

Declaration under Rule of Procedure 103

In the case of...[1]

I...[2] [the officer who (is) (would be) responsible for convening a court-martial to try the accused] [the senior officer on the spot] hereby declare than in my opinion the following exigencies of the service namely...............
....
....
....
render compliance with the following provisions of the Rules of Procedure..............
....
....
....
impracticable.

Signed at........................this...............day of.....................19......
....
(*Signature*)

Notes.

[1]Insert number, rank, name and unit of accused.

[2]Insert rank, name and appointment of officer making the declaration.

Declaration under Rule of Procedure 104

In the case of...[1]

I...[2] [the officer who (is) (would be) responsible for convening a court-martial to try the accused] [the senior officer on the spot] hereby declare that in my opinion the[3]...
....
....
contain(s) information the disclosure of which would or might be directly or indirectly useful to an enemy.

Signed at........................this............day of.......................19......
....
(*Signature*)

Notes

[1]Insert number, rank, name and unit of accused.

[2]Insert rank, name and appointment of officer making the declaration.

[3]Here insert the document(s).

(3) ORDER TO INSPECT BANKERS' BOOKS AND TO TAKE COPIES OF ENTRIES

To the Manager...[1]

IN THE MATTER OF A TRIAL BY (GENERAL) (DISTRICT) COURT-MARTIAL OF NUMBER
....²to be held
at.. on...
WHEREAS I have ordered a Court-Martial to assemble at...............................
on the...day of.......................19......,
for the trial of..
AND WHEREAS application has been made to me by...³
....

IT IS HEREBY ORDERED IN PURSUANCE OF SECTION 7 OF THE BANKERS' BOOKS EVIDENCE
ACT, 1879, AND SECTION 103 OF THE AIR FORCE ACT, 1955 AND RULE 102 OF THE
RULES OF PROCEDURE [AIR FORCE], 1972, MADE THEREUNDER that the said.................³
or (his) (their) representative(s) be at liberty for the purposes of the said court-martial
to inspect and take copies of all entries in the books of.....................................⁴
at.....................................⁵ relating to the account in the name of
....⁶ with the said bank from the...........⁷
day of.............................19...... to the.....................day of
.............................19......, both dates inclusive.
SIGNED AT...
this...........................day of.............................19......

....
An officer authorised to convene courts-martial

Notes

¹Insert the name and address of the Bank.

²Here enter the number, rank, name and unit of the person to be tried.

³Here specify the party to the proceedings making the application.

⁴Here insert the name of the Bank.

⁵Here insert the Branch and Branch address of the Bank.

⁶Here insert the name (and usual address) of the person whose account is to be inspected.

⁷Here insert the material dates.

(4) SUMMONS TO A WITNESS TO ATTEND AT A COURT-MARTIAL

To...¹
WHEREAS a court-martial [has been ordered to assemble at...............................
....................] [has assembled at.....................................] on the ....day of
.............................19...... for the trial of.....................................²
Pursuant to section 103 of the Air Force Act, 1955, and Rule 91 of the Rules of
Procedure (Air Force), 1972, made thereunder YOU ARE HEREBY SUMMONED and required
to attend as a witness at the sitting of the said Court at.....................................
on the...............day of.......................................19...... at.................o'clock
in the...........................noon and to bring with you the documents hereinafter
mentioned, viz:³...
....
and so to attend from day to day until you shall be duly discharged: whereof you shall
fail at your peril.
Given under my hand at.................................on the.............................
day of.....................................19......

....
(*Signature, rank, appointment*)
An officer authorised to convene a court-martial*
President of the Court.*
....⁴ an officer authorised to sign for
....⁵an officer authorised to
convene a court-martial.*

Strike out if not applicable.

Notes

[1]Insert name and address of the person to whom the summons is to be sent.

[2]Insert number, rank, name, and unit of the person to be tried.

[3]Specify the documents which the witness is to bring. The words relating to documents should be deleted if not applicable.

[4]Insert the appointment of the staff officer.

[5]Insert the appointment of the officer for whom the staff officer is signing.

(5) NOTICES REQUIRING ORAL EVIDENCE TO BE GIVEN IN LIEU OF A WRITTEN STATEMENT

Notice by a Commanding Officer

To...[1]

I...[2]Commanding.......................................[3]hereby give notice that I require that.................................[4] shall give oral evidence in lieu of [his] [her] written statement dated.................................at your forthcoming trial by Court-Martial.

....
(*Signature and rank*)
Commanding Officer of the accused.

Date.................................19......

Notice by an accused

To...[2] Commanding...[3]

I...[1] hereby give notice that I require that..............

....[4]

shall give oral evidence in lieu of [his] [her] written statement dated.......................
at my forthcoming trial by Court-Martial.

(*Date*)...................................   ....
(*Signature*)

Notes

[1]Insert number, rank, name and unit of the accused.

[2]Insert rank and name of commanding officer.

[3]Insert unit.

[4]Insert name of witness.

(6) RECORD OF PROCEEDINGS OF A COURT-MARTIAL

PAGE 1

A

RECORD OF PROCEEDINGS OF A COURT-MARTIAL

Proceedings of a.................................[1] Court-Martial held at.......................
on the.................................day of.................................19...... by
order of ....

Commanding...

dated the.................................day of.................................19...

PRESIDENT

MEMBERS

JUDGE ADVOCATE

Trial of...

....

....[2]

The Court comply with Rule of Procedure 26.

....not being available owing to

....

...................................the President appoints...............................a qualified waiting member to take his place.

The accused is brought before the Court.

Prosecutor ....

Defending [officer] [Counsel]..

At......................................hours the trial begins.

The convening order is read in the hearing of the accused, marked...................... signed by the president or judge advocate and attached to the record.

The names of the president and members of the court are read in the hearing of the accused and they severally answer to their names.

Q. Do you object to being tried by me as president, or by any of the officers whose names you have heard read?

A. ....

The proceedings relating to the objection(s) are recorded on pages[3]......................

Notes

[1]Insert "General", "District" or "Field General", as the case may be.

[2]Insert number, rank, name and unit of the accused as given in the charge-sheet.

[3]Strike out if not applicable.

B

SWEARING

PAGE

The president, members of the court and judge advocate are duly sworn.

The [following] officers under instruction [listed on page......] are duly sworn,

Q. Do you object to...as shorthand writer?

A. ....[1]

....is duly sworn as shorthand writer.

Q. Do you object to..as interpreter?

A. ....[1]

....is duly sworn as interpreter.

SPECIAL PLEAS AND OBJECTIONS

The accused offers a plea to the jurisdication under Rule of Procedure 36. The proceedings relating to this plea are recorded on page.........[2].

The accused objects to the.................charge(s) under Rule of Procedure 37. The proceedings relating to his objection(s) are recorded on page.........[2].

The accused offers a plea(s) in bar of trial under Rule of Procedure 38 in respect of the.................charge(s). The proceedings relating to his plea(s) are recorded on page.........[2].

The accused......................applies under Rule of Procedure 39 to be tried separately. The proceedings relating to his application are recorded on page.........[2].

The accused applies under Rule of Procedure 40 to have charges...................... and.............................tried separately. The proceedings relating to his application are recorded on page.........[2].

Notes

[1]If there is an objection the proceedings relating to it should be recorded on a separate numbered page and the fact that this has been done should be recorded in this space with the number of the page.

[2]Strike out if not applicable.

C1

ARRAIGNMENT

The charge-sheet is read to the accused and he is arraigned on each charge.

The charge-sheet is signed by the president or judge advocate and inserted in the record immediately before this page, as page(s)...........

Q. Are you guilty or not guilty of the first[1] charge against you, which you have heard read?

A. ....

Q. Are you guilty or not guilty of the second charge against you, which you have heard read?[1]

A. ....

Q. Are you guilty or not guilty of the third charge against you, which you have heard read?[1]

A. ....

Q. Are you guilty or not guilty of the fourth charge against you, which you have heard read?[2]

A. ....

Q. Are you guilty or not guilty of the fifth charge against you, which you have heard read?[2]

A. ....

Q. Are you guilty or not guilty of the sixth charge against you, which you have heard read?[2]

A. ....

The accused having pleaded guilty to the ....
.............................charge(s) Rule of Procedure 42 is duly complied with in respect of this (these) charge(s)[2]

The accused's pleas to the remaining charges are recorded overleaf[2].

Notes

[1]Strike out "first" if there is only one charge.

[2]Strike out if not applicable.

C2

Q. Are you guilty or not guilty of the seventh charge against you, which you have heard read?

A. ....

Q. Are you guilty or not guilty of the eighth charge against you, which you have heard read?

A. ....

Q. Are you guilty or not guilty of the ninth charge against you, which you have heard read?[1]

A. ....

Q. Are you guilty or not guilty of the tenth charge against you, which you have heard read?[1]

A. ....

Q. Are you guilty or not guilty of the eleventh charge against you, which you have heard read?[1]

A. ....

Q. Are you guilty or not guilty of the twelfth charge against you, which you have heard read?[1]

A. ....

Note

[1] Strike out if not applicable.

D1

PAGE ...

PROCEEDINGS ON PLEA(S) OF NOT GUILTY[1]

Q. Do you wish to apply for an adjournment on the ground that any of the rules relating to procedure before trial have not been complied with, and that you have been prejudiced thereby, or on the ground that you have not had sufficient opportunity for preparing your defence?

A. ....[2]

The prosecutor (makes an opening address shortly outlining the facts) (makes an opening address which is summarized below) (hands in a written address which is read, signed by the president or judge advocate marked.......................and attached to the record).

Notes

[1] Remove this page if there are no pleas of not guilty.

[2] If the accused asks for an adjournment, the proceedings relating to his application should, if necessary, be recorded on a separate page and a record made here that this has been done.

D2

PAGE ...

First witness for the prosecution.   The witnesses for the prosecution are called.

....

being duly sworn[1] says:—

Continued on page ...

Note

[1] When a witness affirms the words "having duly affirmed" should be substituted for the words "being duly sworn", and when a witness is a child who is too young to give evidence on oath the words "without being sworn" should be substituted for the words "being duly sworn".

D3

PAGE ...

PROCEEDINGS ON PLEA(S) OF NOT GUILTY[1]
(*continued*)

The prosecution is closed.

The accused submits under Rule of Procedure 58 that there is no case for him to answer in respect of the.............................charge(s). The proceedings relating to this submission are recorded on pages........

DEFENCE

Rule of Procedure 59 is complied with.

Q.   Do you apply to give evidence yourself on oath or do you wish to make a statement without being sworn?

A.   ....

Q.   Do you intend to call any other person as a witness in your defence?

A.   ....

Q.   Is he a witness as to fact or to character only?

A.   ....

(Where the accused intends to call a witness as to fact, other than himself)[2].

Q.   Do you wish to make an opening address[2].

A.   ....

The accused[2] [makes an opening address which is summarized below] [hands in a written address which is read, signed by the president or judge advocate marked ....and attached to the record].

Notes

[1]Remove this page if there are no pleas of not guilty.

[2]Strike out if the accused does not intend to call witnesses as to fact, other than himself.

D4

PAGE ...

(Where the accused makes a statement without being sworn)[1]

The accused [makes a statement, which is recorded on page......] [hands in a written statement which is read, marked...........................signed by the president or judge advocate and attached to the record].

(Where evidence on oath is given for the defence)[1]

The witnesses for the defence (including the accused, if sworn) are called.

First witness for the defence ....

being duly sworn[2] says:—

Continued on page......

Notes.

[1]Strike out this paragraph if not applicable.

[2]When a witness or the accused affirms, the words "having duly affirmed" should be substituted for the words "being duly sworn" and when a witness is a child who is too young to give evidence on oath, the words "without being sworn" should be substituted for the words "being duly sworn".

D5

PAGE ...

PROCEEDINGS ON PLEA(S) OF NOT GUILTY[1] *(continued)*

The prosecutor [makes a closing address which is summarized on page......] [hands in a closing address which is read, marked..signed by the president or judge advocate, and attached to the record][2].

The accused [makes a closing address which is summarized on page......] [hands in a closing address which is read, marked..signed by the president or judge advocate and attached to the record].[2]

The note of the summing-up of the judge advocate is recorded on page.........[2]

FINDING(S)

The court close to deliberate on their finding(s).

The court find that the accused[3]...

....is:[4]

ANNOUNCEMENT OF FINDING(S)

The court being reopened the accused is again brought before them.

The finding(s) [is] [are] read and (with the exception of the finding(s) of "not guilty")[2] [is] [are] announced as being subject to confirmation.

PROCEEDINGS ON ACQUITTAL ON ALL CHARGES[2]

The accused is released.

Signed at...................................this.....................day of..................19......

Judge Advocate.   President.

Notes.

[1]Strike out this page if not applicable.

[2]Strike out if not applicable.

[3]Insert number, rank, name and unit of the accused as given on the charge-sheet.

[4]Set out the finding on each charge in the appropriate form set out in Schedule 4 to the Rules of Procedure.

E

PAGE ...

PROCEEDINGS ON PLEA(S) OF GUILTY[1]

The accused[2] ....

....

is found guilty of[3]

The finding(s) [is] [are] read in open court and [is] [are] announced as being subject to confirmation.

[The [summary] [abstract] of evidence is read to the court by the prosecutor, marked..........................signed by the president or judge advocate and attached to the record] [the prosecutor informs the court of the facts contained in the [summary] [abstract] of evidence which is marked......................................signed by the president or judge advocate and attached to the record.[4]]

Notes.

[1]Strike out this page if not applicable.

[2]Insert the number, name, rank and unit of the accused as given on the charge-sheet.

[3]Record the finding on each charge of which the accused is found guilty in the appropriate form set out in Schedule 4 to the Rules of Procedure.

[4]Strike out if not applicable.   If this paragraph is struck out, Rule of Procedure 45(2) must be complied with.

F1

PAGE ...

PROCEEDINGS ON CONVICTION

Note: *F.2 should be completed before F.1, if the accused has pleaded not guilty to all charges. F.1 should normally be completed before F.2 if the accused has pleaded guilty to any charge but the president may in his discretion complete F.2 before F.1 if there is no danger of the accused making an inconsistent plea.*

Q. Do you wish to give evidence yourself or to call other witnesses as to your character or in mitigation of punishment?

A. ....

The evidence for the defence as to the accused's character and in mitigation of punishment is recorded on pages....................[1].

Q. Do you wish to address the court in mitigation of punishment?

A. ....

The.................................[makes an address in mitigation of punishment, which is summarized [below] [on page.........]] [hands in an address in mitigation of punishment, which is read, marked..............................signed by the president or judge advocate and attached to the record].[1]

The list of offences which the court have, at the request of the accused, agreed to take into consideration is read to the accused, signed by him, marked.............. ...., signed by the president or judge advocate and attached to the record.[2]

Final question addressed to the accused personally.*

Q. Is there anything further that you wish to say to the court?*

A. ....*

The accused makes a statement which is recorded on page.........*.

The court close to deliberate on sentence.*

*Strike out if F.1 is completed before F.2.

Notes.

[1]Strike out this paragraph if not applicable.

[2]Strike out this paragraph if the accused has not requested other offences to be taken into consideration.

F 2

PAGE ...

PROCEEDINGS ON CONVICTION

Note: F.2 should be completed before F.1 if the accused has pleaded not guilty to all charges.

The prosecutor calls evidence as to the accused's character and record.

....is duly sworn.

Q. Do you produce the Service Record of the accused?

A. I produce ....

Q. Have you compared it with the service books?

A. ....

Q. Do the entries in it correspond with the entries in the service books?

A. ....

The.................................is read, marked..............................signed by the president or judge advocate and attached to the record.

The accused [declines] [elects] to cross-examine this witness [and the cross-examination is recorded on pages.........].

The prosecutor adduces evidence under Rule of Procedure 71(3) which is recorded on pages.........[1].

Final question addressed to the accused personally.*

Q. Is there anything further you wish to say to the court?*

A. ....*

The accused makes a statement which is recorded on page.........*.

The court close to deliberate on sentence.*

*Strike out if F.2 is completed before F.1.

Note.

[1]Strike out this paragraph if the prosecutor does not adduce evidence under Rule of Procedure 71(3).

G

PAGE ...

SENTENCE[1]

"The court (having taken into consideration that he has spent....................days in civil custody and........................days in close arrest and.............................. days in open arrest in connection with the matters for which he is before the court)[2] sentence the accused........................[3]to[4]".

ANNOUNCEMENT OF SENTENCE

The court being re-opened, the accused is again brought before them.

The sentence (and recommendation to mercy[5]) [is] [are] announced in open court; the sentence is announced as being subject to confirmation.

The president announces that the trial is concluded.

Signed at........................this.................day of...............................19......

....
Judge Advocate.   President.

Notes

[1]Remove this page if not applicable.

[2]The words in brackets are to be struck out when the sentence is mandatory e.g. "to be imprisoned for life" where the offence is murder. In all other cases only words which are inapplicable should be deleted.

[3]Insert accused's rank, name, etc. as given on the charge-sheet.

[4]Record the sentence in the appropriate form of words set out in Schedule 5 to the Rules of Procedure. Any recommendation to mercy (see Rule of Procedure 74(4)), recommendation under section 127(4) of the Air Force Act, 1955, restitution order (see section 138 of the Air Force Act, 1955), or order determining a suspended sentence and directing whether the sentences are to run concurrently or consecutively (see section 120 of the Air Force Act, 1955) made by the Court, should be entered on the record immediately after the sentence.

[5]Strike out if not applicable.

H

PAGE ...

CONFIRMATION[1]

Note

[1]For minutes of confirmation see Schedule 4 to Rules of Procedure. Promulgation should be recorded immediately below the minute of confirmation in accordance with Rule of Procedure 95(7).

FINDINGS

Acquittal on all Charges

not guilty of [the charge] [all the charges].

---

not guilty of [the charge] [all the charges], and honourably acquit him thereof.

Acquittal on some but not all Charges

not guilty of the.................[1] charge(s) but is guilty of the.................[1] charge(s).

not guilty of the.................[1] charge(s) and honourably acquit him thereof but is guilty of the.................[1] charge(s).

Conviction on all Charges

guilty of [the charge] [all the charges].

Special Findings

guilty of the.................[1] charge [with the exception of the words......................
.........[2] [with the exception that..[2].

not guilty of the offence *charged* but/is guilty of[3].

No finding on alternative charge

guilty of the..........................charge; the court record no finding on the...........
...............(alternative charge).

Where the accused is unfit to stand his trial.

Unfit to stand his trial.

Acquital by reason of insanity.

Not guilty by reason of insanity.

Notes

[1]Insert the number of the charge or charges as numbered in the charge-sheet.

[2]Specify the exception in detail. This form is appropriate when a special finding is made under Rule of Procedure 66(3).

[3]State the offence of which the accused is found guilty. This form is applicable when a special finding is made under section 98(2) (5) or (6) of the Act.

(8) RECORD OF RECONSIDERATION OF FINDING UNDER RULE 80(5)

The judge advocate advises the court that the finding(s) on the..........................[1] charge(s) [is] [are] contrary to the law relating to the case, and that in his opinion the following finding(s) [is] [are] open to them:—

....
....
....[2]

The court is closed for reconsideration of finding.

The court on reconsideration find that the accused is[3]...............................

....

The finding(s) on reconsideration [is] [are] read in open court and (with the exception of the finding(s) of "not guilty"[4]) [is] [are] announced as being subject to confirmation.

....

Notes

[1]Insert number of charge as numbered in the charge-sheet.

[2]Insert the advice given by the judge advocate.

[3]Set out the finding(s) of the court in the appropriate form(s).

[4]Strike out the words relating to findings of "not guilty" if there is no such finding.

(9) SERVICE RECORD OF ACCUSED
(not applicable to officers)[1]

No..Rank ....

Name...

Unit...Trade..

1. The date of his enlistment is...

2. He is serving on a..
    (*Insert nature and length of engagement*)

3. His present age is...

4. He is (married) and has...children under
    (unmarried)
    (divorced)
    (widowed)
the age of 16 years.

5. His gross basic rate of pay (including additional pay payable on a continuous basis)

is...but he is (*insert forfeitures,
deductions and allotments affecting his pay*)

    ....
    ....
    ....

6. The service which he is allowed to reckon towards discharge or transfer to reserve is.....................................(years)..(days)

7. He is entitled to reckon..
service for the purpose of determining his pension and/or gratuity, etc.

8. He is entitled to the following decorations or awards
....
and.................................acts of gallantry or distinguished conduct by him
are recorded in his conduct sheets.

9. He holds the substantive rank of..
with seniority from.. He has continuously
since...held the acting rank of..............................
....

10. The highest aircraftman rank for which he is qualified is..............................

11. He has been awaiting trial for...................................days since he was first, in connection with any of the matters for which he is before the Court, charged or placed in arrest, of which..
days were spent in civil custody...
days were spent in close arrest and...
days were spent in open arrest.

12. He is not under sentence at the present time.

OR

At the present time he is under sentence of..
beginning on the ....day of.............................19......
but suspended on the......................day of.............................19......
and (not yet put into operation again.)............day of...................19......
    (put into operation again on the)

13. According to his conduct sheets he has been found guilty by his commanding officer, or by the commandant of a military or air force establishment, of the following offences:

Offence	Since Enlistment	In last 12 months
	times	times
	times	times
	times	times

OR

There are no entries in his conduct sheets.

Note.

[1]In the case of officers serving at home, a Form 731 giving details of the officer's service record is prepared by Ministry of Defence on request. In the case of an officer serving overseas, Ministry of Defence on request send details of the officer's service record by signal.

STOKE-ON-TRENT
CITY
LIBRARIES

14. Schedule of offences of which he has been convicted by a court-martial, or of which he has been found guilty during his service by a court other than a court-martial, offences taken into consideration by such courts, offences of which he has been found guilty by an appropriate superior authority and of dispensations with trial under Section 81 of the Air Force Act, 1955, are set out below:—

Description of court, appropriate superior authority or of officer dispensing with trial.	Date and place of trial or summary award by appropriate superior authority or of order dispensing with trial.	Charges upon which found guilty or in respect of which trial was dispensed with and offences taken into consideration.	Sentence of the court, award of appropriate superior authority or order of the authority dispensing with trial.	Punishment remitted (this should not include punishment automatically remitted for good conduct under the Imprisonment and Detention Rules).

I HEREBY CERTIFY that the particulars in this schedule are true extracts from the service books in my custody.

signed this................day of........................19......

Signature...............................

Name, Rank and appointment.

(10) Record of proceedings on revision under section 109 of the act

At..............................[1] on the..............day of...................at..............
hours the court re-assembled by order of......................................[2] the confirming
officer for the purpose of reconsidering their finding(s) on the...........................[3]
charge(s).

Present[4] ....

....

....

The order directing the re-assembly of the court and giving the reasons therefor
is read, marked..............................signed by the president and attached to the
record.

The court having considered the observations of the confirming officer and the whole
of the record of the proceedings do now revoke their finding(s) on the....................
......................[5]charge(s) and find that the accused[6].....................................
is[6]...

....

and [adhere to their sentence] [sentence the accused to[7].....................................

....

in substitution for the original sentence].

or

The court having considered the observations of the confirming officer respectfully
adhere to their finding(s) on the..[3]
charge(s) [and to their sentence] [but sentence the accused...................................[5]
to[7]...in substitution for the original sentence].

or

The court having considered the observations of the confirming officer and the
whole of the record of the proceedings do now revoke their finding(s) on the..............
..........................[3] charge(s) and find the accused.......................................[5]
not guilty of [that] [those] charge(s).[7]

Signed at........................[1] this.......................day of.......................19......

....
Judge Advocate   President

Notes

[1]Insert the name of the place.

[2]Insert the rank, name, appointment, etc., of the confirming officer.

[3]Specify the number(s) of the charge(s) concerned e.g. the 5th charge.

[4]Give the names of the president and members of the court who are present.
If the president is absent the senior member must report to the confirming officer.
If a member is absent and the court is thereby reduced below the legal minimum
the president must report to the confirming officer.

[5]Insert the accused's number, rank, name and unit as given in the charge-sheet.

[6]Set out the finding in the appropriate form set out in Schedule 4.

[7]Set out the new sentence in accordance with the appropriate form set out in
Schedule 5.

(11) Confirmation

Note: *These forms are for guidance only and do not constitute an exhaustive list of all
the possible variations and should be adapted to the circumstances of each case.*

Confirmed.

I confirm the court's finding(s), sentence and order under section 138 of the Air
Force Act, 1955 but [remit...............[1]] [commute..............[2]].

I confirm the court's finding(s) sentence and order under section 138 of the Air Force Act, 1955, but mitigate the sentence so that it shall be as follows:—3

I vary the sentence so that it shall be as follows..and confirm the finding and sentence as so varied.4

I confirm the finding(s), and sentence but [postpone the carrying out of the sentence of.....................until........................5] [suspend the sentence of.................].

I confirm the finding(s) but substitute the sentence of............................for the sentence of the court.6

I substitute a finding of.......................for the finding of the court and substitute the sentence of............................for the sentence of the court.

I substitute a finding of...for the finding of the court and confirm the sentence but [remit.......................1] [commute.......................2]

I substitute a finding of............................for the finding of the court on the ....charge and confirm the finding(s) on the other charge(s) and the sentence.

Not confirmed [on the grounds that..7.

I confirm the finding(s) of the court on the............................charge(s) but do not confirm their finding(s) on the......;.......................charge(s) [on the grounds that ....7]. I confirm the sentence but [remit...........................1] [commute...........................]2

I refer the finding(s) and sentence to............................8for confirmation.

I confirm the finding(s) of the court on the.................................charge(s) and refer the finding(s) on the............................charge(s) and the sentence to......... ....8 for confirmation.

I confirm the finding(s) of the court but refer the sentence to.......................8 for confirmation.

[The record] [Part of the record] of the proceedings of the trial by court-martial which tried...........................at............................on the....................day of....................19.........having been lost, I do not confirm the finding(s) of the court.

Signed at...........................this....................day of....................19......

....9

(*Signature, rank and appointment of confirming officer*)

Notes

1State what part of the sentence is remitted.

2State what the sentence is commuted to.

3This form of words may be used when it is impracticable to use either "remit" or "commute".

4This form of words is appropriate when the court have expressed the sentence informally or incorrectly and the confirming officer desires to put it into the correct legal form.

5Insert the date or event to which the carrying out of the sentence is postponed.

6This form of words is appropriate when the court have passed an illegal sentence on the accused and the confirming officer desires to substitute a legal sentence.

7Where a confirming officer withholds confirmation because he disapproves of the decision of the court on a plea to the jurisdiction or in bar of trial or on any objection to a charge, he should specifically state that he is withholding confirmation for this reason. In other cases the confirming officer is not bound to give his reasons.

8Insert the appointment of the higher authority to whom the matter is to be referred.

⁹The rank and appointment of the confirming officer should be clearly stated after or under his signature.

(12) DETERMINATION BY A CONFIRMING OFFICER OR REVIEWING AUTHORITY OF A SUSPENDED SENTENCE AND DIRECTION THAT SENTENCES ARE TO RUN CONCURRENTLY OR CONSECUTIVELY¹

I.................................[the confirming officer] [the reviewing authority] hereby order the accused to be commited to [imprisonment] [detention] under the sentence passed on him by the court-martial held at...........................on the ......day of ....19......and direct that that sentence and the sentence passed on the accused by [this court-martial] [court-martial held at........................ on.............................day of.................................] shall run [concurrently] [consecutively].

Dated............................19......

....
(*Signature*)

Note

¹When the confirming officer is making the determination the form of words should be inserted in the record of proceedings of the court-martial in the confirming officer's minute of confirmation; When made by a reviewing authority it should follow the minute of promulgation.

(13) DIRECTION UNDER SECTION 127(4) OF THE ACT¹

I..........................the [confirming officer] [reviewing authority] hereby direct that the accused (*insert number, rank, name or other description* (shall not be required to be returned to the United Kingdom until he has served [.........months] [.........years] of the sentence of [imprisonment] [detention, passed on him.

Dated............................19......

....
(*Signature*)

Note

¹When the confirming officer is making the determination this form of words should be inserted in the record of proceedings of the court-martial in the confirming officer's minute of confirmation; when made by a reviewing authority it should follow the minute of promulgation.

(14) RESTITUTION ORDER¹

In accordance with sub-section.....................of section 138 of the Air Force Act' 1955, I............ :...........................² hereby order that................. ....³ be [delivered] [paid] to... ....⁴

Dated.............................19......

....
(*Signature*)

Confirming Officer*
Reviewing Authority*

**Strike out if not applicable*

¹ (*a*) When the confirming officer is making the order this form of words should be inserted in the record of the proceedings of the court-martial in the confirming officer's minute of confirmation: when made by a reviewing authority it should follow the minute of promulgation.

(*b*) Where the conditions set out in section 138(10) of the Act are satisfied, the officer or authority making the order may add at the end of the order: "and I direct that this order shall be carried out forthwith".

₂Insert rank, name and appointment of confirming officer or reviewing authority as the case may be.

2Insert description of article or amount of money, as the case may be.

3Insert name of person to whom restitution is being made.

(15) PROMULGATION

Promulgated and extracts taken at (place).. this...........................day of.................................19.........

....
(Signature, rank and appointment of officer making the promulgation).

SCHEDULE 5   Rules 20, 74
SENTENCES

(1) SENTENCES.

(2) FORFEITURE OF SENIORITY.

(3) CONSECUTIVE SENTENCES OF IMPRISONMENT FOR OFFENCES AGAINST SECTION 70 OF THE ACT.

(4) ORDER THAT SENTENCES ARE TO BEGIN TO RUN ON THE EXPIRY OF SOME OTHER SENTENCE.

(5) DETERMINATION OF A SUSPENDED SENTENCE AND DIRECTION THAT SENTENCES ARE TO RUN CONCURRENTLY OR CONSECUTIVELY.

(6) RECOMMENDATION UNDER SECTION 127(4) OF THE ACT.

(7) RESTITUTION ORDER.

(1) SENTENCES

Note: *The words in the margin should be entered in the right-hand margin of the record of the proceedings of a court-martial opposite the record of the sentence.*

OFFICERS

To suffer death.	Death.
To be imprisoned for......................................	Imprisonment.
To be dismissed with disgrace from Her Majesty's service.	Dismissal with disgrace.
To be dismissed from Her Majesty's service	Dismissal.
(For forms of sentence see (2) *below).*	Forfeiture of seniority.
To be fined £.........	Fine.
To be [severely reprimanded] [reprimanded].	Severe reprimand or reprimand.
To be put under stoppages of pay until he has made good the sum of ....¹ in respect of.................................²	Stoppages.

WARRANT OFFICERS AND NON-COMMISSIONED OFFICERS

To suffer death.	Death.
To be imprisoned for..........................and to be reduced to the ranks.	Imprisonment and reduction to the ranks.
To be dismissed with disgrace from Her Majesty's service and to be be reduced to the ranks.	Dismissal with disgrace
To be dismissed from Her Majesty's service and to be reduced to the ranks.	Dismissal and reduction to the ranks.
To undergo detention for..........................and to be reduced to the ranks.	Detention and reduction to the ranks.

To be dismissed from the Royal Auxiliary Air Force (*non-commissioned officers of the Royal Auxiliary Air Force only*) — Dismissal from R. Aux. AF

To be reduced [to the ranks] [to the rank of.......................]. — Reduction to the ranks or reduction to Disrating.

To be disrated to..........................(*attached naval personnel only*).

To be fined £............................. — Fine.

To be [severely reprimanded] [reprimanded]. — Severe reprimand or reprimand.

To be put under stoppages of pay until he has made good the sum of..........................1 in respect of.............................2 — Stoppages.

AIRMEN

To suffer death. — Death.

To be imprisoned for............................. — Imprisonment.

To be dismissed with disgrace from Her Majesty's service. — Dismissal with disgrace.

To be dismissed from Her Majesty's service. — Dismissal.

To undergo detention for............................. — Detention.

To be dismissed from the Royal Auxiliary Air Force (*men of the Royal Auxiliary Air Force only*). — Dismissal from R. Aux. AF.

To be fined............................. — Fine.

To be put under stoppages of pay until he has made good the sum of.............................1 in respect of.............................2 — Stoppages

Notes

1Insert the amount which has to be made good by stoppages in respect of the charge or article specified.

2Specify the charge or article in respect of which the stoppage is to be imposed. If stoppages are being imposed in respect of more than one charge or article the amount which has to be made good in respect of each charge or article must be stated separately.

(2) FORFEITURE OF SENIORITY
AIR FORCE OFFICERS

To forfeit.........................[months] [years] seniority as a substantive.................. in Her Majesty's air forces

or

To forfeit all seniority as a substantive..in Her Majesty's air forces.

NAVAL OFFICERS

To forfeit.............................[months] [years] seniority as a.......................... in Her Majesty's Fleet.

or

To be placed at the bottom of the list of his rank.

ARMY OFFICERS

To forfeit.............................(months] [years] seniority as a substantive............ ....in Her Majesty's regular forces.

or

To forfeit all seniority as a substantive......................................in Her Majesty's regular forces.

ROYAL MARINE OFFICERS

To forfeit.............................[months] [years] seniority as a.........................
in the corps of Royal Marines.

or

To forfeit all seniority as a......................................in the corps of Royal Marines.

(3) CONSECUTIVE SENTENCES OF IMPRISONMENT FOR OFFENCES AGAINST SECTION 70 OF THE ACT

(*a*) *In cases where the accused is convicted only of offences under s. 70 of the Act.*

To be imprisoned for.....................in respect of the.....................charge, for.....................in respect of the.....................charge, and for.....................
in respect of the.....................charge (*etc, as required*).   These terms of imprisonment are to run consecutively (*or* The terms of imprisonment in respect of the.....................
and.....................charges are to run consecutively with each other/one another but concurrently with the term(s) of imprisonment in respect of the.........................
charge(s)).

(*b*) *In cases where the accused is convicted of offences against s. 70 of the Act and also of one or more other offences against ss. 24 to 69 of the Act.*

To be imprisoned for...............in respect of the...............charge, for...............
in respect of the...............charge and for...............in respect of the.................
charge (*etc, as required, in respect of all the offences against s.70 for which the court desires to award imprisonment*) and to be imprisoned/to undergo detention for............
in respect of the.....................charge(s) (*specifying the charge or charges of offences other than those against s.70 for which the court desires to award imprisonment or detention*).
The terms of imprisonment in respect of the.....................and the.................charges are to run consecutively with each other but concurrently with the term of imprisonment/detention in respect of the.....................charge(s).

(4) ORDER THAT SENTENCES ARE TO BEGIN TO RUN ON THE EXPIRY OF SOME OTHER SENTENCE[1]

The court hereby order that the sentence passed on the accused by this court-martial shall begin to run from the expiry of the sentence of.................................
[months] [years] [imprisonment] [detention] passed upon him by.............................
on...

Note

[1]This form of order is applicable (1) to cases where a sentence of imprisonment or detention is awarded by a court-martial to a person already serving such a sentence awarded by a previous court-martial, and (2) where a sentence of imprisonment or detention is awarded by a court-martial under section 57(2) of the Air Force Act, 1955, to a person whom the same court-martial also sentences to imprisonment or detention in respect of the offence or offences for which he is tried.

(5) DETERMINATION OF A SUSPENDED SENTENCE AND DIRECTION THAT SENTENCES ARE TO RUN CONCURRENTLY OR CONSECUTIVELY[1]

The court hereby order the accused to be committed to [imprisonment] [detention] under the sentence passed on him by the court-martial held at.................................
on the.....................day of.............................19...... and direct that that sentence and the sentence passed on the accused by this court-martial shall run [concurrently] [consecutively].

Note

This form of words should be inserted in the record of proceedings of the court martial in the sentence passed by the court.

(6) RECOMMENDATION UNDER SECTION 127(4) OF THE ACT[1]

The court recommends that the accused.....................................(*number, rank, name or other description*) shall not be required to be returned to the United Kingdom until he has served [...............months] [years...............] of his sentence.

Note

[1]This form of words should be inserted in the record of proceedings of the court-martial in the sentence passed by the court.

(7) Restitution order[1]

In accordance with sub-section..............of section 138 of the Air Force Act, 1955 the court hereby order that............................[2] [be delivered] [paid] to ....[3]

Notes

[1]This form of words should be inserted in the record of the proceedings of the court-martial in the sentence passed by the court.
Where the conditions set out in section 138(10) of the Act are satisfied, the court may add at the end of their order: "and direct that this order shall be carried out forthwith".

[2]Insert the description of the article or the amount of money as the case may be.

[3]Insert the name of person to whom restitution is to be made.

Rule 34   **SCHEDULE 6**
                                Oaths and affirmations

(1) Oaths at Investigations by Commanding Officers and Appropriate Superior Authorities.

(2) Oaths at Courts-Martial.

(3) Scottish Oaths.

(4) Manner of Administering Oaths.

(5) Solemn Affirmations.

(1) Oaths at investigations by commanding officers and appropriate superior authorities

Interpreter

I swear by Almighty God that I will to the best of my ability truly interpret and translate, as I shall be required to do, touching the matter being investigated.

Witness

I swear by Almighty God that the evidence which I shall give at this investigation shall be the truth, the whole truth and nothing, but the truth.

Child or Young Person

I promise before Almighty God that the evidence which I shall give at this investigation shall be the truth, the whole truth, and nothing but the truth.

(2) Oaths at courts-martial

President and members

I swear by Almighty God that I will well and truly try the (accused) (accused persons) before the court according to the evidence, and that I will duly administer justice according to the Air Force Act, 1955, without partiality, favour or affection, and I do further swear that I will not on any account at any time whatsoever disclose or discover the vote or opinion of the president or any member of this court-martial, unless thereunto required in due course of law.

Judge advocate

I swear by Almighty God that I will to the best of my ability carry out the duties of Judge advocate in accordance with the Air Force Act, 1955, and the rules made thereunder and without partiality, favour or affection, and I do further swear that I will not on any account at any time whatsoever disclose or discover the vote or opinion on any matter of the president or any member of this court-martial, unless thereunto required in due course of law.

Officer under Instruction

I swear by Almighty God that I will not on any account, at any time whatsoever disclose or discover the vote or opinion of the president or any member of this court-martial unless thereunto required in due course of law.

Shorthand Writer

I swear by Almighty God that I will truly take down to the best of my power the evidence to be given before this court-martial and such other matters as may be required, and will, when required, deliver to the court a true transcript of the same.

Interpreter

I swear by Almighty God that I will to the best of my ability truly interpret and translate, as I shall be required to do, touching the matter before this court-martial.

Witness

I swear by Almighty God that the evidence which I shall give before this court-martial shall be the truth, the whole truth, and nothing but the truth.

Child or Young Person

I promise before Almighty God that the evidence which I shall give before this court-martial shall be the truth, the whole truth, and nothing but the truth.

(3) SCOTTISH OATHS

The form of Scottish oath shall in each case be the same as the form of oaths set out above, except that for the words "I swear by Almighty God" shall be substituted the words "I swear by Almighty God and as I shall answer to God at the Great Day of Judgment."

(4) MANNER OF ADMINISTERING THE OATH

Christians taking the oath shall, unless female, remove their head-dress and, holding the Bible or New Testament in their right hand, say to or repeat after the person administering the oath the words of the oath. Jews shall take the oath in the same manner except that they shall wear their head-dress and hold the Old Testament in their right hand.

(5) SOLEMN AFFIRMATIONS

The person making a solemn affirmation shall say to or repeat after the person administering the solemn affirmation the words of the appropriate form of oath except that for the words "I swear by Almighty God" he shall substitute the words "I (name in full), do solemnly, sincerely and truly declare and affirm" and for the word "swear" wherever it occurs, the words "solemnly", sincerely and truly declare and affirm.'

SCHEDULE 7   Rule 100
PETITIONS

(1) PETITIONS.

(2) LIST OF PERSONS TO WHOM PETITIONS MAY BE PRESENTED UNDER RULE OF PROCEDURE 100.

(1) PETITIONS

(Petition to confirming officer (before confirmation)

To the Confirming Officer.

I...[1] having been convicted by court-martial on..[2] at ....[3]

and having been sentenced to..
hereby petition against the finding(s) on the...
charge(s)[4] and the sentence[5] on the following grounds:—

....
....
....
....

Signed ....[6]

Dated ....

Appeal Petition to the Air Force Board (*after promulgation*)

To the Air Force Board.

I...[1] having been convicted by court-martial
on ....[1] at ....[3]
and having had the finding(s) and sentence promulgated to me on.........................[7]
hereby petition against the finding(s) on the..............................charge(s)[4]
(and the sentence) [8] on the following grounds:—

....
....
....
....

Signed ....[6]

Dated ....

Note

The appeal petition may if desired be addressed to the Defence Council. The Air
Force Board is however empowered to deal with appeal petitions even if they are so
addressed. (s.1(5) Defence (Transfer of Functions) Act 1964)

Petition to reviewing authority (*after promulgation*)

To..,[9]

I...[1] having been convicted by court-martial
on..[2] at............................[3]
and having been sentenced to..and
having had the finding(s) and sentence promulgated to me on...............................[7]
hereby petition against the finding(s) on the....................................charge(s)[4]
and the sentence on the following grounds:—

....
....
....
....

Signed ....[6]

Dated ....

Notes

[1]Insert the accused's number, rank, name and unit.

[2]Insert the date when accused was convicted.

[3]Insert the place where the trial was held.

[4]The words "the finding(s) on the.......................(charge(s)" should be omitted
if the accused is only petitioning against sentence.

[5]The words "and the sentence" should be omitted if the accused is not petitioning
against sentence.

[6]Petitions should be signed by the accused personally but may if necessary be
signed on his behalf by his representative.

[7]Insert the date when the findings and sentence were promulgated.

[8]The accused may combine a petition against sentence with his appeal petition and if he wishes to do so he should include in his appeal petition the words "and the sentence". Otherwise any reference to the sentence should be omitted from the appeal petition.

[9]Here state the reviewing authority whom it is desired to petition.

(2) LIST OF PERSONS TO WHOM PETITIONS MAY BE PRESENTED UNDER RULE OF PROCEDURE 100

Circumstances	Person to whom a petition may be presented
1. Petitioner serving in or in custody on board H.M. ship.	Captain of the ship.
2. Petitioner in custody on board a ship other than one of H.M. ships.	Officer commanding forces on board.
3. Petitioner serving with an air force or army unit.	Officer commanding the unit.
4. Petitioner confined in naval detention quarters.	Officer in charge of the naval detention quarters.
5. Petitioner confined in air force or military establishment.	Commandant of such establishment.
6. Petitioner confined in a civil prison.	Governor of the prison.
7. Petitioner who is a civilian and is outside the United Kingdom.	Officer commanding at the nearest air-force, naval or army headquarters.

SCHEDULE 8   Rule 107

REVOCATION OF PREVIOUS RULES

Column 1 Regulations revoked	Column 2 References
Rules of Procedure (Air Force) 1956	S.I. 1956/163 (1956 II, p. 2020).
Rules of Procedure (Air Force) (Amendment) Rules 1961	S.I. 1961/2152 (1961 III, p. 3884).
Rules of Procedure (Air Force) (Amendment) Rules 1964	S.I. 1964/1282 (1964 II, p. 2955).
Rules of Procedure (Air Force) (Second Amendment) Rules 1964	S.I. 1964/1854 (1964 III, p. 4045).
Rules of Procedure (Air Force) (Amendment) Rules 1967	S.I. 1967/62 (1967 I, p. 118).
Rules of Procedure (Air Force) (Second Amendment) Rules 1967	S.I. 1967/1466 (1967 III, p. 4149).
Rules of Procedure (Air Force) (Third Amendment) Rules 1967	S.I. 1967/1845 (1967 III, p. 4910).

Column 1	Column 2
Regulations revoked	References
Rules of Procedure (Air Force) (Amendment) Rules 1968	S.I. 1968/1173 (1968 II, p. 3187).
Rules of Procedure (Air Force) (Second Amendment) Rules 1968	S.I. 1968/1921 (1968 III, p. 5213).
Rules of Procedure (Air Force) (Amendment) Rules 1969	S.I. 1969/679 (1969 II, p. 1851).
Rules of Procedure (Air Force) (Amendment) Rules 1970	S.I. 1970/422 (1970 I, p. 1457).
Rules of Procedure (Air Force) (Second Amendment) Rules 1970	S.I. 1970/1731 (1970 III, p. 5652).

The Defence (Transfer of Functions) (No. 2) Order 1964 S.I. 1964/489 (1964 I, p. 794) to the extent of the Amendment to Rules of Procedure (Air Force) 1956 (S.I. 1956/163).

EXPLANATORY NOTE
(This Note is not part of the Rules.)

1. These Rules, which are made under section 103 of the Air Force Act, 1955 make provision with regard to the investigation, trial of, and awarding of punishment for, offences cognisable by court-martial, appropriate superior authorities and commanding officers, and with regard to the confirmation and revision of findings and sentences of courts-martial. They replace, with several important amendments, the Rules of Procedure (Air Force), 1956 (S.I. 1956/163).

2. The principal changes are:—

    (i) Rules 9 and 10 make provision for statements of defence witnesses to be included in the summary of evidence or attached to the abstract of evidence.

    (ii) Rule 12 requires a commanding officer, in appropriate cases, to warn an accused whom he remands for trial by court-martial of the requirements of s 11 Criminal Justice Act, 1967 (notice of alibi).

    (iii) Rule 22 provides that the president of a court-martial will only be supplied with a copy of the summary or abstract of evidence before the trial if a judge advocate is not appointed.

    (iv) Rule 35 gives a court, where an accused has pleaded 'guilty' to a charge, a discretion to defer compliance with Rule 45 until they have arrived at their findings on a subsequent charge sheet.

    (v) Rule 71 requires that, on conviction, evidence of the accused's antecedent history shall include details of all previous findings of guilt by a civil court. This conforms with the practice in the civil courts.

(vi) Rule 81 provides that a judge advocate may determine additional issues in the absence of the court. These issues are a plea in bar of trial, an application to treat a witness as hostile and a submission that the prosecution has not established a *prima facie* case.

(vii) Rule 92 provides that a transcript of the shorthand writer's notes of the proceedings shall not be required where an accused is acquitted unless it is required by the confirming officer.

(viii) Rule 102 allows the convening officer to exercise the powes conferred by s 7 Bankers' Books Evidence Act, 1879.

3. Other minor changes and additions have been made to the Rules and Schedules consequent upon the coming into operation of the Armed Forces Act, 1971.

STATUTORY INSTRUMENTS

1972 No. 421

INDUSTRIAL DEVELOPMENT

LOCAL EMPLOYMENT

The Intermediate Areas and Derelict Land Clearance Areas Order 1972

Made - - - - -	*17th March* 1972
Laid before Parliament - -	*22nd March* 1972
Coming into Operation - -	*22nd March* 1972

The Secretary of State in exercise of his powers under section 1(1) and section 8(6) of the Local Employment Act 1972(**a**) hereby makes the following Order:—

1.—(1) The Interpretation Act 1889(**b**) shall apply to the interpretation of this Order as it applies to the interpretation of an Act of Parliament.

(2) This Order may be cited as the Intermediate Areas and Derelict Land Clearance Areas Order 1972 and shall come into operation immediately after being laid before Parliament.

2. The areas described in Part I of the Schedule to this Order are hereby specified as intermediate areas for the purposes of the Local Employment Act 1972.

3. The Derelict Land Clearance Areas Order 1970(**c**) shall have effect subject to the amendment that the Yorkshire and Humberside Derelict Land Clearance Area and the North West Derelict Land Clearance Area shall be deleted from the Schedule thereto.

4. The Intermediate Areas Order 1970(**d**) shall have effect subject to the amendment that in the Schedule thereto, for the description of the South East Wales Intermediate Area there shall be substituted the description of that Area in Part II of the Schedule to this Order.

Dated 17th March 1972.

John Davies,
The Secretary of State for
Trade and Industry.

(a) 1972 c. 5.   (b) 1889 c. 63.   (c) S.I. 1970/309.   (d) S.I. 1970/308.

SCHEDULE
PART I
NEW INTERMEDIATE AREAS

The Yorkshire and Humberside Intermediate Area consisting of the employment exchange areas of:—

Attercliffe
Barton-on-Humber
Batley
Bradford
Brighouse
Chapeltown
Dewsbury
Driffield
Elland
Gainsborough
Grimsby
Halifax
Harrogate
Haworth
Hebden Bridge
Horncastle
Horsforth
Huddersfield
Keighley
Leeds
Louth
Mablethorpe
Morley
Otley
Pocklington
Ripon
Rothwell
Scunthorpe
Seacroft
Selby
Sheffield
Shipley
Skegness
Skipton
Sowerby Bridge
Spen Valley
Stanningley
Stocksbridge
Tadcaster
Wetherby
Woodhouse
Yeadon (formerly Guiseley)
York

The North West Intermediate Area consisting of the employment exchange areas of:—

Altrincham
Ashton-in-Makerfield
Ashton-under-Lyne
Atherton and Tyldesley
Bamber Bridge
Blackpool
Bolton
Bury
Buxton
Chapel-en-le-Frith
Chester
Chorley
Clitheroe
Congleton
Crewe
Denton
Eccles
Failsworth
Farnworth
Fleetwood
Glossop
Golborne
Heywood
Hindley
Horwich
Hyde
Irlam
Kirkham
Lancaster
Leigh
Levenshulme
Leyland
Littleborough
Lytham
Macclesfield
Manchester
Marple
Middleton
Middlewich
Morecambe
Mossley
Nantwich
New Mills
Newton Heath
Newton le Willows (formerly Earlestown)
Northwich
Oldham and Chadderton
Openshaw
Ormskirk
Preston
Prestwich
Radcliffe
Ramsbottom
Rochdale
Royton
Saddleworth
Salford

The North West Intermediate Area—*continued*

Sandbach	Swinton
Shaw	Thornton Cleveleys
Skelmersdale (excluding that part which lies within the designated area of Skelmersdale New Town)	Warrington
	Westhoughton
	Wigan
Southport	Wilmslow
Stalybridge	Winsford
St. Anne's-on-the-Sea	Withington
Standish	Worsley
Stockport	Wythenshawe
Stretford	

The North Wales Intermediate Area consisting of the employment exchange areas of:—

Buckley	Llandudno
Colwyn Bay	Mold
Flint	Rhyl
Holywell	Shotton

Article 4

PART II

The South East Wales Intermediate Area consisting of the employment exchange areas of:—

Abergavenny (excluding that part which lies outside the Abergavenny Municipal Borough and the Abergavenny Rural District)	Cwmbran
	Llantwit Major
	Monmouth
Barry	Newport
Cardiff	Newport Docks
Chepstow	Penarth

For the purposes of this Schedule the employment exchange areas referred to above are areas for which an employment exchange has been established or maintained for the purposes of the Employment and Training Act 1948(a) as those areas exist on the date on which this Order comes into operation.

EXPLANATORY NOTE

(This note is not part of the Order.)

This Order specifies the areas set out in Part I of the Schedule as intermediate areas for the purposes of the Local Employment Act 1972 in addition to those areas which were so specified by the Intermediate Areas Order 1970 (S.I. 1970/308) and by the Intermediate Areas Order 1971 (S.I. 1971/329). The Order also extends the South East Wales Intermediate Area to include the employment exchange areas of Chepstow and Monmouth.

The Order also amends the Derelict Land Clearance Areas Order 1970 (S.I. 1970/309) by deleting from the Schedule to that Order the areas which are now by virtue of this Order or the Intermediate Areas Order 1971 (S.I. 1971/329) intermediate areas but which were formerly derelict land clearance areas.

(a) 1948 c. 46.

STOKE-ON-Trent
CITY
LIBRARIES

STATUTORY INSTRUMENTS

1972 No. 422

HOUSING, ENGLAND AND WALES
The Housing (Intermediate Areas) Order 1972

Made -	-	-	-	-	*17th March* 1972
Laid before Parliament			-		*22nd March* 1972
Coming into Operation			-		*22nd March* 1972

The Secretary of State for the Environment, in exercise of his powers under section 1(2) of the Housing Act 1971(a) and of all other powers enabling him in that behalf, hereby makes the following order:—

1.—(1) This order may be cited as the Housing (Intermediate Areas) Order 1972 and shall come into operation immediately after being laid before Parliament.

(2) The Interpretation Act 1889(b) shall apply for the interpretation of this order as it applies for the interpretation of an Act of Parliament.

2. The Housing Act 1971 shall apply to works eligible for financial assistance under the provisions of the Housing Act 1969(c) mentioned in the former Act if they are carried out in a local government area which is wholly or partly within an intermediate area specified or described in the Intermediate Areas and Derelict Land Clearance Areas Order 1972(d):

Provided that the Act of 1971 shall not by virtue of this order apply to any works to which it would have applied had this order not been made.

Peter Walker,
17th March 1972. Secretary of State for the Environment.

EXPLANATORY NOTE
(*This Note is not part of the Order.*)

The Housing Act 1971 provides for increased aid from public funds for house and area improvements in local government areas which were, on 23rd June 1971, wholly or partly within development areas or intermediate areas (the designation of these areas is dealt with in section 1 of the Local Employment Act 1972 (c.5)). This order applies the 1971 Act in local government areas (other than those in which it already applies) which are wholly or partly within areas which have become intermediate areas by virtue of the Intermediate Areas and Derelict Land Clearance Areas Order 1972.

(a) 1971 c. 76.
(c) 1969 c. 33.
(b) 1889 c. 63.
(d) S.I. 1972/421 (1972 I, p. 1604).

STATUTORY INSTRUMENTS

1972 No. 428

SOCIAL SECURITY

The National Insurance (Non-participation—Benefits and Schemes) Amendment Provisional Regulations 1972

Made - - -	*20th March* 1972
Laid before Parliament	*24th March* 1972
Coming into Operation	*25th March* 1972

The Secretary of State for Social Services hereby certifies, under section 108(4) of the National Insurance Act 1965(a), that on account of urgency the following regulations should come into operation without delay, and, in exercise of his powers under section 57(4)(b) of that Act, and of all other powers enabling him in that behalf, after submitting a preliminary draft to the National Insurance Advisory Committee, hereby makes the following regulations as provisional regulations: —

Citation and commencement

1. These regulations may be cited as the National Insurance (Non-participation—Benefits and Schemes) Amendment Provisional Regulations 1972 and shall come into operation on 25th March 1972.

Amendment of regulation 3(3) of the National Insurance (Non-participation – Benefits and Schemes) Regulations 1959

2. In regulation 3(3) of the National Insurance (Non-participation—Benefits and Schemes) Regulations 1959(b), as amended(c), after sub-paragraph (b) there shall be added the words—

"and

(c) any scheme or arrangement made or having effect as if made under section 1 or 18 of the Superannuation Act 1972(d) shall be a prescribed means of securing the benefits provided under that scheme or arrangement; and

(d) any scheme or arrangement which, by virtue of subsection (4) of section 56 of the Civil Aviation Act 1971(e), as substituted by section 21 of the said Act of 1972, has effect as if established by virtue of subsection (2) of the said section 56 shall, so long as it remains unamended in any way which adversely affects the security of that scheme or arrangement, be a prescribed means of securing the benefits provided by that scheme or arrangement;

(a) 1965 c. 51.   (b) S.I. 1959/1861 (1959 II, p. 1865).
(c) S.I. 1960/1104, 1961/137 (1960 II, p. 2258; 1961 I, p. 191).
(d) 1972 c. 11.   (e) 1971 c. 75.

and any enactment, regulation or other instrument which immediately before the coming into force of any provision of the Superannuation Act 1972 was prescribed by this paragraph as a means of securing benefits shall, notwithstanding the coming into force of that provision, continue to be a prescribed means of securing benefits, so long as it remains unamended in any way which adversely affects the security of the scheme or arrangement established by it."

Keith Joseph,
Secretary of State for Social Services.

20th March 1972.

EXPLANATORY NOTE

(This Note is not part of the Regulations.)

These Provisional Regulations amend the National Insurance (Non-participation—Benefits and Schemes) Regulations 1959 to take account of the passing of the Superannuation Act 1972. They ensure that any superannuation scheme affected by that Act which was a recognised superannuation scheme for the purposes of Part III of the National Insurance Act 1965 continues to be recognised so long as the security of the scheme is not affected adversely by amendments to it; future schemes made under the Superannuation Act in respect of civil servants and certain other persons will also be recognised.

STATUTORY INSTRUMENTS

1972 No. 429

MEDICAL PROFESSION
The General Medical Council (Registration (Fees) Regulations) Order of Council 1972

<table>
<tr><td>Made</td><td>-</td><td>-</td><td>-</td><td>21st March 1972</td></tr>
</table>

At the Council Chamber, Whitehall, the 21st day of March 1972

By the Lords of Her Majesty's Most Honourable Privy Council

Whereas in pursuance of section 5 of the Medical Act 1969(a) the General Medical Council have made regulations entitled "The Medical Practitioners Registration (Fees) Regulations 1972":

And whereas by subsection (5) of the said section such regulations shall not have effect until approved by Order of the Privy Council:

Now, therefore, Their Lordships, having taken the said regulations into consideration, are hereby pleased to approve the same as set out in the Schedule to this Order.

This Order may be cited as the General Medical Council (Registration (Fees) Regulations) Order of Council 1972.

W. G. Agnew.

SCHEDULE TO THE ORDER

THE MEDICAL PRACTITIONERS REGISTRATION (FEES) REGULATIONS 1972

The General Medical Council in exercise of their powers under section 5 of the Medical Act 1969 hereby make the following Regulations:—

Citation and Commencement

1. These Regulations may be cited as the Medical Practitioners Registration (Fees) Regulations 1972, and shall come into operation on 1st May 1972.

Interpretation

2.—(1) In these Regulations, unless the context otherwise requires:

"the Act of 1956" means the Medical Act 1956(b)

"the Act of 1969" means the Medical Act 1969;

"annual retention fee" means a fee payable by a registered person under Regulation 6(1) or (2);

"the current year" means, in relation to a registered person, the period of twelve months commencing on the most recent anniversary of that person's date of full registration or, if the person is provisionally registered, on the anniversary of his date of provisional registration;

(a) 1969 c. 40. (b) 1956 c. 76.

"due date", in relation to the payment of an annual retention fee by a registered person, is the date on which that fee becomes payable by that person under Regulation 6(3);

"the Overseas List" means the list of that name established in accordance with section 3(2) of the Medical Act 1969;

"the Principal List" means the list of that name established in accordance with section 3(2) of the Medical Act 1969;

"the register" means the register of medical practitioners;

"the Registrar" means the Registrar of the General Medical Council;

"the Registration Committee" means the Committee of that name of the General Medical Council constituted by virtue of the Medical Act 1956, section 1(3) and Schedule 1, paragraph 6(1).

(2) Any reference in these Regulations to a numbered Regulation shall be construed as a reference to the Regulation bearing that number in these Regulations, and any reference to a numbered paragraph shall be construed as a reference to the paragraph bearing that number in the Regulation in which it occurs.

3. The Interpretation Act 1889(a) shall apply to the interpretation of these Regulations as it applies to the interpretation of an Act of Parliament.

Fees for registration

4. The Registrar shall not make any entry in the register until the appropriate fee, if any, prescribed by Regulation 5 has been paid.

5. The appropriate fees for the making of entries in the register shall be:—

(a) On provisional registration under section 17 of the Act of 1956, except in the case of a person who is or has at any time been registered by virtue of any provision of the law of the Republic of Ireland made for purposes similar to the said section 17... ... £10

(b) On provisional registration under section 23 of the Act of 1956 £15

(c) On full registration under section 7 of the Act of 1956

(i) in the case of a person who is or has at any time been provisionally registered under section 17 of the Act of 1956 or by virtue of any provision of the law of the Republic of Ireland made for purposes similar to the said section 17 ... £15

(ii) in the case of any other person £25
except in the case of a person who is already fully registered under section 18 of the Act of 1956, when no fee shall be payable.

(d) On full registration under section 18 of the Act of 1956

(i) in the case of a person who is or has at any time been provisionally registered under section 23 of the Act of 1956 ... £20

(ii) in the case of any other person £35

Annual Retention Fees

6.—(1) Any fully registered person who is not exempted under the provisions of Regulations 7, 8, 9 or 10 shall be liable to pay a fee in respect of the retention of his name in the register in any year subsequent to the year beginning with the date on which he first obtained full registration.

(2) Any provisionally registered person who is not exempted under the provisions of Regulations 7, 8 or 9 shall be liable to pay a fee in respect of the retention of his name in the register in any year subsequent to a period of two years beginning with the date on which he first obtained provisional registration.

(a) 1889 c. 63.

(3) An annual retention fee shall become payable:—

(a) by a fully registered person on the anniversary of the date on which he was first fully registered; and

(b) by a provisionally registered person on the anniversary of the day on which he was first provisionally registered:

Provided that the Regulation shall apply to a person first registered on 29th February as if he had been first registered on 1st March.

(4) Any person whose name is transferred from the Overseas List to the Principal List on his own application shall be liable on transfer to pay an annual retention fee in respect of the current year except in the case of a person who is exempted under the provisions of Regulations 8, 9 or 10.

(5) The annual retention fee shall be £5.

7. Any fully or provisionally registered person who is included in the Overseas List shall be exempt from payment of annual retention fees.

8. Any fully or provisionally registered person who satisfies the Registrar that he has reached the age of 65 years shall be exempt from payment of annual retention fees.

9. Any fully or provisionally registered person who not having reached the age of 65 satisfies the Registration Committee that he is prevented by lasting physical incapacity from rendering services as a medical practitioner for gain shall be exempt from the payment of annual retention fees:

Provided that any person who is exempted under the provisions of this Regulation and who is shown to the satisfaction of the Registration Committee to have rendered services as a medical practitioner for gain subsequently to the granting of the exemption shall cease to be so exempt.

10.—(1) Any person who obtained full registration under section 7 of the Act of 1956 for the first time during the period 1st January 1969 to 30th April 1970 inclusive shall be exempt from payment of an annual retention fee until after 30th April 1973.

(2) Any person who, on 30th April 1970, was provisionally registered in the register and who subsequently obtained full registration on or before 30th April 1972, shall be exempt from payment of an annual retention fee in respect of the full registration for a period of one year from the date on which but for this paragraph such fee would be due.

11.—(1) Except as provided by paragraph (2) of this Regulation, the Registrar shall cause a notice to be sent not less than 7 days before the due date to each fully or provisionally registered person who is liable to pay an annual retention fee.

(2) The persons to whom a notice is required to be sent under paragraph (1) of this Regulation shall not include any person who has completed and returned to the Registrar an order to his bankers to pay to the Registrar money due in respect of his annual retention fee and who has not informed the Registrar that he has cancelled such order.

(3) Where a person is liable under the provisions of Regulations 6 to 10 to pay an annual retention fee and such fee has not, after a period of 28 days from the due date, been received by the Council, the Registrar shall cause a notice, or in the case of a person to whom paragraph (2) of this Regulation does not apply, a further notice, to be sent to that person. In either case the notice shall contain a warning that unless the annual retention fee is received by the Council within a period of 28 days from the date on which the notice was issued, his name may be erased from the register.

(4) Notices sent to a person under paragraphs (1) and (3) of this Regulation shall be sent by post to his registered address.

Erasure after failure to pay annual retention fees

12. Where a fully or provisionally registered person is liable under the provisions of these Regulations to pay an annual retention fee and—

(a) a notice or notices have been sent to him as required by the provisions of

Regulation 11, and

(*b*) a period of 28 days has elapsed from the date of issue of the notice or further notice referred to in Regulation 11(3), and

(*c*) the requisite fee has not been received by the Council,

the Registrar may erase his name from the register.

Voluntary erasure of the name of a person who does not wish to pay annual retention fees

13.—(1) A fully or provisionally registered person may make application for the erasure of his name from the register on the ground that he does not wish to pay, or to continue to pay, annual retention fees.

(2) Such an application shall be in the form prescribed in the Schedule to these Regulations.

(3) On receipt of such an application the Registrar may erase the name of the applicant from the register.

Fees for restoration to the Principal List and the Overseas List

14. The Registrar may refuse to restore to the Principal List or to the Overseas List the name of any person whose name has been erased therefrom by virtue of section 3(5) of the Act of 1969 or section 41(7) of the Act of 1956, or the corresponding enactment repealed by that Act; or by virtue of Regulation 12; or by virtue of Regulation 13; or by virtue of Regulation 8(2) of the Medical Practitioners Registration (No. 2) Regulations 1969(**a**); until that person pays—

(*a*) the appropriate restoration fee (if any) prescribed in Regulation 15, and

(*b*) the retention fee (if any) which if his name had not been so erased would be due from him in respect of the current year.

15.—(1) Except in cases to which paragraphs (2) or (3) apply, the restoration fee referred to in paragraph (*a*) of Regulation 14 shall be £10.

(2) Where it is shown, to the satisfaction of the Registrar, that a person who applies for the restoration of his name to the Principal List or to the Overseas List after erasure by virtue of any of the provisions mentioned in Regulation 14 has either:

(*a*) in any year or years in which his name was not included in the Principal List, rendered any service as a medical practitioner for gain in the United Kingdom as though he were a registered medical practitioner, or

(*b*) in any year or years preceding such erasure, during which his name was included in the Principal List, failed to pay the annual retention fee or fees due from him in respect of that year or those years

the restoration fee shall be the sum of

(i) £10 and

(ii) the amount of any annual retention fees which were due from him in respect of that year or years, or which would have been due from that person if his name had been included in the Principal List in the year or years in question:

Provided that any person who is aggrieved by a decision of the Registrar under this paragraph may appeal to the Registration Committee who shall determine the matter.

(3) In the case of a person whose name has been erased at his own request under Regulation 13 and to whom paragraph (2) does not apply, no restoration fee shall be payable under this Regulation.

Regulations revoked

16.—(1) Subject to paragraph (2) hereof with effect from 1st May 1972, the Medical

---

(**a**) S.I. 1970/47 (1970 I, p. 315).

Practitioners Registration (Fees) Regulations 1969**(a)** as amended by the Medical Practitioners Registration (Fees) (Amendment) Regulations 1970**(b)** (hereinafter together called the earlier Regulations) are hereby revoked.

(2) Notwithstanding anything contained in paragraph (1) hereof any fees due to the Council under or by virtue of the earlier Regulations shall remain due to the Council as though they were payable under these Regulations, and the powers contained in these Regulations in case of non-payment shall apply in the case of such fees.

Given under the official seal of the General Medical Council, this twenty-ninth day of February, nineteen hundred and seventy-two.

(L.S.)

Cohen of Birkenhead,
President.

SCHEDULE TO THE REGULATIONS

Regulation 13

Application for Removal of Name from the Register under Regulation 13 of the Medical Practitioners Registration (Fees) Regulations

I am the person now registered as a medical practitioner under the Medical Acts of the United Kingdom as follows:—

....
(Full Name)

....
(Registration Number)

I am not aware of any proceedings, or of any reason for the institution of any proceedings, which might render me liable to have my name erased from the Register by the Disciplinary Committee.

I request that my name be removed from the Register of Medical Practitioners, on the ground that I do not wish to pay, or to continue to pay, annual retention fees.

Signature of practitioner:..

Present address:..

....

Date: ....

(a) S.I. 1970/467 (1970 I, p. 1562).   (b) S.I. 1970/1986 (1970 III, p. 6482).

EXPLANATORY NOTE
(This Note is not part of the Order.)

The regulations approved by this Order re-enact, with amendments, the existing provisions governing the payment of fees to the General Medical Council in respect of entries in the register of medical practitioners.

The principal purpose of the amendments is to increase the amount of the annual retention fee from £2 to £5.

STATUTORY INSTRUMENTS

1972 No. 430

DEFENCE

The Certificates of Arrest and Surrender (Royal Navy) Regulations 1972

Made - - - -	*20th March* 1972
Coming into Operation	On such date as the Armed Forces Act 1971 comes into force

The Secretary of State for Defence, in exercise of the powers conferred upon him by section 110(3) of the Naval Discipline Act, 1957(a), as amended by the Defence (Transfer of Functions) (No. 1) Order 1964(b), and, by virtue of section 44(1) of the Armed Forces Act 1971(c), by section 103(4) of the Naval Discipline Act, 1957 and of all other powers enabling him in that behalf, hereby makes the following Regulations:

1.—(1) These Regulations may be cited as the Certificates of Arrest and Surrender (Royal Navy) Regulations 1972 and shall come into operation on such date as the Armed forces Act 1971 comes into force.

(2) The Interpretation Act 1889(d) shall apply to the interpretation of these Regulations as it applies to the interpretation of an Act of Parliament.

2. Where, under section 108 of the Naval Discipline Act, 1957, an officer of police causes any person to be delivered into naval custody without being brought before a court of summary jurisdiction, the certificate which is required by subsection (1) of section 110 of that Act to be handed over with him shall be in the form specified in Part I of the Schedule to these Regulations and shall contain the particulars therein set out relating to his surrender.

3.—(1) Where, under section 109 of the Naval Discipline Act, 1957, a court of summary jurisdiction causes any person to be delivered into naval custody, or any person is so delivered after having been committed under that section, the certificate which is required by subsection (2) of section 110 of that Act to be handed over with him shall be in the form specified in Part II of the Schedule to these Regulations and shall contain the particulars therein set out relating to his arrest or surrender and the proceedings before the court.

(2) The fee payable to the clerk of the court in respect of such a certificate as is referred to in paragraph (1) of this Regulation shall be:—

(*a*) in the case of a clerk of a court of summary jurisdiction in Scotland— the sum of thirty three pence; and

(*b*) in any other case the sum of tenpence or in a colony the equivalent amount of local currency.

(a) 1957 c. 53.　　　　　　　　　　(b) S.I. 1964/488 (1964 I, p. 769).
(c) 1971 c. 33.　　　　　　　　　　(d) 1889 c. 63.

4. Where, under section 103 of the Naval Discipline Act, 1957, a person suspected of any offence under Part I of that Act has been arrested under a warrant issued pursuant to subsection (1) of that section, the certificate which is required by subsection (3) to be handed over with him shall be in the form specified in Part III of the Schedule to these Regulations and shall contain the particulars therein set out relating to his arrest.

5. The Certificates of Arrest and Surrender of Deserters and Absentees (Navy) Regulations, 1958**(a)** are hereby revoked.

Dated this twentieth day of March 1972.

Carrington,
One of Her Majesty's Principal Secretaries of State

SCHEDULE

PART I

Certificate in accordance with section 110(1)
of the Naval Discipline Act, 1957

I certify that...(full names)
surrendered himself at...(place) at
.........................(time) on the...........................day of...........................19...
(as being illegally absent from...(ship or naval
establishment)). At the time of his arrest he was $\frac{\text{not wearing the uniform of any of}}{\text{wearing}}$ ....

H.M. naval forces**(b).**

.......................**(c).**

He gave the following particulars/appears to be**(a)**:—

Official number.........................

Rank or rating...........................

Ship or establishment..................

Dated this...........................day of...........................19...

Signature of officer of police in ⎫
charge of police station where   ⎪
the person named above sur-   ⎬ ....
rendered or was taken on sur-   ⎪
render.   ⎭

(a) S.I. 1958/561 (1958 II, p. 2121).
(b) Delete as necessary.
(c) Where the uniform of one of H.M. naval forces was worn here state 'naval uniform', 'Royal Marines uniform' or as the case may require.

Part II

Certificate in accordance with section 110(2)
of the Naval Discipline Act, 1957

I certify that...(full names), whose service particulars are given below, appeared before a court of summary jurisdiction at...............................on the.............................day of................. ....19... in accordance with section 109 of the Naval Discipline Act, 1957, having **(a)**...at..(place), at... ....(time) on the..day of ....19... At the time of his arrest/surrender**(b)** he <u>was not wearing</u> the uniform of any of H.M. naval forces**(b)** was wearing...**(c)** He was committed to civil custody/delivered into naval custody**(b)** in accordance with the said section. The above facts were proved to the satisfaction of the court by the evidence of...(names of witnesses). Opportunity was given to cross-examine the witnesses. ....(name of prisoner) admitted that he illegally absented himself from... (ship or establishment) at...(place), on...(date)**(d)**.

Service particulars of the person named above:—

Official number.......................

Rank or rating..........................

Ship or establishment..................

Dated this......................................day of....................................19... Signature.....................................

Description.......................................

(As to the persons qualified to sign, see Note).

Note

The following persons are authorised to sign under section 33 of the Armed Forces Act 1966:

(1) In England, Wales and the Isle of Man: A Justice of the Peace or Clerk of the Court.

(2) In Scotland: The Clerk of the Court.

(3) In Northern Ireland: A resident magistrate, or the Clerk of Petty Sessions for the petty sessions district in which the court sat.

(4) In Jersey and Guernsey: A magistrate, or a person for the time being authorised to act as a magistrate.

(5) In Alderney: The Chairman of the Court of Alderney, or the person for the time being authorised to act as Chairman of that Court.

(6) In Sark: The Seneschal or the Deputy Seneschal.

(7) In a Colony, Protectorate, or Trusteeship Territory under the United Nations (or territory consisting of two or more such units): A magistrate, or the official (by whatever designation known) who exercises in the Court functions similar to those exercised in England by the clerk of a court of summary jurisdiction.

(a) Insert here 'surrendered to...............' or 'been arrested by...............' as the case required. **(b)** Delete as necessary.
(c) Where the uniform of one of H.M. naval forces was worn here state 'naval uniform', 'Royal Marines uniform' or as the case may require.
(d) Delete if inappropriate.

PART III

Certificate in accordance with section 103(3)
of the Naval Discipline Act, 1957

1. I certify that:

        Official Number.........................

        Rank or rating...........................

        Full Names..............................

        Ship or establishment.................

was arrested at..(place) at.................
..............(time) on the....................................day of...........................19...
under a warrant issued by naval authorities pursuant to section 103(1) of the Naval
Discipline Act, 1957.

2. At the time of his arrest he was:

not <u>wearing</u> the uniform of any of H.M. naval forces**(a)**
was wearing...**(b)**
Dated this..day of...........................19...

        Signature of officer of police⎫

        who causes the above-named per- ⎬ ....

        son to be delivered into naval ⎪

        custody. ⎭

EXPLANATORY NOTE
(*This Note is not part of the Regulations.*)

These Regulations, which replace the Certificates of Arrest and Surrender of
Deserters and Absentees (Navy) Regulations, 1958, prescribe the form of
certificate to be handed over when a naval deserter or absentee, who has surrendered himself to the police, is delivered into naval custody. They also
prescribe the form of certificate to be handed over when a deserter or absentee
is delivered into naval custody as a result of proceedings before a court of
summary jurisdiction (in respect of which certificate the fee payable to the clerk
of the court is also fixed) and, on delivery into naval custody, with a person suspected of any offence under Part I of the Naval Discipline Act, 1957 who has
been arrested under a warrant issued by naval authorities.

(a) Delete as necessary.
(b) Where the uniform of one of H.M. naval forces was worn here state 'naval uniform',
'Royal Marines Uniform' or as the case may require.

STATUTORY INSTRUMENTS

1972 No. 431

CIVIL AVIATION

The Civil Aviation (Notices) (Amendment) Regulations 1972

Made - - -	*20th March* 1972
Laid before Parliament	*27th March* 1972
Coming into Operation	*1st April* 1972

The Secretary of State in exercise of his powers under section 29(4) of the Civil Aviation Act 1971(**a**), and of all other powers enabling him in that behalf hereby makes the following Regulations.

1.—(1) These Regulations may be cited as the Civil Aviation (Notices) (Amendment) Regulations 1972 and shall come into operation on 1st April 1972.

(2) The Interpretation Act 1889(**b**) shall apply for the purpose of the interpretation of these Regulations as it applies for the purpose of the interpretation of an Act of Parliament.

2. For Regulation 3 of the Civil Aviation (Notices) Regulations 1971(**c**) there shall be substituted the following Regulation:—

"3.—(1) The manner of service of a notice for the purposes of section 29(4)(*e*) of the Act shall be either

(*a*) by delivering it to that person; or

(*b*) by leaving it at his proper address; or

(*c*) by post,

and where the person is a body corporate the notice may be served upon the secretary of that body.

(2) For the purposes of this Regulation the proper address of any person shall, in the case of a body corporate, be the registered or principal office of that body and in any other case be the last known address of the person to be served."

Michael Noble,
Minister for Trade,
Department of Trade and Industry.

20th March 1972.

(**a**) 1971 c. 75.   (**b**) 1889 c. 63.
(**c**) S.I. 1971/1686 (1971 III, p. 4611).

EXPLANATORY NOTE

(This Note is not part of the Regulations.)

These Regulations make it possible for a notice under section 29(4)(*e*) of the Civil Aviation Act 1971, permitting a take off or landing to be disregarded for the purposes of a notice under section 29(3) of that Act, to be served by delivery, or by leaving it at a person's address, as well as by post.

STATUTORY INSTRUMENTS

1972 No. 432

SUGAR

The Sugar (Distribution Payments) (No. 3) Order 1972

Made - - - -	*21st March* 1972
Laid before Parliament -	*22nd March* 1972
Coming into Operation -	*23rd March* 1972

The Minister of Agriculture, Fisheries and Food in exercise of the powers conferred upon him by sections 14(5) and 33(4) of the Sugar Act 1956(a), having effect subject to the provisions of section 3 of, and Part II of Schedule 5 to, the Finance Act 1962(b), section 22 of the Finance Act 1964(c) and section 52 of the Finance Act 1966(d) and of all other powers enabling him in that behalf, with the concurrence of the Treasury, and on the advice of the Sugar Board hereby makes the following order:—

1.—(1) This order may be cited as the Sugar (Distribution Payments) (No. 3) Order 1972, and shall come into operation on 23rd March 1972.

(2) The Interpretation Act 1889(e) shall apply for the interpretation of this order as it applies for the interpretation of an Act of Parliament.

2. Notwithstanding the provisions of article 2 of the Sugar (Distribution Payments) (No. 2) Order 1972(f), the rates of distribution payments payable under and in accordance with the provisions of section 14 of the Sugar Act 1956, having effect as aforesaid, in respect of sugar and invert sugar imported or home produced or used in the manufacture of imported composite sugar products shall on and after 23rd March 1972 be those rates specified in the Schedule to this order; and section 10 of the Finance Act 1901(g) (which relates to new or altered customs or excise duties and their effect upon contracts) shall apply accordingly.

In Witness whereof the Official Seal of the Minister of Agriculture, Fisheries and Food is hereunto affixed on 20th March 1972.

(L.S.)

F. M. Kearns,
Authorised by the Minister.

We concur.
21st March 1972.

Walter Clegg,
P. L. Hawkins,
Two of the Lords Commissioners of
Her Majesty's Treasury.

(a) 1956 c. 48.   (b) 1962 c. 44.   (c) 1964 c. 49.   (d) 1966 c. 18.
(e) 1889 c. 63.   (f) S.I. 1972/356 (1972 I, p. 1417).   (g) 1901 c. 7.

SCHEDULE

Part I

Rates of Distribution Payment for Sugar

Polarisation	Rate of Distribution Payment per ton
	£
Exceeding—	
99°	20·000
98° but not exceeding 99°	18·860
97° „ „ „ 98°	18·400
96° „ „ „ 97°	17·920
95° „ „ „ 96°	17·440
94° „ „ „ 95°	16·960
93° „ „ „ 94°	16·480
92° „ „ „ 93°	16·000
91° „ „ „ 92°	15·520
90° „ „ „ 91°	15·040
89° „ „ „ 90°	14·560
88° „ „ „ 89°	14·080
87° „ „ „ 88°	13·680
86° „ „ „ 87°	13·280
85° „ „ „ 86°	12·920
84° „ „ „ 85°	12·560
83° „ „ „ 84°	12·200
82° „ „ „ 83°	11·840
81° „ „ „ 82°	11·520
80° „ „ „ 81°	11·200
79° „ „ „ 80°	10·880
78° „ „ „ 79°	10·560
77° „ „ „ 78°	10. 240
76° „ „ „ 77°	9·920
Not exceeding 76°	9·600

Part II

Rates of Distribution Payment for Invert Sugar

Sweetening matter content by weight	Rate of Distribution Payment per cwt.
	£
70 per cent. or more	0·63
Less than 70 per cent. and more than 50 per cent.	0·45
Not more than 50 per cent.	0·22

EXPLANATORY NOTE

(*This Note is not part of the Order.*)

This order provides for reductions equivalent to £14 per ton of refined sugar in the rates of distribution payment in respect of sugar and invert sugar which become eligible for such payments on and after 23rd March 1972.

STATUTORY INSTRUMENTS

1972 No. 433

SUGAR

The Sugar (Distribution Repayments) (Amendment) (No. 2) Order 1972

Made	-	-	-	-	*21st March* 1972
Laid before Parliament					*22nd March* 1972
Coming into Operation					*23rd March* 1972

The Minister of Agriculture, Fisheries and Food in exercise of the powers conferred upon him by sections 15 and 33(4) of the Sugar Act 1956(a), having effect subject to the provisions of section 3 of, and Part II of Schedule 5 to, the Finance Act 1962(b), section 22 of the Finance Act 1964(c) and section 52 of the Finance Act 1966(d) and of all other powers enabling him in that behalf, an order (e) having been made under section 14 of the said Act, hereby makes the following order:—

1.—(1)This order may be cited as the Sugar (Distribution Repayments) (Amendment) (No. 2) Order 1972, and shall come into operation on 23rd March 1972.

(2) The Interpretation Act 1889(f) shall apply for the interpretation of this order as it applies for the interpretation of an Act of Parliament.

2.—(1) Notwithstanding the provisions of article 3(1) of the Sugar (Distribution Repayments) (Amendment) Order 1972(g) the amount of distribution repayment payable in respect of invert sugar, if the relevant drawback is payable thereon as being invert sugar produced in the United Kingdom from materials on which sugar duty has been paid on or after 23rd March 1972, shall be calculated thereon at the rate applicable to the invert sugar in accordance with the rates prescribed in the Schedule to this order.

(2) Article 2(1) of the Sugar (Distribution Repayments) Order 1972(h) shall apply for the interpretation of this article.

In Witness whereof the Official Seal of the Minister of Agriculture, Fisheries and Food is hereunto affixed on 21st March 1972.

(L.S.)

F. M. Kearns,
Authorised by the Minister.

(a) 1956 c. 48.   (b) 1962 c. 44.   (c) 1964 c. 49.
(d) 1966 c. 18.   (e) S.I. 1972/432(1972 I, p. 1622).   (f) 1889 c. 63.
(g) S.I. 1972/357 (1972 I, p. 1419).   (h) S.I. 1972/67 (1972 I, p. 162).

THE SCHEDULE

RATES OF DISTRIBUTION REPAYMENT FOR INVERT SUGAR

Sweetening matter content by weight	Rate of Distribution Repayment per cwt.
	£
More than 80 per cent.	0·75
More than 70 per cent. but not more than 80 per cent.	0·63
More than 60 per cent. but not more than 70 per cent.	0·45
More than 50 per cent. but not more than 60 per cent.	0·36
Not more than 50 per cent. and the invert sugar not being less in weight than 14 lb. per gallon	0·22

EXPLANATORY NOTE

(*This Note is not part of the Order.*)

This order, which is consequent upon the Sugar (Distribution Payments) (No. 3) Order 1972 (S.I. 1972/432), provides for reductions equivalent to £14 per ton of refined sugar in the rates of distribution repayment, in respect of sugar and invert sugar produced in the United Kingdom from materials which become eligible for distribution payments on or after 23rd March 1972.

STATUTORY   INSTRUMENTS

1972 No. 434

SUGAR

The Composite Sugar Products (Distribution Payments— Average Rates) (No. 3) Order 1972

Made -	-	-	-	21st March 1972
Laid before Parliament-				22nd March 1972
Coming into Operation				23rd March 1972

Whereas the Minister of Agriculture, Fisheries and Food (hereinafter called " the Minister ") has on the recommendation of the Sugar Board made an order (a) pursuant to the powers conferred upon him by section 9(1) of the Sugar Act 1956(b) having effect subject to section 14(8) of that Act and to the provisions of section 3 of, and Part II of Schedule 5 to, the Finance Act 1962 (c), section 22 of the Finance Act 1964(d) and section 52 of the Finance Act 1966(e), providing that in the case of certain descriptions of composite sugar products distribution payments shall be calculated on the basis of an average quantity of sugar or invert sugar taken to have been used in the manufacture of the products and that certain other descriptions shall be treated as not containing any sugar or invert sugar:

And whereas the Minister has by the Sugar (Distribution Payments) (No. 3) Order 1972(f) provided for a change in the rates of distribution payments in respect of sugar and invert sugar which became eligible for such payments on and after 23rd March 1972.

Now, therefore, the Minister on the recommendation of the Sugar Board, and in exercise of the powers conferred upon him by sections 9(1) and 33(4) of the Sugar Act 1956, having effect as aforesaid, and of all other powers enabling him in that behalf, hereby makes the following order:—

1.—(1) This order may be cited as the Composite Sugar Products (Distribution Payments—Average Rates) (No. 3) Order 1972, and shall come into operation on 23rd March 1972.

(2) The Interpretation Act 1889(g) shall apply to the interpretation of this order as it applies to the interpretation of an Act of Parliament.

2. Distribution payments payable on or after 23rd March 1972 under and in accordance with section 14 of the Sugar Act 1956, having effect as aforesaid, in respect of sugar and invert sugar used in the manufacture of the descriptions of imported composite sugar products specified in the second column of Schedule 1 to this order, being goods which are classified in the tariff headings indicated in relation to them in the first column of the said Schedule shall, notwithstanding the provisions of the Sugar (Distribution Payments) (No. 3) Order 1972 and the Composite Sugar Products (Distribution Payments—Average Rates) (No. 2) Order 1972(a) be calculated by reference to the weight of the products and the rates specified in relation thereto in the third column of the said Schedule.

3. Imported composite sugar products other than those of a description specified in Schedules 1 and 2 to this order shall be treated as not containing any sugar or invert sugar for the purposes of distribution payments.

(a) S.I. 1972/358 (1972 I, p. 1421). (b) 1956 c. 48.   (c) 1962 c. 44   (d) 1964 c. 49.
(e) 1966 c. 18.   (f) S.I. 1972/432 (1972 I, p. 1622). (g) 1889 c. 63.

In Witness whereof the Official Seal of the Minister of Agriculture, Fisheries and Food is hereunto affixed on 21st March 1972.

(L.S.)

F. M. *Kearns*,
Authorised by the Minister.

SCHEDULE 1

In this Schedule:—

" Tariff heading " means a heading or, where the context so requires, a subheading of the Customs Tariff 1959 (see paragraph (1) of Article 2 of the Import Duties (General) (No. 7) Order 1971)(a).

Tariff heading	Description of Composite Sugar Products	Rate of Distribution Payment
		Per cwt. £
04.02 ..	Milk and cream, preserved, concentrated or sweetened, containing more than 10 per cent. by weight of added sugar	0·44
17.02 (B) (2) and 17.05 (B)	Syrups containing sucrose sugar, whether or not flavoured or coloured, but not including fruit juices containing added sugar in any proportion:—	
	Containing 70 per cent. or more by weight of sweetening matter	0·63
	Containing less than 70 per cent., and more than 50 per cent. by weight of sweetening matter	0·45
	Containing not more than 50 per cent. by weight of sweetening matter	0·22
17.02 (F) ..	Caramel:—	
	Solid	1·00
	Liquid	0·69
17.04 ..	Sugar confectionery, not containing cocoa ..	0·81
18.06 ..	Chocolate and other food preparations containing cocoa and added sugar:—	
	Chocolate couverture not prepared for retail sale; chocolate milk crumb, liquid ..	0·44
	Chocolate milk crumb, solid	0·54
	Solid chocolate bars or blocks, milk or plain, with or without fruit or nuts; other chocolate confectionery consisting wholly of chocolate or of chocolate and other ingredients not containing added sugar ..	0·44
	Other	0·58

(a) S.I. 1971/1971 (1971 III, p. 5330).

SCHEDULE 1—*continued*

Tariff heading	Description of Composite Sugar Products	Rate of Distribution Payment
		Per cwt. £
19.08 ..	Pastry, biscuits, cakes and other fine bakers' wares containing added sugar:—	
	Biscuits, wafers and rusks containing more than 12½ per cent. by weight of added sugar, and other biscuits, wafers and rusks included in retail packages with such goods.. ..	0·25
	Cakes with covering or filling containing added sugar; meringues	0·33
	Other	0·12
20.01 ..	Vegetables and fruit, prepared or preserved by vinegar or acetic acid, containing added sugar:—	
	Containing 10 per cent. or more by weight of added sugar	0·35
	Other	0·07
20.03 ..	Fruit preserved by freezing, containing added sugar	0·12
20.04 ..	Fruit, fruit-peel and parts of plants, preserved by sugar (drained, glacé or crystallised)	0·65
20.05 ..	Jams, fruit jellies, marmalades, fruit puree and fruit pastes, being cooked preparations, containing added sugar	0·62
20.06 ..	Fruit otherwise prepared or preserved, containing added sugar:—	
	Ginger	0·50
	Other	0·12

SCHEDULE 2

Tariff heading	Description of Composite Sugar Products
17.05 (A) and (B)	Sugar and invert sugar, flavoured or coloured.

EXPLANATORY NOTE

(This Note is not part of the Order.)

This order provides for reductions in the average rates of distribution payments payable in respect of imported composite sugar products of the descriptions specified in Schedule 1 on and after 23rd March 1972. These correspond to reductions in the rates of distribution payment effected by the Sugar (Distribution Payments) (No. 3) Order 1972 (S.I. 1972/432). Provision is also made for certain imported composite sugar products to be treated as not containing any sugar or invert sugar.

STATUTORY INSTRUMENTS

1972 No. 435

AGRICULTURE

The Agricultural Investment (Variation of Rate of Grant) Order 1972

Made - - -	*21st March* 1972
Laid before the House of Commons	*27th March* 1972
Coming into Operation	*10th April* 1972

The Minister of Agriculture, Fisheries and Food, the Secretary of State for Scotland and the Secretary of State for Wales, acting jointly, in pursuance of section 34 of the Agriculture Act 1967(**a**), as read with the Transfer of Functions (Wales) Order 1969(**b**), and of all their other enabling powers, with the consent of the Treasury, hereby make the following order:—

Citation, extent and commencement

1. This order, which may be cited as the Agricultural Investment (Variation of Rate of Grant) Order 1972, shall apply throughout the United Kingdom and shall come into operation on 10th April 1972.

Interpretation

2.—(1) In this order—

"appropriate Minister" means (*a*) in relation to England or Northern Ireland, the Minister of Agriculture, Fisheries and Food; (*b*) in relation to Wales, the Minister of Agriculture, Fisheries and Food and the Secretary of State acting jointly; (*c*) in relation to Scotland, the Secretary of State;

"basic grant" has the same meaning as in section 33 of the Agriculture Act 1967.

(2) The Interpretation Act 1889(**c**) shall apply to the interpretation of this order as it applies to the interpretation of an Act of Parliament.

Variation of rate of grant and non-application of previous order

3.—(1) Subject to the provisions of this article, the amount of any grant under section 33 of the Agriculture Act 1967 which is supplementary to a

---

(**a**) 1967 c. 22. (**b**) S.I. 1969/388 (1969 I, p. 1070).
(**c**) 1889 c. 63.

basic grant under section 1(1) of the Horticulture Act 1960(a) (horticultural improvements) shall, instead of being an amount equal to $1\frac{2}{3}$ per cent., be an amount equal to $6\frac{2}{3}$ per cent. of the cost of expenditure by reference to which the amount of that basic grant is calculated.

(2) This article applies only where the basic grant referred to in the preceding paragraph is paid, as a result of an application submitted to the appropriate Minister for approval on or after 10th April 1972, in respect of the provision of any facility or the supply and installation of any plant or equipment on or after that date; and the Agricultural Investment (Variation of Rate of Grant) (No. 2) Order 1970(b) shall not have effect in relation to a grant which is supplementary to any basic grant paid for the provision of any facility or the supply and installation of any plant or equipment to which this paragraph applies.

In Witness whereof the Official Seal of the Minister of Agriculture, Fisheries and Food is hereunto affixed on 16th March 1972.

(L.S.)

J. M. L. Prior,
Minister of Agriculture, Fisheries and Food.

17th March 1972.

Gordon Campbell,
Secretary of State for Scotland.

Given under my hand on 20th March 1972.

Peter Thomas,
Secretary of State for Wales.

We consent,

Keith Speed,
P. L. Hawkins,
Two of the Lords Commissioners of
21st March 1972.   Her Majesty's Treasury.

(a) 1960 c. 22.   (b) S.I. 1970/1756 (1970 III, p. 5732).

EXPLANATORY NOTE

(This Note is not part of the Order.)

This order, which comes into operation on 10th April 1972 and applies throughout the United Kingdom, increases from $1\frac{2}{3}$ per cent. to $6\frac{2}{3}$ per cent. the rate of supplement paid under section 33 of the Agriculture Act 1967 in respect of expenditure towards which a horticultural improvement grant is made under section 1(1) of the Horticulture Act 1960.

The increased rate applies to improvements which are carried out, and in respect of which applications for approval are submitted, on or after 10th April 1972, and the order provides that the Agricultural Investment (Variation of Rate of Grant) (No. 2) Order 1970 shall not apply to such improvements.

STOKE-ON-TRENT
CITY
LIBRARIES

STATUTORY INSTRUMENTS

1972 No. 436

INCOME TAX

The Income Tax (Small Maintenance Payments) Order 1972

Made - - -	*21st March* 1972
Laid before the House of Commons	*28th March* 1972
Coming into Operation	*6th April* 1972

The Treasury, in exercise of the powers conferred upon them by section 65 of the Income and Corporation Taxes Act 1970(**a**), hereby make the following Order:—

1.—(1) This Order may be cited as the Income Tax (Small Maintenance Payments) Order 1972, and shall come into operation on 6th April 1972.

(2) In this Order, "section 65(1)" means subsection (1) of section 65 of the Income and Corporation Taxes Act 1970 (which specifies certain weekly or monthly payments under an order of a court in the United Kingdom, therein and herein called "small maintenance payments", which are to be payable without deduction of income tax).

(3) The Interpretation Act 1889(**b**) shall apply for the interpretation of this Order as it applies for the interpretation of an Act of Parliament.

2.—(1) The amount specified in paragraph (i)(A) of section 65(1) as that of the maximum weekly rate for small maintenance payments which are payable weekly shall, as respects both payments within paragraph (*a*) of that subsection (payments for maintenance of a party to a marriage or former marriage) and payments within paragraph (*b*) thereof (payments for benefit, maintenance or education of person under 21), be increased from £7·50 to £12.

(2) The amount specified in paragraph (i)(B) of section 65(1) as that of the maximum monthly rate for small maintenance payments which are payable monthly shall, as respects both payments within paragraph (*a*) of that subsection and payments within paragraph (*b*) thereof, be increased from £32·50 to £52.

3. This Order shall not affect payments falling due before 6th April 1973 under an order made before 6th April 1972:

Provided that, where an order so made is varied or revived at any time after 5th April 1972, this Order shall apply in relation to payments falling due under the order after that time.

(**a**) 1970 c. 10. (**b**) 1889 c. 63.

Keith Speed,
P. L. Hawkins,
Two of the Lords Commissioners
of Her Majesty's Treasury.

21st March 1972.

EXPLANATORY NOTE

(This Note is not part of the Order.)

Section 65, Income and Corporation Taxes Act 1970, provides that income tax is not to be deducted at source from certain weekly or monthly payments (called "small maintenance payments") payable under the order of a court in the United Kingdom for the maintenance of a party to a broken marriage or for the benefit, maintenance or education of a person under 21. As the law stands small maintenance payments must be payable weekly at a rate not exceeding £7·50 or monthly at a rate not exceeding £32·50. This Order increases those limits to £12 and £52 respectively. It applies to all payments under orders made after 5th April 1972, to payments under orders varied or revived after that date which fall due after the variation or revival, and otherwise to payments falling due after 5th April 1973 under orders in force at 5th April 1972.

STATUTORY INSTRUMENTS

1972 No. 437

COMMON

The Commons Registration (Disposal of Disputed Registrations) Regulations 1972

Made - - -	*21st March* 1972
Laid before Parliament	*28th March* 1972
Coming into Operation	*18th April* 1972

The Secretary of State for the Environment (as respects England except Monmouthshire) and the Secretary of State for Wales (as respects Wales and Monmouthshire) in exercise of their powers under sections 3(1), 6(2) and 19(1)(*k*) of the Commons Registration Act 1965(a), and of all other powers enabling them in that behalf, hereby make the following regulations:—

Title and commencement

1. These regulations may be cited as the Commons Registration (Disposal of Disputed Registrations) Regulations 1972, and shall come into operation on 18th April 1972.

Interpretation

2.—(1) The Interpretation Act 1889(b) applies for the interpretation of these regulations as it applies for the interpretation of an Act of Parliament.

(2) In these regulations, unless the context otherwise requires,—

"the Act" means the Commons Registration Act 1965;

"General Regulation" followed by a number means the regulation so numbered in the Commons Registration (General) Regulations 1966(c) as amended (**d**);

"Model Entry" followed by a number means the specimen entry so numbered and provided by way of example in Part 1 of the Schedule to these regulations;

"provisional registration" means a registration under section 4 of the Act which has not become final;

"register map" means any map, other than a supplemental map, which, by virtue of any regulation made under the Act, for the time being forms part of a register;

"register unit" bears the meaning assigned to that expression in General Regulation 10;

"supplemental map" bears the meaning assigned to that expression in General Regulation 20.

(a) 1965 c. 64.   (b) 1889 c. 63.
(c) S.I. 1966/1471 (1966 III, p. 3978).
(d) The amending instruments are not relevant to the subject matter of these regulations.

Amendment of registers

3. Where a registration authority is informed under section 6 of the Act that a registration has become final (with or without modifications) or has become void, the authority shall indicate that fact in the register in accordance with Model Entry 27, 28, 29, 30, 31 or 32 as appropriate, with such adaptations and modifications (if any) as the case may require, and shall make any necessary amendment to the register map and any supplemental map.

Transfer of certain entries

4.—(1) Where any land has been registered both as common land and as a town or village green, and the registration authority is informed under section 6 of the Act that one of the registrations of the land has become void, the authority shall cancel in each register the notes made pursuant to paragraph (1) of General Regulation 14 (Double registration of land), and shall transfer from the register wherein the registration of the land has been cancelled to the other register every entry to which this regulation applies, in the following manner:—

(a) every entry shall be allotted a fresh number and shall be dated as of the date when so transferred, but in the left-hand column of the register sheet, below such number and date, shall appear "(Formerly No.......
.... dated .... in Register Unit No.
...............................)";

(b) references to land in column 4 of the rights and ownership sections of the original register containing expressions valid only in relation to that register shall be adapted as necessary; and

(c) the register map shall be amended as necessary.

(2) This regulation applies to every entry mentioned in paragraph (2) of General Regulation 14 except a registration under section 4 of the Act which has become void or has not become final or a note relating to such a registration, and, in the case of a registration which has become final with modifications, applies to that registration with those modifications.

Noting of certain rights registrations

5. Where a registration of a right of common which has become final contains a statement, in whatever terms, that the right is exercisable also over land comprised in another register unit, and the registration of the right as exercisable over that land is cancelled or becomes void, or is modified so as to be exercisable over part only of that land, the registration authority shall enter a note to that effect in the register unit containing the first-mentioned registration, and a cross-reference between the note and the registration.

Area measurement

6.—(1) Where any registration of land, other than a provisional registration, contains no indication of the area of the land, the registration authority shall enter a note of the area in the land section of the register, and shall cancel that note and enter a fresh one whenever there is any alteration in the area.

(2) A note under this regulation shall state the area of the land in hectares to three places of decimals.

Foreshore boundaries

7. Where any land comprised in a registration, other than a provisional registration, was at the date of the registration bounded by the high water mark of medium tides for any distance which, in the opinion of the registration authority, it is practicable to show on the general scale of the register map, the authority may enter a note in the land section of the register substantially in accordance with Standard Entry 9 in Part 2 of the Schedule to these regulations, and, where the authority enters such a note, it shall mark the register map accordingly.

Regulations 2, 7.   SCHEDULE

PART 1

MODEL ENTRIES

No. 27

For land section of register: an example of a registration becoming final with modifications.

No. and date of entry	Description of the land, reference to the register map, registration particulars, etc.
1 2 May 1967 (See entry No. 2 below)	The piece of land called Goose Green containing 2·75 acres or thereabouts in the parish of Lowood, Barset, numbered 617 on the ordnance map (2nd edition, 1907) of that parish, as marked with a green verge line inside the boundary on sheet 2 of the register map and distinguished by the number of this register unit. Registered by the registration authority without application. <div align="right">(Registration provisional.)</div>

No. 27   2
12 June 1972
	The registration at entry No. 1 above, which was disputed, became final on 15 May 1972 with the following modifications:—
	  (*a*) the area to read "2·50 acres or thereabouts";
	  (*b*) the land to the west of the line A-B on the register map (as now hatched black thereon), comprising an area of 0·25 acre, to be removed from the register.

No. 28

For rights section of register: entry for use where a number of disputed registrations have become final without modification. The words "(Registration provisional)" in each of the concerned registration entries must be struck through.

1 No. and date of entry	2 No. and date of application	3 Name and address of every applicant for registration, and the capacity in which he applied	4 Particulars of the right of common, and of the land over which it is exercisable	5 Particulars of the land (if any) to which the right is attached
113 24 May 1972		The registrations at entries were disputed, became final as Nos. 68 and 74 on 24 April 1972, No. 70 on 75, 76 and 77 on 10 May 1972, and Nos. 78, May 1972.	Nos. 68, 70 and 74 follows:— 25 April 1972, Nos.	to 80 above, which 79 and 80 on 11

No. 29

For rights section of register: for use where a registration has become void.   The void entry must be struck through, and a cross-reference to this entry inserted.

1 *No. and date of entry*	2 *No. and date of application*	3 *Name and address of every applicant for registration, and the capacity in which he applied*	4 *Particulars of the right of common, and of the land over which it is exercisable*	5 *Particulars of the land (if any) to which the right is attached*
114 13 Aug. 1972	The registration at entry No. 72, which was disputed, became void on 3 May 1972.			

No. 30

For rights section of register: an example of a disputed registration becoming final with modifications.

| 1
10 Mar.
1967 | 289
4 Mar.
1967 | Jonathan Lotherington, Thatcham Farm, Fursdon, Barset. Owner.

*For modifications on finality see entry No. 103 below | To graze—
(*a*) *20 head of cattle; or
(*b*) *100 sheep: or
(*c*) sheep and cattle together to a limit of *100 gates, each head of cattle counting as 5 gates and each sheep as 1 gate;
over the whole of the land comprised in this register unit except the detached portion to the south of the Grand Junction Canal.
(Registration provisional.) | Thatcham Farm, Fursdon, Barset, comprising O.S. Nos. 284, 285, 287, 301, 302, 302a, 317, 322, 348 and 349 on the O.S. map (2nd edition 1907) of the parish of Fursdon, Barset, and also the land in that parish shown hatched blue on the supplemental map bearing the number of this registration.* |
| 103
4 July
1972 | The registration at entry No. 1 above, which was disputed, became final on 19 June 1972 with the following modifications:—

(*a*) In column 4, for "20 head of cattle" read "16 head of cattle", for "100 sheep" read "80 sheep", and for "100 gates" read "80 gates";

(*b*) In column 5, delete all after "Barset" where that word occurs for the second time. | | | |

Nos. 31 and 32

For ownership section of register.

1 No. and date of entry	2 No. and date of application	3 Name and address of person registered as owner	4 Particulars of the land to which the registration applies
2 18 May 1967	312 10 May 1967	Jesiah Burlinson, Beldon Hall, Dalberry Lees, Barset. (Registration provisional) (See entry No. 5 below)	The part of the land comprised in this register unit lying east of the line A-B and north of the line C-D on the register map.
3 17 June 1968	2001 1 June 1968	The incumbent for the time being of the benefice of St. Peter, Reepham, Barset. (Registration provisional)	The part of the land comprised in this register unit lying east of the line A-B and south of the line C-D on the register map.*
		*For modification on finality see entry No. 6 below	

| No. 31 | 5 20 June 1972 | The registration at entry No. 2, which was disputed, became void on 9 June 1972. | |
| No. 32 | 6 20 June 1972 | The registration at entry No. 3, which was disputed, became final on 9 June 1972 with the following modification:— In column 4 after the word "map" add the words "except the parcel numbered 38c on the ordnance survey map (3rd edition 1930) of the parish of Reepham, Barset.". | |

PART 2

STANDARD ENTRY

No. 9

For Notes, land section of register.

At the date of the registration of the land comprised in this register unit, the boundary of the land between the points marked A-B-C-D on sheet......................of the register map coincided with the high water mark of medium tides.

Peter Walker,
Secretary of State for the Environment

21st March 1972.

Peter Thomas,
Secretary of State for **Wales**

21st March 1972.

EXPLANATORY NOTE

(This Note is not part of the Regulations.)

Under sections 5 and 19 of the Commons Registration Act 1965, if objection is made to a provisional registration of any land as common land or as a town or village green, or of rights of common over or a claim to ownership of such land, or if one such registration conflicts with another, the matter must be referred to a Commons Commissioner.

The ultimate disposal of such registrations will be notified to registration authorities following decisions by Commons Commissioners under section 6 of the Act, and the result of any appeal from such decisions. These regulations provide for the indication of the disposal of these registrations in the registers maintained under the Act. They also provide for consequential matters and for certain minor entries in the registers.

STATUTORY INSTRUMENTS

1972 No. 438

CLEAN AIR

The Smoke Control Areas (Exempted Fireplaces) Order 1972

Made - - - -	*21st March* 1972
Laid before Parliament	*28th March* 1972
Coming into Operation	*18th April* 1972

The Secretary of State for the Environment, in exercise of his powers under section 11(4) of the Clean Air Act 1956(a) and of all other powers enabling him in that behalf, hereby orders as follows:—

Title and commencement

1. This order may be cited as the Smoke Control Areas (Exempted Fireplaces) Order 1972 and shall come into operation on 18th April 1972.

Interpretation

2. The Interpretation Act 1889(b) shall apply for the interpretation of this order as it applies for the interpretation of an Act of Parliament.

Class of fireplace exempted from section 11 of the Clean Air Act 1956

3. The class of fireplace described in column (1) of the schedule hereto shall, subject to the conditions specified in column (2), be exempted from the provisions of section 11 of the Clean Air Act 1956 (which empowers a local authority to declare the whole or any part of their district to be a smoke control area).

SCHEDULE

(1) Class of Fireplace	(2) Conditions
The fireplace known as the Parkray Coalmaster and manufactured by Radiation Parkray Limited.	The fireplace shall be installed, maintained and operated so as to minimise the emission of smoke and in accordance with the manufacturer's instructions. No fuel shall be used other than selected washed coal singles.

(a) 1956 c. 52.　　　　　　　　(b) 1889 c. 63.

Peter Walker,
Secretary of State for the
Environment.

21st March 1972.

EXPLANATORY NOTE
(This Note is not part of the Order.)

Section 11 of the Clean Air Act 1956 empowers local authorities to declare the whole or any part of their district to be a smoke control area in which the emission of smoke is, generally, prohibited.

This order exempts the Parkray Coalmaster Roomheater from the provisions of that section, upon certain conditions as to proper operation.

STATUTORY INSTRUMENTS

1972 No. 440

HOUSING, ENGLAND AND WALES
The Approved Expenditure (Housing Act 1969 Part II) Order 1972

Made - - -	*21st March* 1972
Laid before House of Commons	*23rd March* 1972
Coming into Operation	*28th April* 1972

The Secretary of State for the Environment (as respects England, except Monmouthshire) and the Secretary of State for Wales (as respects Wales and Monmouthshire) in exercise of their powers under section 37(5) (as read with section 86(1)) of the Housing Act 1969(**a**) and of all other powers enabling them in that behalf, with the consent of the Treasury, hereby make the following order: —

1.—(1) This Order may be cited as the Approved Expenditure (Housing Act 1969 Part II) Order 1972 and shall come into operation on 28th April 1972.

(2) The Interpretation Act 1889(**b**) shall apply for the interpretation of this order as it applies for the interpretation of an Act of Parliament.

2. In section 37(4) of the Housing Act 1969 (calculation of approved expenditure of local authorities in respect of general improvement areas) for the amount "£100" there shall be substituted the amount "£200".

Peter Walker,
Secretary of State for the Environment.

21st March 1972.

Peter Thomas,
Secretary of State for Wales.

21st March 1972.

We consent.

Walter Clegg,
P. L. Hawkins,
Two of the Lords Commissioners of
Her Majesty's Treasury.

21st March 1972.

(**a**) 1969 c. 33.   (**b**) 1889 c. 63.

EXPLANATORY NOTE
(*This Note is not part of the Order.*)

This Order increases from £100 to £200 the amount per dwelling which is to be taken into account in calculating the maximum approved expenditure by local authorities under Part II of the Housing Act 1969 in respect of general improvement areas, and towards which contributions may be paid by the Secretaries of State.

STATUTORY INSTRUMENTS

1972 No. 442 (S.32)

EDUCATION, SCOTLAND

The Teachers Superannuation (Family Benefits) (Scotland) Amendment Regulations 1972

Made -	-	-	-	*17th March*	1972
Laid before Parliament				*23rd March*	1972
Coming into Operation				*24th March*	1972

In exercise of the powers conferred on me by section 7 of the Teachers Superannuation (Scotland) Act 1968(a), and of all other powers enabling me in that behalf, and after consultation with representatives of education authorities, teachers and other bodies appearing to me to be likely to be affected as required by section 18(5) of the said Act, and with the consent of the Minister for the Civil Service, I hereby make the following regulations:—

Citation, Commencement and Interpretation

1.—(1) These regulations may be cited as the Teachers Superannuation (Family Benefits) (Scotland) Amendment Regulations 1972 and shall come into operation on 24th March 1972.

(2) The Teachers Superannuation (Family Benefits) (Scotland) Regulations 1971(b) and these regulations may be cited together as the Teachers Superannuation (Family Benefits) (Scotland) Regulations 1971 to 1972.

(3) In these regulations "the 1971 Regulations" means the Teachers Superannuation (Family Benefits) (Scotland) Regulations 1971.

(4) The Interpretation Act 1889(c) shall apply for the interpretation of these regulations as it applies for the interpretation of an Act of Parliament.

Amount of Widow's Pension

2. In paragraph (2) of regulation 44 of the 1971 Regulations—

    (*a*) the word "or" at the end of sub-paragraph (*b*) shall be omitted;

    (*b*) in sub-paragraph (*c*) after "1st May 1971" there shall be inserted "and before 24th March 1972" and at the end of that sub-paragraph there shall be added—

        "or

        (*d*) £153 if her husband, on or after 24th March so ceased or so died."

(a) 1968 c. 12.   (b) S.I. 1971/1775 (1971 III, p. 4813).

(c) 1889 c. 63.

Amount of Short Service Widow's Pension

3. In regulation 47 of the 1971 Regulations—

(a) the word "or" at the end of paragraph (b) shall be omitted;

(b) in paragraph (c) after "1st May 1971" there shall be inserted "and before 24th March 1972 " and at the end of that paragraph there shall be added—
"or
(d) in column (5) thereof in the case of a widow whose husband, on or after 24th March 1972 so ceased or so died:—";
and

(c) there shall be added to the Table as an additional column—
" (5)
Annual Amount
£ 78
£ 90
£ 99
£111
£123
£132
£144"

Amount of Children's Pension

4. In paragraph (1) of regulation 50 of the 1971 Regulations—

(a) the word "or" at the end of sub-paragraph (b) shall be omitted;

(b) in sub-paragraph (c) after "1st May 1971" there shall be inserted "and before 24th March 1972 "and at the end of that paragraph there shall be added—
"or
(d) under letter D, where such contributor, on or after 24th March 1972 so ceased or so died:—"; and

(c) there shall be added to columns (2) and (3) of the Table—

" (2)	(3)
D	D
£ 84	£120
£150	£225
£219	£330
£285	£447"

Gordon Campbell,
One of Her Majesty's Principal
Secretaries of State.

St Andrew's House,
Edinburgh.
15th March 1972.

Consent of the Minister for the Civil Service given under his Official Seal on 17th March 1972.

(L.S.)

K. H. McNeill,
Authorised by the Minister for
the Civil Service.

EXPLANATORY NOTE

(This Note is not part of the Regulations.)

These Regulations amend the Teachers Superannuation (Family Benefits) (Scotland) Regulations 1971 by raising the minimum of a widow's pension and increasing a short service widow's pension and a children's pension which commence after these Regulations come into operation.

STATUTORY INSTRUMENTS

1972 No. 444

EDUCATION, ENGLAND AND WALES

The Raising of the School Leaving Age Order 1972

Laid before Parliament in draft

Made   -   -   -   *22nd March* 1972

Coming into Operation   1*st September* 1972

At the Court of Saint James, the 22nd day of March 1972

Present,

Her Majesty Queen Elizabeth The Queen Mother
Her Royal Highness The Princess Anne

Lord President	**Mr. Amery**
Earl St. Aldwyn	**Chancellor of the Duchy of Lancaster**

Whereas Her Majesty, in pursuance of the Regency Acts 1937 to 1953, was pleased, by Letters Patent dated the fourth day of February 1972, to delegate to the following Counsellors of State (subject to the exceptions hereinafter mentioned) or any two or more of them, that is to say, His Royal Highness The Prince Philip, Duke of Edinburgh, Her Majesty Queen Elizabeth The Queen Mother, His Royal Highness The Prince Charles, Prince of Wales, Her Royal Highness The Princess Anne, Her Royal Highness The Princess Margaret, Countess of Snowdon, and His Royal Highness The Duke of Gloucester, full power and authority during the period of Her Majesty's absence from the United Kingdom to summon and hold on Her Majesty's behalf Her Privy Council and to signify thereat Her Majesty's approval for anything for which Her Majesty's approval in Council is required:

And whereas Her Majesty was further pleased to except from the number of the said Counsellors of State His Royal Highness The Prince Philip, Duke of Edinburgh, His Royal Highness The Prince Charles, Prince of Wales, Her Royal Highness The Princess Anne and Her Royal Highness The Princess Margaret, Countess of Snowdon, while absent from the United Kingdom:

And whereas the Secretary of State for Education and Science and the Secretary of State for Wales are satisfied that it has become practicable to raise to sixteen the upper limit of the compulsory school age:

And whereas a draft of this Order has lain before Parliament for a period of 40 days in accordance with the proviso to section 35 of the Education Act 1944(**a**) and section 6(2) of the Statutory Instruments Act 1946(**b**) and neither House of Parliament has resolved that the draft be not submitted to Her Majesty:

Now, therefore, Her Majesty Queen Elizabeth The Queen Mother and Her Royal Highness The Princess Anne, being authorised thereto by the said Letters Patent, and in pursuance of the said section 35, do hereby, by and with the advice of Her Majesty's Privy Council, on Her Majesty's behalf order, and it is hereby ordered, as follows: —

Citation and commencement

1. This Order may be cited as the Raising of the School Leaving Age Order 1972 and shall come into operation on 1st September 1972.

Raising of the School Leaving Age

2. The definition in section 35 of the Education Act 1944 of the expression "compulsory school age" shall have effect as if for the references therein to the age of fifteen years there were substituted references to the age of sixteen years.

W. G. Agnew.

EXPLANATORY NOTE

(This Note is not part of the Order.)

This Order raises from fifteen to sixteen the upper limit of the compulsory school age.

(**a**) 1944 c. 31.   (**b**) 1946 c. 36.

STATUTORY   INSTRUMENTS

1972 No. 445

CIVIL AVIATION

The Colonial Air Navigation (Amendment) Order 1972

Made - - - -	*22nd March* 1972
Laid before Parliament	*28th March* 1972
Coming into Operation	*1st April* 1972

At the Court of Saint James, the 22nd day of March 1972

Present,

Her Majesty Queen Elizabeth The Queen Mother
Her Royal Highness The Princess Anne

Lord President	**Mr. Amery**
Earl St. Aldwyn	**Chancellor of the Duchy of Lancaster**

Whereas Her Majesty, in pursuance of the Regency Acts 1937 to 1953, was pleased, by Letters Patent dated the fourth day of February 1972, to delegate to the following Counsellors of State (subject to the exceptions hereinafter mentioned) or any two or more of them, that is to say, His Royal Highness The Prince Philip, Duke of Edinburgh, Her Majesty Queen Elizabeth The Queen Mother, His Royal Highness The Prince Charles, Prince of Wales, Her Royal Highness The Princess Anne, Her Royal Highness The Princess Margaret, Countess of Snowdon, and His Royal Highness The Duke of Gloucester, full power and authority during the period of Her Majesty's absence from the United Kingdom to summon and hold on Her Majesty's behalf Her Privy Council and to signify thereat Her Majesty's approval for anything for which Her Majesty's approval in Council is required:

And whereas Her Majesty was further pleased to except from the number of the said Counsellors of State His Royal Highness The Prince Philip, Duke of Edinburgh, His Royal Highness The Prince Charles, Prince of Wales, Her Royal Highness The Princess Anne and Her Royal Highness The Princess Margaret, Countess of Snowdon, while absent from the United Kingdom:

Now, therefore, Her Majesty Queen Elizabeth The Queen Mother and Her Royal Highness The Princess Anne, being authorised thereto by the said Letters Patent, and in pursuance of the powers conferred by the Civil Aviation Act 1949(a) and the Civil Aviation Act 1949 (Overseas Territories) Order 1969(b) and all other powers enabling Her Majesty, do hereby, by and with the advice of Her Majesty's Privy Council, on Her Majesty's behalf order, and it is hereby ordered, as follows:—

1.—(1) This Order may be cited as the Colonial Air Navigation (Amendment) Order 1972 and shall be construed as one with the Colonial Air Navigation Order 1961(c) which Order, as amended by the Colonial Air Navigation (Amend-

---

(a) 1949 c. 67.   (b) S.I. 1969/592 (1969 I, p. 1650).
(c) S.I. 1961/2316 (1961 III, p. 4146).

ment) Order 1962(**a**), the Colonial Air Navigation (Amendment) Order 1963(**b**), the Colonial Air Navigation (Amendment) Order 1965(**c**) and the Colonial Air Navigation (Amendment) Order 1968(**d**) is hereinafter referred to as " the principal Order ".

(2) This Order and the Colonial Air Navigation Orders 1961 to 1968 may be cited together as the Colonial Air Navigation Orders 1961 to 1972.

(3) This Order shall come into operation on 1st April 1972.

2. The principal Order is amended as follows:

(1) In Article 2(16) there are substituted for the words " the Minister " the words " the Civil Aviation Authority ".

(2) (i) In Article 81 after the definition of " Certificate of maintenance " there shall be inserted the following definition:

" ' the Civil Aviation Authority ' refers to the body corporate constituted in accordance with the provisions of section 1 of the Civil Aviation Act 1971(**e**) ";

(ii) the definition of " The Minister " shall be omitted.

W. G. Agnew.

EXPLANATORY NOTE

(This Note is not part of the Order.)

This Order amends the Colonial Air Navigation Order 1961, as previously amended, by replacing the reference to " the Minister " with a reference to the " Civil Aviation Authority ", which assumes its functions on 1st April 1972.

(**a**) S.I. 1962/2597 (1962 III, p. 3485).   (**b**) S.I. 1963/1966 (1963 III, p. 3831).
(**c**) S.I. 1965/588 (1965 I, p. 1845).   (**d**) S.I. 1968/1090 (1968 II, p. 2943).
(**e**) 1971 c. 75.

1972 No. 446

MERCHANT SHIPPING

The Merchant Shipping (Confirmation of Legislation) (Queensland) Order 1972

Made - - - -	*22nd March* 1972
Laid before Parliament	*28th March* 1972
Coming into Operation	*19th April* 1972

At the Court of Saint James, the 22nd day of March 1972

Present,

Her Majesty Queen Elizabeth The Queen Mother
Her Royal Highness The Princess Anne

Lord President	**Mr. Amery**
Earl St. Aldwyn	**Chancellor of the Duchy**
	of Lancaster

Whereas Her Majesty, in pursuance of the Regency Acts 1937 to 1953, was pleased, by Letters Patent dated the fourth day of February 1972, to delegate to the following Counsellors of State (subject to the exceptions hereinafter mentioned) or any two or more of them, that is to say, His Royal Highness The Prince Philip, Duke of Edinburgh, Her Majesty Queen Elizabeth The Queen Mother, His Royal Highness The Prince Charles, Prince of Wales, Her Royal Highness The Princess Anne, Her Royal Highness The Princess Margaret, Countess of Snowdon, and His Royal Highness The Duke of Gloucester, full power and authority during the period of Her Majesty's absence from the United Kingdom to summon and hold on Her Majesty's behalf Her Privy Council and to signify thereat Her Majesty's approval for anything for which Her Majesty's approval in Council is required:

And whereas Her Majesty was further pleased to except from the number of the said Counsellors of State His Royal Highness The Prince Philip, Duke of Edinburgh, His Royal Highness The Prince Charles, Prince of Wales, Her Royal Highness The Princess Anne and Her Royal Highness The Princess Margaret, Countess of Snowdon, while absent from the United Kingdom:

Now, therefore, Her Majesty Queen Elizabeth The Queen Mother and Her Royal Highness The Princess Anne, being authorised thereto by the said Letters Patent, and in pursuance of the powers conferred by section 735 of the Merchant Shipping Act 1894(**a**) and all other powers enabling Her Majesty in that behalf, do hereby, by and with the advice of Her Majesty's Privy Council, on Her Majesty's behalf order, and it is hereby ordered, as follows : —

1.—(1) This Order may be cited as the Merchant Shipping (Confirmation of Legislation) (Queensland) Order 1972.

(2) This Order shall come into operation on 19th April 1972.

2. The Act passed by the Legislature of Queensland entitled " An Act to Amend The Queensland Marine Acts 1958 to 1967 in certain particulars "(**b**) and reserved by the Governor of Queensland for the signification of Her Majesty's pleasure is hereby confirmed.

W. G. Agnew.

EXPLANATORY NOTE

(This Note is not part of the Order.)

This Order made under the Merchant Shipping Act 1894, section 735, confirms an Act passed by the Legislature of Queensland to amend certain provisions of the Queensland Marine Acts 1958 to 1967.

(**a**) 1894 c. 60.   (**b**) The Queensland Marine Act Amendment Act 1971.

STATUTORY INSTRUMENTS

1972 No. 447

MERCHANT SHIPPING
The Merchant Shipping (Tonnage) (Overseas Territories) (Amendment) Order 1972

Made - - - -	*22nd March* 1972
Laid before Parliament	*28th March* 1972
Coming into Operation	*19th April* 1972

At the Court of Saint James, the 22nd day of March 1972

Present,

Her Majesty Queen Elizabeth The Queen Mother
Her Royal Highness The Princess Anne

Lord President	**Mr. Amery**
Earl St. Aldwyn	**Chancellor of the Duchy of Lancaster**

Whereas Her Majesty, in pursuance of the Regency Acts 1937 to 1953, was pleased, by Letters Patent dated the fourth day of February 1972, to delegate to the following Counsellors of State (subject to the exceptions hereinafter mentioned) or any two or more of them, that is to say, His Royal Highness The Prince Philip, Duke of Edinburgh, Her Majesty Queen Elizabeth The Queen Mother, His Royal Highness The Prince Charles, Prince of Wales, Her Royal Highness The Princess Anne, Her Royal Highness The Princess Margaret, Countess of Snowdon, and His Royal Highness The Duke of Gloucester, full power and authority during the period of Her Majesty's absence from the United Kingdom to summon and hold on Her Majesty's behalf Her Privy Council and to signify thereat Her Majesty's approval for anything for which Her Majesty's approval in Council is required:

And whereas Her Majesty was further pleased to except from the number of the said Counsellors of State His Royal Highness The Prince Philip, Duke of Edinburgh, His Royal Highness The Prince Charles, Prince of Wales, Her Royal Highness The Princess Anne and Her Royal Highness The Princess Margaret, Countess of Snowdon, while absent from the United Kingdom:

Now, therefore, Her Majesty Queen Elizabeth The Queen Mother and Her Royal Highness The Princess Anne, being authorised thereto by the said Letters Patent, and in pursuance of the powers conferred by section 6 of the Merchant Shipping Act 1965(a) and all other powers enabling Her Majesty, do hereby, by and with the advice of Her Majesty's Privy Council, on Her Majesty's behalf order, and it is hereby ordered, as follows:—

1. This Order may be cited as the Merchant Shipping (Tonnage) (Overseas Territories) (Amendment) Order 1972 and shall come into operation on 19th April 1972.

(a) 1965 c. 47.

2. The Interpretation Act 1889**(a)** shall apply, with the necessary adaptations, for the purpose of interpreting this Order and otherwise in relation thereto as it applies for the purpose of interpreting, and in relation to, Acts of Parliament.

3. Subject to the provisions of Article 4 of this Order, the provisions of sections 1, 7 and 8(2) and (4) of, and Schedules 1 and 2 to, the Merchant Shipping Act 1965, modified and adapted as in Schedule 1 to the Merchant Shipping (Tonnage) (Overseas Territories) Order 1971**(b)** (hereinafter referred to as " the principal Order "), shall extend to the New Hebrides and Schedule 2 to the principal Order shall accordingly be amended by inserting between the entry " Gilbert and Ellice Islands Colony " and the entry " Seychelles " the words " New Hebrides ".

4. In the definition of " Governor " in Article 2(1) of the principal Order after the words " government of the territory " shall be inserted the words, " and in the case of the New Hebrides means the High Commissioner ".

W. G. Agnew.

EXPLANATORY NOTE

(This Note is not part of the Order.)

The Merchant Shipping (Tonnage) (Overseas Territories) Order 1971 extended to various territories those provisions of the Merchant Shipping Act 1965 which relate to the ascertainment of the tonnage of ships, subject to exceptions, adaptations and modifications specified in Schedule 1 thereto.

This Order extends to the New Hebrides the same provisions subject to the same exceptions, adaptations and modifications and amends the 1971 Order by adding the New Hebrides to the list of territories to which that Order applies.

(a) 1889 c. 63. **(b)** S. I. 1971/383 (1971 I, p. 1175).

STOKE-ON-TRENT
CITY
LIBRARIES

STATUTORY INSTRUMENTS

1972 No. 448

DIPLOMATIC AND INTERNATIONAL IMMUNITIES AND PRIVILEGES

The Second United Nations Conference on the Standardization of Geographical Names (Immunities and Privileges) Order 1972

Made - - - -	*22nd March* 1972
Laid before Parliament	*28th March* 1972
Coming into Operation	*18th April* 1972

At the Court of Saint James, the 22nd day of March 1972

Present,

Her Majesty Queen Elizabeth The Queen Mother
Her Royal Highness The Princess Anne

Lord President	**Mr. Amery**
Earl St. Aldwyn	**Chancellor of the Duchy of Lancaster**

Whereas Her Majesty, in pursuance of the Regency Acts 1937 to 1953, was pleased, by Letters Patent dated the fourth day of February 1972, to delegate to the following Counsellors of State (subject to the exceptions hereinafter mentioned) or any two or more of them, that is to say, His Royal Highness The Prince Philip, Duke of Edinburgh, Her Majesty Queen Elizabeth The Queen Mother, His Royal Highness The Prince Charles, Prince of Wales, Her Royal Highness The Princess Anne, Her Royal Highness The Princess Margaret, Countess of Snowdon, and His Royal Highness The Duke of Gloucester, full power and authority during the period of Her Majesty's absence from the United Kingdom to summon and hold on Her Majesty's behalf Her Privy Council and to signify thereat Her Majesty's approval for anything for which Her Majesty's approval in Council is required:

And whereas Her Majesty was further pleased to except from the number of the said Counsellors of State His Royal Highness The Prince Philip, Duke of Edinburgh, His Royal Highness The Prince Charles, Prince of Wales, Her Royal Highness The Princess Anne and Her Royal Highness The Princess Margaret, Countess of Snowdon, while absent from the United Kingdom:

And whereas the Second United Nations Conference on the Standardization of Geographical Names is to be held in the United Kingdom from 10th to 31st May 1972 and is to be attended by representatives of Her Majesty's Government in the United Kingdom and of the Governments of foreign sovereign Powers:

Now, therefore, Her Majesty Queen Elizabeth The Queen Mother and Her Royal Highness The Princess Anne, being authorised thereto by the said Letters Patent, and in pursuance of the powers conferred by section 6 of the International Organisations Act 1968(a) (hereinafter referred to as the Act) and all other powers enabling Her Majesty, do hereby, by and with the advice of Her Majesty's Privy Council, on Her Majesty's behalf order, and it is hereby ordered, as follows: —

1. This Order may be cited as the Second United Nations Conference on the Standardization of Geographical Names (Immunities and Privileges) Order 1972 and shall come into operation on 18th April 1972.

2. The Interpretation Act 1889(b) shall apply for the interpretation of this Order as it applies for the interpretation of an Act of Parliament.

3.—(1) Except in so far as in any particular case any privilege or immunity is waived by the Governments whom they represent, representatives of the Governments of foreign sovereign Powers at the Second United Nations Conference on the Standardization of Geographical Names shall enjoy: —

 (a) immunity from suit and legal process in respect of things done or omitted to be done by them in their capacity as representatives ;

 (b) while exercising their functions and during their journeys to and from the place of meeting, the like inviolability of residence, the like immunity from personal arrest or detention and from seizure of their personal baggage, the like inviolability of all papers and documents, and the like exemption or relief from taxes (other than customs and excise duties or purchase tax) as is accorded to the head of a diplomatic mission ; and

 (c) while exercising their functions and during their journeys to and from the place of meeting, the like exemptions and privileges in respect of their personal baggage as in accordance with Article 36 of the Vienna Convention on Diplomatic Relations, which is set out in Schedule 1 to the Diplomatic Privileges Act 1964(c), are accorded to a diplomatic agent.

(2) Where the incidence of any form of taxation depends upon residence, a representative shall not be deemed to be resident in the United Kingdom during any period when he is present in the United Kingdom for the discharge of his duties.

(3) Part IV of Schedule 1 to the Act shall not operate so as to confer any privilege or immunity on the official staff of a representative other than delegates, deputy delegates, advisers, technical experts and secretaries of delegations.

(4) Neither this Article nor Part IV of Schedule 1 to the Act shall operate so as to confer any privilege or immunity on any person as the representative of the Government of the United Kingdom or as a member of the official staff of such a representative or on any person who is a citizen of the United Kingdom and Colonies.

W. G. Agnew.

(**a**) 1968 c. 48.   (**b**) 1889 c. 63.   (**c**) 1964 c. 81.

EXPLANATORY NOTE
(This Note is not part of the Order.)

This Order confers privileges and immunities upon the representatives of the Governments of foreign sovereign Powers at the Second United Nations Conference on the Standardization of Geographical Names, which is to be held in the United Kingdom from 10th to 31st May 1972, and upon certain members of their official staffs.

STATUTORY INSTRUMENTS

1972 No. 449

TRUCIAL STATES

The Trucial States (Temporary Provisions) Order 1972

Made - - - -	*22nd March* 1972
Laid before Parliament	*28th March* 1972
Coming into Operation	*1st April* 1972

At the Court of Saint James, the 22nd day of March 1972

Present,

Her Majesty Queen Elizabeth The Queen Mother
Her Royal Highness The Princess Anne

Lord President	**Mr. Amery**
Earl St. Aldwyn	**Chancellor of the Duchy of Lancaster**

Whereas Her Majesty, in pursuance of the Regency Acts 1937 to 1953, was pleased, by Letters Patent dated the fourth day of February 1972, to delegate to the following Counsellors of State (subject to the exceptions hereinafter mentioned) or any two or more of them, that is to say, His Royal Highness The Prince Philip, Duke of Edinburgh, Her Majesty Queen Elizabeth The Queen Mother, His Royal Highness The Prince Charles, Prince of Wales, Her Royal Highness The Princess Anne, Her Royal Highness The Princess Margaret, Countess of Snowdon, and His Royal Highness The Duke of Gloucester, full power and authority during the period of Her Majesty's absence from the United Kingdom to summon and hold on Her Majesty's behalf Her Privy Council and to signify thereat Her Majesty's approval for anything for which Her Majesty's approval in Council is required:

And whereas Her Majesty was further pleased to except from the number of the said Counsellors of State His Royal Highness The Prince Philip, Duke of Edinburgh, His Royal Highness The Prince Charles, Prince of Wales, Her Royal Highness The Princess Anne and Her Royal Highness The Princess Margaret, Countess of Snowdon, while absent from the United Kingdom:

And whereas by the Trucial States Orders 1959 to 1969(a) provision was made for the exercise of Her Majesty's jurisdiction within the territories of the Rulers of Dubai, Sharjah, Ras al Khaimah, Ajman, Umm al Qaiwain, Abu Dhabi and Fujairah:

And whereas Her Majesty has relinquished Her jurisdiction within those territories (which are now comprised in the United Arab Emirates) over all persons and matters formerly subject thereto, except Her jurisdiction therein in relation to certain proceedings commenced under those Orders prior to such relinquishment:

(a) S.I. 1959/1039, 1963/2095, 1969/859 (1959 II, p. 2676; 1963 III, p. 4666; 1969 II, p. 2402).

And whereas it is expedient, in relation to such proceedings, to vest in Her Majesty's Ambassador at Abu Dhabi the powers, authorities and immunities at present vested in the Political Agent in the Trucial States and in Her Majesty's Political Resident in the Persian Gulf:

Now, therefore, Her Majesty Queen Elizabeth The Queen Mother and Her Royal Highness The Princess Anne, being authorised thereto by the said Letters Patent, and in pursuance of the powers conferred by the Foreign Jurisdiction Acts 1890 and 1913(a) and all other powers enabling Her Majesty, do hereby, by and with the advice of Her Majesty's Privy Council, on Her Majesty's behalf order, and it is hereby ordered, as follows:—

1.—(1) This Order may be cited as the Trucial States (Temporary Provisions) Order 1972 and shall be construed as one with the Trucial States Order 1959.

(2) The Trucial States Orders 1959 to 1969 and this Order may be cited together as the Trucial States Orders 1959 to 1972.

(3) This Order shall come into operation on 1st April 1972.

2. The powers, authorities and immunities granted by or under the Trucial States Order 1959, as amended, to the Political Agent in the Trucial States and to Her Majesty's Political Resident in the Persian Gulf shall, in relation to proceedings that have already been commenced before the courts having jurisdiction under the Trucial States Orders 1959 to 1969 but have not been finally disposed of, be vested in Her Majesty's Ambassador at Abu Dhabi.

W. G. Agnew.

EXPLANATORY NOTE

(This Note is not part of the Order.)

Her Majesty has relinquished Her jurisdiction in the Trucial States (which now comprise the United Arab Emirates) except as respects proceedings that have already been commenced before the courts having jurisdiction under the Trucial States Orders 1959 to 1969 but have not been finally disposed of. As respects such proceedings this Order vests in Her Majesty's Ambassador at Abu Dhabi the powers, authorities and immunities hitherto exercisable under those Orders by the Political Agent in the Trucial States and by Her Majesty's Political Resident in the Persian Gulf.

(a) 1890 c. 37; 1913 c. 16.

STATUTORY INSTRUMENTS

1972 No. 450

CIVIL AVIATION

The Civil Aviation Act 1971 (Channel Islands) Order 1972

Made - - -	*22nd March* 1972
Coming into Operation—	
for making orders and regulations	*22nd March* 1972
for all other purposes	*1st April* 1972

At the Court of Saint James, the 22nd day of March 1972

Present,

Her Majesty Queen Elizabeth The Queen Mother
Her Royal Highness The Princess Anne
Lord President
Earl St. Aldwyn
Mr Amery
Chancellor of the Duchy of Lancaster

Whereas Her Majesty, in pursuance of the Regency Acts 1937 to 1953(**a**), was pleased, by Letters Patent dated the 4th day of February 1972, to delegate to the following Counsellors of State (subject to the exceptions hereinafter mentioned) or any two or more of them, that is to say, His Royal Highness The Prince Philip, Duke of Edinburgh, Her Majesty Queen Elizabeth The Queen Mother, His Royal Highness The Prince Charles, Prince of Wales, Her Royal Highness The Princess Anne, Her Royal Highness The Princess Margaret, Countess of Snowdon, and His Royal Highness The Duke of Gloucester, full power and authority during the period of Her Majesty's absence from the United Kingdom to summon and hold on Her Majesty's behalf Her Privy Council and to signify thereat Her Majesty's approval for anything for which Her Majesty's approval in Council is required :

And whereas Her Majesty was further pleased to except from the number of the said Counsellors of State His Royal Highness The Prince Philip, Duke of Edinburgh, His Royal Highness The Prince Charles, Prince of Wales, Her Royal Highness The Princess Anne and Her Royal Highness The Princess Margaret, Countess of Snowdon, while absent from the United Kingdom :

Now, therefore, Her Majesty Queen Elizabeth The Queen Mother and Her Royal Highness The Princess Anne, being authorised thereto by the said Letters Patent and in exercise of the powers conferred by section 66 of the Civil Aviation Act 1971(**b**) do hereby, by and with the advice of Her Majesty's Privy Council, on Her Majesty's behalf order, and it is hereby ordered, as follows : —

(**a**) 1937 c. 16; 1943 c. 42; 1953 c. 1(2 & 3 Eliz. 2).   (**b**) 1971 c. 75.

1.—(1) This Order may be cited as the Civil Aviation Act 1971 (Channel Islands) Order 1972.

(2) This Order shall come into operation forthwith for the purpose of enabling orders and regulations to be made by virtue thereof and on 1st April 1972, for all other purposes.

2.—(1) In this Order the expression "the Channel Islands" means the Bailiwicks of Jersey and Guernsey and the territorial waters adjacent thereto.

(2) The Interpretation Act 1889(**a**) shall apply for the interpretation of this Order as it applies for the interpretation of an Act of Parliament.

3. The provisions of the Civil Aviation Act 1971 shall extend to the Channel Islands with the exceptions and modifications specified in the Schedule to this Order.

W. G. Agnew.

SCHEDULE

EXCEPTIONS AND MODIFICATIONS

PART I

EXCEPTIONS

Sections 3, 4, 6 to 18, 20, 26, 28, 30 to 34, 37 to 60, 61, 65 to 67, Schedules 2, 3, 4, 5, 6, 7, 8, 9.

PART II

MODIFICATIONS

1. Any reference to the Civil Aviation Act 1949(**b**) shall be construed as a reference to that Act as extended to the Channel Islands by the Civil Aviation Act (Channel Islands) Order 1953(**c**) (as amended by the Civil Aviation Act (Channel Islands) Order 1966(**d**)), any reference to the Civil Aviation (Licensing) Act 1960(**e**) shall be construed as a reference to that Act as extended to the Channel Isalnds by the Civil Aviation (Licensing) Act 1960 (Channel Islands) Order 1961(**f**) and any reference to the Civil Aviation Act 1971 shall be construed as a reference to that Act as extended to the Channel Islands by this Order.

2. In section 1, subsection (5) shall be omitted.

3. In section 2(*b*), the words from "the licensing of the provision" to the end of the paragraph shall be omitted.

(**a**) 1889 c. 63.	(**b**) 1949 c. 67.
(**c**) S.I. 1953/393 (1953 I, p. 270).	(**d**) S.I. 1966/688 (1966 II, p. 1546).
(**e**) 1960 c. 38.	(**f**) S.I. 1961/574 (1961 I, p. 1260).

4. In section 5—

    (*a*) in subsection (2)(*b*), in relation to the Bailiwick of Jersey, the words "on summary conviction" shall be omitted;

    (*b*) subsection (3) shall be omitted.

5. In section 19—

    (*a*) in subsection (1) for the words "United Kingdom" there shall be substituted the words "Channel Islands";

    (*b*) subsections (2) and (3) shall be omitted.

6. In section 21—

    (*a*) in subsection (2) for the words "United Kingdom" in the second place where they occur there shall be substituted the words "the Channel Islands";

    (*b*) at the end of subsection (6) there shall be inserted the following words:—

        "In this subsection any reference to the United Kingdom, except where the reference is to a United Kingdom national, shall include a reference to the Channel Islands.".

    (*c*) in subsection (7) for the words "United Kingdom" there shall be substituted the words "Channel Islands".

    (*d*) in subsection (8) in relation to the Bailiwick of Jersey the words "on summary conviction" shall be omitted.

7. In section 24—

    (*a*) in subsection (6) at the end there shall be inserted the words "as in force in the United Kingdom";

    (*b*) in subsection (7) in relation to the Bailiwick of Jersey the words from "on summary conviction" to "conviction on indictment" shall be omitted.

8. In section 27, subsection (1) shall be omitted.

9. In section 29—

    (*a*) for references to the Secretary of State and a designated aerodrome there shall be substituted references to the Board (in the case of the Bailiwick of Guernsey) and to the Committee (in the case of the Bailiwick of Jersey) and an aerodrome respectively;

    (*b*) in subsection (2) for the words "give to the person managing the aerodrome" to the end of the subsection there shall be substituted the following words:—

        "take such steps as may be necessary to secure that facilities for using the aerodrome are withheld to such extent as the Board or the Committee, as the case may be, may determine from aircraft of which the person aforesaid is the operator and from his servants";

    (*c*) in subsection (3) the words following paragraph (*b*) shall be omitted;

    (*d*) in subsection (4)—

        (i) in paragraph (*c*) the words "without prejudice" to "relevant aerodrome" shall be omitted;

        (ii) in paragraph (*d*) for the words "the person managing an aerodrome" and "the aerodrome" there shall be substituted the words "the Board" or "the Committee", as the case may be, and "an aerodrome" respectively;

    (*e*) subsections (5) to (11) shall be omitted.

10. In section 35—

    (*a*) in subsection (1) in paragraph (*a*) after the words "under this Act" there shall be inserted the words "or an aerodrome licence issued by the Committee or the Royal Court of Guernsey, as the case may be";

    (*b*) in subsection (1) in paragraphs (*c*), (*d*) and (ii) for the words "United Kingdom" there shall be substituted the words "the Channel Islands";

(*c*) in subsection (1) at the end there shall be inserted the following words:—

"For references to aerodrome licences issued by the Authority there shall be substituted references to aerodrome licences issued—

(i) in the case of the Bailiwick of Jersey by the Committee;

(ii) in the case of the Bailiwick of Guernsey by the Royal Court of Guernsey";

(*d*) in subsection (4)—

(i) in relation to the Bailiwick of Jersey, in paragraph (*a*) the words "on summary conviction" shall be omitted;

(ii) in relation to the Bailiwick of Jersey in paragraph (*b*) the words from "on summary conviction" to "conviction on indictment" shall be omitted;

(iii) for the words "United Kingdom" where they first apear there shall be substituted the words "Channel Islands".

11. In section 36 in subsection (3) in relation to the Bailiwick of Jersey, the words from "on summary conviction" to "on indictment" shall be omitted.

12. In section 62 subsection (2) and reference in subsection (3) to section 26 shall be omitted.

13. In section 63—

(*a*) the references in subsections (1), (3) and (4) to section 15 shall be omitted;

(*b*) at the end of subsection (1) for the words from "and any statutory instrument" to the end of the subsection there shall be substituted the following words:—

"and any statutory instrument made by virtue of this subsection shall not come into force in the Bailiwick of Jersey or the Bailiwick of Guernsey until it has been registered by the Royal Court of Jersey or the Royal Court of Guernsey, as the case may be".

(*c*) subsection (2) shall be omitted.

14.—(1) In section 64(1)—

(*a*) the definitions of "accounting year", "air navigation services", "the Board", "the initial debt", "land" and "subsidiary" shall be omitted;

(*b*) in the definition of "aerodrome" the references to section 14(1) and Schedule 2 shall be omitted;

(*c*) to the definition of "Air Navigation Order" there shall be added the following words:—

"and shall include an Air Navigation Order as extended to the Bailiwick of Jersey or the Bailiwick of Guernsey as the case may be".

(*d*) after the definition of "the Authority", there shall be inserted the following definition:—

' "the Board" means the Board of Administration of the States of Guernsey;';

(*e*) after the definition of "cargo" there shall be inserted the following definition:—

' "the Committee" means the Harbours and Airport Committee of the States of Jersey;'.

(2) For section 64(2) there shall be substituted the following subsection:—

"For the purposes of this Act a hovercraft, that is to say, a vehicle which is designed to be supported when in motion wholly or partly by air expelled from the vehicle to form a cushion of which the boundaries include the ground, water or other surface beneath the vehicle, is not an aircraft.".

15. In section 68, subsection (1) and, in subsection (2), the reference to section 16 of the Civil Aviation Act 1968(**a**) shall be omitted.

(**a**) 1968 c. 61.

16. In Schedule 10 all paragraphs except paragraph 5 shall be omitted.

17. In Schedule 11 there shall be omitted all references except to section 14 of the Civil Aviation Act 1949 and the Civil Aviation (Licensing) Act 1960.

EXPLANATORY NOTE

(This Note is not part of the Order.)

This Order extends the provisions of the Civil Aviation Act 1971 with exceptions and modifications to the Channel Islands.

STATUTORY INSTRUMENTS

1972 No. 451

CIVIL AVIATION

The Civil Aviation Act 1971 (Isle of Man) Order 1972

Made - - -	*22nd March* 1972
Coming into Operation—	
for making orders and regulations	*22nd March* 1972
for all other purposes	*1st April* 1972

At the Court of Saint James, the 22nd day of March 1972

Present,

Her Majesty Queen Elizabeth The Queen Mother
Her Royal Highness The Princess Anne
Lord President
Earl St. Aldwyn
Mr Amery
Chancellor of the Duchy of Lancaster

Whereas Her Majesty, in pursuance of the Regency Acts 1937 to 1953(a), was pleased, by Letters Patent dated the 4th day of February 1972, to delegate to the following Counsellors of State (subject to the exceptions hereinafter mentioned) or any two or more of them, that is to say, His Royal Highness The Prince Philip, Duke of Edinburgh, Her Majesty Queen Elizabeth The Queen Mother, His Royal Highness The Prince Charles, Prince of Wales, Her Royal Highness The Princess Anne, Her Royal Highness The Princess Margaret, Countess of Snowdon, and His Royal Highness The Duke of Gloucester, full power and authority during the period of Her Majesty's absence from the United Kingdom to summon and hold on Her Majesty's behalf Her Privy Council and to signify thereat Her Majesty's approval for anything for which Her Majesty's approval in Council is required:

And whereas Her Majesty was further pleased to except from the number of the said Counsellors of State His Royal Highness The Prince Philip, Duke of Edinburgh, His Royal Highness The Prince Charles, Prince of Wales, Her Royal Highness The Princess Anne and Her Royal Highness The Princess Margaret, Countess of Snowdon, while absent from the United Kingdom:

Now, therefore, Her Majesty Queen Elizabeth The Queen Mother and Her Royal Highness The Princess Anne, being authorised thereto by the said Letters Patent and in exercise of the powers conferred by section 66 of the Civil Aviation Act 1971(b) do hereby, by and with the advice of Her Majesty's Privy Council, on Her Majesty's behalf order, and it is hereby ordered, as follows:—

(a) 1937 c. 16; 1943 c. 42; 1953 c. 1 (2 & 3 Eliz. 2).
(b) 1971 c. 75.

1.—(1) This Order may be cited as the Civil Aviation Act 1971 (Isle of Man) Order 1972.

(2) This Order shall come into operation forthwith for the purpose of enabling orders and regulations to be made by virtue thereof and on 1st April 1972 for all other purposes.

2. The Interpretation Act 1889(**a**) shall apply for the interpretation of this Order as it applies for the interpretation of an Act of Parliament.

3. The provisions of the Civil Aviation Act 1971 shall extend to the Isle of Man with the exceptions and modifications specified in the Schedule to this Order.

W. G. Agnew.

SCHEDULE

EXCEPTIONS AND MODIFICATIONS

PART I

EXCEPTIONS

Sections 3, 4, 6 to 18, 20, 26, 27(1) and (5), 28 to 34, 37 to 60, 61, 65 to 67, Schedules 2, 3, 4, 5, 6, 7, 8, 9.

PART II

MODIFICATIONS

1. Any reference to the Civil Aviation Act 1949(**b**) shall be construed as a reference to that Act as extended to the Isle of Man by the Civil Aviation Act (Isle of Man) Order 1952(**c**), any reference to the Civil Aviation (Licensing) Act 1960(**d**) shall be construed as a reference to that Act as extended to the Isle of Man by the Civil Aviation (Licensing) Act 1960 (Isle of Man) Order 1961(**e**) and any reference to this Act shall be construed as a reference to the Civil Aviation Act 1971 as extended to the Isle of Man by this Order.

2. In section 1 subsection (5) shall be omitted.

3. In section 2(*b*) the words from "the licensing of the provision" to the end of the paragraph shall be omitted.

4. In section 5 subsection (3) shall be omitted.

5. In section 19—
   (*a*) in subsection (1) for the words "United Kingdom" there shall be substituted the words "Isle of Man";
   (*b*) subsections (2) and (3) shall be omitted.

6. In section 21—
   (*a*) in subsection (2) for the words "United Kingdom" in the second place where they occur there shall be substituted the words "Isle of Man".
   (*b*) at the end of subsection (6) there shall be inserted the following words:—
      "In this subsection any reference to the United Kingdom, except where the reference is to a United Kingdom national, shall include a reference to the Isle of Man";

(**a**) 1889 c. 63. (**b**) 1949 c. 67.
(**c**) S.I. 1952/1032 (1952 I, p. 561). (**d**) 1960 c. 38.
(**e**) S.I. 1961/575 (1961 I, p. 1262).

(c) in subsection (7) for the words "United Kingdom" there shall be substituted the words "Isle of Man".

7. In section 24—

(a) in subsection (6) for the words "of this Act" there shall be substituted the words "of the Civil Aviation Act 1971, as it applies in the United Kingdom";

(b) in subsection (7) for the word "indictment" there shall be substituted the word "information".

8. In section 35—

(a) in subsection (1) in paragraph (a) after the words "under this Act" there shall be inserted the words "or an aerodrome licence issued by the Isle of Man Airports Board";

(b) in subsection (1) in paragraphs (c), (d) and (ii) for the words "United Kingdom" there shall be substituted the words "Isle of Man";

(c) for references to aerodrome licences issued by the Authority there shall be substituted references to aerodrome licences issued by the Isle of Man Airports Board;

(d) in subsection (4)—
 (i) for the word "indictment" there shall be substituted the word "information";
 (ii) for the words "United Kingdom" where they first appear there shall be substituted the words "Isle of Man".

9. In section 36 in subsection (3) for the word "indictment" there shall be substituted the word "information".

10. In section 62—

(a) subsection (2) shall be omitted;

(b) in subsection (3) the words "or 26" shall be omitted.

11. In section 63—

(a) the references in subsections (1), (3) and (4) to section 15 shall be omitted;

(b) at the end of subsection (1) the words from "and any statutory instrument" to the end of the subsection shall be omitted;

(c) subsection (2) shall be omitted.

12. In section 64—

(a) the definitions of "accounting year", "air navigation services", "the Board", "the initial debt", "land" and "subsidiary" shall be omitted;

(b) in the definition of "aerodrome" the references to section 14(1) and Schedule 2 shall be omitted;

(c) to the definition of "Air Navigation Order" there shall be added the following words:—

"and shall include an Air Navigation Order as extended to the Isle of Man".

13. In section 68—

(a) subsection (1) shall be omitted;

(b) in subsection (2) the reference to section 16 of the Civil Aviation Act 1968(a) shall be omitted.

14. In Schedule 10 all paragraphs except paragraph 5 shall be omitted.

15. In Schedule 11—

(a) there shall be omitted all references to any enactment except to section 14 of the Civil Aviation Act 1949 and the Civil Aviation (Licensing) Act 1960;

(a) 1968 c. 61.

(b) for the entry relating to section 10 of the Civil Aviation (Licensing) Act 1960 there shall be substituted the following entry:—

"In section 10 the definition of all expressions except "prescribed" and in that definition all the words after "thereunder"."

EXPLANATORY NOTE

(This Note is not part of the Order.)

This Order extends the provisions of the Civil Aviation Act 1971 with exceptions and modifications to the Isle of Man.

STATUTORY INSTRUMENTS

1972 No. 452

CIVIL AVIATION

The Air Navigation (Jersey) Order 1972

Made - - - -	*22nd March* 1972
Laid before Parliament	*28th March* 1972
Coming into Operation—	
for making regulations	*22nd March* 1972
for all other purposes	*1st April* 1972

At the Court of Saint James, the 22nd day of March 1972

Present,

Her Majesty Queen Elizabeth The Queen Mother
Her Royal Highness The Princess Anne
Lord President
Earl St. Aldwyn
Mr Amery
Chancellor of the Duchy of Lancaster

Whereas Her Majesty, in pursuance of the Regency Acts 1937 to 1953**(a)**, was pleased, by Letters Patent dated the 4th day of February 1972, to delegate to the following Counsellors of State (subject to the exceptions hereinafter mentioned) or any two or more of them, that is to say, His Royal Highness The Prince Philip, Duke of Edinburgh, Her Majesty Queen Elizabeth The Queen Mother, His Royal Highness The Prince Charles, Prince of Wales, Her Royal Highness The Princess Anne, Her Royal Highness The Princess Margaret, Countess of Snowdon, and His Royal Highness The Duke of Gloucester, full power and authority during the period of Her Majesty's absence from the United Kingdom to summon and hold on Her Majesty's behalf Her Privy Council and to signify thereat Her Majesty's approval for anything for which Her Majesty's approval in Council is required:

And whereas Her Majesty was further pleased to except from the number of the said Counsellors of State His Royal Highness The Prince Philip, Duke of Edinburgh, His Royal Highness The Prince Charles, Prince of Wales, Her Royal Highness The Princess Anne and Her Royal Highness The Princess Margaret, Countess of Snowdon, while absent from the United Kingdom:

Now, therefore, Her Majesty Queen Elizabeth The Queen Mother and Her Royal Highness The Princess Anne, being authorised thereto by the said Letters Patent and in exercise of the powers conferred by sections 8, 41, 57, 58, 59 and 61 of the Civil Aviation Act 1949**(b)** (as amended by section 62(1) of the Civil Aviation Act 1971**(c)**), as extended to the Channel Islands by the Civil Aviation

---

(a) 1937 c. 16; 1943 c. 42; 1953 c. 1 (2 & 3 Eliz. 2).
(b) 1949 c. 67.   **(c)** 1971 c.75.

Act (Channel Islands) Order 1953**(a)** (as amended by the Civil Aviation Act (Channel Islands) Order 1966**(b)**) and the Civil Aviation Act 1971 (Channel Islands) Order 1972**(c)** respectively and as further extended by the Civil Aviation Act 1968**(d)**, do hereby, by and with the advice of Her Majesty's Privy Council, on Her Majesty's behalf order, and it is hereby ordered, as follows:—

1.—(1) This Order may be cited as the Air Navigation (Jersey) Order 1972.

(2) This Order shall come into operation forthwith for the purpose of enabling regulations to be made by virtue thereof and on 1st April 1972 for all other purposes.

2. The Air Navigation (Jersey) Order 1966**(e)** is hereby revoked, but any Regulations made by virtue of the provisions of that Order shall remain in force as if they had been made by virtue of the corresponding provisions of this Order.

3.—(1) In this Order the expression "Jersey" means the Bailiwick of Jersey and the territorial waters adjacent thereto.

(2) The Interpretation Act 1889**(f)** shall apply for the interpretation of this Order as it applies for the interpretation of an Act of Parliament.

4. The Air Navigation Order 1972**(g)** shall apply in relation to Jersey with the modifications and adaptations specified in the Schedule to this Order.

W. G. Agnew.

SCHEDULE

Modifications and Adaptations of the Air Navigation Order 1972

1. Any reference to the Civil Aviation Act 1949 shall be construed as a reference to that Act as extended to Jersey by the Civil Aviation Act (Channel Islands) Order 1953 and the Civil Aviation Act (Channel Islands) Order 1966.

2.—(1) Subject to any express substitution made by this Schedule, any reference to the United Kingdom (except in the case of the references specified in the next following sub-paragraph) shall be construed as a reference to Jersey.

(2) The references to the United Kingdom which are not to be construed as references to Jersey are references to Her Majesty's Government in the United Kingdom, to aircraft registered in, or in a country other than, or outside, the United Kingdom, and to a country or state other than the United Kingdom, and references in Article 86(2) and in the definitions in Article 89(1) of "The Commonwealth", "Competent authority", "Contracting State" and "Notified" and in Schedules 9, 11 and 12.

3. Article 1(2) shall be omitted.

4. Article 2(1) shall be omitted.

5. Article 4 shall be omitted.

6. In Article 25(3) the references to the Authority in the first sentence shall be construed as including the Committee.

7. In Article 29(1) for the reference to the Authority in the first sentence there shall be substituted references to the Committee.

(a) S.I. 1953/393 (1953 I, p. 270).　　**(b)** S.I. 1966/688 (1966 II, p. 1546).
(c) S.I. 1972/450 (1972 I, p. 1660).　　**(d)** 1968 c. 61.
(e) S.I. 1966/690 (1966 II p. 1552).　　**(f)** 1889 c. 63.
(g) S.I. 1972/129 (1972 I, p. 366).

8. In Article 39(1)(*b*) after the word "Authority" there shall be inserted the words "or of the Committee".

9. In Article 50(7) after the word "Authority" there shall be inserted the words "or by the Committee".

10.—(1) In Article 61(1) for the reference to the Secretary of State there shall be substituted a reference to the Committee.

(2) In Article 61(3) sub-paragraph (*b*) shall be omitted.

(3) In Article 61(4) for the words from "the competent authority" to the end of the paragraph there shall be substituted the words "the Committee".

(4) At the end of Article 61 there shall be added the following paragraph:—

"(6) The Subordinate Legislation (Jersey) Law 1960 shall apply to regulations made under this Article.".

11. In Article 63(1)—

(*a*) for the words from "the Rules" to "visiting force)" there shall be substituted the words—

"the Rules of the Air and Air Traffic Control (Jersey) Regulations 1967 (as amended) or any Regulations made in substitution of those Regulations, or at any aerodrome or place (not being an aerodrome) at which air traffic control service is provided under the direction of the Committee".

(*b*) in sub-paragraph (*d*)—

(i) for references to the Authority and a Government Department, there shall be substituted references to the Committee;

(ii) for the words "an aerodrome owned or managed by the Authority" there shall be substituted the words "an aerodrome licensed under this order";

(iii) the words "or the Authority" shall be omitted.

12. In Article 65(1) for the references to the Secretary of State there shall be substituted references to the Committee.

13. In Article 66(1) for the reference to the Authority there shall be substituted a reference to the Committee.

14. For Article 67(1) there shall be substituted the following paragraph:—

"(1) An aircraft shall not take off or land at any place in Jersey other than a Government aerodrome or an aerodrome licensed under this Order and in accordance with any condition subject to which the aerodrome may have been notified under Article 68 or licensed under Article 69 of this Order.".

15. For Article 68 there shall be substituted the following Article:—

"68. The Committee may specify, subject to such conditions as it thinks fit, any Government aerodrome as an aerodrome available for the take-off and landing of aircraft or any class of aircraft; and where it has so specified an aerodrome, the Committee shall inform the Authority, who shall cause the information to be notified.".

16.—(1) For Article 69(1) there shall be substituted the following paragraph:—

"(1) The Committee may licence any aerodrome in Jersey subject to such conditions as it thinks fit for the take-off and landing of aircraft or any class of aircraft and may at any time vary, suspend or revoke such a licence.".

(2) Accordingly, in Article 69(2) and (5) for the references to the Authority there shall be substituted references to the Committee and in Article 69(5) for the words "Article 59 of this Order" there shall be substituted the words "paragraph (1) of this Article".

17. Article 71 shall be omitted.

18. In Article 73 for the references to the Secretary of State there shall be substituted references to the States of Jersey and the words "aerodromes owned or managed by the Authority" shall be omitted.

19. In Article 74(1), (2) and (4) for the references to the Authority there shall be substituted references to the Committee and Article 74(3) shall be omitted.

20.—(1) In Article 75(2) for references to the Authority there shall be substituted references to the Committee.

(2) Article 75(4) shall be omitted.

21. For Article 76 there shall be substituted the following Article:—

"76.—(1) The Committee may, with the concurrence of the Finance and Economics Committee of the States of Jersey and subject to such conditions as the Committee thinks fit, by order designate any aerodrome to be a place for the landing or departure of aircraft for the purpose of the enactments for the time being in force relating to customs.

(2) The Committee may, with the concurrence of the Finance and Economics Committee of the States, by order revoke any designation so made.".

22. In Article 79(1) and (2) after the word "Authority" wherever it occurs there shall be inserted the words "the Committee".

23. Article 80 shall be numbered as paragraph (1) of that Article and at the end there shall be added the following paragraph:—

"(2) The Committee shall have the same right of access as the Authority has under this Article save that in relation to the Committee the proviso to paragraph (1) of this Article shall not apply.".

24.—(1) In Article 83(4) the words "on summary conviction" shall be omitted.

(2) In Article 83(5) the words from "on summary conviction" to "on conviction on indictment" shall be omitted.

(3) In Article 83(6) the words "on summary conviction to a fine not exceeding £400 and on conviction on indictment" shall be omitted.

25. For Article 84 and the heading thereto there shall be substituted the following heading and Article:—

"Extent of the Order

84. The provisions of this Order shall apply to all aircraft within Jersey.".

26. In Article 85 for the reference to the Authority there shall be substituted a reference to the Committee.

27. In Article 87 for the reference to the Authority there shall be substituted a reference to the Committee in relation to any provision of this Order where the Committee is substituted for the Authority by this Order and in relation to any regulation made under that provision and the words and figures in parenthesis shall be omitted.

28.—(1) In Article 88(1) the words "Subject to paragraph (2) of this Article" shall be omitted and for the words "a county court" there shall be substituted the words "the Royal Court".

(2) Article 88(2) and (5) shall be omitted.

29. In Article 89(1)—

    (i) in the definition of "Air traffic control unit" for the word "Authority" there shall be substituted the word "Committee";

    (ii) for the definition of "Authorised person" there shall be substituted the following definition:—

        ' "Authorised person" for the purposes of any provision of this Order means—

            (*a*) any police officer; and

            (*b*) any person authorised by the Authority or the Committee either generally or in relation to a particular case or class of cases;';

(iii) for the definition of "the Authority" there shall be inserted the following definition:—

'"the Authority" means the Civil Aviation Authority constituted by section 1 of the Civil Aviation Act 1971, as extended to the Channel Islands by the Civil Aviation Act 1971 (Channel Islands) Order 1972;';

(iv) after the definition of "Commander" there shall be inserted the following definition:—

'"the Committee" means the Harbours and Airport Committee of the States of Jersey;';

(v) the definition of "General lighthouse authority" shall be omitted;

(vi) for the definition of "Government aerodrome" there shall be substituted the following definition:—

'"Government aerodrome" means an aerodrome which is in the occupation of any administration of the States of Jersey';

(vii) for the definition of "Prescribed" there shall be substituted the following definition:—

'"Prescribed" means prescribed by regulations made by the Secretary of State or by the States of Jersey or by the Committee by virtue of this Order, and the expression "prescribe" shall be construed accordingly;'.

30. In Schedule 12, the reference to the Wireless Telegraphy Act 1949(a) shall be construed as a reference to that Act as extended to Jersey by the Wireless Telegraphy (Channel Islands) Order 1952(b).

EXPLANATORY NOTE

(This Note is not part of the Order.)

This Order extends to the Bailiwick of Jersey the provisions of the Air Navigation Order 1972 subject to the modifications and adaptations set out in the Schedule.

(a) 1949 c. 54.   (b) S.I. 1952/1900 (1952 III, p. 3414).

STATUTORY INSTRUMENTS

1972 No. 453

CIVIL AVIATION

The Air Navigation (Guernsey) Order 1972

Made - - - -	*22nd March* 1972
Laid before Parliament	*28th March* 1972
Coming into Operation—	
for making regulations	*22nd March* 1972
for all other purposes	*1st April* 1972

At the Court of Saint James, the 22nd day of March 1972

Present,

Her Majesty Queen Elizabeth The Queen Mother
Her Royal Highness The Princess Anne
Lord President
Earl St. Aldwyn
Mr Amery
Chancellor of the Duchy of Lancaster

Whereas Her Majesty, in pursuance of the Regency Acts 1937 to 1953(**a**), was pleased, by Letters Patent dated the 4th day of February 1972, to delegate to the following Counsellors of State (subject to the exceptions hereinafter mentioned) or any two or more of them, that is to say, His Royal Highness The Prince Philip, Duke of Edinburgh, Her Majesty Queen Elizabeth The Queen Mother, His Royal Highness The Prince Charles, Prince of Wales, Her Royal Highness The Princess Anne, Her Royal Highness The Princess Margaret, Countess of Snowdon, and His Royal Highness The Duke of Gloucester, full power and authority during the period of Her Majesty's absence from the United Kingdom to summon and hold on Her Majesty's behalf Her Privy Council and to signify thereat Her Majesty's approval for anything for which Her Majesty's approval in Council is required:

And whereas Her Majesty was further pleased to except from the number of the said Counsellors of State His Royal Highness the Prince Philip, Duke of Edinburgh, His Royal Highness The Prince Charles, Prince of Wales, Her Royal Highness The Princess Anne and Her Royal Highness The Princess Margaret, Countess of Snowdon, while absent from the United Kingdom:

(**a**) 1937 c. 16; 1943 c. 42; 1953 c. 1 (2 & 3 Eliz. 2).

Now, therefore, Her Majesty Queen Elizabeth The Queen Mother and Her Royal Highness The Princess Anne, being authorised thereto by the said Letters Patent and in exercise of the powers conferred by sections 8, 41, 57, 58, 59 and 61 of the Civil Aviation Act 1949**(a)**, as amended by section 62(1) of the Civil Aviation Act 1971**(b)**, as extended to the Channel Islands by the Civil Aviation Act (Channel Islands) Order 1953**(c)** (as amended by the Civil Aviation Act (Channel Islands) Order 1966**(d)**) and the Civil Aviation Act 1971 (Channel Islands) Order 1972**(e)** respectively and as further extended by the Civil Aviation Act 1968**(f)**, do hereby, by and with the advice of Her Majesty's Privy Council, on Her Majesty's behalf order, and it is hereby ordered, as follows:—

1.—(1) This Order may be cited as the Air Navigation (Guernsey) Order 1972.

(2) This Order shall come into operation forthwith for the purpose of enabling regulations to be made by virtue thereof and on 1st April 1972 for all other purposes.

2. The Air Navigation (Guernsey) Order 1966 **(g)** is hereby revoked, but any Regulations made by virtue of any of the provisions of that Order shall remain in force as if they had been made by virtue of the corresponding provisions of this Order.

3.—(1) In this Order the expression "Guernsey" means the Bailiwick of Guernsey and the territorial waters adjacent thereto.

(2) The Interpretation Act 1889**(h)** shall apply for the interpretation of this Order as it applies for the interpretation of an Act of Parliament.

4. The Air Navigation Order 1972**(i)** shall apply in relation to Guernsey with the modifications and adaptations specified in the Schedule to this Order.

W. G. Agnew.

SCHEDULE

MODIFICATIONS AND ADAPTATIONS OF THE AIR NAVIGATION ORDER 1972

1. Any reference to the Civil Aviation Act 1949 shall be construed as a reference to that Act as extended to Guernsey by the Civil Aviation Act (Channel Islands) Order 1953 and the Civil Aviation Act (Channel Islands) Order 1966.

2.—(1) Subject to any express substitution made by this Schedule, any reference to the United Kingdom (except in the case of the references specified in the next following sub-paragraph) shall be construed as a reference to Guernsey.

(2) The references to the United Kingdom which are not to be construed as references to Guernsey are references to Her Majesty's Government in the United Kingdom, to aircraft registered in, or in a country other than, or outside, the United Kingdom, and to a country or state other than the United Kingdom, and references in Article 86(2), in the definitions in Article 89(1) of "The Commonwealth", "Competent authority", "Contracting State" and "Notified" and in Schedules 9, 11 and 12.

(a) 1949 c. 67.
(b) 1971 c. 75.
(c) S.I. 1953/393 (1953 I, p. 270).
(d) S.I. 1966/688 (1966 II, p. 1546).
(e) S.I. 1972/450 (1972 I, p. 1660).
(f) 1968 c. 61.
(g) S.I. 1966/689 (1966 II, p 1548).
(h) 1889 c. 63.
(i) S.I. 1972/129 (1972 I, p. 366).

3. Article 1(2) shall be omitted.

4. Article 2(1) shall be omitted.

5. Article 4 shall be omitted.

6. In Article 25(3) the references to the Authority in the first sentence shall be construed as including the Board.

7. In Article 29(1) for the reference to the Authority in the first sentence there shall shall be substituted references to the Board.

8. In Article 39(1)(*b*) after the word "Authority" there shall be inserted the words "or of the Board".

9. In Article 50(7) after the word "Authority" there shall be inserted the words "or by the Board".

10.—(1) In Article 61(1) for the reference to the Secretary of State there shall be substituted a reference to the Board.

(2) In Article 61(3) sub-paragraph (*b*) shall be omitted.

(3) In Article 61(4) for the words from "the competent authority" to the end of the paragraph there shall be substituted the words "the Board".

11. In Article 63(1)—

(*a*) for the words from "the Rules" to "visiting force)" there shall be substituted the words—

"the Rules of the Air and Air Traffic Control (Guernsey) Regulations 1967, or any Regulations made in substitution of those Regulations, or at any aerodrome or place (not being an aerodrome) at which air traffic control service is provided under the direction of the Board";

(*b*) in sub-paragraph (*d*) for the references to the Authority and a Government Department there shall be substituted references to the States Civil Service Board and the Board respectively and the words "at a Government aerodrome or at an aerodrome owned or managed by the Authority or" and "or the Authority" shall be omitted.

12. In Article 65(1) for the references to the Secretary of State there shall be substituted references to the Board.

13. In Article 66(1) for the reference to the Authority there shall be substituted a reference to the Board.

14. In Article 67(1) for the words preceding the proviso there shall be substituted the following words:—

"An aircraft engaged on a flight for the purpose of the public transport of passengers or for the purpose of instruction in flying shall not take off or land at any place in Guernsey other than an aerodrome licensed under this Order for the take-off and landing of aircraft so engaged, and in accordance with any condition subject to which the aerodrome may have been so licensed".

15. Article 68 shall be omitted.

16.—(1) In Article 69(1) and (2) for the references to the Authority there shall be substituted references to the Royal Court.

(2) For Article 69(5) there shall be substituted the following paragraph:—

"(5) A licence granted under this Article shall remain in force as may be specified in the licence, but may at any time be varied, revoked or suspended by the Royal Court.".

17. Article 71 shall be omitted.

18. In Article 73 for the references to the Secretary of State there shall be substituted references to the Board and the words "Government aerodromes, aerodromes owned or managed by the Authority" shall be omitted.

19. In Article 74(1), (2) and (4) for the references to the Authority there shall be substituted references to the Board and Article 74(3) shall be omitted.

20.—(1) In Article 75(2) for references to the Authority there shall be substituted references to the Board.

(2) Article 75(4) shall be omitted.

21. For Article 76 there shall be substituted the following Article:—

"76.—(1) The Board may, subject to such conditions as the Board think fit, by order designate any aerodrome to be a place for the landing or departure of aircraft for the purpose of the enactments for the time being in force relating to customs.

(2) The Board may by order revoke any designation so made.".

22. In Article 79(1) and (2) after the word "Authority" wherever it occurs there shall be inserted the words "the Board".

23. In Article 80 after the word "Authority" there shall be inserted the words "the Board" and the proviso shall be omitted.

24. For Article 84 and the heading thereto there shall be substituted the following heading and Article:—

"*Extent of the Order*

84. The provisions of this Order shall apply to all aircraft within Guernsey.".

25. In Article 85 for the reference to the Authority there shall be substituted a reference to the Board.

26. In Article 87 for the reference to the Authority there shall be substituted a reference to the Board in relation to any provision of this Order where the Board is substituted for the Authority by this Order and in relation to any regulation made under that provision and the words and figures in parenthesis shall be omitted.

27.—(1) In Article 88(1) the words "Subject to paragraph (2) of this Article" shall be omitted and for the words "a county court" there shall be substituted the words "the Royal Court sitting as an Ordinary Court".

(2) Article 88(2) and (5) shall be omitted.

28. In Article 89(1)—

    (i) in the definition of "Air traffic control unit" for the word "Authority" there shall be substituted the word "Board";

    (ii) for the definition of "Authorised person" there shall be substituted the following definition:—

        ' "Authorised person" for the purposes of any provision of this Order means—

        (*a*) any police officer; and

        (*b*) any person authorised by the Authority or the Board either generally or in relation to a particular case or class of cases;';

    (iii) for the definition of "the Authority" there shall be substituted the following definition:—

        ' "the Authority" means the Civil Aviation Authority constituted by section 1 of the Civil Aviation Act 1971, as extended to the Channel Islands by the Civil Aviation Act 1971 (Channel Islands) Order 1972;';

    (iv) after the definition of "Beneficial interest" there shall be inserted the following definition:—

        ' "the Board" means the Board of Administration of the States of Guernsey;';

    (v) the definition of "General lighthouse authority" shall be omitted;

    (vi) the definition of "Government aerodrome" shall be omitted;

    (vii) after the definition of "Pilot in command", there shall be inserted the following definition:—

        ' "Police officer" means, in relation to Guernsey, a member of the salaried police force of the Island of Guernsey and also, within the limit of his jurisdiction, a member of the special constabulary of that Island and, in relation to Alderney, a member of any police force which may be established by the States of Alderney and, in relation to Sark, the Constable and the Vingtenier of that Island;';

    (viii) for the definition of "Prescribed" there shall be substituted the following definition:—

        "Prescribed" means prescribed by regulations made by the Secretary of State or the Board by virtue of this Order, and the expression "prescribe" shall be construed accordingly;".

29. In Schedule 2, any reference to a Government aerodrome or an aerodrome owned or managed by the Authority shall be omitted.

30. In Schedule 12, the reference to the Wireless Telegraphy Act 1949(a) shall be construed as a reference to that Act as extended to Guernsey by the Wireless Telegraphy (Channel Islands) Order 1952(b).

    (a) 1949 c. 54.   (b) S.I. 1952/1900 (1952 III, p. 3414).

EXPLANATORY NOTE

(This Note is not part of the Order.)

This Order provides that the provisions of the Air Navigation Order 1972 shall apply, with certain modifications and adaptations, to Guernsey.

STOKE-ON-TRENT
CITY
LIBRARIES

STATUTORY INSTRUMENTS

1972 No. 454

CIVIL AVIATION

The Air Navigation (Isle of Man) Order 1972

Made - - - -	*22nd March* 1972
Laid before Parliament	*28th March* 1972
Coming into Operation—	
for making regulations	*22nd March* 1972
for all other purposes	*1st April* 1972

At the Court of Saint James, the 22nd day of March 1972

Present,

Her Majesty Queen Elizabeth The Queen Mother
Her Royal Highness The Princess Anne
Lord President
Earl St. Aldwyn
Mr Amery
Chancellor of the Duchy of Lancaster

Whereas Her Majesty, in pursuance of the Regency Acts 1937 to 1953**(a)**, was pleased, by Letters Patent dated the 4th day of February 1972, to delegate to the following Counsellors of State (subject to the exceptions hereinafter mentioned) or any two or more of them, that is to say, His Royal Highness The Prince Philip, Duke of Edinburgh, Her Majesty Queen Elizabeth The Queen Mother, His Royal Highness The Prince Charles, Prince of Wales, Her Royal Highness The Princess Anne, Her Royal Highness The Princess Margaret, Countess of Snowdon, and His Royal Highness The Duke of Gloucester, full power and authority during the period of Her Majesty's absence from the United Kingdom to summon and hold on Her Majesty's behalf Her Privy Council and to signify thereat Her Majesty's approval for anything for which Her Majesty's approval in Council is required:

And whereas Her Majesty was further pleased to except from the number of the said Counsellors of State His Royal Highness The Prince Philip, Duke of Edinburgh, His Royal Highness The Prince Charles, Prince of Wales, Her Royal Highness The Princess Anne and Her Royal Highness The Princess Margaret, Countess of Snowdon, while absent from the United Kingdom:

(a) 1937 c. 16; 1943 c. 42; 1953 c. 1 (2 & 3 Eliz. 2).

Now, therefore, Her Majesty Queen Elizabeth The Queen Mother and Her Royal Highness The Princess Anne, being authorised thereto by the said Letters Patent and in exercise of the powers conferred by sections 8, 41, 57, 58, 59 and 61 of the Civil Aviation Act 1949(a), as amended by section 62(1) of the Civil Aviation Act 1971(b), as extended to the Isle of Man by the Civil Aviation Act (Isle of Man) Order 1952(c) (as amended by the Civil Aviation (Isle of Man) Order 1970(d)) and by the Civil Aviation Act 1971 (Isle of Man) Order 1972(e) respectively and as further extended by the Civil Aviation Act 1968(f), do hereby, by and with the advice of Her Majesty's Privy Council, on Her Majesty's behalf order, and it is hereby ordered, as follows:—

1.—(1) This Order may be cited as the Air Navigation (Isle of Man) Order 1972.

(2) This Order shall come into operation forthwith for the purpose of enabling regulations to be made by virtue thereof and on 1st April 1972 for all other purposes.

2. The Air Navigation (Isle of Man) Order 1969(g) is hereby revoked.

3. The Interpretation Act 1889(h) shall apply for the interpretation of this Order as it applies for the interpretation of an Act of Parliament.

4. The Air Navigation Order 1972(i) shall apply in relation to the Isle of Man with the modifications and adaptations specified in the Schedule to this Order.

W. G. Agnew.

SCHEDULE

MODIFICATIONS AND ADAPTATIONS OF THE AIR NAVIGATION ORDER 1972

1. Any reference to the Civil Aviation Act 1949 shall be construed as a reference to that Act as extended to the Isle of Man by the Civil Aviation Act (Isle of Man) Order 1952, as amended.

2.—(1) Subject to any express substitution made by this Schedule and to subparagraph (2) below, any reference to the United Kingdom shall be construed as a reference to the Isle of Man.

(2) The references to the United Kingdom which are not to be so construed are references to Her Majesty's Government in the United Kingdom, to aircraft registered in, or in a country other than or outside, the United Kingdom and to a country or State other than the United Kingdom and references in Article 86(2), in the definitions in Article 89(1) of "The Commonwealth", "Contracting State" and "Notified" and in Schedules 9, 11 and 12.

(a) 1949 c. 67.
(b) 1971 c. 75.
(c) S.I. 1952/1032 (1952 I, p. 561).
(d) S.I. 1970/951 (1970 II, p. 2943).
(e) S.I. 1972/451 (1972 I, p. 1665).
(f) 1968 c. 61.
(g) S.I. 1969/595 (1969 I, p. 1683).
(h) 1889 c. 63.
(i) S.I. 1972/129 (1972 I, p. 366).

3. Article 1(2) shall be omitted.

4. Article 2(1) shall be omitted.

5. Article 4 shall be omitted.

6. In Article 25 at the end of paragraph (3), there shall be added the following words:—

"If the operator has his principal place of business in the Isle of Man, references in the first sentence of this paragraph to the Authority shall include the Board".

7. In Article 29(1) for the word "Authority" in the first sentence there shall be substituted the word "Board".

8. In Article 39(1)(b) after the word "Authority" there shall be inserted the words "or of the Board".

9. In Article 50(7) after the word "Authority" there shall be inserted the words "or by the Board".

10. At the end of Article 59 there shall be added the following paragraph:—

"(6) The foregoing provisions of this Article shall apply in relation to aerodrome licences granted by the Board under Article 69 of this Order as if for references to the Authority there were substituted references to the Board.".

11.—(1) In Article 61(3) paragraph (b) shall be omitted.

(2) In Article 61(4) for the words from "to the competent authority" to the end there shall be substituted the words "to the Board".

(3) After Article 61(5) there shall be added the following paragraph:—

"(6) The foregoing provisions of this Article shall apply in relation to Rules of the Air and Air Traffic Control in the Isle of Man as if for reference to the Secretary of State in paragraph (1) there were substituted a reference to the Board.".

12. In Article 63(1)—

(a) for the words from "the Rules" to "visiting force)" there shall be substituted the words—

"any Rules of the Air and Air Traffic Control Regulations which may be prescribed or at any aerodrome or place (not being an aerodrome) at which air traffic control service is provided under the direction of the Board";

(b) in sub-paragraph (d) for the references to the Authority and a Government Department there shall be substituted references to the Board and the words "at an aerodrome owned or managed by the Authority or" and "or the Authority" shall be omitted.

13. At the end of Article 65 there shall be added the following paragraph:—

"(3) The foregoing provisions of this Article shall apply in relation to areas or routes in the Isle of Man as if for references to the Secretary of State there were substituted references to the Board.".

14. In Article 66(1) for the word "Authority" there shall be substituted the word "Board".

15. In Article 67(1)(a) the words "or an aerodrome owned or managed by the Authority" shall be omitted.

16. For Article 68 there shall be substituted the following Article:—

"68. The Board may specify, subject to such conditions as it thinks fit, any Government aerodrome as an aerodrome available for the take-off and landing of aircraft or any class of aircraft; and where it has so specified an aerodrome, the Board shall inform the Authority who shall cause the information to be notified.".

17.—(1) For Article 69(1) there shall be substituted the following paragraph:—

"(1) The Board may license any aerodrome in the Isle of Man, subject to such conditions as it thinks fit, for the take-off and landing of aircraft or any class of aircraft and may at any time vary, suspend or revoke such licence.".

(2) Accordingly, in Article 69(2) and (5) for the references to the Authority there shall be substituted references to the Board and in Article 69(5) for the words "Article 59 of this Order" there shall be substituted the words "paragraph (1) of this Article".

18. In Article 70 for the word "Authority" in both places where it occurs there shall be substituted the word "Board".

19. In Article 71 for the words "Secretary of State" wherever they occur there shall be substituted the word "Board".

20. In Article 73 for the words "Secretary of State" in both places where they occur there shall be substituted the word "Board", and the words "aerodromes owned or managed by the Authority" shall be omitted.

21. In Article 75(2) and (4) after the word "Authority" wherever it occurs there shall be inserted the words "or the Board".

22.—(1) In Article 76(1) for the words "Secretary of State" there shall be substituted the word "Governor" and the words "with the concurrence of the Commissioners of Customs and Excise and" shall be omitted.

(2) In Article 76(2) for the words "Secretary of State" there shall be substituted the word "Governor" and the words "with the concurrence of the Commissioners of Customs and Excise" shall be omitted.

23. In Article 79 after the word "Authority" wherever it occurs there shall be inserted the words "the Board".

24. In Article 80 after the word "Authority" there shall be inserted the words "the Board" and the words "or aerodrome owned or managed by the Authority" shall be omitted.

25. After Article 82 there shall be inserted the following Article:—

"Fees

82A. The Board may prescribe the fees to be paid in respect of the issue, validation, renewal, extension or variation of any certificate, licence or other document (including an application for, or the issue of a copy of, any such document), or the undergoing of any examination, test, inspection or investigation or the grant of any permission or approval required by, or for the purpose of, this Order or any regulations made thereunder.".

26. In Article 83 in paragraphs (5) and (6) for the word "indictment" there shall be substituted the word "information".

27. For Article 84 and the heading thereto there shall be substituted the following heading and Article:—

"*Extent of the Order*

84. The provisions of this Order shall apply to all aircraft within the Isle of Man.".

28. In Article 87 for the reference to the Authority there shall be substituted a reference to the Board in relation to any provision of this Order where the Board is substituted for the Authority by this Order and in relation to any regulation made under that provision and the words and figures in parenthesis shall be omitted.

29. For Article 88 and the heading thereto there shall be substituted the following heading and Article:—

"*Appeal to Deemster in the Summary Jurisdiction of the High Court of Justice of the Isle of Man*

88.—(1) An appeal shall lie to a Deemster sitting in the Summary Jurisdiction of the High Court of Justice of the Isle of Man from any decision of the Authority that a person is not a fit person to hold a licence to act as an aircraft maintenance engineer, member of the flight crew of an aircraft, air traffic controller or student air traffic controller, and if the Deemster is satisfied that on the evidence submitted to the Authority it was wrong in so deciding, the Deemster may reverse the Authority's decision and the Authority shall give effect to the Deemster's determination:

Provided that an appeal shall not lie from a decision of the Authority that a person is not qualified to hold the licence by reason of a deficiency in his knowledge, experience, competence, skill or physical fitness.

(2) The Authority shall be a respondent to any appeal under this Article.

(3) For purposes of any provision relating to the time within which an appeal may be brought, the Authority's decision shall be deemed to have been taken on the date on which the Authority furnished a statement of its reasons for the decision to the applicant for the licence, or as the case may be, the holder or former holder of it.".

30. In Article 89, in paragraph (1)—

(*a*) in the definition of "Air traffic control unit" for the word "Authority" there shall be substituted the word "Board";

(*b*) in the definition of "Authorised person" after the word "Authority" there shall be inserted the words "the Board or the Governor";

(*c*) for the definition of "the Authority" there shall be substituted the following definition:—

'"the Authority" means the Civil Aviation Authority constituted by section 1 of the Civil Aviation Act 1971, as extended to the Isle of Man by the Civil Aviation Act 1971 (Isle of Man) Order 1972;';

(*d*) after the definition of "Beneficial interest" there shall be inserted the following definition:—

' "Board" means the Isle of Man Airports Board;';

(e) after the definition of "Government aerodrome" there shall be inserted the following definition:—

' "Governor" means the Governor, Lieutenant Governor, Deputy Governor, Deputy Lieutenant Governor and acting Governor or acting Lieutenant Governor of the Isle of Man for the time being;';

(f) in the definition of "Prescribed" after the words "Secretary of State" there shall be inserted the words "or by the Board";

(g) after the definition of "Special VFR flight" there shall be inserted the following definition:—

' "Summary conviction" means conviction subject to and in accordance with the Summary Jurisdiction Acts 1927 to 1960 being Acts of Tynwald, and any Acts amending or consolidating those Acts;'.

31. In Schedule 2 any reference to an aerodrome owned or managed by the Authority and references to Article 4(8) shall be omitted.

32. In Schedule 12 the reference to the Wireless Telegraphy Act 1949(a) shall be construed as a reference to that Act as extended to the Isle of Man by the Wireless Telegraphy (Isle of Man) Order 1952(b).

EXPLANATORY NOTE

(*This Note is not part of the Order.*)

This Order provides that the provisions of the Air Navigation Order 1972 shall apply, with certain modifications and adaptations, to the Isle of Man.

(a) 1949 c. 54.   (b) S.I. 1952/1899 (1952 III, p. 3418).

STATUTORY INSTRUMENTS

1972 No. 455

CIVIL AVIATION

The Air Navigation (Noise Certification) (Amendment) Order 1972

Laid before Parliament in draft

Made - - -	*22nd March* 1972
Coming into Operation	*1st April* 1972

At the Court of Saint James, the 22nd day of March 1972

Present,

Her Majesty Queen Elizabeth The Queen Mother
Her Royal Highness The Princess Anne
Lord President
Earl St. Aldwyn
Mr Amery
Chancellor of the Duchy of Lancaster

Whereas Her Majesty, in pursuance of the Regency Acts 1937 to 1953, was pleased, by Letters Patent dated the fourth day of February 1972, to delegate to the following Counsellors of State (subject to the exceptions hereinafter mentioned) or any two or more of them, that is to say, His Royal Highness The Prince Philip, Duke of Edinburgh, Her Majesty Queen Elizabeth The Queen Mother, His Royal Highness The Prince Charles, Prince of Wales, Her Royal Highness The Princess Anne, Her Royal Highness The Princess Margaret, Countess of Snowdon, and His Royal Highness The Duke of Gloucester, full power and authority during the period of Her Majesty's absence from the United Kingdom to summon and hold on Her Majesty's behalf Her Privy Council and to signify thereat Her Majesty's approval for anything for which Her Majesty's approval in Council is required:

And whereas Her Majesty was further pleased to except from the number of the said Counsellors of State His Royal Highness The Prince Philip, Duke of Edinburgh, His Royal Highness The Prince Charles, Prince of Wales, Her Royal Highness The Princess Anne and Her Royal Highness The Princess Margaret, Countess of Snowdon, while absent from the United Kingdom:

Now, therefore, Her Majesty Queen Elizabeth The Queen Mother and Her Royal Highness The Princess Anne, being authorised thereto by the said Letters Patent, and in pursuance of the powers conferred by section 8 of the

Civil Aviation Act 1949(**a**), as amended(**b**), and section 57 of the said Act of 1949, and all other powers enabling Her Majesty in that behalf, do hereby, by and with the advice of Her Majesty's Privy Council, on Her Majesty's behalf order, and it is hereby ordered, as follows:

Citation and Operation

1. This Order may be cited as the Air Navigation (Noise Certification) (Amendment) Order 1972 and shall come into operation on 1st April 1972.

Interpretation

2.—(1) In this Order "the principal Order" means the Air Navigation (Noise Certification) Order 1970(**c**).

(2) The Interpretation Act 1889(**d**) applies for the purpose of the interpretation of this Order as it applies for the purpose of the interpretation of an Act of Parliament.

Amendment of Air Navigation (Noise Certification) Order 1970

3. The principal Order shall be amended as follows:

(1) Subject to the following paragraph, references to "the Board" wherever they appear in the principal Order (except in Article 1(*a*)) shall be replaced by references to "the Civil Aviation Authority";

(2) In Article 2(1) for the definition of "Prescribed" there shall be substituted:

"'Prescribed' means prescribed by Regulations made by the Secretary of State under this Order";

(3) In Articles 2(2) and 4 proviso (*a*) for "1966 as amended" there shall be substituted "1972";

(4) In Articles 3(1)(*d*)(ii) and 16 after "the Civil Aviation Authority" as substituted by paragraph (1) of this Article, there shall be inserted "after consultation with the Secretary of State";

(5) In Article 4(*a*)(ii) for "the Board of Trade" there shall be substituted "the Secretary of State";

(6) In the heading to Article 5 for "the Board of Trade" there shall be substituted "the Civil Aviation Authority";

(7) In Article 14:

(*a*) in paragraph (3) for "ten pounds" there shall be substituted "£50" and for "twenty pounds" there shall be substituted "£100";

(*b*) for paragraphs (4) and (5) there shall be substituted:

"(4) If any person contravenes Article 12 of this Order he shall be liable on summary conviction to a fine not exceeding £100, or in the case of a second or subsequent conviction for the like offence to a fine not exceeding £200; and on convic-

(**a**) 1949 c. 67.

(**b**) The relevant amendments are section 19 of the Civil Aviation Act 1968 (c. 61) and section 62(1) of the Civil Aviation Act 1971 (c. 75).

(**c**) S.I. 1970/823 (1970 II, p. 2669).   (**d**) 1889 c. 63.

tion on indictment to a fine not exceeding £200 or imprisonment for a term not exceeding 6 months.

(5) If any person contravenes Article 4, 9 or 13 of this Order he shall be liable on summary conviction to a fine not exceeding £400 and on conviction on indictment to a fine or imprisonment for a term not exceeding two years or both."

W. G. Agnew.

EXPLANATORY NOTE

(This Note is not part of the Order.)

This Order amends the Air Navigation (Noise Certification) Order 1970 by substituting the Civil Aviation Authority for the Board of Trade. However, in those provisions which relate to the making of Regulations, the Secretary of State has been substituted for the Board of Trade. The Authority will now be required to consult the Secretary of State before granting exemptions from the Air Navigation (Noise Certification) Order 1970 as now amended. The penalties for failing to comply with the provisions of the Order have been increased by this amendment.

STATUTORY INSTRUMENTS

1972 No. 456

MERCHANT SHIPPING

The Merchant Shipping (Light Dues) Order 1972

Laid before Parliament in draft

Made	-	-	-	*22nd March* 1972
Laid before Parliament			*28th March* 1972
Coming into Operation			*1st April* 1972

At the Court of Saint James, the 22nd day of March 1972

Present,

Her Majesty Queen Elizabeth The Queen Mother
Her Royal Highness The Princess Anne
Lord President
Earl St. Aldwyn
Mr Amery
Chancellor of the Duchy of Lancaster

Whereas Her Majesty, in pursuance of the Regency Acts 1937 to 1953, was pleased, by Letters Patent dated the fourth day of February 1972, to delegate to the following Counsellors of State (subject to the exceptions hereinafter mentioned) or any two or more of them, that is to say, His Royal Highness The Prince Philip, Duke of Edinburgh, Her Majesty Queen Elizabeth The Queen Mother, His Royal Highness The Prince Charles, Prince of Wales, Her Royal Highness The Princess Anne, Her Royal Highness The Princess Margaret, Countess of Snowdon, and His Royal Highness The Duke of Gloucester, full power and authority during the period of Her Majesty's absence from the United Kingdom to summon and hold on Her Majesty's behalf Her Privy Council and to signify thereat Her Majesty's approval for anything for which Her Majesty's approval in Council is required:

And whereas Her Majesty was further pleased to except from the number of the said Counsellors of State His Royal Highness The Prince Philip, Duke of Edinburgh, His Royal Highness The Prince Charles, Prince of Wales, Her Royal Highness The Princess Anne and Her Royal Highness The Princess Margaret, Countess of Snowdon, while absent from the United Kingdom:

Now, therefore, Her Majesty Queen Elizabeth The Queen Mother and Her Royal Highness The Princess Anne, being authorised thereto by the said Letters Patent, and in pursuance of the powers conferred on Her Majesty by section 5 of the Merchant Shipping (Mercantile Marine Fund) Act 1898(a) and all other powers enabling Her Majesty, do hereby, by and with the advice of Her Majesty's Privy Council, on Her Majesty's behalf order, and it is hereby ordered, as follows:—

1.—(1) This Order shall come into operation on 1st April 1972 and may be cited as the Merchant Shipping (Light Dues) Order 1972.

(a) 1898 c. 44.

(2) The Orders listed in Schedule 1 to this Order are hereby revoked.

(3) The Interpretation Act 1889(**a**) shall apply to the interpretation of this Order as it applies to the interpretation of an Act of Parliament and as if this Order and the Orders hereby revoked were Acts of Parliament.

2. For the scale of payments, rules and exemptions relating to the levying of light dues contained in Schedule 2 to the Merchant Shipping (Mercantile Marine Fund) Act 1898, as altered, there shall be substituted the scale of payments, rules and exemptions set out in Schedule 2 to this Order.

W. G. Agnew.

SCHEDULE 1

Column 1 Orders revoked	Column 2 References
Order in Council of 24th July 1901	S.R. & O. 1901/599 (Rev. XIV, p. 676; 1901, p. 254).
Order in Council of 4th July 1908	S.R. & O. 1908/558 (Rev. XIV, p. 678; 1908, p. 647).
Order in Council of 30th July 1919	S.R. & O. 1919/1108 (Rev. XIV, p. 679; 1919 I, p. 1093).
The Merchant Shipping (Light Dues) Order 1935	S.R. & O. 1935/803 (Rev. XIV, p. 680; 1935 I, p. 1187).
The Merchant Shipping (Light Dues) Order 1953	S.I. 1953/392 (1953 I, p. 1065).
The Merchant Shipping (Light Dues) Order 1969	S.I. 1969/386 (1969 I, p. 1067).
The Merchant Shipping (Light Dues) Order 1970	S.I. 1970/639 (1970 I, p. 2064).

SCHEDULE 2
SCALE OF PAYMENTS

1. Home-trade sailing ships: 31p per 10 tons per voyage.
2. Foreign-going sailing ships: 71p per 10 tons per voyage.
3. Home-trade steamers:
   Full rate: 47p per 10 tons per voyage.
   Reduced rate (visiting cruise ships): 24p per 10 tons per voyage.
4. Foreign-going steamers:
   Full rate: 86p per 10 tons per voyage.
   Reduced rate (visiting cruise ships): 48p per 10 tons per voyage.
5. In the place of payments per voyage, the following payments:—

(**a**) 1889 c. 63.

(*a*) for pleasure yachts which the general lighthouse authority is satisfied are ordinarily kept or used outside any of the following countries and territories (including the territorial waters adjacent thereto), namely the United Kingdom, Isle of Man, Republic of Ireland, a payment in respect of any visit of 31p per 10 tons for every period of 30 days or less comprised in such visit ;

(*b*) for tugs and pleasure yachts not included in sub-paragraph (*a*) of this paragraph an annual payment of £3·72 per 10 tons.

RULES

(1) A ship shall not in any year be required to make payments on account of light dues—

(*a*) if the ship is a home-trade ship, for more than ten voyages ; and

(*b*) if the ship is a foreign-going ship, for more than six voyages ; and

(*c*) if the ship makes voyages during the year both as a home-trade and as a foreign-going ship, for more than ten voyages, counting each voyage made as a foreign-going ship as a voyage and a half.

Provided that in any year no steamer shall be required to pay more than £5·16 per 10 tons and no sailing vessel shall be required to pay more than £4·26 per 10 tons.

(2) A ship shall not pay dues both as a home-trade ship and as a foreign-going ship for the same voyage, but a ship trading from a port outside home-trade limits, and discharging cargo or landing passengers or mails at any port within home-trade limits, shall be deemed to be on one voyage as a foreign-going ship, until she has arrived at the last port of discharge of cargo or passengers brought from beyond home-trade limits ; and a ship trading to a port outside home-trade limits, and loading cargo or receiving passengers or mails at any port within home-trade limits, shall be deemed to be on one voyage as a foreign-going ship from the time she starts from the first port of loading of cargo or passengers destined for a port beyond home-trade limits.

(3) The voyage of a home-trade ship shall be reckoned from port to port, but a home-trade ship shall not be required to pay dues for more than three voyages in one month.

(4) The voyage of a foreign-going ship trading outwards shall be reckoned from the first port of lading in the United Kingdom, the Republic of Ireland or the Isle of Man of cargo destined for a port outside home-trade limits.

(5) The voyage of a foreign-going ship trading inwards shall be reckoned from her last port of lading outside home-trade limits to the last port in the United Kingdom, the Republic of Ireland or the Isle of Man at which any cargo laden outside those limits is discharged.

(6) Dues payable per voyage under this Act shall be payable and collected only at ports where a ship loads or discharges cargo or passengers or mails.

(7) The annual payments shall be payable at the commencement of the year in respect of which they are made, provided that a new vessel shall pay only 31p per 10 tons for each month after the commencement of her first voyage till the first of April following.

(8) Every such payment as is referred to in paragraph 5(*a*) of the scale shall be payable at the commencement of the period in respect of which it is made, provided that a vessel shall not in any year be required to pay on account of light dues a sum greater than the sum which such vessel would be liable to pay under paragraph 5(*b*) of the scale.

(9) For the purposes of this Schedule—

(*a*) A ship's tonnage shall be register tonnage reckoned in accordance with the Merchant Shipping Act 1965(**a**) with the addition required in section eighty-five of the Merchant Shipping Act 1894(**b**) as amended by the Mer-

---

(**a**) 1965 c. 47.   (**b**) 1894 c. 60.

chant Shipping Act 1965 with respect to deck cargo, or in the case of an unregistered vessel, the tonnage reckoned in accordance with the Thames measurement adopted by Lloyd's Register.

(b) A year shall be reckoned from 1st April.

(c) In calculating any payment of light dues where the vessel's tonnage is not a multiple of 10 tons, any excess not exceeding 5 tons shall be rounded down and any excess over 5 tons shall be rounded up to the nearest such multiple.

(d) A ship shall be treated as a visiting cruise ship if and only if it makes a call at one or more ports in the United Kingdom, Isle of Man or Republic of Ireland for the purpose of disembarking passengers for a visit ashore and for subsequent re-embarkation (whether or not at the same port) and at no time during that cruise does the ship—

> (a) embark or disembark any other passengers ; or

> (b) load or discharge any cargo or mails—

at any such port.

(e) "Home-trade", in relation to any ship, means employed in trading or going within the following limits, that is to say the United Kingdom, the Channel Islands, the Isle of Man and the Republic of Ireland and the Continent of Europe between the north bank of the River Eider and Brest inclusive ; and "home-trade limits" shall be construed accordingly.

(f) "Foreign-going", in relation to any ship means employed in trading or going between some place or places in the United Kingdom or the Republic of Ireland and some place or places situate beyond the following limits, that is to say the coasts of the United Kingdom, the Channel Islands, the Isle of Man and the Republic of Ireland and the Continent of Europe between the north bank of the River Eider and Brest inclusive.

EXEMPTIONS

There shall be exempted from dues under this Schedule : —

Ships belonging to Her Majesty or to a foreign Government unless carrying cargo or passengers for freight or fares ;

Sailing Ships (not being pleasure yachts) of less than one hundred tons, and all ships of less than twenty tons ;

Vessels (other than tugs or pleasure yachts) when navigated wholly and bona fide in ballast, on which no freight is earned and without any passenger ;

Ships putting in for bunkers, stores, or provisions for their own use on board;

Vessels for the time being employed in sea fishing or in sea fishing service, exclusive of vessels used for catching fish otherwise than for profit ;

Ships putting in from stress of weather or for the purpose of repairing, or because of damage, provided they do not discharge or load cargo other than cargo discharged with a view to such repairs, and afterwards re-shipped ;

Dredgers and hoppers for the time being employed solely in dredging channels or deepening water for or on behalf of a harbour authority or a conservancy authority, within the area in which that authority has jurisdiction, or in disposing within or without such area, otherwise than by way of sale or exchange, of the spoil from such operations ;

Sailing yachts of and above 100 tons, which are not registered in the United Kingdom, Isle of Man, Channel Islands or the Republic of Ireland, and which come into the territorial waters adjacent to the United Kingdom or the Republic of Ireland with the sole object of taking part in yacht racing, so long as such yachts are coming into, remaining in, or leaving such territorial waters solely in connection with such object, and hold a certificate in a form approved by the Secretary of State ;

Ships making voyages entirely performed in waters in respect of which no lighthouse, buoy or beacon is maintained by a General Lighthouse Authority at the expense of the General Lighthouse Fund ;

Yachts in respect of any year ending 31st March during the whole of which they are laid up.

EXPLANATORY NOTE

(This Note is not part of the Order.)

This Order consolidates, with amendments, the scale of payments, rules and exemptions relating to the levying of light dues set out in Schedule 2 to the Merchant Shipping (Mercantile Marine Fund) Act 1898 as previously amended. The current amendments increase the scale of light dues by about 19% overall.

STATUTORY INSTRUMENTS

1972 No. 457 (S.33)

HOUSING, SCOTLAND

The Housing (Improvement of Amenities of Residential Areas) (Scotland) Order 1972

Made - - -	*21st March* 1972
Laid before the Commons House of Parliament	*23rd March* 1972
Coming into Operation	*28th April* 1972

In exercise of the powers conferred upon me by section 59(5) of the Housing (Scotland) Act 1969(a) and of all other powers enabling me in that behalf, I hereby, with the consent of the Treasury, make the following order:—

Citation and Commencement

1. This order may be cited as the Housing (Improvement of Amenities of Residential Areas) (Scotland) Order 1972 and shall come into operation on 28th April 1972.

Interpretation

2.—(1) In this order unless the context otherwise requires, "the Act" means the Housing (Scotland) Act 1969.

(2) The Interpretation Act 1889(b) shall apply for the interpretation of this order as it applies for the interpretation of an Act of Parliament.

3. In section 59(4) of the Act (which provides that the aggregate of any expenditure on the improvement of the amenities of a residential area which the Secretary of State may approve for the purposes of section 59 of the Act shall not exceed the sum arrived at by taking £100 for each of the dwellings

---

(a) 1969 c. 34.   (b) 1889 c. 63.

in the area) there shall be substituted for the sum of £100, the sum of £200.

Gordon Campbell,
One of Her Majesty's Principal
Secretaries of State.

St. Andrew's House,
Edinburgh.
20th March 1972.

We consent.

Tim Fortescue,
Walter Clegg,
Two of the Lords Commissioners of
Her Majesty's Treasury.

21st March 1972.

EXPLANATORY NOTE

(This Note is not part of the Order.)

Section 59 of the Housing (Scotland) Act 1969 provides for the payment of exchequer contributions towards expenses incurred by local authorities under Section 58 of the Act in connection with the improvement of the amenities of predominantly residential areas. By virtue of section 59(4) of the Act the exchequer contribution is calculated on a maximum eligible expenditure of £100 for each dwelling in the area.

This Order increases the maximum eligible expenditure from £100 to £200.

STATUTORY INSTRUMENTS

1972 No. 460

AGRICULTURE

The Livestock and Livestock Products Industries (Payments for Scientific Research) Order 1972

Laid before Parliament in draft

Made - - -	22nd March 1972
Coming into Operation	23rd March 1972

The Minister of Agriculture, Fisheries and Food, the Secretary of State concerned with agriculture in Scotland, and the Secretary of State for Wales, acting jointly, in exercise of the powers conferred on them by section 16 of the Agriculture Act 1967(**a**), as read with the Transfer of Functions (Wales) Order 1969(**b**), and of all other powers enabling them in that behalf, hereby make the following order a draft whereof has been laid before Parliament and approved by resolution of each House of Parliament: —

1.—(1) This order may be cited as the Livestock and Livestock Products Industries (Payments for Scientific Research) Order 1972, and shall come into operation on the day immediately following the day on which it is made.

(2) The Interpretation Act 1889(**c**) shall apply to the interpretation of this order as it applies to the interpretation of an Act of Parliament.

2. For the purpose of providing funds to be applied for the purpose of scientific research which is connected with the livestock industry and the livestock products industry and which is to be carried out by the Agricultural Research Council, the Meat and Livestock Commission (established under Part I of the Agriculture Act 1967) shall make a payment of, or payments amounting in total to, the sum of £215,000 during the twelve months ending with 31st March 1973.

3. The sum to be paid by the Meat and Livestock Commission in accordance with the foregoing provisions of this order shall be paid by them into the Agricultural Research Council Deposit Account, being an account opened by Her Majesty's Paymaster General, such sum to be applied and dealt with by the Agricultural Research Council for the purpose of scientific research to be carried out by them in connection with the livestock industry and the livestock products industry.

(**a**) 1967 c. 22.   (**b**) S.I. 1969/388 (1969 I, p. 1070).
(**c**) 1889 c. 63.

In Witness whereof the Official Seal of the Minister of Agriculture, Fisheries and Food is hereunto affixed on 17th March 1972.

(L.S.)

J. M. L. Prior,
Minister of Agriculture, Fisheries and Food.

Gordon Campbell,
Secretary of State for Scotland.

21st March 1972.

Peter Thomas,
Secretary of State for Wales.

22nd March 1972.

EXPLANATORY NOTE
(This Note is not part of the Order.)

This order requires the making of payments by the Meat and Livestock Commission during the twelve months ending with 31st March 1973 for the purpose of providing funds for the purpose of scientific research, to be carried out by the Agricultural Research Council, in connection with the livestock industry and the livestock products industry.

STOKE-ON-TRENT
CITY
LIBRARIES

STATUTORY INSTRUMENTS

1972 No. 464

INCOME TAX

DOUBLE TAXATION RELIEF

The Transitional Relief for Interest and Royalties paid to Non-Residents (Extension of Period) Order 1972

Laid before the House of Commons in draft

Made - - -	*23rd March* 1972
Coming into Operation	*1st April* 1972

Whereas a draft of this Order was laid before the Commons House of Parliament and approved by resolution:

Now, therefore, the Lords Commissioners of Her Majesty's Treasury, in exercise of the power conferred on them by section 32(1) of the Finance Act 1966(a) hereby make the following Order:—

1. This Order may be cited as the Transitional Relief for Interest and Royalties paid to Non-Residents (Extension of Period) Order 1972.

2. The period referred to in section 32(1) of the Finance Act 1966 as extended by the Transitional Relief for Interest and Royalties paid to Non-Residents (Extension of Period) Orders 1968(b), 1969(c), 1970(d) and 1971(e) shall be further extended to comprise the financial year 1972 in relation to residents in all overseas territories.

3. This Order shall come into force on 1st April 1972.

Walter Clegg,
Keith Speed,
Two of the Lords Commissioners of
Her Majesty's Treasury.

23rd March 1972.

(a) 1966 c. 18. (b) S.I. 1968/455 (1968 I, p. 1166).
(c) S.I. 1969/320 (1969 I, p. 827). (d) S.I. 1970/325 (1970 I, p. 1201).
(e) S.I. 1971/563 (1971 I, p. 1567).

EXPLANATORY NOTE

(This Note is not part of the Order.)

This Order extends by one further year the period during which relief is available under section 32, Finance Act 1966. This section ensures that certain payments to non-residents which are relieved from United Kingdom income tax under a Double Taxation Agreement are not treated as distributions for corporation tax purposes in the hands of the United Kingdom company making them. The relief was originally given for the financial years 1966 and 1967, but provision was made in subsection (1) of the section for the extension of this period. The relief was extended to cover the financial years 1968, 1969, 1970 and 1971 by the Transitional Relief for Interest and Royalties paid to Non-Residents (Extension of Period) Orders 1968, 1969, 1970 and 1971. This Order comes into force on 1st April 1972.

STATUTORY INSTRUMENTS

1972 No. 465

INCOME TAX

DOUBLE TAXATION RELIEF

The Non-Residents' Transitional Relief from Income Tax on Dividends (Extension of Period) Order 1972

Laid before the House of Commons in draft

Made - - - *23rd March* 1972

Coming into Operation *6th April* 1972

Whereas a draft of this Order was laid before the Commons House of Parliament and approved by resolution:

Now, therefore, the Lords Commissioners of Her Majesty's Treasury, in exercise of the power conferred on them by section 31(1) of the Finance Act 1966**(a)** hereby make the following Order:—

1. This Order may be cited as the Non-Residents' Transitional Relief from Income Tax on Dividends (Extension of Period) Order 1972.

2. The period referred to in section 31(1) of the Finance Act 1966 as extended by the Non-Residents' Transitional Relief from Income Tax on Dividends (Extension of Period) Orders 1968**(b)**, 1969**(c)**, 1970**(d)** and 1971**(e)** shall be further extended to comprise the year 1972/73 in relation to dividends paid to residents in those of the overseas territories with the Governments of which the Double Taxation Agreements mentioned in Schedule 9 to the said Act are made and in relation to which the said section 31 can still have effect.

3. This Order shall come into force on 6th April 1972.

Walter Clegg,
Keith Speed,
Two of the Lords Commissioners of
Her Majesty's Treasury.

23rd March 1972.

(a) 1966 c. 18.   (b) S.I. 1968/454 (1968 I, p. 1164).
(c) S.I. 1969/319 (1969 I, p. 825).   (d) S.I. 1970/326 (1970 I, p. 1203).
(e) S.I. 1971/562 (1971 I, p. 1565).

EXPLANATORY NOTE

(This Note is not part of the Order.)

This Order extends by one further year the period during which relief is available under section 31, Finance Act 1966. This section gives relief from United Kingdom income tax on dividends paid by United Kingdom companies to residents of the overseas territories with which the United Kingdom has the Double Taxation Agreements listed in Schedule 9 to the same Act. The relief was originally given for the years 1966/67 and 1967/68, but provision was made for the extension of this period. The relief was extended to cover the years 1968/69, 1969/70, 1970/71 and 1971/72 by the Non-Residents' Transitional Relief from Income Tax on Dividends (Extension of Period) Orders 1968, 1969, 1970 and 1971. This Order comes into force on 6th April 1972.

STATUTORY INSTRUMENTS

1972 No. 466 (S.34)

SOCIAL WORK, SCOTLAND
Residential Establishments (Payments by Local Authorities) (Scotland) Amendment Order 1972

Made - - - -	*22nd March* 1972
Coming into Operation	*1st April* 1972

In exercise of the powers conferred on me by section 90(3) of and paragraph 2(2) of Schedule 7 to the Social Work (Scotland) Act 1968(a), and of all other powers enabling me in that behalf, I hereby make the following order:—

Citation, commencement and interpretation

1.—(1) This order may be cited as the Residential Establishments (Payments by Local Authorities) (Scotland) Amendment Order 1972 and shall come into operation on 1st April 1972.

(2) The Interpretation Act 1889(b) shall apply for the interpretation of this order as it applies for the interpretation of an Act of Parliament.

Increase in rate of payment

2. Article 3 of the Residential Establishments (Payments by Local Authorities) (Scotland) Order 1971(c) (which prescribes weekly payments to be made by local authorities in respect of the expenses of carrying on the establishments which were approved schools immediately before the commencement of Part III of the Social Work (Scotland) Act 1968) shall have effect with the substitution of £20.30 for £16.80.

Gordon Campbell,
One of Her Majesty's Principal
Secretaries of State.

St Andrew's House,
Edinburgh.
22nd March 1972.

EXPLANATORY NOTE
(This Note is not part of the Order.)

This Order amends the Residential Establishments (Payments by Local Authorities) (Scotland) Order 1971 by increasing from £16.80 to £20.30 the weekly payments to be made by local authorities in respect of the expenses of carrying on the establishments which were approved schools immediately before the commencement of Part III of the Social Work (Scotland) Act 1968 and in relation to which functions were transferred to local authorities under section 1(5) of that Act.

(a) 1968 c. 49. (b) 1889 c. 63.
(c) S.I. 1971/249 (1971 I, p. 857).

STATUTORY INSTRUMENTS

1972 No. 467 (S.35)

NATIONAL HEALTH SERVICE, SCOTLAND

HOSPITAL AND SPECIALIST SERVICES

The National Health Service (Appointment of Consultants) (Scotland) Regulations 1972

Made - - -	*22nd March* 1972
Laid before Parliament	*29th March* 1972
Coming into Operation	*1st April* 1972

In exercise of the powers conferred on me by section 14(2) of the National Health Service (Scotland) Act 1947(**a**) as amended by section 9 of the Health Services and Public Health Act 1968(**b**), and of all other powers enabling me in that behalf, I hereby make the following regulations:—

Citation and Commencement

1. These regulations may be cited as the National Health Service (Appointment of Consultants) (Scotland) Regulations 1972 and shall come into operation on 1st April 1972.

Interpretation

2.—(1) In these regulations, unless the context otherwise requires—

"area" means an area of a Regional Hospital Board;

"Committee" means Advisory Appointments Committee;

"consultant in the specialty" means a consultant specialising or who has recently specialised in the branch of medicine or dentistry with which the proposed appointment is concerned;

"Board" means a Regional Hospital Board.

(2) The Interpretation Act 1889(**c**) shall apply for the interpretation of these regulations as it applies for the interpretation of an Act of Parliament and as if these regulations were an Act of Parliament.

Appointments to which the regulations apply

3.—(1) The provisions of these regulations shall apply with respect to the appointment of any medical or dental officer to a post of consultant on the staff of a hospital providing hospital and specialist services other than the appointment of any person in any of the classes specified in regulation 4.

(2) For the purposes of this regulation "appointment" includes any appointment to a post, whether existing or new, and whether whole-time or part-time.

(**a**) 1947 c. 27. (**b**) 1968 c. 46.
(**c**) 1889 c. 63.

Exempted appointments

4.—(1) The classes to which these regulations do not apply are—

   (*a*) professors, readers or other members of a medical or dental department of a university who receive no remuneration (other than a distinction award) from the Board for their hospital appointments;

   (*b*) persons who are primarily engaged in research which necessitates their appointment to the staff of a hospital and who receives no remuneration (other than a distinction award) for that appointment from the Board;

   (*c*) any other person to be appointed to the staff of a hospital who receives no remuneration (other than a distinction award) for that appointment from the Board;

   (*d*) persons to be appointed to locum posts or to posts which are, with the approval of the Secretary of State, limited in duration to a period of two years or less;

   (*e*) redundant officers whose employment, or whose last employment, by a Board in Scotland or by a Board or a Board of Governors of a teaching hospital in England or Wales is, or was, in a post as consultant.

(2) In this regulation "redundant officers" means persons whose employment has been terminated owing to redundancy or other local change of organisation and whose names have at the discretion of the Secretary of State for Scotland, the Secretary of State for Social Services or the Secretary of State for Wales been notified to Boards as officers to whom this regulation applies; and "employment" includes part-time employment whether or not the officer is also employed by any other Board, but does not include employment in a post where the appointment was expressly limited in duration.

Advertisement of vacancy

5.—(1) Where a Board propose to make an appointment to a vacancy in a post to which these regulations apply, they shall place an advertisement in not less than two publications circulating throughout the United Kingdom which are commonly used for similar advertisements relating to the profession concerned. Provided that where such advertisement is not reasonably practicable they shall advertise the vacancy in such other publications as they think appropriate.

(2) Any advertisement shall specify the exact nature of the appointment and the closing date for receipt of applications which shall be not less than one month from the date on which the advertisement is to appear.

National Panel of Specialists

6.—(1) For the purpose of making nominations to the Advisory Appointments Committee constituted under regulation 7 hereof, the Secretary of State shall constitute a National Panel of Specialists consisting of not more than 150 members holding consultant appointments made up as follows:

   (*a*) not more than 35 members nominated jointly by the Universities of Glasgow, Aberdeen, Edinburgh and Dundee;

   (*b*) not more than 100 members nominated jointly by the Royal College of Physicians of Edinburgh, the Royal College of Surgeons of Edinburgh, the Royal College of Physicians and Surgeons of Glasgow, the Royal College of Obstetricians and Gynaecologists, the Royal College of Pathologists, the Royal College of Psychiatrists, the Faculty of

Anaesthetists and the Faculty of Radiologists and such other members of specialist professional bodies as the Secretary of State may from time to time determine; and

(c) not more than 15 members appointed by the Secretary of State.

(2) Of the original members so nominated and appointed one half shall retire on 31st March 1974, and the remainder on 31st March 1976; thereafter members shall serve for a period of four years. Any casual vacancy occurring shall be filled in the same manner as applied at the appointment or nomination of the member vacating office. Except in special circumstances approved by the Secretary of State a member retiring from the Panel shall not be eligible for reappointment until after the lapse of two years from the date of his retiral from the Panel. After retiral from a consultant post in the National Health Service a member of the Panel may complete his term of office unless during this period he attains the age of 70 years, at which age he shall automatically retire.

(3) The Secretary of State shall appoint a Secretary who shall be a registered medical practitioner.

Constitution of Advisory Appointments Committees

7. For the purpose of filling each vacancy in a post to which these regulations apply, the Board making the appointment shall constitute an Advisory Appointments Committee, which shall consist of: —

(1) two persons nominated by that Board;

(2) two persons nominated by any Board of Management concerned; provided that where more than one Board of Management is concerned the Boards of Management shall jointly nominate those two persons;

(3) two consultants in the specialty nominated from among their own number by the members of the National Panel of Specialists constituted in accordance with regulation 6 hereof, at least one of whom shall be from outwith the area; and

(4) in the case of an appointment involving undergraduate teaching duties, six persons nominated by any university concerned; provided that the Board and the university with which the provision of hospital and specialist services in the area is associated may agree that certain appointments carry such limited teaching responsibility as not to justify this representation, in which case the university concerned shall nominate two persons only.

Selection by Committee

8.—(1) The Board shall refer to the Committee all applications received on or before the closing date specified in the advertisement and may also refer an application received after that date if they are satisfied that there is a reasonable explanation for the lateness.

(2) The Committee shall consider all applications so referred to them and may interview suitable persons in order to select from the applicants the person or persons considered by them to be suitable for the appointment and submit the appropriate name or names to the Board showing the order in which the Committee consider them to be most suitable, together with comments which shall include the views of the members nominated from the National Panel of Specialists on the suitability of the candidate(s) for consultant status.

(3) If the Committee consider that none of the applicants is suitable for the appointment they shall so inform the Board.

Appointment by Board

9. An appointment to a vacancy to which these regulations apply shall be made by the Board or, if the Board so delegate, by the appropriate committee of the Board. Neither a Board nor a committee of a Board to which power to make an appointment has been delegated shall make such an appointment except from persons selected by a Committee constituted under regulation 7.

Travelling and subsistence expenses

10. Members of a Committee shall be entitled to receive from the Board such payments in respect of travelling and subsistence expenses as are payable to members of the Board performing an approved duty.

Revocation of Regulations

11. The National Health Service (Appointment of Medical and Dental Officers) (Scotland) Regulations 1948(a) and the National Health Service (Appointment of Medical and Dental Officers) (Scotland) Amendment Regulations 1964(b), 1968(c) and 1969(d) are hereby revoked.

Provided that those regulations shall continue to have effect in relation to any appointment which has been advertised before the coming into operation of these regulations.

Gordon Campbell,
One of Her Majesty's Principal
Secretaries of State.

St. Andrew's House,
Edinburgh.

22nd March 1972.

EXPLANATORY NOTE

(This Note is not part of the Regulations.)

These Regulations consolidate, with amendments, the Regulations in force under section 14 of the National Health Service (Scotland) Act 1947 which provide for the appointment of consultants in the National Health Service.

The main changes are:—

(1) the scope of the Regulations has been clarified; they now apply only to the appointment of consultants;

(2) arrangements for appointment to the National Panel of Specialists are more flexible and ensure a periodical turnover in membership of the Panel;

(3) consultants who become redundant are excluded from the scope of the Regulations.

(a) S.I. 1948/1390 (Rev. XV, p. 854: 1948 I, p. 2311).
(b) S.I. 1964/1454 (1964 III, p. 3382).   (c) S.I. 1968/225 (1968 I, p. 737).
(d) S.I. 1969/257 (1969 I, p. 648).

STATUTORY INSTRUMENTS

1972 No. 468

COAL INDUSTRY
The Coal Industry (Borrowing Powers) Order 1972

Laid before the House of Commons in draft
Made -   -   -   -   *22nd March* 1972
Coming into Operation   *24th March* 1972

The Secretary of State in exercise of his powers under section 1(3) of the Coal Industry Act 1965(**a**) as amended by sections 1(1) and 7(3) of and paragraph 1 of the Schedule to the Coal Industry Act 1967(**b**) and all other powers him enabling hereby makes the following Order, a draft of which has been approved by a resolution of the Commons House of Parliament in accordance with section 1(3) of the said Coal Industry Act 1965:—

1. This Order may be cited as the Coal Industry (Borrowing Powers) Order 1972 and shall come into operation on 24th March 1972.

2. The aggregate amount outstanding in respect of any borrowing mentioned in the said section 1(3) as amended shall not exceed £950 million.

Dated 22nd March 1972.

Nicholas Ridley,
Parliamentary Under Secretary of State,
Department of Trade and Industry.

EXPLANATORY NOTE
(*This Note is not part of the Order.*)

Section 1 of the Coal Industry Act 1965, as amended, empowers the National Coal Board to borrow temporarily or otherwise, subject to an overall limit of £900 million which may be increased to such greater sum not exceeding £950 million as may be specified by the Secretary of State by Order.

This Order increases the limit to the maximum permissible figure of £950 million.

(**a**) 1965 c. 82.   (**b**) 1967 c. 91.

STATUTORY INSTRUMENTS

1972 No. 469

COAL INDUSTRY

The Coal Industry (Accumulated Deficit) Order 1972

Laid before the House of Commons in draft

Made - - - -	*22nd March* 1972
Coming into Operation	*24th March* 1972

The Secretary of State, with the approval of the Treasury, in exercise of his powers under section 3(2) of the Coal Industry Act 1971(**a**) and all other powers him enabling hereby makes the following Order, a draft of which has been laid before and approved by the Commons House of Parliament in accordance with subsection (3) of the said section 3:—

1. This Order may be cited as the Coal Industry (Accumulated Deficit) Order 1972 and shall come into operation on 24th March 1972.

2. The limit imposed by section 1(4) of the Coal Industry Act 1965(**b**), as amended by section 3 of the Coal Industry Act 1971, on the amount of the accumulated deficit in the revenue account of the National Coal Board at the end of any financial year of the National Coal Board shall be increased to £100 million.

Nicholas Ridley,

Dated 22nd March 1972.   Parliamentary Under Secretary of State, Department of Trade and Industry.

We approve the making of this Order

Walter Clegg,

P. L. Hawkins,

Dated 22nd March 1972.   Two of the Lords Commissioners of Her Majesty's Treasury

---

EXPLANATORY NOTE

(This Note is not part of the Order)

Section 1 of the Coal Industry Act 1965, as amended, imposes an overall limit on the amount of the accumulated deficit in the revenue account of the National Coal Board at the end of any financial year of the Board of £75 million which may be increased to such greater sum not exceeding £100 million as may be specified by the Secretary of State by Order.

This Order increases the limit to the maximum permissible figure of £100 million.

(**a**) 1971 c. 16.   (**b**) 1965 c. 82.

STATUTORY INSTRUMENTS

1972 No. 470

SEA FISHERIES

The Herring (North Sea Fishing) Licensing Order 1972

Made - - - -	*23rd March* 1972
Laid before Parliament	*29th March* 1972
Coming into Operation	1 *April* 1972

The Minister of Agriculture, Fisheries and Food, and the Secretaries of State for Scotland and the Home Department (being the Secretaries of State respectively concerned with the sea-fishing industry in Scotland and Northern Ireland), in exercise of the powers conferred on them by sections 4 and 15 of the Sea Fish (Conservation) Act 1967(a) as the latter section is amended by section 22(1) of, and paragraph 38 of Part II of Schedule 1 to, the Sea Fisheries Act 1968(b) and all other powers enabling them in that behalf, hereby make the following order:—

Citation and Commencement

1. This order may be cited as the Herring (North Sea Fishing) Licensing Order 1972 and shall come into operation on 1st April 1972.

Interpretation

2.—(1) In this order—

"the Act" means the Sea Fish (Conservation) Act 1967;

"the North Sea" means the area described in the Schedule to this order.

(2) The Interpretation Act 1889(c) shall apply for the interpretation of this order as it applies for the interpretation of an Act of Parliament.

Appointed Day

3. The appointed day for the purposes of section 4 of the Act (which provides for the licensing of British fishing boats in relation to fishing by way of trade or business in specified areas) in conjunction with this order, is 1st April 1972.

Area, Fish and Periods

4. This order applies only to fishing in the North Sea for herring (clupea harengus) during the periods 1 April to 15 June 1972 (both dates inclusive) and 1 February to 15 June 1973 (both dates inclusive).

(a) 1967 c. 84.   (b) 1968 c. 77.
(c) 1889 c. 63.

Powers of British Sea-fishery Officers

5. For the purposes of the enforcement of section 4 of the Act in conjunction with this order, there are hereby conferred on every British sea-fishery officer all the powers of a British sea-fishery officer under section 8(2) and (3) of the Sea Fisheries Act 1968.

In Witness whereof the Official Seal of the Minister of Agriculture, Fisheries and Food is hereunto affixed on 21st March 1972.

(L.S.)

J. M. L. Prior,
Minister of Agriculture, Fisheries and Food.

21st March 1972.

Gordon Campbell,
Secretary of State for Scotland.

23rd March 1972.

R. Maudling,
Secretary of State for the Home Department.

SCHEDULE

THE NORTH SEA (ARTICLE 4)

The area of sea contained within a line drawn from a position having the co-ordinates of 62° north latitude and 4° west longitude, due south to the north coast of Scotland, thence generally south-eastwards along the north and east coasts of Scotland and the east coast of England, thence westwards along the south coast of England to the meridian of 1° west longitude, thence due south to the coast of France, thence generally in a north-easterly direction along the coasts of France, Belgium, the Netherlands, the Federal Republic of Germany and Denmark to Skagen Point, thence along a rhumb line to the Pater Noster Lighthouse on the coast of Sweden, thence generally in a north-westerly, south-westerly and northerly direction along the coasts of Sweden and Norway to the parallel of 62° north latitude, thence due west to the meridian of 4° west longitude.

EXPLANATORY NOTE

(This Note is not part of the Order.)

Section 4 of the Sea Fish (Conservation) Act 1967 provides that from a day appointed by an order, no British fishing boat registered in the United Kingdom shall be used by way of trade or business for fishing in any area specified in the order except under the authority of a licence granted by one of the Fisheries Ministers.

This order which implements a recommendation of the North-East Atlantic Fisheries Commission appoints 1st April 1972 as the day from which no such fishing boat shall so fish for herring in the North Sea between 1st April and 15th June 1972 and between 1st February and 15th June 1973 (all dates inclusive).

STATUTORY INSTRUMENTS

1972 No. 471

SEA FISHERIES

LANDING AND SALE OF SEA-FISH

The Herring (North Sea) Restrictions on Landing Order 1972

Made - - - -	*23rd March* 1972
Laid before Parliament	*29th March* 1972
Coming into Operation	*1st April* 1972

The Minister of Agriculture, Fisheries and Food, and the Secretaries of State for Scotland and the Home Department (being the Secretaries of State respectively concerned with the sea-fishing industry in Scotland and Northern Ireland), in exercise of the powers conferred on them by sections 6 and 15 of the Sea Fish (Conservation) Act 1967**(a)** as the latter section is amended by section 22(1) of, and paragraph 38 of Part II of Schedule 1 to, the Sea Fisheries Act 1968**(b)** and of all other powers enabling them in that behalf, after consultation with the Secretary of State for Trade and Industry **(c)**, hereby make the following order:—

Citation and Commencement

1. This order may be cited as the Herring (North Sea) Restrictions on Landing Order 1972 and shall come into operation on 1st April 1972.

Interpretation

2.—(1) In this order—

"the Act" means the Sea Fish (Conservation) Act 1967;

"the North Sea" means the area described in the Schedule to this order.

(2) The Interpretation Act 1889**(d)** shall apply for the interpretation of this order as it applies for the interpretation of an Act of Parliament.

Prohibition of Landings

3. The landing in the United Kingdom of herring (clupea harengus) caught in waters comprised in the North Sea during the periods 1st April to 15th June 1972 (both dates inclusive) and 1st February to 15th June 1973 (both dates inclusive) is hereby prohibited.

Exceptions

4. Notwithstanding the prohibition contained in article 3 of this order it shall be lawful to land in the United Kingdom herring caught in the waters and during either of the periods specified in that article, provided that:—

    (*a*) the catching was effected in the course of fishing under the authority of a licence in that behalf issued in pursuance of section 4 of the Act, and the landing of the herring is in accordance with any condition of the licence in that respect,

---

(a) 1967 c. 84.   (b) 1968 c. 77.

(c) For transfer of functions from the Board of Trade to the Secretary of State for Trade and Industry see the Secretary of State for Trade and Industry Order 1970 (S.I. 1970/1537 (1970 III, p. 5293)).   (d) 1889 c. 63.

or (*b*) the herring are comprised in a catch of sea fish of any description, the whole or part of which was taken in waters comprised in the North Sea, and do not exceed in weight one tenth of the total weight of the catch landed in the United Kingdom or, if only part of the catch was taken in the said waters, one tenth of the total weight of that part landed as aforesaid.

Powers of British Sea-Fishery Officers

5. For the purposes of the enforcement of this order there are hereby conferred on every British sea-fishery officer all the powers of a British sea-fishery officer under section 8(2) to (4) of the Sea Fisheries Act 1968.

In Witness whereof the Official Seal of the Minister of Agriculture, Fisheries and Food is hereunto affixed on 21st March 1972.

(L.S.)

J. M. L. Prior,
Minister of Agriculture, Fisheries and Food.

21st March 1972.

Gordon Campbell,
Secretary of State for Scotland.

23rd March 1972.

R. Maudling,
Secretary of State for the Home Department.

SCHEDULE

THE NORTH SEA (ARTICLE 3)

The area of sea contained within a line drawn from a position having the co-ordinates of 62° north latitude and 4° west longitude, due south to the north coast of Scotland, thence generally south-eastwards along the north and east coasts of Scotland and the east coast of England, thence westwards along the south coast of England to the meridian of 1° west longitude, thence due south to the coast of France, thence generally in a north-easterly direction along the coasts of France, Belgium, the Netherlands, the Federal Republic of Germany and Denmark to Skagen Point, thence along a rhumb line to the Pater Noster Lighthouse on the coast of Sweden, thence generally in a north-westerly, south-westerly and northerly direction along the coasts of Sweden and Norway to the parallel of 62° north latitude, thence due west to the meridian of 4° west longitude.

EXPLANATORY NOTE

(This Note is not part of the Order.)

This order which is made under sections 6 and 15 of the Sea Fish (Conservation) Act 1967 implements a recommendation of the North-East Atlantic Fisheries Commission.

It bans the landing in the United Kingdom of herring caught in the North Sea during the periods 1st April to 15th June 1972 and 1st February to 15th June 1973 (all dates inclusive); exemption is provided in respect of herring (*a*) caught under the authority of a licence in that behalf granted under section 4 of the Sea Fish (Conservation) Act 1967 or (*b*) comprised in a catch of sea fish taken in whole or in part in the North Sea and not exceeding 10% of the weight of the catch taken in the North Sea.

STATUTORY INSTRUMENTS

1972 No. 474

NATIONAL HEALTH SERVICE, ENGLAND AND WALES

HOSPITAL AND SPECIALIST SERVICES

The National Health Service (Designation of London Teaching Hospitals) Amendment (No. 2) Order 1972

Made - - - *24th March* 1972

Coming into Operation *31st March* 1972

The Secretary of State for Social Services, in exercise of his powers under sections 11 and 75 of the National Health Service Act 1946(**a**) and of all other powers enabling him in that behalf, and after consultation with the University of London, hereby orders as follows: —

1. This order may be cited as the National Health Service (Designation of London Teaching Hospitals) Amendment (No. 2) Order 1972 and shall come into operation on 31st March 1972.

2.—(1) In this order: —

"the Act" means the National Health Service Act 1946;

"the appointed day" means 31st March 1972;

"the Board of Governors" means the Board of Governors of Westminster Hospital;

"the Hospital Board" means the South West Metropolitan Regional Hospital Board;

"the Management Committee" means the Battersea, Putney and Tooting Group Hospital Management Committee;

"the transferred hospital" means the hospital secondly named in article 3 hereof.

(2) The Interpretation Act 1889(**b**) shall apply to the interpretation of this order as it applies to the interpretation of an Act of Parliament.

3. In column (2) of Schedule 1 to the National Health Service (Designation of London Teaching Hospitals) Order 1957(**c**) as amended(**d**) (which Schedule lists designated London teaching hospitals) after the names of the hospitals listed against the name of the Westminster Hospital in column (1) there shall be added the words "St. John's Hospital S.W.11 (including Westmoor House, 244 Roehampton Lane)".

(**a**) 1946 c. 81. (**b**) 1889 c. 63.
(**c**) S.I. 1957/488 (1957 I, p. 1452).
(**d**) The relevant amending instruments are S.I. 1959/766, 1961/2271, 1962/687, 1966/277 (1959 I, p. 1821; 1961 III, p. 3979; 1962 I, p. 711; 1966 I, p. 745).

4.—(1) All officers of the Hospital Board employed immediately before the appointed day solely at or for the purposes of the transferred hospital shall on that day be transferred to and become officers of the Board of Governors.

(2) All medical and dental officers of the Hospital Board employed immediately before the appointed day partly at or for the purposes of the transferred hospital and partly at or for the purposes of any other hospital shall on that day become officers of the Board of Governors in relation to their work at the transferred hospital and all rights and liabilities under their contract in relation thereto with the Hospital Board shall be transferred to the Board of Governors.

(3) Any other officer of the Hospital Board who is employed immediately before the appointed day partly at or for the purposes of the transferred hospital and who does not receive before that day notice in writing from the Hospital Board that he is not to be transferred to the Board of Governors shall on that day be transferred to and become an officer of the Board of Governors.

(4) Any officer who is transferred to the Board of Governors under this article and whose employment was whole-time shall continue to be subject to the remuneration and other conditions of service applicable to a whole-time officer so long as his employment for both the Hospital Board and the Board of Governors amounts in the aggregate to whole-time employment.

5. On the appointed day there shall be transferred to and vest without further conveyance in the Board of Governors:—

    (a) any property held immediately before the appointed day by the Hospital Board or the Management Committee—

        (i) under section 59 of the Act solely for the purposes of the transferred hospital, and

        (ii) under section 60 of the Act so far as practicable for the purposes of the transferred hospital; and

    (b) any other property held by the Hospital Board or the Management Committee and any rights and liabilities to which either of them were entitled or subject immediately before the appointed day so far as these relate solely to the transferred hospital.

6. On the appointed day capital assets equivalent to assets of the Hospital Endowments Fund with a market value on the 5th July 1948 of such sum as may be determined by agreement between the Hospital Board and the Board of Governors (or in default of agreement such sum, if any, as may be decided by the Secretary of State for Social Services) shall be transferred from the Fund to the Board of Governors.

7. Any action or proceeding or any cause of action or proceeding, pending or existing at the appointed day, by, or against, the Hospital Board or the Management Committee solely in respect of any property, right or liability transferred by this order shall not be prejudicially affected by reason of this order, and may be continued, prosecuted and enforced by, or against, the Board of Governors.

Signed by authority of the Secretary of State for Social Services.

J. S. Orme,
Under Secretary,
Department of Health and Social Security.

24th March 1972.

EXPLANATORY NOTE

(This Note is not part of the Order.)

This Order amends the National Health Service (Designation of London Teaching Hospitals) Order 1957 by including St. John's Hospital, Battersea and Westmoor House, Roehampton in the group of hospitals designated as Westminster Hospital and provides for consequential matters relating to officers and property connected with those establishments.

STATUTORY INSTRUMENTS

1972 No. 475

NATIONAL HEALTH SERVICE, ENGLAND AND WALES

HOSPITAL AND SPECIALIST SERVICES

The National Health Service (Designation of London Teaching Hospitals) Amendment (No. 3) Order 1972

Made - - - -	*23rd March* 1972
Coming into Operation	*1st April* 1972

The Secretary of State for Social Services, in exercise of his powers under sections 11 and 75 of the National Health Service Act 1946(a) and of all other powers enabling him in that behalf, and after consultation with the University of London, hereby orders as follows:—

1. This order may be cited as the National Health Service (Designation of London Teaching Hospitals) Amendment (No. 3) Order 1972 and shall come into operation on 1st April 1972.

2.—(1) In this order:—

"the Act" means the National Health Service Act 1946;

"the appointed day" means 1st April 1972;

"the First Board" means the Board of Governors of Charing Cross Hospital;

"the Second Board" means the North West Metropolitan Regional Hospital Board;

"the Committee" means the Hendon Group Hospital Management Committee;

"the transferred hospital" means the hospital named in Article 3 hereof.

(2) The Interpretation Act, 1889(b), shall apply to the interpretation of this order as it applies to the interpretation of an Act of Parliament.

3. In Column (2) of the First Schedule to the National Health Service (Designation of London Teaching Hospitals) Order 1957(c), as amended (d), (which Schedule prescribes designated London teaching hospitals) opposite the name "Charing Cross Hospital" in column (1) the words "The Kingsbury Maternity Hospital, Honeypot Lane, N.W.9." shall be deleted.

(a) 1946 c. 81. (b) 1889 c. 63.
(c) S.I. 1957/488 (1957 I, p. 1452).
(d) The relevant amending instruments are S.I. 1959/518, 1968/1334 (1959 I, p. 1817; 1968 II, p. 3706).

4.—(1) All officers of the First Board employed immediately before the appointed day solely at or for the purposes of the transferred hospital shall on that day be transferred to and become officers of the Second Board.

(2) All medical and dental officers of the First Board employed immediately before the appointed day, partly at or for the purposes of the transferred hospital and partly at or for the purposes of any other hospital shall on that day become officers of the Second Board in relation to their work at the transferred hospital and all rights and liabilities under their contract in relation thereto with the First Board shall be transferred to the Second Board.

(3) Any other officer of the First Board who is employed immediately before the appointed day partly at or for the purposes of the transferred hospital and who does not receive before that day notice in writing from the First Board that he is not to be transferred to the Second Board shall on that day be transferred to and become an officer of the Second Board.

(4) Any officer who is transferred to the Second Board under this article and whose employment was whole-time shall continue to be subject to the remuneration and other conditions of service applicable to a whole-time officer so long as his employment for both the First Board and the Second Board amounts in the aggregate to whole-time employment.

5. On the appointed day there shall be transferred to and vest without further conveyance in the Committee:—

(*a*) any property held immediately before the appointed day by the First Board

(i) under section 59 of the Act solely for the purposes of the transferred hospital, and

(ii) under section 60 of the Act so far as practicable for the purposes of the transferred hospital; and

(*b*) any other property held by the First Board and any rights and liabilities to which the Board was entitled or subject immediately before the appointed day so far as these relate to the transferred hospital.

6. Any action or proceeding or any course of action or proceeding, pending or existing at the appointed day by, or against, the First Board solely in respect of any property, right or liability transferred by this order shall not be prejudicially affected by reason of this order and may be continued, prosecuted and enforced by or against the Committee.

Signed by authority of the Secretary of State for Social Services.

J. S. Orme,
Under Secretary,
Department of Health and Social Security.

23rd March 1972.

EXPLANATORY NOTE

(This Note is not part of the Order.)

This Order amends the National Health Service (Designation of London Teaching Hospitals) Order 1957 by removing the Kingsbury Maternity Hospital from the group of hospitals designated as a teaching hospital under the name of Charing Cross Hospital and providing for consequential matters relating to officers and property connected with the Kingsbury Maternity Hospital.

STATUTORY INSTRUMENTS

1972 No. 478

LONDON GOVERNMENT

The Greater London Council (Sewerage Area) Order 1972

Made - - -		*21st March* 1972
Coming into Operation		*1st April* 1972

The Secretary of State for the Environment, in exercise of his powers under section 39(1)(*b*) and (2) of the London Government Act 1963(**a**) and of all other powers enabling him in that behalf, hereby makes the following order: —

1.—(1) This Order may be cited as the Greater London Council (Sewerage Area) Order 1972 and shall come into operation on 1st April 1972.

(2) The Greater London Council (Sewerage Area) Orders 1965 to 1971 and this order may be cited together as the Greater London Council (Sewerage Area) Orders 1965 to 1972.

2. The Interpretation Act 1889(**b**) shall apply for the interpretation of this order as it applies for the interpretation of an Act of Parliament.

3.—(1) In this article—

"the relevant boundary maps" mean such of the boundary maps (as defined in the Greater London Council (Sewerage Area) Order 1965(**c**)) as are marked with the numbers 7, 11 to 13, 18, 19, 25, 26, 28, 29 to 36, 46 and 49, together with—

(*a*) such of the boundary maps referred to in the Greater London Council (Sewerage Area) Order 1969(**d**) as are marked with the numbers 14A, 17A, 20A, 21A, 22A, 23A, 24A and 53 to 63; and

(*b*) such of the boundary maps referred to in the Greater London Council (Sewerage Area) Order 1970(**e**) as are marked with the numbers 1B, 2B, 3B, 6B, 8B, 9B, 10B, 27B, 37B, 41B, 45B, 47B, 48B, 50B, 64B, 65B and 66B; and

(*c*) the boundary maps, prepared in duplicate, signed by an Under Secretary in the Department of the Environment and marked "Boundary Map of the Greater London Council (Sewerage Area) Order 1972" which maps are respectively marked with the numbers 43C and 44C.

"the relevant index map" means the index map to the relevant boundary maps, prepared in duplicate, signed by an Under Secretary in the Department of the Environment and marked "Index map of the Greater London Council (Sewerage Area) Order 1972".

(**a**) 1963 c. 33. (**b**) 1889 c. 63. (**c**) S.I. 1965/439 (1965 I, p. 1191).
(**d**) S.I. 1969/512 (1969 I, p. 1420). (**e**) S.I. 1970/520 (1970 I, p. 1718).

(2) On and from 1st April 1972, the sewerage area of the Greater London Council shall comprise the areas within the lines shown coloured red on the relevant boundary maps.

(3) One set of the relevant boundary maps and the relevant index map is deposited and available for inspection at the offices of the Greater London Council, and the other at the offices of the Secretary of State for the Environment.

Signed by authority of the Secretary of State

J. E. Beddoe,
An Under Secretary in the
Department of the Environment

21st March 1972.

EXPLANATORY NOTE

(This Note is not part of the Order.)

This Order redefines the sewerage area of the Greater London Council for the purposes of the London Government Act 1963 from and including 1st April 1972. Section 39(3) of the Act of 1963 requires the Greater London Council to keep a map or other document showing the extent for the time being of the sewerage area, and that map or other document is to be open to inspection by members of the public.

STATUTORY INSTRUMENTS

1972 No. 482

WAGES COUNCILS

The Wages Regulation (Milk Distributive) (England and Wales) (Amendment) Order 1972

Made - - -	*23rd March* 1972
Coming into Operation	*23rd April* 1972

Whereas the Secretary of State has received from the Milk Distributive Wages Council (England and Wales) the wages regulation proposals set out in the Schedule hereto;

Now, therefore, the Secretary of State in exercise of his powers under section 11 of the Wages Councils Act 1959(a), and of all other powers enabling him in that behalf, hereby makes the following Order:—

1. This Order may be cited as the Wages Regulation (Milk Distributive) (England and Wales) (Amendment) Order 1972.

2.—(1) In this Order the expression "the specified date" means the 23rd April 1972, provided that where, as respects any worker who is paid wages at intervals not exceeding seven days, that date does not correspond with the beginning of the period for which the wages are paid, the expression "the specified date" means, as respects that worker, the beginning of the next such period following that date.

(2) The Interpretation Act 1889(b) shall apply to the interpretation of this Order as it applies to the interpretation of an Act of Parliament.

3. The wages regulation proposals set out in the Schedule hereto shall have effect as from the specified date.

Signed by order of the Secretary of State.
23rd March 1972.

J. R. Lloyd Davies,
Assistant Secretary,
Department of Employment.

(a) 1959 c. 69.   (b) 1889 c. 63.

Article 3.

SCHEDULE
HOLIDAYS AND HOLIDAY REMUNERATION

The Wages Regulation (Milk Distributive) (England and Wales) Order 1971(a) (Order M.D. (115)) shall have effect as if in the Schedule thereto:—

1. for paragraphs 16 and 17 there were substituted the following paragraphs:—

"HOLIDAY REMUNERATION

16.—(1) (a) Subject to the provisions of this paragraph, for each customary holiday or day in lieu of a customary holiday, which a worker is entitled to be allowed under this Schedule, he shall be paid by the employer one day's holiday pay as defined in *the appropriate part of* paragraph 21:

Provided, however, that payment of the above-mentioned remuneration is subject to the condition that the worker presents himself for employment at the usual starting hour on the first working day following the holiday or day in lieu, or, if he fails to do so, failure is by reason of the proved illness or injury of the worker or with the consent of the employer, and

Provided also that when two customary holidays on both of which the worker is not required to work occur on successive days or so that no working day intervenes, the above proviso shall apply only to the second customary holiday.

(b) Subject to the provisions of this paragraph, holiday remuneration in respect of any customary holiday or day in lieu of a customary holiday shall be paid by the employer to the worker on the pay day on which the wages for the first working day following the holiday or day in lieu are paid:

Provided that if a worker ceases to be employed before being allowed a holiday in lieu of a customary holiday to which he is entitled the said payment shall be made immediately upon the termination of his employment.

(2) Subject to the provisions of paragraph 17, a worker qualified to be allowed an annual holiday or any days of additional annual holiday under this Schedule shall be paid by his employer one day's holiday pay as defined in *the appropriate part of* paragraph 21 in respect of each day thereof, and in the case of annual holiday such payment shall be made by the employer on the last pay day preceding such annual holiday.

(3) Where under the provisions of paragraph 13 an annual holiday is allowed in more than one period the holiday remuneration shall be apportioned accordingly.

17. Where any accrued holiday remuneration has been paid by the employer to the worker in accordance with paragraph 18 of this Schedule or with Order M.D. (111) or Order M.D. (113) in respect of employment during any of the periods referred to in that paragraph or those Orders respectively, the amount of holiday remuneration payable by the employer in respect of any annual holiday or days of additional annual holiday for which the worker has qualified by reason of employment during the said period shall be reduced by the amount of the said accrued holiday remuneration unless that remuneration has been deducted from a previous payment of holiday remuneration made under the provisions of this Schedule or of Order M.D. (111) or Order M.D. (113)".

2. for the definition "One Day's Holiday Pay" in paragraph 21 there were substituted the following definition:—

"(10) 'ONE DAY'S HOLIDAY PAY' means:—

(a) S.I. 1971/1698 (1971 III, p. 4635).

in relation to customary holidays, the appropriate proportion of the remuneration which the worker would be entitled to receive from his employer at the date of the customary holiday for work for which statutory minimum remuneration is payable, either—

(*a*) for the number of hours normally worked by him for the employer in his normal working week, or

(*b*) for 42 hours,

whichever number of hours is the less, if paid at the appropriate hourly general minimum time rate for that number of hours' work; and

in relation to annual holiday or additional annual holiday—

(*a*) *in the case of a worker who has at 31st March immediately preceding the commencement of the holiday season (or the last holiday season as the case may require) completed 12 months' service with the employer, the appropriate proportion of whichever of the following amounts is the greatest—*

    (*i*) *85% of the average weekly earnings of the worker during the 12 months ended on 5th April immediately preceding the holiday or the termination date, as the case may be, such average weekly earnings to be determined by dividing the total remuneration paid to the worker by the employer during the said 12 months by the number of weeks in respect of which it has been paid; or*

    (*ii*) *the holiday remuneration payable for a week of annual or additional annual holiday under the arrangement in force between the employer and the worker at the date of such holiday or at the termination date as the case may be; or*

    (*iii*) *the remuneration which the worker would be entitled to receive from his employer at the date of the annual holiday or additional annual holiday or at the termination date, as the case may be, for work for which statutory minimum remuneration is payable, either—*

       for the number of hours normally worked by him for the employer in his normal working week, or

       for 42 hours,

       whichever number of hours is the less, if paid at the appropriate hourly general minimum time rate for that number of hours' work;

(*b*) *in the case of any other worker, the appropriate proportion of a week's holiday remuneration as set out in (a)(iii) above.*

In this definition 'appropriate proportion' means where the worker's normal working week is

       5 days—one-fifth; or

       4 days—one-quarter; or

       3 days—one-third."

EXPLANATORY NOTE

(This Note is not part of the Order.)

This Order, which has effect from 23rd April 1972, amends the Wages Regulation (Milk Distributive) (England and Wales) Order 1971 (Order M.D. (115)) by providing a more favourable basis for calculating holiday remuneration for certain workers.

New provisions are printed in italics.

STATUTORY INSTRUMENTS

1972 No. 486

CIVIL AVIATION

The Air Navigation (General) (Guernsey) Regulations 1972

Made - - -	*23rd March* 1972
Coming into Operation	*1st April* 1972

The Secretary of State in exercise of his powers under Articles 9(3), 11(2) and (5), 25(2), 26(1)(*c*), 27(4), 28(1) and (3) and 61 of the Air Navigation Order 1972(**a**), as applied to Guernsey by the Air Navigation (Guernsey) Order 1972(**b**) and of all other powers enabling him in that behalf, hereby makes the following Regulations:

1. These Regulations may be cited as the Air Navigation (General) (Guernsey) Regulations 1972 and shall come into operation on 1st April 1972.

2.—(1) The Air Navigation (General) (Guernsey) Regulations 1966(**c**) are hereby revoked.

(2) The Interpretation Act 1889(**d**) shall apply for the interpretation of these Regulations as it applies for the interpretation of an Act of Parliament.

3. The Air Navigation (General) Regulations 1972(**e**) shall apply in relation to Guernsey as they apply in relation to the United Kingdom with modifications, adaptations and exceptions specified in the Schedule to these Regulations.

4. In these Regulations the expression "Guernsey" means the Bailiwick of Guernsey and the territorial waters thereof.

D. F. Hubback,
A Deputy Secretary,
Department of Trade and Industry.

23rd March 1972.

(**a**) S.I. 1972/129 (1972 I, p. 366).   (**b**) S.I. 1972/453 (1972 I, p. 1674).
(**c**) S.I. 1966/916 (1966 II, p. 2199).   (**d**) 1889 c. 63.
(**e**) S.I. 1972/322 (1972 I, p. 1310).

SCHEDULE

MODIFICATIONS AND ADAPTATIONS OF AND EXCEPTIONS FROM THE
AIR NAVIGATION (GENERAL) REGULATIONS 1972

1. Any reference to the Air Navigation Order 1972 shall be construed as a reference to that Order as applied to Guernsey by the Air Navigation (Guernsey) Order 1972.

2. In Regulation 5(1) for the words "the United Kingdom" there shall be substituted the word "Guernsey".

3. In Regulation 6(4)(*c*) for the words "the United Kingdom" there shall be substituted the word "Guernsey".

4. Regulations 12 and 14 shall be omitted.

5. In Regulation 15, paragraph (3) shall be omitted and in paragraph (4) the words "without prejudice to the requirements of Regulation 14" shall be omitted.

EXPLANATORY NOTE

(*This Note is not part of the Regulations.*)

These Regulations revoke and reproduce the substance of the Air Navigation (General) (Guernsey) Regulations 1966 and substitute the Secretary of State for the Board of Trade.

STATUTORY INSTRUMENTS

1972 No. 487

CIVIL AVIATION
The Air Navigation (General) (Jersey) Regulations 1972

Made - - - *23rd March* 1972
Coming into Operation *1st April* 1972

The Secretary of State in exercise of his powers under Articles 9(3), 11(2) and (5), 25(2), 27(4) and 28(1) and (3) of the Air Navigation Order 1972(a) as applied to Jersey by the Air Navigation (Jersey) Order 1972(b) and of all other powers enabling him in that behalf, hereby makes the following Regulations:

1. These Regulations may be cited as the Air Navigation (General) (Jersey) Regulations 1972 and shall come into operation on 1st April 1972.

2.—(1) The Air Navigation (General) (Jersey) Regulations 1966(c) are hereby revoked.

(2) The Interpretation Act 1889(d) shall apply for the interpretation of these Regulations as it applies for the interpretation of an Act of Parliament.

3. The Air Navigation (General) Regulations 1972(e) shall apply in relation to Jersey as they apply in relation to the United Kingdom with modifications, adaptations and exceptions specified in the Schedule to these Regulations.

4. In these Regulations, the expression "Jersey" means the Bailiwick of Jersey and the territorial waters thereof.

D. F. Hubback,
A Deputy Secretary,
Department of Trade and Industry.

23rd March 1972.

(a) S.I. 1972/129 (1972 I, p. 366).   (b) S.I. 1972/452 (1972 I, p. 1669).
(c) S.I. 1966/917 (1966 II, p. 2201).   (d) 1889 c. 63.
(e) S.I. 1972/322 (1972 I, p. 1310).

SCHEDULE

MODIFICATIONS AND ADAPTATIONS OF AND EXCEPTIONS FROM THE AIR NAVIGATION (GENERAL) REGULATIONS 1972

1. Any reference to the Air Navigation Order 1972 shall be construed as a reference to that Order as applied to Jersey by the Air Navigation (Jersey) Order 1972.

2. In Regulation 5(1) for the words "the United Kingdom" there shall be substituted the word "Jersey".

3. In Regulation 6(4)(*c*) for the words "the United Kingdom" there shall be substituted the word "Jersey".

4. Regulation 12 shall be omitted.

5. Regulations 14 and 15 shall be omitted.

EXPLANATORY NOTE

(This Note is not part of the Regulations.)

These Regulations revoke and reproduce the substance of the Air Navigation (General) (Jersey) Regulations 1966 and substitute the Secretary of State for the Board of Trade.

STOKE-ON-TRENT
CITY
LIBRARIES

STATUTORY   INSTRUMENTS

1972 No. 488

AGRICULTURE

The Price Stability of Imported Products (Rates of Levy) (Cereals) (No. 13) Order 1972

Made -	-	-	-	*24th March* 1972
Coming into Operation				*25th March* 1972

The Minister of Agriculture, Fisheries and Food, in exercise of the powers conferred upon him by section 1(2), (4), (5), (6) and (7) of the Agriculture and Horticulture Act 1964(**a**) and of all other powers enabling him in that behalf, hereby make the following order:—

1. This order may be cited as the Price Stability of Imported Products (Rates of Levy) (Cereals) (No. 13) Order 1972, and shall come into operation on 25th March 1972.

2.—(1) In this order—

" the Principal Order " means the Price Stability of Imported Products (Levy Arrangements) (Cereals) Order 1971(**b**), as amended by any subsequent order and if any such order is replaced by any subsequent order the expression shall be construed as a reference to such subsequent order;

AND other expressions have the same meaning as in the Principal Order.

(2) The Interpretation Act 1889(**c**) shall apply to the interpretation of this order as it applies to the interpretation of an Act of Parliament and as if this order and the orders hereby revoked were Acts of Parliament.

3. In accordance with and subject to the provisions of Part II of the Principal Order (which provides for the charging of levies on imports of certain specified commodities) the rate of levy for such imports into the United Kingdom of any specified commodity as are described in column 2 of the Schedule to this order in relation to a tariff heading indicated in column 1 of that Schedule shall be the rate set forth in relation thereto in column 3 of that Schedule.

4. The Price Stability of Imported Products (Rates of Levy) (Cereals) (No. 11) Order 1972(**d**) and the Price Stability of Imported Products (Rates of Levy) (Cereals) (No. 12) Order 1972(**e**) are hereby revoked.

In Witness whereof the Official Seal of the Minister of Agriculture, Fisheries and Food is hereunto affixed on 24th March 1972.

(L.S.)

M. E. Johnston,
Authorised by the Minister.

(**a**) 1964 c. 28.   (**b**) S.I. 1971/631 (1971 I, p. 1660).   (**c**) 1889 c. 63.
(**d**) S.I. 1972/372 (1972 I, p. 1446).   (**e**) S.I. 1972/400 (1972 I, p. 1493).

SCHEDULE

1. Tariff Heading	2. Description of Imports	3. Rate of Levy
	Imports of:—	per ton £
10.01	Denatured wheat	4·50
	Wheat (other than denatured wheat)..	7·00
10.03	Barley other than barley having a potential diastatic activity of not less than 170 degrees	2·50
10.04	Oats	6·00
10.05	Maize (other than sweet corn on the cob) ..	4·50
10.07	Grain sorghum ..	1·75
11.01	Wheat flours not containing chalk and containing not more than 1 per cent. by weight of fibre at the prescribed standard moisture content	3·25
11.02	Cereal groats, meals, kibbled or cut cereals, rolled, flaked, crushed or bruised cereals and other processed cereals—	
	of barley	5·25
	of oats	8·75
	of maize	5·00

EXPLANATORY NOTE

(This Note is not part of the Order.)

This Order, which comes into operation on 25th March 1972, supersedes the Price Stability of Imported Products (Rates of Levy) (Cereals) (No. 11) Order 1972 and the Price Stability of Imported Products (Rates of Levy) (Cereals) (No 12) Order 1972. It—

(*a*) increases to £3·25 per ton the rate of levy to be charged on imports of wheat flours not containing chalk and containing not more than 1 per cent. by weight of fibre at the prescribed standard moisture content; and

(*b*) reimposes unchanged the remaining rates of levy in force immediately before the commencement of the order.

STATUTORY INSTRUMENTS

1972 No. 489

TOWN AND COUNTRY PLANNING, ENGLAND AND WALES

The Town and Country Planning (Control of Advertisements) (Amendment) Regulations 1972

Made - - -	*23rd March* 1972
Laid before Parliament	*5th April* 1972
Coming into Operation	*1st June* 1972

The Secretary of State for the Environment (as respects England, except Monmouthshire) and the Secretary of State for Wales (as respects Wales and Monmouthshire) in exercise of their powers under sections 34 and 217 of the Town and Country Planning Act 1962(a), and of all other powers enabling them in that behalf, hereby make the following regulations:—

1.—(1) These regulations may be cited as the Town and Country Planning (Control of Advertisements) (Amendment) Regulations 1972, and the Town and Country Planning (Control of Advertisements) Regulations 1969(b) and these regulations may be cited together as the Town and Country Planning (Control of Advertisements) Regulations 1969 and 1972.

(2) These regulations shall come into operation on 1st June 1972.

(3) The Interpretation Act 1889(c) shall apply for the interpretation of these regulations as it applies for the interpretation of an Act of Parliament.

2. At the end of regulation 4 of the Town and Country Planning (Control of Advertisements) Regulations 1969, there shall be added the following proviso:—

"Provided that the display of any advertisement which continues to be displayed with consent deemed to be granted under the said regulations of 1960, may be treated for the purposes of regulation 16 of these regulations as being the display of an advertisement with consent deemed to be granted under these regulations, and, if the display of an advertisement in accordance with the provisions of regulation 12 of the said regulations of 1960 is so treated, the display shall, in addition, be treated for the purposes of these regulations as being the display in accordance with regulation 14 hereof of an advertisement of a specified class; and, where a notice under regulation 16 hereof is served by virtue of this proviso, the consent deemed to be granted shall determine and cease to have effect on the date on which the notice takes effect.".

(a) 1962 c. 38.   (b) S.I. 1969/1532 (1969 III, p. 4962).
(c) 1889 c. 63.

Peter Walker,
Secretary of State for the Environment.

21st March 1972.

Peter Thomas,
Secretary of State for Wales.

23rd March 1972.

EXPLANATORY NOTE

(This Note is not part of the Regulations.)

These Regulations amend the Town and Country Planning (Control of Advertisement) Regulations 1969. The Regulations enable discontinuance notices to be served under regulation 16 of the regulations of 1969 in relation to the display of advertisements which continue to be displayed with consent deemed to be granted under the Town and Country Planning (Control of Advertisements) Regulations 1960 (S.I. 1960/695). (The regulations of 1960 were revoked by the regulations of 1969 subject to a saving, and certain advertisements continue to be displayed with consent deemed to be granted under the regulations of 1960.) Provision is made for the determination of the consent deemed to be granted on the date on which a discontinuance notice takes effect.

STATUTORY INSTRUMENTS

1972 No. 492

AGRICULTURE

GUARANTEED PRICES AND ASSURED MARKETS

The Eggs (Protection of Guarantees) Order 1972

Made - - - -	*23rd March* 1972
Laid before Parliament	*28th March* 1972
Coming into Operation	*2nd April* 1972

The Minister of Agriculture, Fisheries and Food, the Secretary of State for Scotland, the Secretary of State for the Home Department (being the Secretaries of State respectively concerned with agriculture in Scotland and Northern Ireland) and the Secretary of State for Wales, acting jointly, in exercise of the powers conferred upon them by sections 5, 9(4) and 35(3) of the Agriculture Act 1957(a) and section 70 of the Agriculture Act 1967(b), as read with the Transfer of Functions (Wales) Order 1969(c), and of all other powers enabling them in that behalf, hereby make the following order:—

Citation and commencement

1. This order may be cited as the Eggs (Protection of Guarantees) Order 1972, and shall come into operation on 2nd April 1972.

Interpretation

2.—(1) In this order, unless the context otherwise requires—

" the appropriate Minister " means—

(*a*) in relation to England, the Minister of Agriculture, Fisheries and Food;

(*b*) in relation to Scotland and Northern Ireland, respectively, the Secretary of State concerned with agriculture therein; and

(*c*) in relation to Wales—

(i) for the purpose of the making, receipt or recovery of any payment, the Minister of Agriculture, Fisheries and Food;

(ii) for all other purposes, that Minister and the Secretary of State for Wales, acting jointly;

" approved mark " means, in relation to each description of eggs specified in column 1 of the Schedule to this order, the word or words relative to such description specified in column 2 of that Schedule;

" container " means a container which is capable of holding not less than 15 dozen eggs;

" eggs " means eggs in shell laid by domestic fowls in the United Kingdom;

" first quality " means fresh and free from taint, the shells being clean and unstained, sound and of good texture and shape, the contents being free from visible blemish and discolouration, the yolk being central, translucent and faintly but not clearly defined and the white being translucent with the air space not exceeding one-quarter of an inch in depth;

" fresh eggs " means eggs which have not been preserved by cold or chemical storage or any other means;

(a) 1957 c. 57.   (b) 1967 c. 22.   (c) S.I. 1969/388 (1969 I, p. 1070).

" the Minister ", in relation to any part of the United Kingdom, means either the appropriate Minister in relation to that part, or that Minister and any or all of the other Ministers acting jointly;

" the Ministers " means the Minister of Agriculture, Fisheries and Food, the Secretaries of State respectively concerned with agriculture in Scotland and Northern Ireland and the Secretary of State for Wales, acting jointly;

" producer " means a producer of eggs;

" registered packer " means a person whose name is for the time being entered by the Minister in a register kept by him for the purpose;

" registered packing station " means any egg packing station which is for the time being entered by the Minister in a register kept by him for the purpose;

" sale by retail " means any sale to a person buying otherwise than for the purpose of resale but does not include a sale to a caterer for the purposes of his catering business, or a sale to a manufacturer for the purposes of his manufacturing business; and " manufacturing " means using eggs, for the purposes of a trade or business (other than a catering business), in the composition, manufacture or preparation of any other product, and corresponding expressions have corresponding meanings.

(2) The Interpretation Act 1889(a) shall apply to the interpretation of this order as it applies to the interpretation of an Act of Parliament and as if this order and the order hereby revoked were Acts of Parliament.

Marking of containers

3.—(1) Every registered packer shall, as soon as practicable, pack at a registered packing station all eggs to which this article applies in containers, being the containers in which the eggs are to be removed from the registered packing station, and each container shall bear the approved mark relating to the eggs packed therein and shall contain eggs of not more than one weight grade. The approved mark shall appear distinctly and legibly in letters not less than half an inch high and shall be applied by means of stamping with indelible ink or printing or by means of a label affixed to the container, or by more than one of those methods.

(2) This article shall apply to all eggs purchased by a registered packer from a producer or produced by a registered packer and appropriated by him for packing at a registered packing station and which are either of first quality or dirty but otherwise of first quality.

Restriction on sale, etc. and use for hatching of certain eggs

4. No person shall sell, offer or expose for sale or have in possession for sale for hatching or shall use for hatching, or cause or permit to be so used any eggs which are either of first quality or dirty but otherwise of first quality and which he knows or has reason to believe have been purchased by a registered packer from a producer or produced by a registered packer and packed by him at a registered packing station.

Keeping and production of records

5.—(1) Every registered packer shall keep or cause to be kept and shall produce on demand by an authorised officer of the Minister or, in Northern Ireland, of the Ministry of Agriculture for Northern Ireland an accurate record of every purchase, sale and use of fresh eggs by the registered packer, such record to include the following particulars:—

(*a*) the date of each purchase, sale and use;

(a) 1889 c. 63.

(*b*) the name and address of each person from whom he buys and to whom he sells any such eggs;

(*c*) in each case the description or descriptions and number of such eggs bought, sold and used respectively, showing separately (except where this is not reasonably practicable) the number of eggs of each quality and weight grade;

(*d*) the price or prices paid on each purchase and sale;

except that as respects sales by retail of fresh eggs, the record shall include the total number of eggs sold each day and the total daily cash receipts in respect thereof and need not include any other particulars.

(2) If so required by notice in writing served on him by or on behalf of the Minister or the said Ministry, as the case may be, any record which a registered packer is required to keep or cause to be kept in accordance with this article shall be kept or caused to be kept, as the case may be, in such form as shall be prescribed in the notice.

(3) Every person shall retain the record of any transaction and use of eggs which as a registered packer he is or was required to keep or cause to be kept pursuant to this article for two years from the date of such transaction or use.

Right of entry

6. Any authorised officer of the Minister or, in Northern Ireland, of the Ministry of Agriculture for Northern Ireland may at all reasonable times enter upon land used for the production, storage, grading, packing, or sale other than sale by retail of eggs and may inspect and take samples of any eggs found upon land so used.

Right to demand production of books, accounts and records

7. Any authorised officer of the Minister or, in Northern Ireland, of the Ministry of Agriculture for Northern Ireland may require any person concerned by way of trade or business in the production, storage, grading, packing, hatching or sale other than sale by retail of eggs to produce on demand any books, accounts and records in his possession or control relating to the purchase or sale of eggs in the course of the trade or business in which he is concerned.

Service of notices

8.—(1) Any notice required or authorised by this order to be given to or served on any person shall be sufficiently given or served if it is delivered to him personally or left at his last known place of abode or business or sent to him by post in a letter addressed to him at the aforesaid place of abode or business.

(2) Any notice required or authorised by this order to be given to or served on an incorporated company or body shall be sufficiently given or served if given to or served on the secretary or clerk of the company or body. For the purposes of this order and of section 26 of the Interpretation Act 1889, the proper address of such secretary or clerk shall be that of the registered or principal office of the company or body.

Delegation of functions as respects Northern Ireland

9. The functions conferred or imposed on the Minister by this order may be exercised in relation to Northern Ireland by the Minister of Agriculture for Northern Ireland.

Revocation

10. The Eggs (Protection of Guarantees) Order 1971(**a**) is hereby revoked.

(**a**) S.I. 1971/475 (1971 I, p. 1416).

In Witness whereof the Official Seal of the Minister of Agriculture, Fisheries and Food is hereunto affixed on 21st March 1972.

(L.S.)

J. M. L. Prior,
Minister of Agriculture, Fisheries and Food.

Gordon Campbell,
21st March 1972.   Secretary of State for Scotland.

R. Maudling,
Secretary of State for the Home
22nd March 1972.   Department.

Given under my hand on 23rd March 1972.

Peter Thomas,
Secretary of State for Wales.

SCHEDULE   Article 2(1)

APPROVED MARKS FOR CONTAINERS

Column 1		Column 2
Description of eggs		Approved Mark
State or Condition	Weight Grade	
First quality or dirty but otherwise of first quality	Not less than $2\frac{3}{16}$ ounces	LARGE
	Less than $2\frac{3}{16}$ ounces but not less than $1\frac{7}{8}$ ounces	STANDARD
	Less than $1\frac{7}{8}$ ounces but not less than $1\frac{5}{8}$ ounces	MEDIUM
	Less than $1\frac{5}{8}$ ounces but not less than $1\frac{1}{2}$ ounces	SMALL
	Less than $1\frac{1}{2}$ ounces	EXTRA SMALL

EXPLANATORY NOTE

(This Note is not part of the Order.)

This order re-enacts the Eggs (Protection of Guarantees) Order 1971 with modifications providing for an additional weight grade in respect of eggs weighing less than $1\frac{1}{2}$ ounces which eggs are to be eligible in appropriate circumstances for guarantee payments.

STATUTORY INSTRUMENTS

1972 No. 493

PENSIONS

The Comptroller and Auditor General's Pension Regulations 1972

Made - - -	*27th March* 1972
Laid before the House of Commons	*30th March* 1972
Coming into Operation	*20th April* 1972

The Minister for the Civil Service, in exercise of the powers conferred on him by section 13 of the Superannuation Act 1972(a) and of all other powers enabling him in that behalf, hereby makes the following Regulations:—

Citation and commencement

1. These Regulations may be cited as the Comptroller and Auditor General's Pension Regulations 1972, and shall come into operation on 20th April 1972.

Interpretation

2.—(1) In these Regulations—

"the civil service scheme" means the principal civil service pension scheme within the meaning of section 2 of the Superannuation Act 1972 and for the time being in force;

"the Comptroller" means the Comptroller and Auditor General;

"the judicial scheme" means the statutory scheme of pensions and other benefits applicable to the judicial offices listed in Schedule 1 to the Judicial Pensions Act 1959(b).

(2) Any reference in these Regulations to the provisions of any enactment shall be construed, unless the context otherwise requires, as a reference to those provisions as amended by any subsequent enactment.

(3) The Interpretation Act 1889(c) shall apply for the interpretation of these Regulations as it applies for the interpretation of an Act of Parliament.

Election between the judicial and civil service schemes

3. An election under section 13(1) of the Superannuation Act 1972 shall be made within the period of three months beginning with the date on which the person making the election takes office as Comptroller or the date of the coming into operation of these Regulations, whichever is the later, and shall be made in writing addressed to the Minister for the Civil Service.

(a) 1972 c. 11.   (b) 1959 c. 9 (8 & 9 Eliz. 2).
(c) 1889 c. 63.

Comptroller electing for the civil service scheme

4.—(1) This Regulation shall apply to any person appointed to be the Comptroller who elects, or is treated as having elected, for the civil service scheme.

(2) Where—

    (*a*) a person to whom this Regulation applies has before his appointment as Comptroller rendered service to which the civil service scheme applies; and

    (*b*) during that service he has ceased to be employed in an established capacity and become employed in an unestablished capacity in such circumstances that any superannuation allowance or additional allowance granted to him may be increased in accordance with the provisions of section 13 of the Superannuation Act 1965(a),

those provisions shall apply as if his service as Comptroller were service in an unestablished capacity in the civil service of the State.

(3) Where a person to whom this Regulation applies (not being a person to whom paragraph (2) above applies) notifies the Minister for the Civil Service that he desires that on a date specified in the notification the provisions of section 13 of the Superannuation Act 1965 shall apply to him, he shall be treated for the purposes of the civil service scheme as if he had ceased on that date to be employed in an established capacity in the civil service of the State and had immediately re-entered that service to serve in an unestablished capacity.

(4) Any reference in this Regulation to the provisions of section 13 of the Superannuation Act 1965 shall be construed as a reference to those provisions as having effect, by virtue of section 2(12) of the Superannuation Act 1972, as part of the civil service scheme.

Comptroller with other service under the judicial scheme who elects for that scheme

5.—(1) This Regulation shall apply to any person appointed to be the Comptroller who has elected for the judicial scheme and who, either before or after his service as Comptroller, has rendered other service to which the judicial scheme applies:

Provided that this Regulation shall not apply to such person unless either—

    (*a*) that other service has immediately preceded or followed his service as Comptroller, or

    (*b*) he has become eligible for a pension on the termination of the earlier service.

(2) Where, in the case of a person to whom this Regulation applies, his service as Comptroller precedes his other service falling within the judicial scheme, his service as Comptroller shall be aggregated with such other service for the purpose of determining qualification for or the amount of benefit under that scheme.

(a) 1965 c. 74.

(3) Where, in the case of a person to whom this Regulation applies, his other service falling within the judicial scheme precedes his service as Comptroller—

(a) such other service shall be aggregated with his service as Comptroller for the purpose of determining qualification for or the amount of benefit under that scheme;

(b) the amount of the benefit payable under the judicial scheme shall, if it would, when determined in accordance with sub-paragraph (a) above, be less than the amount which would have been payable if, immediately before his appointment as Comptroller, he had retired on the ground of permanent infirmity from the office in which he rendered that other service, be increased up to the last mentioned amount; and

(c) section 4 of the Judicial Pensions Act 1959 (special provisions as to former holders of other judicial offices) shall not apply in relation to him.

Comptroller with other service under the civil service scheme who elects for the judicial scheme

6.—(1) This Regulation shall apply to any person appointed to be the Comptroller who has elected for the judicial scheme and who before his appointment as Comptroller has rendered service to which the civil service scheme applies.

(2) The amount of any annual or lump sum benefit payable under the judicial scheme, in the case of a person to whom this Regulation applies, shall not exceed the difference between the amount of the corresponding benefit granted in his case under the civil service scheme and the amount which would be payable under the judicial scheme if his service falling within the civil service scheme had been service as Comptroller.

(3) Where, in the case of a person to whom this Regulation applies, the lump sum benefit granted under the civil service scheme is greater than the amount of the lump sum which would be payable under the judicial scheme if his service falling within the civil service scheme had been service as Comptroller, a sum equal to one-ninth of the excess shall be deemed to be added, for the purposes of the limit imposed by paragraph (2) above, to the amount of the annual benefit granted under the civil service scheme, and the annual benefit under the judicial scheme shall be reduced accordingly.

(4) Where as a result of the limit imposed by paragraph (2) above no lump sum benefit is payable under the judicial scheme, no widow's or children's pension shall, subject to the following provisions of this Regulation, be granted under that scheme; and where as a result of that limit the amount of the lump sum under the judicial scheme is so reduced that it is insufficient to meet the whole of the contribution falling to be made under section 8 of the Administration of Justice (Pensions) Act 1950(a), any widow's or children's pension shall, subject to the following provisions of this Regulation, be reduced so as to bear to the full amount thereof the same proportion as the contribution made bears to the full contribution falling to be made.

(a) 1950 c. 11 (14 & 15 Geo. 6).

(5) If, within twelve months after the retirement from the office of Comptroller, or the death in such office, of the person in respect of whose service a contribution falls to be made under the said section 8, or within such longer period as the Minister for the Civil Service may allow in any particular case, there is paid to the Minister for the Civil Service a sum which, when added to the contribution (if any) made by a reduction of the lump sum granted in respect of him, is equal to the contribution falling to be made in his case under the said section 8, any widow's or children's pension payable in respect of him may be granted in full.

(6) Where only part of any sum falling to be paid under paragraph (5) above is paid within the period specified therein, any widow's or children's pension shall be reduced so as to bear to the full amount thereof the same proportion as the aggregate contribution made bears to the full contribution falling to be made.

(7) Notwithstanding anything in paragraphs (4) to (6) above, a contribution made by a reduction of a lump sum or a contribution by means of such a payment as is mentioned in paragraph (5) or (6) above, or, where both such contributions are made, the aggregate contribution, shall be ineffective in the case of the person in respect of whose service the contribution falls to be made, unless either a widow's or a children's pension can be paid in respect of his service under the judicial scheme at a rate equal to at least £6·50 per annum, and where a contribution is ineffective—

(a) no widow's or children's pension shall be granted;

(b) the lump sum payable in respect of him shall be increased by the amount of any reduction made in it to provide the contribution; and

(c) the amount of any contribution made by means of such a payment as is mentioned in paragraph (5) or (6) above shall be repaid.

Given under the official seal of the Minister for the Civil Service on 27th March 1972.

(L.S.)

A. W. Wyatt,
Authorised by the Minister
for the Civil Service.

EXPLANATORY NOTE

(This Note is not part of the Regulations.)

Section 13 of the Superannuation Act 1972 revises the terms of the election which holders of the office of Comptroller and Auditor General have the right to make between two pension schemes: the judicial scheme and the civil service scheme. These Regulations prescribe the manner in which the election is to be made. They also contain provisions relating to the application of the civil service scheme to the Comptroller, the aggregation of service as Comptroller under the judicial scheme with other service under that scheme, and the application of the judicial scheme to a Comptroller who has had previous service under the civil service scheme.

STATUTORY INSTRUMENTS

1972 No. 494

PENSIONS

The Parliamentary Commissioner's Pension (Amendment) Regulations 1972

Made - - -	*27th March* 1972
Laid before the House of Commons	*30th March* 1972
Coming into Operation	*20th April* 1972

The Minister for the Civil Service, in exercise of the powers conferred on him by Schedule 1 to the Parliamentary Commissioner Act 1967(**a**), as amended by section 29(1) of, and paragraphs 63 and 64 of Schedule 6 to, the Superannuation Act 1972(**b**), and of all other powers enabling him in that behalf, hereby makes the following Regulations: —

1. These Regulations may be cited as the Parliamentary Commissioner's Pension (Amendment) Regulations 1972, and shall come into operation on 20th April 1972.

2.—(1) In these Regulations "the principal Regulations" means the Parliamentary Commissioner's Pension Regulations 1967(**c**).

(2) The Interpretation Act 1889(**d**) shall apply for the interpretation of these Regulations as it applies for the interpretation of an Act of Parliament.

3. In Regulation 2 of the principal Regulations (Parliamentary Commissioner electing for the civil service scheme) the following paragraph shall be added after paragraph (3): —

"(4) Any reference in this Regulation to the Superannuation Act 1965 or to section 13 of that Act shall be construed as a reference to the provisions of that Act or that section, as the case may be, as having effect, by virtue of section 2(12) of the Superannuation Act 1972, as part of the civil service scheme."

4. In Regulation 5(1) of the principal Regulations (interpretation), for the definition of "the civil service scheme", there shall be substituted the following definition: —

" "the civil service scheme" means the principal civil service pension scheme within the meaning of section 2 of the Superannuation Act 1972 and for the time being in force;".

(**a**) 1967 c. 13.   (**b**) 1972 c. 11.
(**c**) S.I. 1967/846 (1967 II, p. 2525).   (**d**) 1889 c. 63.

Given under the official seal of the Minister for the Civil Service on 27th March 1972.

(L.S.)

A. W. Wyatt,
Authorised by the Minister
for the Civil Service.

EXPLANATORY NOTE

(This Note is not part of the Regulations.)

These Regulations amend the Parliamentary Commissioner's Pension Regulations 1967. The Parliamentary Commissioner has the right to elect, in accordance with those Regulations, between two statutory pension schemes: the judicial scheme and the civil service scheme. Under the Superannuation Act 1972 the statutory civil service scheme is to be replaced by a scheme set out in non-statutory documents. These Regulations make the necessary consequential amendments to the 1967 Regulations.

STATUTORY INSTRUMENTS

1972 No. 495

SAVINGS BANKS

The Trustee Savings Banks (Pensions) (Amendment) Order 1972

Made - - -	*27th March* 1972
Laid before Parliament	*30th March* 1972
Coming into Operation	*20th April* 1972

The Minister for the Civil Service, in exercise of the powers conferred on him by section 82 of the Trustee Savings Banks Act 1969(**a**), as amended by section 29(1) of, and paragraph 76 of Schedule 6 to, the Superannuation Act 1972(**b**), and of all other powers enabling him in that behalf, and after consulting the National Debt Commissioners, hereby makes the following Order: —

1. This Order may be cited as the Trustee Savings Banks (Pensions) (Amendment) Order 1972, and shall come into operation on 20th April 1972.

2. The Interpretation Act 1889(**c**) shall apply for the interpretation of this Order as it applies for the interpretation of an Act of Parliament.

3. In article 2 of the Trustee Savings Banks (Pensions) Order 1970(**d**) (interpretation) the following paragraph shall be added after paragraph (3): —

"(4) Any reference in this Order to any provisions of the Superannuation Act 1965(**e**) shall be construed as a reference to those provisions as having effect, by virtue of section 2(12) of the Superannuation Act 1972, as part of the principal civil service pension scheme within the meaning of section 2 of the said Act of 1972."

4. Article 12 of the Trustee Savings Banks (Pensions) Order 1970 is hereby revoked.

Given under the official seal of the Minister for the Civil Service on 27th March 1972.

(L.S.)

A. W. Wyatt,
Authorised by the Minister
for the Civil Service.

(**a**) 1969 c. 50.   (**b**) 1972 c. 11.
(**c**) 1889 c. 63.   (**d**) S.I. 1970/1056 (1970 II, p. 3289).
(**e**) 1965 c. 74.

EXPLANATORY NOTE

(This Note is not part of the Order.)

This Order amends the Trustee Savings Banks (Pensions) Order 1970. That Order applies, with modifications, to the officers of trustee savings banks certain provisions of the Superannuation Act 1965 relating to widows', children's and dependants' pensions. The Superannuation Act 1972, which enables the civil service pension scheme to be set out in non-statutory documents, repeals those provisions, but provides for them to continue to have effect for the time being as part of the new scheme. This Order makes the necessary consequential amendment to the 1970 Order.

The Order also revokes a provision in the 1970 Order relating to increase of pensions payable by trustee savings banks in Northern Ireland, the provision having been superseded in consequence of the Pensions (Increase) Act 1971 (c.56).

STATUTORY INSTRUMENTS

1972 No. 496

INDUSTRIAL TRAINING

The Industrial Training Levy (Clothing and Allied Products) Order 1972

Made - - -	*26th March* 1972
Laid before Parliament	*7th April* 1972
Coming into Operation	*28th April* 1972

The Secretary of State after approving proposals submitted by the Clothing and Allied Products Industry Training Board for the imposition of a further levy on employers in the clothing and allied products industry and in exercise of his powers under section 4 of the Industrial Training Act 1964(a) and of all other powers enabling him in that behalf hereby makes the following Order: —

Title and commencement

1. This Order may be cited as the Industrial Training Levy (Clothing and Allied Products) Order 1972 and shall come into operation on 28th April 1972.

Interpretation

2.—(1) In this Order unless the context otherwise requires: —

(*a*) "agriculture" has the same meaning as in section 109(3) of the Agriculture Act 1947(b) or, in relation to Scotland, as in section 86(3) of the Agriculture (Scotland) Act 1948(c);

(*b*) "an appeal tribunal" means an industrial tribunal established under section 12 of the Industrial Training Act 1964;

(*c*) "assessment" means an assessment of an employer to the levy;

(*d*) "the Board" means the Clothing and Allied Products Industry Training Board;

(*e*) "business" means any activities of industry or commerce;

(*f*) "charity" has the same meaning as in section 360 of the Income and Corporation Taxes Act 1970(d);

(*g*) "clothing and allied products establishment" means an establishment in Great Britain engaged in the third base period wholly or mainly in the clothing and allied products industry for a total of twenty-seven or more weeks or, being an establishment that commenced to carry on business in the third base period, for a total number of weeks exceeding one half of the number of weeks in the part of the said period commencing with the day on which business was commenced and ending on the last day thereof;

(a) 1964 c. 16.	(b) 1947 c. 48.
(c) 1948 c. 45.	(d) 1970 c. 10.

(*h*) "the clothing and allied products industry" means any one or more of the activities which, subject to the provisions of paragraph 2 of Schedule 1 to the industrial training order, are specified in paragraph 1 of that Schedule as the activities of the clothing and allied products industry;

(*i*) "emoluments" means all emoluments assessable to income tax under Schedule E (other than pensions), being emoluments from which tax under that Schedule is deductible, whether or not tax in fact falls to be deducted from any particular payment thereof;

(*j*) "employer" means a person who is an employer in the clothing and allied products industry at any time in the third levy period;

(*k*) "the industrial training order" means the Industrial Training (Clothing and Allied Products Board) Order 1969(**a**);

(*l*) "the levy" means the levy imposed by the Board in respect of the third levy period;

(*m*) "notice" means a notice in writing;

(*n*) "the third base period" means the period of twelve months that commenced on 6th April 1971;

(*o*) "the third levy period" means the period commencing with the day upon which this Order comes into operation and ending on 31st March 1973.

(2) Any reference in this Order to an establishment that commences to carry on business or that ceases to carry on business shall not be taken to apply where the location of the establishment is changed but its business is continued wholly or mainly at or from the new location, or where the suspension of activities is of a temporary or seasonal nature.

(3) In the case where a clothing and allied products establishment is taken over (whether directly or indirectly) by an employer in succession to, or jointly with, another person, a person employed at any time in the third base period at or from the establishment shall be deemed, for the purposes of this Order, to have been so employed by the employer carrying on the said establishment on the day upon which this Order comes into operation, and any reference in this Order to persons employed by the employer at or from a clothing and allied products establishment in the third base period shall be construed accordingly.

(4) The Interpretation Act 1889(**b**) shall apply to the interpretation of this Order as it applies to the interpretation of an Act of Parliament.

Imposition of the levy

3.—(1) The levy to be imposed by the Board on employers in respect of the third levy period shall be assessed in accordance with the provisions of this Article.

(2) Subject to the provisions of this Article, the levy shall be assessed by the Board in respect of each employer and the amount thereof shall be equal to 0·9 per cent. of the sum (less £25,000) of the emoluments of all the persons employed by the employer at or from the clothing and allied products establishment or establishments of the employer in the third base period.

(**a**) S.I. 1969/1375 (1969 III, p. 4094).   (**b**) 1889 c. 63.

(3) There shall be exempt from the levy—

(*a*) an employer in respect of whom the sum of the emoluments of the persons mentioned in the last foregoing paragraph is less than £26,100;

(*b*) a charity.

(4) Where any persons whose emoluments are taken into account for the purposes of this Article were employed at or from an establishment that ceases to carry on business in the third levy period, the sum of the emoluments of those persons shall be reduced for such purposes in the same proportion as the number of days between the commencement of the said levy period and the date of cessation of business (both dates inclusive) bears to the number of days in the said levy period.

(5) For the purposes of this Article, no regard shall be had to the emoluments of any person wholly engaged—

(*a*) in agriculture; or

(*b*) in the supply of food or drink for immediate consumption.

Assessment notices

4.—(1) The Board shall serve an assessment notice on every employer assessed to the levy.

(2) The amount of an assessment shall be rounded down to the nearest £1.

(3) An assessment notice shall state the Board's address for the service of a notice of appeal or of an application for an extension of time for appealing.

(4) An assessment notice may be served on the person assessed to the levy either by delivering it to him personally or by leaving it, or sending it to him by post, at his last known address or place of business in the United Kingdom or, if that person is a corporation, by leaving it, or sending it by post to the corporation, at such address or place of business or at its registered or principal office.

Payment of the levy

5.—(1) Subject to the provisions of this Article and of Articles 6 and 7, the amount of the assessment payable under an assessment notice served by the Board shall be due and payable to the Board one month after the date of the notice.

(2) The amount of an assessment shall not be recoverable by the Board until there has expired the time allowed for appealing against the assessment by Article 7(1) of this Order and any further period or periods of time that the Board or an appeal tribunal may have allowed for appealing under paragraph (2) or (3) of that Article or, where an appeal is brought, until the appeal is decided or withdrawn.

Withdrawal of assessment

6.—(1) The Board may, by a notice served on the person assessed to the levy in the same manner as an assessment notice, withdraw an assessment if that person has appealed against that assessment under the provisions of Article 7 of this Order and the appeal has not been entered in the Register of Appeals kept under the appropriate Regulations specified in paragraph (5) of that Article.

(2) The withdrawal of an assessment shall be without prejudice to the power of the Board to serve a further assessment notice on the employer.

Appeals

7.—(1) A person assessed to the levy may appeal to an appeal tribunal against the assessment within one month from the date of the service of the assessment notice or within any further period or periods of time that may be allowed by the Board or an appeal tribunal under the following provisions of this Article.

(2) The Board by notice may for good cause allow a person assessed to the levy to appeal to an appeal tribunal against the assessment at any time within the period of four months from the date of the service of the assessment notice or within such further period or periods as the Board may allow before such time as may then be limited for appealing has expired.

(3) If the Board shall not allow an application for extension of time for appealing, an appeal tribunal shall upon application made to the tribunal by the person assessed to the levy have the like powers as the Board under the last foregoing paragraph.

(4) In the case of an assessment that has reference to an establishment that ceases to carry on business in the third levy period on any day after the date of the service of the assessment notice, the foregoing provisions of this Article shall have effect as if for the period of four months from the date of the service of the assessment notice mentioned in paragraph (2) of this Article there were substituted the period of six months from the date of the cessation of business.

(5) An appeal or an application to an appeal tribunal under this Article shall be made in accordance with the Industrial Tribunals (England and Wales) Regulations 1965(**a**) as amended by the Industrial Tribunals (England and Wales) (Amendment) Regulations 1967(**b**) except where the assessment has reference to persons employed at or from one or more establishments that are wholly in Scotland and to no other persons, in which case the appeal or application shall be made in accordance with the Industrial Tribunals (Scotland) Regulations 1965(**c**) as amended by the Industrial Tribunals (Scotland) (Amendment) Regulations 1967(**d**).

(6) The powers of an appeal tribunal under paragraph (3) of this Article may be exercised by the President of the Industrial Tribunals (England and Wales) or by the President of the Industrial Tribunals (Scotland) as the case may be.

Evidence

8.—(1) Upon the discharge by a person assessed to the levy of his liability under an assessment the Board shall if so requested issue to him a certificate to that effect.

(2) The production in any proceedings of a document purporting to be certified by the Secretary of the Board to be a true copy of an assessment or other notice issued by the Board or purporting to be a certificate such as is mentioned in the foregoing paragraph of this Article shall, unless the contrary is proved, be sufficient evidence of the document and of the facts stated therein.

Signed by order of the Secretary of State.

26th March 1972.

Paul Bryan,
Minister of State,
Department of Employment.

(**a**) S.I. 1965/1101 (1965 II, p. 2805).   (**b**) S.I. 1967/301, (1967 I, p. 1040).
(**c**) S.I. 1965/1157 (1965 II, p. 3266).   (**d**) S.I. 1967/302 (1967 I, p. 1050).

EXPLANATORY NOTE

(This Note is not part of the Order.)

This Order gives effect to proposals submitted by the Clothing and Allied Products Industry Training Board to the Secretary of State for Employment for the imposition of a further levy upon employers in the industry for the purpose of raising money towards the expenses of the Board.

The levy is to be imposed in respect of the third levy period commencing with the day upon which this Order comes into operation and ending on 31st March 1973. The levy will be assessed by the Board and there will be a right of appeal against an assessment to an industrial tribunal.

STATUTORY INSTRUMENTS

1972 No. 506

PLANT BREEDERS' RIGHTS
The Plant Breeders' Rights (Fees) Regulations 1972

Made - - -	*24th March* 1972
Laid before Parliament	*5th April* 1972
Coming into Operation	*26th April* 1972

The Minister of Agriculture, Fisheries and Food, the Secretary of State for Scotland and the Secretary of State for the Home Department (being the Secretary of State concerned with agriculture in Northern Ireland), acting jointly, in exercise of the powers vested in them by sections 9(1) and 36 of the Plant Varieties and Seeds Act 1964(a), (extended to Northern Ireland by the Plant Varieties and Seeds (Northern Ireland) Order 1964(b) and to the Isle of Man by the Plant Varieties and Seeds (Isle of Man) Order 1969(c)) and of all other powers enabling them in that behalf, with the approval of the Treasury, hereby make the following Regulations: —

Citation and commencement

1. These Regulations may be cited as the Plant Breeders' Rights (Fees) Regulations 1972 and shall come into operation on 26th April 1972.

Revocation of Previous Regulations

2. The Regulations specified in Schedule 1 to these Regulations are hereby revoked.

Interpretation

3.—(1) In these Regulations unless the context otherwise requires—

"the Act" means the Plant Varieties and Seeds Act 1964;

"the Controller" means the Controller of Plant Variety Rights;

"plant breeders' rights" means rights which may be granted in accordance with Part I of the Act;

"the principal Regulations" means the Plant Breeders' Rights Regulations 1969(d) as amended(e) or any subsequent amendment or re-enactment thereof and other expressions have the same meaning as they have in the Act.

(2) The Interpretation Act 1889(f) shall apply to the interpretation of these Regulations as it applies to the interpretation of an Act of Parliament and as if these Regulations and the Regulations hereby revoked were Acts of Parliament.

(a) 1964 c. 14.
(b) S.I. 1964/1574 (1964 III, p. 3543).   (c) S.I. 1969/1829 (1969 III, p. 5701).
(d) S.I. 1969/1021 (1969 II, p. 2976).
(e) S.I. 1971/1094, 1972/84 (1971 II, p. 3253, 1972 I, p. 244).
(f) 1889 c. 63.

Payment of Fees

4. There shall be paid to the Controller in respect of the matters relating to plant breeders' rights arising under the Act or the principal Regulations—

> (i) a fee on making an application for a grant of plant breeders' rights, being a fee of the amount set out in the third column of Part I of Schedule 2 to these Regulations opposite the reference in the second column of the said Part I to the plant variety of the kind to which the application relates, such fee being payable on making the said application;

> (ii) a fee payable in respect of trials or examination of a plant variety which is the subject of an application for a grant of plant breeders' rights, being a fee of the amount set out in the fourth column of Part II of Schedule 2 to these Regulations opposite the reference in the second column of the said Part II to the plant variety of the kind to which the trials or examination relate, such fee being payable for the trials or examination referred to in the third column of the said Part II and so payable within fourteen days of demand made by the Controller;

> (iii) a fee payable in respect of the continued exercise of plant breeders' rights in a plant variety, being a fee of the amount set out in relation to the particular year of the exercise of such rights in the third to the tenth columns of Part III of Schedule 1 to these Regulations opposite the reference in the second column of the said Part III to the plant variety of the kind for which the rights were granted, such fee being payable on, but not more than three months before, the anniversary of the date of the grant of the rights or within such later period as may have been allowed;

> (iv) the fees payable in respect of the matters referred to in the second column of Part IV of Schedule 2 to these Regulations being the fees of the amounts set out in the fourth column of the said Part IV opposite the respective references to those matters, such fees being payable at the times specified in respect of each such matter in the third column of the said Part IV.

Renewal Fees

5.—(1) The fee payable in respect of the continued exercise of plant breeders' rights in a plant variety (hereinafter referred to as the "renewal fee") shall be paid only by the holder of those rights or by a person acting on his behalf, being either an agent duly authorised in accordance with Regulation 16 of the principal Regulations or a person who shall deliver to the Controller with the fee an authority in writing to pay the same, signed by the holder of the rights.

(2) If any such fee is tendered or paid otherwise than in accordance with the last preceding paragraph, the liability to pay the same shall not be regarded as having been thereby discharged.

(3) In a case where the period for which any plant breeders' rights are exercisable has been terminated in accordance with the principal Regulations on the ground that a renewal fee has not been paid there shall only be recoverable by the Controller such a proportion of the said fee as the period during which the said rights have continued to be enjoyed since the date when the said fee became payable bears to the period of 12 months.

(4) Notwithstanding Regulation 4 of these Regulations and the last preceding paragraph of this Regulation, in a case where the period for which any plant breeders' rights are exercisable has been terminated in accordance with the principal Regulations on the ground that a renewal fee has not been paid and

> (a) the person entitled to exercise those rights shall, not later than 14 days before the date when the said fee became payable, have informed the Controller that he did not propose to exercise any of such rights at any time after such date, and

> (b) such person shall not have exercised any of the said rights during the period beginning with the date when the said fee became payable and ending with the date when the said period was terminated,

the Controller shall not be entitled to recover from such person, by any legal proceedings or otherwise, the said fee or any part thereof.

In Witness whereof the official seal of the Minister of Agriculture, Fisheries and Food is hereunto affixed on 17th March 1972.

(L.S.)

J. M. L. Prior,
Minister of Agriculture, Fisheries and Food.

21st March 1972.

Gordon Campbell,
Secretary of State for Scotland.

22nd March 1972.

R. Maudling,
Secretary of State for the Home Department.

Approved on 24th March 1972.

Tim Fortescue,
Keith Speed,
Two of the Lords Commissioners of
Her Majesty's Treasury.

Regulation 2 **SCHEDULE 1**

Regulations revoked	References
The Plant Breeders' Rights (Fees) Regulations 1968	S.I. 1968/619 (1968 I, p. 1444)
The Plant Breeders' Rights (Fees) (Amendment) Regulations 1969	S.I. 1969/1022 (1969 II, p. 3003)
The Plant Breeders' Rights (Fees) (Amendment) Regulations 1970	S.I. 1970/454 (1970 I, p. 1530)
The Plant Breeders' Rights (Fees) (Amendment) Regulations 1971	S.I. 1971/1102 (1071 II, p. 3280)

Regulation 4

SCHEDULE 2

PART 1

FEES PAYABLE ON AN APPLICATION FOR A GRANT OF PLANT BREEDERS' RIGHTS

No.	Plant Variety	Amount
		£
1.	A wheat, oat, barley, potato, ryegrass or lucerne variety	30
2.	A pea, French bean, runner bean, lettuce, rose, perennial chrysanthemum, perpetual flowering carnation, raspberry, black currant, apple, apple rootstock, pear, pear rootstock, plum, plum rootstock, damson, damson rootstock, strawberry or rhubarb variety	20
3.	A border carnation, pink, narcissus, freesia, gladiolus, dahlia, rhododendron, perennial delphinium, pelargonium, streptocarpus, cymbidium, herbaceous perennial, tree, shrub, woody climber, conifer or taxad variety	15

Part II

Fees Payable in Respect of Trials or examination of a Plant Variety which is the Subject of an Application for a Grant of Plant Breeders' Rights

No.	Plant Variety	Trials or examination for which payable	Amount
			£
1.	A wheat, oat or barley variety	Trials in any one calendar year	75
2.	A potato variety	Trials in any one calendar year	35
3.	A ryegrass or lucerne variety	Trials in any one calendar year	45
4.	A pea, French bean, runner bean or lettuce variety	Trials in any one calendar year	40
5.	A rose variety	Trials in any one calendar year	30
6.	A year-round perennial chrysanthemum variety	(a) Trials in each flowering season in the year 1972	20
		(b) Trials in each flowering season in the year 1973 and in subsequent years	30
7.	A perpetual flowering carnation variety	(a) Trials in the year 1972	20
		(b) Trials in the year 1973 and in any one subsequent calendar year	30
8.	A cymbidium variety	Each examination	20
9.	A rhododendron, delphinium, conifer, taxad, tree, shrub or woody climber variety	(a) Trials in any calendar year in which plants of the variety are being established	10
		(b) Trials in any one calendar year other than one in which plants of the variety are being established	20
10.	A narcissus, freesia, gladiolus, border carnation, pink, dahlia, pelargonium, streptocarpus or herbaceous perennial variety	Trials in any one calendar year	20
11.	A strawberry, raspberry, black currant or rhubarb variety	Trials in any one calendar year	20
12.	An apple, pear, plum or damson variety	(a) Trials in any one calendar year before one or more of the trees undergoing trials comes into fruit	10
		(b) Trials in any one subsequent calendar year	20
13.	An apple rootstock, pear rootstock, plum rootstock or damson rootstock variety	Trials in one calendar year	20

Part III

Fees Payable for the Continued Exercise of Plant Breeders' Rights in a Plant Variety

No.	Plant Variety	Fees payable for the continued exercise of plant breeders' rights during the years indicated below							
		Second year of the exercise of plant breeders' rights £	Third year of the exercise of plant breeders' rights £	Fourth year of the exercise of plant breeders' rights £	Fifth year of the exercise of plant breeders' rights £	Sixth year of the exercise of plant breeders' rights £	Seventh year of the exercise of plant breeders' rights £	Eighth year of the exercise of plant breeders' rights £	Ninth and each subsequent year of the exercise of plant breeders' rights £
1.	A wheat, oat or barley variety	35	50	65	80	90	90	90	90
2.	A potato, ryegrass, lucerne, pea, French bean, runner bean, lettuce, strawberry, raspberry, black currant or rhubarb variety	25	30	35	40	45	45	45	45
3.	A year-round perennial chrysanthemum or perpetual flowering carnation variety	30	35	40	45	50	50	50	50
4.	A perennial chrysanthemum (other than a year-round variety), narcissus, freesia, gladiolus, border carnation, pink, cymbidium, dahlia, rhododendron, pelargonium, perennial delphinium, streptocarpus, herbaceous perennial, conifer, taxad, tree, shrub, woody climber, apple rootstock, pear rootstock, plum rootstock or damson rootstock variety	20	20	25	25	30	30	30	30

PART III—(cont'd.)

FEES PAYABLE FOR THE CONTINUED EXERCISE OF PLANT BREEDERS' RIGHTS IN A PLANT VARIETY

No.	Plant Variety	Fees payable for the continued exercise of plant breeders' rights during the years indicated below							
		Second year of the exercise of plant breeders' rights	Third year of the exercise of plant breeders' rights	Fourth year of the exercise of plant breeders' rights	Fifth year of the exercise of plant breeders' rights	Sixth year of the exercise of plant breeders' rights	Seventh year of the exercise of plant breeders' rights	Eighth year of the exercise of plant breeders' rights	Ninth and each subsequent year of the exercise of plant breeders' rights
		£	£	£	£	£	£	£	£
5.	An apple, pear, plum or damson variety	20	20	25	25	30	35	40	45
6.	A rose variety (only when the fee becomes payable during the year 1972)	25	30	35	40	45	45	45	—
7.	A rose variety, other than a glass-house variety (when the fee be-comes payable after the year 1972)	25	30	35	40	45	45	45	45
8.	A rose variety, being a glasshouse variety (when the fee becomes pay-able after the year 1972)	30	35	40	45	50	50	50	50

Part IV

Fees Payable in Respect of Other Matters

No.	Matter	When payable	Amount
			£
1.	Application for an extension of the period for which plant breeders' rights are exercisable.	On making the application.	10·00
2.	Application for a compulsory licence.	On making the application.	5·00
3.	Application to extend, limit, vary or revoke a compulsory licence.	On making the application.	5·00
4.	Application to amend a document in any application or proceeding.	On making the application.	1·00
5.	Application to rectify an error or omission in the register of plant varieties.	On making the application.	1·00
6.	Application for extension of time for the service or delivery of a document or thing or for the doing of an act.	On making the application.	1·00
7.	Making representations in writing to the Controller, by any person other than the applicant, in connection with any application.	On delivering the representations.	·50
8.	Making representations in writing to the Controller, by any person other than the holder of plant breeders' rights, in connection with a proposal to terminate those rights or to revoke or terminate any extension of such rights.	On delivering the representations.	·50
9.	On attending to be heard by the Controller or by a person appointed by him for the purpose.	Before the hearing.	5·00
10.	The grant of plant breeders' rights in respect of	Before the issue of the document constituting evidence of the grant.	
	(a) a wheat, oat, barley, potato, ryegrass or lucerne variety		20·00
	(b) any other plant variety		30·00

PART IV—(Cont'd.)

FEES PAYABLE IN RESPECT OF OTHER MATTERS

No.	Matter	When payable	Amount
			£
11.	The grant of an extension of the period for which plant breeders' rights are exercisable	Before the issue of the document constituting evidence of the extension.	10·00
12.	The giving of a protective direction.	Before the issue of the document constituting evidence of the giving of the protective direction.	5·00
13.	Application for an extension of the period for payment of a renewal fee.	On making the application.	5·00
14.	Payment of a renewal fee after the expiration of 7 days from the date when it fell due, except in a case where an application has been made for the period for payment to be extended.	On payment of the renewal fee.	2·50
15.	Application for the approval of a substituted name for a plant variety.	On making the application.	5·00
16.	Application for the amendment of the register of plant varieties, except in a case where the plant breeders' rights are transferred to another person.	On making the application.	1·00
17.	Registration of title and amendment of the register of plant varieties on a transfer of plant breeders' rights or a share in such rights.	On making the application for registration.	5·00
18.	Inspection of the register of plant varieties or of a document in the possession of the Controller.	Before the inspection.	·25
19.	Supplying copies of documents, (a) foolscap or smaller, per page (b) larger than foolscap, per page	Before the delivery of the copies.	·10 ·15

PART IV—(*Cont'd.*)

FEES PAYABLE IN RESPECT OF OTHER MATTERS

No.	Matter	When payable	Amount
20.	Supplying a duplicate of a document constituting evidence of a grant of plant breeders' rights or protective direction or of an extension of the period for which plant breeders' rights are exercisable.	On ordering the duplicate.	£ 2·00

EXPLANATORY NOTE
(*This Note is not part of the Regulations.*)

These Regulations, made under the Plant Varieties and Seeds Act 1964, prescribe the fees payable to the Controller of Plant Variety Rights in regard to matters arising out of the application for and granting of plant breeders' rights.

The Regulations revoke the Plant Breeders' Rights (Fees) Regulations 1968 (S.I. 1968/619) as amended. The fees payable for an application for a grant of plant breeders' rights, for trials of a plant variety and for the grant and renewal of rights, are increased. Fees for the renewal of rights are progressively increased during the period of five, and in some cases eight, years in which they are first exercised.

STOKE CITY LIBRARIES

STATUTORY INSTRUMENTS

1972 No. 507

SEEDS

The Plant Varieties (Index) Regulations 1972

Made - - -	*24th March* 1972
Coming into Operation	*26th April* 1972

The Minister of Agriculture, Fisheries and Food, the Secretary of State for Scotland and the Secretary of State for the Home Department (being the Secretary of State concerned with agriculture in Northern Ireland), acting jointly, in exercise of the powers vested in them by section 23A of, and paragraph 5 of Schedule 5 to, the Plant Varieties and Seeds Act 1964(**a**), as amended by Section 43 of, and Schedule 7 to, the Agriculture (Miscellaneous Provisions) Act 1968(**b**) (extended to Northern Ireland by the Plant Varieties and Seeds (Northern Ireland) Order 1964(**c**)) and of all other powers enabling them in that behalf, after consultation with the representatives of such interests as appear to them to be concerned, with the approval of the Treasury, hereby make the following Regulations:—

Citation and commencement

1. These Regulations may be cited as the Plant Varieties (Index) Regulations 1972 and shall come into operation on 26th April 1972.

Revocation of Previous Regulations

2. The Regulations specified in Schedule 1 to these Regulations are hereby revoked.

Interpretation

3.—(1) In these Regulations unless the context otherwise requires—

"the Act" means the Plant Varieties and Seeds Act 1964;

"the gazette" means the gazette published by the Ministers in accordance with section 34 of the Act;

"the Index" means the index of names of plant varieties prepared by the Ministers in accordance with section 20 of the Act;

"injurious weeds" means the weeds specified in Schedule 4 to these Regulations;

(**a**) 1964 c. 14. (**b**) 1968 c. 34.
(**c**) S.I. 1964/1574 (1964 III, p. 3543).

"the Ministers" means the Minister of Agriculture, Fisheries and Food, the Secretary of State for Scotland and the Secretary of State for the Home Department (being the Secretary of State concerned with agriculture in Northern Ireland);

"plant breeders' rights" means rights which may be granted in accordance with Part I of the Act;

"reproductive material" means reproductive material of a plant variety and includes seeds for sowing and seed potatoes;

and other expressions have the same meaning as in the Act.

(2) The Interpretation Act 1889(**a**) shall apply to the interpretation of these Regulations as it applies to the interpretation of an Act of Parliament and as if these Regulations and the Regulations hereby revoked were Acts of Parliament.

Amendment of provisional list or Index

4. Following the publication by the Ministers in the gazette in accordance with paragraph 1 of Schedule 5 to the Act of a provisional list of plant varieties which are within the class of plant varieties to which a section of the Index will relate or of a notice of the coming into force of a section of the Index an application may be made to the Ministers by any person seeking—

(*a*) the addition of the name of a plant variety to,

(*b*) the correction of the name of a plant variety in, or

(*c*) the erasure of the name of a plant variety from
the said provisional list or the said section of the Index as the case may be.

Application for amendment of provisional list or Index

5. An application made in accordance with the last preceding paragraph (hereinafter referred to as "the application") shall be in writing and shall include references to—

(*a*) the particular provisional list or section of the Index to which the application relates;

(*b*) the nature of the application, that is to say whether it seeks an addition to, correction of or erasure from the particular provisional list or section of the Index;

(*c*) in a case where the application seeks a correction or erasure, the name of the plant variety to which the application relates;

(*d*) in a case where the application seeks a correction, the correction which is proposed;

(*e*) the documents, if any, submitted in support of the application; and

(*f*) the grounds relied on in support of the application.

(**a**) 1889 c. 63.

Translations

6. Where any document submitted in support of the application is in a language other than the English language it shall unless the Ministers otherwise direct be accompanied by a complete and adequate translation thereof into the English language.

Lodging of application

7. The application and any documents submitted in support thereof shall be delivered or sent by post in a properly addressed pre-paid letter to the Minister of Agriculture, Fisheries and Food, Murray House, Vandon Street, London, SW1H OAG.

Address for service

8. The person making the application (hereinafter referred to as "the applicant") shall, on or before making the application, give to the Ministers in writing an address within the United Kingdom (hereinafter referred to as his "address for service") which shall be the address at which any notices or other documents may be delivered to or served upon him and he shall be at liberty at any time to give to the Ministers in writing another address which shall thereafter be his address for service in substitution for that previously given.

Information and plant material

9.—(1) Where the application involves the question whether two or more plant varieties are distinct from one another the applicant shall—

(*a*) give to the Ministers such information and produce and deliver to them such documents, records and illustrations as they may from time to time require, and

(*b*) deliver to the Ministers reproductive material of such one or more of the said plant varieties as they shall require for carrying out examinations, tests and trials in the quantity and of the description and quality specified, and packed and in the condition also specified, in Schedule 2 to these Regulations and also such further reproductive and other plant material in such quantity and of such description and quality as shall appear to the Ministers to be required to replace any such material already delivered as may have been damaged in transit or damaged or lost in the course of tests and trials or which is, or has in the course of tests and trials been shown to be, unhealthy or otherwise unsuitable,

being information, documents, records, illustrations and material relevant to the application and in the possession, control or power of the applicant.

(2) Anything required to be given, produced or delivered in accordance with paragraph (1) of this Regulation shall be given, produced or delivered to the Ministers at such place as they shall require within 28 days of demand made by them in writing or within such longer time as they may allow.

Notification of decision

10. The Ministers shall give to the applicant a notice of their decision together with, if the application has been refused, their reasons for such refusal and a sufficient indication of the time within which and manner in which any appeal may be brought.

Fees

11.—(1) Subject to paragraph (2) of this Regulation there shall be paid to the Ministers in respect of the matters set out in the second column of Schedule 3 to these Regulations the fees set out in the fourth column of the said Schedule opposite the respective references to those matters and such fees shall be paid at the times specified in the third column of the said Schedule opposite such references.

(2) The fees prescribed in item No. 1 of the said Schedule 3 for the examination, tests and trials of a plant variety in relation to an application involving the question whether two or more varieties are distinct shall, if at the time of that application an application for a grant of plant breeders' rights in respect of such variety is made or has previously been made, be payable by the applicant only to the extent by which they exceed the amount of any fees which have been paid or which are or will become payable for trials of that variety in connection with a grant of plant breeders' rights.

Failure to supply information etc. or to pay fees

12. If any information, documents, records, illustrations or material shall not have been given, produced or delivered in accordance with Regulation 9 of these Regulations or if any fee payable in accordance with the last preceding Regulation in connection with an application shall not have been paid on the due date, the Ministers shall not be obliged to take any further steps in relation to the application until the requirements of the said Regulation 9 have been complied with or until the fee shall have been paid.

Performance trials

13. Except in a case where section 22 of the Act (which makes provision for the carrying out of performance trials of new plant varieties) has not been brought into force for the class which includes the plant variety which is the subject of an application under these Regulations for the addition of the name of a plant variety to the Index, such application shall be of no effect unless an application for the carrying out of performance trials, made in accordance with Regulations under section 22(10) of the Act, is made in respect of the said variety at the same time as the application under these Regulations.

In Witness whereof the official seal of the Minister of Agriculture, Fisheries and Food is hereunto affixed on 17th March 1972.

(L.S.)

J. M. L. Prior,
Minister of Agriculture, Fisheries and Food.

21st March 1972.   *Gordon Campbell,*
                              Secretary of State for Scotland.

22nd March 1972.   *R. Maudling,*
                              Secretary of State for the Home Department.

Approved on 24th March 1972.

Tim Fortescue,
Keith Speed,
Two of the Lords Commissioners of
Her Majesty's Treasury.

Regulation 2   SCHEDULE 1

Regulations revoked	References
The Plant Varieties (Index) Regulations 1969	S.I. 1969/1027 (1969 II, p. 3030)
The Plant Varieties (Index) (Amendment) Regulations 1970	S.I. 1970/124 (1970 I, p. 558)
The Plant Varieties (Index) (Amendment No. 2) Regulations 1970	S.I. 1970/453 (1970 I, p. 1528)
The Plant Varieties (Index) (Amendment No. 3) Regulations 1970	S.I. 1970/1089 (1970 II, p. 3434)

Regulation 9   SCHEDULE 2

REPRODUCTIVE AND OTHER PLANT MATERIAL TO BE DELIVERED
TO THE MINISTERS

PART I

Wheat, Barley and Oats

Quantity

1.—(1) During the year beginning with the making of the application 500 ears and 14 lb. of seed shall be delivered. Attached to each ear there shall be approximately 1 foot of straw in the case of wheat and 6 inches of straw in the case of barley and oats.

(2) During each of the immediately succeeding years until the completion of the tests and trials there shall be delivered such reproductive and other plant material in such quantity and of such description and quality as shall appear to the Ministers to be necessary or desirable for the proper completion of the tests and trials.

Packing

2. The ears shall be packed in a stiff-sided container, in bundles of 100 each. The seed shall be packed in a suitable container of sufficient strength to withstand mechanical damage during transit.

Quality

3.—(1) *Health*

No ears or seed shall be taken from a crop having more than 1 ear in 5,000 affected with loose smut.

(2) *Purity and germination*

The seed shall be accompanied by a report of a test made at an official seed testing station established under the Seeds Act 1920(a) or a seed testing station licensed under that Act, and made within the 3 months immediately preceding the delivery of the seed stating that in a sample of 8 oz.—

  (a) there were no seeds of injurious weeds and not more than 1% by weight of other impurities, and

  (b) that the percentage of germination was not less than 85.

Dressings and Treatments

4. The seed shall not have been subjected to any fungicidal or insecticidal treatment.

PART II

Potatoes

Quantity

1.—(1) During the year beginning with the making of the application 250 seed tubers shall be delivered.

(2) During each of the immediately succeeding years until the completion of the tests and trials there shall be delivered such reproductive and other plant material in such quantity and of such description and quality as shall appear to the Ministers to be necessary or desirable for the proper completion of the tests and trials.

Packing

2. The seed tubers shall be securely packed in new sacks or other new containers which are capable of withstanding the hazards that may be encountered by perishable produce during transit. The packing material shall be adequate in quantity and quality to protect the tubers from low temperatures which may cause chilling or frosting and from mechanical damage. Where the seed tubers are consigned by rail they shall be sent by passenger train.

Health

3. (a) The seed tubers shall be the produce of a seed crop which did not contain more than—

  (i) 0·05% of rogues, undesirable variations, wildings and bolters;

  (ii) 0·02% with leaf roll or severe mosaic

  (iii) 0·25% with mild mosaic; or

  (iv) 2% with blackleg.

(a) 1920 c. 54.

(b) The seed crop from which the seed tubers were produced shall not have been so affected with any other disease or pest as to render it unsuitable for seed purposes.

(c) The seed tubers shall be accompanied by a Health Certificate issued by the Ministry of Agriculture, Fisheries and Food, the Department of Agriculture and Fisheries for Scotland, the Ministry of Agriculture for Northern Ireland or the Isle of Man Board of Agriculture and Fisheries stating:—

  (i) that on visual examination they were found to be free from signs of wart disease of potatoes (Synchytrium endobioticum (Schilb.) (Perc.));

  (ii) that wart disease of potatoes has not been known to have occurred on the land on which the potatoes were grown; and

  (iii) that representative samples of soil from the land on which the potatoes were grown have been found, on laboratory examination, to be free from potato cyst eelworm (Heterodera rostochiensis Woll).

(d) The seed tubers shall include sufficient virus-free tubers to provide a virus-free nucleus for a reference collection.

Grading and Condition

4. The seed tubers shall be graded so as to be capable of being retained by meshes of a riddle each measuring 1½ inches square and passed by meshes of a riddle each measuring 2 inches square. The seed tubers shall be in sound condition and not be visibly unfit for planting through mecanical damage or attack by any insect, pest or disease or any other condition which would impair subsequent growth. The seed tubers shall be reasonably free from soil.

Dressings and Treatments

5. The seed tubers shall not have been treated with fungicide, pesticide or sprout depressant.

PART III

Peas

Quantity

1.—(1) During the year beginning with the making of the application 6 lb. of seed shall be delivered.

(2) During each of the immediately succeeding years until the completion of the tests and trials there shall be delivered such reproductive and other plant material in such quantity and of such description and quality as shall appear to the Ministers to be necessary or desirable for the proper completion of the tests and trials.

Packing

2. The seed shall be packed in a suitable container of sufficient strength to withstand mechanical damage during transit.

Quality

3.—(1) *Health*
The seed shall be free from serious seed-borne diseases.

(2) *Purity and germination*
The seed shall be accompanied by a report of a test made at an official seed testing station established under the Seeds Act 1920 or a seed testing station licensed under that Act and made within the 3 months immediately preceding the delivery of the seed stating that in a sample of 8 oz.:—

  (a) the percentage of purity was not less than 99, and

  (b) the percentage of germination was not less than 70.

Dressings and Treatments

4. The seed shall not have been subjected to any fungicidal or insecticidal treatment.

Part IV

French Beans

Quantity

1.—(1) During the year beginning with the making of the application 8 lb. of seed shall be delivered.

(2) During each of the immediately succeeding years until the completion of the tests and trials there shall be delivered such reproductive and other plant material in such quantity and of such description and quality as shall appear to the Ministers to be necessary or desirable for the proper completion of the tests and trials.

Packing

2. The seed shall be packed in a suitable container of sufficient strength to withstand mechanical damage during transit.

Quality

3.—(1) *Health*

The seed shall be free from serious seed-borne diseases.

(2) *Purity and germination*

The seed shall be accompanied by a report of a test made at an official seed testing station established under the Seeds Act 1920 or a seed testing station licensed under that Act and made within the 3 months immediately preceding the delivery of the seed stating that in a sample of 1lb.:—

(*a*) the percentage of purity was not less than 99, and

(*b*) the percentage of germination was not less than 60.

Dressings and Treatments

4. The seed shall not have been subjected to any fungicidal treatment.   If the seed has been treated with streptomycin this shall be declared when it is delivered.

Part V

Ryegrass

Quantity

1.—(1) During the year beginning with the making of the application 200 grams of seed shall be delivered.

(2) During each of the immediately succeeding years until the completion of the tests and trials there shall be delivered such reproductive and other plant material in such quantity and of such description and quality as shall appear to the Ministers to be necessary or desirable for the proper completion of the tests and trials.

Each sample delivered shall be accompanied by a written declaration by or on behalf of the applicant, stating the generation to which it belongs.

Packing

2. The seed shall be packed in a suitable container of sufficient strength to withstand mechanical damage during transit.

Quality

3. The seed supplied in the first year shall be accompanied by a report of a test made at an official seed testing station established under the Seeds Act 1920 and made

within the 3 months immediately preceding the delivery of the seed stating that in a sample of 2 oz.:—

    (*a*) the percentage of purity was not less than 97,

    (*b*) the percentage of germination was not less than 80, and

    (*c*) in a purity test there were no seeds of injurious weeds and not more than 0·5% by weight of any other weed seeds.

The seed supplied in subsequent years shall be accompanied in each case by a report of a test made at an official seed testing station as aforesaid or a seed testing station licensed under the Seeds Act 1920, made within the 3 months immediately preceding the delivery of the seed and stating the facts referred to in sub-paragraphs (*a*), (*b*) and (*c*) of this paragraph.

Dressings and Treatments

4. The seed shall not have been subjected to any fungicidal or insecticidal treatment.

Part VI

Lucerne

Quantity

1.—(1) During the year beginning with the making of the application 200 grams of seed shall be delivered.

(2) During each of the immediately succeeding years until the completion of the tests and trials there shall be delivered such reproductive and other plant material in such quantity and of such description and quality as shall appear to the Ministers to be necessary or desirable for the proper completion of the tests and trials.

Each sample delivered shall be accompanied by a written declaration by or on behalf of the applicant, stating the generation to which it belongs.

Packing

2. The seed shall be packed in a suitable container of sufficient strength to withstand mechanical damage during transit.

Quality

3. The seed supplied in the first year shall be accompanied by a report of a test made at an official seed testing station established under the Seeds Act 1920 and made within the 3 months immediately preceding the delivery of the seed stating that in a sample of 2 oz.:—

    (*a*) the percentage of purity was not less than 98,

    (*b*) the percentage of germination together with the percentage of hard seed was not less than 70, and

    (*c*) in a purity test there were no seeds of injurious weeds and not more than 0·5% by weight of any other weed seeds.

The seed supplied in subsequent years shall be accompanied in each case by a report of a test made at an official seed testing station as aforesaid or a seed testing station licensed under the Seeds Act 1920, made within the 3 months immediately preceding the delivery of the seed and stating the facts referred to in sub-paragraphs (*a*), (*b*) and (*c*) of this paragraph.

Dressings and Treatments

4. The seed shall not have been subjected to any fungicidal or insecticidal treatment other than any treatment which has been carried out in order to comply with the requirements of an order made or having effect as if made under the Plant Health Act 1967**(a)** or the Plant Health Act (Northern Ireland) 1967**(b)**.

    (a) 1967 c. 8.   **(b)** 1967 c. 28 (N.I.).

Part VII

Lettuces

1.—(1) During the year beginning with the making of the application 1½ oz. of seed shall be delivered.

(2) During each of the immediately succeeding years until the completion of the tests and trials there shall be delivered such reproductive and other plant material in such quantity and of such description and quality as shall appear to the Ministers to be necessary or desirable for the proper completion of the tests and trials.

Packing

2. The seed shall be packed in a suitable container of sufficient strength to withstand mechanical damage during transit.

Quality

3.—(1) *Health*

The seed shall be free from serious seed-borne diseases.

(2) *Purity and germination*

The seed shall be accompanied by a report of a test made at an official seed testing station established under the Seeds Act 1920 or a seed testing station licensed under that Act and made within the 3 months immediately preceding the delivery of the seed stating that in a sample of 1 oz.:—

(*a*) the percentage of purity was not less than 98, and

(*b*) the percentage of germination was not less than 75.

Dressings and Treatments

4. The seed shall not have been subjected to any fungicidal or insecticidal treatment.

Part VIII

Broad and Field Beans

Quantity

1.—(1) During the year beginning with the making of the application 9 lb. of seed shall be delivered.

(2) During each of the immediately succeeding years until the completion of the tests and trials there shall be delivered such reproductive and other plant material in such quantity and of such description and quality as shall appear to the Ministers to be necessary or desirable for the proper completion of the tests and trials.

Packing

2. The seed shall be packed in a suitable container of sufficient strength to withstand mechanical damage during transit.

Quality

3.—(1) *Health*

The seed shall be free from serious seed-borne diseases.

(2) *Purity and germination*

The seed shall be accompanied by a report of a test made at an official seed testing station established under the Seeds Act 1920(a) or a seed testing station licensed under that Act and made within the 3 months immediately preceding the delivery of the seed stating that in a sample of 1 lb.:—

(a) 1920 c. 54.

(a) the percentage of purity was not less than 98, and

(b) the percentage of germination was not less than 70.

Dressings and Treatments

4. The seed shall not have been subjected to any fungicidal or insecticidal treatment.

Part IX

Runner Beans

Quantity

1.—(1) During the year beginning with the making of the application 9 lb. of seed shall be delivered.

(2) During each of the immediately succeeding years until the completion of the tests and trials there shall be delivered such reproductive and other plant material in such quantity and of such description and quality as shall appear to the Ministers to be necessary or desirable for the proper completion of the tests and trials.

Packing

2. The seed shall be packed in a suitable container of sufficient strength to withstand mechanical damage during transit.

Quality

3.—(1) *Health*

The seed shall be free from serious-borne diseases.

(2) *Purity and germination*

The seed shall be accompanied by a report of a test made at an official seed testing station established under the Seeds Act 1920 or a seed testing station licensed under that Act and made within the 3 months immediately preceding the delivery of the seed stating that in a sample of 1 lb.:—

(a) the percentage of purity was not less than 99, and

(b) the percentage of germination was not less than 60.

Dressings and treatments

4. The seed shall not have been subjected to any fungicidal or insecticidal treatment.

Part X

Timothy, Cocksfoot, Tall Fescue and Meadow Fescue

Quantity

1.—(1) During the year beginning with the making of the application 100 grams of seed in the case of timothy and 200 grams of seed in the case of cocksfoot, tall fescue or meadow fescue shall be delivered.

(2) During each of the immediately succeeding years until the completion of the tests and trials there shall be delivered such reproductive and other plant material in such quantity and of such description and quality as shall appear to the Ministers to be necessary or desirable for the proper completion of the tests and trials.

Packing

2. The seed shall be packed in a suitable container of sufficient strength to withstand mechanical damage during transit.

Quality

3. The seed supplied in the first year shall be accompanied by a report of a test made at an official seed testing station established under the Seeds Act 1920 and

made within the 3 months immediately preceding the delivery of the seed stating that in a sample of 2 oz. (57 grams):—

(*a*) the percentage of purity, in the case of seed of timothy, tall fescue or meadow fescue, was not less than 97 and, in the case of seed of cocksfoot, was not less than 90;

(*b*) the percentage of germination was not less than 80; and

(*c*) in a purity test there were no seeds of injurious weeds and not more than 0·5% by weight of any other weed seeds.

The seed supplied in subsequent years shall be accompanied in each case by a report of a test made at an official seed testing station as aforesaid or a seed testing station licensed under the Seeds Act 1920, made within the 3 months immediately preceding the delivery of the seed and stating the facts referred to in sub-paragraphs (*a*), (*b*) and (*c*) of this paragraph.

Dressings and treatments

4. The seed must not have been subjected to any fungicidal or insecticidal treatment.

SCHEDULE 3   Regulation 11

FEES

No.	Matter	When payable	Amount
1	Examination, tests and trials for one year of a plant variety which is the subject of, or otherwise concerned in, an application involving the question whether two or more varieties are distinct, being	Within 14 days of demand made by the Ministers at the commencement of each year's examination, tests and trials	£
	(*a*) a wheat variety		75
	(*b*) an oat variety		75
	(*c*) a barley variety		75
	(*d*) a potato variety		35
	(*e*) a ryegrass variety		45
	(*f*) a lucerne variety		45
	(*g*) a pea variety		40
	(*h*) a French bean variety		40
	(*i*) a runner bean variety		40
	(*j*) a broad bean or a field bean variety		40
	(*k*) a lettuce variety		40
	(*l*) a timothy variety		45
	(*m*) a cocksfoot variety		45
	(*n*) a tall fescue variety		45
	(*o*) a meadow fescue variety		45
2	Search of the Index of Names of Plant Varieties	Before the search	0·25

Regulation 3   **SCHEDULE 4**

Injurious Weeds

Wild Oat (Avena fatua L. and Avena ludoviciana Durieu)
Dodder (Cuscuta spp.)
Docks and Sorrels (Rumex spp.)
Black grass (Alopecurus myosuroides Huds.)
Couch grass (Agropyron repens (L.) Beauv.)

EXPLANATORY NOTE

(This Note is not part of the Regulations.)

The Plant Varieties and Seeds Act 1964 makes provision for the preparation and maintenance, by the Ministers concerned with agriculture in the United Kingdom, of an Index of Plant Varieties. Only the indexed name of a plant variety may be used to distinguish it from other varieties when it is sold or offered or exposed for sale.

These Regulations re-enact with modifications the Plant Varieties (Index) Regulations 1969 (S.I. 1969/1027) as amended, and the fees payable for the examination, of tests and trials of plant varieties in connection with applications for entries in the Index are, with two exceptions, increased.

STATUTORY INSTRUMENTS

1972 No. 517

DEFENCE

The Army Terms of Service (Amendment) Regulations 1972

Made - - - -	*22nd March* 1972
Laid before Parliament	*7th April* 1972
Coming into Operation	*1st May* 1972

The Defence Council, in exercise of the powers conferred upon them by section 2 of the Armed Forces Act 1966**(a)** and of all other powers enabling them in that behalf, hereby make the following Regulations:—

Citation, Commencement and Interpretation

1.—(1) These Regulations may be cited as the Army Terms of Service (Amendment) Regulations 1972 and shall come into operation on 1st May 1972.

(2) The Interpretation Act 1889**(b)** shall apply to the interpretation of these Regulations as it applies to the interpretation of an Act of Parliament.

(3) In these Regulations "the Principal Regulations" means the Army Terms of Service Regulations 1967**(c)**, as amended **(d)**.

Amendments to the Principal Regulations

2.—(1) The following Regulation shall be substituted for Regulations 4 and 4A of the Principal Regulations:—

"**4.**—(1) Subject to Regulations 7, 10(2) and 11(5), a man, but not a woman, who enlists in the regular army for a term of more than 12 years army service shall have the right exercisable in accordance with Regulation 6—

    (*a*) to be transferred to the reserve at the end of the period of 3 years beginning with the relevant date or, if he enlists under the age of 17 years 6 months, the date of his attaining the age of 18 years or the date of the expiration of his period of training, whichever is the later, or at any time thereafter and

    (*b*) to determine his service at the end of the period of 12 years beginning with the relevant date or at any time thereafter.

(a) 1966 c. 45.   (b) 1889 c. 63.
(c) S.I. 1967/1018 (1967 II, p. 3066).
(d) The relevant amending instrument is S.I. 1971/502 (1971 I, p. 1496).

(2) Subject to Regulations 4(3), 7, 10(2) and 11(5), a woman who enlists in the regular army for a term of more than 12 years army service shall have the right to determine her service in accordance with Regulation 6 at the end of the period of 3 years beginning with the date of her attestation or, if she enlists under the age of 17 years 6 months and revokes any consent given under Regulation 7 pursuant to paragraph (4) thereof, the date of her attaining the age of 18 years or the date of the expiration of her period of training, whichever is the later, or at any time thereafter.

(3) A woman may, after the commencement of these Regulations, be enlisted in army service with the right to determine her service, subject to Regulations 7, 10(2) and 11(5) and in accordance with the provisions of Regulation 6, at the end of the period of 4 years beginning with the date of her attestation, or at any time thereafter and a woman so enlisted shall not have the right conferred by Regulation 4(2).".

(2) The following Regulation shall be substituted for Regulations 6 and 6A of the Principal Regulations:—

"**6.** A right to determine army service and a right to be transferred to the reserve conferred by Regulation 4 shall be exercised by notice in writing given by the person in question to his commanding officer not less than 18 months before the expiration of the period at the end of which his service is to be determined or, as the case may be, he is to be transferred to the reserve.".

(3) Regulation 7 of the Principal Regulations shall have effect as though at the end there were added the following paragraph:—

"(4) Any consent under this Regulation given by a person who has not attained the age of 17 years 6 months may be revoked by notice in writing given by the person in question to his commanding officer not more than 28 days after the attaining by that person of the age of 18 years.".

(4) The following Regulation shall be substituted for Regulations 8 and 8A of the Principal Regulations:—

"**8.**—(1) A man transferred to the reserve in consequence of the exercise of the right conferred by Regulation 4(1)(a) shall serve in the reserve until the expiration of 7 years from the relevant date, unless he has, at the date of his being transferred, completed 6 years army service, when he shall serve in the reserve until the expiration of 12 years from the relevant date.

(2) A man transferred to the reserve under Regulation 5 with the approval of the competent military authority shall serve in the reserve until the expiration of 12 years from the relevant date.".

(5) The Principal Regulations shall have effect as though:—

(a) Regulations 3(3) and 10(2) were omitted and the subsequent paragraphs of those Regulations were numbered respectively (3) and (2) and

(b) In Schedule 2 the words "Regulation 6(2)" in Column 1 and all the words opposite thereto in columns 2 and 3 were omitted.

Saving

3. The amendments effected by these Regulations shall not affect the term of service (either as respects duration, or as respects liability to army service or any liability to serve in the reserve) for which any person who is in army service immediately before the commencement of these Regulations is serving immediately before such commencement.

On behalf of the Defence Council,

G. Johnson Smith,
Michael Carver,
Members of the Defence Council.

Dated 22nd March 1972.

EXPLANATORY NOTE

(This Note is not part of the Regulations.)

These Regulations further amend the Army Terms of Service Regulations by conferring on all persons enlisting for more than 12 years in the regular army after the 1st May 1972 a right to be transferred to the reserve (or in the case of women, to determine service) at any time after 3 years and to determine service at any time after 12 years, provided at least 18 months prior notice has been given to their commanding officer. Provision is made for women on special enlistment to determine their service on similar notice at any time after 4 years. In the case of those under the age of $17\frac{1}{2}$ any consent to be restricted in the exercise of the right to give notice may be revoked within 28 days of reaching the age of 18. Consequential amendments are made to the periods to be served in the reserve and the requirements that persons under the age of $17\frac{1}{2}$ years may not be enlisted or extend their service for a term longer than 12 years are removed.

STATUTORY INSTRUMENTS

1972 No. 518

PROBATION AND AFTER-CARE

The Combined Probation and After-Care Areas Order 1972

Made	- - -	*27th March* 1972

Coming into Operation　　　　　*8th May* 1972

In exercise of the power conferred upon me by section 53(7) of the Courts Act 1971(**a**), I hereby make the following Order: —

1. This Order may be cited as the Combined Probation and After-Care Areas Order 1972 and shall come into operation on 8th May 1972.

2. The Interpretation Act 1889(**b**) shall apply to the interpretation of this Order as it applies to the interpretation of an Act of Parliament.

3. The secretary of the probation and after-care committee for an area specified in the first column in the Schedule to this Order and constituted by the Order referred to opposite thereto in the second column in the Schedule (being an Order made or deemed to have been made under paragraph 1 of Schedule 5 to the Criminal Justice Act 1948(**c**)) shall be, instead of the person appointed or deemed to have been appointed by or under the said Order, the person mentioned opposite thereto in the third column in the Schedule.

R. Maudling,
One of Her Majesty's Principal
Secretaries of State.

Home Office,
　Whitehall.

27th March 1972.

(**a**) 1971 c. 23.　　　　(**b**) 1889 c. 63.　　　　(**c**) 1948 c. 58.

SCHEDULE

Column 1 Probation and After-Care Area	Column 2 Order	Column 3 Secretary of Probation and After-Care Committee
The Bedfordshire Probation and After-Care Area	S.I. 1964/1584	The Clerk of the Bedford County Council
The Berkshire Probation and After-Care Area	S.I. 1951/485	The Clerk of the Berkshire County Council
The Buckinghamshire Probation and After-Care Area	S.I. 1951/1284	The Clerk of the Buckingham County Council
The Cambridgeshire and Isle of Ely Probation and After-Care Area	S.I. 1964/1606	The Clerk of the Cambridge-shire and Isle of Ely County Council
The Cheshire Probation and After-Care Area	S.I. 1969/1054	The Clerk of the Chester County Council
The Cornwall Probation and After-Care Area	S.I. 1955/1882	The Clerk of the Cornwall County Council
The Cumberland Probation and After-Care Area	S.I. 1955/280	The Clerk of the Cumberland County Council
The Derbyshire Probation and After-Care Area	S.I. 1957/1428	The Clerk of the Derbyshire County Council
The Devon, Exeter and Torbay Probation and After-Care Area	S.I. 1967/1031	The Clerk of the Devon County Council
The Dorset Probation and After-Care Area	S.I. 1953/1033	The Clerk of the Dorset County Council
The Durham Probation and After-Care Area	S.I. 1969/37	The Clerk of the Durham County Council
The Essex Probation and After-Care Area	S.I. 1963/2076	The Clerk of the Essex County Council
The Gloucestershire Probation and After-Care Area	S.I. 1952/405	The County Solicitor for Gloucestershire
The Hampshire Probation and After-Care Area	S.I. 1968/371	The Clerk of the Hampshire County Council
The Herefordshire Probation and After-Care Area	S.I. 1954/332	The Clerk of the Herefordshire County Council
The Hertfordshire Probation and After-Care Area	S.I. 1953/1759	The Clerk of the Hertfordshire County Council
The Huntingdon and Peterborough Probation and After-Care Area	S.I. 1964/1615	The Clerk of the Huntingdon and Peterborough County Council
The Kent Probation and After-Care Area	S.I. 1951/1855	The Clerk of the Kent County Council
The Lancashire North Probation and After-Care Area	S.I. 1959/119	The Clerk of the Lancaster County Council

Column 1	Column 2	Column 3
Probation and After-Care Area	Order	Secretary of Probation and After-Care Committee
The Lancashire South-East Probation and After-Care Area	S.I. 1959/119	The Clerk of the Lancaster County Council
The Lancashire South-West Probation and After-Care Area	S.I. 1959/119	The Clerk of the Lancaster County Council
The Leicestershire and Rutland Probation and After-Care Area	S.R. & O. 1927/948	The Clerk of the Leicester County Council
The Lincolnshire Probation and After-Care Area	S.I. 1956/299	The Clerk of the Lincoln, Parts of Lindsey County Council
The Newcastle and Northumberland Probation and After-Care Area	S.I. 1969/268	The Clerk of the Northumberland County Council
The Norfolk Probation and After-Care Area	S.I. 1964/407	The Clerk of the Norfolk County Council
The Northampton and County Probation and After-Care Area	S.I. 1964/319	The Clerk of the Northamptonshire County Council
The Nottingham City and County Probation and After-Care Area	S.I. 1967/1799	The Clerk of the Nottinghamshire County Council
The Oxfordshire Probation and After-Care Area	S.I. 1954/350	The Clerk of the Oxford County Council
The Shropshire Probation and After-Care Area	S.I. 1954/436	The Clerk of the Salop County Council
The Somerset and Bath Probation and After-Care Area	S.I. 1957/395	The Clerk of the Somerset County Council
The Staffordshire Probation and After-Care Area	S.I. 1955/279	The Clerk of the Staffordshire County Council
The Suffolk Probation and After-Care Area	S.I. 1955/383	The County Solicitor for East Suffolk
The Surrey Probation and After-Care Area	S.I. 1950/1794	Such person as the Committee may appoint
The East Sussex Probation and After-Care Area	S.I. 1953/1419	The Clerk of the East Sussex County Council
The West Sussex Probation and After-Care Area	S.I. 1953/1488	The Clerk of the West Sussex County Council
The Warwickshire Probation and After-Care Area	S.I. 1964/389	The Clerk of the Warwickshire County Council
The Westmorland Probation and After-Care Area	S.I. 1962/1213	The Clerk of the Westmorland County Council
The Wiltshire Probation and After-Care Area	S.I. 1953/1441	The Clerk of the Wiltshire County Council
The Worcester City and County Probation and After-Care Area	S.I. 1963/1143	The Clerk of the Worcestershire County Council

Column 1	Column 2	Column 3
Probation and After-Care Area	Order	Secretary of Probation and After-Care Committee
The East Riding and York City Probation and After-Care Area	S.I. 1966/325	The Clerk of the Yorkshire, East Riding, County Council
The North Riding Probation and After-Care Area	S.I. 1953/1411	The Clerk of the Yorkshire, North Riding, County Council
The West Riding Probation and After-Care Area	S.I. 1952/924	The Clerk of the Yorkshire, West Riding, County Council
The Brecknock Probation and After-Care Area	S.I. 1950/1351	The Clerk of the Brecon County Council
The Cardiganshire Probation and After-Care Area	S.R. & O. 1927/974	The Clerk of the Cardiganshire County Council
The Carmarthenshire Probation and After-Care Area	S.I. 1956/1329	The Clerk of the Carmarthenshire County Council
The Flintshire Probation and After-Care Area	S.I. 1953/1587	The Clerk of the Flintshire County Council
The Glamorgan Probation and After-Care Area	S.I. 1966/286	The Clerk of the Glamorgan County Council
The Merioneth Probation and After-Care Area	S.I. 1952/1965	The Clerk of the Merioneth County Council
The County of Monmouth Probation and After-Care Area	S.I. 1952/958	The Clerk of the Monmouthshire County Council
The Montgomeryshire Probation and After-Care Area	S.I. 1964/1634	The Clerk of the Montgomeryshire County Council
The North Wales Probation and After-Care Area	S.R. & O. 1943/1149 (as amended by S.I. 1952/2116)	The Clerk of the Caernarvon County Council
The Pembrokeshire Probation and After-Care Area	S.I. 1954/1552	The Clerk of the Pembroke County Council
The Radnorshire Probation and After-Care Area	S.I. 1964/295	The Clerk of the Radnorshire County Council

EXPLANATORY NOTE

(This Note is not part of the Order.)

Certain Orders constituting combined probation and after-care areas designate or provide for the appointment of a clerk of the peace as secretary of the probation and after-care committee for each such area. Clerks of the peace have been abolished by the Courts Act 1971 and this Order provides for their replacement as secretary of such committees by the person described in column 3 of the Schedule who is, except in three cases, the clerk of the county council.

STOKE-ON-TRENT
CITY
LIBRARIES

STATUTORY INSTRUMENTS

1972 No. 519

PROBATION AND AFTER-CARE

The Combined Probation and After-Care Areas (No. 2) Order 1972

Made	-	-	-	*27th March* 1972
Coming into Operation				*8th May* 1972

In exercise of the power conferred upon me by section 53(7) of the Courts Act 1971(**a**), I hereby make the following Order:—

1. This Order may be cited as the Combined Probation and After-Care Areas (No. 2) Order 1972 and shall come into operation on 8th May 1972.

2. The Interpretation Act 1889(**b**) shall apply to the interpretation of this Order as it applies to the interpretation of an Act of Parliament.

3. For the additional justices, however described, appointed to the probation and after-care committee for an area specified in the first column of the Schedule to this Order by or under the Order referred to opposite thereto in the second column of the Schedule (being an Order made or deemed to have been made under paragraph 1 of Schedule 5 to the Criminal Justice Act 1948(**c**)) there shall be substituted the number of judges of the Crown Court and the number of additional justices who have experience of sitting as members of the Crown Court specified opposite thereto in the third and fourth columns respectively of the Schedule.

R. Maudling,
One of Her Majesty's Principal
Secretaries of State.

Home Office,
Whitehall.
27th March 1972.

(**a**) 1971 c. 23.　　　　(**b**) 1889 c. 63.　　　　(**c**) 1948 c. 58.

SCHEDULE

1	2	3	4
Probation and After-Care Area	Order	Number of judges of the Crown Court	Number of additional justices who have experience of sitting as members of the Crown Court
The Bedfordshire Probation and After-Care Area	S.I. 1964/1584	0	2
The Berkshire Probation and After-Care Area	S.I. 1951/485	1	1
The Buckinghamshire Probation and After-Care Area	S.I. 1951/1284	1	1
The Cambridgeshire and Isle of Ely Probation and After-Care Area	S.I. 1964/1606	0	2
The Cheshire Probation and After-Care Area	S.I. 1969/1054	1	1
The Cornwall Probation and After-Care Area	S.I. 1955/1882	1	1
The Cumberland Probation and After-Care Area	S.I. 1955/280	0	2
The Derbyshire Probation and After-Care Area	S.I. 1957/1428	1	1
The Devon, Exeter and Torbay Probation and After-Care Area	S.I. 1967/1031	1	1
The Dorset Probation and After-Care Area	S.I. 1953/1033	1	1
The Durham Probation and After-Care Area	S.I. 1969/37	1	1
The Essex Probation and After-Care Area	S.I. 1963/2076 (as amended by S.I. 1969/38)	1	2
The Gloucestershire Probation and After-Care Area	S.I. 1952/405	1	1
The Hampshire Probation and After-Care Area	S.I. 1968/371	1	1
The Herefordshire Probation and After-Care Area	S.I. 1954/332	0	2
The Hertfordshire Probation and After-Care Area	S.I. 1953/1759	1	1
The Huntingdon and Peterborough Probation and After-Care Area	S.I. 1964/1615	1	1

1	2	3	4
Probation and After-Care Area	Order	Number of judges of the Crown Court	Number of additional justices who have experience of sitting as members of the Crown Court
The Kent Probation and After-Care Area	S.I. 1951/1855 (as amended by S.I. 1962/2017)	1	1
The Lancashire North Probation and After-Care Area	S.I. 1959/119	1	1
The Lancashire South-East Probation and After-Care Area	S.I. 1959/119	1	1
The Lancashire South-West Probation and After-Care Area	S.I. 1959/119	1	1
The Leicestershire and Rutland Probation and After-Care Area	S.R. & O. 1927/948	0	2
The Lincolnshire Probation and After-Care Area	S.I. 1956/299	1	1
The Inner London Probation and After-Care Area	S.I. 1964/1833	2	0
The North-East London Probation and After-Care Area	S.I. 1964/1834	1	1
The South-East London Probation and After-Care Area	S.I. 1964/1834	1	1
The South-West London Probation and After-Care Area	S.I. 1964/1834	1	1
The Middlesex Probation and After-Care Area	S.I. 1964/1834	1	1
The Manchester and Salford Probation and After-Care Area	S.I. 1969/525	1	1
The Newcastle and Northumberland Probation and After-Care Area	S.I. 1969/268	1	1
The Norfolk Probation and After-Care Area	S.I. 1964/407	1	1
The Northampton and County Probation and After-Care Area	S.I. 1964/319	1	1
The Nottingham City and County Probation and After-Care Area	S.I. 1967/1799	1	1
The Oxfordshire Probation and After-Care Area	S.I. 1954/350	1	1
The Shropshire Probation and After-Care Area	S.I. 1954/436	0	2

1	2	3	4
Probation and After-Care Area	Order	Number of judges of the Crown Court	Number of additional justices who have experience of sitting as members of the Crown Court
The Somerset and Bath Probation and After-Care Area	S.I. 1957/395	1	1
The Staffordshire Probation and After-Care Area	S.I. 1955/279	1	1
The Suffolk Probation and After-Care Area	S.I. 1955/383	1	1
The Surrey Probation and After-Care Area	S.I. 1950/1794	1	1
The East Sussex Probation and After-Care Area	S.I. 1953/1419 (as amended by S.I. 1968/611)	0	2
The West Sussex Probation and After-Care Area	S.I. 1953/1488	1	1
The Warwickshire Probation and After-Care Area	S.I. 1964/389	1	1
The West Midlands Probation and After-Care Area	S.I. 1966/35	1	1
The Westmorland Probation and After-Care Area	S.I. 1962/1213	1	1
The Wiltshire Probation and After-Care Area	S.I. 1953/1441	1	1
The Worcester City and County Probation and After-Care Area	S.I. 1963/1143	0	2
The East Riding and York City Probation and After-Care Area	S.I. 1966/325	0	2
The North Riding Probation and After-Care Area	S.I. 1953/1411	0	2
The West Riding Probation and After-Care Area	S.I. 1952/924	1	1
The Brecknock Probation and After-Care Area	S.I. 1950/1351	0	2
The Cardiganshire Probation and After-Care Area	S.R. & O. 1927/974	0	2
The Carmarthenshire Probation and After-Care Area	S.I. 1956/1329	0	2
The Flintshire Probation and After-Care Area	S.I. 1953/1587	1	1

1	2	3	4
Probation and After-Care Area	Order	Number of judges of the Crown Court	Number of additional justices who have experience of sitting as members of the Crown Court
The Glamorgan Probation and After-Care Area	S.I. 1966/286	1	1
The Merioneth Probation and After-Care Area	S.I. 1952/1965	0	2
The County of Monmouth Probation and After-Care Area	S.I. 1952/958	0	2
The Montgomeryshire Probation and After-Care Area	S.I. 1964/1634	0	2
The North Wales Probation and After-Care Area	S.R. & O. 1943/1149 (as amended by S.I. 1952/2116)	0	3
The Pembrokeshire Probation and After-Care Area	S.I. 1954/1552	0	2
The Radnorshire Probation and After-Care Area	S.I. 1964/295	0	2

EXPLANATORY NOTE

(*This Note is not part of the Order.*)

Under Orders constituting combined probation and after-care areas the probation and after-care committee for each such area includes a specified number of members who hold any one of the offices of chairman, deputy chairman, assistant chairman, or recorder of a court of quarter sessions or are justices appointed to the committee by a court of quarter sessions. Under the Courts Act 1971 courts of quarter sessions have been replaced by Crown Courts. This Order provides for such members to be replaced on each such probation and after-care committee by a specified number of Crown Court judges and a specified number of additional justices who have experience of sitting as members of the Crown Court.

STATUTORY INSTRUMENTS

1972 No. 521

PENSIONS

The Superannuation (Fire and Specified Services) Interchange Rules 1972

Made - - -	*27th March* 1972
Laid before Parliament	*10th April* 1972
Coming into Operation	*1st May* 1972

In exercise of the powers conferred on me by sections 2 and 15 of the Superannuation (Miscellaneous Provisions) Act 1948(**a**), as extended and amended by section 9 of the Fire Services Act 1959(**b**), I hereby make the following Rules:—

Part I

Citation, Operation and Interpretation

1. These Rules may be cited as the Superannuation (Fire and Specified Services) Interchange Rules 1972 and shall come into operation on 1st May 1972.

2.—(1) In these Rules the following expressions have the meanings hereby respectively assigned to them, that is to say:—

"appropriate authority", in relation to specified service, has the meaning assigned to it in Schedule 1;

"the fire authority", in relation to any person, means the authority maintaining the fire brigade from which he retires or has retired as mentioned in Rule 4(1);

"fire brigade" means a fire brigade maintained under the Fire Services Act 1947(**c**);

"the Firemen's Pension Scheme" means the Scheme for the time being in operation under section 26 of the Fire Services Act 1947;

"pension" has the meaning assigned to it by section 17(1) of the Superannuation (Miscellaneous Provisions) Act 1948 except that it does not include an award under the Firemen's Pension Scheme by way of a gratuity or repayment of aggregate contributions;

(**a**) 1948 c. 33.   (**b**) 1959 c. 44.
(**c**) 1947 c. 41.

"pensionable pay" and "pensionable service" have the same meanings as in the Firemen's Pension Scheme;

"Police Pensions Regulations" means the Regulations for the time being in force under section 1 of the Police Pensions Act 1948(a), except that "Isle of Man Police Pensions Regulations" means the Regulations so in force under section 16 of the Police (Isle of Man) Act 1962 (an Act of Tynwald);

"regular fireman" means a member of a fire brigade of a class prescribed by the Firemen's Pension Scheme for the purposes of section 2 of the Fire Services Act 1951(b);

"specified service" has the meaning assigned to it by Schedule 1.

(2) In these Rules, unless the context otherwise requires, any reference to any enactment shall be construed as a reference to that enactment as amended or extended by any subsequent enactment.

(3) In these Rules, unless the context otherwise requires, any reference to a Rule or Schedule shall be construed as a reference to a Rule or Schedule contained therein, any reference in a Rule or Schedule to a paragraph shall be construed as a reference to a paragraph of that Rule or Schedule and any reference in a paragraph to a sub-paragraph shall be construed as a reference to a sub-paragraph of that paragraph.

(4) The Interpretation Act 1889(c) shall apply for the interpretation of these Rules as it applies for the interpretation of an Act of Parliament.

3.—(1) Employment on duties connected with the provision of fire services, otherwise than as a member of a fire brigade, which is treated for the purposes of the Firemen's Pension Scheme as employment as a regular fireman shall be so treated for the purposes of these Rules.

(2) In relation to such employment as is mentioned in paragraph (1) any reference in these Rules to the fire authority shall be construed in like manner as such a reference in the Firemen's Pension Scheme, that is to say, as a reference to the Secretary of State.

PART II

PAYMENT OF TRANSFER VALUES BY FIRE AUTHORITIES

4.—(1) These Rules shall apply in the case of a person who—

(a) retires, or subject to paragraph (2) has retired, from service as a regular fireman without a transfer value becoming payable in his case otherwise than under these Rules;

(b) either was not entitled to a pension under the Firemen's Pension Scheme on so retiring or, if so entitled, has not received any payments in respect of the pension;

(a) 1948 c. 24.
(c) 1889 c. 63.
(b) 1951 c. 27.

(c) enters or has entered specified service (that is to say, such service or employment as is mentioned in Schedule 1) within 12 months of so retiring or within such longer period as may be agreed in the circumstances of his case between the fire authority and the appropriate authority;

(d) within 6 months of 1st May 1972 or 3 months of his entering the specified service, whichever is the later, or within such longer period as may be agreed as aforesaid in the circumstances of his case, notifies the fire authority that he desires these Rules to apply in his case, where, in the specified service he is, or subject to the payment of a transfer value, would be, entitled to reckon service for superannuation purposes by virtue of his service as a regular fireman.

(2) Where a person who retired from service as a regular fireman before 1st May 1972 enters, or before that date has entered, the specified service, these Rules shall apply in his case only with the consent (given at his request) of both the fire authority and the appropriate authority.

5.—(1) Subject to paragraph (2), in respect of a person to whom these Rules apply the fire authority shall pay to the appropriate authority a transfer value calculated in accordance with Schedule 2.

(2) Where the person concerned is subject to any superannuation arrangements specified in the second column of the Table in Schedule 1 but is not employed by the body specified opposite thereto in the first column of that Table, the fire authority shall not be required to, but may, pay a transfer value as aforesaid.

R. Maudling,
One of Her Majesty's Principal
Secretaries of State.

Home Office,
Whitehall.
27th March 1972.

SCHEDULE 1

Specified Service and Appropriate Authorities

1. In these Rules the expressions "specified service" and, in relation thereto, "the appropriate authority" have the meanings hereby respectively assigned to them.

2. Any reference to specified service includes a reference to service as a regular policeman within the meaning of the Police Pensions Regulations and, in relation thereto, "the appropriate authority" means the authority which, for the purposes of those Regulations, is the police authority in relation to the person concerned on the day that these Rules become applicable to him.

3. Any reference to specified service includes a reference to service as a regular policeman within the meaning of the Isle of Man Police Pensions Regulations and, in relation thereto, "the appropriate authority" means the Government of the Isle of Man.

4. Subject as aforesaid, any reference to specified service is a reference to service or employment in which a person is subject to any superannuation arrangements specified in the second column of the following Table (whether or not the person is employed by the body specified in the first column) and, in relation thereto, "the appropriate authority" means the persons having the general management of the arrangements in question.

TABLE

Employing body	Superannuation arrangements
Agricultural Research Council	Industrial Superannuation Scheme
„	Agricultural Research Council Superannuation Scheme 1951
Area Electricity Board	British Electricity Authority Superannuation (Protected Persons) Scheme
„	Electricity Board Superannuation (Protected Persons) Scheme
„	Electricity Supply (Manual Workers) Superannuation Scheme
„	Electricity Supply (Staff) Superannuation Scheme
Area Gas Board	Area Gas Board Protected Persons Superannuation Scheme
„	Area Gas Board Staff Pension Scheme
British Airports Authority	The British Airports Authority Superannuation Scheme
British Broadcasting Corporation	The B.B.C. New Pension Scheme
British Council	British Council Superannuation Scheme
British European Airways Corporation	The Airways Corporations Joint Pension Scheme for General Staff members
British Overseas Airways Corporation	The Airways Corporations Joint Pension Scheme for General Staff members
British Waterways Board	Cheshire County Council Superannuation Fund—Divided
„	Grand Union Canal Company Superannuation Fund
„	Nottingham Corporation Superannuation Fund—Divided
„	Scheme embodied in section 23 of and Schedule 4 to the Regent Canal and Dock Company (Grand Junction Canal Purchase) Act 1928(a)

(a) 1928 c. xcviii.

Employing body	Superannuation arrangements
British Waterways Board (*continued*)	Scheme embodied in the Superannuation Act 1965(a) (as applied to former staff of the Lee Conservancy Board)
Central Electricity Generating Board	British Electricity Authority Superannuation (Protected Persons) Scheme
,,	Electricity Board Superannuation (Protected Persons) Scheme
,,	Electricity Supply (Manual Workers) Superannuation Scheme
,,	Electricity Supply (Staff) Superannuation Scheme
Commonwealth War Graves Commission	The Commonwealth War Graves Commission Superannuation Scheme (1952)
Corporation of Trinity House	Trinity House Service Superannuation Scheme
Crown Agents for Oversea Governments and Administrations	Crown Agents' Pension Scheme
Crown Estate Commissioners	Crown Estate Commissioners Superannuation Scheme
Development Commission	The Development Commission Superannuation Scheme 1940
Electricity Council	British Electricity Authority Superannuation (Protected Persons) Scheme
,,	Electricity Board Superannuation (Protected Persons) Scheme
,,	Electricity Supply (Manual Workers) Superannuation Scheme
,,	Electricity Supply (Staff) Superannuation Scheme
Forestry Commission	The Forestry Commission Superannuation Scheme
Gas Council	Gas Council Staff Pension Scheme
General Lighthouse Authority	General Lighthouse Fund Superannuation Scheme
Horserace Betting Levy Board	Horserace Betting Levy Board Pension Schemes A and B
Independent Television Authority	The Independent Television Authority Staff Superannuation Fund and Staff Life Assurance Scheme
Industrial Training Boards	Industrial Training Boards Pension Fund
Metropolitan Water Board	Metropolitan Water Board Superannuation and Provident Fund Scheme
National Coal Board	National Coal Board Staff Superannuation Scheme

(a) 1965 c. 74.

Employing body	Superannuation arrangements
National Industrial Fuel Efficiency Service	National Industrial Fuel Efficiency Service Superannuation Scheme
National Institute of Agricultural Botany	Industrial Superannuation Scheme
Natural Environment Research Council	Natural Environment Research Council Superannuation Arrangements
North of Scotland Hydro-Electric Board	Hydroboard Superannuation Fund
Port of London Authority	Port of London Authority Pension Fund
Post Office	Post Office Staff Superannuation Scheme
Scottish Agricultural Colleges and Research Institutes	Industrial Superannuation Scheme
Science Research Council	Science Research Council Superannuation Scheme
,,	Principal Non-Industrial Superannuation Scheme of the United Kingdom Atomic Energy Authority
,,	The United Kingdom Atomic Energy Authority's Industrial Superannuation Scheme
South of Scotland Electricity Board	The South of Scotland Electricity Board's Superannuation Scheme
United Kingdom Atomic Energy Authority	The Principal Non-Industrial Superannuation Scheme of the United Kingdom Atomic Energy Authority
,,	Protected Persons Superannuation Scheme of the United Kingdom Atomic Energy Authority
,,	United Kingdom Atomic Energy Authority's Industrial Superannuation Scheme

SCHEDULE 2

TRANSFER VALUES

1.—(1) The sum to be paid by a fire authority under Rule 5 shall be calculated in accordance with this paragraph by reference to the person's adjusted period of service, that is to say, by reference to the period of pensionable service he was entitled to reckon immediately before he ceased to be employed by the said authority adjusted as follows:—

(a) in calculating his adjusted period of service any period by which his pensionable service exceeded 30 years shall be ignored;

(b) where the specified service is such as is mentioned in paragraph 2 or 3 of Schedule 1, any period by which his pensionable service exceeded 20 years but did not exceed 30 years shall be counted twice;

(c) where the specified service is such as is mentioned in paragraph 4 of Schedule 1, the period of his pensionable service not exceeding 30 years shall be increased by a third.

(2) The amounts shown in the second and third columns of Table A or B (as may be appropriate) in relation to an age which corresponds with that of the person concerned—

    (*a*) where he retired from service as a regular fireman more than 12 months before 1st May 1972, on that date, or

    (*b*) in any other case—

        (i) on retirement from service as a regular fireman where within 12 months he entered the specified service as mentioned in Rule 4(1)(*c*), or

        (ii) on entering the specified service where the 12 month time limit mentioned in Rule 4(1)(*c*) is extended thereunder,

are to be multiplied, respectively, by the number of completed years and completed months aggregating less than a year comprised in the person's adjusted period of service.

(3) The sum of the products aforesaid is an amount appropriate in respect of £100 of annual pensionable pay.

(4) The total sum referred to in sub-paragraph (1) is to be calculated proportionately by reference to the annual value of the person's pensionable pay immediately before he retired from service as a regular fireman so, however, that the sum shall not be recalculated on account of any retrospective increase in pay granted after the transfer value has been paid.

(5) The reference in sub-paragraph (2) to Table A or Table B (as may be appropriate) is a reference to—

    (*a*) the following Table A, where the specified service is such as is mentioned in paragraph 2 or 3 of Schedule 1;

    (*b*) the following Table B, where the specified service is such as is mentioned in paragraph 4 of Schedule 1.

TABLE A

TRANSFERS TO POLICE SERVICE

Age in years	Amount for £100 of annual pensionable pay in respect of each completed	
	Year	Month
	£	£
Under 24	19·70	1·65
24	19·70	1·65
25	19·70	1·65
26	19·70	1·65
27	19·70	1·65
28	19·70	1·65
29	19·70	1·65
30	19·75	1·65
31	19·85	1·65
32	20·05	1·65
33	20·30	1·70
34	20·60	1·70
35	21·00	1·75
36	21·45	1·80
37	21·95	1·85
38	22·45	1·85
39	22·95	1·90
40	23·45	1·95
41	23·90	2·00
42	24·35	2·05
43	24·80	2·05
44	25·25	2·10
45	25·65	2·15
46	25·95	2·15
47	26·20	2·20
48	26·40	2·20
49	26·55	2·20
50	26·65	2·20
51	26·70	2·20
52	26·75	2·25
53	26·80	2·25
54	26·85	2·25
55 or more	26·90	2·25

TABLE B

TRANSFERS TO OTHER SERVICE

Age in years				Amount for £100 of annual pensionable pay in respect of each completed	
				Year	Month
				£	£
Under 35	...	...	...	9·00	0·75
35	...	...	...	9·00	0·75
36	...	...	...	9·05	0·75
37	...	...	...	9·10	0·75
38	...	...	...	9·15	0·75
39	...	...	...	9·30	0·75
40	...	...	...	9·45	0·80
41	...	...	...	9·60	0·80
42	...	...	...	9·80	0·80
43	...	...	...	10·00	0·85
44	...	...	...	10·20	0·85
45	...	...	...	10·45	0·85
46	...	...	...	10·65	0·90
47	...	...	...	10·85	0·90
48	...	...	...	11·10	0·90
49	...	...	...	11·35	0·95
50	...	...	...	11·60	0·95
51	...	...	...	11·85	1·00
52	...	...	...	12·15	1·00
53	...	...	...	12·45	1·05
54	...	...	...	12·80	1·05
55	...	...	...	13·20	1·10
56	...	...	...	13·65	1·15
57	...	...	...	14·10	1·15
58	...	...	...	14·55	1·20
59	...	...	...	15·05	1·25

2. The sum to be paid by a fire authority under Rule 5, calculated in accordance with the preceding provisions of this Part of this Schedule, shall be reduced by a sum, subject to paragraph 4(1), equal to the balance outstanding, immediately before the person concerned retired from service as a regular fireman, of any sum he had undertaken to pay by regular instalments in accordance with the relevant provisions of the Firemen's Pension Scheme or so much thereof as has not been deducted from an award payable to him.

3. The sum to be paid by a fire authority under Rule 5, calculated in accordance with the preceding provisions of this Schedule, shall be reduced by a sum, subject to paragraph 4, equal to that of any award paid to him on retirement from service as a regular fireman by way of gratuity or return of aggregate contributions.

4.—(1) For the purposes of paragraphs 2 and 3 the sum which a person had undertaken to pay by regular instalments in accordance with the relevant provisions of the Firemen's Pension Scheme and the sum paid by way of gratuity or return of aggregate contributions to a person who paid pension contributions under that Scheme at a rate related to 6% of his pensionable pay shall, respectively, be deemed to be the sum which he would have undertaken so to pay and the sum which would have been so paid had he paid pension contributions at a rate related to 5% of his pensionable pay.

(2) Where the time limit mentioned in Rule 4(1)(c) is extended thereunder the amount to be deducted under paragraph 3 may be increased by an amount equal to compound

interest thereon at the rate of 3% per annum, with half-yearly rests, in respect of the period beginning with whichever is the later of the two following dates, that is to say—

(a) the first anniversary of the date on which the person ceased to be employed by the fire authority, or

(b) the date on which he was paid his award,

and ending with the date on which he notifies the fire authority as mentioned in Rule 4(1)(d):

Provided that the increase in the amount to be deducted under paragraph 3 shall not exceed a half of the difference between the transfer value which would be payable but for this sub-paragraph and that which would be so payable if paragraph 1(2)(b)(i) applied.

5.—(1) Except in the case of a person who paid pension contributions as a regular fireman at a rate of 1p a week less than the appropriate percentage of his pensionable pay, the sum to be paid by a fire authority under Rule 5, calculated in accordance with the preceding provisions of this Part of this Schedule, shall be reduced by an amount calculated in accordance with paragraph 7.

(2) In relation to a period before 15th February 1971 the reference in this paragraph to 1p a week shall be construed as a reference to 2d. a week.

6.—(1) In the case of a person who was entitled to reckon pensionable service, immediately before his retirement from service as a regular fireman, by virtue of a participating period of relevant employment, the sum to be paid by a fire authority under Rule 5, calculated in accordance with the preceding provisions of this Part of this Schedule, shall be reduced by an amount calculated in accordance with paragraph 7.

(2) In this paragraph the expression "participating period of relevant employment" has the meaning assigned to it by the Firemen's Pension Scheme but, for the purposes of sub-paragraph (1) and for the purposes of the provision applied by paragraph 7(1)(b), a period shall be treated as a participating period of relevant employment notwithstanding that a payment in lieu of contributions (within the meaning of the National Insurance Act 1965 (a)) only fell to be made after the person retired from service as a regular fireman.

7.—(1) The amount specified in the second column of the following Table C in relation to an age which corresponds with that of the person concerned, at the time mentioned in paragraph 1(2), is the amount of the reduction referred to in paragraph 5, or as the case may be, paragraph 6 in respect of each £1 by which the annual value of his pension would be reduced—

(a) under paragraph 1 of Part III of Schedule 1 to the Firemen's Pension Scheme 1971(b) or under the corresponding provision of the Firemen's Pension Scheme for the time being in force, in a case in which paragraph 5 applies;

(b) under paragraphs 2 and 3 of the said Part III or under such corresponding provisions, in a case in which paragraph 6 applies,

in respect of any period beyond the age of 65 years, if he had on retirement from service as a regular fireman been entitled to a pension.

(2) The total reduction is to be calculated proportionately by reference to the amount by which the annual value of such a pension would be so reduced.

(a) 1965 c. 51.   (b) *See* S.I. 1971/145 (1971 I, p. 320).

TABLE C

Age in years				Amount of the reduction in respect of each £1 by which the annual value of a pension would be reduced
				£
Under 24	...	...	...	1·80
24	...	...	...	1·95
25	...	...	...	2·10
26	...	...	...	2·25
27	...	...	...	2·35
28	...	...	...	2·45
29	...	...	...	2·60
30	...	...	...	2·70
31	...	...	...	2·80
32	...	...	...	2·95
33	...	...	...	3·05
34	...	...	...	3·20
35	...	...	...	3·30
36	...	...	...	3·45
37	...	...	...	3·60
38	...	...	...	3·70
39	...	...	...	3·85
40	...	...	...	4·00
41	...	...	...	4·15
42	...	...	...	4·30
43	...	...	...	4·45
44	...	...	...	4·60
45	...	...	...	4·75
46	...	...	...	4·95
47	...	...	...	5·15
48	...	...	...	5·35
49	...	...	...	5·55
50	...	...	...	5·75
51	...	...	...	5·95
52	...	...	...	6·20
53	...	...	...	6·45
54	...	...	...	6·70
55	...	...	...	7·00
56	...	...	...	7·30
57	...	...	...	7·60
58	...	...	...	7·95
59	...	...	...	8·30
60	...	...	...	8·70
61	...	...	...	9·15
62	...	...	...	9·60
63	...	...	...	10·10
64	...	...	...	10·60

EXPLANATORY NOTE

(This Note is not part of the Rules.)

These Rules provide for the payment of transfer values by fire authorities in the case of persons with mixed service who, after being members of fire brigades, have been in police service or such other service as is mentioned in Schedule 1 in which they are (or subject to such payment would be) entitled to reckon their previous fire service for superannuation purposes.

STATUTORY INSTRUMENTS

1972 No. 522

FIRE SERVICES

The Firemen's Pension Scheme (Amendment) Order 1972

Made - - - -	*28th March* 1972
Laid before Parliament	*10th April* 1972
Coming into Operation	*1st May* 1972

In exercise of the powers conferred on me by section 26 of the Fire Services Act 1947**(a)** (read with Article 2(1) of the Minister for the Civil Service Order 1968**(b)**), as amended and extended by section 42 of the Reserve and Auxiliary Forces (Protection of Civil Interests) Act 1951**(c)** and sections 12 and 16(3) of the Superannuation Act 1972**(d),** I hereby, with the approval of the Minister for the Civil Service and after consultation with the Central Fire Brigades Advisory Council and the Scottish Central Fire Brigades Advisory Council, make the following Order:—

1. This Order may be cited as the Firemen's Pension Scheme (Amendment) Order 1972 and shall come into operation on 1st May 1972 and have effect as from 1st April 1972.

2. In this Order any reference to the principal Scheme is a reference to the Firemen's Pension Scheme 1971**(e)**, as amended **(f)**.

3.—(1) For Article 48(1) of the principal Scheme (previous service other than fire or local government service) there shall be substituted the provision set out in Appendix 1 hereto.

(2) The conditions specified in the said Article 48(1) as set out as aforesaid, or in sub-paragraph (*c*) or in sub-paragraph (*d*) thereof, shall be deemed to be satisfied if the conditions specified in the said Article 48(1) as in force immediately before 1st May 1972, or, as the case may be, in sub-paragraph (*b*) or (*c*) thereof, had been satisfied before that date.

4. The provisions of Articles 20, 37 and 38 of the principal Scheme (commutation and allocation of pensions) shall apply in relation to an ill-health pension payable to a part-time fireman under Article 74 thereof and, accordingly, in paragraph (2) of the said Article 74 after the number "19" there shall be inserted the numbers "20, 37, 38".

(a) 1947 c. 41.   **(b)** S.I. 1968/1656 (1968 III, p. 4485).
(c) 1951 c. 65.   **(d)** 1972 c. 11.
(e) *See* S.I. 1971/145 (1971 I, p. 320).
(f) The amending instruments are not relevant to the subject matter of this Order.

5. After Schedule 6 to the principal Scheme there shall be inserted the Schedule set out in Appendix 2 hereto.

R. Maudling,
One of Her Majesty's Principal
27th March 1972.   Secretaries of State.

Approval of the Minister for the Civil Service given under his Official Seal on 28th March 1972.

(L.S.)   *K. H. McNeill,*
Authorised by the
Minister for the Civil Service.

APPENDIX 1

PROVISION SUBSTITUTED FOR ARTICLE 48(1) OF THE PRINCIPAL SCHEME

48.—(1) This Article shall apply in the case of a regular fireman—

(*a*) who before becoming a regular fireman was in such service or employment as is mentioned in Schedule 6A (hereafter referred to in this Article as "former service") by virtue of which he was subject to superannuation arrangements;

(*b*) who last became a regular fireman within 12 months of the termination of his former service or within such longer period as may be agreed, in the circumstances of his case, between the fire authority and the authority specified in Schedule 6A in relation to his former service;

(*c*) in respect of whom such a transfer value relating to his former service as is mentioned in Schedule 6A is paid to the fire authority;

(*d*) who, within 3 months of his becoming a regular fireman or (subject to paragraph 2 of Part I of Schedule 6A) within 6 months of the date specified in Schedule 6A in relation to his former service, whichever is the later, or within such longer period as the fire authority may allow in his case, undertakes to pay in accordance with Schedule 5—

(i) a sum equal to the balance of any liability outstanding immediately before the termination of his former service in respect of payments or contributions he was then making as a condition of reckoning past service as contributing service or otherwise for the purposes of the said superannuation arrangements, being service of which account has been taken in the calculation of the said transfer value, together with

(ii) a sum equal to the amount, if any, by which the said transfer value falls to be reduced on account of any gratuity or award by way of return of contributions made under the said arrangements on the termination of his former service.

APPENDIX 2

SCHEDULE TO BE INSERTED IN THE PRINCIPAL SCHEME

SCHEDULE 6A   Article 48

PART I

CIVIL SERVICE, METROPOLITAN CIVIL STAFFS, EDUCATION, HEALTH, POLICE AND BELFAST FIRE SERVICE

1. This Part shall apply in relation to service or employment—

(*a*) as an established civil servant,

(*b*) in the metropolitan civil staffs within the meaning of section 15 of the Superannuation (Miscellaneous Provisions) Act 1967**(a)**,

(*c*) such as is mentioned in section 2(2)(*e*) and (*ee*) of the Superannuation (Miscellaneous Provisions) Act 1948**(b)** (education service),

(*d*) in respect of which awards may be made under regulations for the time being in force under section 67 of the National Health Service Act 1946**(c)** or section 66 of the National Health Service (Scotland) Act 1947**(d)**,

(*e*) as a regular policeman within the meaning of the regulations for the time being in force under section 1 of the Police Pensions Act 1948**(e)**, (hereinafter referred to as the Police Pensions Regulations), or

(*f*) in the Belfast Fire Force.

2. In relation to the said service or employment Article 48(1)(*d*) shall have effect as if the words "or (subject to paragraph 2 of Part I of Schedule 6A) within 6 months of the date specified in Schedule 6A in relation to his former service, whichever is the later" were omitted.

3. In relation to the said service or employment the transfer value for the purposes of Article 48 shall be one payable under—

(*a*) rules made under sections 2 and 15 of the Superannuation (Miscellaneous Provisions) Act 1948;

(*b*) such regulations as are mentioned in paragraph 1(*d*);

(*c*) the Police Pensions Regulations, or

(*d*) the Scheme for the time being in force under section 13 of the Fire Services (Amendment) Act (Northern Ireland) 1950**(f)**.

4. The specified authority for the purposes of Article 48 shall be—

(*a*) in relation to service or employment as an established civil servant, the Minister for the Civil Service;

(*b*) in relation to service as a regular policeman, the police authority within the meaning of the Police Pensions Regulations;

(*c*) in relation to service in the Belfast Fire Force, the Corporation of the city of Belfast;

(*d*) in relation to any other service or employment, the Secretary of State.

Part II

Other Service or Employment

1. This Part shall apply in relation to such service or employment as is mentioned in paragraphs 3 and 4 of Schedule 1 to the Superannuation (Fire and Specified Services) Interchange Rules 1972**(g)**.

2.—(1) Subject to sub-paragraph (2), in relation to any such service or employment the specified date for the purposes of Article 48 and of paragraph 3(2)(*b*) shall be 1st May 1972.

(2) Where in relation to a particular service or employment no provisions are in operation on 1st May 1972 for the payment of a transfer value to the fire authority, as mentioned in Article 48(1)(*c*), then in relation thereto the specified date for the purposes aforesaid shall be the date on which such provisions first thereafter come into operation.

(a) 1967 c. 28.   **(b)** 1948 c. 33.
(c) 1946 c. 81.   **(d)** 1947 c. 27.
(e) 1948 c. 24.   **(f)** 1950 c. 4 (N.I.).
(g) S.I. 1972/521 (1972 I, p. 1786).

3.—(1) In relation to any such service or employment the transfer value for the purposes of Article 48 shall, subject to sub-paragraphs (2) and (3), be one of the like amount, and calculated in the like manner, as the transfer value which would have been receivable under Part III of the Superannuation (Local Government and Approved Employment) Interchange Rules 1969(a) (as originally made) had the person concerned entered local government employment, within the meaning of those Rules, on the date on which he became a regular fireman and in circumstances in which the said Part III applied.

(2) For the purposes of sub-paragraph (1)—

(a) to the extent that the Table in Schedule 1 to the said Rules of 1969 does not contain entries relating to a particular service or employment, it shall be deemed to do so, and

(b) paragraph 6 of Schedule 1 to the said Rules of 1969 shall have effect as if any references therein to 18th August 1969 and 18th August 1968 were, respectively, references to the specified date and to a date 12 months before the specified date and sub-paragraphs (1)(a) and (b) and (3) were omitted.

(3) In relation to service in which a person is subject to the Isle of Man Police Pensions Regulations, that is to say, the Regulations for the time being in operation under section 16 of the Police (Isle of Man) Act 1962 (an Act of Tynwald) the transfer value shall be one payable under those Regulations.

4. In relation to any such service or employment, the specified authority for the purposes of Article 48 shall be the persons having the general management of the superannuation arrangements to which he was subject in the service or employment in question.

EXPLANATORY NOTE

(This Note is not part of the Order.)

This Order amends the Firemen's Pension Scheme 1971 with effect from 1st April 1972 (retrospective effect is authorised by sections 12 and 16 of the Superannuation Act 1972).

Articles 3 and 5 extend the provisions of the Scheme relating to the reckoning of previous service, where a transfer value in respect of the previous service is paid to the fire authority. The provisions, as extended, apply where the previous service was in the civil service, as a member of the metropolitan police civil staffs or of a police force, in the education or health services, in the Belfast Fire Force or in such other service or employment as is mentioned in paragraphs 3 and 4 of Schedule 1 to the Superannuation (Fire and Specified Services) Interchange Rules 1972.

Article 4 provides that the provisions of the Scheme relating to the commutation or allocation of a pension shall apply to an ill-health pension payable to a part-time fireman.

(a) S.I. 1969/997 (1969 II, p. 2906).

STATUTORY INSTRUMENTS

1972 No. 527 (S. 36)

PENSIONS

The Superannuation (Teaching and Police) Interchange (Scotland) Rules 1972

Made - - - -	*23rd March* 1972
Laid before Parliament	*7th April* 1972
Coming into Operation	*1st May* 1972

ARRANGEMENT OF RULES

PART I

GENERAL

PART II

TRANSFER FROM TEACHING SERVICE TO POLICE SERVICE

PART III

TRANSFER FROM POLICE SERVICE TO TEACHING SERVICE

In exercise of the powers conferred upon me by sections 2 and 15 of the Superannuation (Miscellaneous Provisions) Act 1948(a), as amended by section 11 of the Superannuation (Miscellaneous Provisions) Act 1967(b) and of all other powers enabling me in that behalf, and with the consent of the Minister for the Civil Service, I hereby make the following rules:—

PART I

GENERAL

Citation and Commencement

1. These rules may be cited as the Superannuation (Teaching and Police) Interchange (Scotland) Rules 1972 and shall come into operation on 1st May 1972.

(a) 1948 c. 33.　　　　　　　　(b) 1967 c. 28.

Interpretation

2.—(1) In these rules, unless the context otherwise requires—

" the Act of 1948 " means the Superannuation (Miscellaneous Provisions) Act 1948;

" national service " means, in relation to any person, compulsory national service and service which is relevant service within the meaning of the Reserve and Auxiliary Forces (Protection of Civil Interests) Act 1951(a) and any similar service immediately following relevant service entered into with the consent of the body or person by whom he was last employed before undertaking the service;

" operative date " means the date of the coming into operation of these rules;

" pension " has the meaning assigned to it by the Police Pensions Act of 1948(b);

" police authority " means—

   (a) in relation to a person who has become or becomes a policeman after ceasing to be employed in teaching service, the authority which on the day on which these rules become applicable to him is for the purposes of the Police Pensions Regulations the police authority in relation to him; and

   (b) in relation to a person who has become or becomes employed in teaching service after ceasing to be a policeman, the authority which last was or is treated for the purposes of the Police Pensions Regulations as the police authority in relation to him;

" policeman " means a regular policeman within the meaning of the Police Pensions Regulations;

" Police Pensions Regulations " means the Police Pensions Regulations 1971(c);

" prescribed period " has the meaning assigned to it by rule 3;

" reckonable service " means reckonable service within the meaning of the Teachers Superannuation (Scotland) Act 1968(d);

" the Teachers Regulations of 1957 " means the Teachers (Superannuation) (Scotland) Regulations 1957(e) as amended(f);

" the Teachers Regulations of 1969 " means the Teachers Superannuation (Scotland) Regulations 1969(g) as amended(h);

" the Teachers Schemes " means the Superannuation Scheme for Teachers in Scotland dated 5th June 1919(i) the Superannuation Scheme for Teachers (Scotland) 1926(j) and the Superannuation Scheme for Teachers (Scotland) 1952(k);

" teaching service " means—

   (a) reckonable service; and

(a) 1951 c. 65.   (b) 1948 c. 24.   (c) S.I. 1971/232 (1971 I, p. 700).
        (d) 1968 c. 12.   (e) S.I. 1957/356 (1957 I, p. 733).
(f) S.I. 1958/1595, 1963/2111, 1965/1166, 1966/1229, 1967/1736 (1958 I, p. 1077; 1963 III, p. 4685; 1965 II, p. 3284; 1966 III, p. 3295; 1967 III, p. 4657).
        (g) S.I. 1969/77 (1969 I, p. 133).
        (h) S.I. 1969/659, 1971/1995 (1969 II, p. 1820; 1971 III, p. 5683).
(i) S.R. & O. 1919/1105 (1919 I, p. 688).   (j) S.R. & O. 1926/363 (1926 p. 449).
        (k) S.I. 1952/464 (1952 I, p. 873).

(b) service which for the purposes of the Teachers Regulations of 1969 is service as an organiser;

" the Transfer Value Regulations " means the Local Government Superannuation (Transfer Value) (Scotland) Regulations 1954(a);

" voluntary contributions " means—

(a) in relation to employment in teaching service, additional contributions being paid under regulation 31 of the Teachers Regulations of 1969 in respect of a period of previous employment within the meaning of those provisions and any other contributions being paid by virtue of other rules made under section 2 of the Act of 1948 as a condition of—

(i) making reckonable a period of service not otherwise reckonable;

(ii) increasing the length at which a period of service would otherwise be reckonable; or

(iii) service being increased by the addition thereto of a period; and

(b) in relation to service as a policeman, sums being paid in accordance with Schedule 5 to the Police Pensions Regulations.

(2) Other expressions which have meanings assigned to them by the Teachers Regulations of 1969 or the Police Pensions Regulations shall, unless the context otherwise requires, have the same respective meanings for the purposes of these rules.

(3) Any reference in these rules to any enactment, rules, regulations or other instrument or to provisions thereof shall, unless the context otherwise requires, be construed as a reference to such enactment, rules, regulations or other instrument or to those provisions as amended, modified, extended, applied or replaced by any subsequent enactment, rules, regulations or instrument.

(4) Any reference in these rules to a rule, Part or paragraph shall, unless the context otherwise requires, be construed as a reference to that rule or Part of these rules or to that paragraph of the rule in which the reference occurs, as the case may be.

(5) The Interpretation Act 1889(b) shall apply for the interpretation of these rules as it applies for the interpretation of an Act of Parliament.

Prescribed Period

3.—(1) For the purposes of these rules, subject as provided hereafter in this rule, the expression " prescribed period " shall mean a period of twelve months.

(2) The Secretary of State in the case of a person becoming employed in teaching service and the police authority in the case of a person becoming a policeman may, with the agreement of the other, in any particular case extend the period of twelve months specified in paragraph (1).

(3) In the case of a person who in his new employment is in teaching service—

(a) the period of twelve months specified in paragraph (1) shall be deemed not to expire until six months after the termination of national service in which he became engaged immediately after ceasing to be a policeman; and

(b) no account shall be taken of any period spent by him on a course of study or training undertaken after ceasing to be a policeman if—

(i) before so ceasing (or, if between so ceasing and undertaking the said course he was engaged in national service, before the

(a) S.I. 1954/1256 (1954 II, p. 1736).　　(b) 1889 c. 63.

termination of that service) he gave notice in writing to the police authority of his intention to undertake the said course; and

(ii) the Secretary of State is satisfied that by reason of his having undertaken the said course he is better fitted for employment in teaching service.

PART II

TRANSFER FROM TEACHING SERVICE TO POLICE SERVICE

Application

4. Except as provided hereafter, this Part shall apply to a person who—

(*a*) becomes, or before the operative date became, a policeman within the prescribed period after ceasing to be employed in teaching service;

(*b*) within three months after becoming a policeman or within six months after the operative date, whichever period shall last expire, or within such longer period as the police authority may with the agreement of the Secretary of State in any particular case allow, gives notice in writing to the police authority that he desires this Part to apply to him and furnishes that authority with particulars in writing of his teaching service and of any national service in which he was engaged after ceasing to be employed in teaching service; and

(*c*) pays to the police authority in accordance with regulation 55(1)(*e*) of the Police Pensions Regulations a sum equal to the amount, if any, by which the transfer value payable in respect of him under rule 6 falls to be reduced on account of any sum paid to him by way of repayment of contributions.

Excepted Cases

5. This Part shall not apply to a person who—

(*a*) has received payment of any benefit (other than repayment of contributions) under the Teachers Schemes, the Teachers Regulations of 1957 or the Teachers Regulations of 1969; or

(*b*) last ceased to be employed in teaching service before the operative date, unless—

(i) he is a policeman on the operative date or becomes a policeman after that date and within the prescribed period; and

(ii) the Secretary of State and the police authority agree that this Part shall apply to him.

Transfer Value

6.—(1) In respect of a person to whom this Part applies the Secretary of State shall pay to the police authority a transfer value of an amount calculated in accordance with the following provisions of this rule.

(2) Subject as provided hereafter in this rule, the amount of the transfer value shall be an amount equal to that which would have been payable under the Transfer Value Regulations if the person, at the date when he ceased to be employed in teaching service, had ceased to be a contributory employee under one local authority and had become such an employee under another local authority and had been entitled to reckon as contributing service his reckonable service and his service reckonable for the purposes of Part VII of the Teachers Regulations of 1969 at the length at which it is so reckonable.

(3) For the purposes of paragraph (2) service which is reckoned as contributing service shall be deemed to have been affected or modified in accordance

with regulations applicable to contributing service made under section 110 of the National Insurance Act 1965(a) in like manner and to the like extent, as nearly as may be, as it was affected or modified by other such regulations.

(4) In calculating the amount of a transfer value there shall be excluded—

(*a*) any period of war service within the meaning of the Education (Scotland) (War Service Superannuation) Act 1939(b) and of national service within the meaning of the Teachers Pensions (National Service) (Scotland) Rules 1952(c) in respect of which, at the time the transfer value is paid, the contributions remain unpaid; and

(*b*) any period in respect of which the person was immediately before ceasing to be employed in teaching service paying voluntary contributions and in respect of which, at the time the transfer value is paid, he has not elected to continue to pay such contributions.

(5) The amount of transfer value payable in respect of a person shall be calculated by reference to his age—

(*a*) on the operative date if, having ceased to be employed in teaching service more than twelve months before that date, he became a policeman before that date; or

(*b*) on the date on which he became a policeman if that date is on or after the operative date and more than twelve months after that on which he ceased to be employed in teaching service.

(6) In a case in which the prescribed period exceeds one year the amount of the transfer value payable in respect of any person shall be reduced by an amount equal to the compound interest calculated as in paragraph (7) provided on any sum (including any sum deducted therefrom by reason of liability to income tax arising on its payment) paid to him after he last ceased to be employed in teaching service by way of repayment of contributions (other than voluntary contributions or contributions made for the purpose of securing benefits for his widow, children and other dependants).

(7) For the purposes of paragraph (6)—

(*a*) compound interest shall be calculated on the sum therein mentioned at three per cent per annum with half-yearly rests from the day one year after that on which the person ceased to be employed in teaching service or from the day on which contributions were repaid to him, whichever shall be the later, to the day on which he gave notice to the police authority in accordance with rule 4(*b*); and

(*b*) if the amount of compound interest calculated as aforesaid exceeds a sum equal to one-half of the difference between the amount of the transfer value payable under this rule apart from paragraph (6) and the amount of the transfer value which would have been so payable if calculated by reference to the person's age on ceasing to be employed in teaching service, it shall be reduced to that sum.

Benefits under the Teachers Regulations of 1969

7.—(1) Subject to the provisions of Part III and of interchange rules no payment of any benefit shall be made under the Teachers Regulations of 1969 to or in respect of any person in respect of any service which is taken into account in calculating the amount of a transfer value under rule 6 other than a payment by way of return of voluntary contributions.

(2) In this rule " interchange rules " means rules made under section 2 of the Act of 1948 and includes provisions similar to those of such rules contained in any instrument made under any other Act.

(a) 1965 c. 51.   (b) 1939 c. 96.   (c) S.I. 1952/518 (1952 I, p. 928).

Part III

Transfer from Police Service to Teaching Service

Application

8. Except as provided hereafter, this Part shall apply to a person who—

(a) becomes, or before the operative date became, employed in teaching service within the prescribed period after ceasing to be a policeman;

(b) within three months after becoming employed in teaching service or within six months after the operative date, whichever period shall last expire, or within such longer period as the Secretary of State may with the agreement of the police authority in any particular case allow, gives notice in writing to the Secretary of State that he desires this Part to apply to him and furnishes the Secretary of State with particulars in writing of his service which is pensionable service for the purposes of the Police Pensions Regulations and of any national service in which he was engaged after ceasing to be a policeman;

(c) is a person in respect of whom the Secretary of State receives from the police authority a transfer value calculated in accordance with Schedule 9 to the Police Pensions Regulations;

(d) within three months after becoming employed in teaching service or within six months after the operative date, whichever period shall last expire, or within such longer period as the Secretary of State may in any particular case allow, pays to the Secretary of State a sum equal to the amount, if any, by which the said transfer value falls to be reduced under paragraph 5 of the said Schedule 9.

Excepted Cases

9. This Part shall not apply to a person who last ceased to be a policeman before the operative date unless he is employed on that date in teaching service or the Secretary of State agrees that this Part shall apply to him.

Reckoning of Service

10.—(1) Subject as in paragraph (2) and rule 11 provided, the pensionable service reckonable for the purposes of the Police Pensions Regulations by a person to whom this Part applies immediately before he ceased to be a policeman, increased by one-third, shall be reckoned as reckonable service.

(2) For the purposes of this rule pensionable service reckonable for the purposes of the Police Pensions Regulations shall not include service so reckonable by reason of the payment of voluntary contributions or an undertaking to pay such contributions.

Average Salary

11. For the purpose of calculating under section 4(3) of the Teachers Superannuation (Scotland) Act 1968 the average salary of a person to whom this Part applies whose teaching service after ceasing to be a policeman amounts to less than three years—

(a) such period immediately prior to his ceasing to be a policeman as, together with the period of teaching service, amounts to three years shall be reckoned as teaching service; and

(b) his salary during any period so reckoned shall be his pensionable pay within the meaning of the Police Pensions Regulations for that period.

Voluntary Contributions

12.—(1) A person to whom this Part applies may, within three months of becoming employed in teaching service or within such longer period as the Secretary of State may in any particular case allow, elect to continue to pay voluntary contributions being paid by him immediately before ceasing to be a policeman.

(2) In relation to a person who elects as aforesaid and thereafter pays to the Secretary of State any amounts outstanding in respect of such voluntary contributions at the time at which they would have been payable if he had remained a policeman rule 10 shall have effect as if paragraph (2) thereof were omitted.

(3) The provisions of regulations 31(5)(*b*), (6), (7) and (10) and 37 of the Teachers Regulations of 1969 shall apply to voluntary contributions payable under this rule as if they were additional contributions payable in respect of previous employment within the meaning of those Regulations.

(4) If a person does not elect as aforesaid or if voluntary contributions are repaid to him under regulation 37 of the Teachers Regulations of 1969 as applied by this rule—

(*a*) the period to which such contributions related shall be reckoned for the purposes of the Teachers Regulations of 1969 only to the extent, if any, to which it would have been so reckoned if no such contributions had been made in respect thereof; and

(*b*) the Secretary of State shall repay to the police authority the amount by which the transfer value paid in respect of him was under the Police Pensions Regulations enhanced by reason of the payment by him when a policeman of such contributions.

Commencement of Employment

13. For the purposes of regulation 40(1)(*a*)(ii) of the Teachers Regulations of 1969 the date on which a person to whom this Part applies became a policeman shall be deemed to be a date on which he became employed in teaching service.

Return of Contributions

14.—(1) Where a person to whom this Part applies ceases to be employed in teaching service or dies, then, to any sum to which he or his personal representatives shall be entitled under the Teachers Regulations of 1969 by way of repayment of contributions there shall be added—

(*a*) if pension contributions under the Police Pensions Regulations were related to either 5 per cent or 4·5 per cent of pensionable pay, a sum equal to the amount of the aggregate contributions within the meaning of those Regulations; or

(*b*) if pension contributions under the Police Pensions Regulations were related to 6·25 per cent of pensionable pay, a sum equal to the amount the aggregate contributions within the meaning of those regulations would have been had he paid pension contributions related to 5 per cent of pensionable pay.

(2) The sum to be added under paragraph (1) to that to which a person or his personal representatives shall be entitled shall be—

(*a*) reduced by a sum equal to any sum paid under regulation 37 of the Teachers Regulations of 1969 as applied by rule 12 by way of repayment of voluntary contributions made while a policeman; and

(*b*) increased by compound interest on the amount thereof after any such reduction as aforesaid.

(3) For the purposes of paragraph (2) compound interest shall be calculated in accordance with the provisions of Part IV of the Teachers Regulations of 1969 from the date on which the person became employed in teaching service.

Modification of Contributions and Benefits by reason of National Insurance

15.—(1) In relation to a person to whom this Part applies—

(*a*) the following paragraphs of Schedule 5 to the Teachers Regulations of 1969, that is to say—

paragraph 3 (which provides for the reduction of contributions),

paragraph 5 (which provides for the reduction of benefits by fixed annual amounts specified therein) and

paragraph 6 (which provides for the reduction of benefits in accordance with a table contained therein specifying ages at a given date and annual amounts)

shall not apply if any pension payable to him under the Police Pensions Regulations would not have been subject to any reduction by virtue of paragraph 1(2) of Part III of Schedule 2 to those Regulations;

(*b*) paragraphs 3 and 6 of the said Schedule 5 shall apply if any pension payable to him under the Police Pensions Regulations would have been subject to reduction under paragraph 1(3) of Part III of Schedule 2 to those Regulations; and

(*c*) paragraphs 3 and 5 of the said Schedule 5 shall apply in any other case.

(2) Where, by virtue of paragraph (1)(*b*), paragraph 6 of Schedule 5 to the Teachers Regulations of 1969 applies to a person the date of modification for the purposes of the latter paragraph shall be the date which was in relation to him the appropriate date within the meaning of paragraph 1(3) of Part III of Schedule 2 to the Police Pensions Regulations.

Gordon Campbell,
One of Her Majesty's Principal
Secretaries of State.

St. Andrew's House,
Edinburgh.
22nd March 1972.

Consent of the Minister for the Civil Service given under his Official Seal on 23rd March 1972.

K. H. McNeill,
Authorised by the Minister for
the Civil Service.

(L.S.)

EXPLANATORY NOTE

(This Note is not part of the Rules.)

These Rules relate to the superannuation of persons who transfer from pensionable teaching service in Scotland to pensionable service as a policeman, or vice versa. A policeman becoming a teacher is enabled, if a transfer value is paid to the Secretary of State, to aggregate his service as a policeman (increased by one-third) with his later service as a teacher so that he will receive a single superannuation allowance based on his total service. In the case of a teacher becoming a policeman provision is made for the payment of a transfer value by the Secretary of State to the appropriate police authority in order that a single pension may be paid under the Police Pensions Regulations 1971.

The Rules may have retrospective effect in certain cases under the express powers of, and subject to the safeguards required by, section 2(5) of the Superannuation (Miscellaneous Provisions) Act 1948.

STATUTORY INSTRUMENTS

1972 No. 528 (L.5)

SUPREME COURT OF JUDICATURE, ENGLAND

COUNTY COURTS

The Common Investment Funds (Amendment) Scheme 1972

Made - - -	*24th March* 1972
Laid before Parliament	*11th April* 1972
Coming into Operation	*2nd May* 1972

The Lord Chancellor, in exercise of the powers conferred on him by section 1 of the Administration of Justice Act 1965(**a**), hereby makes the following Scheme: —

1. This Scheme may be cited as the Common Investment Funds (Amendment) Scheme 1972 and shall come into operation on 2nd May 1972.

2. The Interpretation Act 1889(**b**) shall apply to the interpretation of this Scheme as it applies to the interpretation of an Act of Parliament.

3. The Common Investment Funds Scheme 1965(**c**) shall be amended as follows: —

after paragraph 10 of Schedule 1 there shall be added the following paragraph: —

"10A. The Public Trustee shall have power to borrow money in any currency and on such security as he thinks fit for the purpose of purchasing investments authorised by section 1(5) of the Administration of Justice Act 1965."

Dated 24th March 1972.

Hailsham of St. Marylebone, C.

EXPLANATORY NOTE

(This Note is not part of the Order.)

This Scheme amends the Common Investment Funds Scheme 1965 by empowering the Public Trustee to borrow money in any currency to enable him to purchase investments and, if foreign investments, without having to pay a premium for the currency.

(**a**) 1965 c. 2.　　　(**b**) 1889 c. 63.　　　(**c**) S.I. 1965/1467 (1965 II, p. 4303).

STATUTORY INSTRUMENTS

1972 No. 529 (L.6)

BANKRUPTCY, ENGLAND

The Bankruptcy (Amendment) Rules 1972

Made - - -	*22nd March* 1972
Laid before Parliament	*12th April* 1972
Coming into Operation	*3rd May* 1972

The Lord Chancellor, in exercise of the powers conferred on him by section 132 of the Bankruptcy Act 1914(**a**) and with the concurrence of the Secretary of State for Trade and Industry, hereby makes the following Rules: —

1.—(1) These Rules may be cited as the Bankruptcy (Amendment) Rules 1972 and shall come into operation on 3rd May 1972.

(2) The Interpretation Act 1889(**b**) shall apply to the interpretation of these Rules as it applies to the interpretation of an Act of Parliament.

(3) The amendments set out in these Rules shall be made to the Bankruptcy Rules 1952(**c**), as amended(**d**).

2. For Rule 21 there shall be substituted the following rule: —

"Transfer of proceedings by Judge or Registrar of High Court

21. The Judge of the High Court may order the proceedings in any matter under the Act to be transferred from a county court to the High Court; the Judge of the High Court or, where an application for transfer is made by the Official Receiver, a Registrar of the High Court may order the proceedings in any matter under the Act to be transferred from the High Court to a county court."

3.—(1) In paragraph (1) of Rule 70, for the figures "£5 13s 0d", "£6 6s 0d" and "2s 4d" there shall be substituted the figures "£7·05", "£7·85" and "16p" respectively.

(2) This rule shall apply in relation to payments made on or after the date on which these Rules come into operation for attendances and transcripts made on or after the 1st November 1971.

(**a**) 1914 c. 59.   (**b**) 1889 c. 63.
(**c**) S.I. 1952/2113 (1952 I, p. 213).
(**d**) The relevant amending instruments are S.I. 1961/317, 1965/1571, 1969/1162 (1961 I, p. 510; 1965 II, p. 4578; 1969 II, p. 3428).

4. Rule 87 shall be amended as follows:—

(*a*) In paragraph (1), for the words from "in the county court" to the end of the paragraph there shall be substituted the words "be effected by a bailiff of any county court, whether that court has jurisdiction in bankruptcy or not."

(*b*) Paragraph (2) shall be deleted.

Dated 15th March 1972.

Hailsham of St. Marylebone, C.

I concur,

Dated 22nd March 1972.

John Davies,
Secretary of State for
Trade and Industry.

EXPLANATORY NOTE
(*This Note is not part of the Rules.*)

These Rules amend the Bankruptcy Rules 1952. They—

(i) empower a Registrar of the High Court to order the transfer of High Court proceedings to a county court (Rule 2);

(ii) increase the fees payable to shorthand writers for attending the court and making transcripts (Rule 3); and

(iii) provide for the use of county court bailiffs as officers of the court to effect service of process in the High Court (Rule 4).

STATUTORY INSTRUMENTS

1972 No. 530

AGRICULTURE

The Price Stability of Imported Products (Rates of Levy) (Cereals) (No. 14) Order 1972

Made - - - - *29th March* 1972
Coming into Operation *1st April* 1972

The Minister of Agriculture, Fisheries and Food, in exercise of the powers conferred upon him by section 1(2), (4), (5), (6) and (7) of the Agriculture and Horticulture Act 1964(a) and of all other powers enabling him in that behalf, hereby makes the following order:—

1. This order may be cited as the Price Stability of Imported Products (Rates of Levy) (Cereals) (No. 14) Order 1972, and shall come into operation on 1st April 1972.

2.—(1) In this order—

" the Principal Order " means the Price Stability of Imported Products (Levy Arrangements) (Cereals) Order 1971(b), as amended by any subsequent order and if any such order is replaced by any subsequent order the expression shall be construed as a reference to such subsequent order;

AND other expressions have the same meaning as in the Principal Order.

(2) The Interpretation Act 1889(c) shall apply to the interpretation of this order as it applies to the interpretation of an Act of Parliament and as if this order and the orders hereby revoked were Acts of Parliament.

3. In accordance with and subject to the provisions of Part II of the Principal Order (which provides for the charging of levies on imports of certain specified commodities) the rate of levy for such imports into the United Kingdom of any specified commodity as are described in column 2 of the Schedule to this order in relation to a tariff heading indicated in column 1 of that Schedule shall be the rate set forth in relation thereto in column 3 of that Schedule.

4. The Price Stability of Imported Products (Rates of Levy) (Cereals) (No. 13) Order 1972(d) is hereby revoked.

In Witness whereof the Official Seal of the Minister of Agriculture, Fisheries and Food is hereunto affixed on 29th March 1972.

(L.S.)

T. R. M. Sewell,
Assistant Secretary.

(a) 1964 c. 28.   (b) S.I. 1971/631 (1971 I, p. 1660).   (c) 1889 c. 63.
(d) S.I. 1972/488 (1972 I, p. 1728).

SCHEDULE

1. Tariff Heading	2. Description of Imports	3. Rate of Levy
	Imports of:—	per ton £
10.01	Denatured wheat	4·50
	Wheat (other than denatured wheat)..	7·75
10.03	Barley other than barley having a potential diastatic activity of not less than 170 degrees	3·75
10.04	Oats	6·25
10.05	Maize (other than sweet corn on the cob)	5·00
10.07	Grain sorghum	3·50
11.01	Wheat flours not containing chalk and containing not more than 1 per cent. by weight of fibre at the prescribed standard moisture content	1·25
11.02	Cereal groats, meals, kibbled or cut cereals, rolled, flaked, crushed or bruised cereals and other processed cereals—	
	of barley	5·25
	of oats	8·75
	of maize	5·25

EXPLANATORY NOTE

(*This Note is not part of the Order.*)

This order, which comes into operation on 1st April 1972, supersedes the Price Stability of Imported Products (Rates of Levy) (Cereals) (No. 13) Order 1972.

It—

(a) reduces to £1·25 per ton the rate of levy to be charged on imports of wheat flours not containing chalk and containing not more than 1 per cent. by weight of fibre at the prescribed standard moisture content;

(b) increases the rate of levy to be charged on imports of—

    (i) wheat (other than denatured wheat) to £7·75 per ton;

    (ii) barley, other than barley having a potential diastatic activity of not less than 170 degrees to £3·75 per ton;

    (iii) oats, maize (other than sweet corn on the cob), grain sorghum and processed maize within tariff heading 11.02 to £6·25, £5·00, £3·50 and £5·25 per ton respectively, and

(c) reimposes unchanged the remaining rates of levy in force immediately before the commencement of the order.

STATUTORY INSTRUMENTS

1972 No. 531

MERCHANT SHIPPING

SAFETY

The Merchant Shipping (Pilot Ladders) (Amendment No. 2) Rules 1972

Made - - -	*29th March* 1972
Laid before Parliament	*11th April* 1972
Coming into Operation	*1st July* 1972

The Secretary of State, in exercise of his powers under section 427 of the Merchant Shipping Act 1894(**a**) as substituted by section 2 of the Merchant Shipping (Safety Convention) Act 1949(**b**) and amended by section 9 of the Merchant Shipping Act 1964(**c**) and of all other powers enabling him in that behalf, hereby makes the following Rules :—

1.—(1) These Rules may be cited as the Merchant Shipping (Pilot Ladders) (Amendment No. 2) Rules 1972 and shall come into operation on 1st July 1972.

(2) The Interpretation Act 1889(**d**) shall apply to the interpretation of these Rules as it applies to the interpretation of an Act of Parliament and as if these Rules and the Rules hereby revoked were Acts of Parliament.

(3) The Merchant Shipping (Pilot Ladders) (Amendment) Rules 1971(**e**) are hereby revoked.

2. The Merchant Shipping (Pilot Ladders) Rules 1965(**f**) as amended shall be amended as follows :—

(1) The following shall be substituted for Rule 4 :—

"**4.**—(1) Each pilot ladder shall be efficient for the purpose of enabling a pilot to embark and disembark safely and such ladder shall be used only by officials and other persons while a ship is arriving at or leaving a port and for the embarkation and disembarkation of pilots.

(**a**) 1894 c. 60. (**b**) 1949 c. 43.
(**c**) 1964 c. 47. (**d**) 1889 c. 63.
(**e**) S.I. 1971/724 (1971 II, p. 1970). (**f**) S.I. 1965/1046 (1965 I, p. 2536).

(2) Every such pilot ladder shall be so positioned and secured—

    (*a*) that it is clear of any possible discharges from the ship ;

    (*b*) that so far as reasonably practicable it is clear of the finer lines of the ship ;

    (*c*) that each step rests firmly against the ship's side ; and

    (*d*) that the pilot can gain safe and convenient access to the ship after climbing not less than 1·5 metres and not more than 9 metres.

(3) A single length of ladder shall be used capable of reaching the water from the point of access to the ship when the ship is in an unloaded condition and in normal trim with no list.

(4) Whenever the distance from the water to the point of access to the ship exceeds 9 metres, access from the pilot ladder to the ship shall be by means of an accommodation ladder or other equally safe and convenient means.

(5) (*a*) The steps of the pilot ladder shall—

    (i) be of ash, oak, elm, teak or other hard wood of equivalent strength, durability and buoyancy ;

    (ii) each be made in one piece free of knots ;

    (iii) have an efficient non-slip surface ;

    (iv) be not less than 480 millimetres long, 114 millimetres wide, and 25 millimetres in depth excluding any non-slip device or grooving ;

    (v) be equally spaced not less than 305 millimetres nor more than 380 millimetres apart ; and

    (vi) be secured in such a manner that they will remain horizontal.

    (*b*) (i) No pilot ladder shall have more than two replacement steps which are secured in position by a method different from that used in the original construction of the ladder : and any steps so secured shall be replaced as soon as reasonably practicable by steps secured in position by the method used in the original construction of the ladder.

    (ii) When any replacement step is secured to the side ropes of the ladder by means of grooves in the sides of the step, such grooves shall be in the longer sides of the step.

(6) The side ropes of the pilot ladder shall consist of two manilla ropes not less than 60 millimetres in circumference on each side. Each rope shall be left uncovered by any other material and shall be continuous with no joins below the top step.

(7) Two man-ropes of not less than 65 millimetres in circumference, properly secured to the ship, and a safety line shall be kept ready for use if required.

(8) Hard wood battens between 1800 and 2000 millimetres long shall be provided at such intervals as will prevent the pilot ladder from twisting, so however that the lowest batten shall not be lower than the fifth step from the bottom of the ladder and that the interval between any batten and the next shall not exceed 9 steps. Each batten shall be of ash, oak, elm, teak or other hard wood of equivalent strength and durability and shall be made in one piece free of knots.

(9) (*a*) Means shall be provided to ensure safe and convenient passage for the pilot on to, or into, and off the ship between the head of the pilot ladder, or of any accommodation ladder or other appliance provided pursuant to paragraph (4) of this Rule, and the ship's deck.

(*b*) Where such passage is by means of a gateway in the rails or bulwark, adequate hand-holds shall be provided.

(*c*) Where such passage is by means of a bulwark ladder, such ladder shall be securely hooked on to the bulwark rail or landing platform and two hand-hold stanchions shall be fitted at the point of boarding or leaving the ship not less than 700 millimetres or more than 800 millimetres apart. Each stanchion shall be rigidly secured to the ship's structure at or near its base and also at a higher point, shall be not less than 40 millimetres in diameter and shall extend not less than 1200 millimetres above the top of the bulwarks.

(10) A light shall be provided at night so that the pilot ladder overside and also the position where the pilot boards the ship shall be adequately lit. A lifebuoy equipped with a self-igniting light shall be kept ready for use at that position.

(11) Means shall be provided to enable the pilot ladder to be used in accordance with the requirements of this Rule on either side of the ship."

(2) In the Schedule, "Pier" shall be inserted after "Cleethorpes" in column 3 (Partially Smooth Water Areas) relating to the district of Goole in Column 1.

Anthony Grant,
Parliamentary Under Secretary of State,
Department of Trade and Industry.

29th March 1972.

EXPLANATORY NOTE

(This Note is not part of the Rules.)

These Rules amend the Merchant Shipping (Pilot Ladders) Rules 1965, which specify safety requirements for pilot ladders and for appliances designed to ensure safety in their use.

The principal changes made by these Rules are (1) additional requirements relating to the steps and ropes of pilot ladders and to the material of which battens are to be made, and (2) the introduction of new requirements for the securing of bulwark ladders and the fitting of stanchions, and for the provision of a lifebuoy at the position where pilots board the ship. Dimensions are also expressed in metric units.

STATUTORY INSTRUMENTS

1972 No. 532 (S.37)

PENSIONS

The Superannuation (Teaching and Northern Ireland Civil Service) Interchange (Scotland) Rules 1972

Made - - -	*23rd March* 1972
Laid before Parliament	*10th April* 1972
Coming into Operation	*1st May* 1972

In exercise of the powers conferred upon me by sections 2 and 15 of the Superannuation (Miscellaneous Provisions) Act 1948(**a**), as amended by section 11 of the Superannuation (Miscellaneous Provisions) Act 1967(**b**) and of all other powers enabling me in that behalf, and with the consent of the Minister for the Civil Service, I hereby make the following rules:—

PART I

GENERAL

Citation and Commencement

1. These rules may be cited as the Superannuation (Teaching and Northern Ireland Civil Service) Interchange (Scotland) Rules 1972 and shall come into operation on 1st May 1972.

Revocation

2.—(1) The Superannuation (Teaching and Northern Ireland Civil Service) Interchange (Scotland) Rules 1962(**c**) are hereby revoked:

Provided that the rules hereby revoked shall continue to apply in relation to any person who, before 1st February 1969, became employed in contributory service or as a civil servant within the meaning of those rules in like manner as they would have applied if these rules had not been made.

(2) Section 38(2) of the Interpretation Act 1889(**d**) (which relates to the effect of repeals) shall have effect in relation to the rules revoked by this rule as if they were an enactment repealed by an Act.

Interpretation

3.—(1) In these rules, unless the context otherwise requires—

"the Act of 1948" means the Superannuation (Miscellaneous Provisions) Act 1948;

"the Superannuation Acts" means the Superannuation Acts (Northern Ireland) 1967 and 1969(**e**);

(**a**) 1948 c. 33. (**b**) 1967 c. 28.
(**c**) S.I. 1962/864 (1962 I, p. 980). (**d**) 1889 c. 63.
(**e**) 1967 c. 24 (N.I.); 1969 c. 7 (N.I.).

"benefit" means any superannuation benefit payable to or in respect of any person;

"civil servant" means a person serving in an established capacity in the permanent civil service of Northern Ireland;

"contributing service" and "contributory employee" have the same respective meanings as in the Local Government Superannuation (Scotland) Acts 1937 to 1953(**a**);

"the Ministry" means the Ministry of Finance for Northern Ireland;

"national service" means, in relation to any person, service which is relevant service within the meaning of the Reserve and Auxiliary Forces (Protection of Civil Interests) Act 1951(**b**); and any similar service immediately following relevant service entered into with the consent of the Department in which he last served or of the body or person by whom he was last employed before undertaking the service;

"prescribed period" has the meaning assigned to it by rule 4;

"reckonable service" means reckonable service within the meaning of the Teachers Superannuation (Scotland) Act 1968(**c**);

"the Teachers Regulations of 1957" means the Teachers (Superannuation) (Scotland) Regulations 1957(**d**) as amended (**e**);

"the Teachers Regulations of 1969" means the Teachers Superannuation (Scotland) Regulations 1969(**f**) as amended (**g**);

"the Teachers Schemes" means the Superannuation Scheme for Teachers in Scotland dated 5th June 1919(**h**), the Superannuation Scheme for Teachers (Scotland) 1926(**i**) and the Superannuation Scheme for Teachers (Scotland) 1952(**j**);

"teaching service" means—

(*a*) reckonable service; and

(*b*) service which for the purposes of the Teachers Regulations of 1969 is service as an organiser;

"the Transfer Value Regulations" means the Local Government Superannuation (Transfer Value) (Scotland) Regulations 1954(**k**);

"voluntary contributions" means—

(*a*) in relation to employment in teaching service, additional contributions paid or being paid under regulation 31 of the Teachers Regulations of 1969 in respect of a period of previous employment and any other contributions being paid by virtue of other rules made under section 2 of the Act of 1948 as a condition of—

(i) making reckonable a period of service not otherwise reckonable;

(ii) increasing the length at which a period of service would be reckonable; or

(iii) service being increased by the addition thereto of a period; and

---

(**a**) 1937 c. 69; 1939 c. 18; 1953 c. 25.   (**b**) 1951 c. 65.
(**c**) 1968 c. 12.   (**d**) S.I. 1957/356 (1957 I, p. 733).
(**e**) S.I. 1958/1595, 1963/2111, 1965/1166, 1966/1229, 1967/1736 (1958 I, p. 1077; 1963 III, p. 4685; 1965 II, p. 3284; 1966 III, p. 3295; 1967 III, p. 4657).
(**f**) S.I. 1969/77 (1969 I, p. 133).
(**g**) S.I. 1969/659, 1971/1995 (1969 II, p. 1820; 1971 III, p. 5683).
(**h**) S.R. & O. 1919/1105 (1919 I, p. 688).
(**i**) S.R. & O. 1926/363 (1926, p. 449).
(**j**) S.I. 1952/464 (1952 I, p. 873).
(**k**) S.I. 1954/1256 (1954 II, p. 1736).

(*b*) in relation to service as a civil servant, payments being made to the Ministry in respect of any provision contained in rules made under section 33 of the Superannuation Act (Northern Ireland) 1967.

(2) Any reference in these rules to the provisions of any enactment, rules, regulations or other instrument shall, unless the context otherwise requires, be construed as a reference to those provisions as amended, modified, affected or re-enacted by any subsequent enactment, rules, regulations or instrument.

(3) References in these rules to a rule, Part or paragraph shall, unless the context otherwise requires, be construed as references to that rule or Part of these rules, or to that paragraph of the rule in which the reference occurs, as the case may be.

(4) The Interpretation Act 1889 shall apply for the interpretation of these rules as it applies for the interpretation of an Act of Parliament.

Prescribed Period

4.—(1) For the purposes of these rules, subject as provided hereafter in this rule, the expression "prescribed period" shall mean—

(*a*) in the case of a person who, immediately after ceasing to be employed in teaching service or to be a civil servant became engaged in national service, a period of six months after the date of termination of the national service; and

(*b*) in the case of any other person, a period of twelve months after the date on which he ceased to be employed in teaching service or to be a civil servant.

(2) The Secretary of State in the case of a person entering teaching service and the Ministry in the case of a person becoming a civil servant may, with the agreement of the other, in any particular case extend any period specified in paragraph (1).

(3) In reckoning the periods of six months and twelve months specified in paragraph (1) in the case of a person who in his new employment is in teaching service no account shall be taken of any period spent by him on a course of study or training after ceasing to be a civil servant if—

(*a*) his undertaking the said course was approved by the Ministry; and

(*b*) the Secretary of State is satisfied that by reason of his having undertaken the said course he is better fitted for the duties of his new employment.

PART II

TRANSFER FROM TEACHING SERVICE TO CIVIL SERVICE

Application

5.—(1) Except as provided in paragraph (3), this Part shall apply to a person who—

(*a*) on or after 1st February 1969 and within the prescribed period after ceasing to be employed in teaching service becomes or has become a civil servant; and

(*b*) within three months after becoming a civil servant or within such longer period as the Ministry with the agreement of the Secretary of State may in any particular case allow—

(i) notifies the Ministry in writing that he desires this Part to apply to him and furnishes the Ministry with particulars in writing of his teaching service; and

(ii) pays to the Secretary of State an amount determined in accordance with paragraph (2).

(2) The amount to be paid by a person to the Secretary of State under paragraph (1)(*b*)(ii) shall be the aggregate of—

(*a*) any sum paid to him after he last ceased to be employed in teaching service by way of return of contributions (other than voluntary contributions and contributions made or deemed to be made for the purpose of securing benefits for a widow, children or other dependants), together with any interest included therein;

(*b*) any sum deducted from such payment as aforesaid in respect of liability to income tax arising by reason of its payment; and

(*c*) compound interest on the sums specified in sub-paragraphs (*a*) and (*b*) of this rule calculated at the rate of $3\frac{1}{2}$ per cent per annum with yearly rests from the date of the payment to him to the date of the payment by him to the Secretary of State.

(3) This Part shall not apply to a person who has received payment of any benefit (other than repayment of contributions) under the Teachers Schemes, the Teachers Regulations of 1957 or the Teachers Regulations of 1969.

Transfer Value

6.—(1) In respect of a person to whom this Part applies the Secretary of State shall pay to the Ministry a transfer value of an amount calculated in accordance with the following provisions of this rule.

(2) Subject as provided hereafter in this rule the transfer value shall be an amount equal to the transfer value which would have been payable under the Transfer Value Regulations if the person, at the date when he ceased to be employed in teaching service, had ceased to be a contributory employee under one local authority and had become such an employee under another local authority and had been entitled to reckon as contributing service his reckonable service and his service reckonable for the purposes of Part VII of the Teachers Regulations of 1969 at the length at which it is so reckonable.

(3) For the purposes of paragraph (2) of this rule service which is reckoned as contributing service shall be deemed to have been affected or modified in accordance with regulations applicable to contributing service made under section 110 of the National Insurance Act 1965(**a**), or under any provision corresponding thereto contained in an enactment repealed by that Act, in like manner and to the like extent, as nearly as may be, as it was affected or modified by other such regulations.

(4) In calculating the amount of a transfer value there shall be excluded—

(*a*) any period of war service within the meaning of the Education (Scotland) (War Service Superannuation) Act 1939(**b**) and of national service within the meaning of the Teachers Pensions (National Service) (Scotland) Rules 1952(**c**) in respect of which, at the time the transfer value is paid, the contributions remain unpaid; and

---

(**a**) 1965 c. 51. (**b**) 1939 c. 96.
(**c**) S.I. 1952/518 (1952 I, p. 928).

(*b*) any period of previous employment and any period additional to actual service in respect of which the person was immediately before ceasing to be employed in teaching service paying voluntary contributions and in respect of which, at the time the transfer value is paid, contributions are not payable to the Ministry under rules made by the Ministry;

(5) The amount of the transfer value shall, in lieu of being reduced in accordance with the proviso to paragraph 2 of the First Schedule to the Transfer Value Regulations, be reduced by—

(*a*) an amount equal to any sum which remained to be paid by him on his ceasing to be employed in teaching service towards the discharge of a fixed sum as a condition of any period of service being reckoned for the purposes of the Teachers Regulations of 1969; and

(*b*) an amount equal to the capital value of any voluntary contributions which on his ceasing to be employed in teaching service remained to be paid by him in respect of any period not excluded from the calculation of the amount of the transfer value by paragraph (4)(*b*).

(6) In respect of a person who became a civil servant more than twelve months after ceasing to be employed in teaching service or more than six months after ceasing to be engaged in national service, the transfer value shall be calculated by reference to his age on the date on which he became a civil servant.

Benefits under Teachers Regulations

7. Subject to the provisions of Part III and any provisions similar thereto contained in other rules made under the Act of 1948, no payment of any benefit shall be made under the Teachers Regulations of 1969 to or in respect of any person in respect of any service which is taken into account in calculating the amount of a transfer value under rule 6.

PART III

TRANSFER FROM CIVIL SERVICE TO TEACHING SERVICE

Application

8.—(1) Except as provided in paragraph (2) of this rule, this Part shall apply to a person who—

(*a*) on or after 1st February 1969 and within the prescribed period after ceasing to be a civil servant becomes, or has become, employed in teaching service with the consent of the Department in which he was last employed as a civil servant;

(*b*) within three months after becoming employed in teaching service or within such longer period as the Secretary of State with the agreement of the Ministry may in any particular case allow, notifies the Secretary of State in writing that he desires this Part to apply to him and furnishes the Secretary of State with particulars in writing of his service as a civil servant; and

(*c*) is a person in respect of whom the Secretary of State receives from the Ministry a transfer value of an amount calculated in accordance with the provisions of rule 9.

(2) This Part shall not apply to a person who has received payment of any benefit under the Superannuation Acts.

Transfer Value

9.—(1) Subject as provided hereafter in this rule, the transfer value receivable by the Secretary of State from the Ministry in respect of a person to whom this Part applies shall be an amount equal to the transfer value which would have been payable under the Transfer Value Regulations if the person, at the date when he ceased to be a civil servant or ceased to be engaged in national service, as the case may be, had ceased to be a contributory employee under one local authority and had become such an employee under another local authority and had been entitled to reckon his service reckonable for the purposes of the Superannuation Acts as contributing service.

(2) For the purposes of paragraph (1), service reckonable for the purposes of the Superannuation Acts which is to be reckoned as contributing service shall be deemed to have been affected or modified in accordance with regulations applicable to contributing service made under section 110 of the National Insurance Act 1965, or under any provision corresponding thereto contained in an enactment repealed by that Act, in like manner and to the like extent, as nearly as may be, as it was affected or modified in accordance with regulations made under section 103 of the National Insurance Act (Northern Ireland) 1966(**a**), or under any provision corresponding thereto contained in an enactment repealed by that Act.

(3) In respect of a person who became employed in teaching service more than twelve months after ceasing to be a civil servant or more than six months after ceasing to be engaged in national service, the transfer value shall be calculated by reference to his age on the date on which he became employed in teaching service.

Reckoning of Service

10.—(1) In respect of a person to whom this Part applies there shall be reckoned as reckonable service—

> (*a*) the period of service which under rule 9 is reckoned as contributing service for the purpose of calculating the amount of the transfer value payable in respect of him; and

> (*b*) any period in respect of which he was, at the time he ceased to be a civil servant, in course of making payments as a condition of his service reckonable for the purposes of the Superannuation Acts being increased by its addition thereto if—

>> (i) within three months of becoming employed in teaching service or within such longer period as the Secretary of State may in any particular case allow he elects to pay to the Secretary of State sums equal to the aforesaid payments and thereafter pays such sums at the times at which they would have been payable if he had continued to be a civil servant; and

>> (ii) the transfer value paid in respect of him is calculated so as to include the liability of which the Ministry is relieved in respect of that period, reduced by the value of the payments he would have been liable to make if he had continued to be a civil servant.

(2) In relation to any period to which paragraph (1)(*b*) applies—

> (*a*) the provisions of regulations 31(5)(*b*), (6), (7) and (10) and 37 of the Teachers Regulations of 1969 shall apply to the sums payable to the

---

(**a**) 1966 c. 6 (N.I.).

Secretary of State under the said paragraph (1)(b) as if those sums were additional contributions payable in respect of previous employment within the meaning of those regulations; and

(b) if no election to pay those sums is made or if they are repaid under regulation 37 of the Teachers Regulations of 1969, the period shall be reckoned for the purposes of those regulations only to the extent, if any, to which it would have been so reckoned if no payments had been made in respect thereof.

(3) Any period of service of a person to whom this Part applies which under the Superannuation Acts was at the time he ceased to be a civil servant reckonable only for the purpose of calculating the amount of any benefit payable to or in respect of him or only for the purpose of determining whether he was entitled to any pension shall be reckoned only for the corresponding like purpose under the Teachers Regulations of 1969.

Return of Contributions

11.—(1) Where a person to whom this Part applies ceases to be employed in teaching service or dies, then, to any sum to which he or his personal representatives shall be entitled under the Teachers Regulations of 1969 by way of repayment of contributions there shall be added the following sums—

(a) a sum equal to the amount of any contributions paid by him in respect of service which by virtue of this Part is reckoned as reckonable service;

(b) a sum equal to the amount of any voluntary contributions paid by him before becoming employed in teaching service which have either not been returned to him or if returned, have been paid to the Secretary of State and have not subsequently been again returned; and

(c) compound interest on the foregoing sums calculated in accordance with paragraph (2).

(2) For the purposes of paragraph (1) compound interest shall be calculated—

(a) as respects the period ending immediately before the date on which the person became employed in teaching service, in the manner in which such interest, if any, would have been calculated if the occasion for making the calculation had occurred immediately before that date; and

(b) as respects the period beginning with that date, in accordance with the provisions of Part IV of the Teachers Regulations of 1969.

Commencement of Employment

12. For the purposes of regulation 40(1)(a)(ii) of the Teachers Regulations of 1969 the date on which a person to whom this Part applies became a civil servant shall be deemed to be a date on which he became employed in teaching service.

Modification of Contributions and Benefits by reason of National Insurance

13. In relation to a person to whom this Part applies—

(a) the following paragraphs of Schedule 5 to the Teachers Regulations of 1969, that is to say—

paragraph 3 (which provides for the reduction of contributions), paragraph 5 (which provides for the reduction of pensions by fixed annual amounts specified therein) and

paragraph 6 (which provides for the reduction of pensions by annual amounts ascertained by reference to a table and age at a given date)

shall not apply if, on the date on which he ceased to be a civil servant, the National Insurance (Modification of the Superannuation Acts) Regulations (Northern Ireland) 1948(a) did not apply to him; and

(b) paragraphs 3 and 5 of the said Schedule 5 shall apply if, on the date on which he ceased to be a civil servant, the last mentioned Regulations applied to him.

Gordon Campbell,
One of Her Majesty's Principal
Secretaries of State.

St. Andrew's House,
Edinburgh.
22nd March 1972.

Consent of the Minister for the Civil Service given under his Official Seal on 23rd March 1972.

(L.S.)

K. H. McNeill,
Authorised by the Minister for
the Civil Service.

EXPLANATORY NOTE

(This Note is not part of the Rules.)

These Rules continue with minor alterations the arrangements made by earlier Rules for the preservation of superannuation rights upon changes of employment between teaching in Scotland and the Civil Service of Northern Ireland under the provisions of the Superannuation (Teaching and Northern Ireland Civil Service) Interchange (Scotland) Rules 1962 which are revoked.

The Rules may have retrospective effect in certain cases under the express power of, and subject to the safeguards required by, section 2(5) of the Superannuation (Miscellaneous Provisions) Act 1948.

(a) S.R. & O. (N.I.) 1948 No. 91.

STATUTORY INSTRUMENTS

1972 No. 538 (N.I. 1)

NORTHERN IRELAND

The Prosecution of Offences (Northern Ireland) Order 1972

Made - - - -	30*th March* 1972
Coming into Operation -	30*th March* 1972

To be laid before Parliament

At the Court at Windsor Castle, the 30th day of March 1972

Present,

The Queen's Most Excellent Majesty in Council

Whereas it has been made to appear to Her Majesty that by reason of urgency this Order requires to be made without a draft having been approved by resolution of each House of Parliament:—

Now, therefore, Her Majesty, in exercise of the powers conferred by section 1(3) of the Northern Ireland (Temporary Provisions) Act 1972(a), and of all other powers enabling Her in that behalf, is pleased, by and with the advice of Her Privy Council, to order, and it is hereby ordered, as follows:—

Title and commencement

1. This Order may be cited as the Prosecution of Offences (Northern Ireland) Order 1972 and shall come into operation forthwith.

Interpretation

2.—(1) The Interpretation Act (Northern Ireland) 1954(b) shall apply for the interpretation of this Order as it applies for the interpretation of an Act of the Parliament of Northern Ireland.

(2) In this Order—

" deputy Director " means the deputy Director of Public Prosecutions for Northern Ireland appointed under the provisions of this Order;

" Director " means the Director of Public Prosecutions for Northern Ireland appointed under the provisions of this Order;

" documents " includes papers and records of any kind;

" indictable offence " includes any offence which the prosecution may prosecute on indictment;

" initiate " includes institute;

" statutory provision " has the meaning assigned to it by section 1(*f*) of the Interpretation Act (Northern Ireland) 1954;

" transferred provision " has the meaning assigned to it by section 1(*g*) of the Interpretation Act (Northern Ireland) 1954.

(a) 1972 c. 22.   (b) 1954 c. 33 (N.I.).

(3) References in this Order to the Crown shall be construed as including references to any person or authority acting on behalf of the Crown or any Government department or agency and to any member of the Royal Ulster Constabulary acting as such.

Temporary provisions

3.—(1) Nothing in this Order shall be construed as making provision contrary to any provision made by the Northern Ireland (Temporary Provisions) Act 1972 and accordingly, so long as section 1 of that Act has effect, any reference in this Order to the Governor or the Governor acting upon the advice of the Privy Council for Northern Ireland or to a department of the Government of Northern Ireland has effect subject to the provisions of that Act.

(2) So long as section 1 of the said Act has effect, the Director (without prejudice to the validity of anything done by him or on his behalf) shall discharge his functions under the superintendence of the Attorney General and shall be subject to the directions of the Attorney General in all matters including the giving or withholding of any such consent as is mentioned in article 7 of this Order.

Office of the Director of Public Prosecutions for Northern Ireland

4.—(1) The Governor may appoint a Director and a deputy Director of Public Prosecutions for Northern Ireland.

(2) The Director and the deputy Director shall each hold his office during good behaviour but each—

(a) may be removed from his office by the Governor upon the advice of the Privy Council for Northern Ireland;

(b) may at any time at his own request be granted permission by the Governor to resign his office; and

(c) shall unless the Governor by order otherwise directs retire from office at the end of the year of his service therein in which he attains the age of sixty-five years.

(3) The Ministry of Home Affairs after consultation with the Director and with the approval of the Ministry of Finance may appoint such professional and other officers and servants as may be necessary to assist the Director in carrying out the duties of his office.

(4) There shall be paid to the Director and to the deputy Director and to such professional and other officers and servants as aforesaid such salaries or other remuneration and such allowances by way of superannuation or otherwise in respect of their services in that behalf as the Ministry of Finance may determine, and the deputy Director and all such professional and other officers and servants shall in all matters be subject to the direction and control of the Director.

(5) A person shall not be appointed to be Director unless at the date of his appointment he has practised for not less than 10 years either at the Bar of Northern Ireland or as a solicitor of the Supreme Court and a person shall not be appointed to be deputy Director unless at the date of his appointment he has practised for not less than 7 years either at the Bar of Northern Ireland or as a solicitor of the Supreme Court. For the purposes of this paragraph

any period during which a person called to the Bar of Northern Ireland or admitted to practise as a solicitor of the Supreme Court has, after such call or admission, held an appointment under paragraph (3) above may be reckoned either as a period during which he has practised at such Bar or (as the case may be) as a period during which he has practised as such solicitor.

(6) The Director may with the approval of the Ministry of Home Affairs establish and maintain such offices at such place or places in Northern Ireland as he may consider necessary for the due execution of his functions under this Order.

(7) The Director may employ a solicitor to act as his agent in the conduct of any prosecution and the costs of an agent so employed shall be defrayed as part of the expenses incurred in the execution of the duties of the Director.

(8) Any person appointed under paragraph (3) above who is nominated by the Director may do any act or thing which the Director is required or authorised to do by or in pursuance of this Order or of any transferred provision or otherwise, and for the purposes of any criminal or other proceedings a person appointed under paragraph (3) above claiming to act under this paragraph shall until the contrary is proved be deemed to have been duly nominated so to act.

(9) The Director shall not be required to give security and no order shall be made by any court requiring security to be given to him with respect to any proceedings.

(10) Nothing contained in any transferred provision or in any rule of law or practice shall operate to prevent the Director or deputy Director or any person appointed under paragraph (3) above who has been duly admitted to practise at the Bar of Northern Ireland—

(*a*) from prosecuting or carrying on any criminal proceeding whatsoever in any county court or magistrates' court in Northern Ireland; or

(*b*) from exercising a right of audience in any such proceeding;

notwithstanding that he has not been instructed by a solicitor of the Supreme Court.

Functions of the Director

5.—(1) Without prejudice to the operation of the succeeding provisions of this article, it shall be the function of the Director—

(*a*) to consider, or cause to be considered, with a view to his initiating or continuing in Northern Ireland any criminal proceedings or the bringing of any appeal or other proceedings in or in connection with any criminal cause or matter in Northern Ireland, any facts or information brought to his notice, whether by the Chief Constable acting in pursuance of article 6(3) of this Order or by the Attorney General or by any other authority or person;

(*b*) to examine or cause to be examined all documents that are required under article 6 of this Order to be transmitted or furnished to him and where it appears to him to be necessary or appropriate to do so to cause any matter arising thereon to be further investigated;

(*c*) where he thinks proper to initiate, undertake and carry on, on behalf of the Crown proceedings for indictable offences and for such summary offences or classes of summary offences as he considers should be dealt with by him;

(*d*) where a person is in custody charged with or convicted of an offence and application is made to any court for bail, to cause, in such cases as the Director thinks proper, enquiries to be made into the facts and circumstances and if necessary cause such representations to be made regarding the granting of bail as he may think fit including representations as to the sufficiency of the surety or sureties offered and as to the amount of bail;

(*e*) to represent the Crown in any proceedings brought in the county court in respect of any determination or order made by a magistrates' court on or in connection with a summary offence;

(*f*) to represent the Crown in any proceedings before the Court of Criminal Appeal or before the Supreme Court or the House of Lords in a criminal cause or matter;

(*g*) where in the opinion of the Attorney General the public interest so requires, to apply to the High Court in the name and on behalf of the Attorney General for any order of certiorari, mandamus, prohibition or other prerogative order or injunction with respect to any criminal proceedings or any matter arising thereout;

(*h*) when requested in writing by any government department (including a department of the Government of the United Kingdom) to consider the initiating of prosecutions and to initiate, undertake and carry on such prosecutions as he may think proper for offences against any statutory provision in Northern Ireland on behalf of any such department, and to represent that department on any appeal or other subsequent criminal proceedings arising out of or in connection with any such prosecutions.

(2) The Director shall be responsible to the Attorney General for the due performance of the functions of the Director under this Order.

(3) Nothing in this Order shall preclude any person from initiating, undertaking or carrying on any criminal proceedings, but the Director may undertake at any stage the conduct of those proceedings if he thinks fit.

Delivery of informations etc. to Director

6.—(1) Where a person is committed for trial the clerk of the court to which he is so committed shall deliver or cause to be delivered without delay to the Director a copy of all informations, depositions, examinations, statements and recognizances connected with the charge together with copies of all other documents in his custody connected with the charge or, if it is not reasonably practicable to copy such documents, together with particulars thereof, and where a complaint has been laid before a resident magistrate or justice of the peace, whether proceedings have been taken thereon or not, the resident magistrate or justice shall cause to be delivered to the Director copies of all documents in his custody connected therewith on being required by the Director so to do.

(2) Where the circumstances of any death investigated or being investigated by a coroner appear to him to disclose that a criminal offence may have been committed he shall as soon as practicable furnish to the Director a written report of those circumstances.

(3) It shall be the duty of the Chief Constable, from time to time, to furnish to the Director facts and information with respect to—

(*a*) indictable offences alleged to have been committed against the law of Northern Ireland;

(*b*) such other alleged offences as the Director may specify;

and at the request of the Director, to ascertain and furnish to the Director information regarding any matter which may appear to the Director to require investigation on the ground that it may involve an offence against the law of Northern Ireland or information which may appear to the Director to be necessary for the discharge of his functions under this Order.

(4) At the end of section 13(5) of the Police Act (Northern Ireland) 1970(a) there shall be added the words " and shall send copies thereof to the Director of Public Prosecutions for Northern Ireland ".

Consents to prosecutions

7.—(1) In this Article—

" consent provision " means any transferred provision, whether passed before or after the coming into operation of this Order whereby the consent of the Attorney General is required (whether by itself or as an alternative to the consent of any other authority or person) to the initiation or carrying on of proceedings for an offence; but does not include section 8 of the Official Secrets Act 1911(b), section 8(2) of the Official Secrets Act 1920(c) or section 3(2) of the Civil Authorities (Special Powers) Act (Northern Ireland) 1922(d).

(2) Unless the Attorney General otherwise directs, a consent provision passed before the coming into operation of this Order shall be deemed to be complied with as respects the initiation after such coming into operation of proceedings for an offence to which it applies if the consent to the initiation or carrying on of those proceedings is given by the Director.

(3) Without prejudice to anything contained in a consent provision or in any other transferred provision, a consent provision—

(*a*) shall not prevent the issue or execution of a warrant for the arrest of any person for an offence to which the consent provision relates, or the remanding in custody or on bail of any person charged with such an offence; and

(*b*) shall be deemed to be complied with if the consent is produced to the court, in the case of an indictable offence, at any time before the indictment is presented or, in the case of an offence to be tried summarily, at any time before the plea of the accused person is taken.

(4) For the purposes of a consent provision it shall be sufficient to describe the offence to which the consent relates in general terms and—

(*a*) to describe or designate in ordinary language any property or place to which reference is made in the consent so as to identify with reasonable clearness that property or place in relation to the offence; and

(*b*) to describe or designate the accused person or any other person to whom reference is made in the consent in terms which are reasonably sufficient to enable him to be identified in relation to the offence, without necessarily stating his correct name, or his abode, style, degree or occupation.

(5) A consent required by a consent provision may be amended at any time before the arraignment of the accused person or, in the case of a summary trial, before the plea of the accused person is taken, and if at any subsequent stage of a trial it appears to the court that the consent is defective the court may afford the person or authority giving the consent the opportunity of making such amendments as the court may think necessary if the court is satisfied that such amendments can be made without injustice to the accused person.

(6) Any document purporting to be the consent, authorisation or direction of the Director or his deputy to or for the initiation or carrying on of criminal

---

(**a**) 1970 c. 9 (N.I.).   (**b**) 1911 c. 28.   (**c**) 1920 c. 75.   (**d**) 1922 c. 5 (N.I.).

proceedings or criminal proceedings in any particular form, and to be signed by the Director or his deputy, as the case may be, shall be admissible as prima facie evidence without further proof.

Abolition of Office of Crown Solicitor for a county and compensation for certain existing holders thereof

8.—(1) On such day as the Ministry of Home Affairs may by order appoint the Office of Crown Solicitor for any county or place shall be abolished, and the functions of every such Crown Solicitor in connection with criminal proceedings shall thereupon become functions of the Director.

(2) The Ministry of Home Affairs with the approval of the Ministry of Finance may by regulations make provision for the payment by the Ministry of Home Affairs, subject to such exceptions or conditions as may be prescribed by the regulations, of compensation to or in respect of persons who immediately before the day appointed as aforesaid, hold and have held, for such minimum period as may be prescribed by the regulations, part-time office as Crown Solicitor for any county or place.

(3) Where a person who receives compensation pursuant to regulations made under paragraph (2) above is appointed to any post under article 4 of this Order, he shall repay to the Ministry that compensation or such part thereof as the Ministry with the approval of the Ministry of Finance may determine.

(4) Regulations made under paragraph (2) above may include provision as to the manner in which the claim for compensation is to be made, and for the determination of any question arising under the regulations.

Consequential amendments

9.—(1) In sections 73, 96, 97, 106(1) and 120 of, and in paragraph 12 of Schedule 8 to the Electoral Law Act (Northern Ireland) 1962(**a**) (which relates to the prosecution of offences disclosed on election petitions) for the words " The Chief Crown Solicitor " there shall be substituted the words " The Director of Public Prosecutions for Northern Ireland ".

(2) In paragraph 3 of the notes to Schedule 1 to the Parliamentary Commissioner Act (Northern Ireland) 1969(**b**) the words " the Office of the Director of Public Prosecutions for Northern Ireland " shall be added at the end of paragraph (*a*) and in paragraph (*b*) the words " to the administration of the criminal law, or " shall be omitted.

(3) In section 20(3) of the Interpretation Act (Northern Ireland) 1954 for the words " except upon the direction of the Attorney-General " there shall be substituted the words " except by or with the consent of the Attorney-General or the Director of Public Prosecutions for Northern Ireland ".

Amendments as to prosecution of offences against a corporation

10. In section 18(3) of the Criminal Justice Act (Northern Ireland) 1945(**c**) for the words from " a grand jury " to " a true Bill " there shall be substituted the words " an indictment has been presented ".

W. G. Agnew

(a) 1962 c. 14 (N.I.).   (b) 1969 c. 10 (N.I.).   (c) 1945 c. 15 (N.I.).

EXPLANATORY NOTE

(This Note is not part of the Order.)

This Order establishes and makes provision for the office of Director of Public Prosecutions for Northern Ireland.

STOKE-ON-TRENT
CITY
LIBRARIES

STATUTORY INSTRUMENTS

1972 No. 540

CIVIL AVIATION

The British Airports Authority (Traffic Wardens) Order 1972

Made - - - -	*4th April* 1972
Laid before Parliament	*11th April* 1972
Coming into Operation	*1st May* 1972

The Secretary of State, in exercise of his powers under section 9 of the Civil Aviation Act 1968(a) and of all other powers enabling him in that behalf, hereby makes the following Order:

Citation and Commencement

1. This Order may be cited as the British Airports Authority (Traffic Wardens) Order 1972, and shall come into operation on 1st May 1972.

Interpretation

2.—(1) In this Order, unless the context otherwise requires:

"the Authority" means the British Airports Authority;

"the Act of 1967" means the Road Traffic Regulation Act 1967(b) as amended by the Transport Act 1968(c).

(2) The Interpretation Act 1889(d) shall apply for the interpretation of this Order as it applies for the interpretation of an Act of Parliament.

Application of section 81 *of the Act of* 1967

3. Section 81 of the Act of 1967 shall apply in relation to the Authority subject to such adaptations and modifications as are specified in Schedule 1 to this Order.

Application of the Functions of Traffic Wardens Order 1970

4. The Functions of Traffic Wardens Order 1970(e) shall apply in relation to the Authority subject to such adaptations and modifications as are specified in Schedule 2 to this Order.

(a) 1968 c. 61. (b) 1967 c. 76.
(c) 1968 c. 73. (d) 1889 c. 63.
(e) S.I. 1970/1958 (1970 III, p. 6409).

Application of the Functions of Traffic Wardens (Scotland) Order 1971

5. The Functions of Traffic Wardens (Scotland) Order 1971**(a)** shall apply in relation to the Authority subject to such adaptations and modifications as are specified in Schedule 3 to this Order.

Michael Noble,
Minister for Trade,
4th April 1972.   Department of Trade and Industry.

SCHEDULE 1   Article 3

ADAPTATIONS AND MODIFICATIONS OF SECTION 81 OF THE ACT OF 1967

1. Sections 81(1) and (2) shall be omitted.

2. In section 81(3):

(*a*) after the words "by order of the Secretary of State" there shall be inserted "(including an order applied in relation to the Authority by an order made under section 9 of the Civil Aviation Act 1968)";

(*b*) at the end of the first paragraph there shall be added:

"Provided that in any such order no function shall be prescribed as appropriate for discharge by a traffic warden employed by the Authority which is not prescribed in that or any other order as appropriate for discharge by a traffic warden employed by a police authority."

3. In section 81(4A) paragraphs (*a*) and (*b*) shall be omitted.

4. In section 81(5) for the expresssion "A police authority" there shall be substituted the expression "the Authority".

5. After section 81(6) there shall be added the following subsection:

"(6A) In this section unless the context otherwise requires:

"the Authority" means the British Airports Authority;

"traffic warden" means a person appointed by the Authority to discharge, in relation to aerodromes owned or managed by the Authority, functions under this section."

6. Sections 81(7) to (12), shall be omitted.

SCHEDULE 2   Article 4

ADAPTATIONS AND MODIFICATIONS OF THE FUNCTIONS OF TRAFFIC WARDENS ORDER 1970

1. In Article 2 after the definition of "traffic order" there shall be added the following definition:

" "traffic warden" means a person appointed by the British Airports Authority to discharge, in relation to aerodromes owned or managed by that Authority, functions under section 81 of the Act of 1967 as applied to the British Airports Authority."

2. In Article 3 paragraphs 3(2)(*a*) and 3(2)(*b*) shall be omitted.

3. In the Schedule paragraphs 2(1) and 5 shall be omitted.

(a) S.I. 1971/374 (1971 I, p. 1160).

Article 5   SCHEDULE 3

ADAPTATIONS AND MODIFICATIONS OF THE FUNCTIONS OF TRAFFIC WARDENS
(SCOTLAND) ORDER 1971

1. In Article 2 after the definition of "traffic order" there shall be added the following definition:

" "traffic warden" means a person appointed by the British Airports Authority to discharge, in relation to aerodromes owned or managed by that Authority, functions under section 81 of the Act of 1967 as applied to the British Airports Authority."

2. In the Schedule paragraphs 2(1) and 4 shall be omitted.

EXPLANATORY NOTE

(This Note is not part of the Order.)

This Order applies in relation to the British Airports Authority, with adaptations and modifications, section 81 of the Road Traffic Regulation Act 1967 as amended by the Transport Act 1968 (which relates to traffic wardens) and the Functions of Traffic Wardens Order 1970 and the Functions of Traffic Wardens (Scotland) Order 1971 (which prescribe the functions appropriate for discharge by traffic wardens). The Order will enable traffic wardens appointed by the British Airports Authority to discharge at the Authority's aerodromes functions discharged elsewhere by traffic wardens appointed by police authorities.

STATUTORY INSTRUMENTS

1972 No. 550

PENSIONS

The Overseas Service (Pensions Supplement) Regulations 1972

Made - - - -	*5th April* 1972
Laid before Parliament	*14th April* 1972
Coming into Operation	*5th May* 1972

In exercise of the powers conferred on me by sections 5(3) and (4), 11 and 18(2) of the Pensions (Increase) Act 1971(a) and with the approval of the Minister for the Civil Service, I hereby make the following Regulations :—

PART I

CITATION, COMMENCEMENT AND INTERPRETATION

1. These Regulations may be cited as the Overseas Service (Pensions Supplement) Regulations 1972 and shall come into operation on 5th May 1972.

2.—(1) In these Regulations, unless the context otherwise requires, the following expressions have the meanings hereby respectively assigned to them, that is to say :—

" the Act " means the Pensions (Increase) Act 1971 ;

" the Act of " any specified year means the Pensions (Increase) Act of that year ;

" basic pension " means the pension, being a pension to which section 11 of the Act applies, awarded with effect from the date of the officer's retirement (or if it commenced after that date, which would have been so awarded), or in the case of a pension in respect of the services of any person other than the pensioner, the pension first awarded, less the amount of any increase, bonus or other allowance howsoever authorised which may have been included in the amount of the award by virtue of the pension having been determined by reference to conditions existing prior to any specified date ; but excluding in every case any overseas increase ;

" dependent pensioner " means (*a*) a person in receipt of a pension in respect of the service of an officer which is payable either by the government of an overseas territory or in accordance with an enactment, scheme or other instrument specified in Schedule 3 to these Regulations as having been approved by the Secretary of State for purposes of section 11 of the Act, or (*b*) a person in receipt of a pension payable under section 5(1) of the Superannuation (Miscellaneous Provisions) Act 1967(b) in respect of the service of an officer under the government of the former mandated territory of Palestine ;

" notional pension " means the pension which would have been awarded under the Oversea Superannuation Scheme to a person to whom Part III

(a) 1971 c. 56. (b) 1967 c. 28.

of these Regulations applies if the pensionable emoluments taken into account under the Scheme had not been reduced in accordance with the provisions of regulation 21(2) of the Oversea Superannuation Scheme (Consolidation) Regulations 1963 or, in the case of a person in receipt of a pension awarded under any previous Regulations made by the Secretary of State under the Oversea Superannuation Scheme, in accordance with the corresponding provisions of those previous Regulations ;

" overseas increase " means any addition to the amount of basic pension, or the aggregate of two or more such additions, paid by the authority by whom the pension is payable and includes any increase, bonus or allowance (including the restoration of a commuted part of a pension) so paid in respect of that pension howsoever authorised ;

" the Regulations " in Part III of these Regulations means the Oversea Superannuation Scheme (Consolidation) Regulations 1963, and a reference to any provision of those Regulations shall, in the case of a person in receipt of a pension awarded under any previous Regulations made by the Secretary of State under the Oversea Superannuation Scheme, be construed as a reference to the corresponding provision of those previous Regulations ;

" the 1969 Regulations " means the Overseas Service (Pensions Supplement) Regulations 1969(a) ;

" retirement " means the retirement applicable to the computation of a pension in respect of service under the government of an overseas territory.

(2) Unless the context otherwise requires, any reference in these Regulations to any enactment, other than the Act, shall be construed as a reference to that enactment as amended, extended or applied by or under any other enactment.

(3) The Interpretation Act 1889(b) shall apply for the interpretation of and otherwise in relation to these Regulations as it applies for the interpretation of and otherwise in relation to an Act of Parliament and as if these Regulations were an Act of Parliament.

PART II

SUPPLEMENTS IN RESPECT OF OFFICERS' PENSIONS

3. This Part of these Regulations shall apply to any person in receipt of a pension in respect of his own service, being a pension to which section 11 of the Act applies.

4. Subject to the provisions of section 11 of the Act and of these Regulations, the supplement payable to a person to whom this Part of these Regulations applies and who either :—

i. was in receipt of any supplement under the 1969 Regulations, or

ii. becomes eligible for the first time to receive supplements by virtue of section 11(2)(c) of the Act,

and whose pension is determined by reference to emoluments payable by the government of an overseas territory, being an overseas territory specified in Schedule 1 of these Regulations, or by reference to emoluments payable by the Government of the United Kingdom or the Crown Agents for Oversea Governments and Administrations or the Central Office of the Overseas

---

(a) SI 1969/553 (1969 I, p. 1499)   (b) 1889 c. 63.

Audit Department or the Government of the Federation of Rhodesia and Nyasaland or the Government of Egypt, may be of such an amount that when aggregated with any overseas increase paid to him corresponds with the aggregate of the increases, if any, which would be payable under the Act or any order made under section 2 (but not under section 6) of the Act if his basic pension were a pension specified in paragraph 4 of Part I of Schedule 2 to the Act and had begun—

(a) in the case of retirement from service under the government of an overseas territory other than Egypt, on the day immediately following the effective date of the latest general revision of pensionable emoluments in relation to the overseas territory from which he retired which was taken into account in determining the amount of that pension ; or

(b) in the case of retirement from service under the Government of the United Kingdom or the Crown Agents for Oversea Governments and Administrations or the Central Office of the Overseas Audit Department, on the day following the last day of such service ; or

(c) in the case of retirement from service under the Government of Egypt, before the year 1944 :

Provided that

(i) in the case of a pension to which paragraph (a) or (c) of this regulation applies, in determining the amount necessary to bring the basic pension up to the 1969 standard in accordance with section 1 of the Act the multiplier given in Schedule 1 to the Act for the year in which the pension began shall in the case of any such pension which began prior to the date specified in the second column of Schedule 1 to these Regulations be the multiplier applicable to a pension which began in any year up to 1944 ; and

(ii) in the case of a person who was in receipt of any supplement under the 1969 Regulations, any addition which under section 6(5) of the Act would be of the amount prescribed by the Minister for the Civil Service " as corresponding to that of the increase provided for by section 2 of that Act (additional increase for pensioners over 70) " shall not be ascertained by reference to the amount so prescribed but by reference to Schedule 2 to these Regulations ; and

(iii) in the case of a pension of a person who becomes eligible for the first time to receive supplements by virtue of section 11(2)(c) of the Act, section 6 of the Act shall be disregarded.

5. Subject to the provisions of section 11 of the Act and of these Regulations, the supplement payable to a person to whom this Part of these Regulations other than regulation 4 applies and whose pension is determined by reference to emoluments payable by the government of an overseas territory, being an overseas territory specified in Schedule 1 to these Regulations, or by reference to emoluments payable by the Government of the United Kingdom or the Crown Agents for Oversea Governments and Administrations or the Central Office of the Overseas Audit Department or the Government of the Federation of Rhodesia and Nyasaland or the Government of Egypt, may be the amount payable as if regulation 4 of these Regulations except provisos (ii) and (iii) thereof were applicable but subject to the following modifications—

(a) references in regulation 4 to the Act shall be deemed to include references to any order made under section 6 of the Act ;

(*b*) any order made under section 6 of the Act shall be applied as if the pension were a Civil Service pension payable otherwise than under Part II of the Superannuation Act 1965(**a**):

Provided that a pension determined by reference to emoluments payable by the government of an overseas territory specified in Schedule 1 to the Regulations prior to the date specified in the second column of the said Schedule 1 in relation to the country from which a person finally retired, or the pension of a person who retired from the service of the Government of Egypt shall be deemed to have begun prior to 1st April 1947 ;

(*c*) where a pension beginning on or before 16th August 1920 is one that (but for the Act) might have been increased under the Act of 1920(**b**) if the pension were a pension specified in section 1(2) of that Act, the supplement may include the amount which would have been payable under that Act (but disregarding paragraph 3 of Part 1 of the Schedule thereof), if that Act had not been repealed ; and any provision of an order made under section 6 of the Act excluding its application to a pension which qualified for an increase under the Act of 1920 shall be disregarded ;

(*d*) in the case of a pension payable to an officer who retired from the Sudan Civil Service during 1950 the following proportion of the amount of the relevant increase prescribed by order made under section 6 of the Act to correspond with the increase which might (but for the Act) have been granted under the Act of 1944(**c**) shall be reckonable :

(i) Retirement in January 1950	11/12ths
(ii) Retirement in February 1950	10/12ths
(iii) Retirement in March 1950	9/12ths
(iv) Retirement in April 1950	8/12ths
(v) Retirement in May 1950	7/12ths
(vi) Retirement in June 1950	6/12ths
(vii) Retirement in July 1950	5/12ths
(viii) Retirement in August 1950	4/12ths
(ix) Retirement in September 1950	3/12ths
(x) Retirement in October 1950	2/12ths
(xi) Retirement in November 1950	1/12th

6. No supplement shall be payable to a person to whom this Part of these Regulations applies in respect of any pension determined by reference to emoluments payable by the government of an overseas territory, if those emoluments:—

(*a*) in the case of any supplement corresponding to an increase authorised by section 1 (or when relevant section 6) of and Schedule 1 to the Act, derived from a general revision of pensionable emoluments in relation to an overseas territory taking effect on or after 1st April 1970 ; or

(*b*) in the case of any supplement corresponding to an increase authorised by an order under section 2 of the Act, derived from a general revision of pensionable emoluments in relation to an overseas territory taking effect on a date within one year before the end of the review period covered by the order.

(a) 1965 c. 74.   (b) 1920 c. 36.   (c) 1944 c. 21.

PART III

ADDITIONAL SUPPLEMENT IN RESPECT OF PENSIONS OF OFFICERS WHO WERE SPECIAL CONTRIBUTORS TO THE OVERSEA SUPERANNUATION SCHEME

7. This Part of these Regulations shall apply to any person in receipt of a pension payable under the Oversea Superannuation Scheme in respect of his own service who—

(a) is eligible for the payment of a supplement under the provisions of Part II of these Regulations in respect of that pension ;

(b) was a special contributor to the Oversea Superannuation Scheme as provided in regulation 21 of the Regulations ; and

(c) has ceased to contribute to the superannuation scheme operated under the Federated Superannuation System for Universities or such other scheme of a like nature as may have been approved under the provisions of regulation 21(1) of the Regulations, and has become eligible for benefit under that scheme.

8. A special supplement may be paid to any person to whom this Part of these Regulations applies of an amount which when aggregated with the supplement payable under Part II of these Regulations in respect of his pension under the Oversea Superannuation Scheme is equal to the supplement which would have been payable under the said Part II if he had been entitled to a pension of the same amount as his notional pension.

PART IV

SUPPLEMENTS IN RESPECT OF DEPENDENT PENSIONERS

9.—(1) This regulation applies to a dependent pensioner, whose pension is determined wholly or partly by reference to a rate of contributions paid by, and to the age of, an officer from time to time, being the dependent of a person to whom Part II of these Regulations applies, but who does not become eligible for the first time to receive supplements by virtue of section 11(2)(c) of the Act.

(2) Subject to the provisions of section 11 of the Act and of these Regulations the supplement payable in respect of a dependent pensioner to whom this regulation applies shall be assessed in accordance with the provisions of this regulation and may be an amount that corresponds with the aggregate of the amounts which would have been payable under regulation 5 of these Regulations if that regulation had applied to such pensioner and the pension had begun on the date when the period of contributions commenced.

(3) For the purpose of calculating the total supplement payable under this regulation, prior to calculating the reductions, if any, applicable under this regulation, in any case where by virtue of section 6 of the Act the 1971 rate would have been ascertained by reference to an order made under sub-sections (4) and (5) of that section, such order shall be disregarded and the 1971 rate which would have been ascertained by reference to that order shall be ascertained in accordance with the provisions of paragraph (4) of this regulation and the Tables in Schedule 4 to these Regulations.

(4) For the purpose of calculating the total supplement in accordance with the provisions of paragraph (3) of this regulation the 1971 rate shall be : —

(a) if the contributions of the officer in respect of whose service under the government of an overseas territory the pension is payable to the dependent pensioner began before 16th August 1920, the basic pension increased under Tables I to VII inclusive ;

(*b*) if such contributions began on or after 16th August 1920 but before the scheduled date specified in column 2 of Schedule 1 to these Regulations in relation to the territory in question (or in the case of The Gambia, Ghana, Nigeria and Sierra Leone, column 3), the basic pension increased under Tables II to VII inclusive but as if the words in Table II " as increased under Table I " were omitted and as if in Tables III to VII any reference to Table I were omitted ;

(*c*) if such contributions began on or after the scheduled date specified in column 2 of the said Schedule in relation to the territory in question but before the scheduled date specified in column 3, the basic pension increased under Tables III to VII inclusive, but as if in Table III the words " as increased under Tables I and II " were omitted and as if in Tables IV to VII the references to Tables I and II were omitted ;

(*d*) if such contributions began on or after the scheduled date specified in column 3 of the said Schedule in relation to the territory in question but before the scheduled date specified in column 4, the basic pension increased under Tables IV to VII inclusive, but as if in Table IV the words " as increased under Tables I, II and III " were omitted and as if in Tables V to VII the references to Tables I, II and III were omitted ;

(*e*) if such contributions began on or after the scheduled date specified in column 4 of the said Schedule in relation to the territory in question but before the scheduled date specified in column 5, the basic pension increased under Tables V to VII inclusive, but as if in Table V the words " as increased under Tables I, II, III and IV " were omitted and as if in Tables VI and VII the references to Tables I, II, III and IV were omitted ;

(*f*) if such contributions began on or after the scheduled date specified in column 5 of the said Schedule in relation to the territory in question but before the scheduled date specified in column 6, the basic pension increased under Tables VI and VII, but as if in Table VI the words " as increased under Tables I, II, III, IV and V " were omitted and as if in Table VII the references to Tables I, II, III, IV and V were omitted ;

(*g*) if such contributions began on or after the scheduled date specified in column 6 of the said Schedule in relation to the territory in question, the basic pension increased under Table VII but as if the words " as increased under Tables I, II, III, IV, V and VI " were omitted.

(5) Where the officer, in respect of whose service under the government of an overseas territory the pension is payable, left such service or died while in such service, after a scheduled date in relation to that territory, not having completed the full period of contributions prior to that date, the gross amount of the supplement before deduction of any overseas increase but otherwise calculated in accordance with paragraphs (2), (3) and (4) of this regulation shall be reduced : —

(*a*) in the case of an officer who completed the full period of contributions prior to leaving such service or to his death while in such service, in the same proportion that the number of years in respect of which he contributed prior to the scheduled date bears to the total number of years in respect of which he contributed ; and

(*b*) in the case of an officer who died while in such service before completing the full period of contributions, in the same proportion that the number of years in respect of which he contributed prior to the scheduled date bears to the total number of years in respect of which he would have contributed had he continued to contribute until he had completed the full period of contributions ; and

(c) in any other case, in the same proportion that the number of years in respect of which he contributed prior to the scheduled date bears to the number of years in respect of which he contributed during his service under the said government.

(6) The formula which under paragraph (5) of this regulation is appropriate to the circumstances of an officer shall be applied either as in paragraph (7) or paragraph (8) of this regulation.

(7) (a) In relation to the 1969 standard and the other benefits contained in paragraphs (a), (b), (c), (d), (e) and (f) of section 1(1) of the Act or in any order made under section 2 of the Act the formula shall be applied as follows : —

(i) the formula shall be applied successively in relation to each scheduled date before which an officer's full period of contributions had not been completed, in chronological order ;

(ii) in relation to the first scheduled date the formula shall be applied to the proportion of the pension earned prior to that date, and in respect of each other scheduled date to the proportion earned between that scheduled date and the scheduled date immediately before it ; for this purpose a pension shall be deemed to be earned equally by all contributions over the full period of contributions ;

(iii) in relation to the first scheduled date the contributions to be used for the first part of the proportion shall be those made before that scheduled date, and for each other scheduled date shall be those made between that scheduled date and the scheduled date immediately before it ;

(iv) the second part of the proportion is always the full period of contributions ;

(v) to the product of each calculation specified in this paragraph shall be applied the multiplier specified in section 1 of, and Schedule 1 to the Act, or, as the case may be, in an order made under section 2 of the Act, for the year which corresponds to the year mentioned in the scheduled date in relation to which the calculation is made.

(b) For the purposes of this paragraph—

" pension " means

(i) the basic pension, when the formula is applied to a pension in relation to the 1969 standard ;

(ii) the basic pension together with the amount, if any, necessary to bring the rate of that pension up to whichever is the greater of the 1969 standard or the 1971 rate, when the formula is applied to a pension in relation to the other benefits contained in paragraphs (a), (b), (c) (d), (e) and (f) of section 1(1) of the Act ;

(iii) the pension prescribed in sub-head (ii) of this sub-paragraph together with the appropriate amount, if any, accruing under paragraphs (a), (b), (c), (d), (e) and (f) of section 1(1) of the Act, when the formula is applied to a pension in relation to the first order made under section 2 of the Act ;

(iv) the pension prescribed in sub-head (iii) of this sub-paragraph together with the amounts of the increases, if any, payable by virtue of the preceding order or orders made under section 2 of the Act, when the formula is applied to a pension in relation to any subsequent order made under that section.

(8) In relation to the 1971 rate as ascertained under this regulation the formula shall be applied as follows:

(*a*) the formula shall be applied successively in relation to each of the scheduled dates specified in paragraph (9)(*a*) and (*b*) of this regulation before which an officer's full period of contributions had not been completed, in chronological order ;

(*b*) where the officer's full period of contributions had not been completed before 16th August 1920, the formula shall be applied to the increase under Table I ;

(*c*) where the officer's full period of contributions had not been completed before the date specified in column 2 (or in the case of The Gambia, Ghana, Nigeria and Sierra Leone, column 3) of Schedule 1 of these Regulations in relation to the overseas territory in respect of service under the government of which the pension is payable, the formula shall be applied to the increase under Table II ;

(*d*) where the officer's full period of contributions had not been completed before the date specified in column 3 of Schedule 1 to these Regulations in relation to the overseas territory in respect of service under the government of which the pension is payable, the formula shall be applied to the increase under Table III ;

(*e*) where the officer's full period of contributions had not been completed before the date specified in column 4 of Schedule 1 to these Regulations in relation to the overseas territory in respect of service under the government of which the pension is payable, the formula shall be applied to the increase under Table IV ;

(*f*) where the officer's full period of contributions had not been completed before the date specified in column 5 of Schedule 1 to these Regulations in relation to the overseas territory in respect of service under the government of which the pension is payable, the formula shall be applied to the increase under Table V(*a*) and no account shall be taken of Table V(*b*) ;

(*g*) where the officer's full period of contributions had not been completed before the date specified in column 6 Schedule 1 to these Regulations in relation to the overseas territory in respect of service under the government of which the pension is payable, the formula shall be applied to the increase under Table VI ;

(*h*) where the officer's full period of contributions had not been completed before the date specified in column 7 of Schedule 1 to these Regulations in relation to the overseas territory in respect of service under the government of which the pension is payable, the formula shall be applied to the increase under Table VII.

(9) For the purposes of this regulation—

" full period of contributions " means the period during which the officer was required to contribute under any law authorising the payment of the pension to the dependent pensioner in order that such pensioner should qualify for the maximum pension payable under that law ;

" number of years " means the number of complete years, any period of, or exceeding, a half year being treated as a complete year ; and when calculating the number of years before any scheduled date any period less than a half year shall be excluded and added to the period used for the next calculation, or, if it is the last calculation, shall be ignored ;

" scheduled date " means

(a) in relation to all overseas territories mentioned in Schedule 1 to these Regulations and Egypt, 16th August 1920 ; and

(b) in relation to each overseas territory mentioned in Schedule 1 to these Regulations, any date specified in relation to that overseas territory in columns 2 to 7 of that Schedule, provided that in the case of The Gambia, Ghana, Nigeria and Sierra Leone the dates specified in column 3 of the said Schedule shall be used both as dates in that column and also in place of the dates specified in column 2 of the said Schedule ; and

(c) in relation to any overseas territory mentioned in Schedule 1 to these Regulations :—

(i) the date of each general revision of pensionable emoluments in relation to that overseas territory which takes effect from a date later than 1st July 1967 ; and

(ii) the date of the final contribution made by the officer, or the date of his final contribution before retirement from or transfer from the overseas territory under whose enactment, scheme or instrument the pension is payable, whichever is the earlier ;

" Table " or " Tables " means a Table or Tables specified in Schedule 4 to these Regulations.

10.—(1) This regulation applies to a dependent pensioner whose pension is determined wholly or partly by reference to a rate of contributions paid by, and to the age of, an officer from time to time, being the dependent of a person to whom Part II of these Regulations applies and who becomes eligible for the first time to receive supplements by virtue of section 11(2)(c) of the Act.

(2) Subject to the provisions of section 11 of the Act and of these Regulations, the supplement payable in respect of a dependent pensioner to whom this regulation applies shall be assessed in accordance with the provisions of regulation 9 to these Regulations except that section 6 of the Act and any order made under that section shall be disregarded and accordingly paragraphs (3), (4) and (8) and any reference to the 1971 rate in paragraph (7) of regulation 9 shall be disregarded.

11.—(1) Subject to the provisions of section 11 of the Act and of these Regulations, the supplement payable to a dependent pensioner whose pension is determined by reference to emoluments received by an officer during any period of service under the government of an overseas territory, or which would be so determined apart from any provision specifying a fixed sum as the minimum rate of pension, shall be the amount which would have been payable had Part II of these Regulations applied to such pensioner.

(2) (a) No supplement shall be payable to or in respect of a dependent pensioner being a child of the officer in respect of whose service the pension is payable when, if the pension were a children's pension as described in section 52 of the Superannuation Act 1965(a) such pension would not have

_____

(a) 1965 c. 74.

been payable solely by reason of the fact that the dependent pensioner was not in his period of childhood and full-time education as specified in section 84 of the said Act.

(*b*) For the purposes of this paragraph a child of the officer means a child, stepchild, illegitimate child or adopted child of the officer in respect of whose service the pension is payable or of a wife of such officer.

PART V

PERSONS IN RECEIPT OF MORE THAN ONE PENSION

12.—(1) (*a*) Where a person is in receipt of more than one pension in respect of service under any of the governments of the overseas territories specified in Schedule 1 to these Regulations: —

(i) the supplements payable shall not in the aggregate exceed the amount which would be payable if he were in receipt of a single basic pension at a rate equal to the aggregate of his basic pensions and beginning at the time when the earliest of them began, together with an overseas increase at a rate equal to the aggregate of the overseas increases awarded in respect of those pensions:

Provided that for the purposes of determining the amounts which would be payable under the Act or any order under section 2 of the Act in respect of the aforesaid single basic pension the aggregate of his basic pensions shall not include any basic pension which began at a time when, if it were the only basic pension eligible for benefit under these Regulations, it would not have attracted any increase under the Act or under an order under section 2 of the Act ; and

(ii) where the aggregate of the supplements in respect of each of his basic pensions as ascertained apart from this paragraph would exceed the maximum amount authorised under sub-head (i) of this sub-paragraph, the supplement payable in the case of each of such pensions shall be of such amount as, when aggregated with the overseas increase paid in respect of that pension, shall bear the same proportion to the aggregate increases which would be payable under the Act and any orders under section 2 of the Act in respect of the aggregate basic pensions as the basic pension bears to such aggregate:

Provided that where the aggregate of the supplements so determined in respect of all the basic pensions, whether or not such pensions attract benefit under these Regulations, exceeds the maximum amount authorised under sub-head (i) of this sub-paragraph, each such supplement shall be reduced by an amount bearing the same proportion to that supplement as the excess bears to that aggregate.

(*b*) In this paragraph any reference to the basic pensions of a person is a reference to any pension in respect of service under any of the governments of the overseas territories specified in Schedule 1 to these Regulations which is eligible for benefit under these Regulations.

(2) In the application of this regulation to any person who has been granted a pension determined in accordance with section 2 of the Governors' Pensions Act 1957(**a**), any pension in respect of service in the oversea civil service

---

(**a**) 1957 c. 62.

taken into account for the purposes of section 2(2)(*b*) of the said Act shall be regarded—

(*a*) as beginning on the same date as the Governor's pension would be deemed to begin under the Act as modified by regulations, if any, made under section 5(3) of the Act, and

(*b*) as being the basic pension granted for that service notwithstanding that it may include an addition made in accordance with an enactment, scheme, or other instrument providing for the increase of pensions, but the amount of any such addition which is so included shall not be taken into account in determining the overseas increases in respect of that pension.

(3) Where a person is in receipt of more than one pension to which the provisions of regulations 9, 10 or 11 of these Regulations apply, the periods during which the officer in respect of whose service the pensions are payable contributed in respect of those pensions shall be aggregated for the purpose of determining the maximum supplement payable under the provisions of paragraph (1)(*a*) of this regulation:

Provided that where contributions were made in respect of more than one such pension in relation to the same period of service that period shall not be taken into account more than once.

(4) Where a person who is in receipt of a pension to which the provisions of regulations 9, 10 or 11 of these Regulations apply is also in receipt of a pension to which those provisions do not apply, the supplements payable under these Regulations shall not in the aggregate exceed the amount which would be payable if he were in receipt of a single basic pension equal to the aggregate of his basic pensions, together with a single overseas increase at a rate equal to the aggregate of his overseas increases, and if such single basic pension were regarded as a pension to which the provisions of regulations 9, 10 or 11 apply and which was determined by reference to the period of contributions made in respect of the pension actually payable to which the provisions of regulations 9, 10 or 11 apply:

Provided that—

(i) in determining the supplement in respect of the aforesaid single basic pension the amount of any relevant increase to that pension shall not exceed an amount which is equal to the relevant increase which would have been payable in respect of the single basic pension at a rate equal to the aggregate of his basic pensions and beginning at a time when the earliest of them began apart from any basic pension which began at a time when, if it were the only basic pension eligible for benefit under these Regulations, it would not have attracted any such relevant increase, such relevant increase being apportioned among the overseas pensions in the same proportion as the comparable relevant increase in the overseas pension bears to the aggregate of the comparable relevant increases in the overseas pensions ; and

(ii) where a person who is in receipt of a pension to which the provisions of regulations 9, 10 or 11 of these Regulations apply is also in receipt of a pension to which the provisions of none of those regulations apply, the latter pension having been derived from the service of the officer which occurred subsequently to the service giving rise to the former pension, the provisions of the preceding proviso shall not apply.

Part VI

General and Supplemental Provisions

13. Except as otherwise provided in these Regulations, in the application of the Act or any order made under section 6 of the Act for the purpose of determining the supplement payable under these Regulations no regard shall be had to the provisions of section 4, section 8(2) and (3) and the words " and the time when a pension " begins " is that stated in section 8(2) " in the definition of " pension " in section 17(1), of the Act.

14.—(1) Whenever, for the purpose of ascertaining any supplement payable under these Regulations, it is necessary to convert into sterling a basic pension initially payable in a currency other than sterling, the rate of exchange to be taken for the purpose of any such conversion shall be the rate of exchange between that currency and sterling specified in the Public Officers' Agreement concluded between Her Majesty's Government in the United Kingdom and the government of the overseas territory concerned, whether or not that Agreement applies to such basic pension and whether or not it is paid at the rate of exchange specified in that Agreement. Where there is no such Public Officers' Agreement the rate of exchange to be taken shall be:—

(a) in the case of a colony for whose external relations the United Kingdom is responsible or a territory outside Her Majesty's dominions in which Her Majesty has jurisdiction in right of Her Government in the United Kingdom, the current rate of exchange on the date when that instalment of the basic pension to which the supplement relates is payable ;

(b) in the case of each of the following countries the rate of exchange between the currency of that country (by whatever name the country was then known) and sterling in force on the date specified opposite it—

The Arab Republic of Egypt	15th March 1922
The Republic of the Sudan	1st January 1956
The Peoples Democratic Republic of Yemen	30th November 1967
The Federal Republic of Nigeria (other than former Regions thereof)	1st October 1960 ;

(c) in any other case, such date as the Secretary of State shall by regulation specify.

(2) Where on a date when an instalment of the basic pension is payable the rate of the basic pension enjoyed by the pensioner is greater in terms of sterling when ascertained in accordance with the official rate of exchange on that date between the currency in which the basic pension is payable and sterling than the sterling rate of the basic pension calculated in accordance with the preceding paragraph, then for the purpose of ascertaining any supplement payable under these Regulations the difference between the amounts shall be regarded as an overseas increase paid to the pensioner.

15. Where a person has been in receipt of a basic pension in respect of service under a government of an overseas territory specified in Schedule 1 to these Regulations and, in consequence of further service rendered by him to any other government or authority, being service which is reckonable under the law of the first mentioned overseas territory as public service for the purpose of the enactment, scheme or other instrument under which the basic pension is payable, the amount of the basic pension falls to be reduced to the maximum amount which, when account is taken of any pension payable by any other government or authority, may be drawn under the said enactment, scheme or other instrument, then the supplement payable under these Regulations may be further increased up to the amount of supplement which would have been payable if the basic pension had not been so reduced:

Provided that this regulation shall not apply in the case where the further service rendered to any other government or authority is service which has already been taken into account in ascertaining the amount of the basic pension.

16.—(1) In any case where an overseas increase which has been taken into account in determining any supplement payable under these Regulations is revised with retrospective effect such supplement shall be revised accordingly with similar effect and any overpayment made to the pensioner as a result of the revision may be recovered from him.

(2) Where any refund of overpayment as required by paragraph (1) of this regulation is not made within one month of notification no further supplements shall be payable to the pensioner until the amount of the refund so required has been made.

17. Application for a supplement under these Regulations shall be made to the Minister for Overseas Development who may require proof that any person applying for such supplement, or any person on behalf of whom such an application is made, is alive and eligible for such supplement, and no payment shall be made until such proof is furnished.

18. Subject to the provisions of sections 5(4) and 18(2) of the Act, these Regulations shall be deemed to have taken effect from 1st September 1971.

Alec Douglas-Home,
Secretary of State for Foreign
and Commonwealth Affairs.

5th April 1972.

Consent of the Minister for the Civil Service given under his Official Seal on 5th April 1972.

A. W. Wyatt,
Authorised by the Minister for
the Civil Service.

SCHEDULE 1

Regulations 4, 5, 6, 9, 10 and 12

DATES SPECIFIED IN RELATION TO OVERSEAS TERRITORIES
FOR THE PURPOSES OF REGULATIONS 4, 5, 6, 9, 10 AND 12

Col. 1 Overseas Territories	Col. 2	Col. 3	Col. 4	Col. 5	Col. 6	Col. 7
Aden / Federation of South Arabia / Protectorate of South Arabia / People's Democratic Republic of Yemen	1. 1.46	1. 4.53	1. 7.56	1. 7.60	18. 1.63	1. 4.65
Antigua	1. 1.45	1. 1.52	1. 1.56	1. 4.60	1. 4.61	1. 1.65
Bahamas	1. 1.52	1. 1.52	1. 1.56	1. 1.59	1. 4.61	1. 7.64
Barbados	1. 4.48	1. 4.52	1. 4.56	1. 4.61	1. 4.66	
Bermuda	1. 1.52	1. 1.52	1. 7.56	1. 7.60	1. 4.61	1. 1.67
Botswana / Bechuanaland	1. 1.47	1. 7.54	1. 8.58	1. 4.61	1.10.64	
British Antarctic Territory				1. 7.61	1. 7.63	
British Honduras	1. 1.46	1. 7.51	1. 7.56	1. 4.61	1. 7.66	
British Solomon Islands Protectorate	1. 1.46	1. 1.54	1. 4.58	1. 4.61	1.10.65	1. 4.67
British Virgin Islands	1. 1.45	1. 1.52	1. 1.56	1. 4.60	1. 4.61	1. 1.65
Brunei	1. 7.46					
Ceylon	1. 1.63					
Cyprus	1. 1.45	1. 1.53	1. 7.55			
Dominica	1. 1.45	1. 1.52	1. 1.56	1. 4.60	1. 4.61	1. 1.65
East African Community / East African Common Services Organisation / East African High Commission	1. 1.46	1. 1.54	1. 7.56	1. 4.60		
East African Railways and Harbours Administration / Kenya and Uganda Railways and Harbours Administration	1. 1.46	1. 1.54	1. 7.56	1. 4.60		
Eastern Nigeria / Eastern Region of Nigeria	1. 1.46	1. 4.52	1.10.54	1. 4.60		
Employing Authorities Under the Oversea Superannuation Scheme	1. 4.47					
Falkland Islands	1.12.46	1. 4.53	1. 1.57	1. 7.61	1. 7.63	1. 1.66
Federation of Malaysia / Federation of Malaya / Federated Malay States / Malayan Establishment / Malayan Union / Unfederated Malay States / Federal Republic of Nigeria	1. 8.47	1. 1.52	1. 1.55			
Federation of Nigeria / Nigeria	1. 1.46	1. 4.52	1.10.54	1. 9.59		
Fiji	1. 1.46	1. 1.50	1. 1.54	1. 4.61	1. 4.65	1. 4.67
The Gambia	1. 1.46	1.12.53	1. 4.56	1. 1.60	1.11.63	
Ghana / Gold Coast	1. 1.46	1. 4.52	1. 7.57			
Gibraltar	1. 4.46	1. 1.50	1. 1.56	1. 1.60	1. 8.63	1. 7.67
Gilbert and Ellice Islands	1. 1.46	1. 1.50	1. 1.54	1. 4.61	1.10.65	1. 4.67
Grenada	1. 1.45	1. 1.52	1. 1.56	1. 4.60	1. 4.61	1. 1.65
Guyana / British Guiana	1. 1.49	1. 1.54	1. 1.54	1. 4.61	1. 1.64	
Hong Kong	1. 1.47	1. 4.51	1.10.53	1. 7.59	1. 7.63	1. 4.65
Jamaica	1.10.50	1.10.50	1. 4.55	1. 4.58	1. 4.61	

Col. 1 Overseas Territories	Col. 2	Col. 3	Col. 4	Col. 5	Col. 6	Col. 7
Kenya	1. 1.46	1. 1.54	1. 7.56	1. 4.60		
Leeward Islands	1. 1.45	1. 1.52	1. 1.56	1. 4.60	1. 4.61	1. 1.65
Lesotho Basutoland	1. 1.47	1. 7.54	1. 8.58	1. 4.61	1.10.64	
Malawi Nyasaland	1. 1.46	1. 5.53	1. 7.55	1. 4.61	1. 4.63	1. 1.66
Malta	1. 4.48	1.10.53	1. 6.55	1. 4.59	1. 4.66	
Mauritius	1. 7.47	1. 7.50	1. 1.57	1. 4.61	1. 1.64	
Montserrat	1. 1.45	1. 1.52	1. 1.56	1. 4.60	1. 4.61	1. 1.65
Northern Nigeria Northern Region of Nigeria	1. 1.46	1. 4.52	1.10.54	1. 9.59		
Palestine	1. 4.46					
Sabah North Borneo	15. 7.46	1. 1.52	1. 1.56	1. 4.61		
St. Christopher, Nevis and Anguilla	1. 1.45	1. 1.52	1. 1.56	1. 4.60	1. 4.61	1. 1.65
St. Helena	1. 1.52	1. 1.52	1. 4.58	1. 4.61	1. 7.65	
St. Lucia	1. 1.45	1. 1.52	1. 1.56	1. 4.60	1. 4.61	1. 1.65
St. Vincent	1. 1.45	1. 1.52	1. 1.56	1. 4.60	1. 4.61	1. 1.65
Sarawak	1. 7.46	1. 1.52	1.10.54	1. 4.61		
Seychelles	1. 7.47	1. 1.54	1. 1.58	1. 4.61	1. 5.66	
Sierra Leone	1. 1.46	1. 3.53	1. 2.55	1. 4.57		
Singapore Straits Settlements	1. 8.47	1. 1.52	16. 6.53	1. 4.61		
Somali Republic Somaliland Protectorate	1. 1.46	1.10.53	1.10.56			
Sudan	1. 1.50					
Swaziland	1. 1.47	1. 7.54	1. 8.58	1. 4.61	1.10.64	
Tanzania Tanganyika Zanzibar	1. 1.46	1. 1.54	1. 7.56	1. 4.60		
The West Indies Federation	1. 1.46					
Tonga	1.10.49					
Trinidad and Tobago	1. 1.49	1. 1.54	1. 1.59	1. 4.61	1. 1.66	
Turks and Caicos	1.10.50	1.10.50	1. 4.55	1. 4.58	1. 4.61	
Uganda	1. 1.46	1. 1.54	1. 7.56	1. 4.60		
Western Nigeria Western Region of Nigeria	1. 1.46	1. 4.52	1.10.54	1. 4.59		
Western Pacific High Commission	1. 1.46	1. 1.50	1. 1.54	1. 4.61	1.10.65	1. 4.67
Zambia Northern Rhodesia	1. 1.46	1.10.51	1. 1.57	1. 4.61	1. 4.63	

SCHEDULE 2

Regulation 4

AMOUNT OF SUPPLEMENT CORRESPONDING TO ADDITIONAL INCREASE
FOR PENSIONERS OVER 70

Where a pension begins on or before 1st April 1961, and any qualifying condition is satisfied other than one of the conditions specified in section 3(3)(*b*), (*c*) and (*d*) of the Act (which relate to pensioners in receipt of derivative pensione while of an age less than 16 or receiving education or training) the addition to be made to the 1971 rate in accordance with section 6(5) of the Act shall be of the amount which is given by reference to the 1971 rate in the following Table:—

Column 1	Supplement	
	Column 2	Column 3
Pensions beginning		
	1. Normal	2. Small pensions
	£	1971 rate (£)　　×
Up to 1st July 1955　...　...　...　...　...	27·376	124·44　　0·22
Up to 1st April 1956　...　...　...　...　...	27·144	123·38　　0·22
Up to 1st July 1956　...　...　...　...　...	23·072	100·31　　0·23
Up to 1st April 1957　...　...　...　...　...	22·875	99·46　　0·23
Up to 1st July 1957　...　...　...　...　...	18·514	80·50　　0·23
Up to 1st April 1958　...　...　...　...　...	18·354	79·80　　0·23
Up to 1st July 1958　...　...　...　...　...	12·880	53·67　　0·24
Up to 1st April 1959　...　...　...　...　...	12·768	53·20　　0·24
Up to 1st July 1959　...　...　...　...　...	8·778	36·58　　0·24
Up to 1st April 1960　...　...　...　...　...	8·701	36·25　　0·24
Up to 1st July 1960　...　...　...　...　...	4·882	19·53　　0·25
Up to 1st April 1961　...　...　...　...　...	4·838	19·35　　0·25

Column 2 of this Table gives the amount of the supplement for pensions beginning at the time stated in column 1, unless the 1971 rate is less than the figure given in the first division of column 3; if it is less, the amount of the supplement is obtained by multiplying the 1971 rate by the figure given in the second division of column 3.

SCHEDULE 3

Regulation 2

ENACTMENTS, SCHEMES AND INSTRUMENTS APPROVED
FOR THE PURPOSES OF SECTION 11 OF THE ACT

Aden Widows' and Orphans' (United Kingdom) Pension Scheme.

Bahamas Widows' and Orphans' Pension Fund.

Botswana Widows' and Orphans' Pension Fund.

Ceylon Widows' and Orphans' Pension Fund.

East African Railways and Harbours Administration Superannuation Fund.

Ghana Widows' and Orphans' (Overseas Officers) Pension Fund.

Guyana Widows' and Orphans' Pension Fund.

Lesotho Widows' and Orphans' Pension Fund.

Mauritius Widows' and Orphans' Pension Fund.

Overseas Superannuation Scheme.

Sabah Widows' and Orphans' Pension Fund.

Sarawak Widows' and Orphans' Pension Fund.

Seychelles Widows' and Orphans' (Overseas Officers) Pension Fund.

Sierra Leone Widows' and Orphans' Pension Fund.

Somaliland Protectorate Widows' and Orphans' Pension Fund.

Swaziland Widows' and Orphans' Pension Fund.

Zambia Widows' and Orphans' Pension Fund.

SCHEDULE 4

Regulation 9

TABLES FOR CALCULATION OF 1971 RATE

Table I:

Basic Pension		*Increase*
Less than £25		70%
£25 to £25·74	The amount which when added to the basic pension will produce a total of	£42·50
£25·75 to £50		65%
£50·01 to £55	The amount which when added to the basic pension will produce a total of	£82·50
£55·01 to £100		50%
£100·01 to £109·14	The amount which when added to the basic pension will produce a total of	£150
£109·15 to £130		40%
£130·01 to £140	The amount which when added to the basic pension will produce a total of	£182
£140·01 to £200		30%
£200·01 and over		£60

Table II:

Basic pension as increased under Table I	*Increase*
Up to £100	40%
£100·01 to £133·33	£40
£133·34 to £200	30%
£200·01 and over	£60

Table III:

Increase (*a*) is 1/3 of basic pension as increased under Tables I and II or £26, whichever is the less.

Increase (*b*) is 10 per cent. of basic pension only or £100, whichever is the less.

Table IV:

Increase is 12 per cent. of basic pension as increased under Tables I, II and III.

Table V:

Increase (*a*) is 12 per cent. of basic pension as increased under Tables I, II, III and IV.

Increase (*b*) is 25 per cent. of basic pension as increased under Tables I, II, III and IV or £20 whichever is the less.

Table VI:

Increase is 16 per cent. of basic pension as increased under Tables I, II, III, IV and V.

Table VII:

Increase is 18 per cent. of basic pension as increased under Tables I, II, III, IV, V and VI.

EXPLANATORY NOTE

(This Note is not part of the Regulations.)

1. These Regulations, which provide for the payment of supplements on pensions paid to or in respect of certain overseas civil servants, supersede the Overseas Service (Pensions Supplement) Regulations 1969.

2. Part II of these Regulations provides for the payment to an officer of a supplement which, together with any increase or supplement otherwise payable on his pension, corresponds as nearly as may be with the aggregate of the increases which would be payable under the Pensions (Increase) Act 1971 and any orders made under section 2 of that Act (biennial review orders) on a Civil Service pension. Similar provision for the dependants of officers is made in Part IV of the Regulations.

3. Part III of the Regulations provides for the payment of an additional supplement where a pension paid to an officer under the Overseas Superannuation Scheme is of a reduced amount because the contributions to that Scheme in respect of his overseas service were reduced by virtue of his continuing contributions to the Federated Superannuation Scheme for Universities or other similar approved scheme during that overseas service.

4. The provisions of Regulation 14 ensure that account is taken of additions to the value of an overseas pension owing to changes in the rate of exchange between sterling and the currency of an overseas territory.

5. Regulation 15 prevents an overseas pensioner who earns extra pension after normal retirement age from being penalised in certain circumstances because of a rule limiting his pension to two-thirds of his highest pensionable emoluments.

6. These Regulations take effect retrospectively from 1st September 1971, in accordance with the powers contained in sections 5(4) and 18(2) of the Act.

STOKE-ON-TRENT
CITY
LIBRARIES

STATUTORY INSTRUMENTS

1972 No. 551 (S.39)

EDUCATION, SCOTLAND

The Teachers Superannuation (Financial Provisions) (Scotland) Regulations 1972

Made - - - -	*28th March* 1972
Laid before Parliament	*12th April* 1972
Coming into Operation	*3rd May* 1972

ARRANGEMENT OF REGULATIONS

1. Citation and Commencement.
2. Interpretation.
3. Calculation of Salary.
4. Calculation of Average Salary.
5. Financing of Benefits.
6. Teachers Superannuation Account.
7. Actuarial Inquiries.
8. Modification of Regulations.

In exercise of the powers conferred upon me by section 9 of the Superannuation Act 1972(a) and of all other powers enabling me in that behalf, with the consent of the Minister for the Civil Service and after consultation with representatives of education authorities and of teachers and with such representatives of other persons likely to be affected as appear to me to be appropriate, I hereby make the following regulations:—

Citation and Commencement

1.—(1) These regulations may be cited as the Teachers Superannuation (Financial Provisions) (Scotland) Regulations 1972.

(2) These regulations shall come into operation on 3rd May 1972 and shall take effect as from 25th March 1972.

(3) The Teachers Superannuation (Scotland) Regulations 1969 to 1971(b) and these regulations may be cited together as the Teachers Superannuation (Scotland) Regulations 1969 to 1972.

Interpretation

2.—(1) In these regulations, unless the context otherwise requires—

"the Act of 1968" means the Teachers Superannuation (Scotland) Act 1968(c);

(a) 1972 c. 11.
(b) S.I. 1969/77, 659, 1971/1995 (1969 I, p. 133; II, p. 1820; 1971 III, p. 5683).
(c) 1968 c. 12.

"accounting period" means a period for which the teachers superannuation account is to be made up;

"teacher" includes an organiser;

"the Teachers Regulations" means the Teachers Superannuation (Scotland) Regulations 1969 to 1971;

"teachers superannuation account" means the account required to be kept under regulation 6 of these regulations.

(2) These regulations shall be construed as one with the Teachers Regulations.

(3) For the purposes of these regulations the education authority shall be deemed to be the employer of any teacher employed in or in connection with a school maintained by the authority.

(4) Any reference in these regulations to a regulation or paragraph shall, unless the context otherwise requires, be construed as a reference to a regulation of these regulations or to a paragraph of that regulation in which the paragraph occurs as the case may be.

(5) The Interpretation Act 1889(a) shall apply for the interpretation of these regulations as it applies for the interpretation of an Act of Parliament.

Calculation of Salary

3.—(1) For the purposes of the Teachers Regulations the salary of a teacher shall be taken, subject as in this regulation provided, to be the aggregate of the emoluments whether in money or in kind receivable by the teacher in respect of his employment in reckonable service, excluding such moneys and emoluments prescribed in regulation 23(1) of the Teachers Regulations.

(2) The Secretary of State may make a direction, in such cases as he thinks fit, disapplying such exclusion from the salary of a teacher.

(3) Subject as provided in regulation 23(2) of the Teachers Regulations, where a teacher is by reason of sickness receiving less than his full salary then for the purpose of calculating the amounts payable by way of contributions in respect of him the amount which he is so receiving shall be deemed to be his salary.

Calculation of Average Salary

4.—(1) For the purposes of the Teachers Regulations the average salary of a teacher shall be taken, subject as in this regulation provided, to be the average amount of his full salary calculated under regulation 3 in respect of his employment in reckonable service or other prescribed service during the 3 years of such service (whether continuous or not) next preceding the commencement of any annual superannuation allowance or the payment of an additional allowance or gratuity under the Teachers Regulations.

(2) If a teacher has not been employed in reckonable service or other prescribed service for 3 years or more, his average salary shall, except as provided in regulation 55 of the Teachers Regulations, be calculated by reference to the period during which he has been so employed.

(3) If, in the opinion of the Secretary of State, the salary of a teacher has been unreasonably increased in respect of his employment during any period to be taken into account in calculating his average salary, the amount of the salary on

---

(a) 1889 c. 63.

which his average salary is to be computed shall be such as the Secretary of State considers proper.

Financing of Benefits

5.—(1) For the purpose of defraying the cost of the benefits for which the Teachers Regulations provide, contributions shall be paid to the Secretary of State by teachers and their employers in accordance with the provisions of this regulation.

(2) The contributions payable in respect of a teacher by the teacher shall be of an amount equal to 6 per cent of his salary for the time being.

(3) The contributions payable in respect of a teacher by his employer shall be of an amount equal to 6 per cent of the teacher's salary for the time being, together with any supplementary contributions required to be paid under paragraph (4).

(4) Where a report of an actuarial inquiry specifies, in pursuance of regulation 7(3), a rate per cent in relation to supplementary contributions, such contributions shall—

> (*a*) be paid by employers from the beginning of the accounting period next after that in which the report is made until the expiry of the accounting period in which the next subsequent report is made; and
>
> (*b*) be of an amount equal to the rate per cent so specified of the teacher's salary for the time being.

Teachers Superannuation Account

6.—(1) An account shall be kept in accordance with the provisions of this regulation of the revenue and expenditure under these regulations and the Teachers Regulations and such account shall be in continuation of that formerly kept under section 5(1) of the Act of 1968.

(2) The accounting period for which the account is to be made up shall be the period of 12 months beginning on 1st April in each year.

(3) There shall be treated as having been paid into the revenue of the account for each accounting period—

> (*a*) by teachers, the amount of contributions paid by them under regulation 5(2) which are attributable to the period;
>
> (*b*) by the employers of teachers, the amount of contributions (including supplementary contributions) paid by them under regulation 5(3) which are attributable to the period;
>
> (*c*) a sum equal to the expenditure during the period upon superannuation and other allowances attributable to service before 1st June 1922;
>
> (*d*) a sum representing interest calculated in accordance with the provisions of the Teachers Superannuation Account (Rates of Interest) (Scotland) Regulations 1969(**a**);
>
> (*e*) the amount of any balance of revenue over expenditure remaining at the end of the last preceding accounting period; and
>
> (*f*) any other revenue attributable to the period.

(**a**) S.I. 1969/785 (1969 II, p. 2203).

(4) Expenditure upon superannuation and other allowances attributable to service before 1st June 1922 shall be shown separately from expenditure attributable to service on or after 1st June 1922 on allowances, gratuities and re-payment of contributions.

(5) The account shall be kept in such form and prepared in such manner as may be determined by the Secretary of State after consultation with the Treasury.

Actuarial Inquiries

7.—(1) The Government Actuary or the Deputy Government Actuary shall make an actuarial inquiry with respect to the teachers superannuation account at the end of the accounting period ending 31st March 1976 and at the end of every fifth subsequent accounting period.

(2) An inquiry made in pursuance of paragraph (1) shall determine whether the value, at the end of the period for which the inquiry is made, of the expenditure (attributable to service on or after 1st June 1922) required to be included in the teachers superannuation account after the end of that period in respect of teachers who then were employed in reckonable service or had previously been employed in reckonable service exceeds the aggregate of—

(a) the value at the end of that period of the contributions payable after the end of that period in respect of such teachers and of the sums falling to be credited to the teachers superannuation account after the end of that period in accordance with regulation 6(3)(d) and (f); and

(b) the balance of revenue over expenditure remaining in the teachers superannuation account at the end of that period.

(3) Where an actuarial inquiry reveals such a deficiency as is mentioned in paragraph (2), the report of the inquiry shall specify the rate per cent (being a rate of one-quarter of one per cent or a multiple of one-quarter of one per cent) at which supplementary contributions paid by employers of teachers employed in reckonable service would remove the deficiency by the expiry of a period of 40 years beginning with the accounting period next after that in which the report is made.

(4) The report on each actuarial inquiry under this regulation shall be made to the Secretary of State and shall be laid by him before each House of Parliament.

Modification of Regulations

8. References in the Teachers Superannuation Account (Rates of Interest) (Scotland) Regulations 1969 to section 5(1) of, and paragraph 3(d) of Schedule 1 to the Act of 1968 shall be construed as references to the provisions of these regulations which respectively correspond thereto.

Gordon Campbell,
One of Her Majesty's Principal
Secretaries of State.

St Andrew's House,
Edinburgh.
27th March 1972.

Consent of the Minister for the Civil Service given under his Official Seal on 28th March 1972.

(L.S.) *K. H. McNeill,*
Authorised by the Minister for
the Civil Service.

EXPLANATORY NOTE

(This Note is not part of the Regulations.)

These Regulations replace without substantive amendment the provisions of the Teachers Superannuation (Scotland) Act 1968 relating to the calculation of salary and average salary, contributions, accounts and actuarial inquiries which have ceased to have effect on the repeal of that Act by the Superannuation Act 1972.

The Regulations have retrospective effect by virtue of section 12(1) of the Superannuation Act 1972.

STATUTORY INSTRUMENTS

1972 No. 552

INCOME TAX

The Income Tax (Employments) (No. 10) Regulations 1972

Made - - -	*6th April* 1972
Laid before the House of Commons	*13th April* 1972
Coming into Operation	*4th May* 1972

The Commissioners of Inland Revenue, in exercise of the powers conferred upon them by section 204 of the Income and Corporation Taxes Act 1970(a), hereby make the following Regulations: —

1.—(1) These Regulations may be cited as the Income Tax (Employments) (No. 10) Regulations 1972, and shall come into operation on 4th May 1972.

(2) The Interpretation Act 1889 b) shall apply for the interpretation of these Regulations as it applies for the interpretation of an Act of Parliament.

(3) In these Regulations the expression "the Principal Regulations" means the Income Tax (Employments) Regulations 1965(c) as amended(d).

2. Regulations 19 and 29 of the Principal Regulations shall have effect, as regards payments of emoluments made on or after 4th May 1972, as if for any reference to a rate of £8 or more a week there were substituted a reference to a rate of £11 or more a week, and as if for any reference to a rate of £34·50 or more a month there were substituted a reference to a rate of £47 or more a month.

By Order of the Commissioners of Inland Revenue.

A. H. Dalton,
Secretary.

6th April 1972.

EXPLANATORY NOTE

(This Note is not part of the Regulations.)

These Regulations provide for raising the limit of weekly or monthly pay above which an employer has to operate the Pay as You Earn scheme for every employee, to take into account the increased Income Tax allowances proposed in the Finance Bill 1972.

(a) 1970 c. 10.　　　　(b) 1889 c. 63.　　　(c) S.I. 1965/516 (1965 I, p. 1321).
(d) The relevant amending instruments are: S.I. 1966/1373, 1969/170, 688, 1970/666 (1966 III, p. 3691; 1969 I p. 440; II, p. 1859; 1970 II, p. 2166).

STATUTORY INSTRUMENTS

1972 No. 555

SOCIAL SECURITY

The National Insurance (Classification) Regulations 1972

Made - - - -	*6th April* 1972
Laid before Parliament	*17th April* 1972
Coming into Operation	*8th May* 1972

The Secretary of State for Social Services, in conjunction with the Treasury, in exercise of powers under sections 1(3) and 16(1) of the National Insurance Act 1965(a), and of all other powers enabling him in that behalf and for the purpose only of consolidating the regulations hereby revoked, hereby makes the following regulations:—

Citation, commencement and interpretation

1.—(1) These regulations may be cited as the National Insurance (Classification) Regulations 1972, and shall come into operation on 8th May 1972.

(2) In these regulations, unless the context otherwise requires—

"the Act" means the National Insurance Act 1965;

"the Secretary of State" means the Secretary of State for Social Services;

"hospital" means any institution for the reception and treatment of persons suffering from illness or mental defectiveness, any maternity home, and any institution for the reception and treatment of persons during convalescence or persons requiring medical rehabilitation, and includes clinics, dispensaries and out-patient departments maintained in connection with any such institution or home as aforesaid;

"nurse" means any person within the class of persons who under section 1 of the Nurses Agencies Act 1957(b) or section 27 of the Nurses (Scotland) Act 1951(c) and any regulations made thereunder(d) may lawfully be supplied from an agency for the supply of nurses;

and other expressions have the same meanings as in the Act.

(3) References in these regulations to any enactment or regulations shall, except in so far as the context otherwise requires, be construed as including references to such enactment or regulations as amended or extended by or under any other enactment, order or regulations and as including references to any enactment or regulations thereby consolidated.

(4) The rules for the construction of Acts of Parliament contained in the Interpretation Act 1889(e) shall apply in relation to this instrument and in relation to any revocation effected thereby as if this instrument, the regulations revoked by it and any regulations revoked by the regulations so revoked were Acts of Parliament, and as if each revocation were a repeal.

(a) 1965 c. 51.	(b) 1957 c. 16.
(c) 1951 c. 55.	(d) S.I. 1961/1214, 1219 (1961 II, pp. 2412, 2421).
(e) 1889 c. 63.	

Classification of insured persons

2.—(1) For the purposes of the Act, the classification of insured persons shall be modified in accordance with the following paragraphs of this regulation.

(2) Subject to the provisions of paragraphs (3) and (4) of this regulation, every insured person shall, in respect of any employment specified in any paragraph in column (A) of Part I of Schedule 1 to these regulations, be treated as an employed person in so far as he is gainfully occupied in such employment and is not a person specified in the corresponding paragraph in column (B) of that Part.

(3) Subject to the provisions of paragraph (4) of this regulation, every insured person shall, in respect of any employment specified in any paragraph in column (A) of Part II of the said Schedule 1, be treated as a self-employed person in so far as he is gainfully occupied in such employment and is not a person specified in the corresponding paragraph in column (B) of that Part:

Provided that for the purpose of graduated contributions paragraph 13 of that Part shall not apply to the employment of a person on any day or days in any contribution week in continuation of employment by the same employer in which services are or would be rendered normally for more than 8 hours in a week.

(4) Every insured person shall, in respect of any employment specified in any paragraph in column (A) of Part III of the said Schedule 1, be treated as a non-employed person, and any such employment shall be disregarded, in so far as he is not a person specified in the corresponding paragraph in column (B) of that Part.

Employments treated as continuing

3. For the purposes of the Act, the employment of a person shall be treated as continuing in the circumstances specified in Schedule 2 to these regulations.

Special provisions with respect to persons declared by High Court to be included in a particular class of insured persons

4.—(1) Where, under the provisions of the Act relating to references and appeals to the High Court**(a)**, the High Court decides any question as to the class of insured persons in which a person is to be included, and that decision is inconsistent with some previous determination of a question by the Secretary of State**(a)**, then, if the Secretary of State is satisfied that contributions of a prior class have been paid by or in respect of any person by reason of that determination or in the reasonable belief that that determination was applicable, he may, if it appears to him that it would be in the interests of the person by or in respect of whom such contributions have been paid, or of any claimant or beneficiary by virtue of that person's insurance, so to do, direct that that person shall be treated as though he had been included in the class of insured persons corresponding to the contributions paid during any contribution weeks for which contributions of a prior class were so paid before the date on which the decision of the High Court was given, and, if such a direction is given, that person shall be deemed to have been included in that class accordingly for any such weeks.

(2) In any case where the Secretary of State, on new facts being brought to his notice, has revised a determination of a question previously given by him,

---

(a) *See* sections 65(1) and (3), and 73(1) and (4), National Insurance Act 1965.

the provisions of this regulation shall apply with the necessary modifications in the same manner as they apply where the High Court has given a decision inconsistent with a determination previously given by the Secretary of State.

(3) In this regulation the expression "contributions of a prior class" means, in relation to a non-employed person, contributions as an employed or self-employed person and employer's contributions, and, in relation to a self-employed person, contributions as an employed person and employer's contributions.

(4) In the application of this regulation to Scotland, for any reference to the High Court, there shall be substituted a reference to the Court of Session(**a**).

Persons to be treated as employers

5. In respect of any employment specified in any paragraph in column (A) of Schedule 3 to these regulations, the person specified in the corresponding paragraph in column (B) of that Schedule shall for the purposes of the Act be treated as the employer of the employed person concerned.

Effect of Regulations for the purposes of section 43 of the Act

6. The provisions of these regulations shall not have effect for the purpose of the determination of any question whether a person is or is not engaged in a gainful occupation which arises under section 43 of the Act (increase of benefit for adult dependants) or any regulations(**b**) made thereunder.

Revocation and general savings

7.—(1) The regulations specified in column 1 of Schedule 4 to these regulations are hereby revoked to the extent mentioned in column 3 of that Schedule.

(2) Anything whatsoever done under or by virtue of any regulation revoked by these regulations shall be deemed to have been done under or by virtue of the corresponding provision of these regulations, and anything whatsoever begun under any such regulation may be continued under these regulations as if begun under these regulations.

(3) Nothing in paragraphs (2) and (3) of this regulation shall be taken as affecting the general application by regulation 1(4) of these regulations of the rules for the construction of Acts of Parliament contained in section 38 of the Interpretation Act 1889 (effect of repeals) with regard to the effect of revocations.

Keith Joseph,
Secretary of State for Social Services.

30th March 1972.

V. H. Goodhew,
Tim Fortescue,
Two of the Lords Commissioners of Her
Majesty's Treasury.

6th April 1972.

(**a**) *See* sections 65(8) and 73(5), National Insurance Act 1965.
(**b**) *See* S.I. 1967/330 (1967 I, p. 1131).

SCHEDULE 1

Regulation 2

PART 1

Column (A)	Column (B)
Employments in respect of which, subject to the provisions of regulation 2 and to the exceptions in column (B) of this Part, persons are treated as employed persons.	*Persons excepted from the operation of column (A).*
1. Employment under a public or local authority constituted in Great Britain (not being employment under the Crown) notwithstanding that it is not employment under a contract of service.	1. Any person in employment specified in paragraph 1 in column (A) where the service ordinarily performed by the person in that employment (or, if he is employed in more than one such employment or is also employed in an employment specified in paragraph 3 in column (A), the aggregate service performed by him in those employments) is part-time service only or, where that employment is— (*a*) as a medical practitioner or dental practitioner on the list of an Executive Council under the National Health Service Act 1946(**a**), or the National Health Service (Scotland) Act 1947(**b**); (*b*) as a chaplain or other minister of religion; (*c*) otherwise than as an officer or servant of a public or local authority or as a constable.
2. Employment of a medical practitioner or a dental practitioner— (*a*) involving whole-time service in any hospital; or (*b*) in which he is wholly or mainly engaged and is remunerated by salary; or (*c*) being employment by a Regional Hospital Board or a Board of Governors of a Teaching Hospital constituted under the National Health Service Act 1946, where he is employed in any two or more such employments and is wholly or mainly engaged in such employments in the aggregate and is remunerated by salary.	2. None.
3. Employment— (*a*) in England and Wales as superintendent registrar or deputy superintendent registrar, registrar or deputy registrar of births	3. Any person in employment specified in paragraph 3 in column (A) who is not wholly or mainly engaged in such employment or, if he is employed in more than one such employment or is also employed

(**a**) 1946 c. 81.   (**b**) 1947 c. 27.

Column (A)	Column (B)
Employments in respect of which, subject to the provisions of regulation 2 and to the exceptions in column (B) of this Part, persons are treated as employed persons.	*Persons excepted from the operation of column (A).*

and deaths, or registrar or deputy registrar of marriages;
  (*b*) in Scotland as senior registrar, district registrar, or assistant registrar of births and deaths and marriages.

in an employment specified in paragraph 1 in column (A), is not wholly or mainly engaged in such employments in the aggregate.

4. Employment of a nurse (as defined in regulation 1(2)) as nurse for the sick or as midwife, notwithstanding that the employment is not under a contract of service.

4. Any person in employment specified in paragraph 4 in column (A) (other than employment under a public or local authority) in any contribution week in which that person is not exclusively so employed by one employer for at least one day.

5. Employment in Great Britain in plying for hire with any vehicle or vessel the use of which is obtained under any contract of bailment or letting for hire (other than a hire-purchase agreement) in consideration of the payment of a fixed sum or a share in the earnings or otherwise.

5. None.

6. Employment (not being employment under a contract of service)—
  (*a*) as a master or registrar or assistant master or assistant registrar of the Supreme Court of Judicature (including employment as a district registrar or assistant district registrar); or
  (*b*) as a whole-time registrar or whole-time assistant registrar under the County Courts Act 1959(a).

6. Any person in employment as deputy for a person holding any office specified in paragraph 6 in column (A).

7. Employment (notwithstanding that it is not employment under a contract of service) as an office cleaner or in any similar capacity in any premises other than those used as a private dwelling-house.

7. None.

8. Employment, (not being employment under a contract of service or employment in respect of which a person is, under the other provisions of these regulations, treated as an employed person) in which the person employed renders, or is under obligation

8. Any person in employment specified in paragraph 8 of column (A)—
  (*a*) where the service of the person employed is rendered in his own home or on other premises not under the control or management of the person to whom the person

---

(a) 1959 c. 22.

Column (A)	Column (B)
Employments in respect of which, subject to the provisions of regulation 2 and to the exceptions in column (B) of this Part, persons are treated as employed persons.	*Persons excepted from the operation of column (A).*

to render, personal service and is subject to supervision, direction or control, or to the right of supervision, direction or control, as to the manner of the rendering of such service and where the person employed is supplied by or through some third person (including, in the case of a body of persons unincorporate, a body of which the person employed is a member) and—
 	
    (a) where remuneration for such service is paid by or through, or on the basis of accounts submitted by, that third person or in accordance with arrangements made with that third person; or
    (b) where payments, other than to the person employed, are made by way of fees, commission or other payments of like nature which relate to the continued employment in that employment of the person employed.
	employed is supplied (except where such other premises are premises at which the person employed is required, by reason of the nature of the service, to render service); or
	    (b) who is employed as an actor, singer, musician or other entertainer or as a fashion, photographic or artist's model; or
	    (c) in a case where remuneration is not paid by or through, or on the basis of accounts submitted by, that third person—
	      (i) where the person employed has obtained that employment through a third person as part of that third person's activities in which persons seeking employment are introduced to persons requiring their services; and
	      (ii) where as a result of such an introduction the person employed and the person to whom he has been introduced have entered into a contract with each other for the rendering of such service; and
	     (iii) where only the person employed and the person to whom he has been introduced have a direct financial interest in the continued employment in that employment of the person employed.

Part II

Column (A)	Column (B)
Employments in respect of which, subject to the provisions of regulation 2 and to the exceptions in column (B) of this Part, persons are treated as self-employed persons.	*Persons excepted from the operation of column (A).*

9. Employment of a person (not being a pre-1948 contributor within the meaning of the Act (a)) in any employment by virtue of which he would but for the provisions of this paragraph be an employed person, if—
   (*a*) the person is not ordinarily resident in the United Kingdom; and
   (*b*) the employer of that person is not so ordinarily resident, and has no place of business in the United Kingdom.
	9. None.

10. Employment by any one employer as an interviewer for the purpose of obtaining information about habits or opinions of members of the public or any particular category or description of persons, where services in that employment are rendered normally for not more than 28 hours in a contribution week.	10. None.
11. Employment in or about a cathedral, church or other place of religious worship as (*a*) member of the choir, (*b*) organist or other musician, (*c*) precentor, (*d*) beadle, (*e*) caretaker, (*f*) chapel keeper, (*g*) church officer, (*h*) clerk, (*i*) door-keeper, (*j*) pew-opener, (*k*) sacristan, (*l*) sexton or (*m*) verger, including duties incidental to the employment.	11. Any person (not being a person mainly dependent for his livelihood on his earnings from other employment as a self-employed person, or, in the case of employment as a precentor, not being a minister of religion) whose weekly earnings from any one or more of the employments specified in paragraphs 11 and 37 in column (A) include the provision of board and lodging by the employer or are ordinarily more than £5·00.
12. Employment as a sub-postmaster remunerated by scale payment.	12. Any person who renders on the average 18 or more hours' personal service weekly as a sub-postmaster remunerated by scale payment and is not mainly dependent for his livelihood on

---

(a) *See* sections 115 and 117(1) and Schedule 11, para. 17 ibid. and S.I. 1948/612, reg. **2**; 1948/1276, reg. 2 and 1948/1279, reg. 2 (Rev. XVI, p. 18: 1948 I, p. 2834; Rev. XVI, p. 49: 1948 I, p. 2639 and Rev. XVI, p. 63: 1948 I, p. 2685).

Column (A)	Column (B)
Employments in respect of which, subject to the provisions of regulation 2 and to the exceptions in column (B) of this Part, persons are treated as self-employed persons.	*Persons excepted from the operation of column (A).*

	the earnings derived by him from any occupation other than employment under the Post Office.
13. Employment of a person in any capacity by any one employer on any day or days in any contribution week on which that person renders services in that employment where— (*a*) if the employment is in continuation of employment by that employer in which services are or would be rendered normally for more than 8 hours in a week, such services are rendered in that week for not more than 4 hours; or (*b*) in any other case, such services are not rendered in that week for more than 8 hours.	13. Any person employed in any contribution week in any employment specified in paragraph 13 in column (A) which is one of two or more such employments by different employers who carry on business in association, to the extent following:— (*a*) where in the immediately preceding week or weeks the person has been in the employment of any one or more such employers and has rendered or normally would have rendered services in that employment or those employments for more than 8 hours a week in aggregate, in respect of any services rendered by him in such employment or employments in the contribution week in excess of 4 hours in aggregate; (*b*) in any other case, in respect of services rendered by him in such employments in the contribution week in excess of 8 hours in aggregate.
14. Employment of a person— (*a*) in any employment or employments by any one employer; or (*b*) in any employment or employments by two or more employers who carry on business in association, where the weekly earnings (or, where in either case there is more than one such employment, the aggregate weekly earnings) derived therefrom are ordinarily not more than £5·00.	14. Any person employed in one or more of the employments specified in sub-paragraphs (*a*) or (*b*) of paragraph 14 in column (A) in any contribution week in which— (*a*) the earnings include the provision of board and lodging by the employer; or (*b*) the earnings (or, where in either case there is more than one such employment, the aggregate earnings) derived therefrom are more than £5·00.
15. Employment as an agent paid by commission or fees or a share in the profits, or partly in one and partly in another of such ways, where the person so employed is mainly dependent for his livelihood on his earnings from some occupation other than employment as	15. None.

Column (A)	Column (B)
Employments in respect of which, subject to the provisions of regulation 2 and to the exceptions in column (B) of this Part, persons are treated as self-employed persons.	*Persons excepted from the operation of column (A).*
such an agent, or where he is ordinarily employed as such agent by more than one employer, and his employment under no one of such employers is that on which he is mainly dependent for his livelihood.	
16. Employment under a contract of service by the insured person's wife for the purposes of a trade or business.	16. None.
17. Employment under contract of service of a married woman by her husband.	17. None.
18. Employment of a nurse (as defined in regulation 1(2)) as nurse for the sick or as midwife in any contribution week in which the nurse is not exclusively so employed by one employer for at least one day.	18. Any person employed as specified in paragraph 18 in column (A) who is so employed under a public or local authority.
19. Employment by any one employer on a track being a dog racecourse within the meaning of the Betting, Gaming and Lotteries Act 1963(a), involving service only on the days and during the period within which betting on that track by way of bookmaking or by means of a totalisator on the results of dog races is not prohibited by that Act.	19. None.
20. Occasional employment in the operation of a totalisator on an approved horse racecourse within the meaning of the Betting, Gaming and Lotteries Act 1963.	20. None.
21. Occasional employment by any one employer involving planting or sowing, or picking, lifting, gathering, collecting or harvesting, as the case may be, plants or plant produce (including fruit, vegetables, flowers, hops, grain, bulbs, potatoes or any other root crops), or involving any operation ancillary thereto.	21. Any person employed as specified in paragraph 21 in column (A)— (a) who is ordinarily employed in employed contributors' employment or is ordinarily gainfully occupied in agriculture (including horticulture and forestry); and (b) who produces to his employer satisfactory evidence that he is so ordinarily employed or occupied.

(a) 1963 c. 2.

PART III

Column (A)	Column (B)
Employments in respect of which, subject to the exceptions in column (B) of this Part, persons are treated as non-employed persons and their employment therein disregarded.	*Persons excepted from the operation of column (A).*
22. Any employment or employments as a self-employed person (including any employment in respect of which a person is, under these regulations, treated as a self-employed person) where the insured person is not ordinarily gainfully occupied in any such employment or employments or where the weekly earnings (or, where there is more than one such employment, the aggregate weekly earnings) derived therefrom are ordinarily less than £4·00.	22. None.

23. Employment of a person by any one employer in any contribution week—
    (a) on the Sunday where services (not exceeding in length a normal working day) are rendered in that employment only on that day in that week and that person is also employed by the same employer on the Monday of the succeeding contribution week; or
    (b) on the Monday where services (not exceeding in length a normal working day) are rendered in that employment only on that day in that week and that person has also been employed by the same employer only on the Saturday, or on the Friday and the Saturday, and on the Sunday in the preceding contribution week.
	23. None.

24. Employment by the father, mother, grandfather, grandmother, stepfather, stepmother, son, daughter, grandson, grand-daughter, stepson, stepdaughter, brother, sister, half-brother or half-sister of the insured person, in so far as the employment— (a) is employment in a private dwelling-house in which both the insured person and the employer reside; and	24. None.

Column (A)	Column (B)
Employments in respect of which, subject to the exceptions in column (B) of this Part, persons are treated as non-employed persons and their employment therein disregarded.	*Persons excepted from the operation of column (A).*
(b) is not employment for the purposes of any trade or business carried on there by the employer.	
25. Employment by the insured person's wife otherwise than for the purposes of a trade or business whether or not under a contract of service.	25. None.
26. Employment of a married woman (whether or not under contract of service) by, or as partner of, or in any similar association with, her husband.	26. Any person employed as specified in paragraph 26 in column (A) where that employment is in a trade or business and she is ordinarily engaged therein for not less than 24 hours in a contribution week.
27. Employment as a special constable.	27. None.
28. Employment, involving part-time service only, as a member of a fire brigade maintained in pursuance of the Fire Services Act 1947(a).	28. None.
29. Employment, involving part-time service only— (a) in coast-watching for life-saving purposes; (b) in the operation of a life-boat; or (c) in the operation of a rocket or other life-saving apparatus or any gear connected therewith; and in any duties ancillary to such operations.	29. None.
30. Employment, involving part-time service only, in connection with the relief of light keepers or otherwise in attendance upon lighthouses, or in connection with the care or upkeep of minor lights, buoys, beacons, signals or tide-gauges.	30. None.
31. Employment, involving part-time service only, on or in connection with a pasture or grazing held in common under the Small Landholders (Scotland) Acts 1886 to 1931 and the Crofters (Scotland) Acts 1955 and 1961(b) either as a shepherd or other herd.	31. None.

(a) 1947 c. 41.   (b) 1955 c. 21; 1961 c. 58.

Column (A)	Column (B)
Employments in respect of which, subject to the exceptions in column (B) of this Part, persons are treated as non-employed persons and their employment therein disregarded.	*Persons excepted from the operation of column (A).*
32. Employment as secretary or clerk of a society, club, committee, philanthropic institution, school or other similar body or institution, where personal service is ordinarily required only occasionally or outside the ordinary hours of work.	32. None.
33. Employment, involving part-time service only, in the performance of clerical duties after 6 p.m., or outside the ordinary hours of work.	33. None.
34. Employment in any one cotton, woollen, worsted, silk, artificial silk or nylon mill or factory on not more than 2 days in a contribution week as a helper to or substitute for a woman or women regularly employed in spinning, weaving or doubling or in processes incidental thereto.	34. Any person who is employed in employment specified in paragraph 34 in column (A) where the employment is as a helper to or substitute for a woman or women regularly employed in weaving and where in respect of that employment the employer of the said woman or women pays wages or other pecuniary remuneration to the person.
35. Employment as a caretaker in respect of which no wages are paid, or other money payments made, either by the employer or by any other person.	35. None.
36. Employment, involving part-time service only, as a caretaker of, or key-keeper at, ancient monuments.	36. None.
37. Employment— 　(*a*) in or about a cathedral, church or other place of religious worship, as 　　(i) acolyte, 　　(ii) bell-ringer or 　　(iii) organ-blower; or 　(*b*) as (i) bible woman, 　　(ii) lay preacher or 　　(iii) scripture-reader.	37. Any person (not being a person mainly dependent for his livelihood on his earnings from employment as a self-employed person) whose weekly earnings from any one or more of the employments specified in paragraphs 11 and 37 in column (A), excluding any earnings as precentor of a minister of religion, include the provision of board and lodging by the employer or are ordinarily more than £5·00.

Column (A)	Column (B)
Employments in respect of which, subject to the exceptions in column (B) of this Part, persons are treated as non-employed persons and their employment therein disregarded.	*Persons excepted from the operation of column (A).*

38. Employment as a part-time Post Office telephonist (day or night).

39. Employment as an auxiliary postman.

40. Employment as a part-time indoor assistant for postal and telegraph business.

41. Employment as a collector or deliverer of postal letters under allowance.

42. Employment as an occasional messenger on Post Office business.

43. (a) Employment at sittings of the judge or registrar of a county court as an usher or interpreter involving occasional attendance only.
    (b) Employment at sittings of the Sheriff, Police or Justice of the Peace Courts in Scotland as—
        (i) an interpreter involving occasional attendance only; or
        (ii) a Bar Officer or Court Officer.

38 to 57. Any person (not being a person mainly dependent for his livelihood on his earnings from employment as a self-employed person) employed in one or more of the employments specified in paragraphs 38 to 42, 43(b)(ii) and 44 to 57 in column (A) whose weekly earnings in employment by the same employer in any one or more of the employments so specified include the provision of board and lodging by the employer or are ordinarily more than £5·00.

44. Employment, involving part-time service only, under a local savings committee of the National Savings Committee or the National Savings Committee for Scotland in the capacity of clerk, secretary or organiser or in the performance of clerical duties for such a committee.

45. Employment by any public or local authority to act in relief of gymnasium or lavatory attendants or of attendants of a park, playground or other public open space.

46. Employment in England or Wales by a public or local authority or by any company or body responsible for the lighting of any borough or other local area, as a lamp-lighter or extinguisher, whether the employment does or does not include the duty of cleaning or keeping the lamps in order.

Column (A)	Column (B)
Employments in respect of which, subject to the exceptions in column (B) of this Part, persons are treated as non-employed persons and their employment therein disregarded.	*Persons excepted from the operation of column (A).*

47. Employment, involving part-time service only, as a leader, helper or instructor in an institution of further education, including a voluntary youth club or community centre where personal service is required only outside the ordinary hours of work.

48. Employment, involving part-time service only, as a leader, helper or instructor in a play centre established in accordance with section 53(1) of the Education Act 1944(a) or in Scotland in accordance with section 6(1) of the Education (Scotland) Act 1962(b).

49. Employment, involving part-time service only, as—
(a) caretaker of a burial ground, cemetery or crematorium under the control of a burial authority within the meaning of the Burial Acts 1852 to 1906, and the Cremation Acts 1902 and 1952(c);
(b) caretaker of a cemetery or crematorium constructed under any special Act of Parliament;
(c) caretaker of a water-works under the control of a local authority or other water undertaker; or
(d) caretaker of a burial ground, churchyard or crematorium under the control of a local authority in Scotland.

50. Employment under a public or local authority constituted in Great Britain, involving part-time service only, as—
(a) burial ground clerk;
(b) keeper of records of a burial ground;
(c) clerk of a special district committee, not otherwise employed by such a local or public authority;
(d) water or drainage officer;

38 to 57. Any person (not being a person mainly dependent for his livelihood on his earnings from employment as a self-employed person) employed in one or more of the employments specified in paragraphs 38 to 42, 43(b)(ii) and 44 to 57 in column (A) whose weekly earnings in employment by the same employer in any one or more of the employments so specified include the provision of board and lodging by the employer or are ordinarily more than £5·00.

(a) 1944 c. 31.   (b) 1962 c. 47.
(c) 1902 c. 8; 1952 c. 31.

Column (A)	Column (B)
Employments in respect of which, subject to the exceptions in column (B) of this Part, persons are treated as non-employed persons and their employment therein disregarded.	*Persons excepted from the operation of column (A).*

(e) home or domestic help; or
(f) helper in a children's cottage home.

51. Employment by a local education authority or by the managers of a primary school or by the governors of a secondary school, or in Scotland by a public or local authority or by the managers of a State-aided school—

    (a) involving part-time service only, in the cleansing of drains, cesspools, pits or offices in or about any such school; or
    (b) involving attendance on Sundays only, in relief of a school keeper in any such school.

52. Employment of a person undergoing full-time education where the service in that employment is rendered in or about his place of education to the person, body or authority providing the education.

53. Employment, involving part-time service only, in or about a theatre, cinema, music-hall, or any place ordinarily used for public dancing or music or other public entertainment of a like kind as—
    (a) an attendant engaged for the comfort, convenience or safety of the public admitted thereto; or
    (b)—(i) check-taker,
        (ii) money-taker,
       (iii) flyman,
       (iv) property-man,
        (v) stage-hand,
      (vi) supernumerary,
     (vii) lighting operator,
    (viii) call boy or
      (ix) dresser.

54. Employment, involving part-time service only, in the delivery of goods from retail establishments.

38 to 57. Any person (not being a person mainly dependent for his livelihood on his earnings from employment as a self-employed person) employed in one or more of the employments specified in paragraphs 38 to 42, 43(b)(ii) and 44 to 57 in column (A) whose weekly earnings in employment by the same employer in any one or more of the employments so specified include the provision of board and lodging by the employer or are ordinarily more than £5·00.

Column (A)	Column (B)
Employments in respect of which, subject to the exceptions in column (B) of this Part, persons are treated as non-employed persons and their employment therein disregarded.	*Persons excepted from the operation of column (A).*

55. Employment, involving part-time service only, in attendance upon old-age or retirement pensioners or persons in receipt of benefit under the Ministry of Social Security Act 1966(a) where the employer is not—

    (a) the person to whom attendance is given; or

    (b) the person or body carrying on a hospital or accommodation provided under Part III of the National Assistance Act 1948(b) or under the Social Work (Scotland) Act 1968(c) or any other institution, whether maintained out of moneys provided by Parliament or otherwise, in which (as the case may be) the person to whom attendance is given is residing.

56. Employment, involving part-time service only, as a sick visitor by or on behalf of a society or other body providing benefits to its members during sickness, or a branch of any such society or body.

57. Employment in Scotland, involving part-time service only, as a ground officer.

                       38 to 57. Any person (not being a person mainly dependent for his livelihood on his earnings from employment as a self-employed person) employed in one or more of the employments specified in paragraphs 38 to 42, 43(b)(ii) and 44 to 57 in column (A) whose weekly earnings in employment by the same employer in any one or more of the employments so specified include the provision of board and lodging by the employer or are ordinarily more than £5·00.

58. Employment in connection with the recording or counting of votes for the purposes of—

    (a) a Parliamentary or local government election; or

    (b) an election held for the purposes of a society, association or similar body.

                  58. None.

59. Employment in agriculture (including horticulture and forestry) of a person, not being a person who has attained the age of 18 years, who is ordinarily receiving full-time education and is working in such employment from a camp organised by a school in pursuance of arrangements made with

                  59. None.

(a) 1966 c. 20.   (b) 1948 c. 29.
(c) 1968 c. 49.

Column (A)	Column (B)
Employments in respect of which, subject to the exceptions in column (B) of this Part, persons are treated as non-employed persons and their employment therein disregarded.	*Persons excepted from the operation of column (A).*
a County Agricultural Executive Committee or, in Scotland, the Department of Agriculture and Fisheries for Scotland.	
60. Employment, involving part-time service only, by the Ministry of Defence (Air) as a member of the Royal Observer Corps.	60. Any person in employment specified in paragraph 60 in column (A) where he is undergoing training or instruction for a period of not less than 72 consecutive hours.
61. Employment as a member of the National Hospital Service Reserve.	61. Any person in employment specified in paragraph 61 in column (A) where he renders services in that employment for 24 hours or more in a contribution week.
62. Employment, involving part-time service only, by the Ministry of Defence (Navy) as a member of the Royal Naval Auxiliary Service.	62. Any person in employment specified in paragraph 62 in column (A) where he is undergoing training or instruction for a period of not less than 72 consecutive hours.

SCHEDULE 2   Regulation 3

CIRCUMSTANCES IN WHICH EMPLOYMENT IS TREATED AS CONTINUING

Where an insured person is employed as a self-employed person and is ordinarily so employed, that employment shall be treated as continuing unless and until he is no longer ordinarily employed in any gainful occupation in Great Britain (other than an employment specified in Part III of Schedule 1 to these regulations which is to be disregarded):

Provided that—

(a) any week during the whole or part of which he is engaged in an employed contributor's employment shall (subject to the provisions of paragraph (b) of this proviso) not to be taken into account for the purposes of this Schedule;

(b) this Schedule shall cease to apply to a person if and when in a period of 13 consecutive weeks he has been engaged in an employed contributor's employment for 10 of those weeks.

Regulation 5

SCHEDULE 3

EMPLOYMENTS IN RESPECT OF WHICH PERSONS ARE TREATED AS EMPLOYERS

Column (A)	Column (B)
Employments.	*Persons treated as employers.*
1. Employment in Great Britain in plying for hire with any vehicle or vessel the use of which is obtained under any contract of bailment or letting for hire (other than a hire-purchase agreement) in consideration of the payment of a fixed sum or a share in the earnings or otherwise.	1. The person from whom the use of the vehicle or vessel is so obtained.
2. Employment of a casual nature for the purposes of any game or recreation of a person who is engaged or paid for that employment through a club.	2. The club.
3. Employment of a nurse as a nurse for the sick or as a midwife, whether under a contract of service or not, not being employment specified in paragraph 4 in column (B) of Schedule 1 to these regulations, or paragraph 18 in column (A) of that Schedule, where the pecuniary remuneration in respect of that employment is received— (*a*) from, or on the nurse's behalf by, any person carrying on an agency for the supply of nurses within the meaning of the Nurses Agencies Act 1957(**a**) or the Nurses (Scotland) Act 1951(**b**); or (*b*) from any local authority; or (*c*) from any person or body of persons carrying on a hospital.	3. Where the pecuniary remuneration is received on the nurse's behalf by any person carrying on such an agency as is specified in sub-paragraph (*a*) in column (A), the agency, and in any other case, the person or body from whom the pecuniary remuneration is received.
4. Employment of a nurse (as defined in regulation 1(2)) as nurse for the sick or as midwife, whether under contract of service or not, not being employment specified in paragraph 4 in column (B) of Schedule 1 to these regulations, or paragraph 18 in column (A) of that Schedule, where the pecuniary remuneration in respect of the employment is received from a patient or from a third person (not being a person, authority or body specified in sub-paragraphs (*a*), (*b*) and (*c*) of the preceding paragraph in this column) on behalf of such a patient.	4. The patient.

(**a**) 1957 c. 16.   (**b**) 1951 c. 55.

Column (A)	Column (B)
Employments.	*Persons treated as employers.*

5. Employment—
  (*a*) in England and Wales as superintendent registrar or deputy superintendent registrar, registrar or deputy registrar of births and deaths, or registrar or deputy registrar of marriages;
  (*b*) in Scotland as senior registrar, district registrar or assistant registrar of births and deaths and marriages.

5. (*a*) In England and Wales, the local authority in whose employment he is deemed to be an officer for the purposes of the Local Government Superannuation Act 1937(**a**);

(*b*) in Scotland, the council of the county or large burgh within which the whole or the greater part of the registration area of such officer is situate.

6. Employment as a registered dock worker under the Dock Workers (Regulation of Employment) Scheme 1947(**b**) where the dock worker is not one who is engaged by a registered employer under a contract which requires at least one week's notice for its termination.

6. The National Dock Labour Board.

7. Employment as an office cleaner or in any similar capacity in any premises other than those used as a private dwelling-house.

7. (*a*) Where the person employed is supplied by, or through the agency of, some third person and receives his remuneration from, or through the agency of that third person, that third person;
  (*b*) in any other case, the person with whom the person employed contracted to do the work.

8. Employment, whether under a contract of service or not (not being employment specified in paragraph 8 in column (B) of Schedule 1 to these regulations or an employment to which any other paragraph of this Schedule applies) in which the person employed renders or is under an obligation to render personal service and is subject to supervision, direction or control, or to the right of supervision, direction or control, as to the manner of the rendering of such service and where the person employed is supplied by or through some third person (including in the case of a body of persons unincorporate, a body of which the person employed is a member) and—
  (*a*) where remuneration for such service is paid by or through, or on the basis of accounts submitted by, that third person or in accordance with arrangements made with that third person; or

8. (*a*) In England and Wales where the person employed is supplied by or through the agency of a body of persons unincorporate and the person employed is a member of that body, the other members of that body, and in any other case, the third person by whom or through whose agency the person employed is supplied;
  (*b*) in Scotland, the third person by whom or through whose agency the person employed is supplied.

(**a**) 1937 c. 68.
(**b**) *See* S.R. & O. 1947/1189 (Rev. VI, p. 63: 1947 I, p. 535).

Column (A)	Column (B)
Employments.	*Persons treated as employers.*
(*b*) where payments, other than to the person employed, are made by way of fees, commission or other payments of like nature which relate to the continued employment in that employment of the person employed.	

Regulation 7(1)   **SCHEDULE 4**

Column 1 Regulations revoked	Column 2 References	Column 3 Extent of revocation
The National Insurance (Classification) Regulations 1948.	S.I. 1948/1425 (Rev. XVI, p. 95: 1948 I, p. 2738).	The whole regulations.
The National Insurance (Classification) Amendment Regulations 1949.	S.I. 1949/86 (1949 I, p. 2705).	The whole regulations.
The National Insurance (Classification) Amendment (No. 2) Regulations 1949.	S.I. 1949/1518 (1949 I, p. 2706).	The whole regulations.
The National Insurance (Classification) Amendment (No. 2) Regulations 1950.	S.I. 1950/765 (1950 II, p. 10).	The whole regulations.
The National Insurance (Classification) Amendment (No. 3) Regulations 1950.	S.I. 1950/830 (1950 II, p. 12).	The whole regulations.
The National Insurance (Classification) Amendment Regulations 1951.	S.I. 1951/993 (1951 I, p. 1454).	The whole regulations.
The National Insurance (Classification) Amendment Regulations 1952.	S.I. 1952/494 (1952 II, p. 2136).	The whole regulations.
The National Insurance (Classification) Amendment (No. 2) Regulations 1952.	S.I. 1952/1024 (1952 II, p. 2137).	The whole regulations.
The National Insurance (Classification) Amendment (No. 3) Regulations 1952.	S.I. 1952/1454 (1952 II, p. 2139).	The whole regulations.
The National Insurance (Classification) Amendment Regulations 1954.	S.I. 1954/585 (1954 I, p. 1407).	The whole regulations.

Column 1 Regulations revoked	Column 2 References	Column 3 Extent of revocation
The National Insurance (Classification) Amendment Regulations 1957.	S.I. 1957/2175 (1957 I, p. 1623).	The whole regulations.
The National Insurance (Classification) Amendment Regulations 1960.	S.I. 1960/827 (1960 II, p. 2208).	The whole regulations.
The National Insurance (Graduated Contributions and Non-participating Employments—Miscellaneous Provisions) Regulations 1960.	S.I. 1960/1210 (1960 II, p. 2234).	Regulation 13.
The National Insurance (Classification) Amendment Regulations 1961.	S.I. 1961/420 (1961 I, p. 1061).	The whole regulations.
The National Insurance (Classification) Amendment Regulations 1968.	S.I. 1968/1684 (1968 III, p. 4578).	The whole regulations.
The Family Allowances, National Insurance and Industrial Injuries (Post Office Act 1969 Consequential) Regulations 1969.	S.I. 1969/1135 (1969 II, p. 3371).	Regulation 4.
The National Insurance and Industrial Injuries (Classification and Collection of Contributions) Amendment Regulations 1969.	S.I.1969/1362 (1969 III, p. 4069).	Regulations 2 and 3.
The National Insurance (Classification) Amendment Regulations 1970.	S.I. 1970/217 (1970 I, p. 949).	The whole regulations.
The Family Allowances, National Insurance, Industrial Injuries and Miscellaneous Provisions (Decimalisation of the Currency) Amendment (No. 2) Regulations 1970.	S.I. 1970/977 (1970 II, p. 3089).	Regulation 3.
The National Insurance (Classification) Amendment (No. 2) Regulations 1970.	S.I. 1970/1704 (1970 III, p. 5584).	The whole regulations.
The National Insurance and Industrial Injuries (Classification, Contributions and Collection of Contributions) Amendment Regulations 1971.	S.I. 1971/1421 (1971 II, p. 3992).	Regulation 2.
The National Insurance (Classification) Amendment Regulations 1971.	S.I. 1971/1728 (1971 III, p. 4709).	The whole regulations.

EXPLANATORY NOTE

(This Note is not part of the Regulations.)

These Regulations are made for the purpose only of consolidating Regulations hereby revoked and accordingly by virtue of section 108(9)(*c*) of the National Insurance Act 1965 no reference of them has been made to the National Insurance Advisory Committee.

The Regulations modify the classification of certain insured persons in specified employments, by making provision for some persons who would otherwise be employed persons to be treated for the purposes of the National Insurance Act 1965 either as self-employed or non-employed persons, and some persons who would otherwise be self-employed persons to be treated for the same purpose as employed or non-employed persons. Non-employed persons are not reclassified (regulation 2 and Schedule 1).

Provision is made for continuing the status of a self-employed person until the happening of certain specified events (regulation 3 and Schedule 2). Provision is also made for the special classification of persons following a decision of the High Court (or, in Scotland, the Court of Session) or a revised decision of the Secretary of State for Social Services so as to enable the original classification to stand where this would be in the interests of the person concerned (regulation 4).

Regulation 5 and Schedule 3 provide that for the purposes of the National Insurance Act 1965 prescribed persons shall be treated as the employers of persons in certain specified employments. Regulation 6 secures that the provisions of these Regulations by virtue of which certain gainful occupations are disregarded shall not have effect for the purpose of determining, under section 43 of the National Insurance Act 1965, whether an adult dependant, in respect of whom an increase of benefit is claimed, is or is not engaged in a gainful occupation.

STATUTORY INSTRUMENTS

1972 No. 556

EXCHANGE CONTROL

The Exchange Control (Authorised Dealers and Depositaries) (Amendment) Order 1972

Made - - -	*6th April* 1972
Coming into Operation	*18th April* 1972

The Treasury, in exercise of the powers conferred upon them by sections 36(5) and 42(1) of the Exchange Control Act 1947(**a**), hereby make the following Order: —

1.—(1) This Order may be cited as the Exchange Control (Authorised Dealers and Depositaries) (Amendment) Order 1972, and shall come into operation on 18th April 1972.

(2) The Interpretation Act 1889(**b**) shall apply for the interpretation of this Order as it applies for the interpretation of an Act of Parliament.

2. Schedule 2 to the Exchange Control (Authorised Dealers and Depositaries) Order 1972(**c**), shall be amended as follows: —

    (*a*) by inserting the words "Allied Irish Banks Ltd." after the words "Allied Bank International.";

    (*b*) by inserting the words "Crédit Suisse." after the words "Crédit Lyonnais.";

    (*c*) by deleting the words "Dai-Ichi Bank, Ltd., The.";

    (*d*) by deleting the words "Nippon Kangyo Bank Ltd., The."; and

    (*e*) by deleting the words "Standard Bank C.I. Ltd." and substituting the words "Standard & Chase Bank C.I. Ltd."

3. Paragraph 5 of Schedule 3 to the said Exchange Control (Authorised Dealers and Depositaries) Order 1972 shall be amended as follows: —

    (*a*) by inserting the words "Lloyds Bank Executor & Trustee Company (Channel Islands) Ltd." and the words "Midland Bank Finance Corporation (Jersey) Ltd." after the words "First National City Bank (Channel Islands) Ltd."; and

    (*b*) by inserting the words "Slater, Walker (Guernsey) Ltd." after the words "The Royal Trust Company of Canada (C.I.) Ltd."

(**a**) 1947 c. 14.   (**b**) 1889 c. 63.   (**c**) S.I. 1972/132 (1972 I, p. 476).

4. This Order shall extend to the Channel Islands, and any reference in this Order to the Exchange Control Act 1947 includes a reference to that Act as extended by the Exchange Control (Channel Islands) Order 1947(**a**).

Tim Fortescue,
V. H. Goodhew,
Two of the Lords Commissioners
of Her Majesty's Treasury.

6th April 1972.

EXPLANATORY NOTE

(*This Note is not part of the Order.*)

This Order amends the lists of: —

(*a*) the banks and other persons authorised under the Exchange Control Act 1947 to deal in gold and foreign currencies; and

(*b*) those who are entitled to act as authorised depositaries for the purpose of the deposit of securities as required by that Act.

(**a**) S.R. & O. 1947/2034 (Rev. VI, p. 1001: 1947 I, p. 660).

STATUTORY INSTRUMENTS

1972 No. 557

ROAD TRAFFIC

The Road Vehicles Lighting (Standing Vehicles) (Exemption) (General) (No. 2) Regulations 1972

Made - - -	*5th April* 1972
Laid before Parliament	*10th April* 1972
Coming into Operation	*30th April* 1972

The Secretary of State for the Environment, in exercise of his powers under section 10(1) and (4) of the Road Transport Lighting Act 1957(**a**) and of all other enabling powers, and after consultation with representative organisations in accordance with the provisions of section 13 of that Act, as amended by section 264 of, and Schedule 17 to, the Road Traffic Act 1960(**b**), hereby makes the following Regulations: —

Commencement, citation and revocation

1.—(1) These Regulations shall come into operation on 30th April 1972 and may be cited as the Road Vehicles Lighting (Standing Vehicles) (Exemption) (General) (No. 2) Regulations 1972.

(2) The Regulations specified in the Schedule to these Regulations are hereby revoked.

Interpretation

2.—(1) In these Regulations, except where the context otherwise requires, the following expressions have the meanings hereby respectively assigned to them: —

"goods vehicle" means a mechanically propelled vehicle the unladen weight of which does not exceed 30 hundredweight and which is constructed or adapted for use for the carriage of goods or burden of any description;

"motor cycle" means a bicycle or tricycle propelled by mechanical power;

"one-way street" means a road on which the driving of vehicles otherwise than in one direction is prohibited at all times;

"passenger vehicle" means a mechanically propelled vehicle (other than a motor cycle or an invalid carriage) constructed solely for the carriage of passengers and their effects and adapted to carry not more than seven passengers exclusive of the driver;

(**a**) 1957 c. 51.   (**b**) 1960 c. 16.

"pedal cycle" means a pedal bicycle or pedal tricycle, not being in either case propelled by mechanical power;

"road" includes a length of road;

"speed limit", in relation to a road, means a speed limit of 30 miles per hour or a lower speed limit being in either case a speed limit imposed on mechanically propelled vehicles generally by or under any enactment;

"the required lights", in relation to a vehicle, means the lights showing to the front and the lights showing to the rear which, apart from these Regulations, would be required to be shown by that vehicle by the Road Transport Lighting Act 1957;

"trailer" means a vehicle drawn by another vehicle.

(2) The Interpretation Act 1889(**a**) shall apply for the interpretation of these Regulations as it applies for the interpretation of an Act of Parliament, and as if for the purposes of section 38 of that Act these Regulations were an Act of Parliament and the Regulations revoked by Regulation 1 of these Regulations were Acts of Parliament thereby repealed.

Application

3. These Regulations apply to passenger vehicles, goods vehicles and invalid carriages, and to motor cycles and pedal cycles in either case whether or not having a sidecar attached, not being, in the case of any such vehicle, one to which—

(*a*) section 8 of the Road Transport Lighting Act 1957 (which imposes requirements as to lights on vehicles with overhanging or projecting loads) applies; or

(*b*) a trailer is attached.

Parking of vehicles without lights

4.—(1) A vehicle to which these Regulations apply shall, when standing or parked at any place on a road on which a speed limit is in force, be exempted from showing the required lights if—

(*a*) in the case of a road not being a one-way street, the left or near side of the vehicle is as close as may be and is parallel to the edge of the carriageway, and, in the case of a road being a one-way street, the left or near side of the vehicle is as close as may be and is parallel to the left-hand edge of the carriageway or the right or off side of the vehicle is as close as may be and is parallel to the right-hand edge of the carriageway; and

(*b*) no part of the vehicle is within 15 yards from the junction of any part of the carriageway of any highway with the carriageway of the road on which the vehicle is standing or parked, whether that junction is on the same side of the road as that on which the vehicle is standing or parked or not.

Scope of Regulations

5. Nothing in these Regulations shall be taken to authorise any person to cause or permit a vehicle which is exempted by these Regulations from

---

(**a**) 1889 c. 63.

showing the required lights to stand or be parked on a road in any place or for any period in or for which it would be unlawful for the vehicle to stand or be parked.

Signed by authority of the Secretary of State.

John Peyton,
Minister for Transport Industries,
Department of the Environment.

5th April 1972.

SCHEDULE

REGULATIONS REVOKED BY REGULATION 1

Column 1 Regulations revoked	Column 2 References
The Road Vehicles Lighting (Standing Vehicles) (Exemption) (London) Regulations 1955	S.I. 1955/1363 (1955 II, p. 2324).
The Road Vehicles Lighting (Standing Vehicles) (Exemption) (General) Regulations 1956	S.I. 1956/741 (1956 II, p. 2007).
The Road Vehicles Lighting (Standing Vehicles) (Exemption) (General) Regulations 1972.	S.I. 1972/176.

EXPLANATORY NOTE

(This Note is not part of the Regulations.)

These Regulations make new provision with respect to the exemption of certain vehicles when standing or parked on roads from the requirements of the Road Transport Lighting Act 1957 as to the showing of front and rear lights. The Regulations revoke the Regulations (specified in the Schedule) of which those first and secondly so specified make provision generally, and special provision with respect to London, for such exemption (the Regulations thirdly so specified make the same provision as the present Regulations but are revoked because of a procedural defect in their making). The new provisions apply generally to all roads on which a speed limit of 30 mph or less is in force. The classes of vehicle to which the exemption applies and the conditions subject to which it applies are respectively specified in Regulations 3 and 4.

STOKE ... REST
CITY
LIBRARIES

STATUTORY INSTRUMENTS

1972 No. 558

DEFENCE

The Royal Navy Terms of Service (Amendment) Regulations 1972

Made - - -	*7th April* 1972
Laid before Parliament	10*th April* 1972
Coming into Operation	1*st May* 1972

The Defence Council, in exercise of the powers conferred upon them by section 2 of the Armed Forces Act 1966(a) and of all other powers enabling them in that behalf, hereby make the following Regulations:—

Citation, Commencement and Interpretation

1.—(1) These Regulations may be cited as the Royal Navy Terms of Service (Amendment) Regulations 1972 and shall come into operation on the 1st May 1972.

(2) The Interpretation Act 1889(b) shall apply to the interpretation of these Regulations as it applies to the interpretation of an Act of Parliament.

(3) In these Regulations "the Principal Regulations" means the Royal Navy Terms of Service Regulations 1967(c), as amended(d).

Amendments to the Principal Regulations

2.—(1) The following Regulations shall be substituted for Regulations 3A, 3B, 3C, 3D and 3E of the Principal Regulations:—

"Rights to transfer to the reserve

3A. Subject to Regulation 3D, a person in naval service shall, at the end of the period of 9 years beginning with the relevant date and at any time thereafter, have the right exercisable in accordance with Regulation 3C to be transferred to the reserve.

3B.—(1) Without prejudice to the generality of Regulation 3 a person who has attained the age of 17 years 6 months may, after the commencement of these Regulations, be entered in the Royal Navy for a term of not less than 3 years naval service from the relevant date with the right, subject to Regulation 3D and exercisable in accordance with Regulation 3C, to be transferred to the reserve at the end of the period of 3 years beginning with the relevant date or the date of the expiration of his initial period of training, whichever is the later, or at any time thereafter.

(a) 1966 c. 45.   (b) 1889 c. 63.
(c) S.I. 1967/1821 (1967 III, p. 4855).
(d) The relevant amending instrument is S.I. 1971/517 (1971 I, p. 1518).

(2) Subject to Regulation 3D, a person who, after the commencement of these Regulations, is entered in the Royal Navy under the age of 17 years 6 months for a term of naval service expiring on a date falling later than 3 years after the date of his attaining the age of 18 years shall have the right exercisable in accordance with Regulation 3C to be transferred to the reserve at the end of the period of 3 years beginning with the date of his attaining the age of 18 years or the date of the expiration of his initial period of training, whichever is the later, or at any time thereafter provided that the person in question has given notice in writing to his commanding officer not more than 28 days after his attaining the age of 18 years.

3C. A right to be transferred to the reserve conferred by Regulation 3A or 3B shall be exercised by notice in writing given by the person in question to his commanding officer not less than 18 months before the expiration of the period at the end of which he is to be transferred to the reserve.

3D.—(1) A person who, in consideration of—

(*a*) being permitted to undergo a course of instruction of a duration of not less than 8 weeks, or

(*b*) receiving any other benefit or advantage,

consents in writing to be restricted in the exercise of the right conferred by Regulation 3A or 3B shall not exercise such right before the expiration of the appropriate period which shall be specified in such consent and shall begin with the date on which he completes such course of instruction or such other date as is mentioned in such consent.

(2) "The appropriate period" shall be—

(*a*) in relation to permission to undergo a course of instruction, a period of not more than 3 years, and

(*b*) in relation to the receipt of any other benefit or advantage, a period of not more than 6 years.

Service in the reserve

3E. A person transferred to the reserve in consequence of the exercise of a right conferred by Regulation 3A or 3B shall, subject to Regulation 3, serve in the reserve for a period of 3 years from the date of his being transferred thereto.".

(2) In Regulation 4 of the Principal Regulations for the words "the appropriate minimum age" there shall be substituted the words "the age of 17 years 6 months".

Saving

3. The amendments effected by Regulation 2 in so far as they relate to the rights conferred by the substituted Regulation 3B of the Principal Regulations shall not affect the term of service (either as respects duration or as respects liability to naval service or any liability to serve in the reserve) for which any person in naval service is serving immediately before the commencement of these Regulations.

On behalf of the Defence Council,

Peter Kirk,

D. F. Spotswood,

Members of the Defence Council.

Dated 7th April 1972.

EXPLANATORY NOTE

(This Note is not part of the Regulations.)

These Regulations further amend the Royal Navy Terms of Service Regulations 1967 by conferring on all persons entered in the Royal Navy at any time after 9 years a right to be transferred to the reserve provided 18 months prior notice is given to their commanding officer.

Provision is also made for persons over the age of $17\frac{1}{2}$ years to be entered in the Royal Navy after the 1st May 1972 with the right to be transferred to the reserve at any time after 3 years from the end of training (or from age 18 if later) on similar notice being given. Similar rights are conferred on those entering under $17\frac{1}{2}$ years provided they give notice of their intention to take them up within 28 days of reaching the age of 18. Persons may consent, in consideration of "benefits or advantages", e.g. being permitted to undergo courses of instruction, to be restricted in the exercise of the above rights. The period to be served in the reserve is 3 years provided total service does not exceed 12 years.

The amendment made by Regulation 2(2) is necessary to preserve the reference to the age of $17\frac{1}{2}$ years after the raising of "the appropriate minimum age" from that age to 18 years by the Armed Forces Act 1971 (c. 33).

STATUTORY   INSTRUMENTS

1972 No. 567 (C. 9)

CUSTOMS AND EXCISE

The Excise Duties (Gas as Road Fuel) Order 1972

Made - - - -	11*th April* 1972
Laid before the House of Commons	17*th April* 1972
Coming into Operation	3rd *July* 1972

The Lords Commissioners of Her Majesty's Treasury by virtue of the powers conferred on them by section 3 of the Finance Act 1971(**a**) and of all other powers enabling them in that behalf, hereby make the following Order:—

1.—(1) This Order may be cited as the Excise Duties (Gas as Road Fuel) Order 1972.

(2) The Interpretation Act 1889(**b**) shall apply for the interpretation of this Order as it applies for the interpretation of an Act of Parliament.

(3) This Order shall come into operation on 3rd July 1972.

2. Section 3 of the Finance Act 1971 shall come into force on 3rd July 1972.

3. The rate of duty of excise under that section shall be such rate per liquid gallon as is equal to one half of the rate for the time being of excise duty charged on hydrocarbon oil.

V. H. Goodhew,

Tim Fortescue,

Two of the Lords Commissioners of Her Majesty's Treasury.

11th April 1972.

EXPLANATORY NOTE

(This Note is not part of the Order)

This Order brings into force, with effect from 3rd July 1972, section 3 of the Finance Act 1971 which provides for the charge of excise duty on gas for use as fuel in road vehicles.   The Order also provides that the rate of duty chargeable per liquid gallon shall be one-half of the rate of excise duty for the time being chargeable on hydrocarbon oil.

(**a**) 1971 c. 68.   (**b**) 1889 c. 3.

STATUTORY INSTRUMENTS

1972 No. 568

EDUCATION, ENGLAND AND WALES

The Teachers' Superannuation (Financial Provisions) Regulations 1972

Made - - -	*7th April* 1972
Laid before Parliament	*19th April* 1972
Coming into Operation	*30th April* 1972

The Secretary of State for Education and Science, with the consent of the Minister for the Civil Service and after consultation with representatives of local education authorities and of teachers and with such representatives of other persons likely to be affected as appear to her to be appropriate, in exercise of the powers conferred on her by section 9 of the Superannuation Act 1972(**a**) hereby makes the following Regulations: —

Citation and Commencement

1.—(1) These Regulations may be cited as the Teachers' Superannuation (Financial Provisions) Regulations 1972.

(2) These Regulations shall come into operation on 30th April 1972 and shall take effect as from 25th March 1972.

(3) The Teachers' Superannuation Regulations 1967 to 1971 and these Regulations may be cited together as the Teachers' Superannuation Regulations 1967 to 1972.

Interpretation

2.—(1) In these Regulations, unless the context otherwise requires—

"accounting period" means a period for which the teachers' superannuation account is to be made up;

"teacher" includes an organiser, a teacher in an admitted school, a services civilian teacher, a services education officer and a part-time teacher;

"the Teachers' Regulations" means the Teachers' Superannuation Regulations 1967 to 1971; and the "principal Teachers' Regulations" means the Teachers' Superannuation Regulations 1967(**b**); and

"teachers' superannuation account" means the account required to be kept under regulation 6 below.

(2) These Regulations shall be construed as one with the Teachers' Regulations.

(3) For the purposes of these Regulations the local education authority shall be deemed to be the employer of any teacher employed in or in connexion with a school maintained by the authority.

(**a**) 1972 c. 11.   (**b**) S.I. 1967/489 (1967 I, p. 1562).

(4) The Interpretation Act 1889(**a**) shall apply for the interpretation of these Regulations as it applies for the interpretation of an Act of Parliament.

Calculation of Salary

3.—(1) For the purposes of the Teachers' Regulations the salary of a teacher shall be taken, subject as in this regulation provided, to be the sums from time to time paid or payable to him in respect of his employment in reckonable service, excluding any fees and the emoluments specified in regulation 24 of the principal Teachers' Regulations as amended by regulation 6 of the Teachers' Superannuation (Amending) Regulations 1968(**b**) and the Teachers' Superannuation (Amendment) Regulations 1969(**c**).

(2) Where a teacher is by reason of sickness receiving less than his full salary calculated under paragraph (1), then, for the purpose of calculating the amounts payable by way of contributions in respect of him under regulation 5 below, his salary shall be deemed to be the aggregate of—

(*a*) the amount which he is so receiving; and

(*b*) any amount by which his salary has been reduced by reason of entitlement to sickness benefit under the enactments relating to national insurance.

(3) The Secretary of State may direct that any fees or any emoluments specified as aforesaid shall be included in the salary of a teacher.

Calculation of Average Salary

4.—(1) For the purposes of the Teachers' Regulations the average salary of a teacher shall be taken, subject as in this regulation provided, to be the average amount of his full salary calculated under paragraph (1) of regulation 3 above in respect of his employment in reckonable service during the three years of such service (whether continuous or not) next preceding the commencement of any annual superannuation allowance or the payment of an additional superannuation allowance or gratuity under the Teachers' Regulations.

(2) If a teacher has not been employed in reckonable service for three years or more, his average salary shall, except as in regulation 56 of the principal Teachers' Regulations provided, be calculated by reference to the period during which he has been so employed.

(3) If, in the opinion of the Secretary of State, the salary of a teacher has been unreasonably increased in respect of his employment during any period to be taken into account in calculating his average salary, the amount of the salary on which his average salary is to be computed shall be such as shall be determined by the Secretary of State to be proper.

Financing of benefits

5.—(1) For the purpose of defraying the cost of the benefits for which the Teachers' Regulations provide contributions shall be paid to the Secretary of State by teachers and their employers in accordance with the provisions of this regulation.

(2) The contributions payable in respect of a teacher by the teacher shall be of an amount equal to six per cent. of his salary for the time being.

(**a**) 1889 c. 63. (**b**) S.I. 1968/1353 (1968 II, p. 3753).
(**c**) S.I. 1969/80 (1969 I, p. 241).

(3) The contributions payable in respect of a teacher by his employer shall be of an amount equal to six per cent. of the teachers' salary for the time being, together with any supplementary contributions required to be paid under paragraph (4).

(4) Where a report of an actuarial inquiry specifies in pursuance of regulation 7(3) below, a rate per cent. in relation to supplementary contributions, such contributions shall—

(a) be paid by employers from the beginning of the accounting period next after that in which the report is made until the expiry of the accounting period in which the next subsequent report is made; and

(b) be of an amount equal to the rate per cent. so specified of the teacher's salary for the time being.

Teachers' Superannuation Account

6.—(1) An account shall be kept in accordance with the provisions of this regulation of the revenue and expenditure under these Regulations and the Teachers' Regulations and such account shall be in continuation of that formerly kept under section 5(1) of the Teachers' Superannuation Act 1967(**a**).

(2) The accounting period for which the account is to be made up shall be the period of twelve months beginning on 1st April in each year.

(3) There shall be treated as having been paid into the revenue of the account for each accounting period—

(a) by teachers, the amount of contributions paid by them under regulation 5(2) above which are attributable to the period;

(b) by the employers of teachers, the amount of contributions (including supplementary contributions) paid by them under regulation 5(3) above which are attributable to the period;

(c) a sum equal to the expenditure during the period upon superannuation allowances and gratuities attributable to service before the beginning of June 1922;

(d) a sum representing interest calculated in accordance with the provisions of the Teachers' Superannuation Account (Rates of Interest) Regulations 1968(**b**);

(e) the amount of any balance of revenue over expenditure remaining at the end of the last preceding accounting period; and

(f) any other revenue attributable to the period.

(4) Expenditure upon allowances and gratuities attributable to service before the beginning of June 1922 shall be shown separately from expenditure attributable to service after the beginning of June 1922 on superannuation allowances, gratuities and repayment of contributions.

(5) The account shall be kept in the form and prepared in the manner prescribed by the Teachers' Superannuation (Accounts) Regulations 1970(**c**).

(**a**) 1967 c. 12.   (**b**) S.I. 1968/1944 (1968 III, p. 5253).
(**c**) S.I. 1970/1979 (1970 III, p. 6437).

Actuarial Inquiries

7.—(1) The Government Actuary shall make an actuarial inquiry with respect to the teachers' superannuation account at the end of the accounting period ending 31st March 1976 and at the end of every fifth subsequent accounting period.

(2) An inquiry made in pursuance of paragraph (1) shall determine whether the value, at the end of the period for which the inquiry is made, of the expenditure (attributable to service after the beginning of June 1922) required to be included in the teachers' superannuation account after the end of that period in respect of teachers who then were employed in reckonable service or had previously been employed in recognised, contributory or reckonable service exceeds the aggregate of—

(a) the value at the end of that period of the contributions payable after the end of that period in respect of such teachers and of the sums falling to be credited to the teachers' superannuation account after the end of that period in accordance with sub-paragraphs (d) and (f) of regulation 6(3) above; and

(b) the balance of revenue over expenditure remaining in the teachers' superannuation account at the end of that period.

(3) Where an actuarial inquiry reveals such a deficiency as is mentioned in paragraph (2), the report of the inquiry shall specify the rate per cent. (being a rate of one-quarter of one per cent. or a multiple of one-quarter of one per cent.) at which supplementary contributions paid by employers of teachers employed in reckonable service would remove the deficiency by the expiry of a period of forty years beginning with the accounting period next after that in which the report is made.

(4) The report on each actuarial inquiry under this regulation shall be made to the Secretary of State and shall be laid by him before each House of Parliament.

Modification of Regulations

8. References in the Teachers' Superannuation Account (Rates of Interest) Regulations 1968 and the Teachers' Superannuation (Accounts) Regulations 1970 to section 5(1) of, and paragraph 3(1)(d) of Schedule 1 to, the Teachers' Superannuation Act 1967 shall be construed as references to the provisions of these Regulations which respectively correspond thereto.

Given under the Official Seal of the Secretary of State for Education and Science on 6th April 1972.

(L.S.)

Margaret H. Thatcher,
Secretary of State for Education
and Science.

Consent of the Minister for the Civil Service given under his Official Seal on 7th April 1972.

(L.S.)

K. H. McNeill,
Authorised by the Minister for
the Civil Service.

EXPLANATORY NOTE

(This Note is not part of the Regulations.)

These Regulations replace without substantive amendment the provisions of the Teachers' Superannuation Act 1967 relating to the calculation of salary and average salary, contributions, accounts and actuarial inquiries which have ceased to have effect on the repeal of that Act by the Superannuation Act 1972.

The Regulations have retrospective effect from the date of the repeal of the Act of 1967 by virtue of section 12(1) of the Superannuation Act 1972.

S T A T U T O R Y   I N S T R U M E N T S

1972 No. 569

CUSTOMS AND EXCISE

The Anti-Dumping Duty Order 1972

Made - - -	11*th April* 1972
Laid before the House of Commons	17*th April* 1972
Coming into Operation	18*th April* 1972

The Secretary of State, in exercise of the powers conferred upon him by sections 1 and 2 of the Customs Duties (Dumping and Subsidies) Act 1969(**a**), hereby makes the following Order:—

1. This Order may be cited as the Anti-Dumping Duty Order 1972 and shall come into operation on 18th April 1972.

2. There shall be charged on the import into the United Kingdom of any goods of the description set out in the Schedule hereto (being goods classified in the Customs Tariff 1959(**b**) under the heading mentioned in the first column of that Schedule) a duty of customs at the rate mentioned in the third column.

3. Section 2 of the Customs Duties (Dumping and Subsidies) Act 1969 (which allows relief to be given where goods are shown not to have been dumped or where the margin of dumping is less than the amount of the duty) shall apply to the duty imposed by this Order.

Limerick,

Parliamentary Under Secretary of State,
Department of Trade and Industry.

11th April 1972.

SCHEDULE

Relevant Tariff Heading	Description of Goods	Rate of Duty
ex 77.01(B)	Unwrought magnesium originating in the Union of Soviet Socialist Republics.	£62 per tonne

(**a**) 1969 c. 16.   (**b**) *See* S.I. 1971/1971 (1971 III, p. 5330).

EXPLANATORY NOTE

(This Note is not part of the Order)

This Order imposes an anti-dumping duty of £62 per tonne on imports of unwrought magnesium originating in the Union of Soviet Socialist Republics.

The Order applies section 2 of the Customs Duties (Dumping and Subsidies) Act 1969 to the duty.   This section enables relief to be granted where particular goods have not been dumped or the margin of dumping is shown to be less than the amount of duty payable.

STATUTORY INSTRUMENTS

1972 No. 574

ROAD TRAFFIC

The Drivers' Hours (Goods Vehicles) (Exemptions) Regulations 1972

Made - - -	*6th April* 1972
Laid before Parliament	*19th April* 1972
Coming into Operation	*10th May* 1972

The Secretary of State for the Environment, in exercise of his powers under section 96(10) of the Transport Act 1968(a) and of all other enabling powers, and after consultation with representative organisations in accordance with section 101(6) of the said Act of 1968, hereby makes the following Regulations:—

Commencement, citation and revocation

1.—(1) These Regulations shall come into operation on 10th May 1972, and may be cited as the Drivers' Hours (Goods Vehicles) (Exemptions) Regulations 1972.

(2) The Drivers' Hours (Goods Vehicles) (Exemptions) Regulations 1970(b) and the Drivers' Hours (Goods Vehicles) (Exemptions) (Amendment) (No. 3) Regulations 1970(c) are hereby revoked.

Interpretation

2.—(1) In these Regulations, unless the context otherwise requires, "the Act" means the Transport Act 1968 and any other expression which is also used in Part VI of the Act has the same meaning as in that Part of that Act.

(2) Any reference in the Schedule to these Regulations to a numbered section is a reference to the section bearing that number in the Act except where otherwise expressly provided.

(3) Any reference in an entry in column 1 of Parts I or II of the Schedule to these Regulations to an emergency or to a special need is a reference to such a case of emergency or to such a special need as is specified in column 2 in relation to that entry.

(4) Any reference in these Regulations to an enactment or instrument shall be construed, unless the context otherwise requires, as a reference to that enactment or instrument as amended by any subsequent enactment or instrument.

(5) The Interpretation Act 1889(d) shall apply for the interpretation of these Regulations as it applies for the interpretation of an Act of Parliament and as if for the purposes of section 38 of that Act these Regulations were an Act of Parliament and the Regulations revoked by Regulation 1 above were Acts of Parliament thereby repealed.

(a) 1968 c. 73.
(c) S.I. 1970/2014 (1970 III, p. 6538).
(b) S.I. 1970/144 (1970 I, p. 627).
(d) 1889 c. 63.

Exemptions from requirements as to drivers' hours

3. For the purpose of enabling drivers of goods vehicles to deal with the cases of emergency and to meet the special needs specified in Parts I and II of the Schedule hereto such drivers are hereby exempted from the requirements of subsections (1) to (6) of section 96 to the extent specified in column 1 of the said Parts I and II in relation to them, subject, however, to the conditions therein specified or referred to in relation to them.

Signed by authority of the Secretary of State.

6th April 1972.

John Peyton,
Minister for Transport Industries,
Department of the Environment.

SCHEDULE

(See Regulation 3)

PART I

CASES OF EMERGENCY

Column 1	Column 2
Drivers exempted, requirements exempted from and conditions of exemption	Emergencies

A driver who spends time on duty to deal with an emergency—

(1) is exempted from the requirements of section 96(1), (2) and (3) in respect of any working day during which he spends time on such duty, subject to the condition that he does not during that day spend time on duty (otherwise than for dealing with an emergency) for a period of, or periods amounting in the aggregate to, more than 11 hours:

Provided that where a driver spends time on duty to deal with an emergency which interrupts what would otherwise have been an interval for rest between two successive working days, this condition shall not preclude him from subsequently spending not more than 11 hours on duty (of which not more than 10 hours shall be spent in driving vehicles to which Part VI of the Act applies) for other purposes, if he has had, since he was last on duty for such other purposes, two or more intervals for rest which amount in the aggregate to a period of not less than 10 hours;

(2) is exempted from the requirement of section 96(4) in respect of the interval for rest between any working day during which he spends time on such duty and any succeeding working day, subject to the condition that he has between those days an interval for rest of not less than 10 hours, and in such a case subsections (1) to (3) and (8) of section 96 and sub-paragraph (1) above shall, in respect of each of the said working days mentioned above, apply in relation to the driver as if, for the purposes of the expression "working day" in each of those subsections, and in that sub-paragraph, he had had an interval for rest between the said days of not less than 11 hours;

1. Events which—
   (a) cause or are likely to cause such—
      (i) danger to the life or health of one or more individuals or animals, or
      (ii) a serious interruption in the maintenance of public services for the supply of water, gas, electricity or drainage or of telecommunication or postal services, or
      (iii) a serious interruption in the use of roads or airports, or
   (b) are likely to cause such serious damage to property,
as to necessitate the taking of immediate action to prevent the occurrence or continuance of such danger or interruption or the occurrence of such damage.

Column 1	Column 2
Drivers exempted, requirements exempted from and conditions of exemption	Emergencies
(3) is exempted from the requirement of section 96(5) in respect of any working week during which he spends time such duty subject to the condition that he does not during that week spend time on duty (otherwise than for dealing with an emergency) for periods amounting in the aggregate to more than 66 hours;	
(4) is exempted from the requirement of section 96(6) in respect of any working week during which he spends time on such duty— (a) subject to the conditions specified in Part III of this Schedule, and (b) in a case where he spends time on such duty during the last 24 hours of that working week, subject also to the condition that he does not during that period of 24 hours after spending time on duty for dealing with an emergency, spend time on duty for any other purpose.	

PART II

Cases of Special Need

Column 1	Column 2
Drivers exempted, requirements exempted from and conditions of exemption	Special Needs

Post Office

1.—(1) A driver of a goods vehicle which is used for the purposes of the Post Office is exempted from the requirements of—

   (a) section 93(3) in respect of any working day to which this paragraph applies during which the time spent by him on duty is spent wholly or mainly in meeting a special need, subject to the condition that that working day does not exceed 14 hours; and

   (b) section 96(5) and (6) in respect of any working week to which this paragraph applies during which the time spent by him on duty is spent wholly or mainly in meeting such a need, subject, in the case of the exemption from the requirements of—

     (i) section 96(5), to the condition that he is not on duty in that week for periods amounting in the aggregate to more than 66 hours, and

     (ii) section 96(6), to the conditions specified in Part III of this Schedule.

(2) The working weeks to which this paragraph applies are any which fall wholly or partly in the month of December in any year, and the working days to which this paragraph applies are any which fall wholly or partly within any such working week.

Carriage of food and drink

2.—(1) A driver is exempted from the requirements of—

   (a) section 96(3) in respect of any working day to which this paragraph applies during which the time spent by him on duty is spent wholly or mainly in meeting a special need, subject to the condition that that working day does not exceed 14 hours; and

1. Work done wholly or mainly in connection with the handling of mail.

2. Work done wholly or mainly in connection with the carriage of food or drink other than—

   (a) bread;

   (b) milk;

   (c) fodder or feeding stuffs for animals; or

   (d) articles or substances used only as drugs.

Column 1	Column 2
Drivers exempted, requirements exempted from and conditions of exemption	Special Needs

(b) section 96(5) and (6) in respect of any working week to which this paragraph applies during which the time spent by him on duty is spent wholly or mainly in meeting such a need, subject, in the case of the exemption from the requirements of—

    (i) section 96(5), to the condition that he is not on duty in that week for periods amounting in the aggregate to more than 66 hours, and

    (ii) section 96(6), to the conditions specified in Part III of this Schedule.

(2) The working weeks to which this paragraph applies are—

    (a) the working week in which Good Friday falls;

    (b) the working week which immediately precedes that in which the spring bank holiday Monday falls;

    (c) the six working weeks which immediately precede the working week in which the summer bank holiday Monday falls; and

    (d) the working week in which 1st January falls and the two immediately preceding working weeks;

and the working days to which this paragraph applies are any which fall wholly or partly within any such working week.

In this paragraph the expression "bank holiday" means a holiday which is, or is to be observed as, a bank holiday or a holiday under the Bank Holidays Act 1871(a) or the Holidays Extension Act 1875(b), either generally or in the particular locality where the journey or part of the journey takes place.

Carriage of bread

3.—(1) A driver is exempted from the requirements of—   3. Work done wholly or mainly in connection with the carriage of bread.

    (a) section 96(3) in rexpect of any working day to which this sub-paragraph applies during which the time spent by him on duty is spent wholly or mainly in meeting a special need, subject to the condition that that working day does not exceed 14 hours;

(a) 1871 c. 17.   (b) 1875 c. 13.

Column 1	Column 2
Drivers exempted, requirements exempted from and conditions of exemption	. Special Needs

(b) section 96(5) in respect of any working week such as is mentioned in paragraph 2(2) above during which the time spent by him on duty is spent wholly or mainly in meeting such a need, subject to the condition that he is not on duty in that week for periods amounting in the aggregate to more than 66 hours; and

(c) section 96(6) in respect of any working week during which the time spent by him on duty is spent wholly or mainly in meeting such a need, subject to the conditions specified in Part III of this Schedule.

(2) The working days to which sub-paragraph (1)(a) above applies are—

(a) subject to sub-paragraph (3) below, any which fall wholly or partly on a Friday or on a Saturday; or

(b) any which fall wholly or partly within any working week such as is mentioned in paragraph 2(2) above; or

(c) without prejudice to sub-paragraph (b) above, any two each of which falls wholly or partly within a period of 7 days immediately preceding a bank holiday.

In this sub-paragraph the expression "bank holiday" has the same meaning as in paragraph 2 above.

(3) In a case where, by virtue of sub-paragraphs (1) and (2)(a) above, a driver is exempted from the requirements mentioned in the said sub-paragraph (1) in respect of a working day which falls wholly or partly on a Friday, the said sub-paragraph (2)(a) shall apply in his case as if the reference to a Saturday were omitted.

Carriage of milk and liquid egg

4.—(1) A driver is exempted from the requirements of—

(a) section 96(3) in respect of any working day to which this sub-paragraph applies during which the time spent by him on duty is spent wholly or mainly in meeting a special need, subject to the condition that that working day does not exceed 14 hours; and

4. Work done wholly or mainly in connection with the carriage of milk or of liquid egg in bulk.

Column 1	Column 2
Drivers exempted, requirements exempted from and conditions of exemption	Special Needs

(*b*) section 96(5) and (6) in respect of any working week during which the time spent by him on duty is spent wholly or mainly in meeting such a need, subject, in the case of the ex-exemption from the requirements of—

   (i) section 96(5), to the condition that he is not on duty in that week for periods amounting in the aggregate to more than 66 hours, and

  (ii) section 96(6), to the conditions specified in Part III of this Schedule.

(2) The working days to which sub-paragraph (1)(*a*) above applies are any which fall wholly or partly within any working week such as is mentioned in paragraph 2(2) above.

Carriage of animals

5.—(1) A driver is exempted from the requirements of—   **5.** Work done wholly or mainly in connection with the carriage of of animals.

   (*a*) section 96(3) in respect of any working day during which the time spent by him on duty is spent wholly or mainly in meeting a special need, subject to the condition that that working day does not exceed 14 hours;

   (*b*) section 96(4) in respect of the interval for rest between that day and any succeeding working day, subject to the condition that he has between those days an interval for rest of not less than 10 hours; and

   (*c*) section 96(5) and (6) in respect of any working week during which the time spent by him on duty is spent wholly or mainly in meeting such a need, subject, in the case of the exemption from the requirements of—

     (i) section 96(5), to the condition that he is not on duty in that week for periods amounting in the aggregate to more than 66 hours, and

    (ii) section 96(6), to the conditions specified in Part III of this Schedule.

Column 1	Column 2
Drivers exempted, requirements exempted from and conditions of exemption	Special Needs

(2) In any case where a driver is exempted by virtue of paragraph (1)(*b*) above from the requirement of section 96(4), subsections (1) to (3) and (8) of section 96 and the said sub-paragraph (1)(*b*) shall, in respect of each of the said working days mentioned in the said paragraph (1)(*b*), apply in relation to him as if, for the purposes of the expressions "working day" in each of those subsections, and in that sub-paragraph, he had had an interval for rest between the said days of not less than 11 hours.

Carriage of fish and agricultural produce of things used for the repair or replacement of agricultural machinery, of certain materials used in agriculture and of felled trees.

6. A driver is exempted from the requirements of—

    (*a*) section 96(3) in respect of any working day during which the time spent by him on duty is spent wholly or mainly in meeting a special need, subject to the condition that that working day does not exceed 14 hours; and

    (*b*) section 96(5) and (6) in respect of any working week during which the time spent by him on duty is spent wholly or mainly in meeting such a need, subject, in the case if the exemption from the requirements of—

        (i) section 96(5), to the condition that he is not on duty in that week for periods amounting in the aggregate to more than 66 hours, and

        (ii) section 96(6), to the conditions specified in Part III of this Schedule.

6. Work done wholly or mainly in connection with—

    (*a*) the carriage of fish from the place where it has been landed direct to another place, where the carriage takes place immediately after the fish has been landed; or

    (*b*) the carriage of anything produced in the course of agriculture from the place where it is produced (being a place at which the business of agriculture is carried on) direct to another place, where the journey on which the produce is carried commenced during the harvest period for that produce.

For the purposes of this paragraph a journey shall not be treated otherwise than as direct by reason only of any temporary interruption made for the purpose of transferring the produce from one means of transport to another; or

    (*c*) the carriage of anything used for or in connection with the repair or replacement of agricultural machinery (including fuel and lubricants for such machinery) at a time when it is being used in connection with the harvesting of such produce as aforesaid; or

    (*d*) the carriage of agricultural lime, seed or fertilizers, or of fodder or feeding stuffs for animals; or

Column 1	Column 2
Drivers exempted, requirements exempted from and conditions of exemption	Special Needs

| | (*e*) the carriage of trees from any place where they have recently been felled.
In this paragraph "agriculture" has the same meaning as in Part VI of the Act, except that it does not include dairy farming or livestock breeding and keeping, and "agricultural" shall be construed accordingly. |

Blood transfusion service

7. A driver is exempted from the requirement of section 96(3) in respect of any working day during which the time spent by him on duty is spent wholly or mainly in meeting a special need, subject to the conditions that—

    (*a*) that working day does not exceed 14 hours;

    (*b*) he is able to obtain rest and refreshment during that day for a period which is, or for periods which in the aggregate are, not less than the time by which the working day exceeds 10 hours; and

    (*c*) he has not taken advantage of the exemption conferred by this paragraph on more than one previous working day which forms part of the working week of which that day forms part.

7. Work done wholly or mainly in connection with the collection and delivery of blood for the purposes of transfusion.

Distribution of newspapers, magazines and periodicals

8.—(1) A driver is exempted from the requirements of—

    (*a*) section 96(3) in respect of any working day during which the time spent by him on duty is spent wholly or mainly in meeting a special need, subject to the condition that that working day does not exceed 14 hours; and

    (*b*) section 96(4) in respect of the interval for rest between that day and any succeeding working day, subject to the condition that he has between those days an interval for rest of not less than 10 hours.

8. Work done wholly or mainly in connection with the distribution of newspapers, magazines or periodicals to wholesalers or to persons or premises for the purposes of their sale by retail by those persons or at those premises.

Column 1	Column 2
Drivers exempted, requirements exempted from and conditions of exemption	Special Needs

(2) In any case where a driver is exempted by virtue of sub-paragraph (1)(*b*) above from the requirement of section 96(4), subsections (1) to (3) and (8) of section 96 and the said sub-paragraph (1)(*b*), shall, in respect of each of the said working days mentioned in the said paragraph (1)(*b*), apply in relation to him as if, for the purposes of the expression "working day" in each of those subsections. and in that sub-paragraph, he had had an interval for rest between the said days of not less than 11 hours.

Carriage of materials used in building or civil engineering work
   9. A driver is exempted from the requirements of—
    (*a*) section 96(3) in respect of any working day during which the time spent by him on duty is spent wholly or mainly in meeting a special need, subject to the condition that that working day does not exceed 14 hours; and
    (*b*) section 96(5) and (6) in respect of any working week during which the time spent by him on duty is spent wholly or mainly in meeting such a need, subject in the case of the exemption from the requirements of—
      (i) section 96(5), to the condition that he is not on duty in that week for periods amounting in the aggregate to more than 66 hours, and
      (ii) section 96(6), to the conditions specified in Part III of this Schedule.

9. Work done wholly or mainly in connection with the carriage of materials or components used in building or civil engineering work to or from sites where such work is being prepared or carried out.

Furniture removal and carriage of shopfittings
   10. A driver is exempted from the requirement of section 96(3) in respect of any working day during which the time spent by him on duty is spent wholly or mainly in meeting a special need, subject to the condition that that working day does not exceed 14 hours.

10. Work done wholly or mainly in connection with furniture removal (that is to say, the carriage of household furniture and effects from one private residence to another or to or from a place where such furniture and effects are to be or have been put in store) or with the carriage of shopfittings to or from shops.

Column 1	Column 2
Drivers exempted, requirements exempted from and conditions of exemption	Special Needs

Carriage of explosives, radioactive substances and ships' stores

11. A driver is exempted from the requirement of section 96(3) in respect of any working day during which the time spent by him on duty is spent wholly or mainly in meeting a special need, subject to the condition that that working day does not exceed 14 hours.

11. Work done wholly or mainly in connection with—
    (*a*) the carriage of explosives (within the meaning of the Explosives Act 1875**(a)**); or
    (*b*) the carriage of radioactive substances (within the meaning of the Radioactive Substances Act 1948**(b)**); or
    (*c*) the delivery of stores to ships

Carriage of exceptional loads when accompanied by the police

12. A driver is exempted from the requirements of—
    (*a*) section 96(3) in respect of any working day during which the time spent by him on duty is spent wholly or mainly in meeting a special need, subject to the conditions that—
      (i) that working day does not exceed 14 hours, and
      (ii) he is off duty during that day for a period which is, or for periods which in the aggregate are, not less than the time by which that working day exceeds 11 hours; and
    (*b*) section 96(5) and (6) in respect of any working week during which the time spent by him on duty is spent wholly or mainly in meeting such a need, subject, in the case of the exemption from the requirements of—
      (i) section 96(5), to the condition that he is not on duty in that week for periods amounting in the aggregate to more than 66 hours, and
      (ii) section 96(6), to the conditions specified in Part III of this Schedule.

12. Work done wholly or mainly in connection with the carriage of a load where, owing to its dimensions or weight, the vehicle by which it is carried is accompanied for the whole or the greater part of its journey by one or more motor vehicles each driven by a constable in uniform.

(a) 1875 c. 17. **(b)** 1948 c. 37.

Column 1	Column 2
Drivers exempted, requirements exempted from and conditions of exemption	Special Needs

Carriage of goods by sea ferry

13. A driver is exempted from the requirement of section 96(3) in respect of any working day during which the time spent by him on duty duty is spent wholly or mainly in meeting a special need, subject to the conditions that—

    (a) that working day does not exceed 14 hours; and

    (b) he is off duty during that day for a period which is, or for periods which in the aggregate are, not less than the time by which that working day exceeds 11 hours.

13. Work done wholly or mainly in connection with the carriage of goods where the journey on which they are carried—

    (a) involves their being ferried across the sea from one place within Great Britain to another such place, without being removed from the vehicle in which they are carried, and

    (b) is one during the whole of which the vehicle is driven or accompanied by the same driver.

PART III

Conditions applicable to exemptions from section 96(6)

Where any entry in column 1 of this Schedule provides for an exemption from the requirement of section 96(6) in relation to any such working week of a driver as is mentioned in that entry to enable that driver to spend time on duty to meet an emergency or a special need subject to the conditions specified in this Part of this Schedule, the conditions so referred to are the following—

    (i) that the driver has, in respect of each working week in the course of which he has not had such a period off duty as is required by section 96(6), a period of not less than 24 hours for which he is off duty,

    (ii) that any such period is taken within a period of 28 days starting from the beginning of the working week in respect of which he is required to have that period and is taken by him in addition to any other period for which the driver is required by these conditions or by section 96(6) to be off duty in the case of any other working week.

EXPLANATORY NOTE

(This Note is not part of the Regulations.)

These Regulations, which re-enact with amendments the Regulations specified in Regulation 1(2), provide exemptions subject to conditions from the
requirements of section 96(1) to (6) of the Transport Act 1968 (which relates
to permitted driving times and periods of duty) to enable drivers of goods
vehicles to deal with certain cases of emergency and to meet certain special
needs (Regulation 3 and the Schedule). The principal amendments provide—

    (1) for the maximum periods of duty in respect of a working day and a
        working week, and for the minimum interval for rest between working
        days, in cases where a driver is exempted from the said requirements
        for dealing with an emergency (Part 1 of the Schedule); and

    (2) for new exemptions in the cases where work is done in connection with
        the special needs specified in paragraph 9 of Part II of the Schedule
        (carriage of materials used in building or civil engineering work), para-
        graph 11 of that Part (carriage of explosives, radioactive substances,
        and ships' stores) and paragraph 13 thereof (carriage of goods by sea
        ferry).

STOKE-ON-TRENT
CITY
LIBRARIES

STATUTORY INSTRUMENTS

1972 No. 577

MERCHANDISE MARKS

The Motor Vehicles (Designation of Approval Marks) Regulations 1972

Made - - -	*7th April* 1972
Laid before Parliament	*20th April* 1972
Coming into Operation	*11th May* 1972

The Secretary of State for the Environment (hereinafter referred to as "the Secretary of State") in exercise of his powers under section 47(1) of the Road Traffic Act 1962(**a**), as amended by paragraph 4 of Schedule 1 to the Trade Descriptions Act 1968(**b**), and of all other enabling powers and, by virtue of section 52(2) of the Road Traffic Act 1962, after consultation with representative organisations in accordance with section 260(2) of the Road Traffic Act 1960(**c**) hereby makes the following Regulations:—

1.—(1) These Regulations shall come into operation on 11th May 1972 and may be cited as the Motor Vehicles (Designation of Approval Marks) Regulations 1972.

(2) In these Regulations the expression "the International Agreement of 1958" means the Agreement concerning the adoption of uniform conditions of approval and reciprocal recognition of approval for motor vehicle equipment and parts concluded at Geneva on 20th March 1958(**d**), as amended (**e**), to which the United Kingdom is a party (**f**).

(3) The Interpretation Act 1889(**g**) shall apply for the interpretation of these Regulations as it applies for an Act of Parliament, and as if for the purposes of section 38 of that Act these Regulations were an Act of Parliament and the Regulations revoked by regulation 3 of these Regulations were an Act of Parliament thereby repealed.

2.—(1) The Secretary of State hereby designates as an approval mark a marking in the same form as and of a size not less than the marking shown in the diagram in Part I of Schedule 1 to these Regulations subject, however, to the provisions of Part II of that Schedule, the said marking being one for which the International Agreement of 1958 by virtue of the Regulation

---

(**a**) 1962 c. 59. (**b**) 1968 c. 29.
(**c**) 1960 c. 16. (**d**) Cmnd. 2535.
(**e**) Cmnd. 3562.
(**f**) By instrument of accession dated 14th January 1963 deposited with the Secretary General of the United Nations on 15th January 1963.
(**g**) 1889 c. 63.

specified in Part III of that Schedule and annexed to that Agreement makes such provision as is mentioned in section 47(1)(*a*) and (*b*) of the Road Traffic Act 1962 in relation to a motor vehicle part consisting of a fog light.

(2) The Secretary of State hereby designates as an approval mark a marking which is in the same form as and of a size not less than the marking shown in the diagram in Part I of Schedule 2 to these Regulations subject, however, to the provisions of Part II of that Schedule, the said marking being one for which the International Agreement of 1958 by virtue of the Regulation specified in Part III of that Schedule and annexed to that Agreement makes such provision as is mentioned in section 47(1)(*a*) and (*b*) of the Road Traffic Act 1962 in relation to motor vehicle parts consisting of headlights emitting an asymmetrical passing beam or a driving beam or both and equipped with halogen lamps (H_1, H_2, or H_3 lamps).

(3) The Secretary of State hereby designates as an approval mark a marking which is in the same form as and of a size not less than the markings shown in Part I of Schedule 3 to these Regulations subject, however, to the provisions of Part II of that Schedule, the said marking being one for which the International Agreement of 1958 by virtue of the Regulation specified in Part III of Schedule 2 to these Regulations and annexed to that Agreement makes such provisions as is mentioned in section 47(1)(*a*) and (*b*) of the Road Traffic Act 1962 in relation to a motor vehicle part consisting of a halogen (H_1, H_2, or H_3) lamp.

(4) The Secretary of State hereby designates as an approval mark a marking which is in the same form as and of a size not less than the marking shown in the diagram in Part I of Schedule 4 to these Regulations subject, however, to the provision of Part II of that Schedule, the said marking being one for which the International Agreement of 1958 by virtue of the Regulation specified in Part III of that Schedule and annexed to that Agreement makes such provision as is mentioned in section 47(1)(*a*) and (*b*) of the Road Traffic Act 1962 in relation to motor vehicle parts consisting of head lights emitting an asymmetrical passing beam or a driving beam or both and equipped with halogen (H_4) lamps.

(5) The Secretary of State hereby designates as an approval mark a marking which is in the same form as and of a size not less than the marking shown in Part I of Schedule 5 to these Regulations, subject, however, to the provisions of Part II of that Schedule, the said marking being one for which the International Agreement of 1958 by virtue of the Regulation specified in Part III of Schedule 4 to these Regulations and annexed to that Agreement makes such provision as is mentioned in section 47(1)(*a*) and (*b*) of the Road Traffic Act 1962 in relation to a motor vehicle part consisting of a halogen (H_4) lamp.

3. The Motor Vehicles (Designation of Approval Marks) Regulations 1969(**a**) are hereby revoked.

Signed by authority of the Secretary of State.
7th April 1972.

John Peyton,
Minister of Transport Industries,
Department of the Environment.

(**a**) S.I. 1969/200 (1969 I, p. 494).

SCHEDULE 1

PART I

Diagram showing marking

19R-2439

PART II

1. The number shown inside the circle in the marking in the above diagram will be varied, where appropriate, to be the number assigned to each Contracting State party to the International Agreement of 1958 and applying the Regulation specified in Part III of this Schedule.

2. The number which is shown outside the circle in the said marking will be varied, where appropriate, to be the number allotted by a competent authority to distinguish the manufacturer of the motor vehicle part concerned, namely, a fog light.

PART III

Regulation No. 19

UNIFORM PROVISIONS CONCERNING THE APPROVAL OF MOTOR VEHICLE FOG LIGHTS

SCHEDULE 2

PART I

Diagram showing marking

2439

PART II

1. The number shown inside the circle in the marking in the above diagram will be varied, where appropriate, to be the number assigned to each Contracting State party to the International Agreement of 1958 and applying the Regulation specified in Part III of this Schedule.

2. The number which is shown outside the circle in the said marking will be varied, where appropriate, to be the number allotted by a competent authority to distinguish the manufacturer of the motor vehicle parts concerned, namely, headlights emitting an asymmetrical passing beam or a driving beam or both and equipped with halogen lamps (H_1, H_2, or H_3 lamps).

Regulation No. 8

UNIFORM PROVISIONS CONCERNING THE APPROVAL OF MOTOR VEHICLE HEADLIGHTS EMITTING AN ASYMMETRICAL PASSING BEAM OR A DRIVING BEAM OR BOTH AND EQUIPPED WITH HALOGEN LAMPS (H_1, H_2, or H_3 LAMPS) AND OF THE LAMPS THEMSELVES.

SCHEDULE 3

Part I

Diagram showing marking

2439

Part II

1. The number shown inside the circle in the marking in the above diagram will be varied, where appropriate, to be the number assigned to each Contracting State party to the International Agreement of 1958 and applying the Regulation specified in Part III of Schedule 2 to these Regulations.

2. The number which is shown outside the circle in the said marking will be varied, where appropriate, to be the number allotted by a competent authority to distinguish the manufacturer of the motor vehicle part concerned, namely, a halogen (H_1, H_2, or H_3) lamp.

SCHEDULE 4

Part I

Diagram showing marking

20R–2439

Part II

1. The number shown inside the circle in the marking in the above diagram will be varied, where appropriate, to be the number assigned to each Contracting State party to the International Agreement of 1958 and applying the Regulation specified in Part III of this Schedule.

2. The number which is shown outside the circle in the said marking will be varied, where appropriate, to be the number allotted by a competent authority to distinguish the manufacturer of the motor vehicle parts concerned, namely, headlights emitting an asymmetrical passing beam or a driving beam or both and equipped with halogen (H_4) lamps.

Part III

Regulation No. 20

UNIFORM PROVISIONS CONCERNING THE APPROVAL OF MOTOR VEHICLE HEADLIGHTS EMITTING AN ASYMMETRICAL PASSING BEAM OR A DRIVING BEAM OR BOTH AND EQUIPPED WITH HALOGEN LAMPS (H_4 LAMPS) AND OF THE LAMPS THEMSELVES.

SCHEDULE 5
Part I
Diagram showing marking

20R — 2439

Part II
1. The number shown inside the circle in the marking in the above diagram will be varied, where appropriate, to be the number assigned to each Contracting State party to the International Agreement of 1958 and applying the Regulation specified in Part III of Schedule 4 to these Regulations.

2. The number which is shown outside the circle in the said marking will be varied, where appropriate, to be the number allotted by a competent authority to distinguish the manufacturer of the motor vehicle part concerned, namely, a halogen (H_4) lamp.

EXPLANATORY NOTE
(*This Note is not part of the Regulations.*)

Section 47(1) of the Road Traffic Act 1962 enacts that where any International Agreement to which the United Kingdom is a party provides—

(*a*) for markings to be applied to motor vehicle parts of any description to indicate conformity with a type approved by any country,

(*b*) for motor vehicle parts bearing those markings to be recognised as complying with the requirements imposed by the law of another country,

the Secretary of State for the Environment may by Regulations designate the markings as approval marks.

Section 47 of the Road Traffic Act 1962, as amended by Schedule 1 to the Trade Descriptions Act 1968, also provides inter alia that any markings so designated shall be deemed for the purpose of the latter Act to be a trade description and that it shall be an offence under that Act to apply an approval mark without proper authority.

These Regulations designate, for the purposes of the said section 47, as approval marks markings complying with the provisions of Schedule 1, 2, 3, 4 or 5 to these Regulations and in respect of which the International Agreement of 1958 (referred to in the Regulations) and the Regulation specified in Part III of Schedule 1, 2 or 4 to these Regulations make such provision as is mentioned in (*a*) and (*b*) above as respects certain motor vehicle parts. The motor vehicle parts concerned consist of (in the case of a marking complying with Schedule 1) fog lights (in the case of a marking complying with Schedule 2 or 4) headlights and (in the case of a marking complying with Schedule 3 or 5) halogen (H_1, H_2, H_3, or H_4) lamps.

These Regulations also revoke earlier Regulations which designated approval marks in relation to motor vehicle parts consisting of headlights equipped with a halogen (H_1) lamp and of halogen (H_1) lamps.

1972 No. 578

SUGAR

The Sugar (Distribution Payments) (No. 4) Order 1972

Made - - - -	*12th April* 1972
Laid before Parliament -	*12th April* 1972
Coming into Operation -	*13th April* 1972

The Minister of Agriculture, Fisheries and Food in exercise of the powers conferred upon him by sections 14(5) and 33(4) of the Sugar Act 1956(**a**), having effect subject to the provisions of section 3 of, and Part II of Schedule 5 to, the Finance Act 1962(**b**), section 22 of the Finance Act 1964(**c**) and section 52 of the Finance Act 1966(**d**) and of all other powers enabling him in that behalf, with the concurrence of the Treasury, and on the advice of the Sugar Board hereby makes the following order:—

1.—(1) This order may be cited as the Sugar (Distribution Payments) (No. 4) Order 1972, and shall come into operation on 13th April 1972.

(2) The Interpretation Act 1889(**e**) shall apply for the interpretation of this order as it applies for the interpretation of an Act of Parliament.

2. Notwithstanding the provisions of article 2 of the Sugar (Distribution Payments) (No. 3) Order 1972(**f**), the rates of distribution payments payable under and in accordance with the provisions of section 14 of the Sugar Act 1956, having effect as aforesaid, in respect of sugar and invert sugar imported or home produced or used in the manufacture of imported composite sugar products shall on and after 13th April 1972 be those rates specified in the Schedule to this order; and section 10 of the Finance Act 1901(**g**) (which relates to new or altered customs or excise duties and their effect upon contracts) shall apply accordingly.

In Witness whereof the Official Seal of the Minister of Agriculture, Fisheries and Food is hereunto affixed on 11th April 1972.

(L.S.)

E. J. G. Smith,
Authorised by the Minister.

We concur.
12th April 1972.

Tim Fortescue,
V. H. Goodhew,
Two of the Lords Commissioners of
Her Majesty's Treasury.

(**a**) 1956 c. 48.   (**b**) 1962 c. 44.   (**c**) 1964 c. 49   (**d**) 1966 c. 18.

(**e**) 1889 c. 63.   (**f**) S.I. 1972/432 (1972 I, p. 1622).   (**g**) 1901 c. 7.

SCHEDULE

PART I

RATES OF DISTRIBUTION PAYMENT FOR SUGAR

Polarisation	Rate of Distribution Payment per ton
Exceeding—	£
99°	12 ·000
98° but not exceeding 99°	11 ·316
97° ,, ,, ,, 98°	11 ·040
96° ,, ,, ,, 97°	10 ·752
95° ,, ,, ,, 96°	10 ·464
94° ,, ,, ,, 95°	10 ·176
93° ,, ,, ,, 94°	9 ·888
92° ,, ,, ,, 93°	9 ·600
91° ,, ,, ,, 92°	9 ·312
90° ,, ,, ,, 91°	9 ·024
89° ,, ,, ,, 90°	8 ·736
88° ,, ,, ,, 89°	8 ·448
87° ,, ,, ,, 88°	8 ·208
86° ,, ,, ,, 87°	7 ·968
85° ,, ,, ,, 86°	7 ·752
84° ,, ,, ,, 85°	7 ·536
83° ,, ,, ,, 84°	7 ·320
82° ,, ,, ,, 83°	7 ·104
81° ,, ,, ,, 82°	6 ·912
80° ,, ,, ,, 81°	6 ·720
79° ,, ,, ,, 80°	6 ·528
78° ,, ,, ,, 79°	6 ·336
77° ,, ,, ,, 78°	6 ·144
76° ,, ,, ,, 77°	5 ·952
Not exceeding 76°	5 ·760

PART II

RATES OF DISTRIBUTION PAYMENT FOR INVERT SUGAR

Sweetening matter content by weight	Rate of Distribution Payment per cwt.
	£
70 per cent. or more	0 ·38
Less than 70 per cent. and more than 50 per cent.	0 ·27
Not more than 50 per cent.	0 ·13

EXPLANATORY NOTE

(*This Note is not part of the Order.*)

This order provides for reductions equivalent to £8 per ton of refined sugar in the rates of distribution payment in respect of sugar and invert sugar which become eligible for such payments on and after 13th April 1972.

STATUTORY INSTRUMENTS

1972 No. 579

SUGAR

The Sugar (Distribution Repayments) (Amendment) (No. 3) Order 1972

Made - - - -	*12th April* 1972
Laid before Parliament	*12th April* 1972
Coming into Operation	*13th April* 1972

The Minister of Agriculture, Fisheries and Food in exercise of the powers conferred upon him by sections 15 and 33(4) of the Sugar Act 1956(a), having effect subject to the provisions of section 3 of, and Part II of Schedule 5 to, the Finance Act 1962(b), section 22 of the Finance Act 1964(c) and section 52 of the Finance Act 1966(d) and of all other powers enabling him in that behalf, an order (e) having been made under section 14 of the said Act, hereby makes the following order:—

1.—(1) This order may be cited as the Sugar (Distribution Repayments) (Amendment) (No. 3) Order 1972, and shall come into operation on 13th April 1972.

(2) The Interpretation Act 1889(f) shall apply for the interpretation of this order as it applies for the interpretation of an Act of Parliament.

2.—(1) Notwithstanding the provisions of article 2(1) of the Sugar (Distribution Repayments) (Amendment) (No. 2) Order 1972(g) the amount of distribution repayment payable in respect of invert sugar, if the relevant drawback is payable thereon as being invert sugar produced in the United Kingdom from materials on which sugar duty has been paid on or after 13th April 1972, shall be calculated thereon at the rate applicable to the invert sugar in accordance with the rates prescribed in the Schedule to this order.

(2) Article 2(1) of the Sugar (Distribution Repayments) Order 1972(h) shall apply for the interpretation of this article.

In Witness whereof the Official Seal of the Minister of Agriculture, Fisheries and Food is hereunto affixed on 12th April 1972.

(L.S.)

E. J. G. Smith,
Authorised by the Minister.

(a) 1956 c. 48. (b) 1962 c. 44. (c) 1964 c. 49.
(d) 1966 c. 18. (e) S.I. 1972/578 (1972 I, P. 1918). (f) 1889 c. 63.
(g) S.I. 1972/433 (1972 I, p. 1624). (h) S.I. 1972/67 (1972 I, p. 1624).

THE SCHEDULE

RATES OF DISTRIBUTION REPAYMENT FOR INVERT SUGAR

Sweetening matter content by weight	Rate of Distribution Repayment per cwt.
	£
More than 80 per cent.	0·45
More than 70 per cent. but not more than 80 per cent.	0·38
More than 60 per cent. but not more than 70 per cent.	0·27
More than 50 per cent. but not more than 60 per cent.	0·21
Not more than 50 per cent. and the invert sugar not being less in weight than 14 lb. per gallon	0·13

EXPLANATORY NOTE

(*This Note is not part of the Order.*)

This order, which is consequent upon the Sugar (Distribution Payments) (No. 4) Order 1972 (S.I. 1972/578), provides for reductions equivalent to £8 per ton of refined sugar in the rates of distribution repayment, in respect of sugar and invert sugar produced in the United Kingdom from materials which become eligible for distribution payments on or after 13th April 1972.

STOKE-ON-TRENT
CITY
LIBRARIES

STATUTORY INSTRUMENTS

1972 No. 580

SUGAR

The Composite Sugar Products (Distribution Payments—Average Rates) (No. 4) Order 1972

Made - - - -	12*th April* 1972
Laid before Parliament-	12*th April* 1972
Coming into Operation	13*th April* 1972

Whereas the Minister of Agriculture, Fisheries and Food (hereinafter called " the Minister ") has on the recommendation of the Sugar Board made an order (a) pursuant to the powers conferred upon him by section 9(1) of the Sugar Act 1956(b) having effect subject to section 14(8) of that Act and to the provisions of section 3 of, and Part II of Schedule 5 to, the Finance Act 1962 (c), section 22 of the Finance Act 1964(d) and section 52 of the Finance Act 1966(e), providing that in the case of certain descriptions of composite sugar products distribution payments shall be calculated on the basis of an average quantity of sugar or invert sugar taken to have been used in the manufacture of the products and that certain other descriptions shall be treated as not containing any sugar or invert sugar:

And whereas the Minister has by the Sugar (Distribution Payments) (No. 4) Order 1972(f) provided for a change in the rates of distribution payments in respect of sugar and invert sugar which became eligible for such payments on and after 13th April 1972.

Now, therefore, the Minister on the recommendation of the Sugar Board, and in exercise of the powers conferred upon him by sections 9(1) and 33(4) of the Sugar Act 1956, having effect as aforesaid, and of all other powers enabling him in that behalf, hereby makes the following order:—

1.—(1) This order may be cited as the Composite Sugar Products (Distribution Payments—Average Rates) (No. 4) Order 1972, and shall come into operation on 13th April 1972.

(2) The Interpretation Act 1889(g) shall apply to the interpretation of this order as it applies to the interpretation of an Act of Parliament.

2. Distribution payments payable on or after 13th April 1972 under and in accordance with section 14 of the Sugar Act 1956, having effect as aforesaid, in respect of sugar and invert sugar used in the manufacture of the descriptions of imported composite sugar products specified in the second column of Schedule 1 to this order, being goods which are classified in the tariff headings indicated in relation to them in the first column of the said Schedule shall, notwithstanding the provisions of the Sugar (Distribution Payments) (No. 4) Order 1972 and the Composite Sugar Products (Distribution Payments—Average Rates) (No. 3) Order 1972(a) be calculated by reference to the weight of the products and the rates specified in relation thereto in the third column of the said Schedule.

3. Imported composite sugar products other than those of a description specified in Schedules 1 and 2 to this order shall be treated as not containing any sugar or invert sugar for the purposes of distribution payments.

(a) S.I. 1972/434 (1972 I, p. 1626). (b) 1956 c. 48. (c) 1962 c. 44. (d) 1964 c. 49. (e) 1966 c. 18. (f) S.I. 1972/578 (1972 I, p. 1918). (g) 1889 c. 63.

In Witness whereof the Official Seal of the Minister of Agriculture, Fisheries and Food is hereunto affixed on 12th April 1972.

(L.S.)

E. J. G. Smith,
Authorised by the Minister.

SCHEDULE 1

In this Schedule:—

" Tariff heading " means a heading or, where the context so requires, a subheading of the Customs Tariff 1959 (see paragraph (1) of Article 2 of the Import Duties (General) (No. 7) Order 1971)(a).

Tariff heading	Description of Composite Sugar Products	Rate of Distribution Payment
		Per cwt. £
04.02 ..	Milk and cream, preserved, concentrated or sweetened, containing more than 10 per cent. by weight of added sugar	0·26
17.02 (B) (2) and 17.05 (B)	Syrups containing sucrose sugar, whether or not flavoured or coloured, but not including fruit juices containing added sugar in any proportion:—	
	Containing 70 per cent. or more by weight of sweetening matter	0·38
	Containing less than 70 per cent., and more than 50 per cent. by weight of sweetening matter	0·27
	Containing not more than 50 per cent. by weight of sweetening matter	0·13
17.02 (F) ..	Caramel:—	
	Solid	0·60
	Liquid	0·41
17.04 ..	Sugar confectionery, not containing cocoa ..	0·48
18.06 ..	Chocolate and other food preparations containing cocoa and added sugar:—	
	Chocolate couverture not prepared for retail sale; chocolate milk crumb, liquid ..	0·26
	Chocolate milk crumb, solid	0·32
	Solid chocolate bars or blocks, milk or plain, with or without fruit or nuts; other chocolate confectionery consisting wholly of chocolate or of chocolate and other ingredients not containing added sugar ..	0·26
	Other	0·34

(a) S.I. 1971/1971 (1971 III, p. 5330).

SCHEDULE 1—*continued*

Tariff heading	Description of Composite Sugar Products	Rate of Distribution Payment
		Per cwt. £
19.08 ..	Pastry, biscuits, cakes and other fine bakers' wares containing added sugar:—	
	Biscuits, wafers and rusks containing more than 12½ per cent. by weight of added sugar, and other biscuits, wafers and rusks included in retail packages with such goods.. ..	0·15
	Cakes with covering or filling containing added sugar; meringues	0·19
	Other	0·07
20.01 ..	Vegetables and fruit, prepared or preserved by vinegar or acetic acid, containing added sugar:—	
	Containing 10 per cent. or more by weight of added sugar	0·21
	Other	0·04
20.03 ..	Fruit preserved by freezing, containing added sugar	0·07
20.04 ..	Fruit, fruit-peel and parts of plants, preserved by sugar (drained, glacé or crystallised)	0·39
20.05 ..	Jams, fruit jellies, marmalades, fruit puree and fruit pastes, being cooked preparations, containing added sugar	0·37
20.06 ..	Fruit otherwise prepared or preserved, containing added sugar:—	
	Ginger	0·30
	Other	0·07

SCHEDULE 2

Tariff heading	Description of Composite Sugar Products
17.05 (A) and (B)	Sugar and invert sugar, flavoured or coloured.

EXPLANATORY NOTE
(This Note is not part of the Order.)

This order provides for reductions in the average rates of distribution payments payable in respect of imported composite sugar products of the descriptions specified in Schedule 1 on and after 13th April 1972. These correspond to reductions in the rates of distribution payment effected by the Sugar (Distribution Payments) (No. 4) Order 1972 (S.I. 1972/578). Provision is also made for certain imported composite sugar products to be treated as not containing any sugar or invert sugar.

1972 No. 581

WAGES COUNCILS

The Wages Regulation (Road Haulage) Order 1972

Made - - -	*11th April* 1972
Coming into Operation	*24th May* 1972

Whereas the Secretary of State has received from the Road Haulage Wages Council the wages regulation proposals set out in the Schedule hereto;

Now, therefore, the Secretary of State in exercise of his powers under section 11 of the Wages Councils Act 1959(**a**), and of all other powers enabling him in that behalf, hereby makes the following Order: —

1. This Order may be cited as the Wages Regulation (Road Haulage) Order 1972.

2.—(1) In this Order the expression "the specified date" means the 24th May 1972, provided that where, as respects any worker who is paid wages at intervals not exceeding seven days, that date does not correspond with the beginning of the period for which the wages are paid, the expression "the specified date" means, as respects that worker, the beginning of the next such period following that date.

(2) The Interpretation Act 1889(**b**) shall apply to the interpretation of this Order as it applies to the interpretation of an Act of Parliament and as if this Order and the Order hereby revoked were Acts of Parliament.

3. The wages regulation proposals set out in the Schedule hereto shall have effect as from the specified date and as from that date the Wages Regulation (Road Haulage) Order 1970(**c**) shall cease to have effect.

Signed by order of the Secretary of State.

11th April 1972.

J. R. Lloyd Davies,
Assistant Secretary,
Department of Employment.

(**a**) 1959 c. 69.　　　　(**b**) 1889 c. 63.
(**c**) S.I. 1970/1268 (1970 II, p. 4116).

ARRANGEMENT OF SCHEDULE
MINIMUM REMUNERATION AND HOLIDAYS

Article 3

SCHEDULE

The following minimum remuneration and provisions as to holidays and holiday remuneration shall be substituted for the statutory minimum remuneration and provisions as to holidays and holiday remuneration set out in the Wages Regulation (Road Haulage) Order 1970 (hereinafter referred to as "Order R.H.(94)").

STATUTORY MINIMUM REMUNERATION

PART I

REGULAR WORKERS OTHER THAN MILK WORKERS

This Part of this Schedule applies to regular workers (as defined in paragraph 38) other than milk workers (as defined in paragraph 43).

1. Subject to the provisions of this Part and of Parts III and V of this Schedule, the minimum remuneration of regular workers other than milk workers shall be as follows:—

(1) All workers except those employed on the Carriage of Indivisible Loads to whom sub-paragraph (2) of this paragraph applies:—

Occupation	Carrying capacity of vehicle (as defined in paragraph 34)	Age of worker	Remuneration per week	
			Workers whose home depot is situated in the London Area (as defined in para. 35)	Workers whose home depot is situated outside the London Area (as defined in para. 35)
(a) Drivers of vehicles other than (i) tractors not exceeding two tons unladen weight used exclusively for furniture removal work and (ii) tractors which operate from a depot in the London Area (as defined in paragraph 35).	Of 1 ton or less	Under 19 years ... 19 and under 21 years 21 years or over ...	£ 12·43 14·88 18·25	£ 12·33 14·78 18·00
	Over 1 ton and up to and including 5 tons ,, 5 tons ... ... 10 ,, 10 ,, ... 15 ,, 15 ,, ... 18 ,, 18 ,, ... 21 ,, 21 ,, ...	All ages	18·25 18·73 19·10 19·58 20·15 20·63	18·00 18·48 18·85 19·33 19·90 20·38
(b) Drivers of tractors not exceeding two tons unladen weight used exclusively for furniture removal work	—	All ages	18·25	18·00

Occupation	Carrying capacity of vehicle (as defined in paragraph 34)	Age of worker	Remuneration per week	
			Workers whose home depot is situated in the London Area (as defined in para. 35)	Workers whose home depot is situated outside the London Area (as defined in para. 35)
			£	£
(c) Drivers of tractors, other than tractors not exceeding two tons unladen weight used exclusively for furniture work, which operate from a depot in the London Area (as defined in paragraph 35).	Up to and including 8 tons	All ages ...	18·78	—
	Over 8 tons and up to and including 12 tons		19·20	—
	Over 12 tons		19·63	—
(d) Workers in the Furniture Warehousing and Removing Industry employed as:		21 years or over ...		
Foremen			18·20	17·98
Removal packers	—		17·85	17·73
Porters			17·73	17·60
(e) Statutory attendants ...	—	Under 18 years ...	10·62	10·49
(f) Other road haulage workers	—	Under 16 years ...	7·15	7·05
		16 and under 17 years	7·80	7·70
		17 „ „ 18 „	8·55	8·47
		18 „ „ 19 „	11·46	11·31
		19 „ „ 20 „	12·47	12·27
		20 „ „ 21 „	13·75	13·55
		21 years or over ...	17·85	17·70

(2) Workers employed on the Carriage of Indivisible Loads.

(a) Workers on vehicles whilst used in connection with the movement of loads, other than live or dead cattle, which by reason of indivisibility require mechanical loading or unloading equipment carried on the vehicle and operated upon the responsibility of the driver, or

(b) Workers employed on vehicles authorised for the carriage of abnormal indivisible loads as defined in the Motor Vehicles (Authorisation of Special Types) General Order 1969(a):—

Occupation	Class of Vehicle	Carrying capacity of vehicle (as defined in paragraph 34)	Remuneration per week	
			Workers whose home depot is situated in the London Area (as defined in para. 35)	Workers whose home depot is situated outside the London Area (as defined in para. 35)
			£	£
Drivers	Vehicles referred to in (a) above	Over 6 tons and up to and including 10 tons	19·13	18·93
		,, 10 ,, ,, ,, ,, ,, 16 ,,	19·65	19·45
	Vehicles referred to in (b) above	,, 16 ,, ,, ,, ,, ,, 20 ,,	20·43	20·23
		,, 20 ,, ,, ,, ,, 25 ,,	20·75	20·55
		,, 25 ,, ,, ,, ,, 45 ,,	21·08	20·88
		,, 45 ,, ,, ,, ,, 65 ,,	22·70	22·50
		,, 65 ,, ,, ...	23·45	23·25
Mates	Vehicles referred to in (a) above	Over 6 tons and up to and including 16 tons	17·85	17·70
	Vehicles referred to in (b) above	,, 16 ,, ,, ,, ,, 20 ,,	17·98	17·83
		Over 20 tons	18·30	18·15
Heavy brakesmen and steersmen (as defined in paragraph 41).	Vehicles referred to in (b) above	—	19·15	19·00

(a) 1969/344 (1969 I, p. 947).

A worker who on any day is employed in the circumstances specified in this sub-paragraph shall be paid at the rate appropriate to the vehicle for all hours worked by him on that day notwithstanding that he may be employed on other work during some part of that day.

COMPUTATION OF HOURS OF WORK

2. The following provisions shall apply to regular workers, other than milk workers, to whom the guaranteed weekly remuneration provisions apply:—

(1) a five-day worker who works on any day other than Saturday or Sunday shall be deemed to have worked for 8 hours on any such day notwithstanding that he was employed for less than 8 hours;

(2) a six-day worker who works on any day other than Sunday shall, subject to the provisions of paragraph 24 and the proviso to paragraph 44(1)(*a*), be deemed to have worked for 7¼ hours on any day Monday to Thursday, for 7 hours on Friday and for 4 hours on Saturday notwithstanding that he was employed for less than 7¼, 7 or 4 hours respectively:

Provided that a worker who is instructed to report for duty and presents himself for duty but does not commence work shall be deemed to have commenced work.

OVERTIME

3. Subject to the provisions of paragraphs 23, 24 and 44 the following shall be regarded as overtime—

(1) Time worked in excess of 7¼ hours on any day Monday to Thursday and 7 hours on Friday (subject to the proviso to paragraph 44(1)(*a*)) in the case of a six-day worker and in excess of 8 hours on any day Monday to Friday in the case of a five-day worker.

(2) Time worked on Saturdays:—

(*a*) in the case of a six-day worker, in excess of 4 hours, provided that all time worked after 12.30 p.m. by a worker other than a film transport worker shall be regarded as overtime;

(*b*) in the case of a five-day worker, all time worked, provided that a five-day worker who works for less than 4 hours shall be deemed to have worked for 4 hours.

(3) Time worked on Sunday.

A worker who works for less than 5½ hours on Sunday shall be deemed to have worked for 5½ hours:

Provided that a worker whose hours entail a spell of duty commencing on Saturday and finishing on Sunday before 5.30 a.m. or commencing on Sunday after 6.30 p.m. and finishing on Monday, shall not, unless the Sunday duty is less than 3 hours, be deemed to have worked on Sunday in excess of the hours actually worked. If the Sunday duty is less than 3 hours he shall be deemed to have worked 3 hours on Sunday:

Provided also that a worker commencing work on Saturday who finishes work between midnight and 1 a.m. on Sunday shall be deemed to have worked one hour on Sunday.

(4) Time worked in any week in excess of 40 hours.

4.—(1) In determining the time to be regarded as overtime, time worked shall include time deemed to have been worked under the provisions of paragraphs 2, 3(3) and 23.

(2) Time worked on a customary holiday in accordance with paragraph 26(2)(*b*) or paragraph 27(2)(*b*) or on a day in the circumstances set out in the proviso to paragraph 26(4)(*a*) or paragraph 27(4)(*a*), paragraph 26(3) or paragraph 27(3) shall not be included in the calculation of overtime.

(3) When a worker's hours of duty or any part thereof entail employment between 9 p.m. and 6 a.m., a day shall, for the purpose of paragraph 3(1) and paragraph 3(2), be deemed to be any period of 24 hours commencing at 12 noon.

PAYMENT FOR OVERTIME

5. The following are the rates payable for overtime:—

in any week (exclusive of Sunday)	time-and-a-half
on Sunday	double time

Part II
MILK WORKERS

This Part of this Schedule applies to milk workers (as defined in paragraph 43).

6. Subject to the provisions of this Part and of Parts III and V of this Schedule, the minimum remuneration of milk workers shall be as follows:—

Occupation	Carrying capacity of vehicle (as defined in paragraph 34)	Age of worker	Remuneration per week	
			Workers whose home depot is situated in the London Area (as defined in para. 35)	Workers whose home depot is situated outside the London Area (as defined in para. 35)
			£	£
(1) Drivers of vehicles other than tractors which operate from a depot in the London Area (as defined in paragraph 35).	Of 1 ton or less	Under 19 years ...	12·43	12·33
		19 and under 21 years	14·88	14·78
		21 years or over ...	18·25	18·00
	Over 1 ton and up to and including 5 tons	All ages ...	18·25	18·00
	" 5 tons 10		18·73	18·48
	" 10 " 15		19·10	18·85
	" 15 " 18		19·58	19·33
	" 18 " 21		20·15	19·90
	" 21 "		20·63	20·38
(2) Drivers of tractors which operate from a depot in the London Area (as defined in paragraph 35).	Up to and including 8 tons	All ages ...	18·78	—
	Over 8 tons and up to and including 12 tons ...		19·20	—
	Over 12 tons		19·63	—
(3) Statutory attendants ...	—	Under 18 years ...	10·62	10·49
(4) Other road haulage workers ...	—	Under 16 years ...	7·15	7·05
		16 and under 17 years	7·80	7·70
		17 " " 18 "	8·55	8·47
		18 " " 19 "	11·46	11·31
		19 " " 20 "	12·47	12·27
		20 " " 21 "	13·75	13·55
		21 years or over ...	17·85	17·70

SUNDAY WORK

7. A milk worker shall be paid time-and-a-half for 6 hours 40 minutes for any time worked or deemed to have been worked not exceeding 6 hours 40 minutes on Sunday not being the worker's normal day of rest and, thereafter, in accordance with paragraph 11.

COMPUTATION OF HOURS OF WORK

8. A milk worker to whom the guaranteed weekly remuneration provisions apply who works on any day shall be deemed to have worked for 6 hours 40 minutes notwithstanding that he was employed for less than 6 hours 40 minutes:

Provided that a milk worker who is instructed to report for duty and presents himself for duty but does not commence work shall be deemed to have commenced work.

OVERTIME

9. Subject to the provisions of paragraphs 24 and 44 the following shall be regarded as overtime:—

(1) Time worked in excess of 6 hours 40 minutes on any day other than the milk worker's normal day of rest, and all time worked on the milk worker's day of rest.

(2) Time worked in any week in excess of 40 hours.

10.—(1) In determining the time to be regarded as overtime, time worked shall include time deemed to have been worked under the provisions of paragraphs 8 and 23.

(2) Time worked on a customary holiday in accordance with paragraph 26(2)(b) or paragraph 27(2)(b) or on a day in the circumstances set out in the proviso to paragraph 26(4)(a) or paragraph 27(4)(a), paragraph 26(3) or paragraph 27(3) shall not be included in the calculation of overtime.

(3) When a worker's hours of duty or any part thereof entail employment between 9 p.m. and 6 a.m., a day shall, for the purpose of paragraph 9(1), be deemed to be any period of 24 hours commencing at 12 noon.

PAYMENT FOR OVERTIME

11. The following are the rates payable for overtime:—

in any week exclusive of the milk worker's normal day of
rest and Sunday ... ... time-and-a-half

on Sunday not being the milk worker's normal day of rest—
for all time worked in excess of 6 hours 40 minutes ... double time

on the milk worker's normal day of rest—

for any time worked not exceeding 6 hours 40 minutes ... double time for 6 hours 40 minutes

for all time worked in excess of 6 hours 40 minutes ... double time.

PART III

REGULAR WORKERS INCLUDING MILK WORKERS

This Part of this Schedule applies to regular workers including milk workers.

WORKERS TEMPORARILY TRANSFERRED

12. A worker who is temporarily transferred away from his normal home depot and stationed in another locality (beyond reasonable daily travelling distance from his home) for more than one week shall be paid either the rates of wages appropriate to the locality in which his normal home depot is situated, or those appropriate to the new locality in which he has been stationed, whichever is more favourable to the worker.

HOURLY RATE

13. For the purpose of calculating the hourly rates of regular workers, the rates of wages specified in paragraphs 1 and 6 shall be divided by 40.

GUARANTEED WEEKLY REMUNERATION

14.—(1) Notwithstanding the provisions of the other paragraphs of this Schedule, where in any week a worker has performed some road haulage work for the employer and the total remuneration payable for time worked and time deemed to have been worked (excluding overtime and special payments as defined in sub-paragraph (4) of this paragraph) is less than the guaranteed weekly remuneration provided under this paragraph, the minimum remuneration payable to that worker for that week shall, subject to the provisions of this paragraph, be that guaranteed weekly remuneration with the addition of any amount which may be payable in respect of overtime and by way of special payments.

(2) The guaranteed weekly remuneration is the pay for 40 hours, reduced by any time not reckonable by reason of sub-paragraph (3) of this paragraph and excluding special payments, calculated as follows:—

(a) for the time worked and time deemed to have been worked at the rate or rates applicable to such work (but excluding overtime) and

(b) for the remaining time at the time rate normally applicable to the worker.

(3) In calculating the guaranteed weekly remuneration no account shall be taken of

(a) any time during which the worker is at his own request absent from work with leave of the employer, is absent without leave of the employer or on account of sickness or

(b) any time during which the worker is suspended from work following the expiry of any notice given to him in any of the following manners and circumstances:—

(i) flood, snow, ice or other climatic conditions of such a nature as to preclude the operation of the vehicle, provided that not less than 24 hours' notice of the suspension of work shall be given individually to the worker and by the posting of a notice in the depot or other mutually convenient place;

(ii) where the employer is unable to carry on his business by reason of a strike or lock-out, provided that not less than 4 days' notice of such inability is given to the worker;

(iii) where the employer is unable to operate a vehicle or vehicles owing to the restriction of his fuel supply under any enactment or regulation made thereunder, provided that not less than 24 hours' notice of such inability is given to the worker or workers concerned:

Provided that the foregoing notices shall not be given when the worker is away from his home depot, and the suspension shall not operate until the required notice has been given to the worker on his return to his home depot.

(4) For the purposes of sub-paragraphs (1) and (2) of this paragraph:—

(a) in addition to any time deemed to have been worked under the other provisions of this Schedule;

(i) where a worker is allowed a day as a customary holiday or in lieu of a customary holiday or an annual holiday he shall be deemed to have worked the number of hours (excluding overtime) ordinarily worked by him on that day of the week;

(ii) where a worker is required to work on a day of customary holiday he shall be deemed to have worked the number of hours (excluding overtime) ordinarily worked by him on that day of the week notwithstanding that he was employed for less than that number of hours:

Provided that if a worker works on a customary holiday in accordance with the provisions of paragraph 26(2)(b) or paragraph 27(2)(b) or on a day in the circumstances set out in the proviso to paragraph 26(4)(*a*) or paragraph 27(4)(*a*) he shall be deemed only to have worked double the number of hours worked by him on that day (part of an hour being counted as an hour).

(*b*) "Special payments" means the following amounts:—

    (i) Any additional payment for night work payable under paragraph 20.

    (ii) Any amount payable under paragraph 22 (payment for telephoning for instructions whilst off duty).

    (iii) Any subsistence allowance (other than payment for hours during which the worker is deemed to be on duty) payable under paragraph 23.

    (iv) Any amount payable in respect of customary holidays occurring on the worker's weekly half-holiday or, in the case of a five-day worker, on a Saturday, or, in the case of a milk worker, on his normal day of rest, under provisos (*a*), (*b*) and (*c*) of paragraph 26(1) or under provisos (i), (ii) and (iii) of paragraph 27(1).

(5) The provisions of this paragraph shall not apply to a worker whose normal employment in the service of the employer substantially includes other work as well as road haulage work. Such a worker shall be paid in respect of the road haulage work at the appropriate rate for the time actually spent on such work.

A worker not normally a road haulage worker, but who occasionally performs road haulage work, shall be paid the rates of wages appropriate to a road haulage worker for the time actually spent on such work.

Part IV

WORKERS OTHER THAN REGULAR WORKERS

This Part of this Schedule applies to workers other than regular workers.

15. Subject to the provisions of this Part and of Part V of this Schedule, the minimum remuneration of workers other than regular workers shall be the hourly rates applicable to regular workers under Part I or Part II of this Schedule increased by 2p per hour.

GUARANTEED DAY

16. Subject to the provisions of paragraph 24 (relating to the alternative weekly half-holiday) and sub-paragraphs (6) and (7) of paragraphs 26 and 27 (relating to work on customary holidays), a worker other than a regular worker shall be paid not less than the wages due for $7\frac{1}{4}$ hours in respect of work done, or deemed to have been done, by him on any day Monday to Thursday, for 7 hours in respect of work done, or deemed to have been done, on Friday, and not less than the wages due for 4 hours in respect of work done, or deemed to have been done, by him on Saturday:

Provided that—

(1) where a spell of duty commences before midnight and continues thereafter, a worker shall not be entitled, by that fact alone, to two guaranteed payments in respect of that spell of duty;

(2) a worker who is engaged for a day of not less than $7\frac{1}{4}$ hours on any day Monday to Thursday, of not less than 7 hours on Friday, or for not less than 4 hours on Saturday, for work other than road haulage work, but who may perform some road haulage work, shall be paid for the time actually spent on road haulage work at the hourly rate or rates, calculated in accordance with the provisions of paragraph 15; and

(3) a worker who is instructed to report for duty, and presents himself for duty but does not commence work, shall be deemed to have commenced work.

Subject to the provisions relating to overtime, a worker other than a regular worker shall, when the number of hours worked or payable under the guarantee provided in this paragraph, is $7\frac{1}{4}$ on any day Monday to Thursday, 7 on Friday or 4 on Saturday. be paid the wages applicable to a regular worker for $7\frac{1}{4}$ hours, 7 hours or 4 hours as the case may be, plus 16p.

In all other circumstances, he shall be paid at an hourly rate, which is 2p per hour above the hourly rate applicable to the regular worker.

OVERTIME

17. Subject to the provisions of paragraphs 23 and 24, the following shall be regarded as overtime:—

(1) Time worked in excess of 7¼ hours on any day Monday to Thursday, in excess of 7 hours on Friday and in excess of 4 hours on Saturday.

(2) Time worked on Sunday.

A worker who works for less than 5½ hours on Sunday shall be deemed to have worked for 5½ hours:

Provided that a worker whose hours entail a spell of duty commencing on Saturday and finishing on Sunday before 5.30 a.m. or commencing on Sunday after 6.30 p.m. and finishing on Monday, shall not, unless the Sunday duty is less than 3 hours, be deemed to have worked on Sunday in excess of the hours actually worked. If the Sunday duty is less than 3 hours he shall be deemed to have worked 3 hours on Sunday:

Provided also that a worker commencing work on Saturday who finishes work between midnight and 1 a.m. on Sunday shall be deemed to have worked one hour on Sunday.

18.—(1) In determining the time to be regarded as overtime, time worked shall include time deemed to have been worked under the provisions of paragraphs 17(2) and 23.

(2) Time worked on a customary holiday in accordance with paragraph 26(2)(*b*) or paragraph 27(2)(*b*) or on a day in the circumstances set out in the proviso to paragraph 26(4)(*a*) or paragraph 27(4)(*a*) shall not be included in the calculation of overtime.

(3) When a worker's hours of duty or any part thereof entail employment between 9 p.m. and 6 a.m., a day shall, for the purpose of paragraph 17(1), be deemed to be any period of 24 hours commencing at 12 noon.

PAYMENT FOR OVERTIME

19. The following are the rates payable for overtime:—

on any day (other than Sunday)	time-and-a-half
on Sunday	double time.

Part V

ALL WORKERS—ADDITIONAL PROVISIONS

This Part of this Schedule applies to all workers except where otherwise stated.

NIGHT WORK

20. A worker whose hours of duty or any part thereof entail employment between 7 p.m. and 6 a.m. shall be paid the appropriate rates of wages specified in paragraph 1, paragraph 6, or paragraph 15 and, in addition, in each spell of duty, 5p for each hour, or part of an hour, worked between 7 p.m. and 6 a.m. provided that where a spell of duty commences before 7 p.m. and finishes not later than 9 p.m. the additional payment shall not be payable. Where overtime is payable in respect of hours worked between 7 p.m. and 6 a.m., this additional payment remains payable but is not to be included for the purpose of calculating the overtime rate payable in respect of those hours.

TRAVELLING

21. When a worker is required to travel in, or on, or to accompany a vehicle for the purpose of doing road haulage work he shall, in determining the wages payable, be deemed to be engaged on the road haulage work usually performed by him.

TELEPHONING FOR INSTRUCTIONS WHILE OFF DUTY

22.—(1) If a worker during the period between two spells of duty is required to telephone for instructions he shall be paid the wages due for one hour:

Provided that this provision shall not apply when the telephone call is made immediately following a spell of duty.

(2) On each subsequent occasion, during the same period between two spells of duty, on which the worker is required to telephone for instructions he shall be paid the wages due for 4 hours:

Provided that if when telephoning on any such occasion the worker is instructed to commence work within one hour of so telephoning, he shall be paid for one hour instead of the said 4 hours.

(3) The payments to be made under sub-paragraphs (1) and (2) of this paragraph shall be at the rate normally applicable to the worker and shall be in addition to the weekly wages otherwise due to him.

SUBSISTENCE

23.—(1)(a) When a worker's period of rest occurs away from his home depot he shall be paid £1·75 in respect of each period of rest not exceeding 15 hours' continued duration. Subject to the provisions of sub-paragraph (1)(b) of this paragraph, when any such period of rest exceeds 15 hours the worker shall be deemed to be on duty and shall be entitled to be paid (in addition to the £1·75) at the time rate which would be payable if he were actually at work for the period he is resting in excess of 15 hours but not in excess of 24 hours or 23 hours according to whether he is a five- or six-day worker. If the period of rest exceeds 24 or 23 hours, as the case may be, these arrangements will continue to apply until the worker resumes actual duty;

(b) Where, following the first 15 hours of a period of rest for which subsistence is payable, deemed duty or actual duty commences on a Sunday, the worker shall be entitled (in addition to the £1·75) in respect of any deemed and any actual duty performed on the Sunday to not less than the wages due for 9 hours or 8 hours at double time, according to whether he is a five- or six-day worker.

(2) Notwithstanding the provisions of sub-paragraph (1) of this paragraph the following provisions shall apply in the case of a worker who is temporarily transferred away from his normal home depot and stationed in another locality (beyond reasonable daily travelling distance from his home) for more than one week:—

    (a) after payment in respect of the first week in accordance with the provisions of sub-paragraph (1) of this paragraph a worker shall, in respect of the second and subsequent weeks, be paid a weekly subsistence allowance of £8·61 (i.e. £1·23 per day);

    (b) if a worker already on temporary transfer is temporarily transferred to another new station beyond reasonable travelling distance from his home he shall (after payment in respect of the first week at such other new station in accordance with sub-paragraph (1) of this paragraph) be paid, in respect of the second and subsequent weeks, a weekly subsistence allowance of £8·61 (i.e. £1·23 per day);

    (c) for any period of rest occurring away from a new station and from his home, he shall be paid in accordance with the provisions of sub-paragraph (1) of this paragraph and, in respect of any day for which payment is made to the worker under the provisions of that sub-paragraph, the subsistence allowances of £1·23 per day (specified in (a) and (b) above) shall be reduced to £0·95 per day.

ALTERNATIVE WEEKLY HALF-HOLIDAY

24. Where it is the established practice of any section of the industry to allow the weekly half-holiday on any weekday other than a Saturday, and that day is in the case of a six-day worker substituted for Saturday as the worker's weekly half-holiday the provisions of paragraphs 2, 3(1) and (2), 14, 16, 17(1) and 44, shall apply as if in these provisions that day were substituted for "Saturday" and "Saturday" for that day.

MEAL TIMES

25. The hours of work specified are, except for the purpose of paragraph 23, exclusive of meal times.

HOLIDAYS AND HOLIDAY REMUNERATION
CUSTOMARY HOLIDAYS—ENGLAND AND WALES

26.—(1) Subject to the provisions of this paragraph, an employer in England and Wales shall allow the following days as holidays to regular workers to whom paragraphs 1 and 6 apply and who were in his employment on the day immediately prior to the day of holiday:—Christmas Day (or, if Christmas Day falls on a Sunday, such weekday as may be prescribed by national proclamation, or the next following Tuesday), Boxing Day, Good Friday, Easter Monday, Whit Monday (or where another day is substituted therefor by national proclamation, that day), August Bank Holiday and all nationally proclaimed holidays. Where in any place it is not the custom or practice to observe such days as holidays, other days (not fewer in number) may, by agreement between the employer and the worker, be substituted for the above-mentioned days. Each such day (i.e., one of the days specified above or a day substituted therefor—hereafter in this paragraph referred to as a "customary holiday") taken as a holiday shall be paid for on the basis of the wages due for the number of hours (excluding overtime) ordinarily worked by the worker on that day of the week at the time rate normally applicable to the worker:

Provided that—

(a) in addition to the foregoing, in the case of a six-day worker, other than a milk worker, where the customary holiday falls on the worker's weekly half-holiday he shall be paid in respect of that day a sum equivalent to the wages due for 4 hours' work at the rate normally applicable to him;

(b) in the case of a five-day worker, where the customary holiday falls on a Saturday he shall be paid in respect of that day a sum equivalent to the wages due for 8 hours' work at the rate normally applicable to him;

(c) in the case of a milk worker, where the customary holiday falls on the worker's normal day of rest he shall be paid in respect of that day a sum equivalent to the wages due for 6 hours 40 minutes' work at the rate normally applicable to him.

(2) Notwithstanding the foregoing provisions of this paragraph, a regular worker may work for the employer on a customary holiday:—

(a) where by reason of the necessity of maintaining essential services the allowing of a customary holiday is rendered impracticable; or

(b) where the worker will work on the customary holiday for not more than 3 hours during a spell of duty commencing on the day before the customary holiday or ending on the day after the holiday:

Provided that this sub-paragraph shall not apply to women and young persons in whose cases work on the customary holiday would be illegal.

(3)(a) Where a worker works on a customary holiday by virtue of sub-paragraph (2)(a) of this paragraph he shall be paid for work on that day at not less than double the rate appropriate to such work for all time worked by him thereon or for the basic hours for that worker, whichever amount is the greater. For the purpose of this sub-paragraph basic hours means in the case of a milk worker 6 hours 40 minutes, and, in the case of any other worker, the number of hours (excluding overtime) ordinarily worked by him on the day of the week on which the customary holiday falls.

(b) Where a worker works on a customary holiday by virtue of sub-paragraph (2)(b) of this paragraph he shall be paid for work on that day at not less than double the rate appropriate to such work (part of an hour being counted as an hour) and, in addition, an amount equal to the holiday remuneration to which he would have been entitled under the provisions of this order if he had been allowed a customary holiday on that day.

(4)(a) Where a regular worker works on a customary holiday by virtue of the provisions of sub-paragraph (2)(*a*) of this paragraph he shall, within the period of eight weeks immediately following the customary holiday, be allowed a day's holiday (hereafter referred to as "a day in lieu of a customary holiday") on a weekday (other than a weekly half-holiday) on which the worker normally works for the employer:

Provided that if on a weekday which is not a customary holiday or a weekly half-holiday within the said period of eight weeks the worker works for the employer for not more than 3 hours during a spell of duty commencing on the immediately preceding day or ending on the following day and the worker is paid for such work remuneration not less than the remuneration provided for work on a customary holiday under sub-paragraph (3)(*b*) of this paragraph, an employer is not required to allow to a worker a day in lieu of a customary holiday.

(*b*) For each day in lieu of a customary holiday allowed to a worker he shall be paid not less than the holiday remuneration to which he would have been entitled under the provisions of this Schedule if the day had been a customary holiday.

(*c*) For the purposes of this paragraph in the case of a worker who is employed on spells of duty which start before midnight and continue for more than 3 hours after midnight the day in lieu of a customary holiday shall include any period of 24 consecutive hours beginning and ending at noon on a weekday (other than a weekly half-holiday) on which the worker normally works.

(5) The holiday remuneration for a customary holiday or a day in lieu of a customary holiday shall be paid by the employer to the worker not later than the day on which the wages for the first working day following the customary holiday or day in lieu of the customary holiday are paid.

(6) Except as specified in sub-paragraph (7) of this paragraph a worker, other than a regular worker, who is employed on a customary holiday shall be paid for such work at double the rate otherwise appropriate thereto, and, notwithstanding that he may work for less than 7¼ hours on any such day, he shall be paid not less than twice the amount due, under the provisions of paragraph 16, for a guaranteed day of 7¼ hours.

(7) Where a worker, other than a regular worker, works for the employer on a customary holiday for not more than 3 hours during a spell of duty commencing on the immediately preceding day or ending on the following day, he shall be paid for such work at double the rate appropriate to such work, part of an hour being counted as an hour.

CUSTOMARY HOLIDAYS—SCOTLAND

27.—(1) Subject to the provisions of this paragraph, an employer in Scotland shall allow the following days as holidays to regular workers to whom paragraphs 1 and 6 apply and who were in his employment on the day immediately prior to the day of holiday:—

> (*a*) New Year's Day (or the following day if New Year's Day falls on a Sunday) the local Spring Holiday, the local Autumn Holiday, and all nationally proclaimed holidays;
>
> (*b*) Three other days in the course of a calendar year, to be fixed by the employer and notified to the workers not less than 21 days before the holiday;
>
> (*c*) Where in any place it is not the custom or practice to observe the days mentioned in (*a*) above as holidays, other days (not fewer in number) may, by agreement between the employer and the worker, be substituted for the above-mentioned days.

Each such day (i.e., one of the days specified above or a day substituted therefor —hereafter in this paragraph referred to as a "customary holiday") taken as a holiday shall be paid for on the basis of the wages due for the number of hours (excluding overtime) ordinarily worked by the worker on that day of the week at the time rate normally applicable to the worker:

Provided that—

> (i) in addition to the foregoing, in the case of a six-day worker other than a milk worker, where the customary holiday falls on the worker's weekly

half-holiday he shall be paid in respect of that day a sum equivalent to the wages due for 4 hours' work at the rate normally applicable to him;

(ii) in the case of a five-day worker, where the customary holiday falls on a Saturday he shall be paid in respect of that day a sum equivalent to the wages due for 8 hours' work at the rate normally applicable to him;

(iii) in the case of a milk worker, where the customary holiday falls on the worker's normal day of rest he shall be paid in respect of that day a sum equivalent to the wages due for 6 hours 40 minutes' work at the rate normally applicable to him.

(2) Notwithstanding the foregoing provisions of this paragraph, a regular worker may work for the employer on a customary holiday:—

(a) where by reason of the necessity of maintaining essential services the allowing of a customary holiday is rendered impracticable; or

(b) where the worker will work on the customary holiday for not more than 3 hours during a spell of duty commencing on the day before the customary holiday or ending on the day after the holiday:

Provided that this sub-paragraph shall not apply to women and young persons in whose cases work on the customary holiday would be illegal.

(3)(a) Where a worker works on a customary holiday by virtue of sub-paragraph (2)(a) of this paragraph he shall be paid for work on that day at not less than double the rate appropriate to such work for all time worked by him thereon or for the basic hours for that worker, whichever amount is the greater. For the purpose of this sub-paragraph basic hours means, in the case of a milk worker, 6 hours 40 minutes and, in the case of any other worker, the number of hours (excluding overtime) ordinarily worked by him on the day of the week on which the customary holiday falls.

(b) Where a worker works on a customary holiday by virtue of sub-paragraph (2)(b) of this paragraph he shall be paid for work on that day at not less than double the rate appropriate to such work (part of an hour being counted as an hour) and, in addition, an amount equal to the holiday remuneration to which he would have been entitled under the provisions of this order if he had been allowed a customary holiday on that day.

(4)(a) Where a regular worker works on a customary holiday by virtue of the provisions of sub-paragraph (2)(a) of this paragraph he shall, within the period of eight weeks immediately following the customary holiday, be allowed a day's holiday (hereafter referred to as "a day in lieu of a customary holiday") on a weekday (other than a weekly half-holiday) on which the worker normally works for the employer:

Provided that if on a weekday which is not a customary holiday or a weekly half-holiday within the said period of eight weeks the worker works for the employer for not more than 3 hours during a spell of duty commencing on the immediately preceding day or ending on the following day and the worker is paid for such work remuneration not less than the remuneration provided for work on a customary holiday under sub-paragraph (3)(b) of this paragraph an employer is not required to allow a worker a day in lieu of a customary holiday.

(b) For each day in lieu of a customary holiday allowed to a worker he shall be paid not less than the holiday remuneration to which he would have been entitled under the provisions of this Schedule if the day had been a customary holiday.

(c) For the purposes of this paragraph in the case of a worker who is employed on spells of duty which start before midnight and continue for more than 3 hours after midnight the day in lieu of a customary holiday shall include any period of 24 consecutive hours beginning and ending at noon on a weekday (other than a weekly half-holiday) on which the worker normally works.

(5) The holiday remuneration for a customary holiday or a day in lieu of a customary holiday shall be paid by the employer to the worker not later than the day on which the wages for the first working day following the customary holiday or day in lieu of a customary holiday are paid.

(6) Except as specified in sub-paragraph (7) of this paragraph, a worker, other

than a regular worker, who is employed on any of the days mentioned in sub-paragraph (1)(*a*) of this paragraph shall be paid for such work at double the rate otherwise appropriate thereto, and, notwithstanding that he may work for less than 7¼ hours on any such day, he shall be paid not less than twice the amount due, under the provisions of paragraph 17, for a guaranteed day of 7¼ hours.

(7) Where a worker, other than a regular worker, works for the employer on a customary holiday for not more than 3 hours during a spell of duty commencing on the immediately preceding day or ending on the following day, he shall be paid for such work at double the rate appropriate to such work, a part of an hour being counted as an hour.

ANNUAL HOLIDAY, ADDITIONAL ANNUAL HOLIDAY, AND HOLIDAY REMUNERATION

28.—(1) In addition to the holidays provided for in paragraphs 26 and 27 (and subject to the provisions of sub-paragraphs (3) and (6) of this paragraph) an employer shall between the date on which the provisions of this Schedule become effective and 15th October 1972, and in each succeeding year between 1st May and 15th October allow a holiday (hereinafter referred to as an "annual holiday") to every worker in his employment for whom statutory minimum remuneration has been fixed under paragraphs 1, 6 or 15 and who was during the 12 months immediately preceding the commencement of the holiday seas on in that year (hereinafter referred to as the "qualifying period") in his employment for any of the periods of employment specified below, and the duration of a worker's annual holiday shall be related to the period of his employment during the qualifying period as follows:—

Six-day workers		Five-day workers	
Period of employment	Duration of annual holiday	Period of employment	Duration of annual holiday
At least 48 weeks	12 days	At least 48 weeks	10 days
,, ,, 44 ,,	11 ,,	,, ,, 43 ,,	9 ,,
,, ,, 40 ,,	10 ,,	,, ,, 38 ,,	8 ,,
,, ,, 36 ,,	9 ,,	,, ,, 33 ,,	7 ,,
,, ,, 32 ,,	8 ,,	,, ,, 28 ,,	6 ,,
,, ,, 28 ,,	7 ,,	,, ,, 24 ,,	5 ,,
,, ,, 24 ,,	6 ,,	,, ,, 19 ,,	4 ,,
,, ,, 20 ,,	5 ,,	,, ,, 14 ,,	3 ,,
,, ,, 16 ,,	4 ,,	,, ,, 9 ,,	2 ,,
,, ,, 12 ,,	3 ,,	,, ,, 4 ,,	1 day
,, ,, 8 ,,	2 ,,		
,, ,, 4 ,,	1 day		

(2) For the purpose of calculating a period of employment in respect of annual holiday and accrued holiday remuneration "employment" means employment on road haulage work specified in paragraphs 45 to 48 and also employment partly on that work and partly on work other than such road haulage work, and a worker shall be treated as in the employment of the employer when absent from work in any of the following circumstances:—

(*a*) absences of the worker arising from suspension in accordance with paragraph 14(3)(*b*);

(*b*) absences of the worker owing to proved illness or accident up to but not exceeding 16 weeks in the aggregate during the qualifying period;

(*c*) suspension from employment owing to shortage of work or mechanical breakdown up to but not exceeding 16 weeks in the aggregate during the qualifying period;

(*d*) absences of the worker arising from the allowance of holidays provided for in paragraph 26 or paragraph 27 and annual holiday allowed under the provisions of this paragraph and of paragraph 29;

(e) other absences with reasonable cause during the qualifying period;

(f) absence for not more than 7 days during the qualifying period for reasons other than those specified in (a) to (e) above.

(3) Notwithstanding the provisions of sub-paragraphs (1) and (2) of this paragraph, a worker who has been absent for more than 7 days during the qualifying period for reasons other than those specified in (a) to (e) of sub-paragraph (2) of this paragraph shall not be entitled to any annual holiday in respect of such period.

(4) The duration of the worker's annual holiday during the holiday season ending on 15th October 1972, shall be reduced by any days of annual holiday duly allowed to him by the employer under the provisions of Order R.H. (94) between 1st May 1972 and the date on which the provisions of this Schedule become effective.

(5) In this Schedule the expression "holiday season" means in relation to an annual holiday during the year 1972, the period commencing on 1st May 1972 and ending on 15th October 1972, and in relation to each subsequent year, the period commencing on 1st May and ending on 15th October in that year.

(6) Notwithstanding the provisions of sub-paragraphs (1) and (5) of this paragraph, where before 1st October in any holiday season, at the written request of a worker his employer has agreed in writing that the worker shall be allowed after the end of the holiday season and before 1st May in the following year, the annual holiday, or any part thereof, for which he has qualified under this paragraph, any such days of annual holiday may, subject to the provisions of paragraph 33, be allowed in accordance with the agreement and if so allowed shall be treated for the purposes of this Schedule as having been allowed during the holiday season.

29.—(1) Subject to the provisions of this paragraph, in addition to the holidays specified in paragraphs 26, 27 and 28, an employer shall in each year commencing on 1st May allow a further annual holiday (hereinafter referred to as an "additional annual holiday") to every worker in his employment to whom this Schedule applies who has been employed by him at 1st May aforesaid for a continuous period of not less than 3 years (calculated in accordance with the provisions of sub-paragraph 28(2)) and the duration of the additional holiday shall be—

in the case of a six-day worker 6 days

in the case of a five-day worker 5 days

(2) Days of additional annual holiday, which need not be consecutive, shall be allowed on days on which the worker is normally called upon to work for the employer and during the relevant period of 12 months commencing on 1st May at any time either—

(a) on dates agreed between the employer and the worker or his representative at any time before 6th April in that period; or

(b) during the remaining days of that period.

(3) The duration of the worker's additional annual holiday during the 12 months commencing on 1st May 1972, shall be reduced by any days of additional annual holiday duly allowed to him by the employer under the provisions of Order R.H. (94) between 1st May 1972 and the date on which the provisions of this Schedule become effective.

30.—(1) In respect of an annual holiday allowed under paragraph 28, holiday remuneration shall be paid as follows:—

Period of annual holiday Column 1	Holiday remuneration for—		Column 4
	Six-day workers Column 2	Five-day workers Column 3	
12 days	Twice the amount in Col. 4	—	The amount which the worker would be entitled to receive from his employer at the date of the annual holiday for 40 hours' work (exclusive of overtime) at the time rate normally applicable to him under this Schedule.
11 days	One and five-sixths times the amount in Col. 4	—	
10 days	One and two-thirds times the amount in Col. 4	Twice the amount in Col. 4	
9 days	One and a half times the amount in Col. 4	One and four-fifths times the amount in Col. 4	
8 days	One and one-third times the amount in Col. 4	One and three-fifths times the amount in Col. 4	
7 days	One and one-sixth times the amount in Col. 4	One and two-fifths times the amount in Col. 4	
6 days	The amount in Col. 4	One and one-fifth times the amount in Col. 4	
5 days	Five-sixths of the amount in Col. 4	The amount in Col. 4	
4 days	Two-thirds of the amount in Col. 4	Four-fifths of the amount in Col. 4	
3 days	One-half of the amount in Col. 4	Three-fifths of the amount in Col. 4	
2 days	One-third of the amount in Col. 4	Two-fifths of the amount in Col. 4	
1 day	One-sixth of the amount in Col. 4	One-fifth of the amount in Col. 4	

(2) A worker entitled to be allowed an additional annual holiday under paragraph 29 shall be paid by his employer in respect thereof the amount specified in Column 4 of the preceding table.

(3) Holiday remuneration shall be paid on the last pay day preceding an annual holiday or additional annual holiday as the case may be.

Provided that,

(a) (i) where in accordance with the proviso to paragraph 33(1) an annual holiday is allowed in two or three periods; or

(ii) where an additional annual holiday is allowed in more than one period, holiday remuneration shall be apportioned accordingly;

(b) where an additional annual holiday is allowed in more than one period as a day or as days within a week in which the worker also works for the employer, holiday remuneration in respect of that day or those days shall be paid not later than the day on which the wages for the first working day following the day or days of additional annual holiday are paid.

31. Where any accrued holiday remuneration has been paid by the employer to the worker under paragraph 32(1) in respect of any period of employment in the qualifying period preceding the holiday season current when the annual holiday is allowed, the amount to be paid in respect of the period of such holiday is the appropriate amount payable under paragraph 30 less the accrued holiday remuneration previously paid as aforesaid.

32.—(1) Subject to the provisions of this paragraph, where a worker ceases to be employed, the employer shall immediately on the termination of employment (hereinafter referred to as "the termination date") pay to him as accrued holiday remuneration:—

(a) in respect of employment in the 12 months up to 30th April preceding the termination date, a sum equal to the holiday remuneration which would be payable for any days of annual holiday for which he has qualified (except days of annual holiday which he has been allowed or has become entitled to be allowed before the said date) if they were allowed at the time of leaving the employment;

(b) in respect of employment up to 30th April preceding the termination date, a sum equal to the holiday remineration which would be payable for any days of additional annual holiday for which he has qualified (except days of additional annual holiday which he has been allowed or has become entitled to be allowed before the said date) if they were allowed at the time of leaving the employment;

(c) in respect of any employment since 30th April preceding the termination date, of not less than four weeks duration, a sum equal to the holiday remuneration which would have been payable to him if he could have been allowed an annual holiday in respect of that employment at the termination date.

(2) The amount of any accrued holiday remuneration payable in respect of any period of employment shall be reduced by the amount of any previous payment of accrued holiday remuneration in respect of that period made by the employer to the worker under the provisions of this Schedule or of Order R.H. (94).

(3) Accrued holiday remuneration shall not be payable to a worker in respect of a qualifying period during which he was absent for more than seven days for reasons other than those specified in (a) to (e) of paragraph 28(2).

33.—(1) An annual holiday under paragraph 28 shall be allowed on consecutive working days being days upon which the worker is normally called upon to work, and days of holiday shall be treated as consecutive notwithstanding that a Sunday or any of the holidays allowed under paragraph 26 or paragraph 27 intervenes:—

Provided that where the duration of an annual holiday for which a worker is qualified exceeds the period of his normal working week, the holiday may, at the written request of the worker and with the agreement of the employer, be allowed in two or three periods, one of which shall be not less than the period of his normal working week.

(2) An employer shall give to a worker reasonable notice of the commencing date or dates and of the duration of his annual holiday or additional annual holiday if not agreed between them. Such notice may be given individually to a worker or by the posting of a notice in the worker's home depot.

PART VI

DEFINITIONS

Carrying capacity

34.—(1) The carrying capacity of a vehicle is the weight of the maximum load normally carried by the vehicle, and such carrying capacity when so established shall not be affected either by variations in the weight of the load resulting from collections or deliveries or emptying of containers during the course of the journey, or by the fact that on any particular journey a load greater or less than the established carrying capacity is carried.

(2) Where a trailer is attached to the vehicle, the load shall be the loads of the vehicle and trailer combined.

LONDON AREA

35. London Area means the localities named below, and these localities are, unless the context otherwise requires, those defined for local government purposes as at 1st August 1964.

Locality	Local Authority	Locality	Local Authority
City of London		Rainham (see Hornchurch UD)	Parish
Dartford	Borough	Romford	Borough
Dartford—Only Parish of Stone	Rural District	Stone (see Dartford RD) ...	Parish
Gravesend	Borough	Swanscombe	Urban District
Hornchurch—Only Parishes of Rainham, Wennington, and such other parts as are within 2 miles, in a straight line, of the north bank of the River Thames	Urban District	Thurrock—Only that part which is within 2 miles, in a straight line, of the north bank of the River Thames, except those parts which were, prior to 1st April 1936, known as the Parishes of Corringham, Fobbing, Mucking, Stanford-le-Hope, in the Rural District of Orsett	
Metropolitan Police District as existing on 1st August 1964— Except that part of the Borough of Watford which is included therein, and except the UD of Bushey	—		Urban District
Northfleet	Urban District	Wennington (see Hornchurch UD).	Parish

Note: In case of doubt as to the grading applicable to a particular depot, an enquiry should be addressed to the Clerk of the appropriate Local Authority as to the title of the Local Government administrative area, as it existed on 1st August 1964, in which the depot is situated.

Overtime expressions

36. The expressions time-and-a-half and double time mean respectively one and a half times and twice the rate of wages otherwise applicable.

Vehicle

37. Vehicle means a mechanically driven goods vehicle.

Regular worker

38. A regular worker is a worker employed by the week or longer period.

Driver

39. A driver is a worker employed in driving a vehicle and in performing when so required any other road haulage work.

Foremen and removal packers in the Furniture Warehousing and Removing Industry

40.—(1) A foreman in the Furniture Warehousing and Removing Industry is a worker who has charge of a removal and who has authority to issue instructions to two or more persons.

(2) A removal packer in the Furniture Warehousing and Removing Industry is a skilled worker who packs china and other articles.

Heavy brakesman and steersman

41. A heavy brakesman and steersman is a person operating the steering and braking equipment of a heavy trailer used for the carriage of abnormal indivisible loads.

Film transport worker

42. A film transport worker is a worker engaged exclusively in the collection and delivery of films for the cinematograph industry:

Provided that a worker shall not cease to be a film transport worker solely by reason of the fact that he collects from and delivers to cinemas cinematograph accessories and equipment which are carried at the same time as the films are normally carried.

Milk Worker

43. A milk worker is a regular worker who is employed on 6 days a week and who is exclusively engaged in the collection of milk from farms and its delivery to dairies:

Provided that a worker shall not cease to be a milk worker solely by reason of the fact that, exceptionally, he is required to work on the duties specified above on the remaining day of the week.

Ordinary working hours

44. The expression "number of hours (excluding overtime) ordinarily worked by the worker on that day of the week" means—

(1) in the case of a regular worker other than a milk worker:—

(*a*) in respect of a six-day worker (subject to the provisions of paragraph 24), 7¼ hours on any day Monday to Thursday, 7 hours on Friday and 4 hours on Saturday:

Provided that 7¼ hours may be substituted for 7 hours on Friday if 7 hours is substituted for 7¼ hours on one other day from Monday to Thursday.

(*b*) in respect of a five-day worker, 8 hours on any day Monday to Friday:
(2) in the case of a milk worker, 6 hours 40 minutes.

PART VII

WORKERS TO WHOM THIS SCHEDULE APPLIES

45. Subject to the provisions of the following paragraphs, this Schedule applies to workers employed on road haulage work in or from any undertaking or any branch or department of an undertaking being an undertaking, branch or department to any extent engaged in the carriage or haulage of goods of any description by goods vehicles on roads for hire or reward.

46. For the purposes of paragraph 45 goods shall not be deemed to be carried or hauled for hire or reward if:

(1) they are goods sold, used or let on hire or hire-purchase in the course of a trade or business carried on by the undertaking operating the vehicle, and are being delivered or collected in the course of that trade or business; or

(2) they are goods which have been, or are to be, subjected to a process or treatment in the course of a trade or business carried on by the undertaking operating the vehicle, and are being delivered or collected by that undertaking; or

(3) they are goods being delivered or collected by a company in the course of or for the purposes of the trade or business of another company where the company performing the delivery or collection is one engaged in the carriage or haulage of goods by goods vehicles on roads for hire or reward wholly for any company, not being so engaged, associated with it; and for the purposes of this sub-paragraph "company" includes any body corporate and two companies shall be taken to be associated companies if one is a subsidiary of the other (within the meaning of section 154 of the Companies Act 1948**(a)**) or both are subsidiaries of a third company.

(a) 1948 c. 38.

47. A worker is employed on road haulage work—

(1) if he is employed on all or any of the work described in (*a*) to (*e*) below, that is to say:—

    (*a*) driving or assisting in the driving or control of the vehicle;

    (*b*) collecting or loading goods to be carried in or on the vehicle;

    (*c*) attending to goods while so carried;

    (*d*) unloading or delivering goods after being so carried;

    (*e*) acting as attendant to the vehicle;

and who is required to travel on or to accompany the vehicle for the purpose of doing any such work; or

(2) if his time is occupied as specified in (*a*) to (*d*) below, that is to say:—

    (*a*) in doing any work incidental to his employment in work mentioned in sub-paragraph (1) hereof;

    (*b*) in travelling on or accompanying a goods vehicle in connection with his employment in the work so mentioned;

    (*c*) in holding himself under the orders or at the disposal of his employer while waiting in connection with his employment in the work so mentioned;

    (*d*) in waiting (whether overnight or otherwise) in accordance with the instructions of his employer as a necessary consequence of his employment in any of the work so mentioned.

Provided that a person who is employed in loading goods, to be carried in or on a goods vehicle, or in unloading goods after being so carried, and who is required to travel on or to accompany the vehicle partly for that purpose, shall not be regarded as being employed on road haulage work by reason only of that employment, if the main purpose for which he is required to travel on or to accompany the vehicle is that of executing work other than road haulage work after its arrival at his destination.

48. For the purposes of this Schedule—

"goods" includes goods or burden of any description;

"goods vehicle" means a motor vehicle constructed or adapted for use for the carriage or haulage of goods, or a trailer so constructed or adapted;

"road haulage work" includes road haulage work performed by a worker employed by a person carrying on the business of a goods transport clearing house, that is to say, the business of arranging for the mechanical transport of goods by road.

49. This Schedule does not apply to workers:—

(1) for whom or in respect of whose work a minimum rate of wages is, for the time being, fixed by or under any other enactment; or

(2) for whom minimum remuneration has been fixed pursuant to proposals of any other Wages Council established under the Wages Councils Act 1959;

(3) employed by, or by a subsidiary of, a Board established by Section 1 of the Transport Act 1962**(a)** or of the Transport Holding Company, or by, or by a subsidiary of, a New Authority constituted in accordance with Schedule 1 of the Transport Act 1968**(b)**;

(4) employed by the Post Office;

(5) employed for the purposes of funerals.

    (a) 1962 c. 46.   **(b)** 1968 c. 73.

EXPLANATORY NOTE

(This Note is not part of the Order.)

This Order, which has effect from 24th May 1972, sets out the statutory minimum remuneration payable and the holidays to be allowed in substitution for the statutory minimum remuneration and holidays set out in the Wages Regulation (Road Haulage) Order 1970 (Order R.H. (94)), which Order is revoked.

New provisions are printed in italics.

STATUTORY INSTRUMENTS

1972 No. 583

SAVINGS BANKS

The Trustee Savings Banks Regulations 1972

Laid before Parliament in draft

Made - - -	11*th April* 1972
Coming into Operation	1*st May* 1972

ARRANGEMENT OF REGULATIONS

PRELIMINARY

DEPOSIT AND WITHDRAWAL

TRANSFER OF DEPOSITS AND ADDITION OF NAMES

NOMINATIONS

The Treasury, in exercise of the powers conferred upon them by sections 28 and 86 of the Trustee Savings Banks Act 1969(a) and of all other powers enabling them in that behalf, with the concurrence of the National Debt Commissioners, hereby make the following Regulations:—

PRELIMINARY

Citation and Commencement

1. These Regulations may be cited as the Trustee Savings Banks Regulations 1972, and shall come into operation on 1st May 1972.

Interpretation

2.—(1) In these Regulations, unless the context otherwise requires—

"the Commissioners" means the National Debt Commissioners;

"current account deposit" has the meaning assigned to it by section 13(4) of the Trustee Savings Banks Act 1969;

"friendly society" means a friendly society registered under the Friendly Societies Act 1896(b) or a branch registered under that Act of a friendly society so registered;

"government stock" means any stock or securities held by a depositor in a trustee savings bank on a part of the National Savings Stock Register kept by the trustees of a trustee savings bank;

"mentally disordered person", in the application of these Regulations to England and Wales, means a person who is incapable, by reason of mental disorder within the meaning of the Mental Health Act 1959(c), of managing and administering his property and affairs;

"minor" means a person under eighteen years of age;

"receiver", in the application of these Regulations to England and Wales, means, in relation to any act or thing done in respect of a mentally disordered person, a receiver or other person authorised in that behalf under Part VIII of the Mental Health Act 1959;

(a) 1969 c. 50.   (b) 1896 c. 25.
(c) 1959 c. 72.

"savings bank annuity" means an annuity purchased through the medium of a trustee savings bank;

"Treasury Solicitor" means the Solicitor for the affairs of Her Majesty's Treasury;

"trustee savings bank" means any trustee savings bank within the meaning of the Trustee Savings Banks Act 1969;

"trustees" means the trustees and managers of a trustee savings bank.

(2) Any reference in these Regulations to the provisions of any enactment or regulations shall be construed, unless the context otherwise requires, as a reference to those provisions as amended by any other enactment or regulations.

(3) The Interpretation Act 1889(a) shall apply for the interpretation of these Regulations as it applies for the interpretation of an Act of Parliament, and as if these Regulations and the Regulations hereby revoked were Acts of Parliament.

Deposit and Withdrawal

Declaration on opening an account

3.—(1) Subject to the provisions of these Regulations, a depositor, on opening an account in a trustee savings bank, and whenever thereafter required so to do, shall specify his full name, occupation and address, and shall make a declaration in a form approved by the Commissioners.

(2) Subject to the provisions of paragraph (3) below, the declaration shall declare that the person on whose behalf any first deposit is made is not directly or indirectly entitled to any benefit from the funds of any other trustee savings bank, and shall set forth the particulars of any other accounts which he already has, including any joint accounts in which his name appears, in the trustee savings bank receiving the declaration:

Provided that for the purposes of this declaration no account shall be taken of any benefit which the depositor may be entitled to from being a member of a friendly society or of sums which may be derived solely as executor, administrator or other personal representative of any deceased depositor or of sums standing in his name as a trustee either solely or jointly with any other person.

(3) Where an account is opened by a trustee otherwise than under section 30 of the Trustee Savings Banks Act 1969 (under which deposits may be accepted from a person acting as a trustee on behalf of the depositor, the account being in the joint names of the trustee and the depositor), the declaration shall declare that no money belonging to the trust fund from which the first deposit is made is deposited in any other trustee savings bank, and shall set forth the particulars of any other accounts to which moneys belonging to such trust fund are credited in the trustee savings bank receiving the declaration.

(4) For the purposes of paragraph (3) above, so much of the property in the hands of a trustee shall constitute one trust fund as is held on trusts which (as respects the beneficiaries or their respective interests or the purposes of the trust or as respects the powers of the trustee) are not identical with those on which any other property in his hands is held.

(a) 1889 c. 63.

(5) Where a deposit is made by a trustee otherwise than under section 30 of the Trustee Savings Banks Act 1969, he may be described in the account as trustee of a specified trust or as a trustee without specifying a trust.

(6) No entry with respect to any trust, express, implied or constructive, shall be made in the account of any depositor except as provided in paragraph (5) above or except in an account opened by a trustee under section 30 of the Trustee Savings Banks Act 1969, and except as aforesaid no notice of any such trust shall be receivable by the trustees of a trustee savings bank.

(7) The declaration by a depositor applying to open a current account shall declare that he will not operate the account either wholly or partly as a trade or business account.

Withdrawals from accounts of minors

4.—(1) An application for the withdrawal of money deposited by, or in the name of, a minor may be made by the minor, if he has attained the age of seven years.

(2) Upon such application, payment may be made to the minor, and his receipt shall be a good discharge to the trustees for the amount paid to him.

(3) Where it is proved to the satisfaction of the trustees that any deposits in the name of a minor under the age of seven years are urgently needed for the maintenance, education, or benefit of the minor, or that from any other circumstances it is expedient to do so, the trustees may pay the deposits, or any part thereof, to any person who may satisfy the trustees that he will apply such money for the benefit of the minor, and the receipt of such person shall be a good discharge to the trustees for sums so paid.

Withdrawals from accounts of mentally disordered persons

5.—(1) An application for the withdrawal of money deposited in the name of a mentally disordered person shall be made by the receiver.

(2) Upon such application, payment shall be made to the receiver, and his receipt shall be a good discharge to the trustees for the amount paid to him.

(3) Where it is shown to the satisfaction of the trustees that a depositor is a mentally disordered person, and there is no receiver by whom application for withdrawal of deposits standing in the depositor's name may be made, the trustees may, if it is proved to their satisfaction that it is just and expedient so to do, pay the deposits, or any part thereof, to any person whom they shall judge proper to receive the same, and the receipt of such person shall be a good discharge to the trustees for the sum so paid.   ,,

Disability of depositor in trust account

6. Where one of the persons named in a trust account to which section 30 of the Trustee Savings Banks Act 1969 applies has become a mentally disordered person or has become bankrupt, the trustees may in their discretion pay the deposits to the other person named in such account, with or without the concurrence of the receiver or Official Receiver or trustee in bankruptcy (if any) of the person who has become a mentally disordered person or bankrupt, and the receipt of such other person shall be a good discharge to the trustees for the sum so paid.

Withdrawals in case of bankrupts

7. Where either a receiving order has been made in respect of the property of a sole depositor, or a trustee in bankruptcy of the property of a sole depositor has been appointed, the trustees may in their discretion pay the deposits standing in the name of such depositor or any part thereof to the Official Receiver or trustee in bankruptcy on the application of the Official Receiver or trustee in bankruptcy, and upon such evidence of the appointment as the trustees may require, and the receipt of the Official Receiver or trustee in bankruptcy shall be a good discharge to the trustees for the sum so paid.

TRANSFER OF DEPOSITS AND ADDITION OF NAMES

Transfer from one account to another

8.—(1) Any depositor may apply to the trustees for the transfer of deposits (other than current account deposits) standing in his name into the name of any other person entitled to deposit in the trustee savings bank.

(2) The trustees shall be furnished with such evidence as they may require of the title of the depositor to the sums to which the application relates.

(3) Every such application shall be in writing, and be in a form approved by the trustees, and shall state the amount to be transferred, the full name and address of the person into whose name it is desired to transfer the deposits, and particulars of the account (if any) to which the deposits are to be transferred.

(4) A separate record shall be kept of all such applications, each of which shall be approved and signed by a trustee or manager or by some officer of the trustee savings bank specially appointed by the trustees for that purpose.

(5) Upon receiving the application, and upon being satisfied as to the title of the applicant to transfer the deposits to which the application relates, the trustees shall transfer from the account of the applicant to the account of the transferee the sum specified in the application; and the death of the applicant shall not of itself determine the authority given by the applicant for the transfer to be made, but if the trustees receive notice before the transfer is effected that the applicant has died, the transfer shall not be made.

(6) In the event of the transfer being permitted, the application shall be a good discharge to the trustees from the applicant for the sum specified in the application.

Transfer from account of a deceased depositor or a mentally disordered person

9.—(1) Any person who has attained the age of 16 years and to whom any sum due (otherwise than as a current account deposit) to a depositor at the time of his death, or to a depositor who has become a mentally disordered person, may be paid under and in accordance with the provisions of these Regulations, may, subject to the provisions of these Regulations as to death duties, instead of withdrawing such sum, apply to the trustees in writing for the transfer of such sum into his own name or the name of any other person specified in such application.

(2) The provisions of Regulation 8 above shall apply to the transfer of sums under this Regulation so far as those provisions are applicable.

Addition of names to an account

10.—(1) Upon the application of any depositor, the trustees may add the names of other persons in the title of the depositor's account.

(2) Every person whose name is added in the title of an account under this Regulation shall make the declaration required upon the opening of an account.

NOMINATIONS

Power to make nominations

11.—(1) Subject to the provisions of these Regulations, a depositor, being a person who has attained the age of 16 years, may nominate any person to receive any sum not exceeding £500 due to the depositor at his death otherwise than in respect of current account deposits, but a nominator may not have more than one nomination in force at any time.

(2) Every nomination shall be in writing, and may be in a form which may be provided by the trustees; it shall be signed by the nominator in the presence of a witness, and the signature of the nominator shall be attested by the witness.

(3) A nomination shall be of no effect unless it is sent to the trustees during the lifetime of the nominator.

(4) The receipt of a nomination shall be acknowledged by the trustees.

(5) The trustees may in their absolute discretion refuse to accept a nomination received by them, and, upon a notification of the refusal of the trustees to accept a nomination being sent to the nominator, the nomination shall be of no effect.

(6) Every nomination accepted by the trustees shall be registered by them in a book to be kept for the purpose.

(7) A nomination may relate to the whole of the deposits (other than current account deposits) standing in the name of a nominator, or to part only of such deposits.

(8) A nomination shall, subject to the provisions of these Regulations, be deemed to extend to all sums to which a nominator is entitled at the time of his death in respect of government stock or a savings bank annuity, unless the nominator in the nomination expressly excludes any of such sums from the operation of the nomination.

(9) A nomination may be in favour of one person or of several persons, and, in the latter case, may direct that specific sums shall be paid to one or more of the persons named in the nomination, or that the persons named in such nomination may take the property nominated in specified shares, or may give directions to both effects.

(10) A person who witnesses the signature of a nominator to a nomination shall not take any benefit under the nomination.

Revocation of nomination

12.—(1) A nomination shall be revoked—

    (a) by the death of the nominee, or, where there is more than one nominee, of all the nominees, in the lifetime of the nominator;

    (b) so far as relates to the interest thereunder of any nominee (being one of two or more nominees), by the death of that nominee in the lifetime of the nominator, unless the interest of the nominee is disposed of by the nomination;

(*c*) by the marriage of the nominator;

(*d*) by written notice of revocation given in accordance with this Regulation;

(*e*) by a subsequent nomination duly made in accordance with these Regulations by the same nominator;

but a nomination shall not be revoked by any will or by any events or means other than those specified in these Regulations.

(2) A notice of revocation for the purposes of this Regulation shall be signed by the nominator in the presence of a witness, who shall attest the signature of the nominator, and the notice shall be of no effect unless it is sent to the trustees during the lifetime of the nominator.

(3) The receipt of a notice of revocation shall be acknowledged by the trustees, and the notice shall be registered by the trustees in a book to be kept for that purpose in like manner as in the case of a nomination.

(4) Where the trustees have paid money to a nominee in ignorance of the fact that the nominator has married after making the nomination, the receipt of the nominee shall be a valid discharge to the trustees.

Effect of transfer on nomination

13. In the event of the transfer of any deposits from a trustee savings bank to another trustee savings bank or to the National Savings Bank, or from the National Savings Bank to a trustee savings bank, any nomination in force in the bank from which the transfer is made shall cease to apply to the deposits so transferred.

Payment under nomination

14.—(1) Where on the death of a nominator the sums due to him or his estate by the trustees (otherwise than as current account deposits) do not exceed in the whole the sum of £500, and the trustees have no notice of the claim of any creditor of the nominator, the trustees shall, subject to the provisions of these Regulations as to death duties, pay the persons named in any nomination made by the nominator and in force at the time of his death in accordance with the directions of the nomination, and the receipt of any person so named shall be a good discharge to the trustees for the sum so paid, notwithstanding that he has not attained the age of 18 years, if he has attained the age of 16 years.

(2) Where on the death of a nominator the sums due to him or his estate by the trustees (otherwise than as current account deposits) exceed £500, any nomination made by such nominator shall take effect, subject to the provisions of these Regulations as to death duties, as regards any sums not exceeding in the aggregate £500 to which the nomination relates, in like manner as if it were a will of the nominator duly executed, but shall not take effect in any other manner, and a nomination shall not in such case be deemed void because the nominator was a minor at the time such nomination was made.

(3) In any such case as is mentioned in paragraph (2) above, the trustees may, if they have no notice of the claim of any creditor of the nominator, and subject to the provisions of this Regulation, pay any sums not exceeding in the aggregate £500 to which the nomination relates in accordance with the directions of

the nomination, notwithstanding the production of probate of the will of the nominator or letters of administration to his estate.

(4) Where on the death of a nominator the trustees have notice of a claim of any creditor against the estate of the nominator, and the estate, apart from the amount nominated, appears to be insufficient to satisfy the claim, the trustees may in their discretion apply the amount nominated in or towards the satisfaction of the claim; but, subject as aforesaid, any payment made by the trustees to the nominee, whether the amount due to the nominator at his death does or does not exceed £500, shall be a valid payment.

(5) Where any person nominated to receive any sum on the death of a nominator is a minor under the age of 16 years, and it is proved to the satisfaction of the trustees that funds are urgently needed for his maintenance, education, or benefit, the trustees may pay the sum mentioned in the nomination, or any part thereof, to any person who may satisfy the trustees that he will apply such money for the benefit of the minor, and the receipt of such person shall be a good discharge to the trustees for the amount so paid.

(6) Where a nominee dies after the death of the nominator but before any sum has been paid to him as nominee, the provisions of these Regulations shall, subject to the provisions of paragraph (4) of this Regulation, apply to the nominee and to the sum payable to him as nominee as if at the date of his death the deceased nominee were a depositor in the trustee savings bank and the said sum were deposited in his name in a trusteee savings bank account.

Special provisions relating to existing nominations

15.—(1) Nothing in these Regulations shall invalidate or prejudice in any way any nomination made before 25th November 1929, being the date on which the Trustee Savings Banks Regulations 1929**(a)** came into operation, and any such nomination shall continue to be governed (subject nevertheless to the provisions of Regulations 13 and 14(6) above) by the Trustee Savings Banks Regulations 1900**(b)**.

(2) Nothing in these Regulations shall invalidate or prejudice in any way any nomination made on or after 25th November 1929 and before 10th July 1956, being the date on which the Trustee Savings Banks (Amendment) Regulations 1956**(c)** came into operation, and any such nomination shall continue to be governed by the said Regulations of 1929 as originally made.

Death of Depositor

Proof of death

16.—(1) The trustees may require proof to their satisfaction of the death of a depositor.

(2) The trustees may accept as conclusive proof of the death of a depositor and of the date of the death of a depositor such statement or information as the trustees may in their absolute discretion think fit, and a statement or information to their satisfaction that a depositor has not been heard of for a period of seven years or more may be accepted by them as conclusive proof of the death of such depositor.

(a) S.R. & O. 1929/1048 (Rev. XX, p. 584: 1929 p. 1282).
(b) S.R. & O. 1900/629 (1900, p. 795).   (c) S.I. 1956/1066 (1956 II, p. 2194).

(3) Any payment which may be made under these Regulations in reliance on such statement or information as aforesaid shall be a good discharge to the trustees for the sum paid, notwithstanding that the depositor may be in fact alive at the time of such payment.

(4) In this Regulation the expression "depositor" includes any person beneficially interested at any time in the personal estate of a deceased depositor or who, in certain circumstances, would be or would have been beneficially interested at any time in the personal estate of a deceased depositor.

Law applicable on death of depositor

17.—(1) In the event of the death of a depositor, any payment under these Regulations made in accordance with the law of the place in which the depositor resided at the date of his death shall be a good discharge to the trustees for the sum so paid unless express notice in writing that the depositor was domiciled elsewhere shall have been received by the trustees prior to such payment, and for the purposes of this Regulation the trustees may accept as conclusive proof of the place of residence of a depositor at the date of his death such statement or information as they may in their absolute discretion think fit.

(2) In this Regulation the expression "depositor" includes any person beneficially interested at any time in the personal estate of a deceased depositor or who, in certain circumstances, would be or would have been beneficially interested at any time in the personal estate of a deceased depositor.

Payment without a grant of representation

18.—(1) Where the total amount due by the trustees of a trustee savings bank to a depositor at the time of his death does not exceed £500, exclusive of interest, and probate of his will is not, or letters of administration to his estate are not, produced to the trustees within such time as they think reasonable, if such depositor has made no nomination, or so far as any nomination does not extend, the trustees may, without requiring probate of the will or letters of administration to the estate of the depositor, in their discretion pay or distribute the amount so due or any part thereof to or among the following person or persons or any one or more of the following persons (exclusively of the others) who shall in the opinion of the trustees establish a valid claim to the said amount or any part thereof—

(*a*) a person entitled to take out probate of the will of the depositor or letters of administration to his estate;

(*b*) a person who has paid the funeral expenses of the depositor;

(*c*) a creditor of the depositor;

(*d*) a person who has a beneficial interest in the estate of the depositor;

(*e*) a person undertaking to maintain any person who by reason of any incapacity whatsoever (including minority) is unable to give the trustees a legal discharge for the moneys or for a share of the moneys of a deceased depositor due under this Regulation to the person who is unable to give a legal discharge as aforesaid;

(*f*) if the depositor was a British subject and his relatives reside outside the United Kingdom, the Isle of Man and the Channel Islands, such officer or authority as shall appear to the trustees to be suitable to dispose of the amount due in accordance with the appropriate law;

(*g*) if the depositor was a seaman of a foreign country, being a country with which a treaty has been made in respect of the payment of moneys due to seamen, the consular authority of that country;

(*h*) if the depositor was a foreign subject, not being a seaman to whom the provisions of sub-paragraph (*g*) above apply, the consular authority of the country to which the depositor belonged, or such other consular authority as may appear to the trustees to be appropriate, on such assurance as to the ultimate disposition of the amount due as is satisfactory to the trustees;

(*i*) in a case where the estate of the depositor appears to have devolved upon the Crown, the Duchy of Lancaster or the Duchy of Cornwall, the Treasury Solicitor, the Solicitor to the Duchy of Lancaster, or the Solicitor to the Duchy of Cornwall, as the case requires.

(2) The receipt of any person to whom payment may be made under this Regulation or under Regulation 14(6) above shall be a good discharge to the trustees for the sum paid, and any such receipt may be signed by any such person who has attained the age of 16 years, notwithstanding that he has not attained the age of 18 years.

Death duties

19.—(1) Where on the death of a depositor the aggregate value of the specified assets (hereinafter defined) exceeds £3,000, the trustees shall, before making any payment or transfer of a sum standing to the credit of such depositor either alone or jointly with any other depositor whose name was added to the account at the request of the deceased depositor (not being a sum in respect of which it is shown to the satisfaction of the trustees that the deceased depositor had no interest therein otherwise than as a trustee), require the production of a statement from the Commissioners of Inland Revenue to the effect either that no death duties are payable in respect of that sum or that any death duties so payable have been paid:

Provided that the production of such a statement shall not be required—

(*a*) where the payment or transfer is made to or as directed by the legal personal representative of the deceased depositor, or

(*b*) where the deceased depositor was at the time of his death domiciled in Northern Ireland, the Isle of Man or the Channel Islands.

(2) In this Regulation the expression "the specified assets" means the following assets (not being assets in respect of which it is shown to the satisfaction of the trustees that the deceased depositor had no interest therein otherwise than as a trustee):—

(*a*) the total amount (including interest) which, at the date of the death of the depositor, stands to the credit of all accounts in the trustee savings bank in his name alone or in his name jointly with any other person,

(*b*) all stock and securities registered in the name of the deceased depositor alone or in his name and the name of any other person as joint holders on the portion of the National Savings Stock Register kept by the trustees of the trustee savings bank, and

(*c*) the total amount (including any bonus or interest) which would have been repayable (if repayment had been demanded) at the date of the death of the depositor in respect of all savings contracts entered into by him and registered by the trustees of the trustee savings bank under a contractual savings scheme certified by the Treasury in accordance with section 415(2) of the Income and Corporation Taxes Act 1970**(a)**.

(3) For the purposes of this Regulation, the value of the stock and securities referred to in paragraph (2)(*b*) above shall be—

(*a*) in the case of Defence Bonds, National Development Bonds, British Savings Bonds and any other securities which can be held only on the National Savings Stock Register, the nominal capital amount thereof; and

(*b*) in all other cases, the market value thereof at the date of the death of the depositor.

MISCELLANEOUS

Signature of certificate for transfer to another trustee savings bank

20. The certificate required to be furnished for the purpose of the transfer of the account of a depositor from one trustee savings bank to another shall be signed by one trustee or manager, or, in the case of a trustee savings bank open for more than six hours in every week, by a paid officer of the trustee savings bank duly appointed for the purpose by resolution of the trustees:

Provided that the appointment and signature of every officer so appointed shall have been previously certified to the Commissioners by two trustees.

Application to Scotland

21.—(1) In the application of these Regulations to Scotland—

(*a*) any reference to a mentally disordered person shall be construed as a reference to a person who is incapable by reason of mental disorder within the meaning of the Mental Health (Scotland) Act 1960**(b)** of managing and administering his property and affairs;

(*b*) any reference to a receiver in relation to a mentally disordered person shall be construed as a reference to a curator bonis, guardian or tutor;

(*c*) any reference to a receiving order shall be construed as a reference to an award of sequestration;

(*d*) any reference to a trustee in bankruptcy shall be construed as a reference to a judicial factor or trustee appointed under the Bankruptcy (Scotland) Act 1913**(c)**;

(*e*) any reference to probate or letters of administration shall be construed as a reference to confirmation of an executor;

(*f*) any reference to the Treasury Solicitor shall be construed as a reference to the Queen's and Lord Treasurer's Remembrancer.

(2) Where on the death of a depositor domiciled in Scotland, who has made a nomination, the trustees have notice of a claim of any person entitled on the ground of jus relicti, jus relictae or legitim to any part of the moveable estate of such depositor, and such estate, apart from the amount nominated, appears to be insufficient to satisfy such claim, the trustees may in their discretion apply the amount nominated in or towards the satisfaction of such claim, but, subject as aforesaid, any payment made by the trustees to the nominee (irrespective of the amount due to the depositor at his death) shall be a valid payment, and the

(**a**) 1970 c. 10.   (**b**) 1960 c. 61
(**c**) 1913 c. 20.

receipt of the nominee shall be a good discharge to the trustees for the sum so paid.

(3) It shall not be necessary to obtain the sanction of the Treasury to the withdrawal by a Sheriff Clerk of moneys standing in his name as such.

Application to Northern Ireland

22.—(1) These Regulations shall extend to Northern Ireland.

(2) In the application of these Regulations to Northern Ireland—

(a) any reference to a mentally disordered person shall be construed as a reference to a person who, by reason of unsoundness of mind, or of mental disorder within the meaning of the Mental Health Act (Northern Ireland) 1961**(a)**, is or is considered incapable of managing his affairs;

(b) any reference to a receiver in relation to a mentally disordered person shall be construed as a reference to a committee or any other person appointed pursuant to the Lunacy Regulation (Ireland) Act 1871**(b)** and the orders made thereunder to exercise with respect to the estate of such person powers similar to those of a committee;

(c) any reference to a receiving order shall be construed as a reference to an order of adjudication of bankruptcy, or to an order in any arrangement operating by virtue of section 349 of the Irish Bankrupt and Insolvent Act 1857**(c)** to vest a deposit in the Official Assignee alone or jointly with any person;

(d) any reference to the Official Receiver shall be construed as a reference to the Official Assignee in Bankruptcy;

(e) any reference to the Treasury Solicitor shall be construed as a reference to the Chief Crown Solicitor for Northern Ireland;

(f) any reference to the Commissioners of Inland Revenue shall be construed as a reference to the Ministry of Finance for Northern Ireland.

Application to the Isle of Man

23.—(1) These Regulations shall extend to the Isle of Man.

(2) In the application of these Regulations to the Isle of Man—

(a) any reference to a receiver in relation to a mentally disordered person shall be construed as a reference to the committee of the estate of a person found of unsound mind according to the law of the Isle of Man or to a receiver appointed under section 3 of the Mental Diseases Act 1954 of the Isle of Man, as the case may be;

(b) any reference to the Treasury Solicitor shall be construed as a reference to the Attorney-General of the Isle of Man.

Application to the Channel Islands

24.—(1) These Regulations shall extend to the Channel Islands.

(2) In the application of these Regulations to Jersey—

(a) any reference to a mentally disordered person shall be construed as a reference to a person suffering from mental disorder within the meaning of the Mental Health (Jersey) Law 1969;

(a) 1961 c. 15 (N.I.).   **(b)** 1871 c. 22.
(c) 1857 c. 60.

(*b*) any reference to a receiver in relation to a mentally disordered person shall be construed as a reference to a curator;

(*c*) any reference to a receiving order shall be construed as a reference to a declaration of "désastre";

(*d*) any reference to the Official Receiver shall be construed as a reference to Her Majesty's Viscount for Jersey or to an "attourné" appointed in bankruptcy, as the case may be;

(*e*) any reference to the Treasury Solicitor shall be construed as a reference to Her Majesty's Receiver General for Jersey;

(*f*) nominations under Regulation 11 above shall only be made if they are within the testamentary powers of the nominator according to Jersey law;

(*g*) any reference to the age of majority shall be construed as a reference to the age of majority by Jersey law.

(3) In the application of these Regulations to Guernsey, Alderney and Sark—

(*a*) any reference to a mentally disordered person shall be construed as a reference to a person who under any law for the time being in force in any of the Islands of the Bailiwick of Guernsey is a person of unsound mind;

(*b*) any reference to a receiver in relation to a mentally disordered person shall be construed as a reference to a guardian appointed by the Royal Court of Guernsey, the Court of Alderney or the Court of the Seneschal of Sark, as the case may be;

(*c*) any reference to the Treasury Solicitor shall be construed as a reference to Her Majesty's Receiver-General;

(*d*) for Regulation 7 of these Regulations there shall be substituted the following Regulation:—

"7. Where it is shown to the satisfaction of the trustees that any person who is the sole depositor is insolvent, the trustees may, if they think fit, pay the deposits standing in the name of such depositor or any part thereof to any person who makes application in that behalf and who satisfies them that he is a proper person to receive payment."

Revocation and savings

25.—(1) The Regulations specified in the Schedule to these Regulations are hereby revoked.

(2) In so far as any application, declaration, payment, transfer or nomination made, approval, notice or receipt given, document issued, or other thing done, under any Regulations revoked by paragraph (1) above could have been made, given, issued or done under a corresponding provision of these Regulations, it shall not be invalidated by the revocation, but shall have effect as if made, given, issued or done under that corresponding provision.

(3) The mention of particular matters in this Regulation shall be without prejudice to the general application of section 38 of the Interpretation Act 1889 as it applies for the interpretation of these Regulations.

V. H. Goodhew,
Tim Fortescue,
Two of the Lords Commissioners of
Her Majesty's Treasury

10th April 1972.

I concur.

I. de Lisle Radice,
On behalf of the National Debt
Commissioners.

11th April 1972.

SCHEDULE   Regulation 25(1)

Regulations revoked	References
The Trustee Savings Banks Regulations 1929.	S.R. & O. 1929/1048 (Rev. XX, p.584; 1929, p. 1282).
The Trustee Savings Banks (Amendment) Regulations 1956.	S.I. 1956/1066 (1956 II, p. 2194).
The Trustee Savings Banks (Amendment) (No. 2) Regulations 1956.	S.I. 1956/1179 (1956 II, p. 2195).
The Trustee Savings Banks (Amendment) Regulations 1960.	S.I. 1960/2335 (1960 III, p. 3065).
The Trustee Savings Banks (Amendment) Regulations 1961.	S.I. 1961/2414 (1961 III, p.4458).
The Trustee Savings Banks (Amendment) Regulations 1965.	S.I. 1965/573 (1965 I, p. 1794).
The Trustee Savings Banks (Amendment) Regulations 1969.	S.I. 1969/1700 (1969 III, p. 5355).

EXPLANATORY NOTE
(*This Note is not part of the Regulations.*)

These Regulations consolidate with minor amendments the Trustee Savings Banks Regulations 1929 as amended.

STATUTORY INSTRUMENTS

1972 No. 585

INDUSTRIAL DEVELOPMENT

LOCAL EMPLOYMENT

The Intermediate Areas and Derelict Land Clearance Areas (Amendment) Order 1972

Made - - - -	12*th April* 1972
Laid before Parliament	14*th April* 1972
Coming into Operation	14*th April* 1972

The Secretary of State in exercise of his powers under section 1(1), section 8(6) and section 18 of the Local Employment Act 1972(**a**) hereby makes the following Order:—

1.—(1) This Order may be cited as the Intermediate Areas and Derelict Land Clearance Areas (Amendment) Order 1972 and shall come into operation immediately after being laid before Parliament.

(2) The Interpretation Act 1889(**b**) shall apply to the interpretation of this Order as it applies to the interpretation of an Act of Parliament.

2. The Intermediate Areas and Derelict Land Clearance Areas Order 1972(**c**) shall have effect subject to the amendment that the Urban District of Winsford situated within the employment exchange area of Winsford shall cease to form part of the North West Intermediate Area described in Part I of the Schedule to the said Order for the period beginning with the date on which this Order comes into operation and ending with the 1st May 1972 but shall form part of the said North West Intermediate Area on and after the 2nd May 1972.

Dated 12th April 1972.

John Davies,
The Secretary of State for
Trade and Industry.

EXPLANATORY NOTE

(*This Note is not part of the Order.*)

This Order amends the Intermediate Areas and Derelict Land Clearance Areas Order 1972 which came into operation on 22nd March 1972.

Before 22nd March 1972 the Urban District of Winsford, which forms part of the employment exchange area of Winsford, was a locality deemed to be included in the Merseyside Development Area by virtue of the provisions

---

(**a**) 1972 c. 5.   (**b**) 1889 c. 63.   (**c**) S.I. 1972/421.

of section 1(5) and (6) of the Local Employment Act 1972. It was prematurely deprived of its status as such a locality by virtue of its being inadvertently included as part of the North West Intermediate Area on 22nd March 1972 by the Intermediate Areas and Derelict Land Clearance Areas Order 1972.

This Order provides that the Urban District of Winsford shall cease to form part of the North West Intermediate Area for the period from the coming into operation of the Order until 2nd May 1972. On and after that date it will again form part of that Intermediate Area.

STATUTORY INSTRUMENTS

1972 No. 595

HIGHWAYS, ENGLAND AND WALES

The New Street Byelaws (Extension of Operation) Order 1972

Made - - - *13th April* 1972

The Secretary of State for the Environment and the Secretary of State for Wales, in exercise of their respective powers under the proviso to section 312(6) of the Highways Act 1959(**a**), as read with the Secretary of State for Wales and Minister of Land and Natural Resources Order 1965(**b**), and of all other powers enabling them in that behalf, hereby order as follows: —

1. This order may be cited as the New Street Byelaws (Extension of Operation) Order 1972.

2. Any byelaws in force on 30th April 1972, being byelaws remaining in force by virtue of the New Street Byelaws (Extension of Operation) Orders 1962(**c**) and 1967(**d**), shall remain in force until 31st March 1974 or until they are revoked, whichever date is the earlier.

Signed by authority of the Secretary of State for the Environment.

J. Toohey,
An Under Secretary in the
Department of the Environment.

12th April 1972.

Signed by authority of the Secretary of State for Wales.

Owen H. Morris,
An Under Secretary in
the Welsh Office.

13th April 1972.

(**a**) 1959 c. 25.
(**c**) S.I. 1962/645 (S.I. 1962 I, p. 695).
(**b**) S.I. 1965/319 (S.I. 1965 I, p. 785).
(**d**) S.I. 1967/512 (S.I. 1967 I, p. 1684).

EXPLANATORY NOTE

(This Note is not part of the Order.)

1. The Highways Act 1959 repealed certain enactments which had empowered local authorities to make new street byelaws, and provided that existing byelaws made under any of those enactments should cease to have effect on 30th April 1962, unless the Minister of Housing and Local Government extended their period of operation by order under the Act of 1959.

2. That period was extended until 30th April 1972 by the New Street Byelaws (Extension of Operation) Order 1967, and this order further extends it until 31st March 1974.

STATUTORY INSTRUMENTS

1972 No. 597

INDUSTRIAL TRAINING

The Industrial Training (Footwear, Leather and Fur Skin Board) Order 1968 (Amendment) Order 1972

Made - - -	12*th April* 1972
Laid before Parliament	21*st April* 1972
Coming into Operation	15*th May* 1972

The Secretary of State after consultation with the Footwear, Leather and Fur Skin Industry Training Board and with organisations and associations of organisations appearing to be representative respectively of substantial numbers of employers engaging in the activities hereinafter mentioned and of substantial numbers of persons employed in those activities and in exercise of his powers under section 9 of the Industrial Training Act 1964(a) and of all other powers enabling him in that behalf hereby makes the following Order: —

Citation, commencement and interpretation

   1.—(1) This Order may be cited as the Industrial Training (Footwear, Leather and Fur Skin Board) Order 1968 (Amendment) Order 1972 and shall come into operation on 15th May 1972.

   (2) In this Order—

   (*a*) "the Act" means the Industrial Training Act 1964;

   (*b*) "the Board" means the Footwear, Leather and Fur Skin Industry Training Board;

   (*c*) "levy Order" means the Industrial Training Levy (Footwear, Leather and Fur Skin) Order 1969(b) or the Industrial Training Levy (Footwear, Leather and Fur Skin) Order 1971(c);

   (*d*) "the principal Order" means the Industrial Training (Footwear, Leather and Fur Skin Board) Order 1968(d).

   (3) The Interpretation Act 1889(e) shall apply to the interpretation of this Order as it applies to the interpretation of an Act of Parliament and as if this Order and the principal Order were Acts of Parliament.

Amendment of the principal Order

   2. The principal Order shall be amended in accordance with the Schedule to this Order, and accordingly the activities in relation to which the Board exercises the functions conferred by the Act upon industrial training boards shall, in lieu of the activities specified in Schedule 1 to the principal Order, be the activities specified in that Schedule as amended by the Schedule to this Order.

(a) 1964 c. 16.	(b) S.I. 1969/1659 (1969 III, p. 5205).
(c) S.I. 1971/689 (1971 I, p. 1822).	(d) S.I. 1968/1763 (1968 III, p. 4785).
(e) 1889 c. 63.	

Transitional provisions

3.—(1) The chairman and other members of the Board on the day upon which this Order comes into operation shall continue to be members of the Board and to hold and vacate their offices in accordance with the terms of the instruments appointing them to be members.

(2) The provisions of this Order shall not—

(*a*) extend the operation of either levy Order;

(*b*) affect the operation of either levy Order in relation to the assessment of an employer within the meaning of that Order in respect of an establishment that was engaged in the first levy period or the second levy period, as the case may be, wholly or mainly in activities included in the Schedule to the principal Order as amended by the Schedule to this Order;

(*c*) affect the operation of any assessment notice served by the Board under the provisions of either levy Order before the date upon which this Order comes into operation or any appeal or other proceedings arising out of any such notice.

Signed by order of the Secretary of State.

12th April 1972.

Dudley Smith,
Parliamentary Under Secretary of State,
Department of Employment.

Article 2

SCHEDULE

Amendments to the 1968 Order

1. In this Schedule the expression "the Schedule" means Schedule I to the 1968 Order.

2.—(1) Paragraph 2 of the Schedule shall be amended as follows.

(2) For sub-paragraph (*c*)(vi) there shall be substituted the following—
"(vi) any process in the design, manufacture or repair of clothing;".

(3) In sub-paragraph (*c*) immediately after head (viii) there shall be inserted the following—

"(ix) the manufacture of components for footwear by an employer engaged in compounding in relation to plastics materials; or

(x) dealing, as a member (or as a member's nominee) of an international commodity market, in a commodity in which the members of the market deal;".

(4) For sub-paragraph (*d*) there shall be substituted the following—

"(*d*) the activities of an establishment engaged wholly or mainly in business as follows:—

  (i) in banking, finance or insurance; or

  (ii) as a freight forwarder;".

(5) Immediately after sub-paragraph (g) there shall be inserted the following—

  "(h) any activities in agriculture; or

  (i) the activities of a charity.".

3.—(1) Paragraph 3 shall be amended as follows.

(2) For sub-paragraph (a) there shall be substituted the following—

"(a) 'agriculture' has the same meaning as in section 109(3) of the Agriculture Act 1947(**a**) or, in relation to Scotland, as in section 86(3) of the Agriculture (Scotland) Act 1948(**b**);

(aa) 'charity' has the same meaning as in section 360 of the Income and Corporation Taxes Act 1970(**c**);

(ab) 'clothing' means any article of wearing apparel (not being footwear) and, without prejudice to the generality of the foregoing definition, includes—

  (a) headgear;

  (b) neckwear;

  (c) gloves and other handwear;

  (d) surgical belts, trusses and other similar articles;

  (e) braces, garters and suspenders;

  (f) anklets, gaiters, leggings and spats;

  (g) protective clothing of any kind;

  (h) handkerchiefs;

  (i) made-up accessories for articles of wearing apparel such as dress shields, shoulder or other pads, muffs, sleeve protectors and pockets;

  (j) trimmings and adornment for wearing apparel;

  (k) badges;

(ac) 'company' includes any body corporate, and 'subsidiary' has the same meaning as by virtue of section 154 of the Companies Act 1948(**d**) it has for the purposes of that Act;

(ad) 'compounding' in relation to plastics materials means the mixing and processing of raw materials, at least one of which is a polymer or resin, into a homogeneous plastic compound;".

(3) Immediately after sub-paragraph (g) there shall be inserted the following—

"(ga) 'international commodity market' includes a market organised by members of the Baltic Exchange, the London Commodity Exchange, the Grain and Feed Trade Association, the London Metal Exchange or the London Wool Terminal Market Association;".

4. For the Appendix to the Schedule there shall be substituted the following—

"APPENDIX

The activities that would be included in an industry specified in Column 1 hereof by virtue of the industrial training order specified in the corresponding entry in Column 2, if the provisions specified in Column 3 were omitted from that order.

(a) 1947 c. 48.	(b) 1948 c. 45.
(c) 1970 c. 10.	(d) 1948 c. 38.

Column 1	Column 2	Column 3
The wool, jute and flax industry	The Industrial Training (Wool Industry Board) Order 1964 as amended by the Industrial Training (Wool, Jute and Flax Board) Order 1968**(a)**	Schedule 1 Paragraph 1(s)
The iron and steel industry	The Industrial Training (Iron and Steel Board) Order 1964 as amended by the Industrial Training (Iron and Steel Board) Order 1969**(b)**	Schedule 1 Paragraph 1(k)
The construction industry	The Industrial Training (Construction Board) Order 1964 as amended by the Industrial Training (Construction Board) Order 1971**(c)**	Schedule 1 Paragraph 1(k)
The engineering industry	The Industrial Training (Engineering Board) Order 1964 as amended by the Industrial Training (Engineering Board) Order 1971**(d)**	Schedule 1 Paragraph 1(m)
The shipbuilding industry	The Industrial Training (Shipbuilding Board) Order 1964 as amended by the Industrial Training (Shipbuilding Board) Order 1968**(e)**	Schedule 1 Paragraph 1(g)
The ceramics, glass and mineral products industry	The Industrial Training (Ceramics, Glass and Mineral Products Board) Order 1965 as amended by the Industrial Training (Ceramics, Glass and Mineral Products Board) Order 1969**(f)**	Schedule 1 Paragraph 1(p)
The furniture and timber industry	The Industrial Training (Furniture and Timber Industry Board) Order 1965 as amended by the Industrial Training (Furniture and Timber Industry Board) Order 1969 and the Industrial Training (Furniture and Timber Industry Board) Order 1969 (Amendment) Order 1970**(g)**	Schedule 1 Paragraph 1(x)
The man-made fibres producing industry	The Industrial Training (Man-made Fibres Producing Industry Board) Order 1966 as amended by the Industrial Training (Man-made Fibres Producing Industry Board) Order 1969**(h)**	Schedule 1 Paragraph 1(e)
The carpet industry	The Industrial Training (Carpet Board) Order 1966 as amended by the Industrial Training (Carpet Board) Order 1968**(i)**	Schedule 1 Paragraph 1(f)
The knitting, lace and net industry	The Industrial Training (Knitting, Lace and Net Industry Board) Order 1966**(j)**	Schedule 1 Paragraph 1(j)
The cotton and allied textiles industry	The Industrial Training (Cotton and Allied Textiles Board) Order 1966**(k)**	Schedule 1 Paragraph 1(p)

(a) S.I. 1964/907, 1968/898 (1964 II, p. 1928; 1968 II, p. 2376).
(b) S.I. 1964/949, 1969/884 (1964 II, p. 2127; 1969 II, p. 2517).
(c) S.I. 1964/1079, 1971/1766 (1964 II, p. 2384; 1971 III, p. 4784).
(d) S.I. 1964/1086, 1971/1530 (1964 II, p. 2402; 1971 III, p. 4309).
(e) S.I. 1964/1782, 1968/1614 (1964 III, p. 3928; 1968 III, p. 4432).
(f) S.I. 1965/1391, 1969/689 (1965 II, p. 4062; 1969 II, p. 1860).
(g) S.I. 1965/2028, 1969/1290, 1970/1634 (1965 III, p. 5998; 1969 III, p. 3820; 1970 III, p. 5372).
(h) S.I. 1966/143, 1969/1210 (1966 I, p. 257; 1969 II, p. 3545).
(i) S.I. 1966/245, 1968/1882 (1966 I, p. 499; 1968 III, p. 5017).
(j) S.I. 1966/246 (1966 I, p. 506).
(k) S.I. 1966/823 (1966 II, p. 1907).

Column 1	Column 2	Column 3
The agricultural, horticultural and forestry industry	The Industrial Training (Agricultural, Horticultural and Forestry Board) Order 1966 as amended by the Industrial Training (Agricultural, Horticultural and Forestry Board) Order 1970**(a)**	Schedule 1 Paragraph 1(*d*)
The road transport industry	The Industrial Training (Road Transport Board) Order 1966 as amended by the Industrial Training (Road Transport Board) Order 1969 and the Industrial Training (Road Transport Board) Order 1969 (Amendment) Order 1969**(b)**	Schedule 1 Paragraph 1(*p*)
The hotel and catering industry	The Industrial Training (Hotel and Catering Board) Order 1966 as amended by the Industrial Training (Hotel and Catering Board) Order 1969**(c)**	Schedule 1 Paragraph 1(*e*)
The air transport and travel industry	The Industrial Training (Civil Air Transport Board) Order 1967 as amended by the Industrial Training (Air Transport and Travel Industry Board) Order 1970**(d)**	Schedule 1 Paragraph 1(*i*)
The petroleum industry	The Industrial Training (Petroleum Board) Order 1967 as amended by the Industrial Training (Petroleum Board) Order 1970**(e)**	Schedule 1 Paragraph 1(*i*)
The rubber and plastics processing industry	The Industrial Training (Rubber and Plastics Processing Board) Order 1967**(f)**	Schedule 1 Paragraph 1(*k*)
The chemical and allied products industry	The Industrial Training (Chemical and Allied Products Board) Order 1967 as amended by the Industrial Training (Chemical and Allied Products Board) Order 1970**(g)**	Schedule 1 Paragraph 1(*w*)
The paper and paper products industry	The Industrial Training (Paper and Paper Products Board) Order 1968**(h)**	Schedule 1 Paragraph 1(*j*)
The printing and publishing industry	The Industrial Training (Printing and Publishing Board) Order 1968**(i)**	Schedule 1 Paragraph 1(*n*)
The distributive industry	The Industrial Training (Distributive Board) Board) Order 1968 as amended by the Industrial Training (Distributive Board) Order 1970 and the Industrial Training (Distributive Board) Order 1970 (Amendment) Order 1971**(j)**	Schedule 1 Paragraph 1(*h*)

(a) S.I. 1966/969, 1970/1886 (1966 II, p. 2333; 1970 III, p. 6227).
(b) S.I. 1966/1112, 1969/879, 1871 (1966 III, p. 2712; 1969 II, p. 2495; 1969 III, p. 5815).
(c) S.I. 1966/1347, 1969/1405 (1966 III, p. 3669; 1969 III, p. 4132).
(d) S.I. 1967/263, 1970/252 (1967 I, p. 968; 1970 I, p. 983).
(e) S.I. 1967/648, 1970/205 (1967 I, p. 2032; 1970 I, p. 926).
(f) S.I. 1967/1062 (1967 II, p. 3151).
(g) S.I. 1967/1386 ,1970/1743 (1967 III, p. 4049; 1970 III, p. 5706).
(h) S.I. 1968/787 (1968 II, p. 2194).
(i) S.I. 1968/786 (1968 II, p. 2185).
(j) S.I. 1968/1032, 1970/1053, 1971/1876 (1968 II, p. 2709; 1970 II, p. 3273; 1971 III, p. 5109).

Column 1	Column 2	Column 3
The food, drink and tobacco industry	The Industrial Training (Food, Drink and Tobacco Board) Order 1968 as amended by the Industrial Training (Food, Drink and Tobacco Board) Order 1971**(a)**	Schedule 1 Paragraph 1**(g)**
The clothing and allied products industry	The Industrial Training (Clothing and Allied Products Board) Order 1969**(b)**	Schedule 1 Paragraph 1(*j*)
The hairdressing and allied services industry	The Industrial Training (Hairdressing and Allied Services Board) Order 1969**(c)**	Schedule 1 Paragraph 1(*g*)"

EXPLANATORY NOTE

(This Note is not part of the Order.)

This Order amends Schedule 1 to the Industrial Training (Footwear, Leather and Fur Skin Board) Order 1968 which specifies the activities in relation to which the Footwear, Leather and Fur Skin Industry Training Board exercises its functions.

The principal change is the exclusion from the industry of the activities of any establishment engaged wholly or mainly as follows: —

(1) in the manufacture of components for footwear by an employer engaged in compounding in relation to plastics materials; or

(2) in dealing, as a member (or as a member's nominee) of an international commodity market, in a commodity in which the members of the market deal.

The activities of a charity are also excluded from the industry.

(a) S.I. 1968/1033, 1971/648 (1968 II, p. 2721; 1971 I, p. 1709).
(b) S.I. 1969/1375 (1969 III, p. 4094).
(c) S.I. 1969/1634 (1969 III, p. 5133).

STATUTORY INSTRUMENTS

1972 No. 598

SUGAR

The Sugar (Distribution Payments) (No. 5) Order 1972

Made - - - -	14*th April* 1972
Laid before Parliament	17*th April* 1972
Coming into Operation	18*th April* 1972

The Minister of Agriculture, Fisheries and Food in exercise of the powers conferred upon him by sections 14(5) and 33(4) of the Sugar Act 1956(a), having effect subject to the provisions of section 3 of, and Part II of Schedule 5 to, the Finance Act 1962(b), section 22 of the Finance Act 1964(c) and section 52 of the Finance Act 1966(d) and of all other powers enabling him in that behalf, with the concurrence of the Treasury, and on the advice of the Sugar Board hereby makes the following order:—

1.—(1) This order may be cited as the Sugar (Distribution Payments) (No. 5) Order 1972, and shall come into operation on 18th April 1972.

(2) The Interpretation Act 1889(e) shall apply for the interpretation of this order as it applies for the interpretation of an Act of Parliament.

2. Notwithstanding the provisions of article 2 of the Sugar (Distribution Payments) (No. 4) Order 1972(f), the rates of distribution payments payable under and in accordance with the provisions of section 14 of the Sugar Act 1956, having effect as aforesaid, in respect of sugar and invert sugar imported or home produced or used in the manufacture of imported composite sugar products shall on and after 18th April 1972 be those rates specified in the Schedule to this order; and section 10 of the Finance Act 1901(g) (which relates to new or altered customs or excise duties and their effect upon contracts) shall apply accordingly.

In Witness whereof the Official Seal of the Minister of Agriculture, Fisheries and Food is hereunto affixed on 13th April 1972.

(L.S.)

E. J. G. Smith,
Authorised by the Minister.

We concur.
14th April 1972.

V. H. Goodhew,
Tim Fortescue,
Two of the Lords Commissioners of
Her Majesty's Treasury.

(a)·1956 c. 48. (b) 1962 c. 44. (d) 1966 c. 18.
(e) 1889 c. 63 (f) S.I. 1972/578 (1972 I, p. 1918). (g) 1901 c. 7

SCHEDULE

PART I

RATES OF DISTRIBUTION PAYMENT FOR SUGAR

Polarisation	Rate of Distribution Payment per ton
	£
Exceeding—	
99°	6·000
98° but not exceeding 99°	5·658
97° ,, ,, ,, 98°	5·520
96° ,, ,, ,, 97°	5·376
95° ,, ,, ,, 96°	5·232
94° ,, ,, ,, 95°	5·088
93° ,, ,, ,, 94°	4·944
92° ,, ,, ,, 93°	4·800
91° ,, ,, ,, 92°	4·656
90° ,, ,, ,, 91°	4·512
89° ,, ,, ,, 90°	4·368
88° ,, ,, ,, 89°	4·224
87° ,, ,, ,, 88°	4·104
86° ,, ,, ,, 87°	3·984
85° ,, ,, ,, 86°	3·876
84° ,, ,, ,, 85°	3·768
83° ,, ,, ,, 84°	3·660
82° ,, ,, ,, 83°	3·552
81° ,, ,, ,, 82°	3·456
80° ,, ,, ,, 81°	3·360
79° ,, ,, ,, 80°	3·264
78° ,, ,, ,, 79°	3·168
77° ,, ,, ,, 78°	3·072
76° ,, ,, ,, 77°	2·976
Not exceeding 76°	2·880

PART II

RATES OF DISTRIBUTION PAYMENT FOR INVERT SUGAR

Sweetening matter content by weight	Rate of Distribution Payment per cwt.
	£
70 per cent. or more	0·19
Less than 70 per cent. and more than 50 per cent.	0·13
Not more than 50 per cent.	0·06

EXPLANATORY NOTE

(This Note is not part of the Order.)

This order provides for reductions equivalent to £6 per ton of refined sugar in the rates of distribution payment in respect of sugar and invert sugar which become eligible for such payments on and after 18th April 1972.

STATUTORY INSTRUMENTS

1972 No. 599

SUGAR

The Sugar (Distribution Repayments) (Amendment) (No. 4) Order 1972

Made - - - -	14*th April* 1972
Laid before Parliament	17*th April* 1972
Coming into Operation	18*th April* 1972

The Minister of Agriculture, Fisheries and Food in exercise of the powers conferred upon him by sections 15 and 33(4) of the Sugar Act 1956(**a**), having effect subject to the provisions of section 3 of, and Part II of Schedule 5 to, the Finance Act 1962(**b**), section 22 of the Finance Act 1964(**c**) and section 52 of the Finance Act 1966(**d**) and of all other powers enabling him in that behalf, an order (**e**) having been made under section 14 of the said Act, hereby makes the following order:—

1.—(1) This order may be cited as the Sugar (Distribution Repayments) (Amendment) (No. 4) Order 1972, and shall come into operation on 18th April 1972.

(2) The Interpretation Act 1889(**f**) shall apply for the interpretation of this order as it applies for the interpretation of an Act of Parliament.

2.—(1) Notwithstanding the provisions of article 2(1) of the Sugar (Distribution Repayments) (Amendment) (No. 3) Order 1972(**g**) the amount of distribution repayment payable in respect of invert sugar, if the relevant drawback is payable thereon as being invert sugar produced in the United Kingdom from materials on which sugar duty has been paid on or after 18th April 1972, shall be calculated thereon at the rate applicable to the invert sugar in accordance with the rates prescribed in the Schedule to this order.

(2) Article 2(1) of the Sugar (Distribution Repayments) Order 1972(**h**) shall apply for the interpretation of this article.

In Witness whereof the Official Seal of the Minister of Agriculture, Fisheries and Food is hereunto affixed on 14th April 1972.

(L.S.)

E. J. G. Smith,
Authorised by the Minister.

(**a**) 1956 c. 48.   (**b**) 1962 c. 44.   (**c**) 1964 c. 49.
(**d**) 1966 c. 18.   (**e**) S.I. 1972/598 (1972 I, p. 1972).(**f**) 1889 c. 63.
(**g**) S.I. 1972/579 (1972 I, p. 1920).   (**h**) S.I. 1972/67 (1972 I, p. 162).

THE SCHEDULE

RATES OF DISTRIBUTION REPAYMENT FOR INVERT SUGAR

Sweetening matter content by weight	Rate of Distribution Repayment per cwt.
	£
More than 80 per cent.	0·22
More than 70 per cent. but not more than 80 per cent.	0·19
More than 60 per cent. but not more than 70 per cent.	0·13
More than 50 per cent. but not more than 60 per cent.	0·10
Not more than 50 per cent. and the invert sugar not being less in weight than 14 lb. per gallon	0·06

EXPLANATORY NOTE

(*This Note is not part of the Order.*)

This order, which is consequent upon the Sugar (Distribution Payments) (No. 5) Order 1972 (S.I. 1972/598), provides for reductions equivalent to £6 per ton of refined sugar in the rates of distribution repayment, in respect of sugar and invert sugar produced in the United Kingdom from materials which become eligible for distribution payments on or after 18th April 1972.

STOKE-ON-TRENT
CITY
LIBRARIES

STATUTORY   INSTRUMENTS

1972 No. 600

SUGAR

The Composite Sugar Products (Distribution Payments— Average Rates) (No. 5) Order 1972

Made - - - -	14*th April* 1972
Laid before Parliament	17*th April* 1972
Coming into Operation	18*th April* 1972

Whereas the Minister of Agriculture, Fisheries and Food (hereinafter called " the Minister ") has on the recommendation of the Sugar Board made an order (**a**) pursuant to the powers conferred upon him by section 9(1) of the Sugar Act 1956(**b**) having effect subject to section 14(8) of that Act and to the provisions of section 3 of, and Part II of Schedule 5 to, the Finance Act 1962 (**c**), section 22 of the Finance Act 1964(**d**) and section 52 of the Finance Act 1966(**e**), providing that in the case of certain descriptions of composite sugar products distribution payments shall be calculated on the basis of an average quantity of sugar or invert sugar taken to have been used in the manufacture of the products and that certain other descriptions shall be treated as not containing any sugar or invert sugar:

And whereas the Minister has by the Sugar (Distribution Payments) (No. 5) Order 1972(**f**) provided for a change in the rates of distribution payments in respect of sugar and invert sugar which became eligible for such payments on and after April 18th 1972.

Now, therefore, the Minister on the recommendation of the Sugar Board, and in exercise of the powers conferred upon him by sections 9(1) and 33(4) of the Sugar Act 1956, having effect as aforesaid, and of all other powers enabling him in that behalf, hereby makes the following order:—

1.—(1) This order may be cited as the Composite Sugar Products (Distribution Payments—Average Rates) (No. 5) Order 1972, and shall come into operation on 18th April 1972.

(2) The Interpretation Act 1889(**g**) shall apply to the interpretation of this order as it applies to the interpretation of an Act of Parliament.

2. Distribution payments payable on or after 18th April 1972 under and in accordance with section 14 of the Sugar Act 1956, having effect as aforesaid, in respect of sugar and invert sugar used in the manufacture of the descriptions of imported composite sugar products specified in the second column of Schedule 1 to this order, being goods which are classified in the tariff headings indicated in relation to them in the first column of the said Schedule shall, notwithstanding the provisions of the Sugar (Distribution Payments) (No. 5) Order 1972 and the Composite Sugar Products (Distribution Payments—Average Rates) (No. 4) Order 1972(**a**) be calculated by reference to the weight of the products and the rates specified in relation thereto in the third column of the said Schedule.

3. Imported composite sugar products other than those of a description specified in Schedules 1 and 2 to this order shall be treated as not containing any sugar or invert sugar for the purposes of distribution payments.

(**a**) S.I. 1972/580 (1972 I, p. 1922) (**b**) 1956 c. 48. (**c**) 1962 c. 44. (**d**) 1964 c. 49.
(**e**) 1966 c. 18. (**f**) S.I. 1972/598 (1972 I, p. 1972) (**g**) 1889 c. 63.

In Witness whereof the Official Seal of the Minister of Agriculture, Fisheries and Food is hereunto affixed on 14th April 1972.

(L.S.)

E. J. G. Smith,
Authorised by the Minister.

SCHEDULE 1

In this Schedule:—

" Tariff heading " means a heading or, where the context so requires, a subheading of the Customs Tariff 1959 (see paragraph (1) of Article 2 of the Import Duties (General) (No. 7) Order 1971)(a).

Tariff heading	Description of Composite Sugar Products	Rate of Distribution Payment
		Per cwt. £
04.02 ..	Milk and cream, preserved, concentrated or sweetened, containing more than 10 per cent. by weight of added sugar	0·13
17.02 (B) (2) and 17.05 (B)	Syrups containing sucrose sugar, whether or not flavoured or coloured, but not including fruit juices containing added sugar in any proportion:—	
	Containing 70 per cent. or more by weight of sweetening matter	0·19
	Containing less than 70 per cent., and more than 50 per cent. by weight of sweetening matter	0·13
	Containing not more than 50 per cent. by weight of sweetening matter	0·06
17.02 (F) ..	Caramel:—	
	Solid	0·30
	Liquid	0·20
17.04 ..	Sugar confectionery, not containing cocoa ..	0·24
18.06 ..	Chocolate and other food preparations containing cocoa and added sugar:—	
	Chocolate couverture not prepared for retail sale; chocolate milk crumb, liquid ..	0·13
	Chocolate milk crumb, solid	0·16
	Solid chocolate bars or blocks, milk or plain, with or without fruit or nuts; other chocolate confectionery consisting wholly of chocolate or of chocolate and other ingredients not containing added sugar ..	0·13
	Other	0·17

(a) S.I. 1971/1971 (1971 III, p. 5330).

SCHEDULE 1—*continued*

Tariff heading	Description of Composite Sugar Products	Rate of Distribution Payment
		Per cwt. £
19.08 ..	Pastry, biscuits, cakes and other fine bakers' wares containing added sugar:— Biscuits, wafers and rusks containing more than 12½ per cent. by weight of added sugar, and other biscuits, wafers and rusks included in retail packages with such goods.. ..	0·07
	Cakes with covering or filling containing added sugar; meringues	0·09
	Other	0·03
20.01 ..	Vegetables and fruit, prepared or preserved by vinegar or acetic acid, containing added sugar:— Containing 10 per cent. or more by weight of added sugar	0·10
	Other	0·02
20.03 ..	Fruit preserved by freezing, containing added sugar	0·03
20.04 ..	Fruit, fruit-peel and parts of plants, preserved by sugar (drained, glacé or crystallised)	0·19
20.05 ..	Jams, fruit jellies, marmalades, fruit puree and fruit pastes, being cooked preparations, containing added sugar	0·18
20.06 ..	Fruit otherwise prepared or preserved, containing added sugar:— Ginger	0·15
	Other	0·03

SCHEDULE 2

Tariff heading	Description of Composite Sugar Products
17.05 (A) and (B)	Sugar and invert sugar, flavoured or coloured.

EXPLANATORY NOTE

(This Note is not part of the Order.)

This order provides for reductions in the average rates of distribution payments payable in respect of imported composite sugar products of the descriptions specified in Schedule 1 on and after 18th April 1972. These correspond to reductions in the rates of distribution payment effected by the Sugar (Distribution Payments) (No. 5) Order 1972 (S.I. 1972/598). Provision is also made for certain imported composite sugar products to be treated as not containing any sugar or invert sugar.

STATUTORY INSTRUMENTS

1972 No. 603

SOCIAL SECURITY

The National Insurance (Hospital In-Patients) Regulations 1972

Made - - - -	*14th April* 1972
Laid before Parliament	*25th April* 1972
Coming into Operation	*15th May* 1972

The National Insurance Joint Authority, in conjunction with the Treasury, in exercise of powers conferred by section 50(1) of the National Insurance Act 1965(a) and of all other powers enabling them in that behalf, and for the purpose only of consolidating the regulations hereby revoked, hereby make the following regulations:—

PART I

General

Citation, commencement and interpretation

1.—(1) These regulations may be cited as the National Insurance (Hospital In-Patients) Regulations 1972 and shall come into operation on 15th May 1972.

(2) In these regulations, unless the context otherwise requires—

"the Act" means the National Insurance Act 1965;

"the National Health Service Acts" means the National Health Service Acts 1946 to 1968;

"the National Health Service (Scotland) Acts" means the National Health Service (Scotland) Acts 1947 to 1968;

"benefit" means benefit under the Act other than attendance allowance;

"dependency benefit" means that benefit which, apart from these regulations, is payable to a person in respect of another person who is a child or an adult dependant, and includes child's special allowance;

"personal benefit" means that benefit which, apart from these regulations, is payable to a person otherwise than in respect of another person who is a child or an adult dependant, but shall not include earnings-related supplement under section 2 of the National Insurance Act 1966(b) or widow's supplementary allowance under section 4(1) of that Act;

(a) 1965 c. 51.   (b) 1966 c. 6.

"prescribed accommodation" means, in relation to any person, any hospital accommodation or similar accommodation in which that person is residing or has resided either as a patient or inmate or as a person in need of care and attention and wholly or partly at the cost of a local authority, the Secretary of State, or a Hospital Board or a Regional Hospital Board constituted under the National Health Service Acts, or the National Health Service (Scotland) Acts, or any residential accommodation provided for that person under Part III of the National Assistance Act 1948(a); but does not include any such accommodation for any period for which he is or was receiving free in-patient treatment;

"tuberculosis patient" means a person (not being a person under treatment in a hospital or similar institution for the purposes of the Mental Health Act 1959(b) or the Mental Health (Scotland) Act 1960(c)) who is under treatment for tuberculosis of the respiratory system;

and other expressions have the same meaning as in the Act.

(3) For the purposes of these regulations, a person shall be regarded as receiving or having received free in-patient treatment for any period for which he is or has been maintained free of charge while undergoing medical or other treatment as an in-patient—

(a) in a hospital or similar institution maintained or administered under the National Health Service Acts, or the National Health Service (Scotland) Acts, or by or on behalf of the Secretary of State, or by or on behalf of the Defence Council; or

(b) pursuant to arrangements made by the Secretary of State or by a Hospital Board or a Regional Hospital Board constituted under the National Health Service Acts or the National Health Service (Scotland) Acts in a hospital or similar institution not so maintained or administered;

and, for this purpose, a person shall only be regarded as not being maintained free of charge in a hospital or similar institution for any period if he is paying or has paid, in respect of his maintenance, charges which are designed to cover the whole cost of the accommodation or services (other than services by way of treatment) provided for him in the hospital or similar institution for that period.

(4) References in these regulations to any enactment or regulation shall, except in so far as the context otherwise requires, be construed as references to such enactment or regulation as amended or extended by any subsequent enactment, order or regulation and as including references to any enactment or regulation thereby consolidated.

(5) The rules for the construction of Acts of Parliament contained in the Interpretation Act 1889(d) shall apply in relation to this instrument (including any instrument read as one therewith) and in relation to any revocation effected by it as if this instrument, the regulations revoked by it and any regulations revoked by the regulations so revoked were Acts of Parliament, and as if each revocation were a repeal.

(a) 1948 c. 29. (b) 1959 c. 72.
(c) 1960 c. 61. (d) 1889 c. 63.

Part II

Adjustment of benefit

2. The provisions of this Part of these regulations shall have effect subject to the provisions of Part III and Part IV.

Personal benefit

3.—(1) Where the conditions for the receipt of personal benefit by way of sickness benefit, invalidity benefit, widow's allowance, widowed mother's allowance, widow's pension, age addition or retirement pension are satisfied in relation to any person who receives, or has received, continuously, for a period exceeding 8 weeks, free in-patient treatment, the weekly rate of that personal benefit which, but for the provisions of these regulations, would be payable for any period after the first 8 weeks of that treatment shall be reduced subject to and in accordance with the following provisions of these regulations, so however that in the case of a person to whom 2 or more such personal benefits (being benefits by way of retirement pension, age addition, or both), or to whom invalidity pension and invalidity allowance are payable, the weekly rate referred to in this paragraph shall be the aggregate of the weekly rates of those benefits.

(2) In any case in which the provisions of paragraph (1) of this regulation apply in relation to any of the said personal benefits, the weekly rate of any reduction of that personal benefit shall, subject to the provisions of paragraph (3) of this regulation, be determined, for any part of the period of free in-patient treatment which occurs during the 44 weeks next following the first 8 weeks thereof, in accordance with the provisions of regulation 4, and, for any part of the period of that treatment which occurs after the first 52 weeks thereof, in accordance with the provisions of regulation 5 of these regulations.

(3) In any case where a reduction of personal benefit at a rate determined in accordance with the provisions of regulations 4, 5(2), 5(3) or 5(4)(*d*) of these regulations would reduce the rate of that personal benefit, where the beneficiary is a tuberculosis patient, to less than £1·45 a week, or, in any other case, to less than £1·20 a week the reduction of that personal benefit shall not be as so determined but shall be such (if any) as will reduce the rate of that personal benefit, where the beneficiary is a tuberculosis patient, to £1·45 a week, or, in any other case, to £1·20 a week.

4. Where, by virtue of the provisions of regulation 3(2) of these regulations, the weekly rate of any reduction of personal benefit is to be determined for any period in accordance with the provisions of this regulation, that reduction shall be—

  (*a*) for any part of that period during which the beneficiary has a dependant, at the rate of £1·20 a week; and

  (*b*) for any other part of that period, at the rate of £2·40 a week.

5.—(1) Where, by virtue of the provisions of regulation 3(2) of these regulations, the weekly rate of any reduction of personal benefit is to be determined for any period in accordance with the provisions of this regulation, that reduction shall, subject to the following provisions of this regulation, be such (if any) as will reduce the rate of that personal benefit, where the beneficiary is a tuberculosis patient, to £1·45 a week, or, in any other case, to £1·20 a week.

(2) For any part of the period referred to in paragraph (1) of this regulation during which the beneficiary has a dependant and in respect of which an application has been made by the beneficiary to the Secretary of State to pay on behalf of the beneficiary to that dependant, or to some other person who is approved by the Secretary of State and satisfies the Secretary of State that he will apply it for the benefit of that dependant, so much (if any) of the personal benefit as would, but for the provisions of these regulations, be payable to the beneficiary in excess, where the beneficiary is a tuberculosis patient, of £2·65 a week, or, in any other case, of £2·40 a week, the reduction of personal benefit shall be at the rate of £1·20 a week.

(3)(a) For any part of the period of free in-patient treatment which falls within the period of 52 weeks next following the first 52 weeks thereof, and during which the beneficiary has not a dependant or, if the beneficiary has a dependant, in respect of which any such application as is mentioned in paragraph (2) of this regulation has not been made, the reduction of personal benefit shall, subject to the provisions of the next following sub-paragraph, be at the rate of £2·40 a week.

(b) In addition to the reduction of benefit specified in the last foregoing sub-paragraph, so much (if any) of the personal benefit as would, but for the provisions of these regulations, be payable for the said part of the said period in excess, where the beneficiary is a tuberculosis patient, of £3·85 a week, or, in any other case, of £3·60 a week, shall not be payable unless and until the beneficiary is discharged from the hospital or similar institution.

(4) In relation to any beneficiary who is married, the foregoing provisions of this regulation shall have effect subject to the following provisions:—

(a) If the husband or wife of the beneficiary is receiving free in-patient treatment after having received that treatment continuously for a period of not less than 52 weeks, then, notwithstanding the provisions of regulation 11 of these regulations, he or she shall not be regarded as a dependant of the beneficiary.

(b) If—

(i) on a day on which the beneficiary is receiving free in-patient treatment after having received that treatment continuously for a period exceeding 52 weeks, his wife or her husband is receiving free in-patient treatment after having received that treatment continuously for a period which began 52 weeks before that day, and

(ii) as respects the period of free in-patient treatment received by the beneficiary, the provisions of paragraph (3) of this regulation have not applied in relation to any part of that period before that day,

those provisions shall apply as if the part of the period of free in-patient treatment received by the beneficiary next following the first 52 weeks thereof had begun on that day.

(c) Where the benefit in question is personal benefit by way of sickness benefit and the beneficiary is a woman who is receiving free in-patient treatment after having received that treatment continuously for a period of not less than 52 weeks, for any part of the period of that treatment which occurs after the first 52 weeks thereof and for which there is payable to her husband in respect of her any dependency benefit under the Act, the reduction of that personal benefit shall be such (if any) as will reduce the weekly rate thereof, where the beneficiary is a tuberculosis patient, to £1·45 a week, or, in any other case, to £1·20 a week.

(d) If the beneficiary is a man and the benefit in question is personal benefit by way of sickness benefit, invalidity benefit or a retirement pension, or if the beneficiary is a woman and the benefit in question is personal benefit by way of invalidity benefit or a retirement pension, then, for any part of the period of free in-patient treatment received by the beneficiary which occurs after the first 104 weeks thereof and (where the beneficiary is a man) for which the wife of the beneficiary is entitled to a retirement pension by virtue of her own insurance—

(i) notwithstanding the provisions of regulation 11 of these regulations, the wife or husband of the beneficiary shall not be regarded as a dependant of the beneficiary, and

(ii) (where the beneficiary is a man and his wife would, but for the provisions of this sub-paragraph, be regarded as a dependant of the beneficiary) the reduction of the personal benefit in question shall be at the weekly rate of £3·50:

Provided that the provisions of head (i) of this sub-paragraph shall not apply in the case of a beneficiary who is a woman and who is receiving an increase of invalidity pension in respect of her husband and the provisions of head (ii) of this sub-paragraph shall not apply for any period in respect of which any such application as is mentioned in paragraph (2) of this regulation has been made by the beneficiary in relation to any person except his wife who, for that period, is a dependant of the beneficiary.

Special provisions for certain persons entitled to widow's basic pension

6. Where a beneficiary is entitled to a widow's basic pension by virtue of the insurance of her husband who died before 5th July 1951 and to some other benefit to which regulation 3(1) of these regulations relates—

(a) regulation 4 or regulation 5(2) of these regulations shall not require a greater reduction in those benefits than would reduce the aggregate amount payable in respect of them to a sum equal to the aggregate amount which would have been payable in respect of them had they been calculated—

(i) in the case of any benefit other than an invalidity benefit, at the rate appropriate to that beneficiary for the period immediately before 20th September 1971, and

(ii) in the case of invalidity pension, at the rate appropriate to that beneficiary for sickness benefit for that period, and

(iii) in the case of invalidity allowance, at the rate at which it is payable; and

had they been adjusted under the provisions of the National Insurance (Hospital In-Patients) Regulations 1949(a), as amended (b), as in force on 19th September 1971 (invalidity pension and invalidity allowance as so calculated being for this purpose aggregated and treated as sickness benefit);

(b) regulation 5(1) of these regulations shall not operate to permit the aggregate amount payable in respect of those benefits in the case of a tuberculosis patient to exceed £2·50, and in any other case to exceed £2·00.

(a) S.I. 1949/1461 (1949 I, p. 2718).
(b) The relevant amending instruments are S.I. 1957/2077, 1965/40, 1969/1361 (1957 I, p. 1556; 1965 I, p. 47; 1969 III, p. 4048).

Dependency benefit

7.—(1) The provisions of paragraphs (2) to (6) of this regulation shall have effect subject to the provisions of paragraph (7) hereof.

(2) Where, apart from this regulation, the conditions for the receipt by any person (hereafter in this regulation referred to as "the beneficiary") of any dependency benefit under the Act are satisfied as respects a period for which either the beneficiary or the person in respect of whom that dependency benefit is or, apart from this regulation, would be payable (hereafter in this regulation referred to as "the dependant") is receiving free in-patient treatment, that dependency benefit shall be payable subject to and in accordance with the following provisions of this regulation.

(3) In any case (not being a case in which the provisions of the next following paragraph apply) where the beneficiary is married and the dependant is his wife or her husband and is receiving free in-patient treatment after having received that treatment continuously for a period of not less than 8 weeks, the following provisions shall apply:—

(*a*) The weekly rate of the dependency benefit which, but for this regulation, would be payable to the beneficiary in respect of the dependant—

(i) for any part of the period of free in-patient treatment received by the dependant which occurs during the 96 weeks next following the first 8 weeks thereof shall be reduced by £1·20 or by such lesser amount (if any) as will reduce that weekly rate, where the dependant is a tuberculosis patient, to £1·45 a week, or, in any other case, to £1·20 a week; and

(ii) for any part of the period of free in-patient treatment received by the dependant which occurs after the end of 104 weeks beginning with its commencement shall (subject to the provisions of the next following sub-paragraph) be reduced by such an amount (if any) as will reduce that weekly rate, where the dependant is a tuberculosis patient, to £1·45 a week, or, in any other case, to £1·20 a week.

(*b*) Where the beneficiary is a man and the dependant is his wife who is residing with him, the dependency benefit which, but for this sub-paragraph, would be payable to the beneficiary in respect of the dependant for any part of the period of free in-patient treatment received by the dependant which occurs after the end of 104 weeks beginning with its commencement shall not be payable unless the beneficiary is regularly incurring expenditure in respect of the dependant or is regularly making, or causing to be made, some payment to the dependant or to some other person for the benefit of the dependant.

(4) In any case where the beneficiary is married and the dependant is his wife or her husband and each of them is receiving free in-patient treatment after having received that treatment continuously for a period of not less than 52 weeks, the following provisions shall apply:—

(*a*) For any part of the period of free in-patient treatment received by the beneficiary—

(i) which occurs both after the first 52 weeks thereof and during that part of the period of free in-patient treatment received by the dependant which occurs during the 52 weeks next following the first 52 weeks thereof, and

(ii) in respect of which an application has been made by the beneficiary to the Secretary of State to pay on behalf of the beneficiary to the dependant (subject to the dependant's being discharged from the hospital or similar institution and subject also to the provisions of regulation 8 of these regulations) or to some other person who is approved by the Secretary of State and satisfies the Secretary of State that he will apply it for the benefit of a child of the beneficiary's family so much (if any) of the dependency benefit as would, but for this regulation, be payable to the beneficiary in respect of the dependant at a rate in excess, where the dependant is a tuberculosis patient, of £2·65 a week, or, in any other case, of £2·40 a week,

the weekly rate of the dependency benefit which, but for this regulation, would be payable to the beneficiary in respect of the dependant shall be reduced by £1·20 a week or by such lesser amount (if any) as will reduce that weekly rate, where the dependant is a tuberculosis patient, to £1·45 a week, or, in any other case, to £1·20 a week.

(b) For any other part of the period of free in-patient treatment received by the beneficiary which occurs both after the first 52 weeks thereof and during that part of the period of free in-patient treatment received by the dependant which occurs after the first 52 weeks thereof, the weekly rate of the dependency benefit which, but for this regulation, would be payable to the beneficiary in respect of the dependant shall be reduced by such an amount (if any) as will reduce that weekly rate, where the dependant is a tuberculosis patient, to £1·45 a week, or, in any other case, to £1·20 a week.

(c) Any benefit in relation to which, in accordance with sub-paragraph (a) of this paragraph, an application has been made by the beneficiary to the Secretary of State for its payment to the dependant shall not be payable unless and until the dependant is discharged from the hospital or similar institution.

(5) In any case where the dependant is a child and is receiving free in-patient treatment after having received that treatment continuously for a period of not less than 12 weeks, any dependency benefit which, but for this regulation, would be payable to the beneficiary in respect of the dependant shall not be payable unless the beneficiary is regularly incurring expenditure in respect of the dependant or is regularly making, or causing to be made, some payment to the dependant or to some other person for the benefit of the dependant.

(6) In any case (not being a case in which the provisions of paragraph (3)(b) or paragraph (5) of this regulation apply) where, apart from this regulation, the conditions for the receipt by the beneficiary of any dependency benefit under the Act (not being any dependency benefit in relation to which an application has been made in accordance with the provisions of head (ii) of paragraph (4)(a) of this regulation) are satisfied and the beneficiary has received free in-patient treatment continuously for a period exceeding 52 weeks, that dependency benefit, or such part thereof as would be payable but for the provisions of this paragraph, shall not be payable for any part of the period of free in-patient treatment which occurs after the first 52 weeks thereof and in respect of which an application has not been made by the beneficiary to the Secretary of State to pay on behalf of the beneficiary that dependency benefit, or the said part thereof, to the dependant or to some other person who is approved by the Secretary of State and satisfies the Secretary of State that he will apply it for the benefit of the dependant.

(7) In relation to any case where the beneficiary is a married man and the dependant is his wife, the foregoing references to the dependency benefit which, but for this regulation, would be payable for any period shall, as respects any period throughout which the dependant is receiving free in-patient treatment and—

(a) for which personal benefit under the Act by way of sickness benefit is payable to her, or

(b) (where the dependency benefit in question is dependency benefit by way of an increase of a retirement pension) throughout which she is over pensionable age and for which any personal benefit specified in regulation 6(2) of the National Insurance (Overlapping Benefits) Regulations 1972**(a)** is payable to her,

be construed as references to the dependency benefit which, but for the operation of the said regulations of 1972 and the provisions of this regulation, would be payable for that period.

Part III

Supplementary provisions

Benefit payable on discharge from a hospital or similar institution

8.—(1) Where, by virtue of any provision of these regulations, the payment to a person (hereafter in this regulation referred to as "the payee") of any sum by way of benefit is conditional upon the payee's discharge from a hospital or similar institution, that sum (which sum or any part thereof is hereafter in this regulation referred to as "resettlement benefit") shall not be payable unless and until, after the payee's discharge from the hospital or similar institution, the payee proves, in such manner as the Secretary of State shall require, that his discharge therefrom was effected by and with the approval of a person authorised or empowered to discharge him and that he is neither receiving free in-patient treatment nor residing in any prescribed accommodation, and in that event there shall be payable only so much resettlement benefit as is payable in accordance with the provisions of the next following paragraph.

(2) Resettlement benefit shall, during the lifetime of the payee, be payable to him by instalments not exceeding £9·00 a week unless, having regard to the circumstances of any particular case, the Secretary of State decides that payment by other instalments or in one sum is desirable, and any resettlement benefit which, at the payee's death, has not been paid in accordance with this provision shall not be payable:

Provided that—

(a) the payment of any resettlement benefit shall be suspended while the payee is again receiving free in-patient treatment or is residing in any prescribed accommodation; and

(b) where, after an interval of more than 28 days, the payee again receives free in-patient treatment for any period, the amount of any resettlement benefit which, but for the provisions of this paragraph of this proviso, would be payable to him in respect of that period shall be reduced or extinguished by the deduction therefrom of the amount of any resettlement benefit which, at the commencement of that period, either was payable to him and was unpaid, or would have been so payable to him if he had then satisfied the conditions for the receipt thereof.

(a) S.I. 1972/604 (1972 I, p. 1994).

Provisions as to residence

9. For the purposes of Part II and paragraph (*d*) of regulation 11 of these regulations, two spouses shall not be deemed to have ceased to reside together by reason of any absence of either or both of them while receiving medical or other treatment as an in-patient in a hospital or similar institution, notwithstanding that such absence is not temporary and notwithstanding that it commenced before the date on which these regulations come into force.

Adjustment, or further adjustment, of benefit in certain cases

10.—(1) This regulation applies in relation to—

(*a*) any personal benefit by way of sickness benefit, invalidity benefit, widow's benefit or retirement pension (not being personal benefit which, by virtue of an application such as is mentioned in regulation 5(2) of these regulations, is payable on behalf of the beneficiary to or for the benefit of the dependant or any personal benefit which, by virtue of regulation 5(3)(*b*) of these regulations, is not payable unless and until the beneficiary is discharged from a hospital or similar institution) which, but for the provisions of this regulation, would be payable to the beneficiary, and

(*b*) any dependency benefit (not being dependency benefit which, by virtue of an application such as is mentioned in regulation 7(4)(*a*) of these regulations, is payable for the benefit of a child or which, by virtue of such an application and the provisions of regulation 7(4)(*c*) of these regulations, is payable to the beneficiary's wife or husband subject to her or his being discharged from a hospital or similar institution) which, but for the provisions of this regulation, would be payable in respect of the beneficiary's wife or husband,

for a period for which, in the case of personal benefit, the beneficiary or, in the case of dependency benefit, each of the beneficiary and the beneficiary's wife or husband is receiving free in-patient treatment after having received that treatment continuously for a period of not less than 52 weeks; and, in relation to such benefit, the beneficiary or, in the case of dependency benefit, the beneficiary's wife or husband, is hereafter in this regulation referred to as "the patient".

(2) The weekly rate of any benefit in relation to which this regulation applies shall be reduced for any period for which there is in operation a certificate in writing, given by a medical officer who, at the time when it was given, was treating the patient, showing that, in the opinion of that officer, either no sum or no more than a specified weekly sum (being a weekly sum which is less than the weekly rate of that benefit) can be applied by or on behalf of the patient for his personal comfort or enjoyment; and the reduction of the weekly rate of that benefit to be made in accordance with the foregoing provisions of this paragraph shall be such that that benefit is not payable or, as the case may be, it is payable at a weekly rate equal to the weekly sum specified in the certificate.

(3) A certificate such as is referred to in the last foregoing paragraph shall operate from the date on which it is furnished to the Secretary of State and shall continue in operation unless and until either the Secretary of State receives a notice in writing, given by a medical officer who, at the time when it was given, was treating the patient, stating that the certificate is revoked, or another such certificate, relating to the same patient, comes into operation.

(4) In relation to any personal benefit, the foregoing provisions of this regulation shall apply only as respects any period during which the beneficiary is unable to act and benefit to which he is entitled is payable, on his behalf, to the body or authority responsible for the management and control of the hospital or similar institution in which he is receiving treatment and is so payable to that body or authority either as a person or persons empowered to act on behalf of the beneficiary by virtue of an appointment made by the Secretary of State or pursuant to a request made to the Secretary of State by a person so empowered.

(5) Notwithstanding the foregoing provisions of this regulation, any benefit which, by reason only of the application of those provisions, would not be payable to or in respect of the patient shall be payable subject to and in accordance with the following provisions:—

(a) Such benefit shall not be payable unless and until the patient is discharged from the hospital or similar institution.

(b) If, as respects any benefit in relation to which this regulation applies, reductions have been made in accordance with the provisions of paragraph (2) of this regulation for more than 52 weeks, the amount payable in respect of that benefit by virtue of this paragraph shall not exceed the aggregate amount of the reductions so made for the first 52 of those weeks.

(6) If and in so far as an application made in accordance with the provisions of regulation 7(6) of these regulations relates to dependency benefit which would by payable but for any reduction falling to be made in accordance with the provisions of paragraph (2) of this regulation, it shall have effect as if it were an application made by the beneficiary to the Secretary of State for the payment of that dependency benefit to the dependant subject to the dependant's being discharged from the hospital or similar institution and subject also to the provisions of regulation 8 of these regulations.

(7) The references in regulation 7(4) of these regulations to benefit which would be payable but for that regulation, and the reference in paragraph (b) of that regulation to benefit which would be payable but for the provisions of that paragraph, shall be construed as if this regulation had not been made.

Persons constituting "dependants"

11. For the purposes of regulations 4 and 5 of these regulations, a beneficiary shall be regarded as having a dependant for any period if, but only if, for that period either—

(a) any dependency benefit is payable to the beneficiary (or to some other person on his behalf) or, but for the operation of the National Insurance (Overlapping Benefits) Regulations 1972(a) and the provisions of regulation 7 of these regulations would, subject to his satisfying the condition of making a claim therefor, be payable to the beneficiary; or

(b) an increase of benefit would, but for the provisions of regulation 7 of these regulations and subject as aforesaid, be payable to the beneficiary in respect of an adult dependant, if any earnings of that dependant were disregarded otherwise than for the purpose of ascertaining whether or not the beneficiary is or has been wholly or mainly maintaining that dependant; or

(a) S.I. 1972/604 (1972 I, p. 1994).

(c) an increase of benefit would, but for the operation of the said regulations of 1972 and the provisions of regulation 7 of these regulations, and subject as aforesaid, be payable to the beneficiary in respect of his wife for any period in respect of which a retirement pension is payable to her if any earnings of the wife were disregarded; or

(d) a retirement pension is payable to the beneficiary (being the wife of a man to whom a retirement pension is payable in respect of that period) and the beneficiary is residing with her husband; or

(e) in the case of a man to whom a retirement pension is payable by virtue of section 5(1) of the National Insurance Act 1971**(a)** (which relates to retirement pension for persons over 80)—

(i) he is married and is residing with his wife, or

(ii) he has a child or children in his family; or

(f) in the case of a woman to whom a retirement pension is payable by virtue of the said section 5(1)—

(i) she is married and is residing with her husband and he is in receipt of a retirement pension, or

(ii) she has a child or children in her family;

and, in relation to a beneficiary who is regarded as having a dependant by virtue of the provisions of paragraph (a), (b) or (c) of this regulation, a person in respect of whom any dependency benefit is or, but for any provision or condition mentioned in that paragraph would be payable to the beneficiary (or to some other person on his behalf) shall, for the first-mentioned purposes, be regarded as a dependant, and, in relation to a married woman who is regarded as having a dependant by virtue of the provisions of paragraph (d) of this regulation, her husband shall, for those purposes, be regarded as a dependant: and, in relation to a beneficiary who is regarded as having a dependant by virtue of the provisions of paragraph (e) or (f) of this regulation, the spouse, child or children shall, for those purposes, be regarded as a dependant or dependants:

Provided that, if the husband or wife of the beneficiary is temporarily absent from Great Britain for the specific purpose of being treated for incapacity which commenced before he or she left Great Britain, then, when it is being determined for the purposes of the foregoing provisions of this regulation whether any benefit is, or would be, payable, that absence from Great Britain (and any absence of claim for benefit) shall be disregarded.

Two increases of the same benefit to be treated as separate benefits

12. For the purposes of these regulations, in any case where dependency benefit by way of increases of benefit in respect of more than one person (being a child or an adult dependant) is or, but for the provisions of these regulations, would be payable, each of such increases of benefit shall be treated as a separate benefit.

Calculation of periods

13.—(1) For the purpose of calculating any period mentioned in Part II or regulation 16 of these regulations, but for no other purpose, the following provisions of this regulation shall apply:—

(a) 1971 c. 50.

(2) Where a person has entered a hospital or similar institution for the purpose of receiving there medical or other treatment as an in-patient after having ceased to reside in any prescribed accommodation, he shall be regarded as having received free in-patient treatment throughout the period during which he so resided:

Provided that—

    (a) where any such person has ceased to reside in any prescribed accommodation after it has been decided by the appropriate authority that he should be permitted to reside there otherwise than temporarily, the period of that residence (whatever its duration) shall be deemed to have been a period of 52 weeks; and

    (b) where the prescribed accommodation in which any such person has ceased to reside is residential accommodation in premises managed by a voluntary organisation provided for that person under Part III of the National Assistance Act 1948**(a)**, the foregoing provisions of this paragraph and the provisions of the next succeeding paragraph shall not apply in relation to that person unless and until, after having ceased to reside in such accommodation, he shall have received free in-patient treatment for a continuous period exceeding 8 weeks.

(3) Where a person has received (or is regarded under this regulation as having received) free in-patient treatment for 2 or more distinct periods separated by a temporary interval or temporary intervals, he shall be regarded as having received such treatment continuously for a period, equal in duration to the total of such distinct periods, ending on the last day of the latter or last of such periods; and, for this purpose, the expression "temporary interval" means a period not exceeding 28 days.

(4) Any period during which a person has received free in-patient treatment whilst that person was a serving member of the forces (as defined in regulation 1(2) of the National Insurance (Members of the Forces) Regulations 1968**(b)**, as amended **(c)**) shall be disregarded.

Priority of adjustments

14. Except in any case in which the provisions of regulation 7(7) of these regulations apply, where any benefit in relation to which these regulations apply falls to be adjusted in accordance with the provisions of the National Insurance (Overlapping Benefits) Regulations 1972**(d)** the benefit as so adjusted in accordance with those provisions shall be the relevant benefit for the purposes of the provisions of these regulations.

Treatment of age addition in certain cases

15. In a case where age addition would, but for the provisions of this regulation, be payable to a person to whom a retirement pension is not payable, regulations 3, 4 and 5 of these regulations shall not apply so as to reduce that age addition, but where that person is receiving or has received free in-patient treatment continuously for a period exceeding 52 weeks, age addition shall not be payable to that person for any part of that period which falls after the first 52 weeks thereof and during which that person has not a child or children in his or her family or a wife who resides with him.

    (a) 1948 c. 29.   (b) S.I. 1968/827 (1968 II, p. 2228)
    (c) There is no amendment which relates expressly to the subject matter of these Regulations.
    (d) S.I. 1972/604 (1972 I, p. 1994).

PART IV

Transitional provisions, revocations and general savings

16.—(1) In the application of the provisions of these regulations in relation to a person who was receiving (or, by virtue of the provisions of regulation 13, is regarded as receiving) free in-patient treatment immediately before 5th September 1949, those provisions shall, in respect of the period of in-patient treatment then current, or regarded as then current, have effect as if—

(a) in regulation 3(2), for the words "44 weeks" there were substituted the words "52 weeks";

(b) in regulation 3(2) and 3(3) and in regulation 6, for the words "52 weeks" (wherever those words occur) there were substituted the words "60 weeks"; and

(c) in regulation 5(3)(a), for the words "which falls within the period of 52 weeks next following the first 52 weeks thereof" there were substituted the words "which falls within the period of 44 weeks next following the first 60 weeks thereof".

(2) In the application of the said provisions in relation to a person who, immediately before 5th September 1949, had been receiving free in-patient treatment for a continuous period exceeding 60 weeks, those provisions (as modified by paragraph (1) of this regulation) shall have effect as if the period of that free in-patient treatment had commenced 60 weeks before the said date.

(3) In the application of the said provisions in relation to a person who, immediately before 5th July 1948, was entitled to any sum by virtue of the provisions of section 55(3) of the National Health Insurance Act 1936(a) (which related to the payment of benefit under that Act to a person after he had left an institution) and subsequently satisfied the conditions specified in regulation 5(3)(b) for the receipt of any personal benefit to which that sub-paragraph applied, and has been receiving free in-patient treatment throughout the period from that day to the date of his discharge from the hospital or similar institution, it shall be a further condition that there shall be payable only so much (if any) of the amount of that personal benefit as does not exceed the amount (if any) by which £50·00 exceeds the said sum, and that no part of that amount shall become payable until after payment to the beneficiary of the said sum.

17.—(1) The regulations specified in column 1 of the Schedule to these regulations are hereby revoked to the extent mentioned in column 3 of the Schedule.

(2) Anything whatsoever done under or by virtue of any regulation revoked by these regulations shall be deemed to have been done under or by virtue of the corresponding provision of these regulations, and anything whatsoever begun under any such regulation may be continued under these regulations as if begun under these regulations.

(3) Nothing in paragraphs (1)-(2) of this regulation shall be taken as affecting the general application by regulation 1(5) of these regulations of the rules for the construction of Acts of Parliament contained in section 38 of the Interpretation Act 1889 (effect of repeal) with regard to the effect of revocations.

(a) 1936 c. 32.

Given under the official seal of the National Insurance Joint Authority.

(L.S.)   *F. B. Hindmarsh,*
                                        A person authorised by the National Insurance
                                        Joint Authority to act on behalf of the Secretary,
                                            National Insurance Joint Authority.

11th April 1972.

                                                        V. H. Goodhew,
                                                        Tim Fortescue,
                                            Two of the Lords Commissioners
                                                of Her Majesty's Treasury.

14th April 1972.

Regulation 17(1)   SCHEDULE

Regulations revoked (1)	Reference (2)	Extent of revocation (3)
The National Insurance (Hospital In-Patients) Regulations 1949	S.I. 1949/1461 (1949 I, p. 2718)	The whole regulations
The National Insurance (Increase of Benefit, Re-entry into Regular Employment and Miscellaneous Provisions) Regulations 1951	S.I. 1951/1232 (1951 I, p. 1457)	Regulation 20 and Part IX of Schedule A, and regulation 21 in so far as it relates to the National Insurance (Hospital In-Patients) Regulations 1949
The National Insurance (Hospital In-Patients) Amendment Regulations 1952	S.I. 1952/2179 (1952 II, p. 2147)	The whole regulations
The National Insurance (Child's Special Allowance) Regulations 1957	S.I. 1957/1835 (1957 I, p. 1523)	The provisions in the Schedule relating to the National Insurance (Hospital In-Patients) Regulations 1949
The National Insurance (Hospital In-Patients) Amendment Regulations 1957	S.I. 1957/1849 (1957 I, p. 1546)	The whole regulations
The National Insurance (Increase of Benefit and Miscellaneous Provisions) Regulations 1957	S.I. 1957/2077 (1957 I, p. 1556)	Regulations 13, 14 and 15, Parts IV, V and VI of Schedule A
The National Insurance (Hospital In-Patients) Amendment Regulations 1960	S.I. 1960/1283 (1960 II, p. 2163)	The whole regulations
The National Insurance (Widow's Benefit and Miscellaneous Provisions) Regulations 1964	S.I. 1964/297 (1964 I, p. 508)	The provisions in Schedule D relating to the National Insurance (Hospital In-Patients) Regulations 1949, as amended

Regulations revoked (1)	Reference (2)	Extent of revocation (3)
The National Insurance (Over-lapping Benefits and Hospital In-Patients) Amendment Regulations 1966	S.I. 1966/970 (1966 II, p. 2340)	Regulation 3
The Family Allowances, National Insurance, Industrial Injuries and Miscellaneous Provisions (Decimalisation of the Currency) Regulations 1970	S.I. 1970/46 (1970 I, p. 243)	Regulation 10
The National Insurance (Increase of Benefit and Miscellaneous Provisions) Regulations 1971	S.I. 1971/1220 (1971 II, p. 3556)	The provisions in Schedule J relating to the National Insurance (Hospital In-Patients) Regulations 1949, as amended
The National Insurance (Miscellaneous Amendments) Regulations 1971	S.I. 1971/1419 (1971 II, p. 3964)	Regulation 8
The National Insurance (General Benefit and Miscellaneous Amendments) Regulations 1972	S.I. 1972/394 (1972 I, p. 1483).	Regulation 4

EXPLANATORY NOTE

(This Note is not part of the Regulations.)

These Regulations are made for the purpose only of consolidating Regulations hereby revoked, and accordingly, by virtue of section 108(9)(*c*) of the National Insurance Act 1965, no reference of them has been made to the National Insurance Advisory Committee.

The Regulations specify the circumstances in which benefit payable to or in respect of a person under the National Insurance Act 1965 may be adjusted when that person is undergoing medical or other treatment as an in-patient in hospital or similar institution.

Part I of the Regulations contains various definitions; Parts II and III contain provisions relating to the adjustment of benefits; Part IV of, and the Schedule to, the Regulations relate to transitional provisions, revocations and general savings.

STATUTORY INSTRUMENTS

1972 No. 604

SOCIAL SECURITY

The National Insurance (Overlapping Benefits) Regulations 1972

Made - - -	14*th April* 1972
Laid before Parliament	25*th April* 1972
Coming into Operation	15*th May* 1972

The National Insurance Joint Authority, in conjunction with the Treasury so far as relates to matters with regard to which the Treasury have so directed, in exercise of powers conferred by sections 50 and 51 of the National Insurance Act 1965(a) and of all other powers enabling them in that behalf, and for the purpose only of consolidating the regulations hereby revoked, hereby make the following regulations: —

PART I

General

Citation, commencement and interpretation

1.—(1) These regulations may be cited as the National Insurance (Overlapping Benefits) Regulations 1972 and shall come into operation on 15th May 1972.

(2) In these regulations, unless the context otherwise requires—

"the Act" means the National Insurance Act 1965;

"the Industrial Injuries Act" means the National Insurance (Industrial Injuries) Act 1965(b);

"the Act of 1966" means the National Insurance Act 1966(c);

"the deceased" means, in relation to any death benefit, the person in respect of whose death that benefit, apart from these regulations, is payable;

"beneficiary" means the person to whom any benefit, pension or allowance is payable;

"death benefit" means any benefit, pension or allowance (whether under the Act or otherwise) which, apart from these regulations, is payable in respect of the death of any person;

"dependency benefit" means that benefit, pension or allowance (whether under the Act or otherwise) which, apart from these regulations, is payable to a person in respect of another person who is a child or an adult dependant, and includes child's special allowance;

"disablement pension" includes a disablement payment on a pension basis and retired pay or pension in respect of any disablement, wound, injury or disease;

"personal benefit" means that benefit, pension or allowance (whether under the Act or otherwise) which, apart from these regulations, is payable

---

(a) 1965 c. 51.   (b) 1965 c. 52.   (c) 1966 c. 6.

to a person otherwise than in respect of another person who is a child or an adult dependant;

"personal death benefit" means any personal benefit by way of death benefit;

"Personal Injuries Scheme" means any scheme made under the Personal Injuries (Emergency Provisions) Act 1939(a) or under the Pensions (Navy, Army, Air Force and Mercantile Marine) Act 1939(b);

"Pneumoconiosis and Byssinosis Benefit Scheme" means any scheme made under section 5 of the Industrial Injuries and Diseases (Old Cases) Act 1967(c);

"Service Pensions Instrument" means any Royal Warrant, Order in Council or other instrument (not being a 1914-1918 War Injuries Scheme) under which a disablement pension may be paid out of public funds in respect of any disablement, wound, injury or disease attributable to or aggravated by service in the naval, military or air forces of the Crown or in any nursing service or other auxiliary service of any of the said forces or in the Home Guard or in any other organisation established under the control of the Defence Council or under which any pension or allowance may be paid out of public funds to any person after the death of some other person in continuation of any payments made during the lifetime of that person in respect of his service in any of the said forces, services and organisations;

"supplement on account of unemployability" includes an increase, on account of unemployability, of an allowance under any Pneumoconiosis and Byssinosis Benefit Scheme;

"training allowance" means an allowance (whether by way of periodical grants or otherwise) payable, out of public funds, by a Government department to a person for his maintenance, or in respect of any dependant of his, for the period, or part of the period, during which he is following a course of training or instruction provided by, or in pursuance of arrangements made with, that department or approved by that department in relation to him;

"training scheme" means a scheme or arrangement under which a training allowance may be paid, not being a scheme or arrangement under which a training allowance is paid by any Government department to or in respect of a person by reason of the fact that he is following a course of full-time education or is training as a teacher;

"widow's basic pension" and "contributory old age pension" have the same meanings as in the National Insurance (Pensions, Existing Beneficiaries and Other Persons) (Transitional) Regulations 1948(d), as amended(e);

"1914-1918 War Injuries Scheme" means any scheme made under the Injuries in War (Compensation) Act 1914(f) or under the Injuries in War Compensation Act 1914 (Session 2)(g) or under the Injuries in War (Compensation) Act 1915(h) or any Government scheme for compensation in respect of persons injured in any merchant ship or fishing vessel as the result of hostilities during the 1914-1918 War;

and other expressions have the same meanings as in the Act.

(a) 1939 c. 82. (b) 1939 c. 83. (c) 1967 c. 34.
(d) S.I. 1948/55 (Rev. XVI, p. 36: 1948 I, p. 2822).
(e) The relevant amending instruments are S.I. 1949/1151, 1957/1333 (1949 I, p. 2744; 1957 I, p. 1698).
(f) 1914 c. 30. (g) 1914 (5 & 6 Geo. 5) c. 18.
(h) 1915 c. 24.

(3) References in these regulations to any enactment, Scheme, Warrant, order, instrument or regulation shall include references to such enactment, Scheme, Warrant, order, instrument or regulation as amended or extended by any subsequent enactment, Scheme, Warrant, order, instrument or regulation and as including references to any enactment or regulation thereby consolidated.

(4) Where under section 24 of the Industrial Injuries Act (which section provides for the payment in certain cases of an allowance to a woman having the care of a child or children of the family of a person who dies as a result of an industrial accident) there is payable any death benefit, that death benefit shall, for the purpose of these regulations and notwithstanding the provisions of section 30(c) of that Act (which refers to death benefit under the said section 24 as being payable in respect of a child), be treated as personal benefit.

(5) Where under any Personal Injuries Scheme, Service Pensions Instrument or 1914-1918 War Injuries Scheme there is payable to a child any personal benefit by way of a pension, that personal benefit shall, for the purposes of these regulations, be treated as dependency benefit payable to another person in respect of that child.

(6) For the purposes of these regulations, a supplement on account of unemployability shall, notwithstanding that it is payable by way of an increase of a disablement pension or disablement allowance, be treated as a separate benefit, pension or allowance.

(7) The rules for the construction of Acts of Parliament contained in the Interpretation Act 1889(a) shall apply in relation to this instrument (including any instrument read as one therewith) and in relation to any revocation effected by it as if this instrument, the regulation revoked by it and any regulations revoked by the regulations so revoked were Acts of Parliament, and as if each revocation were a repeal.

Part II

Adjustment of benefit where a pension or an allowance is payable out of public funds

Adjustment of personal benefit under the Act where other personal benefit (whether under the Act or otherwise) is payable

2.—(1) Where, for any period, any personal benefit under the Act and one or more of the personal benefits specified in paragraph (5) of this regulation (hereafter in this regulation and in regulation 3 of these regulations referred to as "the specified benefits") or where more than one personal benefit (whether of the same or a different description) under the Act are, or but for this regulation would be, payable to any person, then for that period—

(a) every personal benefit under the Act which is or would be so payable shall, subject to the provisions of regulation 3(1) and to the provisions of regulation 4 of these regulations, be adjusted by reference to each of the specified benefits (if any) payable for that period in accordance with the provisions of paragraphs (2) and (4) of this regulation; and

(b) where (after such adjustment, if any) more than one personal benefit under the Act would be payable for that period, an adjustment between those personal benefits shall, subject to the provisions of regulation 3(2) and (3) of these regulations, be made in accordance with the provisions of paragraphs (3) and (4) of this regulation.

(a) 1889 c. 63.

(2) Where in accordance with paragraph (1) of this regulation any personal benefit under the Act is required to be adjusted for any period by reference to any specified benefit or benefits, then the amount which, but for this regulation, would be payable for that period in respect of that personal benefit under the Act shall be reduced or extinguished by the deduction therefrom of the amount payable for that period in respect of that specified benefit or those specified benefits and, subject to any further adjustment to be made in accordance with paragraph (3) of this regulation, only the balance (if any) shall be payable for that period in respect of that personal benefit under the Act.

(3) Where in accordance with paragraph (1) of this regulation an adjustment between any personal benefits under the Act is required to be made for any period, then the amount payable for that period in respect of those personal benefits shall be the amount which, but for this provision, would be payable for that period in respect of one of those personal benefits (if they would be so payable at equal rates) or that one of them which would be so payable for that period at the higher or highest rate.

(4) Where an adjustment falls to be made in accordance with the provisions of paragraph (2) or paragraph (3) of this regulation and either—

(*a*) one of the benefits in question is widow's basic pension payable to a widow by virtue of the insurance of her husband who died before 5th July 1951 and the other is unemployment benefit, sickness benefit, invalidity benefit or maternity benefit or a specified benefit other than a personal death benefit, or

(*b*) one of the benefits in question is a widow's basic pension or a contributory old age pension and the other is a supplement on account of unemployability payable under the Industrial Injuries Act, any Personal Injuries Scheme, any Service Pensions Instrument or any 1914-1918 War Injuries Scheme, or any Pneumoconiosis and Byssinosis Benefit Scheme,

any such adjustment shall not reduce the aggregate amount payable in respect of the benefits in question to less than the aggregate amount of any invalidity allowance to which the beneficiary may be entitled and the sums which would have been payable in respect of the other benefits had they been calculated at the respective rates appropriate to the period immediately before 20th September 1971 (or, in the case of invalidity pension, had it been calculated at the rate appropriate to sickness benefit for that period) and had no adjustment fallen to be made under this regulation.

(5) The personal benefits referred to in this regulation and in regulation 3 as "the specified benefits" are—

(*a*) any personal benefit by way of injury benefit or a supplement on account of unemployability, or any personal death benefit, under the Industrial Injuries Act;

(*b*) any personal benefit by way of a supplement on account of unemployability under any Pneumoconiosis and Byssinosis Benefit Scheme;

(*c*) any personal benefit by way of a supplement on account of unemployability, or any personal death benefit by way of pension or allowance (not being a grant payable by reason of the beneficiary being in receipt of a pension and being over 65 years of age or a pension or allowance calculated by reference to the necessities of the beneficiary), under any Personal Injuries Scheme or Service Pensions Instrument or any 1914-1918 War Injuries Scheme;

(*d*) any personal benefit under any Personal Injuries Scheme or Service Pensions Instrument or any 1914-1918 War Injuries Scheme, being an additional allowance payable only to a beneficiary who is entitled to a supplement on account of unemployability; and

(*e*) any personal benefit by way of training allowance under any training scheme.

Exceptions to regulation 2

3.—(1) Any personal benefit under the Act which is specified in any paragraph of the first column of Schedule 1 to these regulations shall not be adjusted by reference to any specified benefit in the corresponding paragraph of the second column of the said Schedule.

(2) An adjustment shall not be made between any two personal benefits under the Act of which one is specified in any paragraph of the first column of the said Schedule and the other is specified in the corresponding paragraph of the second column of the said Schedule.

(3) Where, for any period, personal benefits under the Act are, or but for these regulations would be, payable to a widow by way of widow's allowance and retirement pension by virtue of the widow's own insurance, and the widow's allowance, apart from any increase thereof by way of widow's supplementary allowance under section 4(1) of the Act of 1966 is, or but for these regulations would be, payable at a lower weekly rate than the retirement pension, apart from any addition thereto under section 34(1) or section 37(1) of the Act, then the widow's allowance, in so far as it consists of widow's supplementary allowance under the said section 4(1), and the retirement pension, except in so far as it includes any addition under the said section 34(1) or section 37(1), shall not be adjusted by reference to each other.

Further exception to regulation 2

4.—(1) Where, for any period, any personal benefit under the Act by way of retirement pension is, or but for these regulations would be, payable by virtue of her deceased husband's insurance to a widow aged 70 or over who, on 5th July 1948, either—

(*a*) had attained the age of 70 and, immediately before that day, was entitled to an old age pension under the Old Age Pensions Act 1936(**a**), payable by virtue of the Widows', Orphans' and Old Age Contributory Pensions Act 1936(**b**), to her by virtue of her deceased husband's insurance, or

(*b*) attained or had attained the age of 60 and, on her attaining the age of 70, would, but for the repeal of the said Contributory Pensions Act 1936, have been entitled to such an old age pension,

and to whom personal benefit by way of dependants war pension (as defined in paragraph (4) of this regulation) is payable in respect of the death of her deceased husband and was so payable immediately before 5th July 1948, then the amount payable to her for that period in respect of that personal benefit by way of retirement pension shall not, as the result of any adjustment thereof made in accordance with the provisions of regulation 2 of these regulations, be reduced by reference only to that personal benefit by way of dependants war pension below the amount which, but for the said repeal, would have been payable to her for that period in respect of that old age pension.

(**a**) 1936 c. 31.   (**b**) 1936 c. 33.

(2) The foregoing provisions of this regulation shall not apply in relation to any personal benefit under the Act by way of retirement pension payable to a widow in respect of any period before she attained the age of 70.

(3) Where, for any period, the foregoing provisions of this regulation apply in relation to any personal benefit under the Act by way of retirement pension which, in accordance with the provisions of regulation 2 of these regulations, is required to be adjusted by reference to one or more of the personal benefits specified in paragraph (5) of that regulation other than the personal benefit by way of dependants war pension, then that personal benefit by way of retirement pension shall be adjusted for that period first by reference only to the personal benefit by way of dependants war pension and then by reference only to the other personal benefit or personal benefits so specified.

(4) In this regulation the expression "dependants war pension" means any pension or allowance payable out of moneys provided by Parliament at weekly or other periodical intervals to any person—

(a) in respect of the death of some other person attributable to or connected with the service of that other person in the naval, military or air forces of the Crown, or

(b) after the death of some other person in continuation of any payments made during the lifetime of that person in respect of his service in any of the said forces, or

(c) in respect of the death of some other person attributable to or connected with the service of that other person during the 1914-1918 War, or

(d) in respect of the death of some other person, under a scheme made by virtue of the Injuries in War (Compensation) Act 1914(a), the Injuries in War Compensation Act 1914 (Session 2)(b) or under a Personal Injuries Scheme.

Adjustment of dependency benefit under the Act where other dependency benefit (whether under the Act or otherwise) is payable

5.—(1) Subject to the provisions of this regulation, where, for any period, any dependency benefit under the Act is, or but for this regulation would be, payable to any person in respect of a child or an adult dependant, that dependency benefit shall be adjusted—

(a) in the case of dependency benefit in respect of a child, by reference to any other dependency benefit specified in paragraph (2) of this regulation which is payable for that period in respect of that child, or

(b) in the case of dependency benefit in respect of an adult dependant, by reference to any other dependency benefit so specified which is payable for that period to that person in respect of that or any other adult dependant or to any person in respect of that adult dependant,

so that the amount which, but for this regulation, would be payable in respect of that dependency benefit under the Act shall be reduced or extinguished by the deduction therefrom of the amount payable for that period in respect of that other dependency benefit or those other dependency benefits by reference to which the dependency benefit under the Act is required by this regulation to be adjusted and only the balance (if any) shall be payable for that period in respect of that dependency benefit under the Act.

(2) The dependency benefits referred to in paragraph (1)(a) of this regula-

---

(a) 1914 c. 30. (b) 1914 (5 & 6 Geo. 5) c. 18.

tion are any dependency benefit under the Act or the Industrial Injuries Act or any Personal Injuries Scheme or any Service Pensions Instrument or any 1914-1918 War Injuries Scheme or any Pneumoconiosis and Byssinosis Benefit Scheme or any training scheme except any dependency benefit by way of an allowance in respect of a child payable for the purpose of his education.

(3) Notwithstanding the foregoing provisions of this regulation (hereafter in this paragraph referred to as "the said provisions"), in any case where—

(a) two or more dependency benefits are, or but for the said provisions would be, payable for any period in respect of a child included in the family of any person (being a family which includes more than one child); and

(b) one of those dependency benefits is a child's allowance; and

(c) an adjustment of dependency benefits made in accordance with the said provisions would be such that the amount payable for that period in respect of the following benefits, namely—

(i) dependency benefits in respect of the children included in that family, and

(ii) any allowance or allowances for that family under the Family Allowances Act 1965(a),

would be less than the total amount which, after the application of the said provisions, would have been payable for that period in respect of the said benefits if there had not been payable for that period any child's allowance in respect of any child so included, and if the said benefits included every allowance under the said Act which, but for the payment of a child's allowance, would have been payable if it had been claimed,

the said provisions shall not, for that period, be applied in relation to any child's allowance so payable, but the amount which, but for the said provisions, would be payable for that period, by way of a child's allowance in respect of the child, or (if more than one child) the elder or eldest child, so included in respect of whom a child's allowance would be so payable, shall be reduced or extinguished by the deduction therefrom of the amount (if any) by which the said total amount is less than the total amount which, but for the said provisions, would be payable for that period in respect of the said benefits.

(4) The foregoing provisions of this regulation shall not operate to require the making of any adjustment as between two dependency benefits of which one is dependency benefit by way of an increase of benefit under section 43(2)(c) or section 43A(4) of the Act, which is, or but for those provisions would be, payable to a person (hereafter in this paragraph referred to as "the beneficiary") in respect of another person who is employed by, but is not residing with, the beneficiary, and the other is any dependency benefit which is specified in paragraph (2) of this regulation and is, or but for those provisions would be, payable in respect of that other person to some person other than the beneficiary.

Adjustment of dependency benefit where personal benefit is payable

6.—(1) Subject to the provisions of paragraphs (3), (4) and (5) of this regulation, where, for any period, any one or more of the personal benefits specified in paragraph (2) of this regulation is or are payable to any person—

(a) 1965 c. 53.

(*a*) if the weekly rate or the aggregate weekly rate at which that personal benefit or those personal benefits (if more than one) is or are payable for that period (hereafter in this regulation called "the weekly rate of personal benefit") is equal to or exceeds the weekly rate of any dependency benefit under the Act which, apart from this regulation, would be payable for that period (hereafter in this regulation called "the weekly rate of dependency benefit") there shall not be paid in respect of that person for that period any dependency benefit under the Act; and

(*b*) in any other case, there shall not be paid in respect of that person for that period any dependency benefit under the Act at a weekly rate exceeding the difference between the weekly rate of personal benefit and the weekly rate of dependency benefit:

Provided that nothing in this paragraph of this regulation shall require that any dependency benefit shall be adjusted by reason of any one or more personal benefits, in a case where the weekly rate of personal benefit is less than £1·30 a week, below a weekly rate equal to the difference between the weekly rate of personal benefit and £1·30.

(2) The personal benefits referred to in the preceding paragraph of this regulation are any personal benefit specified in regulation 2(5) of these regulations and any personal benefit under the Act.

(3) The provisions of this regulation shall not apply in relation to any dependency benefit by way of an increase of benefit under section 43(2)(*c*) or section 43A(4) of the Act in respect of a person who is employed by, but is not residing with, the beneficiary.

(4) Where any one or more of the personal benefits specified in paragraph (2) of this regulation is or are payable to a married woman for any period throughout which she is over pensionable age, the amount of any dependency benefit under the Act which, but for this regulation, would be payable to her husband in respect of her by way of an increase of a retirement pension for that period shall be reduced or extinguished by the deduction therefrom of the amount or aggregate amount so payable in respect of that personal benefit or those personal benefits for that period.

(5) In any case (not being a case falling within the last foregoing paragraph) where personal benefit under the Act by way of sickness benefit is payable to a married woman for any period at a reduced rate by virtue of the National Insurance (Hospital In-Patients) Regulations 1972(**a**), any dependency benefit under the Act which, but for this regulation, would be payable to her husband in respect of her for that period shall not be adjusted in accordance with the foregoing provisions of this regulation but shall be reduced or extinguished by the deduction therefrom of the amount of that personal benefit.

Dependency benefit under the Act not to be paid to a person to whom a training allowance is payable

7. Where, for any period, any personal benefit by way of training allowance is payable to any person under any training scheme, there shall not be paid to that person for that period any dependency benefit under the Act.

Attendance allowance

8.—(1) Notwithstanding the foregoing provisions of these regulations, no

(**a**) S.I. 1972/603 (1972 I, p. 1979).

adjustment shall be made under those provisions between attendance allowance and any other personal or dependency benefit under the Act, no such benefit shall be adjusted by reference to attendance allowance and attendance allowance shall be adjusted only in accordance with the following provision of this regulation.

(2) Where attendance allowance is payable in respect of any person for any period and any other benefit based on his need for attendance is payable for that period under the Industrial Injuries Act or any Pneumoconiosis and Byssinosis Benefit Scheme, Personal Injuries Scheme, Service Pensions Instrument or 1914-1918 War Injuries Scheme, the attendance allowance shall be adjusted by deducting from it the amount of that other benefit and only the balance (if any) shall be payable for that period in respect of the attendance allowance.

Construction of Part II

9. Nothing in this Part of these regulations shall be construed as requiring either—

(a) that any personal benefit under the Act by way of maternity grant or death grant shall be adjusted, or

(b) that any personal benefit by way of age addition shall be adjusted except by reference to another age addition, or

(c) that any personal benefit or dependency benefit shall be adjusted by reason of personal benefit under the Act by way of maternity grant or death grant, or by reason of any other sum which is payable otherwise than in respect of a period, being payable to any person.

PART III

Miscellaneous provisions

Priority of title to increases of benefit

10. Where, but for any of the foregoing provisions of these regulations, two persons would both be entitled to an increase of benefit under the Act in respect of a third person, the person entitled thereto shall, as between such persons, be determined in accordance with the following order of priority:—

(a) such one of the two persons as may be designated in a written notice to the Secretary of State, signed by the other;

(b) such one of the two persons as the Secretary of State may in his discretion determine, having regard to the circumstances of the case.

Two increases of the same benefit to be treated as separate benefits

11. For the purposes of these regulations, in any case where dependency benefit by way of increases of benefit in respect of more than one person (being a child or an adult dependant) is payable, each of such increases of benefit shall be treated as a separate dependency benefit.

Provisions for adjusting benefit, etc., for part of a week

12.—(1) Where, in accordance with the provisions of these regulations, any benefit under the Act is required to be adjusted for a part only of a week, then, for the purposes of making that adjustment and of determining the amount of that benefit which is payable for the part (if any) of that week for which it is not so required to be adjusted, the amount of the appropriate weekly rate of that benefit and of every benefit by reference to which it is so required to be adjusted (including for this purpose, but for no other purpose, any allowance under the Family Allowances Act 1965 required to be taken into account for the purposes of regulation 5(3) of these regulations) shall, if it is not payable for that week at a daily rate equal to one-sixth of the appropriate weekly rate, for each day of the week excluding Sunday, be deemed to be so payable:

Provided that, if the benefit or one of the benefits so required to be adjusted is unemployment benefit, sickness benefit or invalidity benefit which is, or but for the provisions of these regulations would be, payable to a person in whose case the day to be disregarded in accordance with regulations made under section 20(1)(e) of the Act (Sunday or some other prescribed day to be disregarded for the purpose of unemployment, sickness and invalidity benefit) is a day other than Sunday, the first reference in this paragraph to Sunday shall be construed as a reference to that other day.

(2) In the last preceding paragraph, the expression "appropriate weekly rate" means, in relation to any benefit, the weekly rate at which it would be payable but for the provisions of these regulations.

(3) In this regulation, the expression "benefit" (except in the expressions "unemployment benefit", "sickness benefit" and "invalidity benefit") includes any pension or allowance (whether under the Act or otherwise).

Persons to be treated as entitled to benefit for certain purposes

13. Any person who would be entitled to any benefit under the Act but for these regulations shall be treated as if he were entitled thereto for the purpose of any rights or obligations under the Act and the regulations made thereunder (whether of himself or some other person) which depend on his being so entitled, other than for the purposes of the right to payment of that benefit.

Widow's allowance to be treated as payable for the purposes of widow's supplementary allowance

14. A widow to whom widow's allowance under section 26 of the Act would be payable but for these regulations shall be treated for the purposes of any right to widow's supplementary allowance under section 4(1) of the Act of 1966, but for those purposes only, as if the allowance under the said section 26 was payable.

Revocations and transitional provisions

15.—(1) The regulations specified in column 1 of Schedule 2 to these regulations are hereby revoked to the extent mentioned in column 3 of that Schedule.

(2) Anything whatsoever done under or by virtue of any regulation revoked by these regulations shall be deemed to have been done under or by virtue of the corresponding provision of these regulations, and anything whatsoever begun under any such regulation may be continued under these regulations as if begun under these regulations.

(3) Nothing in paragraphs (1)-(3) of this regulation shall be taken as affecting the general application by regulation 1(7) of these regulations of the rules for the construction of Acts of Parliament contained in section 38 of the Interpretation Act 1889 (effect of repeal) with regard to the effect of revocations.

Given under the official seal of the National Insurance Joint Authority.

(L.S.)   *F. B. Hindmarsh,*
                                 A person authorised by the National
                                 Insurance Joint Authority to act on
                                           behalf of the Secretary,
                                 National Insurance Joint Authority.

11th April 1972.

                                             V. H. Goodhew,
                                              Tim Fortescue,
                                 Two of the Lords Commissioners of
                                           Her Majesty's Treasury.

14th April 1972.

Regulation 3   SCHEDULE 1

Showing in Column 1, by paragraphs, personal benefits under the Act which are not required to be adjusted by reference to any personal benefit shown in the corresponding paragraph of Column 2.

Column 1	Column 2
(1) Widow's basic pension payable to a widow by virtue of the insurance of her deceased husband who died before 5th July 1951.	(1) Invalidity allowance or any increase of unemployability supplement payable by virtue of section 13A of the Industrial Injuries Act.
(2) Invalidity allowance.	(2) Widow's basic pension payable under the Act to a widow by virtue of the insurance of her deceased husband who died before 5th July 1951.
(3) Maternity benefit.	(3) A supplement on account of unemployability payable under the Industrial Injuries Act, any Personal Injuries Scheme, any Service Pensions Instrument or any 1914-1918 War Injuries Scheme, or any Pneumoconiosis and Byssinosis Benefit Scheme.
(4) Unemployment benefit, sickness benefit, invalidity benefit, maternity benefit, or retirement pension— (*a*) in so far as it consists of graduated retirement benefit, or (*b*) in so far as it does not consist of graduated retirement benefit or of an increase under section 34 of the Act if the pension, or that part of it which does not so consist, is not payable wholly or in part by virtue of a husband's contributions or insurance, or (*c*) in so far as it does not consist of a retirement pension payable by virtue of section 1(1) of the National Insurance (Old persons' and widows' pensions and attendance allowance) Act 1970(a) or of section 5(1) of the National Insurance Act 1971(b).	(4) Death benefit by way of pension or allowance payable to a woman as the widow of the deceased under the Industrial Injuries Act, any Personal Injuries Scheme, any Service Pensions Instrument or any 1914-1918 War Injuries Scheme.

(a) 1970 c. 51.   (b) 1971 c. 50.

Column 1	Column 2
(5) Any personal benefit.	(5) Death benefit by way of pension or allowance payable to a person otherwise than as the widow of the deceased under the Industrial Injuries Act, any Personal Injuries Scheme, any Service Pensions Instrument or any 1914-1918 War Injuries Scheme.
(6) Widow's allowance.	(6) Training allowance payable under any training scheme.
(7) Unemployment benefit or sickness benefit in so far as it consists of earnings-related supplement under section 2 of the Act of 1966 (including such supplement when paid with injury benefit under the Industrial Injuries Act pursuant to section 2(7) of the said Act of 1966) and widow's allowance in so far as it consists of widow's supplementary allowance under section 4(1) of that Act.	(7) Injury benefit payable under the Industrial Injuries Act or a supplement on account of unemployability payable under that Act, any Personal Injuries Scheme, any Service Pensions Instrument, any 1914-1918 War Injuries Scheme, or any Pneumoconiosis and Byssinosis Benefit Scheme.
(8) Unemployment benefit or sickness benefit in so far as it consists of earnings-related supplement under section 2 of the Act of 1966 (including such supplement when paid with injury benefit under the Industrial Injuries Act pursuant to section 2(7) of the said Act of 1966).	(8) Widow's benefit payable under the Act.
(9) Widow's benefit payable under the Act.	(9) Unemployment benefit or sickness benefit in so far as it consists of earnings-related supplement under section 2 of the Act of 1966 (including such supplement when paid with injury benefit under the Industrial Injuries Act pursuant to section 2(7) of the said Act of 1966).
(10) Widow's allowance in so far as it consists of widow's supplementary allowance under section 4(1) of the Act of 1966.	(10) Unemployment benefit, sickness benefit, invalidity benefit or maternity allowance payable under the Act, and death benefit by way of pension or allowance payable to a woman as the widow of the deceased under the Industrial Injuries Act.
(11) Unemployment benefit, sickness benefit, invalidity benefit or maternity allowance payable under the Act.	(11) Widow's allowance in so far as it consists of widow's supplementary allowance under section 4(1) of the Act of 1966.
(12) Invalidity pension to which section 3(4) of the National Insurance Act 1971 does not apply.	(12) Invalidity allowance.
(13) Invalidity allowance.	(13) Invalidity pension to which section 3(4) of the National Insurance Act 1971 does not apply.
(14) Any personal benefit under the Act other than invalidity allowance.	(14) Any allowance to which regulation 2(5)(d) of these regulations refers.

Regulation 15

SCHEDULE 2

REGULATIONS REVOKED

Citation (1)	Statutory Instrument (2)	Extent of Revocation (3)
The National Insurance (Overlapping Benefits) Regulations 1948	S.I. 1948/2711 (Rev. XVI, p. 196; 1948 I, p. 2657)	The whole Regulations
The National Insurance (Increase of Benefit, Re-entry into Regular Employment and Miscellaneous Provisions) Regulations 1951	S.I. 1951/1232 (1951 I, p. 1457)	Regulation 21
The National Insurance (Overlapping Benefits) Amendment Regulations 1952	S.I. 1952/422 (1952 II, p. 2194)	The whole Regulations
The National Insurance (Overlapping Benefits) Amendment (No. 2) Regulations 1952	S.I. 1952/526 (1952 II, p. 2196)	The whole Regulations
The National Insurance (Overlapping Benefits) Amendment Regulations 1953	S.I. 1953/756 (1953 I, p. 1367)	The whole Regulations
The National Insurance (Maternity Benefit and Miscellaneous Provisions) Regulations 1954	S.I. 1954/189 (1954 I, p. 1387)	The provision in the second Schedule relating to the National Insurance (Overlapping Benefits) Regulations 1948
The National Insurance (Child's Special Allowance) Regulations 1957	S.I. 1957/1835 (1957 I, p. 1523)	The provision in the Schedule relating to the National Insurance (Overlapping Benefits) Regulations 1948
The National Insurance (Overlapping Benefits) Amendment Regulations 1957	S.I. 1957/1889 (1957 I, p. 1603)	The whole Regulations
The National Insurance (Increase of Benefit and Miscellaneous Provisions) Regulations 1957	S.I. 1957/2077 (1957 I, p. 1556)	Regulation 24
The National Insurance (Overlapping Benefits) Amendment Regulations 1959	S.I. 1959/1290 (1959 II, p. 1875)	The whole Regulations
The National Insurance (Graduated Retirement Benefit and Consequential Provisions) Regulations 1961	S.I. 1961/557 (1961 I, p. 1228)	Part IV of the Second Schedule
The National Insurance (Consequential Provisions) Regulations 1962	S.I. 1962/12 (1962 I, p. 10)	Regulation 7 and Fifth Schedule
The National Insurance (Widow's Benefit and Miscellaneous Provisions) Regulations 1964	S.I. 1964/297 (1964 I, p. 508)	The provision in Schedule D relating to the National Insurance (Overlapping Benefits) Regulations 1948

Citation (1)	Statutory Instrument (2)	Extent of Revocation (3)
The National Insurance (Overlapping Benefits and Hospital In-Patients) Amendment Regulations 1966	S.I. 1966/970 (1966 II, p. 2340)	The whole Regulations except Regulation 3
The National Insurance (Overlapping Benefits) Amendment Regulations 1967	S.I. 1967/562 (1967 I, p. 1776)	The whole Regulations
The Family Allowances, National Insurance, Industrial Injuries and Miscellaneous Provisions (Decimalisation of the Currency) Regulations 1970	S.I. 1970/46 (1970 I, p. 243)	Regulation 9
The National Insurance (Widows' Pensions and Miscellaneous Provisions) Regulations 1970	S.I. 1970/1580 (1970 III, p. 5325)	Regulation 11
The National Insurance (Attendance Allowance) Regulations 1971	S.I. 1971/621 (1971 I, p. 1623)	Regulation 22
The National Insurance (Miscellaneous Amendments) Regulations 1971	S.I. 1971/1419 (1971 II, p. 3964)	Regulation 7
The National Insurance (Miscellaneous Amendments) (No. 2) Regulations 1971	S.I. 1971/1633 (1971 III, p.4496)	Regulation 2
The National Insurance (General Benefit and Miscellaneous Amendments) Regulations 1972	S.I. 1972/394 (1972 I, p. 1483)	Regulation 3

EXPLANATORY NOTE
(*This Note is not part of the Regulations.*)

These Regulations consolidate the National Insurance (Overlapping Benefits) Regulations 1948 and subsequent amending Regulations. They are made for the purpose only of consolidating Regulations hereby revoked and accordingly, by virtue of section 108(9)(*c*) of the National Insurance Act 1965, have not been referred to the National Insurance Advisory Committee.

Part I of the Regulations contains various definitions; Part II of, and Schedule 1 to, the Regulations contain provisions relating to the adjustment of benefit payable under the National Insurance Act 1965 for periods in respect of which certain pensions or allowances (including any other benefit under the 1965 Act) are payable out of public funds; and Part III of, and Schedule 2 to, the Regulations contain miscellaneous provisions including the revocation and transitional provisions.

STATUTORY INSTRUMENTS

1972 No. 605

SOCIAL SECURITY

The National Insurance (Industrial Injuries) (Hospital In-Patients) Amendment Regulations 1972

Made - - -		*17th April* 1972
Laid before Parliament		*25th April* 1972
Coming into Operation		*15th May* 1972

The Industrial Injuries Joint Authority, in exercise of powers conferred by section 33(2)(*a*) of the National Insurance (Industrial Injuries) Act 1965(**a**) and the Secretary of State for Social Services, in exercise of his powers under section 30A of that Act (added by section 10(1) of the National Insurance Act 1971(**b**)) and of all other powers enabling them in that behalf and after reference to the Industrial Injuries Advisory Council hereby make the following regulations: —

Citation, commencement and interpretation

1. These regulations, which may be cited as the National Insurance (Industrial Injuries) (Hospital In-Patients) Amendment Regulations 1972, shall be read as one with the National Insurance (Industrial Injuries) (Hospital In-Patients) Regulations 1971(**c**) (hereinafter referred to as "the principal regulations") and shall come into operation on 15th May 1972.

Amendment of regulation 1 of the principal regulations

2.—(1) In regulation 1(2) of the principal regulations for the words " "the In-Patients Regulations" means the National Insurance (Hospital In-Patients) Regulations 1949 as amended" there shall be substituted the words " "the In-Patients Regulations" means the National Insurance (Hospital In-Patients) Regulations 1972;"(**d**).

(2) In regulation 1(3) of the principal regulations for the words "regulation 1(2A)" there shall be substituted the words "regulation 1(3)".

Amendment of regulation 3 of the principal regulations

3.—(1) In regulation 3(2) of the principal regulations for the words "National Insurance (Overlapping Benefits) Regulations 1948" there shall be substituted the words "National Insurance (Overlapping Benefits) Regulations 1972".

(**a**) 1965 c. 52.
(**c**) S.I. 1971/1440 (1971 III, p. 4052).
(**b**) 1971 c. 50.
(**d**) S.I. 1972/603 (1972 I, p. 1979).

(2) For footnote (**b**) on page 2 of the principal regulations there shall be substituted the following footnote "(**b**) S.I. 1972/604".

(3) In regulation 3(2)(*b*) of the principal regulations for the words "regulation 3(4)" there shall be substituted the words "regulation 3(3)".

Amendment of regulation 4 of the principal regulations

4. In regulation 4 of the principal regulations for the words "regulation 6" there shall be substituted the words "regulation 7", for the words "regulation 6(7)(*b*)" there shall be substituted the words "regulation 7(7)(*b*)" and for the words "the said regulations of 1948" there shall be substituted the words "'the said regulations of 1972".

Amendment of regulation 5 of the principal regulations

5.—(1) In regulation 5(1) of the principal regulations for the words "regulation 6A" wherever they appear there shall be substituted the words "regulation 8", for the words "regulation 6C" wherever they appear there shall be substituted the words "regulation 10", for the words "regulation 8" wherever they appear there shall be substituted the words "regulation 11" and for the words "regulation 9" wherever they appear there shall be substituted the words "regulation 12".

(2) In regulation 5(2) of the principal regulations for the words "regulation 6B" there shall be substituted the words "regulation 9" and for the words "regulation 12" there shall be substituted the words "regulation 13".

(3) In regulation 5(3) of the principal regulations for the words "regulation 8" there shall be substituted the words "regulation 11".

(4) In regulation 5(3)(i) of the principal regulations for the words "National Insurance (Overlapping Benefits) Regulations 1948" there shall be substituted the words "National Insurance (Overlapping Benefits) Regulations 1972".

(5) In regulation 5(3)(ii) of the principal regulations for the words "regulation 8" there shall be substituted the words "regulation 11" and for the words "regulation 6" there shall be substituted the words "regulation 7".

Amendment of regulation 6 of the principal regulations

6. In regulation 6 of the principal regulations for the words "regulation 6(7)" there shall be substituted the words "regulation 7(7)".

Given under the official seal of the Industrial Injuries Joint Authority.

(L.S.)   *N. Hanson,*
                                         Secretary,
                          Industrial Injuries Joint Authority.

17th April 1972.

Signed by authority of the Secretary of State for Social Services.

Paul Dean,
Parliamentary Under-Secretary of State,
Department of Health and Social Security.

17th April 1972.

EXPLANATORY NOTE

(This Note is not part of the Regulations.)

These Regulations are made for the purpose of amending the references in the National Insurance (Industrial Injuries) (Hospital In-Patients) Regulations 1971 to the provisions of the National Insurance (Hospital In-Patients) Regulations consequent upon their consolidation in the National Insurance (Hospital In-Patients) Regulations 1972 and relate principally to the numbering of the regulations.

STATUTORY INSTRUMENTS

1972 No. 606

SOCIAL SECURITY

The National Insurance (Widow's Benefit and Retirement Pensions) Regulations 1972

Made - - - -	*14th April* 1972
Laid before Parliament	*25th April* 1972
Coming into Operation	*15th May* 1972

The National Insurance Joint Authority, in conjunction with the Treasury so far as relates to matters with regard to which the Treasury have so directed, in exercise of powers conferred by sections 33(1), 34(3), 41(4) (as amended by section 1(4)(*a*) of, and Part II of Schedule 1 to, the Family Allowances and National Insurance Act 1967**(a)** and by regulation 10 of the National Insurance (Old Persons' Pensions) Regulations 1970**(b)**) and 45 of, and paragraph 4 (as substituted by regulation 2(4) of the National Insurance (Widows' Pensions and Miscellaneous Provisions) Regulations 1970**(c)**) of Schedule 11 to, the National Insurance Act 1965**(d)**, and the Secretary of State for Social Services in exercise of his powers under sections 31(2), 35 and 75(2) of the said Act of 1965, in each case in exercise of all other powers enabling them in that behalf, and for the purpose only of consolidating the regulations hereby revoked, hereby make the following regulations:—

PART I

General

Citation, commencement and interpretation

1.—(1) These regulations may be cited as the National Insurance (Widow's Benefit and Retirement Pensions) Regulations 1972 and shall come into operation on 15th May 1972.

(2) In these regulations, unless the context otherwise requires—

"the Act" means the National Insurance Act 1965;

"contributions" has the same meaning as in the Act save that it does not include graduated contributions under the Act;

"determining authority" means, as the case may require, an insurance officer appointed under section 68(1) of the Act, or a local tribunal constituted under section 77 of the Act, or the Commissioner;

(**a**) 1967 c. 90. (**b**) S.I. 1970/1280 (1970 II, p. 4168).
(**c**) S.I. 1970/1580 (1970 III, p. 5325). (**d**) 1965 c. 51.

"the Commissioner" means the Chief National Insurance Commissioner appointed under section 9 of the National Insurance Act 1966**(a)** and any other National Insurance Commissioner so appointed, or any Tribunal constituted under subsection (3) of that section;

"the Existing Beneficiaries Regulations" means the National Insurance (Pensions, Existing Beneficiaries and Other Persons) (Transitional) Regulations 1948**(b)**, as amended **(c)**;

"the Existing Contributors Regulations" means the National Insurance (Pensions, Existing Contributors) (Transitional) Regulations 1948**(d)**, as amended**(e)**;

"the New Entrants Regulations" means the National Insurance (New Entrants Transitional) Regulations 1949**(f)**, as amended**(g)**;

and other expressions have the same meanings as in the Act.

(3) References in these regulations to any enactment or regulation shall, except in so far as the context otherwise requires, be construed as references to such enactment or regulation as amended or extended by any subsequent enactment, order or regulation and as including references to any enactment or regulation thereby consolidated.

(4) The rules for the construction of Acts of Parliament contained in the Interpretation Act 1889**(h)** shall apply in relation to this instrument (including any instrument read as one therewith) and in relation to any revocation affected by it as if this instrument, the regulations revoked by it and any regulations revoked by the regulations so revoked were Acts of Parliament, and as if each revocation were a repeal.

PART II

Miscellaneous provisions

Contributions to be disregarded in computing increase of retirement pension

2.—(1) Subject to the provisions of paragraph (2) of this regulation, a contribution paid by a woman over pensionable age in respect of any contribution week for the whole of which—

(*a*) she is entitled to and obtains payment of widow's benefit or a retirement pension by virtue of her husband's insurance; or

(*b*) her husband is entitled, in respect of her, to and obtains payment of, an increase of the weekly rate of retirement pension;

shall be disregarded for the purposes of sections 31(1) and 34(2) of, and paragraph 8(2) of Schedule 11 to, the Act.

(2) This regulation shall not apply—

(*a*) to a woman who became entitled to a retirement pension by virtue of her husband's insurance before 5th August 1957; or

(*b*) in respect of a contribution week for which a woman obtains payment only of—

(**a**) 1966 c. 6.
(**b**) S.I. 1948/55 (Rev. XVI, p. 36: 1948 I, p. 2822).
(**c**) The amending regulations are not relevant to the subject-matter of these regulations.
(**d**) S.I. 1948/612 (Rev. XVI, p. 18: 1948 I, p. 2834).
(**e**) The relevant amending instrument is S.I. 1957/1332 (1957 I, p. 1706).
(**f**) S.I. 1949/352 (1949 I, p. 2737).
(**g**) The relevant amending instrument is S.I. 1957/2147 (1957 I, p. 1694).
(**h**) 1889 c. 63.

(i) a widowed mother's allowance (apart from any increase thereof) at a rate per week not exceeding 30 per cent. of the amount specified in paragraph 8 of Part I of Schedule 3 to the Act; or

(ii) a contributory old age pension.

Special conditions in relation to retirement pensions by virtue of the husband's insurance in the case of women marrying after pensionable age

3. Subject to the provisions of regulation 14 of these regulations, in the application of section 34(1) of, and of paragraph 8(2) of Schedule 11 to, the Act (increase in rate of retirement pension for contributions paid after pensionable age) to a retirement pension payable to a woman by virtue of the insurance of a husband whom she married after attaining pensionable age, contributions paid by the husband for any contribution weeks terminating before the date of the marriage, and contributions paid by him for any contribution weeks terminating both before 5th April 1971 and also before the earliest date on which she would have been entitled to a retirement pension, if she and the husband had both then retired from regular employment, shall not be taken into account except for the purposes of section 34(1)(*b*) of the Act.

Special provisions applying to women who remarry when over pensionable age

4. Where a man dies leaving a widow who remarries after attaining pensionable age, the following provisions shall apply:—

(1) Section 34(1) of, and paragraph 8(2) of Schedule 11 to, the Act (increase in rate of retirement pension for contributions paid after pensionable age) shall apply in relation to her as if she had remained his widow throughout any period after her remarriage for which she is entitled to a retirement pension by virtue of his insurance.

(2) Subject to the provisions of the next following paragraph, paragraph (*b*) of the said section 34(1) shall apply in relation to her as if, throughout any period during the subsistence of that remarriage for which she is entitled to a retirement pension by virtue of her insurance, she had remained the widow of the man whose widow she would have remained but for that remarriage.

(3) If, having remarried after attaining pensionable age, she becomes a widow for a second or subsequent time, the said paragraph (*b*) shall, if she so elects, apply in relation to her as if throughout any period during which she is a widow and is entitled to a retirement pension by virtue of her insurance she were not the widow of her last husband but had remained the widow of any man whose widow she would have remained but for any remarriage after she had attained pensionable age; and, if she has so elected, the said paragraph (*b*) shall continue to apply to her as if she had remained the widow of that man throughout any period, occurring during the subsistence of any remarriage next following the period of her last widowhood, for which she is so entitled to a retirement pension.

Choice of retirement pension by woman

5. A woman who, but for the provisions of section 33(1) of the Act (disentitlement of women to more than one retirement pension for the same period), would be entitled for the same period to more than one retirement pension may, by notice in writing to the Secretary of State, choose from time to time which pension she shall be entitled to for any week commencing after the date on which such notice is so given:

Provided that for any period in respect of which no such notice is given the woman shall be treated as if she had chosen the pension which, excluding any increase for a child, is payable at the higher or highest rate.

Priority between a man and his wife to increase of retirement pension for a child

6.—(1) Where, but for section 41(4)(*b*) of the Act (which prevents a man and his wife both being entitled for the same period to an increase of retirement pension in respect of a child), a man and his wife would, for the same period, both be entitled to an increase under section 40(1) of the Act in respect of the same child or, in respect of different children, to such an increase at the rate applicable to an only, elder or eldest child, or to such an increase at the rate applicable to a second child, the following provisions shall apply:—

(*a*) if and so long as the man and his wife are living together, the man shall, and his wife shall not, be entitled to the increase, or, as the case may be, to the increase at the rate applicable to an only, elder or eldest child or the increase at the rate applicable to a second child;

(*b*) if and so long as they are not living together such one of them shall, and such other of them shall not, be entitled to the increase or, as the case may be, to the increase at the rate applicable to an only, elder or eldest child or the increase at the rate applicable to a second child, as the Secretary of State may in his discretion from time to time determine.

(2) For the purpose of this regulation, a man and his wife shall not be deemed to be living otherwise than together unless they are permanently living in separation either by agreement or under an order of the Court, or one of them has deserted the other and the separation which is incident to the desertion has not come to an end.

Partial satisfaction of contribution conditions and reduced rates of benefit

7.—(1) Where a person would be entitled to widow's benefit or retirement pension but for the fact that the relevant contribution conditions are not satisfied as respects the yearly average of contributions paid or credited, that person shall nevertheless be entitled to benefit in accordance with paragraph (2) or paragraph (3) of this regulation if the yearly average of contributions paid or credited is not less than thirteen.

(2) Where the full weekly rate of widow's benefit (in a case to which paragraph (3) of this regulation does not apply) or retirement pension or increase of retirement pension for an adult dependant under Schedule 3 to the Act (rates of periodical benefits and increases for dependants) is at one of the rates set out at the head of columns (2), (3) and (4) of Schedule 1 to these regulations, then the benefit or pension or increase shall be payable at the reduced rate specified in the appropriate column of the said Schedule 1 which corresponds with the yearly average of contributions paid or credited as shown in column (1) of that Schedule.

(3) In any case in which paragraph (1) of this regulation applies to the widow's pension of such a widow as is mentioned in section 28(3A) of the Act, the pension shall be payable, subject to the provisions of the following paragraph and of regulation 2(1) of the Family Allowances, National Insurance, Industrial Injuries and Miscellaneous Provisions (Decimalisation of the Currency) Regulations 1970**(a)**, as amended**(b)**, at the rate specified in column (3) of Schedule 1

(a) S.I. 1970/46 (1970 I, p. 243).
(b) The amending regulations are not relevant to the subject-matter of these regulations.

to these regulations which corresponds with the yearly average of contributions paid or credited as shown in column (1) of that Schedule subject to a further reduction in accordance with the provisions of the said section 28(3A).

(4) In the case of a woman to whom the foregoing paragraph applies and who would have been entitled to a widow's basic pension or contributory old age pension (these expressions having the same respective meanings in this paragraph as in the Existing Beneficiaries Regulations) had she not become entitled to a widow's pension or a retirement pension payable at a reduced rate by virtue either of section 28(3A) or of the combined effect of sections 28(3A) and 32(3A) of the Act, the weekly rate of the widow's pension or retirement pension (as the case may be) shall be the rate ascertained in accordance with the foregoing paragraph, or the rate of the widow's basic pension or contributory old age pension (as the case may be) to which she would have been entitled, whichever is the greater.

PART III

Provisions relating to re-entry into regular employment after retirement

Election to re-enter employment

8.—(1) Subject to the provisions of this Part of these regulations, in the case of a person of any description specified in the next following paragraph who—

(*a*) has retired for the purposes of the Act from regular employment or has otherwise become entitled to a retirement pension but is, in the case of a woman, under the age of 65 or, in the case of a man, under the age of 70; and

(*b*) elects in the manner and in accordance with the conditions contained in this Part that this Part shall apply in his case;

the Act shall have effect as if that person had not retired or become entitled as aforesaid.

(2) The persons who may so elect are persons of any description who are entitled to retirement pensions, not being—

(*a*) married women who are entitled to retirement pensions by virtue of their husbands' insurance for any period which includes the date upon which their election would take effect in accordance with paragraph (4) of this regulation;

(*b*) persons who are not ordinarily resident in Great Britain; and

(*c*) persons (other than widows who are entitled to retirement pensions by virtue of their husbands' insurance) to whom there apply the provisions either of regulation 4(1)(*a*) of the New Entrants Regulations or regulation 10(1)(*a*) of the Existing Contributors Regulations (retirement pensions of, respectively, certain new entrants and certain existing contributors who entered into insurance while less than ten years under pensionable age):

Provided that, where a husband and wife have both become entitled to retirement pensions by virtue of the husband's insurance, the husband shall not be entitled to elect as aforesaid without the consent of the wife, unless that consent is unreasonably withheld.

(3) Notice of election for the purpose of this Part of these regulations shall be given to the Secretary of State in writing on the form approved by the Secretary of State for the purpose, or in such other manner, being in writing, as the Secretary of State may accept as sufficient in the circumstances of any particular case or class of cases.

(4) Notice under the last foregoing paragraph shall take effect—

(*a*) where the notice does not specify a date as the date of the person's election, on the date on which the notice is given; and

(*b*) where the notice specifies a date, being a date not earlier than the date on which the notice is given and not later than the expiration of 28 days after that date as the date of the person's election, on the date so specified:

Provided that in the case of a man whose wife is entitled to a retirement pension by virtue of his insurance—

(i) if she consents in writing to the election, notice shall not take effect earlier than the date of her consent; and

(ii) if she does not so consent, notice shall not take effect unless the determining authority decides that her consent has been unreasonably withheld, and in that event shall take effect in accordance with the provisions of this paragraph, unless that authority, having regard to all the circumstances of the case, determines that it shall take effect on some later date.

(5) Any such notice, if sent by post, shall be deemed to be given on the date on which it was posted.

Conditions of election

9. The following conditions shall apply to a person making an election for the purpose of the foregoing regulation:—

(*a*) Subject to the provisions of paragraphs (5) and (6) of regulation 10 of the National Insurance (Claims and Payments) Regulations 1971(**a**) (which relate to the adjustment of the commencement and termination of benefit), no retirement pension shall be payable to him, or by virtue of his insurance to his wife, in respect of any period on or after the date of his election and before he subsequently retires for the purposes of the Act from regular employment or dies.

(*b*) If after making his election he subsequently so retires, he shall not thereafter be entitled to make another such election.

(*c*) Where the person is a woman who was entitled to a retirement pension otherwise than by virtue of having retired from regular employment, she shall for the purposes of this Part of these regulations, if she subsequently so retires, cease to be treated as if she had not become entitled to a retirement pension.

(*d*) Where the person is a man whose wife is entitled to a retirement pension by virtue of his insurance and he subsequently retires for the purposes of the Act from regular employment and claims a retirement pension, his claim may be treated as including a claim by the wife for a retirement pension by virtue of his insurance.

(**a**) S.I. 1971/707 (1971 I, p. 1908).

(e) Where the person is a widow to whom there applied the provisions either of sub-paragraph (a) of regulation 4(1) of the New Entrants Regulations or of sub-paragraph (a) of regulation 10(1) of the Existing Contributors Regulations, but who was entitled to a retirement pension by virtue of her husband's insurance, then, notwithstanding in the former case the provisions of paragraph 19(e) of Schedule 11 to the Act (transitional provisions relating to certain women who attained age 50 before 5th July 1948)—

(i) in determining for the purpose of paragraph (a) of this regulation whether she has or has not subsequently retired for the purposes of the Act from regular employment, no account shall be taken of the provisions of sub-paragraph (a) of the said regulations 4(1) and 10(1);

(ii) sub-paragraph (b) and head (iii) of sub-paragraph (c) of the said regulations 4(1) and 10(1) shall not apply as respects any period on or after the date of her election and before she so subsequently retires for the purposes of the Act from regular employment, but as respects any such period she shall, unless she has made an election to such as is referred to in the said sub-paragraph (c), be entitled to pay a contribution as a non-employed person, at the same rate as a woman under the age of 60, for any week for which she is not liable to pay a contribution as an employed or self-employed person.

Special provisions applying after election

10.—(1) In the application of sections 31(1) and 34(1) of, and of paragraph 8(2) of Schedule 11 to, the Act (increases in retirement pensions based on contributions paid as an employed or self-employed person after attaining pensionable age) in relation to contributions paid by a person who has made an election under regulation 8 of these regulations, contributions as an employed or self-employed person paid in respect of any period occurring after pensionable age and before as well as after his first retirement shall be taken into account.

(2) Any woman who makes an election under regulation 8 of these regulations and is not then an insured person shall be treated, for the purpose of her liability to pay contributions as from the date of such election, as if she were an insured person.

(3) In the case of a woman to whom paragraph (e) of regulation 9 of these regulations applies, contributions as an employed or self-employed person paid by virtue of the said paragraph (e) shall not entitle her to any increase in the rate of her retirement pension by virtue of her own insurance under section 31(1) of the Act.

Unemployment, sickness and invalidity benefit in certain cases after election

11.—(1) For the purpose of section 19(3) of the Act (unemployment and sickness benefit for persons over pensionable age), a woman who is entitled to a retirement pension by virtue of her husband's insurance and makes an election under regulation 8 of these regulations shall, if she is unable to satisfy the condition contained in section 19(3)(b) of the Act that on the day for which benefit is claimed she would be entitled to a retirement pension had she retired from regular employment on attaining pensionable age and made the necessary claim, be deemed nevertheless to satisfy that condition.

(2) Where the foregoing paragraph applies to a woman, the references in section 19(3) of the Act to retirement pension shall be construed as referring to the retirement pension to which she was entitled when she made the election.

(3) If a woman who makes an election under regulation 8 of these regulations would, but for the provisions of section 33(1) of the Act (no entitlement to more than one retirement pension in respect of the same period), be entitled for any period which includes the date upon which her election takes effect to retirement pensions by virtue both of her own and her husband's insurance, the references in section 19(3) of the Act to retirement pension shall be construed as referring to the greater of the retirement pensions she would, but for the said provisions, have been entitled when she made the election.

(4) This regulation shall apply for the purposes of the provisions of section 3 of the National Insurance Act 1971(a) (invalidity benefit for chronic sick) in relation to invalidity pension as it applies for the purposes of the said section 19 in relation to sickness benefit.

(5) In this regulation, references to retirement pensions by virtue of a husband's insurance shall not be construed as including references to a retirement pension payable by virtue of section 32(3A) of the Act.

PART IV

Revocations and transitional provisions

Revocation of regulations and general savings

12.—(1) The regulations specified in column 1 of Schedule 2 to these regulations are hereby revoked to the extent mentioned in column 3 of that Schedule.

(2) Anything whatsoever done under or by virtue of any regulation revoked by these regulations shall be deemed to have been done under or by virtue of the corresponding provisions of these regulations, and anything whatsoever begun under any such regulation may be continued under these regulations as if begun under these regulations.

(3) Nothing in paragraph (2) of this regulation shall be taken as affecting the general application by regulation 1(4) of these regulations of the rules for the construction of Acts of Parliament contained in section 38 of the Interpretation Act 1889 (effect of repeal) with regard to the effect of revocations.

Transitional provision relating to certain widows incapable of self-support

13.—(1) Subject to the provisions of paragraph 4 of Schedule 11 to the Act, where a widow would have ceased to be entitled to widow's benefit before 7th January 1957 at a time when she was by reason of any infirmity incapable of self-support and was under pensionable age, she shall, for any subsequent period during which she is incapable of self-support by reason of that infirmity, have the same right (if any) to a widow's pension in respect of the marriage in respect of which she was entitled to the widow's benefit as if the condition in section 28(2) of the Act was satisfied, so however, that if she is under the age of 50, section 28(3A) of the Act shall not apply to that pension.

(2) The following provisions shall apply in the case of a widow who claims a widow's pension by virtue of paragraph (1) of this regulation:—

_____

(a) 1971 c. 50.

(a) the widow shall from time to time, as required by the Secretary of State, furnish evidence by means of a certificate (in such form as the Secretary of State may approve) that by reason of an infirmity she is incapable of self-support, and shall at any time, if so directed by the Secretary of State, submit herself to medical examination by a medical board appointed by him consisting of two or more medical practitioners; and

(b) for the purpose of the determination by the determining authority of any questions as to the nature of the infirmity or whether an infirmity is the same infirmity as that by reason of which the widow was previously incapable of self-support, a certificate given by any such medical board shall be conclusive evidence.

(3) The provisions of the preceding paragraph shall apply in the case of a widow who claims a widow's pension by virtue of regulation 4(2) of the Existing Beneficiaries Regulations, subject to the qualification that, where the claim is made before 5th July 1948, she may (instead of furnishing a certificate in accordance with paragraph (2)(a) of this regulation) elect to have her case submitted to a medical board appointed by the Secretary of State in accordance with the said paragraph (2)(a).

(4) In this regulation, the determining authority shall not include the Commissioner.

Transitional provision relating to retirement pensions by virtue of the husband's insurance in the case of women marrying after pensionable age

14. Any contributions already paid which would have fallen to be taken into account by virtue of paragraph (3) or paragraph (4) of regulation 4 of the National Insurance (Widow's Benefit and Retirement Pensions) Regulations 1948**(a)**, as amended **(b)**, in force immediately before 2nd November 1970 shall be taken into account for the purpose and to the extent mentioned in the said paragraph (3) or paragraph (4) notwithstanding the revocation of those paragraphs by regulation 4(3) of the National Insurance (Widows' Pensions and Miscellaneous Provisions) Regulations 1970**(c)**.

Given under the official seal of the National Insurance Joint Authority.

(L.S.)   *F. B. Hindmarsh,*
A person authorised by the National Insurance
Joint Authority to act on behalf of the Secretary,
National Insurance Joint Authority.

11th April 1972.

Signed by authority of the Secretary of State for Social Services.

Paul Dean,
Parliamentary Under-Secretary of State,
Department of Health and Social Security.

12th April 1972.

V. H. Goodhew,
Tim Fortesque,
Two of the Lords Commissioners
of Her Majesty's Treasury.

14th April 1972.

(a) S.I. 1948/1261 (Rev. XVI, p. 207: 1948 I, p. 2704).
(b) The relevant amending instrument is S.I. 1970/1580 (1970 III, p. 5325).
(c) S.I. 1970/1580 (1970 III, p. 5325).

Regulation 7(2)　　　　　　　SCHEDULE 1

Showing reduced rates of widow's benefit and retirement pension and of increase of retirement pension in respect of an adult dependant

(1)	(2)	(3)	(4)
	Full weekly rate of benefit applicable under Schedule 3 to the National Insurance Act 1965		
Yearly average of contributions paid or credited	£ 8·40	£ 6·00	£ 3·70
	Reduced rate at which benefit payable		
	£	£	£
48—49	8·05	5·76	3·57
46—47	7·70	5·52	3·44
43—45	7·30	5·28	3·27
40—42	6·78	4·48	3·04
37—39	6·16	4·39	2·81
34—36	5·52	3·94	2·50
30—33	4·86	3·47	2·19
26—29	4·20	3·00	1·85
22—25	3·56	2·56	1·55
18—21	2·92	2·09	1·27
13—17	2·24	1·68	1·07

Regulation 12(1)　　　　　　SCHEDULE 2

Regulations revoked (1)	Reference (2)	Extent of revocation (3)
The National Insurance (Widow's Benefit and Retirement Pensions) Regulations 1948	S.I. 1948/1261 (Rev. XVI, p. 207: 1948 I, p. 2704)	The whole regulations
The National Insurance (Increase of Benefit, Re-entry into Regular Employment and Miscellaneous Provisions) Regulations 1951	S.I. 1951/1232 (1951 I, p. 1457)	Regulation 8 and Schedule F; regulation 18 and Part VII of Schedule A
The National Insurance (Increase of Benefit and Miscellaneous Provisions) Regulations 1952	S.I. 1952/2144 (1952 II, p. 2154)	Regulations 4 and 9, and Schedule B
The National Insurance (Widow's Benefit and Retirement Pensions) Amendment Regulations 1953	S.I. 1953/979 (1953 I, p. 1368)	The whole regulations
The National Insurance (Increase of Benefit and Miscellaneous Provisions) Regulations 1955	S.I. 1955/493 (1955 I, p. 1586)	Regulation 5 and Schedule D; regulation 12 and Part V of Schedule A
The National Insurance (Widow's Benefit and Miscellaneous Provisions) Regulations 1956	S.I. 1956/1199 (1956 I, p. 1625)	Regulation 2, regulation 9, Schedule C and Part III of Schedule A

Regulations revoked	Reference	Extent of revocation
(1)	(2)	(3)
The National Insurance (Widow's Benefit and Retirement Pensions) Amendment Regulations 1957	S.I. 1957/1309 (1957 I, p. 1615)	The whole regulations
The National Insurance (Widow's Benefit and Retirement Pensions) Amendment (No. 2) Regulations 1957	S.I. 1957/1949 (1957 I, p. 1620)	The whole regulations
The National Insurance (Increase of Benefit and Miscellaneous Provisions) Regulations 1957	S.I. 1957/2077 (1957 I, p. 1556)	Regulation 6 and Schedule D; regulation 21 and Part XI of Schedule A
The National Insurance (Graduated Contributions and Non-participating Employments—Miscellaneous Provisions) Regulations 1960	S.I. 1960/1210 (1960 II, p. 2234)	In the Schedule, the entries relating to the National Insurance (Widow's Benefit and Retirement Pensions) Regulations 1948
The National Insurance (Increase of Benefit and Miscellaneous Provisions) Regulations 1960	S.I. 1960/2422 (1960 II, p. 2169)	Regulation 6 and Schedule D; regulation 20 and Part XI of Schedule A
The National Insurance (Consequential Provisions) Regulations 1962	S.I. 1962/12 (1962 I, p. 10)	Regulations 2, 3, 4 and 5; Schedules 1, 2 and 3
The National Insurance (Increase of Benefit and Miscellaneous Provisions) Regulations 1963	S.I. 1963/394 (1963 I, p. 424)	Regulation 6 and Schedule C; regulation 15; Part 2 of Schedule J; regulation 23
The National Insurance (Widow's Benefit and Miscellaneous Provisions) Regulations 1964	S.I. 1964/297 (1964 I, p. 508)	Regulation 2 and Schedule A
The National Insurance (Widow's Benefit and Consequential Provisions) Regulations 1964	S.I. 1964/2001 (1964 III, p. 5061)	Regulation 2
The National Insurance (Increase of Benefit and Miscellaneous Provisions) Regulations 1965	S.I. 1965/40 (1965 I, p. 47)	In Schedules A and L, the entries relating to the National Insurance (Widow's Benefit and Retirement Pensions) Regulations 1948; Schedule D
The National Insurance (Increase of Benefit and Miscellaneous Provisions) Regulations 1967	S.I. 1967/1265 (1967 II, p. 3673)	In Schedules A and L, the entries relating to the National Insurance (Widow's Benefit and Retirement Pensions) Regulations 1948; Schedule D
The Family Allowances, National Insurance and Industrial Injuries (Consequential) Regulations 1968	S.I. 1968/524 (1968 I, p. 1246)	Regulation 3

Regulations revoked (1)	Reference (2)	Extent of revocation (3)
The National Insurance (Increase of Benefit and Miscellaneous Provisions) Regulations 1969	S.I. 1969/1361 (1969 III, p. 4048)	In Schedule A, the reference to the National Insurance (Widow's Benefit and Retirement Pensions) Regulations 1948; Schedule D
The Family Allowances, National Insurance, Industrial Injuries and Miscellaneous Provisions (Decimalisation of the Currency) Regulations 1970	S.I. 1970/46 (1970 I, p. 243)	Regulation 6 and Schedule 4
The National Insurance (Widow's Pensions and Miscellaneous Provisions) Regulations 1970	S.I. 1970/1580 (1970 III, p. 5325)	Regulation 4
The National Insurance (Increase of Benefit and Miscellaneous Provisions) Regulations 1971	S.I. 1971/1220 (1971 II, p. 3556)	Schedule D
The National Insurance (Miscellaneous Amendments) Regulations 1971	S.I. 1971/1419 (1971 II, p. 3964)	Regulation 2

EXPLANATORY NOTE

(This Note is not part of the Regulations.)

These Regulations are made for the purpose only of consolidating the Regulations hereby revoked and accordingly, by virtue of section 108(9)(*c*) of the National Insurance Act 1965, no reference of them has been made to the National Insurance Advisory Committee.

These Regulations contain miscellaneous provisions affecting widow's benefit and retirement pensions under the National Insurance legislation. Part I contains various definitions. Part II contains miscellaneous provisions relating to contributions paid after pensionable age, special conditions in relation to retirement pensions by virtue of the husband's insurance in the case of women marrying after pensionable age, the choice of retirement pension by women who would be entitled to more than one retirement pension but for the provisions prohibiting double entitlement, priority as between a man and his wife to an increase of retirement pension for a child, and the payment of benefit at reduced rates in the case of deficient contribution records. Part III contains provisions as to re-entry into regular employment after retirement. Part IV contains provisions as to revocations and transitional provisions.

1972 No. 609

AGRICULTURE

The Price Stability of Imported Products (Rates of Levy) (Eggs) (No. 7) Order 1972

Made	-	-	-	*17th April* 1972
Coming into Operation			*18th April* 1972

The Minister of Agriculture, Fisheries and Food, in exercise of the powers conferred upon him by section 1(2), (4), (5), (6) and (7) of the Agriculture and Horticulture Act 1964 **(a)** and of all other powers enabling him in that behalf, hereby makes the following order:—

1. This order may be cited as the Price Stability of Imported Products (Rates of Levy) (Eggs) (No. 7) Order 1972, and shall come into operation on 18th April 1972.

2.—(1) In this order—

" the Principal Order " means the Price Stability of Imported Products (Levy Arrangements) (Eggs) Order 1970 **(b)** as amended **(c)** and as amended by any subsequent order, and if any such order is replaced by any subsequent order the expression shall be construed as a reference to such subsequent order;

AND other expressions have the same meaning as in the Principal Order.

(2) The Interpretation Act 1889 **(d)** shall apply to the interpretation of this order as it applies to the interpretation of an Act of Parliament and as if this order and the order hereby revoked were Acts of Parliament.

3. In accordance with and subject to the provisions of the Principal Order (which provides for the charging of levies on imports of those eggs and egg products which are specified commodities for the purposes of the Agriculture and Horticulture Act 1964) the rate of general levy for such imports into the United Kingdom of any specified commodity as are described in column 2 of the Schedule to this order in relation to a tariff heading indicated in column 1 of that Schedule shall be the rate set forth in relation thereto in column 3 of that Schedule.

4. The Price Stability of Imported Products (Rates of Levy) (Eggs) (No. 6) Order 1972 **(e)** is hereby revoked.

In Witness whereof the Official Seal of the Minister of Agriculture, Fisheries and Food is hereunto affixed on 17th April 1972.

(L.S.)

B. D. Hayes,
Authorised by the Minister.

(a) 1964 c. 28.　　　(b) S.I. 1970/359 (1970 I, p. 1277).
(c) S.I. 1971/947, 1642 (1971 II, p. 2709; III, p. 4505).　　(d) 1889 c. 63.
(e) S.I. 1972/399 (1972 I, p.1491).

SCHEDULE

1. Tariff Heading	2. Description of Imports	3. Rate of General Levy
	Imports of:—	
04.05	Birds' eggs (*in shell or not in shell*), *fresh, dried or otherwise preserved, sweetened or not, other than egg yolks:* A. Eggs in shell:	(per 120 eggs) *p*
	1. Not exceeding 11 lb. in weight per 120　..	35
	2. Over 11 lb. but not exceeding 12½ lb. in weight per 120　..　　..　　..　　..	35
	3. Over 12½ lb. but not exceeding 14 lb. in weight per 120　..　　..　　..　　..	40
	4. Over 14 lb. but not exceeding 15½ lb. in weight per 120　..　　..　　..　　..	45
	5. Over 15½ lb. but not exceeding 17 lb. in weight per 120　..　　..　　..　　..	50
	6. Over 17 lb. in weight per 120　..　　..	50
	B. Eggs not in shell:	(per ton)
	Whole dried　..　　..　　..　　..　　..	£200
	Whole frozen or liquid　　..　　..　　..	£140

EXPLANATORY NOTE

(*This Note is not part of the Order.*)

This order, which comes into operation on 18th April 1972, supersedes the Price Stability of Imported Products (Rates of Levy) (Eggs) (No. 6) Order 1972. It reduces the rates of general levy on imports of all weight grades of eggs in shell and on imports of dried, frozen or liquid whole egg not in shell.

STATUTORY INSTRUMENTS

1972 No. 611 (S.42)

CLEAN AIR

The Smoke Control Areas (Exempted Fireplaces) (Scotland) Order 1972

Made - - -	*15th April* 1972
Laid before Parliament	*25th April* 1972
Coming into Operation	*17th May* 1972

In exercise of the powers conferred on me by section 11(4) of the Clean Air Act 1956(**a**) and of all other powers enabling me in that behalf, and being satisfied that fireplaces of the class described can be used for burning fuel other than authorised fuels without producing a substantial quantity of smoke, I hereby make the following order:—

Citation and commencement

1. This order may be cited as the Smoke Control Areas (Exempted Fireplaces) (Scotland) Order 1972 and shall come into operation on 17th May 1972.

Interpretation

2. The Interpretation Act 1889(**b**) shall apply for the interpretation of this order as it applies for the interpretation of an Act of Parliament.

Class of fireplace exempted from section 11 *of the Clean Air Act* 1956

3. In Scotland the class of fireplace described in column (1) of the Schedule hereto shall, subject to the conditions specified in column (2), be exempted from the provisions of section 11 of the Clean Air Act 1956 (which empowers a local authority to declare the whole or any part of their district to be a smoke control area).

Gordon Campbell,
One of Her Majesty's Principal
Secretaries of State.

St. Andrew's House,
Edinburgh.

15th April 1972.

(**a**) 1956 c. 52.   (**b**) 1889 c. 63.

SCHEDULE

Article 3

Column 1	Column 2
Class of Fireplace	Conditions
The fireplace known as the Parkray Coalmaster and manufactured by Radiation Parkray Limited	The fireplace shall be installed, maintained and operated so as to minimise the emission of smoke and in accordance with the manufacturer's instructions. No fuel shall be used other than selected washed coal singles

EXPLANATORY NOTE

(This Note is not part of the Order.)

Section 11 of the Clean Air Act 1956 empowers local authorities to declare the whole or any part of their district to be a smoke control area in which the emission of smoke is, generally, prohibited. This Order exempts the Parkray Coalmaster from the provisions of that section, upon certain conditions as to proper operation.

STOKE-ON-TRENT
CITY
LIBRARIES

STATUTORY INSTRUMENTS

1972 No. 620

AGRICULTURE

The Price Stability of Imported Products (Levy Arrangements) (Eggs) (Amendment) Order 1972

Made - - -	*19th April* 1972
Laid before Parliament	*26th April* 1972
Coming into Operation	*1st May* 1972

The Minister of Agriculture, Fisheries and Food and the Secretaries of State respectively concerned with agriculture in Scotland and Northern Ireland, acting jointly in exercise of the powers conferred on them by section 1(2), (4), (6) and (7) of the Agriculture and Horticulture Act 1964(a) and of all other powers enabling them in that behalf, with the approval of the Treasury, hereby make the following order:—

1.—(1) This order may be cited as the Price Stability of Imported Products (Levy Arrangements) (Eggs) (Amendment) Order 1972, and shall come into operation on 1st May 1972.

(2) The Interpretation Act 1889(b) shall apply to the interpretation of this order as it applies to the interpretation of an Act of Parliament.

2. The Price Stability of Imported Products (Levy Arrangements) (Eggs) Order 1970(c) as amended(d) shall be further amended by inserting in paragraph 2 of Part I of the Schedule thereto immediately after the words "the Republic of South Africa" the word "or" and by deleting from that paragraph the words "or the Kingdom of the Netherlands".

In Witness whereof the Official Seal of the Minister of Agriculture, Fisheries and Food is hereunto affixed on 13th April 1972.

(L.S.)

J. M. L. Prior,
Minister of Agriculture, Fisheries and Food.

(a) 1964 c. 28.   (b) 1889 c. 63.
(c) S.I. 1970/359 (1970 I, p. 1277).   (d) S.I. 1971/947, 1642 (1971 II, p. 2709; III, p. 4505).

17th April 1972.

Gordon Campbell,
Secretary of State for Scotland.

18th April 1972.

William Whitelaw,
Secretary of State for Northern Ireland.

Approved 19th April 1972.

V. H. Goodhew,
Tim Fortescue,
Two of the Lords Commissioners of
Her Majesty's Treasury.

EXPLANATORY NOTE

(This Note is not part of the Order.)

This order further amends the Price Stability of Imported Products (Levy Arrangements) (Eggs) Order 1970 to remove the exemption from general levy of imports of liquid, frozen or dried whole egg which has been processed from shell eggs in the Netherlands and consigned to the United Kingdom from that country.

STATUTORY INSTRUMENTS

1972 No. 628

AGRICULTURE

HILL LANDS

The Hill Cattle Subsidy (Breeding Herds) (England and Wales) Payment Order 1972

Made - - -	*20th April* 1972
Laid before Parliament	*27th April* 1972
Coming into Operation	*1st June* 1972

The Minister of Agriculture, Fisheries and Food and the Secretary of State, acting jointly, in pursuance of sections 14(3) and 17 of the Hill Farming Act 1946(**a**), as amended by section 8 of the Livestock Rearing Act 1951(**b**) and as read with the Transfer of Functions (Wales) Order 1969(**c**), and of all their other enabling powers, with the approval of the Treasury, hereby make the following order: —

Citation and commencement

1. This order which may be cited as the Hill Cattle Subsidy (Breeding Herds) (England and Wales) Payment Order 1972, shall come into operation on 1st June 1972.

Interpretation

2.—(1) Unless the context otherwise requires, expressions used in this order shall have the same meanings as in the Hill Cattle (Breeding Herds) (England and Wales) Scheme 1968(**d**), as amended(**e**).

(2) The Interpretation Act 1889(**f**) applies to the interpretation of this order as it applies to the interpretation of an Act of Parliament.

(**a**) 1946 c. 73. For change of title of the Minister, see S.I. 1955/554 (1955 I, p. 1200).
(**b**) 1951 c. 18. (**c**) S.I. 1969/388 (1969 I, p. 1070).
(**d**) S.I. 1968/875 (1968 II, p. 2310). (**e**) S.I. 1971/940 (1971 II, p. 2695).
(**f**) 1889 c. 63.

Amounts of subsidy payments for 1972

3. Subject to the provisions of the Hill Cattle (Breeding Herds) (England and Wales) Scheme 1968, as amended, the amount which may be paid in respect of the year 1972 by way of subsidy payments under that scheme in respect of any animal to which it applies shall be—

(*a*) in the case of an animal comprised in a herd which is an accredited herd on the qualifying day or which subsequently becomes such a herd as a result of a final diagnostic test for brucellosis commenced on or before that day, £29·50;

(*b*) in the case of any other animal, £24·50.

Existing orders not to apply

4. The Hill Cattle Subsidy (Breeding Herds) (England and Wales) Payment Order 1970(**a**), as amended(**b**), shall cease to apply to subsidy payments in respect of the year 1972.

In Witness whereof the Official Seal of the Minister of Agriculture, Fisheries and Food is hereunto affixed on 17th April 1972.

(L.S.)

J. M. L. Prior,
Minister of Agriculture, Fisheries
and Food.

Given under my hand on 18th April 1972.

Peter Thomas,
Secretary of State for Wales.

We approve.
20th April 1972.

P. L. Hawkins,
Tim Fortescue,
Two of the Lords Commissioners
of Her Majesty's Treasury.

(**a**) S.I. 1970/878 (1970 II, p. 2807).　　(**b**) S.I. 1971/941 (1971 II, p. 2697).

EXPLANATORY NOTE

(This Note is not part of the Order.)

This order increases the amount of the hill cattle subsidy payable for the year 1972 under the provisions of the Hill Cattle (Breeding Herds) (England and Wales) Scheme 1968, as amended.

In the case of animals comprised in an accredited herd on the qualifying day in 1972, or in a herd which subsequently becomes accredited as a result of a final diagnostic test for brucellosis commenced on or before that day, the new rate will be £29·50. For other animals to which the scheme applies, the new rate will be £24·50.

STATUTORY INSTRUMENTS

1972 No. 629

AGRICULTURE

HILL LANDS

The Hill Cattle Subsidy (Breeding Herds) (Northern Ireland) Payment Order 1972

Made - - -	*19th April* 1972
Laid before Parliament	*27th April* 1972
Coming into Operation	*1st June* 1972

The Minister of Agriculture, Fisheries and Food, in pursuance of sections 14(3) and 17 of the Hill Farming Act 1946(a), as amended by section 8 of the Livestock Rearing Act 1951(b), and of all his other enabling powers, with the approval of the Treasury, hereby makes the following order: —

Citation and commencement

1. This order, which may be cited as the Hill Cattle Subsidy (Breeding Herds) (Northern Ireland) Payment Order 1972, shall come into operation on 1st June 1972.

Interpretation

2.—(1) Unless the context otherwise requires, expressions used in this order shall have the same meanings as in the Hill Cattle (Breeding Herds) (Northern Ireland) Scheme 1968(c), as amended(d).

(2) In this order, "certified herd" means a herd in respect of which the Ministry of Agriculture for Northern Ireland has issued a brucellosis certificate in accordance with the provisions of an order made under the Diseases of Animals Act (Northern Ireland) 1958(e) in connection with the eradication of that disease, being an order which provides for such certificates to be issued in respect of herds which have been officially tested by that Ministry for the presence of brucella infection, with negative results, or which have been wholly constituted by the transfer of animals from other certified herds or from similar herds in the Republic of Ireland.

(3) The Interpretation Act 1889(f) applies to the interpretation of this order as it applies to the interpretation of an Act of Parliament.

(a) 1946 c. 73. For change of title of the Minister, see S.I. 1955/554 (1955 I, p. 1200).
(b) 1951 c. 18.   (c) S.I. 1968/965 (1968 II, p. 2569).
(d) S.I. 1969/700 (1969 II, p. 1918).   (e) 1958 c. 13 (N.I.).
(f) 1889 c. 63.

Amounts of subsidy payments for 1972

3. Subject to the provisions of the Hill Cattle (Breeding Herds) (Northern Ireland) Scheme 1968, as amended, the amount which may be paid in respect of the year 1972 by way of subsidy payments under that scheme in respect of any animal to which it applies shall be—

(*a*) in the case of an animal comprised in a herd which is a certified herd on the qualifying day, or which subsequently becomes such a herd as a result of a final official test for the presence of brucella infection commenced on or before that day, £29·50;

(*b*) in the case of any other animal, £24·50.

Existing orders not to apply

4. The Hill Cattle Subsidy (Breeding Herds) (Northern Ireland) Payment Order 1970(**a**), as amended(**b**), shall cease to apply to subsidy payments in respect of the year 1972.

In Witness whereof the Official Seal of the Minister of Agriculture, Fisheries and Food is hereunto affixed on 17th April 1972.

(L.S.)

J. M. L. Prior,
Minister of Agriculture, Fisheries
and Food.

We approve,
19th April 1972.

V. H. Goodhew,
Tim Fortescue,
Two of the Lords Commissioners
of Her Majesty's Treasury.

(**a**) S.I. 1970/1445 (1970 III, p. 4705).   (**b**) S.I. 1971/944 (1971 II, p. 2703).

EXPLANATORY NOTE

(This Note is not part of the Order.)

This order increases the amount of the hill cattle subsidy payable for the year 1972 under the provisions of the Hill Cattle (Breeding Herds) (Northern Ireland) Scheme 1968, as amended.

In the case of animals comprised in a certified herd on the qualifying day in 1972, or in a herd which subsequently becomes certified as a result of a final official test for the presence of brucella infection commenced on or before that day, the new rate will be £29·50. For other animals to which the scheme applies, the new rate will be £24·50.

STATUTORY INSTRUMENTS

1972 No. 631

MINES AND QUARRIES

The Coal Mines (Mines Management) Regulations 1972

Made - - -	*20th April* 1972
Laid before Parliament	*1st May* 1972
Coming into Operation	*22nd May* 1972

Whereas in pursuance of Part I of Schedule 2 to the Mines and Quarries Act 1954(a) the Secretary of State has published notice of his intention to make the following regulations and has not received any objection to the draft thereof in respect to which he is required to refer the draft regulations for inquiry and report—

Now, therefore, the Secretary of State in exercise of his powers under section 141 of the Mines and Quarries Act 1954 and sections 1 to 3 of the Mines Management Act 1971(b) and all other powers in that behalf enabling him hereby makes the following regulations—

Citation and Commencement

1. These regulations may be cited as the Coal Mines (Mines Management) Regulations 1972 and shall come into operation on 22nd May 1972.

Interpretation

2.—(1) In these regulations—

"the 1954 Act" means the Mines and Quarries Act 1954 ;

"the 1971 Act" means the Mines Management Act 1971.

(2) The Interpretation Act 1889(c) shall apply to the interpretation of these regulations as it applies to the interpretation of an Act of Parliament.

Mines to which the 1971 Act Applies

3.—(1) Subject to the following provisions of this regulation the following classes and descriptions of mines are hereby prescribed for the purposes of sections 1 and 2 of the 1971 Act—

    (*a*) mines of coal at which the total number of persons employed exceeds seven hundred and fifty ; and

    (*b*) mines of coal where persons are employed below ground on two or more shifts in any period of twenty-four hours for the purpose of getting coal at a face.

(a) 1954 c. 70.   (b) 1971 c. 20.   (c) 1889 c. 63.

(2) The validity of an appointment made by the owner of a mine under section 1(1) of the 1971 Act or of any written instructions given under section 1(2) or for purposes of section 2 shall not be affected by reason of the fact that the total number of persons employed at the mine at any time after the making of the appointment or the giving of the instructions as the case may be falls below seven hundred and fifty-one or by reason of the fact that working below ground on two or more shifts for the purpose of getting coal at a face is occasionally or for short periods suspended.

(3) Where a manager has given a person written instructions under section 1(2) of the 1971 Act he may give him further written instructions notwithstanding that the total number of persons employed at the mine is below seven hundred and fifty-one or working below ground on two or more shifts for the purpose of getting coal at a face is suspended as aforesaid at the time of the further instructions.

(4) Where an appointment has been made by the owner of a mine under section 1(1) of the 1971 Act the owner may make a fresh appointment to replace the person previously appointed and the manager may give the person freshly appointed written instructions under section 1(2) notwithstanding that the total number of persons employed at the mine is below seven hundred and fifty-one or working below ground on two or more shifts for the purpose of getting coal at a face is suspended as aforesaid at the time of the fresh appointment or the instructions.

(5) Where a manager has given an under-manager written instructions for purposes of section 2 of the 1971 Act he may give him or any under-manager appointed by the owner to replace him or any under-manager appointed by the owner in addition to him further written instructions notwithstanding that the total number of persons employed at the mine is below seven hundred and fifty-one or working below ground on two or more shifts for the purpose of getting coal at a face is suspended as aforesaid at the time of the further instructions.

Qualifications of managers' assistants

4.—(1) No person shall be capable of being given, or having, by virtue of instructions under section 1(2) of the 1971 Act any statutory responsibilities of the manager in relation to the construction, installation, maintenance, testing, repair, adjustment, alteration, or examination of any machinery or apparatus, used as, or forming, part of the equipment of the mine, or its fitness for use for the purpose for which it is intended to be used unless he is the holder of a first-class certificate of competency valid with respect to the mine or is qualified to be the mechanical engineer or the electrical engineer for the mine.

(2) No person shall be capable of being given, or having, by virtue of instructions under section 1(2) of the 1971 Act any statutory responsibilities of the manager (other than those mentioned in paragraph (1)) in relation to any part of the mine which is within the jurisdiction of an undermanager, unless he is qualified to be the manager by virtue of section 4(1) of the 1954 Act.

(3) An inspector may by notice served on the manager of the mine exempt it from the application of any provision of this regulation.

5. No person shall, without the approval of an inspector, be capable of being given, or having, by virtue of instructions under section 1(2) of the 1971 Act any statutory responsibilities of the manager at more than one mine.

Provision of copies of instructions to managers' assistants

6. It shall be the duty of the manager of every mine, where written instructions have been given under section 1(2) of the 1971 Act, to ensure that at all times at which persons are employed at the mine there shall be provided in the covered accommodation provided in pursuance of section 135 of the 1954 Act a copy of all the said instructions which are in force ; and all persons employed at the mine shall be entitled to have access to that accommodation for the purpose of inspecting the said documents.

Tom Boardman,
Minister for Industry,
Department of Trade and Industry.

20th April 1972.

EXPLANATORY NOTE

(This Note is not part of the Regulations.)

These regulations prescribe the classes and descriptions of mines to which section 1 (appointment of and giving of statutory responsibilities to managers' assistants) and section 2 (defence for undermanagers required by written instructions from the manager to be on duty at certain times) of the Mines Management Act 1971 apply.

The regulations also provide for qualifications for managers' assistants in certain cases. The regulations further provide for provision in covered accommodation of copies of instructions to managers' assistants under section 1(2).

STOKE-ON-TRENT
CITY
LIBRARIES

STATUTORY INSTRUMENTS

1972 No. 632

TRANSPORT

PENSIONS AND COMPENSATION

The Transport Holding Company (Compensation to Employees) Regulations 1972

Made - - -	*21st April* 1972
Laid before Parliament	*25th April* 1972
Coming into Operation	*19th May* 1972

ARRANGEMENT OF REGULATIONS

PART I

PRELIMINARY

PART II

ENTITLEMENT TO COMPENSATION

PART III

RESETTLEMENT COMPENSATION

[DOE 6475]

TRANSPORT

Part IV

Long-term Compensation

12. Long-term compensation for loss of employment or loss or diminution of emoluments or worsening of position.
13. Conditions for payment of long-term compensation.
14. Factors to be considered in determining payment of long-term compensation.
15. Amount of long-term compensation payable for loss of emoluments.
16. Long-term compensation for diminution of emoluments.
17. Compensation payable to non-pensionable officer on reaching normal retiring age.
18. Date from which long-term compensation is to be payable.

Part V

Retirement Compensation and Payments on Death

19. Entitlement to retirement compensation and other payments.
20. Factors governing payment of retirement compensation.
21. Retirement compensation for loss of a pension payable to pensionable officer on attainment of normal retiring age.
22. Retirement compensation payable to pensionable officer on his becoming incapacitated or reaching minimum pensionable age.
23. Option to take retirement compensation prematurely.
24. Retirement compensation for diminution of pension rights.
25. Pension contributions.
26. Retirement compensation of a person who obtains further pensionable employment.
27. Compensation payable to widow or dependants of a claimant.
28. Compensation where death grant would have been payable.
29. Balances payable to claimant's widow or personal representatives.
30. Intervals for payment of compensation under Part V.

Part VI

Adjustment, Review and Compounding of Compensation

31. Adjustment of compensation where pension is also payable.
32. Reduction of compensation in certain cases.
33. Notification of change of circumstances.
34. Review of awards of long-term or retirement compensation.
35. Compounding of awards.

Part VII

Procedure and Miscellaneous

36. Procedure on making claims.
37. Claimants to furnish information.
38. Procedure on death of claimant.

THE SCHEDULE

Tables mentioned in regulation 2(2).

The Secretary of State for the Environment, in exercise of his powers under section 2(4) of the Transport Holding Company Act 1972(**a**) and of all other enabling powers, hereby makes the following regulations:—

PART I

PRELIMINARY

Citation and commencement

1. These regulations may be cited as the Transport Holding Company (Compensation to Employees) Regulations 1972, shall come into operation on 19th May 1972 and shall have effect from 23rd March 1972.

Interpretation

2.—(1) In these regulations, unless the context otherwise requires, the following expressions have the meanings hereby respectively assigned to them, that is to say:—

"accrued pension", in relation to a pensionable officer who has suffered loss or diminution of pension rights, means—

(*a*) if his last relevant pension scheme provided benefits in which he had a right to participate, the pension to which he would have become entitled in respect of his pensionable service according to the method of calculation, modified where necessary for the purpose of giving effect to these regulations, prescribed by that scheme if, at the date on which he suffered the said loss or diminution, he had attained normal retiring age and complied with any requirement of that scheme as to a minimum period of qualifying service or contribution and completed any additional contributory payments or payments in respect of added years which he was in the course of making; and

(*b*) in any other case, such portion of the pension (if any) of which he had reasonable expectations as the compensating authority consider equitable, having regard to his age, the length of his employment at the date of loss or diminution and all the other circumstances of the case;

"accrued retiring allowance", in relation to a pensionable officer who has suffered loss or diminution of pension rights, means—

(*a*) if his last relevant pension scheme provided benefits in which he had a right to participate, any lump sum payment to which he would have become entitled in respect of his pensionable service according

---

(**a**) 1972 c. 14.

to the method of calculation, modified where necessary for the purpose of giving effect to these regulations, prescribed by that scheme if, at the date on which he suffered the said loss or diminution, he had attained normal retiring age and complied with any requirement of that scheme as to a minimum period of qualifying service or contribution and completed any additional contributory payments or payments in respect of added years which he was in the course of making; and

(b) in any other case, such portion of the lump sum payment (if any) of which he had reasonable expectations as the compensating authority consider equitable, having regard to his age, the length of his employment at the date of loss or diminution and all the other circumstances of the case;

"accrued incapacity pension" and "accrued incapacity retiring allowance" have the same respective meanings as "accrued pension" and "accrued retiring allowance" except that the reference to a person's attaining normal retiring age shall be construed as a reference to his becoming incapable of discharging efficiently the duties of his employment by reason of permanent ill-health or infirmity of mind or body;

"the Act" means the Transport Holding Company Act 1972;

"the Act of 1962" means the Transport Act 1962(**a**);

"the Act of 1968" means the Transport Act 1968(**b**);

"Act relating to National Insurance" includes any such Act of the Parliament of Northern Ireland;

"added years" means years purchased under the provisions of the last relevant pension scheme for the purpose of being reckoned as pensionable service and includes any additional years of service which, having been granted under any enactment or scheme, have subsequently become and are so reckonable under or by virtue of rules made under section 2 of the Superannuation (Miscellaneous Provisions) Act 1948(**c**) or any other enactment;

"additional contributory payments" means—

(a) any additional contributory payments made under a pension scheme as a condition of reckoning any period of employment as service or as a period of contribution for the purposes of the scheme, or, where the scheme provides for the reckoning of non-contributing service, as contributing service for the purposes of the scheme; or

(b) any payments made for the purpose of increasing the length at which any period of service or of contribution would be reckonable for the purpose of calculating a benefit under a pension scheme; or

(c) any payments similar to any of those mentioned in the foregoing sub-paragraphs made in pursuance of rules under section 2 of the Superannuation (Miscellaneous Provisions) Act 1948;

"attributable loss", in relation to a person who suffers loss of employment, or loss or diminution of emoluments or pension rights, or worsening of his position, means any such loss, diminution or worsening as aforesaid which is properly attributable to the happening of the relevant event;

"the Commission" means the British Transport Commission dissolved under the Act of 1962;

(**a**) 1962 c. 46. (**b**) 1968 c. 73.
(**c**) 1948 c. 33.

"the compensating authority" has the meaning assigned to that expression in regulation 4;

"compensation question" means a question arising in relation to these regulations—

(a) as to a person's entitlement to compensation for loss of employment, or for loss or diminution of emoluments or pension rights, or worsening of his position; or

(b) as to the manner of a person's employment or the comparability of his duties;

"emoluments" means any of the following payments or other benefits made to or enjoyed by an officer in respect of services rendered by him as such: —

(a) all salary, wages, fees and other payments of a similar nature for his own use,

(b) all bonuses, allowances, commission, gratuities and special duty and over-time pay, which are of a recurring nature, whether seasonal or otherwise and whether obtaining by law or customary practice,

(c) the money value of all travel privileges, free accommodation, and other allowances in kind, privileges or benefits, whether obtaining by law or customary practice,

but does not include payments for travelling, subsistence, accommodation, engagement of assistance or other expenses in the course of employment or over-time or other payments of a temporary nature; and "net emoluments", in relation to any employment, means the annual rate (modified where necessary in accordance with regulation 40) of the emoluments of that employment less such part of those emoluments as the officer was liable to contribute under a pension scheme, and in relation to any employment which has been lost, the emoluments of which have been diminished or in which the officer has suffered loss or diminution of pension rights or a worsening of his position, the expression means the annual rate of emoluments aforesaid immediately before the loss, diminution or worsening, as the case may be:

Provided that where fees or other variable payments were paid to an officer as part of his emoluments during any period immediately preceding the loss, diminution or worsening the amount in respect of fees or other variable payments to be included in the annual rate of emoluments shall be the annual average of the fees or other payments paid to him during the period of 5 years immediately preceding the loss, diminution or worsening or such other period as the compensating authority may think reasonable in the circumstances;

"enactment" means any Act or instrument made under an Act;

"full-time basis", in relation to the employment of a person on such a basis, means a basis on which that person is required to devote on the average not less than 30 hours per week to that employment during which he is not at liberty to undertake other work in consideration of a fee or remuneration;

"the Holding Company" means the Transport Holding Company;

"the London Board" means the London Transport Board dissolved under the Transport (London) Act 1969(a);

(a) 1969 c. 35.

"long-term compensation" means compensation payable in accordance with the provisions of Part IV of these regulations for loss of employment or loss or diminution of emoluments or worsening of a person's position;

"the material date", in relation to any person who suffers attributable loss, means the date on which he suffers that loss or on which the relevant event happens, whichever date is the earlier;

"minimum pensionable age" means, in relation to a pensionable officer, the earliest age at which, under his last relevant pension scheme, he could have become entitled to a pension, other than a pension payable in consequence of his redundancy or his incapacity to discharge efficiently the duties of his employment by reason of permanent ill-health or infirmity of mind or body;

"national transport authority" means any one of the following:—

(a) the British Railways Board,

(b) the British Transport Docks Board,

(c) the British Waterways Board,

(d) the National Freight Corporation,

(e) the National Bus Company,

(f) the Scottish Transport Group,

(g) the Holding Company;

"national service" means service which is relevant service within the meaning of the Reserve and Auxiliary Forces (Protection of Civil Interests) Act 1951(a) and includes service immediately following such service as aforesaid, being service in any of Her Majesty's naval, military or air forces pursuant to a voluntary engagement entered into with the consent of the person or body under whom an officer held his last relevant employment;

"normal retiring age" means, in the case of a pensionable officer to whom an age of compulsory retirement applied by virtue of his last relevant pension scheme or of the conditions of the employment in which he suffered the attributable loss, that age, and in any other case, the age of 65 years if the officer is a male, or 60 years if the officer is a female;

"officer" includes the holder of any employment whether by virtue of an agreement for the rendering by him of personal services, by appointment, or otherwise but, in relation to the Commission, a national transport authority or the London Transport Executive, does not include a member or director of such body; and "office" shall be construed accordingly;

"pensionable emoluments", in relation to a person who has or had pension rights, means those emoluments which are required in accordance with the provisions of the pension scheme relating to those rights to be taken into account for the purpose of calculating the pension payable to or in respect of him under that scheme;

"pensionable officer", in relation to a person who has suffered attributable loss, means an officer who immediately before such loss had pension rights under a pension scheme;

"pension scheme", in relation to a pensionable officer, means any form of arrangement associated with his employment for the payment of pensions, whether subsisting by virtue of Act of Parliament, trust, contract or otherwise; and "last relevant pension scheme", in relation to a pensionable officer means a pension scheme under which that officer had or has pension rights which were the subject of a loss or diminution properly attributable to the happening of the relevant event;

"reckonable service", in relation to a person, means any period of employment on a full-time basis in any relevant employment and includes any period of war service or national service undertaken on his ceasing to hold any such employment but does not include employment of which account has been taken, or is required to be taken, in calculating the amount of any pension to which he has become entitled;

"relevant employment", in relation to a person who suffers attributable loss, means:—

(a) employment under the Crown, or

(b) employment in the service of the Commission, a national transport authority, the London Board, the London Transport Executive or a subsidiary of any of the foregoing bodies, or

(c) employment in the service of a body which became a subsidiary of the Commission, during any period before the body in question became such a subsidiary, or

(d) employment in the service of a body which has ceased to be a subsidiary of the Holding Company in the circumstances mentioned in section 2(4) of the Act, during any period after such cesser, or

(e) employment by a person whose undertaking or part of whose undertaking was at the date of the passing of the Act carried on by a subsidiary of the Holding Company, being employment in connection with the undertaking or part of the undertaking (as the case may be) which was carried on at that date by such subsidiary, or

(f) employment such as is mentioned in regulation 3(4) (b) or (c) of the British Transport Reorganisation (Compensation to Employees) Regulations 1962(**a**), or

(g) employment preceding any of the foregoing employments, being employment which is reckonable for the purposes of his last relevant pension scheme,

but except as provided in regulations 7(1)(c), 13(1)(c) and 19(2)(c), does not include service in the armed forces of the Crown;

"relevant event", in relation to a person who suffers attributable loss, means the cesser of a body as a subsidiary of the Holding Company in consequence of the sale or other disposal of securities by the Holding Company after the passing of the Act, being the cesser to which the loss is properly attributable;

"resettlement compensation" means compensation payable in accordance with Part III of these regulations for loss of employment;

"retirement compensation" means compensation payable in accordance with the provisions of regulation 21, 22, 23 or 24;

"subsidiary", in relation to the Commission, a national transport authority or the London Transport Executive has the same meaning as in the Act of 1962, and in this connection no account shall be taken of the provisions of section 51(5) of the Act of 1968;

"tribunal" means a tribunal established under section 12 of the Industrial Training Act 1964(**b**) or section 13 of the Industrial Training Act (Northern Ireland) 1964(**c**);

(**a**) S.I. 1962/2834 (1962 III, p. 4051).
(**b**) 1964 c. 16.　　　　　　　(**c**) 1964 c. 18 (N.I.).

"United Kingdom based", in relation to an officer, means that the functions of his office are exerciseable wholly or mainly within the United Kingdom, or that the terms of his office give him a right to be re-employed in the United Kingdom on his return thereto;

"war service" means war service within the meaning of the Local Government Staffs (War Service) Act 1939(**a**), the Teachers Superannuation (War Service) Act 1939(**b**) (or in Scotland, the Education (Scotland) (War Service Superannuation) Act 1939(**c**)), the Police and Firemen (War Service) Act 1939(**d**) or employment for war purposes within the meaning of the Superannuation Schemes (War Service) Act 1940(**e**) and includes any period of service in the First World War in the armed forces of the Crown or in the forces of the Allied or Associated Powers if such service immediately followed a period of relevant employment and was undertaken either compulsorily or with permission of the employer in that employment.

(2) (*a*) Where under any provision of these regulations an annual value is to be assigned to a capital sum or a capital value to an annual amount, the annual or capital value shall be ascertained in accordance with the tables set out in the Schedule to these regulations in so far as they provide for the particular case.

(*b*) For the purpose of determining the application of the said tables the headings and the note to each table shall be treated as a part of the table.

(*c*) Where the said tables do not provide for a case in which an annual value is to be assigned to a capital sum or a capital value to an annual amount, the annual or capital value shall be such as may be agreed between the compensating authority and the person to whom the capital sum or annual amount is payable.

(3) Unless the context otherwise requires, references in these regulations to the provisions of any enactment shall be construed as references to those provisions as amended, re-enacted or modified by or under any subsequent enactment.

(4) References in these regulations to a numbered regulation shall, unless the reference is to a regulation of specified regulations, be construed as references to the regulation bearing that number in these regulations.

(5) References in any of these regulations to a numbered paragraph shall, unless the reference is to a paragraph of a specified regulation, be construed as references to the paragraph bearing that number in the first mentioned regulation.

(6) The Interpretation Act 1889(**f**) shall apply for the interpretation of these regulations as it applies for the interpretation of an Act of Parliament.

PART II

ENTITLEMENT TO COMPENSATION

Persons to whom the regulations apply

3. These regulations shall apply to any person who suffers attributable loss and who—

    (*a*) was employed immediately before the passing of the Act on a full-time basis as a United Kingdom based officer of—

(**a**) 1939 c. 94. (**b**) 1939 c. 95.
(**c**) 1939 c. 96. (**d**) 1939 c. 103.
(**e**) 1940 c. 26. (**f**) 1889 c. 63.

    (i) a national transport authority,

    (ii) the London Transport Executive,

    (iii) a subsidiary of any of the foregoing bodies, or

(*b*) would have been so employed at that time but for any national service on which he was then engaged.

Grounds of entitlement to compensation—Compensating authority

4.—(1) Subject to the provisions of these regulations, any person to whom these regulations apply shall be entitled to have his case considered for the payment of compensation under these regulations, and such compensation shall be determined in accordance with these regulations.

(2) Compensation for attributable loss suffered by a person to whom these regulations apply shall be payable by the Holding Company or, as respects any period after the dissolution of the Holding Company, by such person as may be designated by the Secretary of State by order under section 2(6) of the Act as being the person to whom the liabilities of the Holding Company under section 2(4) of the Act have been transferred in pursuance of section 53 of the Act of 1968, and whichever of them the Holding Company or person aforesaid is required by this regulation to pay such compensation is referred to in these regulations as "the compensating authority".

National service

5.—(1) Any person to whom these regulations apply by virtue of regulation 3(*b*) and who before the expiry of two months after ceasing to be engaged on national service, or if prevented by sickness or other reasonable cause, as soon as practicable thereafter, gives notice to the compensating authority that he is available for employment, shall be entitled—

(*a*) in a case where, in consequence of such cesser as is mentioned in section 2(4) of the Act, he is not given or offered re-employment in his former office or in any reasonably comparable office (whether in the same or in a different service), to have his case considered for payment of compensation for loss of employment, and (if appropriate) for loss or diminution of pension rights, and

(*b*) in a case where, in consequence of any such cesser, he is so re-employed with diminished emoluments, or with loss or diminution of pension rights or worsening of his position as compared with the emoluments, pension rights or position which he would have enjoyed had he continued in his former employment, to have his case considered for payment of compensation for diminution of emoluments, or for loss or diminution of pension rights, or for worsening of his position (as the case may warrant).

(2) The loss of employment which is the cause of a claim for compensation under paragraph (1)(*a*) shall be treated as having occurred on the earlier of the two following dates, that is to say, the date of the refusal of re-employment or a date one month after the date on which the person gave notice that he was available for employment, and the person shall be deemed to have been entitled to the emoluments which he would have enjoyed at such earlier date had he continued in his former employment.

PART III

RESETTLEMENT COMPENSATION

Resettlement compensation for loss of employment

6. The compensating authority shall, subject to the provisions of these regulations, pay resettlement compensation to any person to whom these regulations apply and who satisfies the conditions set out in regulation 7.

Conditions for payment of resettlement compensation

7.—(1) Without prejudice to any other requirement of these regulations, the conditions for the payment of resettlement compensation to any person are that—

(a) he has, before, on, or not later than 10 years after the date of the relevant event, suffered loss of employment which is properly attributable to the happening of the relevant event;

(b) he has not at the date of the loss attained normal retiring age;

(c) he has, for a period beginning 3 years immediately before the material date and ending on the date of the loss, been continuously engaged (disregarding breaks not exceeding in the aggregate 6 months) on a full-time basis in relevant employment; and for this purpose the expression "relevant employment" includes any period of national service immediately following such employment;

(d) he has made a claim for such compensation in accordance with the provisions of Part VII of these regulations not later than—

(i) the end of the period in respect of which resettlement compensation can be payable in his case under the provisions of regulation 9, or

(ii) 13 weeks after the coming into operation of these regulations, whichever is the later;

(e) the loss of employment which is the cause of his claim has occurred for some reason other than misconduct or incapacity to perform such duties as, immediately before the loss, he was performing or might reasonably have been required to perform; and

(f) he has not, subject to paragraph (3), been offered any reasonably comparable employment under the Crown or in the service of a national transport authority, the London Transport Executive or a subsidiary of any of the foregoing bodies.

(2) In ascertaining for the purpose of this regulation whether a person has been offered employment which is reasonably comparable with the employment which he has lost, the following facts shall be disregarded—

(a) the fact that the employment so offered is employment by a body such as is mentioned in paragraph (1)(f) other than the person or body in whose employment he suffered the attributable loss;

(b) the fact that the duties of the employment so offered are duties in connection with activities which did not form part of the activities of that section of the undertaking of the person or body in whose employment he suffered the attributable loss;

(c) the fact that the duties of the employment so offered involve a transfer of his employment from one place to another in the United Kingdom.

(3) No account shall be taken for the purposes of this regulation of an offer of employment where the compensating authority are satisfied—

(a) that acceptance would have involved undue hardship to the person, or

(b) that he was prevented from accepting the offer by reason of ill-health or other circumstances beyond his control.

Amount of resettlement compensation

8.—(1) The amount of resettlement compensation which may be paid to a person shall, for each week for which such compensation is payable, be a sum ascertained by taking two thirds of the weekly rate of the net emoluments which that person has lost and deducting therefrom, in addition to the items mentioned in regulation 32(3) and (4), such of the following items as may be applicable—

(a) unemployment, sickness or injury benefit under any Act relating to National Insurance claimable by him in respect of such week (excluding any amount claimable by him in respect of a dependant); and

(b) two thirds of the net emoluments received by him in respect of such week from work or employment undertaken as a result of the loss of employment.

(2) For the purposes of this regulation the weekly rate of a person's net emoluments shall be deemed to be seven three hundred and sixty-fifths of those emoluments.

Period for payment of resettlement compensation

9. Subject to the provisions of these regulations, resettlement compensation shall be payable to a person only in respect of the period of 13 weeks next succeeding the week in which he lost the employment in connection with which his claim has been made or, in the case of a person who has then attained the age of 45 years, the said 13 weeks and one additional week for every year of his age between the date of his attaining the age of 45 years and the date of the loss of employment, subject to a maximum addition of 13 such weeks.

Additional provisions relating to resettlement compensation

10.—(1) Resettlement compensation shall be payable to a person at intervals equivalent to those at which the emoluments of his employment were previously paid or at such other intervals as may be agreed between the person and the compensating authority.

(2) Resettlement compensation shall be terminated by the compensating authority—

(a) if without reasonable cause the recipient fails to comply with any of the provisions of regulation 11, or

(b) if on being requested to do so, he fails to satisfy the compensating authority that, so far as he is able, he is seeking suitable employment.

Claimant for resettlement compensation to furnish particulars of employment

11. Every person claiming or in receipt of resettlement compensation shall (after as well as before the compensation begins to be paid)—

(*a*) forthwith supply the compensating authority in writing with particulars of any employment which he obtains or of any change in his earnings from any such employment, and

(*b*) if the compensating authority so require, so long as he is out of employment and is not receiving sickness or injury benefit, register with the Department of Employment.

PART IV

LONG-TERM COMPENSATION

Long-term compensation for loss of employment or loss or diminution of emoluments or worsening of position

12. The compensating authority shall, subject to the provisions of these regulations, pay long-term compensation to any person to whom these regulations apply and who satisfies the conditions set out in regulation 13, and this Part of these regulations shall apply to that person.

Conditions for payment of long-term compensation

13.—(1) Without prejudice to any other requirement of these regulations, the conditions for the payment of long-term compensation to any person are that—

(*a*) he has, before, on, or not later than 10 years after the date of the relevant event, suffered loss of employment or loss or diminution of emoluments or worsening of his position, being loss, diminution or worsening (as the case may be) which is properly attributable to the happening of the relevant event;

(*b*) he has not, save as is provided in regulation 17, at the date of such loss, diminution or worsening attained normal retiring age;

(*c*) he has, for a period beginning 8 years immediately before the material date and ending on the date of the attributable loss, been continuously engaged (without a break of more than 12 months at any one time) on a full-time basis in relevant employment; and for this purpose the expression "relevant employment" includes any period of national service immediately following such employment;

(*d*) he has made a claim for such compensation in accordance with the provisions of Part VII of these regulations not later than—

    (i) 2 years after the date on which the loss, diminution or worsening which is the cause of his claim was suffered, or

    (ii) 2 years after the coming into operation of these regulations, or

    (iii) in a case where the claimant could not reasonably have known of the existence of the cause of his claim for compensation at the time when it in fact occurred, 2 years after the first date on which he could reasonably have known of its existence,

whichever is the latest; and

(e) if the cause of the claim for compensation is loss of employment—

  (i) the loss has occurred for some reason other than misconduct or incapacity to perform such duties as, immediately before the loss, he was performing or might reasonably have been required to perform; and

  (ii) he has not been offered any reasonably comparable employment under the Crown or in the service of a national transport authority, the London Transport Executive or a subsidiary of any of those bodies.

(2) If the cause of the claim for compensation is loss of employment paragraphs (2) and (3) of regulation 7 (which relate to offers of employment) shall apply for the purposes of this regulation as they apply for the purposes of regulation 7.

(3) Claims for long-term compensation for loss of employment shall in all respects be treated as claims for such compensation for the loss of emoluments occasioned thereby and the provisions of these regulations shall apply to all such claims accordingly.

(4) Any person to whom this Part of these regulations applies and who, by reason of his position as an officer being worsened, has suffered any loss or injury attributable to the happening of the relevant event, not being a pecuniary loss in respect of which he is entitled to any other compensation or payments under Part IV or V of these regulations, shall, subject to the provisions of these regulations, be entitled to receive in respect of that loss or injury, long-term compensation for the worsening of his position calculated in the following manner, that is to say—

  (a) the pecuniary value of the loss or injury shall be expressed in terms of his net emoluments immediately before his position was worsened,

  (b) such person shall be treated for the purposes of these regulations as a person who has suffered a diminution of emoluments the amount of which is equal to the pecuniary value so expressed, and

  (c) where that person has been awarded any other long-term compensation, as well as compensation for the worsening of his position, the sums payable in respect of that other compensation shall, for the purposes of adjusting, suspending or withholding any long-term compensation under regulation 31 or 32 or both, be aggregated with any sums payable in respect of the compensation for worsening of his position and the payments of the sums so aggregated shall be regarded for those purposes as combined payments under the award of that other long-term compensation and not as separate payments under each of the awards of long-term compensation.

Factors to be considered in determining payment of long-term compensation

14.—(1) For the purpose of determining the amount (subject to the limits set out in these regulations) of long-term compensation (if any) payable under these regulations to any person for loss or diminution of emoluments, the compensating authority shall have regard to such of the following factors as may be relevant, that is to say—

  (a) the conditions upon which the person held the employment which he has lost, or the emoluments of which have been lost or diminished, including in particular its security of tenure, whether by law or practice;

(*b*) the emoluments and other conditions, including security of tenure, whether by law or practice, of any work or employment undertaken by the person as a result of the loss of employment;

(*c*) the extent to which he has sought suitable employment and the emoluments which he might have acquired by accepting other suitable employment offered to him;

(*d*) all the other circumstances of his case:

Provided that if the claimant entered the employment which he has lost or the emoluments of which have been diminished after the passing of the Act, no account shall be taken of that fact for the purpose of this regulation.

(2) In ascertaining for the purposes of paragraph (1)(*c*) whether a person has been offered suitable employment in a case where the cause of the claim for compensation is loss of employment, regulation 7(3) shall apply as it applies for the purpose of ascertaining whether employment is reasonably comparable with employment which has been lost.

Amount of long-term compensation payable for loss of emoluments

15.—(1) Long-term compensation for loss of emoluments shall, subject to the provisions of these regulations, be payable until the normal retiring age or death of a person to whom it is payable, whichever first occurs, and shall not exceed a maximum annual sum calculated in accordance with the provisions of paragraphs (2) to (4).

(2) The said maximum annual sum shall, subject as hereinafter provided, be the aggregate of the following sums, namely—

(*a*) for every year of the person's reckonable service, one sixtieth of the net emoluments which he has lost; and

(*b*) in the case of a person who has attained the age of 40 years at the date of the loss, a sum calculated in accordance with the provisions of paragraph (3) appropriate to his age at that date;

but the said maximum annual sum shall in no case exceed two thirds of the net emoluments which the person has lost.

(3) The sum referred to in paragraph (2)(*b*) shall be—

(*a*) in the case of a person who has attained the age of 40 years but has not attained the age of 50 years at the date of the loss, the following fraction of the net emoluments which he has lost—

(i) where his reckonable service is less than 10 years, one sixtieth for each year of such service after attaining the age of 40 years; or

(ii) where his reckonable service amounts to 10 years but is less than 15 years, one sixtieth for each year of such service after attaining the age of 40 years and one additional sixtieth; or

(iii) where his reckonable service amounts to 15 years but is less than 20 years, one sixtieth for each year of such service after attaining the age of 40 years and two additional sixtieths; or

(iv) where his reckonable service amounts to 20 years or more, one sixtieth for each year of such service after attaining the age of 40 years and three additional sixtieths;

but the sum so calculated shall not in any case exceed one sixth of the said net emoluments;

(*b*) in the case of a person who has attained the age of 50 years but has not attained the age of 60 years at the date of the loss, one sixtieth of the said net emoluments for each year of his reckonable service after attaining the age of 40 years, up to a maximum of 15 years; and

(*c*) in the case of a person who has attained the age of 60 years at the date of the loss, one sixtieth of the said net emoluments for each year of his reckonable service after attaining the age of 45 years.

(4) Where a person has become entitled (whether immediately or prospectively on attaining some greater age) to a pension by way of annual amounts under his last relevant pension scheme, the maximum annual sum referred to in paragraph (1) shall be the maximum sum calculated under paragraphs (2) and (3) as if he had not become so entitled.

(5) Where long-term compensation is payable in respect of any period and resettlement compensation has also been paid in respect of that period, the long-term compensation for that period shall be limited to the amount (if any) by which it exceeds the resettlement compensation paid as aforesaid.

(6) Long-term compensation shall be payable to a person at intervals equivalent to those at which the emoluments of his employment were previously paid or at such other intervals as may be agreed between the person and the compensating authority.

Long-term compensation for diminution of emoluments

16. Long-term compensation for diminution of emoluments in respect of any employment shall, subject to the provisions of these regulations, be awarded and paid in accordance with the following provisions: —

(*a*) the compensation shall consist of an annual sum which shall be payable to a person at intervals equivalent to those at which the emoluments of his employment are or were previously paid or at such other intervals as may be agreed between the person and the compensating authority, and shall, subject to the provisions of these regulations, be payable until normal retiring age or death, whichever first occurs; and

(*b*) the said annual sum shall not exceed the maximum annual sum which could have been awarded under regulation 15 if the person had suffered loss of employment and the loss of emoluments occasioned thereby had been equivalent to the amount of the diminution:

Provided that no compensation shall be payable if the emoluments have been diminished by less than $2\frac{1}{2}$ per cent.

Compensation payable to non-pensionable officer on reaching normal retiring age

17.—(1) Where a person to whom this Part of these regulations applies and who is not a pensionable officer is receiving long-term compensation for loss or diminution of emoluments or worsening of his position and attains normal retiring age, the compensating authority may, if satisfied that the person would have continued to work as an officer for a substantial period beyond normal retiring age, continue to pay compensation to him for the remainder of his life at half its former rate.

(2) Where a person to whom this Part of these regulations applies and who is not a pensionable officer suffers loss or diminution of emoluments, or

worsening of his position, on or after attaining normal retiring age, the compensating authority may, if satisfied that the person, had he not so suffered, would have continued in the normal course of events to work for a substantial period as an officer, pay compensation to him for the remainder of his life at a rate not exceeding one half of that to which he would have been entitled under regulation 15 had he not attained normal retiring age at the date on which he suffered the loss, diminution or worsening, as the case may be.

Date from which long-term compensation is to be payable

18.—(1) Long-term compensation shall be payable with effect from the date of the claim or from any earlier date permitted by the succeeding provisions of this regulation.

(2) Where a claim for long-term compensation is duly made within 13 weeks of the occurrence of the loss or diminution which is the cause of the claim, or within 13 weeks of the coming into operation of these regulations whichever is the later, the award shall be made retrospective to the date on which the loss or diminution occurred.

(3) Where a claim for long-term compensation is made after the expiry of the period mentioned in paragraph (2), the award may, at the discretion of the compensating authority, be made retrospective to a date not earlier than 13 weeks prior to the date on which the claim was made:

Provided that if the compensating authority are satisfied that the failure to make the claim within the period mentioned in paragraph (2) was due to ill-health or other circumstances beyond the claimant's control, the award may be made retrospective to a date not earlier than that on which the loss or diminution occurred.

PART V

RETIREMENT COMPENSATION AND PAYMENTS ON DEATH

Entitlement to retirement compensation and other payments

19.—(1) The compensating authority shall, subject to the provisions of these regulations, pay retirement compensation to any person to whom this Part of these regulations applies, and shall make the other payments for which provision is made in regulations 27 to 29.

(2) This Part of these regulations applies to a pensionable officer who, before, on, or not later than 10 years after the date of the relevant event, has suffered loss or diminution of pension rights which is properly attributable to the happening of the relevant event and who—

    (*a*) is a person to whom these regulations apply;

    (*b*) has not at the date on which the loss or diminution was suffered reached normal retiring age;

    (*c*) has been continuously engaged (without a break of more than 12 months at any one time) on a full-time basis in relevant employment during the period beginning 8 years immediately before the material date and ending on the date of the loss or diminution; and for this purpose the expression "relevant employment" includes any period of national service immediately following such employment.

(3)(*a*) Any claim for retirement compensation or other compensation under this Part of these regulations shall be made in accordance with the provisions of Part VII of these regulations not later than—

    (i) 2 years after the date on which the loss or diminution of pension rights which is the cause of the claim was suffered, or

    (ii) 2 years after the coming into operation of these regulations, or

    (iii) in a case where the claimant could not reasonably have known of the existence of the cause of his claim for compensation at the time when it in fact occurred, 2 years after the first date on which he could reasonably have known of its existence,

whichever is the latest, and

    (*b*) no such compensation as aforesaid shall be payable to or in respect of any claimant before he has reached normal retiring age unless either he had elected to take retirement compensation earlier in accordance with the following provisions of this Part of these regulations or the compensation is compensation payable under regulation 27 or 28.

(4) Retirement compensation and any other such payments as are mentioned in paragraph (1) shall not, however, be paid or made—

    (*a*) to or in respect of a person who has suffered loss or diminution of pension rights which has been occasioned by loss of employment in consequence of the relevant event, if his employment could have been terminated by reason of misconduct or incapacity to perform such duties as, immediately before that loss of employment, he was performing or might reasonably have been required to perform; or

    (*b*) to or in respect of a person who has been offered reasonably comparable employment under the Crown or in the service of a national transport authority, the London Transport Executive or a subsidiary of any of those bodies and who would not have suffered a loss or diminution of pension rights had he accepted that employment; or

    (*c*) to or in respect of a person who has suffered a diminution of pension rights which has been occasioned by a diminution in his pensionable emoluments of less than $2\frac{1}{2}$ per cent.

(5) If the claim results from loss of employment, paragraphs (2) and (3) of regulation 7 (which relate to offers of employment) shall apply for the purposes of this regulation as they apply for the purposes of regulation 7.

(6) References in this Part of these regulations to the date of loss or diminution of pension rights or to the date on which a loss or diminution of pension rights was suffered shall, subject to regulation 5, be interpreted as references to the date on which the loss of employment or emoluments took place or the diminution of emoluments began or the change in the terms of service occurred which occasioned the loss or diminution of pension rights.

Factors governing payment of retirement compensation

20.—(1) Where retirement compensation is payable under any one of regulations 21, 22, 23 and 24, such compensation shall not be payable under any other of those regulations.

(2) For the purpose of determining the amount of any retirement compensation which may, subject to the limits set out in these regulations, be payable thereunder, regard shall be had to the extent of the loss or the diminution of pension rights suffered and also to such of the factors set out in

regulation 14(1) as may be relevant, and in addition the following further factors shall be taken into consideration—

    (a) the terms of any pension scheme associated with any new employment undertaken; and

    (b) the extent to which the person in question has sought pensionable employment, and the terms of any pension scheme which would have applied if he had accepted other suitable employment offered to him.

(3) If a person has attained the age of 40 years at the date on which he suffered loss or diminution of pension rights, the compensating authority, in calculating the amount of the retirement compensation payable to him, shall credit him with additional years of service or an additional period of contribution on the following basis, namely—

    (a) 2 years, whether or not he has completed any years of service after attaining the age of 40 years, and

    (b) 2 years for each of the first 4 completed years of his reckonable service between the date when he attained the age of 40 years and the date of the loss or diminution, and

    (c) one year for each such year of service after the fourth;

but the additional years of service or period of contribution so credited shall not exceed the shortest of the following periods, namely—

    (i) such number of years as, when added to his pensionable service, would amount to the maximum period of such service which would have been reckonable by him had he continued in his employment until attaining normal retiring age, or

    (ii) the number of years of his reckonable service, or

    (iii) 15 years;

and in calculating the amount of any retirement compensation payable to him any period so added shall be aggregated with any years of service or period of contribution entailing reduction of the relevant pension or retiring allowance because of a retirement pension payable under section 30 of the National Insurance Act 1965(a) or section 29 of the National Insurance Act (Northern Ireland) 1966(b).

(4) When retirement compensation is awarded, or when an award is reviewed under regulation 34, the additional compensation payable in consequence of any years of service or period of contribution credited to a person under paragraph (3) may be reduced or withheld to such extent as the compensating authority may think reasonable having regard to the pension scheme (if any) associated with any further employment obtained by him.

(5) If under his last relevant pension scheme the amount of any benefit to which a person might have become entitled could have been increased at the discretion of the body, trustees or other persons administering the pension scheme or of any other body or person, the compensating authority may increase, to an extent not exceeding that to which his accrued pension, accrued retiring allowance, accrued incapacity pension or accrued incapacity retiring allowance might have been increased or supplemented, the corresponding component of any retirement compensation payable to him; and in this connection the compensating authority shall have regard to the terms of any relevant resolutions of such body, trustees or other persons with regard to the increase of benefits and to the provisions of any enactment protecting the interests of that person.

    (a) 1965 c. 51.   (b) 1966 c. 6 (N.I.).

(6) If under his last relevant pension scheme a person would have been entitled to surrender a proportion of any pension which might have become payable to him in favour of his spouse or any dependant, then, if he so desires and informs the compensating authority by notice in writing accordingly within one month after becoming entitled to retirement compensation under these regulations, he may surrender a proportion of so much of the said compensation as is payable by way of an annual sum on the like terms and conditions and in consideration of the like payments by the compensating authority as if the said annual sum were a pension to which he had become entitled under the said pension scheme.

(7) In calculating for the purposes of regulation 21, 22, 23 or 24 the amount of the annual sum which is equal to a person's accrued pension, no account shall be taken of any reduction falling to be made in that pension by reason of the provisions of any Act relating to National Insurance until the person reaches the age at which under his last relevant pension scheme the pension would have been so reduced.

(8) In paragraph (3) the expression "reckonable service" includes any period of employment of which account has been taken or is required to be taken in calculating the amount of any pension to which a person has become entitled under the last relevant pension scheme.

Retirement compensation for loss of a pension payable to pensionable officer on attainment of normal retiring age

21. Subject to the provisions of these regulations, when a person to whom this Part of these regulations applies reaches normal retiring age, the retirement compensation payable to him for loss of pension rights shall be—

(a) an annual sum equal to the amount of his accrued pension, and

(b) a lump sum equal to the amount of his accrued retiring allowance (if any).

Retirement compensation payable to pensionable officer on his becoming incapacitated or reaching minimum pensionable age

22.—(1) Where a person to whom this Part of these regulations applies and who has suffered loss of his pension rights before attaining what would have been his normal retiring age—

(a) becomes incapacitated in circumstances in which, if he had not suffered such loss as aforesaid, he would have become entitled to a pension under his last relevant pension scheme, or

(b) attains the age which, if he had not suffered the said loss, would have been his minimum pensionable age,

he shall be entitled on the happening of either of those events to claim, in lieu of any compensation to which he would otherwise be entitled under these regulations—

(i) in a case where sub-paragraph (a) of this paragraph applies, an annual sum equal to the amount of his accrued incapacity pension and a lump sum equal to the amount of his accrued incapacity retiring allowance (if any), and

(ii) in a case where sub-paragraph (*b*) of this paragraph applies, an annual sum equal to the amount of his accrued pension and a lump sum equal to the amount of his accrued retiring allowance (if any),

subject however to the conditions specified in paragraph (5).

(2) On receipt of a claim under paragraph (1) the compensating authority shall consider whether the claimant is a person to whom that paragraph applies, and within 13 weeks after the date of the receipt of the claim—

(*a*) if they are satisfied that he is not such a person, they shall notify him in writing accordingly; or

(*b*) if they are satisfied that he is such a person, they shall assess the amount of compensation payable to him and notify him in writing accordingly;

and any such notification shall, for the purposes of these regulations, be deemed to be a notification by the authority of a decision on a claim for compensation.

(3) The compensating authority may require any person who makes a claim under paragraph (1)(*a*) to submit himself to a medical examination by a registered medical practitioner selected by that authority, and if they do so, they shall also afford the person an opportunity of submitting a report from his own medical adviser as a result of an examination by him, and the authority shall take that report into consideration together with the report of the medical practitioner selected by them.

(4) If a person wishes to receive compensation under this regulation, he shall so inform the compensating authority in writing within one month from the receipt of a notification under paragraph (2) or, where the claim has been the subject of an appeal, from the decision of the tribunal thereon; and the compensation shall be payable as from the date on which the compensating authority received the claim.

(5) The calculation of compensation under this regulation shall be subject to the following conditions—

(*a*) where the compensating authority, by virtue of regulation 20, have credited the person with additional years of service or an additional period of contribution, no account shall be taken of any additional years or period beyond the number of years which he could have served, had he not lost his employment (in a case where the loss of pension rights was the result of a loss of employment), before the date on which the claim was received by the compensating authority; and

(*b*) if, by reason of any provision of the last relevant pension scheme for a minimum pension or benefit, the amount of any such pension or retiring allowance is in excess of that attributable to the person's actual service, no account shall be taken of any such additional years or period except to the extent (if any) by which they exceed the number of years represented by the difference between his actual service and the period by reference to which the minimum pension or benefit has been calculated; and

(*c*) if the number of years by reference to which an accrued incapacity pension or accrued incapacity retiring allowance is to be calculated is less than any minimum number of years of qualifying service prescribed by the relevant pension scheme, the amount of such pension or retiring allowance shall, notwithstanding any minimum pension or benefit prescribed by the pension scheme, not exceed such proportion of such minimum pension or benefit as the number of years of pensionable service bears to the minimum number of years of qualifying service.

Option to take retirement compensation prematurely

23.—(1) If a person to whom this Part of these regulations applies has suffered a loss of pension rights and loss of employment after attaining the age of 50 years, both losses being attributable to the happening of the relevant event, and so requests the compensating authority by notice in writing, he shall be entitled, as from the date on which the compensating authority receives such notice, to an annual sum equal to the amount of his accrued pension and a lump sum equal to the amount of his accrued retiring allowance (if any), and in that event he shall not be entitled to receive any further payment of long-term compensation after the date on which compensation under this regulation becomes payable:

Provided that—

(i) in calculating the amount of the compensation payable to a person who has given such notice as aforesaid no account shall be taken of any additional years of service or period of contribution credited to him under regulation 20; and

(ii) where the person has claimed long-term compensation, the said notice shall be given not later than 2 years after a decision on the claim has been notified or, where the decision has been reviewed under regulation 34(4), not later than 2 years after the review, or if there has been more than one such review, after the latest.

(2) Regulation 22(2) and (4) shall apply in relation to a notice given under the last foregoing paragraph as it applies to a claim made under paragraph (1) of that regulation.

(3) Where an annual sum is payable under this regulation in respect of any period and resettlement compensation is also payable in respect of that period, the said annual sum shall be limited to the amount (if any) by which it exceeds the resettlement compensation payable as aforesaid.

(4) If a person to whom this Part of these regulations applies has suffered a diminution of pension rights otherwise than by reason of a diminution of his pensionable emoluments and has also suffered a loss of employment after attaining the age of 50 years, such diminution and loss being both attributable to the happening of the relevant event, the provisions of this regulation shall apply and have effect in relation to him in like manner as if he were such a person as is mentioned in paragraph (1) except that the lump sum (if any) referred to in that paragraph shall be reduced by the amount of any pension paid or payable by way of a lump sum under his last relevant pension scheme and except that the annual sum so referred to shall be such annual sum as is therein provided but reduced, on and after the date on which he is first entitled under the said scheme to be paid any instalment of his pension by way of annual amounts, by the amount of each such instalment and paragraph (2) of regulation 24 shall have the like effect in the application of this paragraph as it does in the application of paragraph (1)(*b*) of that regulation.

Retirement compensation for diminution of pension rights

24.—(1) Regulations 21 and 22 shall apply and have effect in relation to a person to whom this Part of these regulations applies and who has suffered a diminution of pension rights as if—

(*a*) where that person has suffered such diminution by reason of a diminution of his pensionable emoluments, the annual sum and the lump sum (if any) payable to him as retirement compensation under those regulations were equal to such an annual sum and such a lump sum (if any) as respectively bear the same ratio to the sums which would be payable under those regulations, had he suffered a loss (instead of a diminution) of pension rights, as the ratio which the amount of the diminution of his pensionable emoluments bears to those emoluments before their diminution, and

(*b*) where that person has suffered diminution of pension rights for any other reason, the annual sum and the lump sum (if any) payable to him as retirement compensation under those regulations were equal to the annual sum and lump sum (if any) which would be payable under those regulations, had he suffered a loss (instead of a diminution) of pension rights, respectively reduced by the amount of any sums payable under his last relevant pension scheme in each year after retirement compensation becomes payable and by the amount of any lump sum paid or payable under that scheme.

(2) In the application of paragraph (1)(*b*) to an officer to or in respect of whom the provisions of any order made under section 2 of the Act have effect so as to secure the payment or payments comprised in his accrued pension rights, the references in that paragraph to his last relevant pension scheme shall include a reference to any arrangements made under that scheme pursuant to such an order and to any arrangements made under that order for the purpose of discharging any liability of a body to make payments prescribed thereby.

Pension contributions

25.—(1) A person entitled to retirement compensation under these regulations for loss of pension rights shall pay to the compensating authority an amount equal to any sum which was paid to him by way of return of pension contributions, including any interest, after ceasing to be employed, and the compensating authority may at his request repay that amount to him at any time before he becomes entitled as aforesaid, but if that amount is not paid to the compensating authority, or is repaid by them to the person, the compensation shall be reduced by an annual amount the capital value of which is equal to the amount of the said contributions.

(2) For the purposes of this regulation the expression "pension contributions" shall include payments made to the pension fund by the person in respect of added years and any additional contributory payments so made by him.

Retirement compensation of a person who obtains further pensionable employment

26. Where a person to whom this Part of these regulations applies, after suffering loss or diminution of pension rights, enters new employment in which he is subject to any pension scheme and thereafter becomes entitled to reckon for the purposes of that scheme any service or period of contribution which falls to be taken into account for the purpose of assessing the amount of any retirement compensation payable to him, his entitlement to retirement compensation shall be reviewed and no retirement compensation shall be payable in respect of such service or period unless the annual rate of the pensionable emoluments to which he was entitled immediately before such loss or diminution exceeds the annual rate on entry of the pensionable emoluments of the new employment by more than $2\frac{1}{2}$ per cent. of such first-mentioned emoluments, and any retirement compensation so payable to him shall, in so far as it is calculated by reference to remuneration, be calculated by reference to the difference between the said annual rates:

Provided that this regulation shall not operate to increase the amount of any retirement compensation payable in respect of loss or diminution of pension rights beyond the amount which would have been payable if the person had attained normal retiring age immediately before he suffered the loss or diminution of pension rights.

Compensation payable to widow or dependants of a claimant

27.—(1) Payments in accordance with this regulation and regulations 28 and 29 shall be made to or for the benefit of the widow, child or other dependant or to the personal representatives of a person to whom this Part of these regulations applies.

(2) If the widow, child or other dependant of that person might, but for the loss or diminution of his pension rights have become entitled to a pension or, as the case may be, to a larger pension under his last relevant pension scheme, the widow, child or other dependant concerned shall be entitled to receive an annual sum equal to the prescribed proportion of any retirement compensation by way of annual amounts payable to the person under regulation 21, 22, 23 or 24 immediately before his death or, if he dies before becoming entitled to receive compensation under any of those regulations, the prescribed proportion of the compensation by way of annual amounts which he would have received under regulation 22 or, as the case may be, under that regulation as applied by regulation 24, had he become entitled thereto immediately before his death:

Provided that—

(i) where any retirement compensation has been surrendered under regulation 20(6) or compounded under regulation 35, any sum payable under this regulation shall be calculated as if such surrender or compounding had not taken place;

(ii) where the pension scheme provides for payment of the pension to any person on behalf of a child or other dependant, any annual sum payable as aforesaid to a child or other dependant shall be paid to that person on behalf of the child or dependant in the like manner and for the like period as is provided in the pension scheme;

(iii) in calculating the sum payable as aforesaid, it shall be assumed that the retirement compensation payable, or which would have been payable, to a person under regulation 21, 22, 23 or 24 had been such sum as would have been payable if the accrued pension or accrued incapacity pension had not been reduced by reason of the provisions of any Act relating to National Insurance;

(iv) where by virtue of a provision of the pension scheme, the annual pension which would have been paid to the widow, child or other dependant but for the loss or diminution of pension rights would not have exceeded, or would not have been less than, or would have been a specified amount, or an amount ascertainable when calculated in like manner as is provided in paragraph (5)(*b*), the aggregate of the annual sum payable under this regulation and any annual pension payable under the pension scheme to the widow, child or other dependant shall correspondingly not exceed, not be less than or shall be equal to that specified amount or, as the case may be, the amount ascertained when so calculated as aforesaid.

(3) Any annual sum payable to or for the benefit of a widow, child or other dependant under this regulation shall cease to be payable in any circumstances in which a corresponding pension under the pension scheme referred to in paragraph (2) would have ceased to be payable.

(4) Except where the compensation has been reduced under regulation 25, compensation payable under this regulation and regulation 28 shall in the aggregate be reduced by an amount the capital value whereof is equal to the amount of any pension contributions as defined in regulation 25(2) returned to the person in respect of whom the compensation is payable and either not paid to the compensating authority or repaid by the compensating authority to him, the compensation under each such regulation being reduced in proportion to the capital value of each amount.

(5) In this regulation "prescribed proportion" means—

(*a*) where provision is made in any last relevant pension scheme of a person to whom this Part of these regulations applies for the pension payable to his widow, child or other dependant to be of such annual amounts as will bear a certain proportion to that person's pension (whether that person's pension is payable to him under that same pension scheme or under another such scheme dealing exclusively with his pension), that certain proportion, and

(*b*) where no such provision is made, the proportion which the annual amounts of the pension to which the widow, child or other dependant of the person in question would have become entitled, in the circumstances mentioned in paragraph (6), (such amounts being calculated in the manner specified in paragraph (7)), bears to the amount of that person's accrued pension or, as the case may be, accrued incapacity pension as assessed for the purpose of calculating his retirement compensation, except that any reduction in the amount of such pension made by reason of the provisions of any Act relating to National Insurance shall, for the purpose of this sub-paragraph, be disregarded.

(6) The circumstances referred to in paragraph (5)(*b*) are that the person to whom this Part of these regulations applies had died immediately before the date on which he suffered the loss or diminution of the pension rights concerned, having then complied with any requirements of the pension scheme as to a minimum period of qualifying service or contribution and completed any additional contributory payments or payments in respect of added years which he was then in the course of making.

(7) The calculation referred to in paragraph (5)(*b*) shall be made on the basis of the method prescribed by the last relevant pension scheme of the person in question for the calculation of benefits for a widow, child or other dependant, but in making that calculation in a case where that person has attained the age of 40 years at the date when he suffered the loss or diminution of pension rights

he shall be credited, unless he is a person who is entitled to retirement compensation under regulation 23, with such number of additional years of service or such period of contribution as was or may be properly credited to him under regulation 20(3) (subject to the provisions of paragraph (5) of regulation 22 if the person in question is entitled to compensation under that regulation) for the purpose of calculating the amount of his retirement compensation:

Provided always that in so crediting him as aforesaid, any number of years of service or period of contribution prescribed by the scheme to be taken into account as a limit in calculating any pension payable to the widow, child or other dependant shall not as a result be exceeded.

Compensation where death grant would have been payable

28.—(1) If the widow or the personal representatives of a person to whom this Part of these regulations applies (in this regulation called "the deceased person") might, but for that person having suffered a loss or diminution of pension rights, have become entitled to a death grant under his last relevant pension scheme, she or they, as the case may be, shall be entitled to receive a sum calculated in accordance with the provisions of this regulation and of regulation 27(4), which sum shall hereafter in this regulation be referred to as "the said sum".

(2) The amount of the said sum shall be ascertained in accordance with the method of calculation of the death grant prescribed by the deceased person's last relevant pension scheme, as modified for the purpose of this regulation by paragraph (3), but in making this calculation in any particular case such of the following assumptions as may be applicable shall be made—

(a) where the deceased person had not been in receipt of retirement compensation, it shall be assumed that he had died immediately before the date on which he suffered the loss or diminution of pension rights;

(b) where the deceased person had been in receipt of retirement compensation, it shall be assumed that he had retired on that date; and

(c) except where the deceased person had been in receipt of retirement compensation under regulation 23, it shall be assumed that on the date on which he suffered the loss or diminution of pension rights he had served for a further period of pensionable service equivalent to the aggregate of any additional years of service or period of contribution credited to him under regulation 20(3), but so however that—

(i) in a case where the deceased person had been in receipt of retirement compensation under regulation 22, such further period shall not exceed the period between the date on which the said loss or diminution was suffered and the date of the claim under that regulation, and

(ii) in any other case such further period shall not exceed the period between the date on which the said loss or diminution was suffered and the actual date of the death of the deceased person.

(3) For the purpose of applying the method of calculation specified in paragraph (2) in a case where the last relevant pension scheme contains a provision to the effect that payment of death grant is to be related to the period which has elapsed from retirement to death, the reference in that provision to such a period shall be treated as a reference to the period which has elapsed from the first accrual of retirement compensation to the actual death of the deceased person.

(4) If the number of years of the deceased person's service or period of contribution is less than the minimum number of years of qualifying service or period prescribed by the pension scheme for the receipt of a death grant, the said sum shall not exceed such proportion of the death grant calculated as aforesaid as the number of years of the person's pensionable service or period of contribution bears to the minimum number of years of qualifying service or period prescribed by the pension scheme.

(5) There shall be deducted from the said sum the amount of any retirement compensation paid to or in respect of the deceased person or, where any part of that compensation has been surrendered under regulation 20(6), the amount which would have been paid but for any such surrender.

(6) Where payment of more than one such sum under this regulation is made in relation to one death, the part of the total amount of retirement compensation to be deducted from each such sum under paragraph (5) shall bear the same proportion to such total amount as the said sum in question bears to the aggregate of such sums paid under this regulation in relation to that death.

(7) For the purpose of calculating any death grant which might be payable under the last relevant pension scheme, an annual sum payable to, or for the benefit of, a widow, child or other dependant under regulation 27 shall be deemed to be a pension payable to, or for the benefit of, the widow, child or dependant, as the case may be.

(8) If the widow or the personal representatives of the deceased person became entitled under his last relevant pension scheme to a smaller death grant than would have been payable had he not suffered a diminution of pension rights attributable to the happening of the relevant event, she or they, as the case may be, shall be entitled to receive a sum calculated in accordance with the foregoing provisions of this regulation modified as follows:—

    (*a*) in a case where the reduction of the death grant has occurred because the diminution of pension rights has been occasioned by the diminution of the deceased person's pensionable emoluments, the amount of the pensionable emoluments to be taken into account for ascertaining the said sum in accordance with paragraph (2) shall be the amount of that diminution, and

    (*b*) in all other cases, the sum payable to the widow or the personal representatives shall be the said sum calculated in accordance with the foregoing provisions of this regulation but reduced by the amount of the death grant to which the widow or the personal representatives became entitled as aforesaid.

Balances payable to claimant's widow or personal representatives

29.—(1) If no annual sum is payable to the widow, child or other dependant of any person under regulation 27 and no sum is payable under regulation 28 and the person dies before he has received in the aggregate by way of retirement compensation a sum equivalent to the amount of any contributions repaid by him under regulation 25, together with compound interest thereon calculated at the rate of 3 per cent. per annum with half-yearly rests up to the date of his death as from the 1st April or 1st October following the half year in which the amount was paid, there shall be paid to his personal representatives the difference between the aggregate amount received by way of retirement compensation as aforesaid and the said equivalent sum.

(2) If an annual sum becomes payable to a widow under regulation 27 and on her re-marriage or death the sum ceases to be payable, and any sum payable to a child or other dependant under that regulation has ceased to be payable, and if the aggregate amount of the payments which were made as aforesaid to her husband by way of retirement compensation and to the widow or personal representatives under regulation 28 is less than a sum equivalent to the amount which would have been payable to the personal representatives under that regulation if no annual sum had been payable under regulation 27, there shall be paid to her or her personal representatives the difference between such aggregate amount and the said equivalent sum.

(3) For the purposes of this regulation a person who has surrendered any part of his retirement compensation under regulation 20(6) shall be deemed to have received during any period the amount of compensation for that period which he would have received but for any such surrender.

Intervals for payment of compensation under Part V

30. Any compensation awarded as an annual sum under this Part of these regulations to or in respect of any person shall be payable at intervals equivalent to those at which the corresponding benefit would have been payable under the person's last relevant pension scheme or at such other intervals as may be agreed between the person entitled to receive the compensation and the compensating authority.

PART VI

ADJUSTMENT, REVIEW AND COMPOUNDING OF COMPENSATION

Adjustment of compensation where pension is also payable

31.—(1) Where any period of service of which account was taken in calculating the amount of any compensation payable under Part IV or V of these regulations is subsequently taken into account for the purpose of calculating the amount of any pension payable to or in respect of any person in accordance with a pension scheme associated with any employment undertaken subsequent to the date on which the attributable loss was suffered which gave rise to the claim for compensation (in this regulation called "the said scheme"), the compensating authority may in accordance with this regulation withhold or reduce the compensation payable in respect of any period for which such pension is being received.

(2) If the part of any pension by way of annual amounts which is attributable to a period of service mentioned in paragraph (1) equals or exceeds the part of any compensation by way of annual amounts which is attributable to the same period, that part of the compensation may be withheld, or if such part of the pension is less than such part of the compensation, the compensation may be reduced by an amount not exceeding such part of the pension.

(3) Where a death benefit is or becomes payable under the said scheme in respect of any person who is for the purposes of regulation 28 called therein the deceased person, any sum payable under that regulation in respect of such a person may be reduced by an amount not greater than the proportion of the death benefit which the period of service mentioned in paragraph (1) bears to the total period of service of which account was taken in the calculation of the death benefit.

(4) In addition to any reduction authorised by paragraph (2) or (3), if, in the circumstances mentioned in paragraph (1), compensation by way of annual amounts is attributable in part to any provision of the said scheme for a minimum benefit or pension, the compensation may be reduced by an amount not exceeding that part.

(5) Where any additional years of service or period of contribution have been credited to a person under regulation 20(3), if the number of such years or such period is equal to or less than the period spent in the subsequent employment mentioned in paragraph (1), the compensation by way of annual amounts may be reduced (in addition to any other reduction authorised by this regulation) by an amount not exceeding that attributable to the additional years or period so credited or, if the number of such years or such period is greater than the period spent in the subsequent employment, by such proportion of that amount as the period spent in the subsequent employment bears to the number of additional years or the period so credited.

(6) Where compensation has been calculated in accordance with regulation 26, the provisions of this regulation shall apply only in relation to such part (if any) of the pension mentioned in paragraph (1) as is attributable to pensionable emoluments in excess of those to which the person was entitled on entering the new employment referred to in regulation 26.

(7) Where long-term compensation is payable to a person in respect of diminution of emoluments or worsening of his position or of both, the provisions of this regulation shall apply only in relation to such part (if any) of the pension as is under the said scheme attributable to his emoluments in the said subsequent employment, being emoluments in excess of those emoluments to which that person was entitled immediately before he suffered the diminution of emoluments or worsening of his position, or if he suffered both, before he suffered whichever was the earlier.

(8) Where retirement compensation is payable to a pensionable officer in respect of diminution of pension rights occasioned by a diminution of pensionable emoluments, the provisions of this regulation shall apply only in relation to such part (if any) of the pension as is attributable to pensionable emoluments in excess of those to which that officer was entitled immediately prior to the diminution of his pension rights.

Reduction of compensation in certain cases

32.—(1) If under a person's last relevant pension scheme any benefit or pension for which the scheme provided would have been subject to reduction or suspension on his taking up other employment specified in that behalf in the scheme, any retirement compensation to which he is entitled for loss or diminution of pension rights shall, where such employment is taken up, be reduced or suspended in the like manner and to the like extent:

Provided that in calculating the amount of the reduction of the compensation in a case where by the provisions of the scheme the amount of the reduction of the benefit or pension is to be related to the emoluments of the employment taken up, the amount of any pension by way of annual amounts payable to the person under his last relevant pension scheme shall be treated as emoluments which shall for the purpose of the calculation be aggregated with the actual emoluments of the said employment.

(2) There shall be deducted from the retirement compensation payable to any person any additional contributory payments remaining unpaid at the date when he suffered loss or diminution of pension rights; and any such payments not recovered at the date of his death shall be deducted from any compensation payable in respect of that person under regulation 27, 28 or 29(2).

(3) Where a person is entitled to compensation under these regulations and the circumstances are such that he is also entitled to—

(a) a redundancy payment under the Redundancy Payments Act 1965(a) or the Contracts of Employment and Redundancy Payments Act (Northern Ireland) 1965(b), or

(b) any similar payment in consequence of the loss of his employment under any contract or arrangement with the body or person by whom he was employed (other than payments by way of a return of contributions under a pension scheme), or

(c) any payment under or by virtue of the provisions of any enactment relating to the reinstatement in civil employment of persons who have been in the service of the Crown,

the compensation which would, apart from this paragraph, become due to the person, whether by instalments or lump sum or both, shall in the aggregate be reduced by the amount of the payments referred to in this paragraph.

(4) Where any resettlement or long-term compensation is payable to or in respect of any person, and that person or his widow, child or other dependant or his personal representatives is or are also entitled (whether immediately or on the person's attaining some greater age) to a pension under that person's last relevant pension scheme, any instalment of such compensation which is payable in respect of any period shall be reduced by the amount of the instalment of such pension which is payable in respect of the same period.

(5) For the purposes of paragraph (4) no account shall be taken of any sum payable in consequence of the surrender by any person of part of his pension under any provision in that behalf in his last relevant pension scheme with a view to obtaining or increasing allowances for his widow, child or other dependant; and the person shall be deemed to have received during any period the amount of pension which he would have received but for any such surrender.

(6) Where in any week a person is entitled to long-term compensation and is also entitled to unemployment, sickness or injury benefit under any Act relating to National Insurance, other than a benefit claimable by him in respect of a dependant, there shall be deducted from the long-term compensation payable for that week a sum equal to the amount by which the aggregate of such National Insurance benefit claimable in respect of that week and the weekly rate at which the long-term compensation would be payable but for this regulation exceeds two thirds of the weekly rate of the net emoluments of the employment which he has lost or in which the emoluments have been diminished:

Provided that this paragraph shall not apply in relation to any such sickness of injury benefit in so far as—

(i) an equivalent sum is deducted from the emoluments of his current employment, and

(ii) such deduction from those emoluments has not occasioned an increase in his long-term compensation.

(7) In paragraph (6) the expression "weekly rate" means seven three hundred and sixty-fifths of the relevant annual rate.

(a) 1965 c. 62.   (b) 1965 c. 19 (N.I.).

Notification of change of circumstances

33. Where—

(*a*) a pensionable officer after suffering any attributable loss enters any new employment referred to in regulation 26 or becomes entitled to any pension on ceasing to hold any such employment, or

(*b*) a person entitled to long-term compensation enters employment the remuneration whereof is payable out of public funds or by any national transport authority or subsidiary thereof, or ceases to hold such employment, or receives any increase in his remuneration in such employment, or

(*c*) a person entitled to retirement compensation enters employment in which the compensation is subject to reduction or suspension under regulation 32, or ceases to hold such employment, or receives any increase in his remuneration in such employment, or

(*d*) a person entitled to long-term compensation starts to receive any benefit, any increase in benefit or any further benefit under any Act relating to National Insurance,

he shall forthwith inform the compensating authority in writing of that fact.

Review of awards of long-term or retirement compensation

34.—(1) The compensating authority shall, within a period of 2 years after the date on which any decision on a claim for long-term or retirement compensation (other than compensation payable under regulation 23) is notified to a claimant under regulation 36 and at intervals of not more than 6 months, review their decision or, where the claim has been the subject of an appeal, the decision of the tribunal, and these regulations shall apply in relation to any such review as they apply in relation to the initial determination of the claim; and on such review, in the light of any material change in the circumstances of the case, compensation may be awarded, or compensation previously awarded may be increased, reduced or discontinued, subject to the limits set out in these regulations:

Provided that where the person to whom the decision relates ceases to hold the employment in which his emoluments were diminished, a review shall be held within 3 months after the date on which he ceases to hold that employment.

(2) After the expiration of the period of 2 years mentioned in paragraph (1), the compensating authority may, at their discretion, carry out reviews in accordance with that paragraph at intervals of not less than 12 months.

(3) The person to whom the decision relates may at any time require the compensating authority to carry out a review in accordance with paragraph (1) if he considers that there has been a change in the circumstances of his case which is material for the purposes of these regulations.

(4) Notwithstanding anything contained in the foregoing provisions of this regulation, the compensating authority shall review a decision (whether of the authority or the tribunal) on a claim for long-term compensation for loss of employment, diminution of emoluments or worsening of a person's position after the expiration of the said period of 2 years if at any time—

(*a*) the person to whom the decision relates becomes engaged in employment (hereinafter referred to as his "current employment") the remuneration whereof is payable out of public funds, or by any national transport authority or subsidiary thereof, and which he has undertaken subsequent to the date on which he suffered the loss, diminution or worsening, and (*b*) the aggregate of the net emoluments of his current employment, any pension or benefit by way of annual amounts payable to him in respect of the employment which he has lost or in which he suffered the diminution or worsening and the long-term compensation payable to him exceeds the net emoluments of the employment which he has lost or, as the case may be, in which he so suffered.

(5) The compensating authority shall further review any decision reviewed under paragraph (4) whenever the net emoluments of the person's current employment are increased.

(6) If on any review under paragraph (4) or (5) the compensation is reduced, it shall not be reduced below the amount by which the net emoluments of the person's current employment, together with any pension or benefit by way of annual amounts payable to him in respect of the employment in which he has suffered the attributable loss, falls short of the net emoluments of the employment in which he suffered that loss.

(7) The compensating authority shall give to a person to whom a decision relates not less than 14 days' notice of any review of that decision to be carried out under this regulation unless the review is carried out at his request.

(8) Nothing in this regulation shall preclude the making of any adjustment of compensation required by regulation 31 or 32.

Compounding of awards

35.—(1) In a case where an annual sum which has been or might be awarded under these regulations does not exceed £35, the compensating authority may, at their discretion, compound their liability in respect thereof by paying a lump sum equivalent to the capital value of the annual sum and, if any lump sum payment has been or might be awarded in addition to such annual sum under regulation 21, 22, 23 or 24, the compensating authority may likewise discharge their liability in respect thereof by an immediate payment.

(2) In any other case, if the person who has been awarded long-term or retirement compensation requests them to do so, the compensating authority may, after having regard to the state of health of that person and the other circumstances of the case, compound up to one quarter of their liability to make payments under the award (other than payments to a widow, child or other dependant under regulation 27) by the payment of an equivalent amount as a lump sum or, where any compensation has been awarded as a lump sum, by increasing that compensation to such equivalent amount; and in calculating for this purpose the liability of the authority to make such payments, account shall be taken of the annual value of lump sum payments of compensation.

(3) The making of a composition under paragraph (2) in relation to an award of long-term or retirement compensation shall not prevent the subsequent making of a composition under paragraph (1) in relation to that award, but, subject as aforesaid, not more than one composition may be made in relation to any award.

Part VII

Procedure and Miscellaneous

Procedure on making claims

36.—(1) Every claim for compensation under these regulations and every request for a review of an award of long-term or retirement compensation shall be made in accordance with this regulation.

(2) Every such claim and request shall be made to the compensating authority in writing, shall set out the grounds on which the claim or request is made and shall state whether any other claim for compensation has been made by the claimant under these regulations.

(3) Resettlement compensation shall be claimed separately from any other form of compensation claimable under these regulations.

(4) The compensating authority shall consider any such claim or request in accordance with the relevant provisions of these regulations and shall notify the person making the claim or request in writing of their decision—

    (*a*) in the case of a claim for resettlement compensation, not later than one month after the receipt of the claim, and

    (*b*) in the case of a claim for, or request for the review of an award of, compensation under Part IV or V of these regulations, not later than 13 weeks after the receipt of the claim or request, and

    (*c*) in any other case, as soon as possible after the decision;

but the decision of the compensating authority shall not be invalidated by reason of the fact that notice of the decision is given after the expiry of the period mentioned in this paragraph.

(5) Every notification of a decision by the compensating authority (whether granting or refusing compensation or reviewing an award, or otherwise affecting any compensation under these regulations) shall contain a statement—

    (*a*) giving reasons for the decision;

    (*b*) showing how any compensation has been calculated and, in particular, if the amount is less than the maximum which could have been awarded under these regulations, showing the factors taken into account in awarding that amount; and

    (*c*) directing the attention of the claimant to his right under regulation 42, if he is aggrieved by the decision, to institute proceedings before a tribunal and giving him the address to which the application instituting such proceedings should be sent.

Claimants to furnish information

37.—(1) Any person claiming or receiving compensation or whose award of compensation is being reviewed shall furnish all such information as the compensating authority may at any time reasonably require; and he shall verify the same in such manner, including the production of books or original documents in his possession or control, as may be reasonably so required.

(2) Any such person shall, on receipt of reasonable notice, present himself for interview at such place as the compensating authority may reasonably require; and any person who attends for interview may, if he so desires, be represented by his adviser.

Procedure on death of claimant

38.—(1) In the event of the death of a claimant or of a person who, if he had survived, could have been a claimant, a claim for compensation under these regulations may be continued or made, as the case may be, by his personal representatives.

(2) Where any such claim is continued or made as aforesaid by personal representatives, the personal representatives shall, as respects any steps to be taken or thing to be done by them in order to continue or make the claim, be deemed for the purposes of these regulations to be the person entitled to claim, but, save as aforesaid, the person in whose right they continue or make the claim shall be deemed for the purposes of these regulations to be such person, and the relevant provisions of these regulations shall be construed accordingly:

Provided that the compensating authority may in any such case extend the period within which a claim is required to be made by regulation 7, 13 or 19.

Calculation of service

39. For the purpose of making any calculation under these regulations in respect of a person's reckonable service, all periods of such service shall be aggregated and, except where reference is made to completed years of service, if the aggregated service includes a fraction of a year, that fraction shall, if it equals or exceeds 6 months, be treated as a year, and shall, in any other case be disregarded.

Temporary variation of emoluments

40. In calculating for the purposes of these regulations the amount of any emoluments lost, or the amount by which any emoluments have been diminished, and in determining the net emoluments, the accrued pension or the accrued retiring allowance of any person who has suffered attributable loss, no account shall be taken of any increase in the amount of the person's emoluments which is due to any temporary allowance made in consequence of the happening of the relevant event and otherwise than in the ordinary course of his employment.

Compensation not assignable

41. Subject to any statutory provision in that behalf, any compensation to which a person becomes entitled under these regulations shall be paid by the compensating authority and shall be payable to, or in trust for, the person who is entitled to receive it, and shall not be assignable:

Provided that, without prejudice to any other right of recovery, any compensation paid in error to a person may be recovered by the compensating authority from him by deduction from any compensation payable to him under these regulations.

Right of appeal from decision of compensating authority

42.—(1) Every person who is aggrieved by any decision of the compensating authority with respect to a compensation question or by any failure on the part of the compensating authority to notify him of any such decision within the appropriate time prescribed by these regulations, may within 13 weeks of the notification to him of the decision or the expiry of the prescribed time, as the case may be, institute proceedings for the determination of the question by a tribunal in accordance with the Industrial Tribunals (Employment and

Compensation) Regulations 1967(a), or in Scotland, the Industrial Tribunals (Employment and Compensation) (Scotland) Regulations 1967(b), or in Northern Ireland, the Industrial Tribunals (Employment and Compensation) Regulations (Northern Ireland) 1967(c) and these regulations; and the tribunal shall determine the question accordingly.

(2) For the purpose of any such proceedings a person or persons may be appointed to sit with the tribunal as assessor or assessors.

(3) The compensating authority shall give effect to the decision of the tribunal subject to any modifications that may be required in consequence of any appeal from that decision on a point of law.

Signed by authority of the Secretary of State.

21st April 1972.

John Peyton,
Minister for Transport Industries
Department of the Environment.

(a) S.I. 1967/361 (1967 I, p. 1205).   (b) S.I. 1967/362 (1967 I, p. 1220).
(c) S.R.&O. (N.I.) 1967 No. 110 (p. 354).

SCHEDULE

TABLE I

Factors by which an annual amount payable for life shall be multiplied to obtain the capital value of that amount.

AGE	FACTOR	
	FEMALE	MALE
Under 35	15·55	15·15
35 and under 40	15·10	14·60
40 and under 45	14·55	13·95
45 and under 50	13·90	13·10
50	13·45	12·55
51	13·25	12·35
52	13·10	12·15
53	12·90	11·90
54	12·70	11·70
55	12·50	11·45
56	12·30	11·25
57	12·10	11·00
58	11·90	10·75
59	11·65	10·50
60	11·40	10·25
61	11·20	10·00
62	10·95	9·70
63	10·70	9·45
64	10·40	9·15
65	10·15	8·90
66	9·90	8·60
67	9·60	8·35
68	9·35	8·05
69	9·05	7·80
70	8·75	7·50

NOTE:—This table is for use in connection with regulation 35(1) and (2) for the compounding of annual retirement compensation which a person is currently entitled to receive under regulation 21, 22, 23 or 24. Where the compensation is payable before age 60 (females), 65 (males) but will be reduced on the attainment of that age (in connection with National Insurance pension) the table should be used in conjunction with Table II, i.e. Table II should be used for valuing that part of the compensation which ceases to be payable at age 60 or 65 as the case may be and this table should be used for valuing the remainder.

TABLE II

Factors by which an annual amount ceasing at 65 (males) or 60 (females) shall be multiplied to obtain the capital value of that amount.

AGE	FACTOR	
	FEMALE	MALE
Under 35	13·40	14·10
35 and under 40	12·25	13·15
40 and under 45	10·70	11·95
45 and under 50	8·65	10·40
50	7·15	9·30
51	6·60	8·90
52	6·00	8·45
53	5·35	7·95
54	4·65	7·50
55	3·90	6·95
56	3·15	6·40
57	2·30	5·85
58	1·45	5·20
59	·50	4·55
60	—	3·85
61	—	3·10
62	—	2·30
63	—	1·40
64	—	·50

NOTE:—This table is for use in connection with regulation 35(1) and (2) for the compounding of any part of annual retirement compensation which will cease to be payable on the attainment of age 60 (females), 65 (males).   Table I should be used in relation to the remainder of such compensation, i.e. the part which is payable for life—see note on that table.

TABLE III

Factors by which an annual amount payable to a widow until death or re-marriage shall be multiplied to obtain the capital value of that amount.

AGE OF WIDOW AT DATE OF WIDOWHOOD	FACTOR	AGE OF WIDOW AT DATE OF WIDOWHOOD	FACTOR
20	6·00	45	11·90
21	6·00	46	12·05
22	6·00	47	12·15
23	6·00	48	12·25
24	6·00	49	12·30
25	6·25	50	12·30
26	6·60	51	12·30
27	6·95	52	12·25
28	7·30	53	12·20
29	7·65	54	12·15
30	8·00	55	12·05
31	8·40	56	11·95
32	8·75	57	11·80
33	9·10	58	11·65
34	9·40	59	11·50
35	9·75	60	11·30
36	10·05	61	11·15
37	10·30	62	10·95
38	10·55	63	10·70
39	10·80	64	10·40
40	11·05	65	10·15
41	11·25	66	9·90
42	11·45	67	9·60
43	11·60	68	9·35
44	11·75	69	9·05
		70	8·75

NOTE:—This table is for use in connection with regulation 35(1) for compounding annual compensation to a widow under regulation 27. It should also be used, where a reduction of compensation under regulation 27(4) falls to be apportioned between the compensation payable under that regulation and under regulation 28, for ascertaining the capital value of annual compensation to a widow.

TABLE IV

Factors by which a lump sum shall be multiplied to obtain an annual amount payable for life equivalent in value.

AGE				FACTOR	
				FEMALE	MALE
Under 35	..	..	..	·0642917	·0660000
35 and under 40	..	..	..	·0662083	·0685000
40 and under 45	..	..	..	·0687083	·0716667
45 and under 50	..	..	..	·0719583	·0763333
50	..	..	..	·0743333	·0796667
51	..	..	..	·0754583	·0809583
52	..	..	..	·0763333	·0822917
53	..	..	..	·0775000	·0840417
54	..	..	..	·0787500	·0854583
55	..	..	..	·0800000	·0873333
56	..	..	..	·0812917	·0888750
57	..	..	..	·0826250	·0909167
58	..	..	..	·0840417	·0930000
59	..	..	..	·0858333	·0952500
60	..	..	..	·0877083	·0975417
61	..	..	..	·0892917	·1000000
62	..	..	..	·0913333	·1030833
63	..	..	..	·0934583	·1058333
64	..	..	..	·0961667	·1092917
65	..	..	..	·0985000	·1123750
66	..	..	..	·1010000	·1162917
67	..	..	..	·1041667	·1197500
68	..	..	..	·1069583	·1242083
69	..	..	..	·1105000	·1282083
70	..	..	..	·1142917	·1333333

NOTE:—This table is for use in connection with regulation 25(1) for ascertaining the annual amount by which retirement compensation under regulation 21, 22 or 23 is to be reduced where a claimant has not paid to the compensating authority an amount equal to any sum paid to him by way of pension contributions or that amount has been repaid to him by the compensating authority at his request. It should also be used in connection with regulation 35(2) for calculating for the purposes of that paragraph the annual value of retirement compensation awarded as a lump sum.

TABLE V

Factors by which a lump sum shall be multiplied to obtain an annual amount payable to a widow until death or re-marriage equivalent in value to that lump sum.

AGE OF WIDOW AT DATE OF WIDOWHOOD	FACTOR	AGE OF WIDOW AT DATE OF WIDOWHOOD	FACTOR
20	·1666667	45	·0840417
21	·1666667	46	·0830000
22	·1666667	47	·0822917
23	·1666667	48	·0816250
24	·1666667	49	·0812917
25	·1600000	50	·0812917
26	·1515000	51	·0812917
27	·1438750	52	·0816250
28	·1370000	53	·0819583
29	·1307083	54	·0822917
30	·1250000	55	·0830000
31	·1190417	56	·0836667
32	·1142917	57	·0847500
33	·1098750	58	·0858333
34	·1063750	59	·0869583
35	·1025833	60	·0885000
36	·0995000	61	·0897083
37	·0970833	62	·0913333
38	·0947917	63	·0934583
39	·0925833	64	·0961667
40	·0905000	65	·0985000
41	·0888750	66	·1010000
42	·0873333	67	·1041667
43	·0862083	68	·1069583
44	·0851250	69	·1105000
		70	·1142917

NOTE:—This table is for use in connection with regulation 27(4) for ascertaining the annual amount by which compensation to a widow is to be reduced in the circumstances described in that paragraph. If a reduction is required to be apportioned between compensation payable under regulations 27 and 28, the capital value of annual compensation to a widow should be ascertained by reference to Table III.

TABLE VI

Table showing, according to the outstanding period of long-term compensation, the factor by which the total amount of long-term compensation to be compounded shall be multiplied in order to obtain the capital value of that amount.

OUTSTANDING NUMBER OF COMPLETE YEARS OF LONG-TERM COMPENSATION	FACTOR	
	FEMALE	MALE
0	·984	·982
1	·952	·948
2	·921	·915
3	·892	·883
4	·864	·854
5	·838	·827
6	·813	·801
7	·789	·777
8	·767	·754
9	·746	·732
10	·726	·712
11	·706	·693
12	·688	·675
13	·670	·657
14	·653	·641
15	·637	·625
16	·621	·610
17	·606	·596
18	·592	·582
19	·578	·569
20	·565	·556
21	·552	·544
22	·540	·532
23	·528	·520
24	·516	·509
25	·505	·499
26	·494	·489
27	·484	·479
28	·474	·469
29	·464	·459
30	·455	·450

NOTE:—This table is for use in connection with regulation 35(1) and (2) for compounding awards of long-term compensation under Part IV of these regulations. The total amount of the annual long-term compensation which is to be compounded must first be calculated, i.e. the amount which the person would receive on account of that compensation or the part of it which is to be compounded, if it were paid until "normal retiring age" (as defined in these regulations). The capital value of that annual long-term compensation will be the total calculated multiplied by the appropriate factor.

EXPLANATORY NOTE

(This Note is not part of the Regulations.)

1. These regulations, made under section 2(4) of the Transport Holding Company Act 1972 (the Act), provide for the payment by the Transport Holding Company or by the authority to whom the responsibilities of the Transport Holding Company are transferred on its dissolution, of compensation to or in respect of any person who suffers loss of employment, or loss or diminution of emoluments or pension rights, or worsening of his position, which is properly attributable to a body ceasing to be a subsidiary of the Transport Holding Company after the passing of the Act. By virtue of section 135(3) of the Transport Act 1968 (as applied by section 2(4) of the Act) the regulations have retrospective effect from 23rd March 1972.

2. Part I of the regulations contains definitions. Part II specifies the persons to whom the regulations apply and the grounds of entitlement to compensation. The regulations apply to persons employed full-time, as United Kingdom based officers, by one of the bodies named in regulation 3(*a*) or who would have been so employed but for being engaged on national service.

3. The compensation payable is—

   (*a*) resettlement compensation for loss of employment (Part III of the regulations);

   (*b*) long-term compensation for loss of employment or loss or diminution of emoluments or worsening of position (Part IV);

   (*c*) retirement compensation for loss or diminution of pension rights (Part V);

   (*d*) payments in respect of a deceased pensionable officer to his widow, child or other dependant or to his personal representatives in circumstances specified in the regulations (Part V).

4. Resettlement compensation is payable for a period not exceeding 26 weeks to officers continuously engaged for at least 3 years (disregarding breaks not exceeding in the aggregate 6 months) in relevant employment before the prescribed date. The qualifying conditions and factors to be considered are set out in regulation 7. The method of calculating the amount of compensation is contained in regulation 8.

5. Long-term and retirement compensation are payable to officers continuously engaged for at least 8 years (without a break of more than 12 months at any one time) in relevant employment before the prescribed date. The qualifying and other conditions for long-term compensation are set out in regulations 13 and 14 and for retirement compensation in regulations 19 and 20.

6. The method of calculating the maximum amount of long-term compensation is laid down in regulations 15 (loss of emoluments) and 16 (diminution of emoluments). This amount is a proportion, not exceeding two thirds of the net emoluments lost or of the amount by which emoluments have been diminished, as the case may be. This compensation is payable from a date determined under regulation 18 and can be payable up to normal retiring age. In the case of a non-pensionable officer, compensation not exceeding one half of the rate of long-term compensation may be paid beyond normal retiring age (regulation 17).

7. Retirement compensation payable to a pensionable officer for loss of pension rights is based upon his accrued pension rights (regulation 21) supplemented in the case of persons aged 40 or over at the date of the loss by the

addition of notional years of service (regulation 20). Provision for retirement compensation (including the concept of additional years) in the case of a pensionable officer who suffers diminution of pension rights instead of a loss is provided by regulation 24 which also lays down the method of calculating the retirement compensation payable in such cases. Retirement compensation is ordinarily payable from normal retiring age but in certain circumstances is payable earlier (regulations 22 and 23).

8. Provision is made for payments to the widow, child or other dependant or to the personal representatives of a claimant who dies where such persons would have derived benefit under the relevant pension scheme (regulations 27 to 29).

9. Part VI of the regulations provides for long-term and retirement compensation to be reviewed and for awards to be varied in the light of changing circumstances (regulation 34). It also contains provisions for the adjustment, suspension and compounding of compensation in certain circumstances.

10. Part VII contains provisions relating to the procedure for making claims and notifying decisions and confers upon a claimant who is aggrieved by a decision on a compensation question or the failure of the compensating authority to notify its decision, a right to refer the question for determination by a tribunal established under section 12 of the Industrial Training Act 1964 or section 13 of the Industrial Training Act (Northern Ireland) 1964.

STATUTORY INSTRUMENTS

1972 No. 638

INDUSTRIAL TRIBUNALS

The Industrial Tribunals (Scotland) (Amendment) Regulations 1972

Made - - -	*20th April* 1972
Laid before Parliament	*28th April* 1972
Coming into Operation	*1st June* 1972

The Secretary of State in exercise of his powers under section 12 of the Industrial Training Act 1964(**a**) and after consultation with the Council on Tribunals hereby makes the following Regulations:—

Citation and commencement

1.—(1) These Regulations may be cited as the Industrial Tribunals (Scotland) (Amendment) Regulations 1972, and the Industrial Tribunals (Scotland) Regulations 1965(**b**) (hereinafter referred to as "the principal Regulations"), the Industrial Tribunals (Scotland) (Amendment) Regulations 1967(**c**), the Industrial Tribunals (Scotland) (Amendment) Regulations 1971(**d**), and these Regulations may be cited together as the Industrial Tribunals (Scotland) Regulations 1965 to 1972.

(2) These Regulations shall come into operation on 1st June 1972.

Interpretation

2. The Interpretation Act 1889(**e**) shall apply to the interpretation of these Regulations as it applies to the interpretation of an Act of Parliament.

Amendment of the principal Regulations

3. For Regulation 3(2) of the principal Regulations there shall be substituted the following—

"(2) The President shall vacate his office at the end of the completed year of service in the course of which he attains the age of seventy-two years."

20th April 1972.

Maurice Macmillan,
Secretary of State for Employment.

(**a**) 1964 c. 16.
(**c**) S.I. 1967/302 (1967 I, p. 1050).
(**e**) 1889 c. 63.
(**b**) S.I. 1965/1157 (1965 II, p. 3266).
(**d**) S.I. 1971/1661 (1971 III, p. 4561).

EXPLANATORY NOTE

(This Note is not part of the Regulations.)

These Regulations amend the Industrial Tribunals (Scotland) Regulations 1965, as previously amended, by providing that the President of the Industrial Tribunals (Scotland) shall vacate his office at the end of the completed year of service in the course of which he attains the age of seventy-two years.

STATUTORY INSTRUMENTS

1972 No. 640

MEDICINES

The Medicines (Exemption from Licences) (Wholesale Dealing) Order 1972

Made - - -	*21st April* 1972
Laid before Parliament	*1st May* 1972
Coming into Operation	*22nd May* 1972

The Secretaries of State respectively concerned with health in England and in Wales, the Secretary of State concerned with health and with agriculture in Scotland, the Secretary of State for Northern Ireland and the Minister of Agriculture, Fisheries and Food, acting jointly, in exercise of their powers under section 15(1) of the Medicines Act 1968(a) (as having effect subject to the provisions of Article 2(2) of, and Schedule 1 to the Transfer of Functions (Wales) Order 1969(b) and section 1(1)(a) of the Northern Ireland (Temporary Provisions) Act 1972(c)) and of all other powers enabling them in that behalf, after consulting such organisations as appear to them to be representative of interests likely to be substantially affected by the following order, hereby make the following order:—

Citation, commencement and interpretation

1.—(1) This order may be cited as the Medicines (Exemption from Licences) (Wholesale Dealings) Order 1972 and shall come into operation on 22nd May 1972.

(2) In this order, unless the context otherwise requires—

"the Act" means the Medicines Act 1968;

"medicinal product" includes substances or articles specified in orders made under section 104 or section 105 of the Act which are for the time being in force and which direct that Part II of the Act shall have effect in relation to such substances or articles as that Part has effect in relation to medicinal products within the meaning of the Act;

and other expressions have the same meaning as in the Act.

(3) Except in so far as the context otherwise requires, any reference in this order to any enactment or order shall be construed as a reference to that enactment or order as the case may be amended or extended by any other enactment or order.

(4) The Interpretation Act 1889(d) applies for the purpose of the interpretation of this order as it applies for the purpose of the interpretation of an Act of Parliament.

(a) 1968 c. 67. (b) S.I. 1969/388 (1969 I, p. 1070).
(c) 1972 c. 22. (d) 1889 c. 63.

Exemption from wholesale dealer's licences

2.—(1) The restrictions imposed by section 8(3) of the Act (restrictions as to wholesale dealing) shall not apply to the sale or offer for sale of a medicinal product by way of wholesale dealing where such sale or offer for sale is either—

    (*a*) by the holder of a product licence which relates to that medicinal product, including such holder of such product licence who is the person who assembled that medicinal product, or

    (*b*) by a person who, not being the holder of such a product licence, assembled that medicinal product, where such assembly was to the order of a person who is the holder of such a product licence,

provided that throughout the period until such sale that medicinal product has not left the premises of any person who either manufactured or assembled that medicinal product being premises which by virtue of the relevant manufacturer's licence the person who so manufactures or, as the case may be, assembles that medicinal product is enabled or authorised to use for the purposes of that licence (hereinafter in this article referred to as "the authorised premises").

(2) For the purposes of this article a medicinal product shall not be regarded as having left the authorised premises whilst that medicinal product is being moved from any of the authorised premises to another, or from one part of the authorised premises to another part, or whilst it is being moved from any of the authorised premises by way of delivery to the purchaser.

Keith Joseph,
Secretary of State for Social Services.

18th April 1972.

Peter Thomas,
Secretary of State for Wales.

19th April 1972.

Gordon Campbell,
Secretary of State for Scotland.

20th April 1972.

21st April 1972.

W. S. I. Whitelaw,
Secretary of State for Northern Ireland.

In witness whereof the official seal of the Minister of Agriculture, Fisheries and Food is hereunto affixed on 21st April 1972.

(L.S.)

J. M. L. Prior,
Minister of Agriculture, Fisheries and Food.

EXPLANATORY NOTE

(This Note is not part of the Order.)

This Order exempts from the restrictions imposed by Section 8(3) of the Medicines Act 1968 as to wholesale dealing in medicinal products except in accordance with a licence granted under that Act, the sale or offer for sale by way of wholesale dealing of a medicinal product by the product licence holder or by the person who assembled that medicinal product to the order of the product licence holder where the product has not left the premises of a licensed manufacturer or assembler throughout the period until the sale of that medicinal product.

STOKE-ON-TRENT
CITY
LIBRARIES

STATUTORY INSTRUMENTS

1972 No. 641

NATIONAL DEBT

The Savings Certificates Regulations 1972

Made - - - -	20*th April* 1972
Laid before Parliament	1*st May* 1972
Coming into Operation	1*st June* 1972

ARRANGEMENT OF REGULATIONS

PRELIMINARY

ISSUE AND PURCHASE OF CERTIFICATES

REPAYMENT OF CERTIFICATES

TRANSFER OF CERTIFICATES AND ADDITION OF NAMES

NOMINATIONS

Payment in case of death

Miscellaneous

The Treasury, in exercise of the powers conferred on them by section 12 of the National Debt Act 1958(a), as amended by section 110 of the Post Office Act 1969(b), and of all other powers enabling them in that behalf, hereby make the following Regulations:—

Preliminary

Citation and commencement

1. These Regulations may be cited as the Savings Certificates Regulations 1972, and shall come into operation on 1st June 1972.

Interpretation

2.—(1) In these Regulations, unless the context otherwise requires—

"amount repayable", in relation to any certificate, includes any interest which has accrued due in respect of that certificate;

(a) 1958 c. 6 (7 & 8 Eliz. 2).   (b) 1969 c. 48.

"certificate" means a certificate issued under the name of a war savings certificate or a national savings certificate by the Treasury through the department of the Postmaster General or under the auspices of the Director of Savings for the purpose of raising money authorised to be raised by any Act;

"friendly society" means a friendly society registered under the Friendly Societies Act 1896(a) or a branch registered under that Act of a friendly society so registered;

"mentally disordered person", in the application of these Regulations to England and Wales, means a person who is incapable, by reason of mental disorder within the meaning of the Mental Health Act 1959(b) of managing and administering his property and affairs;

"multiple certificate" means a certificate representing any number of unit certificates and entitling the holder to receive the aggregate amount of the sums repayable in respect of that number of unit certificates;

"receiver", in the application of these Regulations to England and Wales, means, in relation to any act or thing done in respect of a mentally disordered person, a receiver or other person authorised in that behalf under Part VIII of the Mental Health Act 1959;

"Treasury Solicitor" means the Solicitor for the affairs of Her Majesty's Treasury;

"trustee savings bank" means any trustee savings bank within the meaning of the Trustee Savings Banks Act 1969(c);

"unit certificate" means, in relation to certificates of any series, a certificate issued on payment of the minimum amount for which a certificate of that series is issued.

(2) Any reference in these Regulations to the provisions of any enactment or regulations shall be construed, unless the context otherwise requires, as a reference to those provisions as amended by any other enactment or regulations.

(3) The Interpretation Act 1889(d) shall apply for the interpretation of these Regulations as it applies for the interpretation of an Act of Parliament, and as if these Regulations and the Regulations hereby revoked were Acts of Parliament.

Issue and Purchase of Certificates

Issue, purchase and recording of certificates

3.—(1) Certificates shall be issued at such places as the Director of Savings shall determine and by such persons as he shall authorise.

(2) An application to purchase a certificate shall be made in a manner approved by the Director of Savings, and, for the purposes of any such application, the applicant shall deliver to the Director of Savings such documents and other information in writing as he may require.

(3) The names of all persons who are for the time being holders of certificates shall be recorded by the Director of Savings.

(a) 1896 c. 25.   (b) 1959 c. 72.
(c) 1969 c. 50.   (d) 1889 c. 63.

Persons entitled to purchase and hold certificates

4.—(1) A certificate may be purchased and held by any of the following persons or by any two or more such persons jointly, that is to say—

(*a*) any person who has attained the age of seven years and who is not under any legal disability otherwise than by reason of his age;

(*b*) a friendly society;

(*c*) any other body of persons which the Director of Savings may in his discretion approve for the purpose, either generally or with respect to any particular purchase.

(2) Subject to the provisions of these Regulations, a certificate may be purchased—

(*a*) on behalf of and in the name of a person under the age of seven years, by any other person; and

(*b*) on behalf of and in the name of a mentally disordered person, by his receiver;

and any certificate so purchased shall be deemed to be held by the person on whose behalf it is purchased.

(3) Subject to the provisions of these Regulations, a certificate may be either—

(*a*) purchased and held by a trustee or by two or more trustees jointly; or

(*b*) purchased by a person acting as trustee on behalf of—

(i) any person entitled under sub-paragraph (*a*) of paragraph (1) of this Regulation to purchase and hold a certificate; or

(ii) any person under the age of seven years,

and in the joint names of the trustee and the beneficiary, in which case the certificate shall be held by them jointly:

Provided that no certificate shall be purchased under sub-paragraph (*a*) of this paragraph by a trustee or trustees on behalf of any body of persons (other than a friendly society), whether corporate or unincorporate, without the approval of the Director of Savings, which approval may be either general or limited to a particular purchase.

(4) Where a certificate is purchased and held by a trustee or trustees under sub-paragraph (*a*) of paragraph (3) of this Regulation, he or they may be described in the records kept by the Director of Savings as trustee or trustees of a specified trust or as a trustee or trustees without specifying a trust.

(5) Where a certificate has been purchased on behalf of a person who was, at the date of the purchase, under the age of seven years, the Director of Savings may, at any time after that person has attained the age of seven years, require a specimen of his signature.

Maximum holding of certificates

5.—(1) A person shall not purchase any certificates, or hold any certificates purchased on his behalf under Regulation 4(2) of these Regulations, if the total number of unit certificates which will be held by him immediately after the purchase (whether solely or jointly with any person) will exceed—

(*a*) 500, in the case of certificates issued not later than 31st March 1947 the price of issue of which is less than £1 per unit certificate, and (*b*) 250, in the case of certificates issued not later than 31st March 1947 the price of issue of which is £1 per unit certificate, and

(*c*) 1,000, in the case of certificates issued after 31st March 1947 but not later than 31st January 1951, and

(*d*) 1,400, in the case of certificates issued after 31st January 1951 but not later than 31st July, 1956, and

(*e*) 1,200, in the case of certificates issued after 31st July 1956 but not later than 12th March 1963, and

(*f*) 600, in the case of certificates issued after 12th March 1963 but not later than 27th March 1966, and

(*g*) 1,500, in the case of certificates issued after 27th March 1966 but not later than 4th October 1970, and

(*h*) 1,000, in the case of certificates issued after 4th October 1970.

(2) For the purposes of this Regulation, a person who is a trustee or who holds certificates as a beneficiary jointly with a trustee shall be treated separately in his personal capacity and in his capacity as trustee and in his capacity as such beneficiary, and in either of the last two capacities separately in respect of each separate trust fund; and so much of the property in the hands of a trustee shall be treated as a separate trust fund as is held on trusts which (as respects the beneficiaries or their respective interests or the purposes of the trust or as respects the powers of the trustee) are not identical with those on which other property in his hands is held.

(3) In calculating for the purposes of this Regulation the total number of unit certificates which a person holds, a multiple certificate shall be taken to be such number of unit certificates as is represented by the multiple certificate, but no account shall be taken of any certificate which that person holds and which—

(*a*) was purchased by him or on his behalf out of moneys payable to him on account of a gratuity in respect of service in the 1914-1918 war and formed part of a special issue made in connection with war service gratuities, or

(*b*) has been acquired by him—

(i) as a member of a savings group working under the rules of the Provident Scheme of the National Savings Committee for England and Wales or of the National Savings Committee for Scotland, or

(ii) under the Pensioners' Savings Scheme of the Department of Health and Social Security.

REPAYMENT OF CERTIFICATES

Applications for repayment

6.—(1) Application for payment of the amount repayable in respect of a certificate shall (subject to the provisions of these Regulations relating to payment in the case of special classes of persons) be made by the holder of the certificate in writing in a manner approved by the Director of Savings.

(2) In the case of a multiple certificate, an application may be made for repayment in respect of any number of the unit certificates represented by the multiple certificate.

(3) The holder of a certificate, being a person who has attained the age of seven years, may, subject to the approval of the Director of Savings, authorise any person to apply for or receive on his behalf the amount repayable in respect of the certificate.

Repayment warrants

7.—(1) Except where the Director of Savings otherwise directs, every payment of an amount repayable in respect of a certificate shall be made by a warrant; and accordingly every application for payment of any such amount shall be treated as implying an authority to him to issue a warrant for that amount and to pay it in accordance with the terms of the warrant, and the death of the person who made the application for repayment shall not of itself determine such authority; but if the Director of Savings receives notice that the applicant has died or has countermanded such authority, the Director of Savings shall not issue the warrant or, if it has already been issued, shall take all reasonable steps to stop payment thereof.

(2) The provisions of section 76, subsections (1), (3), (4) and (5) and, so far as it relates to crossed cheques, subsection (6) of section 77, and sections 78, 79, 80 and 81 of the Bills of Exchange Act 1882(a) (which relate to crossed cheques) and of sections 3 and 4 of the Cheques Act 1957(b) (which relate to unindorsed cheques as evidence of payment and to the protection of collecting bankers) shall apply to any crossed warrant issued under these Regulations as if the warrant were a cheque drawn on the Director of Savings by the officer issuing the warrant, but nothing in these Regulations shall make any such warrant negotiable.

(3) An uncrossed warrant shall not be paid until the receipt for the amount thereby payable has been duly signed by the payee or by some person authorised by the payee to receive payment:

Provided that, where such a warrant is paid to a person purporting to be the payee or to be a person authorised by the payee to receive payment, then, notwithstanding that the receipt on the warrant was signed by some person being neither the payee nor a person so authorised, the making of the payment shall be a full discharge to the Treasury and to the Director of Savings for the amount thereof, if it is shown that the payment was made in good faith and without negligence, and that the making of the payment is attributable to some act or omission on the part of the holder of the certificate to which the warrant relates or on the part of the payee or the person so authorised.

(4) Notwithstanding anything in paragraph (3) above, where an uncrossed warrant for the amount repayable in respect of any certificate is made payable to the holder of the certificates, it may be paid to another person who signs the receipt on the warrant and forthwith reinvests the amount of the payment in certificates in the name of the holder of the repaid certificates; and the making of the payment shall be a full discharge to the Treasury and to the Director of Savings for the amount thereof.

(5) Except where the Director of Savings otherwise directs, a warrant shall not be paid until the certificate in respect of which the repayment is to be made has been delivered to the Director of Savings.

(a) 1882 c. 61.   (b) 1957 c. 36.

(6) An uncrossed warrant shall be payable at the place named in the warrant or otherwise in accordance with the directions contained therein, and a crossed warrant shall be payable at the office in London of the Director of Savings or at such other place as he may direct.

(7) For the purpose of determining the amount repayable in respect of a certificate, the payment of the amount repayable thereunder shall be deemed to be effected on the date on which the warrant is issued.

(8) The posting of a letter containing a warrant addressed to any person at the last address furnished by him to the Director of Savings shall, as regards the liability of the Treasury or the Director of Savings, be equivalent to the delivery of the warrant to the person to whom the letter was addressed.

Repayment in case of persons under 7 years of age and mentally disordered persons

8.—(1) Subject to the provisions of this Regulation, no repayment shall be made in respect of a certificate held by a person under the age of seven years.

(2) An application for repayment in respect of a certificate held by a mentally disordered person shall be made by his receiver.

(3) Where it is shown to the satisfaction of the Director of Savings that any person holding, or having an interest in, a certificate is either a person under the age of seven years or a mentally disordered person for whose estate no receiver has been appointed, the Director of Savings may, if he thinks fit, pay the whole or any part of the amount repayable in respect of the certificate to any person who satisfies him that he is a proper person to receive payment.

Repayment in case of certificate held by persons jointly

9.—(1) Application for payment of the amount repayable in respect of a certificate held in the names of two or more persons as joint holders shall be made by all those persons or, in the case of the death of one or more of them, by the survivors:

Provided that—

    (*a*) where one of any joint holders of a certificate, being a trustee for the other or others of them, becomes bankrupt or a mentally disordered person, the application may be made by the other or others of them without the concurrence of the trustee in bankruptcy or the receiver, if any, and the Director of Savings, if he thinks fit, may, without any such concurrence, pay the amount repayable in respect of the certificate in the same manner as if the trustee in question were not one of the holders of the certificate; and

    (*b*) where one of any joint holders of a certificate is the Public Trustee, the application may be made by him alone, and the Director of Savings shall pay the amount repayable in respect of the certificate to the Public Trustee alone.

(2) The joint holders of a certificate may authorise any person, including one of themselves, to act as their agent for the purpose of receiving on their behalf any amount repayable in respect of the certificate.

Repayment to friendly societies, etc.

10.—(1) Any application for payment of the amount repayable in respect of certificates held by a friendly society or any other body of persons, corporate or unincorporate, shall be made by that society or body in the names of the persons specified as the persons authorised to apply for repayment on behalf of the society or body in any direction given to the Director of Savings from time to time by the society or body in a form approved by the Director of Savings or, where no such direction has been given, in the names of such persons as the Director of Savings may approve.

(2) Where, in pursuance of these Regulations, any amount is repayable to any friendly society or other body of persons, whether corporate or unincorporate, a receipt for the amount may be given by any person purporting to be an agent or officer of that society or body authorised to receive the repayment.

Repayment in case of bankrupts

11. Where it is shown to the satisfaction of the Director of Savings that a receiving order has been made against any person who is the sole holder of a certificate, or that a trustee has been appointed in the bankruptcy of any such person, or that an order for the administration in bankruptcy of the estate of a deceased sole holder has been made, the Director of Savings may, if he thinks fit, on an application made in that behalf by the Official Receiver or trustee, pay to the Official Receiver or the trustee, as the case may be, the amount repayable in respect of that certificate.

TRANSFER OF CERTIFICATES AND ADDITION OF NAMES

Transfers and addition of names

12.—(1) Every transfer of a certificate shall be effected by the Director of Savings causing the name of the person to whom the certificate is to be transferred to be recorded as the holder thereof.

(2) The Director of Savings may in his discretion refuse to transfer a certificate, but shall, if he so refuses, forthwith send an intimation of his refusal to the person desiring the transfer:

Provided that nothing in this paragraph shall affect any right of a nominee.

(3) A certificate shall not be transferred except on a written application in that behalf made, in a manner approved by the Director of Savings, by the holder of the certificate, and every such application must, except where the Director of Savings otherwise directs, be accompanied by the certificate to which it relates.

(4) On the receipt of an application duly made for the transfer of a certificate, the Director of Savings, if he is satisfied that the transfer can lawfully be made under these Regulations and ought to be made, shall forthwith cause the certificate to be transferred in accordance with the application, and the death of the applicant shall not of itself determine the authority given by the applicant for the transfer to be made; but if the Director of Savings receives notice before the certificate is transferred that the applicant has died, the transfer shall not be made.

(5) On the application of the holder of a certificate, the Director of Savings may, if he thinks fit and subject to the provisions of these Regulations, cause the names of any persons to be recorded as joint holders of the certificate with the applicant.

(6) Notwithstanding anything in paragraph (3) of this Regulation, where a certificate is held by any person as a trustee jointly with the beneficiary, the Director of Savings may, if he thinks fit, on the application of any person being a holder of the certificate cause the certificate to be transferred either to the beneficiary alone or to the beneficiary and another trustee.

(7) This Regulation shall, so far as applicable, apply, in the event of the death of the holder of a certificate, to the transfer of the certificate, and, in particular, any person to whom the amount repayable in respect of the certificate may be paid in accordance with the provisions of these Regulations may, subject to the provisions of these Regulations, instead of obtaining payment of the amount repayable, apply for the transfer of the certificate into his name or the name of another person.

NOMINATIONS

Power of holder of certificate to nominate

13.—(1) Subject to the provisions of these Regulations, a holder of a certificate, being a person who has attained the age of sixteen years, may make a nomination directing that, on his death, his interest in any certificate then held by him shall devolve in such manner as may, in accordance with the provisions of paragraph (2) of this Regulation, be provided by the nomination.

(2) A nomination may provide—

(*a*) that the interest of the nominator in all certificates held by him at the date of his death shall devolve on any one or more persons specified in the nomination; or

(*b*) that the interest of the nominator in such of those certificates as may be specified in the nomination shall devolve on any nominee or nominees so specified; or

(*c*) where there is more than one nominee, that the interest of the nominator in different certificates shall devolve on different nominees.

Form of nomination

14. Every nomination shall be made in writing in a form approved by the Director of Savings and shall be signed by the nominator in the presence of a witness, and the signature of the nominator shall be attested by the witness.

Validity, retention and acknowledgment of nomination

15.—(1) A nomination shall be of no effect unless it is sent to the Director of Savings during the lifetime of the nominator.

(2) The Director of Savings may in his discretion refuse to accept any nomination received by him, and upon a notification of the refusal of the Director of Savings to accept a nomination being sent to the nominator, the nomination shall be of no effect.

(3) The Director of Savings shall retain every nomination received by him, and shall, as soon as may be after the receipt of a nomination, send to the nominator (whether by post or otherwise) an acknowledgement of the receipt of the nomination and, if the Director of Savings refuses to accept the nomination, a notification of his refusal.

Revocation of nomination

16.—(1) A nomination shall be revoked—

(a) by the death of the nominee or, where there is more than one nominee, of all the nominees in the lifetime of the nominator;

(b) so far as relates to the interest thereunder of any nominee, being one of two or more nominees, by the death of that nominee in the lifetime of the nominator, unless the interest of that nominee is disposed of by the nomination;

(c) by the marriage of the nominator;

(d) by written notice of revocation given in accordance with this Regulation;

(e) subject as hereinafter provided, by a subsequent nomination duly made in accordance with these Regulations by the same nominator, disposing of the nominator's interest in any certificate to which the previous nomination relates;

but a nomination shall not be revoked by any other act, event or means whatsoever:

Provided that a nomination disposing of the nominator's interest in any certificate to which a previous nomination relates shall operate as a revocation of that nomination so far only as it relates to that certificate.

(2) A notice of revocation for the purposes of these Regulations shall be signed by the nominator in the presence of a witness, and the signature of the nominator shall be attested by the witness, and the notice shall be of no effect unless it is despatched to the Director of Savings during the lifetime of the nominator.

(3) Notwithstanding that a nomination has been revoked by the marriage of the nominator, any payment or transfer which, before the marriage comes to the knowledge of the Director of Savings, is made by him in respect of any certificate held by the nominator at the date of his death, being a payment or transfer which would have been a lawful payment or transfer if the nomination had not been so revoked, shall, subject to the provisions of these Regulations for saving the rights of third parties, be as valid as if the nomination had not been so revoked.

Particulars to be furnished by nominator to Director of Savings

17.—(1) A nominator shall, on making a nomination, furnish to the Director of Savings such particulars of the certificates held by him at the date of the nomination as the Director of Savings may require.

(2) Where, by reason of the failure of a nominator to comply with the foregoing requirements of this Regulation, any money payable in respect of all or any of the certificates held by the nominator at the date of his death is paid, or any transfer of such certificates is made, to a person other than the nominee or a

person claiming through him, that payment or transfer shall, subject to the provisions of these Regulations for saving the rights of third parties, be as valid as if the nomination had not been made.

Operation of nomination

18.—(1) On the death of any nominator, the Director of Savings shall, as the nominee or nominees may require, either pay the amount repayable in respect of the certificates which are the subject of the nomination to him or them, or as he or they may direct, or transfer such certificates to him or them:

Provided that—

(*a*) a nominee shall not be entitled under this paragraph to have any certificates transferred to him unless he is entitled under paragraph (1) or (2) of Regulation 4 of these Regulations to hold a certificate;

(*b*) the witness to the signature of a nominator shall not be entitled to take any benefit under the nomination;

(*c*) if, on the death of a nominator, any nominee is under the age of sixteen years, the Director of Savings shall not make any payment or transfer any certificate to, or at the request of, that nominee until he attains that age, but may—

(i) if it is shown to the satisfaction of the Director of Savings that it is expedient that the said amount or any part thereof should be paid and applied for the maintenance or otherwise for the benefit of that nominee, pay the said amount or that part thereof to any person who satisfies the Director of Savings that he will apply it for such purposes as aforesaid; or

(ii) at the request of the nominee, re-invest the said amount or any part thereof in new certificates, which shall then be treated as if they were the certificates which were the subject of the nomination;

(*d*) where it appears to the Director of Savings that the estate of the nominator, apart from the certificates nominated, is insufficient to meet the funeral expenses or satisfy any claims of creditors of the nominator of which the Director of Savings has notice (including, in a case where the nominator was domiciled in Scotland, claims under the Succession (Scotland) Act 1964**(a)** and in respect of jus relicti, jus relictae or legitim), he may, if he thinks fit, apply the amount repayable in respect of the certificates, or any part thereof, in or towards payment of such funeral expenses or in or towards satisfaction of the claim of any person in respect of such funeral expenses paid by that person or of the claims of any such creditors.

(2) Where a nominee dies after the death of the nominator, but before any sum has been paid, or the certificate has been transferred, to him as nominee, the certificate shall, subject to the provisions of these Regulations, be deemed to have been transferred to the nominee immediately before the date of his death.

(3) Notwithstanding any rule of law to the contrary, any nominee to whom a payment may be made under this Regulation may sign a receipt therefor if he has attained the age of sixteen years, and the receipt shall be a valid receipt without the signature of any other person.

(a) 1964 c. 41.

PAYMENT IN CASE OF DEATH

Payment under grant of representation

19.—(1) In the event of the death of the holder of a certificate, the production of probate or letters of administration granted, or having effect as if granted, in respect of personal estate comprising the certificate by a court in the United Kingdom, the Isle of Man or the Channel Islands, or of a certified copy thereof, shall, subject to the provisions of these Regulations, be sufficient authority to the Director of Savings to pay the amount repayable in respect of the certificate, or to transfer the certificate, to the person to whom the grant was made, or as directed by that person.

(2) Where any sum repayable in respect of a certificate is paid, or a certificate is transferred, in purported pursuance of this Regulation, the payment or transfer shall, notwithstanding the invalidity of, or any defect in, the probate or letters of administration, be deemed for the purposes of these Regulations to have been duly made.

(3) Nothing in this Regulation shall affect the operation of any nomination duly made under these Regulations.

Payment without a grant of representation

20.—(1) Where, on the death of any person, being the sole holder of certificates the amount repayable in respect of which does not, at the time of his death, exceed in the aggregate £500, probate of his will or letters of administration to his estate is not or are not produced to the Director of Savings within such time as he thinks reasonable in the circumstances of the case, the Director of Savings, if he thinks fit, may, without requiring probate or letters of administration, pay the amount repayable in respect of those certificates, or any part of that amount—

(a) to a person appearing to the Director of Savings to be entitled to take out probate of the will of the deceased or letters of administration to his estate;

(b) where the deceased has left a will (being a will with respect to which the Director of Savings is satisfied that probate or letters of administration with the will annexed would be granted), to any person to whom the amount repayable or any part thereof would, in the opinion of the Director of Savings, be payable under such will, if probate thereof or letters of administration with the will annexed were granted;

(c) to any person who satisfies the Director of Savings that he is entitled to receive the amount repayable or any part thereof in right of his being—

(i) a person who has paid the funeral expenses of the deceased; or

(ii) a creditor of the deceased; or

(iii) a person who has a beneficial interest in the estate of the deceased;

(d) if the deceased was a British subject and his next of kin appears to the Director of Savings to reside outside the United Kingdom, the Isle of Man and the Channel Islands, to any officer or authority who, in the opinion of the Director of Savings, may properly be entrusted with the duty of distributing the amount repayable;

(*e*) if the deceased was a seaman of a foreign country, being a country with which a treaty has been made in respect of the payment of moneys due to seamen, to the consular authority of that country;

(*f*) if the deceased was a foreign subject, not being a seaman to whom the provisions of the last preceding sub-paragraph apply, to the consular authority of the country to which the deceased belonged, or to such other authority as appears to the Director of Savings to be appropriate, subject in either case to the Director of Savings being satisfied that the amount repayable will be duly distributed;

(*g*) in a case where the estate of the deceased appears to the Director of Savings to have devolved upon the Crown, the Duchy of Lancaster or the Duchy of Cornwall, to the Treasury Solicitor, the Solicitor for the Affairs of the Duchy of Lancaster or the Solicitor for the Affairs of the Duchy of Cornwall, as the case requires:

Provided that where a person to whom any sum may be paid under sub-paragraph (*b*) or (*c*) of this paragraph has died before payment has been made to him, that sum or any part thereof may be paid to any person to whom it might have been paid if the first mentioned person had, immediately before his death, been the sole holder of the certificates in question.

(2) Notwithstanding any rule of law to the contrary, any person to whom a payment may be made under sub-paragraph (*b*) or (*c*) of paragraph (1) of this Regulation or under the proviso to that paragraph may sign a receipt therefor if he has attained the age of sixteen years, and the receipt shall be a valid receipt without the signature of any other person, and where any person to whom a payment may be so made is unable, by reason of his age or for any other reason whatsoever, to give a discharge therefor under these Regulations, the Director of Savings may make the payment to any person who satisfies him that he will apply it for the maintenance or otherwise for the benefit of the first mentioned person.

(3) Subject to the provisions of the last preceding paragraph, the Director of Savings, in making any payment under sub-paragraph (*b*) or (*c*) of paragraph (1) of this Regulation or under the proviso to that paragraph, shall, unless he is of opinion that hardship or inconvenience would be thereby caused, have regard to the rules of law relating to the distribution of the estates of deceased persons, but, if he is of that opinion, may depart from those rules in such manner and to such extent as he considers just.

(4) In this Regulation the expression "will" includes a codicil.

(5) Nothing in this Regulation shall affect the operation of any nomination duly made under these Regulations.

Law applicable on holder's death

21. Where, in the event of the death of the holder of a certificate, any payment in respect of the certificate made under these Regulations is made in accordance with the law of the place where the holder of the certificate resided at the date of his death, that payment shall, unless notice in writing to the effect that the holder was, at that date, domiciled in some other place has been received by the Director of Savings before the payment was made, be deemed for the purposes of these Regulations to have been duly made.

Death duties

22.—(1) Where, on the death of the holder of any certificate (not being a certificate in respect of which it is shown to the satisfaction of the Director of Savings that the deceased holder had no interest therein otherwise than as a trustee), the aggregate value of the specified assets (hereinafter defined) exceeds £3,000, the Director of Savings shall, before making any payment in respect of, or transferring, the certificate, require the production of a statement from the Commissioners of Inland Revenue to the effect either that no death duties are payable in respect of the certificate or that any death duties so payable have been paid:

Provided that the production of such a statement shall not be required—

(a) where the repayment or transfer is made to or as directed by the legal personal representative of the deceased holder, or the Public Trustee, or the Official Receiver, or the trustee in bankruptcy of the estate of the deceased holder;

(b) where the deceased holder was at the time of his death domiciled in Northern Ireland, the Isle of Man or the Channel Islands.

(2) In this Regulation the expression "the specified assets" means the following assets (not being assets in respect of which it is shown to the satisfaction of the Director of Savings that the deceased holder had no interest therein otherwise than as a trustee):—

(a) the total amount which would have been repayable (if repayment had been demanded) at the date of the death of the holder in respect of all certificates recorded in his name alone or in his name jointly with any other person;

(b) the total amount (including interest) which, at the date of the death of the holder, stands to the credit of all accounts in his name alone, or in his name jointly with any other person, in the National Savings Bank;

(c) all stock and securities registered on the National Savings Stock Register at the date of the death of the holder in his name alone or in his name jointly with any other person (not being stock or securities recorded on the parts of the National Savings Stock Register kept by trustee savings banks);

(d) any amount repayable and any other sum payable in respect of all premium savings bonds recorded in the holder's name;

(e) the total amount (including any bonus or interest) which would have been repayable (if repayment had been demanded) at the date of the death of the holder in respect of all savings contracts entered into by him and registered by the Director of Savings under a contractual savings scheme certified by the Treasury in accordance with section 415(2) of the Income and Corporation Taxes Act 1970**(a)**.

(3) For the purposes of this Regulation, the value of the stock and securities referred to in paragraph (2)(c) of this Regulation shall be—

(a) in the case of National Development Bonds, British Savings Bonds and any other securities which can be held only on the National Savings Stock Register, the nominal capital amount thereof; and

(b) in all other cases, the market value thereof at the date of the death of the holder.

(a) 1970 c. 10.

Persons under disability

23. If any person holding, or having an interest in, any certificate is a mentally disordered person or is under legal disability for any other reason except his age alone, anything which under these Regulations is required or authorised to be done by or to the holder of the certificate shall or may be done by or to the receiver or other person having power in law to administer his estate.

Payments into National Savings Bank

24.—(1) Where the Director of Savings is unable for any reason to obtain a valid discharge for any payment falling to be made to any person in respect of a certificate, he may, unless other provision for dealing with the payment has been made by any enactment, open an account in the National Savings Bank in the name of the person to whom the payment is due, and may, until payment can be made to the person entitled thereto, retain the amount due in that account:

Provided that—

(a) if the person to whom the payment is due has an account in the National Savings Bank, the Director of Savings may, if he thinks fit, instead of opening a new account, credit the amount payable to the existing account; and

(b) in the case of an account opened by the Director of Savings—

(i) no sum shall be received by way of deposit for the credit of the account except in pursuance of these Regulations; and

(ii) the regulations requiring a declaration to be made by a depositor in the National Savings Bank shall not apply with respect to any payment into the account by the Director of Savings.

(2) For the purpose of any Order under section 4 of the National Savings Bank Act 1971(a) (which empowers the Treasury by order to limit the amount of deposits in the National Savings Bank) or any Order having effect as if made under that section, regard shall not be had to any sum credited to an account under this Regulation.

Loss of certificates, etc.

25.—(1) The loss or destruction of any document issued by the Director of Savings in pursuance of these Regulations, or by the Postmaster General or the Director of Savings in pursuance of any Regulations revoked by these Regulations, shall be notified in writing to the Director of Savings as soon as practicable by the person entitled to possession of the document.

(2) If it appears to the Director of Savings that any document so issued has been issued in error, lost, destroyed or tampered with, or is in such a condition as to render it desirable that it should be replaced by a new document, he may, subject to the provisions of this Regulation, issue a new document in lieu of the old document to any person who satisfies him that he is entitled to the possession of the document.

(3) The Director of Savings may attach to the issue under this Regulation of any new document such conditions as to indemnity or otherwise as he thinks fit.

(a) 1971 c. 29.

Forfeiture of certificates

26.—(1) Subject to the provisions of this Regulation. if any person—

(*a*) not being a person entitled under Regulation 4 of these Regulations so to do, purchases or holds a certificate; or

(*b*) purchases or holds any certificate in contravention of Regulation 5 of these Regulations (which prescribes the maximum number of unit certificates which may be purchased);

the certificate shall, if the Director of Savings so directs, be forfeited:

Provided that, if in any case in which the Director of Savings has directed the forfeiture of any certificates, he is satisfied that the contravention in question was inadvertent and that in the circumstances forfeiture will cause undue hardship to the person concerned, he may, if he thinks fit, pay to that person or credit to him in the National Savings Bank—

(i) a sum equal to the aggregate amount of the purchase price of the certificates forfeited;

(ii) (in the case of any certificates which the person concerned has purchased or held when he was not entitled so to do under Regulation 4 of these Regulations) such sum by way of interest, not exceeding the amount of interest which had accrued due in respect of those certificates immediately before the forfeiture thereof, as the Director of Savings may determine;

(iii) (in the case of any certificates which the person concerned has purchased or held in contravention of Regulation 5 of these Regulations) interest, at such rate not exceeding the rate of interest for the time being payable on ordinary deposits in the National Savings Bank as the Director of Savings thinks fit, on a sum equal to the purchase price of those certificates, being interest computed in such manner as the Director of Savings, with the approval of the Treasury, may direct.

(2) For the purposes of the foregoing provisions of this Regulation, a multiple certificate shall be taken to be such number of unit certificates as is represented by the multiple certificate.

(3) For the purposes of any Order under section 4 of the National Savings Bank Act 1971 (which empowers the Treasury by order to limit the amount of deposits in the National Savings Bank) or any Order having effect as if made under that section, any sum credited to a person under this Regulation shall, if the Director of Savings so directs, be disregarded.

(4) Notice of any forfeiture under this Regulation shall be sent to the person concerned as soon as may be, and the Director of Savings may require any certificate which might be or is affected to be delivered up to him for the purpose of being either cancelled or altered or otherwise dealt with, as may be necessary to give effect to the provisions of this Regulation.

Persons unable to write

27. Where any document is required by the Director of Savings or by these Regulations to be signed by any person and that person is unable to write, it shall be sufficient for the purposes of these Regulations if the document is marked by that person in the presence of a witness in such manner as the Director of Savings may require.

Rectification of mistakes

28.—(1) Any mistake in any document received from the Director of Savings in pursuance of these Regulations, or from the Postmaster General or the Director of Savings in pursuance of any Regulations revoked by these Regulations, shall, as soon as practicable, be notified in writing to the Director of Savings by the person receiving the document.

(2) If the Director of Savings is satisfied that any transaction effected or thing done, or purporting to have been effected or done, in accordance with these Regulations or any Regulations revoked by these Regulations has been effected or done in error, he may cancel the transaction and may take all such steps as are, in his opinion, necessary to rectify the error, and may for that purpose require the surrender to him of any certificate or other document.

Settlement of disputes

29.—(1) If any dispute arises between the Director of Savings and—

(a) the holder of any certificates, or

(b) a person who is or claims to be the personal representative or next of kin or creditor of a holder, or the trustee in bankruptcy or assignee of a holder who is bankrupt or insolvent, or

(c) a person who claims to be entitled to any certificate,

the matter in dispute shall be referred in writing to the Chief Registrar of Friendly Societies.

(2) On any such reference being made, the Chief Registrar may proceed ex parte on notice in writing sent by post to the Director of Savings, and may administer oaths to any witnesses appearing before him.

(3) The award of the Chief Registrar on any reference under this Regulation shall be final and binding on all parties.

(4) Section 11 of the National Savings Bank Act 1971 (which empowers the Treasury to direct that fees shall be charged on certain awards made by the Chief Registrar of Friendly Societies) shall have effect as if the awards therein mentioned included awards made under this Regulation.

Notice of trust not receivable by Director of Savings

30.—(1) Subject to the provisions of these Regulations, no notice of a trust shall be receivable by the Director of Savings in respect of a certificate.

(2) Neither the Director of Savings nor any person acquiring any interest in a certificate shall, by reason that the certificate is held in the name of any person as trustee (whether jointly with any other person or solely), be affected with notice of any trust or of the fiduciary character of the holder or of any fiduciary obligation attaching to the holding of the certificate.

Exemption from stamp duty

31. No stamp duty shall be charged on—

(a) a warrant for the payment of any amount repayable in respect of a certificate; or

(b) a power of attorney or other document which relates solely to the payment or receipt of any such amount.

Fees for birth, death and marriage certificates

32. Section 10 of the Savings Banks Act 1887(**a**) (which relates to the price of a certificate of birth, death or marriage required for the purpose of the Acts relating to the National Savings Bank), as amended by any Order in force for the time being under section 5 of the Public Expenditure and Receipts Act 1968(**b**), shall apply for the purposes of these Regulations as it applies for the purposes of those Acts, and for the purposes of these Regulations the said section 10 shall have effect as if the holder of a certificate or any person having an interest in a certificate were a depositor in the National Savings Bank.

Indemnity of Treasury, Director of Savings and officers

33.—(1) The Treasury, the Director of Savings and any person acting under his authority shall not be liable in respect of any payment duly made or act duly done in accordance with these Regulations, and any such payment shall, subject to the provisions of these Regulations for saving the rights of third parties, be deemed to have been a valid payment, and the receipt of the person to whom the money was paid shall be a full discharge to the Treasury and the Director of Savings for the amount of the payment.

(2) Where a warrant for payment of any amount repayable in respect of a certificate is issued payable to some person being neither the holder of the certificate nor a person otherwise entitled under these Regulations to receive payment in respect thereof, then, if it is shown that—

(*a*) the warrant was issued in good faith and without negligence; and

(*b*) the issue of the warrant to that person is attributable to some act or omission on the part of the holder or a person so entitled;

the warrant shall, subject to the provisions of these Regulations for saving the rights of third parties, be deemed to have been duly issued to a person so entitled.

Saving of rights of third parties

34. Nothing in these Regulations, or in any Regulations revoked by these Regulations, for the protection of the Treasury, the Director of Savings or the Postmaster General in respect of any act done or any money paid shall operate to prevent the recovery by any person or his representatives of any money lawfully due to him from the person to whom that money was paid by or under the direction of the Director of Savings or the Postmaster General, or from the representatives of that person, or affect the right which any person or his representatives may have in respect of a certificate against a third party.

Form of documents

35. Where any application is required by these Regulations to be made in a manner approved by the Director of Savings, the document in which the application is made shall contain a full and specific statement of the particulars required to be given, and any such document which is required by the Director of Savings to be signed by any person shall be signed by that person.

(**a**) 1887 c. 40.   (**b**) 1968 c. 14.

Evidence of identity, etc.

36.—(1) The Director of Savings shall be entitled to require evidence to be given to his satisfaction of the identity of any person or of the title of any person to any certificates, document or money, or to require evidence that anything purporting to be done in pursuance of these Regulations has been duly done, or otherwise with respect to any matters on which the due exercise of his powers or performance of his duties under these Regulations depends, and the Director of Savings may, for the purpose of obtaining any such evidence, require a statutory declaration to be made by any person.

(2) The Director of Savings may accept as conclusive proof of the death of the holder of a certificate any evidence which establishes to his satisfaction the fact that the holder has not been heard of for a period of seven years or upwards, and, for the purposes of this paragraph, the expression "holder of a certificate" includes any person beneficially interested at any time, whether absolutely or contingently, in the personal estate of the deceased holder of a certificate.

Obligation of secrecy

37.—(1) A person employed in connection with business arising under these Regulations shall not disclose to any person, other than the Director of Savings or a person employed in carrying these Regulations into execution, the name of the purchaser or holder of any certificate, the number of certificates purchased by any person, or the amount repaid in respect of any certificate.

(2) The last foregoing paragraph shall not prevent the disclosure by a person authorised for the purpose by the Director of Savings of information to any person in connection with an offence committed with reference to any certificate or for the purpose of ascertaining whether or not an offence has been so committed.

Saving for rights of joint holders, etc.

38.—(1) Nothing in these Regulations relating to joint holders of certificates shall affect the mutual rights of any joint holders.

(2) Nothing in these Regulations relating to trustees shall as between any trustees or as between any trustee and the beneficiaries under a trust be deemed to authorise the trustees to act otherwise than in accordance with the rules of law applying to the trust and the terms of the instrument (if any) constituting the trust.

Application to Scotland

39. In the application of these Regulations to Scotland—

(*a*) any reference to a mentally disordered person shall be construed as a reference to a person who is incapable by reason of mental disorder within the meaning of the Mental Health (Scotland) Act 1960**(a)** of managing and administering his property and affairs;

(*b*) any reference to a receiver in relation to a mentally disordered person shall be construed as a reference to a curator bonis, guardian or tutor;

(*c*) any reference to a receiving order shall be construed as a reference to an award of sequestration;

(a) 1960 c. 61.

(d) any reference to the Official Receiver shall be construed as a reference to the trustee or judical factor in bankruptcy;

(e) any reference to probate, letters of administration or letters of administration with the will annexed shall be construed as a reference to confirmation of an executor;

(f) any reference to the Treasury Solicitor shall be construed as a reference to the Queen's and Lord Treasurer's Remembrancer;

(g) any reference to the Chief Registrar of Friendly Societies shall be construed as a reference to the Assistant Registrar of Friendly Societies for Scotland.

Application to Northern Ireland

40.—(1) These Regulations shall extend to Northern Ireland.

(2) In the application of these Regulations to Northern Ireland—

(a) any reference to a mentally disordered person shall be construed as a reference to a person who, by reason of unsoundness of mind, or of mental disorder within the meaning of the Mental Health Act (Northern Ireland) 1961**(a)**, is or is considered incapable of managing his affairs;

(b) any reference to a receiver in relation to a mentally disordered person shall be construed as a reference to a committee or any other person appointed pursuant to the Lunacy Regulation (Ireland) Act 1871**(b)** (as amended) and the orders made thereunder to exercise with respect to the estate of such person powers similar to those of a committee;

(c) any reference to a receiving order shall be construed as a reference to an order of adjudication of bankruptcy, or to an order in any arrangement operating by virtue of section 349 of the Irish Bankrupt and Insolvent Act 1857**(c)** to vest a deposit in the Official Assignee alone or jointly with any person;

(d) any reference to the Official Receiver shall be construed as a reference to the Official Assignee in Bankruptcy;

(e) any reference to the Treasury Solicitor shall be construed as a reference to the Chief Crown Solicitor for Northern Ireland;

(f) any reference to the Chief Registrar of Friendly Societies shall be construed as a reference to the Chief Registrar of Friendly Societies or a deputy appointed by him.

Application to the Isle of Man

41.—(1) These Regulations shall extend to the Isle of Man.

(2) In the application of these Regulations to the Isle of Man—

(a) any reference to a receiver in relation to a mentally disordered person shall be construed as a reference to the committee of the estate of a person found of unsound mind according to the law of the Isle of Man or to a receiver appointed under section 3 of the Mental Diseases Act 1954 of the Isle of Man, as the case may be;

(b) any reference to the Treasury Solicitor shall be construed as a reference to the Attorney-General of the Isle of Man.

(a) 1961 c. 15 (N.I.). **(b)** 1871 c. 22.
(c) 1857 c. 60

Application to the Channel Islands

42.—(1) These Regulations shall extend to the Channel Islands.

(2) In the application of these Regulations to Jersey—

(*a*) any reference to a mentally disordered person shall be construed as a reference to a person suffering from mental disorder within the meaning of the Mental Health (Jersey) Law 1969;

(*b*) any reference to a receiver in relation to a mentally disordered person shall be construed as a reference to a curator;

(*c*) the references in Regulation 7(2) of these Regulations to sections 3 and 4 of the Cheques Act 1957 shall be respectively construed as references to article 3 and 4 of the Cheques (Jersey) Law 1957;

(*d*) any reference to a receiving order shall be construed as a reference to a declaration of "désastre";

(*e*) any reference to the Official Receiver shall be construed as a reference to Her Majesty's Viscount for Jersey or to an "attourné" appointed in bankruptcy, as the case may be;

(*f*) any reference to the Treasury Solicitor shall be construed as a reference to Her Majesty's Receiver General for Jersey;

(*g*) a nomination made by a holder domiciled in Jersey of any person to receive any sum due in respect of any certificate held by him at his death shall take effect only as to that portion of his personal estate over which he has power of testamentary disposition according to the law of Jersey, but any payment made to that nominee without notice of the holder's incapacity to dispose of the whole or any portion of the estate nominated shall be a valid payment.

(3) In the application of these Regulations to Guernsey, Alderney and Sark—

(*a*) any reference to a mentally disordered person shall be construed as a reference to a person who under any law for the time being in force in any of the Islands of the Bailiwick of Guernsey is a person of unsound mind;

(*b*) any reference to a receiver in relation to a mentally disordered person shall be construed as a reference to a guardian appointed by the Royal Court of Guernsey, the Court of Alderney or the Court of the Seneschal of Sark, as the case may be;

(*c*) any reference to the Treasury Solicitor shall be construed as a reference to Her Majesty's Receiver-General;

(*d*) any reference to a statutory declaration shall be construed, in relation to Guernsey, as a reference to a declaration on oath before the Bailiff, a jurat, the Magistrate or a Notary Public, in relation to Alderney, as a reference to a declaration on oath before the Court of Alderney, and, in relation to Sark, as a reference to a declaration before the Seneschal;

(*e*) the references in Regulation 7(2) of these Regulations to section 76, subsections (1), (3), (4) and (5) and, so far as it relates to crossed cheques, subsection (6) of section 77, and sections 78, 79, 80 and 81 of the Bills of Exchange Act 1882 shall be respectively construed as references to section 75, subsections (1), (3), (4) and (5) and, so far as it relates to crossed cheques, subsection (6) of section 76, and sections 77, 78, 79 and 80 of the Bills of Exchange (Guernsey) Law 1958, and the references in the said Regulation 7(2) to sections 3 and 4 of the Cheques Act 1957 shall be respectively construed as references to sections 83 and 84 of the Bills of Exchange (Guernsey) Law 1958;

(*f*) for Regulation 11 of these Regulations there shall be substituted the following Regulation:—

"11. Where it is shown to the satisfaction of the Director of Savings that any person who is the sole holder of a certificate is insolvent, the Director of Savings may, if he thinks fit, pay the amount repayable in respect of the certificate to any person who makes application in that behalf and who satisfies him that he is a proper person to receive payment.";

(*g*) in Regulation 29(1)(*b*) of these Regulations the words "or the trustee in bankruptcy or assignee of a holder who is bankrupt or insolvent" shall be deleted;

(*h*) a nomination made by a holder domicilied in the Bailiwick of Guernsey of any person to receive any sum due in respect of any certificates held by him at his death shall take effect only as to that portion of his personal estate over which he has power of testamentary disposition according to the law of the said Bailiwick, but any payment made to the nominee without notice of the holder's incapacity to dispose of the whole or any portion of the estate nominated shall be a valid payment.

Revocation and savings

43.—(1) The Regulations specified in the Schedule to these Regulations are hereby revoked.

(2) In so far as any application, payment, transfer, nomination, reference or award made, approval, authority, direction, notice or receipt given, warrant or document issued, or other thing done, under any Regulations revoked by these Regulations could have been made, given, issued or done under a corresponding provision of these Regulations, it shall not be invalidated by the revocation, but shall have effect as if made, given, issued or done under that corresponding provision.

(3) These Regulations shall not affect the validity of anything done by or in relation to the Postmaster General before 1st October 1969 under the provisions of any Regulations revoked by these Regulations; and anything which at that date was in process of being done under those provisions by or in relation to the Postmaster General may be continued by or in relation to the Director of Savings.

(4) Without prejudice to the last preceding paragraph, where on 1st October 1969 a matter in dispute between the Postmaster General and another stood referred under Regulation 27 of the Savings Certificates Regulations 1933(**a**) to the Chief Registrar of Friendly Societies or a deputy appointed by him or to the Assistant Registrar of Friendly Societies for Scotland, the Director of Savings shall be substituted for the Postmaster General as a party to the reference; and an award made under that Regulation before 1st October 1969 shall bind the Director of Savings.

(5) The mention of particular matters in this Regulation shall be without prejudice to the general application of section 38 of the Interpretation Act 1889 as it applies for the interpretation of these Regulations.

> *V. H. Goodhew*,
> *Tim Fortescue*,
> Two of the Lords Commissioners
> of Her Majesty's Treasury.

20th April 1972.

(**a**) S.R. & O. 1933/1149 (Rev. XV, p. 309: 1933, p. 1406).

2bb

Regulation 43(1)   SCHEDULE

Regulations revoked	References
The Savings Certificates Regulations 1933.	S.R. & O. 1933/1149 (Rev. XV, p. 309; 1933, p. 1406).
The Savings Certificates (Amendment) Regulations 1937.	S.R. & O. 1937/785 (Rev. XV, p. 309: 1937, p. 1723).
The Savings Certificates (Amendment) (No. 2) Regulations 1956.	S.I. 1956/1136 (1956 I, p. 1503).
The Savings Certificates (Amendment) Regulations 1957.	S.I. 1957/1734 (1957 I, p. 1450).
The Savings Certificates (Amendment) (No. 2) Regulations 1960.	S.I. 1960/1981 (1960 I, p. 414).
The Savings Certificates (Amendment) Regulations 1961.	S.I. 1961/1528 (1961 II, p. 3186).
The Savings Certificates (Amendment) (No. 2) Regulations 1963.	S.I. 1963/936 (1963 II, p. 1587).
The Savings Certificates (Amendment) Regulations 1966.	S.I. 1966/216 (1966 I, p. 419).
The Savings Certificates (Amendment) No. 2 Regulations 1968.	S.I. 1968/995 (1968 II, p. 2649).
The Savings Certificates (Amendment) (No. 3) Regulations 1968.	S.I. 1968/1444 (1968 III, p. 4182).
The Savings Certificates (Amendment) (No. 2) Regulations 1969.	S.I. 1969/1334 (1969 III, p. 3969).
The Savings Certificates (Amendment) Regulations 1971.	S.I. 1971/549 (1971 I, p. 1544).

EXPLANATORY NOTE

(This Note is not part of the Regulations.)

These Regulations consolidate with minor amendments the Savings Certificates Regulations 1933 as amended.

STATUTORY INSTRUMENTS

1972 No. 642 (C.10)

SOLICITORS

The Solicitors Act 1965 (Commencement No. 4) Order 1972

Made -   -   -   -   21*st April* 1972

The Lord Chancellor, in exercise of the powers conferred on him by section 30(2) of the Solicitors Act 1965**(a)**, hereby makes the following Order:—

1. This Order may be cited as the Solicitors Act 1965 (Commencement No. 4) Order 1972.

2. The following provisions of the Solicitors Act 1965 shall come into operation on 1st June 1972:—

sections 1 and 2;

Schedule 3, so far as it relates to section 54 of the Solicitors Act 1957**(b)**;

Schedule 4, so far as it relates to sections 3(2) and 40 to 45 of the Solicitors Act 1957.

Dated 21st April 1972.

Hailsham of St. Marylebone, C.

EXPLANATORY NOTE

(This Note is not part of the Order.)

This Order brings into operation on 1st June 1972 the provisions of the Solicitors Act 1965 which extend the powers of the Law Society to make regulations regarding the education and training of those seeking admission as solicitors.

(a) 1965 c. 31.   **(b)** 1957 c. 27.

STATUTORY INSTRUMENTS

1972 No. 644 (C.11)

OFFSHORE INSTALLATIONS

The Mineral Workings (Offshore Installations) Act 1971 (Commencement) Order 1972

Made - - - *21st April* 1972

The Secretary of State in exercise of his powers under section 14(2) of the Mineral Workings (Offshore Installations) Act 1971(**a**) (hereinafter referred to as "the Act") hereby makes the following Order:—

1. This Order may be cited as the Mineral Workings (Offshore Installations) Act 1971 (Commencement) Order 1972.

2. All the provisions of the Act other than sections 4 and 5 shall come into force on 1st May 1972 and sections 4 and 5 of the Act shall come into force on 31st August 1972.

21st April 1972.

Tom Boardman,
Minister for Industry,
Department of Trade and Industry.

(**a**) 1971 c. 61.

STOKE-ON-TRENT
CITY
LIBRARIES

STATUTORY INSTRUMENTS

1972 No. 645

INDUSTRIAL TRAINING

The Industrial Training Levy (Footwear, Leather and Fur Skin) Order 1972

Made - - -	*20th April* 1972
Laid before Parliament	*1st May* 1972
Coming into Operation	*22nd May* 1972

The Secretary of State after approving proposals submitted by the Footwear, Leather and Fur Skin Industry Training Board for the imposition of a further levy on employers in the footwear, leather and fur skin industry and in exercise of his powers under section 4 of the Industrial Training Act 1964(**a**) and of all other powers enabling him in that behalf hereby makes the following Order:—

Title and commencement

1. This Order may be cited as the Industrial Training Levy (Footwear, Leather and Fur Skin) Order 1972 and shall come into operation on 22nd May 1972.

Interpretation

2.—(1) In this Order unless the context otherwise requires:—

(*a*) "agriculture" has the same meaning as in section 109(3) of the Agriculture Act 1947(**b**) or, in relation to Scotland, as in section 86(3) of the Agriculture (Scotland) Act 1948(**c**);

(*b*) "an appeal tribunal" means an industrial tribunal established under section 12 of the Industrial Training Act 1964;

(*c*) "assessment" means an assessment of an employer to the levy;

(*d*) "the Board" means the Footwear, Leather and Fur Skin Industry Training Board;

(*e*) "business" means any activities of industry or commerce;

(*f*) "charity" has the same meaning as in section 360 of the Income and Corporation Taxes Act 1970(**d**);

(**a**) 1964 c. 16.   (**b**) 1947 c. 48.
(**c**) 1948 c. 45.   (**d**) 1970 c. 10.

(*g*) "emoluments" means all emoluments assessable to income tax under Schedule E (other than pensions), being emoluments from which tax under that Schedule is deductible, whether or not tax in fact falls to be deducted from any particular payment thereof;

(*h*) "employer" means a person who is an employer in the footwear, leather and fur skin industry at any time in the third levy period;

(*i*) "footwear, leather and fur skin establishment" means an establishment in Great Britain engaged in the third base period wholly or mainly in the footwear, leather and fur skin industry for a total of twenty-seven or more weeks or, being an establishment that commenced to carry on business in the third base period, for a total number of weeks exceeding one half of the number of weeks in the part of the said period commencing with the day on which business was commenced and ending on the last day thereof;

(*j*) "footwear, leather and fur skin industry" means any one or more of the activities which, subject to the provisions of paragraph 2 of Schedule 1 to the industrial training order, are specified in paragraph 1 of that Schedule as the activities of the footwear, leather and fur skin industry;

(*k*) "the industrial training order" means the Industrial Training (Footwear, Leather and Fur Skin Board) Order 1968(**a**), as amended by the Industrial Training (Footwear, Leather and Fur Skin Board) Order 1968 (Amendment) Order 1972(**b**);

(*l*) "the levy" means the levy imposed by the Board in respect of the third levy period;

(*m*) "notice" means a notice in writing;

(*n*) "the third base period" means the period of twelve months that commenced on 6th April 1970;

(*o*) "the third levy period" means the period commencing with the day upon which this Order comes into operation and ending on 31st March 1973.

(2) In the case where a footwear, leather and fur skin establishment is taken over (whether directly or indirectly) by an employer in succession to, or jointly with, another person, a person employed at any time in the third base period at or from the establishment shall be deemed, for the purposes of this Order, to have been so employed by the employer carrying on the said establishment on the day upon which this Order comes into operation, and any reference in this Order to persons employed by the employer at or from a footwear, leather and fur skin establishment in the third base period shall be construed accordingly.

(3) Any reference in this Order to an establishment that commences to carry on business or that ceases to carry on business shall not be taken to apply where the location of the establishment is changed but its business is continued wholly or mainly at or from the new location, or where the suspension of activities is of a temporary or seasonal nature.

(4) The Interpretation Act 1889(**c**) shall apply to the interpretation of this Order as it applies to the interpretation of an Act of Parliament.

(**a**) S.I. 1968/1763 (1968 III, p. 4785). (**b**) S.I. 1972/597.
(**c**) 1889 c. 63.

Imposition of the levy

3.—(1) The levy to be imposed by the Board on employers in respect of the third levy period shall be assessed in accordance with the provisions of this Article.

(2) Subject to the provisions of this Article, the levy shall be assessed by the Board in respect of each employer and the amount thereof shall be equal to 0·9 per cent. of the sum (less £3,000) of the emoluments of all the persons employed by the employer at or from the footwear, leather and fur skin establishment or establishments of the employer in the third base period.

(3) There shall be exempt from the levy—

(a) an employer in respect of whom the sum of the emoluments of the persons mentioned in the last foregoing paragraph is less than £3,000;

(b) a charity.

(4) Where any persons whose emoluments are taken into account for the purpose of this Article were employed at or from an establishment that ceases to carry on business in the third levy period, the sum of the emoluments of those persons shall be reduced in the same proportion as the number of days between the commencement of the said levy period and the date of cessation of business (both dates inclusive) bears to the number of days in the said levy period.

(5) For the purposes of this Article no regard shall be had to the emoluments of any person wholly engaged in agriculture or in the supply of food or drink for immediate consumption.

Assessment notices

4.—(1) The Board shall serve an assessment notice on every employer assessed to the levy.

(2) The amount of an assessment shall be rounded down to the nearest £1.

(3) An assessment notice shall state the Board's address for the service of a notice of appeal or of an application for an extension of time for appealing.

(4) An assessment notice may be served on the person assessed to the levy either by delivering it to him personally or by leaving it, or sending it to him by post, at his last known address or place of business in the United Kingdom or, if that person is a corporation, by leaving it, or sending it by post to the corporation, at such address or place of business or at its registered or principal office.

Payment of the levy

5.—(1) Subject to the provisions of this Article and of Articles 6 and 7, the amount of the levy payable under an assessment notice served by the Board shall be due and payable to the Board one month after the date of the notice.

(2) The amount of an assessment shall not be recoverable by the Board until there has expired the time allowed for appealing against the assessment by Article 7(1) of this Order and any further period or periods of time that the Board or an appeal tribunal may have allowed for appealing under paragraph (2) or (3) of that Article or, where an appeal is brought, until the appeal is decided or withdrawn.

Withdrawal of assessment

6.—(1) The Board may, by a notice served on the person assessed to the levy in the same manner as an assessment notice, withdraw an assessment if that person has appealed against that assessment under the provisions of Article 7 of this Order and the appeal has not been entered in the Register of Appeals kept under the appropriate Regulations specified in paragraph (5) of that Article.

(2) The withdrawal of an assessment shall be without prejudice to the power of the Board to serve a further assessment notice on the employer.

Appeals

7.—(1) A person assessed to the levy may appeal to an appeal tribunal against the assessment within one month from the date of the service of the assessment notice or within any further period or periods of time that may be allowed by the Board or an appeal tribunal under the following provisions of this Article.

(2) The Board by notice may for good cause allow a person assessed to the levy to appeal to an appeal tribunal against the assessment at any time within the period of four months from the date of the service of the assessment notice or within such further period or periods as the Board may allow before such time as may then be limited for appealing has expired.

(3) If the Board shall not allow an application for extension of time for appealing, an appeal tribunal shall upon application made to the tribunal by the person assessed to the levy have the like powers as the Board under the last foregoing paragraph.

(4) In the case of an assessment that has reference to an establishment that ceases to carry on business in the third levy period on any day after the date of the service of the assessment notice the foregoing provisions of this Article shall have effect as if for the period of four months from the date of the service of the assessment notice mentioned in paragraph (2) of this Article there were substituted the period of six months from the date of the cessation of business.

(5) An appeal or an application to an appeal tribunal under this Article shall be made in accordance with the Industrial Tribunals (England and Wales) Regulations 1965(**a**) as amended by the Industrial Tribunals (England and Wales) (Amendment) Regulations 1967(**b**), except where the assessment relates to persons employed at or from an establishment which is wholly in Scotland and to no other persons, in which case the appeal or application shall be made in accordance with the Industrial Tribunals (Scotland) Regulations 1965(**c**) as amended by the Industrial Tribunals (Scotland) (Amendment) Regulations 1967(**d**).

(6) The powers of an appeal tribunal under paragraph (3) of this Article may be exercised by the President of the Industrial Tribunals (England and Wales) or by the President of the Industrial Tribunals (Scotland) as the case may be.

Evidence

8.—(1) Upon the discharge by a person assessed to the levy of his liability under an assessment the Board shall if so requested issue to him a certificate to that effect.

(**a**) S.I. 1965/1101 (1965 II, p. 2805).   (**b**) S.I. 1967/301 (1967 I, p. 1040).
(**c**) S.I. 1965/1157 (1965 II, p. 3266).   (**d**) S.I. 1967/302 (1967 I, p. 1050).

(2) The production in any proceedings of a document purporting to be certified by the Secretary of the Board to be a true copy of an assessment or other notice issued by the Board or purporting to be a certificate such as is mentioned in the foregoing paragraph of this Article shall, unless the contrary is proved, be sufficient evidence of the document and of the facts stated therein.

Signed by order of the Secretary of State.

20th April 1972.

R. Chichester-Clark,
Minister of State,
Department of Employment.

EXPLANATORY NOTE

(This Note is not part of the Order.)

This Order gives effect to proposals submitted by the Footwear, Leather and Fur Skin Industry Training Board to the Secretary of State for Employment for the imposition of a further levy upon employers in the industry for the purpose of raising money towards the expenses of the Board.

The levy is to be imposed in respect of the third levy period commencing on the day upon which this Order comes into operation and ending on 31st March 1973. The levy will be assessed by the Board and there will be a right of appeal against an assessment to an industrial tribunal.

STATUTORY INSTRUMENTS

1972 No. 646

INDUSTRIAL TRAINING

The Industrial Training Levy (Chemical and Allied Products) Order 1972

Made - - -		*20th April* 1972
Laid before Parliament		*1st May* 1972
Coming into Operation		*1st August* 1972

The Secretary of State after approving proposals submitted by the Chemical and Allied Products Industry Training Board for the imposition of a further levy on employers in the chemical and allied products industry and in exercise of his powers under section 4 of the Industrial Training Act 1964(a) and of all other powers enabling him in that behalf hereby makes the following Order: —

Title and commencement

1. This Order may be cited as the Industrial Training Levy (Chemical and Allied Products) Order 1972 and shall come into operation on 1st August 1972.

Interpretation

2.—(1) In this Order unless the context otherwise requires: —

(*a*) "agriculture" has the same meaning as in section 109(3) of the Agriculture Act 1947(b) or, in relation to Scotland, as in section 86(3) of the Agriculture (Scotland) Act 1948(c);

(*b*) "an appeal tribunal" means an industrial tribunal established under section 12 of the Industrial Training Act 1964;

(*c*) "assessment" means an assessment of an employer to the levy;

(*d*) "the Board" means the Chemical and Allied Products Industry Training Board;

(*e*) "business" means any activities of industry or commerce;

(*f*) "charity" has the same meaning as in section 360 of the Income and Corporation Taxes Act 1970(d);

(*g*) "chemical and allied products establishment" means an establishment in Great Britain engaged in the fifth base period wholly or mainly in the chemical and allied products industry for a total of twenty-seven or more weeks or, being an establishment that commenced to carry on business in the fifth base period, for a total number of weeks exceeding one half of the number of weeks in the part of the said period commencing with the day on which business was commenced and ending on the last day thereof;

(**a**) 1964 c. 16.   (**b**) 1947 c. 48.
(**c**) 1948 c. 45.   (**d**) 1970 c. 10.

(*h*) "the chemical and allied products industry" means any one or more of the activities which, subject to the provisions of paragraph 2 of the Schedule to the industrial training order, are specified in paragraph 1 of that Schedule as the activities of the chemical and allied products industry;

(*i*) "emoluments" means all emoluments assessable to income tax under Schedule E (other than pensions), being emoluments from which tax under that Schedule is deductible, whether or not tax in fact falls to be deducted from any particular payment thereof;

(*j*) "employer" means a person who is an employer in the chemical and allied products industry at any time in the fifth levy period;

(*k*) "the fifth base period" means the period of twelve months that commenced on 6th April 1971;

(*l*) "the fifth levy period" means the period commencing with the day upon which this Order comes into operation and ending on 31st July 1973;

(*m*) "the industrial training order" means the Industrial Training (Chemical and Allied Products Board) Order 1970(**a**);

(*n*) "the levy" means the levy imposed by the Board in respect of the fifth levy period;

(*o*) "notice" means a notice in writing.

(2) In the case where a chemical and allied products establishment is taken over (whether directly or indirectly) by an employer in succession to, or jointly with, another person, a person employed at any time in the fifth base period at or from the establishment shall be deemed, for the purposes of this Order, to have been so employed by the employer carrying on the said establishment on the day upon which this Order comes into operation, and any reference in this Order to persons employed by the employer at or from a chemical and allied products establishment in the fifth base period shall be construed accordingly.

(3) Any reference in this Order to an establishment that commences to carry on business or that ceases to carry on business shall not be taken to apply where the location of the establishment is changed but its business is continued wholly or mainly at or from the new location, or where the suspension of activities is of a temporary or seasonal nature.

(4) Any reference in this Order to persons employed at or from a chemical and allied products establishment shall in any case where the employer is a company be construed as including a reference to any director of the company (or any person occupying the position of director by whatever name he was called) who was, at the material time, in receipt of a salary from the company.

(5) For the purposes of this Order no regard shall be had to the emoluments of a person wholly employed in—

(*a*) the production of textile fibres from polyethylene-terephthalate;

(*b*) agriculture; or

(*c*) the supply of food or drink for immediate consumption.

(**a**) S.I. 1970/1743 (1970 III, p. 5706).

(6) The Interpretation Act 1889(a) shall apply to the interpretation of this Order as it applies to the interpretation of an Act of Parliament.

Imposition of the levy

3.—(1) The levy to be imposed by the Board on employers in respect of the fifth levy period shall be assessed in accordance with the provisions of this Article.

(2) Subject to the provisions of this Order, the levy shall be assessed by the Board in respect of each employer and the amount thereof shall be equal to 1·0 per cent. of the sum (less £50,000) of the emoluments of all the persons employed by the employer at or from the chemical and allied products establishment or establishments of the employer in the fifth base period.

(3) There shall be exempt from the levy—

(a) an employer in whose case the sum of the emoluments of the persons mentioned in the last foregoing paragraph is less than £50,100;

(b) a charity.

(4) Where any persons whose emoluments are taken into account for the purposes of this Article were employed at or from an establishment that ceases to carry on business in the fifth levy period, the sum of the emoluments of those persons shall be reduced for such purposes in the same proportion as the number of days between the commencement of the said levy period and the date of cessation of business (both dates inclusive) bears to the number of days in the said levy period.

Assessment notices

4.—(1) The Board shall serve an assessment notice on every employer assessed to the levy.

(2) The amount of an assessment shall be rounded down to the nearest £1.

(3) An assessment notice shall state the Board's address for the service of a notice of appeal or of an application for an extension of time for appealing.

(4) An assessment notice may be served on the person assessed to the levy either by delivering it to him personally or by leaving it, or sending it to him by post, at his last known address or place of business in the United Kingdom or, if that person is a corporation, by leaving it, or sending it by post to the corporation, at such address or place of business or at its registered or principal office.

Payment of the levy

5.—(1) Subject to the provisions of this Article and of Articles 6 and 7, the amount of the assessment payable under an assessment notice served by the Board shall be due and payable to the Board one month after the date of the notice.

(2) The amount of an assessment shall not be recoverable by the Board until there has expired the time allowed for appealing against the assessment by Article 7(1) of this Order and any further period or periods of time that the Board or an appeal tribunal may have allowed for appealing under paragraph (2) or (3) of that Article or, where an appeal is brought, until the appeal is decided or withdrawn.

_____

(a) 1889 c. 63.

Withdrawal of assessment

6.—(1) The Board may, by a notice served on the person assessed to the levy in the same manner as an assessment notice, withdraw an assessment if that person has appealed against that assessment under the provisions of Article 7 of this Order and the appeal has not been entered in the Register of Appeals kept under the appropriate Regulations specified in paragraph (5) of that Article.

(2) The withdrawal of an assessment shall be without prejudice to the power of the Board to serve a further assessment notice on the employer.

Appeals

7.—(1) A person assessed to the levy may appeal to an appeal tribunal against the assessment within one month from the date of the service of the assessment notice or within any further period or periods of time that may be allowed by the Board or an appeal tribunal under the following provisions of this Article.

(2) The Board by notice may for good cause allow a person assessed to the levy to appeal to an appeal tribunal against the assessment at any time within the period of four months from the date of the service of the assessment notice or within such further period or periods as the Board may allow before such time as may then be limited for appealing has expired.

(3) If the Board shall not allow an application for extension of time for appealing, an appeal tribunal shall upon application made to the tribunal by the person assessed to the levy have the like powers as the Board under the last foregoing paragraph.

(4) In the case of an assessment that has reference to an establishment that ceases to carry on business in the fifth levy period on any day after the date of the service of an assessment notice, the foregoing provisions of this Article shall have effect as if for the period of four months from the date of the service of the assessment notice mentioned in paragraph (2) of this Article there were substituted the period of six months from the date of the cessation of business.

(5) An appeal or an application to an appeal tribunal under this Article shall be made in accordance with the Industrial Tribunals (England and Wales) Regulations 1965(**a**) as amended by the Industrial Tribunals (England and Wales) (Amendment) Regulations 1967(**b**) except where the assessment has reference to persons employed at or from one or more establishments that are wholly in Scotland and to no other persons, in which case the appeal or application shall be made in accordance with the Industrial Tribunals (Scotland) Regulations 1965(**c**) as amended by the Industrial Tribunals (Scotland) (Amendment) Regulations 1967(**d**).

(6) The powers of an appeal tribunal under paragraph (3) of this Article may be exercised by the President of the Industrial Tribunals (England and Wales) or by the President of the Industrial Tribunals (Scotland) as the case may be.

Evidence

8.—(1) Upon the discharge by a person assessed to the levy of his liability under an assessment the Board shall if so requested issue to him a certificate to that effect.

(**a**) S.I. 1965/1101 (1965 II, p. 2805).   (**b**) S.I. 1967/301 (1967 I, p. 1040).
(**c**) S.I. 1965/1157 (1965 II, p. 3266).   (**d**) S.I. 1967/302 (1967 I, p. 1050).

(2) The production in any proceedings of a document purporting to be certified by the Secretary of the Board to be a true copy of an assessment or other notice issued by the Board or purporting to be a certificate such as is mentioned in the foregoing paragraph of this Article shall, unless the contrary is proved, be sufficient evidence of the document and of the facts stated therein.

Signed by order of the Secretary of State.

20th April 1972.

R. Chichester-Clark,
Minister of State,
Department of Employment.

EXPLANATORY NOTE

(This Note is not part of the Order.)

This Order gives effect to proposals submitted by the Chemical and Allied Products Industry Training Board to the Secretary of State for Employment for the imposition of a further levy upon employers in the chemical and allied products industry for the purpose of raising money towards the expenses of the Board.

The levy is to be imposed in respect of the fifth levy period commencing on the day upon which this Order comes into operation and ending on 31st July 1973. The levy will be assessed by the Board and there will be a right of appeal against an assessment to an industrial tribunal.

STOKE-ON-TRENT
CITY
LIBRARIES

STATUTORY INSTRUMENTS

1972 No. 647

SEEDS

The Plant Varieties (Performance Trials) (Amendment) Regulations 1972

Made - - -	*21st April* 1972
Laid before Parliament	*1st May* 1972
Coming into Operation	*22nd May* 1972

The Minister of Agriculture, Fisheries and Food, the Secretary of State for Scotland and the Secretary of State for Northern Ireland, acting jointly, in exercise of the powers vested in them by section 22(10) of the Plant Varieties and Seeds Act 1964(**a**) (extended to Northern Ireland by the Plant Varieties and Seeds (Northern Ireland) Order 1964(**b**)), and of all other powers enabling them in that behalf, with the approval of the Treasury, hereby make the following Regulations:—

Citation and commencement

1. These Regulations may be cited as the Plant Varieties (Performance Trials) (Amendment) Regulations 1972 and shall come into operation on 22nd May 1972.

Amendment of principal Regulations

2. The Plant Varieties (Performance Trials) Regulations 1969(**c**) as amended by the Plant Varieties (Performance Trials) (Amendment) Regulations 1970(**d**) are hereby further amended by substituting for schedule 5 thereto (as substituted by the Plant Varieties (Performance Trials) (Amendment) Regulations 1970) the following schedule:—

(**a**) 1964 c. 14. (**b**) S.I. 1964/1574 (1964 III, p. 3543).
(**c**) S.I. 1969/1028 (1969 II, p. 3041). (**d**) S.I. 1970/1991 (1970 III, p. 6494).

" Regulation 16   SCHEDULE 5

Matter	When Payable	Amount
		£
Performance trials of a plant variety being—	Within 14 days of demand made by the Ministers before the commencement of the performance trials for the particular year.	
(a) a cereal variety		
(i) for the first year		70·00
(ii) for a subsequent year		150·00
(b) a potato variety		
(i) for the first year		50·00
(ii) for a subsequent year		80·00
(c) a Westerwolds ryegrass variety		
(i) for the first year		85·00
(ii) for a subsequent year		85·00
(d) a ryegrass variety other than a Westerwolds ryegrass variety		
(i) for the first year		90·00
(ii) for a subsequent year		160·00"

In Witness whereof the official seal of the Minister of Agriculture, Fisheries and Food is hereunto affixed on 17th April 1972.

(L.S.)   *J. M. L. Prior,*
                    Minister of Agriculture, Fisheries and Food.

                                         Gordon Campbell,
18th April 1972.   Secretary of State for Scotland.

                                       William Whitelaw,
20th April 1972.   Secretary of State for Northern Ireland.

Approved on 21st April 1972.

                                        Tim Fortescue,
                                       V. H. Goodhew,
                          Two of the Lords Commissioners of
                             Her Majesty's Treasury.

EXPLANATORY NOTE

(This Note is not part of the Regulations.)

These Regulations further amend the Plant Varieties (Performance Trials) Regulations 1969 as amended by the Plant Varieties (Performance Trials) (Amendment) Regulations 1970.

A new schedule 5 setting out increased fees payable for performance trials is substituted for the corresponding schedule of the principal regulations.

STATUTORY INSTRUMENTS

1972 No. 648

CUSTOMS AND EXCISE

The Import Duties (Temporary Exemptions) (No. 3) Order 1972

Made - - - -	*24th April* 1972
Laid before the House of Commons	*28th April* 1972
Coming into Operation	*4th May* 1972

The Lords Commissioners of Her Majesty's Treasury, by virtue of the powers conferred on them by sections 3(6) and 13 of the Import Duties Act 1958(a), and of all other powers enabling them in that behalf, on the recommendation of the Secretary of State, hereby make the following Order:—

1.—(1) This Order may be cited as the Import Duties (Temporary Exemptions) (No. 3) Order 1972.

(2) The Interpretation Act 1889(b) shall apply for the interpretation of this Order as it applies for the interpretation of an Act of Parliament.

(3) This Order shall come into operation on 4th May 1972.

2.—(1) Until the beginning of 1st January 1973 or, in the case of goods in relation to which an earlier day is specified in Schedule 1 to this Order, until the beginning of that day, any import duty which is for the time being chargeable on goods of a heading of the Customs Tariff 1959 specified in that Schedule shall not be chargeable in respect of goods of any description there specified in relation to that heading.

(2) The period for which goods of headings of the Customs Tariff 1959 and descriptions specified in Schedule 2 to this Order are exempt from import duty shall be extended until the beginning of 1st January 1973 or, in the case of goods in relation to which an earlier day is specified in that Schedule, until the beginning of that day.

(3) Any entry in column 2 in Schedule 1 or Schedule 2 to this Order shall be taken to comprise all goods which would be classified under an entry in the same terms constituting a subheading (other than the final subheading) in the relevant heading in the Customs Tariff 1959.

(4) For 'the purposes of classification under the Customs Tariff 1959, in so far as that depends on the rate of duty, any goods to which paragraph (1) or paragraph (2) above applies shall be treated as chargeable with the same duty as if this Order had not been made.

3.—(1) Until the beginning of 1st September 1972, in the case of goods of a description specified in paragraph (2) below, any import duty which is for the time being chargeable on goods of heading 85.21(D)(2) of the Customs Tariff 1959—

(*a*) shall not be chargeable if the goods qualify for Commonwealth preference, and

---

(a) 1958 c. 6.   (b) 1889 c. 63.

(b) shall be chargeable at the rate of 3% if, apart from this Order, they would be chargeable at the rate of 10% (the full rate).

(2) Paragraph (1) above applies to goods of the following description, namely, monolithic integrated circuit linear amplifiers having a voltage gain of 75 decibels to 100 decibels and a rated power output of 2·5 milliwatts to 5 milliwatts, of a kind for incorporation in deaf aids, with five connection terminals each side, of a length not exceeding 0·260 inch, of a width, exclusive of terminals, not exceeding 0·150 inch and a thickness not exceeding 0·050 inch.

(3) For the purposes of classification under the Customs Tariff 1959, in so far as that depends on the rate of duty, any goods to which paragraph (1) above applies shall be treated as chargeable with the same duty as if this Order had not been made.

V. H. Goodhew,

Tim Fortescue,

Two of the Lords Commissioners
of Her Majesty's Treasury.

24th April 1972.

SCHEDULE 1

Goods Temporarily Exempt from Import Duty

Tariff Heading	*Description*
29.02	Vinyl chloride (until 4th July 1972)
29.05	Cholesterol (until 4th July 1972)
29.07	4-Chlororesorcinol *di*Sodium 3-hydroxynaphthalene-2,7-disulphonate
29.13	1,5-Dichloroanthraquinone 2,6-Dihydroxyacetophenone
29.14	2-Ethyl-2-hydroxymethylpropanediol triacrylate Undec-10-enoic acid (until 4th July 1972)
29.15	Sodium oxalate
29.22	3-Nitroaniline 2,4,6-Trimethylaniline
29.23	2-(Cyclohexa-1,4-dienyl)glycine 1,3-Diaminopropan-2-ol 2,5-Dimethoxyaniline Ethylenediamine-*NN'*-di-[(2-hydroxyphenyl)acetic acid] Potassium hydrogen 4-amino-5-hydroxynaphthalene-1,3-disulphonate
29.25	*N*-(3-Chloro-*p*-tolyl)-2-methylvaleramide 2-Methyl-1,1-diureidopropane
29.26	DL-Arginine *mono*hydrochloride (until 4th July 1972)
29.29	Benzamido-oxyacetic acid
29.30	1-*iso*Cyanatopropane

Tariff Heading	*Description*

29.35 1-(3-Chlorophenyl)-3-methyl-5-pyrazolone (until 4th July 1972)
Cyanuric acid (until 4th July 1972)
NN-Di*iso*propylbenzothiazole-2-sulphenamide
3-Hydroxyquinaldine-4-carboxylic acid
4-Nitrobenzyl 7-amino-3-methyl-3-cephem-4-carboxylate hydrochloride
Piperazine dihydrochloride

29.37 Sulthiame

29.42 Bamifylline hydrochloride

37.01 Photographic plates on a glass base of flatness 0·001 inch or less per linear inch, of thickness between 0·058 inch and 0·072 inch, of length 2½ inches and of width 2½ inches, with an emulsion on one side and an anti-halation layer either incorporated in the emulsion or on the reverse side: the emulsion being between 5 and 7 micrometres thick, having a spectral sensitivity peak at about 520 nanometres and capable of resolving in excess of 2,000 line pairs per millimetre, and having an average surface contamination per square centimetre of less than 5 particles of a diameter greater than 2 micrometres (until 4th July 1972)

38.19 Prepared catalysts, in the form of spheres, containing silver or silver oxide dispersed in, or deposited on, aluminium oxide or silica or other compounds of silicon, and which contain not less than 7 per cent. by weight and not more than 25 per cent. by weight of total silver calculated as Ag

39.01 Poly-[2,2-di-(4-hydroxyphenyl)propane carbonate] moulding compounds, containing glass fibres which amount to not less than 5 per cent. by weight of the product and not more than 45 per cent. by weight of the product

55.02 Bleached cotton linters not containing more than 3·5 milligrammes per kilogramme by weight of iron or 1·0 milligrammes per kilogramme by weight of copper and yielding, on ignition at a temperature of not less than 800° centigrade and not exceeding 900° centigrade not more than 0·025 per cent. by weight of ash, determined in each case by reference to the dry weight of the linters plus 8·5 per cent. moisture regain

73.15 Cold-rolled non-oriented electrical steel in sheets or coils, whether or not coated, of a width exceeding 500 millimetres and being either:—

(*a*) of a thickness of 0·50 millimetre with guaranteed maximum watts loss per kilogramme at 50 Hz and flux density of 1·0 Tesla of 1·45 watts per kilogramme, or

(*b*) of a thickness of 0·35 millimetre with guaranteed maximum watts loss per kilogramme at 50 Hz and flux density of 1·0 Tesla of 1·25 watts per kilogramme

Hot rolled alloy steel strip in coils, containing not less than 14 per cent. by weight nor more than 18 per cent. by weight of chromium as the major alloying element, and not more than 0·5 per cent. by weight of nickel, of a width of not less than 400 millimetres nor more than 500 millimetres and of a thickness of not less than 3 millimetres nor more than 6 millimetres (until 1st September 1972)

81.04 Chromium, in the form of cathode chips or pellets, which contains not more than 0·10 per cent. by weight of total oxygen, not more than 0·015 per cent. by weight of total aluminium, and not more than 0·001 per cent. by weight of aluminium compounds insoluble in boiling 5N hydrochloric acid and in boiling fuming perchloric acid, and estimated as Al (until 4th July 1972)

Hafnium crystal bars, whole or in pieces 2 inches or less in length, consisting of hafnium wire on which hafnium crystals have been deposited

Tariff Heading   *Description*

85.21   Containers for electronic micro-circuits, consisting of square or rectangular laminations, built up from a bottom sheet of glass, metal, or ceramic composition; from a middle frame of glass with embedded metal alloy leads extending to a lead frame along one, two or all four sides; and from a top sealing frame of glass, metal, or ceramic composition, all three laminae being fused together: each container being provided with a separate solder frame and metal alloy lid for subsequent sealing to the top sealing frame (until 4th July 1972)

88.02   Helicopters of an empty weight of 750 kilogrammes or less, powered by one engine

Helicopters of an empty weight of 2,000 kilogrammes or less, powered by two engines

91.08   Movements for electric clocks of the instrument panel type designed to be permanently mounted in a motor vehicle and to be operated only by a current of not less than 12 volts provided by the battery of the vehicle

SCHEDULE 2

Goods for which Exemption from Import Duty is extended

25.19   Magnesite, dead-burned, containing (*a*) not less than 94 per cent. by weight of magnesium compounds expressed as MgO, (*b*) a total of not more than $1 \cdot 0$ per cent. by weight of aluminium compounds and iron compounds expressed as Al_2O_3 and Fe_2O_3, (*c*) a total of not less than $2 \cdot 5$ per cent. by weight and not more than $5 \cdot 0$ per cent. by weight of calcium compounds and silicon compounds expressed as CaO and SiO_2, and in which the weight of calcium compounds expressed as CaO is not less than $1 \cdot 5$ times the weight of silicon compounds expressed as SiO_2 (until 4th July 1972)

28.18   Magnesium oxide, dead-burned but not fused, of a purity not less than 96 per cent., which contains (*a*) not more than $0 \cdot 05$ per cent. by weight of boron compounds expressed as B_2O_3, (*b*) a total of not more than $0 \cdot 5$ per cent. by weight of aluminium compounds and iron compounds expressed as Al_2O_3 and Fe_2O_3, and (*c*) a total of not less than $1 \cdot 0$ per cent. by weight and not more than $3 \cdot 5$ per cent. by weight of calcium compounds and silicon compounds expressed as CaO and SiO_2, the weight of calcium compounds being not less than $1 \cdot 5$ times and not more than $2 \cdot 5$ times the weight of silicon compounds; and (*d*) of which not less than 35 per cent. by weight is retained by a sieve having a nominal width of aperture of $\frac{3}{16}$ inch (until 4th July 1972)

29.01   Acenaphthene

29.07   2,2-Di-(3,5-dibromo-4-hydroxyphenyl)propane

29.14   Geranyl 5,9,13-trimethyltetradeca-4,8,12-trienoate

29.15   Cyclohexane-1,2-dicarboxylic anhydride (until 4th July 1972)
Naphthalic anhydride

29.16   Cyclandelate (until 1st September 1972)

29.23   4-Amino-5-hydroxynaphthalene-1,3-disulphonic acid

29.27   Tetrachloroisophthalonitrile

29.30   1-Chloro-3-*iso*cyanatobenzene (until 2nd November 1972)
1-Chloro-2-*iso*cyanatoethane
4,4'-Di*iso*cyanato-3,3'-dimethoxybiphenyl

29.31   2-Mercaptoethanol (until 4th July 1972)

29.39   Prednisolone 21-*O*-stearoylglycollate

Tariff Heading	Description

39.03   Regenerated cellulose in the form of sheets not exceeding 430 millimetres by 1,020 millimetres in size, 18 grammes per square metre in weight or 12 micrometres in thickness (until 4th July 1972)

70.20   Glass fibre continuous filament yarn of low alkali borosilicate glass (E glass) (until 1st September 1972)

73.15   Alloy steel coils for re-rolling, which contain not less than 14 per cent. nor more than 18 per cent. by weight of chromium as the major alloying element, and not more than $0 \cdot 5$ per cent. by weight of nickel, and having a width exceeding 500 millimetres but not more than 1,372 millimetres, and a thickness of not less than 3 millimetres nor more than 6 millimetres (until 1st September 1972)

73.19   Hot rolled seamless circular steel tubes of an outside diameter of not less than $19\frac{1}{2}$ inches and not more than $24\frac{1}{2}$ inches, and of a wall thickness of not less than $\frac{7}{16}$ inch and not more than $\frac{5}{8}$ inch (until 4th July 1972)

81.04   Titanium sponge

85.15   The following apparatus for use in aircraft:

(a) very high frequency omni-directional radio range apparatus (VOR), instrument landing system localiser apparatus (ILS/LOC), instrument landing system glide path apparatus (ILS/G.PATH);

(b) very high frequency communication apparatus (VHF/COM) (transmitters, receivers, or combined transmitter/receivers) covering a frequency band of at least 118 to 135·95MHz, with not less than 180 channels and capable of operating in areas where 50 kHz channel spacing is in force;

(c) apparatus combining the functions and capabilities of any of the apparatus specified in (a) and (b) above but excluding apparatus combining any of those functions and capabilities with any other function or capability;

being in each case apparatus of a type approved by the Civil Aviation Authority, at the date of this Order, under Article 14(5) of the Air Navigation Order 1972, for use in aircraft of not more than 5,700 kilogrammes maximum total weight authorised, flying in controlled airspace in accordance with the Instrument Flight Rules as defined in the said Air Navigation Order, but not for use in other aircraft (until 4th July 1972)

EXPLANATORY NOTE

(*This Note is not part of the Order.*)

This Order provides that the goods listed in Schedule 1 shall be temporarily exempt from import duty, and those listed in Schedule 2 shall continue to be exempt from import duty, both until 1st January 1973 or, in the case of certain items, until such earlier day as is specified.

The Order also provides for a reduction, until 1st September 1972, in the duty chargeable on certain monolithic integrated circuit linear amplifiers under heading 85.21 : this temporary reduction is from 10 per cent. to 3 per cent. in the full rate of duty and from 7 per cent. to nil in the Commonwealth rate.

As regards the exemption for equipment for use in aircraft under heading 85.15, apparatus of a type approved by the Civil Aviation Authority is listed in Civil Aviation Publication CAP 208, Airborne Radio Apparatus Vol. 2, published by Her Majesty's Stationery Office. This publication is subject to amendment, and confirmation that apparatus is of a type approved at the date of this Order should be obtained from the Civil Aviation Authority, Controllerate of National Air Traffic Services, Tels.N2(c), 19–29 Woburn Place, London WC1H 0LX.

1972 No. 649

SUGAR

The Sugar (Distribution Payments) (No. 6) Order 1972

Made - - - -	*24th April* 1972
Laid before Parliament -	*25th April* 1972
Coming into Operation -	*26th April* 1972

The Minister of Agriculture, Fisheries and Food in exercise of the powers conferred upon him by sections 14(5) and 33(4) of the Sugar Act 1956(a), having effect subject to the provisions of section 3 of, and Part II of Schedule 5 to, the Finance Act 1962(b), section 22 of the Finance Act 1964(c) and section 52 of the Finance Act 1966(d) and of all other powers enabling him in that behalf, with the concurrence of the Treasury, and on the advice of the Sugar Board hereby makes the following order:—

1.—(1) This order may be cited as the Sugar (Distribution Payments) (No. 6) Order 1972, and shall come into operation on 26th April 1972.

(2) The Interpretation Act 1889(e) shall apply for the interpretation of this order as it applies for the interpretation of an Act of Parliament.

2. Notwithstanding the provisions of article 2 of the Sugar (Distribution Payments) (No. 5) Order 1972(f), the rates of distribution payments payable under and in accordance with the provisions of section 14 of the Sugar Act 1956, having effect as aforesaid, in respect of sugar and invert sugar imported or home produced or used in the manufacture of imported composite sugar products shall on and after 26th April 1972 be those rates specified in the Schedule to this order; and section 10 of the Finance Act 1901(g) (which relates to new or altered customs or excise duties and their effect upon contracts) shall apply accordingly.

In Witness whereof the Official Seal of the Minister of Agriculture, Fisheries and Food is hereunto affixed on 21st April 1972.

(L.S.)

F. M. Kearns,
Authorised by the Minister.

We concur.
24th April 1972.

V. H. Goodhew,
Tim Fortescue,
Two of the Lords Commissioners of
Her Majesty's Treasury.

(a) 1956 c. 48.	(b) 1962 c. 44.	(c) 1964 c. 49.	(d) 1966 c. 18.
(e) 1889 c. 63.	(f) S.I. 1972/598 (1972 I, p. 1972).		(g) 1901 c. 7.

SCHEDULE
PART I
RATES OF DISTRIBUTION PAYMENT FOR SUGAR

Polarisation	Rate of Distribution Payment per ton
	£
Exceeding—	
99°	12·000
98° but not exceeding 99°	11·316
97° ,, ,, ,, 98°	11·040
96° ,, ,, ,, 97°	10·752
95° ,, ,, ,, 96°	10·464
94° ,, ,, ,, 95°	10·176
93° ,, ,, ,, 94°	9·888
92° ,, ,, ,, 93°	9·600
91° ,, ,, ,, 92°	9·312
90° ,, ,, ,, 91°	9·024
89° ,, ,, ,, 90°	8·736
88° ,, ,, ,, 89°	8·448
87° ,, ,, ,, 88°	8·208
86° ,, ,, ,, 87°	7·968
85° ,, ,, ,, 86°	7·752
84° ,, ,, ,, 85°	7·536
83° ,, ,, ,, 84°	7·320
82° ,, ,, ,, 83°	7·104
81° ,, ,, ,, 82°	6·912
80° ,, ,, ,, 81°	6·720
79° ,, ,, ,, 80°	6·528
78° ,, ,, ,, 79°	6·336
77° ,, ,, ,, 78°	6·144
76° ,, ,, ,, 77°	5·952
Not exceeding 76°	5·760

PART II
RATES OF DISTRIBUTION PAYMENT FOR INVERT SUGAR

Sweetening matter content by weight	Rate of Distribution Payment per cwt.
	£
70 per cent. or more	0·38
Less than 70 per cent. and more than 50 per cent.	0·27
Not more than 50 per cent.	0·13

EXPLANATORY NOTE
(*This Note is not part of the Order.*)
This order provides for increases equivalent to £6 per ton of refined sugar in the rates of distribution payment in respect of sugar and invert sugar which become eligible for such payments on and after 26th April 1972.

STATUTORY INSTRUMENTS

1972 No. 650

SUGAR

The Sugar (Distribution Repayments) (Amendment) (No. 5) Order 1972

Made - - - -	24th April 1972
Laid before Parliament	25th April 1972
Coming into Operation	26th April 1972

The Minister of Agriculture, Fisheries and Food, in exercise of the powers conferred upon him by sections 15 and 33(4) of the Sugar Act 1956(**a**), having effect subject to the provisions of section 3 of, and Part II of Schedule 5 to, the Finance Act 1962(**b**), section 22 of the Finance Act 1964(**c**) and section 52 of the Finance Act 1966(**d**) and of all other powers enabling him in that behalf, an order (**e**) having been made under section 14 of the said Act, hereby makes the following order:—

1.—(1) This order may be cited as the Sugar (Distribution Repayments) (Amendment) (No. 5) Order 1972, and shall come into operation on 26th April 1972.

(2) The Interpretation Act 1889(**f**) shall apply for the interpretation of this order as it applies for the interpretation of an Act of Parliament.

2.—(1) Notwithstanding the provisions of article 2(1) of the Sugar (Distribution Repayments) (Amendment) (No. 4) Order 1972(**g**) the amount of distribution repayment payable in respect of invert sugar, if the relevant drawback is payable thereon as being invert sugar produced in the United Kingdom from materials on which sugar duty has been paid on or after 26th April 1972, shall be calculated thereon at the rate applicable to the invert sugar in accordance with the rates prescribed in the Schedule to this order.

(2) Article 2(1) of the Sugar (Distribution Repayments) Order 1972(**h**) shall apply for the interpretation of this article.

In Witness whereof the Official Seal of the Minister of Agriculture, Fisheries and Food is hereunto affixed on 24th April 1972.

(L.S.)

F. M. Kearns,
Authorised by the Minister.

(**a**) 1956 c. 48.
(**d**) 1966 c. 18.
(**g**) S.I. 1972/599 (1972 I, p. 1974).

(**b**) 1962 c. 44.
(**e**) S.I. 1972/649 (1972 I, p. 2127).
(**h**) S.I. 1972/67 (1972 I, p. 162).

(**c**) 1964 c. 49.
(**f**) 1889 c. 63.

THE SCHEDULE

RATES OF DISTRIBUTION REPAYMENT FOR INVERT SUGAR

Sweetening matter content by weight	Rate of Distribution Repayment per cwt.
	£
More than 80 per cent.	0·45
More than 70 per cent. but not more than 80 per cent.	0·38
More than 60 per cent. but not more than 70 per cent.	0·27
More than 50 per cent. but not more than 60 per cent.	0·21
Not more than 50 per cent. and the invert sugar not being less in weight than 14 lb. per gallon	0·13

EXPLANATORY NOTE

(This Note is not part of the Order.)

This order, which is consequent upon the Sugar (Distribution Payments) (No. 6) Order 1972 (S.I. 1972/649), provides for increases equivalent to £6 per ton of refined sugar in the rates of distribution repayment, in respect of sugar and invert sugar produced in the United Kingdom from materials which become eligible for distribution payments on or after 26th April 1972.

STOKE-ON-TRENT
CITY
LIBRARIES

STATUTORY   INSTRUMENTS

1972 No. 651

SUGAR

The Composite Sugar Products (Distribution Payments— Average Rates) (No. 6) Order 1972

Made - - - -	*24th April* 1972
Laid before Parliament-	*25th April* 1972
Coming into Operation	*26th April* 1972

Whereas the Minister of Agriculture, Fisheries and Food (hereinafter called " the Minister ") has on the recommendation of the Sugar Board made an order (**a**) pursuant to the powers conferred upon him by section 9(1) of the Sugar Act 1956(**b**) having effect subject to section 14(8) of that Act and to the provisions of section 3 of, and Part II of Schedule 5 to, the Finance Act 1962 (**c**), section 22 of the Finance Act 1964(**d**) and section 52 of the Finance Act 1966(**e**), providing that in the case of certain descriptions of composite sugar products distribution payments shall be calculated on the basis of an average quantity of sugar or invert sugar taken to have been used in the manufacture of the products and that certain other descriptions shall be treated as not containing any sugar or invert sugar:

And whereas the Minister has by the Sugar (Distribution Payments) (No. 6) Order 1972(**f**) provided for a change in the rates of distribution payments in respect of sugar and invert sugar which became eligible for such payments on and after 26th April 1972.

Now, therefore, the Minister on the recommendation of the Sugar Board, and in exercise of the powers conferred upon him by sections 9(1) and 33(4) of the Sugar Act 1956, having effect as aforesaid, and of all other powers enabling him in that behalf, hereby makes the following order:—

1.—(1) This order may be cited as the Composite Sugar Products (Distribution Payments—Average Rates) (No. 6) Order 1972, and shall come into operation on 26th April 1972.

(2) The Interpretation Act 1889(**g**) shall apply to the interpretation of this order as it applies to the interpretation of an Act of Parliament.

2. Distribution payments payable on or after 26th April 1972 under and in accordance with section 14 of the Sugar Act 1956, having effect as aforesaid, in respect of sugar and invert sugar used in the manufacture of the descriptions of imported composite sugar products specified in the second column of Schedule 1 to this order, being goods which are classified in the tariff headings indicated in relation to them in the first column of the said Schedule shall, notwithstanding the provisions of the Sugar (Distribution Payments) (No. 6) Order 1972 and the Composite Sugar Products (Distribution Payments—Average Rates) (No. 5) Order 1972(**a**) be calculated by reference to the weight of the products and the rates specified in relation thereto in the third column of the said Schedule.

3. Imported composite sugar products other than those of a description specified in Schedules 1 and 2 to this order shall be treated as not containing any sugar or invert sugar for the purposes of distribution payments.

(a) S.I. 1972/600 (1972 I, p. 1976).   (b) 1956 c. 48.   (c) 1962 c. 44.   (d) 1964 c. 49.
(e) 1966 c. 18.   (f) S.I. 1972/649 (1972 I, p. 2127)   (g) 1889 c. 63.

In Witness whereof the Official Seal of the Minister of Agriculture, Fisheries and Food is hereunto affixed on 24th April 1972.

(L.S.)

F. M. Kearns,
Authorised by the Minister.

SCHEDULE 1

In this Schedule:—

" Tariff heading " means a heading or, where the context so requires, a subheading of the Customs Tariff 1959 (see paragraph (1) of Article 2 of the Import Duties (General) (No. 7) Order 1971)(a).

Tariff heading	Description of Composite Sugar Products	Rate of Distribution Payment
		Per cwt. £
04.02 ..	Milk and cream, preserved, concentrated or sweetened, containing more than 10 per cent. by weight of added sugar	0·26
17.02 (B) (2) and 17.05 (B)	Syrups containing sucrose sugar, whether or not flavoured or coloured, but not including fruit juices containing added sugar in any proportion:—	
	Containing 70 per cent. or more by weight of sweetening matter	0·38
	Containing less than 70 per cent., and more than 50 per cent. by weight of sweetening matter	0·27
	Containing not more than 50 per cent. by weight of sweetening matter	0·13
17.02 (F) ..	Caramel:—	
	Solid	0·60
	Liquid	0·41
17.04 ..	Sugar confectionery, not containing cocoa ..	0·48
18.06 ..	Chocolate and other food preparations containing cocoa and added sugar:—	
	Chocolate couverture not prepared for retail sale; chocolate milk crumb, liquid ..	0·26
	Chocolate milk crumb, solid	0·32
	Solid chocolate bars or blocks, milk or plain, with or without fruit or nuts; other chocolate confectionery consisting wholly of chocolate or of chocolate and other ingredients not containing added sugar ..	0·26
	Other	0·34

(a) S.I. 1971/1971 (1971 III, p. 5330).

SCHEDULE 1—*continued*

Tariff heading	Description of Composite Sugar Products	Rate of Distribution Payment
		Per cwt. £
19.08 ..	Pastry, biscuits, cakes and other fine bakers' wares containing added sugar:—	
	Biscuits, wafers and rusks containing more than 12½ per cent. by weight of added sugar, and other biscuits, wafers and rusks included in retail packages with such goods.. ..	0·15
	Cakes with covering or filling containing added sugar; meringues	0·19
	Other	0·07
20.01 ..	Vegetables and fruit, prepared or preserved by vinegar or acetic acid, containing added sugar:—	
	Containing 10 per cent. or more by weight of added sugar	0·21
	Other	0·04
20.03 ..	Fruit preserved by freezing, containing added sugar	0·07
20.04 ..	Fruit, fruit-peel and parts of plants, preserved by sugar (drained, glacé or crystallised)	0·39
20.05 ..	Jams, fruit jellies, marmalades, fruit puree and fruit pastes, being cooked preparations, containing added sugar	0·37
20.06 ..	Fruit otherwise prepared or preserved, containing added sugar:—	
	Ginger	0·30
	Other	0·07

SCHEDULE 2

Tariff heading	Description of Composite Sugar Products
17.05 (A) and (B)	Sugar and invert sugar, flavoured or coloured.

EXPLANATORY NOTE

(*This Note is not part of the Order.*)

This order provides for increases in the average rates of distribution payments payable in respect of imported composite sugar products of the descriptions specified in Schedule 1 on and after 26th April 1972. These correspond to increases in the rates of distribution payment effected by the Sugar (Distribution Payments) (No. 6) Order 1972 (S.I. 1972/649). Provision is also made for certain imported composite sugar products to be treated as not containing any sugar or invert sugar.

STATUTORY INSTRUMENTS

1972 No. 652

AGRICULTURE

The Price Stability of Imported Products (Minimum Import Price Levels) (Milk and Milk Products) (Amendment) Order 1972

Made - - -	*26th April* 1972
Laid before Parliament	*4th May* 1972
Coming into Operation	*1st June* 1972

The Minister of Agriculture, Fisheries and Food and the Secretaries of State respectively concerned with agriculture in Scotland and Northern Ireland, acting jointly in exercise of the powers conferred upon them by section 1(2), (4), (6) and (7) of the Agriculture and Horticulture Act 1964(a) and of all other powers enabling them in that behalf, with the approval of the Treasury, hereby make the following order:—

1. This order may be cited as the Price Stability of Imported Products (Minimum Import Price Levels) (Milk and Milk Products) (Amendment) Order 1972, and shall come into operation on 1st June 1972.

2. The Interpretation Act 1889(b) shall apply to the interpretation of this order as it applies to the interpretation of an Act of Parliament.

3. The Price Stability of Imported Products (Minimum Import Price Levels) (Milk and Milk Products) Order 1971(c) shall be amended by substituting in column 3 of the Schedule thereto—

(*a*) for the minimum import price level (per ton) of £157 specified in relation to such imports as are described in item (A)(2)(*a*) in column 2 of that Schedule in relation to the tariff heading 04.02 indicated in column 1 of that Schedule a minimum import price level (per ton) of £200; and

(*b*) for the minimum import price levels (per ton) of £138 and £157 specified in relation to such imports as are described in items (1) and (2) respectively in column 2 of that Schedule in relation to the tariff heading 23.07 indicated in column 1 of that Schedule minimum import price levels (per ton) of £164 and £200 respectively.

(a) 1964 c. 28. **(b)** 1889 c. 63.
(c) S.I. 1971/857 (1971 II, p. 2474).

In Witness whereof the Official Seal of the Minister of Agriculture, Fisheries and Food is hereunto affixed on 18th April 1972.

(L.S.) *J. M. L. Prior,*
Minister of Agriculture, Fisheries and Food.

Gordon Campbell,
21st April 1972. Secretary of State for Scotland.

William Whitelaw,
25th April 1972. Secretary of State for Northern Ireland.

Approved.

26th April 1972.

P. L. Hawkins,

Tim Fortescue,

Two of the Lords Commissioners of
Her Majesty's Treasury.

EXPLANATORY NOTE

(This Note is not part of the Order.)

This amending order, which comes into operation on 1st June 1972, raises the minimum import price levels for imports into the United Kingdom—

(a) of skimmed milk powder from £157 to £200 per ton;

(b) of animal feedingstuffs containing more than 40 per cent. and not more than 80 per cent. by weight of milk solids from £138 to £164 per ton and of those containing more than 80 per cent. by weight of milk solids from £157 to £200 per ton.

STATUTORY INSTRUMENTS

1972 No. 653

MUSEUMS

The British Museum (Authorised Repositories) Order 1972

Made - - -	*26th April* 1972
Laid before Parliament	*4th May* 1972
Coming into Operation	*1st June* 1972

The Secretary of State for Education and Science with the agreement of the Trustees of the British Museum, in exercise of her powers under section 10(2) of the British Museum Act 1963(**a**), hereby makes the following Order:—

1.—(1) This Order may be cited as the British Museum (Authorised Repositories) Order 1972 and shall come into operation on 1st June 1972.

(2) The Interpretation Act 1889(**b**) shall apply for the interpretation of this Order as it applies for the interpretation of an Act of Parliament.

2. Part I of the Third Schedule to the British Museum Act 1963 as amended(**c**) (authorised repositories for the collections of the British Museum) shall be amended by the addition of the following paragraph:—

"8. Nos. 48-56, Orsman Road, London."

Given under the Official Seal of the Secretary of State for Education and Science on 26th April 1972.

(L.S.)

Margaret Thatcher,
Secretary of State
for Education and Science.

EXPLANATORY NOTE

(*This Note is not part of the Order.*)

This Order adds to the authorised repositories of the British Museum.

(**a**) 1963 c. 24.   (**b**) 1889 c. 63.
(**c**) S.I. 1966/99, 1968/1604, 1970/1956, 1971/82 (1966 I, p. 222; 1968 III, p. 4406; 1970 III, p. 6408; 1971 I, p. 139).

STATUTORY INSTRUMENTS

1972 No. 656

MERCHANT SHIPPING

The Merchant Shipping (Tonnage) (Amendment) Regulations 1972

Made - - -	*26th April* 1972
Laid before Parliament	*9th May* 1972
Coming into Operation	*1st June* 1972

The Secretary of State in exercise of the powers conferred upon him by section 1 of the Merchant Shipping Act 1965(**a**) and of all other powers enabling him in that behalf hereby makes the following Regulations:—

1.—(1) These Regulations may be cited as the Merchant Shipping (Tonnage) (Amendment) Regulations 1972 and shall come into operation on 1st June 1972.

(2) The Interpretation Act 1889(**b**) shall apply for the interpretation of these Regulations as it applies for the interpretation of an Act of Parliament.

2. The Merchant Shipping (Tonnage) Regulations 1967(**c**), as amended(**d**), shall have effect subject to the following further amendments:—

(1) After Regulation 7 there shall be added the following as Regulation 7A:—

"7A—(1) Paragraph (2) of this Regulation applies—

(*a*) to ships registered in the United Kingdom under Part 1 of the principal Act before 1st March 1967 the tonnage of which is to be measured under these Regulations; and

(*b*) to ships previously registered elsewhere than in the United Kingdom which are to be so registered; and

(*c*) to ships registered elsewhere than in the United Kingdom in respect of which application is made for a certificate of British tonnage pursuant to Regulation 3(2).

(2) Without prejudice to the provisions of Regulation 7, space situated on or above the upper deck of a ship to which this paragraph applies, being space—

(*a*) which, in the case of a ship described in sub-paragraph (1)(*a*), was by virtue of openings in it not included in the gross tonnage of the ship under the law in force immediately prior to 1st March 1967(**e**), or

(*b*) which, in the case of a ship described in sub-paragraph

---

(**a**) 1965 c. 47.   (**b**) 1889 c. 63.

(**c**) S.I. 1967/172 (1967 I, p. 283).   (**d**) S.I. 1967/1093 (1967 II, p. 3237).

(**e**) Section 77 of the principal Act and the tonnage regulations of that Act as defined in that section.

1(*b*) or (*c*), was by virtue of there being or having been openings in it not included in the gross tonnage of the ship specified in the national certificate of registry in force in respect of the ship immediately prior to her registry in the United Kingdom or the said application as the case may be,

shall not be included in the gross tonnage of the ship irrespective of whether such openings have been closed or not, if—

> (i) there has been no change since the date on which the tonnage of the ship was last measured in the purpose for which the space is used; and

> (ii) in the case of a ship described in sub-paragraph (1)(*b*) or (*c*), the space is such that it would not, had the ship been registered in the United Kingdom prior to 1st March 1967 with the openings unclosed, have been included in her gross tonnage."

(2) In Regulation 11(3)(*a*) after "Regulation 7" there shall be added "Regulation 7A".

Michael Noble,
Minister for Trade,
Department of Trade and Industry.

26th April 1972.

EXPLANATORY NOTE

(This Note is not part of the Regulations.)

These Regulations amend the Merchant Shipping (Tonnage) Regulations 1967 (the principal Regulations).

They apply to ships registered in the United Kingdom before 1st March 1967 (the date on which the principal Regulations came into force) and to ships registered elsewhere which either are to be transferred to the United Kingdom register or for which application is made for certificates of British tonnage. They permit in the case of such ships the omission from the ship's gross tonnage of the tonnage of certain spaces, situated on or above the upper deck and defined in the Regulations, notwithstanding structural changes in such spaces which would otherwise involve the inclusion of their tonnage in that of the ship.

STATUTORY INSTRUMENTS

1972 No. 659

SUGAR

The Sugar (Distribution Payments) (No. 7) Order 1972

Made - - - -	*27th April* 1972
Laid before Parliament -	*27th April* 1972
Coming into Operation -	*28th April* 1972

The Minister of Agriculture, Fisheries and Food, in exercise of the powers conferred upon him by sections 14(5) and 33(4) of the Sugar Act 1956(a), having effect subject to the provisions of section 3 of, and Part II of Schedule 5 to, the Finance Act 1962(b), section 22 of the Finance Act 1964(c) and section 52 of the Finance Act 1966(d) and of all other powers enabling him in that behalf, with the concurrence of the Treasury, and on the advice of the Sugar Board hereby makes the following order:—

1.—(1) This order may be cited as the Sugar (Distribution Payments) (No. 7) Order 1972, and shall come into operation on 28th April 1972.

(2) The Interpretation Act 1889(e) shall apply for the interpretation of this order as it applies for the interpretation of an Act of Parliament.

2. Notwithstanding the provisions of article 2 of the Sugar (Distribution Payments) (No. 6) Order 1972(f), the rates of distribution payments payable under and in accordance with the provisions of section 14 of the Sugar Act 1956, having effect as aforesaid, in respect of sugar and invert sugar imported or home produced or used in the manufacture of imported composite sugar products shall on and after 28th April 1972 be those rates specified in the Schedule to this order; and section 10 of the Finance Act 1901(g) (which relates to new or altered customs or excise duties and their effect upon contracts) shall apply accordingly.

In Witness whereof the Official Seal of the Minister of Agriculture, Fisheries and Food is hereunto affixed on 26th April 1972.

(L.S.)

E. J. G. Smith,
Authorised by the Minister.

We concur.
27th April 1972.

Tim Fortescue,
Hugh Rossi,
Two of the Lords Commissioners of
Her Majesty's Treasury.

(a) 1956 c. 48.　　(b) 1962 c. 44.　　(c) 1964 c. 49.　　(d) 1966 c. 18.
(e) 1889 c. 63.　　(f) S.I. 1972/649 (1972 I, p. 2127).　　(g) 1901 c. 7.

SCHEDULE

PART I

RATES OF DISTRIBUTION PAYMENT FOR SUGAR

Polarisation	Rate of Distribution Payment per ton
	£
Exceeding—	
99°	10·000
98° but not exceeding 99°	9·430
97° ,, ,, ,, 98°	9·200
96° ,, ,, ,, 97°	8·960
95° ,, ,, ,, 96°	8·720
94° ,, ,, ,, 95°	8·480
93° ,, ,, ,, 94°	8·240
92° ,, ,, ,, 93°	8·000
91° ,, ,, ,, 92°	7·760
90° ,, ,, ,, 91°	7·520
89° ,, ,, ,, 90°	7·280
88° ,, ,, ,, 89°	7·040
87° ,, ,, ,, 88°	6·840
86° ,, ,, ,, 87°	6·640
85° ,, ,, ,, 86°	6·460
84° ,, ,, ,, 85°	6·280
83° ,, ,, ,, 84°	6·100
82° ,, ,, ,, 83°	5·920
81° ,, ,, ,, 82°	5·760
80° ,, ,, ,, 81°	5·600
79° ,, ,, ,, 80°	5·440
78° ,, ,, ,, 79°	5·280
77° ,, ,, ,, 78°	5·120
76° ,, ,, ,, 77°	4·960
Not exceeding 76°	4·800

PART II

RATES OF DISTRIBUTION PAYMENT FOR INVERT SUGAR

Sweetening matter content by weight	Rate of Distribution Payment per cwt.
	£
70 per cent. or more	0·31
Less than 70 per cent. and more than 50 per cent.	0·22
Not more than 50 per cent.	0·11

EXPLANATORY NOTE

(This Note is not part of the Order.)

This order provides for reductions equivalent to £2 per ton of refined sugar in the rates of distribution payment in respect of sugar and invert sugar which become eligible for such payments on and after 28th April 1972.

STATUTORY INSTRUMENTS

1972 No. 660

SUGAR

The Sugar (Distribution Repayments) (Amendment) (No. 6) Order 1972

Made - - - -	*27th April* 1972
Laid before Parliament	*27th April* 1972
Coming into Operation	*28th April* 1972

The Minister of Agriculture, Fisheries and Food, in exercise of the powers conferred upon him by sections 15 and 33(4) of the Sugar Act 1956(a), having effect subject to the provisions of section 3 of, and Part II of Schedule 5 to, the Finance Act 1962(b), section 22 of the Finance Act 1964(c) and section 52 of the Finance Act 1966(d) and of all other powers enabling him in that behalf, an order (e) having been made under section 14 of the said Act, hereby makes the following order:—

1.—(1) This order may be cited as the Sugar (Distribution Repayments) (Amendment) (No. 6) Order 1972, and shall come into operation on 28th April 1972.

(2) The Interpretation Act 1889(f) shall apply for the interpretation of this order as it applies for the interpretation of an Act of Parliament.

2.—(1) Notwithstanding the provisions of article 2(1) of the Sugar (Distribution Repayments) (Amendment) (No. 5) Order 1972(g) the amount of distribution repayment payable in respect of invert sugar, if the relevant drawback is payable thereon as being invert sugar produced in the United Kingdom from materials on which sugar duty has been paid on or after 28th April 1972, shall be calculated thereon at the rate applicable to the invert sugar in accordance with the rates prescribed in the Schedule to this order.

(2) Article 2(1) of the Sugar (Distribution Repayments) Order 1972(h) shall apply for the interpretation of this article.

In Witness whereof the Official Seal of the Minister of Agriculture, Fisheries and Food is hereunto affixed on 27th April 1972.

(L.S.)

E. J. G. Smith,
Authorised by the Minister.

(a) 1956 c. 48.   (b) 1962 c. 44.   (c) 1964 c. 49.
(d) 1966 c. 18.   (e) S.I. 1972/659 (1972 I, p. 2139). (f) 1889 c. 63.
(g) S.I. 1972/650 (1972 I, p. 2129).   (h) S.I. 1972/67 (1972 I, p. 162).

THE SCHEDULE

RATES OF DISTRIBUTION REPAYMENT FOR INVERT SUGAR

Sweetening matter content by weight	Rate of Distribution Repayment per cwt.
	£
More than 80 per cent.	0·37
More than 70 per cent. but not more than 80 per cent.	0·31
More than 60 per cent. but not more than 70 per cent.	0·22
More than 50 per cent. but not more than 60 per cent.	0·18
Not more than 50 per cent. and the invert sugar not being less in weight than 14 lb. per gallon	0·11

EXPLANATORY NOTE

(This Note is not part of the Order.)

This order, which is consequent upon the Sugar (Distribution Payments) (No. 7) Order 1972 (S.I. 1972/659), provides for reductions equivalent to £2 per ton of refined sugar in the rates of distribution repayment, in respect of sugar and invert sugar produced in the United Kingdom from materials which become eligible for distribution payments on or after 28th April 1972.

STATUTORY INSTRUMENTS

1972 No. 661

SUGAR

The Composite Sugar Products (Distribution Payments—Average Rates) (No. 7) Order 1972

Made - - - -	*27th April* 1972
Laid before Parliament-	*27th April* 1972
Coming into Operation	*28th April* 1972

Whereas the Minister of Agriculture, Fisheries and Food (hereinafter called " the Minister ") has on the recommendation of the Sugar Board made an order (a) pursuant to the powers conferred upon him by section 9(1) of the Sugar Act 1956(b) having effect subject to section 14(8) of that Act and to the provisions of section 3 of, and Part II of Schedule 5 to, the Finance Act 1962 (c), section 22 of the Finance Act 1964(d) and section 52 of the Finance Act 1966(e), providing that in the case of certain descriptions of composite sugar products distribution payments shall be calculated on the basis of an average quantity of sugar or invert sugar taken to have been used in the manufacture of the products and that certain other descriptions shall be treated as not containing any sugar or invert sugar:

And whereas the Minister has by the Sugar (Distribution Payments) (No. 7) Order 1972(f) provided for a change in the rates of distribution payments in respect of sugar and invert sugar which became eligible for such payments on and after 28th April 1972.

Now, therefore, the Minister on the recommendation of the Sugar Board, and in exercise of the powers conferred upon him by sections 9(1) and 33(4) of the Sugar Act 1956, having effect as aforesaid, and of all other powers enabling him in that behalf, hereby makes the following order:—

1.—(1) This order may be cited as the Composite Sugar Products (Distribution Payments—Average Rates) (No. 7) Order 1972, and shall come into operation on 28th April 1972.

(2) The Interpretation Act 1889(g) shall apply to the interpretation of this order as it applies to the interpretation of an Act of Parliament.

2. Distribution payments payable on or after 28th April 1972 under and in accordance with section 14 of the Sugar Act 1956, having effect as aforesaid, in respect of sugar and invert sugar used in the manufacture of the descriptions of imported composite sugar products specified in the second column of Schedule 1 to this order, being goods which are classified in the tariff headings indicated in relation to them in the first column of the said Schedule shall, notwithstanding the provisions of the Sugar (Distribution Payments) (No. 7) Order 1972 and the Composite Sugar Products (Distribution Payments—Average Rates) (No. 6) Order 1972(a) be calculated by reference to the weight of the products and the rates specified in relation thereto in the third column of the said Schedule.

3. Imported composite sugar products other than those of a description specified in Schedules 1 and 2 to this order shall be treated as not containing any sugar or invert sugar for the purposes of distribution payments.

(a) S.I. 1972/651 (1972 I, p. 2131).   (b) 1956 c. 48.   (c) 1962 c. 44.   (d) 1964 c. 49.
(e) 1966 c. 18.   (f) S.I. 1972/659 (1972 I, p. 2139).   (g) 1889 c. 63.

In Witness whereof the Official Seal of the Minister of Agriculture, Fisheries and Food is hereunto affixed on 27th April 1972.

(L.S.)

E. J. G. Smith,
Authorised by the Minister.

SCHEDULE 1

In this Schedule:—

" Tariff heading " means a heading or, where the context so requires, a subheading of the Customs Tariff 1959 (see paragraph (1) of Article 2 of the Import Duties (General) (No. 7) Order 1971)(a).

Tariff heading	Description of Composite Sugar Products	Rate of Distribution Payment
		Per cwt. £
04.02 ..	Milk and cream, preserved, concentrated or sweetened, containing more than 10 per cent. by weight of added sugar	0·22
17.02 (B) (2) and 17.05 (B)	Syrups containing sucrose sugar, whether or not flavoured or coloured, but not including fruit juices containing added sugar in any proportion:—	
	Containing 70 per cent. or more by weight of sweetening matter	0·31
	Containing less than 70 per cent., and more than 50 per cent. by weight of sweetening matter..	0·22
	Containing not more than 50 per cent. by weight of sweetening matter	0·11
17.02 (F) ..	Caramel:—	
	Solid	0·50
	Liquid	0·34
17.04 ..	Sugar confectionery, not containing cocoa ..	0·40
18.06 ..	Chocolate and other food preparations containing cocoa and added sugar:—	
	Chocolate couverture not prepared for retail sale; chocolate milk crumb, liquid ..	0·22
	Chocolate milk crumb, solid	0·27
	Solid chocolate bars or blocks, milk or plain, with or without fruit or nuts; other chocolate confectionery consisting wholly of chocolate or of chocolate and other ingredients not containing added sugar ..	0·22
	Other	0·29

(a) S.I. 1971/1971 (1971 III, p. 5330).

SCHEDULE 1—*continued*

Tariff heading	Description of Composite Sugar Products	Rate of Distribution Payment
		Per cwt. £
19.08　..	Pastry, biscuits, cakes and other fine bakers' wares containing added sugar:—	
	Biscuits, wafers and rusks containing more than 12½ per cent. by weight of added sugar, and other biscuits, wafers and rusks included in retail packages with such goods..　　..	0·12
	Cakes with covering or filling containing added sugar; meringues　..　　..　　..　　..	0·16
	Other　..　　..　　..　　..　　..　　..	0·06
20.01　..	Vegetables and fruit, prepared or preserved by vinegar or acetic acid, containing added sugar:—	
	Containing 10 per cent. or more by weight of added sugar ..　　..　　..　　..　　..	0·17
	Other　..　　..　　..　　..　　..　　..	0·03
20.03　..	Fruit preserved by freezing, containing added sugar	0·06
20.04　..	Fruit, fruit-peel and parts of plants, preserved by sugar (drained, glacé or crystallised)　..　　..	0·32
20.05　..	Jams, fruit jellies, marmalades, fruit puree and fruit pastes, being cooked preparations, containing added sugar　　..　　..　　..　　..	0·31
20.06　..	Fruit otherwise prepared or preserved, containing added sugar:—	
	Ginger　..　　..　　..　　..　　..　　..	0·25
	Other　..　　..　　..　　..　　..　　..	0·06

SCHEDULE 2

Tariff heading	Description of Composite Sugar Products
17.05 (A) and (B)	Sugar and invert sugar, flavoured or coloured.

EXPLANATORY NOTE

(*This Note is not part of the Order.*)

This order provides for reductions in the average rates of distribution payments payable in respect of imported composite sugar products of the descriptions specified in Schedule 1 on and after 28th April 1972. These correspond to reductions in the rates of distribution payment effected by the Sugar (Distribution Payments) (No. 7) Order 1972 (S.I. 1972/659). Provision is also made for certain imported composite sugar products to be treated as not containing any sugar or invert sugar.

STOKE-ON-TRENT
CITY
LIBRARIES

STATUTORY INSTRUMENTS

1972 No. 666

MERCHANT SHIPPING

The Merchant Shipping (Dangerous Goods) (Amendment) Rules 1972

Made - - -	*27th April* 1972
Laid before Parliament	*9th May* 1972
Coming into Operation	*31st May* 1972

The Secretary of State in exercise of his powers under section 23 of the Merchant Shipping (Safety Convention) Act 1949(**a**) and of all other powers enabling him in that behalf hereby makes the following Rules:—

1.—(1) These Rules may be cited as the Merchant Shipping (Dangerous Goods) (Amendment) Rules 1972 and shall come into operation on 31st May 1972.

(2) The Interpretation Act 1889(**b**) shall apply to the interpretation of these Rules as it applies to the interpretation of an Act of Parliament.

2. The Merchant Shipping (Dangerous Goods) Rules 1965(**c**), as amended by the Merchant Shipping (Dangerous Goods) (Amendment) Rules 1968(**d**), shall be further amended as follows:—

(1) In Rule 1(2), the following shall be substituted for the definition of "The Blue Book":—

" 'The Blue Book' means the 1966 Report of the Board of Trade Standing Advisory Committee on the Carriage of Dangerous Goods in Ships (Second Edition 1971)."

(2) In Rule 2(2), for "paragraph 3 on page 331 of the Blue Book" there shall be substituted "paragraph 3 of the Introduction to Class 10 in the Blue Book".

(3) In Rule 10(1), for "20 pounds net weight" in sub-paragraph (*b*) there shall be substituted "9 kilogrammes net weight", and for "2,240 pounds" in sub-paragraph (*c*) there shall be substituted "1016 kilogrammes".

(**a**) 1949 c. 43.
(**c**) S.I. 1965/1067 (1965 II, p. 2681).

(**b**) 1889 c. 63.
(**d**) S.I. 1968/332 (1968 I, p. 969).

(4) The following shall be substituted for Schedule 2:—

"SCHEDULE 2

EXPLOSIVES WHICH MAY BE TAKEN ON BOARD PASSENGER STEAMERS

Those explosives

    (i) against which a single asterisk appears in "The United Kingdom Classification List of Military Explosives" or in "The United Kingdom Classification List of United States Visiting Forces Explosives" in Section C of Class 1 of the Blue Book; or

    (ii) which are classified under Class VI, Division I, in the "List of Commercial Explosives" in Section D of Class 1 of the Blue Book."

Michael Noble,
Minister for Trade,
27th April 1972.   Department of Trade and Industry.

EXPLANATORY NOTE

(This Note is not part of the Rules.)

These Rules amend the Merchant Shipping (Dangerous Goods) Rules 1965 as amended by the Merchant Shipping (Dangerous Goods) (Amendment) Rules 1968.

In the place of references in the Rules as amended to the 1966 Report of the Board of Trade Standing Advisory Committee on the Carriage of Dangerous Goods in Ships (The Blue Book), reference is now made to the appropriate passages in the revised 1971 Edition of the Blue Book which incorporates recommendations of the Committee which supersede those of 1966. In addition, references to the weight of explosives given in Imperial units are now expressed in metric units.

The Blue Book may be purchased from H.M. Stationery Office.

STATUTORY INSTRUMENTS

1972 No. 667 (C.12) (S.44)

TOWN AND COUNTRY PLANNING, SCOTLAND

The Town and Country Planning (Scotland) Act 1969 (Commencement No. 4) Order 1972

Made - - - *24th April* 1972

In exercise of the powers conferred on me by section 104 of the Town and Country Planning (Scotland) Act 1969(**a**), I hereby make the following order:—

1.—(1) This order may be cited as the Town and Country Planning (Scotland) Act 1969 (Commencement No. 4) Order 1972.

(2) In this order:—

"the Act" means the Town and Country Planning (Scotland) Act 1969;

"the 1947 Act" means the Town and Country Planning (Scotland) Act 1947(**b**).

2. The provisions of the Act specified in column 1 of the Schedule to this order (which relate to the matters specified in column 2 thereof) shall come into operation in the whole of Scotland on 18th May 1972.

Gordon Campbell,
One of Her Majesty's Principal
Secretaries of State.

St. Andrew's House,
Edinburgh.
24th April 1972.

(**a**) 1969 c. 30.   (**b**) 1947 c. 53.

Article 2

SCHEDULE

Provisions coming into operation on 18th May 1972

Column 1 Provisions of the Act	Column 2 Subject matter of provisions
In Schedule 11 the entry relating to Sections 3 to 9 of the 1947 Act as respects the following provisions:—	Repeal of provisions consequent upon Section 28(*b*) of the Act
Section 3(2) (*b*) and (*c*);	
In section 3(3) the words from "and designated" to "this section";	
In section 3(4) the words from "Provided that" to the end of the subsection;	
In Section 4(3) the words from "Provided that" to the end of the subsection;	
Section 4(5);	
Section 8(5);	
Section 9(5).	

EXPLANATORY NOTE

(This Note is not part of the Order.)

This Order brings into force in the whole of Scotland the repeal of provisions in Part II of the Town and Country Planning (Scotland) Act 1947 relating to designation of land as subject to compulsory acquisition, being provisions which have ceased to have effect by reason of section 28(*b*) of the Town and Country Planning (Scotland) Act 1969.

STATUTORY INSTRUMENTS

1972 No. 668

SOUTH ATLANTIC TERRITORIES

The Falkland Islands (Legislative Council) (Amendment) Order 1972

Made - - - -	*28th April* 1972
Laid before Parliament	*4th May* 1972
Coming into Operation	*25th May* 1972

At the Court at Windsor Castle, the 28th day of April 1972

Present,

The Queen's Most Excellent Majesty in Council

Her Majesty, by virtue and in exercise of the powers vested in Her by the British Settlements Acts 1887 and 1945(**a**), and of all other powers enabling Her in that behalf, is pleased, by and with the advice of Her Privy Council, to order, and it is hereby ordered, as follows:—

Citation, construction and commencement

1.—(1) This Order may be cited as the Falkland Islands (Legislative Council) (Amendment) Order 1972 and shall be construed as one with the Falkland Islands (Legislative Council) Order in Council 1948(**b**), which Order, as amended by the Falkland Islands (Legislative Council) (Amendment) Order in Council 1950(**c**), the Falkland Islands (Legislative Council) (Amendment) Order in Council 1951(**d**), the Falkland Islands (Legislative Council) (Amendment) Order in Council 1955(**e**) and the Falkland Islands (Legislative Council) (Amendment) Order 1964(**f**), is hereinafter referred to as " the principal Order ".

(2) This Order and the principal Order may be cited together as the Falkland Islands (Legislative Council) Orders 1948 to 1972 and shall come into operation on 25th May 1972.

Amendment of section 20 *of the principal Order*

2. Section 20 of the principal Order is amended by substituting for subsection (2) the following subsection—

" (2) No business except that of adjournment shall be transacted if objection is taken by any Member present that there are less than four Members present or that there is no Elected Member present, besides the Governor or other Presiding Member."

W. G. Agnew.

(**a**) 1887 c. 54; 1945 c. 7. (**b**) S.I. 1948/2573 (Rev. VII, p. 591; 1948 I, p. 1018).
(**c**) S.I. 1950/1184 (1950 I, p. 683). (**d**) S.I. 1951/1946 (1951 I, p. 682).
(**e**) S.I. 1955/1650 (1955 I, p. 833). (**f**) S.I. 1964/1397 (1964 III, p. 3204).

EXPLANATORY NOTE

(This Note is not part of the Order.)

This Order further amends the Falkland Islands (Legislative Council) Order 1948 by altering the quorum of the Legislative Council.

STATUTORY INSTRUMENTS

1972 No. 669

DIPLOMATIC AND INTERNATIONAL IMMUNITIES AND PRIVILEGES

The Interim Commission for the International Trade Organization (Immunities and Privileges) Order 1972

Laid before Parliament in draft

Made - - - -	*28th April* 1972
Coming into Operation	*29th April* 1972

At the Court at Windsor Castle, the 28th day of April 1972

Present,

The Queen's Most Excellent Majesty in Council

Whereas a draft of this Order has been laid before Parliament in accordance with section 10 of the International Organisations Act 1968(a) (hereinafter referred to as the Act) and has been approved by a resolution of each House of Parliament:

Now, therefore, Her Majesty, by virtue and in exercise of the powers conferred on Her by section 1 of the Act or otherwise in Her Majesty vested, is pleased, by and with the advice of Her Privy Council, to order, and it is hereby ordered, as follows:—

1. This Order may be cited as the Interim Commission for the International Trade Organization (Immunities and Privileges) Order 1972. It shall come into operation on 29th April 1972.

2. The Interpretation Act 1889(b) shall apply for the interpretation of this Order as it applies for the interpretation of an Act of Parliament.

3. The Interim Commission for the International Trade Organization (hereinafter referred to as the Commission) is an organisation of which Her Majesty's Government in the United Kingdom and the governments of foreign sovereign Powers are members.

4. Officers of the Commission shall have exemption from income tax in respect of salaries and emoluments received by them as officers of the Commission.

W. G. Agnew.

(a) 1968 c. 48.   (b) 1889 c. 63.

EXPLANATORY NOTE

(This Note is not part of the Order.)

This Order confers exemption from income tax upon the officers of the Interim Commission for the International Trade Organization, which was established by a Resolution of the United Nations Conference on Trade and Employment (Cmd. 7375). This exemption is conferred in accordance with an Exchange of Notes between the Government of the United Kingdom of Great Britain and Northern Ireland and the Interim Commission for the International Trade Organization concerning exemption from taxation of officials of the Commission (Cmnd. 4897).

STATUTORY INSTRUMENTS

1972 No. 670

DIPLOMATIC AND INTERNATIONAL IMMUNITIES AND PRIVILEGES

The International Institute for the Management of Technology (Immunities and Privileges) Order 1972

Laid before Parliament in draft

Made - - - -	*28th April* 1972
Coming into Operation	*On a date to be notified in the London, Edinburgh and Belfast Gazettes.*

At the Court at Windsor Castle, the 28th day of April 1972

Present,

The Queen's Most Excellent Majesty in Council

Whereas a draft of this Order has been laid before Parliament in accordance with section 10 of the International Organisations Act 1968(a) (hereinafter referred to as the Act) and has been approved by a resolution of each House of Parliament:

Now, therefore, Her Majesty, by virtue and in exercise of the powers conferred on Her by section 1 of the Act or otherwise in Her Majesty vested, is pleased, by and with the advice of Her Privy Council, to order, and it is hereby ordered, as follows:—

1. This Order may be cited as the International Institute for the Management of Technology (Immunities and Privileges) Order 1972 and shall come into operation on the date on which the Convention on the Establishment of the International Institute for the Management of Technology(b) signed at Paris on 6th October 1971 enters into force in respect of the United Kingdom. This date shall be notified in the London, Edinburgh and Belfast Gazettes.

2. The Interpretation Act 1889(c) shall apply for the interpretation of this Order as it applies for the interpretation of an Act of Parliament.

3. The International Institute for the Management of Technology is an organisation of which Her Majesty's Government in the United Kingdom and the governments of foreign sovereign Powers are members.

4. The International Institute for the Management of Technology shall have the legal capacities of a body corporate.

W. G. Agnew.

(a) 1968 c. 48. (b) Cmnd. 4854. (c) 1889 c. 63.

EXPLANATORY NOTE

(This Note is not part of the Order.)

This Order confers the legal capacities of a body corporate on the International Institute for the Management of Technology, as is required by Article 4 of the Convention on the Establishment of the International Institute for the Management of Technology (Cmnd. 4854) signed at Paris on 6th October 1971.

1972 No. 671 (N.I. 2)

NORTHERN IRELAND

The Appropriation (Northern Ireland) Order 1972

Made - - - -	*28th April* 1972
Laid before Parliament	*1st May* 1972
Coming into Operation	*2nd May* 1972

At the Court at Windsor Castle, the 28th day of April 1972

Present,

The Queen's Most Excellent Majesty in Council

Whereas it has been made to appear to Her Majesty that by reason of urgency this Order requires to be made without a draft having been approved by resolution of each House of Parliament:

Now, therefore, Her Majesty, in exercise of the powers conferred by section 1(3) of the Northern Ireland (Temporary Provisions) Act 1972(a), and of all other powers enabling Her in that behalf, is pleased, by and with the advice of Her Privy Council, to order, and it is hereby ordered, as follows:—

Title and commencement

1. This Order may be cited as the Appropriation (Northern Ireland) Order 1972 and shall come into operation on 2nd May 1972.

Interpretation

2. The Interpretation Act (Northern Ireland) 1954(b) shall apply for the interpretation of the following provisions of this Order as it applies for the interpretation of an Act of the Parliament of Northern Ireland.

Issue and appropriation of moneys for services in Northern Ireland

3.—(1) The sums granted and authorised to be issued by the Consolidated Fund Act (Northern Ireland) 1972(c) out of the Consolidated Fund towards making good the supply granted to Her Majesty, amounting, as appears by that Act and by Schedule (A), in the aggregate to the sum of one hundred and fifty-one million, twenty thousand, two hundred and ninety-seven pounds, may, notwithstanding the prorogation of the Parliament of Northern Ireland by section 1(3) of the Northern Ireland (Temporary Provisions) Act 1972 without the grants having been appropriated, be so issued and are hereby appropriated for the several services and purposes expressed in Schedule (B).

(a) 1972 c. 22.   (b) 1954 c. 33 (N.I.).   (c) 1972 c. 14 (N.I.).

(2) In addition to the sums granted as mentioned in paragraph (1) out of the Consolidated Fund, the sums which, under the Appropriation Acts (Northern Ireland) 1971(a) were authorised to be applied as appropriations in aid for the year ended 31st March 1972, shall be treated as having been increased or, as the case may be, decreased by the sums respectively set forth in columns 3 and 4 of Part II of Schedule (B) in respect of the several services specified in that Part.

(3) This Article shall have effect in relation to any sum issued or appropriated in aid before the commencement of this Order as if this Order had been in force at the time that sum was issued or appropriated.

W. G. Agnew.

(a) 1971 c. 26 and c. 39 (N.I.).

SCHEDULE (A)

Grants out of the Consolidated Fund under the Consolidated Fund Act (Northern Ireland) 1972

	£
For the service of the year ended on 31st March 1971	438,547
For the service of the year ended on 31st March 1972	9,779,750
For the service of the year ending on 31st March 1973	140,802,000
TOTAL	£151,020,297

SCHEDULE (B)

Part I

Excess for Year 1970–71

Sum granted to make good an excess on a certain grant for the year ended on 31st March 1971, viz.:—

Vote	Sum Granted
	£
CLASS III	
No.	
8. Miscellaneous Services (Home Affairs)	438,547

Part II

SCHEDULE of supplementary sums granted, and of the increase or decrease of the sums which were authorised to be applied as appropriations in aid in addition, thereto, to defray the charges of the several services herein particularly mentioned for the year ended on 31st March 1972, viz.:—

	Sums Granted	Appropriations in Aid	
		Increase	Decrease
	£	£	£
CLASS I			
No.			
1. For salaries and expenses of the Senate and of the House of Commons, including contributions to the Contributory Pension Fund for Members of the Commons, expenses related to the Commonwealth Parliamentary Association and a grant in aid	27,000	—	—

	Sums Granted	Appropriations in Aid	
		Increase	Decrease
	£	£	£

CLASS II

No.

1. For the salaries and expenses of the Ministry of Finance ... ... | 10,000 | 25,000 | — |

3. For superannuation, additional allowances, gratuities, compassionate allowances, pensions to widows, children and dependants, insurance premiums under common law, civil pensions and gratuities etc. and contributions under the superannuation scheme for scientific grades | 15,000 | 140,000 | — |

4. For Public Works and Buildings, including the repayment to the Exchequer of certain issues made from the Consolidated Fund to the Capital Purposes Fund, certain expenses in connection with historic monuments and building materials | 470,300 | 41,500 | — |

5. For providing paper, printing, binding, stationery, office supplies, books and office machinery for the public service and for the Houses of Parliament and purchase of publications for sale at the Government Bookshop ... ... | 60,000 | 68,000 | — |

7. For certain grants and grants in aid to institutions and bodies concerned with science, learning and the arts etc., for the refund of selective employment tax to the Post Office and the Ulster Folk Museum and for certain miscellaneous expenses | 303,750 | — | 200,000 |

CLASS III

1. For the salaries and expenses of the Ministry of Home Affairs ... | 43,700 | — | — |

2. For Police Services ... ... | 709,500 | — | — |

3. For the expenses of criminal prosecutions and other law charges, including the expenses of civil litigation ... ... | 58,100 | 4,000 | — |

	Sums Granted	Appropriations in Aid	
		Increase	Decrease
	£	£	£

CLASS III—*continued*

No.

4. For the salaries, allowances and expenses of County Courts, Magistrates' Courts, Coroners and State Pathologist Service, including the repayment to the Exchequer of certain issues made from the Consolidated Fund to the Capital Purposes Fund ... ... | 12,400 | 600 | —

5. For the expenses of prisons and borstal institutions and certain grants in aid ... ... | 320,000 | — | —

8. For certain miscellaneous services and expenses, including certain grants in aid and refunds of selective employment tax to certain public bodies ... ... | 1,042,600 | 3,400 | —

CLASS IV

1. For the salaries and certain expenses of the Ministry of Health and Social Services and a grant in aid | 371,300 | 315,250 | —

2. For employment, training, rehabilitation and resettlement services, including certain grants in aid ... | 50,200 | — | —

3. For the sums payable by the Exchequer to the Northern Ireland National Insurance and Industrial Injuries Funds ... ... | 565,000 | — | —

5. For the payment of non-contributory benefits ... ... | 370,000 | 45,000 | —

7. For hospitals services ... ... | 939,000 | — | 396,000

8. For general health services ... ... | 1,340,000 | — | 170,400

10. For miscellaneous services, including certain grants in aid ... ... | 100 | — | —

CLASS V

1. For the salaries and expenses of the Ministry of Education ... ... | 81,600 | 12,100 | —

2. For expenditure on the items specified in Schedule 6 to the Education Act (Northern Ireland) 1947(a) and grants to the local education authorities including the repayment to the Exchequer of certain issues made from the Consolidated Fund to the Capital Purposes Fund ... | 530,000 | — | —

(a) 1947 c. 3 (N.I.).

	Sums Granted	Appropriations in Aid	
		Increase	Decrease
	£	£	£
CLASS V—*continued*			
No.			
4. For expenditure on pensions, allowances, gratuities, etc. and certain payments to the National Insurance Fund	100	144,900	—
5. For expenditure on university grants, teacher training, Ulster College and on a payment to the Trustees of Magee University College, Londonderry, in consideration of the transfer of certain property to the New University of Ulster ...	1,387,100	—	—
6. For certain educational services and miscellaneous grants including the repayment to the Exchequer of certain issues made from the Consolidated Fund to the Capital Purposes Fund	1,000	—	—
CLASS VI			
2. For the expenses of the Ministry of Agriculture in respect of agricultural and fisheries research and education	100	10,000	—
4. For the expenses of the Ministry of Agriculture in respect of drainage, inland navigation, fishery services and agricultural development, including the repayment to the Exchequer of certain issues made from the Consolidated Fund to the Capital Purposes Fund ...	100	—	—
5. For the expenses of the Ministry of Agriculture in respect of afforestation, including the repayment to the Exchequer of certain issues made from the Consolidated Fund to the Capital Purposes Fund ...	336,000	—	28,000
CLASS VII			
1. For the salaries and expenses of the Ministry of Commerce	49,700	—	20,200

	Sums Granted	Appropriations in Aid	
		Increase	Decrease
	£	£	£

CLASS VII—*continued*

No.

2. For the expenses of the Ministry of Commerce in respect of industrial development services including the repayment to the Exchequer of certain issues made from the Consolidated Fund to the Capital Purposes Fund and certain grants in aid ... ...

	100	55,000	—

3. For certain miscellaneous services and expenses including the repayment to the Exchequer of certain issues made from the Consolidated Fund to the Capital Purposes Fund including certain grants in aid ...

	200,600	8,000	—

CLASS VIII

1. For the salaries and expenses of the Ministry of Development ...

	140,000	10,000	—

2. For housing, planning and related services, including the repayment to the Exchequer of issues made from the Consolidated Fund to the Capital Purposes Fund and a grant in aid ... ...

	343,000	—	—

3. For water supplies and sewerage services, including the repayment to the Exchequer of certain issues made from the Consolidated Fund to the Capital Purposes Fund ...

	100	—	—

5. For the expenses of the Ministry of Development in respect of transport services including the repayment to the Exchequer of certain issues made from the Consolidated Fund to the Capital Purposes Fund

	100	4,000	—

CLASS IX

2. For the salaries and expenses of the Office of the Northern Ireland Commissioner for Complaints ...

	2,200	—	—

TOTAL	£9,779,750	886,750	814,600

PART III

SCHEDULE of sums granted on account of or towards defraying the charges of the several services for which a Vote on Account is required for the year ending 31st March 1973:—

	Sums Granted on Account
	£

CLASS I

No.
1. For the salaries and expenses of the Senate and of the House of Commons, including contributions to the Contributory Pension Fund for Members of the Commons, expenses related to the Commonwealth Parliamentary Association and a grant in aid ... ... | 91,000

2. For the salaries of the department of the Prime Minister, the salaries of the Cabinet Secretariat, and other expenses in connection therewith, including the expenses of the offices of the Privy Council, the Information Service and the Agent for the Government of Northern Ireland in Great Britain ... | 275,000

3. For the salaries and expenses of the department of the Comptroller and Auditor-General ... ... | 34,000

4. For a grant in aid of the Government Hospitality Fund ... | 2,800

5. For the salaries and expenses of the Office of the Northern Ireland Parliamentary Commissioner for Administration ... | 6,000

CLASS II

1. For the salaries and expenses of the Ministry of Finance ... | 1,205,000

2. For the salaries and expenses of the Ministry of Finance in respect of Valuation, General Revaluation, Ordnance Survey and other services ... ... | 431,000

3. For superannuation, additional allowances, gratuities, compassionate allowances, pensions to widows, children and dependants, insurance premiums under common law, civil pensions and gratuities, etc., and contributions under the superannuation scheme for scientific grades ... ... | 383,000

4. For Public Works and Buildings, including the repayment to the Exchequer of certain issues made from the Consolidated Fund to the Capital Purposes Fund, certain expenses in connection with historic monuments and building materials | 2,366,000

5. For providing paper, printing, binding, stationery, office supplies, books and office machinery for the public service and for the Houses of Parliament and purchase of publications for sale at the Government Bookshop ... ... | 212,000

6. For the charge in respect of Secret Services ... ... | 5,000

7. For certain grants and grants in aid to institutions and bodies concerned with science, learning and the arts, etc., for the refund of selective employment tax to the Post Office and the Ulster Folk Museum and for certain miscellaneous expenses | 429,000

	Sums Granted on Account
	£

CLASS III

No.

1. For the salaries and expenses of the Ministry of Home Affairs — 194,000

2. For Police Services ... ... — 5,877,000

3. For the expenses of criminal prosecutions and other law charges, including the expenses of civil litigation ... ... — 96,000

4. For the salaries, allowances and expenses of County Courts, Magistrates' Courts, Coroners and State Pathologist Service, including the repayment to the Exchequer of certain issues made from the Consolidated Fund to the Capital Purposes Fund ... ... — 217,000

5. For the expenses of prisons and borstal institutions and certain grants in aid ... ... — 562,000

6. For the expenses of the Ministry of Home Affairs in connection with remand homes, training schools and the care and protection of children and young persons ... ... — 368,000

7. For civil defence services ... ... — 17,000

8. For certain miscellaneous services and expenses, including certain grants in aid and refunds of selective employment tax to certain public bodies ... ... — 2,062,000

CLASS IV

1. For the salaries and certain expenses of the Ministry of Health and Social Services and a grant in aid ... ... — 1,650,000

2. For employment, training, rehabilitation and resettlement services ... ... — 2,219,000

3. For the sums payable by the Exchequer to the Northern Ireland National Insurance and Industrial Injuries Funds — 3,520,000

4. For the payment of family allowances ... ... — 5,066,000

5. For the payment of non-contributory benefits ... ... — 8,802,000

6. For payments to certain employers who have paid selective employment tax ... ... — 7,286,000

7. For hospitals services ... ... — 16,560,000

8. For general health services ... ... — 6,013,000

9. For expenditure on pensions, allowances, gratuities, etc., and certain payments to the National Insurance Fund ... ... — 100

10. For miscellaneous services, including certain grants in aid ... — 2,497,000

	Sums Granted on Account
	£

CLASS V

No.
1. For the salaries and expenses of the Ministry of Education ... | 361,000

2. For expenditure on the items specified in Schedule 6 to the Education Act (Northern Ireland) 1947, and grants to the local education authorities including the repayment to the Exchequer of certain issues made from the Consolidated Fund to the Capital Purposes Fund ... ... | 15,836,000

3. For miscellaneous grants and services to voluntary schools including the repayment to the Exchequer of certain issues made from the Consolidated Fund to the Capital Purposes Fund ... ... | 2,793,000

4. For expenditure on pensions, allowances, gratuities, etc., and certain payments to the National Insurance Fund ... ... | 100

5. For expenditure on university grants, teacher training, and the Ulster College ... ... | 6,171,000

6. For certain educational services and miscellaneous grants including the repayment to the Exchequer of certain issues made from the Consolidated Fund to the Capital Purposes Fund ... ... | 966,000

CLASS VI

1. For the salaries and expenses of the Ministry of Agriculture ... | 1,121,000

2. For the expenses of the Ministry of Agriculture in respect of agricultural and fisheries research and education ... ... | 830,000

3. For the expenses of the Ministry of Agriculture in respect of improvement of livestock, diseases of animals, agricultural development and credit, and other services including sundry grants in aid ... ... | 252,000

4. For the expenses of the Ministry of Agriculture in respect of drainage, inland navigation, fishery services and agricultural development, including the repayment to the Exchequer of certain issues made from the Consolidated Fund to the Capital Purposes Fund ... ... | 1,401,000

5. For the expenses of the Ministry of Agriculture in respect of afforestation, including the repayment to the Exchequer of certain issues made from the Consolidated Fund to the Capital Purposes Fund ... ... | 815,000

6. For the expenses of the Ministry of Agriculture in respect of agricultural assistance schemes and the Northern Ireland Agricultural Trust ... ... | 1,031,000

	Sums Granted on Account
	£
CLASS VII	
No.	
1. For the salaries and expenses of the Ministry of Commerce ...	451,000
2. For the expenses of the Ministry of Commerce in respect of industrial development services including the repayment to the Exchequer of certain issues made from the Consolidated Fund to the Capital Purposes Fund and certain grants in aid	16,742,000
3. For certain miscellaneous services and expenses, including the repayment to the Exchequer of certain issues made from the Consolidated Fund to the Capital Purposes Fund including certain grants in aid	1,561,000
CLASS VIII	
1. For the salaries and expenses of the Ministry of Development	529,000
2. For housing services and a grant in aid	5,654,000
3. For water supplies and sewerage services, including the repayment to the Exchequer of certain issues made from the Consolidated Fund to the Capital Purposes Fund	1,758,000
4. For Exchequer contributions to local revenues and for the refund of selective employment tax paid by local authorities and certain other bodies	7,988,000
5. For the expenses of the Ministry of Development in respect of transport services including the repayment to the Exchequer of certain issues made from the Consolidated Fund to the Capital Purposes Fund	4,073,000
6. For planning, environmental and related services including the repayment to the Exchequer of issues made from the Consolidated Fund to the Capital Purposes Fund and certain grants in aid	1,693,000
CLASS IX	
1. For the salaries and expenses of the Ministry of Community Relations including extra-statutory grants and payments, grants under the Social Need (Grants) Act (Northern Ireland) 1970(a) and a grant in aid of the Northern Ireland Community Relations Commission	298,000
2. For the salaries and expenses of the Office of the Northern Ireland Commissioner for Complaints	32,000
TOTAL	£140,802,000

(a) 1970 c. 13 (N.I.).

EXPLANATORY NOTE

(This Note is not part of the Order.)

This Order authorises the issue of moneys out of the Consolidated Fund of Northern Ireland and appropriates those moneys for specified services in Northern Ireland, including moneys issued before the coming into operation of the Order.

STOKE-ON-TRENT
CITY
LIBRARIES

STATUTORY INSTRUMENTS

1972 No. 672

CIVIL AVIATION

The Air Navigation (Amendment) Order 1972

Made - - -	*28th April* 1972
Laid before Parliament	*4th May* 1972
Coming into Operation	*25th May* 1972

At the Court at Windsor Castle, the 28th day of April 1972

Present,

The Queen's Most Excellent Majesty in Council

Her Majesty, in exercise of the powers conferred upon Her by sections 8, 57 and 59 of the Civil Aviation Act 1949(**a**), as amended(**b**), and of all other powers enabling Her in that behalf, is pleased, by and with the advice of Her Privy Council, to order, and it is hereby ordered, as follows:

Citation and Operation

1. This Order may be cited as the Air Navigation (Amendment) Order 1972 and shall come into operation on 25th May 1972.

Interpretation

2.—(1) In this Order, "the Principal Order" means the Air Navigation Order 1972(**c**).

(2) The Interpretation Act 1889(**d**) applies for the purpose of the interpretation of this Order as it applies for the purpose of the interpretation of an Act of Parliament.

Amendment of Air Navigation Order 1972

3. The Principal Order shall be amended as follows:

(1) In Article 14(2) for "In the case of aircraft registered in the United Kingdom," there shall be substituted "Without prejudice to paragraph (1) of this Article,"

(2) For Article 18(7) there shall be substituted:

"(7)(*a*) When an aircraft registered in the United Kingdom carries 20 or more passengers on a flight for the purpose of public transport, the crew of the aircraft shall include cabin attendants carried for the purpose of performing in the interest of the safety of passengers duties to be assigned by the operator or the person in command of the aircraft, but who shall not act as members of the flight crew;

(*b*) The Authority may give a direction to the operator of any aircraft registered in the United Kingdom requiring him to include among the crew thereof whenever the aircraft is flying for the purpose of public transport at least one cabin attendant, notwithstanding that the aircraft may be carrying fewer than 20 passengers;

(**a**) 1949 c. 67.
(**b**) The relevant amendment is s.62(1) Civil Aviation Act 1971 (c. 75).
(**c**) S.I. 1972/129 (1972 I. p. 366).   (**d**) 1889 c. 63.

(c) In the case of an aircraft with a total seating capacity of not more than 200, the number of cabin attendants carried on such a flight as is mentioned in sub-paragraph (a) of this Article, shall be not less than one cabin attendant for every 50, or fraction of 50, passengers carried;

(d) In the case of an aircraft with a total seating capacity of more than 200, the number of cabin attendants carried on such a flight as aforesaid, shall be not less than half the number of main exits in the aircraft, and in addition, when more than 200 passengers are carried, one additional cabin attendant for every 25, or fraction of 25, of such passengers:

Provided that, if the number of cabin attendants, calculated in accordance with this sub-paragraph, exceeds the number of main exits in the aircraft, it shall be sufficient compliance with this Article if the number of cabin attendants carried is equal to the number of main exits in the aircraft.

(e) For the purposes of this paragraph a main exit means an exit in the side of the aircraft at floor level intended for the disembarkation of passengers whether normally or in an emergency."

(3) In Article 19(1)(d) "per second" shall be deleted;

(4) In Article 63(1) after "Control or" there shall be inserted "at";

(5) In Schedule 6:

(a) for "apparatus" wherever it appears there shall be substituted "equipment";

(b) in paragraph 1 "registered in the United Kingdom" shall be deleted;

(c) for paragraph 2 there shall be substituted:

"2.   TABLE

Aircraft and Circumstances of Flight	Scale of Equipment Required						
	A	B	C	D	E	F	G
(1) All aircraft within the United Kingdom:							
(a) when flying under Instrument Flight Rules within controlled airspace	A	B					
(b) where required by regulations made under Article 61 of this Order to comply in whole or in part with Instrument Flight Rules in Visual Meteorological Conditions	A*	B*					
(c) when flying within any airspace in respect of which special rules are prescribed by the said regulations in relation to a particular aerodrome, so as to require two-way radio communication with that aerodrome	A*						
(d) when making an approach to landing at an aerodrome notified for the purpose of this sub-paragraph							G*
(2) All aircraft (other than gliders and helicopters) within the United Kingdom when flying at or above flight level 250 and within such controlled airspace as may be notified for the purpose of this sub-paragraph					E*		

Aircraft and Circumstances of Flight	Scale of Equipment Required					
	A	B	C	D	E	F
(3) All aircraft (other than gliders) within the United Kingdom when flying above flight level 100 within controlled airspace and in such other airspace as may be notified for the purpose of this sub-paragraph						F*
(4) All aircraft registered in the United Kingdom, wherever they may be:						
(a) when flying for the purpose of public transport under Instrument Flight Rules:						
(i) while making an approach to landing ..	A	B	C	D		
(ii) on all other occasions	A	B	C			
(b) over 2,300 kg. maximum total weight authorised when flying for the purpose of public transport under Visual Flight Rules	A	B				
(c) not over 2,300 kg. maximum total weight authorised when flying for the purpose of public transport under Visual Flight Rules:						
(i) over a route on which navigation is not effected solely by visual reference to landmarks	A	B				
(ii) over water, beyond gliding distance from any land	A					

*Unless the appropriate air traffic control unit otherwise permits in relation to the particular flight and provided that the aircraft complies with any instructions which the air traffic control unit may give in the particular case."

    (d) in paragraph 3 after Scale D there shall be added:

        "Scale E
        Such type of radio equipment as may be notified as being capable of (a) replying to an interrogation from secondary surveillance radar units on the surface and (b) being set in accordance with such instructions as may be given to the aircraft by the appropriate air traffic control unit.

        Scale F
        Radio equipment capable of providing a continuous indication of the aircraft's distance from the appropriate aeronautical radio stations.

        Scale G
        Radio equipment capable of enabling the aircraft to make an approach to landing using the Instrument Landing System."

    (e) in paragraph 4 after "All aircraft" there shall be inserted "registered in the United Kingdom".

(6) In Schedule 9 Part A 2 in sub-paragraph (c)(ii) of the proviso to the Privileges of the Private Pilot's Licence (Aeroplanes) for "aeroplane" there shall be substituted "aerodrome".

W. G. Agnew.

EXPLANATORY NOTE

(This Note is not part of the Order.)

This Order amends the Air Navigation Order 1972. In addition to some minor and drafting amendments the following changes are made:

(1) Aircraft registered in the United Kingdom which carry 20 or more passengers on a flight for the purpose of public transport are required to carry cabin attendants to perform duties in the interest of the safety of passengers. In the case of aircraft with a total seating capacity of more than 200, the number of cabin attendants now required to be carried must be calculated according to the number of main exits in the aircraft and the number of passengers actually carried (Article 18).

(2) Requirements relating to radio equipment (which previously applied only to aircraft registered in the United Kingdom) are now extended to aircraft registered elsewhere than in the United Kingdom when flying within the United Kingdom. New requirements are also introduced that all aircraft within the United Kingdom, wherever they are registered, must be provided with equipment capable of using the Instrument Landing System (ILS) when they land at notified aerodromes and that all aircraft wherever registered (except gliders) when flying within the United Kingdom above flight level 100 in controlled airspace, must be provided with Distance Measuring Equipment (DME). Provisions relating to the carriage of Secondary Surveillance Transponders (SSR), which were formerly prescribed in regulations, are also incorporated (Schedule 6).

STATUTORY INSTRUMENTS

1972 No. 673

COPYRIGHT

The Copyright (International Conventions) Order 1972

Made - - -	*28th April* 1972
Laid before Parliament	*8th May* 1972
Coming into Operation	*31st May* 1972

At the Court at Windsor Castle, the 28th day of April 1972

Present,

The Queen's Most Excellent Majesty in Council

Her Majesty, by and with the advice of Her Privy Council, and by virtue of the authority conferred upon Her by sections 31, 32 and 47 of the Copyright Act 1956(a) and of all other powers enabling Her in that behalf, is pleased to order, and it is hereby ordered, as follows:—

PART I

Citation, commencement and interpretation

1. This Order may be cited as the Copyright (International Conventions) Order 1972, and shall come into operation on 31st May 1972.

2.—(1) In this Order—

"the Act" means the Copyright Act 1956, as amended by the Design Copyright Act 1968(b) and the Copyright (Amendment) Act 1971(c); and

"material time" means—

> (i) in relation to an unpublished work or subject-matter, the time at which such work or subject-matter was made or, if the making thereof extended over a period, a substantial part of that period;

> (ii) in relation to a published work or subject matter, the time of first publication.

(2) The Interpretation Act 1889(d) shall apply to the interpretation of this Order as it applies to the interpretation of an Act of Parliament and as if this Order and the Orders hereby revoked were Acts of Parliament.

PART II

Protection for literary, dramatic, musical and artistic works, sound recordings, cinematograph films and published editions

3. Subject to the following provisions of this Order the provisions of Parts I and II of the Act (except section 14) and all the other provisions of the Act

---

(a) 1956 c. 74.   (b) 1968 c. 68.
(c) 1971 c. 4.   (d) 1889 c. 63.

relevant to those Parts, shall in the case of any country mentioned in Schedules 1 or 2 hereto apply—

- (a) in relation to literary, dramatic, musical or artistic works, sound recordings, cinematograph films or published editions first published in that country, as they apply to such works, recordings, films or editions first published in the United Kingdom;
- (b) in relation to persons who, at any material time are citizens or subjects of, or domiciled or resident in, that country, as they apply to persons who at such time, are British subjects or are domiciled or resident in the United Kingdom; and
- (c) in relation to bodies incorporated under the laws of that country, as they apply to bodies incorporated under the laws of any part of the United Kingdom.

4.—(1) Subject to the following provisions of this Article, the relevant provisions of Schedule 7 to the Act shall have effect in relation to any work or other subject-matter in which copyright subsists by virtue of this Part of this Order as if for any references therein to the commencement of the Act or any of its provisions or to the date of the repeal of any provision of the Copyright Act 1911(**a**) or of any other enactment there were substituted references to 27th September 1957 (being the date on which the Copyright (International Conventions) Order 1957(**b**) came into operation).

(2) Subject to the following provisions of this Article, in the case of any country mentioned in Schedule 2 hereto in relation to which a date is specified in that Schedule—

- (a) paragraph (1) of this Article shall have effect as if, for the reference to 27th September 1957, there were substituted that date (if different); and
- (b) copyright shall not subsist by virtue of this Part of this Order in any work or other subject-matter by reason only of its publication in such a country before the date so specified.

(3) This Article shall not apply—

- (a) in the case of Ghana, Kenya, Malawi, Mauritius, Nigeria or Zambia; or
- (b) to any work or subject-matter first published in the United States of America, if, immediately before 27th September 1957, copyright under the Copyright Act 1911 subsisted in such work or subject-matter by virtue of either an Order in Council dated 9th February 1920, regulating copyright relations with the United States of America (**c**), or the Copyright (United States of America) Order 1942(**d**), as amended (**e**).

5. The acts restricted by section 12 of the Act as applied by this Part of this Order shall not include—

- (a) causing the recording to be heard in public; or
- (b) broadcasting the recording;

except in the case of the countries mentioned in Schedule 3 to this Order.

6. Where any person has before the commencement of this Order incurred any expenditure or liability in connection with the reproduction or perform-

---

(a) 1911 c. 46.   (b) S.I. 1957/1523 (1957 I, p. 474).
(c) S.R.&O. 1920/257 (1920 I, p. 286).
(d) S.R.&O. 1942/1579 (Rev. IV, p. 963: 1942 I, p. 87).
(e) See S.I. 1950/1641 (1950 I, p. 399).

ance of any work or other subject-matter in a manner which at the time was lawful, or for the purpose of or with a view to the reproduction or performance of a work at a time when such reproduction or performance would, but for the making of this Order, have been lawful, nothing in this Part of this Order shall diminish or prejudice any right or interest arising from, or in connection with, such action which is subsisting and valuable immediately before the commencement of this Order unless the person who, by virtue of this Part of this Order, becomes entitled to restrain such reproduction or performance agrees to pay such compensation as, failing agreement, may be determined by arbitration.

7. Nothing in the provisions of the Act as applied by this Part of this Order shall be construed as reviving any right to make, or restrain the making of, or any right in respect of, translations, if such right has ceased before the commencement of this Order.

Part III

Protection in respect of broadcasts

8. The provisions of section 14 of the Act, so far as they relate to sound broadcasts, and all the other provisions of the Act relevant thereto, other than section 40(3), shall apply, in the case of each of the countries mentioned in Schedule 4 to this Order, in relation to sound broadcasts made from places in any such country by an organisation constituted in, or under the laws of, the country in which the broadcast is made, as they apply in relation to sound broadcasts made from places in the United Kingdom by the British Broadcasting Corporation; so, however, that paragraphs 17 and 18 of Schedule 7 to the Act shall have effect as if for the references therein to the commencement of section 14 there were substituted references to the relevant date set out in the said Schedule 4 (being the date on which the provisions of section 14 of the Act so far as they relate to sound broadcasts were first applied in the case of that country).

9. The provisions of section 14 of the Act, so far as they relate to television broadcasts, and all the other provisions of the Act relevant thereto, other than section 37(4), section 40(3) and Schedule 5, shall apply in the case of each of the countries mentioned in Schedule 5 to this Order, in relation to television broadcasts made from places in any such country by an organisation constituted in, or under the laws of, the country in which the broadcast was made, as they apply in relation to television broadcasts made from places in the United Kingdom by the British Broadcasting Corporation or the Independent Television Authority; so, however, that—

   (*a*) section 24(3)(*c*) of the Act shall have effect as if for the reference to the Corporation or the Authority or any organisation appointed by them there were substituted a reference to any owner or prospective owner of copyright in television broadcasts; and

   (*b*) paragraphs 17 and 18 of Schedule 7 to the Act shall have effect as if for the references therein to the commencement of section 14 there were substituted references to the relevant date set out in Schedule 5 to this Order, (being the date on which the provisions of section 14 of the Act so far as they relate to television broadcasts were first applied in the case of that country).

Part IV

Extensions and revocations

10. Parts I and II of this Order shall extend to the countries mentioned in Schedule 6 to this Order subject to the modifications mentioned in that Schedule and Part III shall extend to Gibraltar and Bermuda subject to the modifications mentioned in Schedule 7 to this Order.

11. The Orders mentioned in Schedule 8 to this Order are hereby revoked insofar as they form part of the law of the United Kingdom or any country mentioned in Schedule 6 to this Order.

W. G. Agnew.

SCHEDULE 1

Countries of the Berne Copyright Union

(The countries indicated with an asterisk are also party to the Universal Copyright Convention.)

Argentina*
Australia* (and Papua, New Guinea, Nauru and Norfolk Island)
Austria*
Belgium*
Brazil*
Bulgaria
Cameroon
Canada*
Ceylon
Chad
Chile*
Congo (Peoples' Republic)
Cyprus
Czechoslovakia*
Dahomey
Denmark*
Fiji*
Finland*
France* (and French territories overseas)
Gabon
Federal Republic of Germany (and Land Berlin)*
Greece*
Hungary*
Iceland*
India*
Republic of Ireland*
Israel*
Italy*
Ivory Coast
Japan*
Lebanon*
Liechtenstein*
Luxembourg*
Madagascar
Mali
Malta*
Mexico*
Monaco*
Morocco
Netherlands* (and Surinam and Netherlands Antilles)

New Zealand*
Niger
Norway*
Pakistan*
Philippines*
Poland
Portugal* (including Portuguese provinces overseas)
Romania
Senegal
South Africa (and South West Africa)
Spain* (and its Colonies)
Sweden*
Switzerland*
Thailand
Tunisia*
Turkey
Uruguay
Vatican City*
Yugoslavia*
Zaire

SCHEDULE 2

COUNTRIES PARTY TO THE UNIVERSAL COPYRIGHT CONVENTION BUT NOT MEMBERS OF THE BERNE UNION

Andorra	27th September 1957
Costa Rica	27th September 1957
Cuba	27th September 1957
Ecuador	27th September 1957
Ghana	—
Guatemala	28th October 1964
Haiti	27th September 1958
Kenya	—
Khmer Republic	27th September 1957
Laos	27th September 1957
Liberia	27th September 1957
Malawi	—
Mauritius	
Nicaragua	16th August 1961
Nigeria	—
Panama	17th October 1962
Paraguay	11th March 1962
Peru	16th October 1963
United States of America (and Guam, Panama Canal Zone, Puerto Rico and the Virgin Islands of the United States of America)	27th September 1957
Venezuela	18th November 1966
Zambia	—

SCHEDULE 3

COUNTRIES IN WHOSE CASE COPYRIGHT IN SOUND RECORDINGS INCLUDES
EXCLUSIVE RIGHT TO PERFORM IN PUBLIC AND TO BROADCAST

Australia
Brazil
Ceylon
Costa Rica
Cyprus
Czechoslovakia
Denmark
Ecuador
Federal Republic of Germany (and Land Berlin)
Fiji
India
Republic of Ireland
Italy
Israel
Mexico
New Zealand
Nigeria
Norway
Pakistan
Paraguay
Spain
Sweden
Switzerland

SCHEDULE 4

COUNTRIES WHOSE ORGANISATIONS ARE PROTECTED IN RELATION TO SOUND BROADCASTS

Brazil	5th November 1965
Congo (Peoples' Republic)	21st May 1964
Costa Rica	19th November 1971
Czechoslovakia	14th August 1964
Denmark	1st July 1965
Ecuador	21st May 1964
Federal Republic of Germany (and Land Berlin)	18th November 1966
Fiji	31st May 1972
Mexico	21st May 1964
Niger	21st May 1964
Paraguay	26th February 1970
Sweden	21st May 1964

SCHEDULE 5

COUNTRIES WHOSE ORGANISATIONS ARE PROTECTED IN RELATION TO TELEVISION
BROADCASTS

Belgium	8th March 1968
Brazil	5th November 1965
Congo (Peoples' Republic)	21st May 1964
Costa Rica	19th November 1971
Cyprus	5th May 1970
Czechoslovakia	14th August 1964
Denmark	1st February 1962
Ecuador	21st May 1964
Federal Republic of Germany (and Land Berlin)	18th November 1966
Fiji	31st May 1972
France	1st July 1961
Mexico	21st May 1964
Niger	21st May 1964
Norway	10th August 1968
Paraguay	26th February 1970
Spain	19th November 1971
Sweden	1st July 1961

SCHEDULE 6

COUNTRIES TO WHICH PARTS I AND II OF THIS ORDER EXTEND

Bahama Islands	11th February 1963
Bermuda	6th December 1962
British Honduras	16th October 1966
Cayman Islands	4th June 1966
Falkland Islands and its Dependencies	10th October 1963
Gibraltar	1st October 1960
Isle of Man	31st May 1959
Montserrat	5th March 1966
Seychelles	10th October 1963
St. Helena and its Dependencies	10th October 1963
Virgin Islands	11th February 1963

Modifications to this Order as extended

1. Article 3 shall have effect as part of the law of any country to which it extends as if for references to the United Kingdom there were substituted references to the country in question.

2. Article 4 shall have effect as part of the law of any country to which it extends as if in paragraphs (1) and (3) there were substituted for "27th September 1957" the date indicated in relation to that country in the preceding provisions of this Schedule (being the date when the Act was first extended to that country).

3. Schedule 2 to this Order shall have effect as part of the law of any such country as if for any date in that Schedule which is earlier than the date mentioned in this Schedule in relation to the relevant country there were substituted that later date.

SCHEDULE 7

MODIFICATIONS OF PART III OF, AND SCHEDULES 4 AND 5 TO, THIS ORDER IN ITS EXTENSION TO BERMUDA AND GIBRALTAR

1. (*a*) In Article 8 the words "other than section 40(3)" shall be omitted;

(*b*) in Article 9 the words "other than section 37(4), section 40(3) and Schedule 5" shall be omitted.

2. Insofar as Part III is part of the Law of Bermuda—

(*a*) in Schedule 4 to this Order, the date mentioned in the second column shall be altered to 23rd August 1969 in the case of every country except Costa Rica, Fiji and Paraguay;

(*b*) in Schedule 5, the names of Belgium, Cyprus, France, Norway and Spain shall be omitted; and

(*c*) the date mentioned in the second column of that Schedule shall be altered to 23rd August 1969 in the case of every country not so omitted except Costa Rica, Fiji and Paraguay.

3. Insofar as Part III is part of the law of Gibraltar—

(*a*) in Schedule 4 to this Order, the date mentioned in the second column shall be altered to 28th October 1966 in the case of every country except Costa Rica, the Federal Republic of Germany (and Land Berlin), Fiji and Paraguay; and

(*b*) in Schedule 5, the date mentioned in the second column shall be altered to 28th October 1966 in the case of every country except Belgium, Costa Rica, Cyprus, the Federal Republic of Germany (and Land Berlin), Fiji, Norway, Paraguay and Spain.

SCHEDULE 8

ORDERS REVOKED

Order	S.I. number and reference
The Copyright (International Conventions) Order 1964	S.I. 1964/690 (1964 II, p. 1319)
The Copyright (International Conventions) (Amendment) Order 1964	S.I. 1964/1194 (1964 II, p. 2773)
The Copyright (International Conventions) (Amendment No. 2) Order 1964	S.I. 1964/1651 (1964 III, p. 3641)
The Copyright (International Conventions) (Amendment) Order 1965	S.I. 1965/1303 (1965 II, p. 3705)
The Copyright (International Conventions) (Amendment No. 2) Order 1965	S.I. 1965/1857 (1965 III, p. 5577)
The Copyright (International Conventions) (Amendment No. 3) Order 1965	S.I. 1965/2159 (1965 III, p. 6327)
The Copyright (International Conventions) (Amendment) Order 1966	S.I. 1966/684 (1966 II, p. 1535)

Order	S.I. number and reference
The Copyright (Gibraltar: Protection of Foreign Broadcasts) Order 1966	S.I. 1966/945 (1966 II, p. 2286)
The Copyright (International Conventions) (Amendment No. 2) Order 1966	S.I. 1966/1185 (1966 III, p. 3171)
The Copyright (International Conventions) (Amendment No. 3) Order 1966	S.I. 1966/1409 (1966 III, p. 3772)
The Copyright (International Conventions) (Amendment) Order 1967	S.I. 1967/877 (1967 II, p. 2617)
The Copyright (International Conventions) (Amendment No. 2) Order 1967	S.I. 1967/1151 (1967 II, p. 3387)
The Copyright (International Conventions) (Amendment) Order 1968	S.I. 1968/1858 (1968 III, p. 4887)
The Copyright (Bermuda: Protection of Foreign Broadcasts) Order 1969	S.I. 1969/743 (1969 II, p. 2027)
The Copyright (International Conventions) (Amendment) Order 1970	S.I. 1970/290 (1970 I, p. 1082)
The Copyright (International Conventions) (Amendment No. 2) Order 1970	S.I. 1970/637 (1970 I, p. 2060)
The Copyright (International Conventions) (Amendment) Order 1971	S.I. 1971/1850 (1971 III, p. 5087)

EXPLANATORY NOTE
(This Note is not part of the Order.)

This Order revokes the Orders mentioned in Schedule 8 (being Orders providing for the protection, in the United Kingdom and the countries to which the Copyright Act 1956 has been extended, of works and other subject-matter originating in other countries party to international copyright conventions) and re-enacts the revoked provisions with minor modifications.

The Order also takes account of—

(*a*) the accession of Fiji to the Berne Union, the Universal Copyright Convention and the International Convention for the Protection of Performers, Producers of Phonograms and Broadcasting Organisations,

(*b*) the confirmation by Mauritius of its adherence to the Universal Copyright Convention and

(*c*) the fact that Western Samoa is no longer a member of the Berne Union.

Parts I and II of the Order are extended to the countries named in Schedule 6, being countries in which the Copyright Act 1956 is in force by virtue of Orders in Council made under that Act. In the case of Bermuda and Gibraltar Part III of the Order, which relates exclusively to sound and television broadcasts, is also extended (with modifications).

STATUTORY INSTRUMENTS

1972 No. 674

HOVERCRAFT

The Hovercraft (General) Order 1972

Made - - - -	*28th April* 1972
Laid before Parliament	*8th May* 1972
Coming into Operation	
(*a*) *Article* 35	*31st May* 1972
(*b*) *Remainder*	*26th June* 1972

ARRANGEMENT OF ORDER

Article

PART III

DUTIES OF OPERATOR AND CAPTAIN

PART IV

SUPPLEMENTARY PROVISIONS

SCHEDULE

At the Court at Windsor Castle, the 28th day of April 1972

Present,

The Queen's Most Excellent Majesty in Council

Her Majesty, in exercise of the powers conferred upon Her by section 1(1)(a), (b),(c),(e),(l),(n),(o) and (p) and by section 1(3) of the Hovercraft Act 1968**(a)**, and of all other powers enabling Her in that behalf, is pleased, by and with the advice of Her Privy Council, to order, and it is hereby ordered, as follows—

Citation and Commencement

1.—(1) This Order may be cited as the Hovercraft (General) Order 1972.

(2)(*a*) Article 35 of this Order shall come into operation on 31st May 1972;

(*b*) The remainder of the Order shall come into operation on 26th June 1972.

(a) 1968 c. 59.

Application

2. This Order applies to hovercraft which are used—

(i) wholly or partly on or over the sea or navigable waters; or

(ii) on or over land to which the public have access or non-navigable waters to which the public have access; or

(iii) elsewhere for the carriage of passengers for reward:

Provided that this Order shall not:

(*a*) apply to hovertrains; nor

(*b*) prejudice the operation of section 19 of the Road Traffic Act 1962**(a)**.

Interpretation

3.—(1) In this Order, unless the context otherwise requires—

"Authorised person" for the purposes of any provision of this Order means—

(*a*) any constable; and

(*b*) any person authorised in writing by the Secretary of State either generally or in relation to a particular case or class of cases;

"Beneficial interest" includes interests arising under contract and other equitable interests;

"The CAA" means the Civil Aviation Authority;

"Captain" means the person who is designated by the operator to be in charge of a hovercraft during any journey, or, failing such designation, the person who is for the time being lawfully in charge of the hovercraft;

"Hovertrains" means hovercraft which are at all times guided by tracks, rails or guides fixed to the ground;

"Military hovercraft" means the naval, military or air force hovercraft of any country and includes—

(*a*) any hovercraft being constructed for the naval, military or air force of any country under a contract entered into by the Secretary of State; and

(*b*) any hovercraft in respect of which there is in force a certificate issued by the Secretary of State that the hovercraft is to be treated for the purposes of this Order as a military hovercraft;

"Navigable water" means any water which is in fact navigable by ships or vessels, whether or not the tide ebbs and flows there, and whether or not there is a public right of navigation in that water;

"Operator" in relation to a hovercraft means the person for the time being having the management of the hovercraft;

"Passenger" means any person carried in a hovercraft, except a person employed or engaged in any capacity on board the hovercraft on the business of the hovercraft;

"Unladen weight" in relation to a hovercraft means the weight of a hovercraft ready for use, excluding the weight of usable fuel, occupants, baggage, cargo, stores, buoyant life-saving equipment, portable fire-fighting equipment, portable emergency equipment and non-permanent ballast;

(a) 1962 c. 59.

"United Kingdom" includes the territorial waters adjacent to the United Kingdom;

"Unqualified person" means a person not qualified in accordance with Article 5(3) to be the holder of a legal or beneficial interest by way of ownership in the hovercraft.

(2) The Interpretation Act 1889(a) shall apply to the interpretation of this Order as it applies to the interpretation of an Act of Parliament.

PART I

REGISTRATION

Hovercraft to be registered

4. Subject to Article 7, a hovercraft shall, if used in the United Kingdom, be registered in the United Kingdom unless—

   (*a*) it is registered in some other country; or

   (*b*) an unqualified person holds a legal or beneficial interest in the hovercraft by way of ownership or share therein, and the Secretary of State consents to its use unregistered in the United Kingdom, subject to such conditions as he thinks fit:

Provided that a hovercraft may also be used unregistered in the United Kingdom if:

   (i) (*a*) it has been issued with an Experimental Certificate in accordance with Article 9, and

   (*b*) it is marked in a manner approved by the Secretary of State; or

   (ii) it has an unladen weight of less than 1,000 kg. and is not used for reward.

Registration of hovercraft in the United Kingdom

5.—(1) The Secretary of State shall be the authority for registration of hovercraft in the United Kingdom.

(2) Subject to the provisions of this Article a hovercraft shall not be registered or continue to be registered in the United Kingdom if it appears to the Secretary of State that—

   (*a*) the hovercraft is registered outside the United Kingdom and that such registration does not cease by operation of law upon the hovercraft being registered in the United Kingdom; or

   (*b*) an unqualified person holds any legal or beneficial interest in the hovercraft by way of ownership or any share therein.

(3) Subject to paragraph (4) of this Article the following persons and no others shall be qualified to be the holder of a legal or beneficial interest by way of ownership in a hovercraft registered in the United Kingdom or a share therein—

   (*a*) the Crown in right of Her Majesty's Government in the United Kingdom;

   (*b*) persons ordinarily resident in the United Kingdom;

   (*c*) bodies incorporated in the United Kingdom and having their principal place of business in the United Kingdom;

_____
(a) 1889 c. 63.

(*d*) firms carrying on business in Scotland;

In this sub-paragraph "firm" has the same meaning as in the Partnership Act 1890**(a)**.

(4) If an unqualified person holds a legal or beneficial interest by way of ownership in a hovercraft or a share therein, or is charterer by demise thereof, the Secretary of State may register the hovercraft in the United Kingdom subject to such conditions as he thinks fit. The Secretary of State may at any time cancel the registration of a hovercraft registered under this paragraph.

(5) Application for the registration of a hovercraft in the United Kingdom shall be made in writing to the Secretary of State and shall include or be accompanied by such particulars and evidence relating to the hovercraft and the ownership and chartering thereof as he may require to enable him to determine whether the hovercraft may properly be registered in the United Kingdom and to issue the certificate referred to in paragraph (7) of this Article.

(6) Upon receiving an application for the registration of a hovercraft in the United Kingdom and being satisfied that the hovercraft may properly be so registered, the Secretary of State shall (or, in the case of an application under paragraph (4) of this Article, may) register the hovercraft, wherever it may be, and shall include in the register the following particulars—

(*a*) the number of the certificate;

(*b*) the registration mark assigned to the hovercraft by the Secretary of State;

(*c*) the name of the constructor of the hovercraft, its type and constructor's number;

(*d*) (i) the name and address of every person who holds a legal interest in the hovercraft by way of ownership or a share therein, or, in the case of a hovercraft which is the subject of a hire-purchase agreement, the name and address of the hirer; and

(ii) in the case of a hovercraft registered in pursuance of paragraph (4) of this Article, an indication that it is so registered, and an indication as to whether the person in whose name it is registered is the owner or charterer by demise.

(7) The Secretary of State shall furnish to the person in whose name the hovercraft is registered (hereinafter in this Article referred to as "the registered owner") a certificate of registration, which shall include the foregoing particulars and the date on which the certificate was issued.

(8) Subject to paragraph (4) of this Article, if at any time after a hovercraft has been registered in the United Kingdom an unqualified person becomes the holder of a legal or beneficial interest in the hovercraft by way of ownership or a share therein, the registration of the hovercraft shall thereupon become void and the certificate of registration shall forthwith be returned by the registered owner to the Secretary of State for cancellation.

(9) Any person who is registered as the owner of a hovercraft registered in the United Kingdom shall forthwith inform the Secretary of State in writing of—

(*a*) any change in the particulars which were furnished to the Secretary of State upon application being made for the registration of the hovercraft;

(a) 1890 c. 39.

(b) the destruction of the hovercraft, or its permanent withdrawal from use;

(c) in the case of a demise chartered hovercraft registered in pursuance of paragraph (4) of this Article, the termination of the demise charter.

(10) Any person who becomes the owner of a hovercraft registered in the United Kingdom shall forthwith inform the Secretary of State in writing to that effect.

(11) The Secretary of State may, whenever it appears to him necessary or appropriate to do so for giving effect to this Order or for bringing up to date or otherwise correcting the particulars entered on the register, amend the register or, if he thinks fit, may cancel the registration of the hovercraft, and shall cancel that registration if he is satisfied that there has been a change in the ownership of the hovercraft.

(12) In this Article references to an interest in a hovercraft do not include references to an interest in a hovercraft to which a person is entitled only by virtue of his membership of a hovercraft club and the reference in paragraph (9) of this Article to the registered owner of a hovercraft includes in the case of a deceased person, his legal personal representative, and in the case of a body corporate which has been dissolved, its successor.

Nationality and registration marks

6.—(1) A hovercraft registered in the United Kingdom shall not be used unless—

(i) it bears prominently and clearly painted or affixed to the craft its nationality and registration marks; and

(ii) the nationality and registration marks together with the name and address of the registered owner are engraved on a fire proof metal plate affixed in a prominent position inside the hovercraft near an entrance.

(2) The nationality mark of a hovercraft registered in the United Kingdom shall be the capital letters "GH" in Roman characters and the registration mark shall be a group of four digits assigned by the Secretary of State on the registration of the hovercraft. The letters and digits shall be without ornamentation and a hyphen shall be placed between the nationality mark and the registration mark.

(3) The nationality and registration marks of a hovercraft shall be used as the sole means of identification of the craft by radio.

Hovercraft registered outside the United Kingdom

7.—(1) A hovercraft registered in a country other than the United Kingdom shall not be used for reward or in connection with a trade or business in or over the United Kingdom, except with the permission of the Secretary of State granted under this Article to the operator or charterer of the hovercraft and in accordance with any conditions to which such permission may be subject.

(2) Nothing in this Article shall apply to the use of a hovercraft for passage through the territorial waters of the United Kingdom.

PART II

CERTIFICATION AND MAINTENANCE

Safety Certificate to be in force

8. A hovercraft registered in the United Kingdom shall not be used unless there is in force in respect thereof a current Safety Certificate issued in accordance with this Order and any conditions subject to which the Certificate was issued are complied with:

Provided that the foregoing prohibition shall not apply to—

(*a*) a hovercraft used in accordance with the conditions of an Experimental Certificate issued by the CAA in respect of that hovercraft; or

(*b*) subject to the prior consent of the CAA and to any conditions subject to which that consent was given, a hovercraft in respect of which a Safety Certificate has previously been in force, which is used solely for the purpose of enabling it to—

(i) qualify for a renewal of a Safety Certificate or a variation of a certificate after an application has been made for such renewal or variation;

(ii) proceed to or from a place at which any inspection or test of the hovercraft is to take place for the purpose referred to in sub-paragraph (i) above; or

(iii) proceed to a place at which repairs can be effected.

Issue and renewal of Experimental Certificates

9.—(1) The CAA may, if satisfied by such investigations relating to the safe use of the hovercraft as it may require, issue in respect of any hovercraft an Experimental Certificate, which shall be subject to the condition that the hovercraft is not to carry any persons other than those engaged on the business of the hovercraft, unless the CAA specifically permits such other persons to be carried in a particular case. The Experimental Certificate shall be issued subject to such further conditions relating to safety as the CAA thinks fit.

(2) The CAA may, if satisfied by such investigations relating to the safe use of the hovercraft as it may require, vary an Experimental Certificate at the request of an applicant. Such variation may be subject to such further conditions relating to safety as the CAA thinks fit.

(3) An Experimental Certificate shall, unless cancelled or suspended, remain in force for such period not exceeding one year as may be specified therein, and may be renewed from time to time by the CAA for such further period not exceeding one year as it thinks fit.

Issue of Type Certificates

10.—(1) The CAA may, if satisfied by such investigations of one or more hovercraft as it may require, or by a study of relevant specifications, or by a combination of investigations and a study of relevant specifications, that individual examples of a particular type of hovercraft would if suitably constructed be capable of safe use, issue a Type Certificate in respect of the type of hovercraft specified in the Certificate.

(2) The CAA may, if satisfied by such investigations as it may require or by a study of relevant specifications, or by a combination of investigations and a study of relevant specifications, that individual examples of an engine, component, instrument, or equipment intended for use in a hovercraft would if suitably constructed safely fulfil the function for which they are intended, issue a Type Certificate in respect of that type of engine, component, instrument, or equipment.

(3) The CAA may, if satisfied by such investigations as it may require, vary a Type Certificate issued under paragraph (1) and (2) of this Article, at the request of an applicant.

(4) A Type Certificate shall remain in force until cancelled or suspended.

Issue of Safety Certificates

11.—(1) The CAA may issue a Safety Certificate in respect of a hovercraft registered in the United Kingdom upon being satisfied that it is fit to be used, having regard, in particular, to—

(*a*) the conformity of the hovercraft, its engines, components, instruments, and equipment to a relevant Type Certificate, and compliance with any conditions subject to which that certificate may have been issued;

(*b*) the results of such investigations of the hovercraft as the CAA may require; and

(*c*) the quality of the hovercraft's construction.

(2) (*a*) Every Safety Certificate may specify such categories as have been applied for and are, in the opinion of the CAA, appropriate to the hovercraft, and the Safety Certificate shall be issued subject to the condition that the hovercraft shall be used only for the purposes indicated in sub-paragraph (*c*) of this paragraph in relation to such categories;

(*b*) The categories referred to in sub-paragraph (*a*) of this paragraph are—

Passenger

Cargo

Special

(*c*) The purposes for which hovercraft may be used are as follows—

Passenger Category:	Carriage of passengers and their baggage, and any other purpose specified in the Certificate.
Cargo Category:	The carriage of cargo generally, or of such cargo as may be specified in the Certificate.
Special Category:	Any purpose specified in the Certificate, but not including the carriage of passengers except as expressly permitted.

(3) The CAA may issue the Safety Certificate subject to such other conditions relating to the safety of the hovercraft as it thinks fit.

(4) The CAA may, having regard to such investigations as it may require, vary a Safety Certificate at the request of an applicant. Such variation may be subject to such other conditions relating to the safety of hovercraft as it thinks fit.

Period of validity of Certificates

12. Subject to the provisions of Articles 11 and 15, a Safety Certificate shall remain in force for such period not exceeding one year as may be specified therein, and may be renewed from time to time by the CAA for such further period not exceeding one year as it thinks fit. A Safety Certificate shall cease to be valid in the event of a hovercraft ceasing to be registered in the United Kingdom.

Maintenance

13. A hovercraft in respect of which a Safety Certificate is in force under this Order shall not be used unless it is maintained in a condition satisfactory to the CAA, and in accordance with arrangements approved by the CAA.

Approvals

14. For the purposes of this Part of this Order the CAA may accept reports furnished to it by a person whom it may for the time being approve either absolutely or subject to such conditions as it thinks fit as qualified to furnish such reports.

Revocation etc., of Certificates etc., and power to prevent hovercraft being used

15.—(1) The CAA may, if it thinks fit, provisionally suspend or vary any Certificate, approval or other document issued, granted or having effect under this part of this Order, pending inquiry into or consideration of the case. Without prejudice to Article 10(3) or 11(4), the CAA may, on sufficient ground being shown to its satisfaction after due inquiry, revoke, suspend or vary any such Certificate, approval or other document.

(2) The holder or any person having the possession or custody of any Certificate, approval or other document which has been revoked, suspended or varied under this Part of this Order shall surrender it to the CAA within a reasonable time after being required to do so by it.

(3) The breach of any condition subject to which any Certificate, approval or other document, has been granted or issued, or which has effect under this Order shall render the document invalid during the continuance of the breach.

(4) If it appears likely to the CAA that a hovercraft is intended or likely to be used—

  (*a*) in such circumstances that any conditions on which the Safety Certificate has been granted are breached;

  (*b*) whilst the approved maintenance arrangements are not adhered to;

  (*c*) whilst materially damaged; or

  (*d*) in such circumstances that the CAA has reason to believe that the hovercraft is or may be unsafe;

the CAA may direct the operator or the captain of the hovercraft that he is not to permit the hovercraft to make the particular journey or any other journey of such description as may be specified in the direction, until the direction has been revoked by the CAA, and the CAA may take such steps as are necessary to detain the hovercraft for a period not exceeding seven days.

(5) In the event of the CAA provisionally suspending any Certificate, approval or other document under paragraph (1), or detaining a hovercraft under paragraph (4) above, the CAA shall, within 48 hours, send to the holder of such Certificate, approval or other document a statement in writing of its reasons.

(6) Notwithstanding paragraph (1) of this Article any document incorporated by reference in any Certificate may be varied on sufficient ground being shown to the satisfaction of the CAA, whether or not after due inquiry.

Inspection of hovercraft

16. The CAA may at any reasonable time inspect a hovercraft or part or equipment thereof in respect of which an Experimental or Safety Certificate—

(a) has been applied for, or

(b) has been issued and is still in force, or

(c) has been issued and has ceased within the preceding period of 3 months to be in force,

and may for that purpose enter any premises where persons are employed in the design, construction, maintenance or storage of the hovercraft, or any hoverport.

International Certificates

17.—(1) The Secretary of State may issue in respect of a hovercraft registered in the United Kingdom such certificates as he deems appropriate, as a result of inspection and survey of the hovercraft by the CAA, under the International Convention for the Safety of Life at Sea**(a)** and the International Convention on Load Lines 1966**(b)** for the purpose of complying with the law of a country other than the United Kingdom.

(2) The Secretary of State may cancel or suspend any certificate issued under this Article where he has reason to believe—

(a) that the certificate has been issued on the basis of inaccurate information; or

(b) that since the issue of the certificate the hovercraft has sustained any material damage or that the condition of the hovercraft or of its equipment does not correspond substantially with the particulars of that certificate.

(3) The Secretary of State may require any certificate, issued under this Article which has expired or been suspended or cancelled to be delivered up as he directs.

PART III

DUTIES OF OPERATOR AND CAPTAIN

Operating Permits

18.—(1) Hovercraft registered in the United Kingdom shall not be used for reward or in connection with a trade or business, otherwise than under and in accordance with a Permit (hereinafter called an "Operating Permit") granted to the operator of the hovercraft under paragraph (2) of this Article. Operating

---

(a) Cmnd. 2812.　　　　　　　　　(b) Cmnd. 3070.

Permits shall be granted with a view to securing the safe operation of the hovercraft. However this Article shall not apply to a hovercraft operating in accordance with an Experimental Certificate issued pursuant to Article 9.

(2) The Secretary of State may grant or renew to any person applying therefor an Operating Permit for the operation of hovercraft of the types and in relation to the areas of operation specified in the Operating Permit for the purposes so specified. The Operating Permit may be granted subject to such conditions as the Secretary of State thinks fit to impose with a view to securing the safe operation of hovercraft and shall remain in force for such time as may be specified in the Operating Permit or until suspended or revoked by the Secretary of State and may be renewed from time to time by the Secretary of State for such further period as he thinks fit. The Secretary of State may vary an Operating Permit on application by the holder.

(3) The conditions to which the Operating Permit may be subject may include, without prejudice to the generality of the foregoing paragraph, conditions in respect of the following matters—

(*a*) crew complement and qualifications;

(*b*) type of hovercraft;

(*c*) area of operation;

(*d*) restrictions with regard to working hours and rest periods of crew;

(*e*) safety arrangements at hoverports or terminal areas;

(*f*) the weather conditions in which the hovercraft may operate;

(*g*) day or night operation;

(*h*) life-saving equipment and procedures;

(*i*) other equipment and procedures necessary for safety of operation;

(*j*) radio and radar;

(*k*) the keeping of records.

Duties of operator

19.—(1) The operator of a hovercraft registered in the United Kingdom or operating unregistered in the United Kingdom in accordance with proviso(i) in Article 4 of this Order shall not permit the hovercraft to be used without first—

(*a*) designating a member of the crew to be captain on that journey;

(*b*) ensuring that a minimum number of the crew corresponding to the complement necessary for the journey are adequately trained for their duties for that journey;

(*c*) ensuring that the safety equipment required to be carried is in working order.

(2) Without prejudice to his other duties under this Order an operator shall at all times take all reasonable precautions at hoverports and terminal areas so as to ensure the safety of persons and property in the hovercraft and on the ground.

(3) An operator shall not permit any hovercraft to be used if he has reason to believe or suspect it is in an unsafe condition.

Duties of captain

20. The captain, before the departure of the hovercraft—

(a) shall take reasonable steps to ensure

(i) that the craft is properly loaded and any cargo adequately secured in the craft;

(ii) that there is adequate supply of fuel; and

(iii) that the craft is in a fit state and that the safety equipment required to be carried is in a fit condition and ready to be used; and

(b) shall satisfy himself that the journey can safely be made, taking into account the latest information available to him as to the route and weather.

Operational records

21.—(1) The captain of every hovercraft registered in the United Kingdom shall ensure that records are kept of the following matters relating to any journey of the hovercraft—

(a) Names of terminal and any intermediate points, and the times of departure from and arrival at such points;

(b) Weather conditions, such as wind, sea condition and visibility experienced;

(c) Any accidents or unusual occurrences on the journey;

(d) Any births or deaths which occur on the journey;

(e) A summary of all communications relating to distress, urgency and safety traffic.

(2) The operator of every hovercraft registered in the United Kingdom shall keep records of—

(a) crew emergency and distress drills (including names of persons present);

(b) the names of all crew aboard a hovercraft on any journey.

(3) The captain or operator, as the case may be, shall within a reasonable time after being requested to do so by an authorised person, cause to be produced to that person the records referred to in paragraphs (1) and (2) above respectively.

(4) (a) The records mentioned above shall be preserved by the operator for at least 12 months after any journey or drill to which they refer;

(b) The records referred to in paragraph (1) of this Article shall be delivered to the operator of the hovercraft to which the records relate by the captain at the time he ceases to be the captain, or when the operator requires their delivery;

(c) A person required to preserve any record by reason of his being the operator of a hovercraft shall, if he ceases to be the operator of the hovercraft continue to preserve the record as if he had not ceased to be the operator, and in the event of his death the duty to preserve the record shall fall upon his personal representative.

Medical equipment

22. A hovercraft registered in the United Kingdom or used unregistered in accordance with proviso (i) in Article 4, shall carry when in use first-aid equipment of good quality, sufficient in quantity having regard to the number of persons on board and the circumstances of the use of the hovercraft, and including the following—

Roller bandages, triangular bandages, absorbent gauze, adhesive plaster, white absorbent lint, cotton wool (or wound dressings in place of the lint and cotton wool), burn dressings, safety pins; haemostatic bandages or tourniquets, scissors; antiseptic, analgesic and stimulant drugs; a handbook on First Aid.

Documents to be carried

23.—(1) A hovercraft registered in the United Kingdom, or operating unregistered in the United Kingdom in accordance with proviso (i) in Article 4 shall, when in operation, carry the following documents or true copies thereof—

(*a*) its Safety Certificate, or Experimental Certificate if any;

(*b*) its certificate of registration if any;

(*c*) any certificate issued to the hovercraft under Article 17.

(2) The Safety Certificate and any certificate issued to the hovercraft under Article 17 or true copies thereof shall be posted in some conspicuous place in the hovercraft.

Notification of casualties

24.—(1) When a hovercraft casualty has occurred, the captain or if the captain is incapacitated, the operator of the hovercraft shall—

(*a*) by the quickest available means, inform the Secretary of State of the happening of the casualty, stating the registration number or identity of the hovercraft and the place where the casualty occurred or is believed to have occurred and, in the case of a hovercraft which is missing, the route it was on; and

(*b*) within 48 hours, or as soon thereafter as possible, transmit to the Secretary of State a report, signed by the captain or operator, of the casualty and of the probable occasion thereof, stating the registration number or identity of the hovercraft and the place where the casualty occurred or is believed to have occurred:

Provided that this Article shall not apply to hovercraft which are less than 1,000 kg. unladen weight and are not used for reward.

(2) For the purpose of this Article a hovercraft casualty shall be deemed to occur when a hovercraft—

(*a*) has sustained, caused or been involved in any accident occasioning loss of life or any serious injury to any person;

(*b*) becomes lost, abandoned, missing or stranded;

(*c*) suffers such damage as the result of any accident that its safety is impaired; or

(*d*) becomes involved in a collision with another hovercraft or ship;

but only when the occurence takes place—

(i) on or over the sea or other navigable water; or

(ii) between the time when any person goes on board the hovercraft for the purpose of making a journey which would involve crossing the sea or other navigable water and the time when it comes to rest at the end of such a journey; or

(iii) during the testing or maintenance of a hovercraft which normally makes journeys on or over the sea or other navigable water

and also only if at the time the occurrence takes place, the hovercraft was registered in the United Kingdom or was operating unregistered in accordance with proviso(i) in Article 4 of this Order or was within the United Kingdom.

PART IV

SUPPLEMENTARY PROVISIONS

Right of access to hoverports

25. The Secretary of State and any authorised person shall have the right of access at all reasonable times to any hoverport and any place where a hovercraft is for the purpose of inspecting any hovercraft or any document which they have power to demand under this Order, and for the purpose of detaining any hovercraft under the provisions of this Order.

Safety of persons and property

26.—(1) A person shall not wilfully or negligently—

(*a*) act in a manner likely to endanger a hovercraft, or any person therein; or

(*b*) go or attempt to go on a journey on a hovercraft without the consent of the captain or other person authorised to give it.

(2) A person shall not—

(*a*) enter a hovercraft when drunk, or be drunk in a hovercraft; or

(*b*) smoke in a place in a hovercraft or at a hoverport where and when smoking is prohibited by notice.

Duty to obey captain

27. Every person in a hovercraft shall obey all lawful commands which the captain may give for the purpose of securing the safety of the hovercraft and of persons or property carried therein, or the safety, efficiency or regularity of navigation.

Power to prevent hovercraft operating

28.—(1) If it appears to the Secretary of State or an authorised person that any hovercraft is intended or likely to be operated—

(*a*) in such circumstances that any provision of Articles 4, 6, 7, 8, 13 or 18 of this Order would be contravened in relation to the journey; or

(*b*) in such circumstances that the journey would be in contravention of any other provision of this Order and be a cause of danger to any person or property whether or not in the hovercraft; or

(*c*) while in a condition unfit for operation whether or not the journey would otherwise be in contravention of any provision of this Order,

the Secretary of State or that authorised person may direct the operator or the captain of the hovercraft that he is not to permit the hovercraft to make the particular journey or any other journey of such description as may be specified in the direction, until the direction has been revoked by the Secretary of State or by an authorised person, and the Secretary of State, or that person may take such steps as are necessary to detain the hovercraft.

(2) For the purposes of paragraph (1) of this Article the Secretary of State or any authorised person may enter upon and inspect any hovercraft.

Revocation etc. of Certificates etc.

29.—(1) The Secretary of State may, if he thinks fit, provisionally suspend any certificate, licence, approval, permission, exemption or other document issued, granted or having effect under this Order other than under Part II, pending inquiry into or investigation of the case. Without prejudice to Article 18(2) of this Order the Secretary of State may on sufficient ground being shown to his satisfaction after due inquiry, revoke, suspend or vary any such certificate, licence, approval, permission, exemption or other document.

(2) The holder or any person having the possession or custody of any certificate, licence, approval, permission, exemption or other document which has been revoked, suspended or varied under this Article shall surrender it to the Secretary of State within a reasonable time after being required to do so by him.

(3) The breach of any condition subject to which any certificate, licence, approval, permission, exemption or other document has been granted or issued, or which has effect under this Order, shall render the document invalid during the continuance of the breach.

Obstruction of persons

30. A person shall not wilfully obstruct or impede any person acting in the exercise of his powers or the performance of his duties under this Order.

Enforcement of directions

31. Any person who fails to comply with any direction given to him by the Secretary of State or by any authorised person under any provision of this Order shall be deemed for the purpose of this Order to have contravened that provision.

Exemption from Order

32. The Secretary of State may exempt from any of the provisions of this Order or any regulations made thereunder any hovercraft or persons or classes of hovercraft or persons, either absolutely or subject to such conditions as he thinks fit.

Penalties

33.—(1) If any provision of this Order is contravened in relation to a hovercraft, the operator of that hovercraft and the captain thereof, shall (without prejudice to the liability of any other person under this Order for that contravention) be deemed for the purposes of sub-paragraphs (3) to (5) of this Article to have contravened that provision unless he proves that the contravention occurred without his consent or connivance and that he exercised all due diligence to prevent the contravention.

(2) If it is proved that an act or omission of any person which would otherwise have been a contravention by that person of a provision of this Order was due to any cause not avoidable by the exercise of reasonable care by that person the act or omission shall be deemed not to be a contravention by that person of that provision.

(3) If any person contravenes any provision of this Order, not being a provision referred to in paragraph (4) or paragraph (5) of this Article, he shall be liable on summary conviction to a fine not exceeding ten pounds; or in the case of a second or subsequent conviction for the like offence to a fine not exceeding twenty pounds.

(4) If any person contravenes any provision specified in Part A of the Schedule to this Order he shall be liable on summary conviction to a fine not exceeding fifty pounds; or in the case of a second or subsequent conviction for the like offence to a fine not exceeding one hundred pounds, or on indictment both to such fine and to imprisonment for a term not exceeding three months.

(5) If any person contravenes any provision specified in Part B of the said Schedule he shall be liable on summary conviction to a fine not exceeding two hundred pounds or, on indictment both to such fine and to imprisonment for a term not exceeding six months.

Crown application

34.—(1) Subject to the following provisions of this Article, the provisions of this Order shall apply to or in relation to hovercraft belonging to or exclusively employed in the service of Her Majesty, as they apply to or in relation to other hovercraft and for the purposes of such application the Government Department or other authority for the time being responsible on behalf of Her Majesty for the operational management of the hovercraft shall be deemed to be the operator of the hovercraft and in the case of a hovercraft belonging to Her Majesty to be the owner of the interest of Her Majesty in the hovercraft:

Provided that nothing in this Article shall render liable to any penalty any Department or other authority responsible on behalf of Her Majesty for the management of the hovercraft.

(2) Save as provided in paragraph (3) of this Article nothing in this Order shall apply to or in relation to any military hovercraft.

(3) Where a military hovercraft is operated by a civilian and is not commanded by a person who is acting in the course of his duty as a member of any of Her Majesty's naval or military or air forces or as a member of a visiting force or international headquarters, Article 20 shall apply on the occasion of that journey.

Fees

35. The Secretary of State may, by regulations made by statutory instrument, require the payment of fees in respect of any matter relating to hovercraft which is specified in this Order, and may prescribe with the approval of the Treasury the amount of any such fee or the manner in which that amount is to be determined, and sections 1, 2 and 3 of the Statutory Instruments Act 1946(a) shall apply to the regulations.

(a) 1946 c. 36.

Extra-territorial effect of the Order

36.—(1) Except where the context otherwise requires, the provisions of this Order—

- (*a*) in so far as they apply (whether by express reference or otherwise) to hovercraft registered in the United Kingdom, shall apply to such hovercraft wherever they may be;

- (*b*) in so far as they apply as aforesaid to other hovercraft shall apply to such hovercraft when they are within the United Kingdom;

- (*c*) in so far as they prohibit, require or regulate (whether by express reference or otherwise) the doing of anything by persons in, or by any of the crew of, any hovercraft registered in the United Kingdom, shall apply to such persons and crew, wherever they may be; and

- (*d*) in so far as they prohibit, require or regulate as aforesaid the doing of anything in relation to any hovercraft registered in the United Kingdom by other persons shall, where such persons are British subjects, apply to them wherever they may be.

(2) Nothing in this Article shall be construed as extending to make any person guilty of an offence in any case in which it is provided by section 3(1) of the British Nationality Act 1948(a) (which limits the criminal liability of certain persons who are not citizens of the United Kingdom and colonies) that that person shall not be guilty of an offence.

W. G. Agnew.

SCHEDULE

Article 33

PENALTIES

PART A: Provisions referred to in Article 33(4); Articles 4, 6, 21, 23, 24 and 30

PART B: Provisions referred to in Article 33(5); Articles 7, 8, 13, 15, 18, 19, 20, 22, 26, 27 and 28

EXPLANATORY NOTE

(This Note is not part of the Order.)

This Order makes provision for the registration, safety certification, maintenance and operational safety of hovercraft. It also includes provision as to ancillary matters affecting the safety of hovercraft and persons and property thereon.

Under the Order the Secretary of State will be the authority for the registration of hovercraft and for issuing Operating Permits, while the Civil Aviation Authority will be the authority for certifying the safe construction of hovercraft.

The Order empowers the Secretary of State to make regulations by Statutory Instrument prescribing fees, with the approval of the Treasury, in respect of matters relating to hovercraft.

(a) 1948 c. 56.

STATUTORY INSTRUMENTS

1972 No. 675

MERCHANT SHIPPING

The Oil in Navigable Waters (Convention Countries) (Saudi Arabia) Order 1972

Made - - -		28*th April* 1972
Laid before Parliament		4*th May* 1972
Coming into Operation		31*st May* 1972

At the Court at Windsor Castle, the 28th day of April 1972

Present,

The Queen's Most Excellent Majesty in Council

Whereas by section 18(3) of the Oil in Navigable Waters Act 1955(a) it is enacted that for the purposes of that section Her Majesty may if satisfied that the government of any country has accepted the International Convention for the Prevention of Pollution of the Sea by Oil 1954, by Order in Council make a declaration to that effect:

And whereas Her Majesty is satisfied that the Government of the Kingdom of Saudi Arabia has accepted the said Convention:

Now, therefore, Her Majesty, in pursuance of the powers conferred on Her by the aforesaid section 18(3) and of all other powers enabling Her in that behalf, is pleased, by and with the advice of Her Privy Council, to order, and it is hereby ordered, as follows:—

1. This Order may be cited as the Oil in Navigable Waters (Convention Countries) (Saudi Arabia) Order 1972 and shall come into operation on 31st May 1972.

2. For the purposes of section 18 of the Oil in Navigable Waters Act 1955 it is hereby declared that the Government of the Kingdom of Saudi Arabia has accepted the International Convention for the Prevention of Pollution of the Sea by Oil 1954.

W. G. Agnew.

(a) 1955 c. 25.

STATUTORY INSTRUMENTS

1972 No. 676

MERCHANT SHIPPING

The Oil in Navigable Waters (Prohibited Sea Areas) (Amendment) Order 1972

Made - - -	*28th April* 1972
Laid before Parliament	*4th May* 1972
Coming into Operation	*31st May* 1972

The Secretary of State, in exercise of his powers under section 2(7) of the Oil in Navigable Waters Act 1955(**a**), as amended by the Oil in Navigable Waters Act 1963(**b**), and of all other powers enabling him in that behalf, hereby makes the following Order:—

1. This Order may be cited as the Oil in Navigable Waters (Prohibited Sea Areas) (Amendment) Order 1972 and shall come into operation on 31st May 1972.

2. The Oil in Navigable Waters (Prohibited Sea Areas) Order 1967(**c**), as amended(**d**), shall have effect subject to the further amendments that:

(*a*) before the words "the United Arab Republic" in paragraph 2(7) of Schedule 1 thereof there shall be added the words "Saudi Arabia,"; and

(*b*) after the word "Kuwait" in paragraph 2(8) of Schedule 1 thereof there shall be added the words "and the eastern coast of Saudi Arabia.".

Michael Noble,
Minister for Trade,
Department of Trade and Industry.

28th April 1972.

EXPLANATORY NOTE

(This Note is not part of the Order.)

Saudi Arabia accepted, with effect from 30th March 1972, the International Convention for the Prevention of Pollution of the Sea by Oil 1954, as amended in 1962.

This Order accordingly amends the Oil in Navigable Waters (Prohibited

---

(**a**) 1955 c. 25.   (**b**) 1963 c. 28.
(**c**) S.I. 1967/709 (1967 II, p. 2142).
(**d**) The amendments do not relate expressly to the subject matter of this Order.

Sea Areas) Order 1967 as amended (which gives effect to the extension of prohibited sea areas introduced by the amendments of the Convention) to include amongst the prohibited sea areas specified by that Order the areas of the Red Sea and Persian Gulf lying within 100 miles from the nearest land along the coasts of Saudi Arabia.

STATUTORY INSTRUMENTS

1972 No. 677

CUSTOMS AND EXCISE

The Import Duties (General) (No. 1) Order 1972

Made - - - -	*28th April* 1972
Laid before the House of Commons	*4th May* 1972
Coming into Operation	*1st July* 1972

The Lords Commissioners of Her Majesty's Treasury, by virtue of the powers conferred on them by sections 1, 2 and 13 of the Import Duties Act 1958(**a**) and of all other powers enabling them in that behalf, on the recommendation of the Secretary of State hereby make the following Order:—

1.—(1) This Order may be cited as the Import Duties (General) (No. 1) Order 1972.

(2) The Interpretation Act 1889(**b**) shall apply for the interpretation of this Order as it applies for the interpretation of an Act of Parliament.

(3) This Order shall come into operation on 1st July 1972.

2. In Schedule 1 to the Import Duties (General) (No. 7) Order 1971(**c**) (which by reference to the Customs Tariff 1959 sets out the import duties chargeable under the Import Duties Act 1958) in subheading (A)(2) of heading 02.01—

(*a*) for the words " 30th June 1972 ", in both places where they occur, there shall be substituted the words " 31st January 1973 "; and

(*b*) for the words " 1st July 1972 ", in both places where they occur, there shall be substituted the words " 1st February 1973 ".

Tim Fortescue,

Hugh Rossi,

Two of the Lords Commissioners
of Her Majesty's Treasury.

28th April 1972.

EXPLANATORY NOTE

(*This Note is not part of the Order.*)

This Order postpones, until 1st February 1973, the increase in import duty on fresh, chilled or frozen mutton or lamb which was due to come into effect on 1st July 1972.

(**a**) 1958 c. 6.   (**b**) 1889 c. 63.   (**c**) S.I. 1971/1971 (1971 III, p. 5330).

STATUTORY INSTRUMENTS

1972 No. 678

AGRICULTURE

The Price Stability of Imported Products (Rates of Levy) (Cereals) (No. 15) Order 1972

Made	-	-	-	28*th April* 1972
Coming into Operation				1*st May* 1972

The Minister of Agriculture, Fisheries and Food, in exercise of the powers conferred upon him by section 1(2), (4), (5), (6) and (7) of the Agriculture and Horticulture Act 1964(a) and of all other powers enabling him in that behalf, hereby makes the following order:—

1. This order may be cited as the Price Stability of Imported Products (Rates of Levy) (Cereals) (No. 15) Order 1972, and shall come into operation on 1st May 1972.

2.—(1) In this order—

" the Principal Order " means the Price Stability of Imported Products (Levy Arrangements) (Cereals) Order 1971(b), as amended by any subsequent order and if any such order is replaced by any subsequent order the expression shall be construed as a reference to such subsequent order;

AND other expressions have the same meaning as in the Principal Order.

(2) The Interpretation Act 1889(c) shall apply to the interpretation of this order as it applies to the interpretation of an Act of Parliament and as if this order and the orders hereby revoked were Acts of Parliament.

3. In accordance with and subject to the provisions of Part II of the Principal Order (which provides for the charging of levies on imports of certain specified commodities) the rate of levy for such imports into the United Kingdom of any specified commodity as are described in column 2 of the Schedule to this order in relation to a tariff heading indicated in column 1 of that Schedule shall be the rate set forth in relation thereto in column 3 of that Schedule.

4. The Price Stability of Imported Products (Rates of Levy) (Cereals) (No. 14) Order 1972(d) is hereby revoked.

In Witness whereof the Official Seal of the Minister of Agriculture, Fisheries and Food is hereunto affixed on 28th April 1972.

(L.S.)

T. R. M. Sewell,
Assistant Secretary.

(a) 1964 c. 28.   (b) S.I. 1971/631 (1971 I, p. 1660).   (c) 1889 c. 63.
(d) S.I. 1972/530 (1972 I, p. 1814).

SCHEDULE

1. Tariff Heading	2. Description of Imports	3. Rate of Levy
	Imports of:—	per ton £
10.01	Denatured wheat	4·50
	Wheat (other than denatured wheat)..	8·50
10.03	Barley other than barley having a potential diastatic activity of not less than 170 degrees	5·75
10.04	Oats	6·50
10.05	Maize (other than sweet corn on the cob)	5·25
10.07	Grain sorghum	3·75
11.02	Cereal groats, meals, kibbled or cut cereals, rolled, flaked, crushed or bruised cereals and other processed cereals—	
	of barley	4·00
	of maize	5·50

EXPLANATORY NOTE

(This Note is not part of the Order.)

This order, which comes into operation on 1st May 1972, supersedes the Price Stability of Imported Products (Rates of Levy) (Cereals) (No. 14) Order 1972.

It—

(a) removes the rates of levy to be charged on imports of—

(i) wheat flours not containing chalk and containing not more than 1 per cent. by weight of fibre at the prescribed standard moisture content under tariff heading 11.01;

(ii) processed oats within tariff heading 11.02,

(b) reduces to £4·00 per ton the rate of levy to be charged on imports of processed barley within tariff heading 11.02,

(c) increases the rate of levy to be charged on imports of—

(i) wheat (other than denatured wheat) to £8·50 per ton;

(ii) barley other than barley having a potential diastatic activity of not less than 170 degrees to £5·75 per ton;

(iii) oats, maize (other than sweet corn on the cob), grain sorghum and processed maize within tariff heading 11.02 to £6·50, £5·25, £3·75 and £5·50 per ton respectively, and

(d) reimposes unchanged the rate of levy to be charged on imports of denatured wheat.

APPENDIX
OF CERTAIN INSTRUMENTS
NOT REGISTERED AS S.I.

Orders in Council,
Letters Patent
and Royal Instructions

relating to the Constitutions etc. of
Overseas Territories or to appeals to the Judicial
Committee,

Royal Proclamations, etc.

BY THE QUEEN

A PROCLAMATION

ELIZABETH R.

MARGARET

Whereas Her Majesty, in pursuance of the Regency Acts 1937 to 1953, was pleased, by Letters Patent dated the fourth day of February, 1972, to delegate to the following Counsellors of State (subject to the exceptions hereinafter mentioned) or any two or more of them, that is to say, His Royal Highness the Prince Philip, Duke of Edinburgh, Her Majesty Queen Elizabeth The Queen Mother, His Royal Highness The Prince Charles, Prince of Wales, Her Royal Highness The Princess Anne, Her Royal Highness The Princess Margaret, Countess of Snowdon and His Royal Highness The Duke of Gloucester, full power and authority during the period of Her Majesty's absence from the United Kingdom to summon and hold on Her Majesty's behalf Her Privy Council, to approve and sign on Her Majesty's behalf any Proclamation relating to the affairs of the United Kingdom, to do on Her Majesty's behalf anything required to be done in relation to any such Proclamation, and further to do on Her Majesty's behalf anything which, by virtue of any statutory or other power, Her Majesty is authorised to do for the safety or good government of the United Kingdom:

And whereas Her Majesty was further pleased to except from the number of the said Counsellors of State His Royal Highness The Prince Philip, Duke of Edinburgh, His Royal Highness The Prince Charles, Prince of Wales, Her Royal Highness The Princess Anne and Her Royal Highness The Princess Margaret, Countess of Snowdon, while absent from the United Kingdom:

And whereas by section 1 of the Emergency Powers Act 1920, as amended by the Emergency Powers Act 1964, it is enacted that if it appears to Her Majesty that there have occurred or are about to occur events of such a nature as to be calculated, by interfering with the supply and distribution of food, water, fuel or light, or with the means of locomotion, to deprive the community or any substantial portion of the community, of the essentials of life, Her Majesty may, by Proclamation, declare that a state of emergency exists:

And whereas the present industrial dispute affecting persons employed in the coal mines and the production and distribution of fuel does, in Our opinion, constitute a state of emergency within the meaning of the said Act of 1920, as so amended:

Now, therefore, We, Elizabeth The Queen Mother and Margaret, Countess of Snowdon, being authorised thereto by the said Letters Patent, and in pursuance of the said Act of 1920, as so amended, and by and with the advice of Her Majesty's Privy Council, do on Her Majesty's behalf hereby declare that a state of emergency exists.

Given at the Court of Saint James this ninth day of March in the year of our Lord nineteen hundred and seventy-two, and in the twenty-first year of Her Majesty's Reign.

GOD SAVE THE QUEEN

GIBRALTAR

The Admiralty Waters (Gibraltar) Order 1972

At the Court of Saint James the 1st day of March 1972

Present,

Her Majesty Queen Elizabeth The Queen Mother
Her Royal Highness The Princess Margaret, Countess of Snowdon
Lord President	**Sir Peter Rawlinson**
Viscount Eccles	**Sir Frederick Lawton**
Mr. Secretary Campbell	

Whereas Her Majesty, in pursuance of the Regency Acts 1937 to 1953, was pleased, by Letters Patent dated the fourth day of February 1972, to delegate to the following Counsellors of State (subject to the exceptions hereinafter mentioned) or any two or more of them, that is to say, His Royal Highness The Prince Philip, Duke of Edinburgh, Her Majesty Queen Elizabeth The Queen Mother, His Royal Highness The Prince Charles, Prince of Wales, Her Royal Highness The Princess Anne, Her Royal Highness The Princess Margaret, Countess of Snowdon, and His Royal Highness The Duke of Gloucester, full power and authority during the period of Her Majesty's absence from the United Kingdom to summon and hold on Her Majesty's behalf Her Privy Council and to signify thereat Her Majesty's approval for anything for which Her Majesty's approval in Council is required:

And whereas Her Majesty was further pleased to except from the number of the said Counsellors of State His Royal Highness The Prince Philip, Duke of Edinburgh, His Royal Highness The Prince Charles, Prince of Wales, Her Royal Highness The Princess Anne and Her Royal Highness The Princess Margaret, Countess of Snowdon, while absent from the United Kingdom:

Now, therefore, Her Majesty Queen Elizabeth The Queen Mother and Her Royal Highness The Princess Margaret, Countess of Snowdon, being authorised thereto by the said Letters Patent, and in exercise of powers enabling Her Majesty in that behalf, do hereby, by and with the advice of Her Majesty's Privy Council, on Her Majesty's behalf order, and it is hereby ordered, as follows: —

Citation

1.—(1) This Order may be cited as the Admiralty Waters (Gibraltar) Order 1972.

(2) This Order shall come into operation on 5th April 1972.

Interpretation

2. The Interpretation Act 1889(a) shall apply to the interpretation of this Order as it applies to the interpretation of an Act of Parliament and as if for the purposes of section 38 of that Act this Order were an Act of Parliament and the Orders revoked by Article 20 of this Order were an Act of Parliament thereby repealed.

Description of Limits

3.—(1) *Admiralty Waters.* All the water area lying between the shore and lines drawn as follows, namely from a point on the high-water line 60 yards south of the root of Rosia Mole in a direction 272° (true) for a distance of 115 yards, thence in a direction 310° (true) for a distance of 290 yards, thence in a direction 322½° (true) continuing along a line 200 yards from and outside the South Mole, " A " Head, " B " Head, the Detached Mole and " C " Head respectively, thence along lines 50 yards from and outside the faced wall of the North Mole, thence along the North Mole to the shore, the boundaries being as delineated on the chart annexed to this Order, shall be deemed to be Admiralty Waters.

(2) *Port Waters.* The water area to the east of the Western Arm of the North Mole extending from low-water mark for a width of 204 yards, the water area extending for a width of 50 yards outside the faced wall of the North Mole, and the water area extending from low-water mark 200 feet eastwards from the two North-East berths on the Detached Mole, which said water areas form part of Admiralty Waters and the boundaries of which are delineated on the chart annexed to this Order, shall be deemed to be Port Waters.

Control of Admiralty Waters

4. Control over Admiralty Waters shall be vested in the Senior Naval Officer (whose title, at the time of making this Order, is the Flag Officer and Port Admiral, Gibraltar) and, with his powers and functions under this Order except those conferred by Article 5, may be exercised on his behalf by the Queen's Harbour Master for Admiralty Waters.

5.—(1) It shall be lawful for the Senior Naval Officer from time to time to make and, when made, to alter or revoke, such regulations in writing as he may deem expedient in respect of the use, order and government of Admiralty Waters and of all vessels therein, including regulations for the exclusion or admission of merchant and other private vessels from and to Admiralty Waters or any part of them, and in respect of the delegation of the duties of Queen's Harbour Master.

(2) All such regulations shall be confirmed by the Secretary of State for Defence and shall be published in the London Gazette and the Gibraltar Gazette, and shall be in force as from the last of the two dates on which they are so published. The production of a copy of either Gazette containing such regulations shall be good and sufficient proof for all purposes of the contents thereof and that the same have been duly made and confirmed in accordance with the terms of this Order.

(a) 52 & 53 Vict. c. 63.

6. Notwithstanding anything in this Order, the Senior Naval Officer may consent to the exercise by the Governor of Gibraltar, or such persons as the Governor may appoint, of his jurisdiction, control, powers and duties under this Order and under any regulations made under this Order, subject to such conditions and modifications as the Senior Naval Officer may think fit, in respect of any vessel or class of vessel other than vessels the property of or under charter to Her Majesty, whilst in Admiralty Waters other than Port Waters, which seeks to enter, leave or make use of Port Waters.

7. The masters of all merchant and other private vessels admitted or to be admitted to Admiralty Waters shall, without prejudice to the provisions of Articles 6 and 10 or any other provision in this Order, be subject to the directions of the Senior Naval Officer in all matters connected with anchoring, mooring, securing or navigation in those waters.

8. If the master or person in charge of any vessel within Admiralty Waters does not moor, anchor, place, secure, move, unmoor or remove the same according to directions given by the Senior Naval Officer or in conformity with any regulations made under this Order, or if there is no person on board of any vessel to attend to such directions, the Senior Naval Officer may cause the vessel to be moored, anchored, placed, secured, moved, unmoored or removed, and for that purpose may cast off, loose, or unshackle, and (if need be) sever any chain or rope of the vessel, first putting on board a sufficient number of persons for the protection of the vessel in case there is not a sufficient number of persons on board to protect the same, and all expenses attending the exercise of these powers shall be paid by the owner or person in charge of the vessel.

9.—(1) The Senior Naval Officer may license pilots for conducting vessels within Admiralty Waters and do all such things as may be necessary or expedient for carrying into effect their powers and duties.

(2) The grant of a licence to a pilot by the Senior Naval Officer shall not impose any liability on the Crown for any loss occasioned by any act or default of the pilot.

10.—(1) Without prejudice to the provisions of this Order, all merchant and other private vessels within Port Waters shall also be subject to such laws as the Legislature of Gibraltar has enacted or may enact for the control of such vessels therein.

(2) The provisions of the Gibraltar Port Ordinance and subsidiary legislation made thereunder and for the time being in force shall (except to such extent as they are inconsistent with the provisions of this Order and regulations made thereunder) apply to every merchant or other private vessel within Admiralty Waters other than Port Waters.

Removal of wrecks and obstructions

11. The Senior Naval Officer may call upon the owner or person in charge of any wreck or other thing of any kind whatsoever, being an obstruction in Admiralty Waters or in or to the approaches thereto, to remove or destroy such wreck or thing, and the owner or person in charge shall forthwith remove or destroy such wreck or thing, and every fragment of such wreck or thing which may arise in course of removal or destruction, to the satisfaction of the Senior Naval Officer.

12. No explosive shall be used for the purpose of destroying any such wreck or thing, without the concurrence of the Senior Naval Officer and in such manner as he may direct.

13.—(1) If the owner or person in charge fails or neglects to remove or destroy such wreck or thing within a reasonable time, to be determined by the Senior Naval Officer, or if in the opinion of the Senior Naval Officer the removal of such wreck or thing is a matter or urgency, the Senior Naval Officer may give notice to the owner or person in charge or to his accredited agent at Gibraltar that on the expiration of a period to be fixed by and stated in such notice the said Senior Naval Officer will remove or destroy such wreck or thing, and on the expiration of such period may proceed to do so.

(2) Should any difficulty be foreseen in effecting service of such notice on the owner or person in charge or on his accredited agent, such notice may be published in the Gibraltar Gazette, and such publication shall be deemed good and valid service thereof.

14. The expenses incurred by the Senior Naval Officer, in the removal or destruction of such wreck or thing and in the temporary lighting, buoying or marking thereof, shall be repaid by the owner or person in charge thereof, and the Senior Naval Officer may detain and, in the case of non-payment of expenses on demand, may sell the wreck or thing and out of the proceeds of the sale pay those expenses and the expenses of the sale, rendering the surplus (if any) to the owner or person entitled thereto on demand, and any deficiency may be recovered as a civil debt from the owner or person in charge.

Provided always that no such sale shall (except in the case of property of a perishable nature) be made until at least seven clear days' notice of the intended sale has been given by advertisement in the Gibraltar Gazette.

15. For the purpose of this Order, the owner of a wreck or thing shall be deemed to be the person owning such a wreck or thing when such wreck or thing becomes an obstruction, notwithstanding any subsequent sale, transfer, or abandonment.

Fines and Penalties

16. The master or person in charge of every merchant or other private vessel within Admiralty Waters shall observe and cause to be observed the provisions of this Order or of any regulation, direction, restriction or condition made or given under this Order, so far as they apply to his vessel, and if any master or other person fails to observe, or cause to be observed, any such provision applying to his vessel, he shall be liable to the penalties prescribed in this Order.

17. Any person contravening any provision, regulation, direction, restriction or condition contained in or for the time being in force under this Order shall be liable on summary conviction to a fine not exceeding £50.

18.—(1) All expenditure incurred and sums recoverable under this Order or any regulation thereunder shall be recoverable in the Gibraltar Court of First Instance notwithstanding that the amount claimed exceeds £300.

(2) Production in the Court of First Instance of a certificate purporting to be signed by the Senior Naval Officer or Queen's Harbour Master that such work was undertaken and/or such expenditure was incurred shall be prima facie proof of the claim.

19. All fines recovered under this Order shall be paid into the general revenues of the Government of Gibraltar for the use of Her Majesty, Her Heirs and Successors.

Revocation

20. The Admiralty Waters (Gibraltar) Orders 1911 to 1960(**a**), dated respectively 22nd March 1911, 27th October 1936 and 3rd August 1960, are hereby revoked.

W. G. Agnew.

(**a**) *See* London Gazette 9.8.60. (No. 42113).

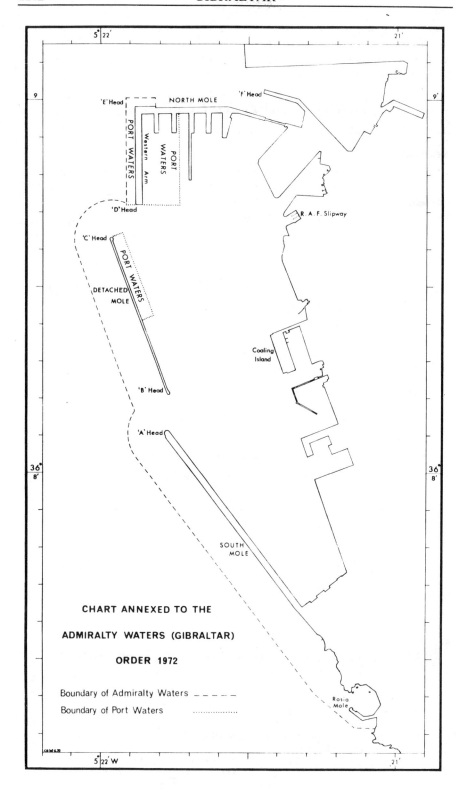

'E' Head
NORTH MOLE
'F' Head

PORT WATERS

Western Arm

PORT WATERS

'D' Head

R. A. F. Slipway

'C' Head

PORT WATERS

DETACHED MOLE

Coaling Island

'B' Head

'A' Head

SOUTH MOLE

CHART ANNEXED TO THE

ADMIRALTY WATERS (GIBRALTAR)

ORDER 1972

Rosia Mole

Boundary of Admiralty Waters ―― ―― ――
Boundary of Port Waters ....

STOKE-ON-TRENT
CITY
LIBRARIES

Modifications to Legislation

Year and Number (or date)	Act or instrument	How affected
1901 599	Merchant Shipping (Mercantile Marine Fund) Act 1898, sch. 2—Amdg. O. in C. 1901 (Rev. XIV, p. 676)	**r.,** 1972/456
1908 558	Merchant Shipping (Mercantile Marine Fund) Act 1898 sch. 2, alteration of exemptions—O. in C. 1908 (Rev. XIV, p. 678.	**r.,** 1972/456
1910 1180	Licensing Rules 1910 (Rev. XI, p. 10)	am., 1972/44
1919 1108	Merchant Shipping Light dues, scale, rules and exemption—Amdg. O. in C. 1919 (Rev. XIV, p. 679)	**r.,** 1972/456
1929 1048	Trustee Savings Bank Regs. 1929 (Rev. XX, p. 584)	**r.,** 1972/583
1933 1149	Savings Certificates Regs. 1933 (Rev. XV, p. 309)	**r.,** 1972/641
1935 803	Merchant Shipping (Light Dues) O. 1935 (Rev. XIV, p. 680)	**r.,** 1972/456
1936 626	County Ct. Rules 1936 (1936 I, p. 282)	am., 1972/208
1937 785	Savings Certificates (Amdt.) Regs. 1937 (Rev. XV, p. 309)	**r.,** 1972/641
1940 1998	Land Charges Rules 1940 (Rev. XI, p. 812)	**r.,** 1972/50
2195	Land Charges (No. 2) Rules 1940 (Rev. XI, p. 813)	**r.,** 1972/50

Year and Number (or date)	Act or instrument	How affected
1943		
683	Welsh Cts. (Oaths and Interpreters) Rules 1943 (Rev. XVI, p. 1107)	am., 1972/97
1944	Education Act 1944 (c. 31)	s. 35 am., 1972/444
1947	Exchange Control Act 1947 (c. 14) ...	sch. 1 am., 1972/386
1659	Police Grant (S.) O. 1947 (Rev. XVIII, p. 189)	am., 1972/24
1948		
1261	National Insurance (Widow's Benefit and Retirement Pensions) Regs. 1948 (Rev. XVI, p. 207)	**r.,** 1972/606
1390	National Health Service (Appointment of Medical and Dental Officers) (S.) Regs. 1948 (Rev. XV, p. 854)	**r.,** 1972/467
1411	Civil Aviation (Births, Deaths and Missing Persons) Regs. 1948 (Rev. I, p. 1302)	am., 1972/323
1425	National Insurance (Classification) Regs. 1948 (Rev. XVI, p. 95)	**r.,** 1972/555
2573	Falkland Is. (Legislative Council) O. in C. 1948 (Rev. VII, p. 591)	am., 1972/668
2711	National Insurance (Overlapping Benefits) Regs. 1948 (Rev. XVI, p. 196)	**r.,** 1972/604
1949		
86	National Insurance (Classification) Amdt. Regs. 1949 (1949 I, p. 2705)	**r.,** 1972/555
1461	National Insurance (Hospital In-Patients) Regs. 1949 (1949 I, p. 2718)	**r.,** 1972/603
1518	National Insurance (Classification) Amdt. (No. 2) Regs. 1949 (1949 I, p. 2706)	**r.,** 1972/555
1950		
765	National Insurance (Classification) Amdt. (No. 2) Regs. 1950 (1950 II, p. 10)	**r.,** 1972/555
830	National Insurance (Classification) Amdt. (No. 3) Regs. 1950 (1950 II, p. 12)	**r.,** 1972/555
1951		
993	National Insurance (Classification) Amdt. Regs. 1951 (1951 I, p. 1454)	**r.,** 1972/555

Year and Number (or date)	Act or instrument	How affected
1951		
1232	National Insurance (Increase of Benefit, Re-entry into Regular Employment and Miscellaneous Provns.) Regs. 1951 (1951 I, p. 1457)	am., 1972/603, 604, 606
1952		
422	National Insurance (Overlapping Benefits) Amdt. Regs. 1952 (1952 II, p. 2194)	r., 1972/604
494	National Insurance (Classification) Amdt. Regs. 1952 (1952 II, p. 2136)	r., 1972/555
526	National Insurance (Overlapping Benefits) Amdt. (No. 2) Regs. (1952 II, p. 2196)	r., 1972/604
559	Public Rights of Way (Applications to Quarter Sessions) Regs. 1952 (1952 II, p. 2318)	am., 1972/93
1024	National Insurance (Classification) Amdt. (No. 2) Regs. 1952 (1952 II, p. 2137)	r., 1972/555
1454	National Insurance (Classification) Amdt. (No. 3) Regs. 1952 (1952 II, p. 2139)	r., 1972/555
2113	Bankruptcy Rules 1952 (1952 I, p. 213)	am., 1972/529
2144	National Insurance (Increase of Benefit and Miscellaneous Provns.) Regs. 1952 (1952 II, p. 2154)	am., 1972/606
2179	National Insurance (Hospitals In-Patients) Amdt. Regs. 1952 (1952 II, p. 2147)	r., 1972/603
1953		
392	Merchant Shipping (Light Dues) O. 1953 (1953 I, p. 1065)	r., 1972/456
756	National Insurance (Overlapping Benefits) Amdt. Regs. 1953 (1953 I, p. 1367)	r., 1972/604
979	National Insurance (Widow's Benefit and Retirement Pensions) Amdt. Regs. 1953 (1953 I, p. 1368)	r., 1972/606
1954		
189	National Insurance (Maternity Benefit and Miscellaneous Provns.) Regs. 1954 (1954 I, p. 1387)	am., 1972/604
585	National Insurance (Classification) Amdt. Regs. 1954 (1954 I, p. 1407)	r., 1972/555
853	Importation of Carcases and Animal Products O. 1954 (1954 I, p. 136)	r., 1972/287

Year and Number (or date)	Act or instrument	How affected
1954		
898	British Transport Commission (Male Wages Grades Pensions) Regs. 1954 (1954 I, p. 175)	am., 1972/51
1955		
255	Ironstone Restoration Fund (Standard Rate) O. 1955 (1955 I, p. 1183)	**r.**, 1971/211
493	National Insurance (Increase of Benefit and Miscellaneous Provns.) Regs. 1955 (1955 II, p. 1586)	am., 1972/606
1363	Road Vehicles Lighting (Standing Vehicles) (Exemption) (London) Regs. 1955 (1955 II, p. 2324)	**r.**, 1972/557
1956		
162	Rules of Procedure (Army) 1956 (1956 I, p. 213)	**r.**, 1972/316
163	Rules of Procedure (Air Force) 1956 (1956 II, p. 2020)	**r.**, 1972/419
580	Certificates of Arrest and Surrender of Deserters and Absentees (Air Force) Regs. 1956 (1956 II, p. 2172)	**r.**, 1972/286
657	Certificates of Arrest and Surrender of Deserters and Absentees (Army) Regs. 1956 (1956 I, p. 363)	**r.**, 1972/318
741	Road Vehicles Lighting (Standing Vehicles) (Exemption) (General) Regs. 1956 (1956 II, p. 2007)	**r.**, 1972/557
1066	Trustee Savings Banks (Amdt.) Regs. 1956 (1956 II, p. 2194)	**r.**, 1972/583
1136	Savings Certificates (Amdt.) (No. 2) Regs. 1956 (1956 I, p. 1503)	**r.**, 1972/641
1179	Trustee Savings Banks (Amdt.) (No. 2) Regs. 1956 (1956 II, p. 2195)	**r.**, 1972/583
1199	National Insurance (Widow's Benefit and Miscellaneous Provns.) Regs. 1956 (1956 I, p. 1625)	am., 1972/606
1655	Registration of Restrictive Trading Agreements (Fees) Regs. 1956 (1956 II, p. 1988)	**r.**, 1972/196
1957		
488	National Health Service (Designation of London Teaching Hospitals) O. 1957 (1957 I, p. 1452)	am., 1972/60, 474, 475
1309	National Insurance (Widow's Benefit and Retirement Pensions) Amdt. Regs. 1957 (1957 I, p. 1615)	**r.**, 1972/606
1734	Savings Certificates (Amdt.) Regs. 1957 (1957 I, p. 1450)	**r.**, 1972/641

Year and Number (or date)	Act or instrument	How affected
1957		
1835	National Insurance (Child's Special Allowance) Regs. 1957 (1957 I, p. 1523)	am., 1972/603, 604
1849	National Insurance (Hospital In-Patients) Amdt. Regs. 1957 (1957 I, p. 1546)	**r.,** 1972/603
1889	National Insurance (Overlapping Bene-fits) Amdt. Regs. 1957 (1957 I, p. 1603)	**r.,** 1972/604
1949	National Insurance (Widow's Benefit and Retirement Pensions) Amdt. (No. 2) Regs. 1957 (1957 I, p. 1620)	**r.,** 1972/606
2077	National Insurance (Increase of Benefit and Misc. Provns.) Regs. 1957 1957 (1957 I, p. 1556)	am., 1972/603, 604, 606
2175	National Insurance (Classification) Amdt. Regs. 1957 (1957 I, p. 1623)	**r.,** 1972/555
1958		
519	Independent Schools Tribunal Rules 1958 (1958 I, p. 1006)	am., 1972/42
561	Certificate of Arrest and Surrender of Deserters and Absentees (Navy) Regs. 1958 (1958 II, p. 2121)	**r.** (1.7.72), 1972/430
1220	Thermal Insulation (Industrial Build-ings) Regs. 1958 (1958 I, p. 1130)	**r.,** 1972/87
1959		
1290	National Insurance (Overlapping Bene-fits) Amdt. Regs. 1959 (1959 II, p. 1873)	**r.,** 1972/604
1507	Welsh Cts. (Interpreters) Rules 1959 (1959 II, p. 2575)	superseded, 1972/97
1861	National Insurance (Non-participation —Benefits and Schemes) Regs. 1959 (1959 II, p. 1865)	am., 1972/428
1960		
	Road Traffic Act 1960 (c. 16) ...	ss. 127, 134, 144 mod., 1972/341
250	Cycle Racing on Highways Regs. 1960 (1960 III, p. 3047)	am., 1972/336
827	National Insurance (Classification) Amdt. Regs. 1960 (1960 II, p. 2208)	**r.,** 1972/555
1210	National Insurance (Graduated Contri-butions and Non-participating Em-ployments—Miscellaneous Provns.) Regs. 1960 (1960 II, p. 2234)	am., 1972/555, 606
1283	National Insurance (Hospital In-Patients) Amdt. Regs. 1960 (1960 II, p. 2163)	**r.,** 1972/603

Year and Number (or date)	Act or instrument	How affected
1960		
1981	Savings Certificates (Amdt.) (No. 2) Regs. 1960 (1960 I, p. 414)	r., 1972/641
2094	Importation of Carcases and Animal Products (Amdt.) O. 1960 (1960 I, p. 298)	r., 1972/287
2335	Trustee Savings Banks (Amdt.) Regs. 1960 (1960 III, p. 3065)	r., 1972/583
2422	National Insurance (Increase of Benefit and Miscellaneous Provns.) Regs. 1960 (1960 II, p. 2169)	am., 1972/606
1961		
	Diplomatic Immunities (Conferences with Commonwealth Countries and the Republic of Ireland) Act 1961 (c.11)	s. 1 am., 1972/114
329	Importation of Carcases and Animal Products (Amdt.) O. 1961	r., 1972/287
420	National Insurance (Classification) Amdt. Regs. 1961	r., 1972/555
557	National Insurance (Graduated Retirement Benefit and Consequential Provns.) Regs. 1961	am., 1972/604
1198	International Tin Council (Immunities and Privileges) O. 1961	r., 1972/120
1528	Savings Certificates (Amdt.) Regs. 1961	r., 1972/641
1837	Certificates of Arrest and Surrender of Deserters and Absentees (Air Force) (Amdt.) Regs. 1961	r., 1972/286
2009	Certificates of Arrest and Surrender of Deserters and Absentees (Army) (Amdt.) Regs. 1961	r., 1972/318
2152	Rules of Procedure (Air Force) (Amdt.) Rules 1961	r., 1972/419
2223	Rules of Procedure (Army) (Amdt.) Rules 1961	r., 1972/316
2316	Colonial Air Navigation O. 1961 ...	am., 1972/445
2414	Trustee Savings Banks (Amdt.) Regs. 1961	r., 1972/583
1962		
	Education (S.) Act 1962 (c. 47)... ...	s. 32(1) am., 1972/59
12	National Insurance (Consequential Provns.) Regs. 1962	am., 1972/604, 606
864	Superannuation (Teaching and N.I. Civil Service) Interchange (S.) Rules 1962	r., 1972/532
2466	Parochial Fees O. 1962	r., 1972/177

Year and Number (or date)	Act or instrument	How affected
1963		
	British Museum Act 1963 (c. 24) ...	sch. 3 Pt. I am., 1972/653
394	National Insurance (Increase of Benefit and Miscellaneous Provns. Regs. 1963	am., 1972/606
911	Importation of Carcases and Animal Products (Amdt.) O. 1963	r., 1972/287
936	Savings Certificates (Amdt.) (No. 2) Regs. 1963	r., 1972/641
1101	Sugar (Distribution Payments and Re-payments) Regs. 1963	r., 1972/69
1964		
73	National Insurance (Industrial Injuries) (Claims and Payments) Regs. 1964	am., 1972/375
297	National Insurance (Widow's Benefit and Miscellaneous Provns.) Regs. 1964	am., 1972/603, 604, 606
489	Defence (Transfer of Functions) (No. 2) O. 1964	am., 1972/316, 419
504	National Insurance (Industrial Injuries) (Benefit) Regs. 1964	am., 1972/393
690	Copyright (International Conventions) O. 1964	r., 1972/673
1006	Rules of Procedure (Army) (Amdt.) Rules 1964	r., 1972/316
1089	Importation of Carcases and Animal Products (Amdt.) O. 1964	r., 1972/287
1194	Copyright (International Conventions) (Amdt.) O. 1964	r., 1972/673
1282	Rules of Procedure (Air Forces) (Amdt.) Rules 1964	r., 1972/419
1454	National Health Service (Appointment of Medical and Dental Officers) (S.) Amdt. Regs. 1964	r., 1972/467
1651	Copyright (International Conventions) (Amdt. No. 2) O. 1964	r., 1972/673
1854	Rules of Procedure (Air Force) (Second Amdt.) Rules 1964	r., 1972/419
1864	Rules of Procedure (Army) (Second Amdt.) Rules 1964	r., 1972/316
2001	National Insurance (Widow's Benefit and Consequential Provns.) Regs. 1964	r., 1972/606
2007	Pensions (Polish Forces) Scheme 1964	am., 1972/95

Year and Number (or date)	Act or instrument	How affected
1965	National Insurance Act 1965 (c. 51) ...	sch. 49(4) am., 1972/166
	Coal Industry Act 1965 (c. 82) ...	s. 1(4) am., 1972/469
40	National Insurance (Increase of Benefit and Miscellaneous Provns.) Regs. 1965	am., 1972/606
321	A.S. (Rules of Ct., consolidation and amdt.) 1965	am., 1972/164
516	Income Tax (Employments) Regs. 1965	am., 1972/552
573	Trustee Savings Banks (Amdt.) Regs. 1965	r., 1972/583
1046	Merchant Shipping (Pilot Ladders) Rules 1965	am., 1972/531
1067	Merchant Shipping (Dangerous Goods) Rules 1965	am., 1972/666
1157	Industrial Tribunals (S.) Regs. 1965 ...	am., 1972/638
1303	Copyright (International Conventions) (Amdt.) O. 1965	r., 1972/673
1373	Building Regs. 1965	r., 1972/317
1467	Common Investment Funds Scheme 1965	am., 1972/528
1500	County Ct. Funds Rules 1965 ...	am., 1972/334
1857	Copyright (International Conventions) (Amdt. No. 2) O. 1965	r., 1972/673
2159	Copyright (International Conventions) (Amdt. No. 3) O. 1965	r., 1972/673
1966	Rating Act 1966 (c. 9)	s. 7(4) am., 1972/112
37	Importation of Carcases and Animal Products (Amdt.) O. 1966	r., 1972/287
216	Savings Certificates (Amdt.) Regs. 1966	r., 1972/641
253	Housing (Prescribed Forms) Regs. 1966	r., 1972/253
667	Origin of Goods (Republic of Ireland) Regs. 1966	am., 1972/338
684	Copyright (International Conventions) (Amdt.) O. 1966	r., 1972/673
689	Air Navigation (Guernsey) O. 1966 ...	r., 1972/453
690	Air Navigation (Jersey) O. 1966 ...	r., 1972/452
916	Air Navigation (General) (Guernsey) Regs. 1966	r., 1972/486
917	Air Navigation (General) (Jersey) Regs. 1966	r., 1972/487
945	Copyright (Gibraltar: Protection of Foreign Broadcasts) O. 1966	r., 1972/673
970	National Insurance (Overlapping Benefits and Hospital In-Patients) Amdt. Regs. 1966	r., 1972/603, 604

Year and Number (or date)	Act or instrument	How affected
1966		
1006	National Insurance and Industrial Injuries (Misc. and Consequential Provisions) Regs. 1966	am., 1972/166
1065	Supplementary Benefit (General) Regs. 1966	am., 1972/330
1144	Building (Second Amdt.) Regs. 1966 ...	**r.**, 1972/317
1185	Copyright (International Conventions) (Amdt. No. 2) O. 1966	**r.**, 1972/673
1409	Copyright (International Conventions) (Amdt. No. 3) O. 1966	**r.**, 1972/673
1449	National Health Service (General Dental Services) (S.) Regs. 1966	am., 1972/96
1967	General Rate Act 1967 (c. 9)	sch. 9 para. 12, 13 am., 1972/81
	Road Traffic Regulation Act 1967 (c. 76)	s. 81 mod., 1972/540
46	Rules of Procedure (Army) (Amdt.) Rules 1967	**r.**, 1972/316
62	Rules of Procedure (Air Force) (Amdt.) Rules 1967	**r.**, 1972/419
172	Merchant Shipping (Tonnage) Regs. 1967	am., 1972/656
225	Antigua Constitution O. 1967 ...	am., 1972/301
293	Pensions (Polish Forces) Scheme (Extension) O. 1967	superseded, 1972/95
313	Industrial Tribunals (Dock Work) Regs. 1967	**r.** (saving), 1972/38
314	Industrial Tribunals (Dock Work) (S.) Regs. 1967	**r.** (saving), 1972/39
330	National Insurance (Unemployment and Sickness Benefit) Regs. 1967	am., 1972/166
359	Industrial Tribunals (Redundancy Payments) Regs. 1967	**r.** (saving), 1972/38
360	Industrial Tribunals (Redundancy Payments) (S.) Regs. 1967	**r.** (saving), 1972/39
361	Industrial Tribunals (Employment and Compensation) Regs. 1967	**r.** (saving), 1972/38
362	Industrial Tribunals (Employment and Compensation) (S.) O. 1967	**r.** (saving), 1972/39
385	Food (Control of Irradiation) Regs. 1967	am., 1972/205
388	Food (Control of Irradiation) (S.) Regs. 1967	am., 1972/307
512	New Street Byelaws (Ext. of Operation) O. 1967	superseded, 1972/595

Year and Number (or date)	Act or instrument	How affected
1967		
562	National Insurance (Overlapping Benefits) Amdt. Regs. 1967	r., 1972/604
606	Importation of Carcases and Animal Products (Amdt.) O. 1967	r., 1972/287
709	Oil in Navigable Waters (Prohibited Sea Areas) O. 1967	am., 1972/676
743	Rules of Procedure (Army) (Second Amdt.) Rules 1967	r., 1972/316
844	National Insurance (Assessment of Graduated Contributions) Regs. 1967	am., 1972/235
846	Parliamentary Commissioner's Pension Regs. 1967	am., 1972/494
877	Copyright (International Conventions) (Amdt.) O. 1967	r., 1972/673
937	National Health Service (General Dental Services) Regs. 1967	am., 1972/82
1018	Army Terms of Service Regs. 1967 ...	am., 1972/517
1151	Copyright (International Conventions) (Amdt. No. 2) O. 1967	r., 1972/673
1265	National Insurance (Increase of Benefit and Miscellaneous Provns.) Regs. 1967	am., 1972/606
1466	Rules of Procedure (Air Force) (Second Amdt.) Rules 1967	r., 1972/419
1469	Rules of Procedure (Army) (Third Amdt.) Rules 1967	r., 1972/316
1570	National Insurance (Determination of Claims and Questions) (No. 2) Regs. 1967	am., 1972/166
1572	Family Allowances (Determination of Claims and Questions) (No. 2) Regs. 1967	am., 1972/167
1645	Building (Third Amdt.) Regs. 1967 ...	r., 1972/317
1767	Exchange Control (Scheduled Territories) O. 1967	r., 1972/386
1793	Importation of Carcases and Animal Products (Amdt.) (No. 2) O. 1967	r., 1972/287
1805	Importation of Carcases and Animal Products (Amdt) (No. 3) O. 1967	r., 1972/287
1821	Royal Navy Terms of Service Regs. 1967	am., 1972/558
1842	Rules of Procedure (Army) (Fourth Amdt.) Rules 1967	r., 1972/316
1845	Rules of Procedure (Air Force) (Third Amdt.) Rules 1967	r., 1972/419
1882	Superannuation (Teaching and N.I. Local Government) Interchange (S.) Rules 1967	r. (saving), 1972/328

Year and Number (or date)	Act or instrument	How affected
1968		
225	National Health Service (Appointment of Medical and Dental Officers) (S.) Amdt. Regs. 1968	r., 1972/467
333	Exchange Control (Scheduled Territories) (Amdt.) O. 1968	r., 1972/386
524	Family Allowances, National Insurance and Industrial Injuries (Consequential) Regs. 1968	am., 1972/606
619	Plant Breeders' Rights (Fees) Regs. 1968	r., 1972/506
716	Police (S.) Regs. 1968	am., 1972/136
987	Redundant Mineworkers (Payments Scheme) O. 1968	am., 1972/335
995	Savings Certificates (Amdt.) No. 2 Regs. 1968	r., 1972/641
1066	Rate Rebates (Limits of Income) O. 1968	superseded, 1972/81
1173	Rules of Procedure (Air Force) (Amdt.) Rules 1968	r., 1972/419
1180	Rules of Procedure (Army) (Amdt.) Rules 1968	r., 1972/316
1399	Exchange Control (Scheduled Territories) (Amdt.) (No. 2) O. 1968	r., 1972/386
1444	Savings Certificates (Amdt.) (No. 3) Regs. 1968	r., 1972/641
1684	National Insurance (Classification) Amdt. Regs. 1968	r., 1972/555
1763	Industrial Training (Footwear, Leather and Fur Skin Bd.) O. 1968	am., 1972/597
1801	Armed Forces (Discharge by Purchase) Regs. 1968	am., 1972/8
1858	Copyright (International Conventions) (Amdt.) O. 1968	r., 1972/673
1862	Inter-Governmental Maritime Consultative Organisation (Immunities and Privileges) O. 1968	am., 1972/118
1898	Rules of Procedure (Army) (Second Amdt.) Rules 1968	r., 1972/316
1921	Rules of Procedure (Air Force) (Second Amdt.) Rules 1968	r., 1972/419
1954	Building Societies (Accounts and Annual Return etc.) Regs. 1968	r., 1972/70
2077	Plant Breeders' Rights (Applications in Designated Countries) O. 1968	am., 1972/403
1969	Housing Act 1969 (c. 33)	s. 37(4) am., 1972/440
	Housing (S.) Act 1969 (c. 34)	s. 59(4) am., 1972/457

Year and Number (or date)	Act or instrument	How affected
1969		
200	Motor Vehicles (Designation of Approval Marks) Regs. 1969	r., 1972/577
233	Rate Support Grant (S.) O. 1969 ...	am., 1972/262
257	National Health Service (Appointment of Medical and Dental Officers) (S.) Amdt. Regs. 1969	r., 1972/467
386	Merchant Shipping (Light Dues) O. 1969	r., 1972/456
595	Air Navigation (Isle of Man) O. 1969	r., 1972/454
639	Building (Fourth Amdt.) Regs. 1969...	r., 1972/317
679	Rules of Procedure (Air Force) (Amdt.) Rules 1969	r., 1972/419
680	Rules of Procedure (Army) (Amdt.) Rules 1969	r., 1972/316
743	Copyright (Bermuda: Protection of Foreign Broadcasts) O. 1969	r., 1972/673
1021	Plant Breeders' Rights Regs. 1969 ...	am., 1972/84
1022	Plant Breeders' Rights (Fees) (Amdt.) Regs. 1969	r., 1972/506
1027	Plant Varieties (Index) Regs. 1969 ...	r., 1972/507
1028	Plant Varieties (Performance Trials) Regs. 1969	am., 1972/647
1038	Food (Control of Irradiation) (S.) Amdt. Regs. 1969	r., 1972/307
1039	Food (Control of Irradiation) (Amdt.) Regs. 1969	r., 1972/205
1135	Family Allowances, National Insurance and Industrial Injuries (Post Office Act 1969 Consequential) Regs. 1969	am., 1972/555
1211	Governor's Pensions (Maximum Amounts) O. 1969	r., 1972/229
1334	Savings Certificates (Amdt.) (No. 2) Regs. 1969	r., 1972/641
1361	National Insurance (Increase of Benefit and Miscellaneous Provns.) Regs. 1969	am., 1972/606
1362	National Insurance and Industrial Injuries (Classification and Collection of Contributions) Amdt. Regs. 1969	am., 1972/555
1532	Town and Country Planning (Control of Advertisements) Regs. 1969	am., 1972/489
1587	Building Societies (Accounts and Annual Return etc.) (Amdt.) Regs. 1969	r., 1972/70
1696	National Insurance (Contributions) Regs. 1969	am., 1972/166

Year and Number (or date)	Act or instrument	How affected
1969		
1700	Trustee Savings Banks (Amdt.) Regs. 1969	**r.,** 1972/583
1713	Remuneration of Teachers (Further Education) O. 1969	**r.,** 1972/255
1746	Civil Aviation (Documentary Evidence) Regs. 1969	**r.,** 1972/187
1780	Remuneration of Teachers (Farm Institutes) O. 1969	**r.,** 1972/276
1970	Finance Act 1970 (c. 24)	s. 35(2) am., 1972/92
	Family Income Supplements Act 1970 (c. 55)	ss. 2, 3 am., 1972/135
46	Family Allowances, National Insurance, Industrial Injuries and Miscellaneous Provns. (Decimalisation of the Currency) Regs. 1970	am., 1972/603, 604, 606
109	Building (Fifth Amdt.) Regs. 1970 ...	**r.,** 1972/317
110	Wages Regulation (Unlicensed Place of Refreshment) O. 1970	**r.,** 1972/264
124	Plant Varieties (Index) (Amdt.) Regs. 1970	**r.,** 1972/507
144	Drivers' Hours (Goods Vehicles) (Exemptions) Regs. 1970	**r.,** 1972/574
198	Fixed Penalty (Procedure) Regs. 1970	am., 1972/333
217	National Insurance (Classification) Amdt. Regs. 1970	**r.,** 1972/555
264	Rules of Procedure (Army) (Amdt.) Rules 1970	**r.,** 1972/316
281	Fiduciary Note Issue (Extension of Period) O. 1970	**r.,** 1972/154
290	Copyright (International Conventions) (Amdt.) O. 1970	**r.,** 1972/673
332	Sugar Beet (Research and Education) (Increase of Contributions) O. 1970	superseded, 1972/105
336	Rate Rebates (Limits of Income) (S.) O. 1970	superseded, 1972/112
359	Price Stability of Imported Products (Levy Arrangements) (Eggs) O. 1970	am., 1972/620
422	Rules of Procedure (Air Force) (Amdt.) Rules 1970	**r.,** 1972/419
453	Plant Varieties (Index) (Amdt. No. 2) Regs. 1970	**r.,** 1972/507
454	Plant Breeders' Rights (Fees) (Amdt.) Regs. 1970	**r.,** 1972/506
467	General Medical Council (Registration (Fees) Regs.) O. of C. 1970	**r.,** 1972/429

Year and Number (or date)	Act or instrument	How affected
1970		
612	Public Service Vehicles (International Circulation) Regs. 1970	r., 1972/341
637	Copyright (International Conventions) (Amdt. No. 2) O. 1970	r., 1972/673
639	Merchant Shipping (Light Dues) O. 1970	r., 1972/456
666	Income Tax (Employments) (No. 5) Regs. 1970	superseded, 1972/552
740	Remuneration of Teachers (Farm Institutes) (Amdt.) O. 1970	r., 1972/276
741	Remuneration of Teachers (Further Education) (Amdt.) O. 1970	r., 1972/255
748	Exchange Control (Scheduled Territories) (Amdt.) O. 1970	r., 1972/386
789	Exchange Control (Purchase of Foreign Currency) O. 1970	am., 1972/137
823	Air Navigation (Noise Certification) O. 1970	am., 1972/455
847	Rate Rebates (Limits of Income) O. 1970	superseded, 1972/81
862	Teachers' Superannuation (Family Benefits) Regs. 1970	am., 1972/360
954	Air Navigation O. 1970	r., 1972/129
977	Family Allowances, National Insurance, Industrial Injuries and Miscellaneous Provisions (Decimalisation of the Currency) Amdt. (No. 2) Regs. 1970	am., 1972/555
1032	Wages Regulation (Perambulator and Invalid Carriage) O. 1970	r., 1972/16
1056	Trustee Savings Banks (Pensions) O. 1970	am., 1972/495
1081	Air Navigation (General) Regs. 1970	r., 1972/322
1082	Rules of the Air and Air Traffic Control Regs. 1970	r., 1972/321
1083	Air Navigation (Restriction of Flying) Regs. 1970	r., 1972/320
1089	Plant Varieties (Index) (Amdt. No. 3) Regs. 1970	r., 1972/507
1209	Fixed Penalty (Procedure) (Amdt.) (No. 4) Regs. 1970	r., 1972/333
1268	Wages Regulation (Road Haulage) O. 1970	r., 1972/581
1288	Export of Goods (Control) O. 1970 ...	am., 1972/89, 266
1329	National Health Service (General Dental Services) Amdt. (No. 2) Regs. 1970	r., 1972/82
1335	Building (Sixth Amdt.) Regs. 1970 ...	r., 1972/317

Year and Number (or date)	Act or instrument	How affected
1970		
1340	National Health Service (General Dental Services) (S.) Amdt. (No. 2) Regs. 1970	am., 1972/96
1372	Diseases of Animals (Approved Disinfectants) O. 1970	am., 1972/242
1442	Air Navigation (Amdt.) O. 1970 ...	r., 1972/129
1448	Rules of the Air and Air Traffic Control (Amdt.) Regs. 1970	r., 1972/321
1449	Air Navigation (General) (Amdt.) Regs. 1970	r., 1972/322
1455	Exchange Control (Scheduled Territories) (Amdt. No. 2) O. 1970	r., 1972/386
1580	National Insurance (Widow's Pensions and Miscellaneous Provns.) Regs. 1970	am., 1972/604, 606
1599	Wages Regulation (Ostrich and Fancy Feathers and Artificial Flowers) O. 1970	r., 1972/9
1704	National Insurance (Classification) (Amdt.) (No. 2) Regs. 1970	r., 1972/555
1731	Rules of Procedure (Air Force) (Second Amdt.) Rules 1970	r., 1972/419
1732	Rules of Procedure (Army) (Second Amdt.) Rules 1970	r., 1972/316
1759	Farm Capital Grant Scheme 1970 ...	am., 1972/368
1805	Farm Capital Grant (S.) Scheme 1970	am., 1972/362
1853	Superannuation (Local Govt. and Approved Employmetn) Interchange (S.) Rules 1970	am., 1972/63
1951	Air Navigation (Second Amdt.) O. 1970	r., 1972/129
1958	Functions of Traffic Wardens O. 1970	am., 1972/540
1981	National Insurance (General Benefit) Regs. 1970	am., 1972/166, 394
1986	General Medical Council (Registration (Fees) (Amdt.) Regs.) O. of C. 1970	r., 1972/429
1995	Air Navigation (General) (Second Amdt.) Regs. 1970	r., 1972/322
2014	Drivers' Hours (Goods Vehicles) (Exemptions) (Amdt.) (No. 3) Regs. 1970	r., 1972/574
1971		
87	Wages Regulation (Dressmaking and Women's Light Clothing) (S.) O. 1971	r., 1972/207
102	Matrimonial Causes Fees. O. 1971 ...	r. (saving), 1972/194
107	Witnesses' Allowances Regs. 1971 ...	am., 1972/49

Year and Number (or date)	Act or instrument	How affected
1971		
145	Firemen's Pension Scheme 1971 ...	am., 1972/522
156	Police Regs. 1971	am., 1972/74, 339
222	Approved Schools and Classifying Centres (Contributions by Local Authies.) Regs. 1971	r., 1972/241
226	Family Income Supplements (General) Regs. 1971	am., 1972/14
249	Residential Establishments (Payments by Local Authies.) (S.) O. 1971	am., 1972/466
271	Air Navigation (General) (Third Amdt.) Regs. 1971	r., 1972/322
274	Import Duty Drawbacks (No. 1) O. 1971	am., 1972/406
304	Therapeutic Substances (Supply of Antibiotics and Chemotherapeutic Substances for Agricultural Purposes) Regs. 1971	am., 1972/190
308	Wages Regulation (Dressmaking and Women's Light Clothing) (E. and W.) O. 1971	r., 1972/168
352	Goods Vehicles (Plating and Testing) Regs. 1971	am., 1972/195
367	Sugar Beet (Research and Education) O. 1971	superseded, 1972/224
374	Functions of Traffic Wardens (S.) O. 1971	am., 1972/540
383	Merchant Shipping (Tonnage) (Overseas Territories) O. 1971	am., 1972/447
384	Foreign Compensation (Financial Provisions) O. 1971	superseded, 1972/302
469	Rate Support Grant (S.) O. 1971 ...	am., 1972/263
470	Rate Support Grant (Increase) (S.) O. 1971	superseded, 1972/262
475	Eggs (Protection of Guarantees) O. 1971	r., 1972/492
477	Exchange Control (Authorised Dealers and Depositaries) O. 1971	r., 1972/132
479	Fixed Penalty (Procedure) (Amdt.) Regs. 1971	r., 1972/333
510	Royal Air Force Terms of Service Regs. 1971	am., 1972/355
517	Royal Navy Terms of Service (Amdt.) Regs. 1971	superseded, 1972/558
549	Savings Certificates (Amdt.) Regs. 1971	r., 1971/641
562	Non-Residents' Transitional Relief from Income Tax on Dividends (Extension of Period) O. 1971	superseded, 1972/465

Year and Number (or date)	Act or instrument	How affected
1971		
563	Transitional Relief for Interest and Royalties paid to Non-Residents (Extension of Period) O. 1971	superseded, 1972/464
621	National Insurance (Attendance Allowance) Regs. 1971	am., 1972/664
702	Family Income Supplements (Computation) Regs. 1971	r., 1972/135
707	National Insurance (Claims and Payments) Regs. 1971	am., 1972/166
724	Merchant Shipping (Pilot Ladders) (Amdt.) Rules 1971	r., 1972/531
845	Wages Regulation (Retail Drapery, Outfitting and Footwear) O. 1971	r., 1972/35
855	Price Stability of Imported Products (Minimum Import Price Levels) (Beef and Veal) O. 1971	r., 1972/254
857	Price Stability of Imported Products (Minimum Import Price Levels) (Milk and Milk Products) O. 1971	am., 1972/652
990	Wages Regulation (Retail Food) (E. and W.) O. 1971	r., 1972/153
1023	Wages Regulation (Retail Food) (S.) O. 1971	r., 1972/165
1028	Exchange Control (Authorised Dealers and Depositaries) (Amdt.) O. 1971	r., 1972/132
1037	Milk (N.I.) O. 1971	am., 1972/366
1038	Milk (G.B.) O. 1971	am., 1972/367
1102	Plant Breeders' Rights (Fees) (Amdt.) Regs. 1971	r., 1972/506
1135	Civil Aviation (Navigation Services Charges) Regs. 1971	am., 1972/188
1220	National Insurance (Increase of Benefit and Miscellaneous Provns.) Regs. 1971	am., 1972/603, 606
1287	Disease of Animals (Approved Disinfectants) (Amdt.) O. 1971	r., 1972/242
1370	Exchange Control (Authorised Dealers and Depositaries) (Amdt.) (No. 2) O. 1971	r., 1972/132
1406	Exchange Control (Scheduled Territories) (Amdt.) O. 1971	r., 1972/386
1419	National Insurance (Miscellaneous Amdts.) Regs. 1971	am., 1972/603, 604, 606
1421	National Insurance and Industrial Injuries (Classification, Contributions and Collection of Contributions) Amdt. Regs. 1971	am., 1972/555

Year and Number (or date)	Act or instrument	How affected
1971		
1426	Remuneration of Teachers (Further Education) (Amdt.) O. 1971	r., 1972/255
1440	National Insurance (Industrial Injuries) (Hospital In-Patients) Regs. 1971	am., 1972/605
1505	Fixed Penalty (Procedure) (Amdt.) (No. 2) Regs. 1971	r., 1972/333
1551	Opencast Coal (Rate of Interest on Compensation) (No. 2)	r., 1972/373
1556	Exchange Control (Scheduled Territories) (Amdt.) (No. 2) O. 1971	r., 1972/386
1566	Exchange Control (Authorised Dealers and Depositaries) (Amdt.) (No. 3) O. 1971	r., 1972/132
1600	Building (Seventh Amdt.) Regs. 1971	r., 1972/317
1631	Wages Regulation (Retail Drapery, Outfitting and Footwear) (Amdt.) O. 1971	r., 1972/35
1633	National Insurance (Miscellaneous Amdts.) (No. 2) Regs. 1971	am., 1972/604
1686	Civil Aviation (Notices) Regs. 1971 ...	am., 1972/431
1698	Wages Regulation (Milk Distribution) (E. and W.) O. 1971	am., 1972/482
1715	Civil Aviation (Rents Charges for Navigation Services) Regs. 1971	am., 1972/108
1728	National Insurance (Classification) Amdt. Regs. 1971	r., 1972/555
1733	Air Navigation (Third Amdt.) O. 1971	r., 1972/129
1750	Air Navigation (General) (Fourth Amdt.) Regs. 1971	r., 1972/322
1751	Rules of the Air and Air Traffic Control (Second Amdt.) Regs. 1971	r., 1972/321
1775	Teachers Superannuation (Family Benefits) (S.) Regs. 1971	am., 1972/442
1839	Diseases of Animals (Approved Disinfectants (Amdt.) (No. 2) O. 1971	r., 1972/242
1850	Copyright (International Conventions) (Amdt.) O. 1971	r., 1972/673
1938	Prices Stability of Imported Products (Rates of Levy) (Eggs) (No. 28) O. 1971	r., 1972/21
1971	Import Duties (General) (No. 7) O. 1971	am., 1972/52, 226, 569, 648, 677
1972	Rules of the Air and Air Traffic Control (Third Amdt.) Regs. 1971	r., 1972/321
2002	Exchange Control (Scheduled Territories) (Amdt.) (No. 3) O. 1971	r., 1972/386
2034	Exchange Control (Authorised Dealers and Depositaries) (Amdt.) (No. 4) O. 1971	r., 1972/132

Year and Number (or date)	Act or instrument	How affected
1971		
2082	Sugar (Rates of Surcharge and Surcharge Repayments) (No. 10) O. 1971	superseded, 1972/1
2083	Composite Sugar Products (Surcharge and Surcharge Repayments—Average Rates) (No. 10) O. 1971	superseded, 1972/2
2154	Price Stability of Imported Products (Rates of Levy) (Cereals) (No. 14) O. 1971	**r.**, 1972/15
1972		
15	Price Stability of Imported Products (Rates of Levy) (Cereals) (No. 1) O. 1972	**r.**, 1972/57
21	Price Stability of Imported Products (Rates of Levy) (Eggs) (No. 1) O. 1972	**r.**, 1972/58
25	Price Stability of Imported Products (Rates of Levy) (Eggs) (No. 2) O. 1972	**r.**, 1972/58
57	Price Stability of Imported Products (Rates of Levy) (Cereals) (No. 2) O. 1972	**r.**, 1972/83
58	Price Stability of Imported Products (Rates of Levy) (Eggs) (No. 3) O. 1972	**r.**, 1972/193
66	Sugar (Distribution Payments) O. 1972	am., 1972/356
67	Sugar (Distribution Repayments) O. 1972	am., 1972/357
68	Composite Sugar Products (Distribution Payments—Average Rates) O. 1972	superseded, 1972/358
83	Price Stability of Imported Products (Rates of Levy) (Cereals) (No. 3) O. 1972	**r.**, 1972/94
94	Price Stability of Imported Products (Rates of Levy) (Cereals) (No. 4) O. 1972	**r.**, 1972/149
129	Air Navigation O. 1972	am., 1972/672
132	Exchange Control (Authorised Dealers and Depositaries) O. 1972	am., 1972/556
146	Exchange Control (Scheduled Territories) (Amdt.) O. 1972	**r.**, 1972/386
149	Price Stability of Imported Products (Rates of Levy) (Cereals) (No. 5) O. 1972	**r.**, 1972/170
160	Electricity (Advertising, Display and Flood Lighting) (Restriction) O. 1972	am., 1972/273

Year and Number (or date)	Act or instrument	How affected
1972		
169	Electricity (Non-Domestic Heating) (Restriction) O. 1972	r., 1972/306
170	Price Stability of Imported Products (Rates of Levy) (Cereals) (No. 6) O. 1972	r., 1972/215
176	Road Vehicles Lighting (Standing Vehicles) (Exemption) (General) Regs. 1972	r., 1972/557
193	Price Stability of Imported Products (Rates of Levy) (Eggs) (No. 4) O. 1972	r., 1972/277
215	Price Stability of Imported Products (Rates of Levy) (Cereals) (No. 7) O. 1972	r., 1972/230
225	Electricity (Directions) O. 1972 ...	r., 1972/305
230	Price Stability of Imported Products (Rates of Levy) (Cereals) (No. 8) O. 1972	r., 1972/299
239	Electricity (Non-Domestic Heating) (Restriction) Amdt. O. 1972	r., 1972/306
240	Electricity (Directions) No. 2 O. 1972	r., 1972/305
245	Electricity (Directions) No. 3 O. 1972	r., 1972/305
265	Electricity (Directions) No. 4 O. 1972	r., 1972/305
273	Electricity (Restrictions) Amdt. O. 1972	r., 1972/306
277	Price Stability of Imported Products (Rates of Levy) (Eggs) (No. 5) O. 1972	r., 1972/399
299	Price Stability of Imported Products (Rates of Levy) (Cereals) (No. 9) O. 1972	r., 1972/347
347	Price Stability of Imported Products (Rates of Levy) (Cereals) (No. 10) O. 1972	r., 1972/372
356	Sugar (Distribution Payments) (No. 2) O. 1972	superseded, 1972/432
357	Sugar (Distribution Repayments) (Amdt.) O. 1972	superseded, 1972/433
358	Composite Sugar Products (Distribution Payments—Average Rates) (No. 2) O. 1972	superseded, 1972/434
372	Price Stability of Imported Products (Rates of Levy) (Cereals) (No. 11) O. 1972	r., 1972/488
394	National Insurance (General Benefit and Miscellaneous Amdts.) Regs. 1972	am., 1972/603, 604
399	Price Stability of Imported Products (Rates of Levy) (Eggs) (No. 6) O. 1972	r., 1972/609

Year and Number (or date)	Act or instrument	How affected
1972		
400	Price Stability of Imported Products (Rates of Levy) (Cereals) (No. 12) O. 1972	**r.,** 1972/488
421	Intermediate Area and Derelict Land Clearance Area O. 1972	am., 1972/585
432	Sugar (Distribution Payments) (No. 3) O. 1972	superseded, 1972/578
433	Sugar (Distribution Repayments) (Amdt.) (No. 2) O. 1972	superseded, 1972/579
434	Composite Sugar Products (Distribution Payments—Average Rates) (No. 3) O. 1972	superseded, 1972/580
488	Price Stability of Imported Products (Rates of Levy) (Cereals) (No. 13) O. 1972	**r.,** 1972/530
530	Price Stability of Imported Products (Rates of Levy) (Cereals) (No. 14) O. 1972	superseded, 1972/678
578	Sugar (Distribution Payments) (No. 4) O. 1972	superseded, 1972/598
579	Sugar (Distribution Repayments) (Amdt.) (No. 3) O. 1972	superseded, 1972/599
580	Composite Sugar Products (Distribution Payments—Average Rates) (No. 4) O. 1972	superseded, 1972/600
598	Sugar (Distribution Payments) (No. 5) O. 1972	superseded, 1972/649
599	Sugar (Distribution Repayments) (Amdt.) (No. 4) O. 1972	superseded, 1972/650
600	Composite Sugar Products (Distribution Payments—Average Rates) (No. 5) O. 1972	superseded, 1972/651
649	Sugar (Distribution Payments) (No. 6) O. 1972	superseded, 1972/659
650	Sugar (Distribution Repayments) (Amdt.) (No. 5) O. 1972	superseded, 1972/660
651	Composite Sugar Products (Distribution Payments—Average Rates) (No. 6) O. 1972	superseded, 1972/661

Index to Part I

SBN 11 840095 9

STOKE-ON-TRENT
CITY
LIBRARIES

HORACE BARKS
Reference Library

HMSO
2parts
413.71
GW